A Step-by-Step Guide to C Programming

[redacted]

A Step-by-Step Guide to C Programming

Jean Paul Corriveau
Saskatchewan Institute of Applied Science and Technology

Prentice Hall
Upper Saddle River, New Jersey   Columbus, Ohio

Library of Congress Cataloging-in-Publication Data
Corriveau, Jean Paul.
A step-by-step guide to C programming / Jean Paul Corriveau.
p. cm.
Includes index.
ISBN 0-13-339946-X
1. C (Computer program language) I. Title.
QA76.73.C15C668 1998
005.13′3—dc21 97-36756
CIP

Cover photo: Lawrence Berkley/Science Source, Photo Researchers
Editor: Charles E. Stewart
Production Coordinator: Custom Editorial Productions, Inc.
Design Coordinator: Julia Zonneveld Van Hook
Text Designer: Custom Editorial Productions, Inc.
Cover Designer: Brian Deep
Production Manager: Laura Messerly
Marketing Manager: Debbie Yarnell

This book was set in Times Roman by Custom Editorial Productions, Inc., and was printed and bound by Banta/Harrisonburg. The cover was printed by Phoenix Color Corp.

Printed in the United States of America

10 9 8 7 6 5 4 3 2 1

ISBN 0-13-339946-X

Prentice-Hall International (UK) Limited, *London*
Prentice-Hall of Australia Pty. Limited, *Sydney*
Prentice-Hall of Canada, Inc., *Toronto*
Prentice-Hall Hispanoamericana, S. A., *Mexico*
Prentice-Hall of India Private Limited, *New Delhi*
Prentice-Hall of Japan, Inc., *Tokyo*
Simon & Schuster Asia Pte. Ltd., *Singapore*
Editora Prentice-Hall do Brasil, Ltda., *Rio de Janeiro*

To my parents,
Monique and Marcel

Preface

Self-taught at C programming, I was soon attracted to its flexibility and terse language. Although rewarding career-wise, the learning process was difficult and frustrating, an experience shared by most students. This is because—putting the C language aside—the logical thinking of computer programming feels unnatural to the uninitiated. On top of this, one has to learn C's cryptic and error-prone language and functions.

THE PURPOSE OF THIS BOOK

Having realized the above, my purpose in writing this book is to ease the learning process for the student. Also, I intend to both facilitate the instructor's lecture preparation and offer the student some assistance in learning C.

Learning is a process that takes place over time, so a book must give the student enough time to understand the material through step-by-step examples. This learning should then be immediately followed by exercises to allow the student to gradually feel comfortable with the material. This book takes this approach.

Based on my experience, current books on this topic capture only the better students, leaving all others stranded. This book offers a helping hand to all.

THE INTENDED AUDIENCE

This book is especially designed for community colleges and technical institutions. It would be ideal for a first course in C programming. It assumes no prior knowledge of computer programming, no math skills, and, most importantly, no prior mental training for formal problem solving. It only assumes some prior general exposure to computers. Nevertheless, the scope of the book is broad and deep enough that it may be used as an introductory course to C as a second programming course.

Finally, the book targets the novice. These students generally show no interest whatsoever in mathematics or science. This is not to say that scientific- and technical-minded students could not benefit from this book; far from that!

WHAT IS DIFFERENT ABOUT THIS BOOK?

With so many C programming books on the market, you are probably still wondering what this book can possibly offer that has not already been seen in other books. I believe that the features described below really set this book apart from others:

- The approach is **informal;** that is, every concept is explained via a practical example rather than abstract ramblings. Except for the general background preparation in Chapter 1, this book contains virtually no theory! Good news for students!
- The explanations are organized as **lecture notes** are. This should facilitate the teacher's task of interpreting the material for the students.
- Almost every example provided is **code complete.** The student may simply key it into the compiler and try it immediately. The student can bring the book to the lab and get right down to business.
- This is a textbook with a **workbook approach.** It adopts a slow pace so that the student can learn at his or her ease. This is assured by the sequence of examples that are immediately followed by exercises that thoroughly test understanding and reinforce learning. Moreover, the book does not move on to new concepts until the student is ready for more. Doing the large number of exercises in this book serves to increase the student's confidence.
- This book uses a **prudent approach;** that is, subject matter is covered only if it is judged that the student is mentally and technically prepared for it. Also, subject matter is covered only to the extent that it is needed at the time.
- This book teaches how to **put segments of codes together,** not just how to use C functions and syntax. By providing exercises that ask the student to add new features to programs from previous exercises, the student inevitably learns how to properly build larger programs. This is taught systematically.
- The students are **guided** in their learning process. Advice as to good programming practices is given in an informal manner. Also, warnings are given about **common errors and traps.** These are pointed out either within the text or within a subsection named "Common Errors and Traps," found at the end of most sections. Many of these common errors are illustrated with a short segment of program that the student may wish to try out in order to experience what the error causes. The intent behind mentioning common errors is not to prevent the students from making mistakes, but rather to teach them to be wary and to teach them to fix these errors when they do come up.
- I/O operations in C are error prone and not at all user friendly. Here, the student is guided in using I/O functions safely, yet without unnecessary technical details. Some instructors prefer to avoid all of these functions and use the objects *cin* and *cout* from C++ instead. To meet their needs, an appendix on C++ I/O objects has been added to the book.
- The evaluation of C expressions is carefully examined with a strong emphasis on the meaning of operator precedence and associativity.
- The use of arrays, both one-dimensional and two-dimensional, is fully examined, as are string variables.
- The creation of user-defined functions and variable scoping are thoroughly explained and illustrated. The importance of and procedure for writing portable functions are heavily stressed.

HOW SHOULD THIS BOOK BE USED?

The instructor is not expected to cover every single page of this book in class. The concepts are covered slowly enough so that students can safely read many parts of it on their own. A possible scenario is as follows:

1. One day, the students are told to read, say, Section 7.1 for the next lecture.
2. During the next lecture, the instructor covers that section in whatever way he or she wishes, and makes sure it is understood. The section will already be structured in a way to test understanding. Then he or she proceeds with another section deemed important to cover in class.
3. If the instructor finds a section too trivial, he or she may simply decide not to cover it at all, but at least it is there for the slower learner to read.

The book is appropriate for weaker students as well as stronger ones.

Finally, the large number of exercises contained in this book may seem intimidating at first. However, students should not feel obligated to do them all. My hope is that the instructor will be able to select some for assignments, homework, in-class exercises, or examination questions.

ACKNOWLEDGMENTS

I would like to thank the following reviewers of this book for their helpful comments and suggestions: Carl C. Hommer, Jr., Purdue University, North Central; Rod Pohl, BDN General Hospital; Robert Shurtleff, Colorado Tech. Also, I appreciate the value that Prentice-Hall saw in my project from the beginning to the end. This project takes its origin from the dissatisfaction that my students expressed with current C books. Some students took active parts in the review of selected chapters, in particular, Scott Dieno, Scott Shymanski, and James Gledhill. It should be noted that James Gledhill also contributed some of the material in Chapters 1 and 13.

Jean Corriveau
Computer Information Systems Department
Saskatchewan Institute of Applied Science and Technology
Moose Jaw, Saskatchewan, Canada

Brief Contents

Contents

Appendixes

1 Background Preparation

OBJECTIVES

This chapter introduces you to the following information:

- An overview of the various components that make up today's typical microcomputer system.
- A general understanding of the microcomputer's internal structure and functions.
- A general understanding of the way software operates.
- The general steps programmers go through to develop computer programs and software.
- A more detailed understanding (but nontechnical) of one of those steps: the translation of a program into machine codes.
- Many good reasons for learning C.

INTRODUCTION

The purpose of this chapter is to teach you about the environment that surrounds the activity of writing computer programs. Learning programming in itself is not enough; the novice programmer needs to know how this activity fits into the broader picture of a computer system. The chapter also presents a discussion on the benefit of learning C, accompanied by an honest discussion of the difficulties that you may face in the process. By the end of this chapter, you should know what is expected of you in order to successfully learn the material in the remainder of the book.

1.1 WHAT IS A COMPUTER SYSTEM?

A computer system is a general-purpose machine that can be programmed to accomplish various tasks, such as word processing, bookkeeping, games, and other activities. To complete its tasks, the machine must possess the following three essential functions:

1. *Input.* The machine must be able to accept the data required to solve a particular task, such as accepting word processing commands from the user. For instance, these could be commands for editing text, loading a file, or inserting a graphic.
2. *Processing.* The processing of the data is performed by the actual software (e.g., word processor) created to solve the specialized task.
3. *Output.* This is the direct outcome from the processing of the data. It consists of the production of the results, such as printing a letter.

1.1.1 FIVE CATEGORIES OF COMPUTERS

Computers systems are divided into five categories: mainframes, minicomputers, supercomputers, microcomputers, and portable computers. Each of these computer types is described in more detail below.

Mainframes. These computers are very fast and usually also the largest in size. They are used for centralized processing and storage by large organizations and governments. Mainframe computers are generally used for business-related activities, but may also be used in engineering and scientific work as well.

Minicomputers. These are midrange computers in speed as well as in size. Their relatively more affordable prices allow many companies to own one or more. Like mainframes, they are mostly used for business-related activities (such as processing payroll), but again, they also have applications in engineering and scientific work.

Computer systems in these two categories can service several users at the same time. These users communicate with the central computer via terminals that can be on location or off location, perhaps far away. The example in Figure 1.1.1 shows four terminals connected to a central computer. This could be the configuration of a computer system at a university. Via the terminal, students log on to the central computer to work on assignments that are then stored in the data storage area. Terminals look somewhat like microcomputers, except that they do not have any computing power of their own. For this reason, they are often referred to as ***dumb terminals.*** They simply serve as a connecting device to the central computer, which is a ***host computer.***

Figure 1.1.1

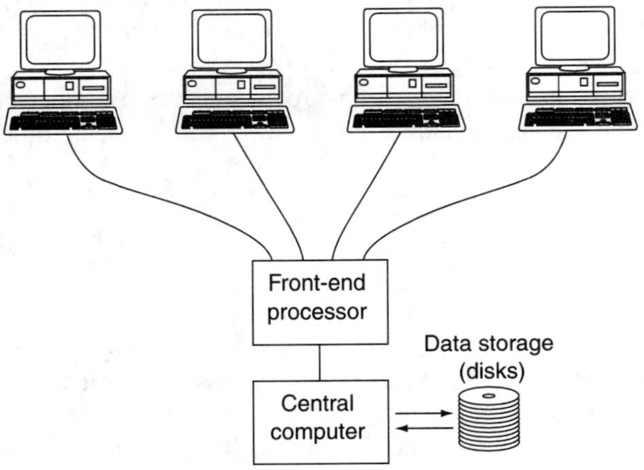

Supercomputers. These are known to be the fastest computers, although not the largest in size. Supercomputers are not designed to optimize access to multiusers and their general-purpose applications. Rather, they are used for specialized tasks that demand top speeds, such as in some areas of scientific research. The activities supercomputers are suited for include simulations, number crunching, and weather prediction.

Microcomputers. These are small computers, also called ***personal computers (PCs).*** They differ from the three categories above in that microcomputers are meant for individual use, not multiusers. In the beginning, microcomputers were expensive and rather sluggish in performance, but now their speed can be quite remarkable, even surpassing some computers in the previous categories. Their prices are quite affordable now, too.

As mentioned, typically microcomputers cannot accommodate multiple users. However, they may be linked together through networks called ***local area networks (LANs).*** In this arrangement, a powerful microcomputer is selected as a ***server. Workstations*** (also called ***clients***) may be connected to this server. The task of a server is to monitor the sharing of various hardware resources (such as printers) among the workstations. The server also acts as a central location where multiple users may store and share data as well as software.

Portable computers. These are very small microcomputers that can be carried around easily. Examples include laptop and notebook computers. Pocket calculators do not fall into this category because they do not have the automated processing capability of portable computers.

1.1.2 THE COMPONENTS OF A TYPICAL MICROCOMPUTER SYSTEM

Since microcomputers are now widespread and are familiar to most people, the discussion in the rest of this section will focus on them rather than computers in general. A microcomputer system is made of input devices, output devices, secondary storage devices, and the computer itself.

Input devices. These devices accept data from the user and pass it on to the computer for processing. Typical input devices include the following components:

- The ***keyboard.***
- The ***mouse,*** which has become standard equipment.
- ***Diskette drives*** or ***hard disk drives.*** Input data is often retrieved from a diskette or a hard disk. The disks themselves are not actually devices, but rather media on which data reside. The disk(ette) drive, which reads this data from the media, is in fact the device.
- ***CD-ROM drive.*** Input data can also be retrieved from a CD-ROM disk. This medium has a huge data storage capacity and has become standard equipment in multimedia systems.

Output devices. These devices receive information from the computer and then display it to the screen, send it to the printer, or store it in some media. The following is a list of typical output devices:

- The ***monitor,*** which is the most essential output device. Without the monitor, no information could ever be visible to the user.
- The ***printer*** is another output device that is quite useful. It causes information from the computer to be printed onto paper. The result is usually called the ***printout*** or ***hard copy.***
- Diskette drives and hard disk drives are output devices as well as input devices, because they are used to store information on disk media in binary form. (The internal computer language is based on the ***binary system***.) The information stored on disk is referred to as a ***soft copy***, or computer ***file,*** as opposed to a hard copy.

Secondary storage devices. These devices are called upon to store information that needs to be kept permanently or for a long period of time. Typical secondary storage devices include the following examples:

- The floppy disk and hard disk.
- A CD-ROM, although data can only be read from this type of disk, not stored on one.

The computer. The three groups of devices described above are called ***peripherals.*** They are parts of the computer system, but not part of the computer itself. The computer is responsible for processing all the information sent to it from the peripherals and to send results back to them. The computer is made of two parts:

1. The ***central processing unit (CPU).*** All the information processing is controlled by this unit.
2. The ***primary storage.*** This contains one or more programs currently being run or waiting to be executed. The CPU grabs these programs one at a time and executes them. The data that these running programs need are also stored in the primary memory. This memory is actually made of two parts, ***Random Access Memory (RAM)*** and ***Read Only Memory (ROM).***

RAM contains programs and data that are removed once their execution terminates. For instance, when you run an application program, it is stored in RAM and the program runs from there. But the program and all the data generated by the program are erased from RAM when the computer power switch is turned off.

The ROM section includes programs and data that are critical to the operation of the computer. Consequently they cannot be removed; they are put in place permanently by the computer manufacturer. Figure 1.1.2 shows the data flow connections between the different storage components and the input and output devices.

Figure 1.1.2

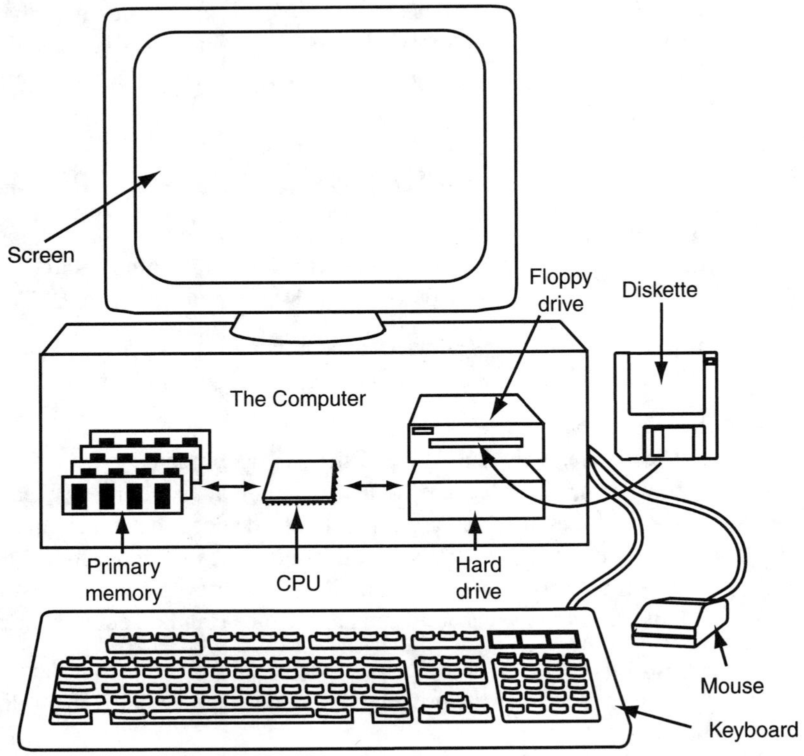

1.1.3 WHAT IS COMPUTER SOFTWARE?

Subsection 1.1.2 described the hardware components of a computer system. But this is really only half the picture. The hardware without software is "lifeless." It is like a cassette player without cassettes.

Integrated programs. Software consists of a group of ***integrated programs*** (along with their data) that tells the hardware what to do. A program is itself a sequence of instructions that the CPU interprets. The software serves as an intermediary between the user and the hardware. To most people, the operation of the computer hardware is complex and incomprehensible. The software lets the programmer or an end user utilize the hardware in a much simpler way. That is, the user does not have to know anything about the internal functions of the hardware. This is one of the roles of the ***operating system (O/S),*** a specialized type of software. The operating system also manages the system's memory, the execution of application programs, and numerous other tasks. Every application software accesses the hardware via the O/S, as illustrated in Figure 1.1.3.

Figure 1.1.3

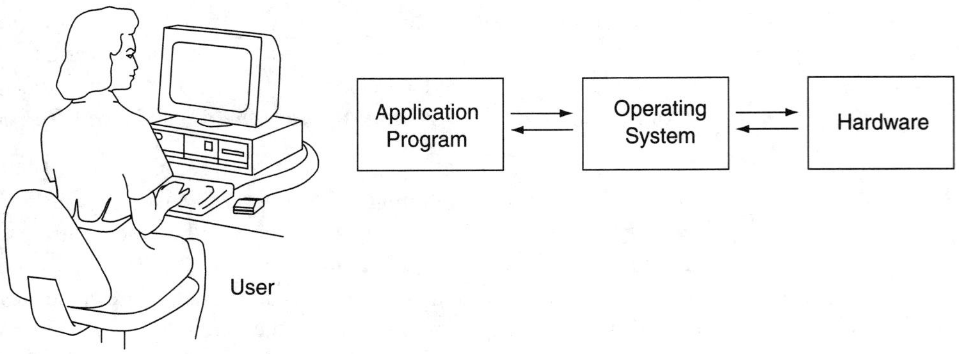

How does the system run a program? If you have used application software before or even played computer games, you basically know how to interact with software. The following three steps will give you a brief and simplified description of how a software program works and how it interacts with the hardware. In this example, the software is a word processing program.

1. The word processor is stored on a diskette, a hard disk, or a CD-ROM. In order to run, the software program must be loaded into RAM (Random Access Memory). The memory is made of cells. Each cell is given an address, much like each house in a city has an address. When the word processor is loaded into RAM, it is moved to a specific location in memory, starting at some cell address determined by the operating system. Let's assume that the software is stored starting at address 2048, as shown in Figure 1.1.4. The software must be in RAM before it can be run. Despite appearances, a software program never runs directly from secondary storage, such as a diskette.

Figure 1.1.4

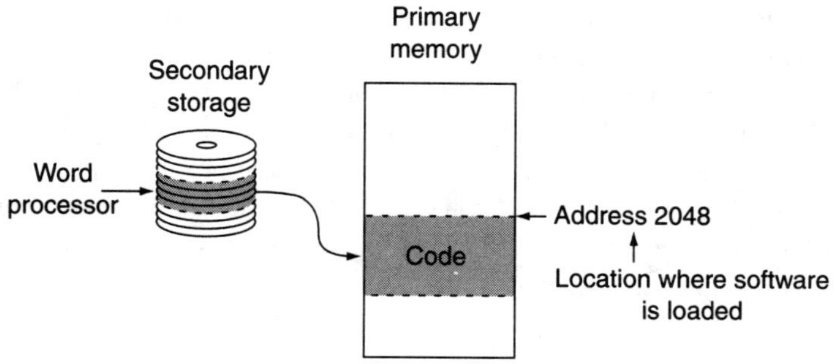

2. Once the program is in RAM, the CPU gives its attention to the word processor. It fetches each of the program's instructions from RAM, one at the time, and executes it (Figure 1.1.5). Each individual instruction performs some low-level hardware task. But as a ***group,*** these instructions perform a specific word processing task, such as underlining text, cut and paste, or search and replace.

Figure 1.1.5

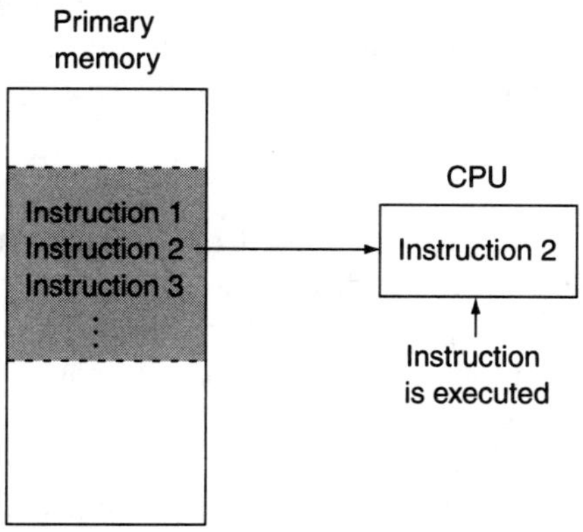

3. When the user exits from the word processor, this software is "removed from RAM." Technically, however, it is not actually removed from the Random Access Memory; the CPU simply no longer acknowledges the word processor's presence in memory. Its space is made available for other software to occupy.

1.2 SKILLS REQUIRED FOR PROBLEM SOLVING*

1.2.1 WHY LEARN ABOUT PROBLEM SOLVING?

Since microcomputers came on the market in the late 1970s, their prices have consistently gone down. For example, in 1979 a complete business microcomputer system with 32K of RAM cost over $5,000. Today a much more sophisticated system costs no more than $1,500—and with

*This section may be skipped if you already have some background in problem solving.

8 MB of RAM. Note that one MB is 1024K, and one K is 1024 bytes. A ***byte*** is the amount of computer memory space that it takes to store one character. So 1024 bytes of memory can store 1024 characters. We will come back to this concept of bytes in Section 3.1.1, and a more technical discussion is included in Appendix E. But you can see that the memory capacity of microcomputers has increased to hundreds of times what it once was, while the price has dropped dramatically. In the same span of time, software programs have also become more sophisticated, but their costs have not decreased at the same pace.

The main reason for the high cost of software programs is that their development has remained lengthy, time consuming, and labor intensive. Programmers are required to follow a methodical approach to ensure success. All software projects, big or small, eventually require their programmers to sit down and write code for the computer. This section is intended to give you an overview of some of the skills involved in the process. The skills introduced here will be instrumental throughout the book.

For bigger projects, however, basic problem-solving skills alone are no longer sufficient. The last subsection is devoted to a quick examination of what else is involved in those situations. A novice who does not learn how to solve simple problems properly will certainly not be able to manage bigger problems. If you have not had much experience in problem solving, pay particular attention to the details in the following subsections. Keep in mind, however, that this is still just an overview of the problem-solving strategy. This whole section does not teach you to write computer programs yet, but prepares your mind for the programming process.

1.2.2 ALGORITHMS: FORMALIZATION OF A SOLUTION

Every day, everyone faces obstacles that need to be tackled and eventually solved, one way or another. The process of seeking a solution to any problem is called ***problem solving,*** and the solution sought is the ***goal.*** Computer programming involves problem solving, but in a broader sense, every person is a problem solver to some degree. What separates programmers from other people is that their solutions have to be formulated in a way that the computer can use.

Consider the noncomputer-related situations below and see how people in general may solve the problems presented. In subsequent subsections, their solutions will be gradually improved to the point that a programmer could code them in the computer.

Example 1.2.1

An American customer, shopping across the border in a Canadian store, purchases a book. The clerk asks for \$41.27 Canadian. The American hands him \$40 American, knowing that American dollars are worth more. The store policy is to return the change in the same currency used for payment by the customer. Suppose the Canadian dollar is worth 0.72 of an American dollar. As soon as the clerk is handed the \$40, he understands that his task (goal) is to give the correct change in American currency.

The clerk has developed a series of four steps that allow him to figure out the correct change to give back to the customer.

1. He calculates the amount the customer has given him in Canadian dollars by dividing \$40 American by 0.72 American dollars per Canadian dollar:

$$\$40 \text{ American} \div 0.72 = \$55.55 \text{ Canadian}$$

2. The cost of the book, \$41.27, is subtracted from the Canadian equivalent of the \$40 American, \$55.55:

$$\$55.55 - \$41.27 = \$14.28$$

3. Now the clerk must convert the amount of change the customer should receive to American dollars by multiplying \$14.28 by 0.72 per Canadian dollar:

$$\$14.28 \times 0.72 = \$10.28 \text{ American}$$

4. The clerk hands \$10.28 American to the customer.

The clerk is a problem solver, since he was able to break down the problem into four smaller problems. Being able to break down the problem into manageable portions constitutes the problem-solving process.

EXERCISE 1.2.1

A family of seven plans to go to the movies this afternoon to see a family movie. The family consists of two boys ages 3 and 4 years old; three girls ages 8, 14, and 22 years old; and both parents. The parents know that the admission prices depend on the following age groups: 0 to 5, 6 to 12, 13 to 17, and adults (18 and over), but they do not know the actual ticket prices. At the counter they inquire about the price of tickets for each age group in order to calculate the total costs. Specify all the steps they will take to reach their goal. List the questions the family will have to ask to solve the problem and give the replies of the theater employee.

Example 1.2.2

The mother of an eight-year-old boy named Eric sends him out to the neighbors to try to sell apples collected from an uncle's farm. The mother gives her son a whole bag of apples and says that if he comes back with at least $15 worth of sales, his allowance for the week will be one third of the sales; otherwise he gets no allowance. Finally she informs Eric that there are plenty of apples to reach the amount of money required, but he must sell them at 30¢ per apple.

Eric understands his goal: to sell at least $15 worth of apples. He also realizes that this goal will be reached only if he is able to accomplish these steps:

1. He must sell enough apples to the neighbors he visits.
2. He has to know how to handle the money he receives. He must be able to count the money he receives from each neighbor who buys apples and add up the money he has collected so far to determine when he reaches $15 in sales.
3. He must determine whether or not he has enough neighbors to offer apples. (He has no control over this part of the problem.)

Assuming that Eric is reasonably good at arithmetic and is a good salesman, there is little doubt of his ability to reach his goal. Consequently, Eric is a problem solver.

What problems are worth solving using a computer? The solutions developed above are still inappropriate and incomplete for the production of computer programs. Before trying to produce a computer program, you should realize that for some types of situations, it may not be possible to develop a computer program at all (at least not completely). For instance, from the two examples above, one may observe that problem-solving situations are in fact a mixture of the following three types:

1. Some problems are solved using formal techniques. For example, precise arithmetic skills are used in a problem such as the currency exchange in Example 1.2.1.
2. Some problems are solved without any formal techniques—they just get resolved through trial and error and experience. In Example 1.2.2, Eric may be able to sell more apples simply by becoming a better salesman with more experience.
3. Some problems are solved using "common sense." For instance, again in Example 1.2.2, Eric knows that his mother's order to go sell apples to the neighbors means that he must go door to door. This fact is so obvious that no thought appears necessary; the deductions are immediate. This is the reason why the three steps in the solution presented were not elaborated any further.

In this book, you will be taught and will be asked to solve problem situations by coding the computer via C programs. No computer can resolve the second type of problem described above, so no problems of that type will be discussed in this book. Problems of the first type are the easiest to code, therefore many of the C programs you will study in this book will be of that complexity. However, you also will have the opportunity to solve much more complex situations of the third type of problem. These can be coded by computer, even though the computer is unable to make even the simplest deductions itself. Indeed, the computer does not have any common sense and does not really know anything. It needs to be told exactly what to do. In this book, you will learn how to give the computer the instructions it needs to solve these more complex type of problems.

Formalize your thought process. Telling the computer exactly what to do involves breaking the solution down into enough steps so the computer can mechanically work out the rest. However, this is easier said than done. The programmer must develop the ability to ***formalize*** his thoughts about the steps to follow in order to solve the problem. Not only does the programmer need to know how to solve the problem, he also needs to be able to tell the computer how to solve it, step by step. This involves the use of formal structures that can then be more easily coded. These formal structures are called ***sequences, decisions,*** and ***loops,*** and the end product is called an ***algorithm.*** These types of structures will be discussed in the next subsection.

Follow strict syntaxes in phrasing a solution. Besides using the basic formal structures mentioned above, the programmer needs to ***code*** the solution into the computer in a language that the computer can understand. The computer does not understand algorithms as presented by humans. This will demand some ability on your part to follow syntaxes of coding and some basic understanding of the way the computer works things out.

The subsection below refers back to Examples 1.2.1 and 1.2.2 to illustrate how to formalize the thought process to create the code the computer needs to solve the problem. The other skill—following strict syntaxes—requires that you know how to write computer programs using a particular programming language. That is the subject of the remaining chapters of this book.

1.2.3 HOW TO FORMALIZE THE THOUGHT PROCESS

In order to formalize a solution, all steps must be specified, even the simplest and most obvious ones. Remember, we are working toward solutions that will eventually be coded in the computer. Think of the computer as a robot that needs to be told everything. Also, the solution presented in the form of an algorithm must be generalized enough; otherwise its applicability is limited. Let us now look back at the two solutions outlined earlier to illustrate these concepts and the use of the three formal structures: sequences, decisions, and loops.

Sequence of instructions. The example below refers back to the situation described in Example 1.2.1 to illustrate the concept of how to properly sequence the instructions for the computer.

Example 1.2.3

Let's make a first attempt at formalizing the steps:

1. Look at the amount of money handed to you by the customer.
2. Calculate the Canadian equivalent with the equation:

$$\$40 \text{ American} \div 0.72 = \$55.55 \text{ Canadian}$$

3. Look at the price of the book.
4. Calculate the change with the equation:

$$\$55.55 - \$41.27 = \$14.28$$

5. Calculate the American equivalent for this change with the equation:

$$\$14.28 \text{ Canadian} \times 0.72 = \$10.28 \text{ American}$$

6. Give that amount of change to the customer.

Look at steps 1 and 3. They appear to be too obvious to mention, but keep in mind that you are now assuming that a robot clerk may be asked to follow these steps. No question about it, he will now be able to handle this transaction with the customer. But what if the next customer comes in to buy a book with a different price? The robot clerk will not realize that it is only a matter of changing the numbers—he can only deal with a book priced $41.27. Yes, this is how dumb the computer is. So steps 2, 4, and 5 are still not formalized and generalized enough. Let's revise the steps one more time:

1. Look at the amount of MONEY HANDED to you by the customer.
2. Calculate the Canadian equivalent with the equation:

$$\text{MONEY HANDED} \div 0.72 = \text{CAN EQUIVALENT}$$

3. Look at the PRICE of the book.
4. Calculate the change with the equation:

$$\text{CAN EQUIVALENT} - \text{PRICE} = \text{CHANGE}$$

5. Calculate the US EQUIVALENT for this change with the equation:

$$\text{CHANGE} \times 0.72 = \text{US EQUIVALENT}$$

6. Give the US EQUIVALENT to the customer.

The information processed by this algorithm is indicated in uppercase letters in order to make it stand out. This type of information is called a ***variable,*** because it can stand for any number. The choice for the name of a variable is arbitrary but must reflect the meaning of the information it represents. The set of instructions in steps 1 through 6 is called a ***sequence of instructions.*** Now the robot clerk will be able to use this algorithm to handle any books, but only if the customer is American. This restriction will be relaxed in Example 1.2.4 below.

In most cases, you will find that there is more than one way to phrase the instructions for a particular problem—no precise rules are imposed. Just make sure the steps are simple enough to follow and that variables are used where necessary.

EXERCISES 1.2.2

1. Formalize the steps you developed for Exercise 1.2.1 by working out an algorithm for the problem. The algorithm must work for any change in ticket prices for the various age groups; you can assume that the age group divisions remain the same and it is the same family trying to work out the total cost of the movie tickets.
2. Generalize the algorithm further so that it will work for any number of people in the family. This is only a matter of including instructions such as "look at how many KIDS BETWEEN 6 AND 12 there are." Generalize the formula that calculates the total cost.
3. A laboratory technician has only a Fahrenheit thermometer, but he wants to record temperatures in the centigrade and Kelvin scales also. Provide him with an algorithm to show how to do this. Use the following conversion formulas:

$$\text{centigrade} = 5/9 \times (\text{Fahrenheit} - 32)$$
$$\text{Kelvin} = \text{centigrade} + 273$$

4. Design an algorithm that can be used to calculate the grade of a student, given that three tests were taken:

Test 1	out of 20;	counts for 10% of final grade
Test 2	out of 50;	counts for 15% of final grade
Final exam	out of 100;	counts for 75% of final grade

For example, suppose that the student scored 15 on test 1, 42 on test 2, and 72 on the final exam. The final grade is calculated as:

$$\text{final grade} = (15/20) \times 10 + (42/50) \times 15 + (72/100) \times 75$$

The decision structure. To illustrate the decision structure, let's introduce a modification to the algorithm we developed in Example 1.2.3.

Example 1.2.4

The customer could have been a Canadian instead, in which case no currency exchange needs to be calculated. Suppose this Canadian customer handed the clerk $45. Let's add the steps to take this new case into account. Here is the new algorithm:

1. Look at the amount of MONEY HANDED to you by the customer.
2. **If the MONEY HANDED to you by the customer is American, do steps 2.1 to 2.5.**
   2.1. Calculate the Canadian equivalent with the equation:

$$\text{MONEY HANDED} \div 0.72 = \text{CAN EQUIVALENT}$$

   2.2. Look at the PRICE of the book.
   2.3. Calculate the change with the equation:

$$\text{CAN EQUIVALENT} - \text{PRICE} = \text{CHANGE}$$

2.4. Calculate the U.S. equivalent for this change with the equation:

$$\text{CHANGE} \times 0.72 = \text{US EQUIVALENT}$$

2.5. Give the US EQUIVALENT to the customer.

Otherwise, do steps 2.6 to 2.8.

2.6. Look at the PRICE of the book.
2.7. Calculate the change with the equation:

$$\text{MONEY HANDED} - \text{PRICE} = \text{CHANGE}$$

2.8. Give the CHANGE to the customer.

Note that the steps under the "if" instruction are numbered 2.1 through 2.8. This is to indicate that those instructions are part of a decision formulated at step 2. The instructions are indented to serve as a visual aid, to make it clear that these steps are dependent on the "if" instruction in step 2, which is called a ***decision instruction.*** Again note that the variables appear in uppercase in every instruction that refers to their information.

EXERCISES 1.2.3

1. A salesman receives a commission of 10% on all sales if he has sold at least $10,000 worth of merchandise in a given period, but only 8.5% if his sales are below $10,000. Write an algorithm to show him how to figure out his commission.
2. Modify the algorithm you developed in Exercises 1.2.2, 2 so that it will take the following situation into account: On Tuesday the ticket prices are the same for all age groups; on all other days of the week they are as described previously.
3. Construct an algorithm that calculates the quotient a/b if it exists. If the quotient does not exist (i.e., when b is 0), an appropriate message should be produced instead.

The selection structure. This structure is made up of an embedded group of decision structures. An example of the selection structure will be delayed until Example 1.2.12.

The loop structure. Let's look back at Example 1.2.2 to illustrate this concept.

Example 1.2.5

In the example about selling apples, the information in steps 1 through 3 implies that Eric will attempt to sell apples as long as he has not collected $15, unless there are no more neighbors left to visit. Since the computer is unable to make this deduction, it will have to be made into an explicit set of instructions the computer can understand. The loop begins with the instruction shown in bold in this detailed algorithm.

1. **As long as less than $15 has been collected and there are still some neighbors to visit, do steps 1.1 to 1.4.**
   1.1. Go to a neighbor not visited yet.
   1.2. Attempt to sell apples by asking how many apples they want.
   1.3. Count the NUMBER OF APPLES they request.
   1.4. If they buy apples, do steps 1.4.1 to 1.4.4.
      1.4.1. Give them that NUMBER OF APPLES.
      1.4.2. Count the amount of MONEY MADE by doing the arithmetic:

$$\text{NUMBER OF APPLES} \times 30¢ \text{ per apple} = \text{MONEY MADE}$$

      1.4.3. Collect the MONEY MADE.
      1.4.4. Add this MONEY MADE to the rest of the money collected so far.

2. If at least $15 was collected, do step 2.1.
   2.1. Receive allowance from mother, calculated with the equation:

   money collected ÷ 3 = allowance

   Otherwise, do step 2.2.

   2.2. Receive no allowance.

Step 1 in the algorithm above is called a ***loop (repetition) instruction.*** This means that the instructions within it (steps 1.1 to 1.4) are repeated as long as the conditions are met—that is, as long as the money collected is less than $15 **and** there are still neighbors to visit. The loop is terminated when either $15 or more is collected **or** all neighbors have been asked to buy apples. If the former is true, Eric collects his allowance; otherwise, he does not. This is the logic expressed by step 2. Note that step 2.2 must be included or the algorithm would not specify what to do if less than $15 was collected.

EXERCISES 1.2.4

1. Modify the algorithm you developed for Exercise 1.2.2, 4 to accommodate a list of students along with their marks. The algorithm will be used to calculate the final grade of each student. (***Hint:*** Add a loop instruction.)
2. Modify the algorithm you developed for Exercise 1.2.3, 1 to accommodate a list of salesmen along with their sales. Change the algorithm as needed to calculate the commission of all the salesmen.

1.2.4 THE IMPORTANCE OF FOLLOWING A STRICT SYNTAX

The formalization of an algorithm is incomplete if it does not adopt a strict and consistent syntax. Let's look at some guidelines. The algorithm in Example 1.2.5 will be used to illustrate this point.

Use verbs to indicate the actions to be performed. In each instruction, you should use a verb that clearly indicates the action that will be performed in that step. For instance, the verbs "calculate," "look," and "do" indicate specific actions. Use the same verbs consistently to write the same types of instructions.

Use variables to indicate relationships among instructions. Once more, note that variables are used in every instruction where the information they refer to is needed. This is important because variables illustrate the relationships between the instructions. For instance, it is clear that the instructions in steps 1.4.2, 1.4.3, and 1.4.4 in Example 1.2.5 all relate to each other because the variable MONEY MADE is referred to in each. Those three instructions could just as easily have been formulated as shown in Figure 1.2.1. Any reasonably intelligent person would still understand that they relate to each other, but the computer will not see the relationship, because it cannot make the assumptions a reasonably intelligent person can make. The association among the instructions must be made absolutely clear to the computer, by referring to the same variable with the same name in each instruction. Proper use of variables is crucial in programming.

Figure 1.2.1

1.4.2. Count the amount of money given by doing the arithmetic:
   NUMBER OF APPLES × 30¢ per apple
1.4.3. Collect the money.
1.4.4. Add that amount to the money collected so far.

Use variables to generalize an algorithm. This was explained in Subsection 1.2.3, but it can be illustrated again here. Our algorithm for selling apples and collecting an allowance now works only when apples are priced at 30¢ each and when $15 is the total amount that needs to be collected. Variables could be used instead in order to make the algorithm even more flexible and general in use (Figure 1.2.2).

Figure 1.2.2

1. **Ask mother the COST PER APPLE.**
2. **Listen to her answer.**
3. **Ask mother how much MONEY TO COLLECT for the allowance.**
4. **Listen to her answer.**
5. As long as less than MONEY TO COLLECT is collected and there are still some neighbors to visit, do steps 5.1 to 5.4.
   5.1. Go to a neighbor not visited yet.
   5.2. Attempt to sell apples by asking how many apples they want.
   5.3. Count the NUMBER OF APPLES requested.
   5.4. If they buy apples, do steps 5.4.1 to 5.4.4.
      5.4.1. Give them that NUMBER OF APPLES.
      5.4.2. Count the amount of MONEY MADE by doing the arithmetic:

      NUMBER OF APPLES × COST PER APPLE = MONEY MADE

      5.4.3. Collect the MONEY MADE.
      5.4.4. Add MONEY MADE to the money collected so far.
6. If at least MONEY TO COLLECT was collected, do step 6.1.
   6.1. Receive allowance from mother, calculated as:

   money collected ÷ 3 = allowance

   Otherwise, do step 6.2:

   6.2. Receive no allowance.

Look at steps 1 to 4, indicated in bold in Figure 1.2.2. By beginning the algorithm with instructions that ask for the cost per apple and the money to collect, the algorithm can be used for any cost per apple and any money to collect; the algorithm is more generalized. This is a quality good computer programs have.

Use arithmetic and relational operators. This algorithm still can be improved. The instructions in steps 5.2, 5.3, and 5.4 are related to one another; they share information about the number of apples sold to a particular neighbor. Yet no variables are used in steps 5.2 and 5.4 to make this relationship with step 5.3 explicit, hence it would certainly be overlooked by a computer. A similar argument can be made about the instructions in steps 5, 5.4.4, 6, and 6.1. The instructions in these steps all have the amount of money collected in common, but the relationship among these steps is not obvious to a computer. Figure 1.2.3 is a revised algorithm for this problem with all the related instructions made explicit.

Figure 1.2.3

1. Ask mother the COST PER APPLE.
2. Listen to her answer.
3. Ask mother how much MONEY TO COLLECT for the allowance.
4. Listen to her answer.
5. As long as the **MONEY COLLECTED < MONEY TO COLLECT** and there are still some neighbors to visit, do steps 5.1 to 5.4.
   5.1. Go to a neighbor not visited yet.
   5.2. Attempt to sell apples by asking the NUMBER of APPLES the neighbor wants.
   5.3. Count the **NUMBER OF APPLES** they ask for.
   5.4. If **NUMBER OF APPLES > 0,** do steps 5.4.1 to 5.4.4.
      5.4.1. Give them that NUMBER OF APPLES.
      5.4.2. Count the amount of MONEY MADE by doing the arithmetic:

      NUMBER OF APPLES × COST PER APPLE = MONEY MADE

      5.4.3. Collect the MONEY MADE.
      5.4.4. Add MONEY MADE to the **MONEY COLLECTED** so far.
6. If the **MONEY COLLECTED ≥ MONEY TO COLLECT,** do step 6.1.
   6.1. Receive ALLOWANCE from mother, calculated as:

   MONEY COLLECTED ÷ 3 = ALLOWANCE

   Otherwise, do step 6.2:

   6.2. Receive no ALLOWANCE.

Note that relational symbols, such as the less than symbol (<), are used inside some conditions, such as MONEY COLLECTED < MONEY TO COLLECT. This serves to abbreviate the algorithm a little, and makes the algorithm even easier to read. We now have an algorithm that contains many of the ideas used in computer programming. This greatly facilitates its translation into code for a computer program.

EXERCISES 1.2.5

1. Look back at your solutions for the following exercises and revise them if they do not follow a strict syntax as described in this subsection:
   a. Exercises 1.2.3, 2 and 3
   b. Exercises 1.2.4, 1 and 2
2. A Catholic priest's income comes solely from the collection at Sunday mass. Suppose that the following fictional procedure exists to indicate how much money he can keep; the rest of the collection is sent to missionaries. Every week, the priest must report to the bishop the maximum income that he is allowed to keep for that week and verify how much he will keep as income and how much money the missionaries will receive. Here is the algorithm he is accustomed to follow:

   1. As long as the collection bag is not empty and the maximum income is not reached, do step 1.1.
      1.1. If it there is paper money greater than $5, do step 1.2.1.
         1.2.1. Put money in the bag for the missionaries.
         Otherwise, do step 1.2.2.
         1.2.2. Keep it!
   2. Tell the bishop how much money you kept.
   3. Tell the bishop how much the missionaries will receive.

   This priest is so busy that he decides to have his altar boy do this task for him from now on. But he is worried that the boy may misunderstand the procedure, so he asks you to introduce variables and possibly additional instructions (i.e., to formalize the algorithm). Try to generalize the algorithm as much as possible.
3. Generalize the family situation of Exercise 1.2.3, 2 to make it applicable to all families going to the movies, not just the one in the exercise. The theater employee needs to ask his manager for the maximum number of people the theater can seat and for the maximum capacity of the cash register. The employee accepts families until the theater is full or the cash register is full. Work out the algorithm.
4. Judy, a college student, is being offered a summer job by a prospective employer. Before accepting she wants to know how much money the job will bring. The algorithm below shows the steps involved.

   1. Judy asks for the HOURLY RATE of pay.
   2. Judy listens to the answer from the employer.
   3. Then Judy asks for the number of HOURS OF WORK per week.
   4. Judy listens to the answer from the employer.
   5. Judy asks for the number of WEEKS OF WORK offered.
   6. Judy listens to the answer.
   7. Finally Judy takes out her calculator and finds the AMOUNT OF INCOME:
      HOURLY RATE × HOURS OF WORK × WEEKS OF WORK

   Since Judy used variables in the algorithm, it appears to be adequately generalized. Actually it is not. Can you see what still makes it very limited? (***Hint:*** Note the explicit mention of the name "Judy.") Suggest a modification that makes the algorithm more general.

1.2.5 SOME TYPICAL BUSINESS-BASED ALGORITHMS

The problems solved so far are not really typical of the kinds of business problems solved and coded in computers. Now let's now look at some operations often found in business software. These operations could easily be carried out using a spreadsheet software package, for instance. The algorithms presented below for these operations are only briefly explained. You are encouraged to study them carefully before moving on.

Example 1.2.6 Counting the Number of Records

A teacher wants to know how many students she has in her class list and then wants to record that number at the bottom of the list. An algorithm to perform this task is shown below. A variable called a ***counter*** is used to count how many students there are as each record is looked up.

1. Initialize the COUNT OF STUDENTS to 0.
2. As long as the end of the list is not reached, do steps 2.1 to 2.3.
   2.1. Look at the student record.
   2.2. Increase the COUNT OF STUDENTS so far by 1.
   2.3. Go to the next record.
3. Record the COUNT OF STUDENTS at the bottom of the list.

The instruction in step 1 is obvious. No student records have been looked up yet, so the count should start at 0, of course. But remember that the robot teacher or the computer would not know that. So it must be mentioned.

Example 1.2.7 Calculating Averages

A store owner wants to calculate the average number of people coming in the store per day. He has kept track with a list of the number of customers each day for the past four weeks. The average is arrived at by summing up (adding up) the number of customers for each day and then dividing the sum by how many days the list was kept. Therefore the algorithm may go as follows:

1. Start the SUMMATION at 0.
2. Initialize the COUNT OF DAYS summed up to 0.
3. As long as the end of the list is not reached, do steps 3.1 to 3.4.
   3.1. Look at the NUMBER in the list.
   3.2. Add the NUMBER to the SUMMATION.
   3.3. Increase the COUNT OF DAYS summed up so far by 1.
   3.4. Go to the next number.
4. Calculate the AVERAGE with the following formula:

SUMMATION / COUNT OF DAYS

The instructions in steps 1 and 2 are obvious, but again, they must be included for the same reasons mentioned in Example 1.2.6. If you look back at Example 1.2.5, you will see that it involved this same type of summation operation, summing the amount of money made from neighbors. Consequently, its final algorithm lacked one instruction: "The MONEY COLLECTED starts at 0." This instruction should be added to the algorithm before the loop instruction.

Example 1.2.8 Finding the Maximum Number from a List

Now the same store owner wants to know the maximum number of people that came in to the store in one day, and which day it was. The day is identified by its order within the list; for example, day number 20 is the 20th record in the list. The algorithm for this operation is as follows:

1. Assume the MAXIMUM is 0.
2. Assume the DAY OF THE MAXIMUM is day 1.
3. Initialize the COUNT OF DAYS to 0.
4. As long as the end of the list is not reached, do steps 4.1 to 4.4.
   4.1. Look at the NUMBER in the list.
   4.2. If the NUMBER > MAXIMUM so far, do steps 4.2.1 and 4.2.2.
      4.2.1. This NUMBER is now the current MAXIMUM.
      4.2.2. The current DAY OF THE MAXIMUM is now given by COUNT OF DAYS.
   4.3. Increase the COUNT OF DAYS so far by 1.
   4.4. Go to the next number.
5. MAXIMUM is the number desired.

In the first exercise on the next page you will work through this algorithm.

EXERCISES 1.2.6

1. Work through the algorithm presented in Example 1.2.8 line by line using the data in the table at left below. As you do, fill in the table to the right. The first few records (days) have already been filled in for you.

List of Days	
Day Recorded	Number of People
Mon, May 4	6
Tue, May 5	19
Wed, May 6	51
Thu, May 7	44
Fri, May 8	49
Sat, May 9	102
Mon, May 12	28
Tue, May 13	63
Wed, May 14	77
Thu, May 15	30

Fill-in Table			
Count of Days	Number	Maximum	Day of the Maximum
0	none	0	1*
1	6	6	1**
2	19	19	2
3	51	51	3
4	44	51	3
5	49	51	3

*Before starting the algorithm.
**After NUMBER is looked up.

2. The same store owner wants to know the minimum number of people that came in one day and which day it was (for example, the eighth day). Write the algorithm.
3. An algorithm is required to determine the average weight, age, and height of the students at a school. There is a list of students available that includes the name, weight, age, and height of each student in the school. Write the algorithm.
4. At an auto parts store, a record is prepared each day with the total amount of sales for that day and the record for each day is included in a list. Write an algorithm to determine the number of days when total sales were below $1,000.
5. The XYZ Paper Company awards its top salesman of the year with a month's holiday in Bermuda (all expenses paid). XYZ records each salesman's yearly total and salesman number in a list. Each branch office sends these records to the head office, where the winner is picked by computer. Write an algorithm that outlines how the computer finds the winner.

Now let's look at a few more examples.

Example 1.2.9 Real Estate Application

A real estate agent is asked to evaluate the straight-line yearly depreciation of properties given on a list. This list contains the following information for each property: property item number, initial cost of the property, estimated value when it becomes useless (scrap value), and estimated number of years of use of property (years of life). The yearly depreciation is found with the following formula:

$$\text{Yearly Depreciation} = \frac{\text{Initial Cost} - \text{Scrap Value}}{\text{Years of Life}}$$

He is asked to record the yearly depreciation for each property on the list. Below is an algorithm that will help him in his task.

1. As long as the end of the list is not reached, do steps 1.1 to 1.4.
   1.1. Look at the INITIAL COST, the SCRAP VALUE, and the YEARS OF LIFE of the property.
   1.2. Figure out the YEARLY DEPRECIATION with the formula:

   (INITIAL COST – SCRAP VALUE) / YEARS OF LIFE

   1.3. Record this YEARLY DEPRECIATION back on the list.
   1.4. Go to the next property.

Example 1.2.10 Searching a Record in a List

The next day, a property owner comes in and wants to know the yearly depreciation of her property. The real estate agent simply needs to look up her property item number in the list and read off its depreciation. The algorithm may be written as follows:

1. Ask the person for his or her PROPERTY ITEM NUMBER.
2. Look up that PROPERTY ITEM NUMBER in the list.
3. Read off its YEARLY DEPRECIATION.
4. Tell the person the YEARLY DEPRECIATION for his or her property.

Example 1.2.11 Removing Records

The agent's boss asked him to remove all properties with an estimated number of years of use over 100 years and put them in another list called TO SCRAP. All those properties have been bought from the owners by the real estate company and will either be transformed into museums or demolished. All the other properties go in a new list called TO KEEP. The algorithm to do this might be written as follows:

1. Ask the boss the YEARS OF USE OVER for the limit.
2. Listen to his answer.
3. As long as the end of the list is not reached, do steps 3.1 and 3.2.
   - 3.1. Look on the record at the YEARS OF LIFE of the property in the list.
   - 3.2. If the YEARS OF LIFE > YEARS OF USE OVER, do steps 3.2.1 and 3.2.2.
     - 3.2.1. Remove the property from the list.
     - 3.2.2. Put the property in the TO SCRAP list.

     Otherwise, do steps 3.2.3 and 3.2.4.

     - 3.2.3. Remove the property from the list.
     - 3.2.4. Put the property in the TO KEEP list.
   - 3.3. Go to the next record.

EXERCISES 1.2.7

1. Modify the algorithm in Example 1.2.9 so that the agent will also be able to figure out the number of properties found on the list and the average yearly depreciation.
2. The XYZ Paper Company handles exactly 50 different kinds of paper products. They do not produce the paper products themselves, but order them from Japan. Using an algorithm, show the logic involved in the decision to reorder an item when the stock on hand plus that on order is below the reorder point. Each record contains the paper product number, the number on hand, the number on order, and the reorder point. An order report will include all items below the reorder point.
3. Each record in a list contains three entries: an employee name, a rate of pay, and a number of hours worked in the week. Write an algorithm to calculate each employee's pay and then record the paycheck amount back to the list. Overtime occurs when an employee works more than 40 hours in one week and it is paid at time and a half the regular rate. All employees earning over $500 in one week get a bonus equal to 1.8% of their gross pay. A sample of the type of input and output data is as follows:

Employee List

Name	Rate	Hours	Recorded Pay
DOE	5	40	200.00
LUKE	20	60	1425.20
SAM	10	50	559.90
MATT	5	50	275.00

Now let's look at a situation that requires a ***selection*** structure in the algorithm. As mentioned earlier, a selection structure consists of embedded decision structures. Example 1.2.12 below illustrates this.

Example 1.2.12 Classifying Records

Continuing with the real estate records we were working with in Example 1.2.11, the boss further wants to subdivide the TO KEEP list of properties. The properties will be classified according to their initial cost:

- Properties with an initial cost of less than $40,000 will be put in a list called CHEAP.
- Those with an initial cost greater than or equal to $40,000, but less than or equal to $85,000, will be put in a list called AFFORDABLE.
- Those that cost greater than $85,000, but less than or equal to $120,000, will be put in a list called EXPENSIVE.
- Properties with an initial cost greater than $120,000 will be put in a list called LUXURIOUS.

Here is an algorithm that makes this task feasible:

1. As long as the end of the TO KEEP list is not reached, do steps 1.1 and 1.2.
   1.1. Look at the INITIAL COST of the property from the record in the list.
   1.2. If the INITIAL COST < $40,000, do steps 1.2.1 and 1.2.2.
      1.2.1. Remove the property from the TO KEEP list.
      1.2.2. Put the property in the CHEAP list.

      Otherwise, if the INITIAL COST ≥ $40,000 but ≤ $85,000, do steps 1.2.3 and 1.2.4.

      1.2.3. Remove the property from the TO KEEP list.
      1.2.4. Put the property in the AFFORDABLE list.

      Otherwise, if the INITIAL COST > $85,000 but ≤ $120,000, do steps 1.2.5 and 1.2.6.

      1.2.5. Remove the property from the TO KEEP list.
      1.2.6. Put the property in the EXPENSIVE list.

      Otherwise, if the INITIAL COST > $120,000, do steps 1.2.7 and 1.2.8.

      1.2.7. Remove the property from the TO KEEP list.
      1.2.8. Put the property in the LUXURIOUS list.
   1.3. Go to the next record.

The instruction in step 1.2 is a ***selection*** structure. It is called so because the series of decision structures that make it up indicate which list to select for storing the property. Note that it guarantees that one and **only one** pair of instructions 1.2.1 through 1.2.8 will be selected and performed. (Can you explain why?)

A keen reader might notice some redundancy in the algorithm. The instruction starting with "Remove the property" always needs to be done, regardless of the property; so it does not depend on any one of the decision instructions. It can therefore be taken out of them and moved immediately above the instruction in step 1.2.

In the last decision instruction, **if the INITIAL COST > $120,000, do steps 1.2.7 and 1.2.8**, is not needed. It is implied whenever the instructions in steps 1.2.7 and 1.2.8 are reached. (Do you understand why?) These two changes result in the reduced algorithm in Figure 1.2.4. As you can see, the instruction to remove the property from the TO KEEP list (step 1.2.1 in the previous algorithm) has been moved out of the selection structure, and the last condition has been removed from the revised algorithm.

Figure 1.2.4

1. As long as the end of the TO KEEP list is not reached, do steps 1.1 to 1.3.
   1.1. Look at the INITIAL COST of the property in the list.
   1.2. Remove the property from the TO KEEP list.
   1.3. If the INITIAL COST < $40,000, do step 1.3.1.
      1.3.1. Put the property in the CHEAP list.

      Otherwise, if the INITIAL COST ≥ $40,000 but ≤ $85,000, do step 1.3.2.

      1.3.2. Put the property in the AFFORDABLE list.

      Otherwise, if the INITIAL COST > $85,000 but ≤ $120,000, do step 1.3.3.

      1.3.3. Put the property in the EXPENSIVE list.

      Otherwise, do step 1.3.4.

      1.3.4. Put the property in the LUXURIOUS list.

EXERCISES 1.2.8

1. A merchandise company classifies its products by weight as follows:

Class A	Over 12 lbs.
Class B	5 to 12 lbs.
Class C	Less than 5 lbs.

   An employee will use this table to classify a truckload of products. Using an algorithm, show her the logic for determining into which class to place each item, given its weight.

2. Write an algorithm that reads the final grade of the student from Exercise 1.2.2, 4 and then records the letter grade based on the following table:

Final Grade	**Letter Grade**
80 to 100	A
70 to 79	B
60 to 69	C
0 to 59	F

3. A teacher wants to modify the marks obtained in an examination as follows:
   - If the mark is less than or equal to 70, then it is increased by 7%.
   - If the mark is between 71 and 95 inclusive, then it is increased by 3%.
   - Otherwise, there is no change in the mark.
   a. Write an algorithm that reads each student's examination marks and modifies them accordingly.
   b. Using your algorithm, incorporate the solution to modify the mark recorded for the student in question 2 above.

4. A student is accepted into an electronics course if either of the following is true:
   - His or her average is 80 or higher.
   - His or her average is 70 or higher and his or her mark in physics is 90 or higher.

   Write an algorithm that shows how to determine acceptance of freshmen from a list. The list includes the name of a student, the student's average, and his or her physics mark.

5. Each record in an NHL team listing contains the name of an NHL player along with his plus/minus number. The team coach has been asked by the general manager to find how many players are in the negative, positive, or zero plus/minus categories. Write an algorithm that shows the coach what to do.

6. The ABC Insurance Company wants a report produced from their payroll records. One of the fields on the payroll record is the yearly salary field. This company wants to know how many of their employees fall into the following categories:
   a. Yearly salary less than $10,000
   b. Yearly salary greater than or equal to $10,000 and less than $20,000
   c. Yearly salary greater than or equal to $20,000 and less than $45,000
   d. Yearly salary greater than $45,000

   Write the algorithm that shows how to proceed.

7. Write an algorithm to simulate a metric converter. Your algorithm should be able to convert from kilometers to miles, kilograms to pounds, and liters to quarts. The algorithm should first ask for the type of conversion involved, i.e., whether it will be a conversion of distance, weight, or volume. It should then proceed to ask the appropriate metric value and convert it to the correct imperial value. Use the following conversion factors:

   1 kilometer = 0.621388 mile
   1 kilogram = 2.2046 pounds
   1 liter = 0.877193 quarts

8. Each data record in a list of employees contains the following fields: Employee Number, Years' Experience, Position Code, Weekly Pay. Each employee will receive a Christmas bonus based on the following criteria:

Position Code	**Bonus**
1	One week's pay
2	Two weeks' pay, to a maximum of $700
3	One and a half weeks' pay

Employees with more than 10 years' experience are to receive an additional $100; employees with less than two years' experience receive half the usual bonus. Write an algorithm that calculates the Christmas bonuses and records the amount of each back to the list.

9. An accounts receivable department holds a list of customer records that includes the account number, amount due, and date due of total payment. Write an algorithm to compute the total amount due and percentage of the total amount of receivables that are:
   - Less than 30 days past due
   - Past due between 31 and 60 days
   - Past due over 60 days

   Include in your output the number of accounts in each category. The first input value will be today's Julian date (i.e., the day from January 1).

   For example:

Account Number	Amount Due	Date Due
1168	$1495.67	145
2196	$3211.16	15
3485	$1468.12	130
3612	$1896.45	98
7184	$ 5.48	126
8621	$ 965.10	75
9142	$ 613.50	105

   Assuming today's Julian date to be 155, your algorithm should produce the following output:

Accounts Past Due	Number of Accounts	Total Amount Due	Percent of Total Amount
Less than 30 days	3	$2969.27	30.752
30 to 60 days	2	$2509.95	25.995
Over 60 days	2	$4176.26	43.253
	7	$ 9655.48	100.00

1.2.6 SUMMARY: A GENERAL APPROACH TO DEVELOPING AN ALGORITHM

We have seen many algorithms already. For beginners, developing algorithms may still remain puzzling. Unfortunately there is no magic recipe that can be used to derive an algorithm for any situation. However, there are five questions that can be answered for any situation and may help in the development of an algorithm:

1. What is required?
   Indicate the goal of the algorithm or what it produces (i.e., its ***output***).
2. What is available to solve the problem?
   Indicate the information needed to solve the problem (i.e., the ***input*** needed).
3. What calculations are required?
   Indicate the formulas needed.
4. What decisions may need to be made?
   Indicate the *if* instructions (including the ***selection*** ones)
5. What steps are repeated?
   Indicate the instructions involved within a ***loop.***

   For example, here are two situations that automatically require a loop:
   a. When there is information that must be summed up or accumulated or collected.
   b. When data must be counted.

Let's look back at the apple sales in Example 1.2.5 to illustrate how an algorithm can be developed using these questions. First answer each of the five questions listed above for this case.

1. What is required?
   An allowance of one-third of the sales

2. What is available to solve the problem?
   Apples
   Neighbors
3. What calculations are required?
   Count money made from a neighbor
   Count amount of money made so far
4. What decisions may need to be made?
   If enough money has been made
   If there are any more neighbors left to visit
   If the neighbor bought apples
5. What steps are repeated?
   Collect and count amount of money made from a neighbor, if apples were sold
   Add this to the money collected so far

Once you have answered these questions for any situation that requires an algorithm, it should become clearer to you how to go about developing the algorithm. Success is not guaranteed, though—much practice is needed. You will get a lot of practice in this book.

1.2.7 PROBLEM SOLVING WITH MORE COMPLEX SITUATIONS

There are some problems that are too big or too complex to solve by directly using the methods shown in the previous subsections; too many little steps would be required and the programmer would get lost in a web of codes.

For example, consider the following situation. The real estate company mentioned earlier wants to develop a software to achieve the following tasks:

1. Have a menu-driven system that allows the user (an agent or secretary) to select a choice from a list of commands:
   a. Ask the computer to generate a list of all properties for sale. The list would also indicate the number of properties, the properties with the maximum and minimum market value, and the average market value of all the properties.
   b. Generate a list of properties for sale for each of the four groups: cheap properties, affordable properties, expensive properties, and luxurious properties. Each of these lists should also contain the other information as mentioned in (a) above.
   c. Query to find a particular property from any of the four lists.
2. Have a graphical user interface (GUI) so that the user can communicate with the system with a mouse device and the information will be presented in nice colors, with pie graphs, histograms, and other illustrative data types.

A programmer could not code this system directly as we have done so far. Yet the thought process still remains the same, breaking down the problem in more manageable problems and looking at how the parts relate to each other. Notice that many of the tasks demanded in this particular example have already been formulated in the form of an algorithm in Subsection 1.2.5, including counting the number of properties, finding the maximum/minimum, and looking for a particular property. There are only two new tasks to code, creating the GUI and the menu.

Structure charts. Once you have broken down the tasks and recognize what problems need to be solved, it is only a matter of putting the separate algorithms (tasks) you already know how to accomplish together with the new tasks in a way that makes them relate to each other in a logical way. A ***structure chart*** is often used to help illustrate the overall relationships between tasks and make it easier for the viewer to grasp these relationships. The structure chart in Figure 1.2.5 represents the relationships between tasks in our problem.

Each rectangle represent a task. This chart shows that the system will need to be partitioned into two smaller subsystems: the "GUI" and the "Menu." However, it looks like the menu subsystem will still be too big, so it will be partitioned in three smaller, more manageable portions: the "List," the "List by groups" and the "Look up" programs. The algorithms for "count," "average," and "max/min" exist already, and will constitute the three partitions of the subsystems "List" and "List by groups."

Figure 1.2.5

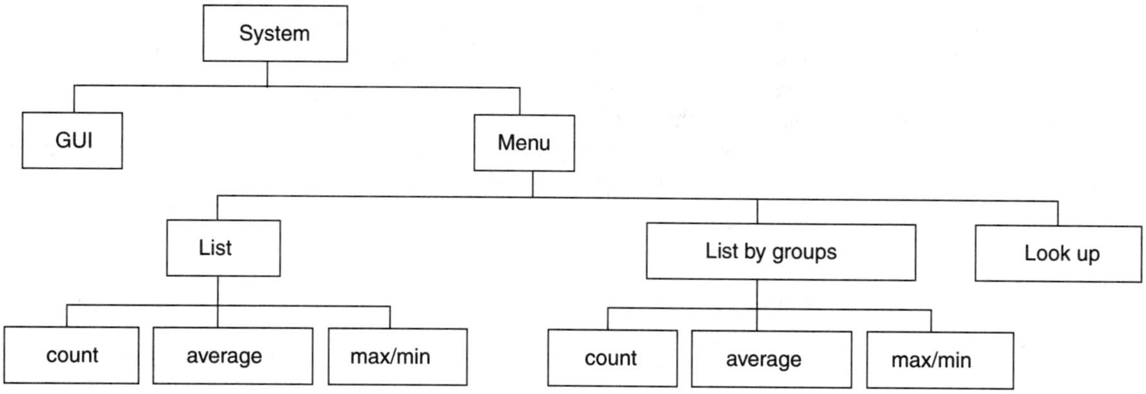

Once this structure chart is set up, it is a matter of developing all the algorithms, starting with the smallest subsystems and then moving up to the bigger ones by putting the smaller ones together. This way, eventually you can put the whole system together, and get the program up and running. You will see in Chapters 10, 11, and 12 how structure charts are used to help partition a big task into smaller ones, and you will learn how to put together small C programs, which will be lots of fun!

Programming teams. The particular problem at hand here has now become so big that the development of the algorithms and programs are only one of the many phases of development of the system. At this level of complexity, many people are involved in the development, not just a single programmer. These other people may be department managers, company employees, business owners, and so forth. Even though these people may have a limited knowledge of software development, they need to be involved because they are the ones who will use the system in the end. The key problem-solving decisions are now made by ***systems analysts,*** not programmers. Systems analysts study what the users want, set up the big picture (e.g., structure charts), and then hand down the work of coding to programmers.

All the activities briefly discussed in this subsection make up what is called the ***systems analysis and design*** of a system. Many books are written every year on this topic and some may be found at your local library or college library, or you may be interested enough in the subject to take a course to learn more about it.

1.3 TOOLS REQUIRED TO WRITE COMPUTER PROGRAMS

1.3.1 CREATING THE COMPUTER PROGRAM

A skill brought up in Section 1.2, the ability to follow proper syntaxes of coding, deals with the use of codes from a computer language to change an algorithm into a workable computer program, or in other words, the translation of the algorithm into a computer program. The specific syntaxes used depend on the programming language selected. For example, BASIC, Clipper, and C all have different syntaxes. Unlike algorithms, the instructions must follow **precise** rules, dictated by the chosen programming language. The ability to follow proper syntaxes is an important skill that will be reinforced throughout this book.

Once the translation is complete, the programmer typically creates the computer program using a type of software called an ***editor.*** Most C compiler packages today provide their own editor.

1.3.2 TRANSLATION OF THE COMPUTER PROGRAM INTO MACHINE CODE

The next step is to translate the program into machine code. To do this, you need some knowledge of machine language, assembler language, compilers, and linkers. Each of these are introduced on the next page with a brief explanation of what they do.

Machine language. Strictly speaking, the computer does not understand a computer program, whether it is written in Pascal, Clipper, FORTRAN, or C. This is because the instructions in those languages, although in code form, still contain some words of the English language, which the computer does not understand. The only language the computer understands is ***machine language.*** The programmer must therefore translate the program that he or she wrote into machine language so the computer can recognize the codes.

For instance, the following simple program, written in the C computer language, displays the message "Hello" to the screen when executed:

```
#include <stdio.h>

main()
{
   printf("Hello");
}
```

At this time, you are not expected to understand how the program works. But you can recognize some of the words as being actual words in the English language. Now look at the same program translated into the shortest amount of code in machine language that a programmer could come up with for that program (when run on the MS-DOS operating system):

```
BA 01 0D B4 09 CD 21 B4 4C B0 00 CD 21 48 65 6C 6C 6F 0D 0A 24
```

Needless to say, you cannot readily recognize any of this seemingly meaningless sequence of digits and letters. Don't worry, you are not expected to understand it. The purpose of this illustration is to show that machine coding is dreadful, even to the best programmers in the world, and therefore is rarely attempted.

Assembler language. Because it was apparent how difficult direct machine coding was a long time ago, a software translator called an ***assembler*** was invented. The assembler freed programmers from having to code in machine language. All they had to do was write an assembly program. For instance, here is an assembly program (for the MS-DOS operating system) that does the same thing as the C program above:

```
SEGMENT   COM    WORD PUBLIC 'CODE'
ASSUME    CS:COM, DS:COM, ES:COM, SS:COM
          ORG          100H
ENTRY:    MOV          DX, OFFSET MSG
          MOV          AH, 9
          INT          21H
          MOV          AH, 4CH
          MOV         AL, 0
          INT         21H
MSG       DB          "Hello", 13, 10, '$'
ENDS
END       ENTRY
```

Even though this program consists of some familiar English words, like *WORD* and *MOV*e, it still remains obscure—and long. This level of programming is therefore called ***low-level programming,*** as opposed to ***high-level programming,*** like Pascal or BASIC programming.

Clearly, translation into machine codes is tedious and error prone. Assembly coding is better in comparison but it is still unfriendly and assumes the programmer knows computer architecture well.

Compilers. A software program called a ***compiler*** was then later invented to let the programmer code using a friendly computer language—a high-level language—rather than assembly language. The compiler translates a program like the C program above into machine codes automatically. (Strictly speaking, the C language allows ***mid-level programming***, not high-level).

For the sake of illustration, the screen in Figure 1.3.1 shows the user interface seen with the Borland C compiler.

Figure 1.3.1

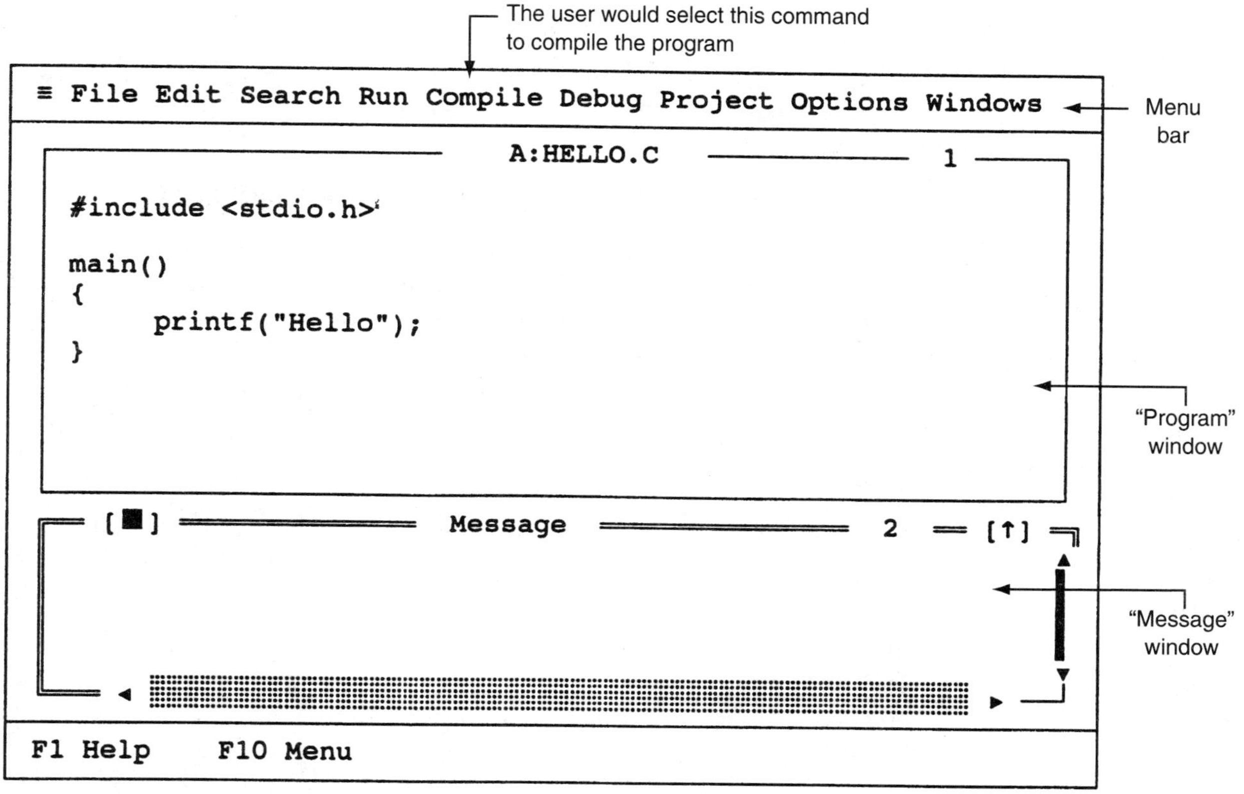

There are two windows in the user interface screen:

1. The "program" window (an editor), shown here with a C program called HELLO.C in it. This is the name of the file in which the program is stored; the file is on a diskette.
2. The "message" window may hold various compilation warnings or errors messages. For example, if the compiler finds something wrong with the program when the user compiles it, information about the error will be displayed in the message window.

The request for compilation is issued with the menu command **Compile**. At this time, you are not required to understand any other parts of this interface other than what has been explained in this subsection.

Linkers. Quite often, another type of software is needed to complement the task of the compiler. This is known as the ***linker***. In most cases, the compiler alone is unable to translate a program completely. A more detailed explanation of compilers and linkers is in Section 1.4.

In summary, you should know that a good ***C compiler package*** now comes with the following types of software:

- An editor to type the program in a file.
- A compiler to translate the program in machine code.
- A linker to complete the translation, when necessary.
- A loader to run the program.
- And, as you shall see, many other goodies!

1.3.3 RUNNING THE PROGRAM

The steps used to run a program differ from one compiler package to another, but running a program basically means loading it into the computer memory from the disk or diskette where it is stored. In Borland C, the user selects the **Run** menu command.

1.4 CAPABILITIES AND LIMITATIONS OF COMPILERS*

This section is devoted to an explanation of how compilers and linkers work and will discuss their capabilities and limitations. This discussion will be useful because if you aspire to become a good C programmer, you should acquire some basic knowledge about how compilers and linkers work and understand their limitations.

1.4.1 HOW COMPILERS AND LINKERS WORK—AN ANALOGY

Since the novice computer user is unlikely ever to have used a compiler, let alone having pondered what makes it tick, analogies will be used to explain how it works instead. Remember that this analogy is meant to explain the functionality of compilers in general, not just those used in C. Also remember that it is an **analogy**, not a similarity. Recall that a compiler and a linker are software tools that team up to translate a program into machine language. The series of examples below will illustrate the functionality of compilers and linkers.

Example 1.4.1

Recall Example 1.2.3, the one with the bookstore clerk. Suppose that one morning his manager gave him the following two instructions to follow as each customer comes to the counter with a purchase:

1. The customer reads off the COST for her purchase.
2. She pays that COST.

These instructions are quite easy to follow, unless the clerk is unable to read English. Assume the clerk is French. Luckily the store has a machine (an automatic language translator) that can do the translation. The analogy here is that this machine is a compiler and a linker, French is the computer machine language, and the algorithm is the program, as shown in Figure 1.4.1.

Figure 1.4.1

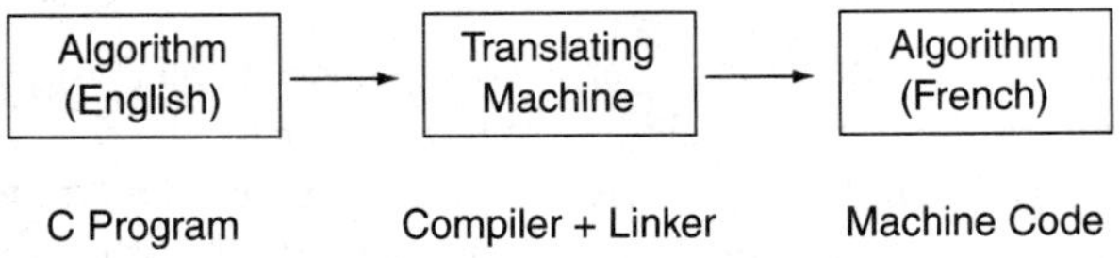

Let's use this translating machine to illustrate how compilers and linkers work. Here are the two steps that the machine performs to translate the instructions:

1. Once the instructions are fed into the machine, they are broken down according to English grammar—according to the grammar of the programming language in the case of computers—to verify that the instructions follow the grammar correctly:

The customer	reads off	the COST for her purchase
She	pays	that COST
Subject	Verb	Direct Object

   The machine is able to break down the instructions, since it knows that "reads off" and "pays" are verbs. Therefore these verbs are said to be ***built in*** to the compiler. The proper conjugation of the verbs is also checked.
2. The words are then translated into French:

Le client	lit	le PRIX de son achat
Elle	paie	ce PRIX
Subject	Verb	Direct Object

*Subsections 1.4.1 and 1.4.2 may be skipped if you already have some experience with compilers and linkers.

It should be noted that actual automatic language translators function on a much more complex level than these two steps indicate. However, you should understand that the analogy needs to be kept simple in order to be effective.

Example 1.4.2

This example shows that sometimes two more steps are needed to fully translate a sentence from English to French. Suppose the instructions the manager gave to the bookstore clerk were written as follows:

1. The customer verifies the COST for her purchase.
2. She pays that COST.

To translate these sentences, the machine still proceeds to break down the instructions first, to check the grammar the same way as illustrated above in step 1. However, the translating machine does not have unlimited knowledge of words—this is especially true of real compilers. For instance, suppose it does not know the verb "verifies" because this verb is not built in to the compiler.

The machine proceeds with the translation anyway (step 2), except that the verb "verifies" cannot be translated yet because the compiler does not know it.

Le client	<u>verifies</u>	le PRIX de son achat
Elle	paie	ce PRIX
Subject	Verb	Direct Object

Therefore two additional steps are needed to terminate the translation:

3. The provider of the instructions must also include the English conjugation rules of the verb "verifies" and their French translations. A sample of the information that needs to be provided to the translating machine is as follows:

English Verb Conjugation: "verify"

Present Tense	Past Tense	Future Tense
verify	verified	will verify
verify	verified	will verify
verifies	verified	will verify
verify	verified	will verify
verify	verified	will verify
verify	verified	will verify

French Translation: "vérifier"

Present Tense	Past Tense	Future Tense
vérifie	vérifiais	vérifierai
vérifies	vérifiais	vérifieras
vérifie	vérifiait	vérifiera
vérifions	vérifiions	vérifierons
vérifiez	vérifiiez	vérifierez
vérifient	vérifiaient	vérifieront

4. Then the machine **links** this definition with the incomplete translation:

Le client	vérifie	le PRIX de son achat
Elle	paie	ce PRIX

The translation is now complete.

Steps 3 and 4 are performed by the ***linker.*** Once this process is done, the translation is complete. Note that the compiler does not know about this link taking place—the compiler is only involved in steps 1 and 2. This observation is important because it limits the error-checking capabilities of compilers, and that is the subject of the next subsection.

1.4.2 ERROR-CHECKING CAPABILITIES—AN ANALOGY

Let us now look at the error-checking capabilities and limitations that compilers tend to have. As mentioned before, automatic language translators really are quite sophisticated. Compilers, on the other hand, are primitive in comparison and have a much smaller vocabulary. Let's look at some different types of errors they may be able to detect and others that they may not be unable to detect, still using our analogy.

Example 1.4.3

Compilers do well at checking for misspellings. For example, the following instructions show misspelled words underlined:

1. The costomer reads off the COST for her purshace.
2. She pays that COST.

Any compiler can detect simple spelling errors like these.

Example 1.4.4

Consider now a more difficult situation. Suppose the instructions are written as follows:

1. The customer verify the COST for her purchase.
2. She pay that COST.

Remember that we had assumed that the verb "verify" is not built in to the compiler. Therefore, it is impossible for it to realize that "verify" is conjugated incorrectly in the first instruction, yet it is able to do so for the verb "pay," since that word is built in to the compiler. In computer terms, this means that the first instruction would fail, even though the compiler would **not** have flagged an error! This kind of situation happens a lot with C programming.

Example 1.4.5

This example contains syntactic errors as underlined:

1. Reads off the customer the COST her purchase.
2. She pays, that COST.

In the first instruction, the subject and the verb are reversed and the word "for" is missing before the word "her." The second instruction contains a comma where none should be. Compilers are able to check for syntactic errors and correct them quite well.

Unfortunately, compilers fall short at checking ***semantics***, which pertains to the meaning of the words. It is necessary to check the semantics in order to verify the relationship between objects, which then makes it easier to check that proper grammar has been used. All compilers are capable of some semantic checking, but with limited capacity. Consider the examples below.

Example 1.4.6

Here is a type of semantic error few compilers are capable of detecting:

1. The customer reads off the COST for his purchase.
2. She pays that COST.

The words "his" and "she" conflict in gender. Compilers are largely unable to see relationships between instructions; therefore any relationship must be made explicit by the use of carefully chosen variables.

Example 1.4.7

An equally difficult type of error to detect is the following:

1. The customer reads off the COST for her purchase.
2. She pays that amount.

Most compilers, if not all, are unable to realize that the word "amount" refers to the COST. The use of the variable COST would eliminate this ambiguity, which is why the second instruction should be written as follows:

2. She pays that COST.

For this reason, you can see that the importance of choosing variables carefully cannot be emphasized too much.

Example 1.4.8

As a final example, many compilers are unable to detect the kind of error in the first instruction below:

1. The <u>cloud</u> reads off <u>the customer</u>.
2. She pays that COST.

The first instruction makes no sense at all, but the grammar is still correct. Compilers are incapable of understanding the context of an algorithm; **it only does what the programmer tells it to do**. Remember this!

The analogies in this subsection should serve to make you realize that computer languages do not understand English words too well and they do not understand English grammar at all. Furthermore, compilers cannot guess what the programmer wants to do unless he codes the instructions according to the strict grammar and rules dictated by the computer language.

1.4.3 A FEW CAUTIONS ABOUT C COMPILERS

The C programming language has many similarities to high-level languages like BASIC or Pascal. They all are third-generation languages, all allow for structured programming, and all are capable of general-purpose programming.

These similarities are somewhat deceiving, however. BASIC was developed as a tool for programming business applications (usually by beginners). Pascal was developed for educational purposes, to teach computer users how to program, and therefore it is a language that is still directed toward beginners. The C language was developed by engineers at the AT&T Bell Laboratories in the early 1970s. It was intended to be used by knowledgeable programmers and engineers, and was never meant for beginners. Now in the 1990s the C programming language has become popular in the business world. Consequently it tends to the language of choice for a first programming course in colleges and universities.

The emergence of C in the business world may give the impression to the novice programmer that the C language is just as capable and friendly at developing business applications with relatively ease as are Clipper, FoxPro, and numerous other packages. But this is not so, because C originated in a engineering environment and was never meant to be used in a business setting. More importantly, it was never designed to be used by beginners.

The C compiler is consequently not designed for the beginner either. It is more primitive than other compilers in that it does not assist the programmer as much in detecting errors. This is why the language is classified as mid-level, not high-level. To give you a feel for C's weaknesses at detecting errors, let's go back to the same analogy we used in Subsections 1.4.1 and 1.4.2.

Example 1.4.9

As mentioned previously, all compilers are capable of some semantic checking, but their capacity for finding this type of error is limited. For example, many compilers would be able to detect the errors in the following set of instructions:

1. The customer <u>read</u> off the COST for her purchase.
2. She <u>pay</u> that COST.

However, it is unlikely that a C compiler would detect these errors. This is because the C compiler does not know many verbs—only a few are built in to the compiler. This implies that the linker will likely end up linking the wrong conjugation of "read" and "pay," which could lead to having the translated instructions interpreted incorrectly. In computer terms, the program would fail, yet the compiler would not have served a warning.

Example 1.4.10

Consider the following instructions:

1. The customers reads off the COST for her purchase.
2. They pays that COST.

These grammatical errors will likely remain undetected by the C compiler, again because it knows only a few verbs, so it is unable to check whether the subject and the verb agree properly.

Example 1.4.11

Another example that would be difficult for the C compiler to detect is as follows:

1. Reads off the customer the COST for her purchase.
2. She pays that COST.

Here the subject and verb are switched in the first instruction, yet there are some C compilers that might not be able to detect these kinds of obvious errors. Some C compilers have weak type-checking. However, most do very well.

The verbs in C that are not built in are called ***functions.*** It is important to point out that some C compiler packages are better than others at helping the user detect errors, even though they may all follow the ANSI C standard. For example, the C++ compiler packages, which all include an ANSI C compiler, do well checking errors. There will be more about the C++ programming language in the next subsection.

But even ANSI C compiler packages are not always totally compatible. Many functions provided by those packages are not guaranteed ANSI C functions, such as those used to display geometric figures or to control the screen. However, many functions provided **are** guaranteed ANSI C. All the functions that will be covered in the book are in that group—they are located in what is called the ***standard libraries.*** You will learn more about standard libraries in Section 12.4.

The point is that learning structured programming using the C language is tricky—it is much more than simply being able to understand the development of algorithms, which was covered in Section 1.2. You will need to understand some details about the C compiler in order to help it do what it does not bother to check itself. Luckily this book recognizes this challenge and provides numerous sections that list common errors and traps to alert you to problems and pitfalls in C programming.

In summary, C programming presents two major challenges to the novice programmer:

1. The error-checking capabilities are limited. For the most part, C compilers are capable of checking only misspelling and incorrect syntax.
2. The compiler knows few verbs, so it is unable to check if the instructions make sense or not. The C functions *printf()* and *scanf()* that will be covered in Chapter 2 are two examples that can often cause problems. Numerous times the C compiler will report no errors or problems with a program using these functions, yet the program fails. In this book, you will be warned whenever those situations may occur. Since the compiler is not smart, the programmer will have to be!

Novice programmers—even those with a background in programming—feel vulnerable when faced with a C program that fails badly for no apparent reason. This book realizes this vulnerability and helps you before it turns into frustration. This book respects your learning process whereas many other books tend to emphasize respect for the power of the C language instead.

Look at the information in Table 1.4.1. It lists only a sample of verbs and keywords provided by various computer languages.

In the C language column, strictly speaking, **none** of the input or output verbs are built in to the compiler. So they really should not be in the table at all. But those verbs (and numerous others) have become part of the standard "equipment" that now is included with all ANSI C compilers. In

Table 1.4.1

Operation	Computer Language					
	C	**Pascal**	**BASIC**	**FORTRAN**	**COBOL**	**Clipper**
Input Verbs	scanf() getc() getchar() gets() fscanf()	READ READLN GET	INPUT READ/ DATA GET	READ/ FORMAT	READ ACCEPT	INPUT @ GET MENU TO FREAD ()
Processing Verbs	if/else for while do = strcpy() strstr()	IF/ELSE FOR WHILE REPEAT :=	IF/ELSE FOR = INT() INSTR()	IF/ELSE DO WHILE/ DO = INT()	IF/ELSE PERFORM = MOVE STRING	IF/ELSE DO WHILE = SUBSTR()
Output Verbs	printf() putchar() puts() fprintf() putc()	WRITE WRITELN PUT	PRINT PRINT/ USING PUT	WRITE/ FORMAT PRINT	WRITE DISPLAY	? @ SAY FWRITE()

fact this provision has become part of the ANSI C standard. Only some of the processing verbs (very few of them) are truly built in to the C language.

In Pascal, BASIC, FORTRAN, COBOL, and Clipper compilers, **all** the verbs are built in. So it is to be expected that these compilers are much more capable of detecting errors than C compilers—and this is a fact. Nevertheless, among these languages, C is the language of choice today. Why? There are many reasons, and we will look at some of them in the subsection below.

1.4.4 WHY LEARN C?

You may find the information in the previous subsection rather discouraging and may be about to close the book and give up on learning C programming. This would be premature decision, as this subsection explains.

There are many good reasons for learning C, and the following is a list of just a few of them:

1. Although it is a mid-level language, C is more flexible than high-level programming languages in that it offers many more functions than other languages (as Table 1.4.1 suggests). This means a wider variety of program types may be written using C. For example, Clipper or COBOL should only be used for business applications.
2. C is more efficient in that it interfaces easily with low-level programming such as bit manipulations, assembly language programming, and direct communication with the hardware. All these are possible because the semantics of C are closer to machine language. It must be remarked that some of these capabilities involve non-ANSI C standard programming.
3. C is increasingly being used for business, engineering, and scientific applications.
4. C is widely available to anyone. It can be run on most microcomputers, which are becoming more affordable.
5. C programs are portable from one machine to another. It is only a matter of recompiling the program on the receiving machine, if that machine runs with a different operating system. However, this benefit is no longer guaranteed when the program contains non-ANSI C codes.
6. On the one hand, the learning curve for C may be steep, as the previous two subsections suggest. On the other hand, knowing C programming will give you a respectable "status." Contrary to what some C book authors may claim, it is **not** easy to learn C and **not** everyone can learn it (at least to a level of effectiveness acceptable in the real world).

7. It has many of the same characteristics as other friendlier computer languages like Clipper or BASIC. So in that respect, it makes no difference which one to select, but because of all the advantages, it is better to learn C.

The emergence of object-oriented software development packages have taken some attention away from C (or C++), but C still remains the third-generation language of choice.

1.4.5 WHY NOT LEARN C++ INSTEAD (OR FIRST)?

It is clear that C++ is gaining popularity in the academic world and in business and industry. Without going into details, here is a sample of reasons that favor C++:

1. C++ is a superset of the C language. This means that one can write C programs using a C++ compiler, but the reverse is almost impossible. C++ supports all the features of C, plus much more, hence the ++ after the C. It is possible to learn and use C using a C++ compiler.
2. C++ detects more errors than a C compiler.
3. C++ offers relatively user-friendly objects, as opposed to their function counterparts in C. Less technical computer knowledge is needed to program in C++ when those objects are used. These objects can be included in a C program, but then the program is no longer a C program, but rather a "better C" program with C++ features in it.
4. C++ allows programming at a more abstract level, which makes possible the creation of programs that are more general in use by the introduction of data abstraction. This approach to programming is called ***object-oriented programming (OPP)*** and can be considered a "higher level" of programming than C.

These attractive advantages make it easy to conclude that, yes, C++ should or could be learned first. Some highly skilled professionals with a good deal of expertise, such as researchers and university professors, share this opinion. As a college educator, however, I still believe that learning C++ first is a mistake for these reasons:

1. Because the main power of C++ (and what differentiates it from C) is its ability to write abstract programs using OPP, all books on C++ necessarily cover all the techniques and features surrounding OPP, such as building objects. Unfortunately, numerous concepts need to be explained to do this—and those concepts are not simple, to say the least. In comparison, the concepts you need to learn in order to program in C are simpler and less numerous.
2. The demand for C programmers will remain steady—not all programming is becoming OPP, and will not for some time yet.
3. Teaching "better C," as mentioned in (3) in the list of advantages of C++ above, seems like a good compromise. However, it gives you the impression that "better C" is in fact C, and this would be a mistake from the point of view of computer education. Also, as stated above, there is still a lot of demand for C programming, so programmers are still expected to know the features of C anyway.
4. In addition, instruction in "better C" teaches the student to use objects, not to build them. As reason (1) in this list infers, learning C++ means learning to **build** objects. So learning "better C" is not at all the same as learning C++.
5. C++ compilers are not readily or widely available in all well-known operating systems environment, such as VMS under VAX.
6. Referring back to (1) in the list of reasons that favor C++, it seems to suggest that one might as well learn C++, since C is part of it. Then (2) in that same list leads us to conclude that a C++ compiler detects more errors in a C program than a C compiler would. However, this is **not** so—a C++ compiler only detects more errors in a **C++** program—its compiler does not know any more about the functions used in C programs than a C compiler.

The point is made. True, programming in C++ is more flexible and perhaps more interesting than programming in C, but these are only advantages if the learning process is enjoyable and tailored to your readiness to process the information. It will do no good for you to switch to learning C++ instead of using this book to learn C programming, for instance, and then be overwhelmed by the material required to learn C++.

Still undecided whether to learn C or C++? Let me give you some arguments from my own experience:

1. To a novice who has never programmed before, learning C++ first would be strenuous and frustrating and really impossible.
2. To a person with programming knowledge, but no experience in C, learning C++ first would be a definite challenge but might be possible (just perhaps) only if the student has a good inclination toward programming in the first place.
3. To an experienced programmer, but one not knowledgeable in C, learning C++ first would be interesting, maybe even more so than C, but it would not be any easier.

Let's hope these arguments have convinced you to give the C programming language a chance. The next chapter will introduce you to some of the basic functions of C, and you can see for yourself that the reasons and advantages given here for learning C hold true.

2 Input/Output Operations

OBJECTIVES

This chapter introduces you to the following information:

- The function *scanf()*, the most typical function employed to read data from the keyboard into a program. You will learn how to read numbers.
- The function *printf()*, the most typical function employed to display numbers, messages, and text to the screen.
- The codes used to display data to the screen in different formats.
- A typical function used for reading data from a file.
- A typical function used for storing data and text in a file.

INTRODUCTION

Input/output operations allow the user to interact with a program and they handle user files as well. These are the most essential kinds of operations so we will cover them first. Input/output operations in C are provided by functions. Unfortunately these functions are difficult to program and use, essentially due to the compiler's limited error-checking capabilities with functions, which was mentioned in Chapter 1. A lot of things can easily go wrong, and the reader will be warned of the many pitfalls. Learning about the functions used to control input/output operations will require you to absorb a lot of technical information that may seem complicated, but it is necessary to understand the operations.

Chapter 2 does not emphasize problem solving as much as some technical details of the language, which will hit some readers like a cold shower! However, once you pick up the basic skills here, you will be prepared for later chapters that emphasize problem solving and program development. This chapter will guide you carefully through the technical maze.

2.1 DISPLAYING MESSAGES WITH *printf()*

2.1.1 THE *printf()* STATEMENT

It's time to write our first C program. It simply will display a message to the screen when it is run.

Example 2.1.1

We are going to write a C program that produces the following message to the screen:

Hello. Salut. Ciao.

The program below does this. The superscript numbers after each line refer to the *Explanations* that follow, and are not part of the program.

```
#include <stdio.h>[1]

main()[2]
{[3]
      printf("Hello. Salut. Ciao.");[4]
}[3]
```

Explanations

1. All C functions are located in special computer files called ***libraries.*** When a program needs to call a C function, such as *printf()* here, the directive *#include <stdio.h>* must be present at the **very top** of the program. This is called a ***preprocessor directive*** and it enables the compiler to find the function *printf()* in the proper library. This command is required for numerous other C functions, such as *scanf()*. Every single program in this book will need it.
2. The word *main()* marks the beginning of the C code. The parentheses to the right of *main* are always required.
3. The open and close braces, { and }, are always necessary and must surround the code (here a single *printf()* call).
4. *printf()* is called a ***function.*** It is used to display a message such as some ordinary text. This message must be surrounded with **double** quotation marks. The *printf()* ***statement*** consists of everything up to but **excluding** the semicolon. Figure 2.1.1 summarizes the syntax of the *printf()* statement.

Figure 2.1.1

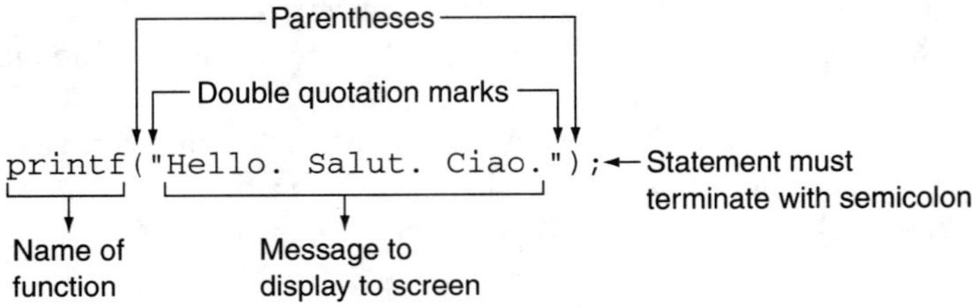

Note that the name of the function *printf()* must be in lowercase letters; this applies to *main()* and *#include* also. This is because all C compilers are ***case sensitive:*** lowercase and uppercase letters are **not** considered the same.

When you run this program, the compiler may give a warning message saying that a *return* statement is needed. Do not be concerned, because this message will never prevent any one of your programs or any of the ones in this book from running normally. However, should you prefer to avoid this message every time, then insert the line in bold type below at the end of all the C programs:

```
#include <stdio.h>

main()
{
      printf("Hello. Salut. Ciao.");
      return (0);
}
```

You do not need to understand the *return* statement at this time. It will be covered in Section 10.4.

EXERCISES 2.1.1

Every *printf()* below contains at least one error. Identify each error.

1. `print "Hello there."`
2. `printf('Hello you');`
3. `Printf("Tic tac toe");`

A C program may consist of multiple statements, and every one must be terminated with a semicolon. To illustrate, consider the example below.

Example 2.1.2

Let's write a program to display the three lines below:

Cze the future!
I C C there
So C now. Don't be a CC

Three calls to a *printf()* function should do the job:

```
#include <stdio.h>

main()
{
      printf("Cze the future!");
      printf("I C C there");
      printf("So C now. Don't be a CC");
}
```

This seems simple enough, but surprisingly here is the resulting display when you run this program:

Cze the future!I C C thereSo C now. Don't be a CC

All three *printf()* statements output their message on the same line. This happens because *printf()* never skips to a new line unless you tell it to do so. A special escape sequence coded for that purpose is explained in the next subsection.

2.1.2 SOME USEFUL ESCAPE SEQUENCES

The problem encountered in the program above is fixed with the use of an ***escape sequence.*** There are various such sequences. This subsection only covers some of the more commonly used escape sequences.

How to skip to a new line. Each *printf()* in the program above simply needs to be told to move the cursor to the next line after each statement's message is displayed:

```
#include <stdio.h>

main()
{
      printf("Cze the future!\n");
      printf("I C C there\n");
      printf("So C now. Don't be a CC\n");
}
```

The *\n* after each of the statements you want to print to screen tells each *printf()* to move the cursor to the next line after its message is displayed. The symbol \ is an ***escape character.*** Technically *\n* tells the compiler to escape from what *n* usually means (which would simply be to display the letter *n*) and instead *n* means go to a new line. Note that there must not be any space between the \ and the *n*.

The *\n* need not be at the end of the message. It may be anywhere within it as long as the end result is the one desired. For instance, consider the example below.

Example 2.1.3

The program below produces the exact same output as the previous program, yet each *\n* is placed in a different location within the messages:

```
#include <stdio.h>

main()
```

```
{
     printf("Cze the future!");
     printf("\nI C C there\n");
     printf("So C now. Don't be a CC\n");
}
```

Can you see why it produces the same output?

Example 2.1.4

Because the escape sequence *\n* may be placed anywhere within the double quotation marks, all three lines may be displayed using a single *printf()* statement:

```
#include <stdio.h>

main()
{
    printf("Cze the future!\nI C C there\nSo C now. Don't be a CC\n");
}
```

The *\n* after each of the phrases that will print to screen instructs the computer to display each phrase on a new line.The disadvantage here is that the message given to *printf()* is now quite long and it is harder to read.

EXERCISES 2.1.2

1. Is there anything wrong with the statement below?

   ```
   printf(\n"That's it");
   ```

2. Write a program to display the following message exactly:

   The latest estimate of the earth's area
   place the fertile regions
   at 33,000,000 "s.m.".

   Write the program in two different ways:
   a. Use three *printf()* statements.
   b. Use only one *printf()* statement.
3. Use one *printf()* statement to display the following title:

   Project #1
   Title: "Working with C"
   Year: 1998

4. Use six *printf()* statements to display the message in Example 2.1.4 exactly the same as it appeared in the example.

A useful application of *\n* is for double spacing a message that takes up several lines. Simply use two *\n* escape sequences in a row to produce the double spacing, as shown in the example below.

Example 2.1.5

The program below displays the same message as in Example 2.1.4, but double spaced:

```
#include <stdio.h>

main()
{
    printf("Cze the future!\n\nI C C there\n\nSo C now. Don't be a CC\n");
}
```

The double \n escape sequences between the phrases will cause the program to skip a line, so the output will be double spaced:

Cze the future!

I C C there

So C now. Don't be a CC

How to display double quotation marks. Displaying a double quotation mark as part of the message requires the use of an escape sequence as well. To see why, consider the example below.

Example 2.1.6

Let us write a program to display the message:

Celine Dion sings "Falling into You" in concert

The solution seems simple:

```
#include <stdio.h>

main()
{
      printf("Celine Dion sings "Falling into You" in concert");
}
```

Yet the compiler will complain at the double quotation marks **within** the message to be displayed because it is confused as to which one of the double quotation marks actually terminates the message. To avoid this ambiguity, simply precede the conflicting double quotation mark with a backslash as shown below:

```
printf("Celine Dion sings \"Falling into You\" in concert");
```

As mentioned previously, the prefix \ is called an escape character and technically indicates to the compiler to escape from what a particular character usually means (i.e., the double quotation mark means the end of the message) and display it to the screen instead. Then the rest of the message is displayed normally. Note that there must not be any space between \ and ".

How to display a percent sign. Displaying a percent sign as part of the message also requires the use of an escape sequence. To see how, consider the example below.

Example 2.1.7

Suppose we wish to display the following message:

The notation 25% means 25 percent

You first might write a simple program:

```
#include <stdio.h>

main()
{
      printf("The notation 25% means 25 percent");
}
```

Surprisingly, although the compiler will not complain, this program will not run properly. For instance, the output might come out as follows:

The notation for 25

The rest of the message would be missing. Some compilers might display the whole message, but leave out the percent symbol:

The notation for 25 means 25 percent

The reason for this weird behavior is that the symbol % bears a special meaning when used within *printf()*, which will be explained more completely in the next section. For now, just be aware that simply putting the symbol % in a program message will not display the percent sign. If you want to display a percent sign in an output line, its special meaning must be cancelled with the \ escape character, as shown below:

```
printf("The notation 25\% means 25 percent");
```

The prefix \ technically indicates to the compiler to escape from what % usually means and to display the character % to the screen instead. There must not be any space between \ and %.

Another way to cancel the special meaning of % is to put two percent symbols next to each other:

```
printf("The notation 25%% means 25 percent");
```

EXERCISES 2.1.3

1. Is there anything wrong with the statement below?

   ```
   printf("That"s it");
   ```

   Discuss the difference between the statement above and the following statement:

   ```
   printf("that''s it");
   ```

2. Write a C program that calls a single *printf()* for each line below:

   The contracted form of "I do not" is "I don't"
   Lucy got 91% on her test.
   Lucy got "91%" on her test.
   The symbol %% could be used to mean per thousand
   A "" means empty message

3. How would you write a *printf()* statement to display the following message?

   No space between \ and ", please

2.1.3 DISPLAYING LONG MESSAGES

Example 2.1.4 showed that a single *printf()* may be used to display multiple lines of text. In that case the *printf()* fitted nicely on a single line, but had the message been any longer, it would not have. For instance, suppose the message you wanted to display was as follows:

Cze the future!
I C C there
So C now.
Don't be a CC
Enjoy programming
--From a friend

A single use of *printf()* would force the message to wrap around in the program code line:

```
printf("Cze the future!\nI C C there\nSo C now. Don't be a CC\n Enjoy
programming\n--From a friend");
```

The result is confusing and ugly. In addition, wrapping a text message to the next line causes a syntax error. Of course, it is better to use six *printf()*s, one for each line. Nevertheless, should you wish to remain with this single *printf()*, it needs reorganizing and the following two examples show two proper methods to do so.

Example 2.1.8

Break up the long message into six smaller ones:

```
#include <stdio.h>

main()
```

```
{
     printf("Cze the future!\n"
            "I C C there\n"
            "So C now.\n"
            "Don't be a CC\n"
            "Enjoy programming\n"
            "--From a friend");
}
```

Each smaller message is enclosed in its own set of double quotation marks. Any information surrounded by double quotation marks is called a ***string.*** Therefore this *printf()* displays a message made up of six strings. Note the \n at the end of each string.

Some compilers may not allow the solution described above. If this is your case, use the method shown in the example below.

Example 2.1.9

Break up the long message as shown above, but also include a format string:

```
#include <stdio.h>

main()
{
    printf("%s%s%s%s%s%s", [1]
           "Cze the future!\n", [2]
           "I C C there\n", [2]
           "So C now.\n, " [2]
           "Don't be a CC\n, " [2]
           "Enjoy programming\n", [2]
           "--From a friend");
}
```

Explanations

This solution is almost identical to the previous one. The two differences are explained below, and the numbers refer to the superscript numbers at the end of the lines in the program:

1. The first string, "%s%s%s%s%s%s", is called a ***format string.*** It consists of ***format codes,*** percent symbols (%). These codes are **not** text, and do not show on the output. They are used to carry out the process of displaying the six messages that follow the format string. Note that one such % must be specified for each string below it: there are six strings following the format string, so there must be six % codes in the format string. Much more will be said about format strings in Sections 2.2 and 2.4 and Subsection 18.1.4.
2. A comma is used to separate each of the strings.

EXERCISES 2.1.4

1. Is there anything wrong with the statement below?

   ```
   printf("This message has",
          "more than one line
           but will not work");
   ```

2. Write a program to display the following message exactly, using one *printf()* statement with three strings inside it:

   The latest estimate of the earth's area
   place the fertile regions
   at 33,000,000 "s.m.".

3. Use a single *printf()* statement to display the long text below. Provide a solution for each method illustrated above:

   Notice that more than one statement can be put on one
   line, or one statement can be written across lines.
   Except for messages contained within double quotation marks.

2.1.4 COMMON ERRORS AND TRAPS

1. Forgetting to put the *#include <stdio.h>* directive at the top of the program. Some compilers will complain about this omission in the form of a warning. For example, for the program in Example 2.1.9, the warning might be "No prototype found for *printf()*". Despite this, the program might still run well. Other compilers, however, will **not** complain, but the program will **not** run well. Do not take any chances: put the *#include <stdio.h>* in all your programs. Including it in the program also helps the compiler detect errors.
2. Putting a semicolon at the end of the *#include* directive:

   ```
   #include <stdio.h>;
   ```

   Only ***statements*** end with a semicolon. Since *#include* is not a statement (it is a preprocessor directive), the compiler will complain. More is said about preprocessor directives in Sections 2.3.4 and 12.4 and in Appendix C.
3. Using uppercase letters where only lowercase letters should be used:

   ```
   #INCLUDE <stdio.h>

   Main()
   {
       PRINTF("Hello. Salut. Ciao.");
   }
   ```

   Remember, C is case sensitive, so uppercase letters will be interpreted differently than lowercase letters by the compiler. In this example, the compiler will complain about INCLUDE and Main but not necessarily about PRINTF. (Can you see why?)
4. Forgetting the semicolon at the end of a statement:

   ```
   #include <stdio.h>

   main()
   {
       printf("Hello. Salut. Ciao.")
   }
   ```

   The semicolon is missing at the end of the *printf()* line and the compiler will issue a syntax error message due to the omission.
5. Surrounding the message within a *printf()* with single quotation marks:

   ```
   #include <stdio.h>

   main()
   {
       printf('Hello. Salut. Ciao.');
   }
   ```

   Because there are single quotation marks around the message to be displayed, the compiler will likely complain. **Single quotation marks and double quotation marks have entirely different meanings in C.** Never mix them up. In a *printf()* message, double quotation marks must be used.
6. Omitting one of the double quotation marks surrounding the message in *printf()*:

   ```
   #include <stdio.h>

   main()
   ```

```
{
    printf("Hello. Salut. Ciao.);
    printf(Hello. Salut. Ciao.");
}
```

In this example, there are missing double quotation marks at the end of the first *printf()* statement and at the beginning of the second *printf()* statement. The compiler will definitely complain about this.

7. Forgetting to include *\n* within the message of a *printf()* statement when you want to move to the next line. The *printf()* statement will not cause the message to display on a new line by itself; you have to tell it to do so by using *\n*.
8. Placing the *\n* escape sequence outside the message:

```
#include <stdio.h>

main()
{
    printf("Cze the future!"\n);
    printf(\n"I C C there\n");
    printf("So C now. Don't be a CC\n");
}
```

The compiler will complain because of errors in this program. (Can you tell at which lines?) The *\n* escape sequence should always be within the double quotation marks, because it is part of the message.

9. Using a forward slash instead of a backward slash as the escape character:

```
#include <stdio.h>

main()
{
    printf("Cze the future!/n");
    printf("/nI C C there/n");
    printf("So C now. Don't be a CC/n");
}
```

The compiler would not complain, but the output would be as follows:

Cze the future!/n/n C C there/nSo C now. Don't be a CC/n

Do you understand why?

10. Forgetting the \ symbol before a double quotation mark when attempting to display the quotation mark as part of a message:

```
printf("Celine Dion sings "Falling into You" in concert");
```

The result of this error was discussed in Subsection 2.1.2 above.

11. Forgetting the \ symbol before a percent symbol (%) when attempting to display the percent symbol as part of a message:

```
printf("The notation 25% means 25 percent");
```

The result of this error also was discussed in Subsection 2.1.2.

12. In the context of a *printf()* statement, attempting to display a long message comprised of multiple strings by separating the strings with commas when none should be there:

```
#include <stdio.h>

main()
{
    printf("Notice that more than one statement can be put on one\n",
           "line, or one statement can be written across lines.\n",
           "Except for messages contained within double quotes.\n");
}
```

The commas after the double quotation marks at the end of the first two lines in the *printf()* statement should not be used. The compiler will **not** complain, but the display would be as follows:

```
Notice that more than one statement can be put on one
```

The other lines will not show. The explanation of this strange result in the display is beyond us for now, however.

2.2 PROGRAM INTERACTION WITH THE USER

In the previous section, the *printf()* function only let the computer send information to the user. A function named *scanf()* lets the user enter information into the program. This function provides a way for the user to interact with the computer program. In this section, you will learn about the basic tools necessary to write simple C programs incorporating *scanf()* to allow user interaction with the programs. This section also teaches you more about how to use variables.

2.2.1 AN INTRODUCTORY EXAMPLE

In Chapter 1, there was an algorithm that was created to help a college student named Judy calculate the total salary she would receive in a summer job. Here again is that algorithm from Exercise 1.2.5, 4:

1. Judy asks for the HOURLY RATE of pay.
2. Judy listens to the answer from the employer.
3. Then Judy asks for the number of HOURS OF WORK per week.
4. Judy listens to the answer from the employer.
5. Judy asks for the number of WEEKS OF WORK offered.
6. Judy listens to the answer.
7. Finally Judy takes out her calculator and finds the AMOUNT OF INCOME:

$$\text{HOURLY RATE} \times \text{HOURS OF WORK} \times \text{WEEKS OF WORK}$$

The example below shows how a C program may be written based on this algorithm.

Example 2.2.1

Judy decides to write a program in C that will do these calculations for her. The program will contain a sequence of *scanf()* statements to ask her for the hourly wage, the total hours of work per week, and the number of weeks of work. Then the program will calculate the total income for the summer and display it using the function *printf()*. Here is an example of a run of the program we want to create:

```
Enter the hourly wage > 7.05↵
Enter the total work hours per week > 35↵
Enter the number of weeks of work > 10↵

You will make $ 2467.50 this summer
```

The Enter key (represented by the symbol ↵) must be pressed after each number is entered. Now look below at the program code Judy developed. Remember, the superscript numbers are not part of the program code; they refer to the *Explanations* that follow.

```
#include <stdio.h>

main()
{[1]
    float hourly_rate;[2]
    int hours_per_week;[2]
    float total_income;[2]
    int num_weeks;[2]
```

```
    printf("Enter the hourly wage > ");[3]
    scanf("%f", &hourly_rate);[3]
    printf("Enter the total work hours per week > ");[3]
    scanf("%d", &hours_per_week);[3]
    printf("Enter the number of weeks of work > ")
    scanf("%d", &num_weeks);[3]
    total_income = hourly_rate * hours_per_week * num_weeks;[3]
    printf("You will make $ %.2f this summer", total_income);[3]
}
```

Explanations

1. Section 2.1 mentioned that the program's ***code*** goes within the open and close braces, { and }. In the program above, the code includes all the lines between the braces.
2. In this program, the code is made up of two sections. The first four lines include the ***declaration of variables.***
3. The rest of the lines are the ***executable code.*** The executable code and the declaration of variables both are explained in more detail below.

Declaration of variables. This section consists of variables that are necessary to receive the data from the user:

```
float hourly_rate;
int   hours_per_week;
```

The first declaration tells the compiler that the programmer intends to use the variable called *hourly_rate*. The compiler will reserve a cell in the computer memory for that variable, so that a number can be put in it later. This variable also is said to be of type *float*, meaning that it will contain fractional numbers (also called ***real numbers***), such as 62.81, –155.3, or even 12.00. The second declaration tells the compiler that the variable *hour_per_week* is of type *int,* which stands for integers (also called ***whole numbers***). Figure 2.2.1 shows the four cells allocated once all variables are declared in the first section of the program code.

Figure 2.2.1

hourly_rate	hours_per_week	total_income	num_weeks
?	?	?	?

The question marks are used to indicate that no data has been stored in the cells yet. Also note the easy one-to-one correspondence between the variables of this C program and that of the algorithm. This was one motive for introducing variables in the algorithms in Chapter 1 (Section 1.2). Note that variables of the same type may be declared at the same time. Thus the four variables could have been declared with only two declaration statements:

```
float hourly_rate, total_income;
int   hours_per_week, num_weeks;
```

Executable codes. This section includes all the codes that make the program perform the work, such as codes that read the information from the user, process it, and display the result. This section is always the most complex and is usually made of at least three parts as described below.

1. Codes to ask the user to enter data. This is done with *printf()* statements:

   ```
   printf("Enter the hourly wage > ");
   ```

   This displays the message within the double quotation marks on the computer screen. In this case, the message is called a ***prompt,*** because it is used to prompt the user for input.
2. Codes to accomplish the actual reading of the data. The program reads the user data with *scanf()* statements:

   ```
   scanf("%f", &hourly_rate);
   ```

This function simply lets the user enter the requested information in the variable *hourly_rate*. The cursor will be positioned next to the prompt, and pauses until the user inputs the data:

```
Enter the hourly wage > _
```

The cursor position is indicated by the underscore character in the line of code above. Once the data is entered at the prompt, the user must press the Enter key. Only then will the number be *scan*ned and put in the variable named *hourly_rate*. The screen then displays the following information:

```
Enter the hourly wage > 7.05↵
_
```

The cursor (again indicated by the underscore character) has moved to the next line, ready to display the next prompt. Every time the Enter key is pressed, the cursor moves to the next line. Note carefully the syntax of the *scanf()* function in Figure 2.2.2.

Figure 2.2.2

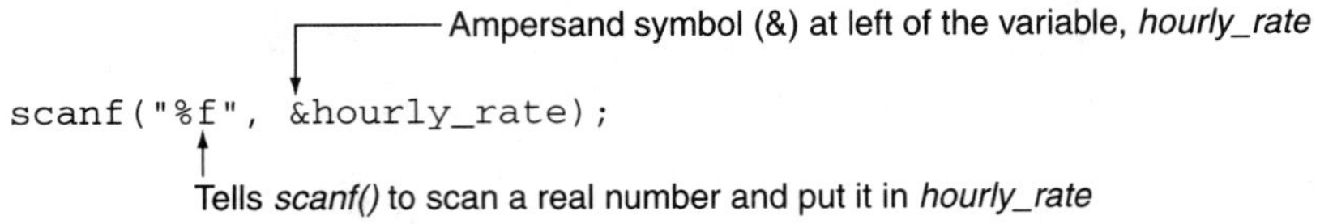

A complete explanation of the purpose of the ampersand symbol (&) is included in Section 11.2 in the discussion of arguments by reference. The special code "%f" is called a ***format string.*** A format string is **always** needed to tell *scanf()* how to scan the data provided by the user. For instance, in *scanf("%d", &hours_per_week)*, the format string "*%d*" instructs *scanf()* to scan an integer. (Many more data types exist; some others will be covered in Chapter 3.) Once all the *scanf()* statements have been reached and executed, the contents of the cells are filled, as shown in Figure 2.2.3.

Figure 2.2.3

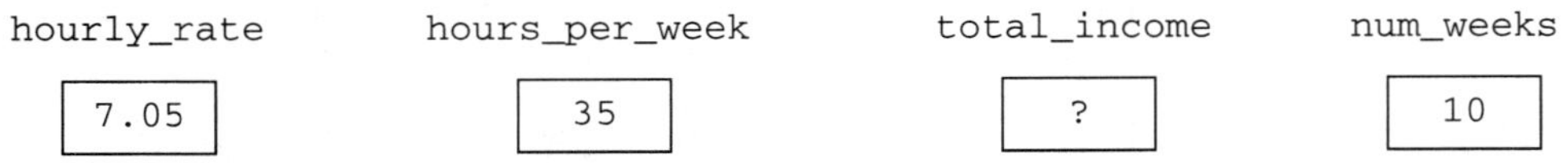

Note that the box representing the cell for variable *total_income* does not contain anything yet. It will once the statement explained below is executed.

3. Codes to manipulate the data. In this case the manipulation relates to the following calculation:

   *total_income = hourly_rate * hours_per_week * num_weeks;*

   This simply performs the calculation:

   \$7.05/hour × 35 hours/week × 10 weeks

   The result of the calculation, \$2467.50, is placed inside the variable named *total_income*. Note that the multiplication symbol in C is the asterisk (*). The equal sign (=) is used to tell the program to put the result of the calculation in the variable to the left of where it appears, in the variable *total_income*. Figure 2.2.4 shows exactly how this statement is executed.

Figure 2.2.4

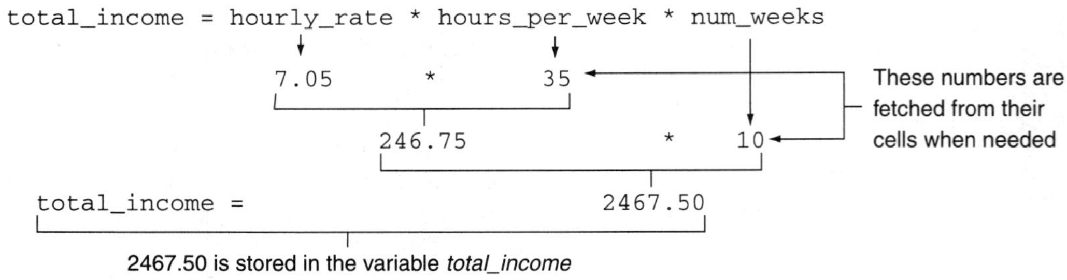

The equal sign symbol (=) always takes the number calculated to its right, here 2467.50, and puts it in the variable to its left. For this reason it is called an ***assignment*** operator.

Displaying the results. In this case, the total income calculated is displayed with the *printf()* statement, as shown in Figure 2.2.5.

Figure 2.2.5

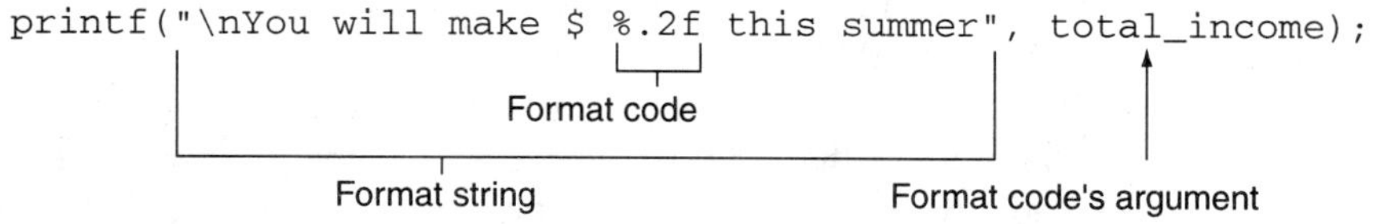

Notice that, just like *scanf()*, this function call is made of two parts: the format string and the variable whose value is to be displayed.

The format string contains the message to be displayed, but also it contains codes starting with percent symbols (%) called ***format codes.*** Here it contains only one format code, *%.2f.* This code inserts the content of the variable *total_income*, 2467.50, inside the message. Only then is the message displayed. Figure 2.2.6 shows how it all works.

Figure 2.2.6

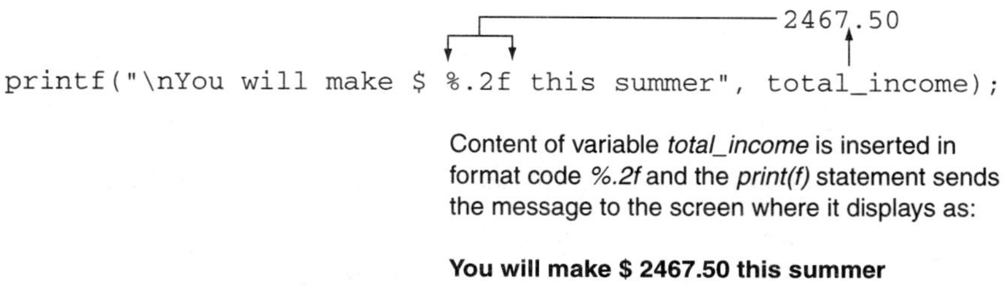

The *.2* in *%.2f* ensures that two digits are displayed after the decimal point. The symbol *\n* at the beginning of the message forces the cursor to move to the next line before the text of the message is displayed on the screen.

The importance of using the correct format code for its argument cannot be emphasized enough. Fortunately, it is easy to learn. With *scanf()*, simply use *%d* to scan a whole number and use *%f* to scan a real number. Similarly, with *printf()*, you also would use *%d* to display a whole number and *%f* to display a real number (*%.2f* is used above to display the result to two decimal places). Section 2.4 will show how to display numbers in many different ways by coding the format codes in diverse ways.

EXERCISES 2.2.1

1. Remove the symbol *\n* from the *printf()* statement in Figure 2.2.6 above and run the program. Observe how the display changes and explain why it changes.
2. Find all the errors in the following code:

```
#include <stdio.h>

main()
     printf("Enter your date of birth,
          (e.g., Aug 21, 1961 would be entered as 08 21 61) ");
     int month day year;
     scanf(month, day, year);
     age = 1994 - year
     printf("You are ", age, " old");
}
```

3. Write a program that asks the user to enter the dimensions in centimeters of a file cabinet (i.e., its height, width, and depth) and to calculate its volume (i.e., height × width × depth) and then display it.
   a. Assume the dimensions are obtained to the closest centimeter. For example, if the exact dimensions are 137.1 by 47.7 by 81.5 centimeters, assume instead that the values 137, 48, and 82 are entered.
   b. Rewrite the program to assume the dimensions are to the closest millimeter (e.g., 137.12, 47.78, and 81.51).
4. A waitress is paid $5.09 per hour, and the rest of her income comes from tips. Write a program that prompts the waitress to enter the number of hours worked and the total amount of tips made including the cents. Then have the program display the waitress's total income.
5. Write a program for the algorithm that is the answer to Exercise 1.2.2, 2. The program will need to provide prompts that ask the user to enter the price of tickets for each age group and then how many people there are in each group. Should there be no people in a particular age group, the user simply types in 0.

2.2.2 DISPLAYING MORE THAN ONE NUMBER AT A TIME

A single *printf()* may be coded to display more than one number at the time. The example below shows how.

Example 2.2.2

Suppose that we want to run the program in Example 2.2.1 as follows:

```
Enter the hourly wage > 7.05↵
Enter the total work hours per week > 35↵
Enter the number of weeks of work > 10↵

You will make $ 2467.50 in 10 weeks this summer
```

The *printf()* that displays the last line needs to display both the total income and the number of weeks worked. This function call needs to be modified with format codes as follows:

```
printf("You will make $ %.2f in %d weeks this summer",
        total_income, num_weeks);
```

The format codes *%.2f* and *%d* format the display of the variables *total_income* and *num_weeks* respectively.

EXERCISES 2.2.2

1. Reduce the sequence of *printf()* statements below to a single statement:

```
printf("The winning numbers ");
printf("for the lottery");
printf("%d, %d, %d followed by ", num1, num2, num3);
printf("%d, %d, %d", num4, num5, num6);
printf("\nand the bonus is %d\n", bonus);
```

2. Write a program that reads in three real numbers and displays the summation. Example:

```
Enter a number > 12.4
Enter another one > –9.8309
Enter yet another > 31.01

The summation of 12.4, –9.8309, and 31.01 is 33.5791
```

3. Suppose you have the following variables:

```
int   age,    kids;
float height, weight;
```

Given these variables, which of the following *printf()* statements will fail, and at which format code?

```
printf("Dave lives on %dth street", street);
printf("He is %d years old, %d meters tall and %f pounds",
       age, height, weight);
printf("He has %d kids", kids);
```

4. In Subsection 2.1.4 above, *Common Errors,* there was a program in (12) that used double quotation marks incorrectly:

```
#include <stdio.h>

main()
{
   printf("Notice that more than one statement can be put on one\n",
          "line, or one statement can be written across lines.\n",
          "Except for messages contained within double quotes.\n");
}
```

The use of the quotation marks in the program is inappropriate, yet the compiler does not complain, and the display is as follows:

Notice that more than one statement can be put on one

The other lines of the message do not show. Provide an explanation of this strange result.

2.2.3 READING MORE THAN ONE NUMBER AT A TIME

A single *scanf()* may also read more than one number at the time. However, this practice should be avoided because it makes the program more error prone. Nevertheless, since most books on C programming cover such a practice, it will be covered here as well, with a few warnings along the way. (See Subsection 2.2.6, *Common Errors and Traps.*) Consider the example below now.

Example 2.2.3

Let's change the program from Example 2.2.2 so that the data is entered all on one line as shown below:

Enter the hourly wage,
   the total work hours per week and
   the number of weeks of work > 7.05 35 10↵

You will make $ 2467.50 in 10 weeks this summer

Here is the program with modifications indicated in bold:

```
#include <stdio.h>

main()
{
     float hourly_rate;
     int   hours_per_week;
     float total_income;
     int   num_weeks;

     printf("Enter the hourly wage,\n"
```

```
            "the total work hours per week and\n"
            "the number of weeks of work > ");
    scanf("%f%d%d", &hourly_rate, &hours_per_week, &num_weeks);

    total_income = hourly_rate * hours_per_week * num_weeks;

    printf("You will make $ %.2f in %d weeks this summer",

            total_income, num_weeks);
}
```

In the *scanf()* statement, the format codes act upon their respective arguments as explained earlier in this section; that is, the first format code (*%f*) scans the number into the variable *hourly_rate*, the second format code (*%d*) scans the number into the variable *hours_per_week,* and the final format code, (*%d*), scans the number into the variable *num_weeks*:

```
scanf("%f%d%d", &hourly_rate, &hours_per_week, &num_weeks);
```

EXERCISES 2.2.3

1. Reduce the sequence of *scanf()* statements below into a single one:

```
scanf("%d", &var1);
scanf("%f%d", &var2, &var3);
scanf("%f", &var4);
```

2. Modify the program in Exercise 2.2.2, 2 so that the data is entered all on one line as follows:

   Enter three numbers > 12.4 – 9.8309 31.01

Note that the *scanf()* statement in the example above wants to read **all** three numbers in **one scan** of the input. The example below uses the program from Example 2.2.3 again to show the significance of this fact.

Example 2.2.4

Suppose you enter only the first number, 7.05, and then press Enter. Section 2.1 explained that once the user presses Enter, *scanf()* scans the input. This is true **only** when *scanf()* is coded to accept just one number. In the call above, there are three format codes within the *scanf()*. So it will wait until the user enters three numbers **and then** the Enter key is pressed before moving on. For example, the display in Figure 2.2.7 results when the user carelessly presses Enter many times in between the numbers: *scanf()* did not budge until the user pressed the Enter key for the last time, after all three numbers were entered.

Figure 2.2.7

Enter the hourly wage,
the total work hours per week and
the number of weeks of work > 7.05↵
↵
↵
35↵
↵
10↵

scanf() did not read any numbers until all three numbers were entered

---

EXERCISES 2.2.4

1. Assume the following variables:

```
int   street, age, pounds, weight;
float height;
```

Which of the following *scanf()* statements will fail, and at which format codes?

```
scanf("%d", &street);
scanf("%d%d%f", &age, &height, &weight);
scanf("%d", &kids);
```

2. Assume the following:

```
int   a;
float b;
```

Find the errors in the following codes, if any:

a. `scanf("%d", &b);`
b. `scanf("f", &b);`
c. `scanf("%f", &a);`
d. `scanf("%d%f", &b, &a);`
e. `scanf(a, b);`
f. `scanf(&a);`

2.2.4 BE WARY OF *scanf()*

Subsection 1.4.3 mentioned that *printf()* and *scanf()* are not really part of the compiler. The implication is that the compiler is limited in helping you code these functions without errors. As a result, undetected errors easily creep up on the unwary programmer. The purpose of the next two subsections is to warn you of possible pitfalls. This subsection will cover problems that may occur when programming with *scanf()* and the next subsection will deal with difficulties that may arise when using *printf()*.

Typing input data incorrectly. The person who enters the data at the prompt must ensure that it is entered correctly. This is crucial. For instance, if the user incorrectly types data that *scanf()* is waiting for, the program will fail unexpectedly as the example below shows.

Example 2.2.5

Using the program from Example 2.2.1, suppose the input was mistyped as follows:

Enter the hourly wage > 7.05↵
Enter the total work hours per week > #5↵
Enter the number of weeks of work >

You will make $ 0 this summer

In the second input line, #5 was typed instead of 35 for the total work hours per week. As a result, the program did not let the user enter any number at the final prompt, and the program displayed "garbage" as output. Keying just one number incorrectly, #5 instead of 35, caused quite a stir, as you can see.

First of all, the user was not given the opportunity to reenter the number correctly. This is because the *scanf()* function that was supposed to scan the #5 failed. It was expecting a number, and # is not a number, so it panicked and quit. Then the program did not wait for the user to enter the number of weeks of work. Since the *scanf()* function above it failed, the *scanf()* for the number of weeks of work panicked as well and failed too. Consequently no numbers were stored in the variables, accounting for the income calculation being bogus.

The reason for this chain of failures of *scanf()* functions is beyond us for now, but it is fully explained in Appendix F. The lesson to remember here is that the *scanf()* function does **not** give the user the opportunity to edit data that is entered incorrectly. This function is therefore highly unfriendly, yet it is still the most sophisticated ANSI C function for input. And this particular idiosyncracy of *scanf()* is only the tip of the iceberg. It gets worse. There are numerous and obscure ways in which the *scanf()* function can fail.

EXERCISE 2.2.5

Still using the program from Example 2.2.1, suppose a careless user entered the hourly wage incorrectly. He got the following run:

Enter the hourly wage > &2↵
Enter the total work hours per week > Enter the number of weeks of work >

You will make $ 0 this summer

How do you explain the strange behavior of the program and the resulting display?

Using the wrong format code. Using a format code of the wrong type for its corresponding argument leads to execution errors. Four examples are provided to illustrate this.

Example 2.2.6

In the program below the format code *%f* is incorrect; it should be *%d*:

```
#include <stdio.h>

main()
{
      int age;

      printf("Enter the age > ");
      scanf("%f", &age); /* conflicting types */
      printf("age = %d\n", age);
}
```

Surprisingly, the compiler will not complain about this type of error. But when the program is run, it will crash and an error message such as "Floating point format not linked" will appear. Can you guess why this type of message appears? The actual error message differs depending on the compiler.

Example 2.2.7

In the program below the format code *%d* is incorrect; it should be *%f*:

```
#include <stdio.h>

main()
{
      float height;

      printf("Enter the height > ");
      scanf("%d", &height); /* conflicting types */
      printf("height = %f\n", height);
}
```

This program will compile correctly but a bogus number will be stored in *height*. Example:

Enter the height > 1.79
height = 0.000000

This type of error also causes the input mechanism used by *scanf()* to become unstable (the technical reasons for this are fully explained in Appendix F). Consequently, equally serious errors may occur if *scanf()* is called again.

Example 2.2.8

The errors illustrated above should not be taken lightly. If your program uses multiple *scanf()* statements and one of them is incorrect, the devastating effects on the program can become mind-boggling and frustrating. Consider the example below in which the first *scanf()* is incorrect:

```
#include <stdio.h>

main()
{
     float height;
     int   age;

     printf("Enter the height > ");
     scanf("%d", &height); /* conflicting types */
     printf("Enter the age > ");
     scanf("%d", &age); /* this one is correct */
     printf("\nage = %d\n", age);
     printf("height = %f\n", height);
}
```

Here is an example of a run:

Enter the height > 1.79↵
Enter the age >

age = 7077
height = 0.000000

As seen above, the *scanf()* function used to input the first entry failed (because its corresponding format code was incorrect). This caused the *scanf()* in the second line to panic, and it did not let the user enter data, resulting in bogus numbers in the output lines (7077 and 0.000000). When one *scanf()* fails, all the others after it will most likely fail too—a "snowball" effect takes place. Again, the exact explanations for the failures are given in Appendix F.

A program that uses a single *scanf()* can also cause similar troubles when it is coded to read multiple numbers, as the example below illustrates.

Example 2.2.9

In the program below, a single *scanf()* reads three numbers:

```
#include <stdio.h>

main()
{
     float hourly_rate;
     int   hours_per_week;
     float total_income;
     int   num_weeks;

     printf("Enter the hourly rate,\n"
            "the total work hours per week and\n"
            "the number of weeks of work > ");
     scanf("%d%d%d", &hourly_rate, &hours_per_week, &num_weeks);
     printf("\nhourly rate = %f, hours a week = %d, weeks = %d",
          hourly_rate, hours_per_week, num_weeks);
}
```

Here is an example of a run:

Enter the hourly rate,
the total work hours per week and
the number of weeks of work > 12.50 35 8

hourly rate = 0.000000, hours a week = 7076, weeks = 4912

All the numbers are wrong. What happened? The number for *hourly_rate* was not scanned correctly because its format code should be *%f*. In turn, this made the scanning of the following two numbers fail—**even though their format codes are correct.** In fact, if there were other *scanf()* statements following, they would all fail too. The "snowball" effect mentioned earlier would continue through the entire program.

In summary, the failure of a *scanf()*, for whatever reason, affects its own execution, and then usually goes on to affect the execution of **all** of the other ***scanf()*** calls thereafter, even if they are correct. For this reason, you must carefully check and double-check all your scanf() statements, and make sure that you enter the input data correctly, as *scanf()* expects it. It's better to be safe than sorry.

EXERCISE 2.2.6

Assuming that the user does not mistype any numbers during the input, which of the following *scanf()* calls would likely fail, and for which variables?

```
int     num1, num2, num3, num4;
float   num5, num6;
scanf("%d%f", &num2, &num5);
scanf("%f", &num1);
scanf("%d%d%d", &num3, &num4, &num6);
```

2.2.5 BE WARY OF *printf()*

This subsection illustrates a few ways that *printf()* may function inexplicably.

Using a wrong format code. When you use the wrong type of format code for the type of argument in the program code, you can expect execution errors. Consider the following two examples.

Example 2.2.10

In the program below, the format codes in both *printf()* statements are incorrect:

```
#include <stdio.h>

main()
{
     int      age;
     float    height;

     age = 21;     /* put number 21 in variable age */
     height = 1.79; /* put number 1.79 in variable height */

     printf("age = %f\n", age);
     printf("height = %d\n", height);
}
```

In both of the *printf()* statements above, the format code type conflicts with the type of argument used in the statement. The compiler will **not** complain about this, but the execution of the program will cause erroneous displays. For instance, the screen might display the following output:

```
age = 0.660000
height = 0.000000
```

These results do not indicate that the variables *age* and *height* now contain the numbers 0.66 and 0.00—in fact, the content of the variables never changed. What the results **do** indicate is that the *printf()* statements were unable to display the variables' content, hence bogus numbers resulted.

Erroneous execution tends to get even worse when the program is to display more than one item at a time, as the example below illustrates.

Example 2.2.11

In the program below, the second and third *printf()* statements are incorrect because the format code type conflicts with the type of argument used in the statements:

```
#include <stdio.h>

main()
{
     int      age;
     float    height;

     age = 21;    /* put number 21 in variable age */
     height = 1.79; /* put number 1.79 in variable height */

     printf("age = %d, height = %f\n", age, height);
     printf("age = %f, height = %d\n", age, height);
     printf("age = %f, height = %f\n", age, height);
     printf("age = %d, height = %f\n", age, height);
}
```

Again the compiler will **not** complain about the conflicts between the format codes and the arguments, but the execution of the program will cause erroneous displays:

age = 21, height = 1.790000
age = –0.000000, height = 16380[1]
age = –0.000000, height = 0.660000[2]
age = 21, height = 1.790000[3]

Explanations

1. The numbers on the second line are totally incorrect, due to the fact that both format codes are wrong in the corresponding *printf()*.
2. The third line is also bogus. However, in the corresponding *printf()*, the type of the second format code, *%f*, is **not** in conflict with its arguments. Its display on the third line is wrong regardless. The reason is that since the first format code is in conflict (hence the display of its argument being wrong), the display of the second argument will also be wrong—**even if its format code is correct!** In fact, if there had been more arguments following, they would have all displayed incorrect output as well. For instance, assume a third variable *float weight* and the following *printf()* call:

   ```
   printf("age = %f, height = %f\n, weight = %f", age, height, weight);
   ```

   Even though only the first format code is incorrect—the next two are both correct with regard to their corresponding arguments—**all three** of the outputs displayed with this *printf()* statement will be incorrect.
3. Note that the fourth line in the display above is correct. The erroneous *printf()* statements do not affect later *printf()* statements that are correct.

In summary, the failure of a *printf()*, in whatever way, affects itself but will not have an impact on any other *printf()* call thereafter.

EXERCISE 2.2.7

Assume the variables below contain some number:

```
int   num1, num2, num3, num4;
float num5, num6;
```

Which of the following *printf()* calls would likely fail, and for which variables?

```
printf("%d%f", num2, num5);
printf("%f", num1);
printf("%d%d%d", num3, num4, num6);
```

2.2.6 COMMON ERRORS AND TRAPS

1. Forgetting to declare a variable. For example, if the variable *hourly_rate* in Example 2.2.1 had not been declared, then an error message such as "Declaration for variable "hourly_rate" not found" would have displayed. (The actual message varies among compilers.)
2. Declaring a variable in the wrong section:

```
#include <stdio.h>

main()
{
        int hourly_rate;

        printf("Enter the hourly wage > ");
        scanf("%d", &hourly_rate);

        int hours_per_week;
        printf("Enter the total work hours per week > ");
        scanf("%d", &hours_per_week); in

        int num_weeks;
        printf("Enter the number of weeks of work > ");
        scanf("%d", &num_weeks);
}
```

The two lines indicated in bold are in the wrong place; they should be in the declaration section at the top of the program code. The compiler will complain.

The error above is fairly easy to fix because the compiler complains about it. Unfortunately, there are numerous errors that a C compiler is unable to detect and so does not warn the programmer about. For that reason, I call them ***traps.*** Undetected traps cause ***bugs*** in a program. These manifest themselves sometimes in obscure ways.

The following eight traps illustrate various ways that *scanf()* and *printf()* may fail if not coded correctly. The unwary programmer is guaranteed to spend countless hours trying to locate these traps when they do come up, unless he or she takes note of this list.

3. Using an ampersand symbol (&) with an argument of *printf()*:

```
printf("You will work $ %d hours this summer", &num_hours);
```

The ampersand symbol applies to *scanf()* only. The compiler will not complain about this error. When the program is executed, it will display the proper message, but the number for the hours will be totally wrong. For example, if the variable *num_hours* contains the number 347, the display may be some garbage number:

You will make $ –12 this summer

The term ***garbage*** is often used to express the fact that the number is bogus or meaningless.

4. Forgetting the ampersand symbol (&) in front of the variable to receive data:

```
printf("Enter the hourly wage > ");
scanf("%d", hourly_rate);
printf("The variable hourly_rate contains %f", hourly_rate);
```

The & is missing in front of the variable *hourly_rate* (in line two). The compiler will **not** complain about this omission. When the program is executed, it will show the prompt and let the user enter the data, say 7.05. Then unpredictable things may happen:

- The program may continue normally, but the number 7.05 will not be stored in the variable *hourly_rate*. Instead, the display might well be:

  The variable hourly_rate contains 0

  Can you figure out why?
- The program may ***crash*** at the point where the symbol is missing; that is, the program will be terminated immediately by the operating system—the *printf()* following the *scanf()* will not even be reached. A crash may cause serious troubles, especially when the program is run on an operating system that does not guarantee memory protection, such as MS-DOS.

5. Forgetting the format string, such as *%f*, in the *scanf()* call:

```
printf("Enter the hourly wage > ");
scanf(&hourly_rate);
```

   In the second line, the format string *%f* is missing (it should appear before *&hourly_rate*). The compiler **may not** complain about this error, but most will. When the program is executed, it will display the prompt but the *scanf()* will fail badly and the program will probably crash. Sometimes the ampersand symbol (&) is also forgotten: *scanf(hourly_rate)*. In this case, the compiler will most likely complain.
6. Forgetting the *%f* code in the *printf()* statement:

```
printf("You will make $ this summer", total_income);
```

   The *%f* format code should follow the dollar sign in the message, but has been omitted here. The compiler will **not** complain. When the program is executed, it will display the message, but the number will be missing. (Do you understand why?)

   You will make $ this summer

7. Forgetting the % symbol in the *printf()* statement:

```
printf("You will make $ f this summer", total_income);
```

   The % symbol is missing (between the dollar sign and the *f*), but the compiler will **not** complain. When the program is executed, it will display the message, but the number will be missing. Instead, the letter *f* will appear in its place. (Do you know why?)

```
You will make $ f this summer
```

8. Forgetting the % code in the *scanf()*:

```
scanf("d", &hourly_rate);
```

   The % code is missing (from in front of the *d*). The compiler will **not** complain about this omission, but when the program is executed, the *scanf()* will be unable to read the data and the program may even crash.
9. Using the wrong format code with *printf()* or *scanf()*. These traps were covered extensively in Subsections 2.2.4 and 2.2.5.
10. Using format codes in places other than in the format string of a *printf()*. People who already know another computer language tend to fall in this trap. For example, look at the following program:

```
#include <stdio.h>

main()
{
      float hourly_rate;
      int   hours_per_week;
      float total_income;
      int   num_weeks;

      printf("Enter the hourly rate,\n"
             "the total work hours per week and\n"
             "the number of weeks of work > ");
      scanf("%f%d%d", &hourly_rate, &hours_per_week, &num_weeks);

      printf("\nhourly rate = %f, ", hourly_rate,
```

```
                " hours a week = %d, ", hours_per_week,
                " weeks = %d", num_weeks);
}
```

The second *printf()* is used incorrectly. As a result, the display generated is:

Enter the hourly rate,
the total work hours per week and
the number of weeks of work > <u>12.50 35 8</u>

hourly rate = 12.500000,

The hourly rate displays, but the hours per week and the number of weeks did not show following it. What happened? Simply this: the second *printf()* did not receive its arguments in the order it expected them. It expected to receive the format string followed by the first data, then the second data, and so forth. In the correct code below, the first line includes the format string, and the second line includes the list of data to display:

```
printf("\nhourly rate = %f, hours a week = %d, weeks = %d",
        hourly_rate, hours_per_week, num_weeks);
```

Instead it received the information in this order: first format string, first data, followed by second format string, second data, followed by third format string, third data, as shown below:

```
printf("\nhourly rate = %f, ", hourly_rate,
       " hours a week = %d, ", hours_per_week,
       " weeks = %d", num_weeks);
```

A *printf()* must have only one format string. It must be placed at the beginning of the *printf()* and must contain all the format codes. All the other arguments must be data only. In the *printf()* statement above, all the additional format strings and their data were ignored. (Can you see why?)

2.3 PROGRAM LAYOUT AND PRESENTATION

C compilers are quite flexible when it comes to allowing the programmer to groom his program. This section presents some ways to do just that.

2.3.1 PROPER USE OF WHITE SPACE

A ***white space*** can be any of the following:

- A blank space produced with the space bar
- A tab produced with the Tab key
- A blank line produced with the Enter key

Places where spaces are ignored. White space can be inserted in many places in the program to make it more readable and better looking. In most cases, the addition of blank lines or space will not affect the run of the program.

Example 2.3.1

The following program illustrates good places to insert white space. Remember, the superscript numbers refer to the *Explanations* below; they are not part of the program.

```
#include <stdio.h>
1
main()
{2
3    float 4hourly_rate;
3    int   4hours_per_week;
3    float 4total_income;
3    int   4num_weeks;
5
```

```
3     printf("Enter the hourly wage,\n"
6            "the total work hours per week and\n"
6            "the number of weeks of work > ");
3     scanf("%f%d%d", &hourly_rate, &hours_per_week, &num_weeks);
7
3     total_income = hourly_rate *[8] hours_per_week *[8] num_weeks;
7
3     printf("You will make $ %.2f in %d weeks this summer",
6             total_income,[9] num_weeks);
}[2]
```

Explanations

1. Leave at least one blank line between the *#include* statement and *main()*. Also place *main()* on its own line.
2. Put the open and close braces each on their own separate line. This way they are easy to locate, and it is easy to ensure that all the code is within the braces.
3. The block of code within the braces should be ***indented*** a few spaces. This is the single most important use of white space. In later chapters, the programs will gradually consist of more than one block of code (within braces). At that point, it will become essential to indent sections of the code to make it easier to read.
4. Line up all the variables so that they are easy to read and to ensure that they are all declared.
5. Leave at least one blank line to separate the variable declaration section from the code.
6. Indent the arguments of *printf()* when they continue on the next line. This makes the name of the function stand out.
7. You may want to use blank lines to space out the code. They can be used to create a visual separation between the codes that read the data, the codes that do the calculations, and the codes that display the result. The blank lines make it easy to distinguish the different codes and make the program that much easier to read.
8. Leave a space between an operator and its operand(s). For example, in the line of code below, there is a space before and after each multiplication operator (*):

   ```
   total_income = hourly_rate * hours_per_week * num_weeks;
   ```

   instead of running all the code and operators together, as shown below:

   ```
   total_income=hourly_rate*hours_per_week*num_weeks;
   ```

9. Leave a space between a comma and the argument next to it. This applies to the *scanf()* statements as well, and anywhere else there is a comma. For example, in the line of code below, a space has been added after each comma:

   ```
   int hourly_rate, hours_per_week, total_income, num_weeks;
   ```

   instead of running the code together as shown below:

   ```
   int hourly_rate,hours_per_week,total_income,num_weeks;
   ```

This book will follow the guidelines set out above for use of white space. You may prefer to deviate from these guidelines, and are welcome to do so. Keep in mind, however, that your programs must remain easy to read.

EXERCISES 2.3.1

1. Reorganize the following program to meet the grooming guidelines above. The program is already free of syntax errors.

   ```
   #include <stdio.h>
   main() {
   int  goal_1;
   int     goal_2;
      int goal_3;
   ```

```
int  total_goals;
printf("Enter number of goals in period 1 > ");
scanf("%d",&goal_1);
printf("Enter number of goals in period 2 > ");
scanf("%d",&goal_2);
printf("Enter number of goals in period 3 > ");
scanf("%d",&goal_3);
total_goals=goal_1+goal_2+goal_3;
printf("The team scored %d goals in the game",total_goals);}
```

2. Rewrite the following program in a more readable way.

```
#include <stdio.h>
 main
 (
 ){printf
 ("Hello. there\n")
 ;}
```

3. Rewrite the following program in a more readable way.

```
#include <stdio.h>
main
() {int num; printf("This is"); printf(
" a program"
); printf
(
"that does not "); printf              (
            "look too good."              );
    printf("Enter a number > "); scanf(
"%d", &num); printf      (      "Echoed is number %d",
       num);
}
```

Places where spaces are not ignored. White space is not ignored by the compiler everywhere in the program—there are exceptions. These include the following:

- Within strings (i.e., within double quotation marks)
- Within function names
- Within variable names
- Within reserved words (*int* is an example of a reserved word that you have seen already)

Example 2.3.2

Suppose that additional white space is inserted in the program we looked at in Example 2.3.1, as shown below:

```
#include <stdio.h>

main()
    {
     f l o a t[1] hourly_rate;
     int hours per week;[2]
     float total_income;
     int num_weeks;

     print f[3]("Enter the hourly wage > ");
     scanf("%f", &hourly_rate);
     printf("Enter the total work hours per week[2] > ");
     scanf("%d", &hours per week);
     printf("Enter the number of weeks of work > ");
     scan f[3]("%d", &num_weeks);
```

```
    total_income = hourly_rate * hours_per_week * num_weeks;
    printf("You    will    make $ %.2f    this    summer",[4]

    total_income);
}
```

Explanations

The compiler will complain about the improper use of white space in a lot of places:

1. The spaces within *f l o a t* will cause a syntax error. No spaces are allowed in a reserved word.
2. No spaces are allowed within a variable name; the underscore character is generally used within a variable to indicate a space, such as *hours_per_week.* Using a space instead will cause a syntax error.
3. No spaces are allowed within a function name; *scanf, printf,* and other functions must be typed without spaces to avoid syntax errors.
4. The extra spaces within the message in the double quotation marks will show on the screen, but this is not a syntax error.

In summary, white space can be used in programs to enhance readability, but be careful not to add spaces where they will cause syntax errors or affect the run of the program:

- Within strings—they will not cause syntax errors but may affect the run of the program. In Example 2.3.2, for instance, the display would be affected. (Can you explain why?)
- Within function names spaces always cause syntax errors.
- Within variable names spaces always cause syntax errors.
- Within reserved words spaces always cause syntax errors.

2.3.2 COMMENTS

In addition to white space when used properly, ***comments*** may be inserted in a program to make it easier to understand. A comment is typically used to explain, in plain English, the purpose of a program or a portion of the code. An example of how to use comments effectively in a program is shown below. First take a look at a few things you should know about using comments:

- The beginning of a comment must be indicated by a slash mark and an asterisk with no space between the symbols (/*) and the end of the comment must be followed by an asterisk and then a slash mark (*/).
- A comment may be one line or may run to more lines.
- By default, nested comments are not allowed. They can be used only when you announce to the compiler your intent to use them. The way to express this intent depends on the compiler used.
- A comment cannot be inserted within a variable name, function name, or reserved word:

  ```
  int total/* of */goals
  ```

  This not allowed by the compiler, since *total_goals* is a variable. Comments may be inserted almost anywhere else. (The meaning of reserved words will be explained in Subsection 2.3.3.)
- The compiler ignores all comments. Comments are only inserted for program documentation in order to assist the programmer or user, and do not affect the run of the program.

Example 2.3.3

Below is the program from Example 2.3.1 with comments added. The comments are indicated in bold and their use is explained below the program. These types of comments are typical, and usually are required as part of any software development project.

```
#include <stdio.h>

/* Program information:
    Written by: Jean Corriveau
    Date: March 30 1994
```

```
        Purpose: This program calculates the income for a
                 prospective job. A priori, it asks for the
                 hourly rate, the number of hours of work
                 per week, and the number of such weeks.
*/1

main()
{
        /* This is the variable declarations section */2
        float hourly_rate; /* pay per hour */3
        int   hours_per_week; /* hours of work per week */3
        float total_income; /* total income over the summer */3
        int   num_weeks; /* number of weeks of work */3

        /* This is the executable code section */2

         /* Ask the user the necessary information */2

        printf("Enter the hourly wage > ");
        scanf("%f", &hourly_rate);
        printf("Enter the total work hours per week > ");
        scanf("%d", &hours_per_week);
        printf("Enter the number of weeks of work > ");
        scanf("%d", &num_weeks);

         /* calculate the total income over the summer */2
        total_income = hourly_rate * hours_per_week * num_weeks;

         /* display the total income to the screen */2
        printf("You will make $ %.2f this summer", total_income);
}
```

Explanations

1. This comment covers multiple lines and describes what the program is all about. It also identifies the author and when the program was written. Note that the whole comment block is delimited by a single pair of /* and */ markers. As you can see, one set of markers can delimit the entire comment, no matter how long it is. It is not necessary to delimit each line of the comment block separately.
2. Comments are used to explain the purpose of blocks of statements, and sometimes of individual statements.
3. Comments should also be used to explain the meaning of each variable.

Not every line of code needs to be accompanied by a comment. Often a line is self-explanatory. Refrain from inserting too many comment lines in your programs because numerous comments may clutter up an otherwise readable program. For this reason, most examples in this book contain few comments, if any at all. Instead, explanations of different parts of the code will continue to be provided in a section directly after the program called *Explanations*. You have already encountered lists of explanations of program code that refer back to superscript numbers in the code. Remember that the numbers refer only to the explanations and are not part of the program itself. This system should enable you to concentrate on the actual code, unobstructed by comments, while still providing a means of explaining new or difficult aspects of the program.

EXERCISES 2.3.2

1. Insert appropriate comments into the program that you groomed previously in Exercise 2.3.1, 1.
2. What will the following *printf()* statements display, if anything? Check each statement for syntax errors.

a. `printf("/* is this a comment? */");`
b. `/* printf("is this a comment?"); */`
c. `/* printf("/* is this a comment? */"); */`

2.3.3 USE DESCRIPTIVE VARIABLE NAMES

Variable names always should be descriptive of the kind of information they contain.

Example 2.3.4

The following program will do the same thing as the one presented in Example 2.3.1, but the variables are no longer descriptive:

```
#include <stdio.h>

main()
{
     /* This is the variable declarations section */

     float hr; /* pay per hour */
     int   hpw; /* hours of work per week */
     float ti; /* total income over the summer */
     int   nw; /* number of weeks of work */

     /* This is the executable code section */

     /* Ask the user the necessary information */

     printf("Enter the hourly wage > ");
     scanf("%d", &hr);
     printf("Enter the total work hours per week > ");
     scanf("%d", &hpw);
     printf("Enter the number of weeks of work > ");
     scanf("%d", &nw);

     /* calculate the total income over the summer */

     ti = hr * hpw * nw;

     /* display the total income to the screen */

     printf("You will make $ %.2f this summer", ti);
}
```

Use your imagination when choosing descriptive variable names. However, you should keep in mind some naming rules:

- The variable name can only begin with a letter or an underscore character (_). Many of the internal variables used by the compiler start with an underscore. You should then refrain from naming your own variables that way.
- The variable name can contain only letters, underscore characters, or numbers. Any other character is invalid.
- The variable name cannot be a reserved word. Reserved words have special meanings and are for the exclusive use of the compiler. Examples of reserved words include *int, float, if,* and *while.*
- The variable name should not contain more than 31 characters. If it does, the additional characters will be ignored.

Table 2.3.1 illustrates some legal and illegal variable names.

Table 2.3.1

Valid Names	Invalid Names	Explanations
my_age	my age	Spaces not allowed; use _ to simulate a space
name1	name 1	Spaces not allowed
name_1	1name	Name must begin with a letter
dollars	$dollars	$ sign not allowed
pct	pct%	% sign not allowed
Int	int	*int* is a reserved word, but Int is not
FLOAT	float	*float* is a reserved word, but FLOAT is not (Why?)
Very_long_variable	Very_long_variable!	! character not allowed

A few observations are in order here:

1. When a variable is made up of more than one word, join them with underscore characters. Another practice that is becoming popular is to start each word with an uppercase letter, such as *VeryLongVariable*.
2. Variables may be declared in uppercase letters, such as *NUM_HOURS*. Remember that this variable is not the same as *num_hours*, because C is case sensitive.
3. Stay away from C reserved words. Table 2.3.2 lists all existing reserved words in ANSI C.

Table 2.3.2

ANSI C Reserved Words			
auto	*double*	*int*	*struct*
break	*else*	*long*	*switch*
case	*enum*	*register*	*typedef*
char	*extern*	*return*	*union*
const	*float*	*short*	*unsigned*
continue	*for*	*signed*	*void*
default	*goto*	*sizeof*	*volatile*
do	*if*	*static*	*while*

Make sure that you do not name your variables using any of the reserved words. Some compilers may have additional reserved words such as *asm, far, fortran, huge, interrupt, near,* and *pascal.* But these are not ANSI C standard reserved words. Note that function names are **not** reserved words, so *printf()* and *scanf()* are not reserved words. This is simply because they are not integral parts of the compiler.

EXERCISES 2.3.3

1. Which of the following variable names are invalid and why?

   a. *2rdn* b. *for* c. *_final*
   d. *sales tax* e. *sys$in* f. *level1*
   g. *For* h. *a1b2c3* i. *assign.1*

2. Do you see anything potentially wrong with the following declarations?

```
int         this_long_variable_is_meant_to_hold_a_number,
            this_long_variable_is_meant_to_hold_an_age;
```

2.3.4 THE *#define* PREPROCESSOR DIRECTIVE

When you submit a C program to the compiler, it goes through a preprocessor before the actual compilation takes place. (This is more fully explained in Section 12.4.) The preprocessor manipulates the program text by executing any directives that the program may contain. These ***preprocessing directives*** are positioned on lines beginning with the character #. Once manipulated, the program text is then handed down to the compiler for the actual compilation.

We have been using the *#include* directive already. Another directive, *#define*, may be used to attach a meaning to a literal, such as a number.

Example 2.3.5

Consider the program below. It asks for the weight of an object in kilos, then displays its conversion in pounds.

```
#include <stdio.h>

#define KILO_TO_POUND 2.2046[1]

main()
{
     float pound, kilo;

     printf("Enter the weight of the object in kilo > ");
     scanf("%f", &kilo);
     pounds = kilo * KILO_TO_POUND;[2]
     printf("The conversion is %f kilo\n", kilo);
}
```

Explanations

1. This directive defines the ***symbolic constant*** *KILO_TO_POUND* to stand for the number *2.2046*. Note the syntax:

   ```
   #define KILO_TO_POUND 2.2046
   ```

   The # character precedes the directive, *define,* which is followed by the symbolic constant, *KILO_TO_POUND,* and then the number it stands for follows it.
2. Wherever the symbolic constant *KILO_TO_POUND* appears, the preprocessor replaces it with the number *2.2046*, and then the expression is passed down to the compiler. For example, in the following line of code, *KILO_TO_POUND* will be replaced by 2.2046:

   ```
   pounds = kilo * KILO_TO_POUND;
   ```

   Then the resulting code will be compiled:

   ```
   pounds = kilo * 2.2046;
   ```

Note that the symbolic constant in the example above is in capital letters, but it does not have to be; lowercase does just as well, as shown in the following code:

```
#include <stdio.h>

#define kilo_to_pound 2.2046

main()
{
     float pound, kilo;

     printf("Enter the weight of the object in kilo > ");
     scanf("%f", &kilo);
```

```
    pounds = kilo * kilo_to_pound;
    printf("The conversion is %f kilo\n", kilo);
}
```

But now the symbolic constant *kilo_to_pound* looks like a variable. Yet it is **not** one, and the difference is quite important. You cannot change the value of a symbolic constant, such as changing *KILO_TO_POUND* to *2.3,* for example:

```
KILO_TO_POUND = 2.3;
```

Can you see why? It is important to distinguish symbolic constants from variables, so it is a good practice to define symbolic constants in capital letters to prevent them from being confused with variables.

A symbolic constant also may be defined for other purposes than that shown above. Consider the example below.

Example 2.3.6

Suppose that you do not like the reserved word *float*, and prefer the word *REAL*. The directive *#define* may be used to replace it. The program below illustrates what you need to do:

```
#include <stdio.h>

#define KILO_TO_POUND 2.2046
#define REAL          float

main()
{
    REAL pound, kilo;

    printf("Enter the weight of the object in kilo > ");
    scanf("%f", &kilo);
    pounds = kilo * KILO_TO_POUND;
    printf("The conversion is %f kilo\n", kilo);
}
```

EXERCISES 2.3.4

1. Explain how the new *#define* directive in the program above accomplishes the task it was created to do.
2. Consider the program segment below:

```
main()
{
    float circum, width, length;

    width = 15.3;
    length = 4.8;
    circum EQUALS 2 TIMES (width PLUS length);
}
```

   What *#define* statements are necessary for the program to compile correctly?
3. Consider the program below:

```
#include <stdio.h>

#define SUM 21.09 + 3.5

main()
{
```

```
        int sum;

        sum = SUM / 2;
        printf("The average of 21.09 and 3.5 is %d", sum);
}
```

a. The symbolic constant and the variable appear to have the same name. Is this actually the case? Will the program compile correctly?
b. If the program does compile, will it correctly calculate the average of the two numbers 21.09 and 3.5?
c. If it will not compile, suggest a simple rectification while still preserving the symbolic constant *SUM*.

2.3.5 COMMON ERRORS AND TRAPS

1. Putting spaces within a variable, as illustrated in this section.
2. Delimiting a portion of code as a comment by mistake:

```
#include <stdio.h>

main()
{
        :
        :
        :

        /* Ask the user the necessary information

        printf("Enter the hourly wage > ");
        scanf("%d", &hourly_rate);
        printf("Enter the total work hours per week > ");
        scanf("%d", &hours_per_week);
      :
      :
}
```

In the program above, the comment was never closed with a final */ delimiter. This will result in all the code following the actual comment to become a part of the comment. In other words, the lines following the comment are no longer codes.

3. Thinking that the *#define* directive is the same as an assignment statement:

```
#define RATE = 0.035
```

2.4 NUMBER OUTPUT FORMATTING

Section 2.2 showed you how to read and display numbers. This section will explain how special numbers can be added to the format codes *%d* and *%f* to format numbers to the screen display in various ways. The format code *%.2f* in the program in Example 2.2.1 is an example of number output formatting.

When a programmer is asked to produce a program to generate marketing reports, for instance, he may be required to format the data to the screen in various ways. The *printf()* function provides techniques to do this kind of formatting, and this section elaborates on the techniques. We will look at using format codes to display real numbers and integers.

2.4.1 DISPLAYING REAL NUMBERS

The four examples below explain how to format real numbers for display.

Example 2.4.1

Recall the *printf()* statement from the program in Example 2.2.1. In the program below, the format code *%.2f* has been changed to *%12.3f:*

```
printf("You will make $ %12.3f this summer", total_income);
```

If we assume that the *total_income* variable contains 2467.50, the display will be as follows:

You will make $ _ _ _ _ 2467.500 this summer

Note that the display zone for the number is 12 spaces wide (including the decimal point), and there are 3 digits after the decimal point. (***Note:*** The _ character indicates a blank space in the display.)

Now let's assume that the *total_income* variable contains a different amount, 27.1327. The display will be as follows:

You will make $ _ _ _ _ _ _ 27.133 this summer

As you can see, the display zone is again 12 spaces wide, and there are again 3 digits after the decimal point. The number has been rounded off to the third place after the decimal point.

The area of the output line occupied by the number is called a ***display zone.*** In the format code *%12.3f,* 12 stands for the ***width*** of the display zone and 3 stands for the ***precision,*** the number of digits to display after the decimal point.

Should a number require more than the 12 spaces, this *printf()* simply will give it all the space it needs. For instance, assuming *total_income* contains –246701044.5802, the display will be as follows:

You will make $ –246701044.580 this summer

The entire display zone here is 14 spaces wide (including the decimal point and the negation sign), with 3 digits again after the decimal point (truncated from the 4 digits after the decimal point in the number contained in the variable).

The number codes in the *printf()* statement that control the width and/or the precision may be omitted from the format code, as the three examples below show.

Example 2.4.2

In the *printf()* statement below, the code for the display zone width is omitted, which causes *printf()* simply to give it exactly the space the number needs.

```
printf("You will make $ %.3f this summer", total_income);
```

Assuming *total_income* contains 2467.50, the display will be as follows:

You will make $ 2467.500 this summer

The display zone is 8 spaces wide (including the decimal point); because there is a code for the precision, 3, there are 3 digits after the decimal point.

Now let's assume that the *total_income* variable contains 27.1327. The display will be as follows:

You will make $ 27.133 this summer

The display zone is now only 6 spaces wide, and still has 3 digits after the decimal point (rounded off), because 6 spaces are all that are needed to display this number, including the decimal point, in accordance with the format codes in the *printf()* statement.

Example 2.4.3

The precision may be omitted, too. If this code is omitted, *printf()* **always** displays 6 digits after the decimal point:

```
printf("You will make $ %12f this summer", total_income);
```

If we assume that the *total_income* variable contains 2467.50, the display will be as follows:

You will make $ _ 2467.500000 this summer

The display zone is 12 spaces wide (including the decimal point), as indicated by the number 12 in the format code. There are 6 digits after the decimal point since no code for the precision was included in the *printf()* statement.

Now let's assume that the *total_income* variable contains 27.1327. The display will be as follows:

You will make $ _ _ _ 27.132700 this summer

The display zone is 12 spaces wide (including the decimal point), and there are 6 digits after the decimal point, the default display when no format code for the precision is given.

Example 2.4.4

When both width and precision are omitted, the width of the print zone defaults to whatever space is needed to display the number and the precision is always 6 digits. The example below illustrates the default display zone:

```
printf("You will make $ %f this summer", total_income);
```

If the *total_income* variable contains 2467.50, the display will be as follows:

You will make $ 2467.500000 this summer

The display zone is 12 spaces wide (including the decimal point) to allow the entire number to display with 6 digits after the decimal point (the default precision).

Now let's assume that the *total_income* variable contains 527.1327. The display will be as follows:

You will make $ 527.132700 this summer

To display this entire number, the display zone is 13 spaces wide (including the decimal point), with 6 digits after the decimal point (the default precision).

EXERCISES 2.4.1

Suppose the argument to a *printf()* is the number –702.0166. Indicate the format code required in order to have each of the following numbers displayed in the display zone:

1. –702.0
2. _ _ – 702.01660
3. _ _ _ _ – 702.0167
4. –702.02

Rules for the format code *%f*. To summarize the discussion about formatting output for real numbers, Table 2.4.1 lists the format code rules, using *%7.3f* as an example.

Table 2.4.1

Format Code	Meaning	Default (when no code is specified)
%7.3f — f	Displays the argument as a *float* number.	None; the code *f* is always needed.
%7.3f — .3	Display 3 digits after the decimal point. If the argument has less than 3 digits, zeros will display in the rest of the spaces. If the argument has more than 3 digits, the display will round off to 3 decimal places or truncate the number.	Displays 6 digits after the decimal point.
%7.3f — 7	Creates a display zone width of 7 spaces. If the argument needs more spaces, the display zone will expand as necessary to show the number correctly. If the argument needs less spaces, the display zone will fill with **leading** blank spaces.	Uses whatever display zone width is needed in order to show the number correctly.
%7.3f — %	Indicates the beginning of the format codes for the argument.	None; the code % is always needed.

Table 2.4.2 shows many more examples illustrating the output formatting rules for real numbers:

Table 2.4.2

Argument	%f	%.3f	%8.3f	%4.2f	%5.0f
27.5	27.400000	27.400	_ _27.400	27.40	_ _ _27
–27.5	–27.400000	–27.400	_–27.400	–27.40	_ _–27
0.6277	0.627700	0.628	_ _ _0.628	0.63	_ _ _ _1
1.3	1.300000	1.300	_ _ _1.300	_1.3	_ _ _ _1
5901	Garbage	Garbage	Garbage	Garbage	Garbage

2.4.2 DISPLAYING WHOLE NUMBERS

The output formatting rules for integers are similar to the ones for real numbers; therefore, only two examples will be presented to explain how to format whole number output.

Example 2.4.5

Consider the statement below, in which codes for both the display zone width and the precision are included:

```
printf("Judy will work %7.5d weeks", 14);
```

The display is as follows:

Judy will work _ _00014 weeks

The special numbers in the format code create a display zone 7 spaces wide, and there are 3 leading zeros because the 5 in *%7.5d* causes the output to display 5 digits. Since the number 14 has only 2 digits, three leading zeros are displayed to fill 5 digits. Some business applications like to display numbers with leading zeros. The Supplementary Exercises at the end of this section will cover such an application.

Example 2.4.6

Now consider the statement below, in which the precision code is omitted:

```
printf("Judy will work %6d weeks", 14);
```

The display is as follows:

Judy will work _ _ _ _14 weeks

The display zone is 6 spaces wide, and since the precision code is omitted, no leading zeros are needed.

Table 2.4.3 illustrates other examples of the output formatting rules for whole numbers.

Table 2.4.3

Argument	%d	%.4f	%8.4f	%8d
27	27	0027	_ _ _ _0027	_ _ _ _ _ _27
–27	–27	–0027	_ _ _–0027	_ _ _ _ _–27
62771	62771	62771	_ _ _62771	_ _ _62771
5.901	Garbage	Garbage	Garbage	Garbage

Rules for the format code *%d*. To summarize the discussion about formatting output for whole numbers, Table 2.4.4 lists the format code rules, using *%7.3d* as an example.

Table 2.4.4

%7.3d

Format Code	Meaning	Default (when no code is specified)
d	Displays the argument as an *int* number.	None; the code *d* is always needed.
.3	Displays 3 leading digits. If the argument has less than 3 digits, the display zone will fill with **leading** zeros in the rest of the spaces. If the argument has more than 3 digits, all the digits in the number will display.	Displays all the numbers in the argument; displays no leading zeros.
7	Creates a display zone width of 7 spaces. If the argument needs more spaces, the display zone will expand as necessary to show the number correctly. If the argument needs less spaces, the display zone will fill with **leading** blank spaces.	Uses whatever display zone width is needed in order to show the number correctly.
%	Indicates the beginning of the format codes for the argument.	None; the code % is always needed.

EXERCISES 2.4.2

Suppose the argument to a *printf()* is the number –702. Indicate the format code required in order to have each of the following numbers displayed in the display zone:

1. –702
2. _ _–702
3. _ _ _ _ –00702
4. –00000702

2.4.3 DISPLAYING HUGE NUMBERS AND TINY NUMBERS

Very large or very small numbers can become quite awkward to express and display. Two examples are given below to illustrate how to deal with problems in displaying very large and very small numbers.

Example 2.4.7

As part of a physics class experiment, the teacher asks students to write a program that calculates the average growth rate of hair in meters per second. They found that hair grew 13.4 millimeters in 54 days. That is 13.4 / 1000 = 0.0134 meters. There are 60 × 60 × 24 = 86400 seconds in one day, so there are 86400 * 54 = 4665600 seconds in 54 days. The average growth rate is therefore 0.0134 / 4665600 = 0.000000002872 millimeters per second. Displaying this number is obviously awkward at best. An easier notation is needed to deal with such a small number: ***exponential notation.*** Here is a program that calculates this same average and illustrates the use of exponential notation.

```
#include <stdio.h>

main()
{
   int   days;
   float millimeters, meters, growth;

   printf("Enter the growth in millimeters and the time span in days > ");
   scanf("%f%d", &growth, &days);
   meters = millimeters / 1000;
```

```
    growth = meters / (86400 * days);
    printf("The average growth rate is = %e", growth);
}
```

Note the format code (in bold type) needed to display a number in exponential notation.

The display is as follows:

Enter the growth in millimeters and the time span in days > 13.4 54
The average growth rate is 2.872e–9

The number *2.872e–9* represents the exponential notation of 0.000000002872. It simply means 2.872 multiplied by 10^{-9}, as shown in the following equation:

2.872e–9
$2.872 \times 10^{-9} = 0.000000002872$

This type of notation is rarely encountered in business applications, except when some kind of statistical analysis is required for sales or financial forecasting, for example.

Example 2.4.8

The program below calculates the speed in kilometers per second of any moving thing:

```
#include <stdio.h>

main()
{
     float distance, seconds, speed;

     printf("Enter distance covered > ");
     scanf("%e", &distance);
     printf("How many seconds > ");
     scanf("%e", &seconds);

     speed = distance / seconds;

     printf("The speed is %e km/second", speed);
}
```

Note the format code in *scanf()*: it allows the program to read numbers in exponential notation. Here are two examples of a run. The first calculates the speed of a meteor, the second that of an ant.

Enter distance covered > 15
How many seconds > 1.5
The speed is 1.000000e+1 km/sec

Enter distance covered > 2.3e–5
How many seconds > 3.5
The speed is 6.571429e–06 km/sec

Note that in the first run the use of the exponential notation was unnecessary because the result is the number 10, which is neither very big nor very small. But in the second run, the exponential notation is useful. The problem is that the format code *%e* always displays in exponential notation.

We need some way of letting the computer decide the best way to display a number. The format code *%g* does just that—it gives the computer control over how to display the number. Let's change the *%e* code in the program above to a *%g* code:

```
printf("The speed is %g km/second", speed);
```

Now look at the output when we run the program again a few times:

Enter distance covered > 15
How many seconds > 1.5
The speed is 10 km/sec

```
Enter distance covered > 2.3e–5
How many seconds > 3.5
The speed is 6.571429e–06 km/sec

Enter distance covered > 24
How many seconds > 2.2
The speed is 10.909091 km/sec
```

You can see that the resulting display for the different runs is much better than in the previous examples. When the *%g* code is used, the computer displays the output using exponential notation only when necessary, if the number is very large or very small.

EXERCISES 2.4.3

1. Express the following numbers in C:
   a. 4.209×10^4 b. 0.037106 c. -7.401×10^{-25}
2. An unruly student has been given the task of counting the total number of words contained in all the books in his school library. He is sure that nobody knows the exact answer, so he proceeds to make an estimate. He knows that the library has 21 stacks, each with 5 shelves. By examining a few shelves, he estimates the number of books per shelf to be 60. By flipping through a few books, he estimates the number of words per page at 1000 and the number of pages per book at 320. Therefore there are $1000 \times 320 = 320000$ words per book. There are $60 \times 5 = 300$ books per stack; this makes $300 \times 21 = 6300$ books in all. Finally there are $6300 \times 320000 = 2016000000$ words in the library.

   Because the answer is such a large number, exponential notation can be used. The number 2016000000 in exponential notation would be written as 2.016×10^9. Even though this huge number is a whole number, it has to be stored in a variable of type *float* in order for it to be expressible in exponential notation in the computer. Write a program to solve this problem in a more general sense. The program should ask for the number of stacks, the number of shelves per stack, the average number of pages per book, and the average number of words per page. When all these numbers are input into the program, it should display the result in exponential notation.

2.4.4 COMMON ERRORS AND TRAPS

None of the errors listed in this subsection will cause the compiler to complain, yet the program will not work well when the programmer makes one of these errors.

1. Forgetting the *%* code in a *printf()*:

   ```
   printf("You will make $ 5.2f this summer", total_income);
   ```

   The *%* symbol is missing in front of the *5,* and while the compiler will **not** complain, the output will be as follows. (Can you see why?)

   ```
   You will make $ 5.2f this summer
   ```

2. Specifying numbers in the format code of a *scanf()*:

   ```
   scanf("%7.2f", &hourly_rate);
   ```

   The numbers in front of the *f* are not needed and should not be included in this format code. The compiler will **not** complain, but when this *scanf()* is run, the resulting number may be unpredictable. Although numbers are allowed in the format codes of a *scanf()*, it is advised that numbers be used **only** with *printf()*.
3. Confusing the number codes. For example, in the code *%7.2f*, a programmer may mistakenly think that the *7* refers to the number of digits before the decimal point. For instance, when a programmer is asked to write a *printf()* to display the number 8305.51, the following *printf()* is sometimes mistakenly written:

   ```
   printf("%4.2f", 8305.51);
   ```

Although the output will be correct, the format code *%4.2f* tells the program to allocate 4 spaces to the entire **display zone,** not just the digits before the point. The correct format code should be *%7.2f.* In this code, the *7* sets the display zone—all the digits before and after the decimal point, plus the decimal point itself—to 7.

SUPPLEMENTARY EXERCISES 2.4

1. Suppose two variables, *num1* and *num2,* contain the numbers 275 and 16 respectively. Code a *printf()* call in four different ways so that each time the following output is produced exactly:

   000275.016

   The two variables must be used once and only once, but additional arguments may be used too, if necessary. Here is one solution:

```
printf("%d%d%d%7.3f", 0, 0, 0, num1 + num2 / 1000.0);
```

2. Complete the following table. Each line refers to a *printf()* call. For example, the first line refers to *printf("%5.2f", 83.6).* The vertical bars in the last column are there for the sole purpose of clearly showing the width of the print zone. Also wherever a (d) appears, it stands for the default number for the code.

<table>
<tr><th>Format Code</th><th>Print Zone</th><th>Precision</th><th>Given in List</th><th>Shown in Output</th></tr>
<tr><td>%5.2f</td><td>5</td><td>2</td><td>83.6</td><td>|83.60|</td></tr>
<tr><td>______</td><td>7</td><td>2</td><td>83.6</td><td>| 83.60|</td></tr>
<tr><td>______</td><td>9</td><td>6 (d)</td><td>83.6</td><td>|83.000000|</td></tr>
<tr><td>%5f</td><td>______</td><td>______</td><td>83.6</td><td>|83.000000|</td></tr>
<tr><td>%.4f</td><td>______</td><td>______</td><td>83.6</td><td>|83.0000|</td></tr>
<tr><td>%f</td><td>______</td><td>______</td><td>83.6</td><td>______</td></tr>
<tr><td>%5.2f</td><td>5</td><td>2</td><td>83.689</td><td>______</td></tr>
<tr><td>______</td><td>______</td><td>______</td><td>–83.6</td><td>|–83.60|</td></tr>
<tr><td>%7.2f</td><td>7</td><td>2</td><td>–83.6</td><td>______</td></tr>
<tr><td>%9f</td><td>______</td><td>6 (d)</td><td>–83.6</td><td>______</td></tr>
<tr><td>%5f</td><td>______</td><td>______</td><td>–83.6</td><td>______</td></tr>
<tr><td>%.4f</td><td>______</td><td>______</td><td>–83.6</td><td>|–83.0000|</td></tr>
<tr><td>%f</td><td>______</td><td>______</td><td>–83.6</td><td>|–83.000000|</td></tr>
<tr><td>%5.2f</td><td>6 (d)</td><td>2</td><td>–83.689</td><td>______</td></tr>
<tr><td></td><td></td><td>leading zeros</td><td></td><td></td></tr>
<tr><td>%8d</td><td>______</td><td>0</td><td>196</td><td>| 196|</td></tr>
<tr><td>%1d</td><td>______</td><td>0</td><td>196</td><td>______</td></tr>
<tr><td>%.5d</td><td>______</td><td>______</td><td>196</td><td>______</td></tr>
<tr><td>%10.2d</td><td>______</td><td>______</td><td>23041</td><td>______</td></tr>
</table>

3. Find the errors in the following codes, if any. Also indicate which problems the compiler will not be able to detect.
   a. `printf("%d," 14);`
   b. `printf("%5d", 14.5);`
   c. `printf("%6.2f", 25);`
   d. *`printf("number=", 37.8);`*
   e. `printf("%3.3f", 14.53);`
   f. `printf("%2d, %6f", 0.41, 6.6);`
   g. `printf("%2d", 18760);`
   h. `printf(923.8);`
   i. `printf("7.3d", 65);`
   j. `printf("%5.2f + %6d", 41, 6);`
   k. `printf("%3.8", 3.8);`
4. Write a program to produce the following grocery receipt:

```
At:  ABC Grocery Store
     125 Main Street
     Some City, XY

Terminal: 0055                  Operator: 00000122

Date: 12/09/94                  Time: 17:34:07

Items bought:

Meat @ 8.95 a pound             $ 25.09
Dairy products                  $  8.21
Cereals                         $ 12.99
Desserts                        $  3.48

Total:                          $ 49.77
Received:                       $ 50.00
Change:                         $  0.23

                 THANK YOU!
```

The information is usually retrieved from electronic equipment like a laser scanner. Of course, we will need to assume all the data is keyed in by the checkout clerk:

```
Enter the date (day, month, year) > 12 09 94
Enter the time (hours, minutes, seconds) > 17 34 07
Enter the terminal code > 55
Enter the operator code > 122
Enter the weight of meat in pounds and cost per pound > 2.803 8.95
Enter the total cost of the dairy products > 8.21
Enter the total cost of the cereals > 12.99
Enter the total cost of the desserts > 3.48
Total cost is $ 49.77

Enter money received > 50.00
The change is 0.23
     :
     :  ——— Grocery receipt produced here
     :
```

Note that the user must enter the time and date of the purchase. This is dreadfully impractical. It is better to let the computer figure out these things. Unfortunately, this would require functions that we are not prepared to use at this point.

2.5 I/O OPERATIONS WITH FILES*

Data can also be read from a file rather than from the keyboard. Similarly data can be stored as output to a file instead of displayed to the screen.

2.5.1 ESSENTIAL AND ELEMENTARY FILE HANDLING

In this book, the action of opening a file, reading from a file, storing data into a file, and closing a file will be called ***file handling. File processing*** will refer to the processing of data from and to a file. The example below illustrates the basics of file handling.

* This section may be skipped without loss of continuity.

Example 2.5.1

Let's refer back to the program in Example 2.2.2 again. Suppose that the hourly rate, the hours per week of work, and the total number of weeks of work are stored in a file named JOB.DAT using a text editor instead of being entered at prompts on the screen. The data might be stored as follows:

7.05 35 10

The first number is the rate of pay, the next is the hours per week of work, and the last is the number of weeks of work. The program reads this data from the file, processes it, and calculates the total income expected. Let's store this income figure to a file named INCOME.OUT. The advantage of storing this information is that Judy can refer to it later, perhaps to send it to a printer, without having to run the program again. This data flow may be pictured as shown in Figure 2.5.1.

Figure 2.5.1

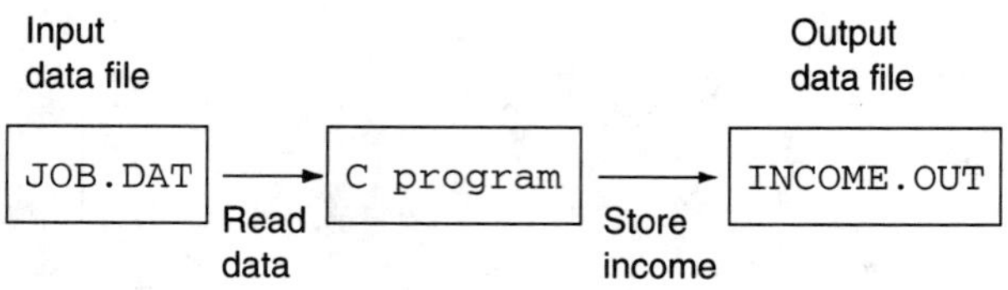

The program will process the file as follows:

1. Open the input file JOB.DAT.
2. Create an output file called INCOME.OUT.
3. Read the data from the input file.
4. Calculate the total income.
5. Store this figure into the output file.
6. Close the file JOB.DAT.
7. Close the file INCOME.OUT.

As you can see, there are four operations possible with files:

1. Opening a file
2. Reading from a file (record by record in this case)
3. Writing to a file
4. Closing a file

Other operations that can be performed on files exist as well, but they are not relevant at this time.

Here is the program with the changes made to the program from Example 2.2.2 in bold. Explanations referring to the superscript numbers follow the program.

```
#include <stdio.h>

main()
{
    float hourly_rate;
    int   hours_per_week;
    float total_income;
    int   num_weeks;
    FILE * input_file;[1]
    FILE * output_file;[1]

    input_file = fopen("JOB.DAT", "r");[1]
    output_file = fopen("INCOME.OUT", "w");[1]

    fscanf(input_file, "%f", &hourly_rate);[2]
    fscanf(input_file, "%d", &hours_per_week);[2]
    fscanf(input_file, "%d", &num_weeks);[2]
```

```
    total_income = hourly_rate * hours_per_week * num_weeks;

    fprintf(output_file, "You will make $ %.2f in %d weeks this summer\n",[3]
    num_weeks, total_income);[3]
    fclose(input_file);[4]
    fclose(output_file);[4]
}
```

Explanations

1. Declaring a file pointer and opening a file. A ***file pointer*** variable **must** be declared **before** any file operation is possible. Also the file must be opened **before** anything can be read from it (or written to it). The declaration of a file pointer variable and the opening of a file are illustrated in Figure 2.5.2.

   In the program code shown in Figure 2.5.2, the *fopen()* function searches for the file JOB.DAT in the current directory and then opens it. Note that it searches in the current directory **only.** If the file is not found there, the *fopen()* call could fail. The ***current directory*** is the directory from which the program is run.

Figure 2.5.2

Declaration / **Opening a File**

```
FILE *   input_file;        input_file = fopen("JOB.DAT", "r");

FILE *   output_file;       output_file = fopen("INCOME.OUT", "w");
```

"r" indicates a ***permissible mode*** of ***reading.*** This file cannot be written to.

"w" indicates a ***permissible mode*** of ***writing*** to the file. This file cannot be read from.

File name (must be within double quotation marks) to open. The name must follow the host operating system's naming rules.

Name of the C function that opens the file. This function returns a *FILE* pointer into *output_file* and *input_file* respectively. These file pointers identify (point to) the file named INCOME.OUT and JOB.DAT respectively.

Variables to hold the pointers to the files above. The variables *output_file* and *input_file* identify the files INCOME.OUT and JOB.DAT respectively.

Name of a file pointer variable. It must be provided to **all** file operations.

File type declaration statement (requires the statement *#include <stdio.h>*). Note the asterisks that must be present.

2. Reading data from a file. The function *fscanf()* reads the data from the input file specified by the variable *input_file*. Note the syntax shown in Figure 2.5.3.

Figure 2.5.3

```
fscanf(input_file, "%f", &hourly_rate);
```

Function name	File pointer variable	Format string	Variable to receive the data

This function works **exactly** the same way as *scanf()*, except that its name is *fscanf()* and that its first argument is the file pointer variable that identifies the input file to read data from. Note that the program no longer prompts the user for data from the screen—the data comes from the file JOB.DAT.

3. Storing data into a file. The function *fprintf()* stores the data to the output file specified by the variable *output_file*. Note the syntax shown in Figure 2.5.4.

Figure 2.5.4

Format string

```
fprintf(output_file, "You will make $ %.2f in %d weeks this summer\n",
num_weeks, total_income);
```

Function name — File pointer variable — Data to output to the file

This function works **exactly** the same way as *printf()*, except that its name is *fprintf()* and that its first argument is the file pointer variable that identifies the input file to write data to.

4. The function *fclose()* closes a file as specified by the file pointer variable passed to it:

```
fclose(input_file)
```

The file pointer variable for the file to close is *input_file* in the *fclose()* statement above. This same function is used to close either an input or output file. Only one file can be closed at a time—a separate call to *fclose()* is necessary for each file to close. Remember that the file pointer variable must always be provided to a file-handling function.

EXERCISES 2.5.1

1. In the program in Example 2.5.1 above, show how the sequence of three *fscanf()*s may be reduced to a single one.
2. Change the programs below so that the data is read from an input file and the results are stored in an output file rather than input from the keyboard and output to the screen:
   a. Exercises 2.2.1, 3
   b. Exercises 2.2.1, 5
   c. Exercises 2.2.2, 2; the data is stored on separate lines.
   d. Exercises 2.2.3, 2; the data is all stored on the same line.
   e. Example 2.4.7

2.5.2 COMMON ERRORS AND TRAPS

1. Forgetting to surround the file name with double quotation marks when *fopen()* is called:

```
input_file = fopen(JOB.DAT, "r");
```

The compiler will definitely complain about this omission.

2. Surrounding the file name and/or the permissible mode with single quotation marks when *fopen()* is called:

```
input_file = fopen('JOB.DAT', 'r');
```

The compiler will likely complain—but some may not and so will let the program run. Disaster would eventually prevail, however.

3. Forgetting to specify the permissible mode when *fopen()* is called:

```
input_file = fopen("JOB.DAT");
```

The permissible mode "r" or "w" is missing from the line above, and the compiler will definitely complain about the omission.

4. Opening a file with the wrong permissible mode. There are two different situations in which this can happen.
   Situation 1:

```
input_file = fopen("JOB.DAT", "w");
```

   In this case, the “w” should have been “r” and in this case the compiler will **not** complain because it has no way of knowing at that time whether the programmer intends to read from the file or write to it. The input file will simply be overwritten. Then when the first *fscanf()* is reached, such as the one below, the program may not complain at all, but the variables will contain nothing meaningful.

```
fscanf(input_file, "%f%f%d%d", &minimum, &hourly_rate,
                               &hours_per_week, &num_weeks)
```

   Situation 2:

```
output_file = fopen("INCOME.OUT", "r");
```

   In this case, the “r” should have been “w” and again the compiler will **not** complain. However, when the first *fprintf()* is reached, such as the one shown below, the program may not complain at all, but nothing will be output to the file.

```
fprintf(output_file, "Take the job.\n");
```

5. Attempting to open an input file that does not exist or cannot be found. For example, suppose the file JOB.DAT does not exist. When the program is run, the instruction shown below will fail:

```
input_file = fopen("JOB.DAT", "r");
```

   But the operating system will not complain and will let the program continue. Disaster would likely occur when the *fscanf()* is encountered in the program.
6. Forgetting to specify the file pointer variable in a function call to *fscanf()* or *fprintf()*:

```
 :
 :
 fscanf("%f%f%d%d", &minimum, &hourly_rate,
                    &hours_per_week, &num_weeks);
 :
 :
 fprintf("You will make $ %.2f this summer\n", total_income);
```

   The file pointer variables were omitted in both the *fscanf()* call and the *fprintf()* call above. The compiler will probably complain, but it depends on the compiler—the program might continue anyway. As a result, however, there would be problems running the program later.
7. Using *scanf()* and *printf()* instead of *fscanf()* and *fprintf()*:

```
 :
 :
 scanf(input_file, "%f%f%d%d", &minimum, &hourly_rate,
                  &hours_per_week, &num_weeks);
 :
 :
 printf(output_file, "You will make $ %.2f this summer\n",
                     total_income);
```

   The compiler will probably complain. Again this depends on the compiler—some do not complain at all and let the program run. The results will be unpredictable, however. In the case of *scanf()*, the program might wait for input. In the case of *printf()*, the program probably would **not** crash, but dreadful garbage would appear on the screen.

3 Arithmetic and Data Types

OBJECTIVES

This chapter introduces you to the following information:

- Some technical considerations regarding the data types covered in Chapter 2.
- The basic arithmetic operators used to perform calculations.
- A brief discussion of ASCII codes, a method of storing individual characters in memory, and an explanation of how to perform operations on them.

INTRODUCTION

The manipulation of data in arithmetic calculations is based on the same arithmetic concepts learned in grade school. However, due to the way data is represented and the way these arithmetic operations are implemented in the computer, we will need to discuss data manipulation a little more. This chapter will guide you through the process of working with data in calculations using the computer.

As in Chapter 2, this chapter does not emphasize problem solving as much as some technical details of the language. Once you have learned the basic skills, you will be ready for the later chapters that emphasize problem solving and program development.

You are encouraged to read about the input mechanism in Appendix F, located at the end of the book, before proceeding with the next chapters. The input mechanism is a hidden process that conveys input data from the keyboard to your program. A good understanding of this process will be beneficial as you begin to learn about data manipulation.

3.1 DATA TYPES AND QUALIFIERS FOR ARITHMETIC

As mentioned in Section 2.2.1, data is stored in "cells" within the memory. This is a simplified explanation of the storage mechanism, and to become a good C programmer, you need to acquire a more elaborate knowledge of memory than this. This section provides a more complete explanation of how data is stored in the memory of a computer.

3.1.1 STORAGE OF DATA IN MEMORY

The declaration statement of a variable tells the compiler four things:

1. The name of the variable
2. The type of the variable
3. The size of its cell in memory
4. The storage class

The first three elements of the declaration statement will be explained in this section. The fourth, the storage class, is not covered, but Appendix D will give you a brief overview of storage class designations.

The size is expressed in a unit called a ***byte.*** Essentially, one byte is the amount of space required to store one single character, like a letter of the alphabet or a punctuation mark. A more technical discussion of bytes is given in Appendix E.

Variables occupy cells of different sizes, depending on their types. (As an analogy, consider two different types of living things, an elephant and a human being—an elephant occupies more space than a human, and the amount of space each occupies depends on its type.) A bigger cell also can contain larger numbers than a smaller cell. (To continue with the same analogy, an elephant also is heavier than a human.) For example, a variable of type *int* always occupies 2 bytes and can hold numbers as big as 32767 exactly, whereas a variable of type *float* always occupies 4 bytes and can hold immense numbers, as big as approximately 10^{38}. To illustrate, Table 3.1.1 shows two declarations, along with the size of the memory cell occupied by each.

Table 3.1.1

Declaration	In Memory	Number of Bytes
int age_mine;	*age_mine*	2 bytes
float height;	*height*	4 bytes

In addition, a qualifier may accompany the type declaration of a variable. For example, in Table 3.1.2, the qualifier *long* tells the compiler to make the cell for *age_country* twice as large as for *age_mine*, even though both are of the same type, *int.* (Referring back to the analogy described previously, two living things of the same type can differ widely in size; for example, one human can be twice as large as another one.)

The keyword *long* does not indicate a new type. In both examples in Table 3.1.2, the type is *int.* A ***type*** tells the compiler in what form to store the data in the cell. So the data for an *int* variable is stored in a different form than that for a *float* variable. This is because a different coding scheme is used. (In the analogy we have been using, this would compare to the observation that elephants and humans are different species.)

Table 3.1.2

Declaration	In Memory	Number of Bytes
int age_mine;	*age_mine*	2 bytes
long int age_country;	*age_country*	4 bytes

Example 3.1.1

Now let's look at a specific example. The program below sets three variables of different types to the same value:

```
#include <stdio.h>

main()
{
      int        whole_num;
      long int   long_num;
      float      real_num;

      whole_num = 32;
      long_num = 32;
      real_num = 32.0;
}
```

These cells are stored in memory:

long_num	*whole_num*	*real_num*
32	32	32.0

The first two numbers are stored using the same coding method. The second and third numbers, even though they have the same value, will be stored using different coding methods.

EXERCISE 3.1.1

Given the declarations below, how many bytes will each variable occupy?

```
float    hours, weight;
long int seconds, length;
int      minutes, hours;
```

3.1.2 MAXIMUM AND MINIMUM VALUES OF DATA TYPES

As a C programmer, you need to be aware of the maximum and minimum values each data type allows, and therefore you need to know the number of bytes a variable occupies. Subsection 3.1.5 below illustrates a common trap that testifies to the need for this awareness. Table 3.1.3 shows the maximum and minimum values for various data types and the byte allocation for each of the data types. Other data types exist, but they are rarely used.

Table 3.1.3

Type/Qualifiers	Bytes	Maximum	Minimum
*char**	1	127	–128
int	2	32767	–32768
long int	4	2147483647	–214783648
unsigned char	1	255	0
unsigned int	2	65535	0
unsigned long int	4	4294967295	0
float	4	3.40282×10^{38}	1.17549×10^{-38}
		-3.40282×10^{38}	-1.17549×10^{-38}
		(these are rounded off)	
double	8	1.79769×10^{308}	2.22507×10^{-38}
		-1.79769×10^{308}	$-2.22507 \times 10^{-308}$
		(these are rounded off)	

* Some compilers use the maximum 255 and the minimum 0 for *char.* For those compilers, the qualifier *signed* must be added to enforce acceptance of negative numbers: *signed char some_var.* This is usually the only time the *signed* qualifier is needed.

A variable declared with the qualifier *unsigned* can only store positive numbers. You may not be able to remember the maximum and minimum size for each data type, but you should remember the magnitude of each type.

EXERCISES 3.1.2

1. Indicate all the possible data types that could be used for the variables below in order to receive the following information correctly:
   a. The age of a customer
   b. The distance in whole kilometers between any two cities

c. The distance in kilometers, including fractions of a kilometer, between any two cities
d. The speed of light (about 3×10^8 meters/second) as a whole number
e. The speed of light (about 3×10^8 meters/second) as a real number
f. The outside temperature in Celsius
g. The outside temperature in Kelvin
h. The age of the universe (about 10^{16} years)
i. The monthly Canadian deficit (assuming the yearly deficit is exactly $44 billion)

2. Suppose you compile the following program with compiler A:

```
#include <stdio.h>

main()
{
        char  answer;

        printf("Enter a number > ");
        scanf("%d", &answer);
        printf("Echoed %d\n", answer);
}
```

Then you run the program and get the following screen display:

```
Enter a number > 147
Echoed 147
```

Next you compile and run the same program with compiler B and run the program. The screen display from the program run is as follows:

```
Enter a number > 147
Echoed –8091
```

This time you get the wrong display. What could have caused the difference?

3. Consider the following two advertisements for computers for sale in the classified ads:

USED COMPUTER: 8088 microcomputer, 8 MHz, 640K RAM, 20-MB HD. Asking $120.

BARGAIN! 486 microcomputer, 50 MHz, 8-MB RAM, 220-MB HD. Asking $1300.

The 640K and the 8-MB specifications mean the amount of space (in bytes) in the internal memory of the computer, where programs are run. The 20-MB HD and the 220-MB HD mean the amount of space (again in bytes) in the hard disk, where files are stored.
The letter K is used to represent 1024 bytes, so 64K is equivalent to 64×1024 bytes = 65536 bytes. In turn, the letters MB stand for 1024K, so 6 MB is equivalent to $6 \times 1024K = 6144K = 6144 \times 1024$ bytes = 6291456 bytes. Now answer the following questions for each computer:
a. How many bytes can be stored in the internal memory?
b. How many bytes can be stored on the hard disk?
c. A typewritten page contains about 1500 characters. How many copies of one page could be stored on the hard disk?
d. A spreadsheet on the hard disk contains a table of numbers. Assume that the data of the first column are stored as *floats*, the second as *long ints*, the third as *doubles*, and the fourth as *unsigned ints*. (***Note:*** The real method of storage is quite different.) The table is 156 rows deep. How many copies of this spreadsheet could be stored in memory?

3.1.3 SYSTEM DEPENDENCIES

The maximum and minimum values in Table 3.1.3 assumed the use of Borland C with MS-DOS. This observation is significant because the size of a data type (and therefore its maximum and minimum) depends on the environment it is in. Three factors influence the data type size:

1. The computer (specifically the CPU) being used
2. The type and qualifier
3. The compiler used to run the program

The *sizeof* operator. The compiler provides an operator, *sizeof*, that can be used by the programmer to find out for sure the size of a data type in a particular environment. For example, the following *printf()* displays the number of bytes occupied by a *long int* data. This statement will work regardless of the environment.

```
printf("Data type long int occupies %d bytes\n", sizeof(long int));
```

In this statement, *sizeof* is the operator and *long int* represents the data type. Note that *sizeof* is **not** a function, even though it looks like one. As a matter of fact, the parentheses are not really needed: *sizeof long int* would do just the same.

Predefined symbolic constants. Knowing the amount of space a particular piece of data occupies does not reveal immediately its minimum and maximum. It is possible to calculate them, but it would require a level of mathematical knowledge that is beyond us at this point. C does not have an operator to calculate the minimum and maximum size of a data type. Instead it provides symbolic constants that represent them, listed in Table 3.1.4.

Table 3.1.4

	Symbols	
Type/Qualifiers	**Maximum**	**Minimum**
char	SCHAR_MAX	SCHAR_MIN
int	INT_MAX	INT_MIN
long int	LONG_MAX	LONG_MIN
unsigned char	UCHAR_MAX	0
unsigned int	UINT_MAX	0
unsigned long int	ULONG_MAX	0
float	FLT_MAX	FLT_MIN
double	DBL_MAX	DBL_MIN

These symbolic constants stand for the same number types as the ones presented earlier (in Table 3.1.3). When a symbolic constant is used in a program, the following directives must be included as well, at the **top** of the program:

- Use *#include <limits.h>* for all symbolic constants pertaining to *char*s and *int*s
- Use *#include <float.h>* for all symbolic constants pertaining to *float*s and *double*s

An example is presented in Exercise 3.1.3, 2 below.

EXERCISES 3.1.3

1. Try the program below on your computer, and observe the values:

```
#include <stdio.h>

main()
{
   printf("Data type char occupies %d bytes\n", sizeof(char));
   printf("Data type int occupies %d bytes\n", sizeof(int));
   printf("Data type long int occupies %d bytes\n", sizeof(long int));
   printf("Data type unsigned char occupies %d bytes\n",
          sizeof(unsigned char));
   printf("Data type unsigned int occupies %d bytes\n",
          sizeof(unsigned int));
   printf("Data type unsigned long int occupies %d bytes\n",
          sizeof unsigned(long int));
```

```
    printf("Data type float occupies %d bytes\n", sizeof(float));
    printf("Data type double occupies %d bytes\n", sizeof(double));
}
```

2. Try the program below on your computer, and observe the values:

```
#include <stdio.h>
#include <limits.h>
#include <float.h>

main()
{
    printf("Data type char has max = %d and min = %d\n",
            SCHAR_MAX, SCHAR_MIN);
    printf("Data type int has max = %d and min = %d\n",
            INT_MAX, INT_MIN);
    printf("Data type long int has max = %ld and min = %ld\n",
            LONG_MAX, LONG_MIN);
    printf("Data type unsigned char has max = %d and min = 0\n",
            UCHAR_MAX);
    printf("Data type unsigned int has max = %u and min = 0\n",
            UINT_MAX);
    printf("Data type unsigned long int has max = %lu and min = 0\n",
            ULONG_MAX);
    printf("Data type float has max = %g and min = %g\n",
            FLT_MAX, FLT_MIN);
    printf("Data type double has max = %g and min = %g\n",
            DBL_MAX, DBL_MIN);
}
```

Note some new format codes used here, including *%ld, %u,* and *%lu*. These are explained in the subsection coming up next.

3. Why was the format code *%g* used in the program above? To help you answer this, modify the program in two ways:
   a. Change each *%g* with a *%f* and run the program.
   b. Change each *%g* with a *%e* and run the program.
   Note the slightly different displays caused by the changes to the program.

Before closing this subsection, we should observe that the declarations for some data types can be shortened. Examples include the following:

long	some_var;	means the same as	*long int*	some_var;
unsigned long	some_var;	means the same as	*unsigned long int*	some_var;

In other words, the keyword *int* may be omitted from the declarations.

3.1.4 FORMAT CODES WITH QUALIFIERS

Displaying data (with *printf()*) that are declared with a qualifier may require a qualifier in the format code as well. Table 3.1.5 shows the format codes to use for each type of argument.

Similarly, when reading (with *scanf()*) into variables declared with qualifiers, the format codes to use are listed in Table 3.1.6.

The format codes *%i* and *%li* are not specified by ANSI C, but nonetheless they are widely used now. The proper use of these format codes should require no explanations. The format codes that have an "*l*" between the percent sign and the next letter work the same as those without the "*l*", but they are for larger numbers. For example, *%lf* works the same as *%f,* except *%lf* is used for bigger numbers. You may ignore the format code *%c* for now. Its purpose will be covered in Section 3.3.

Table 3.1.5

Argument Data Type	Format Code to Use
int	%*d* or %*i*
long	%*ld* or %*li*
unsigned	%*u*
long unsigned	%*lu*
char	%*c*
	%*d* or %*i*
float	%*f*
	%*g*
	%*e*
double	%*f* or %*lf*
	%*g* or %*lg*
	%*e* or %*le*

Table 3.1.6

Argument Data Type	Format Code to Use
int	%*d* or %*i*
long	%*ld* or %*li*
unsigned	%*u*
long unsigned	%*lu*
char	%*c*
	%*d* or %*i*
float	%*f*
	%*g*
	%*e*
double	%*lf*
	%*lg*
	%*le*

EXERCISES 3.1.4

1. Indicate all the possible data types that could be used for the variables below in order to read the data correctly and then to display the data correctly:
   a. The age of a customer
   b. The distance in whole kilometers between any two cities
   c. The distance in kilometers, including fractions of a kilometer, between any two cities
   d. The speed of light (about 3×10^8 meters/second) as a whole number
   e. The speed of light (about 3×10^8 meters/second) as a real number
   f. The outside temperature in Celsius
   g. The outside temperature in Kelvin
   h. The age of the universe (about 10^{16} years)
   i. The monthly Canadian deficit (assuming the yearly deficit is exactly $44 billion)
2. For the following declarations, write a *scanf()* function call to read data into them:
   a.
   ```
   int    month, year;
   float  avg;
   ```
   b.
   ```
   double        volt1, volt2;
   float         res;
   unsigned int  age;
   ```
3. Write declaration statements for variables to hold the data from Exercise 3.1.2, 1 and include appropriate *printf()* and *scanf()* function calls.

3.1.5 COMMON ERRORS AND TRAPS

1. Overflowing or underflowing a variable. ***Overflowing*** means attempting to store a number that is too big to fit in the cell of a variable. ***Underflowing*** means attempting to store a number that is too small to fit in the cell of a variable. This happens when a number is so tiny that the hardware is simply unable to code it.

   Since overflowing is a more common error, the following program illustrates an overflow problem. The program prompts for the user's weekly salary and displays the yearly salary.

```
#include <stdio.h>

main()
{
    int  week_sal, year_sal;

    printf("Enter your weekly salary > ");
    scanf("%d", &week_sal);

    year_sal = week_sal * 49;   /* 52 weeks minus 3 weeks vacation */

    printf("Yearly salary = $ %d\n", year_sal);
}
```

   Here is an example of the display when the program is run:

   Enter your weekly salary > <u>680</u>
   Yearly salary = $ –32216

   The yearly salary is totally wrong. Yet it appears that the code is correct. The clue to this mystery lies in the memory cells of the variables:

week_sal	year_sal
680	-0

   A bogus number has been stored in the variable *year_sal*. Where did it come from? It was calculated using the following equation:

   year_sal = *week_sal* * 49

   Since 680 was entered at the prompt that requested the user's weekly salary, that number was used to calculate the yearly salary in the equation:

   yearly_sal = 680 * 49
   yearly_sal = 33320

   The maximum number an *int* type variable is able to store is 32767. The value calculated here, 33320, is therefore too big to fit in the cell for *year_sal*. So when the equal sign tries to put it in its cell, the cell "cracks open," causing the number to be damaged so that a bogus number is displayed. Technically the error does not really happen this way, but the analogy is good enough.

   The only change needed in the program code to resolve the problem is to change the declaration for the variable to the following:

```
long int  year_sal;
```

   The cell is now big enough so that the number 33320 will fit in the allotted space. In fact, the declaration *unsigned int year_sal;* would do just as well. (Can you explain why?)

   This sort of error does not come up often. However, a programmer unaware of the potential problems it can cause may spend a considerable amount of time trying to detect it when it does come up. The programmer should make an estimate of how big the values of the variables will be before writing the program or running it.

2. Using an incorrect qualifier code (or omitting one) in the format code. Consider the program above (after it was corrected):

```
#include <stdio.h>

main()
{
    int         week_sal;
    long int    year_sal;

    printf("Enter your weekly salary > ");
    scanf("%d", &week_sal);

    year_sal = week_sal * 49;   /* 52 weeks minus 3 weeks vacation */

    printf("Yearly salary = $ %d\n", year_sal);
}
```

When you run the corrected program, you will see the following display:

Enter your weekly salary > 680
Yearly salary = $ –32216

Despite the fact that the error in the declaration has been corrected, the result is still wrong. This time, it is the *printf()* that failed. The format code *%ld* should be used when the argument is of the type *long int*:

```
printf("Yearly salary = %ld\n", year_sal);
```

The format code *%ld* must be used in the *printf()* statement for a *long int* argument. Only then will the display be correct.

SUPPLEMENTARY EXERCISES 3.1

1. The owner of the ABC Manufacturing Company has set up a new system that uses a test to determine the upcoming yearly salary increases of its employees. The test has three parts:
   a. Aptitude. Each question is worth 5 points. There are 40 questions.
   b. Interest in the work. Each question is worth 3 points. There are 30 questions.
   c. Depth of knowledge. Each question is worth 2 points. There are 30 questions.
   In all three parts, 2 points are deducted for each wrong answer and no points are deducted for questions left unanswered. A clever mathematician, hired by the company, discovered that when the total score obtained by an employee is multiplied by the employee's daily salary, the result gives a good estimate of the salary increase the employee deserves.

   The same mathematician developed the following program to calculate the salary increase from the test results for each employee. Unfortunately, she made numerous little coding errors that she could have easily avoided if she had read Section 3.1 in this book. Locate all the places where the program has the potential to malfunction and explain what is wrong with the code. No lines of code must be removed but some do need fixing.

```
#include <stdio.h>

main()
{
      int               corr, wrong, blank, increase;
      unsigned char     score1, score2, score3;
      long int          temp;
      float             total_score;
      char              daily;
```

```
    printf("For the aptitude test:"
           "Enter the number of:");
    printf("  a. correctly answered questions > ");
    scanf("%d", &corr);
    printf("  b. wrongly answered questions > ");
    scanf("%d", &wrong);
    printf("  c. questions left blank > ");
    scanf("%d", &blank);

    score1 = corr * 5 - wrong * 2;
    temp = score1;
    printf("Score obtained in this test = %d\n", temp);

    printf("For the interests test:"
           "Enter the number of:");
    printf("  a. correctly answered questions > ");
    scanf("%d", &corr);
    printf("  b. wrongly answered questions > ");
    scanf("%d", &wrong);
    printf("  c. questions left blank > ");
    scanf("%d", &blank);

    score2 = corr * 3 - wrong * 2;
    temp = score2;
    printf("Score obtained in this test = %d\n", temp);

    printf("For the knowledge test:"
           "Enter the number of:");
    printf("  a. correctly answered questions > ");
    scanf("%d", &corr);
    printf("  b. wrongly answered questions > ");
    scanf("%d", &wrong);
    printf("  c. questions left blank > ");
    scanf("%d", &blank);

    score3 = corr * 2 - wrong * 2;
    temp = score3;
    printf("Score obtained in this test = %d\n", temp);

    total_score = score1 + score2 + score3;

    printf("Enter the employee's daily salary > ");
    scanf("%d", &daily);
    increase = daily * total_score;
    printf("The employee deserves $ %d in increase\n",
           increase);
}
```

3.2 ARITHMETIC OPERATORS AND EXPRESSIONS

In this section, we will look more closely at the standard arithmetic operators, addition (+), subtraction (–), multiplication (*), and division (/). In addition, the use and applications of one other arithmetic operator, the modulus (%), will be covered in this section.

3.2.1 SOME WELL-KNOWN BINARY AND UNARY OPERATORS

You are probably quite familiar with the uses of the addition, subtraction, and multiplication operators, and you have seen examples of how these operators are used in program codes. At this point, only the division and modulus operators require further explanation. The division operator returns the *quotient* of a division problem, whereas the modulus operator returns the ***remainder*** from a division problem.

Example 3.2.1

Consider the division problem 26 divided by 7. We know that 7 will go into 26 three times, because 7 × 3 = 21. So 3 is the quotient and the remainder is consequently 5 because 26 – 21 = 5.

The C expression to find the quotient in this problem, which we just found was 3, is 26 / 7. In this expression, the symbol / is the symbol for the division operator.

The C expression to find the remainder in this problem, which we determined was 5, is 26 % 7. In this expression, the symbol % is the symbol for the modulus operator.

The following list gives other examples of the result determined by an expression using the modulus operator to find the remainder as opposed to the division operator to find the quotient:

12 % 5 returns the remainder of 12 divided by 5, which is 2
12 / 5 returns the quotient of 12 divided by 5, which is 2

27 % 3 returns the remainder of 27 divided by 3, which is 0
27 / 3 returns the quotient of 27 divided by 3, which is 9

22 % 7 returns the remainder of 22 divided by 7, which is 1
22 / 7 returns the quotient of 22 divided by 7, which is 3

3 % 7 returns the remainder of 3 divided by 7, which is 3
3 / 7 returns the quotient of 3 divided by 7, which is 0

6 % 7 returns the remainder of 6 divided by 7, which is 6
6 / 7 returns the quotient of 6 divided by 7, which is 0

Both operators can have some useful applications in C programming, as will be seen throughout this book.

The numbers on either sides of the operator are called ***operands.*** An operator that requires two operands is said to be ***binary.*** Look at the following example:

12 % 5

The modulus operator (%) is a binary operator because it requires two operands, in this case 12 and 5.

An operator that requires only one operand is said to be ***unary.*** The ***negation*** operator is an example of a unary operator. It simply changes its operand to negative, and requires only one operand, as shown in the following example:

–34

More must be said about the use of the unary negation operator when its operand is a variable. Suppose that the variables *a* and *b* are declared, *int a, b* and *a = 5*. The expression *b = –a* takes the value in the variable *a*, 5, makes it negative (i.e., –5), and then stores the result in the variable *b*. It is important to realize that the value inside the variable *a* **remains** 5.

There is also a ***positive*** sign unary operator:

+34

This unary operator is rarely used, since a number is always positive by default.

3.2.2 PRECEDENCE OF ARITHMETIC OPERATORS IN EXPRESSIONS

If a program includes the declaration *int result;* and the expression *result = 31 + 6 / 2 – 83 % 5 * –2;* the compiler must decide which of the operators to apply first, second, and so on. Rules of precedence for each of the operators are necessary and are shown in Table 3.2.1.

Table 3.2.1

Operator (in order of priority)	Associativity
– (unary)	Right to left
* / %	Left to right
+ – (binary)	Left to right

Table 3.2.1 indicates that the multiplication operator (*), the division operator (/), and the modulus operator (%) have equal priority, and that their priority is higher than the binary operators for addition (+) and subtraction (–). The unary negation operator (–) has the highest priority. Operators of higher priority are applied first. Before working out the evaluation of the expression above, let us look at three simpler ones.

Example 3.2.2

Consider the expression *8 – 4 * –2*. It involves three operators, and here is the order in which the operators are applied:

Action	*8 – 4 * –2*
Apply the unary operator (-) first:	*–2*
Apply the multiplication operator (*) second:	*4 * –2 = –8*
Apply the subtraction operator (–) third:	*8 – –8 = 16*

16 is the result of the expression *8 – 4 * –2*

Example 3.2.3

Consider the expression *8 – 4 * 2 + –12*. It involves four operators. Note that the binary operators for subtraction (–) and addition (+) have equal priority. This causes confusion: which one should be applied first? The answer is that in the event that two operators with equal priority are used in an expression, the associativity column of Table 3.2.1 indicates which operator to apply first. The rule of associativity for addition and subtraction is from left to right, meaning that evaluation involving these operators goes from left to right. Here is how the expression *8 – 4 * 2 + –12* is evaluated:

Action	*8 – 4 * 2 + –12*
Apply the unary negation operator (–) first:	*–12*
Apply the multiplication operator (*) second:	*4 * 2 = 8*
Apply the subtraction (–) and addition (+) operators from left to right, solving the subtraction problem first:	*8 – 8 = 0*
Then solve the addition problem:	*0 + –12 = –12*

–12 is the result of the expression *8 – 4 * 2 + –12*

When an expression has more than one binary operator with the same level of priority, the associativity rule causes the operator to the left to be applied first. When there are two or more unary operators, however, the operator to the right is applied first. Let us look at another example that requires the use of the associativity rules.

Example 3.2.4

In the expression below, all the operators have the same level of priority, so the rules of associativity must be used throughout.

Action	*8 – 4 + 2 – 12*
Left to right, apply the subtraction operator first:	*8 – 4 = 4*
Apply the next operator to the right (addition):	*4 + 2 = 6*
Apply the final operator (subtraction):	*6 – 12 = –6*

–6 is the result of the expression *8 – 4 + 2 – 12*

EXERCISES 3.2.1

Evaluate the following expressions:

1. 15 * 4 / 2 % 4 * 7
2. 15 + 4 – 6 – 21 + 2
3. 15 * –4 / 2 + 7 * 3

Example 3.2.5

We are now ready to evaluate the expression presented at the beginning of this subsection:

*result = 31 + 7 / 2 – 83 % 5 * –2*

The unary operator (at the far right of the expression) is applied first:

–2

According to the table of priority, the division operator (/), the modulus operator (%) and the multiplication operator (*) must be applied next. Remember, they are applied in order from left to right, according to the rules of associativity. First solve the division operation:

7 / 2 = 3

Next solve the operation using the modulus, to find the remainder in a division problem:

83 % 5 = 3

The result of this operation (3) is used in the multiplication operation:

3 * –2 = –6

The addition (+) and subtraction (–) operations are lowest in priority, and these operators are applied last, from left to right, according to the rules of associativity. The result of the division operation is added to the number 31 first:

31 + 3 = 34

Then the result of that operation is used in the final subtraction problem:

34 – –6 = 40

The result of the expression *31 + 7 / 2 – 83 % 5 * –2* is 40.

Example 3.2.6

The expression below uses the same operands as the example above, but different operators have been used. The order in which the operators are applied is therefore different, according to the rules for priority and associativity of the operators.

*result = 31 – 7 * 2 + 83 / 5 % 2*

Look for the multiplication (*), division (/), and modulus (%) operators first. Do the calculations using these operators in order from left to right, starting with the multiplication operation:

7 * 2 = 14

Now apply the division operator:

83 / 5 = 16

Next do the calculation with the modulus operator:

16 % 2 = 0

When these highest priority operators have been applied, you can move on to the subtraction (–) and addition (+) operations. Again, apply the operators in order from left to right, so the subtraction operation is first:

31 – 14 = 17

Use this result in the final addition operation:

17 + 0 = 17

The result of the expression *31 – 7 * 2 + 83 / 5 % 2* is 17.

EXERCISES 3.2.2

1. Evaluate the following expressions, assuming the declaration *int result;*:
   a. *result = 31 / 6 % 2 + 83 – 5 * 2*
   b. *result = 112 / 5 / 2 % 6 * 3*
   c. *result = –6 * 7 % 2 + –3*
2. Write a program that prompts the user to enter a social insurance number, reads the number into the program, and they displays it as shown below:

   Enter an S.I.N. > 207962454
   The S.I.N. entered is 207-962-454

   Work out two solutions using the following criteria:
   a. Read the entry into a single number. Then separate it into the three parts shown by using a series of remainder and division operations.
   b. Read the entry into three separate variables. This requires the format string of the *scanf()* to indicate how many digits to scan for each number. For instance, the *scanf("%4d%3d%2d", &num1, &num2, &num3)* would store 2079 into *num1*, 624 into *num2*, and 54 into *num3*.

3.2.3 CHANGING THE PRECEDENCE OF OPERATORS

The precedence of an operator can be changed temporarily in the evaluation of an expression by simply putting the particular operation within a set of parentheses. Parentheses have the highest priority of all operators, as shown in Table 3.2.2.

Table 3.2.2

Operator (in order of priority)	Associativity
()	Left to right
– (unary)	Right to left
* / %	Left to right
+ – (binary)	Left to right

Example 3.2.7

Let's change the order of evaluation of the expression in Example 3.2.6 as follows:

$$result = (31 - 7) * 2 + 83 / (5 \% 2)$$

Even though none of the operands nor the operators in the expression have changed, the evaluation changes completely. The operation within parentheses at the far left of the expression is evaluated first:

$$(31 - 7) = 24$$

Next the second operation in parentheses, from left to right, is evaluated:

$$(5 \% 2) = 1$$

After the two operations within parentheses have been completed, the operators next in order of priority are applied, in this case the multiplication (*) and division (/) operators. From left to right, the multiplication operation is evaluated first:

$$24 * 2 = 48$$

Next the division operator is applied:

$$83 / 1 = 83$$

The addition operator (+) is the last to be applied:

$$48 + 83 = 131$$

The result of the expression $(31 - 7) * 2 + 83 / (5 \% 2)$ is 131. The addition of two sets of parentheses changed the order of evaluation of the operations in this expression, and so the result of the expression is very different from the expression in Example 3.2.6.

Example 3.2.8

A different arrangement of parentheses results in the evaluation of the operations in yet another order, and a different result is found for the expression, as shown below.

$$result = 31 + (7 / 2 - (83 \% 5 * 2))$$

Open the outer set of parentheses first:

$$7 / 2 - (83 \% 5 * 2)$$

Evaluate the expression within the inner set of parentheses from left to right:

$$83 \% 5 = 3$$
$$3 * 2 = 6$$

Then evaluate the expressions within the outer set of parentheses:

$$7 / 2 = 3$$
$$3 - 6 = -3$$

This leaves only one expression left to evaluate:

$$31 + -3 = 28$$

The result of the expression $31 + (7 / 2 - (83 \% 5 * 2))$ is 28.

EXERCISES 3.2.3

Evaluate the following expressions, assuming the declaration *int result*:

1. $result = 31 / (6 \% 2) + (83 - 5) * 2$
2. $result = 112 / ((5 / 2) \% 6) * 3$
3. $result = -(6 * 7 \% 2) + -3$

3.2.4 MIXING DATA TYPES AND IMPLICIT CONVERSION

All the expressions we have examined so far involve only integers. When other data types are mixed with integers, the order of precedence of the operators remains the same, but sometimes the way individual operators function may change slightly. Let's take a look at an example using mixed data types.

Example 3.2.9

The following program calculates and displays the average of two student test grades, 86 and 97.

```
#include <stdio.h>

main()
{
        int    mark1, mark2;
        int    total, average;

        mark1 = 86;
        mark2 = 97;
        total = mark1 + mark2;
        average = total / 2;
        printf("The average mark is %d\n", average);
}
```

The program's output will be:

The average mark is 91

Yet the exact average is 91.5. The .5 was dropped, **not** by the *printf()*, but by the division in *average = total / 2*. Remember the division operator returns the quotient and drops the remainder. How then can we retain and display the decimal part of the answer (.5)? Three modifications to the program are needed:

1. Change the type of the variable *average* to *float*.
2. Divide the variable *total* by 2.0 instead of 2.
3. Change the format code within the *printf()* from *%d* to *%.1f*.

Here is the new program (with changes in bold and explanations below):

```
#include <stdio.h>

main()
{
        int    mark1, mark2;
        int    total;
        float[1] average;

        mark1 = 85.5;
        mark2 = 97.0;
        total = mark1 + mark2;
        average = total / 2.0[2];
        printf("The average mark is %.1f[3]\n", average);
}
```

When the revised program is run, the following line now displays:

The average mark is 91.5

Explanations

1. Since the variable *average* is declared as *float*, it is able to receive and store the fractional part of the division. If its declaration remained *int*, then it would not able to receive the number 91.5 (*float*). Consequently, the fractional part of 91.5 would have been lost ***(truncated);*** that is, the result would be converted from a *float* number to an *int* number. You will not even be aware that the conversion occurs, so it is termed an ***implicit*** conversion. Such conversions occur due to a ***type mismatch*** between two entities (here *average* was declared as data type *int* but the result of *total / 2.0* required a *float* data type). In summary, if we had used *int average* in the program, the expression would have been evaluated as follows:

   average = total / 2.0
   183 / 2.0 = 91.5
   average = 91.5

   At this point, the compiler realizes a type mismatch has occurred, and truncates the number, dropping the .5:

   average = 91

   The result 91 is the number that is stored in the cell for the variable *average.*
2. The evaluation of the expression *average = total / 2.0* is as follows:

   average = total / **2.0**;
   183 / 2.0 = 91.5
   average = 91.5

   The 2.0 is a real number. Having a real number involved in the division tells the compiler that the fractional part of the division must be kept. So rather than returning only the quotient, the division operator will return the exact result of the division.
3. The format code *%.1f*, as you recall, ensures that only one number is displayed after the decimal point.

Another situation leading to a mismatch of types between the evaluation of the expression and the variable on the left side of the assignment operator would occur if the declaration was changed to *float average* but the 2.0 had remained 2:

average = total / **2**
183 / 2 = 91
average = 91

Since the variable *average* was declared as a data type *float*, at this point a fractional part .0 will be attached to the variable *average*, so its cell will contain 91.0, which is not longer an *int*eger.

EXERCISES 3.2.4

1. Consider the following segment of code:

```
int  res;
res = 15 / 4;
```

Which of the following results will be stored in the variable *res*?
a. 3
b. 4
c. 4.0
d. 3.0
e. 3.7
f. 3.75

2. Answer the question above for the following expression:

```
res = 15.0 / 4;
```

3. Consider the following segment of code:

```
printf("%.0f", 17.61);
```

Which of the following results will be displayed?
a. 17.61
b. 17.0
c. 17.1
d. 17.
e. 17
f. 18.0
g. 18.
h. 18

4. Consider the following segment of code:

```
printf("%d", 15 / 4);
```

Which of the following results will be displayed? (***Hint:*** Look at the first entry in Subsection 3.2.7, *Common Errors and Traps.*)
a. 3
b. 4
c. 4.0
d. 3.0
e. 3.7
f. 3.75
g. None of the above

5. Consider the following segment of code:

```
printf("%.0f", 15 / 4);
```

Which of the following results will be displayed?
a. 3
b. 4
c. 4.0
d. 3.0

e. 3.7
f. 3.75
g. None of the above

6. What result would each of the following programs display?

a.
```
#include <stdio.h>

main()
{
        int   mark1, mark2;
        float total, average;

        mark1 = 86;
        mark2 = 97;
        total = mark1 + mark2;
        average = total/2;
        printf("The average mark is %f\n", average);
}
```

b.
```
#include <stdio.h>

main()
{
        int    mark1, mark2;
        float  total;
        double average;

        mark1 = 86;
        mark2 = 97;
        total = mark1 + mark2;
        average = total/2;
        printf("The average mark is %lf\n", average);
}
```

c.
```
#include <stdio.h>

main()
{
        int    mark1, mark2;
        float  total;
        double average;

        mark1 = 86.4;
        mark2 = 97.6;
        total = mark1 + mark2;
        average = total/2;
        printf("The average mark is %lf\n", average);
}
```

d.
```
#include <stdio.h>

main()
{
        float  mark1, mark2;
        int    total;
        float  average;

        mark1 = 86.4;
        mark2 = 97.6;
        total = mark1 + mark2;
        average = total/2;
        printf("The average mark is %f\n", average);
}
```

The operator rules of conversion. We have just seen an example of a simple expression, *total / 2.0*, where one operand of the division problem is data type *int* and the other is *float.* (Strictly speaking it is data type *double*. We will learn more about that particular data type later.) The result of the division is data type *float* (again it is really *double*). It is important to be able to know what the type of the result of any expression will be. This is because the variable on the left side of the assignment operator will receive this evaluation. So that variable had better be of the same type as the result of the expression, or else some information may be lost due to a type mismatch, as was illustrated in the Example 3.2.9 above. Luckily there are simple rules that govern the type of the result of an operation. These rules are listed in Table 3.2.3.

Table 3.2.3*

Data Types for the Addition Operator (+), Subtraction Operator (–), and Multiplication Operator (*)

Operand Data Type		Result Data Type
Operand 1	**Operand 2**	
int	*int*	*int*
int	*double*	*double*
int	*float*	*double*
float	*double*	*double*
(and vice versa)		

Data Types for the Division Operator (/)

Operand Data Type		Result Data Type
Operand 1	**Operand 2**	
int	*int*	*int* (truncation)
int	*double*	*double*
int	*float*	*double*
float	*double*	*double*
(and vice versa)		

Data Types for the Modulus Operator (%)

Operand Data Type		Result Data Type
Operand 1	**Operand 2**	
int	*int*	*int*
(No other data types are allowed with the % operator)		

* Qualifiers may be used with the data types listed (e.g., *unsigned int*).

Example 3.2.10

Consider the declaration *int result* and the expression *result = 31 + 7.0 / 2 – 83 % 5 * 2*. While we evaluate it, let's also keep track of the data types received by the values as they are calculated (Figure 3.2.1). In the figure, the letter *i* stands for *int* and *d* stands for *double* data types.

Figure 3.2.1

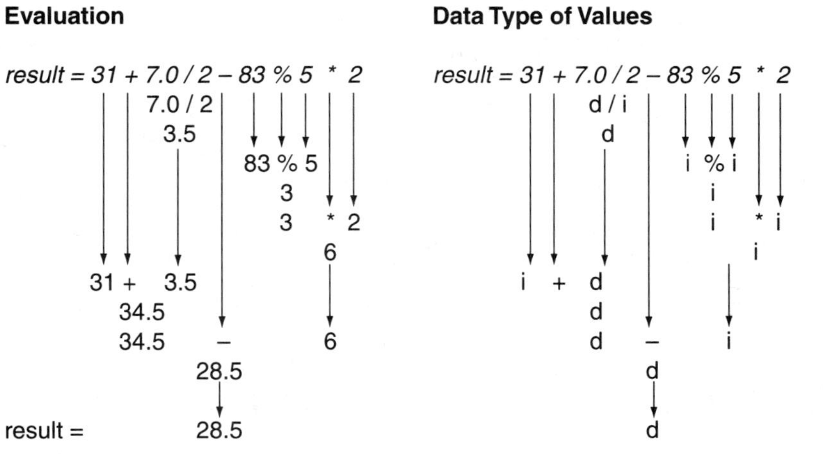

The expression *31 + 7.0 / 2 – 83 % 5 * 2* evaluates to 28.5, but 28 will be stored in *result*. This is due to a type mismatch again: the variable *result* is data type *int*. It would be better to make the variable *result* data type *float* (or *double*). Once this change is made, 28.5 will be stored in *result*.

Earlier it was mentioned that in the expression *total / 2.0,* the number 2.0 is actually data type *double.* Also in *31 + 7.0 / 2 – 83 % 5 * 2,* the number 7.0 is data type *double.* What is the explanation for this? You might think it would be data type *float,* but it is not, because the C compiler always stores a real number literal in a cell of type *double.*

The rules outlined in Table 3.2.3 above show the existence of a hierarchy of the data types from lowest to highest as follows:

char → *int* → *long* → *float* → *double*

char ↑ lowest; *double* ↑ highest

The data type of the result of an operation is always the highest of the two operands. For instance, observe in Figure 3.2.1 that the result of the operation *7.0 / 2* is data type *double*. Then immediately after that, the result of the operation *31 / 3.5* is also data type *double*. This is the highest data type, and it continues through the remaining operations, making the whole expression evaluate to type *double*. The data type of the end result of an expression is simply the highest one from the data types of the results obtained by each operation.

Example 3.2.11

Note that the remainder operator (%) accepts only integer types. If one of its operand is not an integer, it is **not** converted to an integer; instead, the operation simply fails! For example, in the following expression, the compiler will complain about the operand *5.0,* which is not an integer, but is used with the modulus operator:

*result = 31 + 7 / 2 – 83 % 5.0 * 2;*

83 % ERROR!

EXERCISES 3.2.5

1. Evaluate the expressions below, assuming the following declarations:

```
int     result;
float   var1, var2;
long    var3;
double  var4;
var1 = 5.1; var2 = 3.71; var3 = 83; var4 = 10.3;
```

a. `result = 31 / 6 % 2 + var3 - var1 * 2;`
b. `result = var3 / 5 / 2 % 6 * var2;`
c. `result = -6 * 7 % 2 + -var4;`
d. `result = -6.3 * 7 % 2 + 3;`

2. Evaluate the same expressions above again, assuming the declaration *float result.*
3. The following program is supposed to accept a temperature in Fahrenheit and display the equivalent in centigrade:

```
#include <stdio.h>

main()
{
        float       F, C;

        printf("Enter the degrees in Fahrenheit > ");
        scanf("%f", &F);
        C = 5/9 * (F - 32);
        printf("The centigrade is %f\n", C);
}
```

Here is an example of a run:

Enter the degrees in Fahrenheit > 41
The centigrade is 0.000000

The centigrade should be 5 degrees. Find the error in the program and correct it.

4. A real estate agent is asked to evaluate the straight-line yearly depreciation of a property. The following information is to be read into the program: property item number, original price of the property (*Initial Cost*), estimated value when it becomes useless (*Scrap Value*), and estimated number of years of use of property (*Years of Life*). The yearly depreciation is found with the formula:

$$\text{Yearly Depreciation} = \frac{\text{Initial Cost} - \text{Scrap Value}}{\text{Years of Life}}$$

Write a program that reads in the necessary information and displays the yearly depreciation. Note that the depreciation will likely have a fractional part that should be preserved.

5. Write a program that calculates the grade of a student in a course, given that three tests were taken by the student:

Test 1	out of 20;	counts for 10% of final grade
Test 2	out of 50;	counts for 15% of final grade
Final exam	out of 100;	counts for 75% of final grade

For example, suppose the student scores 15 on test 1, 42 on test 2, and 72 on the final exam. The final grade is calculated as follows:

$$\text{final grade} = (15/20) \times 10 + (42/50) \times 15 + (72/100) \times 75$$

Be wary of implicit conversions. Most books about C programming make light of implicit conversions and are content to simply cover the rules. Yet unwanted implicit conversions can create a lot of havoc in a computer program. They sneak in "from behind" and force the programmer to a merciless battle in the darkness of the night! The following program will serve to further warn you to look out for implicit conversions in your programs.

Example 3.2.12

The program below calculates the total weight of the contents of a wheelbarrow. There are two boxes in the wheelbarrow: one contains bricks that weigh 1200 grams each; the other contains rods weighing 650 grams each.

```
#include <stdio.h>

main()
{
      int       box1, box2;
      long      weight;

      printf("Enter the number of bricks in the box one > ");
      scanf("%d", &box1);
      printf("Enter the number of rods in the box two > ");
      scanf("%d", &box2);

      weight = box1 * 1200 + box2 * 650;
      printf("The total weight is %ld grams\n", weight);
}
```

This is an example of a run:

Enter the number of bricks in the box one > 24
Enter the number of rods in the box two > 41
The total weight is grams –10086

The total weight is completely bogus, yet the program is clearly correct—or is it? Let's see what happened. The expression is evaluated as shown in Figure 3.2.2, and the results are compared with the data types taken by the corresponding values (*i* represents *int*).

Figure 3.2.2

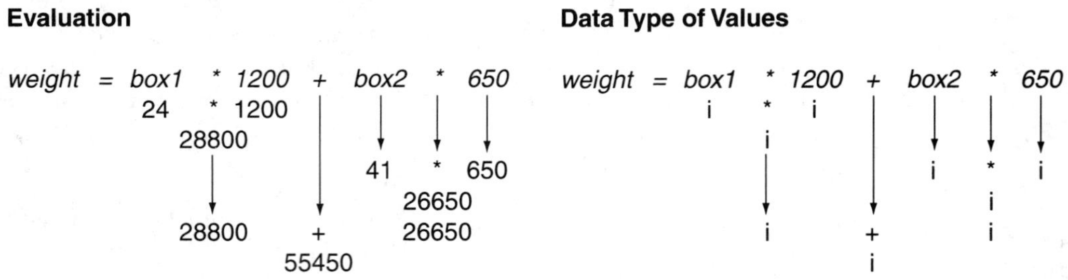

The cell allocated for the end result is of type *int*, but the result (55450) is too big to fit in a cell of type *int*. This is the problem, and there are three methods to solve this problem:

1. One solution is to avoid the problem by performing the calculation in three steps. Use two more *long int* variables and store the results of the multiplication operations into them as shown:

```
long int  temp1, temp2;
temp1 = box1 * 1200;
temp2 = box2 * 650;
weight = temp1 + temp2;
```

   The numbers resulting from the multiplication operations are 28800 and 26650 as calculated above, and both operations are of type *int.* (Do you understand why?) Consequently, there will not be any loss of information.
2. Another solution is to declare the variables *box1* and *box2* of type *long int*, even though their values would never exceed more than 100 or so. The idea is to guarantee that the result of all operations in the expression *box1 * 1200 + box2 * 650* will be stored in a cell of type *long int.*

   Each of the first two methods described above has a flaw:

   - The first method fails if either box contains more items than expected. For example, should there be 36 bricks in box 1, the multiplication gives 42200, which does not fit in the cell.
   - The second method never fails, but declaring the variables *box1* and *box2* of type *long int* seems to suggest there may be huge number of items in the boxes, which is slightly misleading to the user of the program.

3. The final method to solve the problem avoids both of these drawbacks. Simply insert an uppercase letter *L* immediately to the right of the constants 1200 and 650. This tells the C compiler to store these constants in a cell of type *long int*, not *int.* In the following expression, you can see that this ensures the result will be stored in a cell that is large enough.

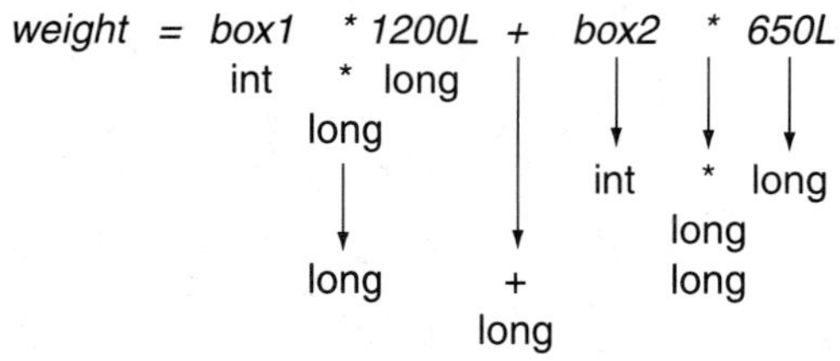

   A number of data type *int* multiplied by a *long* number results in a *long* number because of the hierarchy shown earlier: *long int* is a "higher" type than *int.*

EXERCISES 3.2.6

1. Explain completely how the two solutions adopted for the wheelbarrow problem will work and implement them in your computer.

2. Here is a solution to Exercise 2.4.3, 2. Remember that the answer is to be displayed in exponential notation:

```
#include <stdio.h>

main()
{
        int pages_per_book, words_per_page, shelves_per_stack,
            books_per_shelf, stacks_in_lib;
        unsigned long int            total_words;

        printf("Enter the number of words per page and\n"
               "       the number of pages per book > ");
        scanf("%d%d", &words_per_page, &pages_per_book);
        printf("Enter the number of books per shelf,\n"
               "       the number of shelves per stack and\n"
               "       the number of stacks > ");
        scanf("%d%d%d", &books_per_shelf, &shelves_per_stack,
                        &stacks_in_lib);

        total_words = words_per_page * pages_per_book *
                      books_per_shelf * shelves_per_stack *
                      stacks_in_lib;

        printf("There are %e words in the library.", total_words);
}
```

This program compiles correctly but every time the program is run, it displays the following:

There are

Then it "crashes" the computer! Find what is causing this problem and fix it.

3.2.5 THREE SIMPLE APPLICATIONS TO USE IMPLICIT CONVERSIONS

The example in the previous subsection explains that unwanted implicit conversions can be troublesome. However, when well applied, implicit conversions can be quite useful. Let's look at three applications.

Example 3.2.13

Section 2.2 warned more than once about the dangers of selecting the wrong type of format codes in both the *scanf()* and the *printf()* statements. Unfortunately, no matter how careful the programmer is, the outcome of a program also depends on the cautious entering of the data by the user. For instance, consider the prompt provided by the *printf()* below:

```
int       temp;

printf("Enter your average for the year > ");
scanf("%d", &temp);      /* read as an integer */
```

It is likely that the user would enter a fractional number for the average. This would then cause subsequent calls to *scanf()* to fail. The program must take the possibility of the user entering a fractional number into account. The idea is to always have the program read the data as a real number, then convert to a whole number when it is necessary. Let's change the code for the prompt above as follows:

```
float     temp;

printf("Enter your average for the year > ");
scanf("%f", &temp);        /* read as a real number */
year_avg = temp;           /* implicit conversion into an integer */
```

Now here is the whole program:

```
#include <stdio.h>

main()
{
        int          year_avg;
        float        class_avg;
        float        temp;

        printf("Enter your average for the year > ");
        scanf("%f", &temp);
        year_avg = temp;

        printf("Enter your class average > ");
        scanf("%f", &class_avg);

        printf("Echoed: year average = %d, class average = %f",
                year_avg, class_avg);
}
```

Now it no longer matters whether the user enters the average as a whole number or a real number; either way, the *scanf()* call won't crash. Unfortunately, this method has its limitations: for instance, it fails if the user mistypes a number as illustrated in Subsection 2.2.4. Another limitation is that ANSI C does not guarantee proper results when a *float* number is assigned an *int* variable. In other words, some compilers may fail when faced with this situation (although I am not aware that this has ever been a problem).

Example 3.2.14

You can write another small but useful program using what you have learned so far. The C language does not have a function that will accept a number such as 41.837 and then **truncates** to the one-hundredth (i.e., 41.83); or to the one-tenth (i.e., 41.8); or to the unit (i.e., 41). Here is a program that does just that:

```
#include <stdio.h>

main()
{
        float                answer;
        float                truncated;
        unsigned long int temp;

        printf("Enter a positive number to truncate > ");
        scanf("%f", &answer);

        temp = answer * 100;
        truncated = temp / 100.0;
        printf("%f truncated to the one-thousandth is %.2f\n",
              answer, truncated);
        temp = answer * 10;
        truncated = temp / 10.0;
        printf("%f truncated to the one-hundredth is %.1f\n",
              answer, truncated);
        temp = answer;
        truncated = temp;
        printf("%f truncated to the one-tenth is %.0f\n",
              answer, truncated);
}
```

The exercises on the following page give you an opportunity to study this program.

EXERCISES 3.2.7

Verify that the program in Example 3.2.14 is correct and then answer the following questions:

1. Why divide by *100.0* and *10.0*? Why not just *100* and *10*?
2. Why was the type *unsigned long int* chosen for the variable *temp*? Why not just *int*?
3. Explain the purpose of the following two statements:

```
temp = answer;
truncated = temp;
```

4. Could you replace the last three statements with this single *printf()* statement?

```
printf("%f truncated to the one-tenth is %.0f\n,
      answer, answer);
```

5. Is it possible to use only one expression of the two below and still produce the desired effect (i.e., truncation)?

```
temp = answer * 10;
truncated = temp / 10.0;
```

Now let's look at one last application.

Example 3.2.15

The C language also does not have a function that will accept a number such as 41.837 and then **round off** the number to the nearest hundredth (41.84), the nearest tenth (41.8), or nearest unit (42). However, we can run the following program to round off a number:

```
#include <stdio.h>

main()
{
      float               answer;
      float               rounded;
      unsigned long int   temp;

      printf("Enter a positive number to round off > ");
      scanf("%f", &answer);

      temp = answer * 100 + 0.5;
      rounded = temp / 100.0;
      printf("%f rounded to the nearest one-hundredth is %.2f\n",
            answer, rounded);
      temp = answer * 10 + 0.5;
      rounded = temp / 10.0;
      printf("%f rounded to the one-tenth is %.1f\n",
            answer, rounded);
      temp = answer + 0.5;
      rounded = temp;
      printf("%f rounded to the nearest unit is %.0f\n",
            answer, rounded);
}
```

The exercises below give you an opportunity to study this program.

EXERCISES 3.2.8

1. Verify that simply adding 0.5 to a number as shown in the program above will round off the number.

2. Is it possible to replace the two expressions below with only one and still produce the desired effect (i.e., round off the number)?

```
temp = answer * 10 + 0.5;
truncated = temp / 10.0;
```

3. Rewrite the program in Exercise 2.2.1, 3 to make it round off the centimeter value entered, rather than having the user do it. The user would enter the dimensions in exact centimeters, such as 27.52.

3.2.6 THE CAST OPERATOR: AN EXPLICIT CONVERSION

The following program will simply round off a number. Look at it carefully:

```
#include <stdio.h>

main()
{
        float        answer;
        int          temp;

        printf("Enter a number > ");
        scanf("%f", &answer);

        temp = answer + 0.5;
        printf("Rounded off = %d\n", temp);
}
```

The only reason for using the assignment in *temp = answer + 0.5* is that it converts the value inside *answer* into an integer (and rounds it off, too). The ***cast*** operator can convert the value without the need for an assignment statement. Let's take a look at how the cast operator can be used in a program.

Example 3.2.16

The program below does the same thing as the one above, except that it uses a cast operator (rather than an assignment operator) to round off the value. Hence it uses one less statement and one less variable.

```
#include <stdio.h>

main()
{
        float        answer;

        printf("Enter a number > ");
        scanf("%f", &answer);

        printf("Rounded off = %d\n", (int) (answer + 0.5));
}
```

The *printf()* statement does all the work. The cast operator is *(int)* and its operand is *(answer + 0.5)*. Look at how the expression is evaluated, assuming the variable *answer* contains 26.93:

```
printf( "Rounded off = %d\n", (int) (answer + 0.5))
                                    (26.93 + 0.5)
                                        27.08
                              (int)     27.08
printf("Rounded off = %d\n",               27     );
```

The number 27 is displayed. So, as you can see, the cast operator *(int)* converts its operand to an integer. If the cast operator is *(unsigned int)*, then it will convert its operand into a *unsigned int* type, and so on.

In the first program, the conversion of 27.08 was hidden by the assignment operator, hence it is called an **implicit** conversion. In the second program, the conversion of 27.08 is done **explicitly** with the cast operator. Note that the cast operator is an unary operator with the same precedence as the unary minus operator (Table 3.2.4), and that it actually **truncates** its operand rather than rounding it off.

Table 3.2.4

Operator (in order of priority)		Associativity
()		Left to right
– (unary)	cast operator **(type)**	Right to left
* / %		Left to right
+ – (binary)		Left to right

Example 3.2.17

Whenever an assignment operator is used solely to convert a value, the cast operator can be used instead, cutting down on how many statements and variables are needed. To illustrate, let's see if we can reduce the three statements below into only one:

```
temp = answer * 10 + 0.5;
rounded = temp / 10.0;
printf("%f rounded to the one-tenth is %.1f\n,
      answer, rounded);
```

By using a cast operator, we can rewrite the same code into one statement:

```
printf("%f rounded to the one-tenth is %.1f\n",
      answer, (int) (answer * 10 + 0.5) / 10.0);
```

To see why this works, let's evaluate the expression inside the *printf()*. Remember that the cast operator has the same precedence as the unary minus:

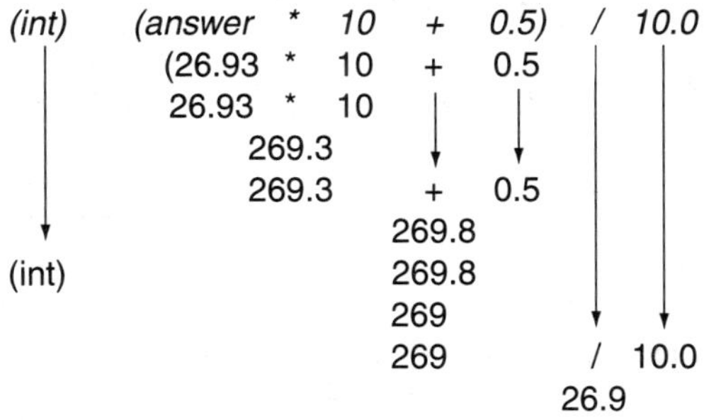

Note that the cast operator *(int)* truncates 269.8 to 269. In practice, the cast operator is not often used; the programmer is usually satisfied with the implicit conversions.

EXERCISES 3.2.9

1. Evaluate the following expressions:
   a. `(int) 26.8`
   b. `(int) 26.93 * 10 + 0.5 / 10.0`
   c. `(int) (26.8 * (float) 10 / (int) 10.0)`

2. Is there anything wrong with the following expressions?
   a. `(signed char) 227`
   b. `(unsigned int) -30982`
   c. `(long int) 1.4e+25`
3. Use cast operators to fix the problem discussed in the wheelbarrow problem in Example 3.2.12.

3.2.7 COMMON ERRORS AND TRAPS

1. Thinking that the format code is capable of properly converting its respective argument when there is mismatch of type between the argument and the format code. For instance, consider the program below, in which the format code in the *printf()* is *%d,* in an attempt to display only the integer part of *average*:

```
#include <stdio.h>

main()
{
    int   mark1, mark2;
    int   total;
    float average;

    mark1 = 86;
    mark2 = 97;
    total = mark1 + mark2;
    average = total / 2.0;
    printf("The average mark is %d\n", average);
}
```

   The data type of the format code (*%d*) does not match the data type of its argument (*average*). So will the value of *average* convert to data type *int*? No! Format codes do not work like expressions: data types do **not** mix! Thus the format code *%d* will not be able to convert the value of *average* to an integer, so the output will be bogus. However, the compiler will **not** complain about this mismatch.
2. Forgetting that C does not warn the user of situations that cause implicit conversions. This can cause obscure errors as illustrated in Subsection 3.2.4.
3. Trying to divide by zero. This is a basic principle of arithmetic—it simply cannot be done, regardless of the computer or the compiler.

SUPPLEMENTARY EXERCISES 3.2

1. A survey was conducted to predict student enrollment in the computer information system department of a particular college by the year 2000. These are the results of the survey, by age distribution:

Group	Age	Number of Students
1	19	190
2	20	654
3	21	989

   You have been asked to write a program that finds the average age of the three groups. The average is found by using the following formulas:

$$\begin{aligned}\text{total age} = {} & (\text{number students in group 1}) \times 19 + \\ & (\text{number students in group 2}) \times 20 + \\ & (\text{number students in group 3}) \times 21\end{aligned}$$

total students = (number students in group 1) +
(number students in group 2) +
(number students in group 3)

average = total age / total students

Use the following variables: *num_group1*, *num_group2*, *num_group3*, *total_age*, *total_std*, and *average*. Write a program for each of the following data type requirements:

Program	num_groups	total_age	average
# 1	*int*	*int*	*int* (truncate fraction out)
# 2	*int*	*int*	*int* (round off to nearest unit)
# 3	*int*	*int*	*float*
# 4	*nt*	*float*	*int* (truncate fraction out)
# 5	*float*	*float*	*int* (round off to nearest unit)
# 6	*int*	*float*	*int* (round off to nearest 0.01)

You must decide what type the variable *total_std* should be for each of these programs. Some *int*eger variables also may need qualifiers for some of these programs or for all of them—be careful!

Have the program output the *average* variable content in floating point format with 4 digits after the point. How can you do this when *average* is declared as data type *int*? (***Note:*** The exact average is 20.43589744 . . .)

2. Write a program that will produce a credit card bill similar to the following example:

CREDIT CARD BILL

Date	Location	Amount
01/08/99	Sears	$ 20.77
01/09/99	Safeway Grocery Store	$ 61.02
01/11/99	Toyota	$ 272.81
01/27/99	Coles Bookstore	$ 55.12
01/31/99	Interest Charged	$ 0.00
01/31/99	Payment from Last Month's Bill	$ 308.91

Account Number	Owed on Last Bill	Credits	Debits This Month	New Amount Owed
4510	$ 308.91	– $ 308.91	+ 409.72	$ 409.72

Interest Rate	Credit Limit	Minimum Payment
17.5%	$ 4000	$ 20.49

The bill will print after the following information is provided by the user:

Enter your expenses for this month > 20.77 61.02 272.81 55.12
How much do you owe from last month's bill? >.308.91
Enter your payment > 308.91
What is this month's interest rate? > 17.5
Enter your credit card number > 4510

For simplicity's sake, make the (unrealistic!) assumption that exactly four expenses are made on the credit card each month, from the same locations and on the same dates. Also assume that the credit card number is always four digits long. The total amount owed is this month's expenses plus last month's unpaid portion (if applicable). In the example above, there is no unpaid portion. So no interest is charged, and the total amount owed is simply this month's expenses. Here is another example in which only a portion of last month's expenses were paid:

CREDIT CARD BILL

Date	Location	Amount
01/08/99	Sears	$ 222.99
01/09/99	Safeway Grocery Store	$ 120.00
01/11/99	Toyota	$ 33.92
01/27/99	Coles Bookstore	$ 7.75
01/31/99	Interest Charged	$ 16.52
01/31/99	Payment from Last Month's Bill	$ 800.00

Account Number	Owed on Last Bill	Credits	Debits This Month	New Amount Owed
4510	$ 2001.51	– $ 800.00	+ 401.18	$ 1602.69

	Interest Rate	Credit Limit	Minimum Payment
	16.5%	$ 4000	$ 80.13

The following information is provided by the user:

Enter your expenses for this month > 222.99 120.00 33.92 7.75
How much do you owe from last month's bill? > 2001.51
Enter your payment > 800.00
What is this month's interest rate? > 16.5
Enter your credit card number > 4510

Exactly 1201.51 of last month's bill is unpaid (2001.51 – 800.00 = 1201.51). So an additional amount of 16.52 in interest is added to this month's expenses. This is calculated by using the formula 1201.51 × (0.165 / 12). Note that the minimum payment is always 5% of the total amount owed.

3. On a weekly basis, all the clerks at the XYZ Company are required to submit time cards showing the number of hours they worked on each particular project. The company currently has four projects in process. The information on the card must be arranged as follows:

Employee No.	**Hours for Projects 1–4**	**Wage per Hour**	**No. of Dependents**
810	2.5 31.5 5.0 1.0	13.09	3

The employees all give their time cards to their boss, who inserts a sheet in each clerk's file that lists the hours spent on projects:

Employee #810	**Projects**			
	1	**2**	**3**	**4**
Hours Worked	2.5	31.5	2.0	1.0

The boss is not interested in the rest of the information on the time cards. The cards are then passed to the human resources department where the payroll administrator calculates the total wages owed to each clerk for the week and puts a sheet like the one below in each clerk's file:

Employee #810	Number of hours worked		37.0
	Wage per hour		13.09
	Salary		484.33
	Deductions:		
		Tax (30%)	145.30
		Pension (5%)	24.22
		Union dues (1%)	4.84
		Unemployment insurance (2%)	9.69
		Total	184.05
	SALARY		$300.28

The accounting department is notified and issues checks for each clerk. The check for Employee #810 would look similar to the following:

> XYZ COMPANY
>
> Paid to the order of Employee #810,
>
> The amount of $300.28

Now your task is to computerize this procedure.

a. Write a program that prompts the user for all the information at the screen, and then displays the information on each of the sheets above on the screen.
b. Change the program so it will read the employee information from a file named WORK.DAT and then store the sheets in the files BOSS.DAT, HR.DAT, and CHECK.DAT respectively instead of displaying the information to the screen. (Review Section 2.5 on file handling if necessary.)

4. A business owner wrote the program below to figure out her net profit for the year, given the number of sales, profit per sale, advertising expenses, and operating costs:

```
#include <stdio.h>

main()
{
        int    qty_sales, profit_per_sale;
        double op_cost;
        double net_profit, ad_cost;

        printf("Enter the gross profit per sale "
               "and the number of sales > ");
        scanf("%d%d", &profit_per_sale, &qty_sales);
        printf("Enter the advertising and operating costs > ");
        scanf("%f%f", &ad_cost, &op_cost);
        printf("\n\n     Sales       Advertising Costs     Net Profit");

        net_profit = qty_sales * profit_per_sale - ad_cost - op_cost;

        printf("\n\n     %4.2lf           %4.2lf                  %4.2lf",
               qty_sales, ad_cost, net_profit);
}
```

She ran the program:

```
Enter the gross profit per sale and the number of sales > 500 100
Enter the advertising and operating costs > 1000 10000

Sales       Advertising Costs          Net Profit
0.00        7.8804012392789e+115       0.00
```

She was surprised by the outcome, and wondered what caused the program to generate these wild numbers. Point out where the trouble spots are in her program and then fix the problems.

3.3 THE CHARACTER DATA TYPE

So far, we have only covered how to read numbers. You might be wondering how to read information that does not consist of numbers, such as names of people, cities, and so on. There is a good reason why this issue has been delayed: reading of these data types, called ***character strings,*** requires a detailed study of the following two subjects:

1. The input mechanism that governs the functionality of *scanf()* (and other input functions)
2. Strings (one-dimensional arrays of characters)

These two topics are much too complex to be completely (or even partially) covered now. However, because business applications use character strings a lot, we should at least skim the surface of this data type now.

3.3.1 READING AND DISPLAYING CHARACTERS

Character strings consist of a sequence of characters. Let's see how individual characters are read in a program and displayed.

Example 3.3.1

Consider the program in Example 2.2.1 that calculates a student's summer income. We can modify the program so that it asks for the user's initials as well. With this modification, here is an example of a run of the new program:

Enter your initials > JPC↵
Enter the hourly wage > 7.05↵
Enter the total work hours per week > 35↵
Enter the number of weeks of work > 10↵

JPC, You will make $ 2467.50 this summer

Now take a look at the new program (the modifications are shown in bold):

```
#include <stdio.h>

main()
{
    float  hourly_rate;
    int    hours_per_week;
    float  total_income;
    int    num_weeks;
    char   letter1, letter2, letter3;[1]

    printf("Enter your initials > ");
    scanf("%c%c%c", &letter1, &letter2, &letter3);[2]
    printf("Enter the hourly wage > ");
    scanf("%f", &hourly_rate);
    printf("Enter the total work hours per week > ");
    scanf("%d", &hours_per_week);
    printf("Enter the number of weeks of work > ");
    scanf("%d", &num_weeks);

    total_income = hourly_rate * hours_per_week * num_weeks;

    printf("%c%c%c,[2] You will make $ %.2f this summer",
           letter1, letter2, letter3,[2] total_income);
}
```

Explanations

1. Note the declaration of the three variables of type *char*. Recall from Subsection 3.1.2 that *int* variables occupy 2 bytes and *char* variables occupy 1 byte. Since all letters or any other single character occupy only 1 byte each in memory, the data type *char* is chosen here instead of *int*.

The use of *int* is would be perfectly acceptable, but the cells would be unnecessarily large. (***Note:*** In some computers, the *int* variable occupies 4 bytes. For the sake of illustration, throughout this book we will always assume that the *int* variable occupies 2 bytes.)

2. The format code *%c* is the one to use to both read a **single** character and to display a **single** character. The three *%c* codes in the *scanf()* tell it to scan three characters, in this case the letters J, P, and C. Hence the following variables will contain the letters of the initials:

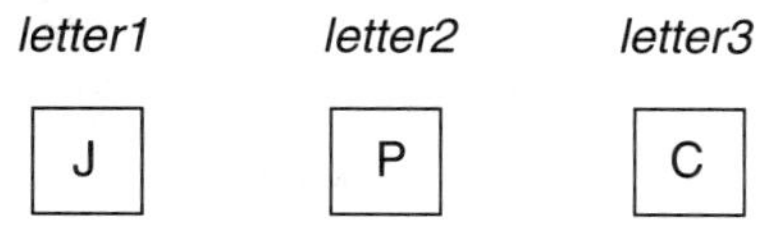

The variables have small cells because they are declared as data type *char*.

EXERCISE 3.3.1

Write a program that reads in a name of four letters, such as Mike, and displays it backwards so it reads as ekiM.

3.3.2 BE WARY OF *scanf()*—AGAIN!

You have been warned a few times already about the erratic behavior of the function *scanf()*. Well, when reading characters, *scanf()* can make you completely crazy! Your programs will exhibit lots of bizarre behavior if the characters are not entered **exactly** as *scanf()* expects them. Let's look at two examples that illustrate some of the problems you may encounter.

Example 3.3.2

Let's rerun the program above and at the prompts, we'll enter the initials, each separated by a space:

Enter your initials > J P C↵
Enter the hourly wage > 7.05↵
Enter the total work hours per week > 35↵
Enter the number of weeks of work > 10↵

J P, You will make $ 2467.50 this summer

The output includes a blank space between the first two initials, and the last initial is missing. Why did this happen, and where did that blank space come from?

This mysterious blank space is the one that was keyed in after the J at the prompt that asked for the user's initials as input. A blank space **is** a character, so *scanf()* scanned the space into the program as a character. It then read the P—and that made three characters read in, so it simply **ignored the rest!**

You must remember that there are two significant differences between reading numbers and reading characters:

1. When reading characters, *scanf()* stops scanning as soon as the user presses the correct number of keys (in this case three keys) followed by the Enter key. It doesn't matter what keys are pressed; the spacebar counts as key, for example. (There are exceptions, but never mind that for now!) The *scanf()* function **does** skip spaces when reading numbers, but it **never** skips spaces when reading characters—unless you tell it otherwise. You can tell the program to skip spaces by modifying the format string slightly. Just insert one space between each *%c* format code:

```
scanf("%c %c %c", &letter1, &letter2, &letter3);
```

The space in between each code does not indicate that the user **must** put a space between each of the initials, but rather that spaces will be ignored **if** they are keyed.

2. The other main difference between reading numbers and characters is that when reading numbers, you can press the Enter key any time between entry of the numbers, and the numbers still will be scanned only when **all** the numbers required by the *scanf()* statement are entered and then Enter is pressed one last time. (This was demonstrated in Example 2.2.4.) But, when reading characters, *scanf()* terminates scanning as soon as the user presses the required number of keys—any keys—followed by the Enter key.

Example 3.3.3

The program run below shows what happens when the Enter key is pressed before all three initials are entered:

Enter your initials > J↵
P↵
Enter the hourly wage > 7.05↵
Enter the total work hours per week > 35↵
Enter the number of weeks of work > 10↵

J↵
P, You will make $ 2467.50 this summer

The user did not even have time to press the final letter C—*scanf()* quit before the last letter could be keyed. It is easy to see why: the first three keys entered were J, ↵, and P, so the *scanf()* read in those three characters and ignored the rest. Then the *printf()* statement output those first three keys since those were the ones read into the variables. Look at the output above and you will see that echoing the ↵ character caused the cursor to move to the next line.

The program will allow the user to press the Enter key at any place during the input only if **every** *%c* code in the program is preceded by an escape sequence, *\n*:

```
scanf("\n%c\n%c\n%c", &letter1, &letter2, &letter3);
```

The *\n* escape sequences do not indicate that the user **must** press Enter before each initial, but only that the user **may** press Enter any time during the input. In fact, this format string also allows the user to space out the initials, just like we did with spaces between the format codes in Example 3.3.2. This second solution is therefore more general and more flexible, so the best advice to avoid big headaches when reading characters is to **always** precede a *%c* code with a *\n* escape sequence.

At this point, we could digress to a detailed discussion of how the input mechanism of *scanf()* actually works. However, this information is covered completely in Appendix F at the end of the book, and you can refer to that explanation as necessary.

EXERCISES 3.3.2

1. Consider the *scanf()* call below:

```
scanf("\n%c%c\n%c", &c1, &c2, &c3)
```

If *c1*, *c2*, and *c3* are *char* variables, what would be stored in these variables if the user keyed in the following keys exactly?

a. ↵ ↵ w ↵ e↵	b. r qu↵	c. h↵ ↵ t↵	d. uye↵

2. Modify the solution of Supplementary Exercise 3.2, 3a so that the program also prompts the user to enter the initials of the employee (e.g., KJT). Since the XYZ Company has many divisions across the country, modify the program so it also prompts the user to enter the location (province or state) where the employee works (e.g., CA). This new information will be displayed for the boss and for the human resources and accounting departments.

3. In a similar fashion, modify the solution of Supplementary Exercise 3.2, 3b to make file WORK.DAT include the following information, as shown:

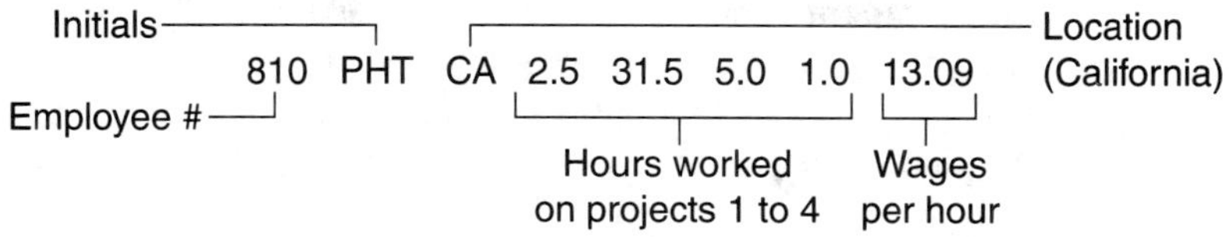

The departments will process this file the same way, except that the new information will also be stored in the other files they generate.

3.3.3 SPECIFYING CHARACTER DATA IN A PROGRAM

Just as a number literal can be specified in a program, the same can be done with a character, as shown in the example below.

Example 3.3.4

Suppose the program at the beginning of this section did not ask the user to enter the initials but instead put the initials into the variables itself. The program would have to be modified as shown below (with the changes shown in bold):

```
#include <stdio.h>

main()
{
    float  hourly_rate;
    int    hours_per_week;
    float  total_income;
    int    num_weeks;
    char   letter1, letter2, letter3;

    letter1 = 'J'; letter2 = 'P'; letter3 = 'C';
    printf("Enter the hourly wage > ");
    scanf("%f", &hourly_rate);
    printf("Enter the total work hours per week > ");
    scanf("%d", &hours_per_week);
    printf("Enter the number of weeks of work > ");
    scanf("%d", &num_weeks);

    total_income = hourly_rate * hours_per_week * num_weeks;

    printf("%c%c%c, You will make $ %.2f this summer",
            letter1, letter2, letter3, total_income);
}
```

The assignment operator in *letter1 = 'J'* still does the same thing it did with numbers: it takes whatever is on its right side and puts it in the variable to the left side. So in this case, it puts the letter J into the variable *letter1*. The notation 'J' on the right side simply means the character J.

Note that this new program is no longer flexible in the choice of the initials. Every time this program is run, the initials JPC will be used. The initials can change only if the program is changed. In programming, this kind of rigidity is never welcome. Therefore the program in Example 3.3.1, where the user is prompted to key in the initials, is a much better solution.

There are better ways to use characters in programs than the ones we have looked at in these examples. Numerous other uses of characters in programs are included in the rest of the book, especially in Chapters 18 to 20.

EXERCISES 3.3.3

Write a program that displays the message *Tic Tac Toe*. You must reserve one variable for each different character. For instance, the letter T needs a single variable that will be used each time the uppercase T appears in the phrase; you do not need to reserve three separate variables for the three appearances of the character. Write the program in two ways:

1. The program prompts the user to enter the message.
2. The message is assigned within the program.

3.3.4 A BRIEF INTRODUCTION TO ASCII CODES

In Example 3.3.1, the format codes scanned letters. Actually, a digit may be read as a character, too—and for that matter, any other character you can key can be scanned as a character. For instance, the program in Example 3.3.1 could have been run with the initials JP2 as shown in the following run:

Enter your initials > JP2↵
Enter the hourly wage > 7.05↵
Enter the total work hours per week > 35↵
Enter the number of weeks of work > 10↵

JP2, You will make $ 2467.50 this summer

The initials are stored in memory as shown below:

letter1	*letter2*	*letter3*
'J'	'P'	'2'

The quotation marks are not stored, of course. They are only shown here to emphasize that the data is of type *char*. The **character** '2' is stored in the cell quite differently than the **number** *2*. It is stored as an ASCII code. You may wonder what an ASCII code is. Well, each keystroke generates a code that is sent to the computer. This code identifies which character was entered from the keyboard. Of course, each character must be assigned a unique code. The American Standard Code for Information Interchange (ASCII) decided on the ***ASCII character codes sequence*** shown in Table 3.3.1.

For instance, find the letter 'g' in Table 3.3.1, and look at the ASCII code to its right—its ASCII code is 103. Table 3.3.1 only lists some of the ASCII codes; a complete list of ASCII codes is included in Appendix A. If you refer to the complete ASCII code table, you can determine that the characters JP2 would be stored in memory as shown below:

letter1	*letter2*	*letter3*
74	81	50
'J'	'P'	'2'

The numbers in the boxes represent the ASCII codes for each character, and the letters represented by the codes are shown below each box. So the character '2' is stored as the number 50, not 2. To store the input '2' as a number, it must be scanned with the format code *%d*. For instance, suppose that input is 6:

scanf("%c", &num) stores the input 6 as the character '6' (i.e., as number 54)
scanf("%d", &num) stores the input 6 as the number 6

The concept of reading numbers as characters instead of as numbers may seem strange to you, but you probably have been exposed to this before. For example, if you type the key 3 while using a word processor, the 3 is stored as a character; however, if you type the same key while using a spreadsheet, the 3 is stored as a number. Much more will be said about the *char* type in Section 13.6.

Table 3.3.1

Character	ASCII Code	Character	ASCII Code	Character	ASCII Code
space	32	0	48	A	65
!	33	1	49	B	66
"	34	2	50	C	67
#	35	3	51	D	68
$	36	4	52	E	69
%	37	5	53	F	70
&	38	6	54	G	71
'	39	7	55	H	72
(	40	8	56	I	73
)	41	9	57	etc.	etc.
*	42	:	58	a	97
+	43	;	59	b	98
,	44	<	60	c	99
-	45	=	61	d	100
.	46	>	62	e	101
/	47	?	63	f	102
		@	64	g	103

EXERCISES 3.3.4

The following ten programs each ask the user to input data. To the right of each program is a prompt with the input data entered. After each input, indicate the data that will be stored in the variable *x*. Should the *scanf()* fail, write GARBAGE in the variable *x* instead.

Program | **Prompt and Input**

1.
```
#include <stdio.h>

main()
{
        int  x;
        printf("Enter the data: ");
        scanf("%d", &x);
}
```
Enter the data: t↵

2.
```
#include <stdio.h>

main()
{
        char  x;
        printf("Enter the data: ");
        scanf("%c", &x);
}
```
Enter the data: 7↵

3.
```
#include <stdio.h>

main()
{
        int  x;
        printf("Enter the data: ");
        scanf("%c", &x);
}
```
Enter the data: t↵

4.
```
#include <stdio.h>

main()
```

```
{
        char  x;
        printf("Enter the data: ");
        scanf("%d", &x);
}
```

Enter the data: 3↵

5.
```
#include <stdio.h>

main()
{
        char  x;
        printf("Enter the data: ");
        scanf("%d", &x);
}
```

Enter the data: 74↵

6.
```
#include <stdio.h>

main()
{
        char  x;
        printf("Enter the data: ");
        scanf("%c", &x);
}
```

Enter the data: 74↵

7.
```
#include <stdio.h>

main()
{
        int  x;
        printf("Enter the data: ");
        scanf("%c", &x);
}
```

Enter the data: the↵

8.
```
#include <stdio.h>

main()
{
        char  x;
        printf("Enter the data: ");
        scanf("%d", &x);
}
```

Enter the data: 230↵

9.
```
#include <stdio.h>

main()
{
        char  x;
        printf("Enter the data: ");
        scanf("%c", &x);
}
```

Enter the data: ↵

10.
```
#include <stdio.h>

main()
{
        char  x;
        printf("Enter the data: ");
        scanf("%c", &x);
}
```

Enter the data: ↵↵

3.3.5 THE *getchar()* AND *putchar()* FUNCTIONS

The function *getchar()* has a very simple mechanism: it reads the next character keyed in and assigns it to a variable. The following two examples illustrate how it works and how the function *putchar()* works as well.

Example 3.3.5

This program reads in the abbreviation of a state or province name and echoes it to the screen:

```
#include <stdio.h>

main()
{
    char abr1, abr2;
    printf("Enter the abbreviation for a state > ");
    abr1 = getchar();[1]
    abr2 = getchar();

    printf("The state is ");
    putchar(abr1);[2]
    putchar(abr2);
}
```

Here is an example of a run of the program:

Enter the abbreviation for a state > TX↵
The state is TX

Explanations

1. The function *getchar()* reads the first key pressed, which is T here, and the assignment operator assigns it to the variable *abr1*. Unlike the *scanf()* function, no format string can be used with *getchar()*. As this implies, the *getchar()* function is unable to skip over blank spaces, interpret the *\n* escape sequence, or anything else that is usually done with a format string. The *getchar()* function also cannot read numbers.
2. The function *putchar()* displays a character given to it to the screen at the exact location where the cursor happens to be at the moment. The *putchar()* function cannot be used to display numbers, or even messages. For instance, the following statement is impossible in C programming:

```
putchar("Enter the abbreviation for a state")
```

The example above does not illustrate fully how these two new functions work. Look at the example below to learn more about *getchar()* and *putchar()*.

Example 3.3.6

Let's modify the program in Example 3.3.5 so that it will also read a two-letter abbreviation for the country as well as the state or province abbreviation. Look at the example of a run below:

Enter the abbreviation for a state > SK↵
Enter the abbreviation for the country > CA↵
The state is SK, CA

This is the modified program that creates the output above:

```
#include <stdio.h>

main()
{

    char abr1, abr2, country1, country2;

    printf("Enter the abbreviation for a state > ");
    abr1 = getchar();
    abr2 = getchar();
    printf("Enter the abbreviation for the country > ");
    getchar();[1]
    country1 = getchar();
    country2 = getchar();
```

```
        printf("The state is ");
        putchar(abr1);
        putchar(abr2);
        putchar(',');²
        putchar(' ');²
        putchar(country1);²
        putchar(country2);²
}
```

Explanations

1. It is important to realize that **before** the second datum can be read (i.e., the country abbreviation), the Enter key still remains in the input buffer. So it must be read with a single call to *getchar()*. Since the Enter serves no purpose in the program, it is not assigned to a variable. However, only after the Enter character is read by the *getchar()* can the country be read in.
2. These four *putchar()* statements serve to display a comma followed by a space and then the country abbreviation, as in ", CA". These *putchar()* statements perform the same objective as the following statement:

```
printf(", %c%c", country1, country2)
```

EXERCISES 3.3.5

1. Introduce the functions *getchar()* and *putchar()* in appropriate places in the program from Example 3.3.1.
2. What would be the output of the program in question 1 if the input was provided as shown in Example 3.3.2? Example 3.3.3?
3. Rewrite the program in Example 3.3.5 above with *scanf()* and *printf()* as follows:
   a. Use two *scanf()* and two *printf()* statements.
   b. Use one *scanf()* and one *printf()* statement.
4. What is the output produced by the program below?

```
#include <stdio.h>

main()
{
        putchar('a');
        putchar('b');
        printf("Msg1");
        putchar('\n');
        putchar('c');
        putchar('d');
        putchar('e');
        putchar('\n');
        printf("Msg2\n");
}
```

   A single *printf()* statement is sufficient to produce the output in the program above. What is it?
5. Consider the program below:

```
#include <stdio.h>

main()
{
        char c1, c2, c3;

        printf("Enter three characters: ");
        c1 = getchar();
        printf("\nmsg1");
```

```
        c2 = getchar();
        printf("\nmsg2");
        c3 = getchar();
        printf("\nc1 = %c, c2 = %c, c3 = %c\n", c1, c2, c3);
}
```

Which of the runs below could have been obtained as a result of running this program?

a. Enter three characters: h5i↵
   msg1
   msg2
   c1 = h, c2 = 5, c3 = i

b. Enter three characters: h5i↵
   msg1
   msg2
   c1 = h, c2 = 5, c3 = i

c. Enter three characters: h5i↵
   msg1
   msg2
   c1 = h, c2 = 5, c3 = i

d. Enter three characters: h↵
   msg1
   5↵
   msg2
   i↵
   c1 = h, c2 = 5, c3 = i

e. Enter three characters: h↵
   msg1
   5↵
   msg2
   i↵
   c1 = h, c2 = 5, c3 = i

f. Enter three characters: h↵
   msg1
   msg2
   5↵
   c1 = h, c2 = ↵
   , c3 = 5

6. Indicate the program(s) below that is/are equivalent to the program in the question above. ***Equivalent*** means that given the exact same input, entered the same way, both programs will run the same way.

a.
```
#include <stdio.h>

main()
{
        char c1, c2, c3;

        printf("Enter three characters: ");
        scanf("%c", &c1);
        printf("\nmsg1");
        scanf("%c", &c2);
        printf("\nmsg2");
        scanf("%c", &c3);
        printf("\nc1 = %c, c2 = %c, c3 = %c\n", c1, c2, c3);
}
```

b.
```
#include <stdio.h>

main()
{
        char c1, c2, c3;
```

```
        printf("Enter three characters: ");
        scanf("%c%c%c", &c1, &c2, &c3);
        printf("\nmsg1 ");
        printf("\nmsg2 ");
        printf("c1 = %c, c2 = %c, c3 = %c\n", c1, c2, c3);
}
```

c.
```
#include <stdio.h>

main()
{
      char c1, c2, c3;

      printf("Enter three characters: ");
      scanf("\n%c", &c1);
      printf("\nmsg1");
      scanf("\n%c", &c2);
      printf("\nmsg2");
      scanf("\n%c", &c3);
      printf("\nc1 = %c, c2 = %c, c3 = %c\n", c1, c2, c3);
}
```

7. Consider a program that performs the task below:

   How many CDs did you buy? 6↵
   How much per unit? 12.55↵
   How much money in your pocket? 91.70↵
   You have $ 75.30 left

   For simplicity, assume that the money amounts are always entered with two digits before and after the decimal point.
   a. Write a program for it that uses *scanf()* and *printf()* statements.
   b. Given the knowledge that you obtained in this section, can a solution be worked out that uses only *getchar()* and *putchar()* calls to read and display the data?

3.3.6 COMMON ERRORS AND TRAPS

1. Omitting the single quotation marks around a character data:

```
#include <stdio.h>

main()
{
    char   letter1, letter2, letter3;

    letter1 = J; letter2 = P; letter3 = C;
    :
    :
    printf("%c%c%c\n", letter1, letter2, letter3);
}
```

   The single quotation marks are missing around the letters J, P, and C, and so the compiler will complain that the **variables** *J, P,* and *C* are not declared. It thinks these characters are variables. (Can you explain why?)

   The following errors may remain undetected by the compiler:

2. Not preceding a format code *%c* with an escape sequence *\n* in the format string of a *scanf()*. The consequences of this omission were explained in Section 3.3.
3. Putting a word (or more than one character) within a set of single quotation marks:

```
#include <stdio.h>

main()
```

```
{
    char   initials;

    initials = 'JPC';
    printf("initials = %c\n", initials);
}
```

Some compilers allow no more than two characters within single quotation marks, others allow up to four. But you are **strongly** advised to always have only one character within the single quotation marks. In any case, the display will be affected as shown:

```
initials = J
```

Only the first letter will show. Can you see why?

4. Using double quotation marks in place of single quotation marks:

```
#include <stdio.h>

main()
{
    char   letter1, letter2, letter3;

    letter1 = "J"; letter2 = "P"; letter3 = "C";


    printf("Initials = %c%c%c\n", letter1, letter2, letter3);
}
```

Single quotation marks **must** be used around the characters. The compiler probably will complain about the double quotation marks around the letters in this program and will display an error message such as "Invalid implicit pointer conversion." It is important to remember that **double and single quotation marks have entirely different meanings.**

Some C compilers have weak type checking and will not see this error at all. In such a case, the display will be dreadfully meaningless. For example, this is what my computer displayed when I tried to run the program above:

```
Initials = ♦♠
```

Figure that one out!

5. Thinking that *putchar()* can display numeric data. For instance, when asked to display a number, such as 65, the code *putchar(65)* is mistakenly attempted.
6. Thinking that *putchar()* can display character strings, such as *putchar("Hello!")*.
7. Thinking that *putchar()* requires a format string, such as in *putchar("%c", 'a')*.

4 Introduction to Decision Structures

OBJECTIVES

This chapter introduces you to the following information:

- How to code programs that are flexible enough to perform various actions, depending on what the user requests.
- The use of basic statement structures (such as *if/else*) that make the above possible.
- An overview of the arithmetic of logic.

INTRODUCTION

Chapters 2 and 3 covered applications that were intentionally elementary and limited in their practical uses. The programs were rigid in that they could only read, calculate, and display. The emphasis was in teaching the necessary technical knowledge about C so that you can produce small programs to read, display, and manipulate data effectively without falling victim to the intricacies of the language.

Clearly, a program is useful only if it offers alternatives to the user: the user should be in control. For example, a good computer game allows the player to start a new game or save a game on disk or play different games—the player has a lot of choices in what to do next. This chapter will cover the basis for making a more flexible program that is better able to interact with the user. This will be done by adding conditions to a program so that it performs one or more actions. Now that most necessary technical details have been dealt with, we will begin to concentrate entirely on problem solving. As we cover new program features, we will revisit many of the examples from Chapters 2 and 3 and rewrite existing code with the new features in mind. This approach will help you understand better how simpler pieces of code are assembled to make more complex programs.

4.1 THE *if* STATEMENT

Statements in a program are normally executed in sequence, as those covered in Chapters 2 and 3. However, most programs require alteration of this normal sequential flow of logic due to the users' varying needs. The C compiler uses the *if/else* and *if* statements for that purpose. This section covers the *if* statement.

4.1.1 THE SYNTAX AND LOGIC OF *if* STATEMENTS

Relational operators. Let us study the syntax of the *if* statement and explain how it works with Example 4.1.1.

Example 4.1.1

Modern cars have a warning mechanism that lets a driver know that the car is low on gas. For example, if the gas level goes down to, say, five liters or less, a signal might sound, and the message "Low on Gas!" might appear on the dashboard display. The following program simulates such a warning system:

```
#include <stdio.h>

main()
{
      float      level;

      printf("Enter the amount of gas left > ");
      scanf("%f", &level);
      if (level <= 5)
      {
            printf("LOW ON GAS!!!\n");
      }
}
```

Upon reading the gas level, the *if* statement checks whether the car has five liters or less left. If so, the warning message is displayed; otherwise nothing at all happens. Observe the syntax of the *if* statement:

```
if (level <= 5)
{
     printf("LOW ON GAS!!!\n");
}
```

The keyword *if* must be in lowercase letters, and the condition (in this case, "level <= 5") next to it must ***always*** be surrounded with parentheses. The symbol <= means "less than or equal to." So *if (level <= 5)* literally means "if the gas level is less than or equal to five liters." The *if* statement offers only one alternative: do some action or do nothing at all. In this case, if the condition is true, the *printf* statement will be executed.

The operator <= is said to be a ***binary operator*** since it compares two operands. For example:

```
level <= 5
```

The first operand, *level,* is compared to the second operand, *5.* Note that there must not be any spaces separating the < and =. For instance, *level < = 5* is a syntax error. The operator <= is a member of the class of ***relational*** operators. Table 4.1.1 lists the other relational operators that we will see in this chapter. They are all binary operators.

Table 4.1.1

Operator	Meaning
<=	Less than or equal to
>=	Greater than or equal to
==	Exactly equal to
!=	Not equal to
>	Strictly greater than
<	Strictly less than

Compound statements within an *if* statement. Of course, more than one statement may be placed within the braces, as Example 4.1.2 shows.

Example 4.1.2

Suppose the car in question consumes 9.5 liters per 100 kilometers. It is possible to add a feature to our warning system, i.e., to indicate the maximum distance the car can go before running out of gas:

```
if (level <= 5)
{
        printf("LOW ON GAS!!!\n");
        printf("Maximum running distance left = %f",
                (100/9.5) * level);
}
```

Note that the two statements within the *if* statement are surrounded with braces. Also, each statement within the braces terminates with a semicolon, as always. These braces serve to create a ***block*** of statements (also called a ***compound*** statement). If the condition *level <= 5* is true, the block is selected and executed; otherwise, it is skipped. Executing a block simply means executing the statements inside it.

We have already seen one use of braces, the *main()* block:

```
main()
{
    :
    :
    :
}
```

In this case, the three colons represent the sequence of statements making up the program. The use of braces tells the program to execute all of the statements within the block.

EXERCISES 4.1.1

1. Write a program that displays the warning "You must pay the minimum monthly payment" on a customer's credit card bill if last month's minimum payment was not met. Suppose the minimum payment was $10.
2. Write a program that reads in an employee's initials and the number of hours worked in the week. Overtime pay is at time and a half and occurs after 40 hours of work. The program will first calculate the regular pay, then add on the overtime pay, if any.

4.1.2 THE SEQUENCE OF *if* STATEMENTS

By using multiple *if* statements, a program can do more interesting tasks than the ones shown in the previous section. The one kind of multiple *if* statements we consider here are sequences of *if* statements. Consider Example 4.1.3.

Example 4.1.3

Let us write a program to simulate a metric converter. It will be able to convert from kilometers to miles, kilograms to pounds, and liters to quarts. The program will ask the user the metric value, along with the type of conversion involved, i.e., whether it is a conversion of distance (d), weight (w), or volume (v). Then it will convert into the correct standard measure.* Use the following conversion factors:

1 kilometer = 0.6214 mile
1 kilogram = 2.2046 pounds
1 liter = 0.8772 quart

*Standard measure refers to the imperial system of measurement.

Here are two examples of a run. Each entry consists of the metric value followed by a letter representing the conversion type:

Enter the metric value and type of conversion (lowercase) > 10 d
The standard value is 6.21 miles

Enter the metric value and type of conversion (lowercase) > 20.5 v
The standard value is 19.98 quarts

Note that the conversion type must be entered as a lowercase 'd', 'w', or 'v'. Also, the standard measure must be rounded off to two decimals. Following is the new program:

```
#include <stdio.h>

main()
{
   float          metric, standard;
   char           conv_type;

   printf("Enter the metric value and type of conversion (lowercase) > ");
   scanf("%f %c", &metric, &conv_type);

   if (conv_type == 'd')
   {
        standard = 0.6214 * metric;
   }
   if (conv_type == 'w')
   {
        standard = 2.2046 * metric;
   }
   if (conv_type == 'v')
   {
        standard = 0.8772 * metric;
   }

   printf("The standard value is %.2f quarts", standard);
}
```

sequence of *if* statements

Remember that the format code *%.2f* rounds off to the nearest one-hundredth. Also, note the format string in the *scanf(): "%f %c"*. (Why is a space needed? Actually, the format code *"%f\n%c"* would have been better. Why?)

The *if* statement (and the *if/else* statement presented in Section 4.3) belongs in the class of ***control structures*** because it controls the flow of logic by providing an alternate action, depending on a condition. These structures are specifically called ***decision structures.*** (Chapter 7 will cover another kind of control structure: the ***loop.***)

When a program uses control structures, there is usually more than one way to code that program. For instance, the following solution is just as acceptable as the one above (modifications are shown in bold):

```
#include <stdio.h>

main()
{
   float          metric, standard, conv_factor;
   char           conv_type;

   printf("Enter the metric value and type of conversion (lowercase) > ");
   scanf("%f %c", &metric, &conv_type);

   if (conv_type == 'd')
   {
        conv_factor = 0.6214;
   }
```

```
    if (conv_type == 'w')
    {
          conv_factor = 2.2046;
    }
    if (conv_type == 'v')
    {
          conv_factor = 0.8772;
    }
    standard = conv_factor * metric;

    printf("The standard value is %.2f quarts", standard);
}
```

In fact, this solution is better. Why? The first solution shows the calculation performed inside the *if* statements. This seems to suggest that the decision to **calculate** a conversion depends on the conversion type. However, this is not so; a conversion is **always** performed, regardless of the conversion type. What truly depends on the conversion type is the ***conversion factor.*** Therefore, the calculation should be taken out of the *if* statements in order to make that clear. This clarity provides a visual aid that may come in handy with large programs. Subsection 4.3.2 will show that both solutions have a somewhat inefficient logic. A better solution will be provided at that time.

EXERCISES 4.1.2

1. Write a program that uses a sequence of *ifs* to tell whether a number is positive, negative, or zero.
2. Write a program that shows the ability to add, subtract, and multiply numbers. Here are two examples of a run:

   Enter the operation > 6 + 2.7
   The result = 8.7

   Enter the operation > 2.03 - 6
   The result = -3.97

   The program simply needs to read the first operand, the operator, and the second operand. Then it compares the operator with '+', '–', and '*'. Upon finding the correct operator, it performs the operation. You will need a sequence of three *ifs*.
3. Write a program that converts temperatures from Fahrenheit to Celsius or vice versa, depending on the unit provided. Two examples:

   Enter the temperature and the unit > 13 c
   The temperature is 55.4 in Fahrenheit

   Enter the temperature and the unit > -25 f
   The temperature is -31.7 in Celsius

   Assume the units are always entered in lowercase letters.
4. A bank wants a program that determines the yearly interest earned on a guaranteed investment certificate (GIC), given the number of years. If the investment is for five years, the interest is 8.2% per year; if it is for one year, the interest is 5%. The interest earned is paid yearly and is never reinvested. Determine the amount of interest earned per year. For example:

   Enter the amount to invest > 2000
   For a one-year GIC or a five-year GIC ? > 5
   We will pay you $ 164 interest per year.

5. Write a program that accepts as input the length and width of a table, along with the unit of measurement used. The program then outputs the length and width in meters. It also displays the area in meters squared (rounded off to the nearest one-hundredth). Use a sequence of *ifs* for this task. Here is an example of a run:

   Enter the length and width of the table > 524 316
   What is the unit used: (m)eters, (d)ecimeters, (c)entimeters? c

Length = 5.24 meters, width = 3.16 meters
Surface area = 16.56 meters squared

Assume the units are always entered in lowercase letters.

6. Modify the program in question 5 so that the length and the width may be entered in different units. The display should look like the following:

 Enter the length and width of the table
 along with the unit used:
 (m)eters, (d)ecimeters, (c)entimeters > <u>524 c 3.16 m</u>

 Length = 5.24 meters, width = 3.16 meters
 Surface area = 16.56 meters squared

 (***Hint:*** Use two sequences of *if*s.)

7. Write a program that prompts the user to enter information about a day, a month, and a year as numerals. The complete date is then displayed, with the month converted to text. For example:

 Enter the day (1 to 31) > <u>21</u>
 Enter the month (1 to 12) > <u>8</u>
 Enter the year (1900 to 1999) > <u>1961</u>

 The date is August 21, 61

 You will need a sequence of *if*s to determine which month should be displayed. Assume the data is always entered within the ranges indicated. Note that the year is displayed without the prefix 19. This is easy to accomplish: simply use the remainder operator with 100 as the divisor. Example: 1961 % 100 gives you 61.

Let us look at a last typical application of a sequence of *if*s.

Example 4.1.4

Write a program that finds the largest number of goals scored in a period in a game of hockey. There are three periods in hockey. Here are examples of three runs:

Enter the scores for the three periods > <u>3 8 1</u>
The largest score in a period is 8

Enter the scores for the three periods > <u>3 3 8</u>
The largest score in a period is 8

Enter the scores for the three periods > <u>3 3 3</u>
The largest score in a period is 3

Following is the code that accomplishes these runs:

```
#include <stdio.h>

main()
{
        int n1, n2, n3, max_so_far;

        printf("Enter the scores for the three periods > ");
        scanf("%d%d%d", &n1, &n2, &n3);

        max_so_far = n1;          /* assume n1 is the biggest */
        if (n2 > max_so_far)
        {
              max_so_far = n2;   /* now n2 is the biggest so far */
        }
        if (n3 > max_so_far)
        {
              max_so_far = n3;   /* finally n3 is the biggest */
```

```
    }
    printf("The largest score in a period is %d", max_so_far);
}
```

The first number is assumed to be the largest; then it is compared to the second number. The larger of the two is in turn compared to the third number before the largest of the three is displayed.

EXERCISES 4.1.3

1. Note that the conditions in the program in Example 4.1.4 do not include equality. Does that mean that the program will not work if two or all three numbers are equal?
2. Write a program similar to the one above that:
   a. finds the smallest of three numbers.
   b. finds the smallest of four numbers.
   c. finds the smallest of five numbers.
   You will find that a new *if* statement must be added for each additional number—if there are 20 numbers, 20 *if* statements will be needed. This is clearly undesirable. Luckily, a program may be coded in a way that it can find the largest number in a sequence of numbers of any size. In fact, this was done in Example 1.2.8. A loop was used, and only one *if* instruction was needed. (Unfortunately, you will have to wait until Chapter 7 to see how to write loops in C. Have patience.)
3. Write a program that calculates the holiday bonus of a salaried employee. The bonus is one-half the weekly salary up to $300.
4. Modify the program in Example 4.1.4 so that it also tells which period had the highest score. (***Hint:*** Use the idea presented in the algorithm in Example 1.2.8.)
5. Write a program that calculates an employee's holiday bonus, given the employee's position within the company. The program will ask for the employee's initials, years of experience, position code, and weekly pay. The employee is assigned a bonus based on the following rules:

Job Type	Job Code	Bonus
Secretary	1	Half a week's pay to a maximum of $200
Programmer	2	One week's pay to a maximum of $500
MIS manager	3	One and a half pay weeks' to a maximum of $600
Engineer	4	Two and a half pay weeks' pay to a maximum of $900

6. Add the following features to the question above. An employee with more than ten years' experience is to receive an additional $100; an employee with less than two years' experience will receive half the usual bonus

---

4.1.3 THE NEGATION OPERATOR

We have seen the relational operators == and != (meaning "not equal to"). We have also seen other relational operators, such as >. It is natural to think that C may also use the relational operator !>, meaning "not greater than." For instance, in Example 4.1.4, a programmer could easily have thought of checking if *max_so_far* is **not** greater than *n2,* instead of checking if *n2* is greater than *max:*

```
if (max_so_far !> n2)
{
    max_so_far = n2;   /* now n2 is the biggest so far */
}
```

Nice try, but the C language does not have such an operator. Instead, it provides the ***negation*** operator !, which is used to negate another operator. Here is how it would be used with the *if* statement above:

```
if (!(max_so_far > n2))
{
      max_so_far = n2;   /* now n2 is the biggest so far */
}
```

The *if* condition above reads: "not [indicated by !] *max_so_far* greater than *n2* [indicated by the parenthetical *(max_so_far > n2)*]" which is a bit awkward to read. It means the same as *"max_so_far* is **not** greater than *n2*." Here are two examples that illustrate how the condition is evaluated:

```
!(max_so_far > n2)                  !(max_so_far > n2)
 (     3       > 7 )                 (     5       > 3 )
       3       > 7                         5       > 3
          false                               true
!         false                     !         true
  true                                 false
```

The negation operator turns whatever is true to false, and vice versa, so "!false" is equivalent to true. Note that the negation operator is a unary operator, and it belongs to the class of ***logical*** operators. Table 4.1.2 shows the precedence of C operators.

Table 4.1.2

Operator	Associativity
()	Left to right
!	Right to left
>= <= > <	Left to right
== !=	Left to right

You now see why the parentheses are necessary in *!(max_so_far > n2)*. If they were omitted, the expression would be:

```
!max_so_far > n2
```

Since the value of *max_so_far* is 3, this expression indicates a logical negation (!) of 3, which is meaningless. (Still, the C language does not mind working with something that does not make sense, so it is important that the programmer have plenty of sense.) Other examples of the negation operator will be presented throughout this chapter.

EXERCISES 4.1.4

Modify the conditions below so that the negation operator is used once and only once:

1. `b != 3`
2. `a >= b`
3. `c == d`
4. `!(!(a != c))`

4.1.4 COMMON ERRORS AND TRAPS

Programmers often make common errors when writing *if* statements. Follow these rules to avoid errors.

1. Do not forget to surround the condition of an *if* statement with parentheses. For instance, in the following example, in the first line parentheses are missing around *level <= 5*.

```
if  level <= 5
{
      printf("LOW ON GAS!!!\n");
      printf("Maximum running distance left = %f",
              (100/9.5) * level);
}
```

The compiler will complain in the form of a syntax error.

2. Do not mistake the assignment operator (=) for the equality relational operator (==). For instance, in the following example, the incorrect operator is used in the line *if (currency = 'C')*.

```
#include <stdio.h>

main()
{
     char currency;

     printf("Enter the currency > ");
     scanf("\n%c", &currency);

     if (currency = 'C')
     {
     printf("That's Canadian\n");
     }
     if (currency == 'A')
     {
     printf("That's American\n");
     }
}
```

Although the compiler will not complain about the incorrectly written line, every time the program is run, it will think the currency is Canadian regardless of the input. Here are examples of two runs:

Enter the currency > C
That's Canadian

Enter the currency > A
That's Canadian

However, in the second run, the currency is actually American. Clearly, the program always thinks that the condition *currency = 'C'* is true. The exact explanation for this weird behavior will be given in Chapter 13. For now, suffice it to say that when the assignment operator is used in place of the equality relational operator, the program usually evaluates the condition as true.

3. Do not terminate the line containing the keyword *if* with a semicolon. For instance, in the example below, a semicolon placed at the end of the first line will terminate the *if* statement.

```
if (level <= 5);
{
      printf("LOW ON GAS!!!\n");
      printf("Maximum running distance left = %f",
              (100/9.5) * level);
}
```

Although the compiler will not complain simply because the syntax is correct, the misplaced semicolon terminates the *if* statement. Hence, the statements within the braces no longer belong to this *if* statement. This implies that these statements are always to be executed, regardless of the *if* condition.

4. Do not forget the braces around the block of statements under the *if*. For example:

```
if (level < 5)
      printf("LOW ON GAS!!!\n");
      printf("Maximum running distance left = %f",
              (100/9.5) * level);
```

The compiler will not complain since the syntax is valid. Yet when the program is run, the maximum running distance left will always be displayed, regardless of the level of gas left (Why do you think this is true?), whereas the message "Low on Gas" continues to be displayed only when expected.

5. Do not put the negation operator outside the parentheses of the condition. For example:

```
if !(max_so_far > n2)
{
      max_so_far = n2;
}
```

The compiler will complain of a syntax error because the *if* condition must be surrounded by parentheses and the negation operator is part of this condition. Therefore, the negation symbol must be within the parentheses:

```
if (!(max_so_far > n2))
```

4.2 TECHNICAL CONSIDERATIONS WHEN COMPARING DATA

The comparison of integers is simple and intuitive. In C, however, the underlying mechanism for the comparison of characters and real numbers is a little trickier. Consequently, the purpose of this section is to provide some detailed explanations.

4.2.1 COMPARING CHARACTERS

Example 4.2.1 explains the comparison of characters.

Example 4.2.1

Let us write a program that simply reads two letters and displays an error message if they are not entered in alphabetical order. Here is an example of a run:

Enter two letters > f c
They are not in alphabetical order

Here is the program that results in this run:

```
#include <stdio.h>

main()
{
      char      ch1, ch2;
      printf("Enter two letters > ");
      scanf("\n%c\n%c", &ch1, &ch2);

      if (ch1 > ch2)
      {
            printf("They are not in alphabetical order");
      }
}
```

The condition *ch1 > ch2* uses the normal alphabetical order to determine its veracity. The letter 'a' is the "smallest" letter and the letter 'z', is the "largest". Also the letter 'A' is the "smallest" letter and the letter 'Z' is the "largest." So the letter in *ch1* is larger than the letter in *ch2* if the letter in *ch1* comes **after** the letter in *ch2* in the alphabet. Here are two examples of how the condition *ch1 > ch2* evaluates:

ch1 > ch2	*ch1 > ch2*
'f' > 'c'	'F' > 'C'
true	true

Keep in mind that the C programming language is ***case-sensitive,*** so the letter 'F' is **not** equal to 'f'. This means that the program above will not work if lowercase and uppercase letters are mixed.

EXERCISES 4.2.1

Are the following true or false?

1. `'u' >= 'z'`
2. `'e' == 'E'`
3. `'U' >= 'Z'`

4.2.2 COMPARING REAL NUMBERS

Comparing real numbers can be trickier than comparing whole numbers. Example 4.2.2 shows why and offers solutions.

Example 4.2.2

A physical education teacher makes his students run on a track one at the time. He uses a computer program that takes in the distance covered by the student and the time taken to cover it. A message indicates if the boy ran faster than last year's class record. Assume last year's record was 7.15 meters/second. Following is the program for this situation:

```
#include <stdio.h>

main()
{
      float  distance, time;

      printf("Enter the distance covered > ");
      scanf("%f", &distance);
      printf("Enter the time taken > ");
      scanf("%f", &time);

      if (distance / time > 7.15)
      {
            printf("The boy went faster than last year's record.");
      }
}
```

Before signalling the first boy to run, the instructor decides to test his program by entering the simple data 7.15 meters and one second. This is 7.15 meters/second, which is obviously **not** more than last year's record, so no message should appear. Yet to his dismay he saw:

Enter the distance covered > 7.15
Enter the time taken > 1
The boy went faster than last year's record.

Clearly the message is in error. The instructor keeps his cool and immediately modifies the program so that it displays the calculated speed to see if that is correct:

```
#include <stdio.h>

main()
{
      float  distance, time;

      printf("Enter the distance covered > ");
      scanf("%f", &distance);
      printf("Enter the time taken > ");
      scanf("%f", &time);

      printf("The speed is %f\n", distance / time); /* is speed OK ? */
```

```
        if (distance / time > 7.15)
        {
                printf("The boy went faster than last year's record.");
        }
}
```

A new run reveals nothing wrong:

Enter the distance covered > 7.15
Enter the time taken > 1
The speed is 7.150000
The boy went faster than last year's record.

The speed is calculated correctly as 7.15, yet the computer still thinks it is not equal to 7.15. At this point, the teacher thinks his computer is possessed and loses his cool. He is about to smash it on the track just as the computer teacher passes by. She proceeds to give him an explanation for this weird behavior (of the computer program, that is). She modifies the *printf()* as follows:

```
printf("The speed is %.20f\n", distance / time);
```

Her substitution of the expression *%.20f\n* (which indicates that the first 20 decimals are to be displayed) for the previously used expression *%f\n* unveils the mystery when a the program is run again:

Enter the distance covered > 7.15
Enter the time taken > 1
The speed is 7.15000009536743200000
The boy went faster than last year's record.

A look at all of those decimals tells him something is still wrong. The computer calculated the speed as:

distance / time
  7.15 / 1
  7.15 + a long series of extra decimals

The correct answer is obviously 7.15, but the computer was unable to divide accurately because it stored the number 7.15 in memory inaccurately as 7.150000095367432. Why? Because the memory cell is too small to contain all those decimals, causing the number in it to be damaged (a common error mentioned in Chapter 3).

What should our baffled teacher do now? Answer: simply give the variable *distance* a bigger memory cell by declaring it *double.* Following is the new program. Note that the format codes within *scanf()* are changed to *%lf* and changes are in bold type.

```
#include <stdio.h>

main()
{
        double  distance, time;

        printf("Enter the distance covered > ");
        scanf("%lf", &distance);     /* note format code %lf */
        printf("Enter the time taken > ");
        scanf("%lf", &time);

        printf("The speed is %.20f\n", distance / time);
        if (distance / time > 7.15)
        {
        printf("The boy went faster than last year's record.");
        }
}
```

A new run show the following:

Enter the distance covered > 7.15
Enter the time taken > 1
The peed is 7.15000000000000000000

The number 7.15 is now stored accurately.

The purpose of this example is not to conclude that the type *double* should always be used instead of *float*—some numbers cannot be stored accurately in *double* cells either. Simply remember that comparisons of real numbers may very well fail **when both operands are equal.** Other than this case, the comparison should never fail.

EXERCISES 4.2.2

1. Consider the code below:

```
main()
{
        float       num1, num2;

        printf("Enter two numbers in ascending order > ");
        scanf("%f%f", &num1, &num2);
        if (num1 > num2)
        {
                printf("Wrong! The input is not in ascending order);
        }
}
```

   a. Can you come up with data that will make the program fail?
   b. If you find data that will make the program fail, modify the program so that it will work properly.

2. Consider the code below:

```
main()
{
        char       num1, num2;

        printf("Enter two numbers in ascending order > ");
        scanf("%d%d", &num1, &num2);

        if (num1 > num2)
        {
                printf("Wrong! The input is not in ascending order);
        }
}
```

   a. Can you come up with data that make the program fail?
   b. If you answered (a) positively, modify the program so it will work properly. (***Hint:*** See Subsection 3.1.2.)

4.2.3 ARITHMETIC WITHIN A CONDITION

Consider Example 4.2.3 to learn about arithmetic calculations within a condition.

Example 4.2.3

The following program simply asks the user to enter the number of newspapers sold by a newsstand for each day of the week. If sales are too low, an appropriate message is displayed.

```
#include <stdio.h>

main()
{
        int day1, day2, day3, day4, day5;
```

```
        printf("Enter the number of newspapers sold\n"
               "for each day of the week > ");
        scanf("%d%d%d%d%d", &day1, &day2, &day3, &day4, &day5);
        if (day1 + day2 + day3 + day4 + day5 < 40)
        {
            printf("Alert. Sales sagging.\n");
        }
}
```

Note the use of the addition operators within the *if* condition. Let us examine how this condition is evaluated. The arithmetic operators have a higher priority than the relational operators, so the expression will be evaluated as follows (assume the numbers entered were 19 5 9 7 22):

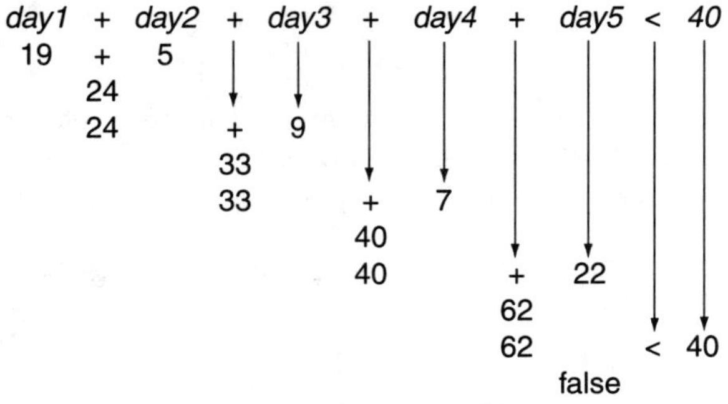

The condition evaluates to false, so no alert message is displayed. This example shows that C does not view a relational operator any differently than an arithmetic operator. It blindly refers to the precedence table to evaluate an expression.

EXERCISES 4.2.3

Evaluate the conditions below:

1. a == 7 + b * 6, where a = –5 and b = –2
2. b + 9 – a * 11 != 2 * b / 5, where a = –3, b = 36

4.3 THE *if/else* STATEMENT

4.3.1 THE SYNTAX AND LOGIC OF THE *if/else* STATEMENT

The *if* statement offers one alternative only: do some action or do nothing at all. The *if/else* offers two alternatives. The following two examples explain those alternatives.

Example 4.3.1

Section 2.2 started off with the implementation in C of an algorithm from Section 1.2. That program calculated Judy's summer income. At the time the goal was simply to calculate summer income. It was implicitly assumed she would take the job. What if she didn't? The algorithm did not address that issue. It would be useful for the program to advise Judy to take the job or not, based on the income calculated. This leads to the improved algorithm below (changes appear in bold type):

1. **Judy derives an acceptable MINIMUM INCOME, based on her upcoming school year expenses.**
2. Judy asks for the HOURLY RATE of pay.
3. Judy listens to the answer from the employer.
4. Then Judy asks for the number of HOURS OF WORK per week.
5. Judy listens to the answer from the employer.
6. Judy asks for the number of WEEKS OF WORK offered.

7. Judy listens to the answer.
8. Finally, Judy takes out her calculator and finds the AMOUNT OF INCOME to be:

HOURLY RATE × HOURS OF WORK × WEEKS OF WORK

9. If the AMOUNT OF INCOME ≥ MINIMUM INCOME, do step 9.1:
   9.1 Take the job.
   Otherwise, do step 9.2:
   9.2 Look someplace else for a job.

(The details for instruction 1 will be explained in Supplementary Exercises 6.1, 6 and 7.) Following is the new program with the changes from the solution in Section 2.2 in bold type.

```
#include <stdio.h>

main()
{
   float  hourly_rate;
   int    hours_per_week;
   float  total_income;
   int    num_weeks;
   float  minimum;

   printf("Enter the minimum income acceptable > ");
   scanf("%f", &minimum);
   printf("Enter the hourly wage > ");
   scanf("%f", &hourly_rate);
   printf("Enter the total work hours per week > ");
   scanf("%d", &hours_per_week);
   printf("Enter the number of weeks of work > ");
   scanf("%d", &num_weeks);

   total_income = hourly_rate * hours_per_week * num_weeks;

   if (total_income >= minimum) /* if this is true, do next two steps */
   {

   printf("Take the job.\n");
   printf("You will make $ %.2f this summer\n", total_income);
   }
   else   /* otherwise, do the following step */
   {
   printf("Look someplace else for a job.\n");
   }
}
```

Note the new statement: an *if/else* statement:

```
if (total_income >= minimum)  /* if this is true, do next two steps */
```

This statement says "if the *total_income* is greater than or equal to the *minimum* income acceptable, then take the job and display the summer income; otherwise, do not take the job." Here is the syntax:

```
if (total_income >= minimum)[1]
{
      printf("Take the job.\n");[2]
      printf("You will make $ %.2f this summer\n", total_income);[2]
}
else
{
      printf("Look someplace else for a job.\n");[3]
}
```

Explanations

1. Note the parentheses around the condition.
2. If the condition is true, execute these two statements.
3. Otherwise (that is, if the condition is false), execute this statement.

The *if* and the *else* constitute a statement **together:** an **else cannot** be a statement without an *if,* whereas an *if* may be used without an *else.* To summarize, the general mechanism of the *if/else* is illustrated in Figure 4.3.1.

Figure 4.3.1

```
if (condition)
{
     :
     :
     :
}
else
{
     :
     :
     :
}
     :
     :
```

One and only one of the two blocks is guaranteed to be reached and executed.

EXERCISES 4.3.1

1. Modify the *if/else* in Example 4.3.1 so that the condition is
   a. !(total_income < minimum)
   b. total_income < minimum
2. Is there anything wrong with the following code segments?
   a.
   ```
   if (answer == 'y')
   {
          printf("Fine!");
   }
          printf("Continue");
   else
   {
          printf("Oops!");
   }
   ```
   b.
   ```
   if x >= 0;
          printf("x is positive");
          x = 0;
   else;
          printf("x is negative");
          x = -x;
   ```
3. What will the following two programs display?
   a.
   ```
   x = 2;
   y = 8;
   if (x+2 > y)
   {
          printf("one");
   }
   ```

```
    else
    {
            printf("two");
    }
```

b.
```
if (x < x)
    {
            printf("Failure");
    }
    else
    {
            printf("Good machine");
    }
```

4. Write a program that advises whether or not to trade in your car. If the difference in dollar value between the trade-in and the new car is less than $14,000, buy the car; otherwise, do not. The program will ask for the dollar value of both cars.
5. Write a C program for the algorithms developed in the following exercises:
   a. Exercise 1.2.3, 1
   b. Exercise 1.2.3, 2
   c. Exercise 1.2.3, 3

Let us look at a few more examples.

Example 4.3.2

A psychologist wants to conduct apptitude tests on all students of an elementary school. A different test is written for each age. The program below checks whether or not two given students should take the same test.

```
#include <stdio.h>

main()
{
     int       age1, age2;

     printf("Enter the two students' ages > ");
     scanf("%d%d", &age1, &age2);
     if (age1 != age2)
     {
            printf("They cannot write the same test");
     }
     else
     {
            printf("They may write the same test");
      }
}
```

Example 4.3.3

A very common application of the *if/else* is to write a program that takes two numbers and displays them in ascending order. Here are two examples of a run:

Enter two numbers > <u>97 21</u>   Enter two numbers > <u>35 36</u>
In ascending order: 21 97   In ascending order: 35 36

This is easily done with an *if/else* statement:

```
main()
{
```

```
	int	num1, num2;

	printf("Enter two numbers > ");
	scanf("%d%d", &num1, &num2);

	if (num1 > num2)
	{
		printf("In ascending order: %d %d", num2, num1);
	}
	else
	{
		printf("In ascending order: %d %d", num1, num2);
	}
}
```

Note that a run of the program might look like this:

Enter two numbers > <u>97 21</u>
In ascending order: <u>21 97</u>

This gives the impression that the values inside the variables *num1* and *num2* are changed to 21 and 97, respectively. Of course, you will see in the program that this is not so. The values in memory do not change order.

Example 4.3.4

Suppose we are to order the two numbers above **in memory**, and then display them on the screen. If *num1* is larger than *num2,* their contents should be swapped, i.e., the content of *num1* will be put in *num2* and vice versa; otherwise, no swapping is necessary. Following is the program that accomplishes this task (changes appear in bold type):

```
#include <stdio.h>

main()
{
	int	num1, num2, hold;

	printf("Enter two numbers > ");
	scanf("%d%d", &num1, &num2);
	if (num1 > num2)
	{
		hold = num1;
		num1 = num2;
		num2 = hold;
	}
	printf("In ascending order: %d %d", num1, num2);
}
```

In the preceding example, the statements that perform the swapping of the two numbers are:

```
hold = num1;
num1 = num2;
num2 = hold;
```

Figure 4.3.2 shows the code that swaps two numbers, assuming *num1* contains 97 and *num2* contains 21. The idea is analogous to the task of exchanging the contents of a glass of beer with the contents of a glass of liquor; to make the exchange, a third glass is obviously needed. The variable *hold* serves a similar purpose. This swapping technique is frequently used in computer programs.

Figure 4.3.2

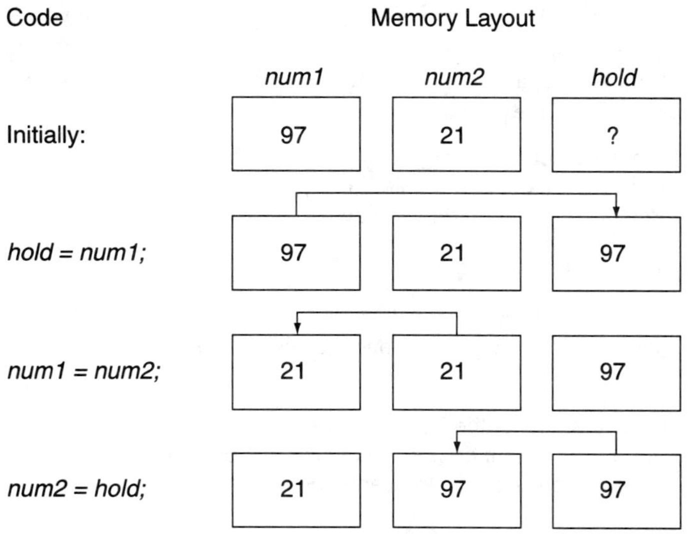

EXERCISES 4.3.2

1. Modify the program of Example 4.3.4 so that it orders numbers in descending order.
2. Modify the program of Example 4.3.2 so that the condition is *age1 == age2*.
3. Extend the swapping program of Example 4.3.4 so that it orders three numbers. Use simple *if* statements only. (***Hint:*** swapping may be needed up to three times.)
4. Write a program that reads in three letters and displays them in alphabetical order. For example:

   ```
   Enter two letters > f c
   ```

   The method of swapping letters is similar to the one of swapping numbers. (***Hint:*** Use the swapping program developed in question 3 above and refer to the Example 4.2.1.)
5. Write a program that determines an employee's pay given the number of hours worked. If the hours worked were no more than 40, the employee is paid $9.12 an hour; otherwise, the employee is paid at time and a half for the overtime. Besides the number of hours worked, the program will read in the employee's initials.
6. Modify the program in question 5 above as follows. The program will read the rate of pay, rather than assuming that it is $9.12. Also, if the employee earns more than $500.00, a bonus of 1.8% of the employee's gross pay is added.
7. Write a program that echoes the information the user enters back to the screen in text form. Here are examples of two runs:

   ```
   What are your initials? HWA
   How many children do you have? 3
   HWA has 3 children.

   What are your initials? UYT
   How many children do you have? 1
   UYT has one child.
   ```

   The numbers are echoed as numerals, except for the number 1, which is echoed as the word *one*. The word *child* is used if there is only one child; otherwise, *children* is used. Assume everyone has at least one child.
8. Modify the program above slightly so it asks the user's gender. For example:

   ```
   What are your initials? HWA
   Are you a male or a female? (m=male, f=female) f
   How many children do you have? 3

   Ms. HWA has 3 children.
   ```

The title will be either *Ms.* or *Mr.,* depending on the gender. (***Hint:*** You need two *if/else* statements. Display the message in two steps: the initials and title first, then the number of children.)

9. Improve the program in question 8 above so that it will handle the case of a person who has no children. For example:

    What are your initials? OLI
    Are you a male or a female? (m=male, f=female) m
    How many children do you have? 0

    Mr. OLI has no children.

10. Design a C program for the algorithm in Example 1.2.4. Your program will need the cost of the book, the amount of money received, and the type of currency. Here are two examples of a run:

    Enter the cost of the book > 41.27
    Enter the amount of money paid by the customer > 40
    Enter the currency (C for Canadian, A for American) > A

    The change is $ 10.28

    Enter the cost of the book > 41.27
    Enter the amount of money handed by the customer > 45
    Enter the currency (C for Canadian, A for American) > C

    The change is $ 3.73

    Assume the user always enters the currency as a capital letter and that the letter is never mistyped.

11. Modify the program in question 10 above so that all data are entered at the same time, and so that the currency in which the change is given is indicated. For example:

    Enter the amount of money handed by the customer,
    the currency (C for Canadian, A for American),
    the cost of the book > 45 C 41.27

    The change is $ 3.73 Canadian

4.3.2 *if/else* CHAINS

Let's return to Example 4.1.3 for a moment. Following is the sequence of *if*s used there:

```
if (conv_type == 'd')
{
      conv_factor = 0.6214;
}
if (conv_type == 'w')
{
      conv_factor = 2.2046;
}
if (conv_type == 'v')
{
      conv_factor = 0.8772;
}
standard = conv_factor * metric;

printf("The standard value is %.2f quarts", standard);
```

This solution is inefficient (both logically and in terms of how much CPU time it requires): all three conditions are always evaluated, even though only one of them is ever true. For instance, if the conversion type is 'w', the program still evaluates the next two conditions, even though they cannot possibly be true. The last two conditions are ***alternatives*** that should be considered only when the first one is false. This is precisely what the *if/else* chain allows. Example 4.3.5 shows how this works.

Example 4.3.5

The following segment of code produces the same results as the one in Example 4.1.3, although the logic differs (changes are shown in bold type):

```
if (conv_type == 'd')
{
      conv_factor = 0.6214;[1]
}
else if (conv_type == 'w')
{
      conv_factor = 2.2046;[2]
}
else if (conv_type == 'v')
{
      conv_factor = 0.8772;[3]
}
standard = conv_factor * metric;

printf("The standard value is %.2f quarts", standard);
```

Explanations

1. Alternative 1
2. Alternative 2
3. Alternative 3

Alternative 1, which will be reached only if the conversion factor is 'd', implies that the condition *conv_type == 'w'* will be evaluated only if the condition *conv_type == 'd'* is false. Similarly, the condition *conv_type == 'v'* will be evaluated only if the condition *conv_type == 'w'* is false **and** the condition *conv_type == 'v'* is false. This *if/else* chain therefore ensures that conditions are not evaluated unless necessary.

Another way to phrase this explanation is: if the condition of a given *if* is false, evaluate the condition of the next *if* below; otherwise, get out of the chain structure. This structure consists of all the *if/else*s and is called an **if/else *chain.*** This chain looks very much like the sequences of *if*s discussed in Subsection 4.1.2, but they work very differently.

A mutually exclusive sequence of *if* statements. Note that all conditions in the *if/else* chain must be mutually exclusive; that is, no two conditions may be true at the same time.

Example 4.3.6

In Example 4.3.5 all *else* keywords were accompanied by a condition. This is not required. For instance, suppose the user mistyped the letter indicating conversion type. To alert the program to such an instance, we might decide that *conv_type* should be set to 0. The *if/else* chain should check that possibility with the following code (changes are shown in bold type):

```
if (conv_type == 'd')
{
      conv_factor = 0.6214;[1]
}
else if (conv_type == 'w')
{
      conv_factor = 2.2046;[2]
}
```

```
else if (conv_type == 'v')
{
      conv_factor = 0.8772;[3]
}
else
{
      printf("Invalid conversion type.\n");[4]
      conv_type = 0;[4]
}
standard = conv_factor * metric;

printf("The standard value is %.2f quarts", standard);
```

Explanations

1. Alternative 1
2. Alternative 2
3. Alternative 3
4. Alternative 4

Application: Checking ranges. The above *if/else* chain was simple. The conditions involved consisted only of checking equalities. The logic of an *if/else* chain becomes a little trickier when inequalities are involved. Consider Example 4.3.7.

Example 4.3.7

Suppose we want to write a program that simply assigns a letter grade given the mark (the numerical score) obtained by a student on a test, based on the following policy:

Mark Range	Letter Grade
80–100	A
70–79	B
60–69	C
0–59	F

The program follows. Note that the *printf()* is not inserted in each *if* statement. Its action has nothing to do with the mark, so it is called **after** the *if/else* chain (recall that Example 4.1.3 did the same):

```
#include <stdio.h>

main()
{
      char      letter;
      int       mark;

      printf("Enter the mark > ");
      scanf("%d", &mark);

      if (mark >= 80)
      {
            letter = 'A';
      }
      else if (mark >= 70)[1]
      {
            letter = 'B';
      }
      else if (mark >= 60)[1]
      {
            letter = 'C';
```

```
    }
    else[2]
    {
        letter = 'F';
    }
    printf("The letter grade is %c\n", letter);
}
```

Explanations

1. This statement seems to suggest that if the mark is greater than or equal to 70, the letter is a B. Something seems wrong here: a mark greater than or equal to 80 should get an A, not a B. But remember how the *if/else* chain works: the condition *mark >= 70* is reached only if the condition above it, *mark >= 80,* is not true. The same could be said about the next condition: *mark >= 60.*
2. No condition is needed with this *else.* This *else* is reached only when all three conditions above it are false. Hence, the letter must be an F. No further checking is needed.

EXERCISES 4.3.3

1. Does each pair of codes below produce the same output, given the same value of variable *num*?

a. **Code 1**

```
if (num == 1)
{
   printf("msg 1");
}
else if (num == 2)
{
   printf("msg 2");
}
else if (num ==3)
{
   printf("msg 3");
}
```

Code 2

```
if (num == 1)
{
      printf("msg 1");
}
if (num == 2)
{
      printf("msg 2");
}
if (num == 3)
{
      printf("msg 3");
}
```

b. **Code 1**

```
if (num == 1)
{
   printf("msg 1");
}
else if (num == 2)
{
   printf("msg 2");
}
else if (num == 3)
{
   printf("msg 3");
}
else
{
   printf("msg 4");
}
```

Code 2

```
if (num == 1)
{
      printf("msg 1");
}
if (num == 2)
{
      printf("msg 2");
}
if (num == 3)
{
      printf("msg 3");
}
else
{
      printf("msg 4");
}
```

c. **Code 1**

```
if (num <= 1)
{
   printf("msg 1");
```

Code 2

```
if (num <= 1)
{
      printf("msg 1");
```

```
}
else if (num <= 2)
{
   printf("msg 2");
}
else if (num <= 3)
{
  printf("msg 3");
}
```

```
}
if (num == 2)
{
      printf("msg 2");
}
if (num == 3)
{
      printf("msg 3");
}
```

2. Is there anything wrong logically with the *if/else* chains below?

a.
```
if (num == 1)
{
  printf("msg 1");
}
else if (num > 0)
{
  printf("msg 2");
}
else
{
  printf("msg 3");
}
```

b.
```
if (num > 0)
{
      printf("msg 1");
}
else if (num == 1)
{
      printf("msg 2");
}
else
{
      printf("msg 3");
}
```

3. Redo the exercises below using an *if/else* chain in each, instead of a sequence of *if*s:
   a. Exercise 4.1.2, 1
   b. Exercise 4.1.2, 2
   c. Exercise 4.1.2,3
   d. Exercise 4.1.2, 4
   e. Exercise 4.1.2, 6
   f. Exercise 4.1.2, 7
   g. Exercise 4.1.3, 5
   h. Exercise 4.1.3, 6
4. Modify the program of question 3 (a) above so that division (/) is allowed. The program must also check whether division is possible (it is not possible if the divisor is 0). For example:

   Enter the operation > 5.8 / 0
   Cannot divide by 0

5. Suppose a taxation department wants a civil status entry program that presents the following menu:

   Tax Information System
   Select your civil status:
     (M) Married
     (S) Single
     (W) Widowed
     (D) Divorced

   Enter here > S

   You must fill out form TX-113-2

   The status is entered as a code letter, which is entered in uppercase letters only. Then the program simply displays the tax form that individual is to file. The forms are as follows:

Married	TX-120-9
Single or widowed	TX-113-2
Divorced	TX-121-7

   Write a program that accomplishes this task. Also, the program should indicate so if the user enters an invalid letter code.

6. Modify the program of Exercise 3.3.2, 2(b) as follows. The method of income tax calculation has been revised, and the base rate of 30% now may be reduced by the number of dependents:

1 dependent	reduce base rate by 5%
2 dependents	reduce base rate by 12%
3 dependents	reduce base rate by 25%
4 dependents	reduce base rate by 35%
5 dependents or more	reduce base rate by 45%

The number of dependents must be placed in the file WORK.DAT:

```
810 PHT CA 2.5 31.5 5.0 1.0 13.09 3
```

Initials (PHT); Employee # (810); Location (California) (CA); # hours for projects 1 to 4 (2.5 31.5 5.0 1.0); Wages per hour (13.09); # of dependents at home (3)

4.3.3 COMMON ERRORS AND TRAPS

Programmers often make common errors when writing *if* statements. Follow these rules to avoid errors.

1. Do not terminate the line containing the keyword *if* with a semicolon. For example:

```
if (total_income >= minimum);
{
    printf("Take the job.\n");
    printf("You will make $ %.2f this summer\n", total_income);
}
else
{
    printf("Look someplace else for a job.\n");
}
```

The compiler will complain that the *else* does not have an *if* associated with it. Why? Because the misplaced semicolon terminated the *if/else* statement **before** the compiler saw the keyword *else*, so the *else* is no longer part of an *if/else* statement, and that constitutes a syntax error.

2. Do not terminate the line containing the keyword *else* with a semicolon. For example:

```
if (total_income >= minimum)
{
    printf("Take the job.\n");
    printf("You will make $ %.2f this summer\n", total_income);
  }
 else;
  {
      printf("Look someplace else for a job.\n");
  }
```

The compiler will **not** complain about this code. Why? Because there is no syntax error. Indeed, the misplaced semicolon terminated the *if/else* statement **after** the compiler saw the *else*, so the *else* is indeed part of an *if/else* statement.

The program will not run well, though: the message "Look someplace else." will be displayed every time, regardless of the condition. This is because its *printf()* is not part of the *if/else*, so it is not affected by the condition.

3. Do not think that a condition must be specified for the *else* block also. For example:

```
if (total_income >= minimum)
{
     printf("Take the job.\n");
```

```
        printf("You will make $ %.2f this summer\n", total_income);
}
else if (total_income < minimum)
{
        printf("Look someplace else for a job.\n");
}
```

This condition [*else/if ([total_income < minimum)*] is redundant because it is implied when the program reaches the *else* block. Indeed the *else* block is reached only if the condition *total_income >= minimum* is false, that is when *total_income < minimum.*

4. Do not forget the braces around a block of statements. For example:

```
if (total_income >= minimum)
        printf("Take the job.\n");
        printf("You will make $ %.2f this summer\n", total_income);
else
        printf("Look someplace else for a job.\n");
```

The compiler will complain that the *else* does not have an *if.* Why? Because the **first** semicolon encountered acted as a termination of the *if/else* statement, so the *else* is now without an *if.*

5. Do not use an *if/else* statement unnecessarily. For example, when asked to write a program that calculates the holiday bonus of an employee, given that it is half a week's pay to a maximum of $300, novices sometimes offer the following solution:

```
bonus = weekly / 2;
if (bonus > 300)
{
            bonus = 300;
}
else
{
            bonus = bonus;
}
```

This is fine, except that the *else* part does nothing at all. It should be removed. Section 5.2 will discuss further when to use and when not to use an *if/else.*

6. Do not mix up the *if/else* chain and a sequence of *if*s. For example:

Sequence of *if*s	*vs.*	*if/else* chain

```
if (condition1)                     if (condition1)
{                                   {
        ......                      ......
}                                   }
if (condition2)                     else if (condition2)
{                                   {
        ......                      ......
}                                   }
if (condition3)                     else if (condition3)
{                                   {
        ......                      ......
}                                   }
```

These two structures do **not** have the same logic. In the first one, **all** *if* statements are reached, whereas in the second one, this is never guaranteed and depends on the conditions as explained in Subsection 4.3.2.

7. Do not mention a condition in the last *else* of an *if/else* chain when it is not logically necessary. For example:

```
printf("Enter your grade: ");
scanf("%d", &grade);

if (grade > 90)
```

```
{
     printf("Mighty good.\n");
}
else if (grade > 70)
{
     printf("Not bad.\n");
}
else if (grade <= 70)
{
     printf("Not good.\n");
}
```

The last condition is redundant since the program can only reach that point when the grade is indeed less than or equal to 70.

SUPPLEMENTARY EXERCISES 4.3

1. Improve the program from Supplementary Exercise 2.4, 4, so that the program will ask which type of meat was bought. Assume one and only one type is bought from this list:

Ground beef	at 3.95	a pound
Sirloin	at 8.95	a pound
Chicken	at 10.05	a pound
Fish	at 7.10	a pound

If the customer doesn't pay enough money he or she will be charged for the difference at the end of the month. Following is an example of a run (changes are in bold type):

At: ABC Grocery Store
125 Main Street
Some City, XY

Terminal: 0055   Operator: 00000122

Date: 12/09/94   Time: 17:34:07

Items bought:

Meat Sirloin	
@ 8.95/pound	*$ 25.09*
Dairy products	$ 8.21
Cereals	$ 12.99
Desserts	$ 3.48
Total:	$ 49.77
received:	$ 45.00
Charged:	**$ 4.77**

THANK YOU!

Enter the time (hours, minutes, seconds) > 17 34 07
Enter the date (day, month, year) > 12 09 94
Enter the terminal code > 55
Enter the operator code > 122
Enter the weight of meat in pounds > 2.803
(G)round beef, (S)irloin, (C)hicken or (F)ish? S
Enter the total costs of the dairy products > 8.21
Enter the total costs of the cereals > 12.99
Enter the total costs of the desserts > 3.48

Total cost is $ 49.77

Enter money received > 45.00
> This is not enough money.
You will be charged $ 4.77 at the end of the month.
:
:
:

The grocery slip is produced at the end of the run.

2. Improve the program from Supplementary Exercise 3.2, 2, as follows. If the user did not pay any of last month's payment, the credit card bill will issue the warning "No payment made last month." If the user paid less the minimum payment, the warning "Did not pay enough last month" will appear. In this case, interest will be charged on the unpaid portion of the minimum. For example, the bill below is taken from Supplementary Exercise 3.2, 2, with changes in bold type:

CREDIT CARD BILL

Date	Location	Amount
08/01/96	Sears	$ 20.77
09/01/96	Safeway Grocery Store	$ 61.02
11/01/96	Toyota	$ 272.81
27/01/96	Coles Bookstore	$ 55.12
31/01/96	Interest Charged	$ **54.07**
31/01/96	Payment from Last Month's Bill	$ **0.00**

Account Number	Owed on Last Bill		Credits		Debits This Month	New Amount Owed
4510	$ 308.91	–	$ **0.00**	+	409.72	$ **718.63**

Interest Rate	Credit Limit	Minimum Payment
17.5%	$ 4000	$ **35.95**

Comments:
No payments made last month

Note that interest has been charged on the $308.91 at 17.5%. This bill will be produced after the information below is provided by the user:

Enter your expenses for this month > 20.77 61.02 272.81 55.12
How much do you owe from last month's bill? 308.91
Enter your payment > **0.00**
What is this month's interest rate? > 17.5
Enter your credit card number > 4510

3. Further improve the program in question 2 above. If the payment for the month is larger than the credit limit, a notification will appear on the bill. For example, the bill below illustrates in bold this new feature:

CREDIT CARD BILL

Date	Location	Amount
08/01/96	Sears	$ 1178.09
09/01/96	Safeway Grocery Store	$ 500.11
11/01/96	Toyota	$ 4902.88
27/01/96	Coles Bookstore	$ 11.99

31/01/96	Interest Charged			$ **453.79**
31/01/96	Payment from Last Month's Bill			$ 308.91
Account Number	Owed on Last Bill	Credits	Debits This Month	New Amount Owed
4510	$ 308.91 –	$ **308.91** +	$ **7046.86**	$ **7046.86**
	Interest Rate	Credit Limit	Minimum Payment	
	17.5%	$ 4000	$ **352.34**	

Comments:
Your expenses this month are above the credit limit.
Interest is charged on the amount above this limit.

Note that interest has been charged at 17.5% on the amount \$6,593.07 – \$4,000.00 = \$2,593.07 above the \$4,000 credit limit. So the debit is actually \$6,593.07 + \$453.79 = \$7,046.86. This bill will be produced after the information below is provided by the user:

Enter your expense for this month > **1178.09 500.11 4902.88 11.99**
How much do you owe from last month's bill? 308.91
Enter your payment > **308.91**
What is this month's interest rate? > 17.5
Enter your credit card number > 4510

4. A state wishes to computerize the scoring at its diving competition. Each diver receives a score (out of 10) from five judges. These scores are then entered into the computer by the final judge. For example:

Diving Competition

Enter the diver's ID > 245901621
Enter the diver's city code> 24
Enter the score given by each judge> 7.7 8.1 9.2 6.3 8.5
What was the degree of difficulty? 1.4

The diver's ID is his or her social security number. The overall score is obtained as follows: all five scores are added (this total is 39.8). The highest and the lowest scores are always assumed to be skewed, or inaccurate, so they are dropped. This gives a score of $39.8 - (6.3 + 9.2) = 24.3$. Then this score is multiplied by the degree of difficulty. The degree of difficulty ranges from 1.00 to 1.67. In this case, the degree of difficulty is 1.4, so the calculation is $24.3 \times 1.4 = 34.02$. Finally, this number is divided by 5, resulting in an overall score of 6.8.

A report will then be sent to the scoreboard operator screen, which then displays the overall score:

Report to Scoreboard Operator

Display the score obtained: 6.8

Also, a report such as the following one is sent to the media:

Report to the Media

Event: Diving competition
Diver ID: 245901621, City code: 24

Scores given by each judge were:

```
1   2   3   4   5          Final score
7.7 8.1 9.2 6.3 8.5  --->  6.8
```

Of course, it would be more realistic to display the name of the diver and the name of the city in which he or she lives, but this requires string handling operations, which are not covered until Chapter 18.

4.4 THE *switch* STATEMENT

Situations calling for *if/else* chains are quite common, so a special statement, the *switch,* exists in C that makes programming such chains easier.

4.4.1 CONVERTING AN *if/else* CHAIN INTO A *switch* STATEMENT

A typical example of the use of an *if/else* chain is the implementation of ***menus.*** Consider Example 4.4.1.

Example 4.4.1

Let us revisit the civil status entry program of Exercises 4.3.3, 5. Here is a solution (that you may have found):

```
#include <stdio.h>

main()
{
    char civil_code;

    printf("%s%s%s%s%s%s%s",
        "                 Tax Information System\n\n",
        "                 Select your civil status:\n\n",
        "                 (M)     Married\n",
        "                 (S)     Single\n",
        "                 (W)     Widowed\n",
        "                 (D)     Divorced\n\n",
        "                Enter here > ");
    scanf("\n%c", &civil_code);

    if (civil_code == 'M')
    {
       printf("\nYou must fill out form TX-120-9\n");
    }
    else if (civil_code == 'S')
    {
       printf("\nYou must fill out form TX-113-2\n");
    }
    else if (civil_code == 'W')
    {
       printf("\nYou must fill out form TX-113-2\n");
    }
    else if (civil_code == 'D')
    {
       printf("\nYou must fill out form TX-121-7\n");
    }
    else

    {
       printf("\nInvalid code.");
    }
}
```

Now let us convert it to a *switch* statement.

Syntax and logic of a *switch* statement. As mentioned earlier, situations requiring the use of *if/else* chains are so common that the C compiler provides a specially designed statement structure for those situations: the *switch* statement. The *if/else* chain above is easy to convert into a *switch* statement, as shown in Figure 4.4.1.

Figure 4.4.1

```
switch(civil_code) 1
{2
   case 'M':3
         printf("\nYou must fill out form TX-120-9\n");
         break;
   case 'S': case 'W':
         printf("\nYou must fill out form TX-113-2\n");
         break;
   case 'D':
         printf("\nYou must fill out form TX-121-7\n");
         break;
   default:
         printf("\nInvalid code.");
         break;
}4
```

Explanations

1. Note that the syntax of a *switch* statement requires parentheses around the controlling expression.
2. This brace denotes the beginning of the *cases.*
3. 'M' is the label of the first case. Labels can be either a character or a whole number; real numbers and variables are not allowed.
4. This brace denotes the end of both the *cases* and the *switch* statement.

The *switch* statement tries to find a match between the ***controlling expression*** and the ***labels.*** If it finds a match for 'M', it executes the statements following *case 'M':* until reaching the statement *break.* This causes the program to jump to the end of the *switch* statement, hence skipping everything else. If it does not find a match for "M', it checks with "S' or "W', and so on. If it finds no match, then the program will inevitably reach the *default* keyword, at which point it will execute the statements under it.

Note that the *switch* statement is in fact a block of statements because of the **mandatory** use of braces. Also the sequence of statements under each *case* does *not* require braces, even when there is more than one statement. Finally, each sequence of statements must terminate with a *break* statement.

Since C compilers ignore white spaces, the *switch* statement can be arranged differently, such as listing the *cases* on separate lines:

```
switch(civil_code)
{
   case 'M':
      printf("\nYou must fill out form TX-120-9\n");
      break;
   case 'S':
   case 'W':
      printf("\nYou must fill out form TX-113-2\n");
      break;
   case 'D':
      printf("\nYou must fill out form TX-121-7\n");
      break;
   default:
      printf("\nInvalid code.");
      break;
}
```

The general mechanism of the *switch* is illustrated in Figure 4.4.2.

Figure 4.4.2

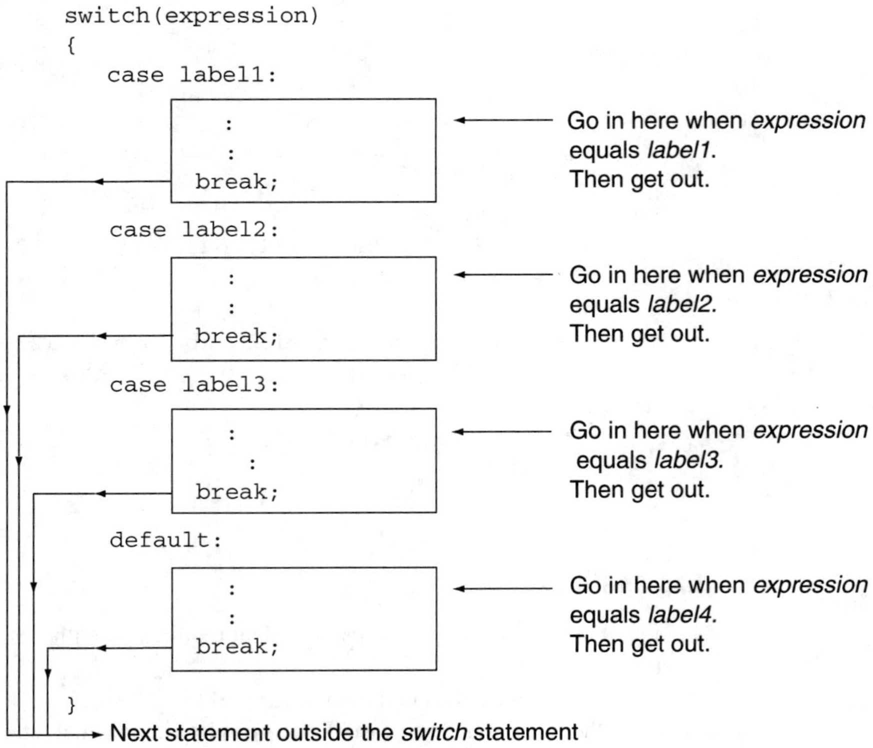

Note that the *break* statement is optional after a sequence of statements under the *default.* It will not make a difference. (Why do you think that is true?) The *default* case is also optional. There may be situations where it is not needed, although it is usually included.

Of course a *switch* statement can be used to find a match with numbers instead of characters, as shown in Example 4.4.2.

Example 4.4.2

Suppose the menu from Exercise 4.3.3, 5, was changed to:

Tax Information System

Select your civil status:

(1) Married
(2) Single
(3) Widowed
(4) Divorced

Enter here > 2

You must fill out form TX-113-2

The program would be changed to (modifications are shown in bold type):

```
#include <stdio.h>

main()
{
    int civil_code;

    printf("%s%s%s%s%s%s%s",
        "               Tax Information System\n\n",
```

```
    "                Select your civil status:\n\n",
    "                 (1)      Married\n",
    "                 (2)      Single\n",
    "                 (3)      Widowed\n",
    "                 (4)      Divorced\n\n",
    "                Enter here > ");
  scanf("%d", &civil_code);

  switch(civil_code)
  {
    case 1:
         printf("\nYou must fill out form TX-120-9\n");
         break;
    case 2: case 4:
         printf("\nYou must fill out form TX-113-2\n");
         break;
    case 3:
         printf("\nYou must fill out form TX-121-7\n");
         break;
    default:
         printf("\nInvalid code.");
         break;
  }
}
```

EXERCISES 4.4.1

1. Convert this *if/else* chain to a *switch* statement:

```
if (number == 1)
{
    printf("Have a good breakfast");
}
else if (number == 2)
{
    printf("Have a nice lunch");
}
else if (number == 3)
{
    printf("Have a copious supper");
}
else if (number == 4)
{
    printf("Have a copious supper");
}
else if (number == 5)
{
    printf("Have a copious supper");
}
```

2. Convert this *switch* statement to an *if/else* chain:

```
switch(watts)
{
    case 40:
            duration = 2500;
            break;
```

```
    case 100:
            duration = 2000;
            break;
    case 1000:
            duration = 2500;
            break;
    default:
            duration = 0;
            break;
}
```

3. Modify the program in Example 4.4.1 so that either the letter or the number may be entered. The menu is now:

   Tax Information System

   Select your civil status:

   (1) (M)arried
   (2) (S)ingle
   (3) (W)idowed
   (4) (D)ivorced

   Enter here > 2

   You must fill out form TX-113-2

   For instance, both the number *2* and the letter *S* would select 'single'. There is a little hitch: numbers are read with the format code *%d*, while letters are read with *%c*. Why not use two *scanf()*s?

```
int      number;
char     ch;

printf("Enter here > ");
scanf("%d", &number);
scanf("\n%c", &ch);
```

   Obviously, this will not do. (Why do you think that is true?) There must be only one *scanf()*. (***Hint:*** Read the number as a character).

4. Modify each exercise below so that a *switch* statement is used instead of an *if/else* chain.
   a. Exercises4.3.3, 3a
   b. Exercise 4.3.3, 3b
   c. Exercise 4.3.3, 3c
   d. Exercise 4.3.3, 3d
   e. Exercise 4.3.3, 3e
   f. Exercise 4.3.3, 3f
   g. Exercise 4.3.3, 3g
   h. Exercise 4.3.3, 3h
   i. Exercise 4.3.3, 6
5. Improve the program in (4b) above so that it will detect if the operator is invalid. For example:

   Enter the operation > 5.8 x 0.1
   The operator 'x' is invalid.

6. A student has been given the task of writing a program that offers a list of games that can be played depending on the number of players available. Following is a list of cases:
   1. Solitaire games can be played by one player only.
   2. Cribbage can be played by two, three, or four players.
   3. Othello can be played by two players only.
   4. Poker can be played by four players only.
   5. Street hockey can be played by six, eight, or ten players.

Here is the program he came up with:

```
main()
{
    int players;

    printf("How many players are there? ");
    scanf("%d", &players);
    printf("Here are the games that may be played "
           "with %d players:\n", players);
    switch(players)
    {
     case 1:
        printf("\nSolitaire games");
        break;
     case 2: case 3: case 4:
        printf("\nCribbage");
        break;
     case 2:
        printf("\nOthello");
        break;
     case 4:
        printf("\nPoker");
        break;
     case 6: case 8: case 10:
        printf("\nStreet hockey");
        break;
     default:
        printf("\nDon't know");
        break;
    }
}
```

a. Unfortunately, the logic of this program is wrong. To prove it, show the output produced when
   1. there are two players.
   2. there are four players.

b. Fix the program's logic by reorganizing the case structure.

4.4.2 COMMON ERRORS AND TRAPS

Programmers often make common errors when writing *switch* statements. Follow these rules to avoid errors.

1. Do not think that the numbers used with the *case* keyword mean the numerical order of the cases. For example:

```
switch(university_year)
{
        case 1:     printf("Freshman");
                            break;
        case 2:     printf("year 2");
                            break;
        case 3:     printf("year 3");
                            break;
        case 4:     printf("Graduating");
                            break;
}
```

Remember that the numbers are labels checked against the controlling expression *university_year* to determine which case to pick. They have nothing to do with the order in which these cases are listed. For example, the following statement would work just as well:

```
switch(university_year)
{
     case 3:     printf("year 3");
                          break;
     case 1:     printf("Freshman");
                          break;
     case 2:     printf("year 2");
                          break;
     case 4:     printf("Graduating");
                          break;
}
```

2. Do not attempt to code a *switch* statement in which the controlling expression and/or the labels are real numbers. For example:

```
float coin;

printf("Enter the value of the coin in dollars > ");
scanf("%f", &coin);
switch(coin)
{
    case 0.01: printf("It's a penny");
                         break;
    case 0.05: printf("It's a nickel");
                         break;
    case 0.10: printf("It's a dime");
                         break;
    case 0.25: printf("It's a quarter");
                         break;
    default:   printf("Don't know this one");
}
```

The compiler will complain. Luckily, there are ways to get around this difficulty with *float* numbers. If the coin value absolutely must remain a *float,* then the program must temporarily convert the value into an integer using a cast operator:

```
switch((int) (coin * 100))
{
    case 1:  printf("It's a penny");
                     break;
    case 5:  printf("It's a nickel");
                     break;
    case 10: printf("It's a dime");
                     break;
    case 25: printf("It's a quarter");
                     break;
    default: printf("Don't know this one");
}
```

3. Do not forget the *break* statements. For example:

```
switch(civil_code)
{
    case 1:
          printf("\nYou must fill out form TX-120-9\n");
    case 2: case 4:
          printf("\nYou must fill out form TX-113-2\n");
```

```
    case 3:
          printf("\nYou must fill out form TX-121-7\n");
    default:
          printf("\nInvalid code.");
}
```

The compiler will **not** complain, yet assuming *civil_code* is 2, the display will look like this:

```
You must fill out form TX-113-2
You must fill out form TX-121-7
Invalid code.
```

The *break* statement causes the program to jump out of the *switch* statement when the case of *civil_code* is equal to 2. If it is not present, the *switch* statement simply covers all the cases until it reaches a *break* or the end of the *switch* statement.

4. Do not forget the braces. For example:

```
switch(civil_code)
    case 1:
      printf("\nYou must fill out form TX-120-9\n");
      break;
    case 2: case 4:
      printf("\nYou must fill out form TX-113-2\n");
      break;
    case 3:
      printf("\nYou must fill out form TX-121-7\n");
      break;
    default:
      printf("\nInvalid code.");
```

This constitutes a syntax error and the compiler will **definitely** complain.

5. Do not put a semicolon on the *switch* line or on a *case* line. For example:

```
switch(civil_code);
{
    case 1;
      printf("\nYou must fill out form TX-120-9\n");
      break;
    case 2; case 4;
      printf("\nYou must fill out form TX-113-2\n");
      break;
    case 3;
      printf("\nYou must fill out form TX-121-7\n");
      break;
    default;
      printf("\nInvalid code.");
      break;
}
```

This constitutes a syntax error and the compiler **definitely** will again complain.

6. Do not think that a *switch* statement can check more than one type of information. To illustrate, revisit Exercise 4.4.1, 5h. Following is the correct program code:

```
int      job_code, experience;
float    weekly, bonus, limit, ratio;

printf("Enter the job code and experience > ");
scanf("%d%d", &job_code, &experience);
printf("Enter the weekly salary > ");
scanf("%f", &weekly);

switch(job_code)1
```

```
{
    case 1: ratio = 0.5;
        limit = 200;
        break;
    case 2: ratio = 1;
        limit = 500;
        break;
    case 3: ratio = 1.5;
        limit = 600;
        break;
    case 4: ratio = 2;
        limit = 900;
        break;
}
bonus = ratio * weekly;
if (bonus > limit)
{
    bonus = limit;
}
if (experience > 10)²
{
    bonus = bonus + 10;
}
else if (experience < 2)
{
    bonus = bonus / 2;
}
    printf("The holiday bonus is %.2f\n", bonus);
```

Explanations

1. *Switch* can only act on job codes, not years of experience.
2. This case must be checked outside the *switch* statement.

The bonus depends on:

- the job code being a 1, 2, 3, or 4.
- the experience being either less than two years or ten years and over.

There are six cases here. It may be tempting to put all of these cases under a common *switch* statement, but that is not possible. The fact that the bonuses also depend on the experience cannot be checked within the same *switch* statement that checks job codes. The experience will have to be checked after as shown in the solution above.

5 Decision Structures: More Complex Issues

OBJECTIVES

This chapter introduces you to the following information:

- More complex conditions that will allow you to broaden the range of applicability of your programs.
- A typical application: the checking of a data range.

INTRODUCTION

This chapter is a continuation of Chapter 4 and includes a slightly more involved programming discussion.

5.1 COMPOSITE CONDITIONS

Composite conditions, which are a combination of individual conditions, are called ***logical*** expressions. Just like arithmetic expressions, composite conditions consist of operators and operands. They allow the development of more complex programs than the ones seen thus far.

5.1.1 THE || LOGICAL OPERATOR

In Example 4.3.5 it was stated that the conversion type must be entered as lowercase 'd', 'w', or 'v'. This restriction is irritating for the user. It is obviously better that the program allows uppercase entries as well. In other words, the program should be ***case-insensitive.*** To this end, the conditions need to be changed, as shown in Example 5.1.1.

Example 5.1.1

The new condition for converting in distance is that the conversion type be entered as either 'd' or 'D'. This is called a ***composite condition*** because more than one thing must be checked. Other composite conditions involve checking the weight and volume. Here is our new program, with the changes shown in bold type:

```
#include <stdio.h>

main()
{
```

```
    float           metric, standard, conv_factor;
    char            conv_type;

    printf("Enter the metric value and type of conversion > ");
    scanf("%f\n%c", &metric, &conv_type);

    if (conv_type == 'd' || conv_type == 'D') /* conversion type is */
    {                                          /* 'd' or 'D' */
          conv_factor = 0.6214;
    }
    else if (conv_type == 'w' || conv_type == 'W')
    {
          conv_factor = 2.2046;
    }
    else if (conv_type == 'v' || conv_type == 'V')

    {
          conv_factor = 0.8772;
    }
    standard = conv_factor * metric;

    printf("The standard value is %.2f quarts", imperial);
}
```

The composite condition *conv_type* == *'d'* || *conv_type* == *'D'* means "conversion type is equal to 'd' OR equal to 'D'." The symbol || stands for OR and is an operator member of the class of logical operators, just like the operator + is a member of the class of arithmetic operators. This composite condition is in fact an expression, just like the ones covered in Section 3.2, so its evaluation is governed by the same rules, and the precedence of its operators must be known before evaluating it. The rules of precedence for logical operators are listed in Table 5.1.1

Table 5.1.1

Operator	Associativity
>= <= > <	Left to right
== !=	Right to left
&&	Left to right
||	Left to right

Evaluation of a composite condition. Our composite condition is then evaluated from left to right. For instance, assuming *conv_type* is 'D', the evaluation is as shown in Figure 5.1.1.

Figure 5.1.1

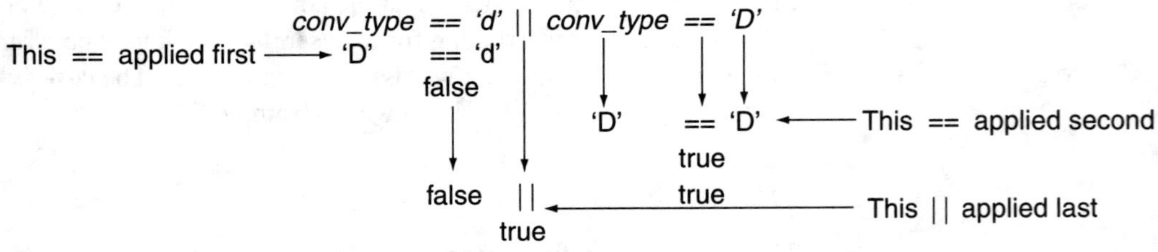

The composite condition evaluates to true. This does not mean that both comparisons are true. As long as one of the two is true, the composite condition is true. Note that || is a binary operator; its first operand is *conv_type* == *'d'* and its second is *conv_type* == *'D'*.

Let's look at another example. Assuming *conv_type* is 'v', the expression is evaluated as in Figure 5.12.

Figure 5.1.2

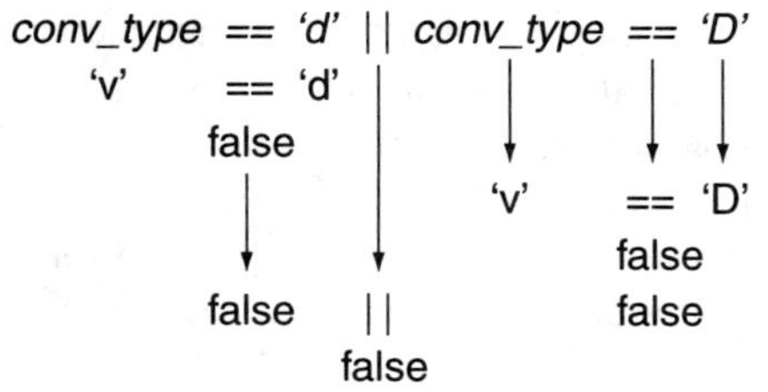

The condition is false because neither comparison is true. There are two other possibilities: the first comparison is true and the second is false, or both comparisons are true.

Truth table of the OR operator. Table 5.1.2 is a ***truth table*** that summarizes the possibilities and their results. A truth table indicates the valid values the operands can take from the operation's results.

Table 5.1.2

Operand 1	||	Operand 2	Result*
true	||	true	true
true	||	false	true
false	||	true	true
false	||	false	false

*As long as one operand is true, the composite condition is true.

Finally, note that there must never be a space between the vertical bars in ||. For example, the following would be a syntax error:

conv_type == 'd' | | conv_type == 'D'

EXERCISES 5.1.1

1. Evaluate the following expressions:

```
a >= 2 || a < 6
a == 2 || b != a || b <= -9
```

   a. Assuming that *a* contains 5 and *b* contains –5
   b. Assuming that both *a* and *b* contain –2
2. Simplify the following expressions:
   a. `a >= 2 || a > 6`
   b. `a == b || a > b`
3. a. In Exercise 4.3.2, 9, it was assumed that the letter for the gender was always entered as a lowercase character. How would the condition of the *if/else* need to be modified if this assumption is removed?
   b. In Exercise 4.3.2, 10, it was assumed that the letter for the currency was always entered as an uppercase character. How would the condition of the *if/else* need to be modified if this assumption is removed?
   c. In Exercise 4.3.3, 5, it was assumed that the letter for the civil status was always entered as an uppercase character. How would the condition of the *if/else* need to be modified if this assumption is removed?
4. Modify the program of Exercise 4.4.1, 5e so that the program will flag an error if the entry is not one of 'c', 'C', 's', 'D', 'm', or 'M'.
5. Write a C expression for the following composite conditions:
   a. A person is heavier than 60 kilograms or more than 20 years old.
   b. A car has been driven less than 40,000 km or costs less than $14,500.

6. Country XYZ is searching for good candidates for an upcoming astronaut training program. To be accepted, a candidate must be a graduate of a physics or engineering course at a college or university. Write a program that determines if a given person is eligible. The program must ask for all necessary information.
7. Use a *switch* statement in all three programs for question 3 above.
8. Convert the following *if/else* chain to a *switch* statement:

```
if (number == 1)
{
	printf("Have a good breakfast");
}
else if (number == 2)
{
	printf("Have a nice lunch");
}
else if ((number == 3) || (number == 4) || (number == 5))
{
	printf("Have a copious supper");
}
```

9. Convert the following *switch* statement into an *if/else* chain:

```
switch(watts)
{
	case 40: case 60:
		duration = 2500;
		break;
	case 100:
		duration = 2000;
		break;
	case 1000:
		duration = 2500;
		break;
	default:
		duration = 0;
		break;
}
```

10. Revisit Example 4.4.1: Suppose a student wrote the following version of that program:

```
if (civil_code == 'M' || civil_code =='S' ||
    civil_code == 'W' || civil_code == 'D')
{
    switch(civil_code)
    {
      case 'M':
             printf("\nYou must fill out form TX-120-9\n");
             break;
      case 'S': case 'W':
             printf("\nYou must fill out form TX-113-2\n");
             break;
      case 'D':
             printf("\nYou must fill out form TX-121-7\n");
             break;
    }
}
else
{
    printf("\nInvalid code.");
}
```

Is this a good solution?
11. Use an *if/else* chain in the solution for Exercise 4.4.1, 4.

5.1.2 THE && LOGICAL OPERATOR

The following two examples illustrate the use and syntax of the && operator.

Example 5.1.2

A temporary secretarial employment agency wants a program that calculates the amount of money earned by its contractors, who are paid $12.39 per hour on weekdays and time and a half on weekends. The program asks for the day of the week worked and the number of hours the person worked.

```
#include <stdio.h>

main()
{
        int       hours, day;
        float     pay;

        printf("Enter the day worked (Sunday = 1, Monday = 2, etc) > ");
        scanf("%d", &day);
        printf("Enter the number of hours > ");
        scanf("%d", &hours);

        if (day >= 2 && day <= 6)       /* is it a weekday ? */
        {
                pay = 12.39 * hours;
        }
        else
        {
                pay = 12.39 * 1.5 * hours;
        }
        printf("The pay is %.2f\n", pay);
}
```

The composite condition *day >= 2 && day <= 6* means: "The day of the week is between day 2 ***and*** 6, ***inclusive.***" The symbol && stands for AND and is a member of the class of ***logical*** operators. Note that there must never be a space in &&. The following would be a syntax error:

day >= 2 & & day <= 6

Evaluation of a composite condition. The composite condition above is evaluated as shown in Figure 5.1.3 (assuming the entry for *day* is 4).

Figure 5.1.3

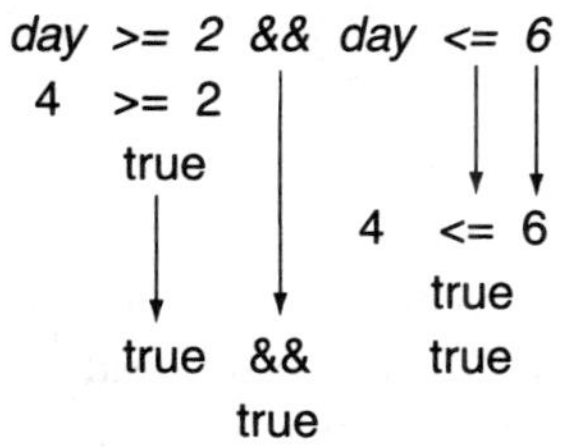

The condition evaluates to true, which is possible only when ***both*** operands, *day >= 2* and *day <= 6*, are true. Note that && is also a binary operator.

Assuming the entry for *day* is 7, the composite condition would be evaluated as in Figure 5.14.

Figure 5.1.4

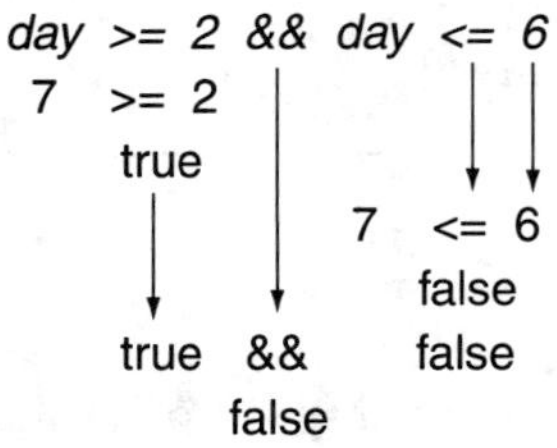

Truth table of the AND operator. The truth table for && is shown in Table 5.1.3.

Table 5.1.3

Operand 1	&&	Operand 2	Result*
true	&&	true	true
true	&&	false	false
false	&&	true	false
false	&&	false	false

*As long as one operand is false, the composite condition is false.

Logical relationship between an AND and an OR. If you compare the truth table in Table 5.1.3 with the truth table of the || operator (Table 5.1.2), you can see that the logic of && is the logical negation of ||. To illustrate this (and its significance), consider Example 5.1.3.

Example 5.1.3

We want a program that determines whether or not a TV channel is accessible through the local cable. The cable company offers channels numbered from 2 to 35. The solution would look like this:

```
#include <stdio.h>

main()
{
      int channel;

      printf("Enter a TV channel > ");
      scanf("%d", &channel);

      if (channel >= 2 && channel <= 35)
      {
           printf("This channel can be accessed through cable");
      }
      else
      {
           printf("This channel may be accessed only "
                  "through satellite");
      }
}
```

Let us now discover the exact relation between the AND and the OR operators. If the channel number is ***not*** between 2 AND 35 inclusive, then it must be either less than 2 OR greater than 35. The *if/else* could be coded as shown below. Changes from the previous program are shown in bold.

```
if (channel < 2 || channel > 35)
{
     printf("This channel may be accessed only "
```

```
                "through satellite");
}
else
{
     printf("This channel can be accessed through cable");
}
```

Note that the two blocks of *printf()* statements have been switched. Another way to code this is by using the negation operator covered in Subsection 4.1.3:

```
if (!(channel >= 2 && channel <= 35))
{
     printf("This channel may be accessed only "
               "through satellite");
}
else
{
     printf("This channel can be accessed through cable");
}
```

The last two *if/else* statements are equivalent, so the expressions:

```
channel < 2 || channel > 35
```

and

```
!(channel >= 2 && channel <= 35)
```

are equivalent. These show that the || operator is the logical negation of &&, and vice versa.

Examples 5.1.2 and 5.1.3 show the most common use of the logical operator &&: checking ranges of values. (Section 5.3 will expand on this type of application.)

EXERCISES 5.1.2

1. Evaluate the following expressions:

```
a >= 2 && a < 6
a == 2 && b != a && b <= -9
```

   a. Assuming that *a* contains 5 and *b* contains –5
   b. Assuming that both *a* and *b* contain –2
2. Simplify the expression *a >= 2 && a > 6.*
3. Does the following expression make sense?

   a == b && a > b

4. Recode the *if/else* of Example 5.1.2 so that the condition uses the || logical operator instead.
5. Country ABC is searching for good candidates for an upcoming astronaut training program. To be accepted, a candidate must be a university graduate and in good health. Write a program that determines if a given person is eligible.
6. Write a C expression for the following composite conditions:
   a. A person is heavier than 60 kilograms and more than 20 years old.
   b. A car has been driven less than 40,000 km and costs less than $14,500.
   c. How would you phrase the logical negation of both statements above?
7. a. Are the expressions *channel < 2 || channel > 35* and *!(channel >= 2 && channel <= 35)* in Example 5.1.3 equivalent? (***Hint:*** Try all of the possible logical values of the comparisons.)
   b. Prove that the expressions *!(channel < 2) && !(channel > 35)* and *channel >= 2 && channel <= 35* are equivalent. (***Hint:*** Try all of the possible logical values of the comparisons.)
8. a. Change this sequence of *if*s to a single *if/else.*

```
if (a > 6 && b <= a && c == 10)
{
```

```
        a = 0; b = 0; c = 0;
}
if (a <= 6)
{
        a = -1; b = -1; c = -1;
}
if (b > a)
{
        a = -1; b = -1; c = -1;
}
if (c != 10)

{
        a = -1; b = -1; c = -1;
}
```

b. Can the following be changed to an *if/else?*

```
if (a > 6 && b <= a && c == 10)
{
        printf("good enough");
}
if (a <= 6)
{
        printf("no good");
}
if (b > a)
{
        printf("no good");
}
if (c != 10)
{
        printf("no good");
}
```

9. Of *a, b, c,* and *d* below, which examples share the same logic as the following code:

```
if (a > 5 && a <= 25)
{
        printf("Life is cool");
}
else
{
        printf("Life is hot");
}
```

a.
```
if (a < 5 && a >= 25)
{
        printf("Life is hot");
}
else
{
        printf("Life is cool");
}
```

b.
```
if (a <= 5 && a > 25)
{
        printf("Life is hot");
}
else
```

```
  {
        printf("Life is cool");
  }
c. if (a <= 5 || a > 25)
  {
        printf("Life is hot");
  }
  else
  {
        printf("Life is cool");
  }
d. if (!(a > 5 && a <= 25))
  {
        printf("Life is hot");
  }
  else
  {
        printf("Life is cool");
  }
```

One more example is worth a look:

Example 5.1.4

Let us redo Example 4.1.4 using composite conditions (the changes are shown in bold):

```
#include <stdio.h>

main()
{
      int n1, n2, n3, max;

      printf("Enter the score for the three periods > ");
      scanf("%d%d%d", &n1, &n2, &n3);

      if (n1 >= n2 && n1 >= n3)  /* is n1 at least as big as n2 and */
      {                          /* at least as big as n3 ? */
            max = n1;
      }
      else if (n2 >= n1 && n2 >= n3)
      {
            max = n2;
      }
      else if (n3 >= n1 && n3 >= n2)
      {
            max = n3;
      }
      printf("The largest score in a period is %d", max_so_far);
}
```

The logic of the conditions is obvious. Note, though, that all of the comparisons are done twice. For example, *n1* and *n2* are compared in the first two composite conditions. Of course, this is inefficient. "Who cares?" one might reply! The code is intuitive and it works. This attitude of coming up with an easy and quick solution with no regard for efficiency and elegance is sometimes called ***brute-force coding.*** Occasionally, programmers do resort to such practices because they produce code quickly; programming time is expensive. Nevertheless, brute-force coding is usually not a good idea. The program in Example 4.1.4 is in fact probably the best one for finding the largest number among three.

EXERCISES 5.1.3

1. Would the program in Example 5.1.4 still work correctly if the equalities were not checked? For example:

```
if (n1 > n2 && n1 > n3)
{
     max = n1;
}
else if (n2 > n1 && n2 > n3)
{
     max = n2;
}
else if (n3 > n1 && n3 > n2)
{
     max = n3;
}
```

   If not, specify the cases when it fails.
2. Modify the program in Example 5.1.4 so that it finds the largest of four numbers.

5.1.3 MIXING ARITHMETIC IN CONDITIONS

Arithmetic operations may be mixed into a logical expression, as you will see in Example 5.1.5.

Example 5.1.5

We want to write a program that calculates the amount of points obtained by a particular country in the Olympic Games. Three points are granted for a gold medal, two for a silver medal, and one point for a bronze medal. The program will also announce if the team is on the "Honor Roll," collecting at least 100 points or collecting more gold medals than silver and bronze medals together. Here is the program:

```
#include <stdio.h>

main()
{
        int b_ct, s_ct, g_ct;

        printf("Enter the number of medals won:\n");
        printf("Bronze > ");
        scanf("%d", &b_ct);
        printf("Silver > ");
        scanf("%d", &s_ct);
        printf("Gold > ");
        scanf("%d", &g_ct);

        if (b_ct + s_ct * 2 + g_ct * 3 >= 100 || g_ct > s_ct + b_ct)

        {
             printf("This team is on the \"Honor Roll"\"");
        }
}
```

Note that the *if* condition includes arithmetic operations. When such operations are involved in a logical expression, it is important to understand how C will evaluate it. A look at the order of precedence of the operators involved here is necessary (Table 5.1.4).

Table 5.1.4

Operator	Associativity
()	Left to right
– (unary)	Right to left
* / %	Left to right
()	Left to right
+ – (binary)	Lleft to right
>= <= > <	Left to right
== !=	Left to right
&&	Left to right
||	Left to right

Arithmetic operators have a higher priority than relational operators. These in turn have a higher priority than the logical operators. Thus, the evaluation of the composite condition is shown in Figure 5.1.5 (suppose *g_st* is 6, *s_ct* is 1, *b_ct* is 4).

Figure 5.1.5

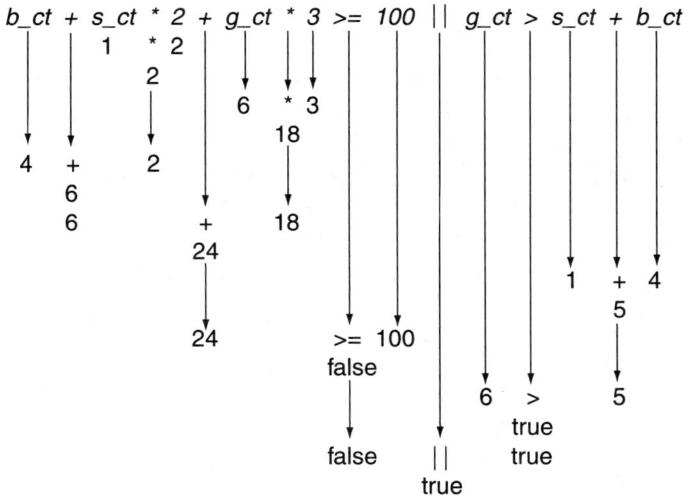

This team would be included on the "Honor Roll."

It may be a good idea to insert parentheses to enhance the readability of this rather long composite condition, even though none are needed (in this case):

*(b_ct + s_ct * 2 + g_ct * 3 > 100) || (g_ct > s_ct + b_ct)*

This is better, isn't it?

EXERCISES 5.1.4

1. Evaluate the following expression if *a* is 5, *b* is –7, and *c* is 12.

   *3 + a / b >= c * a - 2 && a * b - 8 != -c / a*

2. The condition in the program above introduces so many arithmetic operations that it is difficult to read it. Reduce its length, thereby making it easier to read. (***Hint:*** Use a ***temporary variable*** to hold the calculation of the total number of points obtained.)

5.1.4 COMPOSITE CONDITIONS OF MULTIPLE RELATIONAL OPERATORS

The || and the && logical operators allow programmers to make up more complex conditions. When these two operators are used together, the programs can handle even more complex situations than the ones so far. Sometimes the increased complexity is necessary, as Examples 5.1.6, 5.1.7, and 5.1.8 show.

Example 5.1.6

Suppose the temporary secretarial employment agency in Example 5.1.2 uses a coding system to quickly identify the qualification of each secretary they send out. The code consists of three characters, a letter and two numerals. The letter denotes the area of expertise (M = medical secretary; L = law secretary), and the numerals stand for the typing speed (must be within 40 and 120, inclusive). For example, the code M65 stands for a medical secretary who types 65 words per minute.

Codes like these always feel foreign, so errors in typing them or reading them often occur. For this reason, the agency wants a program that verifies the correctness of the entry. Clearly, if the first entry, the area of expertise, is not an 'M' OR 'm' OR 'L' OR 'l', OR if the second entry, the typing speed, is not within 40 AND 120 inclusive, then the code will be erroneous. Here is the program, with changes from the previous program shown in bold type:

```
#include <stdio.h>

main()
{
        char    ex;
        int     sp;

        printf("Enter the contractor's qualification code > ");
        scanf("\n%c%d", &ex, &sp);

        if ((ex == 'M' || ex == 'm' || ex == 'L' || ex == 'l') &&
              (sp >= 40 && sp <= 120))
        {
                printf("The code is valid");
        }
        else
        {
                printf("The code is INVALID");
        }
}
```

The composite condition says that the expertise must be one of the following entries: 'M', 'm', 'L', OR 'l', AND that the typing speed must be within 40 and 120, inclusive. These conditions present two drawbacks: the conditions are long and complex, and the programmer must always remember to check both upper- and lowercases entries. This could easily be overlooked in a long program in which the checking of the expertise code is performed in multiple places.

It is therefore advisable to simplify the *if/else* condition. The trick is to convert the letter representing the expertise to uppercase as soon as it is read in. Then the program need only check the entry against uppercase letters. There is a C function named *toupper()* that converts letters to uppercase characters. It is found in the header file *ctype.h*. The line *#include <ctype.h>* must be typed in at the top of the program when *toupper()* is used. Following is the new program, with changes shown in bold:

```
#include <stdio.h>
#include <ctype.h>

main()
{
        char   ex, ex_up;
        int    sp;
```

```
        printf("Enter the contractor's qualification code > ");
        scanf("\n%c%d", &ex, &sp);
        ex_up = toupper(ex);

        if (ex_up == 'M' || ex_up == 'L') && (sp >= 40 && sp <= 120))
        {
            printf("The code is valid");
        }
        else
        {
            printf("The code is INVALID");
        }
}
```

The function *toupper()* in *ex_up = toupper(ex)* makes an uppercase copy of the character from *ex* and places it in *ex_up*. The variable *ex* is not altered. Now the condition will be evaluated correctly, as shown in Figure 5.1.6 (assume *ex* is 'M' and *sp* is 23).

Figure 5.1.6

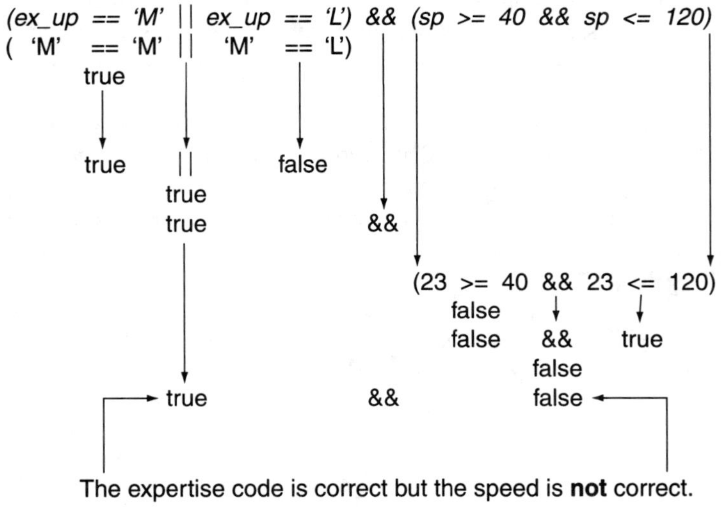

The composite condition is therefore false, as expected.

EXERCISES 5.1.5

1. Re-evaluate the expression in Figure 5.1.6 with and without the parentheses, when *ex* is 'L' and *sp* is 23. Are the parentheses necessary? (***Hint:*** Refer to the order of precedence of the operators in Section 5.1.1.)
2. How would the condition in the program in Figure 5.1.6 need to be changed if the two alternatives were switched?

```
if (______________________________________________)
{
    printf("The code is INVALID");
}
else
{
    printf("The code is valid");
}
```

   a. Assume that you cannot use the negation unary operator. (***Hint:*** Refer to Example 5.1.3.)
   b. Show how easily this question could be answered if you could use the negation unary operator.

3. a. Replace the composite conditions in the following programs with the function *toupper()*:
      1. Example 5.1.1
      2. Exercise 5.1.1, 3
      3. Exercise 5.1.1, 4
   b. Redo (a) but with the function *tolower()*. This function simply converts an uppercase letter to lowercase.
4. Shorten the following code to one *if* statement:

```
if (a > 5 && a < 10)
{
        printf("good day");
}
if (a >= 50)
{
        printf("good day:);
}
```

5. Due to a lack of funding, countries XYZ (from Exercise 5.1.1, 6) and ABC (from Exercise 5.1.2, 5) have merged their upcoming astronaut training programs. The criteria have been combined; now a candidate must meet the requirements of both countries. Write a program that determines the eligibility of a given person under this new arrangement.

In Example 5.1.6 it was clear that parentheses were needed in the composite condition to surround the sequence of OR operations. Sometimes, though, it is unclear which operations the parentheses should surround, or whether parentheses are needed at all. Since the presence or absence of parentheses affects the logic, this is important to ascertain. Consider Example 5.1.7.

Example 5.1.7

A student is asked to write a program that advises the user to dress warmly if it rains and it gets colder or the barometer falls. Here is her solution:

```
#include <stdio.h>

main()
{
        char  rain, colder, baro_falls;

        printf(Does it rain? (y/n) ");
        scanf("\n%c", &rain);
        printf(Is it getting colder? (y/n) ");
        scanf("\n%c", &colder);
        printf(Is the barometer falling? (y/n) ");
        scanf("\n%c", &baro_falls);

        if (rain == 'y' && colder == 'y' || baro_falls == 'y')
        {
                printf("Dress warmly");
        }
        else
        {
                printf("Still summer weather");
        }
}
```

The composite condition of the *if/else* has a confusing logic. It could be interpreted as follows:

Dress warmly if:

- it rains

AND

- it gets colder OR the barometer falls.

In this case, the condition should be expressed as:

rain == 'y' && (colder == 'y' || baro_falls == 'y')

Parentheses are necessary. (Why do you think that is the case?) But then, perhaps, the composite condition is intended to mean:

Dress warmly if either:
- it rains AND it gets colder

OR
- the barometer falls.

In this case, the composite condition would be:

(rain == 'y' && colder == 'y') || baro_falls == 'y'

Note that parentheses are not really necessary (Why is that true?), but should still be used for clarity's sake.

EXERCISES 5.1.6

1. Verify that the following conditions do not have the same logic.

   rain == 'y' && colder == 'y' || baro_falls == 'y'
   rain == 'y' && (colder == 'y' || baro_falls == 'y')

   (***Hint:*** Find one set of values for which one condition evaluates to true, the other to false, or vice versa.)
2. The following situation can be interpreted in two ways. Write a logical expression for each.

   A person is heavier than 60 kilograms and is 20 years of age or taller than 1.8 meters.

There may be situations that call for a long and complex composite condition. In such cases, it may be a good idea to break down the condition into smaller ones by using an *if/else* chain. Example 5.1.8 illustrates that solution.

Example 5.1.8

Revisit Example 5.1.5. Suppose the Olympic Committee decided to stiffen the requirements for acceptance of teams on the Honor Roll. Now the team must meet at least one of the following requirements:

1. The team collected at least 100 points.
2. It collected more gold medals than silver and bronze medals together.
3. It collected between 80 and 99 points inclusive and won gold medal(s) in at least six different disciplines.

The first two requirements are the same as before, but the third one is new. Here is the new program with changes shown in bold type:

```
#include <stdio.h>

main()
{
     int b_ct, s_ct, g_ct, points, num_disc;

     printf("Enter the number of medals won:\n");
     printf("Bronze > ");
     scanf("%d", &b_ct);
     printf("Silver > ");
```

```
        scanf("%d", &s_ct);
        printf("Gold > ");
        scanf("%d", &g_ct);
        printf("How many different disciplines with at least one gold? ");
        scanf("%d", &num_disc);
        points = b_ct + s_ct * 2 + g_ct * 3;
        if (points >= 100 ||
            g_ct > s_ct + b_ct ||
            num_disc >= 6 && (points >= 80 && points < 100))
        {
            printf("This team is on the \"Honor roll\"");
        }
}
```

Again, the composite condition is long, but now each condition is placed on a separate line to ease the reading. Perhaps you will prefer the following solution, which breaks up the long composite condition:

```
if (points >= 100)
{
    printf("This team is on the \"Honor Roll\"");
}
else if (g_ct > s_ct + b_ct)
{
    printf("This team is on the \"Honor Roll\"");
}
else if (num_disc >= 6 && (points >= 80 && points < 100))
{
    printf("This team is on the \"Honor Roll\"");
}
```

EXERCISES 5.1.7

1. A programmer looks at the program in Example 5.1.8 and instead develops the following version. He has broken the composite condition into three smaller conditions by using a sequence of three *if* statements:

```
if (points >= 100)
{
      printf("This team is on the \"Honor Roll\"");
}
if (g_ct > s_ct + b_ct)
{
      printf("This team is on the \"Honor Roll\"");
}
if (num_disc >= 6 && (points >= 80 && points < 100))
{
      printf("This team is on the \"Honor Roll\"");
}
```

Answer the following questions:

a. The logic of the code above differs slightly from the one in Example 5.1.8. Explain.

b. While still keeping the three *if* statements, suggest a modification to assure that both programs agree, yet do not use an *if/else* chain.

2. a. Modify the program in question 1b above so that it will also tell how many of the three conditions have been met.

b. Can the solution in Example 5.1.8 that uses an *if/else* be modified to tell how many of the three conditions have been met while preserving the *if/else?* If so, provide a solution. If not, explain.

3. Add the following feature to the original program in Example 5.1.8: Have the program issue the message 'This team did not meet the requirements' if the team is not put on the Honor Roll.
   a. Can this feature be added to the second program in Example 5.1.8 (the one with an *if/else* chain)?
   b. Can this feature be added to the program in question 1b above?
4. A teacher wants to modify a set of exam marks as follows:
   a. If a mark is less than or equal to 70, then it will be increased by 7%.
   b. If a mark is between 71 and 95 inclusive, then it will be increased by 3%.
   c. Otherwise, the mark will not change.

   Write a program that reads in a mark and modifies it with these points.
5. A student is accepted into an electronics course if any of the following is true:
   a. His or her average is 90 or higher.
   b. His or her average is 70 or higher and his or her physics mark is 85 or higher.
   c. His or her physics mark is 95 or higher but the average is at least 50.

   Write a program that determines a student's acceptance status. The initials of a student, his or her average, and his or her physics mark must be provided. A letter of acceptance or rejection is to be produced for each student as shown below:
   If the student is rejected:

```
Enter the student's initials > JPC
                     average > 78
                physics mark > 81

Dear Mr. JPC:

We are sorry to inform you that your average of 78 and your physics mark of 81 have not met
our requirements.

Try again!
                                                        Ms. Principal
```

   If the student is accepted:

```
Enter the student's initials > PKL
                     average > 54
                physics mark > 96

Dear Ms. PKL:

We are pleased to inform you that your average of 54 and your physics mark of 96 have met
our requirements.

Welcome!
                                                        Ms. Principal
```

6. You probably coded a solution to the question above with an *if/else* chain. It turns out that this chain may be shortened to one single *if/else* statement. Implement this change.
7. Improve the program in Exercise 4.3.1, 4, that advises whether or not to trade your car. If the difference in dollar value between the trade-in and the new car is less than $14,000 and the price of the new car is less than $18,000 or the trade-in is more than $3,000, buy the car; otherwise, do not buy the car. The program will ask for the dollar value of both cars.
8. The bank in Exercise 4.1.2, 4, now offers cashable GICs. Their interest rates are lower, however. For a one-year GIC, the rate is 3.7%; for a five-year, it is 6.9%. Modify the program so that it also will ask if the investor wants to purchase a cashable GIC or not. There are now four cases altogether. Use an *if/else* chain with composite conditions.
9. Modify Supplementary Exercise 4.3, 1, so that the type of meat may be entered in lower- or uppercase letters, regardless. Also no credit is given if the amount owed is more than $50.

5.1.5 COMMON ERRORS AND TRAPS

Programmers often make common errors when writing *if/else* chains. To guard against errors, follow these rules:

1. Do not omit the variable in the second operand of a composite condition. For example:

```
if (conv_type == 'd' || 'D')
{
     conv_factor = 0.6214;
}
```

   This composite condition literally translates as: conversion type equals 'd' or 'D'. While in plain English this is good phrasing, in the C language, it is not. The variable to be compared must be mentioned for **every comparison.**

   Surprisingly, the compiler does not see this omission as a syntax error; therefore it will **not** complain! Yet the *if* statement won't work. Here is what will happen: the composite condition will always be evaluated as true, regardless of the conversion type. (Why is this? The reason is so technical that it is delayed until Chapter 13.)

2. Do not use only a single vertical bar for the OR operator. For example:

```
if (conv_type == 'd' | conv_type == 'D')
{
    conv_factor = 0.6214;
}
```

   The | should be the || operator. The compiler will not complain because the single vertical bar **is** a valid operator (called the ***OR bise-wise operator***). It does not perform quite the same operation as ||, though. In this case, this *if* statement will probably work as is, but avoid using this single vertical bar operator in place of the OR operator.

3. Do not omit the variable in the second operand of &&. This would produce a syntax error similar to the one in (1) above.

4. Do not use a single & for the AND operator. For example:

```
if (day >= 2 & day <= 6)
{
    pay = 12.39 * hours;
}
else
{
    pay = 12.39 * 1.5 * hours;
}
```

   The compiler will not complain because the single & **is** a valid operator (called the ***AND bise-wise operator***). It does not perform quite the same operation as &&, though. This *if* statement will probably work as is, but the functionality of this operator is not as close to && as | is to ||, so definitely avoid using the single & operator.

5.2 PROGRAM LAYOUT AND PRESENTATION

As pointed out in Chapter 2, a program should be presented in an easily readable form. Section 2.3 showed some grooming guidelines, and this section adds a few more. When coding a program with decision structures, it is even more important that it be well organized.

5.2.1 GROOMING *if/else* AND ONE-WAY *if* STATEMENTS

Because the C compiler ignores white spaces, you are free to arrange an *if/else* statement any way you wish. Nonetheless, Figure 5.2.1 illustrates a few grooming tips to follow, numbered in order of importance.

Figure 5.2.1

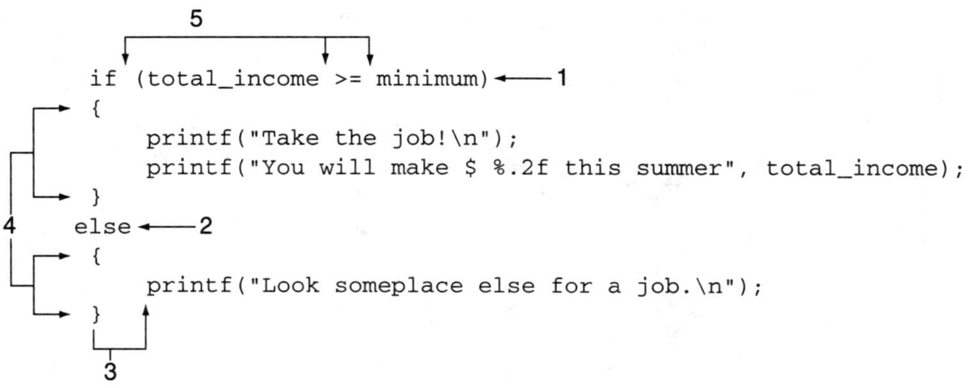

Explanations

1. Place the keyword *if* and its condition on the same line.
2. Place the keyword *else* on a separate line by itself.
3. Indent *printf()* statements **within** *if* or *else* conditions by a few blank spaces.
4. Always surround the blocks of statements with braces.
5. Leave spaces where indicated around operators.

Section 4.1 showed that braces must always be used. There is one exception: if there is ***one*** single statement within the block, the braces may be omitted. Back in Example 4.1.3, the following would be acceptable:

```
if (conv_type == 'd')
       conv_factor = 0.6214;
if (conv_type == 'w')
       conv_factor = 2.2046;
if (conv_type == 'v')
       conv_factor = 0.8772;
```

Since the C compiler ignores white spaces, the following would also be acceptable:

```
if (conv_type == 'd') conv_factor = 0.6214;
if (conv_type == 'w') conv_factor = 2.2046;
if (conv_type == 'v') conv_factor = 0.8772;
```

The elimination of the braces makes the code a little shorter, but it is still easy to read the logic. When eliminated improperly, though, the lack of braces makes the program's logic harder to follow. You have not seen enough to convince you, yet the simple *if/else* statement of Example 4.3.1 will give you an idea. The following would be acceptable by the C language syntax as well:

```
if (total_income >= minimum)
{
    printf("Take the job!\n");
    printf("You will make $ %.2f this summer", total_income);
}
else
    printf("Look someplace else for a job.\n");
```

or even

```
if (total_income >= minimum)
{
    printf("Take the job!\n");
    printf("You will make $ %.2f this summer", total_income);
}
else printf("Look someplace else for a job.\n");
```

Now, suppose this last *if/else* statement was involved in a long program. Its *else* could easily be overlooked during a walk-through. Therefore this *if/else* could easily be mistaken for an *if* without an *else*. Bad mistake! Consequently, you are strongly encouraged to use the braces **at all times.**

EXERCISES 5.2.1

1. Rearrange the *if/else* statement below so that it follows the grooming guidelines:

```
if(a>b) {
printf("a is greater than b");
b = a;
} else a = b;
```

2. a. Are the following structures syntactically correct and equivalent to an *if/else* chain?

1.
```
if (conv_type == 'd')
    conv_factor = 0.6214;
else if (conv_type == 'w')
    conv_factor = 2.2046;
else if (conv_type == 'v')
    conv_factor = 0.8772;
else
{
   printf("Invalid!\n");
   conv_type = 0;
}
```

2.
```
if (conv_type == 'd')
{
    conv_factor = 0.6214;
}
    else if (conv_type == 'w')
         {
             conv_factor = 2.2046;
         }
         else if (conv_type == 'v')
              {
                  conv_factor = 0.8772;
              }
              else
              {
                  printf("Invalid conversion type!\n");
                  conv_type = 0;
              }
```

3.
```
if (conv_type == 'd')  conv_factor = 0.6214;
else if (conv_type == 'w')  conv_factor = 2.2046;
else if (conv_type == 'v')  conv_factor = 0.8772;
else
{
    printf ("Invalid!\n");
    conv_type = 0;
}
```

   b. If all are equivalent, which one offers better readability?

3. Proper use of symbolic constants can enhance the readability of a program. Symbolic constants were first covered in Subsection 2.3.4; review that section before trying the following:
   a. The following segment is the same metric converter program you've seen throughout this subsection, except that symbolic constants have been added. Determine what *#define* directives are needed to ensure that this segment compiles correctly.

```
main()
{
     float          metric, standard;
     char           conv_type;

     printf("Enter the metric value and type of conversion "
            "(lowercase) > ");
     scanf("%f %c", &metric, &conv_type);
      if (conv_type == 'd')
             conv_factor = KMS_TO_MILES;
      else if (conv_type == 'w')
             conv_factor = KGS_TO_POUNDS;
      else if (conv_type == 'v')
             conv_factor = LITERS_TO_GALLONS;
      standard = conv_factor * metric;

      printf("The standard value is %.2f quarts", standard);
}
```

b. What *#define* statement is needed to ensure that the following segment will compile correctly? Discuss whether using the symbolic constant *EQ* is a good practice.

```
main()
{
      int  a, b;

      printf("Enter two numbers > ");
      scanf("%d%d", &a, &b);
      if (a EQ b)
      {
             printf("They are the same");
      }
      else
      {
             printf("They are different");
      }
}
```

5.2.2 CHOOSING A DECISION STRUCTURE TO USE

Now that three decision structures have been covered (the *if,* the *if/else,* and the *switch* statements), you may be wondering which of these decision structures are right for a given situation. Unfortunately, there is no magic recipe for deciding which to use. The following questions may help you choose:

1. Is there an indication of different actions required that depend on some condition? If yes, then an *if/else* or an *if* or a *switch* statement is needed. Which one? This may be determined by the next two questions.
2. Is there an indication that an action is required if the condition is met and that no action is required otherwise? If yes, an *if* statement is appropriate, since no *else* part is needed.
3. Is there an indication that an action is required if the condition is met and that some other action is required otherwise? If yes, an *if/else* statement is appropriate.
4. Is there an indication of the need for a sequence of conditions, each calling for specific actions? If so, an *if/else* chain or a *switch* statement is needed. Which one? This is answered in Subsection 5.3.3.

With the help of these general guidelines and the numerous programs you have seen, you should be able to sort out which decision structure to use.

5.2.3 KEEPING THE DECISION STRUCTURES SIMPLE

It turns out that situations requiring an *if/else* statement or chain or a *switch* statement are much more common that those requiring simple *if*s. You may have realized that the logic of an *if/else* statement is slightly more complex than that of an *if* statement. Therefore a programmer should try to avoid using an *if/else* wherever a simple *if* statement will do, and even should consider avoiding the use of a simple *if* statement whenever it is not really necessary.

Unfortunately the reduction of an *if/else* to an *if* often is not achievable. (The reduction to no decision statement at all is very hard and rarely worth the effort!) Nevertheless, let us look at two situations that, at first, suggest that an *if/else* statement should be used when, through careful rearranging of the logic, a simple *if* statement or even no *if* at all will do! The resulting programs will be simpler and just as easy to follow. Later on in this subsection, an example will show where the elimination of the *if/else* makes the program more complex. The key idea is to keep the program simple, one way or the other.

Example 5.2.1 shows a situation where the elimination of the *if/else* is appropriate.

Example 5.2.1

Suppose that your teacher wants you to write a program that reads in the mark (numerical score) obtained for your assignment. The program also asks if it was handed in late, in which case, the mark is adjusted by a late penalty rate entered by the teacher. Following are sample runs of the program:

```
Enter the mark > 71
Is it late? (yes = 1, no = 0) > 1
Enter the correction factor > 0.20
The new mark is 56
```

Note that result of this first run, 56, is truncated.

```
Enter the mark > 83
Is it late? (yes = 1, no = 0) > 0
The new mark is 83
```

Figure 5.2.2 shows a solution that uses an *if/else* statement.

Figure 5.2.2

```
#include <stdio.h>

main()
{
    int   mark, new_mark;
    char  late;
    float correction_factor;

    printf("Enter the mark > ");
    scanf("%d", &mark);
    printf("Is it late? (yes = 1, no = 0) > ");
    scanf("%d", &late);
    if (late == 1)
    {
        printf("Enter the correction factor > ");
        scanf("%f", &correction_factor);
        new_mark = mark - mark * correction_factor;
        printf("The new mark is %d\n", new_mark);
    }
    else
    {
        printf("The new mark is %d\n", mark);
    }
}
```

The elimination of the *if/else* in this figure proceeds in three steps, as we will see in the following explanations.

Find what is in common in both alternatives. It is clear that the display of the new mark is common to both alternatives. Figure 5.2.3 shows the proof.

Figure 5.2.3

```
if (late == 1)
{
    printf("Enter the correction factor > ");
    scanf("%f", &correction_factor);
    new_mark = mark - mark * correction_factor;
    printf("The new mark is %d\n", new_mark);
}
else
{
    new_mark = mark;
    printf("The new mark is %d\n", new_mark);
}
```

The addition of the new statement (shown in bold type) is evidence that the latter two *printf()*s appear in both cases, so the display does not depend on the condition *late == 1* and, therefore, should be taken out of the *if/else* statement. This move can be called ***factoring out*** the *printf()* and always simplifies the logic a little. Figure 5.2.4 shows the result.

Figure 5.2.4

```
if (late == 1)
{
    printf("Enter the correction factor > ");
    scanf("%f", &correction_factor);
    new_mark = mark - mark * correction_factor;
}
else
{
    new_mark = mark;
}
printf("The new mark is %d\n", new_mark);
```

This last *printf()* has been factored out of the *if/else* statement. We have already seen some programs where an instruction was factored out, such as in Example 4.1.3.

EXERCISE 5.2.2

Factor out as many statements as possible:

```
if (net_income < 27000)
{
      printf("Hello!");
      printf("You are eligible for a child tax credit");
      printf("Enter the number of children > ");
      scanf("%d", &children);
      ctc_credit = 200 * children;
      tax = net_income * 0.17 - ctc_credit;
      printf("The tax will be %f\n", tax);
}
else
{
      printf("Hello!");
```

```
        printf("You are eligible for a child tax credit");
        ctc_credit = 200;
        tax = net_income * 0.17 - ctc_credit;
        printf("The tax will be %f\n", tax);
}
```

Try to see if one alternative can be eliminated. Revisit Example 5.2.1. If the assignment is not late, then nothing really needs to be done: the current mark will remain the new mark, so the *else* part is not really needed. It can be eliminated by **assuming** that the mark will not need to be changed (i.e., the assignment is not late) before checking if the assignment is late. Thus the code can be changed as shown in Figure 5.2.5 (change appears in bold type).

Figure 5.2.5

```
new_mark = mark;    /* assume the mark will not change */
if (late == 1)      /* if late, change the mark */
{
    printf("Enter the correction factor > ");
    scanf("%f", &correction_factor);
    new_mark = mark - mark * correction_factor;
}
printf("The new mark is %d\n", new_mark);
```

The *if/else* statement has been reduced to a simple *if* statement! The method of elimination of the *else* (i.e., assuming the occurrence of one alternative before reaching the *if* statement) is typical.

EXERCISES 5.2.3

1. Simplify the following code. Is an *if/else* really necessary? Is a simple *if* even necessary?

```
if (weekly / 2 > 300)
{
        bonus = weekly / 2;
        printf("Receive a bonus of %f\n", bonus);
}
else
{
        bonus = 300;
        printf("Receive a bonus of %f\n", bonus);
}
```

2. Eliminate the *else* in the following code:

```
if (net_income < 27000)
{
        printf("Hello!");
        printf("You are eligible for a child tax credit");
        ctc_credit = 200 * children;
        tax = net_income * 0.17 - ctc_credit;
}
else
{
        printf("Hello!");
        printf("You are eligible for a child tax credit");
        ctc_credit = 200;
        tax = net_income * 0.17 - ctc_credit;
}
```

3. Reduce the *if/else* in Example 5.1.2 to a simple *if* statement. Is it a good idea to do that?

Verify whether an expression can replace the *if* statement. Continuing with our example: as of now, the *if* statement *cannot* be eliminated, no matter how hard we try. But upon reformulating the input prompts, this can be achieved. Let us start the program from scratch, as Example 5.2.2 explains.

Example 5.2.2

Suppose the screen displays in Example 5.2.1 are changed as shown in these two sample runs:

Enter the mark > 71
Enter the correction factor **(0 if not late)** > 0.20
The new mark is 56

Enter the mark > 83
Enter the correction factor **(0 if not late)** > 0
The new mark is 83

The change is that the user is always asked for a correction factor, regardless of whether or not the assignment is late. A nonzero correction factor will obviously mean that the assignment is late; otherwise, it is not late. This suggests the program in Figure 5.2.6.

Figure 5.2.6

```
main()
{
    int   mark, new_mark;
    float correction_factor;

    printf("Enter the mark > ");
    scanf("%d", &mark);
    printf("Enter the correction factor (0 if not late) > ");
    scanf("%f", &correction_factor);
    if (correction_factor != 0)
    {
        new_mark = mark - mark * correction_factor;
        printf("The new mark is %d\n", new_mark);
    }
    else
    {
        printf("The new mark is %d\n", mark);
    }
}
```

Now let us simplify its logic. It is appropriate to eliminate the *else* part and arrive at the simplified code in Figure 5.2.7.

Figure 5.2.7

```
new_mark = mark;    /* assume the new mark will remain the same */
if (correction_factor != 0)
{
    new_mark = mark - mark * correction_factor;
}
printf("The new mark is %d\n", new_mark);
```

The assignment *new_mark = mark* is equivalent to assuming that the correction factor will remain 0. The expression within the *if* is reached only when the correction factor is not 0. Let us observe what it would boil down to when a correction factor of 0 is entered (Figure 5.2.8).

Figure 5.2.8

```
new_mark = mark – mark * correction_factor
                 mark *     0
                            0
                 mark –     0
                      mark
new_mark =            mark
```

The entry 0 indicates the assignment is not late. The expression boils down to no change in the mark, as would be expected. This clearly shows that this expression can be used regardless of whether or not the assignment is late. Consequently, the *if* statement can be eliminated. The final program is shown in Figure 5.2.9.

Figure 5.2.9

```
main()
{
    int   mark, new_mark;
    float correction_factor;

    printf("Enter the mark > ");
    scanf("%d", &mark);
    printf("Enter the correction factor (0 if not late) > ");
    scanf("%f", &correction_factor);
    new_mark = mark - mark * correction_factor;
    printf("The new mark is %d\n", new_mark);
}
```

In conclusion, the expression in bold is effectively equivalent to the *if/else* statement with which we started. Impressive! You might object that the elimination of the *if* statement has been made possible only because some input prompts were changed. One might not want to change the prompts. If that is the case, then the *if* statement would have to stay, and there is nothing wrong with that.

The purpose of this example of eliminating *if/else* statements and a simple *if* statement is not to conclude that decision statements should be avoided, but rather that sometimes they can be avoided and should be. Keep in mind that the more complex the logic of the *if/else,* the more complex the arithmetic of the expression that replaces it will be. This in turn makes the program harder to understand, prompting the following two questions:

1. When should you eliminate an *if/else?*
   a. When its equivalent arithmetic expression remains simple and intuitive
   b. When this expression is also at least as simple as the *if/else* from which it came
2. Why eliminate an *if/else?*
   a. The more *if/else*s there are, the longer the program and possibly the more complex the logic.

Refrain from being too fancy. In the case of the previous example, the final solution is better. The elimination of an *if/else* statement is not always a good move, though. Example 5.2.3 shows how the elimination of the *if/else* leads to a more complex program.

Example 5.2.3

A nutritionist has discovered a formula (totally fictional) that tells the time it takes for a chicken dish or a beef dish to cook. The user only needs to know the weight of the dish.

```
#include <stdio.h>

main()
{
      float          weight, cook_time;
      int            meat_type;

      printf("Is it (1) beef or (2) chicken? ");
      scanf("%d", &meat_type);
      printf("Enter the weight of the meat > ");
      scanf("%f", &weight);

      if (meat_type == 1)
      {
            cook_time = 40 + weight * 0.2;
      }
```

```
        else
        {
              cook_time = 20 + weight * 0.15;
        }
        printf("The dish will take %.0f minutes to cook", cook_time);
}
```

This *if/else* can be reduced to a simple *if* as shown in Figure 5.2.10.

Figure 5.2.10

```
cook_time = 20 + weight * 0.15; /* assume a chicken dish */
if (meat_type == 1)
{
        cook_time = 40 + weight * 0.2;
}
```

This simple *if* statement is equivalent to the *if/else.* Its logic is not any more complex, just more confusing. Indeed, why assume the dish will be chicken? This is not a fair assumption. In eliminating the *else* in Example 5.2.1's program, the programmer also made the assumption that the assignment was not late. That was a fair assumption, though, since most assignments are usually on time. In Example 5.2.3, the *if/else* should be kept. Nevertheless, for the sake of illustration, let us reduce the simple *if* down to an expression, as shown in Figure 5.2.11. Changes are shown in bold type.

Figure 5.2.11

```
#include <stdio.h>

main()
{
        float           weight, cook_time;
        int             meat_type;

        printf("Is it (1) beef or (2) chicken? ");
        scanf("%d", &meat_type);
        printf("Enter the weight of the meat > ");
        scanf("%f", &weight);
        cook_time = (meat_type-1) * (20 + weight * 0.15) -
                    (meat_type-2) * (40 + weight * 0.2);
        printf("The dish will take %.0f minutes to cook", cook_time);
}
```

Try it, it works, but is it ever confusing and unnatural! Chapter 13 will cover other techniques for the elimination of an *if/else* statement.

EXERCISES 5.2.4

1. A salesman receives a commission of 10% on all sales if he has sold at least $10,000 worth of merchandise in a given period, but only 8.5% if his sales are below $10,000. Write a program with an *if/else* that figures his commission and displays it.
2. a. Is it possible to reduce the *if/else* in question 1 to a simple *if* statement?
   b. Is it possible to reduce the *if/else* in question 1 to an expression?
   c. In either (a) or (b), is the resulting program any simpler?
3. Can the *if/else* of Example 4.3.1 be reduced to a simple *if?* To an expression?
4. A student provides the solution below to Exercise 4.4.1, 5g:

```
#include <stdio.h>

main()
{
        int       job_code;
```

```
    float    weekly, bonus;

    printf("Enter the job code > ");
    scanf("%d", &job_code);
    printf("Enter the weekly salary > ");
    scanf("%f", &weekly);

    switch(job_code)
    {
       case 1: bonus = weekly / 2;
               if (bonus > 200)
               {
                   bonus = 200;
               }
               else
               {
                   bonus = bonus;
               }
               printf("The holiday bonus is %.2f\n", bonus);
               break;
       case 2: bonus = weekly;
               if (bonus > 500)
               {
                   bonus = 500;
               }
               else
               {
                   bonus = bonus;
               }
               printf("The holiday bonus is %.2f\n", bonus);
               break;
       case 3: bonus = weekly * 1.5;

               if (bonus > 600)
               {
                   bonus = 600;
               }
               else
               {
                   bonus = bonus;
               }
               printf("The holiday bonus is %.2f\n", bonus);
               break;
       case 4: bonus = weekly * 2;
               if (bonus > 900)
               {
                   bonus = 900;
               }
               else
               {
                  bonus = bonus;
               }
               printf("The holiday bonus is %.2f\n", bonus);
               break;
       }
}
```

This program works well. However, its logic is unnecessarily complex. Indeed:

a. The *else*s are totally unnecessary. (Why?)
b. The *printf()*s clearly should be factored out of the *switch* statement. (Why is that the case?)
c. Even though the *if* statement is not exactly the same for all cases, the action of checking the limit of the bonus is common to all. Therefore, this action should be factored out of the *switch* statement. (How can this be done?)

d. Similarly, even though the calculation of the bonus is not exactly the same for all cases, it needs to be calculated for all. Therefore this action is common to all and should be factored out of the *switch* statement. (How can this be done?)

Based on these observations, come up with a much simplified solution.

With more practice and experience, you will be better able to detect the pieces of codes that can and should be simplified. This skill is one that good programmers possess, but it is not one about which novices should worry. Nevertheless, it is educational to know that a program's logic should be kept simple.

5.3 CHECKING RANGES OF VALUES

In Example 4.3.7 we saw an application involving checking ranges of marks. Let us now look at many other such applications.

5.3.1 CHECKING RANGES WITH NUMBERS

Explicit vs. implicit range checking. A C program can check a range of numbers ***explicitly,*** that is, with lines of code that clearly are written to do the checking. A program can also check a range ***implicitly,*** in which case the way the range is checked is not expressed directly in the program's code. Example 5.3.1 has an example of implicit range checking.

Example 5.3.1

Let us revisit Example 4.3.7. Here is the *if/else* chain again:

```
if (mark >= 80)
{
        letter = 'A';
}
else if (mark >= 70)
{
        letter = 'B';
}
else if (mark >= 60)
{
        letter = 'C';
}
else
{
        letter = 'F';
}
```

Remember that if the program reaches, say, the line *letter = 'C',* then the condition *mark >= 60* must obviously be true. It follows from the logic of the *if/else* chain that the conditions *mark >= 70* and *mark >= 80* must be false. Therefore the mark must be between *mark >= 60* and *mark < 70.* The condition *mark >= 60* checks the ***lower boundary*** and *mark < 70* checks the ***upper boundary*** of the range. These two conditions are said to be ***boundary conditions.*** Because the range is not explicitly coded, it is said to be an ***implicit range checking.*** Most beginners have difficulty with this and prefer range checking to be done explicitly, as shown below:

```
if (mark >= 80 && mark <= 100)
{
        letter = 'A';
}
else if (mark >= 70 && mark <= 79)
{
        letter = 'B';
}
```

```
else if (mark >= 60 && mark <= 69)
{
        letter = 'C';
}
else
{
        letter = 'F';
}
```

The ranges of marks are immediately noticeable. Note the absence of a condition with the last *else.* Indeed none is needed. (Why is that the case?)

Be wary of boundary conditions. Regardless of whether you choose implicit or explicit range checking, the boundary conditions must be expressed carefully, as Example 5.3.2 explains.

Example 5.3.2

Suppose now that the variable *mark* in Example 5.3.1 is declared as *float* and read in with *scanf("%f", &mark)* (i.e., marks with a fractional part are allowed). Now the program is run with the mark 69.5:

Enter a mark > <u>69.5</u>
The letter grade is F

The letter grade obtained, F, is obviously wrong. How did this happen? The number "fell through the cracks" of the *if/else* logic. Solution: The cracks must be "sealed" by carefully covering all boundary cases. The following *if/else* does that by providing "airtight" logic:

```
if (mark >= 80 && mark <= 100)
{
        letter = 'A';
}
else if (mark >= 70 && mark < 80)   /* logical negation of mark >= 80 */
{
        letter = 'B';
}
else if (mark >= 60 && mark < 70)   /* logical negation of mark >= 70 */
{
        letter = 'C';
}
else if (mark < 60)   /* logical negation of mark >= 60 */
{
        letter = 'F';
}
```

The rule for "airtight" logic is that the upper boundary of one condition must be the **logical negation** of the lower boundary of the **previous** condition, as shown in Figure 5.3.1.

Figure 5.3.1

Lower boundary

```
if (mark >= 80 && mark <= 100)
{
        letter = 'A';
}
if (mark >= 70 && mark < 80)
{
        letter = 'B';
}
```

Upper boundary

The upper boundary is the logical negation of the lower boundary.

Marks are usually integers, though, so the declarations *int mark* and *scanf("%d", &mark)* are more appropriate. Even so, follow "airtight" logic at all times. It also keeps the bugs out!

EXERCISES 5.3.1

1. The local water company charges homeowners one of the following, whichever applies:
   a. A flat rate of $15 for usage up to 1,000 c.m. (cubic meters)
   b. 1.8¢ per c.m. for usage over 1,000 c.m. and up to 2,000 c.m.
   c. 2¢ per c.m. for usage over 2,000 c.m. and up to 3,000 c.m.
   d. A flat rate of $70 for usage over 3,000 c.m.

   The program below calculates the water charge for a home owner. Indicate the places where the code overlooks or overlaps boundary cases. Fix the code in those places.

```
main()
{
      float usage;
      float charge;

      printf("Enter the water usage > ");
      scanf("%f", &usage);

      if (usage < 1000)
      {
           charge = 15.00;
      }
      else if (usage >= 1001 && usage <= 2000)
      {
           charge = 0.018 * usage;
      }
      else if (usage > 2000 && usage < 3001)
      {
           charge = 0.02 * usage;
      }
      else
      {
           charge = 70.00;
      }
      printf("The water charge is %.2f\n", charge);
}
```

2. A post office classifies the parcels they receive in three groups:

   Group A, less than one pound
   Group B, between one and three pounds, inclusive
   Group C, over three pounds

   Write a program that simply reads in the weight of a parcel and determines its group.
3. Shorten the following conditions:
   a. *num == 1 || num == 2 || num == 3 || num == 4 || num == 5*
   b. *num != 1 && num != 2 && num != 3 && num != 4 && num != 5*
4. Improve the program of Exercise 4.3.3, 3f so that the ranges are also verified. If the data is out of range, the program will display an error message and bring the data within range using the remainder operator: *month = (month - 1) % 12 + 1.* For example:

   Enter the day (1 to 31) > 32
   Day out of range. Changed to 1
   Enter the month (1 to 12) > -1
   Month out of range. Changed to 11
   Enter the year (1900 to 1999) > 0

Year out of range. Changed to 1999

The date is November 1, 99

5. Modify the above program so that the year is accepted with or without the prefix 19 but is still displayed with the prefix 19. Hence the following is accepted:

   Enter the day (1 to 31) > 7
   Enter the month (1 to 12) > 1
   Enter the year (1900 to 1999) > 18
   The date is January 7, 1918

   This means that the acceptable range for the year is effectively 0 to 99 or 1900 to 1999.
6. Modify the program of Exercise 4.4.1, 5c so that the program will flag an error if the temperature entered is not within the range –50 and 60 or that the unit is not 'c', 'C', 'f', or 'F'.
7. Write a program that calculates the taxes owed to the government. The gross income, the deductions, and the income tax already paid are required. The amount of tax depends on the net income (income after deductions) as follows:

Net Income	**Tax Rate**
0 to 27,000	17%
27001 to 50,000	26%
50,001 and up	29%

   Here is an example of a run:

   Enter the gross income $ 41098.01
   Enter the deductions $ 3208.81
   Taxes already paid $ 9517.55

   You owe $ 333.64

8. Write a program for an accounts receivable department. A penalty is assessed for all accounts that are overdue. Here are the rates of penalty:
   a. Less than 30 days past due: the penalty rate is 5%
   b. Past due between 31 and 60 days: the penalty rate is 12%
   c. Past due more than 60 days: the penalty rate is 21%
   The program will read in the amount due and the number of days overdue. Then it will issue a penalty, if one applies.
9. A weather forecasting office wishes to offer the public a program that advises them on timing outdoor activities. If the probability of precipitation is more than 40%, they advise people not to go out. But a humidity index between 30 and 70 is acceptable. Finally, a temperature between 15° C and 28° C is acceptable. Write the program. Following are two examples of a run:

   Likelihood of precipitation? 0.1
   Humidity index? 45
   Temperature? 24

   You may engage in outdoor activities

   Likelihood of precipitation? 0.45
   Humidity index? 45
   Temperature? 24

   You had better stay home

10. a. Improve the program above so that it checks the input against the acceptable ranges and gives a message if the range is violated. For example:

   Likelihood of precipitation? 10
   Should be within 0.0 and 1.0
   Humidity index? 45
   Temperature? 120
   Should be within –50 and +60

   You had better stay home

b. Of course, the advice is not worth much if the input data is invalid. Modify the program so that it will not bother giving advice if any one of the entries is out of range. For example:

```
Likelihood of precipitation? 10
Should be within 0.0 and 1.0
Humidity index? 45
Temperature? 120
Should be within –50 and +60

No advice possible due to invalid inputs
```

5.3.2 CHECKING RANGES WITH CHARACTERS

Application: Checking character classification. Many character-handling applications make use of character range checking. The following examples illustrate the two most common applications.

Example 5.3.3

The following program checks if the entered letter is a lowercase or uppercase character. Assume the character entered is always a letter.

```
#include <stdio.h>

main()
{
   char letter;

   printf("Enter a letter > ");
   scanf("\n%c", &letter);

   if (letter >= 'a' && letter <= 'z')     /* is the letter between */
   {                                       /* 'a' and 'z', inclusive ? */
         printf("Lowercase");
   }
   else
   {
         printf("Uppercase");
   }
}
```

Example 5.3.4

The following program checks if the user entered an alphabet letter or not.

```
#include <stdio.h>

main()
{

      char      ch;

      printf("Enter a letter > ");
      scanf("\n%c", &ch);

      if ((ch >= 'a' && ch <= 'z') || (ch >= 'A' && ch <= 'Z'))
      {
            printf("Yes! It's a letter");
      }
      else
```

```
        {
                printf("It's NOT a letter");
        }
}
```

Figure 5.3.2 explains the condition of the *if/else*.

Figure 5.3.2

`(ch >= 'a' && ch <= 'z')`	`||`	`(ch >= 'A' && ch <= 'Z')`
The character is within 'a' **and** 'z', i.e., it is a lowercase letter.	OR	The character is within 'A' **and** 'Z', i.e., it is an uppercase letter.

As you can see, both cases must be checked. If the character does not fall in either range, then it cannot be a letter.

The *islower()* and *isalpha()* C functions. There is an ANSI C standard library that already contains functions to check what the two applications in Examples 5.3.3 and 5.3.4 do. The program in Example 5.3.5 includes them. The changes are in bold type.

Example 5.3.5

Revisit Example 5.3.3. The C function *islower(letter)* returns true if *letter* is a lowercase letter; otherwise, it returns false. Following is the new program that uses the function:

```
#include <stdio.h>
#include <ctype.h>

main()
{
        char        letter;

        printf("Enter a letter > ");
        scanf("\n%c", &letter);

        if (islower(letter))
        {
                printf("Lowercase");
        }
        else
        {
                printf("Uppercase");
        }
}
```

Note the need for the directive *#include <ctype.h>*. The function *islower()* is declared in it.

Example 5.3.6

Revisit Example 5.3.4. The C function *isalpha(ch)* returns true if *ch* is a letter; otherwise, it returns false. Following is the new program that uses this function:

```
#include <stdio.h>
#include <ctype.h>

main()
{

        char        ch;

        printf("Enter a character > ");
```

```
        scanf("\n%c", &ch);

        if (isalpha(ch))
        {
                printf("Yes! It's a letter");
        }
        else
        {
                printf("It's NOT a letter");
        }
}
```

Again, note the need for the directive *#include <ctype.h>*.

EXERCISES 5.3.2

1. How would the composite condition in Example 5.3.4 evaluate if the parentheses were not used?
2. How would the composite condition in Example 5.3.4 need to be changed if the two alternatives were switched? Do not use the logical negation operator to make the changes.

```
if (______________________________________________)
{
        printf("It's NOT a letter");
}
else
{
        printf("Yes! It's a letter");
}
```

3. How would the condition in Example 5.3.6 need to be changed if the two alternatives were switched?

```
if (______________)
{
        printf("It's NOT a letter");
}
else
{
        printf("Yes! It's a letter");
}
```

5.3.3 RANGE CHECKING AND *switch* STATEMENTS DON'T MIX!

Section 4.4 seems to suggest that an *if/else* chain and a *switch* statement are equivalent. Not so! For instance, consider the following code:

```
#include <stdio.h>

main()
{
        char letter;
        int  mark;

        printf("Enter the mark > ");
        scanf("%d", &mark);

        if (mark >= 80 && mark <= 100)
```

```
        {
                letter = 'A';
        }
        else
        if (mark >= 70 && mark < 80)
        {
                letter = 'B';
        }
        else
        if (mark >= 60 && mark < 70)
        {
                letter = 'C';
        }
        else
        {
                letter = 'F';
        }
        printf("The letter grade is %c\n", letter);
}
```

Can there be an equivalent *switch* statement for it? No, as the explanation in (2) of *Common Errors and Traps* in Subsection 5.3.4 explains.

Remember, a *switch* statement can always be converted to an *if/else* chain, whereas an *if/else* chain can be converted into a *switch* statement only when *individual* values, not ranges of values, are to be checked.

EXERCISES 5.3.3

1. Can a *switch* statement be coded for the following?
   a. Exercise 5.1.7, 5.
   b. Exercise 5.3.1, 2.
   c. Exercise 5.3.1, 5.
   d. Exercise 5.3.1, 6.
   e. Exercise 5.3.1, 7.

   If so, write the programs.
2. Is it possible to use a *switch* statement for the following situations? If so, write the code:
   a. Use these criteria to determine the severity of the penalty for drunk driving:

0.08 to 0.010	$500 fine
0.11 to 0.15	One month in jail
0.16 to 0.20	Six months in jail
Over 0.20	One year in jail

   b. An individual makes financial decisions depending on these interest rates:

From 0% to just under 4.2%	Stock market or bonds
From 4.2% to 8%	Stock market
From just over 8% to 12.5%	Money market
Over 12.5%	Money market or bank

3. Devise solutions to questions 2a and 2b that use an *if/else* chain.

5.3.4 COMMON ERRORS AND TRAPS

Programmers often make the following common errors when writing programs that check a range of values.

1. Do not overlook (or overlap) boundary cases, as was illustrated early in this section. This can cause some of the most difficult bugs to trace, because the logic may not fail for a long time.

However, proper testing of a program should be able to spot these errors. Section 6.2 will discuss some useful debugging and testing techniques.

2. Do not think that a *switch* statement can always be found for any *if/else* chain. For example, novices often use the following *switch* statement for the *if/else* chain presented in Example 5.3.1:

```
switch (mark) [1]
{
   case (mark >= 80 && mark <= 100): [2]
            letter = 'A';
            break;
   case (mark >= 70 && mark <= 80): [2]
            letter = 'B';
            break;
   case (mark >= 60 && mark <= 70): [2]
            letter = 'C';
            break;
   default:
            letter = 'F';
            break;
}
```

Explanations

1. The controlling expression is *mark.*
2. The compiler will complain at these lines, because they include syntax errors. The *switch* statement can only compare **labels** against the controlling expression, not logical expressions (or any other expressions).

6 Putting It All Together

OBJECTIVES

This chapter introduces you to the following information:

- The procedure for systematically writing complex programs from simpler ones.
- The procedure for systematically debugging and testing your programs.

INTRODUCTION

In Chapters 4 and 5 you studied various decision structures and saw that a program may include many of them. In fact, decisions structures may be put together in many arrangements, such as a decisions structure within other decisions structures. These are called ***nested decision structures***, which is the main subject of this chapter.

6.1 NESTED DECISION STRUCTURES

As we saw in Section 5.1, composite conditions allow the development of logically more complex programs. They have limits, though. Often a situation calls for more than one *if/else* structure and those may need to be organized in more complex ways than the simple sequential order shown so far. In this section, we will study two-level and three-level decision structures. It is easy to generalize to other levels after that.

6.1.1 TWO-LEVEL DECISION STRUCTURES

Two-level decision structures involve one decision structure within another. This subsection includes four examples of two-level decision structures.

Example 6.1.1

In Example 5.3.3, the program checked if a letter was lowercase or uppercase. It assumed that the character typed in was a letter, but what if it was not? Clearly, the program should first check if the character is a letter. If so, it will then check the letter's case. Following is the new code that performs that function (with changes in bold type):

```
#include <stdio.h>
#include <ctype.h>

main()
```

```
{
      char      ch;

      printf("Enter a letter > ");
      scanf("\n%c", &ch);
if (isalpha(ch))          /* outer if/else */
{
      if (islower(ch))    /* inner if/else */
      {
            printf("Lowercase");               Block C
      }                                                         Block A
      else
      {
            printf("Uppercase");               Block D
      }
}
else
{
      printf("It is not a letter");                             Block B
}
```

This program has two levels of *if/else*s: the outer one and the inner one (the one inside Block A). The inner *if/else* is said to be ***nested*** within the outer *if/else.* Note that the two *if*s are **not** in sequence; the inner *if* is reached only if the outer *if*'s condition is true. If the condition of Block A of the outer *if/else* is true, it is executed; otherwise, Block B is executed. If the condition of the outer *if/else* is true, then either Block C or Block D will be reached, depending of the condition of the inner *if/else.*

EXERCISES 6.1.1

1. Write a program that orders a list of three numbers in ascending or descending order, depending on the user's request. A run might look like this:

   Enter three numbers ? 8 −9 1
   (A)scending or (D)escending? d
   8 1 −9

   (***Hint:*** See the solution to Example 4.1.4.)
2. A student developed the sequence of *if*s below as a solution for Example 6.1.1. He claims that the sequence is logically identical to the code shown in the example. Is he right?

```
#include <stdio.h>
#include <ctype.h>

main()
{
      char      ch;

      printf("Enter a letter > ");
      scanf("\n%c", &ch);

      if (isalpha(ch) && islower(ch))
      {
            printf("Lowercase");
      }
      if (isalpha(ch) && !islower(ch))
      {
            printf("Uppercase");
      }
      if (!isalpha(ch))
      {
```

```
                printf("It is not a letter");
            }
    }
```

Which of the two programs represents better programming practice?

Example 6.1.2

Consider the temporary secretarial employment agency (Section 5.1) again. Suppose the agency now wishes to combine two programs, the one that calculates the pay (Example 5.1.2) and the one that checks the qualification code (Example 5.1.6). The user first enters the qualification code. If that code is valid, the user will then enter the day worked and the number of hours; otherwise the program quits. The new code would look like this:

```
#include <stdio.h>

main()
{

    int     hours, sp;
    char    day, ex, ex_up;
    float   pay;

    printf("Enter the contractor's qualification code > ");
    scanf("\n%c%d", &ex, &sp);
    ex_up = toupper(ex);

    /* Check if the code is valid */

if ((ex == 'M' || ex == 'L' && (sp >= 40 && sp <= 120))
{
    printf("Enter the day worked (Sunday = 1, Monday = 2, etc) > ");
    scanf("%d", &day);
    printf("Enter the number of hours >);
    scanf("%d", &hours);
    if (day >= 2 && day <= 6)                              Block
    {                                                        A
        pay = 12.39 * hours;                  Inner              Outer
    }                                         if/else            if/else
    else                                      (nested)
        pay = 12.39 * 1.5 * hours;
    }
    printf("The pay is %.2f\n", pay);
}
else
{                                                    Block
    printf("The code is INVALID\n");                   B
}
```

The situation has become too complex for a single *if/else* to cover all the different possibilities. A second (inner) *if/else* is needed within the outer one, giving us two levels of *if/else*s. If the condition of the outer *if/else* is true, Block A is executed; otherwise Block B is executed.

Following are three possible results of running this program. Each run depends on what input the program receives.

Enter the contractor's qualification code > <u>L79</u>
Enter the day worked (Sunday = 1, Monday = 2, etc) > <u>6</u>
Enter the number of hours > <u>4</u>
The pay is 49.56

Enter the contractor's qualification code > <u>X45</u>
The code is INVALID

Enter the contractor's qualification code > M17
The code is INVALID

Remember to indent the compound statements. The program in Examples 6.1.2 illustrates the importance of the grooming tips in Subsections 5.2.1 and 2.3.1. If you ignored them, the program might look like this:

```
#include <stdio.h>
main() {
int hours, sp;
char day, ex;
float pay;
printf("Enter the contractor's qualification code > ");
scanf("\n%c%d",&ex,&sp);
if((ex=='M'||ex=='L')&&
  (sp>=40&&sp<=120))     {
printf("Enter the day worked (Sunday = 1, Monday = 2, etc) > ");
scanf("%d",&day);
printf("Enter the number of hours > ");
scanf("%d",&hours);
if (day>=2&&day<=6)  pay=12.39*hours;
else
pay=12.39*1.5*hours;
printf("The pay is %.2f\n",pay);
}
else  printf("The code is INVALID");
}
```

Ugly! Students often seek help in debugging programs that look this way, and just as often, the error is obvious and would have been avoided in properly entered code.

EXERCISES 6.1.2

1. Rewrite the program in Example 6.1.2 so that Blocks A and B are reversed (i.e., Block A is in the *else* and Block B is in the *if*). Of course this will require a change in the condition.
2. Improve the program in Example 5.1.3 by adding code that detects if the channel is invalid and displays a message accordingly. The channel is invalid when it is less than 2 or greater than 99.
3. In Exercise 5.1.1, 3b, it was assumed that the programmer never mistyped the letter. If the letter is invalid, the program indicates so and does not calculate any change. If this assumption is removed, how would the program need to be modified? Following are two examples of how the new program might run, given particular input:

   Enter the cost of the book > 41.27
   Enter the amount of money paid by the customer > 40
   Enter the currency (C for Canadian, A for American) > a

   The change is $ 10.28

   Enter the cost of the book > 41.27
   Enter the amount of money paid by the customer > 40
   Enter the currency (C for Canadian, A for American) > G

   The currency is invalid.

4. In the program for Exercise 5.1.1, 3a, make a change similar to that of question 3 above to check the gender of the person and the number of children entered by the user. (The number must be within 0 and 12.) For example:

   What are your initials? HWA
   Are you a male or a female? (m=male, f=female) w
   How many children do you have?–2

   Invalid input.

5. Improve the invalidity message above so that it also explains what information was entered incorrectly. For example:

   What are your initials? HWA
   Are you a male or a female? (m=male, f=female) w
   How many children do you have? –2

   Invalid input.
   The gender 'w' does not exist.
   The number of children is outside the range.

   (***Hint:*** You will need two *if* statements within the outer *else.*)

Know where to add new code. As illustrated so far, nested *if/else* structures often occur as new features are added to a program. It is thus important to understand where to insert the new corresponding codes. Consider Example 6.1.3.

Example 6.1.3

Back to the temporary secretarial agency from Example 6.1.2: Currently all employees are paid the same rate. Now that employees' individual qualifications are known, the rate should depend on these qualifications. It was decided that a medical secretary's rate should be 15% higher than that of a law secretary. The rate is further increased or decreased given the typing speed:

40 to 69	Decrease by 10%
70 to 99	Remain the same
100 to 120	Increase by 18%

The basic rate is still $12.39. Figure 6.1.1 shows the new program with changes in bold.

Figure 6.1.1

```
#include <stdio.h>

main()
(
    int      hours, sp;
    char     day, ex, ex_up;
    float    pay, rate;

    printf("Enter the contractor's qualification code > ")'
    scanf("\n%c%d", %ex, %sp);
    ex_up = toupper(ex);

    if ((ex == 'M' || ex == 'L') && (sp >= 40 && sp <= 120))
    {
        /* Ask for the information */

        printf("Enter the day worked (Sunday = 1, Monday = 2, etc) > ");
        scanf("%d", &day);
        printf("Enter the number of hours > ");
        scanf("%d", &hours);

        /* Figure out the rate of pay, given the information */

        rate = 12.39;
        if (ex_up == 'M')
        {
            rate = rate + rate * 0.15;   /* increase by 15% */
        }
        if (sp >= 40 && sp <= 59)
        {
            rate = rate - rate * 0.10;
        }
```

Block A

New code

```
        else if (sp >= 100 && sp <= 120)
        {
            rate = rate + rate * 0.18;
        }

        /* Calculate the pay */

        if (day >= 2 && day <= 6)
        {
             pay = rate * hours;
        }
       else
        {
            pay = rate * 1.5 = hours;
        }
        printf("The pay is %.2f\n", pay);
    }
    else
Block {
  B      printf("The code is INVALID\n");
    }
{
```

This program shows that many *if/else* and *if* statements can be inserted within a block. Why was the sequence of *if/else*s (shown in bold) inserted within Block A? After all, the solution in Figure 6.1.2 works just as well with the new code placed immediately after the relevant information (qualification code).

Figure 6.1.2

```
printf("Enter the contractor's qualification code > ")'
scanf("\n%c%d", %ex, %sp);
ex_up = toupper(ex);

/* Figure out the rate of pay, given the information */

rate = 12.39;                                               ┐
if (ex_up == 'M')                                           │
{                                                           │
      rate = rate + rate * 0.15;  /* increase by 15% */     │
}                                                           │
if (sp >= 40 && sp <= 59)                                   ├ New
{                                                           │ code
      rate = rate - rate * 0.10;                            │
}                                                           │
else if (sp >= 100 && sp <= 120)                            │
{                                                           │
      rate = rate + rate * 0.18;                            │
}                                                           ┘
if ((ex == 'M' || ex == 'L') && (sp >= 40 && sp <= 120))
{

     /* Ask for the information */

     printf("Enter the day worked (Sunday = 1, Monday = 2, etc) > ");
     scanf("%d", &day);
     printf("Enter the number of hours > ");
     scanf("%d", &hours);

     /* Calculate the pay */

     if (day >= 2 && day <= 6)
     {
         pay = rate * hours;
```

```
    }
    else
    {
        pay = rate * 1.5 = hours;
    }
    printf("The pay is %.2f\n", pay);
}
else
{
    printf("The code is INVALID\n");
}
{
```

Both solutions are equally good. The only fault of the latter solution is that since the rate of pay is calculated **prior** to checking the validity of the qualification code, should this code be invalid, then the calculated rate of pay would be wrong. It is better to calculate the pay rate **after** it is known that the qualification code is valid. So the first solution is preferable.

EXERCISES 6.1.3

Are the solutions below equivalent to the two solutions in Figure 6.1.1 and Figure 6.1.2?

1.
```
rate = 12.39;
if ((ex == 'M' || ex == 'L') && (sp >= 40 && sp <= 120))
{
    printf("Enter the day worked (Sunday = 1, Monday = 2, etc) > ");
    scanf("%d", &day);
    printf("Enter the number of hours > ");
    scanf("%d", &hours);

    if (sp >= 40 && sp <= 59)
    {
        rate = rate - rate * 0.10;
    }
    else if (sp >= 100 && sp <= 120)
    {
        rate = rate + rate * 0.18;
    }
    if (ex_up == 'M')
    {
        rate = rate + rate * 0.15;
    }
    if (day >= 2 && day <= 6)
    {
        pay = rate * hours;
    }
    else
    {
        pay = rate * 1.5 * hours;
    }
    printf("The pay is %.2f\n", pay);
}
else
{
    printf("The code is INVALID\n");
}
```

2.
```
rate = 12.39;
if ((ex == 'M' || ex == 'L') && (sp >= 40 && sp <= 120))
```

```
{
    printf("Enter the day worked (Sunday = 1, Monday = 2, etc) > ");
    scanf("%d", &day);
    printf("Enter the number of hours > ");
    scanf("%d", &hours);

    if (ex_up == 'M')
    {
        rate = rate + rate * 0.15;
    }
    else if (sp >= 40 && sp <= 59)
    {
        rate = rate - rate * 0.10;
    }
    else if (sp >= 100 && sp <= 120)

        rate = rate + rate * 0.18;
    }
    if (day >= 2 && day <= 6)
    {
        pay = rate * hours;
     }
    else
    {
        pay = rate * 1.5 * hours;
    }
    printf("The pay is %.2f\n", pay);
}
else
{
    printf("The code is INVALID\n");
}
```

3. (***Hint:*** To answer this one, first you may need to read Subsections 6.1.3 and 6.1.4.)

```
rate = 12.39;
if ((ex == 'M' || ex == 'L') && (sp >= 40 && sp <= 120))
{
    printf("Enter the day worked (Sunday = 1, Monday = 2, etc) > ");
    scanf("%d", &day);
    printf("Enter the number of hours > ");
    scanf("%d", &hours);

    if (ex_up == 'M')
    {
        rate = rate + rate * 0.15;
    }
    else
    {
        if (sp >= 40 && sp <= 59)
        {
            rate = rate - rate * 0.10;
        }
        else
        {
            if (sp >= 100 && sp <= 120)
            {
                rate = rate + rate * 0.18;
            }
```

```
            }
        }
        if (day >= 2 && day <= 6)
        {
            pay = rate * hours;
        }
        else
        {
            pay = rate * 1.5 * hours;
        }
        printf("The pay is %.2f\n", pay);
    }
    else
    {
        printf("The code is INVALID\n");
    }
```

Example 6.1.4

You may work out a solution to Example 4.1.4 by using two levels of *if/else*s. The idea is to check if *n1* is greater than *n2*. If it is, check if *n1* is also greater than *n3*. If so, then *n1* is the largest number; otherwise *n3* is the largest. Following is the code for this problem:

```
#include <stdio.h>
main()
{
     int n1, n2, n3, max;

     printf("Enter the score for the three periods > ");
     scanf("%d%d%d", &n1, &n2, &n3);


     if (n1 > n2)
     {
            if (n1 > n3)
            {
                   max = n1;
            }
            else
            {
                   max = n3;
            }
      }
      else
      {
            if (n2 > n3)
            {
                   max = n2;
            }
            else
            {
                   max = n3;
            }
     }
     printf("The largest score in a period is %d", max_so_far);
}
```

(***Note:*** The solution in Example 4.1.4 is certainly simpler.)

EXERCISE 6.1.4

Note that the program in Example 6.1.4 never checks the equality of the numbers. Does that mean that the program will not work correctly if two of the numbers (or all three) are the same?

6.1.2 WHOSE *else* IS IT?

Needless to say, multiple levels of *if/elses* can easily lead to confusion. To examine further that confusion, let us revisit the **original** program of Example 5.2.1. Let us simplify the illustration by assuming that the correction factor is always 20%. Also, instead of asking for a correction factor, the program will ask whether or not to penalize the student if the assignment is late. Following are examples of two runs, each of which depends on the input received by the program:

Enter the mark > 71
Is it late? (yes = 1, no = 0) > 1
If late, do you wish to penalize? (y/n) > y
The new mark is 56

Enter the mark > 83
Is it late? (yes = 1, no = 0) > 1
If late, do you wish to penalize? (y/n) > n
The new mark is 83

Figure 6.1.3 shows the solution with which to start.

Figure 6.1.3

```
#include <stdio.h>

main()
{
     int     mark, new_mark;
     char    late, answer;

     printf("Enter the mark > ");
     scanf("%d", &mark);
     printf("Is the assignment late? (y=1, n=0) > ");
     scanf("%d", &late);
     printf("If late, do you wish to penalize? (y/n) > ");
     scanf("\n%c", &answer);
     if (late == 1)
     {
         if (answer == 'y' || answer == 'Y')
         {
               new_mark = mark - mark * 0.20;
         }
         else
         {
               new_mark = mark;
         }
}
else
{
           new_mark = mark;
}
printf("The new mark is %d\n", new_mark);
```

There are two levels of *if/elses* in this example. Clearly the outer *if/else* can be reduced to a simple *if* by using the technique shown in Subection 5.2.3:

```
new_mark = mark;    /* assume that the mark will not change */
if (late == 1)
{
    if (answer == 'y' || answer == 'Y')
    {
         new_mark = mark - mark * 0.20;
    }
    else
    {
         new_mark = mark;
    }
}
```

Let us call this Solution 1. Next, each block contains only one statement so you can eliminate the braces (although this is not recommended):

```
if (late == 1)
    if (answer == 'y' || answer == 'Y')
         new_mark = mark - mark * 0.20;
    else
         new_mark = mark;
```

Now the confusion: Let us move the keyword *else* to the far left.

```
if (late == 1)
    if (answer == 'y' || answer == 'Y')
         new_mark = mark - mark * 0.20;
else
         new_mark = mark;
```

The *else* keyword now appears to be associated with the outer *if.* Careful! Do not let appearances confuse you, for this structure has the same logic as the code in Figure 6.1.4.

Figure 6.1.4

```
if (late == 1)
{
    if (answer == 'y' || answer == 'Y')
    {
         new_mark = mark - mark * 0.20;
    }
}
else
{
     new_mark = mark;
}
```

This solution—let us call it Solution 2—does **not** have the same logic as Solution 1. So where did we go wrong? Clearly, moving the *else* to the far left does not change the logic; the *else* is still associated with the inner *if.*

Figure 6.1.4 shows that the use of braces, even when not strictly needed, enhances the clarity of the logic. In the absence of braces, the compiler will always pair up the *else* to the latest *if* it encounters.

EXERCISES 6.1.5

1. Which *if* will the *else* be associated with?

```
if (a > 10)
     if (b > a)
     {
```

```
            printf("b is greater than a and 10");
      }
else
     printf("a is less than 10");
```

2. What will be displayed by the following code?

```
if (i == 1)
   if (j == 2)
      printf("First message");
else
   printf("Second message");
   printf("Third message");
```

a. if *i* contains 1, *j* contains 1?
b. if *i* contains 1, *j* contains 2?
c. if *i* contains 5, *j* contains 2?

3. Match the nested *if/else* constructs below that express equivalent logic.

a.
```
if (sp >= 40)i m
        if (sp <= 60)
              rate = 0.20;
else
        rate = 0.10;
```

b.
```
if (sp >= 40)
{
        if (sp <= 60)
              rate = 0.20;
}
else
{
        if (sp > 60)
              rate = 0.10;
}
```

c.
```
if (sp >= 40)
{
      if (sp <= 60)
            rate = 0.20;
}
else
            rate = 0.10;
```

d.
```
if (sp >= 40)
      if (sp <= 60)
            rate = 0.20;
```

e.
```
if (sp >= 40 && sp <= 60)
      rate = 0.20;
```

6.1.3 THREE-LEVEL DECISION STRUCTURES

If C allows a two-level decision structure, it is a fair guess that a three-level structure is possible. Example 6.1.5 illustrates such a structure.

Example 6.1.5

Let us add one more feature to the program in Example 6.1.3. The program already responds with an error message when a user enters an incorrect qualification code. However, it would be more user-friendly if it also specified exactly what was entered incorrectly, as shown in the following examples:

```
Enter the contractor's qualification code > x45
The code is INVALID
The secretarial expertise 'x' does not exist.

Enter the contractor's qualification code > M17
The code is INVALID
The typing speed is too low.

Enter the contractor's qualification code > M173
The code is INVALID
The typing speed is unrealistic.
```

Following is the program (the top part is the same as in Example 6.1.3, so it is not repeated here):

```
if ((ex_up == 'M' || ex_up == 'L') && (sp >= 40 && sp <= 120))1
{
     /* Ask for the information */

     printf("Enter the day worked (Sunday = 1, Monday = 2, etc) > ");
     scanf("%d", &day);
     printf("Enter the number of hours > ");
     scanf("%d", &hours);

     /* Figure out the rate of pay, given the information */

     rate = 12.39
     if (ex_up == 'M')2
     {
            rate = rate + rate * 0.15;
     }
     if (sp >= 40 && sp <= 59)
     {
            rate = rate - rate * 0.10;
     }
     if (sp >= 100 && sp <= 120)
     {
            rate = rate + rate * 0.18;
     }

     /* Calculate the pay */

     if (day >= 2 && day <= 6)
     {
            pay = rate * hours;
     }
     else
     {
            pay = rate * 1.5 * hours;
     }
     printf("The pay is %.2f\n", pay);
}
else
{
     printf("The code is INVALID\n");
     if (ex_up != 'M' && ex_up != 'L')2
{
     printf("The secretarial expertise '%c' does not exist.", ex);4
}
else
{
     if (sp < 40)3
     {
          printf("The typing speed is too low.");
     }
     else
     {
          printf("The typing speed is unrealistic.");
     }
}
}
```

Explanations

This program clearly contains three levels of *if/else*s.

1. Level 1 starts here.
2. Indicates level 2 *if/else* constructs.
3. Level 3 starts here.
4. Take a second look at the first run of the program. The letter 'x' appears in lowercase, the same case in which it was read, even though the program converted the 'x' to an uppercase letter with the *toupper()* function. The trick is simply a matter of using the variable *ex* rather than *ex_up* to display the letter.

EXERCISES 6.1.6

1. In the code in Example 6.1.5, should there not be a test for *(sp > 120)* as well?

```
if (sp < 40)
{
    printf("The typing speed is too low.");
}
else if (sp > 120)
{
    printf("The typing speed is unrealistic.");
}
```

2. The program in Example 6.1.5 has one serious flaw. To discover the flaw, find out what message the program will display for the following input, where both entries are invalid:

   Enter the contractor's qualification code > H143

   Both entries are invalid, yet the program flags an error for only one of them. Modify the code so that both error messages will appear when both entries are wrong.
3. Add code to the program of Example 6.1.5 so that it checks that the entry for the day is between 1 and 7, inclusive. If the day is invalid, the program will quit immediately after explaining the reason.
4. What will be displayed by this nested *if/else* structure?

```
if (num == 5)
{
      printf("writer");
      if (num == 1)
             printf("poet");
      else
             printf("singer");
}
else
{
      if (num != 5)
      {
             printf("biologist");
             if (num < 10)
                    printf("professor");
             else
                    printf("researcher");
      }
      else
      {
             printf("CIA agent");

      }
}
```

a. Given that, what is displayed when *num* contains 5? When *num* contains 2? When *num* contains 12?
b. Some portions of the code are redundant. Simplify this nested *if/else* structure.

5. Improve the invalidity message of Exercise 6.1.2, 5, so that the error message pertaining to the range of number of children is made more precise. If the number is below 0, the message will be "This number of children is impossible." If it is above 12, the message will be "This number of children is too high."
6. Modify the program in (5) further. After the data have been validated, the program will ask if the person has a spouse. If so, it will ask for the initials, but not the gender, for it will assume that the spouse is of the opposite gender. If the person has no spouse, the final message will include the verb *has;* otherwise, the message will use *have.* (Also note the gender in the final prompt for input below):

```
What are your initials? DXJ
Are you a male or a female? (m=male, f=female) m
How many children do you have? 2
Do you have a spouse? (y/n) y
What are her initials? KPM

Mr. DXJ and Ms. KPM have 2 children.
```

6.1.4 N-LEVEL DECISION STRUCTURES

Example 6.1.6

Blackjack is a card game in which a player is dealt two playing cards initially. The object is to gather cards with face values that add up to a number that is as close to 21 as possible without going over. Players may ask to be dealt up to three additional cards before finishing a hand.

Write a program to simulate this game. For the purposes of this program, a player will be able to draw no more than three cards in all, and face cards will have the following values: jack = 11, queen = 12, king = 13. An ace = 1. Here are two examples of program runs:

```
Do you want a card ? (y/n) y
The card drawn is an 8
Do you want another card ? (y/n) y
The card drawn is a 13
Do you want another card ? (y/n) n

You totalled 21. Congratulations!
```

```
Do you want a card ? (y/n) y
The card drawn is a 1
Do you want another card ? (y/n) y
The card drawn is a 12
Do you want another card ? (y/n) y
The card drawn is a 9

You totalled 22. Too high!
```

The user is given the choice of drawing one, two, three, or no cards at all. (Drawing no cards should be an option in any computer game to accommodate someone who decides not to play after all!) Assume the replies are always given in lowercase letters. Following is the code, along with an explanation:

```
#include <stdio.h>
#include <stdlib.h>
main()
{
    int      card1, card2, card3;
    char     answer;

    printf("Do you want a card ? (y/n) ");
```

```
    scanf("\n%c", &answer);

    card1 = 0;                          /* assume the answer is no */
    if (answer == 'y')
    {
        card1 = rand() % 13 + 1;        /* generate a card randomly */
        printf("The card drawn is a %d\n", card1);
        if (answer == 'y')              /* ask for a second card ONLY */
        {                               /* if a first card was accepted */
            printf("Do you want another card ? (y/n) ");
            scanf("\n%c", &answer);
            card2 = 0;                  /* assume the answer is no */
            if (answer == 'y')
            {
                card2 = rand() % 13 + 1;    /* generate a card randomly */
                printf("The card drawn is a %d\n", card2);
                if (answer == 'y')      /* ask for a third card ONLY */
                {                       /* if a second card was accepted */
                    printf("Do you want another card ? (y/n) ");
                    scanf("\n%c", &answer);
                    card3 = 0;          /* assume the answer is no */
                    if (answer == 'y')
                    {
                        card3 = rand() % 13 + 1;    /* generate a card */
                        printf("The card drawn is a %d\n", card3);
                    }
                }
            }
        }
    }
    printf("You totalled %d. ", card1 + card2 + card3);
    if (card1 + card2 + card3 < 21)
    {
        printf("Too low!");
    }
    else if (card1 + card2 + card3 > 21)
    {
        printf("Too high!");
    }
    else
    {
        printf("Congratulations!");
    }
}
```

Talk about a long sequence of *if*s—five in a row with the condition *answer == 'y'*. Yet all of them are necessary; if the user answers "no" to any question, all of the subsequent questions and displays should be skipped. The test *answer == 'y'* is performed each time the question "Do you want another card? (y/n)" is posed.

Suppose the game was modified to allow drawing up to 10 additional cards. This means that the sequence of *if*s would need to be 10 long! Luckily, there is a way around this: code a ***loop*** in which the testing of the answer is coded only once. (Sadly, loops are not covered until Chapter 7.)

Note also the code that generates the card numbers:

```
card1 = rand() % 13 + 1
```

The function *rand()* returns a ***random*** integer number that is anywhere from 0 to RAND_MAX, which is at least INT_MAX (see Subsection 3.1.3 for this symbolic constant). So then the expression would evaluate as either of the two examples in Figure 6.1.5.

Figure 6.1.5

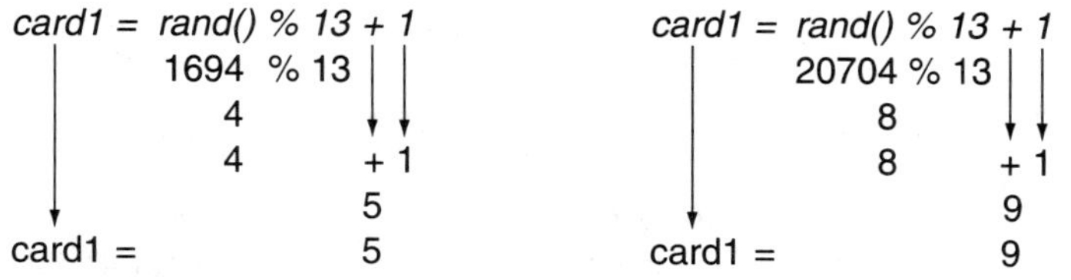

The line *#include <stdlib.h>* must be typed in whenever this *rand()* function is used. This function is often used in computer games of all sorts. Note the use of the remainder operator. The random function cannot be used alone to generate random card numbers between 1 and 13, inclusive, because the range of numbers it generates would be too large. The remainder operator ensures that the range of numbers is reduced to 0 to 12, inclusive. For example:

0 % 13 returns 0	1 % 13 returns 1	2 % 13 returns 2
3 % 13 returns 3	4 % 13 returns 4	5 % 13 returns 5
6 % 13 returns 6	7 % 13 returns 7	8 % 13 returns 8
9 % 13 returns 9	10 % 13 returns 10	11 % 13 returns 11
12 % 13 returns 12		
13 % 13 returns 0	14 % 13 returns 1	15 % 13 returns 2
16 % 13 returns 3	17 % 13 returns 4	18 % 13 returns 5
19 % 13 returns 6	20 % 13 returns 7	21 % 13 returns 8
22 % 13 returns 9	23 % 13 returns 10	24 % 13 returns 11
25 % 13 returns 12		
26 % 13 returns 0	27 % 13 returns 1	
28 % 13 returns 2	29 % 13 returns 3	

EXERCISES 6.1.7

1. Although the logic of the two programs below seems similar, they produce different results. Explain.

   a.
```
int  card;

card = rand();
if (card == 1)
{
     printf("Ho! Got an ace\n");
}
else if (card >= 11 && card <= 13)
{
     printf("Lucky! Got a face card\n");
}
else
{

     printf("You got the number %d\n", card);
}
```

   b.
```
if (rand() == 1)
{
     printf("Ho! Got an ace\n");
}
else if (rand() >= 11 && rand() <= 13)
{
     printf("Lucky! Got a face card\n");
}
```

```
else
{
    printf("You got the number %d\n", rand());
}
```

2. Change the embedding of the *if* statements in Example 6.1.6 to a sequence of *if* statements.
3. Improve the program in question 2 further. As of now, nothing prevents the user from drawing a card unnecessarily. For example, the following run allows the user to draw another card even though the player already has blackjack (21 points).

   Do you want a card ? (y/n) y
   The card drawn is an 8
   Do you want another card ? (y/n) y
   The card drawn is a 13
   Do you want another card ? (y/n) y
   The card drawn is a 9

   You totalled 30. Too high!

   At any time, when the total is either greater than or equal to 21, or greater, make the program quit instead of asking the question.
4. A final modification: The user is allowed to refuse to play the game by not drawing any cards. Unfortunately the program still gives a total:

   Do you wish a card ? (y/n) n

   You totalled 0. Too low!

   Change the program so that it skips absolutely everything when the user does not draw any cards.
5. Using the program below, show that an *if/else* chain is nothing more than a special form of a multilevel *if/else* structure. (***Hint:*** Show that this program is logically the same as an *if/else* chain solution of it.)

```
#include <stdio.h>

main()
{
    char civil_code;

    printf("Enter the individual's civil code: ");
    scanf("\n%c", &civil_code);

    if (civil_code == 'M' || civil_code == 'm')
    {
        printf("Individual is married.");
    }
    else
    {
        if (civil_code == 'S' || civil_code == 's')
        {
            printf("Individual is single.");
        }
        else
        {
            if (civil_code == 'W' || civil_code == 'w')
            {
                printf("Individual is widowed.");
            }
        }
    }
}
```

6. Improve the program in Exercise 5.1.7, 7, further. If the difference is less than $14,000, do as before, but if the difference is greater than or equal to $14,000, and if the financing is less than 7% for exactly four years, then buy. If the financing is equal to or more than 7%, then buy only if it is for less than three years; otherwise do not buy. Use nested *if/else*s or simple *if* statements.
7. Improve the program in Exercise 5.1.7, 6, so that if the program finds an input data outside the acceptable range, it will flag an error and quit immediately. Use embedded *if/else*s.
8. Improve the program in question 6 above so that if the program finds invalid input data, it will flag an error and quit immediately. Use embedded *if/else*s.
9. Improve the program in Exercise 5.1.1, 4, so that if the program finds an error in the unit of measure, it will flag an error and quit immediately. Use embedded *if/else*s.
10. In the program in Exercise 5.1.7, 8, use nested *if/else*s instead of an *if/else* chain.
11. Modify the program in Exercise 5.3.1, 5, so that the program terminates as soon as it finds data out of range.
12. Modify the program in Exercise 5.3.1, 6, so that the program terminates as soon as it finds data out of range.
13. Modify the program in Exercise 5.1.1, 4, so that the program terminates as soon as it finds data out of range.
14. Modify the program in Exercise 5.1.7, 9, so that the program terminates as soon as it finds data out of range. The ranges are as follows:

Data	**Range**
Terminal code	At least 2 digits, but no more than 4 digits
Operator code	At least 3 digits, but no more than 8 digits
Weight of meat	0 to 15 pounds
Type of meat	G, g, S, s, C, c, F, f
Cost of dairy products	$0 to $200
Cost of cereal products	$0 to $100
Cost of desserts	$0 to $60
Money received	$0 to $600

15. In the program above, when a 0 is entered for the Cost of desserts field, for example, the slip still lists

```
Desserts          $ 0.00
```

Of course, when none was bought, nothing should be listed. Modify the program so that only the items bought will show on the slip.

16. Improve the program from Exercise 5.1.7, 5, so that the gender of the person is taken into account:
    a. The prompts refer to "his" or "her."
    b. The letter addresses "Ms." for a woman and "Mr." for a man.
    c. The user enters "Mr." for a male and "Ms." for a female.

    A run might look like this:

```
Enter the student's initials > Mr. JPC
                 his average > 78
            his physics mark > 81

Dear Mr. JPC:

We are sorry to inform you that your average of 78 and your physics mark of 81 have not met
our requirements.

Try again!
                                                        Ms. Principal
```

17. Improve the above program so that the letter differs depending on the context:
    a. If the student is accepted, the letter should emphasize the accomplishment and downplay the lower grade, if there is one. A grade is considered too low if it is less than 70.
    b. If the student is rejected, the letter should explain why and emphasize an accomplishment, if there is one. An accomplishment is a score of more than 79.

c. A score between 80 and 89, inclusive, will receive the qualifier "good"; a score between 90 and 95, inclusive, will receive the qualifier "very good"; a score of more than 95 will receive the qualifier "excellent."

d. The verb *have* will be conjugated as "has" or "have," to agree with the subject.

Following are some possible runs of this program:

```
Enter the student's initials > Ms. TRH
                 her average > 54
           her physics mark > 96

Dear Ms. TRH:

We are pleased to inform you that your excellent physics mark of 96 has met our
requirements.

          Welcome!
                                                        Ms. Principal

Enter the student's initials > Mr. JPC
                 his average > 92
           his physics mark > 51

Dear Mr. JPC:

We are pleased to inform you that your very good average of 92 has met our requirements.

          Welcome!
                                                        Ms. Principal

Enter the student's initials > Mr. CXL
                 his average > 63
           his physics mark > 51

Dear Mr. CXL:

We are sorry to inform you that your average of 63 and your physics mark of 51 have not met
our requirements.

Try again!
                                                        Ms. Principal

Enter the student's initials > Mr. HHF
                 his average > 97
           his physics mark > 40

Dear Ms. HHF:

We are sorry to inform you that your physics mark of 40 has not met our requirements,
despite your excellent average of 97.

Try again!
                                                        Ms. Principal
```

18. Modify the program in question 11 so that it also gives a choice for displaying the date. For example:

```
Enter the day (1 to 31) > 7
Enter the month (1 to 12) > 1
Enter the year (1900 to 1999 > 18

How do you wish to display the date?
(a)  Verbalized
```

(b) DD/MM/YY
(c) MM/DD/YY
(d) DD-MMM-YY
(e) MMM-DD-YY
Enter selection > d

The date is 07-Jan-18

Enter the day (1 to 31) > 19
Enter the month (1 to 12) > 26

The month is out of range

6.1.5 COMMON ERRORS AND TRAPS

Do not forget either an opening brace or closing brace. The following errors are quite easy to make, and even easier if you do not indent the blocks of statements. The compiler will definitely flag an error. However, these examples show that the actual nature of the error message differs depending on where the brace is missing. What is the meaning of each error message below?

1.
```
if (n1 > n2)
{
        if (n1 > n3)
        {
                max = n1;
        }
        else
        {
                max = n3;
}
```

The error message flagged here would be "Compound statement missing a }."

2.
```
if (a == b)
{
        if (a > 6)
        {
                a = 6;
        else
        {
                a = a + 1;
        }
}
```

The error message flagged here would be "Misplaced *else.*"

3.
```
if (n1 > n2)
{
        if (n1 > n3)
        {
                max = n1;
        }
        else
                max = n3;
        }
}
```

The error message flagged here would be "Unexpected }."

SUPPLEMENTARY EXERCISES 6.1

1. Write a program to simulate the logical process a car driver must go through in order to decide whether or not to cross an intersection. Clearly, if the light is green, he crosses. If he wishes to turn left, he may do so only if no car is coming on the cross street. If the light is red, he stops, and then waits for the greenlight unless he is in the right lane and wishes to turn right. Following are examples of results this program might produce:

   What is the color of the light? (r=red, g=green) r
   Are you in the right lane? (y/n) y
   Do you plan on turning right? (y/n) y

   You may turn right.

   What is the color of the light? (r=red, g=green) r
   Are you in the right lane? (y/n) y
   Do you plan on turning right? (y/n) n

   You must wait for the green light.

   What is the color of the light? (r=red, g=green) g
   Are you in the right lane? (y/n) y

   You may cross the intersection or turn right.

2. How would you need to modify the program to take into account pedestrians?
3. Write a program that plays a guessing game in which the computer randomly generates a number between 1 and 52; each number represents a card in the deck. The player is allowed three guesses. If a guess is too high or too low, the program will display a message with that information. Of course, as soon as the player finds the number, the program quits. Running the program might produce one of the following displays:

   I selected my number. Try to guess.
   Guess #1 >> 41
   Too high
   Guess #2 >> 22
   Too low
   Guess #3 >> 30
   Too high

   Sorry! The number was 28

   Guess #1 >> 41
   Too low
   Guess #2 >> 45
   Right on!

4. Improve the program in question 3 to allow the player to quit guessing at any time:

   I selected my number. Try to guess. Enter –1 to quit.
   Guess #1 >> 41
   Too high
   Guess #2 >> –1

   Chicken!

5. Improve this program further. If the player enters –1, the program will ask for confirmation. Also, the program will interpret the player quitting at the first guess as the player not wanting to play after all. The program will then issue a different message. Following are examples of what a programmer might see after running the program:

   I selected my number. Try to guess. Enter –1 to quit.
   Guess #1 >> 41
   Too high
   Guess #2 >> –1
   Are you sure you want to give up (y/n) y

   Chicken!

```
I selected my number. Try to guess. Enter –1 to quit.
Guess #1 >> –1
Are you sure you do not want to play (y/n) y

Maybe next time!

I selected my number. Try to guess. Enter –1 to quit.
Guess #1 >> 41
Too high
Guess #2 >> –1
Are you sure you want to give up (y/n) n
Guess #2 >> 8
Too high
Guess #3 >> 2
Right on!
```

6. Example 4.3.1 asks the user to enter the minimum acceptable income. The algorithm indicated that this number is arrived at based on Judy's school expenses. No specific information was given about those expenses, however. Now let's look at the expenses in more detail.

   The minimum income is the amount that covers all expenses, with no surplus. Suppose the average of all expenses at a state university is $5,499. Students also may apply for financing from the government to augment their minimum income. The average cost of expenses increases due to the following factors:

   - If the student goes to a college in California or New York, the basic cost increases by 9%; otherwise the costs increase by 3%.
   - If the student is enrolled in science or engineering, the cost increases a further 5%; otherwise there is no further increase.

   Note that these increase apply to the basic costs. Assume that the student always takes residence in the city where the college is located. Here is how the program will interact with the user now:

```
Questions on expenses:
   Where is the college: (C)alifornia, (N)ew York, or (O)ther? > C
   Are you enrolled in (S)cience, (E)ngineering, or (O)ther? > O
Questions on income:
   Did you apply for financing? (y/n) y
   How much will you receive? 4100
   Enter the hourly wage > 7.05
   Enter the total work hours per week > 35
   Enter the number of weeks of work > 10

Advice:
   Take the job!
   You will make $ 2467.50 this summer
```

   The expenses will increase by $5499 × 9% = $494.91 because the school is in California. So the expenses will be $5499 + $494.91 = $5993.91. This also represents the minimum income acceptable. The actual income will be: $4100 + $2467.50 = $6567.50. Since this is greater than the minimum income required to cover the expenses, the student is advised to take the job.

   Make the necessary modifications to the program to create the output shown above.

7. The factors above did not explain what causes the increases. Let's itemize the expenses. The expenses consist of college fees, the cost of books, the rent, and the cost of food. Modify the program above, given this more precise description of the factors:

   - If the student goes to a college in California or New York, the college fees increase by 13%, the rent goes up by 23%, and the cost of food goes down by 19%; otherwise the cost of food goes up by 13%.
   - If the student is enrolled in science or engineering, the cost of books increases by 18% and the fees increase by an extra 14%.

   You will need a variable for each of the four types of cost. Also these increases are from the state averages of $1,451 for the college fees, $2,380 for the rent, $399 for the books, and $1,269 for the food, for a total of $5,499. To illustrate how the increases affect the expenses, let us go through the calculations with the run example from the previous question:

   - The fees are increased by $1451 × 13% = $188.63.
   - The rent is increased by $2380 × 23% = $547.40.

- The food costs are decreased by \$1269 × 19% = \$241.11.
- The overall increase is \$188.63 + \$547.40 \$241.11 = \$494.92. (***Note:*** This number does not quite match the increase in expenses of \$494.91 from question 6. This is due to percentages that were rounded off).

So the expenses will be \$5499 + \$494.92 = \$5993.92. This represents the minimum income acceptable. The actual income will be: \$4100 + \$2467.50 = \$6567.50. Since this is greater than the minimum income, the student is advised to take the job.

Make the modifications necessary to the program to calculate the changes in expenses. Note that the changes are all internal. The screen display does not change.

6.2 DEBUGGING AND TESTING PROGRAMS

After having fixed all of the syntax errors in a program, you will still find that it rarely runs according to plan the first time. In fact, there exists a rule of thumb among programmers: If a program works the first time that it is run, there must be a bug in it!

You certainly realize by now that multiple levels of decision structures in a program increase its complexity, manyfold and the complexity of testing it, manyfold. Thus, the development of a program must be methodical and the testing must follow the same principles. This advice should be taken even more seriously with C programming because the compiler helps very little in detecting errors (as was explained in Section 1.4 and illustrated many times in Chapter 2 with the bizarre "mood swings" of *printf()*s and *scanf()*s!).

Anyone—especially a software company—worries at the thought of releasing a software product that may fail under certain circumstances. Consequently, in the real world much software development time (as much as 50%) is spent on debugging and testing. This is time well spent because an improperly tested program may leave a few bugs that are extremely difficult to detect but may cause disastrous failures.

At this point it should be made clear that ***debugging*** a program means investigating what causes it to malfunction, whereas ***testing*** a program means verifying whether it works as intended or not. If it does not, then debugging takes place, and the program is retested. The goal of testing is to eventually prove beyond any doubt that the program works by running it with carefully selected test data. The purpose of this section is to illustrate the concepts mentioned here and to guide you toward applicability.

In contrast to the above approach, novice (and not-so-novice) programmers often form the following bad habits that drive them into debugging before testing:

1. They put codes together with no clear planning or understanding of the situation. Good problem-solving skills (as briefly covered in Section 1.2) would help here.
2. They run the program **before** they have sufficient reason to believe it may work.
3. Consequently, they obtain the wrong results.
4. They go back to the program and change a few things, often blindly, because they do not have an understanding of the meaning of the wrong results. (In C, the cause of wrong results may be quite subtle, as you'll see in Subsection 6.2.1.)
5. As a result, the behavior of the program gets worse.
6. Frustration sets in!

6.2.1 DEBUGGING A PROGRAM

Let us now discuss how to debug a program, since this procedure is simpler than testing. Students often struggle when trying to find a bug (and its cause) in their program. They assume that the bug must be due to wrong logic in a decision structure or a group of them. It seems to be a natural tendency to check there. However, in C a bug may lurk in places that one rarely thinks about. For instance, a bug may be caused by:

1. An operator mistyping
2. Missing braces
3. Data type conflict
4. The wrong location of data in I/O operations such as a *printf()* or a *scanf()*

Most compilers are smart enough to automatically "kill" type 3 and 4 bugs, but not C! This chapter (and Chapters 2 and 3) pointed out many of these last two kinds of bugs. This subsection includes three examples that illustrate how to locate bugs. There are three general approaches to debugging: backward debugging, forward debugging, and using *printf()*s to debug a program. We will look at examples of debugging using each method.

Backward debugging. The example below illustrates backward debugging.

Example 6.2.1

One tiny little bug has been inserted in the program below taken from Example 6.1.3:

```
#include <stdio.h>
#include <ctype.h>

main()
{
    int     hours, sp;
    char    day, ex, ex_up;
    float   pay, rate;

    printf("Enter the contractor's qualification code > ");
    scanf("\n%c%d", &ex, &sp);
    ex_up = toupper(ex);

    if ((ex_up == 'M' || ex_up == 'L') && (sp >= 40 && sp <= 120))
    {
        /* Ask for the information */
        printf("Enter the day worked (Sunday = 1, Monday = 2, etc) > ");
        scanf("%d", &day);
        printf("Enter the number of hours > ");
        scanf("%d", &hours);

        /* Figure out the rate of pay, given the information */

        rate = 12.39;
        if (ex_up == 'M')
        {
            rate = rate + rate * 0.15;   /* increase by 15% */
        }
        if (sp >= 40 && sp <= 59)
        {
            rate = rate - rate * 0.10;
        }
        if (sp >= 100 && sp <= 120)
        {
            rate = rate + rate * 0.18;
        }

        /* Calculate the pay */

        if (day >= 2 && day <= 6)
        {
            pay = rate * hours;
        }
        else
        {
            pay = rate * 1.5 * hours;
        }
        printf("The pay is %.2d\n", pay);
```

```
        }
        else
        {
            printf("The code is INVALID");
        }
}
```

When you run the program, you obtain:

Enter the contractor's qualification code > L79
Enter the day worked (Sunday = 1, Monday = 2, etc) > 6
Enter the number of hours > 4
The pay is 00

A pay of $0! In debugging, the tendency of many programmers seems to be to carefully verify the logic of the nested *if/elses*. Although there could be something wrong there, a more successful procedure is to trace back the logic step-by-step **backward:**

1. Verify the *printf()* that displayed the erroneous data.
2. If that function call is correct, check the instruction that was performed just before it.
3. If that instruction is correct, check the instruction that was performed just before it.
4. Repeat step 3 until you find the bug.

This way, you will immediately see that the error is in the *printf():*

```
printf("The pay is %.2d\n", pay);
```

The expression %.2d\n should have been typed as %.2f\n.

Forward debugging: Garbage in, garbage out! Most importantly, the backward debugging procedure should be preceded by a check of the *scanf()* that reads the data. If it failed, the data read in it is likely wrong, which would certainly lead to bad output. Remember this principle: garbage in, garbage out. It is quite simple to verify if a *scanf()* reads data correctly: it is only a matter of placing a *printf()*, which displays this data immediately after the *scanf()*.

Insert debugging *printf()*s here and there. The two examples below will serve to illustrate this method.

Example 6.2.2

Suppose that the temporary secretary agency of Example 6.1.3 now services schools. The letter code 'S' is given to secretaries assigned to schools. Suppose further that these secretaries are paid exactly the same wages as medical secretaries. The new program simply takes this new code into account:

```
#include <stdio.h>
#include <ctype.h>

main()
{
    int     hours, sp;
    char    day, ex_up;
    float   pay, rate;

    printf("Enter the contractor's qualification code > ");
    scanf("\n%c%d", &ex, &sp);
    ex_up = toupper(ex);

    if ((ex_up == 'M' || ex_up == 'L' || ex_up == 'S') &&
        (sp >= 40 && sp <= 120))
    {
       /* Ask for the information */

       printf("Enter the day worked (Sunday = 1, Monday = 2, etc) > ");
```

```
        scanf("%d", &day);
        printf("Enter the number of hours > ");
        scanf("%d", &hours);

        /* Figure out the rate of pay, given the information */

        rate = 12.39;
        if (ex_up == 'M' || ex_up = 'S')
        {
            rate = rate + rate * 0.15;  /* increase by 15% */
        }
        if (sp >= 40 && sp <= 59)
        {
            rate = rate - rate * 0.10;
        }
        else if (sp >= 100 && sp <= 120)
        {
            rate = rate + rate * 0.18;
        }

        /* Calculate the pay */

        if (day >= 2 && day <= 6)
        {
            pay = rate * hours;
        }
        else
        {
            pay = rate * 1.5 * hours;
        }
        printf("The pay is %.2f\n", pay);
    }
    else
    {
        printf("The code is INVALID\n");
    }
}
```

When you run the program, you obtain:

Enter the contractor's qualification code > L79
Enter the day worked (Sunday = 1, Monday = 2, etc) > 6
Enter the number of hours > 4
The pay is 56.99

The program seems fine, and so does the output, but: The pay should be \$12.39 x 4 = \$49.56, yet we got \$56.99! Since the *printf()* is now correct, verify the instructions before it. Instead of checking only one of them at the time, it is faster to check many of them by inserting *printf()* debugging statements in the locations where there is a ***potential for action,*** in particular where variables have a ***potential of changing values.*** The debugging *printf()*s are shown in bold in Figure 6.2.1.

Figure 6.2.1

```
printf("Enter the contractor's qualification code > ");
scanf("\n%c%d", &ex, &sp);
printf("Debugging: ex = %c, sp = %d\n", ex, sp);     /* check the input */
ex_up = toupper(ex);

if ((ex_up == 'M' || ex_up == 'L' || ex_up == 'S') &&
   (sp >= 40 && sp <= 120))
{
   /* Ask for the information */
```

```
    printf("Enter the day worked (Sunday = 1, Monday = 2, etc) > ");
    scanf("%d", &day);
    printf("Enter the number of hours > ");
    scanf("%d", &hours);
    printf("Debugging: day = %d, hours = %d\n", day, hours);     /* check */
                                                                  /* input */
    /* Figure out the rate of pay, given the information */
    rate = 12.39;
    if (ex_up == 'M' || ex_up = 'S')
    {
        rate = rate + rate * 0.15;   /* increase by 15% */
    }
    printf("Debugging: rate = %f\n", rate);              /* check the logic */
    if (sp >= 40 && sp <= 59)
    {
        rate = rate - rate * 0.10;
        printf("Debugging: rate = %f\n", rate);          /* check the logic */
      }
      else if (sp >= 100 && sp <= 120)
      {
        rate = rate + rate * 0.18;
        printf("Debugging: rate = %f\n", rate);          /* check the logic */
    }
    /* Calculate the pay */

    if (day >= 2 && day <= 6)
    {
        pay = rate * hours;
    }
    else
    {
        pay = rate * 1.5 * hours;
    }
    printf("The pay is %.2f\n", pay);
}
else
{
    printf("The code is INVALID\n");
}
```

After running the program again, you will see the following display. Note that the debugging information on the second and fifth lines show that the data are read correctly.

Enter the contractor's qualification code > L79
Debugging: ex = L, sp = 79
Enter the day worked (Sunday = 1, Monday = 2, etc) > 6
Enter the number of hours > 4
Debugging: day = 6, hours = 4
Debugging: rate = 14.248500
Debugging: rate = 14.248500
Debugging: rate = 14.248500
The pay is 56.99

Notice also that on the sixth line, the rate was changed after the *if* statement that checked the expertise. This was not supposed to happen. After a closer look, we find an error in the composite condition:

```
if (ex_up == 'M' || ex_up = 'S')
```

The single = symbol should be two = symbols. Remember you learned in Section 4.1.4; *Common Errors and Traps,* that in this case the condition is always evaluated as true. The evaluation of the statement is shown in Figure 6.2.2.

Figure 6.2.2

```
ex_up == 'M'  ||  ex_up = 'S'
    'L' == 'M'
     false
              ||  ex_up = 'M'
                      true
     false    ||      true
            true
```

The composite condition will always evaluate to true. That is the problem—it will always cause the rate of pay to be increased by 15%.

Example 6.2.3

Refer back to Example 4.2.2. The teacher was the victim of an obscure bug. The procedure that he followed to solve it was akin to the one shown above:

1. The message "The boy went faster than last year's record." was not supposed to display when the student's time was slower than the record.
2. He verified the formula *distance / time* within the condition by inserting a debugging *printf( ).*
3. Nothing wrong was revealed.
4. In this case this was because not enough decimal digits were shown. Once this was changed, the bug was revealed.

For most of us, the debugging procedures illustrated in this subsection suffice. For much larger programs, this method may not guarantee that all bugs will be found. For this reason, software development companies usually rely on more formal methods of testing and debugging. Many of those are too complex to discuss here, so the next two subsections will only present the simplest concepts in the techniques of testing.

6.2.2 BUILDING A SET OF TEST DATA

As mentioned before, testing should be done before debugging. Fortunately, the principle behind testing the logic of a program (of any magnitude of complexity) is simple: every logical path must be tested. This implies that the set of test data must allow the program to run through every single logical path that exists. Every *if/else* or *if* statement creates two logical paths: one path for when the condition is true, the other for when the condition is false. Each must be tested. (Analogy: Every component of a new car must be proven to work before the car is released to a dealer.) To illustrate, let us look back at two examples from Section 6.1.

Example 6.2.4

Here is the *if/else* structure for Example 6.1.1:

```
if (isalpha(ch))
{
     if (islower(ch))
     {
          printf("Lowercase");
     }
     else
     {
          printf("Uppercase");
     }
}
else
```

```
{
     printf("It is not a letter");
}
```

The outer *if/else* creates two logical paths: one leads to the inner *if/else,* the other displays the message "It is not a letter." The inner *if/else* also creates two logical paths: the first one displays the message "Lowercase," the other displays the message "Uppercase." Each path leads to an action of displaying some message. Of course, which path is taken is determined by the conditions. The tree in Figure 6.2.3 illustrates all possible logical paths.

Figure 6.2.3

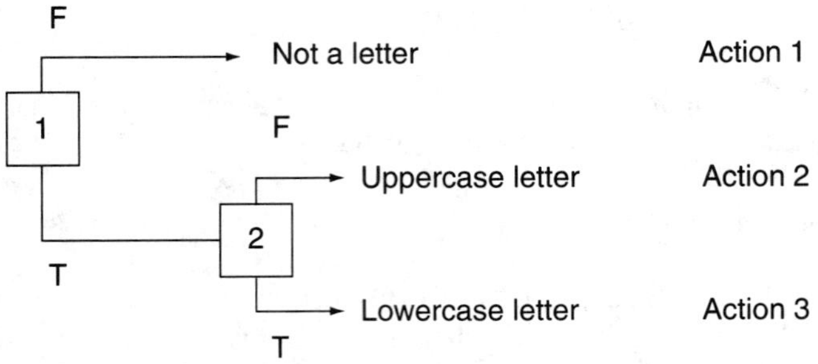

where

1 refers to the condition *if (isalpha())*
2 refers to the condition *if (islower())*
F stands for the condition being false
T stands for the condition being true

There are three paths leading to three actions; therefore, there needs to be three test data. Which ones?

1. Action 1 is reached if condition 1 is false, i.e., when *isalpha()* is false. Therefore test data 1 will be a character other than a letter.
2. Action 2 is reached if condition 1 is true **and** if condition 2 is false, i.e., when *islower()* is false. So test data 2 will be an uppercase letter.
3. Action 3 is reached if condition 1 is true **and** if the condition 2 is true, i.e., when *islower()* is true. So test data 3 will be a lowercase letter.

Therefore, for example, the program could be tested with the following set of test data: @, U, k. It would be unnecessary to test the program any more than that, for we have proven that these three test data constitute a complete test.

Example 6.2.5

The method above is used here just as it was for Example 6.1.3. Here is the *if/else* structure again:

```
if ((ex == 'M' || ex == 'L') && (sp >= 40 && sp <= 120))
{
     /* Ask for the information */

     printf("Enter the day worked (Sunday = 1, Monday = 2, etc) > ");
     scanf("%d", &day);
     printf("Enter the number of hours > ");
     scanf("%d", &hours);

     /* Figure out the rate of pay, given the information */

     rate = 12.39;
     if (ex == 'M')
     {
          rate = rate + rate * 0.15;   /* increase by 15% */
     }
     if (sp >= 40 && sp <= 59)
```

```
        {
            rate = rate - rate * 0.10;
        }
        else if (sp >= 100 && sp <= 120)
        {
            rate = rate + rate * 0.18;
        }

        /* Calculate the pay */

        if (day >= 2 && day <= 6)
        {
            pay = rate * hours;
        }
        else
        {
            pay = rate * 1.5 * hours;
        }
        printf("The pay is %.2f\n", pay);
}
else
{
        printf("The code is INVALID\n");
}
```

Because this program is more complex, it has more paths and actions, so we will step through the method in tabular form. Thus you will be able to use the method to build a set of test data for any program.

Make a list of the conditions. Make a list of all of the conditions in the program along with the set of data that makes them true or false.

For example, in Table 6.2.1, condition 1 is false when *ex* is neither M nor L **and** below 40 or above 120.

Table 6.2.1

#	Condition of the *if* Statement	Set of Data			Path
		ex	*sp*	*day*	
1	(ex_up == 'M' || ex_up == 'L') && (sp >= 40 && sp <= 120)	M or L	40 to 120		true
		neither M nor L	below 40 or above 120		false
2	ex_up == 'M'	M			true
		not M			false
3	sp >= 40 && sp <= 59		40 to 59		true
			below 40 or above 59		false
4	sp >= 100 && sp <= 120		100 to 120		true
			below 100 or above 120		false
5	day >= 2 && day <= 6			2 to 6	true
				not within 2 and 6	false

Present all logical paths possible in the form of a tree. The tree for this example will depict the logical paths to the nine possible actions, as shown in Figure 6.2.4. The numbers refer to the conditions in Figure 6.2.4.

Figure 6.2.4

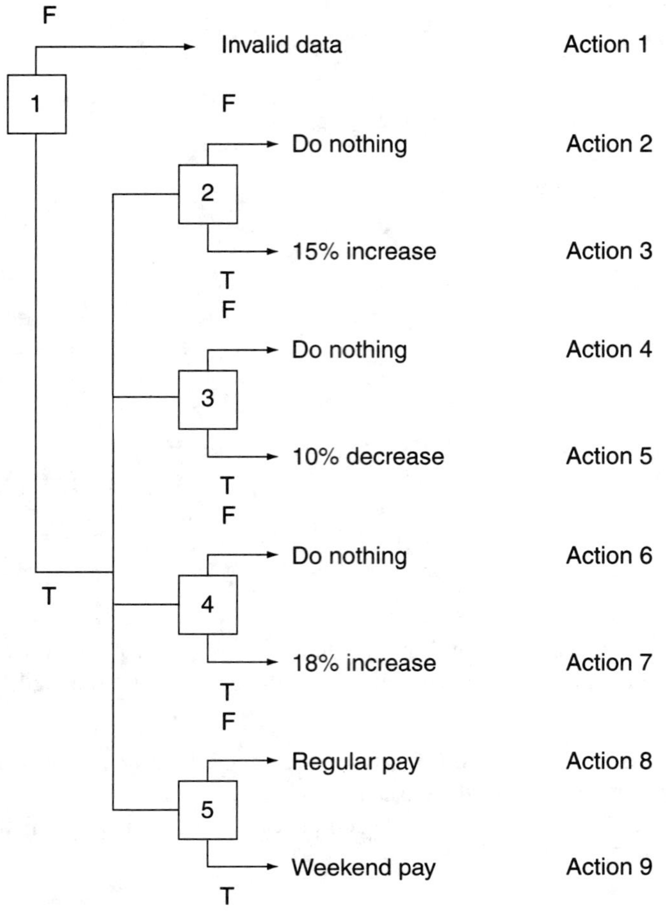

Determine the sets of test data that lead to each action. This step puts the previous two steps together. Again, this is best done in tabular form as shown in Table 6.2.2:

In the Logical Path column of the table, the notation *cd* stands for condition, *F* stands for false, and *T* stands for true. For example, cd 1 T, cd 2 F means the "logical path for which the condition 1 is true **and** condition 2 is false." This leads to action 2, as the tree shows. The notations in the Set of Values column serve to determine the data in the Test Data column that lead to a particular action. Take action 4: The logical path leading to it is cd 1 T, cd 3 F and the set of values that make the program follow that path are that the expertise must be 'M' or 'L' and the speed must be above 59 and no more than 120. Here is how this is so:

- For the *ex_up* variable, the logical path is cd 1 T. The set of values 'M' or 'L evaluates as "Condition 1 being true implies that the expertise must be 'M' or 'L.' "
- For *sp* variable, there are two logical paths. The first path logical path is cd 1 T and the set of values is 40 to 120. The other logical path is cd 3 F and the set of values is below 40 or above 59. The two paths can be evaluated as "condition 1 being true implies that the speed must be within 40 to 120 AND condition 3 being false implies that the speed must be below 40 OR above 59." Together these two conditions imply that the speed must be above 59 and no more than 120.

Select a test data to reach each action. The Test Data column lists the **set** of test data for each action. Only one member of each of these sets is needed for a test run. A sample of a set of test data for all nine actions is shown below:

	ex_up	*sp*	*day*
Test data for action 1	P	35	
Test data for action 2	L	60	

Test data for action 3	M	60	
Test data for action 4	M	100	
Test data for action 5	L	55	
Test data for action 6	L	82	
Test data for action 7	M	111	
Test data for action 8	M	71	1
Test data for action 9	L	71	5

It would be a good idea to test the program with lowercase letters as well, at least once, just to make sure that the function call *ex_up = toupper(ex)* works.

The above set of data constitutes a complete test. If the test is not successful, then either of the following is true:

1. Some condition in the table developed earlier is wrong.
2. Some logical path in the tree is wrong.

Table 6.2.2

Action	Logical Path	Set of Values *ex*	*sp*	*day*	Test Data
1	cd 1 F	– cd 1 F: neither M nor L	– cd 1 F: below 40 or above 120		any expertise other than m, M, l, or L speed below 40 or above 120
2	cd 1 T, cd 2 F	– cd 1 T: M or L – cd 2 F: not M	– cd 1 T: 40 to 120		expertise l or L speed within 40 and 120
3	cd 1 T, cd 2 T	– cd 1 T: M or L – cd 2 T: M	– cd 1 T: 40 to 120		expertise m or M speed within 40 and 120
4	cd 1 T, cd 3 F	– cd 1 T: M or L	– cd 1 T: 40 to 120 – cd 3 F: below 40 or above 59		expertise m, M, l, or L speed 60 to 120
5	cd 1 T, cd 3 T	– cd 1 T: M or L	– cd 1 T: 40 to 120 – cd 3 T: 40 to 59		expertise m, M, l, or L speed 40 to 59
6	cd 1 T, cd 4 F	– cd 1 T: M or L	– cd 1 T: 40 to 120 – cd 4 F: below 100 or above 120		expertise m, M, l, or L speed 40 to 99
7	cd 1 T, cd 4 T	– cd 1 T: M or L	– cd 1 T: 40 to 120 – cd 4 T: 100 to 120		expertise m, M, l, or L speed 100 to 120
8	cd 1 T, cd 5 F	– cd 1 T: M or L	– cd 1 T: 40 to 120	– cd 5 F: other than 2 to 6	expertise m, M, l, or L speed 40 to 120 day other than 2 to 6
9	cd 1 T, cd 5 T	– cd 1 T: M or L	– cd 1 T: 40 to 120	– cd 5 T: 2 to 6	expertise m, M, l, or L speed 40 to 120 day 2 to 6

If nothing is wrong there, then some other code is wrong. This could be any of the following:

3. A *printf()* or a *scanf()*
4. A mistyped operator
5. A data type conflict
6. A bug akin to UFO phenomenons!

EXERCISES 6.2.1

Apply the method of constructing the test data on the programs below:

1. Example 6.1.2
2. Example 6.1.5
3. Exercise 6.1.1, 1
4. Exercise 6.1.2, 2
5. Exercise 6.1.2, 5
6. Exercise 6.1.7, 6
7. Supplementary Exercise 6.1, 1
8. Supplementary Exercise 6.1, 5
9. Supplementary Exercise 6.1, 7
10. Exercise 6.1.7, 15
11. Exercise 6.1.7, 7
12. Exercise 6.1.7, 18

6.2.3 TESTING A PROGRAM

After the set of test data is chosen, it is run on the program to be tested. Let us look at some examples.

Example 6.2.6

In the case of Example 6.2.4, it is easy to tell if the program works. Indeed, here are the three runs fed with the set of test data:

```
Enter a letter > @        Enter a letter > U     Enter a letter > k
It is not a letter        Uppercase              Lowercase
```

The display clearly shows that the program works. It is easy to see what logical path the program chose.

Example 6.2.7

If the set of test data for Example 6.2.5 was fed into the program, it would not immediately be apparent that the data had worked. The following examples show this problem.

```
Enter the contractor's qualification code > L79
Enter the day worked (Sunday = 1, Monday = 2, etc) > 6
Enter the number of hours > 4
The pay is 49.56

Enter the contractor's qualification code > m104
Enter the day worked (Sunday = 1, Monday = 2, etc) > 7
Enter the number of hours > 7
The pay is 176.54
```

The display does not show the entire logical path taken by the program, but it does show that the program went into condition 1. Nevertheless, a manual calculation of the pay for the first run ($4 \times 12.39 = 49.56$) strongly suggests that the program did not go into conditions 2 to 4. This implies that the program worked. Similarly a calculation by hand of the pay for the second run ($7 \times 12.39 \times 1.15 \times 1.18 \times 1.5 = 176.54$) strongly suggests that the program did go into conditions 2 to 4. This implies that the program worked.

This approach of testing by hand is nowhere near foolproof. When programs are very complex, it is not clear from the display alone what logical path the program took, and the calculations by hand may be complex. Following are two foolproof methods of testing a program.

Insert testing statements. In this method, the program code is slightly modified to help the testing as much as possible. In particular, the display from the run should somehow indicate the logical path it takes, in its entirety. To this end, there should be a *printf()* in every *if* and *else* to indicate to the tester whether or not the program went there.

Example 6.2.8

For instance, the following program shows (in bold) the places where testing *printf()*s could be inserted. Testing statements should also be inserted for all input operations and function calls, such as *toupper()*.

```
#include <stdio.h>
#include <ctype.h>

main()
{
    int     hours, sp;
    char    day, ex_up;
    float   pay, rate;

    printf("Enter the contractor's qualification code > ");
    scanf("\n%c%d", &ex, &sp);
    printf("Testing: ex = %c, sp = %d\n", ex, sp);
    ex_up = toupper(ex);
    printf("Testing: ex_up = %c, sp = %d\n", ex_up, sp);

    if ((ex_up == 'M' || ex_up == 'L') && (sp >= 40 && sp <= 120))
    {
        /* Ask for the information */

        printf("Enter the day worked (Sunday = 1, Monday = 2, etc) > ");
        scanf("%d", &day);
        printf("Enter the number of hours > ");
        scanf("%d", &hours);
        printf("Testing: day = %d, hours = %d\n", day, hours);

        /* Figure out the rate of pay, given the information */

        rate = 12.39;
        if (ex_up == 'M')
        {
            rate = rate + rate * 0.15;  /* increase by 15% */
            printf("Testing: Increase pay by 15%%, rate = %.2f", rate);
        }
        if (sp >= 40 && sp <= 59)
        {
            printf("Testing: Decrease pay by 10%%, rate = %.2f", rate);
            rate = rate - rate * 0.10;
        }
        else if (sp >= 100 && sp <= 120)
        {
            printf("Testing: Increase pay by 18%%, rate = %.2f", rate);
            rate = rate + rate * 0.18;
        }

        /* Calculate the pay */
```

```
            if (day >= 2 && day <= 6)
            {
                printf("Testing: Regular pay");
                pay = rate * hours;
            }
            else
            {
                printf("Testing: Weekend pay");
                pay = rate * 1.5 * hours;
            }
            printf("The pay is %.2f\n", pay);
        }
        else
        {
            printf("The code is INVALID");
        }
}
```

Let us now run the program again with two runs. The first goes through condition 1 only. The last three lines of the second run go through conditions 2, 4, and 5.

```
Enter the contractor's qualification code > L79
Testing: ex = L, sp = 79
Enter the day worked (Sunday = 1, Monday = 2, etc) > 6
Enter the number of hours > 4
Testing: day = 6, hours = 4
The pay is 49.56

Enter the contractor's qualification code > m104
Testing: ex = m, sp = 104
Enter the day worked (Sunday = 1, Monday = 2, etc) > 7
Enter the number of hours > 7
Testing: day = 7, hours = 7
Testing: Increase pay by 15%, rate = 14.25
Testing: Increase pay by 18%, rate = 16.81
Testing: Weekend pay
The pay is 176.54
```

The numbers and logical paths taken are correct; it is now clear that the program works for this one test data. It now must be run through the whole set of test data listed earlier.

There are two main disadvantages to this method of testing: (1) the program is modified by the insertion of testing instructions, and (2) the testing instructions could be mistyped and have bugs themselves. In fact, that very thing happened with the debugging of the program in Example 4.2.2: the debugging *printf()* used the format code *%f,* which was incorrect. The following method does not have these drawbacks.

Issue debugging commands from the compiler. Most commercial C packages have testing and debugging features that can be used without having to tamper with the program code. For example, the Borland C compiler introduced in Subsection 1.3.2 has a "Debug" command in the menu. As the program runs, the programmer can, at any time, inspect the values of the variables. This method is therefore much more flexible. It is not necessarily faster in a case of a program with numerous bugs. Using this method or the other is probably a matter of taste.

EXERCISE 6.2.2

Insert testing *printf()*s in the programs in Exercises 6.2.1 and run them with the set of test data constructed there.

---

7 Introduction to the *while* Loop

OBJECTIVES

This chapter introduces you to the following information:

- The procedure for using the *while* loop in writing programs that repeatedly run a sequence of actions.
- Ways for a user to control how often these actions should be performed.
- The creation of tables.

INTRODUCTION

Most examples from Chapter 6 were small, practical applications. However, remember that their sequences of instructions were executed only once. Of course, this restriction is totally unacceptable. A good program must possess the ability to execute a group of actions quickly and as often as the user wishes. This is the purpose of loop statements.

7.1 AN INTRODUCTION TO THE *while* LOOP

The simplest loops are coded to execute a sequence of instructions a fixed number times. Let us take a look at those first.

7.1.1 THE MECHANISM OF LOOPS

Example 7.1.1 explains what a ***loop*** is and how it works.

Example 7.1.1

Look back at Example 3.3.1: Suppose a prospective employer has many different positions available. Those jobs vary in description and responsibilities; therefore, each pays a different hourly wage, requires a different number of hours worked per week, and has a different duration. Furthermore, suppose the employer is offering five different jobs. Judy will have to rerun the program in order to determine the amount of money to expect for each job over the summer. This is cumbersome and not user-friendly. It would be better to modify the program so that it will rerun itself for each job. A ***loop*** is the best tool for this task. A loop would produce the following program runs for Judy.

Income calculation for job number 1:

```
Enter your initials > JPC
Enter the hourly wage > 7.05
```

Enter the total work hours per week > 35
Enter the number of weeks of work > 10

JPC, You will make $ 2467.50 this summer

Income calculation for job number 2:

Enter your initials > JPC
Enter the hourly wage > 9.31
Enter the total work hours per week > 30
Enter the number of weeks of work > 8

JPC, You will make $ 2234.40 this summer

The run would continue, asking the same questions for three more jobs. Below is the new program with a *while* loop. The changes to the code from Example 3.3.1 are in bold.

```
#include <stdio.h>

main()
{
    float   hourly_rate;
    int     hours_per_week;
    float   total_income;
    int     num_weeks;
    char    letter1, letter2, letter3;
    int     counter;

    counter = 1;
    while (counter <= 5)[1] /* execute the code below 5 times */
    {
        printf("Income calculation for job number %d:\n\n", counter);[2]
        printf("Enter your initials > ");
        scanf("\n%c\n%c\n%c", &letter1, &letter2, &letter3);
        printf("Enter the hourly wage > ");
        scanf("%f", &hourly_rate);
        printf("Enter the total work hours per week > ")'
        scanf("%d", &hours_per_week);
        printf("Enter the number of weeks of work > ");
        scanf("%d", &num_weeks);

        total_income = hourly_rate * hours_per_week * num_weeks;

        printf("%c%c%c, You will make $ %.2f this summer\n\n",
                letter1, letter2, letter3, total_income);
        counter = counter + 1;
    }[3]
}
```

Code from Example 3.3.1

Figure 7.1.1 shows how the loop is executed.

Figure 7.1.1

1. A counter variable is set to 1.
2. The condition of entry in the loop is evaluated. In this case the condition is *counter<=5.*
3. If the evaluation is true, do the steps 3.1 to 3.3 below.
   3.1. Execute the statement(s) within the braces.
   3.2. Increment the counter by 1.
   3.3. Go back to step 2 above.
   If the condition is false, do the following step:
   3.4. Get out of the loop.

The loop will be executed five times. The explanations below refer to the superscript numbers in the program code and describe how the loop works and some loop syntax issues.

Explanations

1. The loop condition counter <= 5 must be within parentheses, just as with the *if* statement. The loop condition is sometimes called an ***entry condition,*** because it determines whether or not the program will enter (execute) the loop. Also the name of the variable serving as a counter does not have to be *counter;* any other descriptive name will do.
2. Note the use of the new statement within the loop:

```
printf("Income calculation for job number %d:\n\n", counter);
```

   Its purpose is to clearly separate the output for each job on the display.
3. The sequence of statements within the loop must always be contained within braces.

EXERCISES 7.1.1

1. In Example 7.1.1, what do the two \ns added to the following line do?

```
printf("%c%c%c, You will make $ %.2f this summer\n\n",
```

   How would the display have looked like if the \ns were not there?
2. In the same example, suppose the *counter* had been initialized to 0 instead of 1. How would the condition of the loop need to be changed? Would other changes be needed?
3. Suppose the *counter* had been incremented on the fourth line of the following code instead of at the end of the loop. Would the program's execution have been affected in any way?

```
counter = 1;
while (counter <= 5)
{
     counter = counter + 1;
     printf("Income calculation for job number %d:\n\n", counter);
     printf("Enter your initials > ");
     scanf("\n%c\n%c\n%c", &letter1, &letter2, &letter3);
     :
     :
     printf("%c%c%c, You will make $ %.2f this summer\n\n",
            letter1, letter2, letter3, total_income);
}
```

4. The sequence of statements below simply echoes back to the screen what the user entered on four occasions. Change this code into a loop.

```
printf("Enter a character > ");
scanf("\n%c", &ch);
printf("Echo is %c\n", ch);
printf("Enter a character > ");
scanf("\n%c", &ch);
printf("Echo is %c\n", ch);
printf("Enter a character > ");
scanf("\n%c", &ch);
printf("Echo is %c\n", ch);
printf("Enter a character > ");
scanf("\n%c", &ch);
printf("Echo is %c\n", ch);
```

5. Use a loop to improve the program of Example 3.2.12 (the one that calculates the total weight two boxes in a wheelbarrow; one box contains bricks each weighing 1,200 grams, the other contains rods each weighing 650 grams). This time, make the program calculate the weight of eight individual wheelbarrows. Your output might look like this:

   Wheelbarrow 1:
   Enter the number of bricks in box one > 24
   Enter the number of rods in box two > 41
   The total weight of wheelbarrel 1 is 55450 grams

```
Wheelbarrel 2:
Enter the number of bricks in box one > 51
Enter the number of rods in box two > 7
The total weight of wheelbarrel 2 is 65750 grams

:
:
```

6. Write a loop that displays the numbers 0 to 9 as follows:
   a. Horizontally, on the same line
   b. Vertically, one per line
   c. Vertically, one per line, double spaced
7. Write a loop that displays the numbers 9 to 0, in descending order, all on the same line.
8. Example 7.1.1 asks for the initials for every job. Since it is the same person who is a prospect for all of these jobs, initials should be requested only once. How do you make the necessary modifications? (***Hint:*** Ask for the name before going into the loop.)
9. Add a loop to the program of Exercise 2.2.1, 4, so it will process information about eight waitresses.
10. Write a program that uses a loop to display the following text:

```
Pizza special: five bucks!
               five bucks!
               five bucks!
               five bucks!
               five bucks!
               five bucks!
               five bucks!
```

11. Write a program that uses a loop to accept ten individual values in gallons. Each value entered is immediately converted to liters using the following formula:

$$\text{liters} = 3.785 \times \text{gallons}$$

The resulting number of gallons is then displayed.

7.1.2 CALCULATING THE NUMBER OF LOOP EXECUTIONS

You may have realized that the number of times a loop is executed depends on three factors:

1. The condition for continued looping (e.g., *counter <= 5*)
2. The incremental increase of the counter every time the loop is executed (e.g., *counter = counter + 1*)
3. The value to which the *counter* is set **before** initially entering the loop (e.g., *counter = 1*)

Should any of these factors change, the number of times the loop is executed would also change. To understand this concept, try Exercises 7.1.2.

EXERCISES 7.1.2

1. How many times will the following loops execute?

a.
```
ctr = 0;
while (ctr < 20)
{
   printf("%d\n", ctr);
   ctr = ctr + 3;
}
```

b.
```
ctr = 20;
while (ctr > 1)
{
   ctr = ctr - 4;
   printf("%d\n", ctr);
}
```

c.
```
ctr = 1;
while (ctr <= 20)
{
   printf("%d\n", ctr);
   ctr = ctr + 2;
}
```

d.
```
ctr = 1;
while (ctr == 1)
{
   printf("%d\n", ctr);
   ctr = ctr - 1;
}
```

e.
```
ctr = 0;
while (ctr == 5)
{
    printf("%d\n", ctr);
    ctr = ctr + 1;
}
```
2. For each of the five loops above:
   a. What is the first number displayed? The last number displayed?
   b. What is the value of *ctr* after the loops terminate?
3. For each of the five loops, suppose the *printf()* was switched with the counter incrementation/decrementation.
   a. What is the first number displayed? The last number displayed?
   b. What is the value of *ctr* after the loops terminate?

It is fairly easy to figure out the answers for Exercise 7.1.2, 1. This would all be much tricker if the loop boundaries were wide apart and the incrementation of the counter was a value other than one. For example, how many times will this loop execute?

```
ctr = 5;
while (ctr < 4821)
{
    printf("%d\n", ctr);
    ctr = ctr + 3;
}
```

This can no longer be figured out by hand; it must be calculated. Since the incremental increase is 3, an estimate is simple to compute:

$$\frac{4821}{3} = 1607 \text{ times}$$

Deriving a formula. Figure 7.1.2 shows how a formula is arrived at that calculates the exact answer:

Figure 7.1.2

1. Perform a few loops by hand and keep track of the value of *ctr:*

ctr	5	8	11	14	17	20
loop	1st	2nd	3rd	4th	5th	6th

2. Notice a pattern that relates the loop number to its respective counter value:

Loop	**Value of *ctr***		**Pattern**		
1st	5	=	5	=	$5 + 0 \times 3$
2nd	8	=	$5 + 3$	=	$5 + 1 \times 3$
3rd	11	=	$8 + 3$	=	$5 + 2 \times 3$
4th	14	=	$11 + 3$	=	$5 + 3 \times 3$
5th	17	=	$14 + 3$	=	$5 + 4 \times 3$
6th	20	=	$17 + 3$	=	$5 + 5 \times 3$

Given the equation – 1 = counter value, the general pattern would look like this:

5 + counter value × 3
5 + (loop number – 1) × 3

The initial counter value is 5 and the increment is 3.

3. Extrapolate to the boundary value of *ctr* (here, 4,821):

Loop	**Value of *ctr***		**Pattern**
x^{st}	4821	=	$5 + (x - 1) \times 3$

It is now only a matter of solving this equation for *x.*

Solve for x in the equation in Figure 7.1.2, as follows:

$$x = \frac{4821 - 5}{3} + 1 = 1606.33 \text{ times}$$

Therefore, the loop will execute 1,606 times. It is a simple matter to deduce the general formula:

$$\text{number of loop executions} = \frac{\text{upper boundary} - \text{lower boundary}}{\text{step size}} + 1$$

The performance of a software program can be influenced greatly by its loops; especially if embedded loops (see Section 9.2) are involved. Although this may not be required from a programmer, she should have a "feel" for how many times a loop may execute. A highly skilled software developer may be capable of carrying out a ***performance analysis*** of her product, but this demands skills far beyond those required here.

EXERCISES 7.1.3

1. Verify the formula obtained by using the boundaries of the loops of Exercise 7.1.2, 1. The answers should be the same as the ones you found manually.
2. Using the method explained in Section 7.1.2, calculate the number of times the following loops will execute:

a.
```
ctr = 0;
while (ctr < 8109)
{
    printf("%d\n", ctr);
    ctr = ctr + 5;
}
```
b.
```
ctr = 47283;
while (ctr > 1)
{
    ctr = ctr - 4;
    printf("%d\n", ctr");
}
```
c.
```
ctr = 79;
while (ctr <= 2002)
{
    printf("%d\n", ctr");
    ctr = ctr + 2;
}
```

3. For each of the three loops in the question above:
   a. What is the first number displayed? The last number displayed?
   b. What is the value of *ctr* after the loops terminate?

7.1.3 COMMON ERRORS AND TRAPS

There are a number of errors that programmers make when entering loops in their code. Many of those errors are illustrated below using the program from Example 7.1.1.

1. Do not forget to surround the loop condition with parentheses. For example, if you enter

```
while counter <= 5
{
      :
      :
      :
}
```

   the compiler will complain about the lack of parentheses.
2. Do not put a semicolon at the end of the line containing the *while* loop. If you enter

```
while (counter <= 5);
{
      :
      :
      :
}
```

   the compiler will **not** complain, but the statements within the loop will be executed only **once.**

This is because the semicolon terminates the loop, so the block of statements after it is not part of the loop.

3. Do not forget to increment the counter within the loop. Look at the following code:

```
counter = 1;
while (counter <= 5)
{
     printf("Income calculation for job number %d:\n\n", counter);
       :
     :
     printf("%c%c%c, You will make $ %.2f this summer\n\n",
               letter1, letter2, letter3, total_income);
}
```

The line *counter = counter + 1;* is missing just above the end brace. Of course, this causes the sequence of statements within the loop to be executed forever—an ***infinite loop.*** The way to stop an infinite loop depends on the operating system. Often, pressing Ctrl-C or Ctrl-Y does the trick, but not always. Sometimes you may have to reboot the computer. (This is sometimes the case with an MS-DOS system.)

4. Do not increment the counter outside the loop, instead of within. This will also cause an infinite loop. (Why do you think this happens?)

```
while (counter <= 5)
{
     printf("Loop\n");
}
counter = counter + 1;
```

5. Do not forget to initialize the counter before going into the loop. Look at the following code:

```
while (counter <= 5)
{
     :
     :
     counter = counter + 1;
}
```

The line *counter = 1;* is missing as the first line of the program code. If a variable is not initialized, the compiler usually enters a 0 in it. If that happened in the above code, this loop will execute six times instead of five. Some compilers put nothing in a variable that the programmer does not initialize. In that case, the loop executes an unpredictable number of times.

6. Do not use an *if* statement when a *while* statement is more appropriate. For example, some novices would write the following program for Example 7.1.1:

```
counter = 1;
if (counter <= 5)
{
    :
    :
    counter = counter + 1;
}
```

Block of statements

The *if* statement in the second line should be a *while* statement. The confusion arises from the one mechanism that both statements have in common: If the condition is evaluated as true, then the block of statements is executed; otherwise, the block of statements is skipped. The difference, of course, is that the *if* statement executes the block of statements only once, whereas the *while* loop executes it repeatedly, until it finds the condition to be false.

7. Do not execute a loop one too many times or one too few times. For example, suppose you wrote the following loop:

```
counter = 1;
while (counter < 15)
{
```

```
        printf("Hello there!\n");
        counter = counter + 1;
    }
```

This loop will execute 14 times. Minor changes can make it loop 13 times or 15 times. (How does that happen?)

7.2 USING A CONTROL VARIABLE

One serious drawback to all the programs in Section 7.1 is that the user has no control over the number of times a loop is executed. For instance, the program in Example 7.1.1 **always** expects data for five jobs. What if later there are fewer or more jobs available? Loops should be flexible enough to let the user execute it any number of times. There are two methods for doing this: using a control variable or using a sentinel. Here we will discuss control variables.

7.2.1 WHAT IS A CONTROL VARIABLE?

Let's revisit Example 7.1.1 for this discussion. The best way to learn about control variables is through an example.

Example 7.2.1

To improve the usability of this program code it would be better if the program asks how many jobs there are to process before going into the loop. Then the loop would execute that number of times. For example, if the user wants to process 15 jobs, the run would begin like this:

Calculate the income for how many jobs? 15
Income calculation for job number 1:

Enter your initials > JPC
Enter the hourly wage > 7.05
Enter the total work hours per week > 35
Enter the number of weeks of work > 10

JPC, You will make $ 2467.50 this summer

Income calculation for job number 2:

Enter your initials > JPC
Enter the hourly wage > 9.31
Enter the total work hours per week > 30
Enter the number of weeks of work > 8

JPC, You will make $ 2234.40 this summer

The run would continue, asking the same questions for 13 more jobs. The program for this run would look like the following code (changes from Example 7.1.1 appear in bold):

```
#include <stdio.h>

main()
{
    float  hourly_rate;
    int    hours_per_week;
    float  total_income, sum_income;
    int    num_weeks;
    int    num_jobs;     /* control variable */
    char   letter1, letter2, letter3;
    int    counter;
    counter = 1;
```

```
    printf("Calculate the income for how many jobs? ");
    scanf("%d", &num_jobs);
    while (counter <= num_jobs)
    {
        printf("Income calculation for job number %d:\n\n", counter);
        printf("Enter your initials > ");
        scanf("\n%c\n%c\n%c", &letter1, &letter2, &letter3);
        printf("Enter the hourly wage > ");
        scanf("%f", &hourly_rate);
        printf("Enter the total work hours per week > ");
        scanf("%d", &hours_per_week);
        printf("Enter the number of weeks of work > ");
        scanf("%d", &num_weeks);

        total_income = hourly_rate * hours_per_week * num_weeks;

        printf("%c%c%c, You will make $ %.2f this summer\n\n",
                letter1, letter2, letter3, total_income);
        counter = counter + 1;
    }
}
```

The loop condition is now *counter <= num_jobs.* If the number 15 is entered in this variable, the loop will execute 15 times; if the number 8 is entered in this variable, the loop will execute 8 times, and so on. The variable *num_jobs* is called a ***control variable*** because it controls how many times the loop is executed.

EXERCISES 7.2.1

1. Make the program of Exercise 7.1.1, 5, more flexible by allowing the user to enter the number of wheelbarrows to weigh.
2. Make the program of Exercise 7.1.1, 9, more flexible by allowing the user to enter the number of waitresses.
3. Make the program of Exercise 7.1.1, 11, more flexible by using a control variable.

7.2.2 SOME COMMON APPLICATIONS OF LOOPS

In this subsection you will learn about two of the most common uses of loops.

Calculating summations and averages. For this very common and typical application consider Example 7.2.2.

Example 7.2.2

Example 1.2.7 showed the algorithm for the calculation of averages. Now apply that algorithm to finding the average pay offered for the jobs in Example 7.2.1. The modification involves simply introducing a summation variable. Figure 7.2.1 provides the instructions for calculating the average.

Figure 7.2.1

1. A *counter* variable is set to 1.
2. A *summation* variable (also called an ***accumulator***) is set to 0.
3. As long as the condition *counter <= num_jobs* is true, do steps 3.1 through 3.3.
    3.1 Calculate the total income.
    3.2 Add the *total_income* to the summation variable *sum_income.*
    3.3 Increment the *counter* by 1.
4. Calculate the *average* as *sum_income / num_jobs.*

Following is the new program, with modifications shown in bold:

```
#include <stdio.h>

main()
{
    float  hourly_rate;
    int    hours_per_week;
    float  total_income, sum_income; /* summation of the income */
    int    num_weeks;
    int    num_jobs;
    char   letter1, letter2, letter3;
    int    counter;
    float  average;

    counter = 1;
    sum_income = 0;
    printf("Calculate the income for how many jobs? ");
    scanf("%d", &num_jobs);
    while (counter <= num_jobs)
    {
        printf("Income calculation for job number %d:\n\n", counter);
        printf("Enter your initials > ");
        scanf("\n%c\n%c\n%c", &letter1, &letter2, &letter3);
        printf("Enter the hourly wage > ");
        scanf("%f", &hourly_rate);
        printf("Enter the total work hours per week > ");
        scanf("%d", &hours_per_week);
        printf("Enter the number of weeks of work > ");
        scanf("%d", &num_weeks);

        total_income = hourly_rate * hours_per_week * num_weeks;

        printf("%c%c%c, You will make $ %.2f this summer\n\n",
                letter1, letter2, letter3, total_income);
        sum_income = sum_income + total_income;
        counter = counter + 1;
    }
    average = sum_income / num_jobs;
    printf("\nThe average income is $ %.2f\n", average);
}
```

Study this program code before attempting Exercises 7.2.2.

EXERCISES 7.2.2

1. In the program in Example 7.2.2:
   a. The expression *average = sum_income / num_jobs* serves to calculate the average. Suggest another equivalent expression that would involve this *counter* variable.
   b. If the *counter* had initially been set to 0, would the formula in (a) need to be changed?
   c. Note that the variables *counter* and *sum_income* needed to be initialized prior to entering the loop. Why is the variable *average* not initialized as well?
2. Improve the program of Exercise 7.2.1, 1, so it also calculates the average weight of all of the wheelbarrows' contents.
3. a. Write a loop that displays the average of the numbers from 1 to 9, inclusive.
   b. Modify the program so that the user may enter the limit (i.e., use a control variable).

4. a. Write a loop that lets the user enter any ten numbers, one at a time (i.e., have the program prompt for each), after which the program calculates the average and the sum.
   b. Modify the program so that the user may enter the number of numbers to be entered (i.e., use a control variable).
5. Modify the program of Exercise 7.2.1, 2, so it calculates the average number of hours worked and the average income made from tips for all eight waitresses.
6. The following sequence of instructions asks the user for four numbers and displays the sum of the numbers. Reduce the sequence into a loop.

```
printf("Enter the score for period 1: ");
scanf("%d", &score1);
printf("Enter the score for period 2: ");
scanf("%d", &score2);
printf("Enter the score for period 3: ");
scanf("%d", &score3);
printf("Enter the score for period 4: ");
scanf("%d", &score4);
sum = score1 + score2 + score3 + score4;
printf("The sum of scores is %d", sum);
```

7. Change the following embedded *if/else* structure into a loop:

```
float     num1, num2, num3, num4;
int       counter;

counter = 0;
printf("Enter a number (-1 to terminate): ");
scanf("%f", &num1);
if (num1 != -1)
{
    counter = 1;
    printf("Enter a number (-1 to terminate): ");
    scanf("%f", &num2);
    if (num2 != -1)
    {
        counter = 2;
        printf("Enter a number (-1 to terminate): ");
        scanf("%f", &num3);
        if (num3 != -1)
        {
            counter = 3;
            printf("Enter a number (-1 to terminate): ");
            scanf("%f", &num4);
            if (num4 != -1)
            {
                counter = 4;
            }
            else
            {
                num4 = 0;
            }
        }
    }
}
printf("The sum of the %d numbers is %f\n",
        counter, num1 + num2 + num3 + num4);
```

8. a. Modify the program of Exercise 3.2.5, 6, so that it processes 30 students and the average grade of the class.

b. Modify the program so that the user may enter how many students' grades are to be entered, i.e., use a control variable.

9. a. Write a program to calculate the number of points that eight players score when they each throw three darts. A sample run might look like this:

   Player 1: Enter the points scored for each dart > 18 2 20
   You scored 40 points
   Player 2: Enter the points scored for each dart > 60 40 5
   You scored 105 points
   :
   :
   Player 8: Enter the points scored for each dart > 19 3 7
   You scored 29 points

   b. Modify the program so that the user may enter the number of players to be entered (i.e., use a control variable).

Generating tables. Business applications usually have the ability to produce tables, such as those in financial statements. This subsection includes techniques and examples for producing some simple tables.

Example 7.2.3

A very simple application of loops is one that generates a table of squares and cubes for the numbers from, say, 1 to 10 (e.g., 5^2 is $5 \times 5 = 25$ and 5^3 is $5 \times 5 \times 5 = 125$). Here is a program with that function.

```
#include <stdio.h>

main()
{

        int       num;

        num = 1;
        printf("     Number                        Square          Cube\n"
              "     ------                        ------          ----\n\n");

        while (num <= 10)
        {
               printf("     %d                            %d              %d\n",
                        num, num * num, num * num * num);
               num = num + 1;
        }
}
```

Note the spaces within the format string of the printf()s. The spaces are used to line up the columns. (Unfortunately this did not work to perfection; a later subsection provides information on lining up columns correctly.) Following is the table produced by the above code:

```
0         1         2         3         4         5         6
0123456789012345678901234567890123456789012345678901234567890

     Number                        Square          Cube
     -----                         ------          ----
     1                             1               1
     2                             4               8
     3                             9               27
     4                             16               64
     5                             25               125
     6                             36               216
```

```
7                    49                   343
8                    64                   512
9                    81                   729
10                    100                  1000
```

Note that column numbers always start at 0, not 1.

EXERCISES 7.2.3

1. Modify the program in Example 7.2.3 so that a table is produced
   a. from 10 down to 1.
   b. from 100 down to 10, in increments of 5. Is any change needed in the *printf()?*
2. Write a program that generates a table of Fahrenheit and Celsius equivalents:
   a. From –5° to 30° Fahrenheit. Round off the Celsius equivalents.
   b. From –40° to 90° Fahrenheit at five-degree intervals. Round off the Celsius equivalents to the nearest tenth of a degree. (***Hint:*** Revisit Example 3.2.15.)
   c. Make the program in (b) above more flexible by letting the user specify the boundaries.
3. a. Write a program that produces a table showing the metric equivalents of measurements from 1 to 50 feet. The formula is:

   $$\text{feet} = 3.28 \times \text{meters}$$

   (Do not worry if the columns do not line up perfectly.)
   b. Make the program more flexible by letting the user specify the upper boundary.

Example 7.2.4

In January 1994 William put $10,000 in a retirement fund paying 8.5% interest per year. He now wants to know how much money his fund will contain in 20 years and the interest made every year, and he'd like to see this information in the form of a table. Here is the program that performs this task:

```
#include <stdio.h>

main()
{
     int        year
     float      fund, interest;

     fund = 10000;
     year = 1994;
     printf("      Year                 Interest      Fund\n"
           "      ----                 --------      ----\n\n");
     while (year < 1994+20)   /* in 20 years */
     {
           interest = fund * 0.085;      /* the interest for the year */
           fund = fund + interest;
           printf("       %d                %.2f             %.2f\n",
                  year, interest, fund);
           year = year + 1;
      }
}
```

Note that the variable *year* is used as a counter, even though it does not begin at 1. Also, the loop condition excludes equality. (Why do you think that is the case?) Following is the table produced by the program above:

```
Year        Interest        Fund
----        --------        ----

1994        850.00          10850.00
1995        922.25          11772.25
```

```
1996         1000.64          12772.89
1997         1085.70          13858.59
  :             :                :
  :             :                :
2010         3135.41          40022.62
2011         3401.92          43424.55
2012         3691.09          47115.63
2013         4004.83          51120.46
```

Again, notice that neither the last column nor the decimal points line up. (This will be fixed in a future exercise.)

Example 7.2.5

William now wants to know in what year his investment will double, or reach $20,000. The table is to terminate at that year. Only the loop condition needs to be changed to accomplish this task:

```
#include <stdio.h>

main()
{
     int        year
     float      fund, interest;

     fund = 10000;
     year = 1994;
     printf("     Year             Interest             Fund\n"
            "     ----             --------             ----\n\n");
     while (fund < 20000)
     {
           interest = fund * 0.085;     /*  the interest for the year */
           fund = fund + interest;
           printf("      %d              %.2f              %.2f\n",
                  year, interest, fund);
           year = year + 1;
      }
}
```

The code works if the fund (an *accumulator* variable) is less than $20000. If that is true, the program will continue to calculate and accumulate the interest; otherwise, it will stop. Here the variable *fund* is the control variable. This is our first case in which the loop entry condition did not check a counter.

EXERCISES 7.2.4

1. a. Improve the program in Example 7.2.4 so that the initial investment amount and the interest rate is entered by the user. Here is an example of the desired output:

   ```
   Enter the amount to invest > 25000
   Enter the interest rate of the fund > 6.75

   Year      Interest      Fund
   ----      ------        ----
   ```

   b. Make a similar improvement to the program in Example 7.2.5.
2. a. An airplane travels at 450 kilometers per hour. Make a table that shows the distance the plane will cover at intervals of five minutes for the next two hours.
   b. Generalize the program by letting the user enter the interval and the time range.
3. a. Write a program that asks the user to enter a number until the sum of the entered numbers exceeds 100.
   b. Generalize the program by letting the user enter the upper boundary.
4. Write a program that shows the depreciation of a house trailer year by year. The purchase price was $69,500, and the real estate company estimates that the depreciation rate is 3.7% per year. The owner wants to produce a table incremented by years that shows the current property value

a. for the next 35 years.
b. until it goes down to the scrap value of $25,000.
   Write a program for each.
c. Let the user enter the number (i.e., use a control variable). Do this for both (a) and (b).

5. a. A microchip manufacturer notices that 3.7% of the chips produced each week are defective and must be discarded. Currently the weekly production is 27,900 chips (including the defective chips). The weekly production increases by 0.6% every week due to improving economic conditions. Write a program that tabulates the weekly production for a year. All numbers must be rounded up. The table begins this way:

Week	Good Chips	Defective	Defective Accumulated to Date
1	26868	1032	1032
2	27029	1038	2070
3	27190	1045	3115
4	27353	1051	4166
5	27517	1057	5223
6	27681	1064	6287

   b. How many chips will be lost one year from now?
   c. Generalize the program by letting the user enter the value for the rate of bad chips, the weekly production, and the weekly production increase.

6. a. The manufacturer in question 5 was in debt $1,105,000 two years ago. Luckily, the economy bounced back in week 1 of the table above. As a result, the manufacturer promises to rehire employees as soon as the company is out of debt. Assume the manufacturer uses the entire revenue from the 0.6% growth in the economy to pay back the debt. Knowing that each good chip brings in $121.23, produce a table that determines which week the callback of employees will occur. The table begins as follows:

Week	Good Chips	Growth in Chip Production	Debt Remaining
1	26868	0	$ 1105000.00
2	27029	167	$ 1084771.25
3	27190	168	$ 1064421.37
4	27353	169	$ 1043950.37
5	27517	170	$ 1023358.25
6	27681	171	$ 1002645.00

   b. Generalize the program by letting the user enter the value for the rate of economic growth, the debt, and the revenue per chip.

7. a. Assuming that the world population increases by 90 million people per year, determine the projected world population by the year 2020. Assume the population is 5.5 billion in 1994.
   b. Generalize the program by letting the user enter the current population, the growth rate, and the target year.

Using format codes to line up columns. As you undoubtedly noticed, the columns do not line up in any of the tables produced so far. Example 7.2.6 demonstrates how to fix this.

Example 7.2.6

Let us reconsider Example 7.2.3 and examine a method that ensures that the columns line up. Let us produce the same table again in these specific columns:

```
0         1         2         3         4         5         6
0123456789012345678901234567890123456789012345678901234567890

          Number                 Square           Cube
          ------                 ------           ----
               1                      1              1
               2                      4              8
```

```
   3                9               27
   4               16               64
   5               25              125
   6               36              216
   7               49              343
   8               64              512
   9               81              729
  10              100             1000
```

Most C compilers include functions that allow the user to display a number or text at any specific line and column. This would make our task easy. Unfortunately, those functions are not ANSI C standard. So instead, we must inform C of all the spaces needed to line up the columns by using format codes—no spaces are inserted within the *printf()*. To proceed, visualize each line of the table to consist of six separate display zones, with the respective format codes. The display zones and corresponding format codes are illustrated in Figure 7.2.2.

Figure 7.2.2

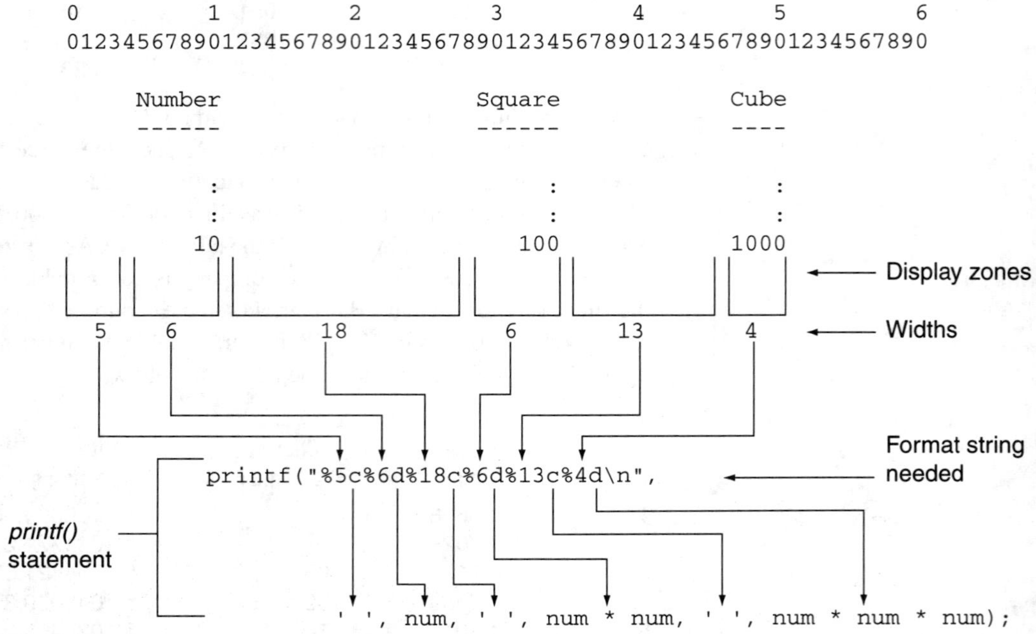

The numbers in the format codes correspond exactly to the widths of their respective display zones. These same zones also apply to the header, but the type of the format codes will differ (Figure 7.2.3).

Figure 7.2.3

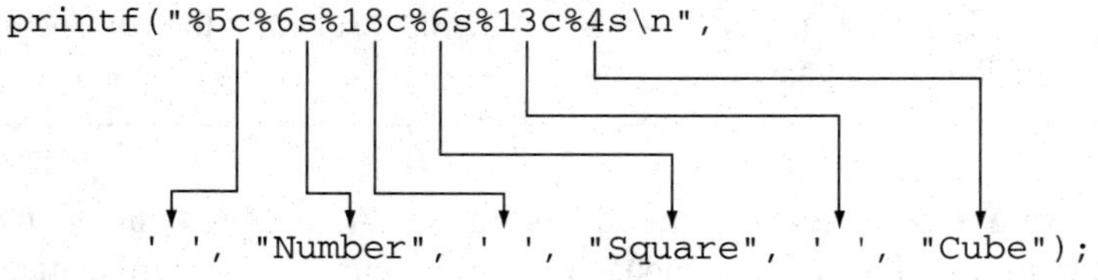

Here, finally, is the program, with the format codes to align the display zones correctly indicated in bold type:

```
#include <stdio.h>

main()
{
        int      num;

        num = 1;
        printf("%5c%6s%18c%6s%13c%4s\n",
```

```
                ' ',   "Number",  ' ',    "Square",  ' ',   "Cube"),
        printf("%5c%6s%18c%6s%13c%4s\n",
                ' ',   "------",  ' ',    "------",  ' ',   "----"),
        while (num <= 10)
        {
            printf("%5c%6d%18c%6d%13c%4d\n",
                   ' ', num, ' ', num, ' ', num,  ' ',
                   num * num * num);
            num = num + 1;
        }
}
```

The columns will now line up—guaranteed—since each line will be produced using the same widths.

Example 7.2.7

Note that the program above produces a table in which the numbers are aligned at the right of their columns. The number can just as easily be aligned at the left:

```
0         1         2         3         4         5         6
0123456789012345678901234567890123456789012345678901234567890
     Number                  Square             Cube
     ------                  ------             ----
     1                       1                  1
     2                       4                  8
     3                       9                  27
     4                       16                 64
     5                       25                 125
     6                       36                 216
     7                       49                 343
     8                       64                 512
     9                       81                 729
     10                      100                1000
```

The changes to be applied to the program are quite simple. The format codes *%6d, %6d,* and *%4d* in the following code:

```
printf("%5c%6d%18c%6d%13c%4d\n",
        ' ', num, ' ', num, ' ', num, ' ',
        num * num * num);
```

simply need to be changed to:

```
printf("%5c%-6d%18c%-6d%13c%-4d\n",
        ' ', num, ' ', num, ' ', num, ' ',
        num * num * num);
```

The minus signs instruct *printf()* to left-align the numbers within their print zones.

EXERCISES 7.2.5

1. The columns for the table in Example 7.2.6 can be formed with three display zones instead of six. The three zones have widths of 11, 24, and 17 spaces, respectively.

```
0         1         2         3         4         5         6
0123456789012345678901234567890123456789012345678901234567890
     Number                  Square             Cube
     ------                  ------             ----
          :                       :                :
          :                       :                :
         10                     100             1000
```

How should the format string be coded?

2. Improve the program in Example 7.2.5 so that the table lines up as follows

```
0         1         2         3         4         5         6
0123456789012345678901234567890123456789012345678901234567890

          Year               Interest             Fund
          ----               --------             ----
```

3. Modify the format strings in the program in Example 7.2.4 so that the columns and decimal points line up correctly.
4. Modify the programs in the exercises below so that the columns line up perfectly:
   a. Exercise 7.2.4, 4(c)
   b. Exercise 7.2.4, 5(c)

7.2.3 VALIDATING A CONTROL VARIABLE'S BOUNDARIES

Since the execution of a loop is determined by the control variable, it is important that the variable's value be validated before entering the loop. Otherwise the loop will execute the wrong number of times. The following example shows what can happen.

Example 7.2.8

As we have seen, the use of a control variable allows a loop to be executed any number of times, including not at all. This is a special case that all the programs of this section (7.2) did not yet address. For instance, if the user in Example 7.2.1 did not want to enter any job information, the code would produce this display:

Calculate the income for how many jobs ? 0
Divide by zero

The error message came from the computer hardware. It explains that an attempt was made to divide by 0 (which the hardware cannot do). Look back at the program in Example 7.2.1. This error appears in the following statement:

```
average = sum_income / (counter - 1);
```

Such an error causes the system to terminate the program immediately. A good program should verify if the division is possible **before** carrying it out. An *if/else* statement is now in order (shown in bold type):

```
   counter = 1;
   sum_income = 0;
   printf("Calculate the income for how many jobs? ");
   scanf("%d", &num_jobs);
   while (counter <= num_jobs)
   {
       printf("Income calculation for job number %d:\n\n", counter);
       printf("Enter your initials > ");
       scanf("\n%c\n%c\n%c", &letter1, &letter2, &letter3);
       :
       :
       sum_income = sum_income + total_income;
       counter = counter + 1;
       printf("Do you have another job to process? (y/n) ");
       scanf("\n%c", &answer);
}
if (counter > 1)        /* Can a division be carried out? */
{
       average = sum_income / (counter - 1);
       printf("\nThe average income is $ %.2f\n", average);
}
```

```
else
{
        printf("\nNo average calculated\n");
}
```

If the division cannot be done, the program will go to the *else* part of the statement. The message it displays is more informative than the message generated by the computer hardware.

EXERCISES 7.2.6

1. Note that the test is *counter > 1*, not *counter > 0*. This is because if the variable *counter* was a 1, the program never went into the loop. But it seems as though, the program should have gone through the loop once if the counter was 1. Make the changes necessary to the program to make that happen.
2. One solution to the example above is started below. Simply fill in the blanks appropriately:

```
counter = 1;
sum_income = 0;
printf("Calculate the income for how many jobs? ");
scanf("%d", &num_jobs);
if (_______________)
{
          ________________________________
          ________________________________
          ________________________________

          :
          :
}
else
{
          printf("\nNo average calculated\n");
}
```

3. Modify the program in each exercise below so that the program will display an appropriate message if the user enters 0 in the control variable.
   a. Exercise 7.2.2, 2
   b. Exercise 7.2.2, 5
   c. Exercise 7.2.2, 9(b)
   d. Exercise 7.2.4, 1. The amount to invest is the control variable.
   e. Exercise 7.2.4, 2(b). The time range is the control variable.

Example 7.2.9

Revisit Example 7.2.1. Should the user enter an invalid number by mistake for the number of jobs to process, say –2, the loop will never be executed. If the user enters too large a number, say 200, the loop will run too often. In any case, a good program should always warn of invalid input, and then should repeatedly ask the user to reenter the number of times to loop until the number is reasonable. For instance, this interaction is safer:

Calculate the income for how many jobs? <u>150</u>
The response is invalid
Calculate the income for how many jobs? <u>–2</u>
The response is invalid
Calculate the income for how many jobs? <u>5</u>

Income calculation for job number 1:

Enter your initials > <u>JPC</u>

```
Enter the hourly wage > 7.05
Enter the total work hours per week > 35
Enter the number of weeks of work > 10

JPC, You will make $ 2467.50 this summer
              :
              :
```

Here is how this can be done (the new lines of code are shown in bold type):

```
counter = 1;
sum_income = 0;
printf("Calculate the income for how many jobs? ");
scanf("%d", &num_jobs);
while (num_jobs < 0 || num_jobs > 50) /* if number is not valid */
{
     printf("The response is invalid\n");
     printf("Calculate the income for how many jobs? ");
     scanf("%d", &num_jobs);
}
while (counter <= num_jobs)
{
     printf("Income calculation for job number %d:\n\n", counter);
     printf("Enter your initials > ");
     scanf("\n%c\n%c\n%c", &letter1, &letter2, &letter3);
     :
     :    — Same as in the Example 7.1.1
     :
     counter = counter + 1;
     }
     if (num_jobs > 0)
     {
          average = sum_income / num_jobs;
          printf("\nThe average income is $ %.2f\n", average);
     }
     else
     {
          printf("\nNo jobs were processed");
     }
}
```

Every single example presented from now on should include a validation check of the control variable's range. However, for the sake of keeping programs short, this will be left out.

EXERCISES 7.2.7

Include a validity check of the control variable in the programs below:

1. Exercise 7.2.2, 2
2. Exercise 7.2.2, 5
3. Exercise 7.2.2, (b)
4. Exercise 7.2.2, (b)
5. Exercise 7.2.4, 1
6. Exercise 7.2.4, 2(b)

7.2.4 MISTYPING INPUT DATA WHILE IN A LOOP

Once again it is time to warn you about *scanf()*'s erratic behavior, this time when called within a loop.

Example 7.2.10

Consider the following program, which repeatedly prompts the user for numbers. The user tells how many numbers to prompt for:

```
sum = 0;
counter = 0;
printf("How many numbers will you enter? ");
scanf("%d", &num);
while (counter < num)
{
     printf("Enter a grade > ");
     scanf("%f", &grade);
     sum = sum + grade;
     counter = counter + 1;
}
average = sum / counter;
printf("\nThe average grade is %.2f\n", average);
```

Should a number be mistyped, the program panics:

How many numbers will you enter? 6
Enter a grade > 72
Enter a grade > 51
Enter a grade > (9
Enter a grade > Enter a grade > Enter a grade >
The average grade is 17.57

When the data entry was mistyped, the *scanf()* failed, and the remaining three calls to *scanf()* failed as well. (Rremember Subsection 2.2.4, which said that once a *scanf()* call fails, the subsequent calls fail, too.) The average is incorrect as a result. Note that all three prompts appear on the same line as a result of their respective *scanf()*'s failure.

EXERCISE 7.2.8

In Example 7.2.10, suppose the user had entered all the numbers at the same prompt by mistake. This is what would happen:

How many numbers will you enter? 4
Enter a grade > 72 51 63 12
Enter a grade > Enter a grade > Enter a grade >
The average grade is 49.50

The last three prompts appear on the same line, and no numbers can be entered! How do you explain that?

7.2.5 COMMON ERRORS AND TRAPS

Many of the errors below are illustrated using Example 7.2.2.

1. Do not forget to initialize the accumulator (such as *sum_income*) before going into the loop. If you forget to do so, the summation in the accumulator could be incorrect.
2. Do not sum up the accumulator outside the loop; do it within instead. For example:

```
counter = 1;
sum_income = 0;
while (counter <= 5)
{
        :
        :
        counter = counter + 1;
}
```

```
sum_income = sum_income + total_income;
average = sum_income / 5;
printf("\nThe average income is $ %.2f\n", average);
```

Here the line *sum_income = sum_income + total_income* should be in the loop, but it is outside the loop, causing only the **las**t income to be summed up.

3. Do not forget to sum up the accumulator within the loop. If you forget to to so, the accumulator will remain 0.
4. Do not fail to understand the different purposes of a counter versus an accumulator. Novices sometimes make the following mistake:

```
while (counter <= 5)
{
        :
        :
        sum_income = sum_income + 1;
        counter = counter + 1
}
```

Placing a + *1* instead of + *total_income* on the *sum_income* line is due to the following misinterpretation: add one income to the summation of incomes. The purpose of a counter is to ensure that the loop executes the correct number of times. The purpose of an accumulator is to sum up specific information (a quantity) each time a loop is executed.

5. Do not calculate the average within the loop. For example:

```
counter = 1;
sum_income = 0;
while (counter <= 5)
{
        :
        :
        sum_income = sum_income + total_income;
        average = sum_income / 5;
        counter = counter + 1;
}
printf("\nThe average income is $ %.2f\n", average);
```

The line *average = sum_income / 5;* should be outside the loop. The calculation of the average is an operation that makes sense only **after** all incomes are summed up. Incidently, the above program will still display the average correctly!

6. Do not put the code that produces a header inside the loop. For example:

```
fund = 10000;
year = 1994;
while (fund < 20000)
{
        printf("       Year              Interest        Fund\n"
                "       ----              --------        ----\n\n");
        interest = fund * 0.085;     /* the interest for the year */
        :
        :
}
```

Of course this code will cause the header to be displayed for every line in the table. Only the code that needs to be repeated should be within the loop. The code that produces the header should be left outside the loop.

7.3 USING A SENTINEL

Although the control variable allows the user to execute a loop any number of times, there may still be one disadvantage to its use. For instance, in Example 7.2.1 the user needs to know how many times he wants to loop **before** going into the loop. Suppose the user expects to process eight jobs, but only five are found. The loop would be executed three additional times unnecessarily. This section discusses a technique that uses a sentinel to allow the user to terminate a loop at any time.

7.3.1 WHAT IS A SENTINEL?

The ***sentinel*** is simply specific data that the user enters at the time she wants to exit the loop. The sentinel can be provided in two different forms, as shown in the following examples:

Sentinels in the form of a question. Example 7.3.1 shows how this method works.

Example 7.3.1

Let us modify the program of Example 7.2.1 so it uses a sentinel. We want the program to produce the following display. Notice how a response to a single prompt terminates the loop.

```
Do you have any jobs to process? (y/n) y
Income calculation for job number 1:

Enter your initials > JPC
Enter the hourly wage > 7.05
Enter the total work hours per week > 35
Enter the number of weeks of work > 10

JPC, You will make $ 2467.50 this summer

Do you have another job to process? (y/n) y
Income calculation for job number 2:

Enter your initials > JPC
Enter the hourly wage > 9.31
Enter the total work hours per week > 30
Enter the number of weeks of work > 8

JPC, You will make $ 2234.40 this summer
Do you have another job to process? (y/n) n

The average income is $ 2350.95
```

The sentinel here is the answer 'n' to the final question. Following is the program that implements this example, with modifications shown in bold type:

```
#include <stdio.h>

main()
{
    float  hourly_rate;
    int    hours_per_week;
    float  total_income, sum_income;
    int    num_weeks;
    char   letter1, letter2, letter3, answer;
    int    counter;
    float  average;

    counter = 1;
    sum_income = 0;
    printf("Do you have any jobs to process? (y/n) "); [1]
    scanf("\n%c", &answer);
    while (answer == 'y') [2]
    {
        printf("Income calculation for job number %d:\n\n", counter);
        printf{"Enter your initials > ");
        scanf("\n%c\n%c\n%c", & letter1, & letter2, & letter3);
```

```
            printf("Enter the hourly wage > ");
            scanf{"%f", &hourly_rate);
            printf("Enter the total work hours per week > ");
            scanf("%d", &hours_per_week);
            printf("Enter the number of weeks of work > ");
            scanf("%d", &num_weeks);

            total_income = hourly_rate * hours_per_week * num_weeks;

            printf("%c%c%c, You will make $ %.2f this summer\n\n",
                   letter1, letter2, letter3, total_income);
            sum_income = sum_income + total_income;
            counter = counter + 1;[3]
            printf("Do you have another job to process? (y/n) ");[4]
            scanf("\n%c", &answer);[4]
        }
        average = sum_income / (counter - 1);
        printf("\nThe average income is $ %.2f\n", average);
}
```

Explanations

1. The program asks if the user wants to loop at all. This must obviously be asked *before* going into the loop.
2. The loop is executed as long as the answer to the question is 'y'.
3. Note that the *counter* is no longer needed to ensure that the loop is executed a specific number times. It is still needed for the calculation of the average, though.
4, The question is also asked at the bottom of the loop. This ensures that the program gives the user the opportunity to get out of the loop at any time.

Sentinels in the form of invalid data. Sentinels in the form of a question have an obvious drawback: It is rather annoying to have to answer the question repeatedly. Luckily, the sentinel does not need to be a yes/no question, as the following examples show.

Example 7.3.2

Instead of a question, invalid initials could be used to tell the program to terminate looping. An invalid initial is one that is not a letter. The folllowing run illustrates this:

```
To terminate processing jobs, type invalid initials
Income calculation for job number 1:

Enter your initials > JPC
Enter the hourly wage > 7.05
Enter the total work hours per week > 35
Enter the number of weeks of work > 10

JPC, You will make $ 2467.50 this summer

Income calculation for job number 2:

Enter your initials > JPC
Enter the hourly wage > 9.31
Enter the total work hours per week > 30
Enter the number of weeks of work > 8

JPC, You will make $ 2234.40 this summer
Income calculation for job number 3:

Enter your initials > 000

The average income is $ 2350.95
```

As a result of the invalid initials entered (000), the loop terminated. These characters indicate the end of data input. Following is the program that accomplishes this, with the modifications shown in bold type:

```
#include <stdio.h>
#include <ctype.h>

main()
{
    float  hourly_rate;
    int    hours_per_week;
    float  total_income, sum_income;
    int    num_weeks;
    char   letter1, letter2, letter3;
    int    counter;
    float  average;

    counter = 1;
    sum_income = 0;
    printf("To terminate processing jobs, type invalid initials\n");  <---- 1
    printf("Income calculation for job number %d:\n\n", counter);   --+
    printf("Enter your initials > ");                                 |-2
    scanf("\n%c\n%c\n%c", &letter1, &letter2, &letter3);            --+
    while (isalpha(letter1) && isalpha(letter2) && isalpha(letter3)) <---- 3
    {
        printf("Enter the hourly wage > ");
        scanf("%f", &hourly_rate);
        printf("Enter the total work hours per week > ");
        scanf("%d", &hours_per_week);
        printf("Enter the number of weeks of work > ");

        total_income = hourly_rate * hours_per_week * num_weeks;

        printf("%c%c%c, You will make $ %.2f this summer\n\n",
                letter1, letter2, letter3, total_income);
        sum_income = sum_income + total_income;
        counter = counter + 1;
        printf("Income calculation for job number %d:\n\n", counter); --+
        printf("Enter your initials > ");                               |-4
        scanf("\n%c\n%c\n%c", &letter1, &letter2, &letter3);          --+
    }
    average = sum_income / (counter - 1);
    printf("\nThe average income is $ %.2f\n", average);
}
```

Explanations

1. A message must be displayed that explains to the user how to terminate the loop.
2. Since the initials were chosen to receive the sentinel, the **first** initials must be asked for **before** entering the loop. This way the loop can then check if these first initials are the sentinel. The program would then never enter the loop. (The program must allow for the possibility that the user does not want to run the loop after all.)
3. This condition ensures that the loop is executed as long as all three initials are letters.
4. The code that asks for the initials must be typed into the program twice. The first occurrence is for the sole purpose of reading the very first initials, as was explained in (2) above. The second occurrence is for all subsequent initials.

It is important to remember that the sentinel value must be one that represents an ***invalid data item.***

EXERCISES 7.3.1

1. How would the program in Example 7.3.2 interact with the user if
   a. segment 2 was ignored?

b. segment 4 was ignored?
c. segment 4 was misplaced at the top of the loop (the first segment within the loop)?

2. The program in Example 7.3.2 was run with these results:

   Do you have any jobs to process? (y/n) n
   Divide by zero

   a. Explain the result.
   b. Suggest an improvement to the code so that the user will be presented instead with the message "No job processed" in such a situation.

3. Make the program for Exercise 7.2.2, 9(a), more flexible by using a sentinel to terminate the loop by:
   a. Entering a value of negative points for the first dart throw
   b. Entering a negative value at any one of the three dart throws
   c. Asking whether or not to process another player

   Write a solution for each.

4. Make the program for Exercise 7.2.2, 8(a), more flexible by using a sentinel to terminate the loop by:
   a. Entering a negative number for the first mark
   b. Entering a negative number fort any one of the marks
   c. Asking whether or not to process another student

   Write a solution for each.

Example 7.3.3

Write a program that lets the user enter students' grades until an invalid one is entered. At that point the average of the grades is displayed. An invalid grade is one that is less than 0 or greater than 100. Following is the program:

```
#include <stdio.h>

main()
{
      float  grade, sum, average;
      int    counter;

      sum = 0;
      counter = 1;
      printf("Enter an invalid grade to terminate the loop\n\n");
      printf("Enter a grade > ");
      scanf("%f", &grade);
      while (grade >= 0 && grade <= 100)   /* is the grade valid? */
      {
            sum = sum + grade;
            counter = counter + 1;
            printf("Enter a grade > ");
            scanf("%f", &grade);
}
average = sum / (counter - 1);
printf("\nThe average grade is %.2f\n", average);
}
```

Note that the loop condition ensures that the loop terminates as soon as a mark outside the valid range is entered.

EXERCISES 7.3.2

1. In Examples 7.3.2 and 7.3.3, the variables *sum_income* and *sum* must be divided by *counter – 1* rather than *counter.*
   a. Explain why.

b. Suggest a minor change in the program that would eliminate the need to subtract the from the counter.
2. Improve the program of Exercise 7.1.1, 5, so it uses a sentinel to terminate the loop by
   a. Asking whether or not to continue looping
   b. Entering an invalid number of bricks (i.e., less than 0 or greater than 99)
   Provide a solution for each.
3. Improve the program of Exercise 7.1.1, 9, so it uses a sentinel to terminate the loop by:
   a. Asking whether to continue looping or not
   b. Entering a negative number of hours or entering a negative value for tips income
   Provide a solution for each.
4. A computer store needs an inventory system for its software products. Write a program that asks the user to enter the following information for each software package:

   The product identification number (e.g., 7047)
   The inventory at the beginning of this month
   The number of copies received this month
   The number of copies sold this month

   The user will enter this information for each product and the new inventory will be displayed immediately (new inventory = inventory at the beginning of this month + copies received this month – copies sold this month). Once a negative identification is input, a summary of the total number of copies received and the total number of copies sold will be displayed.
5. Modify the programs below to accommodate the special case of never looping:
   a. Example 7.3.1
   b. Example 7.3.2
   c. Example 7.3.3
   d. Exercise 7.3.1, 3
   e. Exercise 7.3.1, 4
   f. Exercise 7.3.2, 2
   g. Exercise 7.3.2, 3

7.3.2 ENTERING A LIST OF NUMBERS

So far, all of our loops have prompted for each individual data entry (see Example 7.3.3). Sometimes it may be more convenient to have all numbers entered at once. This subsection explains how to do this and gives examples.

Example 7.3.4

Revisit Example 7.3.3. Suppose we want to enter all the grades at once and terminate with the sentinel –1. Our display might look like this:

Enter a list of grades terminated by a –1:

61 76 63 92 50 80 70 43 79 –1↵

The average grade is 68.22

The following program will do just that:

```
sum = 0;
counter = 0;
printf("Enter a list of grades terminated by a -1:\n\n");
scanf("%f", &grade);1
while (grade != -1)2
{
     sum = sum + grade;
     counter = counter + 1;
     scanf("%f", &grade)3
}
average = sum / counter;
printf("\nThe average grade is %.2f\n", average);
```

Explanations

1. This *scanf()* is intended to capture the first number of the list, which in this case is 61.
2. The loop is executed until the number –1 is scanned.
3. This *scanf()* captures all of the other numbers, one number per loop.

Note that the prompt has been removed from within the loop, for it is no longer desirable to have it there. Even though the *scanf()* is called separately for each grade, all grades can still be entered all at once. Why? Remember Example 2.2.4: the numbers that were input are scanned (captured) only when the Enter key is pressed. So, in the run above, the first number, 61, will be scanned by the first *scanf()* when the Enter key is pressed, which occurs only after all numbers have been entered. Then the numbers that follow will be scanned, one per loop.

EXERCISES 7.3.3

1. What might happen in the example above if the user forgot to enter the sentinel value –1?

   Enter a list of grades terminated by a –1:

   61 76 63 92 50 80 70 43 79↵

2. What might happen in the example above if the user entered some of the numbers on separate lines?

   Enter a list of grades terminated by a –1:

   61 76↵
   63↵
   92 50 80 70 43 79↵

EOF: A built-in sentinel for input. Entering a number such as –1 is a rather awkward way to indicate the end of a list of data. Its presence suggests that it is itself a member of the list, when it is only meant to signal the list's end. It turns out that all operating systems possess a built-in sentinel value: the EOF (end-of-file) signal. This sentinel is produced by pressing a combination of keys: in MS-DOS and VMS, the key combination is the Ctrl-Z; in UNIX, it is Ctrl-D. The following example illustrates how to use the EOF sentinel Ctrl-Z.

Example 7.3.5

Let us modify the program in Example 7.3.4 above so that the user simply presses Ctrl-Z instead of –1 to indicate the end of the list of grades. We want to see the following display:

Enter a list of grades terminated by pressing CTRL-Z:

61 76 63 92 50 80 70 43 79 CTRL-Z↵

The average grade is 68.22

Note that the Enter key still needs to be pressed. Also keep in mind that some compilers require that Enter be pressed before as well as after Ctrl-Z. Here is the new program, with modifications shown in bold caps:

```
signed char  flag;[1]

sum = 0;
counter = 0;
printf("Enter a list of grades terminated by pressing CTRL-Z:\n\n");
flag = scanf("%f", &grade);
while (flag != EOF)[2]
{
```

```
        sum = sum + grade;
        counter = counter + 1;
        flag = scanf("%f", &grade);
}
average = sum / counter;
printf("\nThe average grade is %.2f\n", average);
```
[3]

Explanations

1. The symbol EOF is actually a symbolic constant for the number –1. Consequently, the variable *flag* has to be declared as a *signed char,* not just *char.*
2. For a program to detect the end of the list, it is only a matter of checking the value inside the variable *flag* against EOF. Note that the name of the variable can be any other descriptive name.
3. After the very first number is read in, this *scanf()* reads every other number, one at a time. Then it detects the Ctrl-Z. This is interpreted as meaning ***end of list*** (***end of file*** if the list was read from a file; more on that in Section 8.2). When the *scanf()* reaches it, the symbol EOF returns to the program, as shown in Figure 7.3.1:

Figure 7.3.1

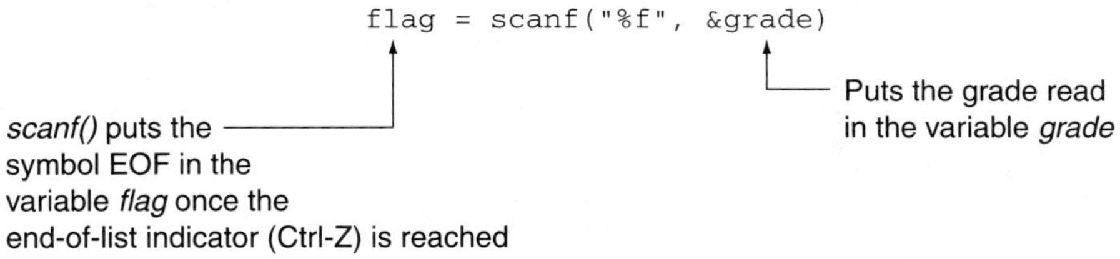

EXERCISES 7.3.4

1. How might the program in Example 7.3.5 react if the Ctrl-Z and the Enter keys were switched?

   Enter a list of grades terminated by pressing CTRL-Z:

   61 76 63 92 50 80 70 43 79↵CTRL-Z

2. In Example 7.3.5, shouldn't the variable *char ch,* as well as the variable *flag,* be made *signed?* Explain.

Be wary of Ctrl-Z while reading in a loop. Be careful when using Ctrl-Z. Not only does it mean end of list, it also closes the keyboard input mechanism (until you exit the program). This implies that *scanf()* is no longer able to accept input from then on. Consider Example 7.3.6:

Example 7.3.6

Revisit Example 7.3.5. Suppose that we are now asked to enter a list of grades for two classmates so the program can compare the students' grades:

Enter a list of grades for classmate 1. Terminate by pressing CTRL-Z:

61 76 63 92 50 80 70 43 79 CTRL-Z↵

The average grade is 68.22
Enter a list of grades for classmate 2. Terminate by pressing CTRL-Z:

81 71 66 78 40 75 25 CTRL-Z↵

The average grade is 62.38
Classmate 1 is better

The modifications seem quite simple: Use two loops in sequence, one for each classmate:

```
signed char  flag;
float  avg1, avg2;
sum = 0;
counter = 0;
printf("Enter a list of grades for classmate 1."
       "Terminate by pressing CTRL-Z:\n\n");
flag = scanf("%f", &grade);
while (flag != EOF)      /* check if the CTRL-Z is read */
{
     sum = sum + grade;
     counter = counter + 1;
     flag = scanf("%f", &grade);
}
avg1 = sum / counter;
printf("\nThe average grade is %.2f\n", avg1);
sum = 0;
counter = 0;
printf("Enter a list of grades for classmate 2."
       "Terminate by pressing CTRL-Z:\n\n");
flag = scanf("%f", &grade);
while (flag != EOF)      /* check if the CTRL-Z is read */
{
     sum = sum + grade;
     counter = counter + 1;
     flag = scanf("%f", &grade);
}
avg2 = sum / counter;
printf("\nThe average grade is %.2f\n", avg2);
if (avg1 > avg2)
{
     printf("Classmate 1 is better\n");
}
else
{
     printf("Classmate 2 is better\n");
}
```

An unexpected problem occurs when the program is run:

Enter a list of grades for classmate 1. Terminate by pressing CTRL-Z:

61 76 63 92 50 80 70 43 79 CTRL-Z↵

The average grade is 68.22
Enter a list of grades for classmate 2. Terminate by pressing CTRL-Z:
The average grade is 0.00
Classmate 1 is better

What happened? The program did not let the user enter the list for the second classmate! This is due to the Ctrl-Z, which disabled *scanf()*, so it couldn't read any more numbers. The second loop was skipped. To reactivate the input mechanism, simply insert the statement *fflush(stdin)* after the first loop. Only then will the program work correctly. This function also clears the input buffer. (The input mechanism is explained in detail in Appendix 6.) A note of warning is in order here: although ASCII C standard, the *fflush(stdin)* function does not work with some compilers as described here.

7.3.3 ENTERING A LIST OF CHARACTERS: A SENTENCE

A list of data is not restricted to numbers; it may consist of characters. A sentinel also must be provided to indicate the end of the list of characters, and Ctrl-Z may be used. Whereas numbers have to be read with *scanf()*, characters may be read with *scanf()* or *getchar()*. Consider the following example.

Example 7.3.7

We want to write a program that reads in a sentence and echoes the letters spaced out. The sentence must be terminated with Ctrl-Z. For example:

```
Enter a sentence > I think, therefore I am! CTRL-Z↵
I think, therefore I am!
```

Here is the program:

```
#include <stdio.h>

main()
{
    char        ch;
    signed char flag;

    printf("Enter a sentence > ");
    flag = scanf("%c", &ch);

    while (flag != EOF)
    {
        printf("%c ", ch);      /* space out the letters */
        flag = scanf("%c", &ch);
    }
}
```

EXERCISES 7.3.5

1. Run the program in Example 7.3.7. Type the same sentence, and then press Enter instead of Ctrl-Z. The line will be echoed correctly, and the cursor will wait for more input. Explain why.
2. Note that the format string *"%c"* in the *scanf()* does not have a *\n*. Yet Example 3.3.3 advised you to always precede *%c* with a *\n*. However, it also said that the presence of a *\n* also makes the *scanf()* ignore all spaces in the input. Here, we wish to read in the spaces. To understand the effect of the *\n*, change the format strings of the *scanf()*s to *"\n%c"*. Run the program.
3. The presence of the qualifier *signed* is absolutely necessary. If it is omitted, the user could never terminate the program, despite pressing Ctrl-Z. Remove the qualifier, run the program, and explain what happens. (***Hint:*** The symbol EOF is equal to –1.)
4. Modify Example 7.3.7 so that the letters are echoed in uppercase, one per line. Use the function *toupper()*.
5. The function *getchar()* also recognizes the Ctrl-Z combination. When it detects those keystrokes, it returns EOF, just as *scanf()* does. Knowing this, introduce the function *getchar()* (as well as *putchar()*) into the program in Example 7.3.7.

As seen thus far, the combination of Ctrl-Z and the Enter key signals to the program to accept the keyed data. This method is error prone and not userfriendly. Indeed, it leads to confusion, as illustrated in Exercise 7.3.5, 1. Most software uses a more intuitive Enter keystroke. For instance, the following run in the program of Example 7.3.7 is better:

```
Enter a sentence > I think, therefore I am!↵
I t h i n k ,   t h e r e f o r e   I   a m !
```

Example 7.3.8 shows how this improvement may be accomplished.

Example 7.3.8

The necessary modifications are quite simple. Indeed, it is only a matter of reading each character until the Enter keystroke is reached. The modified program is shown below, with changes in bold type:

```
#include <stdio.h>

main()
{
     char          ch;

     printf("Enter a sentence > ");
     scanf("%c", &ch);
     while (ch != '\n')     /* check for the Enter keystroke */
     {
     printf("%c ", ch);       /* space out the letters */
     scanf("%c", &ch);
     }
}
```

Note that the condition of the loop is now *ch != '\n'*, not *flag != EOF*. The variable *flag* is no longer needed. Nothing else needs changing.

The last two examples introduced you to string processing, a very practical field in computer programming. Chapters 18 to 20 have more to say about string processing.

EXERCISES 7.3.6

1. Would the following program work the same as the one above? Explain.

```
#include <stdio.h>

main()
{
     char          ch;
     signed char flag;

     printf("Enter a sentence > ");
     flag = scanf("%c", &ch);
     while (flag != '\n')
 {
           printf("%c ", ch);
           flag = scanf("%c", &ch);
     }
}
```

2. Devise a solution to Example 7.3.8 that uses *getchar()*s and *putchar()*s instead.
3. a. Will the solution in Example 7.3.8 still work if the user enters Ctrl-Z anyway?
   b. If not, then make the necessary modifications.
4. Consider the following loop. It simply echoes every character entered, capitalizing the vowels:

```
char x;

printf("> ");  /* just a prompt for input */
while (scanf("%c", &x) != EOF)
{
     switch(x)
     {
           case 'a': case 'e': case 'i':
           case 'o': case 'u':
```

```
                x = toupper(x);
                break;
            default:
                break;
        }
        printf("\n%c\n", x);
        printf("> ");
}
printf("End");
```

a. Are the following statements true or false?
   1. *printf("%d", x);* and *putchar(x);* would produce the same output.
   2. The loop terminates if Enter is pressed.
   3. The loop terminates if Ctrl-Z is pressed (followed by Enter).

b. Which of the following screens correspond(s) correctly to a **complete** run of the above code: (User inputs are underlined, ↵ stands for Enter key being pressed or echoed, and ^Z stands for the key combination Ctrl-Z.

1.
```
>a
A
> b
b
> ^Z↵
End
```

2.
```
>ABC↵
A
>
B
>
C
>
↵

>^Z↵
End
```

3.
```
> abcDe↵
AbcDE↵
> ^Z↵
End
```

4.
```
> a↵
A
>
↵

> B↵
B
>
↵

> ^Z↵
End
```

5.
```
> AB↵
A
B
↵

> ↵
End
```

5. Rewrite the above loop with the functions *getchar()* and *putchar()* only. The program must still do the same thing as the one above.

7.3.4 COMMON ERRORS AND TRAPS

There are a number of mistakes programmers make when using sentinels:

1. Do not mistakenly think that the EOF symbolic constant has been read into the argument (here *grade*) to the *scanf()*. That is:

   ```
   flag = scanf("%f", &grade)
   ```

   Mistakenly, the student programmer then proceeds to check against the variable *grade* for the presence of the sentinel:

   ```
   while (grade != EOF)
   {
       .....

   }
   ```

   This is all wrong. The symbolic constant EOF is stored in the variable *flag* when the end-of-list indicator (Ctrl-Z) is reached, so the presence of the end-of-list indicator must be checked with the variable *flag*.

2. Do not position the *scanf()* call at the wrong end of the loop. For example, the following mistake is often made when coding a loop in the context of a control variable:

```
counter = 1;
printf("How many numbers will you enter? ");
scanf("%d", &num);
while (counter <= num)
{
      sum = sum + grade;
      counter = counter + 1;
      printf("Enter a grade > ");
      scanf("%f", &grade);
}
average = sum / counter;
```

The *printf()* statement in the eighth line should be at the beginning of the loop. How will the program behave as written? The mistake is due to a mix-up in the coding of a loop in the context of a sentinel, where the *scanf()* call is indeed made at the bottom of the loop:

```
counter = 0;
printf("Enter an invalid grade to terminate the loop\n\n");
printf("Enter a grade > ");
scanf("%f", &grade);
while (grade >= 0 && grade <= 100)
{
      sum = sum + grade;
      counter = counter + 1;
      printf("Enter a grade > ");
      scanf("%f", &grade);
}
average = sum / (counter - 1);
```

The mistake is sometimes made in the other direction as well: the *scanf()* call is made at the beginning of the loop in the context of a sentinel, instead of at the bottom. In this case, how would the program behave?

7.4 LOOP LAYOUT AND PRESENTATION

7.4.1 GROOMING THE *while* STATEMENT

The procedures layout of loops is similar to that for decision statements. Because the C compiler ignores white spaces, the programmer is free to arrange a *while* statement any way she wishes. Nonetheless Figure 7.4.1 illustrates a few grooming tips, numbered in order of importance.

Figure 7.4.1

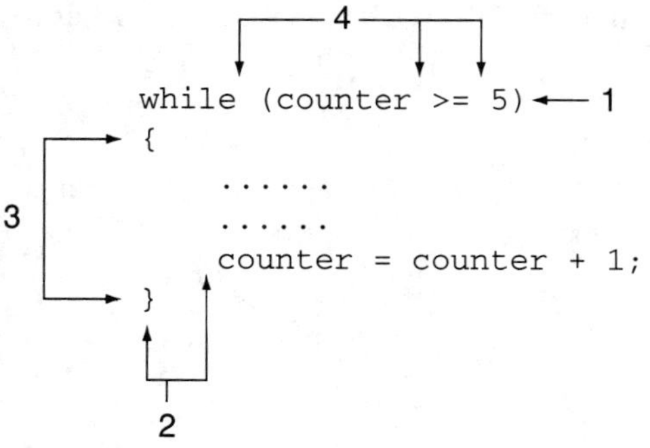

Explanations

1. The word *while* and its loop condition should always be on the same line.
2. Indent the block of statements within the loop by a few blank spaces.

3. Always surround the block of statements with braces.
4. Leave spaces where indicated in the loop condition.

7.4.2 WHEN TO USE A LOOP AND WHAT BELONGS IN IT

When is a loop necessary? Unlike decision statements, there is a magic recipe that can be used to decide about using loops in any situation. It is only a matter of answering the first question below:

1. Is there an indication of actions required to be performed repeatedly?
   If yes, use a loop; otherwise, do not.
2. If a loop is needed, what actions/instructions should be put in it?
   Include the actions that are repeated, leaving all others outside the loop.

The first question requires no more explanation because numerous examples were provided in previous sections. There have also been numerous examples illustrating the second, some of which are reconsidered below.

Example 7.4.1

In Example 7.2.3, the instructions that produce the header were kept outside the loop because the header needs to be produced only once.

Example 7.4.2

In Example 7.2.2, the instruction for calculating the average was kept outside the loop because the calculation of the average is to be done only once, after the loop.

Example 7.4.3

In Example 7.2.1, the user is prompted for the control values only once, before the loop.

This principle is quite simple, yet students sometimes overlook it.

EXERCISE 7.4.1

The following sequence of statements simply echoes back to the screen whatever data the user enters. Change the sequence into a loop. What instructions should go within the loop? Before the loop? After?

```
printf("Enter data as specified and they will be echoed:\n");
printf("Enter a character > ");
scanf("\n%c", &ch);
printf("Echo is %c\n", ch);
printf("Enter a character > ");
scanf("\n%c", &ch);
printf("Echo is %c\n", ch);
printf("Enter a character > ");
scanf("\n%c", &ch);
printf("Echo is %c\n", ch);
printf("Enter a character > ");
scanf("\n%c", &ch);
printf("Echo is %c\n", ch);
printf("Enter a number > ");
scanf("%d", &num);
printf("Echo is %d\n", num);
```

---

8 More Complex Applications of *while*

OBJECTIVES

This chapter introduces you to the following information:

- Many more applications of loops with increasing complexity.
- Practical processing of data files and report creation.

INTRODUCTION

This chapter simply continues where Chapter 7 left off, offering you greater flexibility in the use of the *while* loop.

8.1 DECISION STATEMENTS WITHIN A LOOP

None of the loops in Chapter 7's examples includes decision statements. This limits their applicability. This section, therefore, gives you options for using *while* in more complex situations. The use of decision statements within loops is identical to the approach presented in Chapters 4, 5, and 6, so much of this will seem familiar to you.

8.1.1 GENERAL APPLICATIONS

The following example shows how to place an *if/else* statement within a loop structure.

Example 8.1.1

Suppose that the program in Example 4.3.1 is needed to process information for five jobs. It is appropriate then to insert this program within a loop (as was done in Subsection 7.1.1). Following is the new program with changes shown in bold type:

```
#include <stdio.h>

main()
{
    float  hourly_rate;
    int    hours_per_week;
    float  total_income;
    int    num_weeks;
    float  minimum;
```

```
    int     counter;

    counter = 1;
    while (counter <= 5)
    {
        printf("Income calculation for job number %d:\n\n", counter);
        printf("Enter the minimum income acceptable > ");
        scanf("%f", &minimum);
        printf("Enter the hourly wage > ");
        scanf("%f", &hourly_rate);
        printf("Enter the total work hours per week > ");
        scanf("%d", &hours_per_week);
        printf("Enter the number of weeks of work > ");
        scanf("%d", &num_weeks);

        total_income = hourly_rate * hours_per_week * num_weeks;
        if (total_income >= minimum)
        {
             printf("Take the job!\n");
             printf("You will make $ %.2f this summer\n",
                     total_income);
         }
         else
         {
             printf("Look someplace else for a job.\n");
         }
         counter = counter + 1;
    }
}
```

The *if/else* decision statement is embedded within the loop, just like the rest of the code.

The following examples illustrate some interesting applications of loops involving decision statements.

Finding the maximum number from a list. Consider Example 8.12 for this typical application.

Example 8.1.2

Let us write a program for the algorithm of Example 1.2.8, which finds the maximum number in a list. Here is the algorithm again:

1. Set the MAXIMUM at 0.
2. Set the DAY OF THE MAXIMUM at day 1.
3. Initialize the COUNT OF DAYS to 0.
4. As long as the end of the list is not reached, do steps 4.1 to 4.3.
   - 4.1. Look at the next NUMBER in the list.
   - 4.2. If the NUMBER > MAXIMUM so far, do steps 4.2.1 and 4.2.2:.
     - 4.2.1. This NUMBER is now the current MAXIMUM
     - 4.2.2. The current DAY OF THE MAXIMUM is now given by COUNT OF DAYS.
   - 4.3. Increase the COUNT OF DAYS so far by 1.
5. The number desired is MAXIMUM.

Instruction 4 is not precise enough to be coded. Although you might know what "the end of the list" means, the computer does not. Consequently, let us mark the end of the list with the sentinel EOF. Here is what you might see during a sample run of the program:

```
Enter a list of the number of people for each day.
End the list by pressing CTRL-Z:
6 19 51 44 49CTRL-Z↵

The maximum number of people in one day is 51 which occurred on day 3
```

Following is a program for this display:

```
#include <stdio.h>

main()
{

   int    maximum, day_of_max, count_of_day, number;
   signed char flag;

   maximum = 0;
   count_of_day = 0;
   day_of_max = 1;
   printf("Enter a list of the number of people for each day.\n"
          "End the list by pressing CTRL-Z:\n");
   flag = scanf("%d", &number);
   while (flag != EOF)
   {
      if (number > maximum)       /* keep track of the maximum number */
         {
            maximum = number;
            day_of_max = count_of_days;
         }
         count_of_day = count_of_day + 1;
         flag = scanf("%d", &number);
   }
   printf("\nThe maximum number of people in one day is %d "
          "which occurred on day #%d",  maximum, day_of_max);
}
```

This solution is entirely based on the algorithm in Example 1.2.8 (which was explained in that section). Take the time to study this solution on your own before attempting Exercises 8.1.1.

EXERCISES 8.1.1

1. Modify the program in Example 8.1.2 so that it also finds the smallest number of people in a day and the day associated with that number.
2. Write a program that asks the user to enter two numbers and then displays the maximum number. The program repeates this action until the user enters a negative number.
3. Introduce a loop to the program in Exercise 4.1.1, 1, so that any number of credit card holders may be processed. In addition, change the minimum allowable payment to be 10% of the amount owed or $10, whichever is more.
4. a. Improve the program in Exercise 4.3.2, 9, so that the program loops until the user enters the invalid initial 000.
   b. Add code so that the average number of children (per parent) is displayed.
   c. Add code so that the program displays the number of females and the number of males.
   d. Add code so that the program displays the average number of children per male as well as the average number of children per female.
5. Improve the correct program at the end of Example 4.2.2 so that it processes any number of students. A sample run might produce the following display:

   Do you wish to start the program? (y/n) y

   Enter the distance covered > 100
   Enter the time taken > 14.4
   The speed is 6.94 meters/second
   Do you wish to continue? (y/n) y

   Enter the distance covered > 80
   Enter the time taken > 10.9

The speed is 7.34 meters/second
The boy went faster than last year's record

Do you wish to continue? (y/n) y

Enter the distance covered > 100
Enter the time taken > 13.9
The speed is 7.19 meters/second
The boy went faster than last year's record

Do you wish to continue? (y/n) n

Before going into the loop, the record will be set at the time mentioned in Example 4.2.2, or 7.15. Within the loop, the program will compare the student's speed to that record. If the speed is faster than the record, the program will display an appropriate message.

6. Modify the program above so that the speed is compared with the most recent record instead of last year's record. A sample run might look like this:

Do you wish to start the program? (y/n) y

Enter the distance covered > 100
Enter the time taken > 14.4
The speed is 6.94 meters/second
Do you wish to continue? (y/n) y

Enter the distance covered > 80
Enter the time taken > 10.9
The speed is 7.34 meters/second
The boy went faster than the latest record

Do you wish to continue? (y/n) y
Enter the distance covered > 100
Enter the time taken > 13.9
The speed is 7.19 meters/second

Do you wish to continue? (y/n) n

The program compares the user's latest entry with the previous record entered.

7. Modify the program in Example 7.2.9 so that the program displays a more precise error message, as illustrated in the following example of a run:

Calculate the income for how many jobs ? 150
The response is too high
Calculate the income for how many jobs? –2
The response is too low
Calculate the income for how many jobs? 5
Income calculation for job number 1:

Enter your initials > JPC
:
:
:

8. Modify the program in Exercise 7.2.7, 4, to find the winner among all players (i.e., the player who scored the most points).
9. A teacher asks a girl a series of true/false questions. For each, she enters into the computer the letter *T* for true or the letter *F* for false. The program then reports how many were answered true, how many were answered false, and how many questions were asked. Here is the program:

```
#include <stdio.h>
#include <stdlib.h>

main()
{
     int counter, sum_t, sum_f;
```

```
        char answer, cont;

        sum_t = 0; sum_f = 0; counter = 0;
        cont = 'Y';

        while (cont == 'Y')
        {
                printf("Enter your answer: (T)rue, (F)alse > ");
                scanf("\n%c", &answer);
                answer = toupper(answer);
                if (answer == 'T')
                {
                        sum_t = sum_t + 1;
                }
                else
                {

                        sum_f = sum_f + 1;
                }
                counter = counter + 1;
                printf("Type 'Y' if there is another question > ");
                scanf("\n%c", &cont);
                cont = toupper(cont);
        }
        printf("%d questions were answered true,\n"
               "%d questions were answered false,\n"
               "%d questions were asked", sum_t, sum_f, counter);
}
```

The variable *counter* is used to count up the total number of questions asked. This is simply *sum_t* + *sum_f*, so the variable *counter* is not necessary. Make changes to eliminate it.

10. a. Revisit Example 7.3.8. Remember that you cannot readily eliminate the need for pressing Ctrl-Z for a list of numbers such as the following:

    Enter a list of grades. Then press the Enter key:

    <u>61 76 63 92 50 80 70 43 79↵</u>

    The average grade is 68.22

    What is the challenge here that must be overcome?

    b. Let us now overcome the challenge! The method presented in Example 7.3.8 can still be used. It simply needs extra codes. Develop a solution based on the following algorithm:

    Have a *scanf()* read in a single character at a time, skipping all blanks. If the character read is *\n* instead of a digit, then the program will go to end of the list and simply quit the loop. In this case, read the second digit of the number. Remember that *getchar()* reads the digits as characters, so you need to find the numeric value of the character digit. For instance, *6* would be changed to the number 6. Use a *switch* statement for that purpose, a *case* for each digit. Finally put the two digits together into a number using the formula *number = digit1 * 10 + digit2*. (Note that Chapter 18 includes easier ways to implement a solution that the one suggested here.)

11. The program in the question above works well only if all grades consist of two digits. Change the program to account for:
    a. grades from 0 to 9.
    b. grades equal to 100.

    Be careful; this is tricky.

Text processing. Actually, Example 7.3.7 was our first (simplistic) application of text processing. Let us look at other examples.

Example 8.1.3

Modify Example 7.3.7 so that the sentence is compressed (i.e., all unnecessary spaces are removed). But now let's do it in French! Example:

```
Enter a sentence > Je      pense  ,  donc     je suis    !↵
Je pense, donc je suis!
```

The trick here is to display the first space following a word and then ignore other spaces (if any) immediately following up to the next word. This process is then repeated for the other words. Following is the new program, with changes bold type:

```
#include <stdio.h>
#include <stdlib.h>

main()
{
  char        ch, prev_ch;

  printf("Enter a sentence > ");
  scanf("%c", &ch);
  prev_ch = 'x';[1]
  while (ch != '\n')
  {
    if (!(isspace(ch) && isspace(prev_ch)))[2] /* if this is the NOT the */
    {                                          /* second space in a row */
        printf("%c", ch);
    }
    prev_ch = ch;[3]                   /* a new character will be read, so */
    scanf("%c", &ch);                          /* ch is previous to it */
  }
}
```

Explanations

1. Initially, the variable *prev_ch* must be set to any character that is not a space. Here it is set to *x*, but it could be set to any other nonspace character.
2. This *if* condition checks if the last two characters read, *ch* and *prev_ch,* are **both** spaces. If they are not spaces, then *ch* is displayed; otherwise, it is not. The function *isspace(ch)* returns true if the character in *ch* is a space, otherwise it returns false. You may check for yourself that the condition of the *if* does indeed check if two spaces follow. Note that when the function *isspace()* is used, the line *#include <stdlib.h>* is necessary.
3. Prior to reading the next character, the character *ch* must be set to become the new previous character *prev_ch.*

To illustrate how this program works, consider Table 8.1.1. Note that in the output column, the symbol _ stands for a space.

Table 8.1.1

Input buffer	Variables *prev_ch*	*ch*	Output
Je pense , donc je suis !↵	'x'	'J'	J
Je pense , donc je suis !↵	'J'	'e'	Je
Je pense , donc je suis !↵	'e'	' '	Je_
Je pense , donc je suis !↵	' '	' '	Je_
Je pense , donc je suis !↵	' '	' '	Je_
Je pense , donc je suis !↵	' '	' '	Je_
Je pense , donc je suis !↵	' '	'p'	Je_p

You may wish to complete this example as an exercise.

EXERCISES 8.1.2

1. Actually, strictly speaking, the function *isspace()* returns a true condition if the character is a white space (a blank space, a Tab, or an Enter keystroke). How will the above program compress the sentences below where the Tab or Enter keys were keyed within it?
   a. Note that every time you press the Tab key, a large space shows up on the screen:

      Enter a sentence > Je TAB pense , donc TAB TAB je suis!

   b. Note results when you press the Enter key:

      Enter a sentence > Je pense ,
      donc je↵
      suis!↵

2. Modify the program in Example 7.3.7 so that it removes all nonalphabetic characters from the sentence, and it no longer spaces out the sentence. For example:

   Enter a sentence > Je pense 100 fois, donc je suis!↵
   Je pense fois donc je suis

3. Modify the program in Example 7.3.7 so that it reverses the case of each letter and no longer spaces out the sentence. For example:

   Enter a sentence > Je PENSE, donc je SUIS!↵
   jE pense, DONC JE suis!

4. Modify the program in Example 7.3.7 so that the sentence is collapsed, meaning all white spaces are removed. For example:

   Enter a sentence > Je pense, donc je suis!↵
   Jepense,doncjesuis!

5. Modify the program in Example 7.3.7 so that the first letter of each word is capitalized and the remaining letters are lowercase. For example:

   Enter a sentence > Je pense, donc Je SUIS!↵
   Je Pense, Donc Je Suis!

6. Write a program that accepts a sentence and counts the number of letters, the number of digits, the number of punctuation marks, and the number of spaces in that sentence.
7. Run the program for Example 8.1.3 with the sentence below:

   Enter a sentence > Je pense, donc Je suis!↵

   a. What do you see after running the program?
   b. Suggest a simple modification to the program so that all leading spaces are eliminated.

Investment planning. We have seen some examples of program related to investment planning previously. Below is another example with decision statemtns embedded within a loop.

Example 8.1.4

Let us revisit the solution of Exercise 7.2.4, 1(b), which was based on Example 7.2.5. Suppose that William now wants to know the year and the month that his investment will double. A new column for the month is needed. Also, the table is to be double spaced. Since now the loop must calculate the interest by the month, not the year, the month (no longer the year) must be incremented for every execution of the loop. The modifications to be made. Explanations follow.

```
int      year, month; [1]
float    fund, interest, rate, goal;

month = 1;     /* month 1 is January */
year = 1994;
printf("Enter the amount to invest > ");
```

```
scanf("%f", &fund);
goal = 2 * fund;
printf("Enter the interest rate of the fund > ");
scanf("%f", &rate);
printf("%4s%5c%5s%5c%8s%5c%8s\n",2
        "Year", ' ', "Month", ' ', "Interest", ' ', "Fund");
printf("%4s%5c%5s%5c%8s%5c%8s\n\n",
        "----", ' ', "-----", ' ', "--------", ' ', "----");
while (fund < goal)
{
     interest = fund * rate / 12;3
     fund = fund + interest;
     printf("%4d%5c%5d%5c%8.2f%5c%8.2f\n\n",4
               year, ' ', month, ' ', interest, ' ', fund);
     month = month % 12 + 1;5
     if (month == 1)
     {
        year = year + 1;
     }
}
```

Explanations

1. Two counters are now needed: one for counting the years and one for keeping track of the months.
2. New codes have been added to the *printf()* statements to include a column for the month.
3. Since the interest calculation is now divided by 12, since interest now is accumulated by the month now.
4. New codes have been added to the *printf()* to include a column for the month.
5. The month begins at 1. The statement *month = month % 12 + 1* will increment it all the way to 12. The next time this statement is reached, the month will be set back to 1.

Running this program might produce the following output:

```
Enter the amount to invest > 5000
Enter the interest rate of the fund > 0.15

Year      Month     Interest       Fund
----      -----     --------       ----

1994          1        62.50    5062.50

1994          2        63.28    5125.78

1994          3        64.07    5189.85

1994          4        64.87    5254.73

1994          5        65.68    5320.41

1994          6        66.51    5386.92

1994          7        67.34    5454.25

1994          8        68.18    5522.43

1994          9        69.03    5591.46

1994         10        69.89    5661.35
```

```
1994      11        70.77      5732.12

1994      12        71.65      5803.77

1995       1        72.55      5876.32

1995       2        73.45      5949.77

1995       3        74.37      6024.15
:
:
:
1998       5       119.24      9658.44

1998       6       120.73      9779.17

1998       7       122.24      9901.41

1998       8       123.77     10025.17
```

Example 8.1.5

Let us improve the program above so that the month will be displayed as a word. For instance:

```
Enter the amount to invest > 5000
Enter the interest rate of the fund > 0.15

Year         Month    Interest        Fund
----         -----    --------        ----

1995       January       63.28     5125.78

1995      February       64.07     5189.85

1995         March       64.87     5254.73

1995         April       65.68     5320.41

1995           May       66.51     5386.92

1995          June       67.34     5454.25

1995          July       68.18     5522.43
:
:
:
1999         April      119.24     9658.44

1999           May      120.73     9779.17

1999          June      122.24     9901.41

1999          July      123.77    10025.17
```

More space is needed in the "Month" column to make room for the month names. The column width will now be increased from five to eight spaces. Following is the modified program, with changes shown in bold type:

```
year = 1994;
printf("Enter the amount to invest > ");
```

```
scanf("%f", &fund);
goal = 2 * fund;
printf("Enter the interest rate of the fund > ");
scanf("%f", &rate);
printf("%4s%5c%8s%5c%8s%5c%8s\n",
       "Year", ' ', "Month", ' ', "Interest", ' ', "Fund");
printf("%4s%5c%8s%5c%8s%5c%8s\n\n",
       "----", ' ', "-----", ' ', "--------", ' ', "----");
while (fund < goal)
{
   interest = fund * rate / 12;      /* the interest for the month */
   fund = fund + interest;
   switch(month)                     /* which month is it? */
   {
      case 1: printf("%4d%5c%8s%5c%8.2f%5c%8.2f\n\n",
                     year, ' ', "January", ' ', interest, ' ', fund);
              break;
      case 2: printf("%4d%5c%8s%5c%8.2f%5c%8.2f\n\n",
                     year, ' ', "February", ' ', interest, ' ', fund);
              break;
               :
               :
               :
     case 12: printf("%4d%5c%8s%5c%8.2f%5c%8.2f\n\n",
                     year, ' ', "December", ' ', interest, ' ', fund);
              break;
   }
   month = month % 12 + 1;
   if (month == 1)
   {
       year = year + 1;
   }
}
```

Study this program carefully. Note that the use of a *switch* statement within the loop is anatural choice for this task.

EXERCISES 8.1.3

1. Include a loop in the program for Exercise 4.4.1, 5(b), so that the user enters expressions until he wants to stop. The following display is an example:

   Enter the operation > <u>6 + 2.7</u>
   The result = 8.7
   Another expression? (y/n) <u>y</u>
   Enter the operation > <u>2.03 – 6</u>
   The result = <u>–3.97</u>
   Another expression? (y/n) <u>n</u>

2. Include a loop in the program for Exercise 4.3.2, 9, so that the user may process information for more than one parent. Use a sentinel to terminate the loop. Provide a solution for each of the following tasks:
   a. The user is asked a question about whether or not to continue.
   b. Invalid initials will be entered to terminate the loop.
3. Include a loop in the program in Exercise 4.4.1, 5(a), so that the user may enter more than one number. Use a sentinel in the form of a question about whether or not to continue to terminate the loop.

4. Include a loop in the program in Example 4.1.4 so that the user may enter the scores for multiple games. Use a sentinel in the form of a question about whether or not to continue to terminate the loop.
5. Include a loop in the program in Example 4.1.4 so that the user may enter civil codes several times. Use the *switch* statement as part of your solution, and use a sentinel in the form of a question about whether or not to continue to terminate the loop.
6. Modify the program in question 5 above so that entering an invalid civil code terminates the loop. (Of course, this implies that the civil code no longer needs to be checked in the *if/else* chain.)
7. Place the program in Example 5.1.2 within a loop. The loop will be terminated by:
   a. entering an invalid day.
   b. entering an invalid day or invalid hours.
   c. asking a question about whether or not to continue.
   Provide a solution for each.
8. Place the program in Example 5.1.3 within a loop. The loop will be terminated by asking a question about whether or not to continue.
9. Place the program in Example 5.1.6 within a loop. The loop will be terminated by asking a question about whether or not to continue.
10. Place the program in Example 5.3.1 within a loop. The loop will be terminated by:
    a. entering an invalid mark.
    b. asking a question about whether or not to continue.
    Provide a solution for each.
11. Place the program in Example 6.1.2 within a loop. The loop will be terminated by asking a question about whether or not to continue.
12. Place the program in Exercise 6.1.1, 1, within a loop. The loop will be terminated by asking a question about whether or not to continue.
13. Place the program in Exercise 6.1.2, 5, within a loop. The loop will be terminated by asking a question about whether or not to continue. In addition, the program will sum up (for valid entries only, of course), the total number of children, the total number of males, and the total number of females.
14. Place the program in Example 6.1.4 within a loop. The loop will be terminated by asking a question about whether or not to continue.
15. Place the program in Exercise 6.1.5, 6, within a loop. The loop will be terminated by asking a question about whether or not to continue.
16. Place the program for Exercise 4.4.1, 6, within a loop. The loop will be terminated by asking a question about whether or not to continue.
17. Place the corrected program at the end of Exercise 5.2.4, 4, within a loop. The loop will be terminated by:
    a. asking a question about whether or not to continue.
    b. entering an invalid job code.
    Provide a solution for each.
18. Include a loop in the program in Exercise 6.1.7, 12. The loop terminates when the user answers *no* to the question about whether or not to continue. Should any input be incorrect such as the temperature range or the degree notation, the program does not terminate. Instead, it rejects the request and moves on to the next request.
19. Include a loop in the program in Exercise 4.3.2, 5. Develop two solutions. The loop terminates when the user:
    a. enters a negative number of hours worked.
    b. answers *no* to the question about whether or not to continue.
20. Include a loop in the program in Exercise 5.3.1, 2. Develop two solutions. The loop terminates when the user:
    a. enters a negative weight.
    b. answers *no* to the question about whether or not to continue.
21. Include a loop in the program for Exercise 6.1.6, 9. The loop terminates when the user answers *no* to the question about whether or not to continue. Should any input be incorrect, the program does not terminate. Instead, it rejects the request and moves on to the next request.
22. Include a loop in the program in Exercise 4.4.1, 5(f). The loop terminates when the user answers *no* to the question about whether or not to continue.

23. Include a loop in the program in Exercise 5.1.7, 9. The loop terminates when the checkout clerk answers *no* to the question, "Is there another customer waiting?" The checkout clerk enters the date, the terminal, and the operator codes before looping. Do not ask for the time.
24. Improve the program from question 23 above so that the validity of the input is checked (see Exercise 6.1.7, 14). Use embedded *if/elses*. Should any input be incorrect, the program does not terminate. Instead, it rejects the request and moves on to the next customer's information. Also, implement the special case expressed in Exercise 6.1.7, 15.
25. Modify the program in Exercise 7.3.1, 4 so that it counts
    a. the number of students who failed test 1.
    b. the number of students who failed test 2.
    c. the number of students who failed the final exam.

    Any one of these tests is considered failed if a grade is less than 50%. Provide a single solution for all three counts.
26. Modify the program in question 25 above so that it also counts the number of students that failed the course. Devise a program for each one of the following assumptions:
    a. A course failure results if the final grade is less than 60%.
    b. A course failure results if the final grade is less than 60% or the student failed the final exam.
    c. A course failure results if the student failed any one test or final exam.
27. Include a loop in the program in Exercise 5.1.7, 7. The loop terminates when the user answers *no* to the question about whether or not to continue.
28. Improve the solution above by following the specifications in Exercise 6.1.7, 8. Should any input be incorrect, the program does not terminate. Instead, it rejects the request and moves on to the next request.
29. Include a loop in the program in Exercise 6.1.7, 10. The loop terminates when the user answers *no* to the question about whether or not to continue.
30. Include a loop in the program in Exercise 6.1.7, 9. The loop terminates when the user answers *no* to the question about whether or not to continue. Should any input be incorrect, the program does not terminate. Instead it rejects the request and moves on to the next request.
31. Include a loop in the program in Exercise 5.1.7, 6. Develop two solutions. The loop terminates when the user:
    a. enters all numeric initials.
    b. answers *no* to the question about whether or not to continue.
32. Improve the solution for question 31 above so that any incorrect input (input outside the acceptable range) prompts the program to reject the request and move on to the next request instead of terminating.
33. Include a loop in the program in Exercise 5.3.1, 7. The loop terminates when the user answers *no* to the question about whether or not to continue.
34. Include a loop in the program in Exercise 6.1.7, 11. The loop terminates when the user answers *no* to the question about whether or not to continue. Should any input be incorrect, the program does not terminate. Instead it rejects the request and moves on to the next request.
35. Include a loop in the program in Supplementary Exercise 6.1, 1. The loop terminates when the user answers *no* to the question about whether or not to continue.
36. Include a loop in the program in Supplementary Exercise 6.1, 2. The loop terminates when the user answers *no* to the question about whether or not to continue.
37. Include a loop in the program in Supplementary Exercise 6.1, 5. The loop terminates when the user answers *no* to the question about whether or not to continue.
38. Include a loop in the program in Supplementary Exercise 6.1, 6. The loop terminates when the user answers *no* to the question about whether or not to continue.
39. Include a loop in the program in Supplementary Exercise 6.1, 7. The loop terminates when the user answers *no* to the question about whether or not to continue.
40. Include a loop in the program in Exercise 6.1.7, 16. Develop two solutions. The loop terminates when the user:
    a. enters all numeric initials.
    b. answers *no* to the question about whether or not to continue
41. Improve the program in question 40 above by following the specifications in Exercise 6.1.7, 17.

8.1.2 MENU-DRIVEN INTERFACES

Loops make menu-driven programming possible and useful. A menu-driven program is one that allows the user to select from a list by simply pressing a key. (See Example 8.1.6.)

Example 8.1.6

Revisit Example 4.4.1. We want to use the menu from the example. A new option, "Quit," has been added to allow a user to terminate the program. Following is a look at the new display:

Tax Information System

Select your civil status:

(M) Married
(S) Single
(W) Widowed
(D) Divorced
(Q) Quit

Enter here > S

You must fill out the form TX-113-2

The user may return to the menu repeatedly and select another option. The program for this task is shown below, with new coded in bold type:

```
#include <stdio.h>
#include <conio.h>

main()
{
     char civil_code;

     civil_code = ' ';1
     while (civil_code != 'Q' && civil_code != 'q')2
     {
          clrscr();3
          printf("%s%s%s%s%s%s%s",
                 "                TAX INFORMATION SYSTEM\n\n",
                 "                Select your civil status:\n\n",
                 "                (M)      Married\n",
                 "                (S)      Single\n",
                 "                (W)      Widowed\n",
                 "                (D)      Divorced\n",
                 "                (Q)      Quit\n\n",
                 "               Enter here > ");

          scanf("\n%c", &civil_code);

          switch(civil_code)
          {
            case 'M': case 'm':
                    printf("\nYou must fill out form TX-120-9\n");
                    break;
            case 'S': case 's': case 'W': case 'w':
                    printf("\nYou must fill out form TX-113-2\n");
                    break;
```

```
            case 'D': case 'd':
                    printf("\nYou must fill out form TX-121-7\n");
                    break;
            case 'Q': case 'q':
                    break;4
            default:
                    printf("\nInvalid code.\n");
                    break;
        }
    }
    printf("\nGood bye!");    /* program should quit gracefully */
}
```

Explanations

1. This line is a necessary trick. The loop must be entered **at least once** in order to display the menu. By setting *civil_code* to ' ', the loop is guaranteed to be entered. Note that setting *civil_code* to ' ' is arbitrary; it could be set to anything except *'Q'* or *'q'*.
2. The menu should be displayed as long as the user does not press a *'Q'* or a *'q'*.
3. The function *clrscr()* clears the screen in order to redisplay the menu for each execution of the loop. This function is not ANSI C. Its name differs across compilers. Also, the line *#include <conio.h>* is needed when *clrscr()* is called. Again, this may differ for other compilers.
4. If the user enters a *'Q'* or a *'q'*, the program will not immediately quit the loop. The loop will eventually be terminated once the loop entry condition is rechecked. Why is the action of quitting the loop delayed? Because the entry condition is what should decide whether or not to continue looping. This is good programming practice.

EXERCISES 8.1.4

1. To understand the importance of clearing the screen before displaying the menu, remove the *clrscr()* command, run the program, and explain what happens.
2. Develop a menu interface for Exercise 4.4.1, 5(g). Following is an example showing what the menu should look like:

   The Job Classifications

   (1) Secretary
   (2) Programmer
   (3) MIS Manager
   (4) Engineer
   (5) Quit

   Enter your job classification > 2
   Enter your weekly salary > 510
   Your Christmas bonus is 500.00

3. Modify the program in question 2 above so that the user may either enter the job code or the first letter of the job title. For instance, to choose Engineer, the user can key in the letter 'E' or 'e' as well as the number '4'.

8.1.3 KEEP THE BODY OF THE LOOP SIMPLE

As mentioned in Subsection 7.4.2, users often mistakenly insert instructions in the loop that need to be executed only once. Another common mistake is to include redundant decision statements within a loop, as Example 8.1.7 shows.

Example 8.1.7

Suppose we want to use the program in Example 5.1.6 repeatedly until the qualification code is invalid. This invalid data serves as the sentinel. Once the sentinel is detected, an appropriate message is displayed, and the program quits. It seems natural to simply place the program in Example 5.1.6 within a loop, as follows:

```
printf("Enter the contractor's qualification code > ");
scanf("\n%c%d", &ex, &sp);
ex_up = toupper(ex);
while ((ex_up == 'M' || ex_up == 'L') && (sp >= 40 && sp <= 120))
{
     if ((ex_up == 'M' || ex_up == 'L') && (sp >= 40 && sp <= 120))[1]
     {
        printf("\nThe code is valid");
     }
     else[2]
     {
        printf("\nThe code is INVALID");
     }
     printf("\nEnter the contractor's qualification code > ");
     scanf("\n%c%d", &ex, &sp);
}
```

Explanations

Much of the code is redundant.

1. The *if* condition is not needed because it checks the exact same thing that the *while* entry condition checks. There is no need to check the same thing twice.
2. The *else* part is never reached because its placement within the loop tells the program that the qualification code is valid. It cannot be invalid.

   In light of these observations, the program can be reduced to the following:

```
printf("Enter the contractor's qualification code > ");
scanf("\n%c%d", &ex, &sp);
ex_up = toupper(ex);
while ((ex_up == 'M' || ex_up == 'L') && (sp >= 40 && sp <= 120))
{
      printf("\nThe code is valid");
      printf("\nEnter the contractor's qualification code > ");
      scanf("\n%c%d", &ex, &sp);
}
printf("The code is INVALID");
```

EXERCISES 8.1.5

1. A student was asked to write a program that accepts up to ten grades or stops when an entry is invalid. An invalid grade is one that is less than 0 or greater than 100. For each number entered, if the number is valid, the message "The mark is valid" is displayed. Otherwise, the message "An invalid mark has been entered" is displayed. After the loop has quit, the program displays either "Ten valid marks have been entered" or "An invalid mark has been entered," depending on the situation. Following is the program that the student developed.

   ```
   count = 1;
   printf("Enter a mark: ");
   scanf("%d", &mark);
   ```

```
while (count <= 10 && (mark >= 0 && mark <= 100))
{
      if (mark >= 0 && mark <= 100)
      {
          printf("The mark is valid\n");
      }
      else
      {
          printf("An invalid mark has been entered\n");
      }
      printf("Enter a mark: ");
      scanf("%d", &mark);
}
if (count == 10)      /* if 10 marks were entered */
{
      printf("Ten valid marks have been entered");
}
if (mark < 0 || mark > 100)
{
      printf("An invalid mark has been entered");
}
```

Show how this solution, although in working order, can be simplified. (***Hint:*** The *else* part is not needed, since the loop will not continue if a mark is invalid. In fact, even the *if* is not needed. The two *if*s after the loop may be changed to an *if/else.*)

2. Some loops below may be simplified by either eliminating the *if* or the *else.* Which ones should be eliminated and how? (***Hint:*** Do not change what the loops do; just simplify their logic.)

a.
```
scanf("%d%d", &a, &b);
while (a > 10 && b < 6)
{
      if (a > 10 && b < 6)
      {
            printf("More...");
      }
      else

      {
            printf("That's it");
      }
      scanf("%d%d", &a, &b);
}
```

b.
```
scanf("%d%d", &a, &b);
while (a > 10 || b < 6)
{
      if (a > 10 && b < 6)
      {
            printf("Both...");
      }
      else
      {
            printf("Not both...");
      }
      scanf("%d%d", &a, &b);
}
```

c.
```
scanf("%d%d", &a, &b);
while (a > 10 || b < 6)
{
      if (a > 10)
```

```
        {
              printf("Met first");
        }
        if (b < 6)
        {
              printf("Met second");
        }
        scanf("%d%d", &a, &b);
  }
```

d.
```
  scanf("%d%d", &a, &b);
  while (a > 10 && b < 6)
  {
        if (a > 10)
        {
              printf("Met first");
        }
        if (b < 6)
        {
              printf("Met second");
        }
        scanf("%d%d", &a, &b);
        }
```

SUPPLEMENTARY EXERCISES 8.1

1. Example 6.1.6 allowed only one player to play blackjack. Of course, in reality there may be up to four players. After the initial hands are dealt, each player, in turn, is offered a card. Then each player is offered another card. Eventually, none of the players will want more cards. The implementation of this situation clearly calls for a loop. In fact, it calls for embedded loops and the use of arrays. Embedded loops will be covered in Section 9.2 and arrays are beyond this discussion. Consequently, it is impossible to implement this solution at this time.

   Instead, modify the game so that the solution for Example 6.1.6 may be easily included within a loop in the following way. Have the program offer the first player up to three cards and then display her score. Do the same for the second player, and so on. Implement this solution.
2. a. Write a program that reverses the digits of an integer number and displays them in words. For example:

   Enter a number > 2057
   The digits in reverse are:
   Seven, Five, Zero, Two

   Implement the algorithm as follows: First, extract the last digit, 7, with the operation *2057 % 10.* Second, eliminate this digit with the operation *2057 / 10,* which gives you 205. The loop will continue until all numbers have been extracted. To display each digit as text, use a *switch* statement within the loop.

   b. Modify the program above so that the word 'and' will precede the last word:

   Enter a number > 2057
   The digits in reverse are:
   Seven, Five, Zero, and Two

3. Validating the input data is a vital part of any user-friendly software. This is why you have been asked many times since Chapter 4 to write programs that verify the user's input. No matter how clever and professional the internals of a software program are, it is all worthless if the input portion of the software does not:
   a. check the validity of the user's input, such as being within the ranges of valid values.
   b. let the user know about bad input.
   c. allow the user to reenter the data correctly.

Suppose that we wish to create an arithmetic calculator. The program will read in an arithmetic expression, evaluate it, and display the result. It will be able to perform all four arithmetic operations. Following are sample displays that illustrate various situations in which the input is invalid:

```
Enter an arithmetic operation > 5 / 0
Cannot divide by zero. Enter again.
Enter an arithmetic operation > 5 / 2.5
Result =  2.00

Enter an arithmetic operation > -3 > 9
Operation > is unknown. Enter again.
Enter an arithmetic operation > -3 / 9
Result = -0.33
```

Both of the examples illustrate a validation check of the first kind.

```
Enter an arithmetic operation > $ * 2
Failed to read data item #1. Enter again.

Enter an arithmetic operation > 4 * @
Failed to read data item #3. Enter again.

Enter an arithmetic operation > 4 * 2
Result =  8.00
```

This example shows a validation check of the second kind. The *scanf()* that reads erroneous input such as *$ * 2* will fail because it expects a number where the *$* is. As a result, the program will "crash" and likely leave the user puzzled. To prevent a crash, the program must detect that *scanf()* failed and take corrective action. To this end, we will use a handy feature of *scanf()* that, after called, always returns the number of data items successfully read in. For example, when executing the following statement, the program:

```
printf("Enter age, education level, and salary > ");
read_success = scanf("%d%d%f", &age, &educ, &salary);
```

- will store 0 in the variable *read_success* if reading the age fails (reading the data items following it would therefore fail also).
- will store 1 in the variable *read_success* if reading the education level fails (reading the data items following it would therefore fail also).
- will store 2 in the variable *read_success* if reading the salary fails (reading the data items following it would therefore fail also).
- will store 3 in the variable *read_success* if all data items are read successfully.
- will store EOF in the variable *read_success* if it detects Ctrl-Z.

Once the failure is detected, the function *fflush(stdin)* should be called to clear the input buffer. (This function was first used in Example 7.3.6.) The outline of the algorithm that checks the validity of an arithmetic expression is as follows:

1. Enter an arithmetic operation.
2. As long as either the *scanf()* failed
   or the operator is invalid
   or a division by zero is attempted,
   do steps 2.1 to 2.4.
   - 2.1. If *scanf()* failed, do step 2.1.1.
     - 2.1.1. Issue the appropriate error message.
   - 2.2. If the operator is wrong, do step 2.2.1.
     - 2.2.1. Issue the appropriate error message.
   - 2.3. If division by zero is attempted, do step 2.3.1.
     - 2.3.1. Issue the appropriate error message.
   - 2.4. Reenter the arithmetic operation.
3. The operation is now valid; evaluate it.
4. Display the answer.

Now, write a C program to implement this algorithm.

8.2 APPLICATIONS INVOLVING FILES

File handling was first covered in Section 2.5, but we could not discuss a few useful applications at that time. Practical applications of file handling are possible only with loop structures. This section will discuss some typical applications of file processing.

8.2.1 SEQUENTIAL FILE PROCESSING

Although various types of files exist, the only type discussed in this book includes ***text files.*** Information is stored sequentially in these files, meaning that the information is read and processed in the order that it is stored. Consider Example 8.2.1.

Example 8.2.1

Back in Example 8.1.1, it may have been more convenient to enter all the necessary information for all the jobs in a data file using an ***editor.*** Then the program would process all the jobs in one batch. The data might be stored as shown in Figure 8.2.1.

Figure 8.2.1

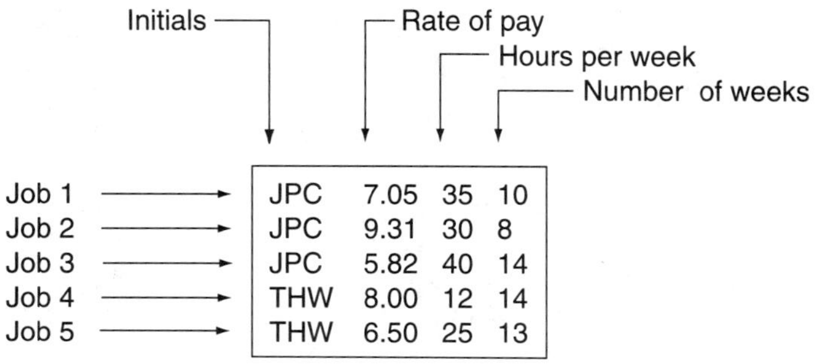

Suppose this data is stored in a file called JOBS.DAT. After Judy had collected the data for each job, she could go home and feed this file into the program. The program could then display the appropriate advice for each job. We also wish to store those advice messages in a file called ADVICE.OUT so that Judy can refer to them later or send them to a printer. This data flow may look like Figure 8.2.2.

Figure 8.2.2

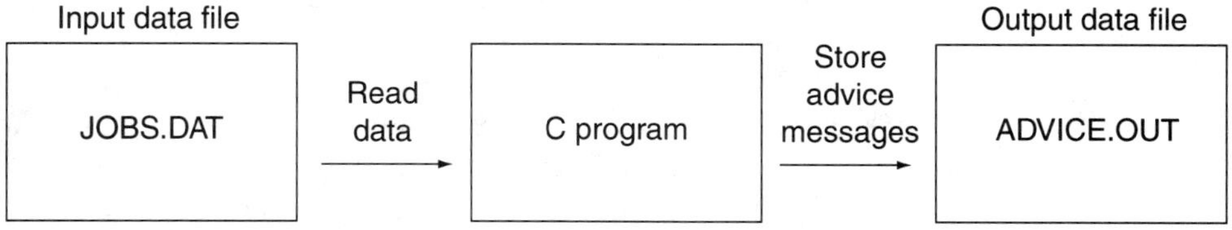

Following is the program. Changes from Example 8.1.1 are shown in bold.

```
#include <stdio.h>

main()
{
      float     hourly_rate;
      int       hours_per_week;
      float     total_income;
      int       num_weeks;
      float     minimum;
      int       counter;
      char      i1, i2, i3;
      FILE *    input_file;    /* declare file pointer variables for */
      FILE *    output_file;   /* both input and output files */

      input_file = fopen("JOBS.DAT", "r");     /* open both files */
```

```
    output_file = fopen("ADVICE.OUT", "w");
    counter = 1;
    while (counter <= 5)
    {
        printf("Income calculation for job number %d:\n\n", counter);

        /* read a record from the file */
        fscanf(input_file, "\n%c\n%c\n%c%f%f%d%d", &i1, &i2, &i3,
                           &minimum, &hourly_rate,
                           &hours_per_week, &num_weeks);

        total_income = hourly_rate * hours_per_week * num_weeks;

        if (total_income >= minimum)
        {
            fprintf(output_file, "Take the job!\n");
            fprintf(output_file,
                       "%c%c%c, You will make $ %.2f this summer\n",
                       i1, i2, i3, total_income);
        }
        else
            fprintf(output_file, "Look someplace else for a job.\n");
        }
        counter = counter + 1;
    }
    fclose(input_file);
    fclose(output_file);
}
```

Note that no prompts are sent to the screen since the data is now pulled from the file JOBS.DAT.

EXERCISE 8.2.1

Modify the program in Example 7.3.4 so that it reads the list of grades from a file named LIST.DAT and stores the average in a file named AVG.OUT.

Checking for the end-of-file indicator. The program in Example 8.2.1 assumes that the file contains five records. Usually, a program does not know ahead of time how many records a file contains. Instead it keeps on reading until it finds a sentinel, which indicates the end of the file. Exercise 8.2.1 above showed that terminating the file with an invalid number does the trick. In general, though, that is a poor method. Luckily, there is an easier way.

At the time that a file is saved, an ***end-of-file (EOF)*** marker is automatically stored at the end of the file by the operating system. This built-in end-of-file indicator is much like a sentinel; hence it is a natural choice for indicating the end of a list of numbers (rather than using an invalid number as in Example 7.3.4). So the –1 simply may be taken out of the file LIST.DAT.

To illustrate the procedure of checking the end-of-file marker, assume a file named IN.DAT with the data:

```
6 3 87 0 21
```

To process this file, we need a loop that reads one number at a time. This loop will continue until the program detects the end-of-file sentinel. There are two possible implementations in C for this task, as shown in the following examples.

Example 8.2.2

Let us revisit the program for Exercise 8.2.1. Each time that *fscanf()* is called, an invisible pointer moves along the file, scanning the data as *fscanf()* demands it. Once this pointer sits at the end-of-file marker, *fscanf()* returns the value EOF. This statement puts EOF in the variable *flag* only when the end-of-file marker is reached:

```
flag = fscanf(ifp, "%d", &num)
```

The indicator *&num* puts the number read in the variable *num.*

For the program to detect the end-of-file, it is only a matter of checking the value inside the variable *flag*. Following is the new program with changes shown in bold type:

```
#include <stdio.h>

main()
{
    int     sum, num, flag;
    FILE  * ifp, * ofp;     /* file pointer variables */

    ifp = fopen("in.dat", "r");
    ofp = fopen("ans.out", "w");
    sum = 0;
    flag = fscanf(ifp, "%d", &num);
    while (flag != EOF)    /* is it the end of file? */
    {
        sum = sum + num;
        flag = fscanf(ifp, "%d", &num);
    }
    fprintf(ofp, "The sum is %d.\n", sum);
    fclose(ifp);
    fclose(ofp);
}
```

Example 8.2.3

The C language provides a function named *feof()* that also checks for the end of the file. When called, *feof()* returns a condition of true if it detects the end-of-file indicator; otherwise, the condition is false. It is obviously meant to be used in a *if* or *while* condition. Here is how the program above would change with this new function:

```
#include <stdio.h>

main()
{
    int    sum, num;
    FILE * ifp, *ofp;       /* file pointer variables */

    ifp = fopen("in.dat", "r");
    ofp = fopen("ans.out", "w");
    sum = 0;
    fscanf(ifp, "%d", &num);
    while (!feof(ifp))    /* loop while end of file not reached */
    {
            sum = sum + num;
            fscanf(ifp, "%d", &num);
    }
    fprintf(ofp, "The sum is %d.\n", sum);
    fclose(ifp);
    fclose(ofp);
}
```

Both programs include the exact same logic, but the former checks the end-of-file (EOF) marker explicitly, and the latter example does this implicitly.

EXERCISES 8.2.2

1. Modify the program in Exercise 8.2.1 so that the program reads grades until reaching the end of the file. Provide two solutions:
   a. Use the EOF symbol (as in Example 8.2.2).
   b. Use the function *feof()*.
2. a. Steve, a college freshman, objects to the solution in Example 8.2.3, explaining that *fscanf()* is called before the end-of-file indicator is checked with *feof()*. Therefore the program will fail if the file is empty. Is he right?
   b. Trying to prove his point, Steve comes up with the following program (which is almost identical to the one in Example 8.2.3):

```
main()
{
        int     sum, num;
        FILE   * ifp, * ofp;

        ifp = fopen("in.dat", "r");
        ofp = fopen("ans.out", "w");
        sum = 0;
        while (!feof(ifp))
        {
                fscanf(ifp, "%d", &num);
                sum = sum + num;
        }
        fprintf(ofp, "The sum is %d.\n", sum);
        fclose(ifp);
        fclose(ofp);
}
```

   He runs his program with the file IN.DAT, which still contains the data 6 3 87 0 21. To his surprise, his program stores the incorrect answer: "The sum is 138." instead of the correct total, 117. Track down the problem and explain.

8.2.2 THREE RULES CONCERNING PERMISSIBLE MODES

There are three rules about permissible modes that you should keep in mind when using files. (To review permissible modes, see Subsection 2.5.1.)

Reading data. If the file contains input data, then use permissible mode *"r"* (read-only). If the file does not exist or cannot be found, then the function *fopen()* will return a NULL value in the file pointer variable. (This special value is useful as you will see in the next subsection.)

Storing data in a new file. If the file is to receive output data, use permissible mode *"w"* (write-only). Should the file not yet exist, it will be created. If the file exists already, it will be reset. (All data that was in it originally probably will be deleted, but this depends on the host operating system. For example, in VAX/VMS the original file is not reset, and a new version of the file is created instead.)

Appending data to an existing file. If the file already contains data, and new data is to be added to it, use permissible mode *"a"*. Should the file not yet exist, it will be created. If the file exists, it will **not** be reset. The data already there will **not** be deleted, and the new data will be appended.

8.2.3 CHECKING FOR THE EXISTENCE OF A FILE

Revisit the program in Example 8.1.1. Suppose the program is run from a subdirectory named MISC, but the input file JOBS.DAT was located in a subdirectory named JOBS. The input file is therefore not in the current directory. Consequently, the *fopen()* function will be unable to find the file JOBS.DAT. Surprisingly, the operating system will not complain and the program will continue to run anyway, without an open input file. As a result, the program could very well behave strangely. This is clearly not desirable.

A good program should trap or capture the error before it reaches the operating system, thereby preventing a possible disaster. To this end, the program should check if the input and output files are open **before** proceeding. Following is an example of this point.

Example 8.2.4

Let us improve the program of Example 8.2.2 so that it first checks if the input file exists. How? The *fopen()* returns the value NULL when it fails to open a file:

```
ifp = fopen("in.dat", "r")
```

The variable *ifp* receives the value NULL **if** the file cannot be opened. Thus, it is only a matter of checking the variable *ifp* before moving on. If the value returned is NULL, the program should notify the user of an error and take an alternative action. Otherwise, the program simply continues. The following program uses this feature and is **much** safer than the one in Example 8.2.2:

```
#include <stdio.h>

main()
{
    int     sum, num, flag;
    FILE * ifp;     /* file pointer variables */
    FILE * ofp;

    ifp = fopen("in.dat", "r");
    if (ifp == NULL) [1]
    {
       printf("Could not open input file\n");
    }
    ofp = fopen("ans.out", "w");
    if (ofp == NULL) [1]
    {
       printf("Could not open output file\n");
    }
    if (ifp != NULL && ofp != NULL) /* both files opened correctly ? */ [2]
    {
      sum = 0;
      flag = fscanf(ifp, "%d", &num);
      while (flag != EOF)   /* is it the end of file ? */
      {
          sum = sum + num;
          flag = fscanf(ifp, "%d", &num);
      }
      fprintf(ofp, "The sum is %d.\n", sum);
      fclose(ifp);
      fclose(ofp);
    }
}
```

Explanations

1. These instructions check if the files opened correctly. If not, an error message is displayed.
2. It is pointless to continue the program if a file could not be opened, so all the file processing is included within the *if* statement and is reached only if both files can be opened.

These safety features should always be used, yet they are usually omitted in most of this book's examples for the sake of shorter programs.

EXERCISES 8.2.3

1. Modify the program in Exercise 7.3.2, 3(b), so the data is now read from a file called WAITS.HRS. Also the sentinel will now be EOF. Assume the data is entered one line per waitress. Check for the existence of the file.
2. Modify the program in Exercise 8.1.1, 4, so that the data is read from a file called PARENTS.KDS. Also, the sentinel will now be EOF. Assume the data is entered one line per parent. Check for the existence of the file.
3. Would the programs in questions 1 and 2 above need to be modified if the data have been entered on the same line, instead of one waitress per line and one parent per line?
4. Improve the solution for Exercise 4.4.1, 5(i) so that it processes more than one employee. Place the information for each employee on separate lines.

8.2.4 STORING REPORTS IN A FILE

The production of reports is very common in business applications. Three activities often connected with the production of reports are: I/O file operations, looping, and page feeds. Following is an example of these activities.

Example 8.2.5

Let us improve the program from Example 8.1.5 so that the display is sent to a file. The report should have 50 lines per page with a header at the top of each page. Here is the new program, with changes in bold:

```
#include <stdio.h>

main()
{
      int      year, month, line;
      float    fund, interest;
      FILE *   report;

      report = fopen("report.out", "w");[1]
      year = 1994;
      printf("Enter the amount to invest > ");
      scanf("%f", &fund);
      goal = 2 * fund;
      printf("Enter the interest rate of the fund > ");
      scanf("%f", &rate);
      line = 1;[2]
      fprintf(report, "%4s%5c%8s%5c%8s%5c%8s\n",
              "Year", ' ', "Month", ' ', "Interest", ' ', "Fund");
      fprintf(report, "%4s%5c%8s%5c%8s%5c%8s\n\n",
              "----", ' ', "-----", ' ', "--------", ' ', "----");
      while (fund < goal)
      {
          interest = fund * rate / 12;
          fund = fund + interest;
          switch(month)
          {
             case 1: fprintf(report, "%4d%5c%8s%5c%8.2f%5c%8.2f\n\n",
                              year, ' ', "January", ' ', interest, ' ', fund);
                     break;
             case 2: fprintf(report, "%4d%5c%8s%5c%8.2f%5c%8.2f\n\n",
                              year, ' ', "February", ' ', interest, ' ', fund);
```

```
                break;
                  :
                  :
                  :
          case 12: fprintf(report, "%4d%5c%8s%5c%8.2f%5c%8.2f\n\n",
                         year, ' ', "December", ' ', interest, ' ', fund);
                 break;
        }
        line = line + 2;3
        if (line > 50)4
        {
            fprintf(report, "\f");5
            fprintf(report,
                    "       Year     Month          Interest          Fund\n"
                    "       ----     -----          --------          ---- \n\n");
            line = 1;6
        }
        month = month % 12 + 1;
        if (month == 1)
        {
            year = year + 1;
        }
    }
    fclose(report);
}
```

Explanations

1. This is the file that will contain the report. All *printf()*s simply need to be changed to *fprintf()*s.
2. The counter variable *line* is needed to keep track of how many lines are occupied on the current page of the report. The text page starts at line 1.
3. A record is reported, and then the counter *line* is incremented by 2, accounting for the double spacing.
4. Once the line count exceeds 50, a new page must be started.
5. The new page is created by sending the escape sequence \f to the file. When the file is sent to the printer, this character will force a ***form feed,*** and the printer will eject a new page.
6. The header is again stored on the new page. Then the line count is set back to 1.

Note that this program does not send the report to the printer directly. It saves it to a file, which then may be sent to a printer.

EXERCISES 8.2.4

1. Modify the program in Exercise 8.2.3, 1, so that a report containing the following columns is stored in a file called WAITS.OUT:

```
0123456789012345678901234567890123456789012345678901234567890

Waitress ID     Number of        Salary         Tips        Total
               Hours Worked                   Received      Income
```

2. Modify the program inf Exercise 8.2.3, 2, so that a report containing the following columns is stored to the screen:

```
01234567890123456789012345678901234567890123456789012345678901234567

Parent's      Gender       Number of      Counts of
Initials                   Children     Males    Females        Children
```

8.2.5 READING A FILE OF A FIXED FORMAT

Let us revisit Example 8.2.1. Suppose Judy used a database such as *Clipper* to store the data for all interviews. She wanted to feed this data to her C program, but she encountered a problem: her program can only read text files and *Clipper* database files are **not** of that type. So she must use *Clipper's* file conversion utility to change the file data into text. Figure 8.2.3 shows what she obtained in the conversion.

Figure 8.2.3

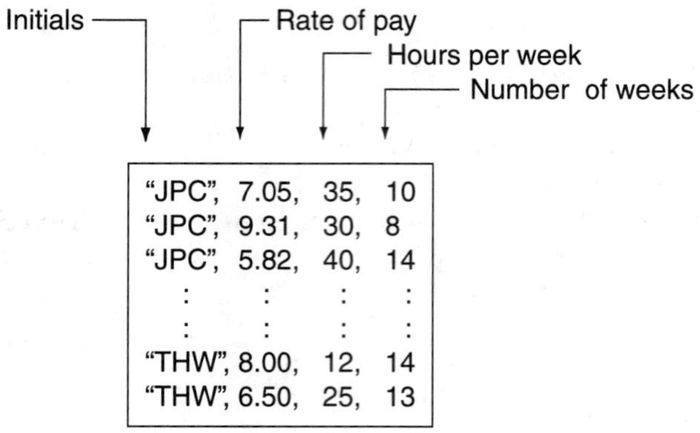

Clipper automatically surrounded the initials with double quotes and separate each data by a comma. These extra characters are a nuisance to Judy. She does not need them read into the C. Luckily, it is easy to tell *fscanf()* to ignore those extra characters. Simply mention them in the format string at the **exact** location that they are expected to appear on the record, as shown in Figure 8.2.4.

Figure 8.2.4

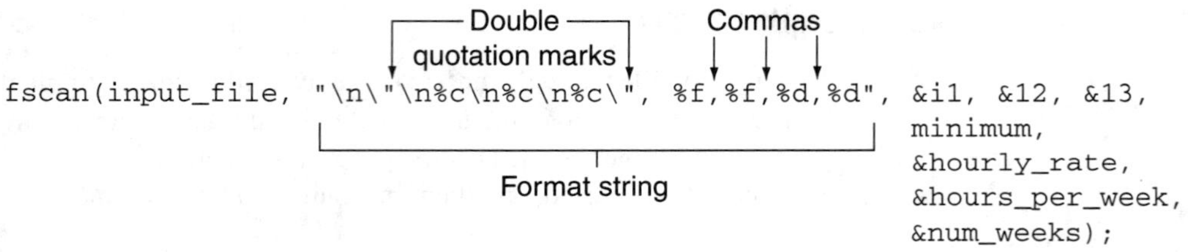

As *fscanf()* scans the record, it skips **all** of the characters in it that are mentioned in the format string and reads only the data corresponding to the format codes. Also:

1. It skips the newline characters. If there are blank lines, they will be ignored.
2. It ignores doubles quotation marks and commas.

Remember, though, that if the format string and the input record do not match **exactly,** the reading may very well fail: double quotation marks, commas, and newlines must appear where expected. In this context, the format string is really a ***template*** specifying the format of the records.

Note the *\n* in front of the format string that precedes the opening double quotation mark of the character sting:

```
fscanf(input_file, "\n\"\n%c\n%c\n%c\", %f,%f,%d,%d", &i1, &i2, &i3,
```

It has the same purpose as do those *\ns* placed before the *%c:* it ensures that the newline character located at the end of the preceding line (before the first double quotation mark of the next line of data) will be skipped when the *fscanf()* is read by the program.

EXERCISES 8.2.5

Suppose the lines of the file refered to above (from Example 8.2.1) were arranged in these formats:

1. "JPC" : 9.31 : 30 : 8
2. <JPC> 9.31 30 8

3. J-P-C 9.31 30 8
4. JPC, $9.31, 30 8

For each, what would the correct format string be to ensure that only the initials and numbers are read in?

8.2.6 COMMON ERRORS AND TRAPS

Do not forget to include code in a loop that checks for the end-of-file marker. For example:

```
fscanf(ifp, "%d", &num);
while (num >= 0)    /* is it the end of the list? */
{
   sum = sum + num;
   fscanf(ifp, "%d", &num);
}
```

Should there not be a number less than 0 in the list, this loop will never stop—the *fscanf()* will try to read past the end-of-file marker.

SUPPLEMENTARY EXERCISES 8.2

1. Improve the program in Exercise 8.1.3, 41, so that all of the letters are stored in a file called LETTERS.LIS. Sending this file to the printer should produce only one letter per page.
2. Improve the program in Exercise 8.1.3, 24, so that all receipts are stored in a file called RECEIPTS.LIS. Sending this file to the printer produces only one receipt per page.
3. Simulate the processing of credit card bills in Supplementary Exercise 4.3, 3, in the following way. Credit charges will be stored in a file named CREDITS.LIS as follows:

   ```
   4510
   20.77 61.02 272.81 55.12
   1178.09 500.11 4902.88 11.99
   661.66 11.52 221.45 78.50
   ```

   The first line consists of the account number, and the following lines each contain the four purchases for a month. The program will read each line, display the credit card bill as in Supplementary Exercise 4.3, 3, and then ask the credit account holder how much he wants to pay toward the month's balance. The unpaid amounts and interest will be automatically accumulated toward the next month's bill. Then the next line will be read, and the process will start over. The interest rate will fluctuate from month to month with the random formula

   *pow(-1, rand() % 2) * ((rand() % 2) + (rand() % 10)/10.0) + 16.00,*

   where 16.00 is the interest to start. Include the directives *#include <stdlib.h>* and *#include <math.h>* at the top of your program. For the dates of the purchases, produce the day randomly from 0 to 31; the month will start at 1 and be incremented every month; the year will start at 1996.
4. Improve the program in question 3 above so that any number of purchases may be made. The list will be terminated with a –1. Following is an example:

   ```
   4510
   20.77 61.02 272.81 55.12 -1
   1178.09 500.11 4902.88 11.99 161.72 81.50 31.03 -1
   11.52 78.50 -1
   ```

   Since the names of the businesses can no longer be assumed as the four used so far, change their names to

   ```
   01/08/96   Purchase location 1                 $    20.77
   01/09/96   Purchase location 2                 $    61.02
   ```

```
01/11/96   Purchase location 3                     $  272.81
01/27/96   Purchase location 4                     $   55.12
01/31/96   Interest charged                        $   54.07
01/31/96   Payment from last month's bill          $    0.00
```

5. As explained in Subsection 8.2.5, the format string of *scanf()* can be made to read a file of a fixed format. The same technique may apply to reading from the screen. Take for instance the DOS *time* command:

   C:\> time
   Current time is 9:38:52.52a
   Enter new time: 10:38:52.52a
   C:\>

   There are five parts in the time format: the hour, minutes, seconds, hundredth of seconds, and A.M. or P.M. The time must be entered in that exact format, or the message "Invalid time" will appear and the user will be asked to reenter the time. Write a program that simulates this time command. Since you have not been taught how to obtain the current time with C, have the program instead generate a random time using the *rand()* function. You will need to call it for each part of the time format.
6. Develop a program similar to the one in question 5 above for the DOS *date* command. It runs as follows:

   C:\> date
   Current date is Fri 02-30-1996
   Enter new date (mm-dd-yy): Thu 02-29-1996
   C:\>

9 Other Kinds of Loops

OBJECTIVES

This chapter introduces you to the following information:

- The *for* and the *do/while* loop structures
- The similarities and differences of each kind of loop
- The procedure for coding embedded loops

INTRODUCTION

This chapter offers you more tools for using C: the *for* loop, the *do/while* loop, and embedded loops, or loops within loops. You will also learn in what situations each loop is appropriate.

9.1 THE *for* STATEMENT

From the numerous examples shown in Chapters 7 and 8, we know the following:

1. A loop requires a counter to indicate the desired number of times that it will execute.
2. A loop requires a counter and an accumulator when calculating an average from a list of numbers.

The *for* loop is ideal for these tasks because it simplifies the logic of the loop for those situations. Let's first take a look at the *for*'s syntax.

9.1.1 *for:* AN ABBREVIATED FORM OF A *while* LOOP

Following are some examples that illustrate how a *for* loop is constructed.

Example 9.1.1

Let us convert the *while* loop in Example 7.1.1 into a *for* loop. Figure 9.1.1 compares the two loops graphically.

Figure 9.1.1

The *while* loop:

```
counter = 1;            <------ Executed first

while (counter <= 5)    <------ Executed second
```

```
{
    :
    :     ─── Executed third (same as solution in Subsection 7.1.1)
    :

    counter = counter + 1;  ←── Executed last, then return to step 2
}
```

The *for* loop:

```
      Executed first     Executed second     Executed last, then return to step 2
for (counter = 1 ; counter <= 5 ; counter = counter + 1)
{
    :
    :  ─── Executed third (same as solution in Subsection 7.1.1)
    :
}
```

Note carefully the order of execution of the different parts of the *for* loop. Following is the complete solution, with the *for* header shown in bold type:

```
#include <stdio.h>

main()
{
    float   hourly_rate;
    int     hours_per_week;
    float   total_income;
    int     num_weeks;
    char    letter1, letter2, letter3;
    int     counter;

    for (counter = 1; counter <= 5; counter = counter + 1)
    {
        printf("Income calculation for job number %d:\n\n", counter);
        printf("Enter your initials > ");
        scanf("\n%c\n%c\n%c", &letter1, &letter2, &letter3);
        printf("Enter the hourly wage > ");
        scanf("%f", &hourly_rate);
        printf("Enter the total work hours per week > ");
        scanf("%d", &hours_per_week);
        printf("Enter the number of weeks of work > ");
        scanf("%d", &num_weeks);

        total_income = hourly_rate * hours_per_week * num_weeks;

        printf("%c%c%c, You will make $ %.2f this summer\n\n",
        letter1, letter2, letter3, total_income);
    }
}
```

The code within the inner braces comes from Subsection 7.1.1. Note that parentheses are not required on either side of the entry condition, *counter <= 5:*

```
for (counter = 1; counter <= 5; counter = counter + 1)
```

This first line of the loop is called the ***header.*** It consists of three parts, the initialization of the counter, the entry condition, and the incrementation or decrementation of the counter. These parts **must** be separated by semicolons, as shown in Figure 9.1.2.

Figure 9.1.2

```
for (counter = 1;¹ counter <= 5;² counter = counter + 1)³
```

Explanations

1. Initialization
2. Entry condition
3. Counter incrementation/decrementation

Even if one of these three parts is left empty, the semicolons must remain. Note that the header does not terminate with a semicolon, and, as a visual aid, the three parts may be placed on separate lines:

```
for (counter = 1;
     counter <= 5;
     counter = counter + 1)
```

Using the comma operator. More than one statement may be placed within each part of the header, as Example 9.1.2 shows. It also shows that the condition of a *for* loop need not involve a counter; it can involve an accumulator instead.

Example 9.1.2

Let us change the *while* loop of the program in Example 8.1.4 into a *for* loop. Here is the program again:

```
#include <stdio.h>

main()
{
       int      year, month;
       float    fund, interest, rate, goal;

       month = 1;¹
       year = 1994;¹
       printf("Enter the amount to invest > ");
       scanf("%f", &fund);
       goal = 2 * fund;
       printf("Enter the interest rate of the fund > ");
       scanf("%f", &rate);
       printf("%4s%5c%5s%5c%8s%5c%8s\n",
               "Year", ' ', "Month", ' ', "Interest", ' ', "Fund");
       printf("%4s%5c%5s%5c%8s%5c%8s\n\n",
               "----", ' ', "-----", ' ', "--------", ' ', "----");
       while (fund < goal)¹
       {
           interest = fund * rate / 12;
           fund = fund + interest;
           printf("%4d%5c%5d%5c%8.2f%5c%8.2f\n\n",
                   year, ' ', month, ' ', interest, ' ', fund);
           month = month % 12 + 1;
           if (month == 1)
           {
               year = year + 1;
           }
       }
}
```

The lines indicated by a superscript number 1 will be moved into the *for* header. Following is the revised program. The bold type indicates the change from the last version:

```
int       year, month;
float     fund, interest, rate, goal;

printf("Enter the amount to invest > ");
scanf("%f", &fund);
goal = 2 * fund;
printf("Enter the interest rate of the fund > ");
scanf("%f", &rate);
printf("%4s%5c%5s%5c%8s%5c%8s\n",
       "Year", ' ', "Month", ' ', "Interest", ' ', "Fund");
printf("%4s%5c%5s%5c%8s%5c%8s\n\n",
       "----", ' ', "-----", ' ', "---------", ' ', "----");
for (month = 1, year = 1994; fund < goal; )
{
    interest = fund * rate / 12;
    fund = fund + interest;
    printf("%4d%5c%5d%5c%8.2f%5c%8.2f\n\n",
           year, ' ', month, ' ', interest, ' ', fund);
    month = month % 12 + 1;

    if (month == 1)
    {
        year = year + 1;
    }
}
```

When writing a *for* header, remember the following three points. Refer to the code below as you review these points.

```
for (month = 1, year = 1994; fund < goal; )
```

1. The condition does not have to check a counter. Here *(fund < goal;)* it checks the fund against the goal.
2. The third part (after the final semicolon) is left empty.
3. Two statements have been inserted within the first part of the *for* header *(month = 1, year = 1994;)*. They must be separated with a comma, **not** a semicolon.

Why were the statements *month = 1* and *year = 1994* moved into the *for* header, while other statements such as *goal = 2 * fund* were not? Indeed, how do we decide which statements should be moved into a *for* header? (See Subsection 9.1.3 for the answer to these questions.)

Finally, keep in mind that the *for* loop performs the **exact** same task as the *while* loop does; only the presentation differs. Therefore the material covered in Chapters 7 and 8 applies here too.

EXERCISES 9.1.1

1. In *for (month = 1, year = 1994; fund < goal;),* why do you think that the semicolon cannot be used to terminate statements within the first part of the header?
2. Revisit any programs from Chapters 7 and 8, and replace the *while* statement in each with a *for* loop. In particular, try the following questions:
   a. Exercise 7.2.1, 1
   b. Exercise 7.2.1, 2
   c. Exercise 7.2.1, 3
   d. Exercise 7.2.2, 2
   e. Exercise 7.2.2, 5
   f. Exercise 7.2.3, 2
   g. Exercise 7.2.4, 1
   h. Exercise 7.2.5, 2
   i. Exercise 8.1.1, 4

Application: Pausing to continue. The example below illustrates this common and trivial application.

Example 9.1.3

A software product usually starts with an introductory screen. It might show a title, the author, and a brief explanation of the purpose of the software. For example, Example 8.1.1's program might include the following start-up screen:

Summer Job Income Calculator

by

Judy

This program calculates the summer income for five jobs, given the number of hours per week, the wages, and the number of weeks of work for each.

The screen would then pause for, say, five seconds, and then it would continue on. How do you make a program pause? An empty *for* loop seems a good candidate for this task:

```
for (ctr=1; ctr < 8000; ctr = ctr + 1)
{
}
```

or

```
for (ctr=1; ctr < 8000; ctr = ctr + 1) ;
```

There is no code in the loop (which is terminated by the final semicolon). This causes the program to sit idle for a number of seconds (it is not possible to predict how many seconds). This approach might be acceptable if the program is run on a single-user operating system, such as MS-DOS, but it is a poor solution on a multi-user operating system, such as UNIX or VMS. The loop makes the CPU sit idle while other programs wait to be executed. A better solution is to suspend the execution for five seconds and then make it active again. Most C compilers include a function that allows this, as shown in the following example:

```
sleep(5);    /* Put the program to sleep for 5 seconds */
```

Note that the function's name differs across compilers, and it is not ANSI C standard.

9.1.2 INCREMENTATION AND SUMMATION OPERATORS

Because the incrementation of a counter and the summation of an accumulator are very common operations, the C language has two special operators to make these operations easier to code, as shown in Example 9.1.4.

Example 9.1.4

The following program is similar to that for Example 7.2.2, except that this one uses a *for* loop. Remember that the program assumes that the information for at least one job will be entered. Bold type denotes the changes in this version:

```
#include <stdio.h>

main()
{
    float  hourly_rate;
    int    hours_per_week;
    float  total_income, sum_income; /* summation of the incomes */
    int    num_weeks;
    int    num_jobs;
```

```
    char   letter1, letter2, letter3;
    int    counter;
    float  average;

    counter = 1;
    sum_income = 0;
    printf("Calculate the income for how many jobs? ");
    scanf("%d", &num_jobs);
    for (counter = 1, sum_income = 0;
         counter <= num_jobs;
         sum_income += total_income, counter++)
    {
        printf("Income calculation for job number %d:\n\n", counter);
        printf("Enter your initials > ");
        scanf("\n%c\n%c\n%c", &letter1, &letter2, &letter3);
        printf("Enter the hourly wage > ");
        scanf("%f", &hourly_rate);
        printf("Enter the total work hours per week > ");
        scanf("%d", &hours_per_week);
        printf("Enter the number of weeks of work > ");
        scanf("%d", &num_weeks);

        total_income = hourly_rate * hours_per_week * num_weeks;

        printf("%c%c%c, You will make $ %.2f this summer\n\n",
                letter1, letter2, letter3, total_income);
    }
    average = sum_income / num_jobs;
    printf("\nThe average income is $ %.2f\n", average);
}
```

Figure 9.1.3 shows the *for* header and points out the operators that allow shortcuts in the code.

Figure 9.1.3

```
for (counter = 1, sum_income = 0;
     counter <= num_jobs;
     sum_income += total_income, counter++)
```

The operator += tells the program to add the the content of *total_income* to the accumulator *sum_income.* The end result is the same as *sum_income = sum_income + total_income.*

The operator ++ in *counter++* tells the program to add 1 to *counter.* The end result is the same as *counter = counter + 1.*

Other shortcut operators exist for subtraction and decrementation. The operator –= in *sum_income –= total_income* tells the problem to subtract the content of *total_income* from the accumulator *sum_income.* The end result is the same as *sum_income = sum_income – total_income.* The operator – – in *counter– –* tells the program to subtract 1 from *counter.* The end result is the same as *counter = counter – 1.*

Note that in *counter– –,* the operator may just as easily be placed on the left side: – –counter. It works the same on either side (this is also the case for the operator ++). In general, this observation is not true, though, as will be seen in Chapter 13.

EXERCISE 9.1.2

Introduce the shortcut operators discussed above where appropriate in each program produced in Exercise 9.1.1, 2.

9.1.3 WHEN SHOULD A *for* LOOP BE USED?

A *for* loop should be used when:

1. There is a counter to initialize and increment/decrement.
2. There is an accumulator to initialize and to use in the loop.

A *for* loop is probably unnecessary in all other situations. Consider the following two examples.

Example 9.1.5

Write a program that lets the user enter weights in pounds and displays them in kilograms. Simply divide the pounds by 2.2046. The end of input will be indicated by entering a negative weight. Following is what the solution would look like using a *while* loop:

```
#include <stdio.h>

main()
{
    float  pounds;

    printf("Enter an invalid weight to terminate the loop\n\n");
    printf("Enter a weight in pounds > ");
    scanf("%f", &pounds);
    while (pounds >= 0)
    {
          printf("The weight in kilograms is %.2f\n", pounds / 2.2046);
          printf("Enter a weight in pounds > ");
          scanf("%f", &pounds);
    }
}
```

A solution using a *for* loop would look like this:

```
printf("Enter an invalid weight to terminate the loop\n\n");
printf("Enter a weight in pounds > ");
scanf("%f", &pounds);
for ( ; pounds >= 0; )
{
    printf("The weight in kilograms is %.2f\n", pounds / 2.2046);
    printf("Enter a weight in pounds > ");
    scanf("%f", &pounds);
}
```

The first and third parts of the *for* header are empty because there is no counter to initialize and no counter to increment/decrement. Therefore, in this case the *for* loop adds no advantage over the *while* loop and the *while* loop is sufficient.

Example 9.1.6

Modify Example 9.1.5's program above so that it displays the summation of the weights in pounds and in kilograms. As soon as a negative weight is entered, the loop will terminate. Following is the revised code, with changes in bold:

```
float  pounds, sum;

printf("Enter an invalid weight to terminate the loop\n\n");
printf("Enter a weight in pounds > ");
scanf("%f", &pounds);
for (sum = 0; pounds >= 0; sum += pounds)
{
     printf("The weight in kilograms is %.2f\n", pounds / 2.2046);
```

```
        printf("Enter a weight in pounds > ");
        scanf("%f", &pounds);
}
printf("Total weight in pounds = %.2f\n", sum);
printf("Total weight in kilograms = %.2f\n", sum / 2.2046);
```

A *for* loop is now advantageous because the header clearly indicates a summation of pounds:

```
for (sum = 0; pounds >= 0; sum += pounds)
```

The segment *sum = 0* initializes the summation, while *sum += pounds* sums up the pounds for each loop execution.

EXERCISES 9.1.3

1. Revisit the following programs and rewrite each *while* statement into a *for* loop:
   a. Exercise 7.3.2, 2
   b. Exercise 7.3.2, 3
   c. Exercise 8.1.1, 6
   d. Exercise 8.1.2, 2
   e. Exercise 8.1.2, 4
   f. Exercise 8.1.3, 2
   g. Exercise 8.1.3, 4
   h. Exercise 8.1.3, 5
   i. Exercise 8.1.3, 6
   j. Exercise 8.1.3, 11
   k. Exercise 8.1.3, 14
   l. Supplementary Exercise 8.1, 2
   m. Exercise 8.2.4, 1
   n. Exercise 8.2.4, 2
2. a. Write a program that produces the following sequence of numbers:

   0, 1, 1, 2, 3, 5, 8, 13, 21, 34, 55, 89, 144, and so on

   One number will be displayed for each execution of the loop. Each number in the sequence is obtained from the addition of the previous two, except for the first two numbers, which must be displayed before entering the loop. The sequence is called a Fibonacci sequence.

   b. A solution can be worked out so that only the *printf()* remains inside the body of a *for* loop. How?

Proper layout of a *for* loop. A *for* loop must be put together properly, or it will offer no advantage over the *while* loop. Consider the following examples.

Example 9.1.7

The following two programs do the same thing:

```
ctr = 0;                          ctr = 0;
for ( ; ctr < 10; )               while (ctr < 10)
{                                 {
      printf("Flash");                  printf("Flash");
      ctr++;                            ctr++;
}                                 }
```

However, parts 1 and 3 of the *for* header, the initialization and counter incrementation, respectively, are missing from the program at left above. This negates the purpose for such a loop.

Example 9.1.8

The header should **not** include statements other than those that initialize a counter or an accumulator, check a condition, or increment/decrement a counter or sum into an accumulator. There is usually no practical reason for other statements (this is not entirely true, but may be assumed true for our purposes). For example, the following program does the exact job that the programs above did. (Why do you think that is true?)

```
ctr = 0;
for (ctr = 0; ctr < 10; printf("Flash"), ctr++) ;
```

But the presence of the *printf()* in the third part of the header goes against the purpose of the third part.

EXERCISE 9.1.4

Discuss the use of the *for* header in Example 9.1.2. Could other statements be included in it? If so, would it be appropriate?

9.1.4 COMMON ERRORS AND TRAPS

Programmers commit a few common errors when creating for loops:

1. Do not think that the three parts in the *for* loop header are executed in sequence, with initialization always first, entry second, incrementation/decrementation third, and statements fourth. The correct sequence is:

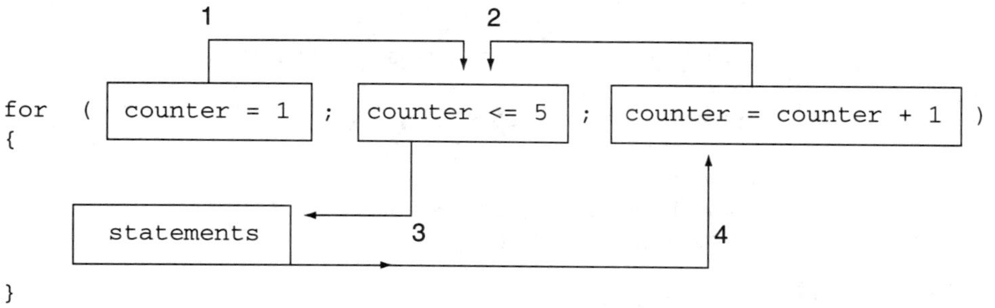

   The reason for this confusion is most likely caused by a misinterpretation of the purpose of the semicolons in the *for* header. They separate the three parts of the header, but they are **not** statement terminators.

2. Do not terminate the *for* loop header with a semicolon. For example, in the following code, the last semicolon terminates the loop:

```
for (counter = 1; counter <= 5; counter = counter + 1);
{
      :
      :
      :
}
```

   The statements within the braces (shown as :) are no longer part of the loop. (Why do you think this is so?) Consequently, they will be executed only once.

3. Do not terminate the third part of the header with a semicolon. For example, in the following code, note the semicolon inside the closing parentheses:

```
for (counter = 1; counter <= 5; counter = counter + 1;)
{
      :
      :
      :
}
```

   Within the header, the semicolon's purpose is to separate the three parts. It does not signal the end of the statement *counter = counter + 1,* as it would anywhere else. The presence of this third semicolon indicates to the compiler that there are four parts. This constitutes a syntax error.

4. Do not use commas instead of semicolons to separate the three parts of the *for* loop header, as in this example:

```
for (counter = 1, counter <= 5, counter = counter + 1)
{
        :
        :
        :
}
```

A comma should be used only to separate statements **within** a single part of the header. It is the three parts of the *for* header that are separated with semicolons.

SUPPLEMENTARY EXERCISE 9.1

Write a program that monitors the level of hot water in a water tank in a home. The program will ask how much water is initially loaded in the tank. Then the house's occupants will enter how much water they use. They will do this until the user wants to stop monitoring the family's water use (i.e., terminate the loop). Should the level of the water drop below a minimum capacity (entered at initialization time), the program will send a warning and advise the user to refill the tank. Following is a sample run of the program:

Enter the amount of liters loaded > 350
Enter the minimum capacity acceptable > 50

Monitoring started. Enter a negative amount to terminate.
Enter the amount used > 23.6
Enter the amount used > 101.2
Enter the amount used > 140.73
Enter the amount used > 57.06
WARNING The level of the water is LOW
Do you wish to refill now (y/n)? y
        Enter how much > 200
Enter the amount used > 9.01
Enter the amount used > –1
Monitoring stopped.

9.2 EMBEDDED LOOPS: APPLICATIONS

Embedded loops are simply loops within loops. Numerous applications require them. Following are some examples for the use of embedded loops.

9.2.1 DRAWING PATTERNS

Drawing patterns on the screen, as in Example 9.2.1, is a simple and entertaining way to come to like *for* loops!

Example 9.2.1

Write a program that displays a rectangle, the size of which is requested by the user. The program display might look like this:

```
Enter the size of the rectangle > 4 8
********
********
********
********
```

Following is the program that accomplishes this task. Study it carefully.

```
#include <stdio.h>

main()
{
      int i, j, width, height;

      printf("Enter the size of the rectangle > ");
      scanf("%d%d", &height, &width);

      /* display the rectangle */

      for (i = 1; i <= height; ++i)
      {
            /* display a line of stars */

            for(j = 1; j <= width; ++j)
            {
                  printf("*");
            }
            printf("\n");
      }
}
```

Inner loop (embedded): `for(j = 1; j <= width; ++j) { printf("*"); }`

Outer loop: `for (i = 1; i <= height; ++i) { ... }`

EXERCISES 9.2.1

1. Modify the program in Example 9.2.1 so that the rectangle begins at column 30. For example:

```
********
********
********
↑
Column 30
```

2. Use solely embedded loops to display the flag of the United States:

```
**********--------------------------
**********--------------------------
**********--------------------------
**********--------------------------
------------------------------------
------------------------------------
------------------------------------
```

   Hint: Use a sequence of two loops. The first one displays the first four lines, the second the remaining lines. Moreover, the first loop will execute two embedded loops: one for the stars, another for the dashes.

3. a. Write a program that uses embedded loops to produce the following rectangle:

```
**************************
*                        *
*                        *
*                        *
*                        *
*                        *
*                        *
**************************
```

   b. Modify the program in (a) so that the user must enter the dimensions of the rectangle.

c. Modify (b) so that the program verifies the validity of the dimensions. If they are invalid, the program repeatedly asks the user to reenter them until they are valid.

4. a. Write a program that uses embedded loops to produce the following cross:

```
+       +
 +     +
  +   +
   + +
    +
   + +
  +   +
 +     +
+       +
```

b. Modify (a) so the user enters the dimensions. Assume the dimensions are always odd numbers. Why? because the cross is constructed slightly differently when the dimensions are even numbers:

```
+       +
 +     +
  +   +
   + +
   + +
  +   +
 +     +
+       +
```

c. Modify (a) so the user enters the dimensions of the cross. Assume the dimensions are always even numbers.

d. Modify the programs from (b) and (c) so that the loop will work regardless of the parity of the dimensions.

e. Include code in both programs to verify the validity of the dimensions. If they are invalid, the program repeatedly asks the user to reenter the dimensions until the entered information is judged to be valid.

5. Modify the program from question 4 above so that numbers are displayed instead of plus signs in the cross. Example:

```
4       4
 3     3
  2   2
   1 1
   1 1
  2   2
 3     3
4       4
```

6. a. Write a program to produce a subtraction table of size 5:

```
 -  | 0   1   2   3   4
 -- |-------------------
 0  | 0  -1  -2  -3  -4
 1  | 1   0  -1  -2  -3
 2  | 2   1   0  -1  -2
 3  | 3   2   1   0  -1
 4  | 4   3   2   1   0
```

b. Generalize the program so that it can produce a table of up to size 10.

c. Include code that verifies the validity of the table size that the user requests.

9.2.2 READING MULTIPLE LISTS OF NUMBERS

Example 9.2.2 illustrates the concept of reading multiple lists of numbers.

Example 9.2.2

Let us write a program that adds up the scores at a baseball game and determines the winner. This is done for all the games played that day. The user first enters the number of games, and then enters the scores. Let us assume that a game always consists of nine full innings, even if there is a tie. A sample run of the program might yield the following display.

```
Enter number of games > 2

Enter the scores for the visitors: 0 0 0 2 0 1 0 0 1
The total score for the visitors is 4
Enter the scores for the home team: 1 0 0 2 2 0 0 0 3
The total score for the home team is 8
Home team won

Enter the scores for the visitors: 0 2 0 0 1 0 4 4 0
The total score for the visitors is 11
Enter the scores for the home team: 2 2 3 0 5 1 0 0 0
The total score for the home team is 13
Home team won
```

Following is the program that produced the display above.

```
#include <stdio.h>

main()
{
     int   i, j, num_games, score, total;

     printf("Enter number of games > ");
     scanf("%d", &num_games);

     /* Process all the games */

     for (i = 1; i <= num_games; ++i)
     {
          printf("\n\nEnter the scores for the visitors; "):
          for (total = 0, j = 1; j <=9; ++j)
          {
               scanf("%f", &score);                               — 1
               total = total + score;
          }
          printf("The total score for the visitors is %d\n", total);
          printf("Enter the scores for the home team: ");
          for (total = 0, j = 1; j <= 9; ++j)
          {
               scanf("%f", &score);                               — 2
               total = total + score;                                 — 4
          }
          print("The total score for the home team is %d\n", total);
          if (total_home > total_visitors)
          {
               printf("Home team won");
          }
          else if (total_home < total_visitors)
          }                                                       — 3
          else
          {
               printf("It is a tie");
          }
     }
}
```

Explanations

1. A *for* loop is needed to read in the scores for the visiting team. Note that the loop is executed nine times, once for each inning. A summation variable named *total* is used to accumulate the scores.
2. Similarly a *for* loop is needed to read in the scores for the home team. The same summation variable *total* is used to accumulate the scores for the visiting team as well. A different variable could have been used, but that is not necessary. (Why do you think that is so?)
3. An *if/else* chain decides which team won.
4. The outer *for* loop ensures that the user enters scores for *num_games,* the number of games.

EXERCISES 9.2.2

1. The use of the += operator would be appropriate in the program in Example 9.2.2. Introduce it in the inner loops. Then move the expression inside the *for* header, giving the body of the loop the statement *scanf("%f", &score).*
2. Write a program that reads the scores of a team of four bowlers playing five-pin games, adds the scores, and displays the total score for the team. There are ten frames in a game and a score for a single fram can range from 0 to 15 inclusive. Following is a sample run of the program:

   Enter the score of each frame for bowler 1:
   8 15 15 10 10 8 12 15 15 7
   Enter the score of each frame for bowler 2:
   2 10 10 5 3 15 13 10 2 7
   Enter the score of each frame for bowler 3:
   15 15 12 15 12 15 15 15 15 12
   Enter the score of each frame for bowler 4:
   10 8 12 15 15 7 12 3 5 12
   The team totalled 432 points

3. Redo the question above, but this time, have the data read from a file, ten frames per line.
   a. Use a *fscanf()* to read a player's scores all ten frames at one time.
   b. Use a *fscanf()* to read a player's scores only one frame at a time.
4. Improve the program in question 3 above so that the program checks if the scores are valid. (Remember the range for the scores is 0 to 15.) If the program finds a score to be invalid, it will store an error message in the file ERROR.LIS. For instance, should the score for bowler 2 at frame 7 be incorrect, the following message will be stored in the error file:

   Bowler 2: Your score for frame 7 is incorrect.
   It has been reset to 0.

5. Consider the following code segment:

```
for (i=1; i < 6; ++i)
{
        printf("Enter 3 numbers > ");
        for (j=0, sum=0; j <= 3; j++, sum += num)
        {
                scanf("%d", &num);
        }
        printf("The sum of the 3 numbers is %d\n", sum);
}
```

   a. Eliminate the inner loop.
   b. Does the resulting program have a better style and readability?
6. Consider the following code segment (which is almost the same as that for question 5):

```
for (i=1; i < 6; i++)
{
        printf("Enter %d numbers > ", i);
        for (j=0, sum=0; j <= i; j++, sum += num)
        {
                scanf("%d", &num);
```

```
        }
        printf("The sum of the %d numbers is %d\n", i, sum);
}
```

Can the inner loop be eliminated?

7. Generalize the program in Example 9.2.2 so that it can accept any number of innings (e.g., overtime innings in case of a tie). The user presses Ctrl-Z to indicate the end of each game. A sample run of the program might produce the following display:

```
Enter number of games > 2
Enter the scores for the visitors: 0 0 1 0 4 0 0 0 0 0 0 1
The total score for the visitors is 6
Enter the scores for the home team: 1 0 0 0 1 3 0 0 2 0 0 0
The total score for the home team is 7
Home team won

Enter the scores for the visitors: 6 2 0 0 0 2 0 0 1
The total score for the visitors is 11
Enter the scores for the home team: 1 0 0 1 3 0 0 2 1
The total score for the home team is 8
Visitors won
```

8. While using the solution for Exercise 8.1.1, 10, eliminate the need to press Ctrl-Z in the program above. For this to work, assume that no inning will have a score above 99—a pretty safe assumption!
9. Overtime innings are played only if the first nine innings ended in a tie. Question 8 above does not ask to check that. Modify its program further so that the result of a game will be ignored if:
   a. Overtime innings were entered when the first nine innings did **not** result in a tie.
   b. Overtime innings were **not** entered when the first nine innings did indeed result in a tie. For example:

```
Enter number of games > 2

Enter the scores for the visitors: 0 0 1 0 4 0 1 0 0
The total score for the visitors is 6
Enter the scores for the home team: 1 0 0 0 1 3 0 0 1
Error! Overtime innings should have been played—game ignored.

Enter the scores for the visitors: 6 2 0 0 0 2 0 0 1 2
The total score for the visitors is 11
Enter the scores for the home team: 1 0 0 1 3 0 0 2 1 0
Error! Overtime innings should NOT have been played—game ignored.
```

   Hint: Use additional summation variables for the total scores for the first nine innings only.
10. Generalize the solution to Exercise 8.1.1, 10 so that numbers of any magnitude may be entered. This will require an inner loop to scan each digit of each number.
11. Revisit Supplementary Exercise 8.2, 5, where the user is asked to enter a time in the format HH:MM:SS.SSa, such as 10:38:52.92a. In that exercise, the user had to enter all parts making up the time format. However, to be exact, in DOS the user may omit parts of this time format. For instance, the user may enter the time as follows:

```
C:\> time
Current time is 9:38:52.92a
Enter new time: 10
C:\>
```

   This user simply advanced the hour so that the time shows as 10:38:52.92a. Here, all parts of the time format have been omitted except the hour (10). All omitted parts do not change value. To illustrate this further, consider the example below in which only the hour and the minutes have been entered:

```
C:\> time
Current time is 9:38:52.92a
Enter new time: 10:45p
C:\>
```

   In this case, the time will change to 10:45:52.92p.

Generalize the solution for Supplementary Exercise 8.2, 5, to meet these new requirements. It would be difficult to achieve this with the *scanf()* function as coded in Supplementary Exercise 8.2, 5. Instead, have the program read one character from the input at the time. (***Hint:*** Base your solution on the technique employed in Exercise 8.1.1, 10.)

9.2.3 EXTRACTING WORDS FROM A SENTENCE

Example 9.2.3 illustrates the concept of extracting words from a sentence.

Example 9.2.3

Revisit Exercise 7.3.6, 2, the program which is based on Example 7.3.8. This time the program should echo each word, one per line, and ignore all nonletter characters. For example:

```
Enter a sentence > Je pense, donc je suis!
Je
pense
donc
je
suis
```

Following is the program that will accomplish this task:

```
#include <stdio.h>
#include <stdlib.h>

main()
{
    char        ch;

    printf("Enter a sentence > ");
    ch = getchar();
    while (ch != '\n')
    {
        while (isspace(ch) && (ch != '\n'))  /* skip spaces to next word */
        {
            ch = getchar();
        }
        if (ch != '\n')
        {
            putchar(ch);
            ch = getchar();
            while (!isspace(ch) && (ch != '\n'))     /* display the word */
            {
                putchar(ch);
                ch = getchar();
            }
            putchar('\n');                          /* skip to next line */
        }
    }
}
```

Note that the check *ch != '\n'* is needed throughout. Indeed, the sentence could end **any** place in the program's logic. The rest of the program is left for you to study.

EXERCISES 9.2.3

1. Modify the program from Example 9.2.3 so that the user may press Ctrl-Z as well to terminate the sentence. Also use *scanf()* and *printf()* throughout.
2. Change the logic of the program in Example 9.2.3 so that letters are no longer displayed. Instead, punctuation marks are displayed, one per line.

9.2.4 ELIMINATION OF EMBEDDED *if/else* STATEMENTS

This section shows that some very specific types of embedded *if/else* statements may be generated when transformed into a loop. Example 9.2.4 explains this.

Example 9.2.4

Let us generalize the blackjack game described in Supplementary Exercise 8.1, 1. Suppose the player can now draw more than three cards; in fact, he or she can draw any number of cards (assume that a deck is bottomless). Keep in mind that the solution in Supplementary Exercise 8.1, 1, involved embedded *if/elses*, one for each card. It seems now that an endless embeddedness of *if/elses* is needed! Of course, such a construct does not exist. The trick is to use a loop that repeatedly draws a card until the user wants to stop. Following is the new program with changes appearing in bold:

```
#include <stdio.h>
#include <stdlib.h>

main()
{

     int       card, sum_cards, player;
     char      answer;

     for (player = 1; player <= 4; player++)[1]
     {
          printf("\nPlayer %d's turn to play:\n\n");
          printf("Do you wish a card ? (y/n) ");
          scanf("\n%c", &answer);
          sum_cards = 0;
          while (answer == 'y')[2]
          {
               card = rand() % 13 + 1;
               printf("The card drawn is a %d\n", card);[3]
               sum_cards = sum_cards + card;[3]
               printf("Do you want another card ? (y/n) ");[4]
               scanf("\n%c", &answer);[4]
          }
          printf("You totalled %d. ", sum_cards);
          if (sum_cards < 21)
          {
               printf("Too low!");
          }
          else if (sum_cards > 21)
          {
               printf("Too high!");
          }
          else
          {
               printf("Congratulations!");
          }
     }
     printf("\nEnd of the game! -- good bye!");
}
```

Explanations

1. A counter, *player,* is used to determine when to stop the outer loop.
2. A *while* loop replaces the embedded *if/else* construct. However, the condition *answer == 'y'* remains.
3. The variables *card1, card2,* and *card3* are replaced by the single variable *card,* which is repeatedly accumulated into the variable *sum_cards.* This summation variable is **absolutely** necessary. (Why do you think this is so?)
4. A sentinel (in the form of a question) is used to determine when to stop the inner loop.

EXERCISES 9.2.4

1. Modify the program in Example 9.2.3 so that the text is read from a file, one character at a time.
2. Modify the program in Exercise 9.2.2, 9, further. When the scores of a game are found to be incorrect, the program will invite the user to reenter the scores instead of ignoring the game. This will require three embedded loops!
3. Make modifications to the programs in Exercise 7.2.4, 1 so that a user can produce multiple tables. The program will prompt the necessary data for each table.

9.3 THE *do/while* STATEMENT

Almost all examples of loops described thus far give the user the choice of skipping the loop altogether. This is done either through the use of a control variable or a sentinel. Most real-life situations call for this flexibility. Sometimes, though, the loop must be entered at least once. This was the case for the menu-driven interface in Example 8.1.6: the menu had to be produced at least the first time. The *while* and the *for* loop can easily suit such situations. Nevertheless, the C language includes a loop called *do/while* that is meant just for these sorts of situations.

9.3.1 NOT QUITE A *while* LOOP!

The *do/while* works exactly like a *while* loop, except that the entry condition is tested **at the bottom** of the loop instead of at the top. This ensures that the loop is entered at least once and all statements within the loop are executed **at least once.** The following example illustrates this loop.

Example 9.3.1

Revisit Example 7.3.1. If the user answers no to the very first prompt, then the loop will not be entered. Let us assume that there will always be at least one job to process. Thus, the first prompt is no longer needed and a *do/while* loop becomes appropriate. Following is the new program. Modifications appear in bold.

```
#include <stdio.h>

main()
{
    float  hourly_rate;
    int    hours_per_week;
    float  total_income, sum_income;
    int    num_weeks;
    char   letter1, letter2, letter3, answer;
    int    counter;
    float  average;

    counter = 1;
    sum_income = 0;
    do[1]
    {
        printf("Income calculation for job number %d:\n\n", counter);[2]
        printf("Enter your initials > ");
        scanf("\n%c\n%c\n%c", &letter1, &letter2, &letter3);
        printf("Enter the hourly wage > ");
        scanf("%f", &hourly_rate);
        printf("Enter the total work hours per week > ");
        scanf("%d", &hours_per_week);
```

```
        printf("Enter the number of weeks of work > ");
        scanf("%d", &num_weeks);

        total_income = hourly_rate * hours_per_week * num_weeks;

        printf("%c%c%c, You will make $ %.2f this summer\n\n",
                letter1, letter2, letter3, total_income);
        sum_income = sum_income + total_income;
        counter = counter + 1;
        printf("Do you have another job to process? (y/n) ");
        scanf("\n%c", &answer);
    }
    while (answer == 'y');[3,4]
    average = sum_income / (counter - 1)
    printf("\nThe average income is $ %.2f\n", average);
}
```

Explanations

1. Just before entering the loop, the question “Do you have any jobs to process? (y/n)” is deleted, because it is no longer needed there.
2. The block of instructions within the loop remains identical to the one with the *while* loop. However, note that the loop condition (explanation 3) is placed at the bottom of the block of instructions. This means that the block of instructions is executed, and then the loop condition is tested to see if the loop should be executed again. This guarantees that the instructions are reached at least once. This is different from a *while* loop, in which the loop condition is tested before the block of instructions is executed. The possibility exists that the instructions within the loop may not need to be executed at all in a *while* loop.
3. The entry condition is checked at the **bottom** of the loop.
4. The loop statement must terminate with a semicolon. This is not the case with a *while* loop.

EXERCISES 9.3.1

1. Revisit Example 7.1.1. Since the loop will run five times, it certainly loops at least once, so a *do/while* loop is more appropriate. Implement this.
2. How many times will the following loops execute?

a.
```
ctr = 0;
do
{
   printf("%d\n", ctr);
   ctr = ctr + 3;
}
while (ctr < 20);
```

b.
```
ctr = 20;
do
{
   ctr = ctr - 4;
   printf("%d\n", ctr);
}
while (ctr > 1);
```

c.
```
ctr = 0;
do
{
   printf("%d\n", ctr);
   ctr = ctr + 1;
}
while (ctr == 5);
```

d.
```
ctr = 1;
do
{
   printf("%d\n", ctr);
   ctr = ctr + 2;
}
while (ctr <= 20);
```

e.
```
ctr = 1;
do
{
   printf("%d\n", ctr);
   ctr = crt - 1;
}
while (ctr == 1);
```

3. For each of the five loops in question 2 above:
   a. What is the first number displayed? the last number displayed?
   b. What is the value of *ctr* after the loops terminate?
4. For each of the five loops, suppose the *printf()* was switched with the counter incrementation/decrementation.
   a. What is the first number displayed? The last number displayed?
   b. What is the value of *ctr* after the loops terminate?
5. Change the loop in the program from Example 8.1.6 into a *do/while* loop.
6. Modify the following loop into a *do/while* loop:

```
printf("enter some number: ");
scanf("%d", &num);
while (num > 0)
{
    printf("Good. Once again...");
    printf("enter some number: ");
    scanf("%d", &num);
}
```

   Was it worth the effort?
7. Modify the following loop into a *while* loop:

```
do
{
    printf("Enter a student ID > ");
    scanf("%d", &id);

    if (id < 9000 || id > 9999)
    {
          printf("The ID is invalid\n");
          printf("Enter a student ID > ");
          scanf("%d", &id);
    }
}
while (id < 9000 || id > 9999);
```

   Is the resulting loop simpler?
8. The two loops below do exactly the same thing: each repeatedly asks the user to enter a number until it is positive. A negative number is considered invalid. Discuss whether the *while* or *do/while* loop is more appropriate.
   a.
```
do
{
      printf("Input a positive number: ");
      scanf("%d", &num);
      if (num < 0)
      {
          printf("\nERROR: Negative value not allowed!\n\n");
      }
}
while (num < 0);
```
   b.
```
printf("Input a positive number: ");
scanf("%d", &num);
while (num < 0)      /* num < 0 tested only once per loop */
{
      printf("\nERROR: Negative value not allowed!\n\n");
      printf("Input a positive number: ");
      scanf("%d", &num);
}
```

9. The two loops below do exactly the same thing: each asks the user to enter three numbers. Discuss whether the *while* or *do/while* loop is more appropriate:

a.
```
printf("Enter the score for each period:\n");
count = 1;
while (count <= 3)
{
        printf("Period %d >> ", count);
        scanf("%d", &num);
        count++;
}
```

b.
```
printf("Enter the score for each period:\n");
count = 1;
do
{
        printf("Period %d >> ", count);
        scanf("%d", &num);
        count++;
}
while (count <= 3);
```

10. The two loops below do exactly the same thing: they generalize the situation in question 10 above. The user is asked to enter the number of periods played. Discuss whether the *while* or *do/while* loop is more appropriate:

a.
```
printf("How many periods were there (enter 0 if no game) ? ");
scanf("%d", &periods); /* assume the user does not enter */
count = 1;             /* a negative number */
while (count < =periods)
{
        printf("Period %d >> ", count);
        scanf("%d", &num);
        count++;
}
```

b.
```
printf("How many periods were there (enter 0 if no game) ? ");
scanf("%d", &periods);
count = 0;
do
{
        if (count <= periods)
        {
                printf("Period %d >> ", count);
                scanf("%d", &num);
        }
        count++;
}
while (count < periods);
```

11. The two loops below do exactly the same thing as those in question 11 above except that a sentinel indicates the end of the periods. Discuss whether the *while* or *do/while* loop is more appropriate:

a.
```
printf("Enter a list of scores (enter a negative number to stop):\n");
printf("Period 1 >> ");
scanf("%d", &num);
count = 0;
while (num >= 0)
{
        count++;
        printf("Period %d >> ", count);
        scanf("%d", &num);
}
```

b.
```
printf("Enter a list of scores (enter a negative number to stop):\n");
printf("Period 1 >> ");
scanf("%d", &num);
count = 0;
do
{
        if (num >= 0)
        {
                count++;
                printf("Period %d >> ", count);
                scanf("%d", &num);
        }
}
while (num >= 0);
```

9.3.2 COMMON ERRORS AND TRAPS

Forgetting the semicolon at the end of a *do/while* loop is a common mistake made by programmers. For example:

```
do
{
        :
        :
        :
}
while (counter <= 5)
```

If the semicolon is missing at the end of the loop, the compiler will complain. Do not confuse this loop's syntax with that of the *while* loop.

10 User-Defined Functions

OBJECTIVES

This chapter introduces you to the following information:

- How to define and use your own functions.
- The procedure for using the various techniques for passing data to user-defined functions and for having them send back data.
- An introduction to local variables and when to use them.
- How to develop programs using the top-down approach, a systematic and logical method of developing programs.
- The method for defining your own library of functions.

INTRODUCTION

We have already encountered and used functions such as *printf(), scanf(),* and *clrscr().* Precoded and stored in libraries by the compiler manufacturer, these functions may consist of just a few lines [e.g., *clrscr()*] or hundreds of lines of C code [e.g., *printf()*]. In this chapter, you will learn to write your own functions. Actually, you have already been writing functions: *main()* is a function that the program immediately calls when execution is initiated.

The *main()* function is only one part of a program; the programmer may also add his or her own functions. Defining functions offers many advantages. Four of these are listed below and will be made clear in this chapter:

1. User-defined functions may help to reduce the length of a program. This is why the function *printf()* is already provided by the compiler manufacturer. If *printf()* did not exist, you would need to provide all the codes necessary to send messages to the screen, and you would have to do this every single time a *printf()* would otherwise have been called! This would make for an unbearably long program.
2. User-defined functions contribute to the readability of program code, partly because functions make a program shorter.
3. Functions are a natural tool when top-down design is used to build a program. This is because the point of top-down design is to break up a large task into smaller tasks, which can in turn be subdivided into yet even smaller tasks. All of these tasks can easily be coded as functions. Top-down design encourages the creation of modular programs.
4. Finally, when defined correctly, user-defined functions may be used by any program, and the code does not need to be retyped every time.

10.1 STRUCTURE CHARTS AND FUNCTIONS

10.1.1 TOP-DOWN DESIGN APPROACH

Remember that the use of functions is a natural choice in a program coded with the top-down design. Top-down design, in which a large task is broken into smaller tasks, is best illustrated using ***structure charts.*** These charts were introduced in Subsection 1.2.7. The chart given there is too complex to reuse here, so we will look at much simpler situations instead.

Example 10.1.1

Let us write a program that displays the following house:

```
         ^
      /     \
   /           \
/                 \
-------------------
|                 |
|     ------      |
|     |    |      |
|     |    |      |
-------------------
```

Of course this simply requires a sequence of *printf()*s:

```c
#include <stdio.h>

main()
{
    printf("          ^         \n");
    printf("       /     \\      \n");   /* Note that double backslashes */
    printf("    /           \\   \n");          /* are needed to display */
    printf(" /                 \\ \n");                 /* a single one. */
    printf(" ------------------- \n");
    printf(" |                 | \n");
    printf(" |      -----      | \n");
    printf(" |      |   |      | \n");
    printf(" |      |   |      | \n");
    printf(" ------------------- \n");
}
```

Let us now develop another solution using the top-down approach, breaking down the main task into smaller ones. Drawing the house can be broken into two smaller tasks:

Task 1: Draw the roof.
Task 2: Draw the main floor.

This is best illustrated and explained in the form of a structure chart, as shown in Figure 10.1.1.

Figure 10.1.1

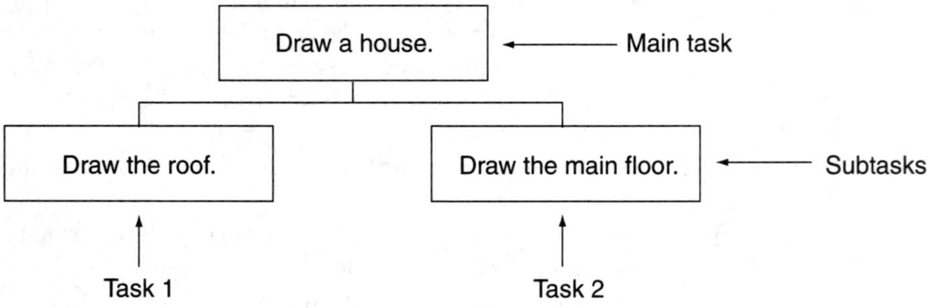

Once a structure chart is designed, the next step is to write a C program that reflects it. Subsection 10.1.2 explains how to proceed.

10.1.2 DEFINING YOUR OWN C FUNCTIONS

In order to develop a C program, you must define a function to accomplish each task: (1) a function named *roof()* to draw the roof, (2) a function named *main_floor()* to draw the main floor, and (3) the function *main()* to execute the first two functions. Let us now look at how a C function is defined.

Function definitions and calls. The process of writing a function is called the ***definition.*** The action of using or executing a function [e.g., *printf()*] is called a ***function call.*** Following is the program from Example 10.1.1, which we can use to illustrate these concepts:

```
#include <stdio.h>

/* First, define the functions */

void roof(void)
{                                                              
    printf("          ^          \n");   
    printf("        /   \\        \n");   Function
    printf("      /       \\      \n");   definition
    printf("    /           \\ \n");
}

void main_floor(void)
{
    printf("    ------------------- \n");                        1
    printf("   |                  | \n");
    printf("   |      |---|       | \n");   Function
    printf("   |                  | \n");   definition
    printf("   |                  | \n");
    printf("    ------------------- \n");

}

/* Second, call the functions above in the main() function */

main()
{
    roof();         /* a function call */                        2
    main_floor();  /* a function call */
}
```

Explanations

1. All of the user-function definitions should be placed above the function *main()*. Strictly speaking, they may also be placed below that function, but at a price: the use of the function would become a little more complex. We will avoid this completely until Section 12.1.
2. This is the definition of the "main" function. It consists of calls to the functions defined above it.

The execution of the program always begins at *main()*. When the function *roof()* is called, the following happens:

1. The execution is passed to the function *roof()*.
2. The lines of code defined within it are immediately executed, thereby displaying the roof.
3. Once this is terminated, the execution goes back to *main()* and continues with a call to the function *main_floor()*.

Figure 10.1.2 summarizes the mechanism of a function call and the return from that call:

Figure 10.1.2

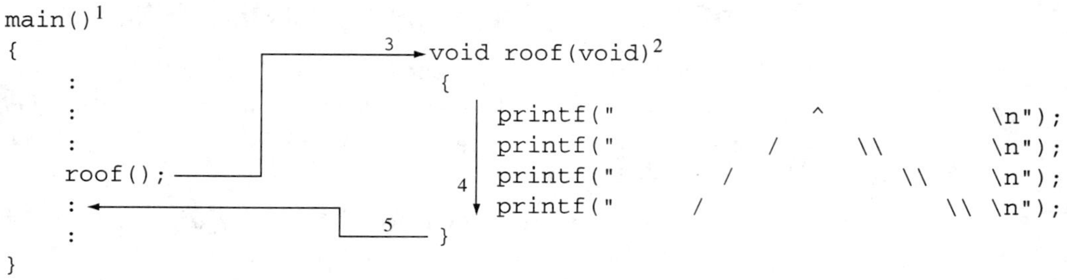

Explanations

1. This is the calling function.
2. This is the called function.
3. After executing *roof(),* the program moves to the called function.
4. The program is executed.
5. The program returns from the called function.

The function that calls another function is said to be the ***calling function*** and of course the function it calls is said to be the ***called function.*** Here *main()* is the calling function and *roof()* is the called function.

Note carefully the components of a function definition, as shown in Figure 10.1.3.

Figure 10.1.3

```
void roof(void)1
{
    printf("          ^          \n");2
    printf("        /   \\        \n");
    printf("      /       \\      \n");
    printf("    /           \\ \n");
}
```

Explanations

1. This line is the function header.
2. These four lines comprise the function body.

The function entry point. The function header is the ***entry point*** into the function; that is, it is the location where execution begins when the function is called. (The keyword *void* mentioned in the header will be defined in Sections 10.2 and 10.4.) Note that the function header must **not** be terminated with a semicolon.

The function body. The function body, which contains all of the code that makes up the function, must always be enclosed in braces. The function body may consist of any C statements, examples of which will be provided shortly.

The function call. Note the function syntax of a function call:

```
roof();
```

Parentheses are required. They indicate to the compiler that *roof* refers to a function name rather than a variable name, or something else.

At this point, you may be thinking that the introduction of functions made the code in Example 10.1.1 unnecessarily complex to read. Indeed! The usefulness of functions will become clearer later, but the following two examples may help to shed some light.

Example 10.1.2

Improve the program of Example 10.1.1 so that the user may draw a tower by choosing the number of upper stories (above the main floor) to display. For example:

Enter the number of upper stories > 2

```
              ^
          /       \
      /               \
  /                       \
 -------------------------
 |                       |
 |       ------          |
 |       |    |          |
 |       ------          |
 |                       |
 -------------------------
 |                       |
 |       ------          |
 |       |    |          |
 |       ------          |
 |                       |
 -------------------------
 |                       |
 |       ------          |
 |       |    |          |
 |       ------          |
 |                       |
 -------------------------
```

The task of drawing this house can be broken into three smaller tasks, as shown in the structure chart in Figure 10.1.4.

Figure 10.1.4

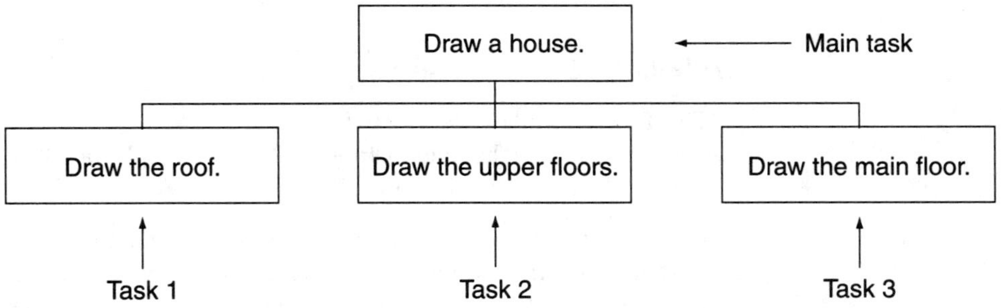

In Example 10.1.1, a function was already coded for Tasks 1 and 3, so we may simply reuse them here instead of writing them. A new function, drawing the upper floor, will be coded for Task 2. Let us name that function *upper_floor()*. The program will then look like this (the new code appears in bold type):

```
#include <stdio.h>

/* First, define the functions */

void roof(void)
{
    print("              ^
    print("          /       \\          \n");
    print("      /               \\      \n");
    print("  /                       \\  \n");
}

void upper_floor(void)
{
    print("    -------------------- \n");
    print("    |       -----       | \n");
    print("    |       |   |       | \n");
    print("    |       -----       | \n");
    print("    |                   | \n");
}

void main_floor(void)
{
```

```
    print("     -------------------  \n");
    print("     |                  |  \n");
    print("     |       -----      |  \n");
    print("     |       |   |      |  \n");
    print("     |       |   |      |  \n");
    print("     -------------------  \n");
}
```

```
/* Second, call the functions above in the main() function */

main()
{
    int  num_up_floors:
    print("Enter the number of upper stories > ");
    scanf("%d", &num_up_floors);
    roof();[1]

    for ( ; num_up_floors > 0; num_up_floors--)[2]
    {
       upper_floor();
    }
    main_floor();[3]
}
```

Explanations

1. This function call displays a roof.
2. The *for* loop calls the function *upper_floor()* to display a series of upper floors.
3. Finally, the main floor is drawn.

It is now possible to see a few advantages of defining functions. In the program above, functions kept the *main()* short and easier to read, and they served as a self-documentation of the program—the name of the functions appearing in the *main()* spell out their tasks—so it is important to choose descriptive function names.

Example 10.1.3

Suppose you were assigned to write a program that displays the face of a smiling person as shown below:

```
      vvvvvvvvvvvvvvvv
  / vvvvvvvvvvvvvvvvvv \
  |   vvvvvvvvvvvvvv    |
  |                     |
  |                     |
  |   -----   -----     |
 (|     +       +       |)
  |         |           |
   \    \______/       /
     \                /
       \_____________/
```

The structure chart in Figure 10.1.5 shows how this task can be broken apart.

Figure 10.1.5

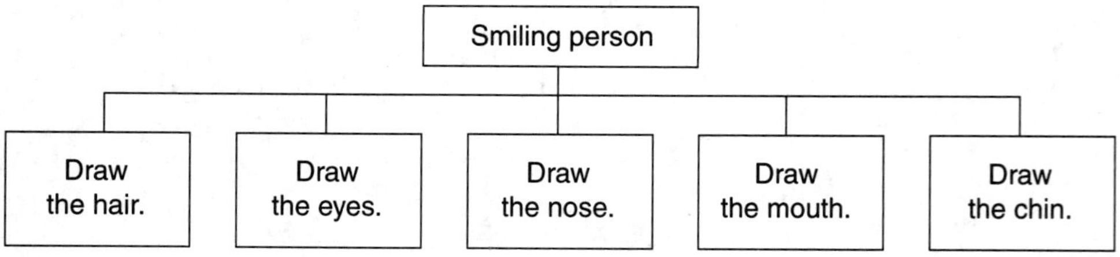

In words, the structure chart in Figure 10.1.5 says:

Task 1: Draw the hair [to be executed by a user-defined function named *hair()*].
Task 2: Draw the eyes [to be executed by a user-defined function named *eyes()*].
Task 3: Draw the nose [to be executed by a user-defined function named *nose()*].
Task 4: Draw the mouth [to be executed by a user-defined function named *mouth()*].
Task 5: Draw the chin [to be executed by a user-defined function named *chin()*].

Following is the program that puts these tasks together to display the smiling face:

```
#include <stdio.h>

void hair(void)
{
    printf("          vvvvvvvvvvvvvvvv   \n");
    printf("       / vvvvvvvvvvvvvvvvvv  \\\n");
    printf("       |   vvvvvvvvvvvvvv  | \n");
}

void eyes(void)
{
    printf("       |                   |  \n");
    printf("       |   -----  -----    |  \n");
    printf("      (|     +      +      |) \n");
}

void nose(void)
{
    printf("       |         |         | \n");
}

void mouth(void)
{
    printf("         \    \_____/      / \n");
    printf("          \              /   \n");
}

void chin(void)
{
    printf("            \___________/    \n");

}

main()
{
    hair();
    eyes();
    nose();
    mouth();
    chin();
}
```

For the sake of convenience, from this point on, structure charts will show actual function names, instead of descriptions of the tasks. For example, the structure chart in Figure 10.1.4 becomes the chart shown in Figure 10.1.6.

Figure 10.1.6

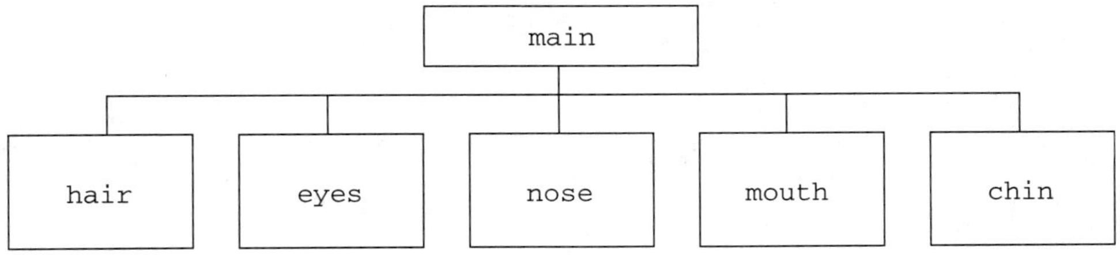

EXERCISES 10.1.1

1. Find and fix all of the errors in the following program:

```
#include <stdio.h>

main()
{
    show_msg();
}

show_msg();
     printf("Today's schedule is:\n\n");
     printf("a. get up at 7:30am\n");
     printf("b. skip breakfast\n");
     printf("c. Work all day\n\n");
     printf("d. Go home\n\n");
```

2. Break the following program into four function calls: *product_name(), author(), features(),* and *release_note()*. Of course, a definition must also be provided for each function.

```
main()
{
     printf("\n\n      The ABC software product\n\n");
     printf("                 Written by\n\n");
     printf("                  your name\n\n\n");
     printf("    This software helps you forecast the\n");
     printf("    performance of the market. It features:\n\n");
     printf("       1. a database of the TSE indexes this year\n\n");
     printf("       2. an inference engine\n\n");
     printf("       3. a knowledge base\n\n");
     printf("       4. slide presentations\n\n");
     printf("\n\nNOTE: This product will be released in 1999\n\n");
}
```

3. Introduce a function named *show_menu()* in the program in Exercise 9.3.1, 5. Its purpose is to display the menu only, and the prompting for the choice remains in the *main()*.
4. Introduce a loop to the program in Example 10.1.2 so that the user is given the opportunity to draw more than one tower. Make the program clear the screen before each tower is drawn. For example:

   Enter the number of upper stories (enter 0 to terminate drawing) > 5

   A house with six stories is drawn and then the screen is cleared.

   Enter the number of upper stories (enter 0 to terminate drawing) > 1

   A house with two stories is drawn and then the screen is cleared.

   Enter the number of upper stories (enter 0 to terminate drawing) > 0

5. Improve the program of Example 10.1.3 so that along with the original face, the following faces may be displayed on request:

```
      vvvvvvvvvvvvvvv
   / vvvvvvvvvvvvvvvvvvv \
   |   vvvvvvvvvvvvvv    |
   |                     |
   |    __         __    |
   |      \       /      |
  (|     * \     / *     |)
   |         |           |
    \       (___)       /
      \               /
        \___________/

        Angry face
```

```
      vvvvvvvvvvvvvvv
   / vvvvvvvvvvvvvvvvvvv \
   |   vvvvvvvvvvvvvv    |
   |                     |
   |      /       \      |
  (|    / -       - \    |)
   |         |           |
    \      _______      /
      \  /         \  /
        \___________/

         Sad face
```

The user uses the following menu to request which one to display:

```
Do you wish:
  the (H)appy face
  the (S)ad face
  the (A)ngry face
  to (Q)uit
Enter the choice >
```

The screen is cleared, the chosen face appears, and the menu reappears. Since the shape of the hair, the nose, and the chin is common to all faces, use the same functions as in the Example 10.1.3. Different functions must be defined for each face's eyes and mouth. Build a program in two steps:

a. Construct the structure chart.
b. Write the program.

6. Write a program that reads in a phrase and creates a vertical banner for it. For example:

```
Enter a phrase > Hi! Joe

**************
       *
       *
**************

****** *

* *********

****
*
*
**************

******
*    *
*    *
******

******
*  * *
*  * *
*  ***
```

The program will use the function *getchar()* to read in each character, one at the time. Then it will call the appropriate function to display the letter. For instance, the letter 'A' could be drawn by a function named *A()*, the letter 'a' by a function named *a()*, and so on. (Note the case sensitivity.) The *main()* will consist of a very long *switch()* statement, one case for each letter.

7. Write a program that reads in a message and displays it in Morse code. Following is a table of Morse code:

A .-	B -...	C -.-.	D -..	E .	F ..-.
G --.	H	I ..	J .---	K -.-	L .-..
M --	N -.	O ---	P .--.	Q --.-	R .-.
S ...	T -	U ..-	V ...-	W .--	X -..-
Y -.--	Z --..				

Here is a sample run:

```
Enter a message: meet here
Morse code: -- . . -  .... . .-. .
```

Note that the message should be converted to uppercase characters and then to Morse code, which consists of dots (use the periord character) and dashes (use the hyphen character). As in the question above, the program will define a function for each letter in which the Morse code is displayed.

10.1.3 COMMON ERRORS AND TRAPS

Programmers commit a few common errors when including user-defined functions in programs. Use the following information to avoid these errors.

1. Never omit the parentheses in the function header. For example:

```
void roof
{
     printf("              ^              \n");
     printf("          /       \\         \n");
     printf("      /               \\     \n");
     printf("  /                       \\ \n");
}
```

   The compiler will complain because *(void)* is missing at the end of the first line.
2. Do not terminate the function header with a semicolon. For example:

```
void roof(void);
{
     printf("              ^              \n");
     printf("          /       \\         \n");
     printf("      /               \\     \n");
     printf("  /                       \\ \n");
}
```

   The compiler will complain because the function lacks a definition. (Why do you think that is so?)
3. Never omit the parentheses on a function call. For example:

```
roof;
```

   The compiler will complain because the *()* is missing after *roof.*

10.2 ARGUMENT PASSING BY VALUE

The functions discussed in Section 10.1 were very limited in use. In the following example, the function *main_floor()* does not allow data to be passed to it.

```
void main_floor(void)
{
     printf("    -------------------  \n");
     printf("    |                  | \n");
     printf("    |      -----       | \n");
     printf("    |      |   |       | \n");
     printf("    |      |   |       | \n");
     printf("    -------------------  \n");

}
```

In the first line, the second occurence of the keyword *void* (in parentheses) indicates that no arguments (data) may be passed inside the function from the outside. Data passed to a function are called ***arguments.*** Of course, functions are more flexible and can be used in a variety of ways when they accept arguments. For example, the call to *printf()* in Figure 10.2.1 includes four arguments.

Figure 10.2.1

```
printf("Sum of %d and %d is %d\n",¹ num1,² num2,³ sum⁴);
```

Explanations

1. First argument
2. Second argument
3. Third argument
4. Fourth argument

When *printf()* is given arguments that differ from these, it displays a different message; hence the function's versatility. In this section, we will explore the mechanism of ***argument passing.*** Nearly all books prefer the term ***parameter passing,*** but this term is misleading. It suggest that the parameter is passed to the function; the truth is that the argument is passed to the function. Parameters and arguments are not the same thing. (All this will soon become clear!)

10.2.1 THE MECHANISM OF ARGUMENT PASSING

Example 10.2.1 shows the mechanism of passing data to a function.

Example 10.2.1

Let us improve the program of Example 10.1.1 so that a user can draw a house made from any of the materials shown in Figure 10.2.2.

Figure 10.2.2

```
          ^                                 ^
      /       \                         /       \
  /               \                 /               \
/                   \             /                   \
---------------------            ---------------------
|                   |            [                   ]
|        -----      |            [        -----      ]
|        |   |      |            [        |   |      ]
|        |   |      |            [        |   |      ]
---------------------            ---------------------
```

Clapboard   Bricks

```
          ^                                 ^
      /       \                         /       \
  /               \                 /               \
/                   \             /                   \
---------------------            ---------------------
/                   \            (                   )
/        -----      \            (        -----      )
/        |   |      \            (        |   |      )
/        |   |      \            (        |   |      )
---------------------            ---------------------
```

Siding   Logs

The program will ask for the type of wall desired. For example:

What material are the walls made of?
(Type | | for clapboard, [] for bricks,
/\ for siding, and () for logs)   >>> /\

A house with siding walls would then be drawn. Following is the new program, with modifications from the original program shown in bold:

```
#include <stdio.h>

/* First, define the functions */

void roof(void)
{
    printf("          ^          \n");
    printf("      /       \\      \n");
    printf("   /             \\   \n");
    printf(" /                 \\ \n");
}

/* This function declares two parameters */
```

```
void main_floor(char left_wall, char right_wall)[1]
{
    printf("      -------------------      \n")
    printf("      %c                     %c \n", left_wall, right_wall);
    printf("      %c        -----        %c \n", left_wall, right_wall);
    printf("      %c        |   |        %c \n", left_wall, right_wall);
    printf("      %c        |   |        %c \n", left_wall, right_wall);
    printf("      -------------------      \n");

}

/* Second, call the functions above in the main() function */

main()
{
    char   mat_l, mat_r;

    roof();

    printf("What material are the walls made of?\n"
           "      (Type || for clapboard, [] for bricks,\n'
           "             /\ for siding, and () for logs)      >>> ");
    scanf("\n%c\n%c", &mat_l, &mat_r);

    main_floor(mat_l, mat_r);[2]
}
```

Explanations

1. Note the syntax of the header of the function *main_floor()*, as shown in Figure 10.2.3. The parameters indicate the type of data that the function expects to receive from the outside.

Figure 10.2.3

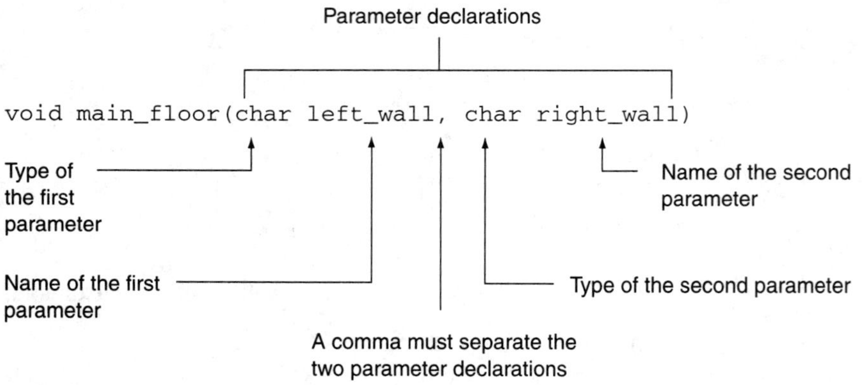

2. Note how *main()* makes a call to this function, as shown below:

   The function call is:

```
main_floor(mat_l, mat_r);
```

The data from *mat_l,* the first argument to the function *main_floor(),* is copied to the first parameter *left_wall.* This is essentially the assignment *left_wall = mat_l.*

The data from *mat_r,* the second argument to the function *main_floor(),* is copied to the second parameter right_wall. This is essentially the assignment *right_wall = mat_r.*

The resulting function is now:

```
void main_floor(char left_wall, char right_wall)
```

The arguments *mat_l* and *mat_r* are said to be passed ***by value*** because their contents (values) are copied (passed) into the parameters of the function *main_floor().* Figure 10.2.4 summarizes the mechanism of argument passing.

Figure 10.2.4

```
main()¹                                    void main_floor(int left_wall, right_wall)²
{                                          {
     :                                        printf("      -------------------  \n");
     :                                        printf("      %c                   %c \n",
     :                                               left_wall, right_wall);
     :                                        printf("      %c      -----        %c \n",
     :                                               left_wall, right_wall);
     main_floor(mat_1, mat_r):                printf("      %c      ¦   ¦        %c \n",
                                                     left_wall, right_wall);
     :                                        printf("      %c      ¦   ¦        %c \n",
     :                                               left_wall, right_wall);
     :                                        printf("      -------------------  \n",
     :                                     }
}
```

Explanations

1. This is the calling function.
2. This is the called function.
3. These arrows represent the action of the data being copied to the parameters.
4. These arrows represent the direction in which the program is executed.

In a structure chart, the data that is passed to the function *main_floor()* should be shown with an arrow pointing toward the called function, as shown in Figure 10.2.5.

Figure 10.2.5

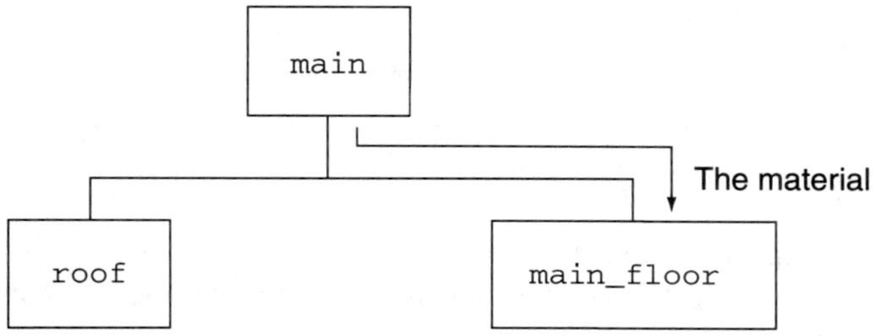

EXERCISES 10.2.1

1. Give the function header for each of the following functions. (Do not code the function body.)
   a. A function named *power()* that takes in two integer arguments *base* and *exponent* and displays the result.
   b. A function named *repeat()* that takes in a character argument *ch* and an integer argument *times,* which is the number of times the character is to be displayed.
2. Modify the program in Example 10.2.1 so that it presents a menu as follows:

   There are four types of materials:
   1. clapboard
   2. bricks
   3. siding
   4. logs

   Enter your choice for the walls > <u>3</u>

   The program will also display the message "No house drawn" if the choice is invalid. [***Hint:*** include a *switch* statement in *main()* that will call *main_floor()* with the appropriate arguments.]
3. Improve the program in Example 10.1.2 so that a tower of any one of the four materials may be drawn. [***Hint:*** Use a *switch()* statement for calling *upper_floor()* with the appropriate material and one for calling *main_floor()* with the appropriate material; i.e., there should be two *switch()* statements in the *main()*.]

In the house-building program, the function *main_floor()* accepted arguments of type *char.* Of course, a function may be defined to accept parameters of other types, as Example 10.2.2 illustrates.

Example 10.2.2

Let us write a function named *star_line()* that is designed to display a line of stars. The user simply indicates the number of stars desired. For example:

```
Enter the length of the line of stars > 21

********************
```

Following is the program:

```
#include <stdio.h>

void star_line(int num)[1]
{
      for ( ; num > 0; num--)
      {
         printf("*");
      }
      printf("\n");
}

main()
{
     int len;

      printf("Enter the length of the line of stars > ");
      scanf("%d", &len);
      star_line(len);[2]
}
```

Explanations

1. This is the definition of the function *star_line().* The length of the line to draw is passed to it.
2. The content of the variable *len* is passed as the argument. Figure 10.2.6 shows how this information is passed to the function *star_line().*

Figure 10.2.6

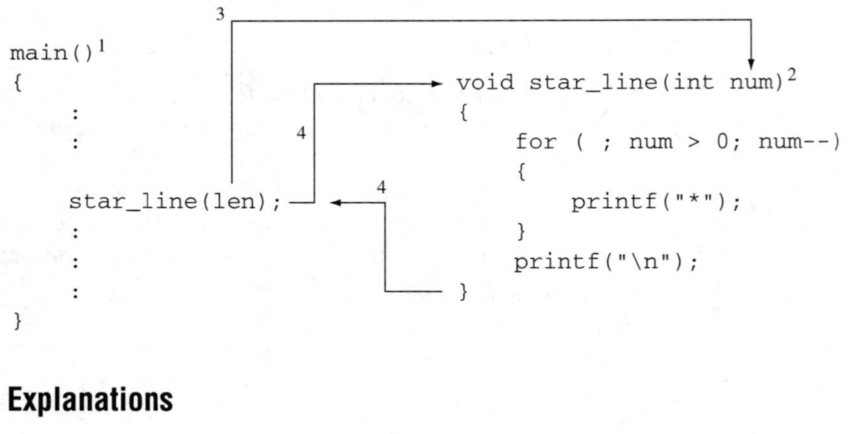

Explanations

1. This is the calling function.
2. This is the called function.
3. This arrow represents the passing of the information (21) to the function *(int num).*
4. These arrows represent the direction in which the program is executed.

The parameter is a copy of the argument. Note that the argument's name is *len,* whereas its corresponding parameter's name is *num.* The names do not have to match up. In fact, the argument and the parameter are **not** the same object at all. To fully understand this, it is best to look at the memory layout of the variables before, during, and after the function call. Before the function call to *star_line()*, only the variable *len* exists, and its content is 21.

At the time that the execution of the function *star_line()* is initiated, memory space is allocated to its code and variables, hence to the parameter *num* as well, as shown in Figure 10.2.7.

Figure 10.2.7

Then the value of the argument *len* is copied to the parameter *num,* as shown in Figure 10.2.8.

Figure 10.2.8

Then the loop executes and decrements the variable *num* all the way down to 0, but the value of *len* **does not** change (Figure 10.2.9). Eventually the function terminates. It is removed from memory, as is its parameter *num.* The execution returns to *main()* with the value of *len* unchanged, at 21.

Figure 10.2.9

While the parameter *num*'s value was reduced to 0, its corresponding argument *len*'s value remains unchanged at 21. This clearly proves that it is the **value** of the argument that is copied down the function *star_line(),* **not** the actual variable. The content of *num* is like a photocopy of *len*'s content; when the photocopy is made, the original is not affected or changed.

EXERCISES 10.2.2

1. What will the following program display?

```
#include <stdio.h>

void stuff(int num)
{
     printf("num = %d\n", num);
     num = 99;
     printf("num = %d\n", num);
}

main()
{
```

```
    int num;

    num = 11;
    printf("num = %d\n", num);
    stuff(num);
    printf("num = %d\n", num);
    stuff(66);
    printf("num = %d\n", num);
}
```

2. Modify the function *upper_floor()* from Example 10.1.2 so that it takes as its argument the number of upper floors to draw. Then it—instead of the *main()*—draws them. This simply requires a counter that will be decremented down to 0, as was done with *star_line()*. Also, change the name to *upper_floors()*. The *main()* should become:

```
main()
{
    int   num_up_floors;

    printf("Enter the number of upper stories > ");
    scanf("%d", &num_up_floors);
    roof();
    upper_floors(num_up_floors);
    main_floor();
}
```

3. a. Write a function named *repeat()* that accepts two arguments: one is a character, the other is the number of times that this character is to be displayed. For example, *repeat('-', 80)* would display a line of dashes. The cursor remains on that line, and does not move to the next line.
   b. Include the function *repeat()* in a working program. Have the program ask for the arguments.
4. Modify the program in Example 9.2.1 so that it uses the *repeat()* function from question 3.
5. a. Use only the *repeat()* function in a program that displays the contour of a box. For example:

```
***********************
*                     *
*                     *
*                     *
***********************
```

   b. Include the *repeat()* function in a working program. Have the program ask for the arguments.
6. a. Use the *repeat()* function in a program that displays a thick contour of a box. For example:

```
***********************
***                 ***
***                 ***
***                 ***
***********************
```

   The thickness of the contour is specified by the user.
   b. Include the *repeat()* function in a working program. Have the program ask for the arguments.
   c. Introduce data validation to the program, which must ensure that the thickness is valid. If it is not valid, the user is asked again for a valid value.

Multiple parameters of different types. A function may accept arguments of different types, as Example 10.2.3 shows.

Example 10.2.3

Let us define a function named *total()* that accepts a number of items bought and the cost of each item. It then displays the total cost. The program will run as follows:

Enter the number of items bought > <u>61</u>
Enter the cost of each item > <u>2.01</u>
The total cost is   122.61

Here is a program that illustrates how the function *total()* may be coded and used:

```
#include <stdio.h>

/* function definition */

void total(int qty, float unit_cst)[1]
{
    printf("The total cost is %8.2f\n", qty * unit_cst);
}

main()
{
     int   items;
     float cost;

     printf("Enter the number of items bought > ");
     scanf("%d", &items);
     printf("Enter the cost of each item > ");
     scanf("%f", &cost);

     total(items, cost);[2]
}
```

Explanations

1. The function header for *total()* has two parameters; one is of type *int*, the other of type *float*. Indeed, the parameters do not have to be of the same type.
2. The corresponding arguments are sent into the function.

Figure 10.2.10 illustrates the function call and return.

Figure 10.2.10

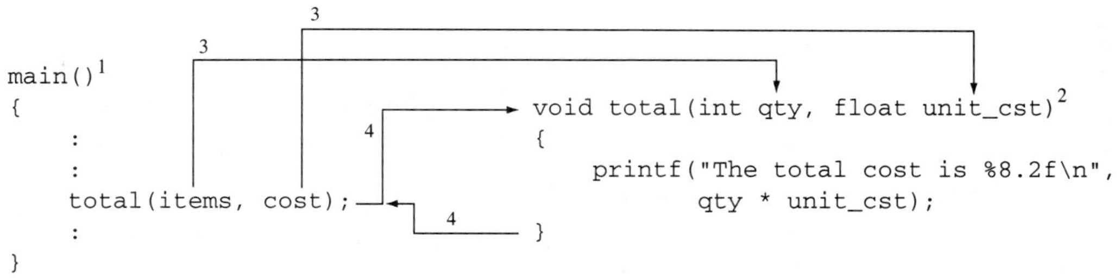

Explanations

1. This is the calling function.
2. This is the called function.
3. These arrows represent the copying of arguments, 61 to *qty* and 2.01 to *unit_est.*
4. These arrows represent the execution of the program.

EXERCISES 10.2.3

1. a. Write a function named *multi()* that displays the result from the multiplication of its three arguments. The arguments are real numbers. For example: *multi(5.0, 9.3, 7.03).*
   b. Include the function in a working program. Have the program ask for the arguments repeatedly until the user wants to stop.
2. a. Write a function named *square()* that displays the square of its argument. The argument is a real number.

b. Include the function in a working program. Have the program ask for the arguments.

3. a. Write a function named *cube()* that displays the cube of its argument. The argument is a real number.

   b. Include the function in a working program. Have the program ask for the arguments.

4. a. Suppose that the function *total()* had been defined as follows:

```
void total(int items, float cost)
{
   printf("The total cost is %8.2f\n", items * cost);
}
```

Note that the parameters now share the same names as the variables in the *main()*. Does that mean they are the same variables? Explain.

b. Suppose that the function is changed to the following:

```
void total(int items, float cost)
{
   printf("The total cost is %8.2f\n", items * cost);
   items = 0;
   cost = 0.00;
}
```

Would the variables *items* and *cost* in *main()* be reset to 0, too?

What codes can go into the function body? As mentioned in Section 10.1, a function body may consist of any C statements, as Example 10.2.4 illustrates.

Example 10.2.4

The following program reads in two numbers and displays them in ascending order:

```
#include <stdio.h>

void asc_order(float n1, float n2)             /* function definition */
{
    if (n1 > n2)
    {
        printf("In ascending order: %d %d\n", n2, n1);
    }
    else
    {
        printf("In ascending order: %d %d\n", n1, n2);
    }
}

main()
{
    int num1, num2;

    printf("Enter two numbers > ");
    scanf("%d%d", &num1, &num2);

    asc_order(num1, num2);          /* function call */
}
```

The function *asc_order()* includes an *if/else* statement to display two numbers in ascending order. Any code that we placed inside the *main()* in Chapter 9 can also be placed in another function of your own making.

EXERCISES 10.2.4

1. Introduce another function named *display_tx()* to the program in Exercise 10.1.1, 3. This function will simply consist of the *switch()* statement that lists all of the possible civil codes. This means that the civil code must be passed to the function.
2. a. Write a function called *even()* that displays the message "This argument is even" or "This argument is odd" depending on the parity of the argument. (***Hint:*** Use the remainder operator.)
   b. Include the function in a working program. Have the program ask for the argument.
3. Introduce a function named *print_advice()* in the program in Example 4.3.1. This function displays the appropriate message regarding accepting the job. The income calculated and the minimum income acceptable are passed to it.
4. a. Write a function named *absolute()* that displays the absolute value of the argument passed to it. For example, the absolute value of –9.52 is 9.52, and the absolute value of 178.2184 is 178.2184. Declare the parameter of type *double.*
   b. Include the function in a working program. Have the program ask for the argument.
5. a. Write a function named *find_max()* that displays the largest of two arguments passed to it. Declare the parameters of type *double.*
   b. Include the function in a working program. Have the program ask for the arguments.
6. The following program provides two numbers randomly generated. The user attempts to sum them, and the program verifies the sum. This continues until the user fails to answer correctly.

```
#include <stdio.h>
#include <stdlib.h>

main()
{
     int num1, num2, answer;

     do
     {
          num1 = rand();
          num2 = rand();
          printf("What is the addition of %d and %d ?\n ",
               num1, num2);
          scanf("%d", &answer);
          if (answer == num1 + num2)
          {
               printf("You are right!\n");
          }
          else

          {
               printf("You are wrong!\n");
          }
     }
     while (answer == num1 + num2);
}
```

Write a function named *display_msg()* that takes in as arguments both numbers and the user's answer and then displays the appropriate message. Then use that function in this program.

10.2.2 BE WARY OF PARAMETER/ARGUMENT MISMATCHES

You may declare parameters of any type, but it is important that the type of the arguments and **corresponding** parameters match. Otherwise, the program may behave strangely, as the program in Example 10.2.5 shows.

Example 10.2.5

Consider a slight modification to Example 10.2.3. Suppose the programmer made a mistake and declared the parameter *cost* of *total()* as an *int* instead of a *float*. The following program shows the error in bold type:

```
#include <stdio.h>

void total(int qty, int unit_cst)
{
   printf("The total cost is %8.2f\n", qty * unit_cst);
}

main()
{
     int   items;
     float cost;

     printf("Enter the number of items bought > ");
     scanf("%d", &items);
     printf("Enter the cost of each item > ");
     scanf("%f, &cost);

     total(items, cost);
}
```

What effect will this have on the argument passing? At the time of the function call to *total()*, an implicit conversion will occur. Assume the argument has a content of 2.01 for the unit cost. The implicit conversion will occur as shown in Figure 10.2.11.

Figure 10.2.11

Function call: `total(items, cost);`

cost is declared of type *float*. 2.01 is passed down to the parameter *cost*, declared of type *int*, so a type conversion occurs. As a result, 2 will be stored in the parameter *unit_cst*, not 2.01.

Function header: `void total(int qty, int unit_cst)`

The same type conversion rules discussed in Subsection 3.2.4 apply here as well. Consequently, the fractional part of the cost will be lost when 2.01 is passed to the parameter.

EXERCISES 10.2.5

1. In the program in Exercise 10.2.3, 1, what would have happened with the call *multi(5, 9.3, 7.03)?*
2. Suppose your program includes the function header *void fcn(int a, char b, float c)*.
   a. What would be stored in the parameters with the call *fcn(–3304.0, 513, 9)?*
   b. Would the code below produce the same result as in (a) above?

```
int   vi;
char  vc;
float vf;

vi = -3304.0;
vc = 513;
vf = 9;
fcn(vi, vc, vf);
```

10.2.3 TESTING A USER-DEFINED FUNCTION, PART 1

Before a user-defined function is put into production, its correctness should be thoroughly tested. ***Unit test drivers*** (other authors may use a different terminology here) may be written for this purpose. Basically, the procedure for writing unit test drivers consists of including the userdefined function in a program designed to test that function exclusively. Without realizing it, this is what you have been doing all along. Now let us discuss this issue a little more formally.

Example 10.2.6

Let us write a unit test driver for the function *total()* in Example 10.2.5, which had a bug in it. The unit test driver should run with a loop so that the user may try all combinations of values of quantity of items and costs to test *total()*. Thus, if a bug exists, it is likely to surface. Following is a good unit test driver for *total()*.

```
#include <stdio.h>
#include <stdlib.h>

void total(int qty, int unit_cst) [1]
{
    printf("Testing: qty = %d, unit_cost = %f\n", qty, unit_cost); [2]
    printf("The total cost is %8.2f\n", qty * unit_cst);
}

main()
{
    int   items;
    float cost;
    char  ans;

    do
    {
        printf("Enter the number of items bought > "); [3]
        scanf("%d", &items);
        printf("Enter the cost of each item > ");
        scanf("%f, &cost);
        total(items, cost);
        printf("End of the test drive (y/n) ? "); [4]
        scanf("\n%c", &ans);
        ans = toupper(ans);
    }
    while (ans == 'N');
}
```

Explanations

1. The program bug is *int.*
2. Note that a testing *printf()* is inserted into the function *total()*. It displays the values received by the two parameters. The purpose of this *printf()* is to verify if the arguments are passed correctly to the function.
3. This first part of the loop performs a particular test of the function *total()*.
4. This second part of the loop asks if more testing should be performed. Following is an example of a run:

```
Enter the number of items bought > 2
Enter the cost of each item > 5.0
Testing: qty = 2, unit_cost = 5.000000
The total cost is     10.0
End of the test drive (y/n) ? n
Enter the number of items bought > 61
Enter the cost of each item > 2.01
Testing: qty = 61, unit_cost = 2.000000
The total cost is     122
End of the test drive (y/n) ? y
```

Two tests are performed. The first testing message, in lines 3: in line 3, tells you that the two arguments were sent correctly to the function *total()*, accounting for the correct total cost calculated. Test 1 is fine.

For the second test message shown in line 8, the input is 61 items at $2.01 each. The total cost should be $122.61, yet the test reveals $122. Something is wrong! The testing message makes it clear that the second argument, the cost per unit, was sent incorrectly into the parameter. After looking at *total()*'s code, the culprit is found to be a parameter type that does not match that of its argument.

EXERCISES 10.2.6

1. Run a unit test driver on the following functions:
   a. *main_floor()* d. *star_line()* g. *repeat()*
   b. *multi()* e. *square()* h. *cube()*
   c. *asc_order()* f. *even()* i. *absolute()*
2. Rewrite the loop in Example 10.2.6 using a *while* loop.

10.2.4 PASSING FILE POINTERS TO A FUNCTION

Remember that any data type may be passed to a function, and this includes passing file pointers. The passing of a file pointer is conceptually equivalent to passing a number or a character, but in practice it proves to be a little more error prone. Example 10.2.7 illustrates a typical situation in which a file pointer must be passed to a function.

Example 10.2.7

It is a fact that the standard *fclose()* function can make the program crash or behave weirdly if it attempts to close either a nonexisting file or a file that was not opened in the first place. In either situation, the file pointer [produced by *fopen()*] would be a NULL.

Realizing the precarious nature of *fclose()*, a keen programmer may prefer to write a function, named say, *close_safely()*, that accepts a file pointer and closes its file only if the pointer is not NULL; otherwise, it will display the message "File not opened or does not exist." Let us incorporate that function in the program of Example 8.2.4. Following is the program we obtain, with changes shown in bold:

Type of the parameter (file pointer)

```
#include <stdio.h>

void close_safely(FILE * fp)
{
    if (fp != NULL)         /* can the file be closed safely? */
    {
        fclose(fp);
    }


    else
    {
         printf("File not opened or does not exist\n");
    }
}

main()
{
    int     sum, num, flag;
    FILE * ifp;      /* file pointer variables */
    FILE * ofp;

    ifp = fopen("in.dat", "r");
```

```
    if (ifp == NULL)
    {
        printf("Could not open input file\n");
    }
    ofp = fopen("ans.out", "w");
    if (ofp == NULL)
    {
        printf("Could not open output file\n");
    }
    if (ifp != NULL && ofp != NULL) /* both files opened correctly ? */
    {
        sum = 0;
        flag = fscanf(ifp, "%d", &num);
        while (flag != EOF)    /* is it the end of file ? */
{
            sum = sum + num;
            flag = fscanf(ifp, "%d", &num);
        }
        fprintf(ofp, "The sum is %d.\n", sum);
    }
    close_safely(ifp);
    close_safely(ofp);
}
```

Note the parameter to the function *close _safely: FILE * fp*. The parameter name is *fp,* and it is a file pointer. This is indicated by its type, *FILE* *. The asterisk is part of the type. In Chapter 11, when we study the use of this asterisk, the need for it will become clearer.

EXERCISES 10.2.7

1. a. Write a function named *are_opened()* that accepts two file pointers and returns 1 if both files are opened, and returns a 0 in all other cases.
   b. Use that function in program in the Example 10.2.7.
2. a. Write a function named *window()* that will accept a file pointer. This function will display the content of the file from a column number specified by the parameter *left* to a column number specified by the parameter *right* (only that window of the file is shown on the screen). The file will be read one character at a time without echoing until reaching the left column. This will require a loop. A second loop will read and display each character within the window. Finally, a third loop will read the remaining characters on the line. An outer loop is necessary to process each line in a similar fashion. Assume that the window specifications are always valid. Choose any text file that you currently possess in your computer system. A sample run might look like this:

   Enter the window to view > <u>5 22</u>

   Text will
   be shown in
   this area.

   Column 5 Column 22

   b. Remove the assumption made in (a). This implies that the user may inadvertently enter window parameters out of range.

10.2.5 COMMON ERRORS AND TRAPS

Programmers commit a few common errors when passing by value. Use the following information to avoid these errors.

1. Always specify the type for each parameter. For example:

```
void main_floor(char left_wall, right_wall)
{
    printf("      -------------------      \n");
    printf("     %c                       %c \n", left_wall, right_wall);
    printf("     %c        -----          %c \n", left_wall, right_wall);
    printf("     %c        |   |          %c \n", left_wall, right_wall);
    printf("     %c        |   |          %c \n", left_wall, right_wall);
    printf("      -------------------      \n"");
}
```

Even though both parameters have the same type, that type must be mentioned for each parameter (unlike **variable** declarations). Here, the type is not specified for *right_wall*. However, the compiler will **not** complain because when a type declaration is missing, the compiler automatically defaults to *int*. This would not cause the program above to malfunction anyway. (Why do you think that is so?)

2. Watch for a mismatch of types between a parameter and its argument. This can lead to very subtle bugs caused by implicit conversions. Perhaps the simplest way to avoid or to detect such errors is to echo to the screen all parameters during a unit test drive.
3. Do not omit arguments. For example:

```
void fcn(int a, char c)
{
        :
        :
}


main()
{
        :
        fcn(7);
        :
}
```

The compiler will complain because an argument is missing in *fcn(7);*. All parameters must have a matching argument. Since there were two parameters, there must be two arguments.

4. Do not think that the argument is passed to the parameter. This is probably the most common error. In reality, it is the **value** of the argument that is passed (or copied) to the parameter. The argument and the parameter are **not** the same object.
5. Do not confuse the meaning of the terms ***argument*** and ***parameter.*** Arguments are the data listed along with the function call and are passed to the parameters of the function called. Parameters are often referred to as ***formal arguments.***

10.3 LOCAL VARIABLES

main() is simply a function, no different than any others. Since variables may be declared within *main(),* the same can be done with user-defined functions. These variables are said to be ***local*** variables.

10.3.1 WHAT IS A LOCAL VARIABLE?

It is most important to understand the scope and implications for local variables. The following examples will make this clear.

Example 10.3.1

Revisit Example 10.2.2. A counter could be used within the function *star_line()* to keep track of the number of stars displayed instead of decrementing the parameter. Following is the resulting program (changes are shown in bold type):

```
#include <stdio.h>

void star_line(int num)
{
      int  counter;     /* a local variable */

      for (counter=0; counter < num; counter++)
      {
         printf("*");
      }
      printf("\n");
}

main()
{
     int len;    /*a local variable */

      printf("Enter the length of the line of stars > ")
      scanf("%d", &len);
      star_line(len);
}
```

The variable *counter* is declared **within** the function *star_line()* because it is only meant to be used within that function. This is also true for the variable *len* within *main()*. When variables are declared within a function, they are said to be ***local*** variables because they can only be used within the function that declares them. No other functions can use them. Therefore the function *main()* cannot use the variable *counter* and the function *star_line()* cannot use the variable *len.*

Visibility and implications. Local variables are ***visible*** (and therefore ***accessible***) only from within the function that declares them. The area of the program that can see or access a particular variable is called its ***scope.*** For example, the scope of the variable *counter* is simply the inside of the function *star_line().*

Note that because parameters are also declared within the function, their scope is local as well. Think of each function as a room, and each local variable as a person within that room. Within a particular room, only the persons inside it can be seen, as shown in Figure 10.3.1.

Figure 10.3.1

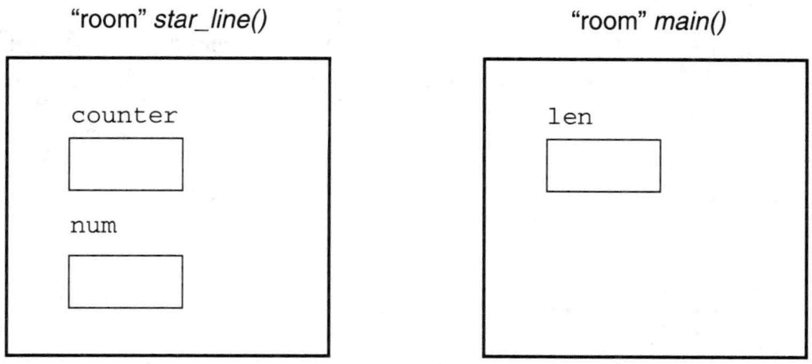

Since the visibility of a local variable is limited to a single function, this enables multiple functions to use the same variable **name** for their own local variables without affecting each other. Example 10.3.2 illustrates this.

Example 10.3.2

Let us write a program that draws the letter 'C' to the size specified by the user. For example:

Enter the size of the letter C > 4

```
****
*
*
****
```

The function *star_line()* displays the horizontal stars and a new function named *star_border()* displays the vertical ones. Following is the program with new code shown in bold type:

```
#include <stdio.h>

void star_line(int num)
{
     int  counter;    /* a local variable */

     for (counter=0; counter < num; counter++)
     {
        printf("*");
     }
     printf("\n");
}

void star_border(int num)
{
     int  counter;    /* a local variable */

     for (counter=0; counter < num; counter++)
     {
        printf("* \n");
     }
}

main()
{
    int len;

     printf("Enter the size of the letter C > ");
     scanf("%d", &len);
     star_line(len);
     star_border(len);
     star_line(len);
}
```

You see that both *star_* functions use a local variable of the same name: *counter.* Nonetheless, these are **not** the same variable. This can be seen with the memory layout of all variables, as shown in Figure 10.3.2.

Figure 10.3.2

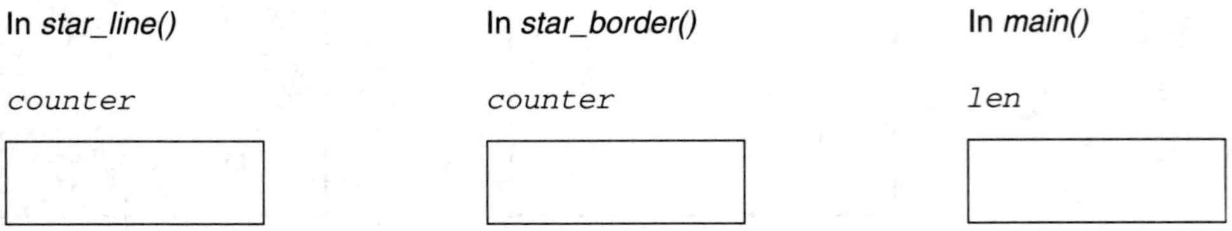

Although they share the same name, the two variables *counter* do not occupy the same cell. This is like two people with the same name who are not the same person. Note that the parameters also share the same name, yet they are different entities.

EXERCISES 10.3.1

1. Consider the following program:

```
void square(void)
{
     printf("square is %d\n", x * x);
```

```
}

main()
{
     int x;

     x = 6;
     square();
}
```

a. The compilation will fail. Indicate where this will happen.

b. Given what you have been taught thus far, suggest a way to make the program work.

2. What is the scope of each variable in the following program?

```
void fcn1(int num, float res)
{
     int c;
     :
     :
}

void fcn2(void)
{
     char c, d;
     :
     :
}

main()
{
     long int  i;
     float     res;
     char      c;

     fcn2();
     fcn1(7, res);
}
```

3. Consider the following program:

```
#include <stdio.h>

void stuff(void)
{
     int num;

     printf("num = %d\n", num);
     num = 99;
     printf("num = %d\n", num);
}

main()
{
     int num;

     num = 11;
     printf("num = %d\n", num);
     stuff();
     printf("num = %d\n", num);
}
```

a. What will this program display?

b. Now suppose that the definition of *stuff()* is changed to

```
void stuff(int num)
{
        printf("num = %d\n", num);
        num = 99;
        printf("num = %d\n", num);
}
```

and its call is changed to *stuff(11)*. What will the display look like?

4. In Exercise 10.2.1, 2, the function *main_floor()* may be defined another way. Instead of checking the user's choice of material within the *main()*, this could be done within the *main_floor()* function. That is, the *switch* statement could be moved within *main_floor()*, and *main()* would pass the user's choice of material (1 to 4) to it. Complete the following sketch of the solution.

```
#include <stdio.h>

void roof(void)
{
      printf("              ^             \n");
      printf("           /     \\          \n");
      printf("        /           \\       \n");
      printf("     /                 \\    \n");
}

void main_floor(_____________________)
{
      ______________________________

      switch(material)
      {
       case 1: left_wall = ____; right_wall = ____;
               break;
       case 2: _______________; ________________;
               break;
       case 3: _______________; ________________;
               break;
       case 4: _______________; ________________;
               break;
      }
       printf("     -------------------      \n");
       printf("     %c                  %c \n", left_wall, right_wall);
       printf("     %c       -----      %c \n", _________, __________);
       printf("     %c       |   |      %c \n", _________, __________);
       printf("     %c       |   |      %c \n", _________, __________);
       printf("     -------------------      \n");
}

main()
{
       _________________________

       printf("There are four types of materials::\n");
       printf("1. clapboards\n");
       printf("2. bricks\n");
       printf("3. sidings\n");
       printf("4. logs\n");
       printf("Enter your choice for the walls > ");
       scanf("%d", &material);
       if (_________________________________)
       {
            roof();
```

```
            main_floor(______________);
        }
        else
        {
            printf("No house drawn");
        }
}
```

5 a. Write a function called *fraction()* that displays the fractional part of the argument. (***Hint:*** Assign the parameter to a local integer variable. This will automatically extract the integer part. Then subtract this from the original number to find the fractional part.)

b. Design a unit test driver for this function.

6. a. Write a function named *swap()* that swaps the value of two arguments given to it and displays them. Note that the arguments themselves will not be swapped. (Why is this the case?) (***Hint:*** This is exactly what the program in Example 4.3.4 does.)

   b. Design a unit test driver for this function.

7. Design a unit test driver to verify each of the following functions:

   a. Write a function named *round()* that rounds off the number sent to it to the nearest unit and displays it. (Refer to Example 3.2.15 to remind yourself how to round off a number.)

   b. Modify the function above so that it rounds off to the nearest one-tenth or one-hundredth or one-thousandth. For example, *round(20.968, 2)* will give the message "20.968 rounded to the nearest one-hundredth is 20.97".

   c. The function will fail if the number is negative. For example, *round(–3.6)* will display –3 instead of –4. To fix this, if the number is negative, the function should subtract, not add, 0.5. Make the necessary modifications.

8. a. Write a function named *roll_dice()* that simulates the rolling of two dice and displays the outcome on the screen. Use the formula *1 + rand() % 6* to generate the number for each die.

   b. Design a unit test driver for this function.

9. Design a unit test driver to verify each of the following functions:

   a. Recall in Exercise 9.2.1, 1, where the program drew rectangles filled with stars. Based on it, write a function named *draw_rect()* that accepts as argument the size of a rectangle and then displays it.

   b. Improve the function so that it accepts a third argument, the character used to fill the rectangle.

10. a. Write a function named *find_max()* that displays the largest of three numbers passed through the parameters.

    b. Design a unit test driver for this function.

11. a. Use the *star_line()* function developed in this section to produce histograms for stationery items sold. Following is a sample run:

    ```
    Enter the number of pencils sold > 27
     PENCILS: *************************** 27
    Enter the number of erasers sold > 15
     ERASERS: *************** 15
    Enter the number of rulers sold > 4
     RULERS: **** 4
    ```

    Note the numbers that follow the histograms.

    b. Modify the program so that the user specifies the item sold. For example:

    ```
    Enter the name of the item and how many sold > pencils 27
     PENCILS: *************************** 27
    Enter the name of the item and how many sold > erasers 15
     ERASERS: *************** 15
    Enter the name of the item and how many sold > rulers 4
     RULERS: **** 4
    ```

    (***Hint:*** Use *getchar()* to read and echo each letter (in uppercase characters) of the item's name. Once a space is detected, use *scanf()* to read the number, and then call *star_line()* to display the histogram. Finally, echo the number beside it.)

10.3.2 COMMON ERRORS AND TRAPS

Programmers often make common errors when using local variables. Use this information to avoid these errors.

1. Do not forget that a local variable cannot be used outside itself. For example:

```
void double(void)
{
        printf("calculation = %f\n", n * n);
}

main()
{
        float n;

        scanf("%f", &n);
        double();
}
```

   In the function *double()*, the compiler will likely complain that the variable *n* is not declared, unless it finds a global declaration outside the function. (Why? Global declaration is covered in Section 12.3.)

2. Declaring a variable of the same name within both the called and the calling function is not in itself an error, but it is an error when they are in fact meant to be the **same** variable. For example, see line 3 below:

```
void double(void)
{
        float n;

        printf("calculation = %f\n", n * n);
}

main()
{
        float n;

        scanf("%f", &n);
        double();
}
```

   Here, the value of *n* should be passed to the function *double()* instead.

3. Do not declare the same variable as parameter and local. For example:

```
void double(float n)
{
        float n;

        printf("calculation = %f\n", n * n);
}

main()
{
        float n;

        scanf("%f", &n);
        double();
}
```

   Again, the *n* in line 3 inside the function *double()* should be removed.

10.4 THE RETURN STATEMENT

We have seen so far that data can be sent down to functions via parameters. However, Section 10.3 showed that a function's code and data (local variables) cannot be seen by other functions, cannot see other codes and local variables, thereby making it impossible to send data back out. This restrictive one-way communication between functions makes them impractical to use. Luckily, methods exist to ensure two-way communication. Following are the methods that we will cover in this and following chapters:

1. Share the results from within a function to the outside. This may be done in two ways:
   a. Use the *return* statement to share the value of internal data, e.g., from local variables (see Section 10.4.1).
   b. Send data out through parameters by reference (see Section 11.2).
2. Use variables that may be shared among functions (see Section 12.2).

10.4.1 THE MECHANISM OF THE RETURN STATEMENT

Example 10.4.1 shows how to send data back out from a function.

Example 10.4.1

The function *total()* in Example 10.2.3 could be made to calculate the total without displaying any message. Then *total()* would send the total cost to *main()*, which would then produce the message. This is what the following program does (changes from the earlier program are shown in bold type):

```
#include <stdio.h>

float total(int qty, float unit_cst)2
{
    return qty * unit_cst;1
}

main()
{
    int   items;
    float cost, owe;

    printf("Enter the number of items bought > ");
    scanf("%d", &items);
    printf("Enter the cost of each item > ");
    scanf("%f", &cost);

    owe = total(items, cost);

    printf("You owe $ %8.2f\n", owe);
}
```

The program still produces the exact same run as in Example 10.2.3:

```
Enter the number of items bought > 61
Enter the cost of each item > 2.01
You owe $   122.61
```

Explanations

1. Note the *return* statement. It does three things:
   a. It evaluates the expression given to it, here *qty * unit_cst.*
   b. Then the result, 122.61, is "stored" in the function name *total.*

c. The execution goes back to the calling function. At this point, the assignment operator takes over and assigns the number 122.61 (that was "put" into the function name *total*) to the variable *owe:*

owe = *total(items, cost)*
owe = 122.61

When involved in an expression, the function name can be viewed as a variable name holding a value.

2. Note the keyword is now *float,* not *void.* This keyword indicates the type of the data (here, total cost is *float*) that the calling function receives from *total().* In other words, it is the type of the data that the function *total()* sends back to *main().* Then this data is assigned to the variable *owe.* Figure 10.4.1 summarizes this.

Figure 10.4.1

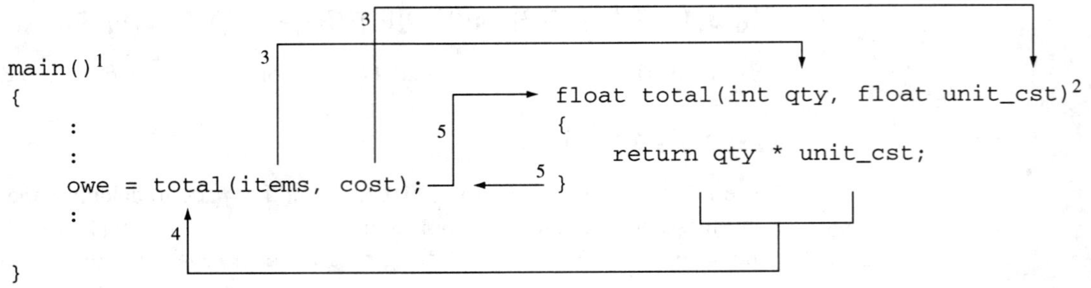

Explanations

1. This is the calling function.
2. This is the called function.
3. These arrows represent the action of arguments being copied: 61 to *qty* and 2.01 to *unit_cst.*
4. This arrow represents the action of the product of *return qty * unit_cst* (61 * 2.01), which is 122.61, being stored in the function.
5. These arrows represent the direction in which the program is executed.

EXERCISES 10.4.1

1. Modify the function *multi()* developed in Exercise 10.2.3, 1, so that the result is returned instead of displayed. The *main()* will display it.
2. Modify the function *square()* developed in Exercise 10.2.3, 2, so that the result is returned instead of displayed. The *main()* will display it.
3. Modify the function *cube()* developed in Exerciss 10.2.3, 3, so that the result is returned instead of displayed. The *main()* will display it.
4. Use the functions in questions 2 and 3 above to produce a table of the squares and cubes of numbers from –10 to 10.
5. Modify the function *show_menu()* from Exercise 10.1.1, 3, so that the action of asking for a choice is moved within it. The user's answer will be stored in a local variable, and its value will then be returned to *main().*
6. As stated in Subsection 2.1.1, the *return* statement is always needed at the end of the *main()* function. Otherwise, a warning message may appear. Suggest a reason that this statement is needed.

Example 10.4.2

Consider the following program which simply reads in a list of numbers ended by pressing Ctrl-Z. The sum is then displayed.

```
#include <stdio.h>

main()
{
      float       num, sum;
      signed char flag;

      sum = 0;
      printf("Enter a list of numbers:\n");
      flag = scanf("%f", &num);
      while (flag != EOF)
      {
            sum += num;
            flag = scanf("%f", &num);
      }
      printf("The sum is %f\n", sum);
}
```

The explanation for Example 10.4.1 said that functions that return a value may be regarded as variables containing a value. Therefore, any place a variable appears in an expression, a function may also appear (as long as it returns data). Consequently the temporary variable *flag* in the *while* condition above may be replaced by the value returned by the call to *scanf()* directly. This makes the following changes (shown in bold type):

```
#include <stdio.h>

main()
{
      float   num, sum;

      sum = 0;
      printf("Enter a list of numbers:\n");
      while (scanf("%f", &num) != EOF)
      {
            sum += num;
      }
      printf("The sum is %f\n", sum);
}
```

Note that there is now only one *scanf()*, and it is part of the condition. Only one *scanf()* is needed because the condition is reached as the loop is entered. It is then reached after each execution of the loop. Thus, both solutions are logically the same.

EXERCISES 10.4.2

What would be the effect of the following programs?

1.
```
sum = 0;
printf("Enter a list of numbers:\n");
while (scanf("%f", &num) != EOF)
{
      sum += num;
      scanf("%f", &num);
}
printf("The sum is %f\n", sum);
```

2.
```
sum = 0;
printf("Enter a list of numbers:\n");
scanf("%f", &num);
```

```
while (scanf("%f", &num) != EOF)
{
      sum += num;
}
printf("The sum is %f\n", sum);
```

Example 10.4.3

Let us modify the program in Exercise 10.2.4, 5 so that the maximum number found is returned to the *main()* instead of being displayed. Following is the resulting program:

```
#include <stdio.h>

float find_max(float num1, float num2)
{
    if (num1 > num2)
    {
       return num1;
    }
    else
    {
       return num2;
    }
}

main()
{
    float num1, num2, max;

    printf("Enter two numbers > ");
    scanf("%f%f", &num1, &num2);

    max = find_max(num1, num2);
    printf("The largest number is %f\n", max);
}
```

Although two *return* statements appear in the function *find_max()*, only one will be reached.

Now that we've seen numerous examples and exercises, we know that a function header may be made of three parts: the data return type, the function name, and the list of parameters. (The data return type is also termed the ***function type.***) For example, in the following function header:

float find_max(float num1, float num2)

the data return type is *float,* the function name is *find_max,* and the list of parameters is *(float num1, float num2).*

EXERCISES 10.4.3

1. What will the following program display?

```
int echo(int num)
{
   return num / 2;
   return num * 2;
}

main()
{
```

```
    int num;

    num = echo(6);
    printf("echo is %f", num);
    num = echo(8);
    printf("echo is %f", num);
}
```

2. Modify the function *absolute()* developed in Exercise 10.2.4, 4, so that the absolute value is returned instead of displayed. The *main()* will now display it.
3. Write a unit test driver for each of the following functions after they are defined:
   a. Modify the function *even()* in Exercise 10.2.4, 2 so that the letter 'E' is returned if the argument is even, and the letter 'O' appears in all other cases.
   b. Modify the function again so that a 1 is returned if the argument is even, and a 0 is returned in all other cases.
4. After defining each function below, write a unit test driver for each:
   a. Write a function named *ispass()* that receives a mark in the range of 0 to 100 and returns a 1 if it is a passing mark or a 0 in all other cases. The lowest passing mark is also passed as an argument.
   b. Modify the function again so that it returns 'P' for a passing mark or 'F' for a failing mark.
5. The following program provides two randomly generated numbers. The user attempts to sum them, and the program verifies the sum's correctness. This continues until the user enters a wrong answer. Following is the program. It is almost identical to the one in Exercise 10.2.4, 6, except for the bold type:

```
#include <stdio.h>
#include <stdlib.h>

main()
{
     int   num1, num2, answer;
     char  more;
     do
         {
           num1 = rand();
           num2 = rand();
           printf("What is the addition of %d and %d ?\n ",
                     num1, num2);
           scanf("%d", &answer);
           if (answer == num1 + num2)
           {
                   printf("You are right!\n");
                   more = 1;
           }
           else
           {
                   printf("You are wrong!\n");
                   more = 0;
           }
     }
     while (more == 1);
}
```

   Write a function named *display_msg()* that takes in as arguments both numbers and the user's answer and then displays the appropriate message. It then returns a 1 if the answer is correct and returns a 0 in all other cases.
6. Revisit Example 8.1.2 and introduce a function named *update_max()* to the program. This function will be called every time that a number is read in. It will compare that number against the current maximum and update that maximum if necessary. The maximum, changed or not, is returned.

10.4.2 BE WARY OF RETURNED DATA TYPE MISMATCHES

An implicit conversion may occur when data is sent through the *return* statement. Sometimes that is useful; other times, it is not. Consider Example 10.4.4.

Example 10.4.4

Let us revisit Example 10.4.1. Suppose that the type of the function was coded as *int* by mistake, as shown in bold in the following program:

```
int total(int qty, float unit_cst)
{
   return qty * unit_cst;
}
```

The rest of the program remains the same. Assuming 61 items and $2.01 per item, Figure 10.4.2 shows what happens from the time of the function call to the time of function return.

Figure 10.4.2

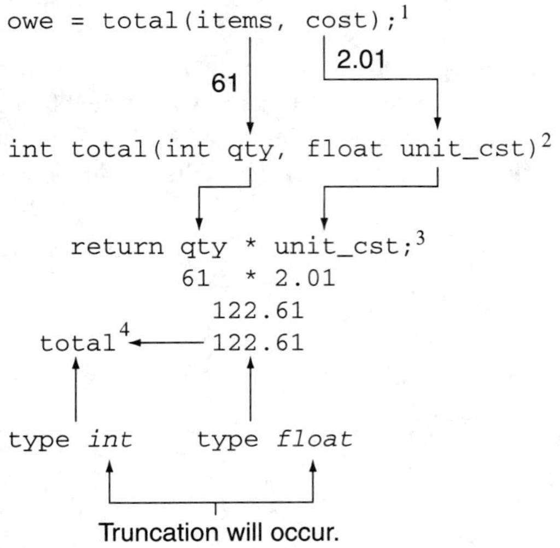

Explanations

1. Function call
2. Function header
3. Return statement, followed by the evaluation
4. Result "assigned" to function name

The result will be converted to 122 and stored in the function *total.* Finally, the assignment statement will store 122 in the variable *owe:*

owe = total(items, cost);
owe = 122

Even though *owe* is of type *float,* the function *total()* is of type *int* (i.e., it always returns an integer).

Example 10.4.5

Implicit conversion may occur in yet another way. Suppose now that the function type for *total()* is corrected to *float,* as shown in the following program code:

```
float total(int qty, float unit_cst)
{
   return qty * unit_cst;
}
```

Now suppose that the type of the variable *owe* in the *main()* is mistakenly changed to *int:*

```
main()
{
    int   items;
    float cost;
    int   owe;

    printf("Enter the number of items bought > ");
    scanf("%d", &items);
    printf("Enter the cost of each item > ");
    scanf("%d", &cost);

    owe = total(items, cost);

    printf("You owe $ %8.2f\n", owe);
}
```

Figure 10.4.3 shows what happens from the time of the function call to the time of function return.

Figure 10.4.3

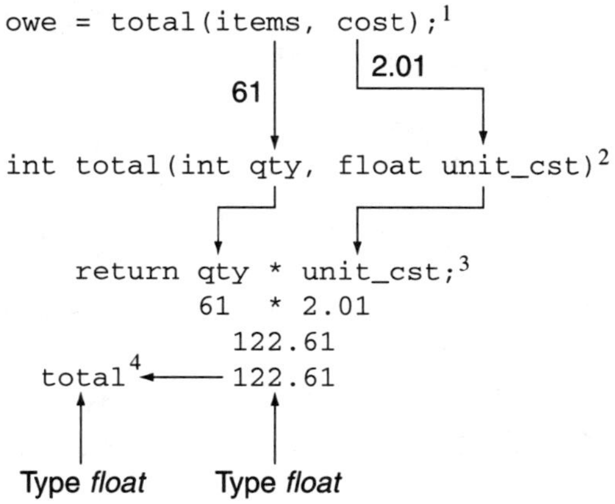

Explanations

1. Function call
2. Function header
3. Return statement, followed by the evaluation
4. Result "assigned" to function name

The correct result, 122.61, is "stored" in the function *total.* So far, so good! But finally, the assignment statement will store the integer 122, not 122.61, into the variable *owe.* (Why?)

Explicit conversions. Because implicit conversions may lead to unwanted side effects, some programmers may prefer to indicate explicitly where type conversions occur. As we saw in Subsection 3.2.6, this is accomplished with the cast operator. For instance, the implicit conversion made with the function call above is made explicit with the use of *int.* In the following line of code:

```
owe = (int) total(items, cost)
```

(int) means this will convert the number returned by the function to an integer. With the function call in Example 10.2.5, the conversion looked like this:

```
owe = total(items, (int) cost)
```

Here, *(int)* means this will convert the cost to an integer, and then pass that to the parameter.

EXERCISES 10.4.4

1. Discuss all of the implicit conversions that occur with the following pieces of code that call arithmetic operations (covered in detail in Subsection 10.4.4):

a.
```
int  num;

num = fabs(7538);
```

b.
```
int   num;
float result;

num = -825;
result = labs(num);
```

2. For both (a) and (b) above, show the conversions explicitly by using the cast operator.
3. Use the following function to answer the questions below:

```
int increment(int num, int step)
{
        return num + step;
}
```

What would be returned by the function with the following calls? Also, what would be stored in the variables *int num* and *float fl* shown below?

a. *increment*(6, 8.3)
b. *num* = *increment*(6, 8.3)
c. *increment*(6.0, 8)
d. *fl* = *increment*(6.0, 8.9)

4. Consider the following programs:

```
float find_avg_1(int size)
{
        float sum;
        int   i;

        for (sum = 0, i = 0; i < size; sum += size + 0.25, i++) ;
        return sum / size;
}

int find_avg_2(int size)
{
        float sum;
        int   i;

        for (sum = 0, i = 0; i < size; sum += size + 0.25, i++) ;
        return sum / size;
}

main()
{
        int    vi;
        float  vf;

        vi = find_avg_1(5);
        vf = find_avg_2(5);
}
```

For each function call in *main()*, answer the following questions:

a. To what value will the *return* statement evaluate its expression?
b. What value will the function *find_avg()* return?
c. What value will be stored in the variable to the left?

10.4.3 TESTING A USER-DEFINED FUNCTION, PART 2

Section 10.2.3 stressed the importance of testing the correctness of argument passing. Just the same, the value returned by a function should be tested. This is easy to do, as shown in Example 10.4.6.

Example 10.4.6

Following is a unit test driver for the function *total()* as defined in Example 10.4.1 (changes are shown in bold type). Note that a *printf()* is still needed to test argument passing.

```
#include <stdio.h>

float total(int qty, float unit_cst)
{
   printf("Testing: received in total(): qty = %d, unit_cost = %f\n",
          qty, unit_cost);
   printf("Testing: sending from total(): total = %f\n",
          qty * unit_cst);
   return qty * unit_cst;
}

main()
{
    int   items;
    float cost, owe;
    char  ans;

    do
    {
        printf("Enter the number of items bought > ");
        scanf("%d", &items);
        printf("Enter the cost of each item > ");
        scanf("%f, &cost);
        owe = total(items, cost);
        printf("You owe $ %8.2f\n", owe);
        printf("End of the test drive (y/n) ? ");
        scanf("\n%c", &ans);
        ans = toupper(ans);
    }
    while (ans == 'N');
}
```

No further explanations are needed. Run this program and observe!

EXERCISES 10.4.5

Suppose that you run the unit test driver in Example 10.4.6 and that the two *printf()*s in the function *total()* reveal nothing wrong.

1. Can it be immediately concluded that the function *total()* is free of errors? Explain.
2. With a function definition in general, what errors (if any) can escape the testing of the parameters and the returned value?

10.4.4 AN OVERVIEW OF SOME ARITHMETIC FUNCTIONS

An ANSI C compiler comes with a set of arithmetic functions, some of which are commonly used. Following is a list of those:

double ceil(double n)
: Returns the smallest integer larger than *n*. For example, *ceil(51.4)* is 52.

double floor(double n)
: Returns the largest integer smaller than *n*. For example, *floor(51.9)* is 51.

double fabs(double n)
: Returns the absolute value of *n*. For example, *fabs(–2127.92)* is 2127.92.

double fmod(double a, double b)
    Returns the remainder of *a* divided by *b*. For example, *fmod(19.2, 5.1)* is 3.9.

double pow(double a, double b)
    Returns the value of a^b.

double sqrt(double a)
    Returns the square root of *a*.

When any one of these functions is used, the line *#include <math.h>* must be placed at the top of the program. Other arithmetic functions require the line *#include <stdlib.h>* instead. Following are two of them:

int abs(int n)
    Returns the absolute value of *n*. For example, *abs(–51)* is 51.

long int labs(long int n)
    Returns the absolute value of *n*. For example, *labs(–219827)* is 219827.

Let us now look at a ways to use some of these functions.

Example 10.4.7

Let us evaluate the following expression.

```
pow(5.1, 3.2) + fabs(-9.02) * ceil(26.01)
                 9.02
                 9.02        * 27
                        243.54
183.749
183.749        +        243.54
           427.289
```

Example 10.4.8

Let us evaluate the following expression.

```
pow(2.05 + fabs(-3.05), 3.2)
     2.05 + fabs(3.05)
           3.05
    2.05 + 3.05
        5.1
pow(    5.1           , 3.2)
183.749
```

EXERCISES 10.4.6

1. Evaluate the following expressions.
   a. *floor(7.5) / pow(2.1, 1.5) * labs(–22751)*
   b. *fabs(ceil(–93.02) – abs(–728)) * sqrt(5)*
   c. *floor(pow(9–abs(–4), ceil(sqrt(5)))*
2. Is there anything wrong with these statements?
   a. *printf("absolute value = %d\n", fabs(4–13));*
   b. *printf("floor = %d\n", floor(32.568));*
   c. *printf("absolute value = %f\n", labs(5));*
3. You may remember from high school algebra that negative numbers do not have square roots. For example, should a program contain the expression *sr = sqrt(–5),* garbage would be stored in the variable, or worse, the program may crash. For each function below, write a unit test driver to ensure their correctness:
   a. Write a function named *issqrt()* that returns 1 if the argument has a square root or returns 0 in all other cases.

b. Write a function named *safe_sqrt()* that returns the square root of the argument, if one exists, and returns FLT_MAX if it does not exist.

c. Modify the function *safe_sqrt()* so that in addition to returning FLT_MAX, it displays the message "imaginary number" when no square root of the argument exists.

4. a. Modify the *round()* function in Exercise 10.3.1, 7(b), so that it returns the rounded number instead of displaying the message. The message will be displayed by the *main()*.

   b. Write a unit test driver for this function.

5. The following program is supposed to raise a base to the exponent entered by the user. That is, it calculates $base^{exponent}$. For instance, $2^4 = 16$.

```
#include <stdio.h>

long power(int a, long b)
{
        float total;
        int   ctr;

        total = a;
        for (ctr=0; ctr < b1; ctr++)
        {
                total = total * a;
        }

        return total;
}

main()
{
        unsigned long res;
        long base, exp;

        printf("Enter a base and an exponent > ");
        scanf("%ld%ld", &base, &exp);
        res = power(base, exp);
        printf("%ld raised to exponent %d is %ld\n", base, exp, res);
}
```

Although the logic here is absolutely flawless, the user found that the program never works! For example, here is the response with a simple input:

```
Enter a base and an exponent > 2 4
2 raised to exponent 4 is 1048576
```

Can you find what is wrong with this program? Careful! There is more than just one bug!

6. a. Write a function named *ceiling()* that returns the smallest integer not less than the argument. For example *ceiling(19.2)* is 20.

   b. Write a unit test driver for this function.

7. a. Write a function named *floor()* that returns the largest integer not greater than the argument. For example *floor(19.2)* is 19.

   b. Write a unit test driver for this function.

8. a. Write a function named *divisible()* that determines if the first argument is divisible by the second one. If so, 'y' is returned; otherwise 'n' is returned.

   b. Modify the function above so that it returns 1 if the argument is divisible and 0 if it is not.

9. Write a function named *quotient()* that returns the quotient of the first argument divided by the second one. Both arguments are of type *float*. For example, *quotient(19.2, 3.5)* is 5.

10. Write a function named *remainder()* that returns the remainder of the first argument divided by the second one. Both arguments are of type *float*. For example, *remainder(19.2, 3.5)* is 1.7; 3.5 * 5 + 1.7 = 19.2.

11. Modify the function *fraction()* from Exercise 10.3.1, 5, so that the fractional part is returned.

12. a. Write a function named *isprime()* that returns a 1 if its argument *num* is a prime number, or otherwise returns a 0. Remember that a number is prime if it is not divisible by any number

except 1 and itself. For example, 13 is prime, but 14 is not. (***Hint:*** Use a loop that runs from the divisor 2 all the way to *num* itself.)

b. The loop in (a) is unnecessarily slow. Make the loop run from the divisor 2 to *sqrt(num)*. Going farther is pointless. (Why is that so?)

13. Write a program that uses the function *isprime()* (from question 12 above) to find all twin primes in the range of 1 to 10,000. Twin primes are odd numbers that are next to each other. For instance, the numbers 3 and 5 are twin primes. In fact the numbers 5 and 7 are also twin primes.
14. Write a function named *sum_divs()* that returns the sum of the divisors of the argument. For example, the divisors of 12 are 1, 2, 3, 4, 6, 12 and their sum is 28, so *sum_divs(12)* returns 28.

10.4.5 RETURNING A FILE POINTER

Returning a file pointer from a function is conceptually equivalent to returning a number or a character. In practice, though, it proves to be a little more error prone. Example 10.4.9 illustrates a typical situation in which a file pointer is returned from a function.

Example 10.4.9

Let us continue with Example 10.2.7. Recall from Subsection 8.2.3 that the *fopen()* does not warn the user of a failure to open a file. Consequently, additional codes had to be included in the program in Example 8.2.4 (duplicated in Example 10.2.7) to ensure that the files IN.DAT and ANS.OUT were opened safely. Let us now move those codes inside user-defined functions.

Specifically, let us write a function named *open_input_safely()* that will display an appropriate message when the input file named IN.DAT cannot be opened; otherwise, it sends back the file pointer variable. Similarly, a function named *open_output_safely()* will be defined for the output file named ANS.OUT. The program in Example 10.2.7 changes to the following, with changes in bold type:

```
#include <stdio.h>

FILE * open_input_safely(void) [1]
{
   FILE * fp; [2]

   fp = fopen("in.dat", "r");
   if (fp == NULL)
   {
      printf("Could not open input file\n");
   }
   return fp; [3]
}

FILE * open_output_safely(void)
{
   FILE * fp;

   fp = fopen("ans.out", "w");
   if (fp == NULL)
   {
      printf("Could not open output file\n");
   }
   return fp;
}

void close_safely(FILE * fp)
{
```

```
    if (fp != NULL)        /* can the file be closed safely? */
    {
       fclose(fp);
    }
    else
    {
       printf("File not opened or does not exist\n");
    }
}

main()
{
    FILE * ifp;
    FILE * ofp;
    int    sum, flag, num;

    ifp = open_input_safely();4
    ofp = open_output_safely();
    if (ifp != NULL && ofp != NULL) /* both files opened correctly ? */
    {
       sum = 0;
       flag = fscanf(ifp, "%d", &num);
       while (flag != EOF)    /* is it the end of file ? */
       {
            sum = sum + num;
            flag = fscanf(ifp, "%d", &num);
       }
       fprintf(ofp, "The sum is %d.\n", sum);
       close_safely(ifp);
       close_safely(ofp);
    }
}
```

Explanations

1. The *FILE* * located here indicates that the function returns a file pointer. The asterisk is important.
2. A local variable is absolutely needed to hold the file pointer returned by *fopen()*.
3. The value of the file pointer is sent back to the *main()*, whether or not it is NULL.
4. The function call takes the file pointer sent back by the *return* statement and stores it in the file pointer variable *ifp*.

   Similar explanations can be made about the function *open_output_safely()*.

EXERCISES 10.4.7

1. Discuss why a local variable is needed in both *open_input_safely()* and *open_output_safely()* to temporarily hold the file pointer until it can be returned.
2. Improve the program in Exercise 10.2.7, 2, so that the file is opened and closed safely.

10.4.6 USE ONE *return* STATEMENT ONLY

Notice that most functions presented in this section have the form shown in Figure 10.4.4. The *return* statement is placed at the end of the function's code, and a single *return* statement is used. This arrangement turns out to be advantageous, as Example 10.4.10 illustrates.

Figure 10.4.4

```
data_return_type  function_name(list of parameters)
{
        :     ┐
        :     ├── Variable declarations
        :     ┘
        :     ┐
        :     ├── Executable codes
        :     ┘
        return statement;
}
```

Example 10.4.10

The program in Example 10.4.3 has two *return* statements but can easily be modified to use a single *return* statement. The only way to achieve this is to use a local variable, as shown in the following program. Note the single return at the end.

```
float find_max(float num1, float num2)
{
    float max;

    if (num1 > num2)
    {
       max = num1;
    }
    else
    {
       max = num2;
    }
    return max;
}
```

For the sake of programming style. By having a *return* statement at the bottom of the function, it is easy to recognize that this function returns the content of the variable *max*. Also, because there is only one *return* in the whole function, it is clear that the function is exited at that location (recall that a function can only exit via a *return* statement). A wellstructured function should have only one ***exit point.*** Why? Well, imagine a function with numerous *return* statements. It would be hard to know where the functions exit. This is like trying to track down a shoplifter when there are many exits in a store. Where is he or she going to exit? It is much easier to understand and debug a function with a single *return.*

A function cannot return multiple values. Reconsider Example 10.4.1. Currently the function returns the total cost for the purchase. Suppose that a sales tax of 5% is now required and must be returned. Since a single *return* statement sends back only one number, it seems natural to use two *return* statements, as follows:

```
float total(int qty, float unit_cst)
{
   return qty * unit_cst;    /* return the total cost, */
                             /* excluding sales tax */
   return qty * unit_cst * 0.05; /* return the amount of sales tax */
}
```

Unfortunately, this cannot work because a *return* statement returns the execution back to the calling function. Therefore the second *return* statement will never be reached. A function can only return **one** datum through the *return* statement. When more than one datum is to be sent back to the calling program, the *return* statement is clearly not sufficient. Data need to be sent back via a technique called ***argument by reference.*** This technique will be covered in Section 11.2. For now, consider the following alternative method.

Example 10.4.11

The only way (for now) to return two data is to simply define **two** separate functions: one that returns the total costs, and another that returns the amount of sales tax. Following is the solution, with new code shown in bold type:

```
#include <stdio.h>

float total_owed(int qty, float unit_cst)
{
   return qty * unit_cst;     /* return the total cost, */
                              /* excluding sales tax */
}

float total_taxed(int qty, float unit_cst)
{
   return qty * unit_cst * 0.05; /* return the amount of sales tax */
}

main()
{
    int   items;
    float cost, owe, tax;

    printf("Enter the number of items bought > ");
    scanf("%d", &items);
    printf("Enter the cost of each item > ");
    scanf("%f", &cost);

    owe = total_owed(items, cost);
    tax = total_taxed(items, cost);
    printf("You owe $ %8.2f and $ %8.2f for taxes\n", owe, tax);
}
```

Of course, this method is not at all satisfactory, but it will have to do for now.

10.4.7 COMMON ERRORS AND TRAPS

Use the following guidelines to help you avoid common programming errors.

1. Do not omit the type of the function. For example:

```
find_max(float num1, float num2)
{
    if (num1 > num2)
    {
       return num1;
    }
    else
    {
       return num2;
    }
}
```

The compiler will **not** complain that the return type is missing in the first line. Instead, it will assume that the function type is *int,* which will cause trouble here. (Why?)

2. Do not use the *void* type for a function that returns a value. For example:

```
void find_max(float num1, float num2)
{
    if (num1 > num2)
```

```
    {
        return num1;
    }
    else
    {
        return num2;
    }
}
```

Recall that *void* means that the function does not return (or does not have the ability to return) a value. Yet the compiler will probably **not** complain that, in this case, *void* should be *float.* However, when the program is run, and a statement such as *max = find_max(num1, num2)* is executed, the number returned into *max* will likely be garbage.

3. Do not forget to use a *return* statement to return a value. For example:

```
float total(int qty, float unit_cst)
{
    float tot_sale;

    tot_sale = qty * unit_cst;
}
```

The statement *return tot_sale* is missing. Yet the compiler might not complain. Of course, when a statement such as *owe = total(items, cost)* is encountered, nothing will be stored in the variable *owe.*

4. Do not use the *return* statement to attempt to return more than one datum. For example:

```
int add_n_diff(int num1, int num2)
{
        int add, diff;

        add = num1 + num2;
        diff = num1  num2;
        return ( add, diff );
}
```

The *return* statement can only return a single datum, not two, as requested here.

SUPPLEMENTARY EXERCISES 10.4

1. a. Write a function named *in_seconds()* that has three arguments: a number of hours, minutes, and seconds. The total number of seconds is then returned. For example, *in_seconds(3, 40, 5)* returns 13,205 seconds. Be careful! The number of total seconds has the potential of being much bigger.
   b. Write a unit test driver for this function.
2. a. Write a function named *random()* that returns a random number between 0 and a maximum value provided by the argument. For example: *random(49).*
   b. Write a unit test driver for this function.
3. a. Improve the function in the question above so that it returns a random number between the range provided by two arguments. For example: *random(15, 31).*
   b. Write a unit test driver for this function.
4. Write a function named *even_rand()* that returns a random even number between 0 and the limit set by the argument. (***Hint:*** Loop until such an even number is found. Use the remainder operator to test for "evenness.")
5. Write a function named *odd_rand()* that returns a random odd number between 0 and the limit set by the argument. (***Hint:*** Loop until such an odd number is found. Use the remainder operator to test for "oddness.")

6. Write a function named *hypotenuse()* that calculates the length of the hypotenuse of a right triangle, given the lengths of the sides as arguments. For example, given the following right triangle:

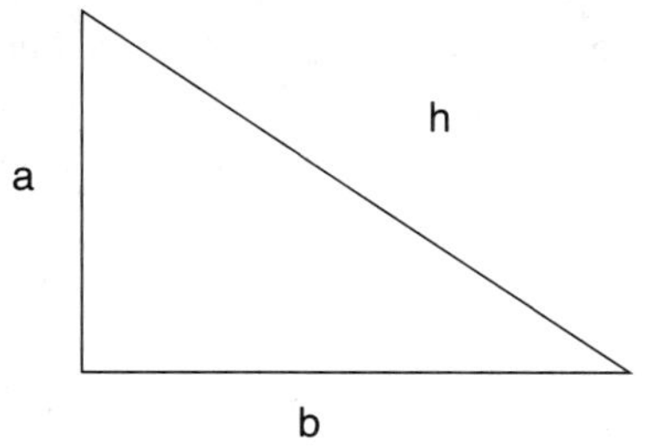

The length of the hypotenuse is found using the formula $a^2 + b^2 = h^2$.

7. a. Define a function named *convert()* that converts an argument in centigrade to Fahrenheit. The formula is $F = (^9/_5)C + 32$.
   b. Use this function in a program that produces the table:

```
Fahrenheit      Centigrade

      32.00            0.00
      41.00            5.00
      50.00           10.00
        :               :
        :               :
     212.00          100.00
```

8. Write a unit test driver for the following functions to ensure that they work:
   a. Write a function named *F_or_C()* that receives two arguments. The first is a temperature in Fahrenheit if the second argument is 'f', otherwise, if the second argument is 'c,' it is a temperature in Celsius. Then the appropriate conversion is calculated. Should the second argument be other than f or c, the function displays an error message.
   b. Improve the function so that it accepts the second argument in uppercase letters as well.
9. Write a program that prompts the user to enter an arithmetic expression. The program then evaluates it. For example:

   Enter an arithmetic expression > 81 – 23.6
   The answer is 57.4

   The *main()* will call a different function for each operation. Both operands will be passed to the function and it will return the result, which *main()* will then display.
10. Write a function named *my_scan()* that reads in an integer and returns it. For example: *num = my_scan()*. You will need a local variable.
11. Write a function named *reverse()* that takes in as argument a number and returns the number with its digits reversed. For example, the number 5801 would be returned as the number 1085.
12. Write a function named *arithm_seq()* that displays an arithmetic sequence. Following is an example of such a sequence:

    3, 5, 7, 9, 11, 13

    It will also return the sum of the terms. Each number is generated using the formula *3 + 2 * counter,* where the counter runs from 0 to 5. Your function must be able to generate any sequence. To this end, it needs a starter value, here 3, and a step value, here 2. The general formula to generate a number is:

```
starter + step * counter
```

    The function needs a third argument: the number of terms to generate.

13. Write a function named *geo_seq()* that displays a geometric sequence. Here is an example of such a sequence:

1, 3, 9, 27, 81, 243

It will also return the sum of the terms. Each number is generated using the formula *pow(3, counter),* where the counter runs from 0 to 5. Your function must be able to generate any sequence. To this end, it simply needs the base, here 3, and the number of terms to generate. The general formula to generate a number is *pow(base, counter).*

11 More Complex Issues About Functions

OBJECTIVES

This chapter introduces you to the following information:

- How to properly use the technique of sending data back out of a function via parameters by reference.
- How to manipulate pointers. Pointer manipulation will be necessary since pointers are involved in the passing of arguments by reference.

INTRODUCTION

Because of the topic's complexity, some textbooks do not cover pointers this early in the course; however, with C an early discussion of this type is necessary to the understanding of later topics. Don't worry; you will be carefully guided through it all.

11.1 POINTER VARIABLES

This section discusses a special kind of variable: the pointer variable. The mechanism of the pointer is fairly complex. Programs in any language make use of pointers, and luckily, most languages hide these pointers from the programmer. In C, unfortunately, pointers are explicitly involved in the passing of arguments by reference, which will be discussed in the next section. On a more positive note, this variable type can enhance the flexibility and speed of a program. Most C programs make use of them.

11.1.1 MEMORY LAYOUT AND ADDRESSES

Section 3.1 mentioned that each variable occupies some space in memory. Just like each house in a city has an address, each cell in memory has an address. Once variables are declared, they are immediately given space in memory.

Example 11.1.1

Consider the following declarations:

```
int    num1, num2;
float  weight, height;
char   i1, i2;
```

and these initializations:

```
num1 = 5;          num2 = 12;
weight = 67.09;    height = 1.71;
i1 = 'H';          i2 = 'P';
```

Let us assume the same storage requirements as in Section 3.1, 1 byte for a *char,* 2 bytes for an *int,* and 4 bytes for a *float.* Assume that the variable *num1* is stored at address 4300, and that the others follow at the addresses indicated in Figure 11.1.1.

Figure 11.1.1

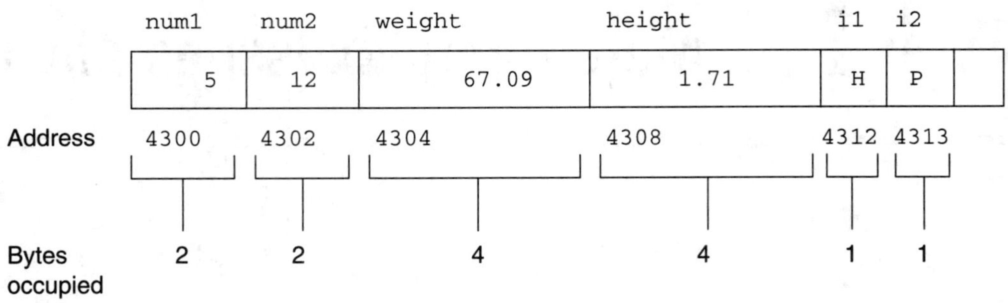

Note that the variable *num2* starts at address 4302, not 4301. Why? Because each byte in memory has an address: *num1* occupies 2 bytes, respectively, at addresses 4300 and 4301; *num2* also occupies 2 bytes, respectively, at addresses 4302 and 4303; *weight* occupies 4 bytes, respectively, at addresses 4304, 4305, 4306, and 4307; and so on.

When an assignment instruction, such as *weight = 67.09,* is executed, the computer automatically places 67.09 at the location indicated by the address 4304. This is where the variable *weight* resides.

11.1.2 THE MECHANISM OF POINTERS

In all the assignment statements listed above, the location of the cell is referred to automatically. That is, there is no need to tell the program to store 67.09 at address 4304. The computer knows where the variable *weight* is located. The address reference is said to be ***implicit.*** Sometimes a program needs to make an **explicit** address reference to a variable (as will be seen shortly). This is done using ***pointer variables.*** These variables manipulate cell addresses, much like an *int* variable manipulates integers. Example 11.1.2 illustrates the pointer mechanism.

Example 11.1.2

Let us accomplish the assignment *weight = 67.09* by using an explicit address reference. This requires the declaration of a pointer variable in addition to the variable *weight,* as shown below.

```
float    weight;           /* data variable */
float  * weight_addr;      /* pointer variable */
```

The asterisk in line 2 indicates that the variable *weight_addr* is a pointer variable. It is of type *float,* meaning that it is meant to contain the **address** of a *float* variable. It cannot hold the address of a variable of any other type.

Finding out the address of a variable. Suppose that the variable *weight_addr* resides at address 4308. Remembering that the variable *weight* resides at address 4304, at this point, the memory layout looks like Figure 11.1.2. The arrow indicates that the pointer variable *weight_addr* is meant to point to a *float* variable, **any** *float* variable, although currently it does not point to any data.

Figure 11.1.2

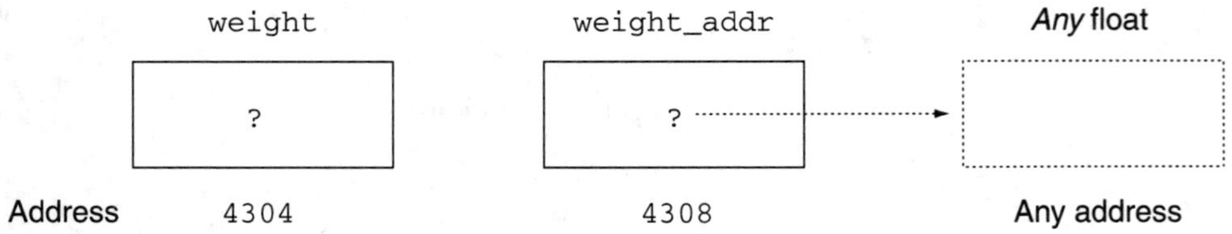

When *weight_addr* is given the address of the variable *weight,* it automatically points to it. This is accomplished in two steps, contained in a single expression, as shown in Figure 11.1.3.

Figure 11.1.3

```
weight_addr = &weight[1]
                4304
weight_addr = 4304[2]
```

Explanations

1. The & operator is called the ***address operator;*** hence it returns the address of the variable *weight,* 4304.
2. This address is then put into the pointer variable *weight_addr.*

The memory layout is now as shown in Figure 11.1.4. Note the dotted arrow pointing toward the variable *weight.* This shows that the variable *weight_addr* ***points*** to the variable *weight.* The solid arrow shows the copying of the address to the variable *weight_addr.*

Figure 11.1.4

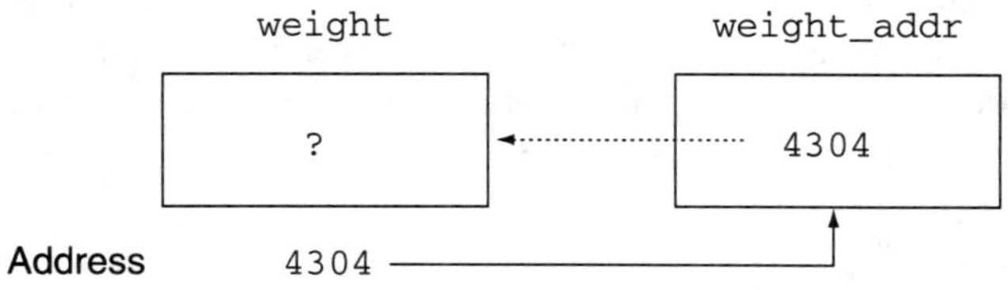

Explicit address dereferencing. Now the number 67.09 is to be stored in the variable *weight.* We will do this via an explicit address reference, i.e., a ***reference*** to the pointer *weight_addr.* This is accomplished in two steps in a single expression, as shown in Figure 11.1.5.

Figure 11.1.5

```
*weight_addr = 67.09;[1]
*4304
weight[2]
weight       = 67.09[3]
```

Explanations

1. The asterisk (*) at the beginning of this line is called the ***dereferencing operator.*** Its operand must be a pointer variable. It tells the pointer to go to the cell to which it is pointing; that is, go to the cell whose address is 4304.
2. The variable *weight* at that cell resides.
3. The computer places the number 67.09 in the variable *weight.*

The memory layout now looks like Figure 11.1.6.

Figure 11.1.6

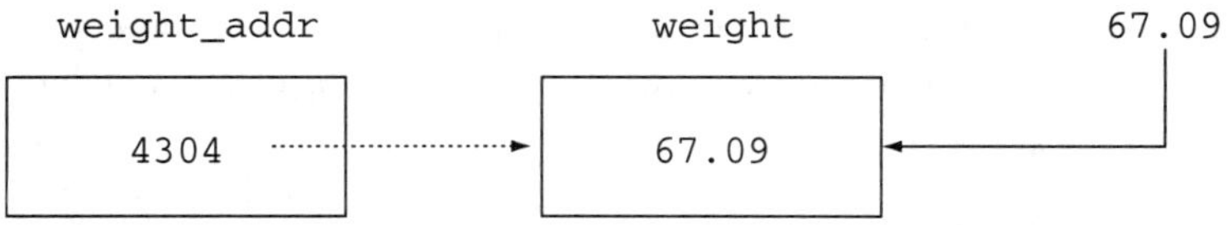

As seen in earlier figures, the dashed arrow in Figure 11.1.6 indicates pointing, while the solid arrow indicates copying. In effect, the assignment **weight_addr = 67.09* is absolutely identical to the assignment *weight = 67.09,* simply because **weight_addr* **is** the variable *weight,* even though it does not look like it. In the latter case, the CPU performs the address referencing for you; in the former case, you do the address referencing yourself.

Thus, via an explicit address referencing, four statements were needed to store a number in a variable, whereas with implicit referencing only two were needed as shown in Table 11.1.1.

Table 11.1.1

Explicit Addressing	Implicit Addressing
`float    weight;`	`float    weight;`
`float  * weight_addr;`	
	`weight = 67.09;`
`weight_addr = &weight;`	
`*weight_addr = 67.09;`	

Why learn about pointers? Now you may be thinking that pointer variables are not useful. In truth, they are quite useful and powerful. The next section will discuss one of the most useful and common applications of pointers, arguments by reference.

11.1.3 POINTER VARIABLES AS MAILPERSON

A pointer variable works very much like a mail delivery person. The address operator & corresponds to the mailperson looking at the address where a parcel is to be delivered. The dereferencing operator * corresponds to the mailperson going to that address. The assignment operator = corresponds to the mailperson putting the parcel in the mailbox. Just as a mailperson goes from one address to another, a pointer variable may be made to point to one variable and then to another one. Consider Example 11.1.3.

Example 11.1.3

The cell address to which a pointer variable points may be changed in the course of a program. For example, consider the following slightly more complex program:

```
#include <stdio.h>

main()
{
     int   miles, dist, temp;
     int * int_addr;                       /* declare a pointer to an int */

     dist = 41;
     miles = 12;

     int_addr = &miles;                   /* make int_addr point to miles */
     temp = *int_addr;
     printf("The value pointed to by int_addr is %d\n\n", temp);

     int_addr = &dist;                    /* make int_addr point to dist */
     temp = *int_addr;
     printf("The value pointed to by int_addr is %d\n", temp);
}
```

For our example, assume that the variable *miles* is at address 5000, and the others follow. After the variables have been declared and initialized, the memory layout looks like Figure 11.1.7. Notice

Figure 11.1.7

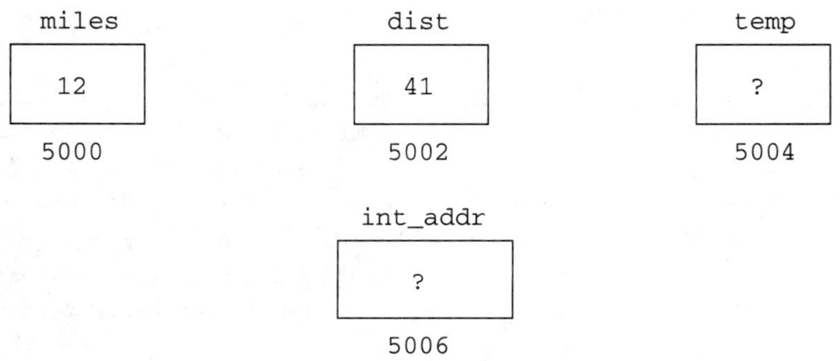

that a pointer variable such as *int_addr* occupies more space than an integer; it may be 4 bytes or more, depending on the computer system. The *sizeof* operator may be used to find out for sure. For example, the following returns the size of a pointer to an integer. Note the asterisk:

```
sizeof(int *)
```

Now back to the program. The first statement *int_addr = &miles* puts the address of *miles* into the pointer variable *int_addr,* causing *int_addr* to point to the variable *miles,* as shown in Figure 11.1.8. Remember that the dashed arrow denotes pointing while the solid arrow shows copying. As you can see, the pointer now looks at the variable *miles*.

Figure 11.1.8

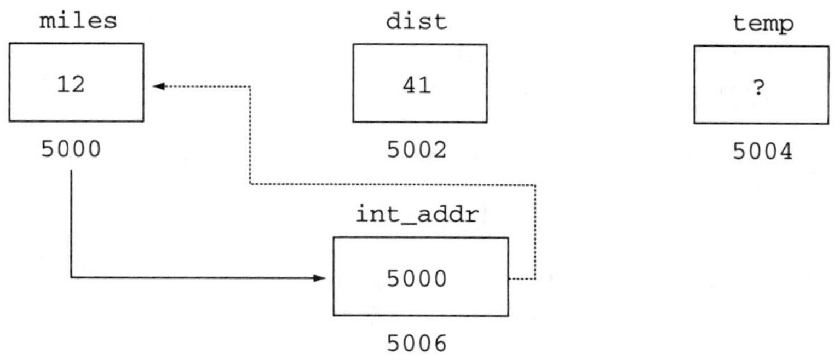

The statement *temp = *int_addr* does two things:

1. The dereferencing operator * tells the pointer *int_addr* to go to the cell at which it is looking, i.e., *miles*.
2. Once there, the assignment operator takes the content of *miles* and assigns it to the variable *temp*, as shown in Figure 11.1.9.

Figure 11.1.9

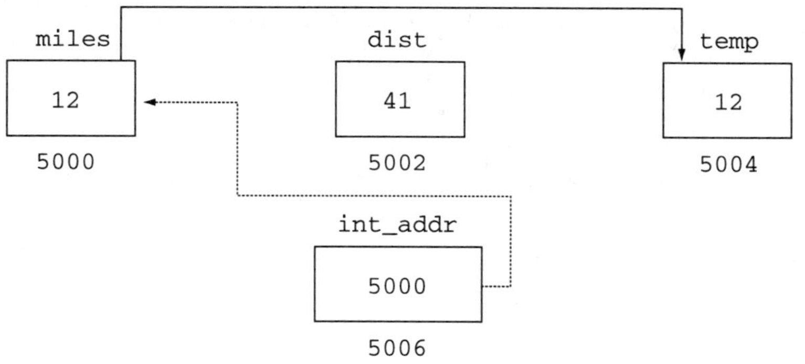

Finally, the *printf()* statement displays the number 12. Next the statement *int_addr = &dist* places the address of *dist*, i.e., 5002, into the pointer variable *int_addr*, thereby making *int_addr* look at *dist,* as Figure 11.1.10 shows.

Figure 11.1.10

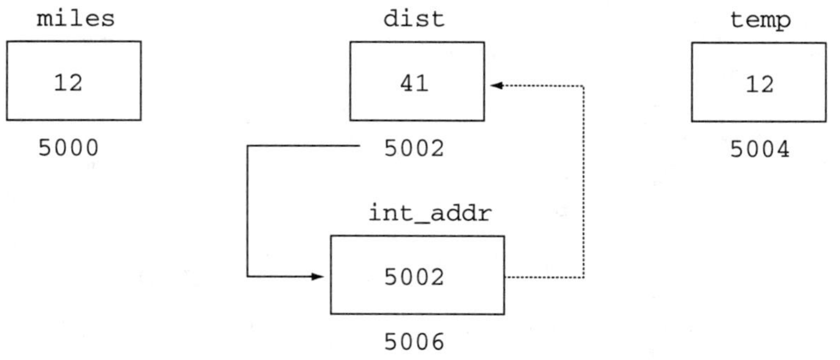

The memory layout in Figure 11.1.11 results from the next statement, *temp = *int_addr:* The number 41 will finally be displayed by the *printf()*.

Figure 11.1.11

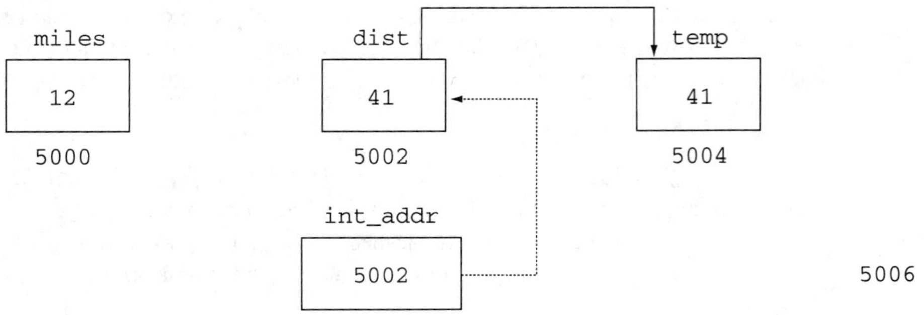

EXERCISES 11.1.1

1. Show the memory layout after each of the following statements.

```
int      num1, num2;
float    f1;
float *  f_ptr;
int   *  i_ptr;

f1 = 51.42;
i_ptr = &num2;
*i_ptr = 66;
f_ptr = &f1;
num1 = num2 + *i_ptr * *f_ptr;
f_ptr = &f2;
num1 = num2 + *i_ptr * *f_ptr;
```

   Careful! Do not confuse the multiplication and the dereferencing operators.
2. In question 1 above, shorten the program by eliminating the use of pointer variables.
3. Find the error in the following statements.
   a.
   ```
   char ch, ptr,

   ch = 'a';
   ptr = &ch;
   ```
   b.
   ```
   char ch;
   char * ptr;

   ch = 'T';
   ptr = ch;
   ```
4. Write a simple program that finds the size in bytes that pointers to integers *(int),* to long integers *(long int),* to *char,* and to *float* values require. Do they all require the same space?
5. What is displayed by the following code?

```
float f1, f2;
float * ptr1;
float * ptr2;

ptr1 = &f1;
ptr2 = &f2;
*ptr2 = *ptr1;
printf("f1 = %f, f2 = %f\n", f1, f2);
printf("*ptr1 = %f, *ptr2 = %f\n", *ptr1, *ptr2);
ptr2 = ptr1;
printf("*ptr1 = %f, *ptr2 = %f\n", *ptr1, *ptr2);
```

6. Consider the following code:

```
char   c1, c2, tmp;
char * c1_addr;
char * c2_addr;
```

```
c1 = 'A';
c2 = 'B';
*c1_addr = &c1;
*c2_addr = &c2;
tmp = *c1_addr;
*c1_addr = *c2_addr;
*c2_addr = tmp;
```

Draw the memory layout after all statements are executed. Assume the following addresses:

Variable	Address
c1	3000
c2	3004
tmp	3008
c1_addr	3012
c2_addr	3016

7. The examples in this section have assumed arbitrary addresses. The exact addresses never mattered. Nevertheless, there is a format code that can be used to display real addresses: *%p*. For instance, the following displays the address of variable *height:*

```
printf("variable height resides at %p", &height);
```

The actual format of the address displayed differs across systems. On your system, find the actual addresses of all the variables in the program in question 2 above.

11.1.4 COMMON ERRORS AND TRAPS

The following information will help you avoid common programming errors.

1. Do not omit the dereferencing operator in an expression. As shown in the program for Exercise 11.1.1, 1:

```
i_ptr = 66;      or      i_ptr = num2;
```

The compiler would complain when encountering this code.

2. Do not make a pointer variable point to a variable of the wrong type. For example:

```
float * ptr;
int     a;

ptr = &a;
```

The compiler will complain about this code also.

11.2 ARGUMENTS BY REFERENCE

Section 10.4 explained that a function is limited to returning only one datum with the *return* statement. Besides the use of the *return* statement, there exists another way that a function may send data back to the calling function: via an argument by reference. With this approach, multiple data may be sent back, which is quite handy. (The bad news is that this technique uses variable pointers.)

Note that nearly all books prefer the term ***parameter by reference*** instead of ***argument by reference.*** This term is misleading. As will be seen in this section, it is actually the argument that is sent by reference (but we will continue to call the parameter associated to this argument a ***parameter by reference***).

11.2.1 THE MECHANISM OF ARGUMENTS BY REFERENCE

Example 11.2.1

Let us fix the problem encountered with the function *total()* in Example 10.4.11. Remember that the problem was that the function could not be coded to return two values. Both the total cost and the sales tax amounts should simply be sent back via arguments by reference. There is no longer a need for two functions. Following is the new program, with changes shown in bold type:

```
#include <stdio.h>

void total(int qty, float unit_cst, float * owe_addr, float * tax_addr)
{
   *owe_addr = qty * unit_cst;
   *tax_addr = qty * unit_cst * 0.05;
}

main()
{
    int   items;
    float cost, owe, tax_owe;

    printf("Enter the number of items bought > ");
    scanf("%d", &items);
    printf("Enter the cost of each item > ");
    scanf("%d", &cost);

    total(items, cost, &owe, &tax_owe);

    printf("You owe $ %8.2f, with tax %8.2f\n", owe, tax_owe);
}
```

In Figure 11.2.1, observe how the arguments of *total()* are passed to their respective parameters.

Figure 11.2.1

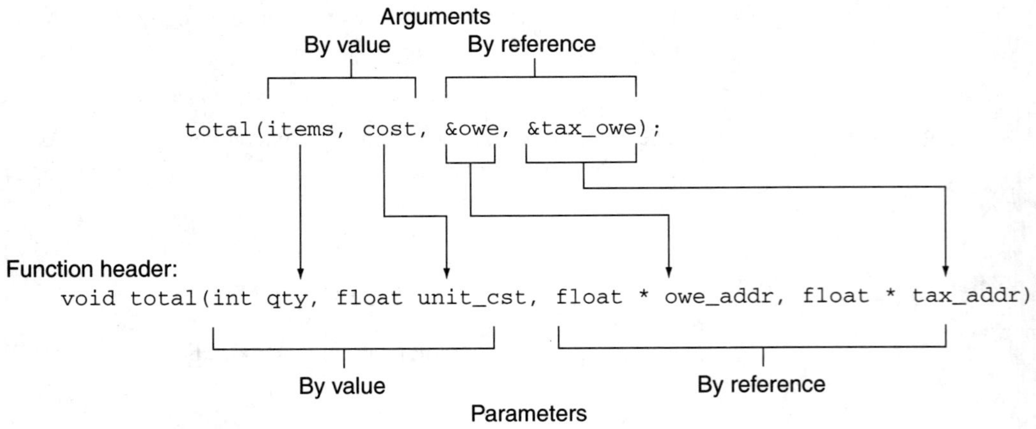

The passing of the first two arguments, *items* and *cost,* require no explanation; they are passed by value, as explained in Section 10.2. For the last two arguments, the addresses of the variables *owe* and *tax_owe* are passed to the parameters *owe_addr* and *tax_addr.* Both of them are of type *float* *; i.e., they are pointer variables. At the time that the arguments are passed, the memory layout looks like Figure 11.2.2. Solid arrows indicate copying taking place.

Figure 11.2.2

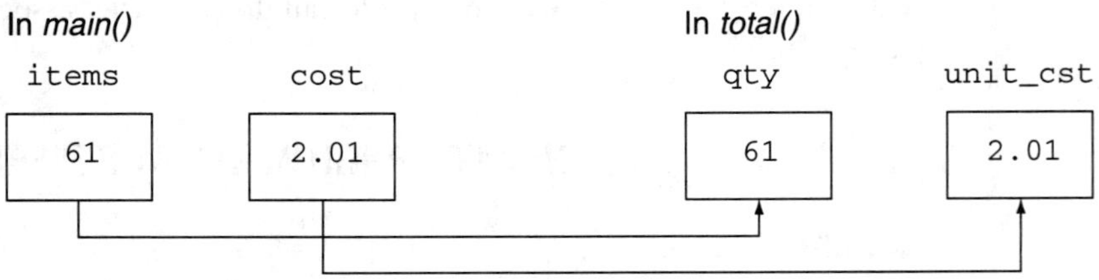

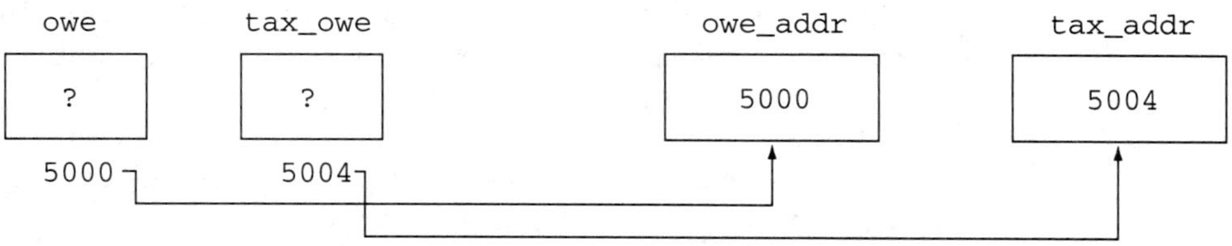

This address passing causes the two pointers, *owe_addr* and *tax_addr,* to look at the variables *owe* and *tax_owe* respectively, as shown in Figure 11.2.3. Dashed arrows indicate pointing taking place.

Figure 11.2.3

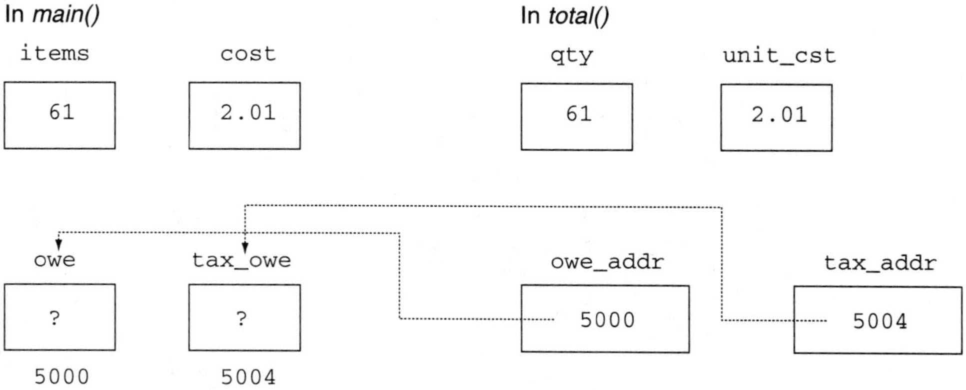

Next, the two statements within the function are executed:

```
*owe_addr = qty * unit_cst;
*tax_addr = qty * unit_cst * 0.05;
```

The results of these calculations, 122.61 and 6.13, will be placed in the variables *owe* and *tax_owe,* respectively, via the pointer references **owe_addr* and **tax_addr,* as Figure 11.2.4 illustrates.

Figure 11.2.4

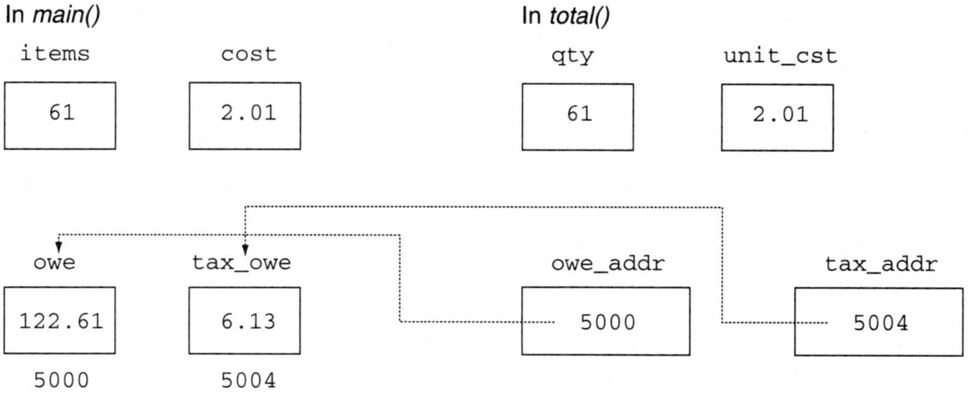

Visibility considerations. Note that the two statements above are in effect equivalent to the following two:

```
owe = qty * unit_cst;
tax_owe = qty * unit_cst * 0.05;
```

Yet the variables *owe* and *tax_owe* are not visible within *total().* (Why do you think that is so?) How was the function *total()* able to use these two variables if it could not see them? The answer, of course, is that the function *total()* knew the addresses of *owe* and *tax_owe.* It could then reach out and store values in them, even though it could not see them. This is the same principle used in telephone communications. You cannot see the person at the other end of the line, but exchange of communication is possible because you dialed that person's phone number—an address.

Note also that the type of the function *total()* is *void.* This is because it no longer sends anything back with the *return* statement. Of course, arguments by reference and the *return* statement can coexist, as Example 11.2.2 below will show.

Note that it does not matter in what order the parameters of *total()* are declared. Here, the parameters by value were declared first, and the parameters by reference were declared second. Just as easily, they could have been declared in this order:

```
void total(int qty, float * owe_addr, float unit_cst, float * tax_addr)
```

Then, the arguments would have to be sent as follows:

```
total(items, &owe, cost, &tax_owe)
```

EXERCISES 11.2.1

1. For the following two programs, draw the memory layout for each variable and draw the situation of *find_max* at the time of call and at the time of return. Make up some address values.

   a.
```
int find_max (int x, int y)
{
        int max;

        if (x > y)
        {
                max = x;
        }
        else
        {
                max = y;
        }
        return max;
}

main()
{
        int max, x, y;

        max = find_max(x, y);
}
```

   b.
```
void find_max (int x, int y, int *max)

{
        if (x > y)
        {
                *max = x;
        }
        else
        {
                *max = y;
        }
}

main()
{
        int x, y, max;

        find_max(x, y, &max);
}
```

2. A novice programmer looks at the function from Example 11.2.1:

```
void total(int qty, float unit_cst,
           float * owe_addr, float * tax_addr)
{
    *owe_addr = qty * unit_cst;
    *tax_addr = qty * unit_cst * 0.05;
}
```

and figures that the solution below will work as well:

```
void total(int qty, float unit_cst,
           float owe, float tax_owe)
{

    float * owe_addr;
    float * tax_addr;

    owe_addr = &owe;           /* gives pointer to variable owe */
    tax_addr = &tax_owe;       /* gives pointer to variable tax_owe */
    *owe_addr = qty * unit_cst;
    *tax_addr = qty * unit_cst * 0.05;
}
```

Is she right? Explain.

3. Modify the program in Exercise 10.4.3, 6, so that the function *update_max()* no longer uses a *return* statement. Instead the data will be sent by reference.

11.2.2 CHOOSING A METHOD TO SEND BACK DATA

We now have two ways to send data out of a function: with the *return* statement, or with an argument by reference. So which one should you use for a given situation? This subsection covers three examples to help shed some light on this question.

Example 11.2.2

Back in Example 11.2.1, the programmer may decide to use the *return* statement to send back the total cost owed and use a parameter by reference to send back the tax owed. The definition of the function *total()* then needs to change to the following (changes are in bold type):

```
float total(int qty, float unit_cst, float * tax_addr)
{
   *tax_addr = qty * unit_cst * 0.05;
   return qty * unit_cst;                 /* return total cost */
}
```

Note that the function type must now be *float.* (Why is that so?) The function call must become:

```
owe = total(items, cost, &tax_owe);
```

The program will still run in the same way. However, there is really no good reason for sending the total cost owed through the *return* statement and sending the tax owed via the argument by reference. Indeed, why send them out differently? They should both be sent back using the same route, i.e., using arguments by reference.

EXERCISES 11.2.2

1. Write a function header for each function description below.
   a. A function named *sum_avg()* that takes in three numbers and sends back their sum and average via arguments by reference

b. A function named *sum_avg()* that takes in three numbers and sends back their sum with the *return* statement and their average via an argument by reference
2. Modify the function *multi()* developed in Exercises 10.4.1, 1, so that the result is sent back by reference.
3. Modify the function *square()* used in Exercise 10.4.1, 2, so that the result is sent back by reference.
4. Modify the function *cube()* used in Exercise 10.4.1, 3, so that the result is sent back by reference.
5. Modify the function *show_menu()* from Exercise 10.4.1, 5, so that the user's choice is sent back by reference.
6. Consider the following program:

```
void sum_n_ave(float n1, n2, float * sum, float * ave)
{
        *sum = n1 + n2;
        *ave = *sum / 2;
}

main()
{
        float sum, ave;

        sum_n_ave(18, 6, &sum, &ave);
        printf("sum = %f, ave = %f\n", sum, ave);
}
```

a. What will be displayed by this program?
b. Discuss the common use of the variable names *sum* and *ave* in both functions. Are they the same variable? Is it wise to use the same name?
c. To what are the two statements within the function equivalent?
7. Modify the function *round()* in Exercise 10.4.6, 4, so that the result is sent back by reference.
8. Modify the function *in_seconds()* in Supplementary Exercise 10.4, 1, so that the result is sent back by reference.
9. Modify the function *ceiling()* in Exercise 10.4.6, 7, so that the result is sent back by reference.
10. Modify the function *floor()* in Exercise 10.4.6, 8, so that the result is sent back by reference.
11. Modify the function *random()* in Supplementary Exercise 10.4, 2, so that the result is sent back by reference.
12. Modify the function *even_rand()* in Supplementary Exercise 10.4, 4, so that the result is sent back by reference.
13. Modify the function *odd_rand()* in Supplementary Exercise 10.4, 5, so that the result is sent back by reference.
14. Modify the function *hypotenuse()* in Supplementary Exercise 10.4, 6, so that the result is sent back by reference.
15. Modify the function *convert()* in Supplementary Exercise 10.4, 7, so that the result is sent back by reference.
16. Modify the function *F_or_C()* in Supplementary Exercise 10.4, 8, so that the result is sent back by reference.
17. Modify the program in Supplementary Exercise 10.4, 9, so that all results are sent back by reference.
18. Modify the function *divisible()* in Exercise 10.4.6, 9, so that the result is sent back by reference.
19. Modify the function *quotient()* in Exercise 10.4.6, 10, so that the result is sent back by reference.
20. Modify the function *remainder()* in Exercise 10.4.6, 11, so that the result is sent back by reference.
21. Modify the function *fraction()* in Exercise 10.4.6, 12, so that the result is sent back by reference.

22. Modify the function *reverse()* in Supplementary Exercise 10.4, 11, so that the result is sent back by reference.
23. Modify the function *sum_divs()* in Exercise 10.4.6, 15, so that the result is sent back by reference.
24. Write a function named *liquid()* that accepts a quantity value (in volume) in pints and sends back by reference the equivalent in gallons, quarts, and pints.
25. Write a function named *time()* that accepts a quantity value in seconds and sends back by reference the equivalent in days, hours, minutes, and seconds.
26. Write a function named *days()* that accepts a quantity value in days and sends back by reference the equivalent in years, months, and days.
27. Write a function named *money()* that accepts a quantity value in cents and sends back by reference the equivalent in dollars, quarters, dimes, nickels, and pennies.
28. Write a program that asks for an amount of time in seconds and displays the equivalent in years, months, days, hours, minutes, and seconds. Use the functions *time()* and *days()* above.
29. Given the function *sum_n_ave()* in question 5 above, what would be the effect of the following expressions? Assume the declarations *float x, y* and that *x* contains the number 25:
    a. *sum_n_ave(x, x, &x, &y);*
    b. *sum_n_ave(x, x, x, y);*
    c. *sum_n_ave(&x, &x, &x, &y);*
30. a. Explain why the address operator is needed in the *scanf()*, as in *scanf("%d", &items)* and *scanf("%d", &costs)*.
    b. Explain why the omission of the address operator in the statement *scanf("%d", costs)* would cause the variable to contain garbage or perhaps even make the program crash. (***Hint:*** You may wish to read Subsection 11.2.5 on common errors and traps first.

A few more examples will help make application of parameter by reference clearer.

Example 11.2.3

Let us write a function called *swap()* that swaps the contents of two variables passed to it. This function will then be used in the program in Example 4.3.4. Here is that program again:

```
#include <stdio.h>

main()
{
        int      num1, num2, hold;

        printf("Enter two numbers > ");
        scanf("%d%d", &num1, &num2);

        if (num1 > num2)
        {
                hold = num1;
                num1 = num2;
                num2 = hold;
        }
        printf("In ascending order: %d %d", num1, num2);
}
```

Since this segment does the swapping, it will make up the definition of *swap()*. With the introduction of this function, this program becomes the following (changes are in bold type):

```
#include <stdio.h>

void swap(int * num1_addr, int * num2_addr)
{
```

```
        int  hold;1

        hold = *num1_addr;
        *num1_addr = *num2_addr;
        *num2_addr = hold;
}

main()
{
        int     num1, num2;

        printf("Enter two numbers > ");
        scanf("%d%d", &num1, &num2);

        if (num1 > num2)
        {
              swap(&num1, &num2);2
        }
        printf("In ascending order: %d %d", num1, num2);
}
```

Explanations

1. Note that the variable *hold* is now local to the function *swap()* instead of *main()*. Indeed, its declaration must be moved to where the variable is needed.
2. The two variables are passed by reference, not by value, using *swap()*. The function *swap()* needs to know where the variables *num1* and *num2* reside in memory so that their contents can be swapped.

Example 11.2.4

Let us modify the program in Example 10.4.3 so that the maximum number found is sent back to *main()* by reference. The needed changes are shown in bold type:

```
#include <stdio.h>

void find_max(float num1, float num2, float * max_addr)
{
     if (num1 > num2)
     {
        *max_addr = num1;
     }
     else
     {
        *max_addr = num2;
     }
}

main()
{
     float num1, num2, max;

     printf("Enter two numbers > ");
     scanf("%f%f", &num1, &num2);

     find_max(num1, num2, &max);
     printf("The largest number is %f\n", max);
}
```

Note that the type of the function *find_max()* is changed to *void*. (Why is that so?)

EXERCISES 11.2.3

1. Change the *absolute()* function from Exercise 10.4.3, 2, so that the result is sent back by reference.
2. Change the *even()* function from Exercise 10.4.3, 3, so that the result is sent back by reference.
3. Change the *ispass()* function from Exercise 10.4.3, 4, so that the result is sent back by reference.
4. Change the *display_msg()* function from Exercise 10.4.3, 5, so that the result is sent back by reference. Also define a function named *generate_operands()* that will generate both operands and send them back by reference.
5. a. Write a program that calls the *swap()* function in Example 11.2.3 three times in order to sort three numbers, 9, 2, 1.

If you enter:	*This is what happens:*
9, 2, 1	9 and 2 are swapped.
2, 9, 1	9 and 1 are swapped.
2, 1, 9	2 and 1 are swapped.
1, 2, 9	This is displayed.

   b. How many calls to *swap()* are needed to ensure the sorting of four numbers?
6. Suppose that the *swap()* function had been mistyped as the following:

```
void swap(int * num1_addr, int * num2_addr)
{
    int  hold;

    hold = num1_addr;
    num1_addr = num2_addr;
    num2_addr = hold;
}
```

   a. Most compilers encountering this code would issue error messages. Can you see where?
   b. Assuming you use a compiler that would not issue any errors, discuss the effect of the call *swap(&num1, &num2)* on the variables' content.
7. Write a function called *find_minmax()* that accepts three numbers and sends back the largest and the smallest ones. Since more than one datum is to be sent back, both should be sent via arguments by reference.
8. A function does not reside in memory for the entire run of a program that calls it. Instead, the function is stored in memory only when it is called. When it terminates and returns, all of its memory (code and variables) is released; i.e., the function no longer exists in memory. This has implications that you now need to discover using the following functions:

```
#include <stdio.h>

int * find_max(int a, int b)
{
    if (a > b)
    {
        return &a;
    }
    else
    {
        return &b;
    }
}

int * find_avg(int a, int b)
{
    int  temp;

    temp = (a + b) / 2;
    return &temp;
}
```

```
main()
{
    int num1, num2, * ptr;
    printf("Enter two numbers: ");
    scanf("%d%d", &num1, &num2);
    ptr = find_max(num1, num2);
    printf("The maximum is %d\n", *ptr);
    ptr = find_avg(num1, num2);
    printf("The average is %d\n", *ptr);
}
```

The functions *find_max()* and *find_avg()* take in the values of *num1* and *num2* and return the **address** (rather than the **value**) of the variable where the maximum and the average, respectively, are stored.

a. Returning the address of a cell rather than simply its value is not wrong; some ANSI C functions do it that way. However, the functions *find_max()* and *find_avg()* illustrate a very poor way of accomplishing this. Explain what it is.
b. Suggest a safer solution that still returns the address.

11.2.3 READING INPUT DATA INTO A FUNCTION'S PARAMETER

You have to be a little careful when using *scanf()* within a function, particularly when a parameter is concerned. Example 11.2.5 explains.

Example 11.2.5

Let us write a Pascal-like function named *readln()* to read a single integer. Should there be any other data on the line, they will be ignored—exactly as the Pascal command *READLN* works. For example, given the input:

Enter the number of items bought > 27 blah joe

The following segment will read the number 27 into the variable items and ignore the rest.

```
printf("Enter the number of items bought > ");
readln(&items);
```

Now here is the function definition for *readln()*:

```
void readln(int * items_addr)
{

     scanf("%d", items_addr);
     fflush(stdin);
}
```

Note that the address operator is left out of the *scanf()* call. Indeed, *scanf()* expects an address to a variable; since the parameter *items_addr* received the address *&items*, it already contains the address of the variable *items*. Therefore, the symbol & is not needed a second time. It is important to remember this.

EXERCISES 11.2.4

1. If the function *readln()* was defined as:

```
void readln(int items)
{
      scanf("%d", &items);
      fflush(stdin);
}
```

will the following code produce the same effect as that in Example 11.2.5?

```
printf("Enter the number of items bought > ");
readln(items);
```

2. Is the use of address referencing in the following program necessary?

```
void display(int * a)
{
        printf("a = %d\n", *a);
}

main()
{
        int   x;

        x = 10;
        display(&x);
}
```

3. What output will the following program produce?

```
void calculate(int a, int * b, int * c)
{
        *c = 8 + *b - a;
}

void boss(int * x, int * y)
{
      int z;

      z = 12;
      calculate(*y, &z, x);
}

main()
{
      int w, z;

      z = 7;
      boss(&w, &z);
      printf("w = %d, z = %d\n", w, z);
}
```

4. Modify the function *show_menu()* from Exercise 10.4.1, 5, so that the user's answer is sent back by reference. The call will be made in the form *show_menu(&answer).*

11.2.4 PASSING FILE POINTERS BY REFERENCE

Passing a file pointer by reference to a function is conceptually equivalent to passing a number or a character by reference. In practice, though, it proves to be a very error-prone practice. Example 11.2.6 illustrates a typical situation in which a file pointer is passed to a function by reference.

Example 11.2.6

Example 10.4.9 used the *return* statement to send back the file pointers to the *main()*. Let us now modify the definition of *open_input_safely()* and *open_output_safely()* so that the file pointers are each sent back via an argument by reference. That is, for instance, the call to *open_input_safely()* must look like this:

```
open_input_safely(&ifp);
```

The address operator & indicates that the argument is sent by reference. Of course, the function now needs a parameter by reference. It is natural to attempt to solve this by entering the following:

```
void open_input_safely(FILE * fp)
```

void is correct, but is the statement *FILE * fp* correct? Indeed, the presence of an asterisk has thus far always indicated a parameter by reference. Unfortunately, this is incorrect here.

A pointer to a pointer. To see why the above is incorrect, let us observe what is actually sent to the parameter *fp*. Since the variable *ifp* is declared as *FILE * ifp* in *main()*, it is meant to point to a file, as shown in Figure 11.2.5.

Figure 11.2.5

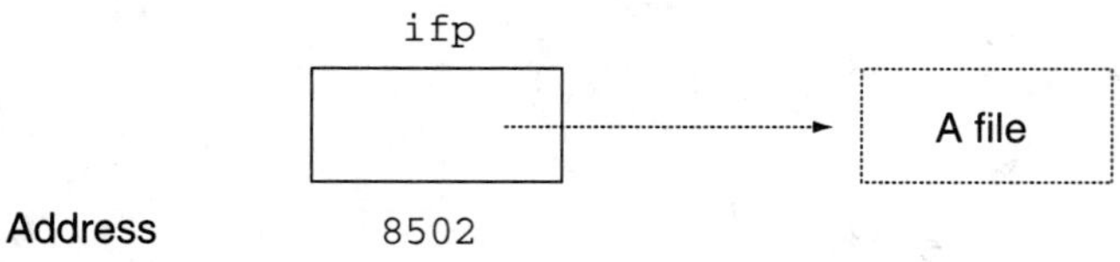

Assume the variable *ifp* is at address 8502. Then the argument *&ifp* (the address of *ifp*) is sent to the parameter *fp*, as Figure 11.2.6 illustrates. As before, the dashed arrow denotes pointing, while the solid arrow indicates copying.

Figure 11.2.6

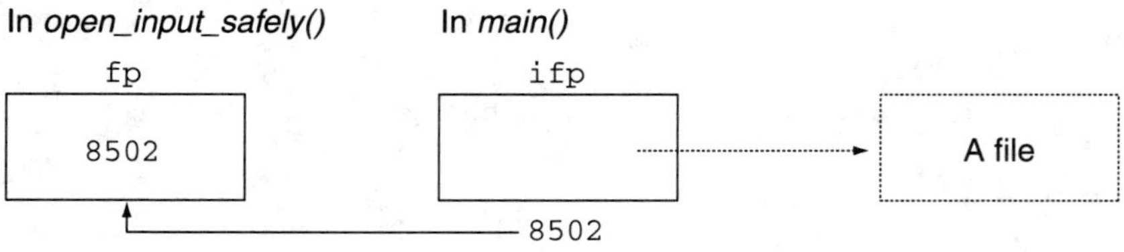

As shown in Figure 11.2.7, the parameter now points to *ifp*, which in turn points to a file.

Figure 11.2.7

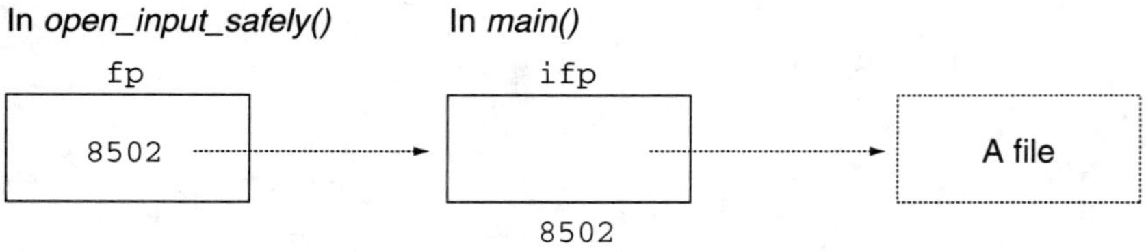

You see now that the parameter *fp* is a pointer to a pointer, i.e., a two-level pointer to the file. Therefore this parameter must be declared as:

```
void open_input_safely(FILE ** fp)
```

Note that two asterisks are needed. The complete correct definition of the function is then:

```
void open_input_safely(FILE ** fp)
{
    *fp = fopen("in.dat", "r");
    if (*fp == NULL)
    {
        printf("Could not open input file\n");
    }
}
```

Note the necessary use of the asterisk within the function's code:

```
*fp = fopen("in.dat", "r");
```

The asterisk tells the pointer *fp* to go where it is pointing, i.e., to the variable *ifp*, as shown in Figure 11.2.8.

Figure 11.2.8

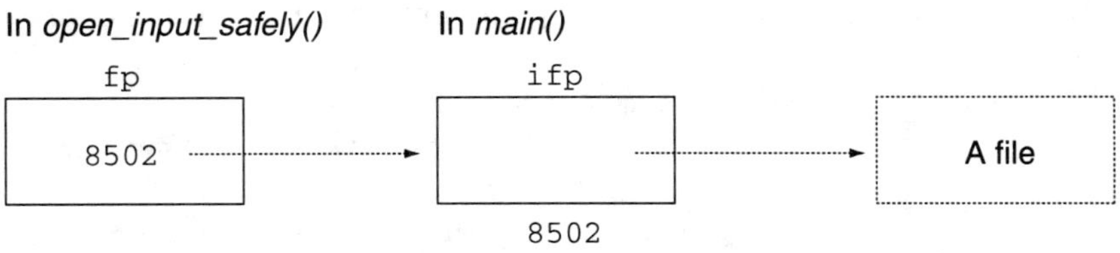

This move ensures that the assignment statement will store the file pointer [produced by *fopen()*] into the variable *ifp*. In other words, this statement is, in effect, identical to the following:

```
ifp = fopen("in.dat", "r");
```

***fp is** the variable *ifp* (recall that Subsection 11.1.2 discussed this equivalence). Finally, here is the entire program with changes from Example 10.4.9 in bold:

```
#include <stdio.h>

void open_input_safely(FILE ** fp)
{
    *fp = fopen("in.dat", "r");
    if (*fp == NULL)
    {
          printf("Could not open input file\n");
    }
}

void open_output_safely(FILE ** fp)
{
    *fp = fopen("ans.out", "w");
    if (*fp == NULL)
    {
          printf("Could not open output file\n");
    }
}

void close_safely(FILE * fp)
{
    if (fp != NULL)       /* can the file be closed safely? */
    {
          fclose(fp);
    }
    else
    {
          printf("File not opened or does not exist\n");
    }
}

main()
{
    FILE * ifp;
    FILE * ofp;
    int    sum, flag, num;

    open_input_safely(&ifp);
    open_output_safely(&ofp);
    if (ifp != NULL && ofp != NULL) /* both files opened correctly ? */
    {
          sum = 0;
          flag = fscanf(ifp, "%d", &num);
```

```
        while (flag != EOF)    /* is it the end of file ? */
        {
            sum = sum + num;
            flag = fscanf(ifp, "%d", &num);
        }
        fprintf(ofp, "The sum is %d.\n", sum);
        close_safely(ifp);
        close_safely(ofp);
    }
}
```

EXERCISES 11.2.5

1. Describe the memory layout as the following lines are executed:

```
char    c1;
char *  p1;
char *  p2;
char ** pp1;

c1 = 'A';
p1 = &c1;
pp1 = &p1;
p2 = *pp1;
*p2 = 'B';
```

2. What is wrong with the following codes?

a.
```
int     num;
int *   p1;
int **  pp1;

num = 61;
pp1 = &p1;
printf("%d", **pp1);
```

b.
```
int    num;
int *  p1;
int    p2;

num = 61;
p1 = &num;;
p2 = &p1;
```

c.
```
int     num;
int *   p1;
int **  pp1;

num = 61;
p1 = &num;
pp1 = &p1;
printf("%d", *pp1);
```

3. Following is a program that uses a function named *find_max()*. That function requires three arguments, and the first two arguments are variables sent by reference. Depending on which variable is largest, its **address** is sent by reference into the third argument. Simply fill in the blanks.

```
void find_max(____________________________________________)
{
      ________________________;    /* declare a local variable */
      if (_______________________)
```

```
        {
                __________________________;
        }
        else

        {
                __________________________;
        }
        return ________________;
}

main()
{
        int  num1, num2;
        ______________________; /* declare variable largest_addr */

        printf("Enter two numbers > ");
        scanf("%d%d", &num1, &num2);
        find_max(&num1, &num2, &largest_ptr)
        printf("Largest number = %d\n", ___________);
}
```

4. The following function calculates the average of its two arguments and returns the address to the location where the answer is:

```
void find_avg(int a, int b, int ** avg_addr)
{
     int  temp;

     temp = (a + b) / 2;
     avg_addr = &temp;
}
```

Can you see something very wrong with this code? (***Hint:*** Refer to Exercise 11.2.3, 8.)

11.2.5 COMMON ERRORS AND TRAPS

Use the following information to avoid making common programming errors.

1. Do not omit the dereferencing operator in an assignment. For example:

```
void total(int qty, float unit_cst,
           float * owe_addr, float * tax_addr)
{
     *owe_addr = qty * unit_cst;
     tax_addr = qty * unit_cst * 0.05;
}
```

The * is missing at the beginning of the *tax_addr* statement. A compiler may not complain, but if it does not, the value inside the variable pointer *tax_addr* will be changed to whatever the right side evaluates to. For example:

tax_addr = *qty* * *unit_cst* * 0.05;
61 * 1.2 * 0.05
73.2 * 0.05
tax_addr = 3.66

As a result, the pointer will point to the cell at address 3.66, which makes no sense. C will thus convert this number into an existing address, the location of which could be anywhere in memory, even in locations where the user is not supposed to be. Consequently, unpredictable and very undesirable things may happen!

2. Do not omit the address operator in an argument by reference. For example, the call *total(items, cost, &owe, tax_owe);* will cause the content of *tax_owe* (not its address) to be assigned to its parameter pointer *tax_addr.* So, assuming that the variable *tax_owe* contains 0, this pointer will point to the cell at address 0, which is a location reserved to the operating system. Therefore, at the statement [within the function *total()*] **tax_addr = qty * unit_cst * 0.05;*, the program will crash without any explanation.
3. Do not think that the asterisk * is part of the pointer variable name. For example:

```
int  *ptr;
int  num;

ptr = &num;
*ptr = 25;
```

Novice programmers tend to consider **ptr* to be the variable name. In fact, the variable name is *ptr* and its type is *int **. Perhaps, because the asterisk is always next to the variable, it suggests that it is part of the name. This visual deception is emphasized when more than one pointer variable is declared at once. For example:

```
float *a, *b, *c;
```

By the way, pointer and nonpointer variable declarations may be mixed, as in:

```
float *a, *b, *c, n, m;
```

4. Do not think that a parameter declared with an asterisk is automatically one by reference. The truth is that it is the presence of an address operator with the argument that determines the method of passing.

SUPPLEMENTARY EXERCISES 11.2

1. Make a function named *validate()* in the program in Supplementary Exercise 8.1, 3. It will accept as argument the addresses of the operator and the two operands. This function will repeatedly ask for input until it is valid. The actual calculation of the arithmetic operation is done outside this function. For example, the following program asks for an arithmetic operation and then evaluates it. It uses the function *validate():*

```
main()
{
      float   opd1, opd2, result;
      char    opr;

      validate(&opd1, &opd2, &opr);
      switch(opr)
      {
      case '+': result = opd1 + opd2;   break;
      case '-' : result = opd1 - opd2;   break;
      case '*': result = opd1 * opd2;   break;
      case '/': result = opd1 / opd2;   break;
      }
      printf("Result = %6.2f\n", result);
}
```

2. Make a function named *validate()* with a different interpretation than in the question above. It will not repeatedly ask for input; it will only verify the validity of the input and display a message if it is wrong. If the message is wrong, *validate()* will return a 0; otherwise it will return a 1. The actual reading of the data will be done outside this function. Also, the number of data successfully read needs to be passed to *validate()*. Finally, since the data is read outside *validate()*, this function no longer needs the addresses of the operator and of the operands. For example, the following program asks for an arithmetic operation and then evaluates it:

```
main()
{
        float   opd1, opd2, result;
        char    opr, read_success;
        do
        {
                printf("Enter an arithmetic operation > ");
                read_success = scanf("%f\n%c%f", &opd1, &opr, &opd2);
        }
        while (validate(read_success, opd1, opd2, opr) == 0);

        switch(opr)
        {
        case '+': result = opd1 + opd2;   break;
        case '-' : result = opd1 - opd2;   break;
        case '*': result = opd1 * opd2;   break;
        case '/': result = opd1 / opd2;   break;
        }
        printf("Result = %6.2f\n", result);
}
```

3. a. Write a function named *throw()* that simulates the throw of a dart at a board. It will use the function *rand()* twice to generate the angle of hit and the distance from the center. For example:

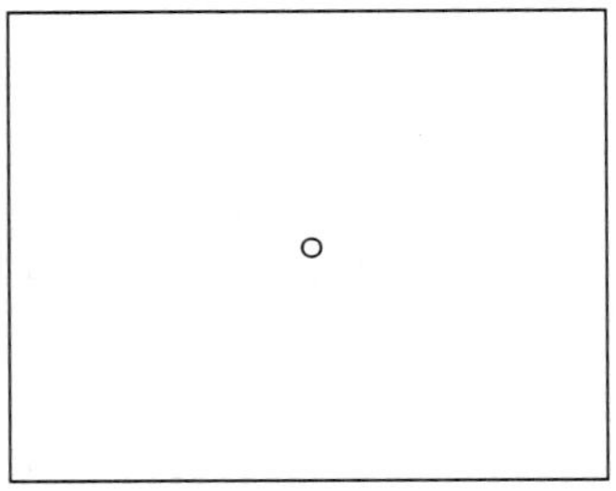

Both the angle and the distance from the center will be sent back by reference.

b. Improve the function so that the diameter of the board will be passed to the function. Using it, the function will return a 1 if it hits the target board and a 0 if it misses.

12 Building Programs with Multiple-Function Definitions

OBJECTIVES

This chapter introduces you to the following information:

- Nested function calls, which are calls occuring within other calls.
- Four criteria for the systematic development of large programs.
- Write functions that are portable across applications (a very important skill to acquire!).
- Global variables.
- Libraries of functions.

INTRODUCTION

In the previous two chapters, you have learned to define and use your own functions. Also, you have learned about the different techniques of passing information to and from functions. So far the emphasis has been largely on the technical aspects of definitions and use.

Even after you understand the techniques, you still will not have totally covered the subject of user-defined functions. Two issues often remain unclear at this stage. First, a student may start writing programs made of numerous function definitions. This presents some challenges that will be illustrated and discussed in this chapter. Second, it may still be unclear to many students as to why or in which situations it is advantageous to define functions. So this chapter will address the question of when to use user-defined functions.

The chapter also includes a discussion of global variables. When writing large programs, the use of global variables often comes up, either on purpose or by accident. Many books frown upon discussing global variables in an introductory course. However, it is better for you to know why the use of global variables should (almost) always be avoided, rather than for you to use them accidentally and then live with the consequences.

12.1 NESTED FUNCTION CALLS

In all previous examples and exercises, the calling function was always *main()*. Of course, any one function *X()* may be a calling function, so long as it calls another function *Y()*. It's as simple as that! The call to function *Y()* is termed a ***nested function call.*** This section puts together every feature about functions encountered so far. Also, you will see that the same program can be rearranged in various ways and still obtain the same results.

12.1.1 THE ORDER OF THE FUNCTION DEFINITIONS

In the context of nested function calls, the order in which the functions are **called** will determine the correct order in which they have to be **defined.** This ordering is important for the proper compilation of the program.

Example 12.1.1

Reconsider the program in Example 10.2.1. Let us rewrite it differently to illustrate the concept of a nested function call. Specifically, let us call a separate function for each type of house:

- Call the function *floor_clapboard()* to draw a house of clapboard.
- Call the function *floor_bricks()* to draw a house of bricks.
- Call the function *floor_siding()* to draw a house of siding.
- Call the function *floor_logs()* to draw a house of logs.

The function *main_floor()* will call the appropriate *floor_* function, depending on the material sent to it. The structure chart now looks like Figure 12.1.1.

Figure 12.1.1

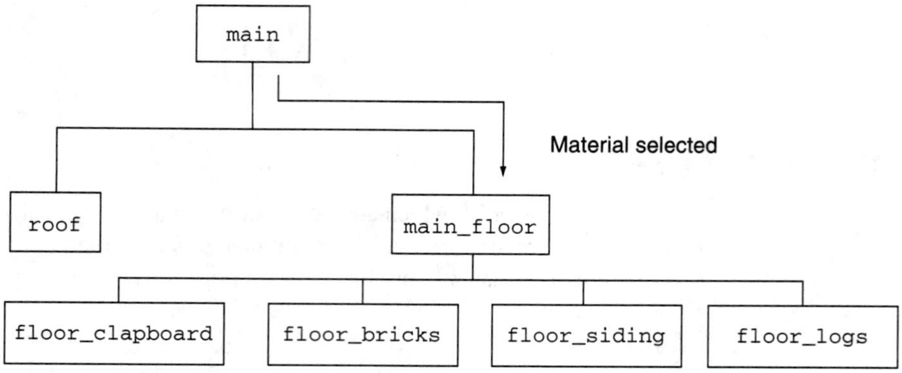

The resulting program is now a little more complicated. Changes appear in bold type in the following program:

```
#include <stdio.h>

/* First, define all the functions */

void roof(void)
{
    printf("           ^           \n");
    printf("         /     \\       \n");
    printf("      /           \\    \n");
    printf("    /                \\ \n");
}


void floor_clapboards(void)[2]
{
    printf("      -------------------- \n");
    printf("                           \n");
    printf("             -----         \n");
    printf("      |      |   |       | \n");
    printf("      |      |   |       | \n");
    printf("      |------------------| \n");
}     |                          |

void floor_brick(void)[1]
{
```

```
    printf("     ------------------- \n");
    printf("     [                 ] \n");
    printf("     [      -----      ] \n");
    printf("     [      |   |      ] \n");
    printf("     [      |   |      ] \n");
    printf("     ------------------- \n");
}

void floor_siding(void)[1]
{
    printf("     ------------------- \n");
    printf("     /                 \ \n");
    printf("     /      -----      \ \n");
    printf("     /      |   |      \ \n");
    printf("     /      |   |      \ \n");
    printf("     ------------------- \n");
}

void floor_log(void)[1]
{
    printf("     ------------------- \n");
    printf("     (                 ) \n");
    printf("     (      -----      ) \n");
    printf("     (      |   |      ) \n");
    printf("     (      |   |      ) \n");
    printf("     ------------------- \n");
}

void main_floor(char left_wall, char right_wall)
{
    switch(left_wall)
    {
       case '|': floor_clapboards();[2]
                 break;
       case '[': floor_bricks();[2]
                 break;
       case '/': floor_sidings();[2]
                 break;
       case '(': floor_logs();[2]
                 break;
        default: printf("No house drawn");
    }
}
/* Second, call the functions above in the main() function */

main()
{
    char   mat_l, mat_r;

    roof();

    printf("What material are the walls made of?\n"
           "     (Type || for clapboards, [] for bricks,\n"
           "           /\ for siding and () for logs)      >>> ");
    scanf("\n%c\n%c", &mat_l, &mat_r);

    main_floor(mat_l, mat_r);
}
```

Notice that this program shows that the *main()* is much more concise than in the previous version, and also much easier to read.

Explanations

1. These definitions **must** appear before the one for *main_floor()*. There is a good reason for this. When a function makes a call to another function, it naturally has to look for its definition. The C language requires this look to be in an upward direction. Think of these functions like people in different rooms, connected by a one-way hallway. These people can only look one way up the hallway. Figure 12.1.2 shows this analogy graphically as it relates to the way C works.

Figure 12.1.2

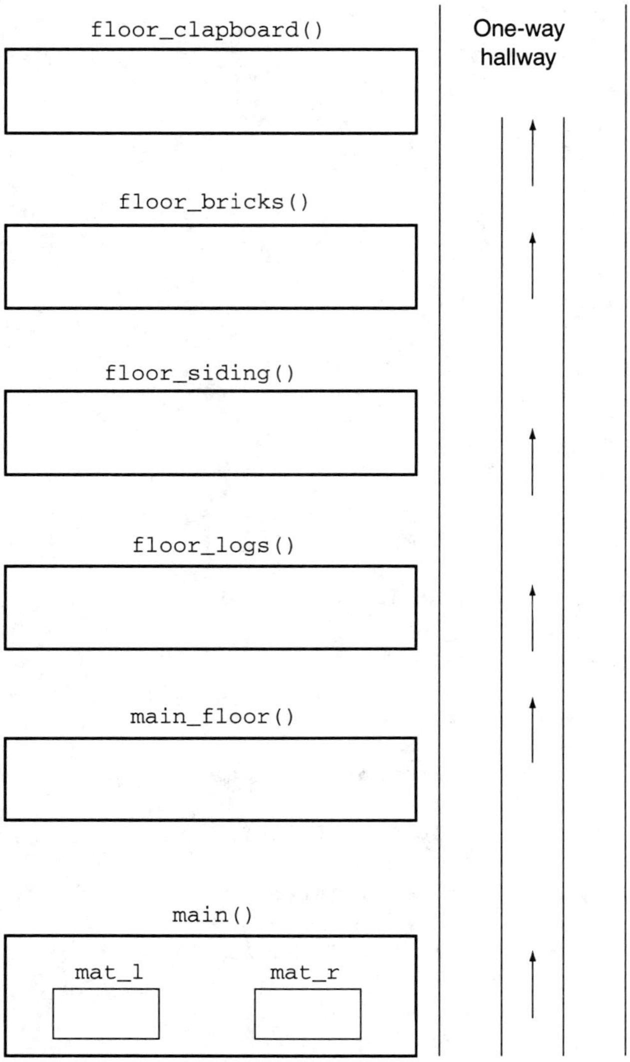

2. Definitions must precede the calls ***(the "define-before-call" rule).*** These *floor_* function calls are nested ones, because they occur within the function *main_floor()*, which is itself called by *main()*. The C compiler always expects the definition of a function to precede any instance of a call to it. Consequently, all those *floor_* function calls must be placed **after** their respective definitions. This implies that the definition for *main_floor()* must follow that of the *floor_* functions. Otherwise, the compiler will generate warnings.

EXERCISES 12.1.1

1. Reorder the sequence of the function definitions below so that the compiler will not complain when the program is tested:

```
void fcn1(void)
{
```

```
        int a;

        a = 9;
        fcn3(a);
        fcn2(a+1);
}

float fcn2(float c)
{
        fcn3(c);
        return c;
}

void fcn3(float x)
{
        printf("x = %f\n", x);
}
main()
{
        float x;

        x = 10;
        fcn3(2 * x);
}
```

2. Rewrite the program in Example 12.1.1 without user-defined functions. Which version is better?
3. a. Revisit Exercise 11.2.1, 3. Define an additional function named *lookup()* that consists of the loop that searches the maximum number. That number will then be returned to *main()*.
   b. The function *lookup()* must now find the minimum number as well. Define a function named *update_min()* for that purpose.

Example 12.1.1 was rather simple. To better appreciate the implications that the "define-before-call" rule has for the order of function definitions, consider the much more complex Example 12.1.2.

Example 12.1.2

Let us introduce the following functions into the program from Supplementary Exercise 4.3, 4:

read_scores(): This function will ask for the diver's social security number as his or her identification number, city, scores from all five judges, and degree of difficulty. All this information is sent back by reference.

report_to_media(): This function will display the report for the media as explained in Supplementary Exercise 4.3, 4, to the screen. All necessary information will have to be sent to this function.

report_to_scoreboard(): In a similar fashion, this function will display the report for the scoreboard operator as explained in Supplementary Exercise 4.3, 4, to the screen. The diver's I.D. and the city code do not need to be passed to this function.

calc_score(): This function calculates the overall score, given the five individual scores and the degree of difficulty. Both of the above functions need to call this function.

find_high_low(): This function is called by *calc_score()* to find the highest and the lowest scores. The function *calc_score()* then eliminates these scores.

make_reports(): This function simply calls on the functions *report_to_scoreboard()* and *report_to_media()* to generate the reports.

Figure 12.1.3 is a structure chart that illustrates the functions hierarchy and the data passed around.

Figure 12.1.3

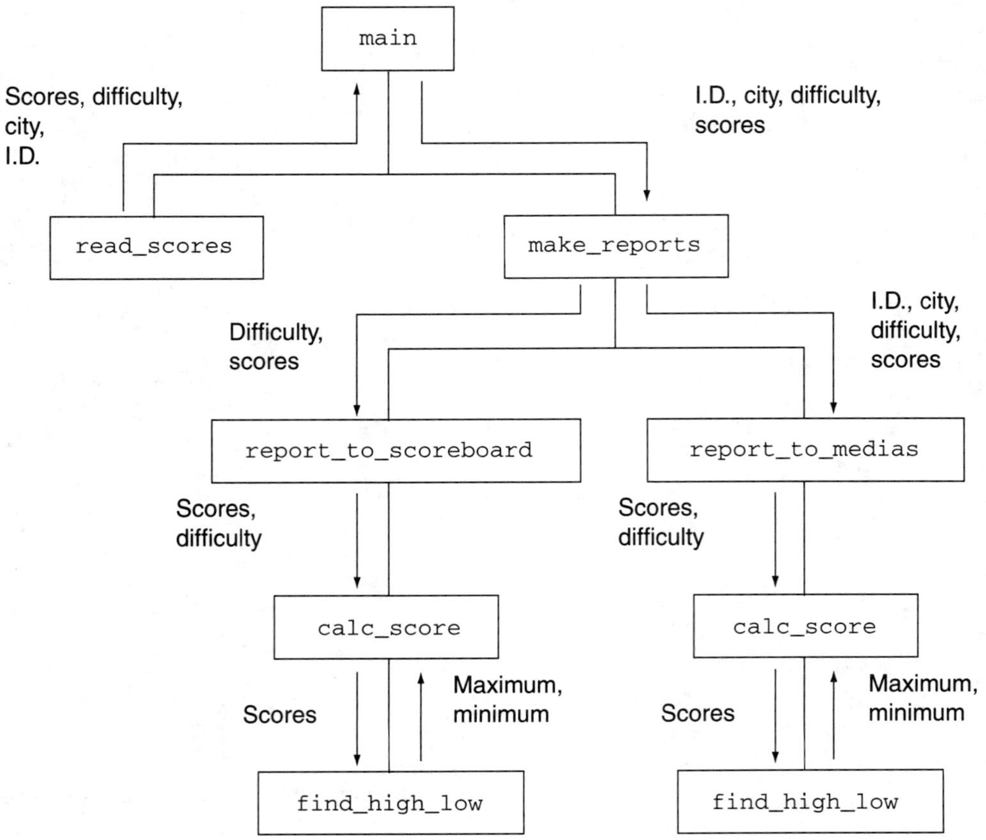

Following is the program based on this structure chart:

```
#include <stdio.h>

void read_scores(long * idp, int * cityp,
                 int * s1p, int * s2p, int * s3p, int * s4p, int * s5p,
                 float * diffp)[1]
{
     printf("          Diving Competition\n\n");
     printf("Enter the diver's I.D. > ");
     scanf("%ld", idp);[2]

     printf("Enter the diver's city code > ");
     scanf("%d", cityp);[2]

     printf("Enter the score given by each judge > ");
     scanf("%f%f%f%f%f", s1p, s2p, s3p, s4p, s5p);[2]

     printf("What was the degree of difficulty? ");
     scanf("%f", diffp);[2]
}

void find_high_low(float s1, float s2, float s3, float s4, float s5,
                   float * highp, float * lowp)[3]
{
     *highp = s1;
     if (s2 > *highp) *highp = s2;
     if (s3 > *highp) *highp = s3;
     if (s4 > *highp) *highp = s4;
```

```
     if (s5 > *highp) *highp = s5;
     *lowp = s1;
     if (s2 < *lowp) *lowp = s2;
     if (s3 < *lowp) *lowp = s3;
     if (s4 < *lowp) *lowp = s4;
     if (s5 < *lowp) *lowp = s5;[4]
}

float calc_score(float s1, float s2, float s3, float s4, float s5,
                 float diff)
{
     float max, min, total;

     find_high_low(s1, s2, s3, s4, s5, &max, &min);[5]
     total = (s1 + s2 + s3 + s4 + s5) - (max + min);
     return (total * diff) / 5;
}

void report_to_scoreboard(float s1, float s2, float s3, float s4, float s5,
                          float diff)
{
     float final_score;
     printf("           Report to Scoreboard Operator\n\n");
     final_score = calc_score(s1, s2, s3, s4, s5, diff);
     printf("Display the score obtained: %5.1f\n", final_score);
}

void report_to_media(long id, int city,
                      float s1, float s2, float s3, float s4, float s5,
                      float diff)
{
     float final_score;

     printf("           Report to the Media\n\n");
     printf("Event: Diving Competition\n");
     printf("Diver I.D.: %ld, City code: %d\n\n", id, city);

     final_score = calc_score(s1, s2, s3, s4, s5, diff);
     printf("Scores given by each judge were:\n\n");
     printf("%5d%5d%5d%5d%5d%s\n", 1, 2, 3, 4, 5, " Final score");
     printf("%5.1f%5.1f%5.1f%5.1f%5.1f    -->%5.1f\n",
            s1, s2, s3, s4, s5, final_score);
}

void make_reports(long id, int city,
                  float s1, float s2, float s3, float s4, float s5,
                  float diff)
{
     report_to_scoreboard(id, city, s1, s2, s3, s4, s5, diff);
     report_to_media(id, city, s1, s2, s3, s4, s5, diff);
}

main()
{

    long   id;
```

```
    int     city;
    float   s1, s2, s3, s4, s5;
    float   diff;

    read_scores(&id, &city, &s1, &s2, &s3, &s4, &s5, &diff);6
    make_reports(id, city, s1, s2, s3, s4, s5, diff);6
}
```

Explanations

1. Note the order of the function definitions. The function *read_scores()* may safely be defined anywhere above the *main()*, here at the top of the program. The location does not matter because:
   a. It does not call any user-defined functions.
   b. It is not called by any function other than *main()*.
2. Note that these variables are not preceded by an address operator. This is because the corresponding arguments are sent by reference (see Example 11.2.5).
3. The function *find_high_low()* is called by the function *calc_score()*, so its definition must precede that of *calc_score()*.
4. This sequence of *ifs* simply locates the largest and the smallest scores. Then these two are sent back by reference to the function *calc_score()*.
5. This statement and the two that follow remove the largest and the smallest scores from the total scores. Then the result is divided by 5. (This is how the overall score is arrived at according to the description in Supplementary Exercise 4.3, 4.)
6. The *main()* does very little work itself. The function *read_scores()* places the information into its arguments, because these are sent by reference. Then the function *make_reports()* receives these same arguments by value. The *main()* should be kept short, and yet descriptive. These are two advantages of defining functions. (More will be said about this in Section 12.2.)

EXERCISES 12.1.2

1. In Example 12.1.2 above, justify the location of the function definitions for *calc_score()*, *report_to_scoreboard()*, *report_to_media()*, and *make_reports()*.
2. a. Consider a program with the following calls to user-defined functions:
   - Function *x()* calls function *a()* and function *y()*, which calls function *z()*.
   - *main()* calls function *y()* as well as functions *a()*, *b()*, and *c()*.
   - Function *y()* also calls function *b()*.

   Give an outline of the proper order in which these functions may be defined.
   b. Are there other possible orders in which the functions may be defined?
   c. It was mentioned in Section 10.1 that all user-defined function definitions should precede the *main()*. Use the functions here to justify this statement.
   d. Are there any definitions that could safely be placed after the *main()?*
3. a. Along the lines of Example 12.1.1, make the necessary changes to the program in Exercise 10.3.1, 4.
   b. The *main()* function in the program obtained in (a) above may be made more concise by defining a function to execute the menu. Define a function named *menu()* that asks for the desired material. The user's answer is then sent back to the *main()* from *menu()*. It, in turn, sends the answer down to the *main_floor()* function to draw the house. Draw a structure chart before writing the program.
   c. Alternatively, the function *menu()* could send back the user's choice via a parameter by reference. Make the necessary modifications.
4. The solution for Exercise 10.2.1, 3, is rather long and clumsy. There is no need for two *switch* statements to test the material twice. There are many ways to eliminate this redundancy. Here is one we invite you to implement:

   Define a function named *tower()* that accepts as argument the number of floors to draw (including the main floor) and the material. This function will be called from the *main()*. Then the function *tower()* will call one of the following functions, depending on the material:

tower_clapboard(), *tower_bricks()*, *tower_siding()*, or *tower_logs()*. Each of these receives as argument the number of floors to draw.

5. a. Rewrite the function *even_rand()* in Supplementary Exercise 10.4, 4, so that it makes use of the function named *even()* developed in Exercise 10.4.3, 3(b).
   b. Incorporate these functions into a working program.
6. Write a function named *order()* that accepts three numbers by reference and orders them. Inside it, *order()* uses the *swap()* function developed in Example 11.2.3. (***Hint:*** Revisit the program in Exercise 11.2.3, 5.)
7. a. Rewrite the function *sum_divs()* in Exercise 10.4.6, 14, so that it uses the *divisible()* function developed in Exercise 10.4.6, 8b.
   b. Rewrite the function *sum_divs()* in Exercise 10.4.6, 14, so it uses the *remainder()* function developed in Exercise 10.4.6, 10.
   c. A number is said to be ***perfect*** if the sum of its divisors equals the number itself. For example, the sum of the divisors of 6 is 1+2+3=6. Write a function named *isperfect()* that returns 1 if an argument is perfect, or 0 if it is not perfect. It will call the function *sum_divs()*, which calls the function *remainder()*.

12.1.2 RECURSIVE FUNCTION CALLS

Recursive function calls are a special type of nested calls in which the function calls itself. Example 12.1.3 shows how this works.

Example 12.1.3

Let us write a recursive function named *sequence()* that displays the sequence 1, 5, 9, 13. First, here is a nonrecursive solution:

```
void sequence(void)
{
      int number;

      for (number=1; number <= 13; number += 4)
      {
            printf("%d", number);
       }
}

main()
{
      sequence();
}
```

You can see that this program does the job. Now here is a version that uses a recursive function:

```
void sequence(int number)
{
      if (number <= 13)
      {
            printf("%d", number);
            sequence(number + 4);     /* calls itself */
      }
 }

main()
{
      sequence(1);
}
```

A series of five calls to *sequence()* will be triggered by the initial one in the *main()*. Figure 12.1.4 shows how it all unfolds.

Figure 12.1.4

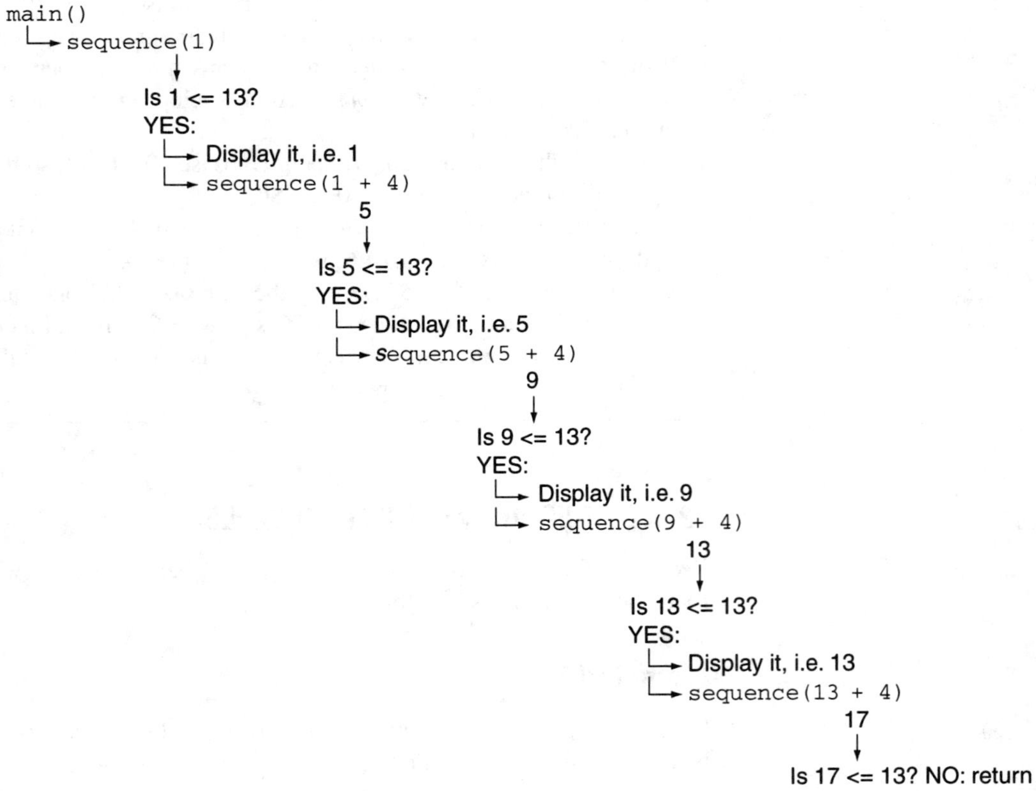

As Figure 12.1.4 shows, the embedded calls occur in the following order: *sequence(1), sequence(1 + 4), sequence(5 + 4), sequence(9 + 4),* and *sequence(13 + 4).* Then the return from this last call, *sequence(13 + 4),* causes all the other embedded calls to return in the reverse order: *sequence(9 + 4), sequence(5 + 4), sequence(1 + 4), sequence(1).*

When should recursive functions be used? Note these characteristics about the programs in Example 12.1.3:

1. The recursive solution does not have a loop. The loop is implicit and occurs every time the function calls itself. Indeed, the rule of thumb is that the nonrecursive solution contains a loop, but the recursive solution does not.
2. The condition in the *for* loop header of the nonrecursive solution and the condition in the *if* of the recursive solution are the same. The presence of this *if* is very important. Its omission inevitably leads to endless recursive calls. How bad is that? Recall from Example 10.2.2 that at the time of a call, the function is given memory space. The memory is released only after the function terminates. The absence of an *if* statement prevents each recursive function call from terminating. Consequently, endless recursive calls will eventually eat up all memory. Some systems may show an error message such as "Stack overflow." Not only will your program crash, it may also crash the operating system (such as MS-DOS)!

These characteristics are typical of recursive vs. nonrecursive solutions. Choosing to define recursive functions instead of nonrecursive ones offers two main advantages:

1. The code of recursive functions is often shorter than its nonrecursive counterpart.
2. For certain type of problems, it is easier to devise a recursive solution rather than a nonrecursive one. Recursive codes are also more intuitive.

Despite these appealing advantages, consider these two disadvantages:

1. In Example 12.1.3, you see five embedded calls. This means that five instances of the function *sequence()* sit in memory until they eventually terminate in the order 5, 4, 3, 2, and 1. Imagine if the function were to generate the first 100 terms of the series!

2. The task of making a function call requires some amount of CPU time. Since recursive functions have the potential of making numerous calls, they slow down a program. Software developers usually avoid developing recursive functions for this reason.

EXERCISES 12.1.3

1. a. Write a recursive function that generates the series 23, 17, 11, 5, –1.
   b. Write an equivalent nonrecursive solution.
2. Is there anything wrong with the following function definition? If so, what effect will it have on the computer system?

```
void sequence(int x)
{
      sequence(x - 2);
      printf("%d", x);
}
```

3. In Example 12.1.3, what would be displayed if the *printf()* was moved after the recursive call, as shown below?

```
void sequence(int number)
{
      if (number <= 13)
      {
            sequence(number + 4);
            printf("%d", number);
      }
}

main()
{
      sequence(1);
}
```

4. Write a recursive function that produces the following display:

```
\\\\\\\\\\\\
\\\\\\\\\\
\\\\\\\\
\\\\\\
\\\\
\\
```

5. Modify the function in question 4 above so that the figure looks like this:

```
\\\\\\\\\\\\
\\\\\\\\\\//
\\\\\\\\////
\\\\\\//////
\\\\////////
\\//////////
```

6. a. What would the following program display?

```
int count(int n)
{
      if (n > 1)
      {
            return 1 + count(n - 1);
      }
      else
```

```
        {
                return 1;
        }
}

main()
{
        printf("Count is %d\n", count(12));
}
```

b. What would the display look like if all the *return* statements were replaced with *printf()*s [e.g., *return 1 + count(n – 1)* is changed to *printf("%d", 1 + count(n – 1)*]? Make the necessary changes to the program.

c. Since a *return* statement causes a function to terminate, the absence of *return* statements in (b) should spell trouble. Does it? Explain.

7. What would the following program display?

```
int fib(int n)
{
        if (n == 1 || n == 2)
        {
                printf("%d", 1);
        }
        else
        {
                printf("%d", fib(n - 1) + fib(n - 2));
        }
}

main()
{
        fib(6);
}
```

8. Develop a nonrecursive solution for questions 4, 5, 6, and 7 above.

12.1.3 FUNCTION PROTOTYPES

Section 12.1.1 explained that function calls must always precede their respective definition. Therefore, it is important that function definitions be ordered correctly. This demands the programmer's careful attention and is further complicated and confusing when nested functions calls occur. Fortunately, there is a way around this complication: use function prototypes. When placed at the top of the program, they allow the programmer to place the function definitions anywhere, with no particular consideration to ordering. Example 12.1.4 illustrates this further.

Example 12.1.4

Let us insert function prototypes into the program of Example 12.1.2, as shown here (changes appear in bold type):

```
#include <stdio.h>

void read_scores(long *, int *,[1]
                 int *, int *, int *, int *, int *,
                 float *);
void make_reports(long, int,
                  float, float, float, float, float,
                  float);
void report_to_scoreboard(long, int,
                          float, float, float, float, float,
```

```
                              float);
void report_to_medias(long, int,
                       float, float, float, float, float,
                       float);
float calc_score(float, float, float, float, float,
                  float);
void find_high_low(float, float, float, float, float,
                    float *, float *);

main()2
{

    long   id;
    int    city;
    float  s1, s2, s3, s4, s5;
    float  diff;

    read_scores(&id, &city, &s1, &s2, &s3, &s4, &s5, &diff);
    make_reports(id, city, s1, s2, s3, s4, s5, diff);
}

void read_scores(long * idp, int * cityp,
                 int * s1p, int * s2p, int * s3p, int * s4p, int * s5p,
                 float * diffp)
    {
      printf("          Diving Competition\n\n");
      printf("Enter the diver's I.D. > ");
      scanf("%ld", idp);

      printf("Enter the diver's city code > ");
      scanf("%d", cityp);

      printf("Enter the score given by each judge > ");
      scanf("%f%f%f%f%f", s1p, s2p, s3p, s4p, s5p);

      printf("What was the degree of difficulty? ");
      scanf("%f", diffp);
}

void make_reports(long id, int city,
                  float s1, float s2, float s3, float s4, float s5,
                  float diff)
{
      report_to_scoreboard(id, city, s1, s2, s3, s4, s5, diff);
      report_to_media(id, city, s1, s2, s3, s4, s5, diff);
}

void report_to_scoreboard(float s1, float s2, float s3, float s4, float s5,
                          float diff)
{
      float final_score;

      printf("           Report to Scoreboard Operator\n\n");
      final_score = calc_score(s1, s2, s3, s4, s5, diff);
      printf("Display the score obtained: %5.1f\n", final_score);
}

void report_to_media(long id, int city,
                     float s1, float s2, float s3, float s4, float s5,
                     float diff)
```

```
        float final_score;

        printf("          Report to the Media\n\n");
        printf("Event: Diving Competition\n");
        printf("Diver I.D.: %ld, City code: %d\n\n", id, city);

        final_score = calc_score(s1, s2, s3, s4, s5, diff);
        printf("Scores given by each judge were:\n\n");
        printf("%5d%5d%5d%5d%5d%s\n", 1, 2, 3, 4, 5, " Final score");
        printf("%5.1f%5.1f%5.1f%5.1f%5.1f     -->%5.1f\n",
                s1, s2, s3, s4, s5, final_score);
}

float calc_score(float s1, float s2, float s3, float s4, float s5,
                 float diff)
{
        float max, min, total;

        find_high_low(s1, s2, s3, s4, s5, &max, &min);
        total = (s1 + s2 + s3 + s4 + s5) - (max + min);
        return (total * diff) / 5;
}

void find_high_low(float s1, float s2, float s3, float s4, float s5,
                   float * highp, float * lowp)
{
        *highp = s1;
        if (s2 > *highp) *highp = s2;
        if (s3 > *highp) *highp = s3;
        if (s4 > *highp) *highp = s4;
        if (s5 > *highp) *highp = s5;
        *lowp = s1;
        if (s2 < *lowp) *lowp = s2;
        if (s3 < *lowp) *lowp = s3;
        if (s4 < *lowp) *lowp = s4;
        if (s5 < *lowp) *lowp = s5;
}
```

Explanations

1. The list in bold starting at this line includes a function prototype for each user-defined function definition contained in this program. It is important to take note of the difference in syntax between a function prototype and a function header. Following is the function prototype for the function *find_high_low():*

   ```
   void find_high_low(float, float, float, float, float,  float *, float *);
   ```

   and its corresponding function header:

   ```
   void find_high_low(float s1, float s2, float s3, float s4, float s5,
                      float * highp, float * lowp)
   ```

   Note the information in parentheses in both statements. While the function prototype lists only the **type** of the parameters, the function header also lists their **names.** Also note that the function prototype **must** end with a semicolon, but the function header does not need one.

   The purpose of a function prototype is to announce to the compiler your intention to use a function. Basically, a function header announces a **definition** whereas a function prototype is a **declaration** of intent of use, exactly like a variable declaration. This is the reason why a function prototype must terminate with a semicolon.
2. It was mentioned in Section 10.1 that user-defined functions should precede the *main( ).* This is true only if function prototypes are not used. As you can see here, the *main()* is defined first.

Some programmers prefer to place the *main()* at the top of the program and define all the functions below it.

Note that the order of the function definitions is as follows: the *main()* is placed first, followed by the functions it calls. These are in turn followed by the functions they call. This ordering ensures that the last functions, here *find_high_low(),* are the ones that do not call any other user-defined functions. Some programmers like this ordering, which is **exactly** the opposite that in Example 12.1.2.

EXERCISES 12.1.4

1. Code the function prototypes for the following function headers:
   a. *int pension(float amt, int months, float interest, long * error_code)*
   b. *FILE * openfile(int id, char * success)*
2. a. In Example 12.1.1, force the use of function prototypes in the following way: move the definition of *main()* to the top of the program (preceded by *#include <stdio.h>* of course) and follow it with the definition for *main_floor()* and the remaining function definitions.
   b. Pick any programs from this and previous sections and force the use of prototypes; that is, move the function definitions after their call.
3. Rewrite the program in Example 12.1.4 without user-defined functions. Which version is better?
4. a. Reconsider Exercise 12.1.2, 2. If function prototypes were placed at the top of the program, what are all of the possible orders in which the functions could be defined?
   b. Suppose that these function prototypes were mistakenly placed just above the *main()*. What are all of the possible orders in which the functions could be defined?

12.1.4 COMMON ERRORS AND TRAPS

The following information will help you avoid common programming errors.

1. Do not place a function call before its definition.
2. Do not mix the syntax and meaning of a function prototype with a function definition.
3. Do not place a function definition within another function. For example:

```
void fcn1(void)
{
        void fcn2(void)
        {
                .
                .
        }
        .
        fcn2();
}
```

Languages like Pascal allow this, but C does not.

12.2 WHEN SHOULD I DEFINE FUNCTIONS?

You have now written many programs with user-defined functions. No doubt you know how to define and call them. However, up until now you have been in controlled situations: you were often told what functions to define and the arguments that each should accept. What if you were presented with a problem and asked to write a program from scratch? What functions should be defined? What arguments are needed? How should the data be sent from one function to another?

There is no magic recipe that determines when a function should be defined for a given situation. Nevertheless, this section presents four criteria for developing programs with user-defined functions accompanied with examples to gain some insight about this important issue. These criteria aim at helping the programmer to write code that is:

1. free of logic errors and bugs
2. readable
3. immediately usable by any program, with no changes necessary
4. easy to modify
5. easy to develop

These qualities become important when a program increases in size.

This section stresses ***modular programming.*** Modularity is the grouping of logically related units of code and data in a way that the details of implementation are hidden from other sections of the program. This important topic could not easily be discussed in previous sections due to technicalities about functions that you needed to understand first.

12.2.1 DEFINE FUNCTIONS WHEN AN OPERATION CAN BE DESCRIBED AS A DISTINCT TASK

Example 12.2.1

The following program finds the largest number from a list entered by the user. This program is first written without functions. Some functions will be added subsequently.

```
#include <stdio.h >

main()
{

     int        cnt, n;
     float      max, x;

     printf("The maximum value will be computed.\n");
     printf("How many numbers do you wish to enter? ");
     scanf("%d", &n);
     while (n <= 0)
     {                                                                  Task
          printf("\nERROR: A positive integer is required.\n\n");        1
          printf("How many numbers do you wish to enter? ");
          scanf("%d", &n);
     }
     printf("\nEnter %d real numbers: ", n);
     scanf("%f", &x);
     max = x;
     for (cnt = 1; cnt < n; cnt++)
     {
          scanf("%f", &x);
          if (max < x)                                                  Task
          {                                                              2
               max = x;
          }
     }
     printf("The maximum value: %f\n", max);                            Task
}                                                                        3
```

Let us now break up this program into functions. There are four general steps to follow:

Step 1: Look for distinct tasks. This step consists simply of recognizing that the *main()* is made up of distinct tasks. There are three in the program above. You must decide which ones are worth placing within a function. Usually, tasks that are made up of more than one line may be considered; here Tasks 1 and 2, but not Task 3, are eligible. Let us name the function for Task 1 *enter_list_size(),* and for Task 2 *enter_list().* Task 3 will remain within *main().* Note that the function names should reflect the tasks that they carry out.

Step 2: Study the scope of the variables' uses. It must be determined which variables should be declared locally to each new function. The rule is simple: if a variable's purpose is solely local to the task, it should be declared locally. Here the variables *cnt* and *x* are only used in Task 2, so their declarations should be within the function *enter_list()*.

Step 3: Determine if any data need to be shared among functions. You must decide which data the functions need to send to each other via parameters and/or *return* statements. This can be tricky in general, but the decision is not complex here. You can see that Task 2 needs the variable *n* from Task 1. Also Task 3 [which is within *main()*] needs to print the maximum number found, so the variable *max* must be sent back to *main()*. All of this data communication is better illustrated with the structure chart shown in Figure 12.2.1.

Figure 12.2.1

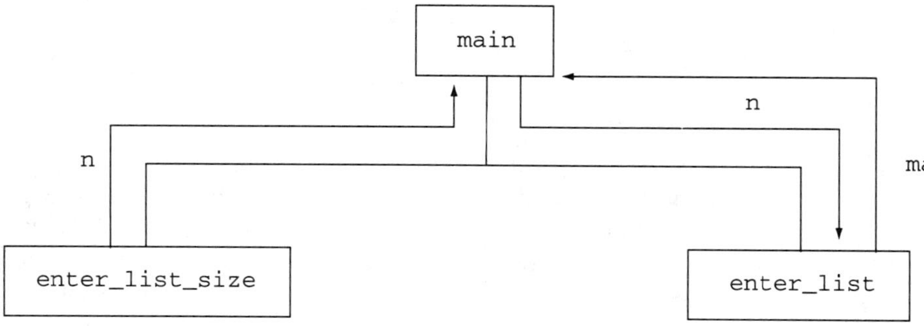

Step 4: Decide what technique will accomplish this sharing. It is best to send the value of *n* from *enter_list_size()* to *main()* via a *return* statement and to send the value of *max* from *enter_list()* to *main()*. Obviously, the value of *n* is passed to *enter_list()* through a parameter. Finally, these two variables are declared local to *main()*. The new program should look like this:

```
#include <stdio.h>

int enter_list_size(void)
{
     int n;

     printf("How many numbers do you wish to enter? ");
     scanf("%d", &n);
     while (n <= 0)
     {
          printf("\nERROR: A positive integer is required.\n\n");
          printf("How many numbers do you wish to enter? ");
          scanf("%d", &n);
     }
     return n;
}

float enter_list(int size)
{
     int    cnt;
     float  x, max;

     printf("\nEnter %d real numbers: ", size);
     scanf("%f", &x);
     max = x;
     for (cnt = 1; cnt < size; ++cnt)
     {
          scanf("%f", &x);
          if (max < x)
          {
```

```
                max = x;
            }
        }
        return max;
}

main()
{
        int     n;
        float   max;

        printf("The maximum value will be computed.\n");
        n = enter_list_size();
        max = enter_list(n);
        printf("The maximum value: %f\n", max);
}
```

Study this program carefully before moving on, keeping in mind the four steps we went through to obtain this solution. Note that we did not use a single global variable. ***Global variables*** are the opposite of local variables. They are declared outside functions, and are visible in the whole program. Make every effort to eliminate or reduce the use of global variables. (Exercise 12.3.1, 3, hints at a drawback of global variables, and other significant reasons for not using them will be provided in Subsection 12.2.3.)

EXERCISES 12.2.1

1. Consider the following program, which is the same as in Example 12.2.1, except that the variables are declared in different places:

```
#include <stdio.h>

void enter_list_size(void)
{
     printf("How many numbers do you wish to enter? ");
     scanf("%d", &n);
     while (n <= 0)
     {
          printf("\nERROR: A positive integer is required.\n\n");
          printf("How many numbers do you wish to enter? ");
          scanf("%d", &n);
     }
}

void enter_list(int size)
{
     int cnt;

     printf("\nEnter %d real numbers: ", size);
     scanf("%f", &x);
     max = x;
     for (cnt = 1; cnt < size; ++cnt)
     {
          scanf("%f", &x);

          if (max < x)
          {
```

```
                    max = x;
            }
        }
}

main()
{
        int     n;
        float   max, x;

        printf("The maximum value will be computed.\n");
        enter_list_size();
        enter_list(n);
        printf("The maximum value: %f\n", max);
}
```

When compiled, three error messages are generated that indicate the following problems: (1) the variable *n* is not declared in the function *enter_list_size()*, (2) the variable *x* is not declared in *enter_list()*, and (3) the variable *max* is not declared in *enter_list()*.

a. Explain these errors.

b. Without changing the function definitions at all, how can you make this program work?

2. Modify the function definitions above slightly so that the content of the variables *n, x,* and *max* are always sent back through parameters by reference.

3. a. In the *main()* above, the value from *enter_list_size()* could just as well be sent directly to the function *enter_list()* instead of through the variable *n.* In other terms, this variable is not strictly needed, nor is the variable *max.* Suggest a change to the code of *main()* so that the need for these variables is eliminated.

   b. Is the code that results from (a) above better than before? Explain.

12.2.2 DEFINE FUNCTIONS WHEN A PROGRAM IS TOO LONG

Example 12.2.2

Revisit Example 6.1.5. Suppose that it now repeatedly asks for user input until the user requests to stop. Therefore, the program requires a loop:

```
#include <stdio.h >
#include <ctype.h >

main()
{
    int     hours, sp;
    char    day, ex, ex up, ans;
    float   pay, rate;

    printf("Do you wish to enter a contractor's qualification code ? ");
    scanf("\n%c", &ans);
    ans = toupper(ans);

    while (ans == 'Y')
    {
        printf("Enter the contractor's qualification code > ");
        scanf("\n%c%d", &ex, &sp);

        ex up = toupper(ex);
        if ((ex up == 'M' || ex up == 'L') && (sp >= 40 && sp <= 120))
        {
            /* Ask for the information */
```

```
        printf("Enter the day worked (Sunday = 1, Monday = 2, etc.)    ");   Task C
        scanf("%d", &day);
        printf("Enter the number of hours > ");
        scanf("%d", &hours);

        /* Figure out the rate of pay, given the information */

        rate = 12.39;
        if (ex up == 'M')
        {
            rate = rate + rate * 0.15;
        }
        if (sp >= 40 && sp <= 59)                Task D
        {
            rate = rate - rate * 0.10;
        }
        if (sp >= 100 && sp <= 120)
        {
            rate = rate + rate * 0.18;
        }

        /* Calculate the pay */

        if (day >= 2 && day <= 6)
        {
            pay = rate * hours;
        }
        else
        {
            pay = rate * 1.5 * hours;
        }
        printf("The pay is %.2f\n", pay);                                   Task A
    }
    else
    {
        printf("The code is Invalid\n");
        if (ex up != 'M' && ex up != 'L')
        {
            printf("The secretarial expertise '%c' does not exist.", ex);
        }
        else
        {
            if (sp < 40)                                                      Task B
            {
                printf("The typing speed is too low");
            }
            else
            {
                printf("The typing speed is unrealistic");
            }
        }
    }
    printf("Do you wish to enter a contractor's qualification code ? ");
    scanf("\n%c", &ans);
    ans = toupper(ans);
  }
  printf("\nDone!");
}
```

Clearly, this program has become too large, and begs to be broken up into smaller tasks. To proceed, simply go through the four steps from the previous subsection. Some of these steps are left to you as an exercise:

Step 1: The distinct tasks in this program are identified above. (Of course, a program may be partitioned into different tasks than the ones selected here.) Choose a name for each task, such as *calculate()* for Task A; *specify_error()* for Task B; *read_data()* for Task C; and *set_rate()* for Task D. The *main()* will call them all in a logical sequence.

Step 2: Determine which variables should be declared locally to each function.

Step 3: Determine what data is to be sent back and forth among these five functions. The structure chart in Figure 12.2.2 illustrates the communication of data.

Figure 12.2.2

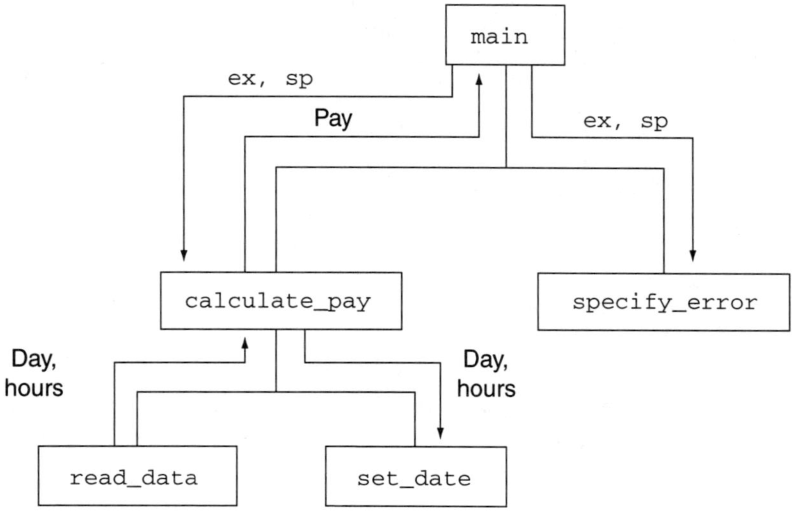

Step 4: Determine which technique to use to pass and send back the data to and from the functions.

Finally, our program looks like this:

```
#include <stdio.h>
#include <ctype.h>

void read_data(int * day_ptr, int * hours_ptr)
{
    printf("Enter the day worked (Sunday = 1, Monday = 2, etc.) > ");
    scanf("%d", day_ptr);
    printf("Enter the number of hours > ");
    scanf("%d", hours_ptr);
}

float set_rate(char ex_up, int sp)
{
    float  rate;

    rate = 12.39;
    if (ex_up == 'M')
    {
        rate = rate + rate * 0.15;
    }
    if (sp >= 40 && sp <= 59)
    {
        rate = rate - rate * 0.10;
    }
```

```
    if (sp >= 100 && sp <= 120)
    {
        rate = rate + rate * 0.18;
    }
    return rate;
}

float calculate(char ex_up, int sp)
{
    float pay, rate;
    int   day, hours;

    read_data(&day, &hours);
    rate = set_rate(ex_up, sp);
    if (day >= 2 && day <= 6)
    {
        pay = rate * hours;
    }
    else
    {
        pay = rate * 1.5 * hours;
    }
    return pay;
}

void specify_error(char ex, char ex_up, int sp)
{
    if (ex_up != 'M' && ex_up != 'L')
    {
        printf("The secretarial expertise '%c' does not exist.", ex);
    }
    else
    {
        if (sp < 40)
        {
            printf("The typing speed is too low");
        }
        else
        {
            printf("The typing speed is unrealistic");
        }
    }
}

main()
{
    int     sp;
    char    ex, ex_up, ans;
    float   pay;

    printf("Do you wish to enter a contractor's qualification code ? ");
    scanf("\n%c", &ans);
    ans = toupper(ans);
    while (ans == 'Y')
    {
        printf("Enter the contractor's qualification code > ");
        scanf("\n%c%d", &ex, &sp);
        ex_up = toupper(ex);

        if ((ex_up == 'M' || ex_up == 'L') && (sp >= 40 && sp <= 120))
```

```
        {
            pay = calculate(ex_up, sp);
            printf("The pay is %.2f\n", pay);
        }
        else
        {
            printf("The code is Invalid\n");
            specify_error(ex, ex_up, sp);
        }
        printf("Do you wish to enter a contractor's qualification code ? ");
        scanf("\n%c", &ans);
        ans = toupper(ans);
    }
    printf("\nDone!");
}
```

The *main()* is still long, perhaps too long, but note again that not a single global variable is used. Study this program carefully before moving on.

EXERCISES 12.2.2

1. Annotate the program above for steps 1 to 4, and add explanations.
2. a. Explore other ways that the program could have been partitioned, i.e., go through steps 1 to 4 again.
   b. The *main()* is a little too large. Suggest a way of making it smaller.

12.2.3 DEFINE FUNCTIONS WHEN AN OPERATION SERVES MORE THAN ONE PROGRAM

Reusability. You might be interested in displaying your name as the author on programs you write, as shown below.

```
This program was written by
        your name
          :
          :
          :
```

Since this operation would be needed for all programs, it should be performed via a user-defined function call. This way, the code to display the author's name is needed only once, but this same code may be called from any number of programs. This is the idea behind ***reusability*** of a function.

Example 12.2.3

Revisit the program in Example 3.3.1. Here the function that displays the author's name is named *show_author():*

```
#include <stdio.h>

void show_author(void)
{
    printf("This program was written by\n");
    printf("            your name\n\n");
}

main()
{
    float  hourly_rate;
```

```
    int    hours_per_week;
    float  total_income;
    int    num_weeks;
    char   letter1, letter2, letter3;

    /* function call to show_author() */
    show_author();

    printf("Enter your initials > ");
    scanf("\n%c\n%c\n%c", &letter1, &letter2, &letter3);
    printf("Enter the hourly wage > ");
    scanf("%f", &hourly_rate);
    printf("Enter the total work hours per week > ");
    scanf("%d", &hours_per_week);
    printf("Enter the number of weeks of work > ");
    scanf("%d", &num_weeks);

    total_income = hourly_rate * hours_per_week * num_weeks;

    printf("%c%c%c, You will make $ %.2f this summer",
            letter1, letter2, letter3, total_income);
}
```

Portability. The function *show_author()* may be called from any one of your programs, as long as its definition is brought in as well. A function that can be used in a multitude of programs is said to be ***reusable.*** However, a friend could not use this function as is; the name in *show_author()* must be changed to his name. Thus, the function is not fully ***portable.*** Passing the name as an argument would suffice to make the function portable. This would be done as follows:

```
void show_author(char name[])
{
     printf("This program was written by\n");
     printf("          %s\n\n", name);
}
```

Unfortunately, we should not explore this solution yet, for it involves passing string variables, which will not be covered until Chapter 18. (If you have a burning desire to know how to do this, read Sections 18.1, 18.2, and 19.1 to get started.)

12.2.4 CRITERIA TO MAKE FUNCTIONS FULLY PORTABLE

The issues regarding portability of functions are quite important in software development. Let us explore three common criteria for making a function portable.

Send data through parameters. Consider Example 12.2.4 below.

Example 12.2.4

The function below simply draws 15 stars on the screen:

```
void stars(void)
{
      int  ctr;

      for (ctr = 0; ctr < 15; ctr++)
      {
            printf("*");
      }
```

```
        printf("\n");
}
```

This function is certainly reusable. (Why is that so?) However, it is not portable, because when called (in any program), it always displays 15 stars. What if the programmer wants to draw fewer or more stars? Now compare this with the function named *star_line()* in Example 10.2.2:

```
void star_line(int num)
{
        for ( ; num > 0; num--)
        {
                printf("*");
        }
        printf("\n");
}
```

This function can be used in any program, because the program only needs to pass the number of stars desired. In this chapter, we have seen many other functions that are also portable in this way.

Eliminate I/O operations within a function. Usually, it is essential that a function accept arguments to be portable, but this requirement is not always enough, as Example 12.2.5 shows.

Example 12.2.5

Consider the function named *total()* in Example 10.2.3:

```
void total(int qty, float unit_cst)
{
        printf("The total cost is %8.2f\n", qty * unit_cst);
}
```

Although this function accepts arguments bearing any values, it is still not fully portable. This is because the message that it produces is not necessarily the one that the calling program wants. (In fact, the calling program may not want a message at all!) In either case, the function cannot be used without changes; hence, it is not portable. It is best to have the function simply calculate the total cost and then send that back to the calling function, as shown below:

```
float total(int qty, float unit_cst)
{
        return qty * unit_cst;[1]
}

main()
{
        int   items;
        float cost, sum;

        printf("Enter the number of items bought > ");
        scanf("%d", &items);
        printf("Enter the cost of each item > ");
        scanf("%f", &cost);

        sum = total(items, cost);
        printf("You owe %.2f\n", sum);[2]
}
```

Explanations

1. The function *total()* does not assume any messages. It simply sends back the total cost.
2. The calling program can create its own message.

EXERCISES 12.2.3

1. In Example 12.2.5 above, although the function *star_line()* is more portable than the function *stars()*, is it nonetheless fully portable?
2. Discuss the degree of portability of the following functions:
   a.
```
void close(FILE * fp)
{
        if (fp == NULL)
        {
                printf("Oops! cannot close this file\n");
        }
        else
        {
                fclose(fp);
        }
}
```
   b.
```
float div(float a, float b)
{
        if (b == 0)
        {
                return FLT_MAX;      /* largest float number */
        }
        else
        {
              return a / b;
        }
}
```

Eliminate global variable references. Another factor that limits a function's portability is the presence of global variables. Global variables also make program debugging and maintenance more error prone. Consider Example 12.2.6 below. (Global variables are discussed in detail in Section 12.3 but this will give you a preview of the problems associated with them.)

Example 12.2.6

Exercise 12.3.1, 3, uses the function *power()* to illustrate the effect of a global variable when used within a function. The function there is:

```
int power(void)
{
        res = 1;
        for (i=1; i < exp; i++)
        {
                res = res * base;
        }
        return res;
}
```

This function is clearly not portable. It does not have parameters to receive the base and the exponent. Let us include some:

```
int power(int base, int exp)
{
      res = 1;
      for (i=1; i < exp; i++)
      {
              res = res * base;
```

```
    }
    return res;
}
```

This is better! Now this function works for any base and exponent. Unfortunately, the variables *i* and *res* are not declared locally. Consequently, this function relies on the host (calling) program to declare them, of course, globally. (Why is that so?)

Not only should a portable function work for any input, it must be viewed as a black box; i.e., the user should not need to know anything about the mechanism inside the function. Clearly, the function *power()* violates this principle. The remedy is simple. Since the variables *i* and *res* have a local use only, they should be declared within the function:

```
int power(int base, int exp)
{
      int   i;
      long  res;

      res = 1;
      for (i=1; i < exp; i++)
      {
            res = res * base;
      }
      return res;
}
```

This function is now fully portable. Here is how the *main()* would be coded to use it:

```
main()
{
      int  base, exp, i;
      long result;

      for (i=1; i < 5; i++)
      {
            printf("Enter the base and exponent > ");
            scanf("%d%d", &base, &exp);
            result = power(base, exp);
            printf("%d to the power of %d is %ld\n",
                  base, exp, result);
      }
      printf("Done!");
}
```

Note that both *main()* and *power()* utilize a variable *i*. However, no side effects will result because all variables are declared locally. This is the way most ANSI C functions are designed. Some do use global variables, but they are clearly documented.

In general, global variables are **not** a good way of sharing data among functions. Passing data by value and by reference and the *return* statement are preferred, for they guarantee that side effects do not occur. Note that none of the examples in this section has used global variables. That is the way it should be!

12.2.5 DEFINE FUNCTIONS WHEN AN OPERATION IS USED TWO OR MORE TIMES

This section discusses the last of four criteria for writing user-defined functions. There are two situations in which a task is used two or more times:

1. A specific task is performed in two or more programs. The function that performs this task must be portable, as discussed above.
2. A specific task is performed in two or more places within a same program.

Either situation suggests the definition of a function. Example 12.2.7 illustrates.

Example 12.2.7

The following program asks the user to enter the rank number of the spouses of military officers. The ranks are as follows:

Rank Number	Title
1	lieutenant
2	captain
3	major
4	colonel
5	general

This program assumes that both spouses are in the armed forces. The program simply echoes the officers' titles for those ranks. It does this repeatedly until an invalid rank is entered.

```
#include <stdio.h>

main()
{
      int  rank1, rank2;

      printf("Enter the rank for both spouses: ");
      scanf("%d%d", &rank1, &rank2);

      printf("Spouse 1 is a(n) ");
      switch(rank1)
      {
         case 1:   printf("lieutenant\n");
                   break;
         case 2:   printf("captain\n");
                   break;
         case 3:   printf("major\n");
                   break;
         case 4:   printf("colonel\n");
                   break;
         case 5:   printf("general\n");
                   break;
         default:  printf("imposter!\n");
                   break;
      }
      printf("Spouse 2 is a(n) ");
      switch(rank2)
      {
         case 1:   printf("lieutenant\n");
                   break;
         case 2:   printf("captain\n");
                   break;
         case 3:   printf("major\n");
                   break;
         case 4:   printf("colonel\n");
                   break;
         case 5:   printf("general\n");
                   break;
         default:  printf("imposter!\n");
                   break;
      }
      while (rank >= 1 && rank <= 5)
      {
            printf("Enter the rank for both spouses: ");
            scanf("%d%d", &rank1, &rank2);
```

```
            printf("Spouse 1 is a(n) ");
            switch(rank1)
            {
               case 1:  printf("lieutenant\n");
                        break;
               case 2:  printf("captain\n");
                        break;
               case 3:  printf("major\n");
                        break;
               case 4:  printf("colonel\n");
                        break;
               case 5:  printf("general\n");
                        break;
               default: printf("imposter!\n");
                        break;
            }
            printf("Spouse 2 is a(n) ");
            switch(rank2)
            {
               case 1:  printf("lieutenant\n");
                        break;
               case 2:  printf("captain\n");
                        break;
               case 3:  printf("major\n");
                        break;
               case 4:  printf("colonel\n");
                        break;
               case 5:  printf("general\n");
                        break;
               default: printf("imposter!\n");
                        break;
            }
      }
}
```

You will surely agree that this program is nuts! There is absolutely no need to repeat the same *switch* statement four times. That code should be placed within a function, as shown below. Then that function should simply be called four times. Following is the resulting:

```
#include <stdio.h>

void display_title(int rank, int spouse_number)
{
      printf("Spouse %d is a(n) ", spouse_number);
      switch(rank)
      {
         case 1:   printf("lieutenant\n");
                   break;
         case 2:   printf("captain\n");
                   break;
         case 3:   printf("major\n");
                   break;
         case 4:   printf("colonel\n");
                   break;
         case 5:   printf("general\n");
                   break;
         default:  printf("imposter!\n");
                   break;
      }
}
```

```
main()
{
      int  rank1, rank2;

      printf("Enter the rank for both spouses: ");
      scanf("%d%d", &rank1, &rank2);
      display_title(rank1, 1);
      display_title(rank2, 2);

      while (rank >= 1 && rank <= 5)
      {
            printf("Enter the rank for both spouses: ");
            scanf("%d%d", &rank1, &rank2);
            display_title(rank1, 1);
            display_title(rank2, 2);
      }
}
```

This is much better!

EXERCISES 12.2.4

1. Consider the program in Example 12.2.7 above. Note that the *main()* still has some codes repeated, twice in fact. For instance, you might argue that the *printf()* and the *scanf()* could have been put in a function, too. This could be done in one of two ways:
   a. Placing them both in a new function, named, say, *ask_rank()*
   b. Placing them both in the already existing function *display_title()* (The ranks would now be asked in separate calls to *display_title().)*

   Implement both (a) and (b) and discuss which of these is preferable. Perhaps the solution of Example 12.2.7 is best?
2. Continuing with question 1 above, another modification of the *main()* might be simply to put all the duplicated codes into a new function, named, say, *ask_and_display()*. The resulting *main()* would be reduced to:

```
main()
{
      int  rank1, rank2;

      ask_and_display(______________________);
      while (rank >= 1 && rank <= 5)
      {
            ask_and_display(____________________);
      }
}
```

   a. Fill in the blanks above, and write a proper definition for the function *ask_and_display()*.
   b. Discuss which of the solutions implemented in question 1 above and in this question is preferable. Perhaps the solution of Example 12.2.7 is best?

SUPPLEMENTARY EXERCISES 12.2

Modular programming was defined at the beginning of this chapter. Review that discussion as needed while doing the following exercises. Along with each solution, draw its structure chart.

Finally, although the questions are specific about which functions to define, some may specify only ***a few*** of the arguments that should be passed to them. It is left to you to decide if more are needed, and which one(s) are needed.

1. Modularize the program in Example 9.2.4. Do this as indicated below. In all cases, do not declare global variables.
   a. Modularize the program any way you wish.
   b. Modularize the program by defining the following functions:

   play(): This function will ask if the player wants to draw a card until the player wants to stop. It has no parameters but returns the sum of the cards drawn.

   message(): This function will display the messages "Too low!", "Too high!", or "Congratulations!" It takes as argument the summation mentioned above.

   draw(): This function will simulate the drawing of a card with the *rand()* library function. It has no parameters but returns the number drawn.

2. Modularize the program obtained in Exercise 9.2.2, 7. Do this as indicated below. In all cases, do not declare global variables.
   a. Modularize the program any way you wish.
   b. Modularize the program by defining the following functions:

   read_innings(): This function will read the scores for all innings. The total score will then be returned. This function will be called for each team. Since the prompt differs slightly for home and visitor teams, an argument will be sent to tell the function which prompt to use. The argument 'v' will stand for visitor, 'h' will mean home team.

   read_nine_innings(): This function will be called by *read_innings()*. It keeps track of the scores for the first nine innings only. The total score is sent back.

   error(): This function determines if an error in the scores is found. If overtime should have been played, it returns the error code 1; if overtime should **not** have been played, it returns the error code 2; if no error was found, 0 is returned.

   display_error(): This function displays an appropriate message corresponding to the error code passed to it. If 0 is passed, nothing is displayed.

   winner(): This function announces the winner, unless an error was found in the scores. Then an appropriate message is displayed. This function calls *error()* and *display_error()*.

3. Modularize the program obtained from Supplementary Exercise 8.2, 2. Do this as indicated below. In all cases, do not declare global variables.
   a. Modularize the program any way you wish.
   b. Modularize the program by defining the following functions:

   open_safely(): This function will open the file RECEIPTS.LIS safely. The file pointer is sent back by reference.

   close_safely(): This function will close the file RECEIPTS.LIS safely.

   ask_terminal(): This function asks for the terminal code. If an invalid response is given, it returns 0; otherwise, 1 is returned.

   ask_operator(): This function asks for the operator code. If an invalid response is given, it returns 0; otherwise, 1 is returned.

   ask_meat(): This function asks for the weight of the meat purchased. If the response is valid, it calls *ask_meat_type()*. In either case, if an invalid response is given, 0 is returned; otherwise, 1 is returned.

   ask_meat_type(): This function asks for the meat type. If an invalid response is given, it returns 0; otherwise, 1 is returned.

   ask_dairy(): This function asks for the cost of dairy products purchased. If an invalid response is given, it returns 0; otherwise, 1 is returned.

   ask_cereals(): This function asks for the cost of the cereals purchased. If an invalid response is given, it returns 0; otherwise, 1 is returned.

   ask_desserts(): This function asks for the cost of desserts purchased. If an invalid response is given, it returns 0; otherwise, 1 is returned.

   pay_up(): This function calculates the total cost, displays it, and asks for payment. Then the change or credit is calculated and displayed. This function sends the total cost and change/credit back by reference.

produce_receipt(): This function produces the amount of receipts and stores it in the file RECEIPTS.LIS. In addition to the file pointer, many other arguments need to be passed to it.

4. Modify and improve the modularity of the program in Example 10.4.9. Do this as indicated below. Do not declare global variables. Define the following new functions, besides existing ones:

   find_sum(): This function will be called from *main()*. It will read the input file, sum up the numbers, and store the result in the output file. Both files pointers must be passed to this function.

   exist(): This function accepts the input and output file pointers and returns a 1 if the files that they point to exist; otherwise it returns a 0. This function is called from the *main()*.

5. Let us add some requirements to Example 10.4.9. Suppose that you are to calculate the average of the list of numbers as well. Do this as indicated below. Do not declare global variables. Define the following new functions, besides the existing ones.

   calculate_stats(): This function will be called from *main()*. It will read the input file and sum up the numbers. This sum and the average will then be sent back by reference.

   report_stats(): This function will store the sum and the average into the output file, which is also passed to this function.

   exist(): This is defined the same way as in question 4 above.

6. (Skip this question if you chose to skip Section 11.2.4.) Let us make more changes to the program in question 4 above. Modify the definitions of the following existing functions:

   open_input_safely(): This function will now send the file pointer back by reference.

   open_output_safely(): This function will now send the file pointer back by reference.

   Define the following new functions:

   open_files(): This function will accept as argument by reference both the file pointers for the input and the output file. Then it will open them by calling the already existing functions *open_input_safely()* and *open_output_safely()*.

   close_files(): This function will accept as argument the file pointers for both the input and the output files. Then it will close them by calling the already existing function *close_safely()* (from Example 10.4.9) once for each file.

   Functions *open_files()* and *close_files()* are called from the *main()*.

7. Modularize the program obtained from Exercise 8.2.3, 4. Do this as indicated below. In all cases, do not declare global variables.
   a. Modularize the program any way you wish.
   b. Modularize the program by defining the following functions:

   open_input_safely(): This is the same as in Example 10.4.9, except that the file is WORK.DAT.

   open_output_safely(): This is the same as in Example 10.4.9, except that a number is also passed to it telling which file to open:

1	open BOSS.DAT
2	open HR.DAT
3	open ACCOUNT.DAT

   close_safely(): This is the same as in Example 10.4.9.

   Define the following new functions:

   are_files_open(): This function checks if all files are open. If so, the number 1 is returned; otherwise, 0 is returned.

   calc_net_income(): This function calculates the net income, given the number of hours worked and the wages per hour.

   calc_deducts(): This function calculates all of the deductions from the net income. Each deduction is sent back via an argument by reference.

   report_to_boss(): This function produces an employee's report for his or her boss. This report is stored in a file named BOSS.DAT.

   report_to_HR(): This function produces an employee's report for the human resources department. It is stored in a file named HR.DAT. This function will call the functions *calc_net_income()* and *calc_deducts()*.

report_to_accounting(): This function produces an employee's report for the accounting department. It is stored in a file named ACCOUNT.DAT.

read_record(): This function reads a record from the file WORK.DAT and sends back all of the data by reference.

process(): This function simply runs through the file WORK.DAT, one record at a time. It will call the functions *report_to_boss(), report_to_HR(), report_to_accounting(),* and *read_record().*

8. Modularize the program obtained from Supplementary Exercise 8.2, 4. Do this as indicated below. In all cases, do not declare global variables.
   a. Modularize the program any way you wish.
   b. Modularize the program by defining the following functions:

   open_input_safely(): This is the same as in Example 10.4.9, except that it will open the file CREDITS.LIS.

   close_safely(): This is the same as in Example 10.4.9.

   ask_payment(): This function asks the user how much she wishes to contribute toward this month's payment (which shows on the credit card bill). The payment is returned.

   show_purchases(): This function reads the purchase costs from the file CREDITS.LIS and displays them as part of the credit card bill.

   interest_rate(): This function calculates the interest rate for the month's bill. The rate is returned.

   calculate_interest(): This function calculates the interest charges on the unpaid portion of the month's bill. The interest is returned.

   display_bill(): This function displays a credit card bill. It calls the functions *show_purchases(), calculate_interest(),* and *interest_rate().* Note that the latter two functions do not display anything on the bill; they only perform the calculations.

   process_file(): This function simply runs through the file CREDITS.LIS, one record at a time. It calls the functions *display_bill()* and *ask_payment().*

   The *main()* calls the functions *open_input_safely(), display_bill(),* and *close_safely().*
9. For each solution in questions 1 to 8, move the function definitions around to enforce the need for function prototypes.

12.3 GLOBAL VARIABLES

As opposed to local variables, global variables may be used by any one function in a program; there is no concern of visibility. In truth, some restrictions may apply, though, as this section will clarify.

12.3.1 BE WARY OF GLOBAL VARIABLES!

To a novice programmer, global variables are tempting. Following are illustrations of the two main situations in which these variables appear to be the right approach.

Example 12.3.1

Section 6.2 stressed the importance of testing the logic of a program before putting it into production (or submitting it to your teacher!). Subsection 10.4.3 stressed the importance of testing the passing of data to and from functions. Testing *printf()*s are placed in the program and then removed when the program's correctness is verified.

Now suppose that new requirements come in, forcing new features and codes to be added to the working program. The revised program has to be retested. This may imply that many of the testing *printf()*s (previously removed) may need to be restored for the new testing procedure. This is time consuming.

A better approach would be to leave these testing *printf()*s in the program permanently. When a testing procedure is asked for, a logical toggle will simply turn them on. Then when the program is in the production phase, the toggle will turn them off. To illustrate, let us insert some of these toggles into the program of Example 12.2.2. For the sake of a short illustration, testing *printf()*s have been placed only for verifying the passing of data to and from functions, not for the detailed logic. Therefore, the following is only an outline of the entire program, with changes shown in bold type:

```
#include <stdio.h>
#include <ctype.h>

char testing;[1]

void read_data(int * day_ptr, int * hours_ptr)
{
   if (testing == 'y')
   {
      printf("Testing: Received in read_data(): day = %d, hours = %d\n",
             *day_ptr, *hours_ptr);
   }
   :
   :
   :
   if (testing == 'y')
   {
      printf("Testing: Sent from read_data(): day = %d, hours = %d\n",
             *day_ptr, *hours_ptr);
   }
}

float set_rate(char ex_up, int sp)
{
   float  rate;

   if (testing == 'y')
   {
      printf("Testing: Received in set_rate(): ex_up = <%c>, sp = %d\n",
             ex_up, sp);
   }
   :
   :
   :
   if (testing == 'y')
   {
      printf("Testing: Sent from set_rate(): rate = %f", rate);
   }
   return rate;
}

float calculate(char ex_up, int sp)
{
   float pay, rate;
   int   day, hours;

  if (testing == 'y')
  {
     printf("Testing: Received in calculate(): ex_up = <%c>, sp = %d\n",
            ex_up, sp);
  }
  :
```

```
    :
    :
    if (testing == 'y')
    {
       printf("Testing: Sent from calculate(): pay = %f", pay);
    }
    return pay;
}
void specify_error(char ex, char ex_up, int sp)
{
    if (testing == 'y')2
    {
       printf("Testing: Received in calculate(): "
              "ex = <%c>, ex_up = <%c>, sp = %d\n", ex, ex_up, sp);
    }
    :
    :
    :
}

main()
{
    int      sp;
    char     ex, ex_up, ans;
    float    pay;

    printf("Is this run for testing (y/n)? ");
    scanf("\n%c", &testing);3
   :
   :
   :
   printf("\nDone!");
}
```

Explanations

1. The variable *testing* is the toggle. Note that it is declared at the **top** of the program, and **outside** of all the functions [including *main()*]. These are the two criteria that make this variable visible to all functions. Therefore, this variable may be shared.
2. Note that all testing *printf()*s are surrounded by an *if (testing == 'y')* to ensure that they are activated only when testing is indeed requested. Now why was the variable *testing* declared globally? There are two reasons:
   a. It is easily visible and accessible in all functions.
   b. It is visible everywhere, hence it does not need to be passed to any functions. Therefore, no function headers and function calls need to be modified for the sole purpose of testing.
3. A 'y' or an 'n' is stored into the variable *testing,* depending on whether or not testing is requested.

Another situation that invites a novice programmer to use global variables is illustrated in Example 12.3.2.

Example 12.3.2

Example 12.1.2 had an obvious drawback: too much data had to be passed around to functions. More precisely, it can be seen that the diver's I.D., city code, and the five scores are passed to almost all functions. Consequently, the function headers are unpleasant to read. For instance:

```
void report_to_media(long id, int city,
                     float s1, float s2, float s3, float s4, float s5,
                     float diff)
```

This is too much! Why not declare all these variables globally? This way, all functions can see these variables, so there's no need to pass them through parameters. The program becomes much simpler:

```
#include <stdio.h>

long   id;
int    city;
float  s1, s2, s3, s4, s5;
float  diff;[1]

void read_scores(void)[2]
{
    printf("          Diving Competition\n\n");
    printf("Enter the diver's I.D. > ");
    scanf("%ld", &id);[3]

    printf("Enter the diver's city code > ");
    scanf("%d", &city);[3]

    printf("Enter the score given by each judge > ");
    scanf("%f%f%f%f%f", &s1, &s2, &s3, &s4, &s5);[3]

    printf("What was the degree of difficulty? ");
    scanf("%f", &diff);[3]
}

void find_high_low(float * highp, float * lowp)[4]
{
   *highp = s1;
   if (s2 > *highp) *highp = s2;
   if (s3 > *highp) *highp = s3;
   if (s4 > *highp) *highp = s4;
   if (s5 > *highp) *highp = s5;
   *lowp = s1;
   if (s2 < *lowp) *lowp = s2;
   if (s3 < *lowp) *lowp = s3;
   if (s4 < *lowp) *lowp = s4;
   if (s5 < *lowp) *lowp = s5;[5]
}
float calc_score(void)
{
    float max, min, total;

    find_high_low(&max, &min);
    total = (s1 + s2 + s3 + s4 + s5) - (max + min);
    return (total * diff) / 5;
}

void report_to_scoreboard(void)
{
    float final_score;

    printf("           Report to Scoreboard Operator\n\n");
    final_score = calc_score();
    printf("Display the score obtained: %5.1f\n", final_score);
}

void report_to_media(void)
```

```
{
      float final_score;

     printf("          Report to the Media\n\n");
     printf("Event: Diving competition\n");
     printf("Diver I.D.: %ld, City code: %d\n\n", id, city);

     final_score = calc_score();
     printf("Scores given by each judge were:\n\n");
     printf("%5d%5d%5d%5d%5d%s\n", 1, 2, 3, 4, 5, " Final score");
     printf("%5.1f%5.1f%5.1f%5.1f%5.1f     -->%5.1f\n",
             s1, s2, s3, s4, s5, final_score);
}

void make_reports(void)
{
      report_to_scoreboard();
      report_to_media();
}

main()
{
    read_scores();[5]
    make_reports();
}
```

Explanations

1. These variables were moved from **within** the *main()* to the global scope. They are now visible in all functions. This was not the case before. This is why they had to be passed to nearly all functions.
2. Very few function calls still need to define parameters. (Why is that so?) This is why all parameters are *void,* except for the function *find_high_low().*
3. All functions can access the global variables **directly.**
4. The function *find_high_low()* chose to have a couple of variables, *max* and *min,* passed to it. This was a wise choice, since these two variables are of local interest only and not needed in most functions.
5. Very few functions still require arguments.

The introduction of global variables allowed a considerably simplified program.

EXERCISES 12.3.1

1. What will the following program display?

```
int  a;

void show1(void)
{
      a = 10;
      printf("a = %d\n", a);
}

void show2(int a)
{
      a = 20;
      printf("a = %d\n", a);
}
```

```
main()
{
        int  a;

        a = 5;
        printf("a = %d\n", a);
        show1();
        printf("a = %d\n", a);
        show2();
        printf("a = %d\n", a);
}
```

2. Move all of the variables (i.e., *a, x, y, t, m,* and *n*) in the following program to the global scope. What implication does this have on the function headers and local variables?

```
#include <stdio.h>

int calt1(int a)
{
        return a + 5;
}

void calt2(float x, int y)
{
        int  t;

        t = x / y;
        printf("t = %d\n", t);
}

main()
{
        int  m, n;

        n = 12;
        m = calt1(n);
        printf("m = %d\n", m);
        calt2(n, m);
}
```

3. After you complete this question, you will realize why global variables should be avoided. The following program calculates exponential numbers five times:

```
#include <stdio.h>

int  i;            /* Globals */
int  base, exp;
long res;

int power(void)
{
        res = 1;
        for (i=1; i < exp; i++)
        {
                res = res * base;
        }
        return res;
}

main()
{
```

```
        int  result;

        printf("This program will calculate five exponential numbers:\n\n");
        for (i=1; i < 5; i++)
        {
              printf("Enter the base and exponent > ");
              scanf("%d%d", &base, &exp);
              result = power();
              printf("%d to the power of %d is %d\n",
                      base, exp, result);
        }
        printf("Done!");
}
```

Here is an example of output from this program:

```
This program will calculate five exponential numbers:

Enter the base and exponent: 3 4
81 to the power of 4 is 81
Enter the base and exponent: 2 10
1024 to the power of 10 is 1024
Done!
```

This program obviously does not run properly. Lines 2 and 4 display wrong answers, and the program quits after only two calculations. What is the problem? How can it be fixed? Suggest a remedy.

4. Reconsider Example 12.3.1. Move the definition of all of the variables so that they are visible in all functions. What impact does this have on the program?

12.3.2 SO WHEN ARE GLOBAL VARIABLES APPROPRIATE?

The introduction of global variables to the programs in Examples 12.3.1 and 12.3.2 above is appealing. This appeal is quite deceiving, though, and is truly a two-edged sword! The pitfall illustrated in Exercise 12.3.1, 3, shows perfectly well one drawback of using global variables: they cause side effects. Functions should not have side effects, especially if they are to be portable. Even when global variables appear to be the right choice, there is almost always a better way that avoids using them.

Following are the three main reasons that students are inclined to use global variables:

1. "I use global variables in order to cut down on the number of arguments to functions." This was illustrated in Example 12.3.2. This is **never** a good reason for switching to global variables. Chapters 14 and 21 will show you that arrays and structures, respectively, are a much more stylish and safe approach to reducing the quantity of arguments.
2. "I use global variables because then I do not need to worry about variable scoping." This is the worst reason possible. Actually, even here, the issue of variable scoping may need a look as the subsections below will explain.
3. "I use global variables because there are some variables that I need nearly everywhere." This was illustrated in both Examples 12.3.1 and 12.3.2. This is usually not a good reason, but it depends on the nature of the variables in question. If the variables have a very special purpose, then making them global might be fine. For instance, the purpose of the variable *testing* in Example 12.3.1 is solely for turning the testing procedure on and off—a special purpose. Keep in mind, though, that the functions that use this variable are not fully portable. If they are called into another program, problems will arise if that new program already uses the variable *testing* for some other purpose. So what is the solution if you still want the variable *testing* to remain global? Clearly document its special use so that programmers will not use it for something else. A good example of this practice is the global variable *errno* declared in the header file *stdlib.h* of most C compiler packages. This variable is assigned a number whenever a system call error occurs. For instance, when *fopen()* fails to find the file to open, the variable *errno* receives a value of 2.

Now you see the clear message: do not use global variables! However, if you are a daredevil, you will still be tempted to use them. (In that case, better read the rest of this section!)

12.3.3 BE WARY OF THE DIFFERENT LEVELS OF GLOBAL VARIABLES

When you do use global variables, you must take care that they all are declared at the **top** of the program; otherwise their "globalness" will be weakened. Example 12.3.3 illustrates this.

Example 12.3.3

In Example 12.3.1, suppose the variable *testing* was inadvertently declared at the location shown in bold type below (much of the code is left out), instead of at the top of the program:

```
#include <stdio.h>
#include <ctype.h>

void read_data(int * day_ptr, int * hours_ptr)
{
    if (testing == 'y')
    :
    :
    :
}

char testing;

float set_rate(char ex_up, int sp)
{
    float  rate;

    if (testing == 'y')
    :
    :
    :
}
float calculate(char ex_up, int sp)
{
    float pay, rate;
    int   day, hours;

    if (testing == 'y')
    :
    :
    :
}

void specify_error(char ex, char ex_up, int sp)
{
    if (testing == 'y')
    :
    :
    :
}

main()
{
    int     sp;
```

```
    char    ex, ex_up, ans;
    float   pay;

    printf("Is this run for testing (y/n)? ");
    scanf("\n%c", &testing);
    :
    :
    :
    printf("\nDone!");
}
```

The compilation of this program will fail within the function *read_data()*. The compiler will complain that the variable *testing* is not defined there. This is because global variables are only visible to the functions defined **below** them. That is, here only the functions *set_rate(), calculate(), specify_error()*, and *main()* can see the variable *testing*.

Declaration must precede the reference. Functions can only look upwards for global variable definitions. Think of functions like people in different rooms, where the hallway is one way. These people can only look in that direction for global variables. A similar situation was illustrated previously in Figure 12.1.2.

EXERCISE 12.3.2

Consider the program skeleton below and fill in the table to the right. Do not concern yourself with what is inside the functions.

```
#include <stdio.h>

int  a, b;

void  fcn_one(void)
{
      int b;
      .....
}

int c;

void  fcn_two(void)
{
      .....
}

int d;

void  fcn_three(void)
{
      .....
}

main()
{
      fcn_two();
      fcn_three();
}
```

Global variable	Functions that can see the variable
a	
b	
c	
d	

12.3.4 BE WARY OF MASKING GLOBAL VARIABLES

There is another situation that limits the visibility of a global variable: when it is masked from view within a function. This can happen in two ways, as you will see in Example 12.3.4.

Example 12.3.4

Let us write a program for Exercise 9.2.1, 2., to display the flag of the United States:

```
**********--------------------
**********--------------------
**********--------------------
**********--------------------
------------------------------
------------------------------
------------------------------
```

The program will use a function named *star_line()* to draw the stars for each line, and a function named *dash_line()* to draw the dashes for each line. Following is the program:

```
#include <stdio.h>

int  ctr;                /* global counter variable */

void star_line(void)
{
        for (ctr=1; ctr <= 10; ctr++)        /* uses the global counter */
        {
                printf("*");
        }
}

void dash_line(int ctr)
{
        for ( ; ctr > 0; ctr--)              /* uses the parameter, */
        {                                    /* NOT the global counter */
                printf("-");
        }
}
main()
{
        int  ctr;

        for (ctr=1; ctr <= 4; ctr++)         /* uses the local counter */
        {
                star_line();                 /* draw 10 stars */
                dash_line(20);               /* draw 20 dashes */
                printf("\n");
        }
        for (ctr=1; ctr <= 3; ctr++)         /* uses the local counter */
        {
                dash_line(30);               /* draw 30 dashes */
                printf("\n");
        }
}
```

Note that the compiler looks for the closest declaration. All three functions need a counter, so a global one named *ctr* has been declared that can be used by all of them. Unfortunately, the function *dash_line()* has a parameter that is also named *ctr.* When that function is being executed, whenever a reference to *ctr* is made, it will search for the closest definition, i.e., the parameter. It will therefore never bother going outside the function to look for a global definition for *ctr.* This means that the global variable of the same name is not visible within this function: it is ***masked.*** Clearly, the use of variables here is poorly designed. Nonetheless, this program works. It was presented here solely to explain the technique of masking global variables.

EXERCISES 12.3.3

Suppose the local declaration of *ctr* in *main()* is removed from the program in Example 12.3.4.

1. Will the program still compile?
2. If yes, will it still run correctly?

Masking global variables, or equivalently, using global and local variables of the same name, is rarely a good idea. It can easily lead to confusing code. Although in the program for Example 12.3.4, a counter is needed in all functions, its purpose differs in each. Therefore, a local counter should be declared in each function. Here is a better use of variables for the previous program, with changes shown in bold type:

```
#include <stdio.h>

void star_line(void)
{
        int ctr;

        for (ctr=1; ctr <= 10; ctr++)        /* uses a local counter */
        {
                printf("*");
        }
}

void dash_line(int length)     /* uses a parameter of a different name */
{

        for ( ; length > 0; length--)
        {
                printf("-");
        }
}

main()
{
        int  ctr;

        for (ctr=1; ctr <= 4; ctr++)         /* uses the local counter */
        {
                star_line();
                dash_line(20);
                printf("\n");
        }
        for (ctr=1; ctr <= 3; ctr++)         /* uses the local counter */
        {
                dash_line(30);
                printf("\n");
        }
}
```

The same variable name, *ctr,* is still used in two functions. This is acceptable, as long as there is no global variable of the same name.

EXERCISES 12.3.4

1. Consider the following program:

```
#include <stdio.h>

int b;

void func1(int a)
{
    int i;

    i = 2;
    printf("in func1: a = %d, i = %d\n", a, i);
    a = 3;
    printf("in func1: a = %d\n", a);
    printf("in func1: b = %d\n", b);
    b = 4;
}

int c;
void func2(int b, int i)
{
    printf("in func2: b = %d, i = %d\n", b, i);
    b = 5;
    c = 10;
}

int d;

main()
{
    int i;
    int a;

    b = 1;    c = 8;     d = 9;
    i = 6;    a = 7;
    func1( i );
    printf("in main: a = %d, i = %d, b = %d\n", a, i, b);
    func2( a, i );
    printf("in main: a = %d, i = %d, b = %d, c = %d\n", a, i, b, c);
    func2( i, a );
    printf("in main: a = %d, i = %d, b = %d, c = %d\n", a, i, b, c);
}
```

Answer the following questions about this program:

a. In which functions are the global variables *a, b, c,* and *d* visible?

b. What output will this program produce?

2. Review the following program and fill in the table below. For each global variable, list the functions that can:

a. see that variable; i.e., the variable is visible within a function

b. reach that variable, i.e., its memory location is known there

Remember that a variable may be reachable and yet not visible.

It is totally irrelevant what the functions do, so the code within them is omitted.

```
#include <stdio.h>

int  a, b;
```

```
void  fcn_one(void)
{
      int b;

      .....
}

int c;

void  fcn_two(int * c, int * f)
{
      int a;

      .....
}

int d;

void  fcn_three(int a, int c)
{
      .....
}


main()
{
      int a;

      fcn_two(&c, &d);
      fcn_three(c, b);
}
```

Global variable	Functions that can: See the variable	Reach the variable
a		
b		
c		
d		

12.3.5 COMMON ERRORS AND TRAPS

Use the following information to avoid common programming errors:

1. Do not place the declaration of a global variable in the wrong place, preventing its visibility to functions above it.

2. Do not unintentionally mask a global variable that is needed within a function. This may happen when a parameter and a local variable of the same name are declared.
3. Do not use global variables unjustifiably!

12.4 LIBRARIES OF FUNCTIONS

Any C compiler comes with numerous predefined functions. We have seen some already, such as *printf()*, *getchar()*, and *toupper()*. These functions are classified (by their type of use) into groups called ***libraries.*** This makes their use and retrieval much easier. Functions stored in libraries are usually the ones needed most often. Based on the discussion in the previous section, these functions must be highly portable.

This section explores in more detail libraries and how to use them. It also briefly discusses how to create your own libraries of functions.

12.4.1 HEADER FILES AND LIBRARIES

Libraries of functions are provided to ease the development of your programs. Examples of libraries that are available with most C compilers include:

1. Standard input/output library functions such as *scanf()* and *printf()*
2. Mathematical library functions such as *sqrt()* and *fabs()*
3. String library functions, which are used to read, display, store, and process such data as people's names and city names (Read more about those in Chapter 18.)
4. Screen-handling library functions, which serve such functions as manipulating the cursor

Of course, there are numerous other libraries. When you wish to use such functions, you must first announce your intention to the compiler. For example, you announce your intention to use *printf()* or *scanf()* with the line *#include <stdio.h>*. This directive inserts the file *stdio.h* in your program **before** it is compiled. For this reason, the directive is termed a ***preprocessor*** directive. The file *stdio.h* is called a ***header file.*** We have already encountered other header files. Table 12.4.1 lists the C functions that have been used so far in this book, with the respective headers that need to be inserted:

Table 12.4.1

Function	Header file in which the function is declared	ANSI C standard?
printf()	*stdio.h*	Yes
scanf()	*stdio.h*	Yes
clrscr()	*conio.h* (differs across compilers)	No
toupper()	*stdlib.h*	Yes
tolower()	*stdlib.h*	Yes
isalpha()	*stdlib.h*	Yes
islower()	*stdlib.h*	Yes

These header files include declarations (function prototypes) for the functions in the left column and many other functions. These declarations only tell the compiler that you intend to use the functions. Their actual definitions are added to your program later, during the linking. To illustrate this process, let us consider a program that uses *toupper()*, *printf()*, and *scanf()* in some way. The program goes through three steps:

1. Prepreprocessing
2. Compiling
3. Linking

The flow chart in Figure 12.4.1 details each step.

Figure 12.4.1

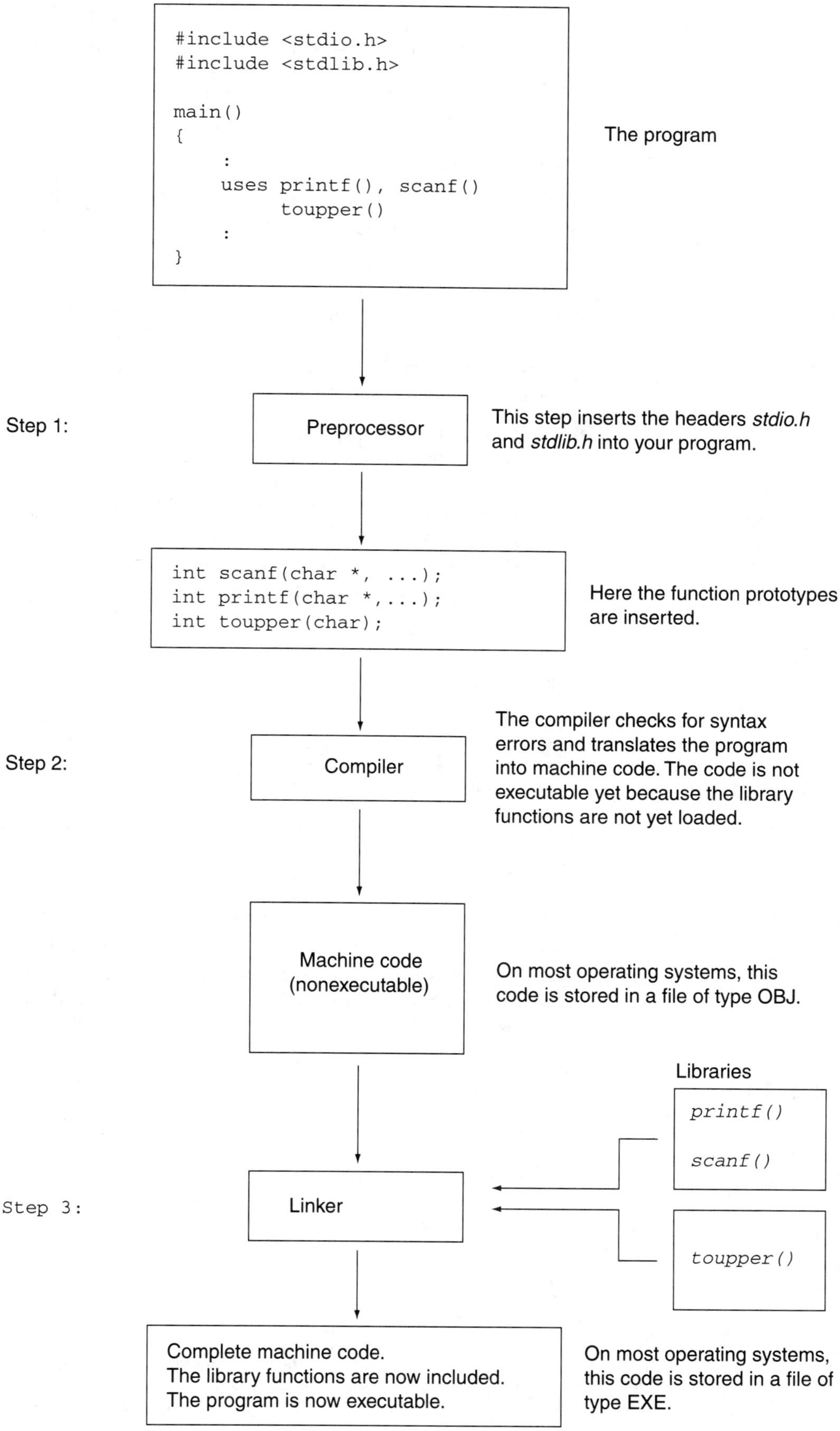

12.4.2 STANDARD LIBRARIES VS. NONSTANDARD LIBRARIES

A subset of all of the libraries, called the ***standard libraries,*** consists of the libraries included by all ANSI C compilers. The other libraries may very well differ across compilers. For example, the following libraries that most C compilers provide are non-ANSI standard:

- Screen-handling library functions, which serve such functions as manipulating the cursor
- Graphics library functions, which can be used, for example, to draw geometric figures in a multitude of colors
- Windowing library functions, which allow for the development of Windows®-based programs

Other nonstandard libraries may come from third-party software companies. These often provide specialized libraries, such as image processing libraries, business math libraries, and accounting libraries.

Creating your own libraries. You can also create your own libraries, just like the professionals! C compilers come with features that allow this. The exact steps to follow in order to produce a user-based library differ across compilers, so we will not go into them here, but let's look at an example. Suppose that you wish to create a library of functions for image processing. This would certainly require such functions as:

- A function named *enlarge()* to enlarge an image
- A function named *shrink()* to shrink an image
- A function named *enhance()* to sharpen an image
- A function named *contour()* to highlight the shapes within an image
- A function named *load()* to load an image in memory
- A function named *store()* to save an image to disk

You may decide to store definitions of all of these functions in a file named IMAGES.C. This program would be compiled and then stored in a library, as shown in Figure 12.4.2.

Figure 12.4.2

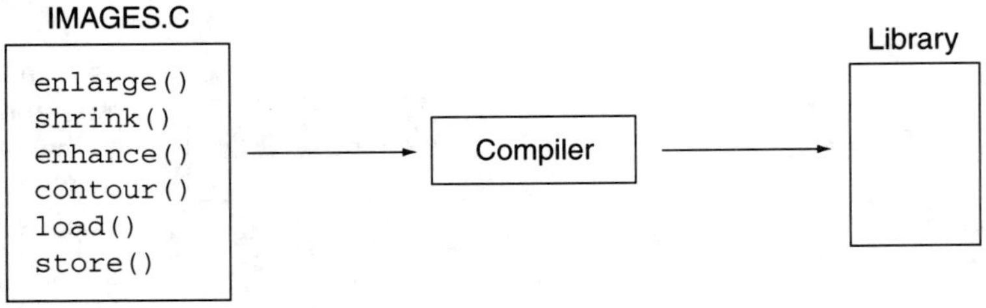

Now suppose that a programmer proceeds to write a program called, say, PROCESS.C, to process an image. She would need to use some of the functions in this library. These functions would simply be called in a logical sequence from the program in PROCESS.C. Since the definitions of the library function are **not** in the file PROCESS.C, this file must include the function declarations (so that the compiler knows that they will be called), as shown in Figure 12.4.3.

Figure 12.4.3

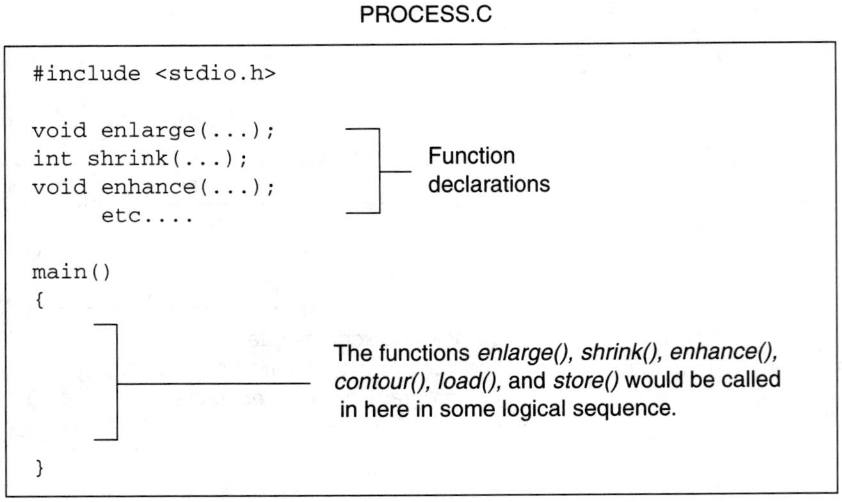

However, since these declarations may very well be needed again in other programs, it is best to store them in a header file named, say, IMAGES.H. (This is the reason for the existence of the header file *stdio.h* and others.) Then the programmer would use the *#include* preprocessor command to include these declarations in the program PROCESS.C, as shown in Figure 12.4.4. Note the double quotation marks in the *#include* command, as opposed to the angle brackets (i.e., *<stdio.h>*). Brackets indicate that the header file is provided by the compiler manufacturer, while double quotation marks indicate that the header file is provided by a third-party provider, or perhaps by the programmer.

Figure 12.4.4

PROCESS.C

```
#include <stdio.h>
#include "images.h"

main()
{

}
```

The functions *enlarge(), shrink(), enhance(), contour(), load(),* and *store()* would be called in here in some logical sequence.

13 Technical Details About Some Operators and Data Types

OBJECTIVES

This chapter introduces you to the following information:

- In-depth discussion of the technical aspects and uses of operators covered initially in Chapters 2 and 3 and again in Chapter 5.
- A new operator: the conditional operator.
- A detailed coverage of ASCII codes.
- Operations with ASCII codes and characters.

INTRODUCTION

Chapter 3 and subsequent chapters introduced you to C expressions. You may then be wondering: why should you cover this again? In those earlier chapters, we intentionally stayed away from revealing to you the complete picture simply because problem-solving skills were more important. However, now much more needs to be explained about operators in C. To begin, consider the following facts:

1. All operators in C are regarded in the same way; that is, they all require one or more operands, they all produce a result, and they all have a precedence of operation.
2. Various kinds of data types can be mixed together in arithmetic operations, including the characters.

These facts suggest that operators in C are quite flexible. Indeed, they are, and this has interesting implications, as we will see later in this chapter. Unfortunately, this flexibility comes with numerous traps for an unwary programmer, which was one very good reason for staying away from all of this until now!

Table 13.1.1 shows the precedence for all of the operators that we have covered so far. This table also includes those that will be discussed in this chapter. At times, we will refer back to this table.

Table 13.1.1

Operator	Description	Type	Associativity
()	Parentheses	Unary	Left to right
++ --	Increment and decrement	Unary	Right to Left
–	Arithmetic negation	Unary	
!	Logical negation	Unary	
(type)	Cast operator	Unary	
sizeof	Size (in bytes)	Unary	
&	Address of	Unary	
*	Dereference	Unary	
* / %	Arithmetic	Binary	Left to right
+ –	Arithmetic	Binary	Left to right
< <= > >=	Relational	Binary	Left to right
== !=	Relational	Binary	Left to right
&&	Logical AND	Binary	Left to right
||	Logical OR	Binary	Left to right
? :	Conditional	Ternary	Right to left
= += -=	Assignment	Binary	Right to left
*= /=	Assignment	Binary	

13.1 THE ASSIGNMENT OPERATORS

Besides the usual assignment operator =, the C language provides many other assignment operators. We will look at those most commonly used.

13.1.1 THE USUAL ASSIGNMENT OPERATOR

The assignment operator requires two operands. For instance, in the following statement:

```
age = 27
```

the assignment has two operands: the variable *age* and the number 27. Two actions take place:

1. The operand 27 is stored in the variable *age.*
2. This number constitutes the result of the operation in the same way that, say, the operation 6 + 9 returns the result 15.

Note that the operand to the left must be a variable. For example, the statement *5 = 27* would be illegal because it would tell C to store 27 in the constant 5, which makes no sense.

Because the assignment operator is no different in nature than any other operator, it may be used at any place in an expression, not just to the far left. This has interesting implications as the following three examples illustrate.

Example 13.1.1

The assignment operator is allowed to initialize more than one variable at the time. For instance, the following expression is valid even though it has more than one assignment operator: *result = a = b = 8.* Here is how this expression works. Remember from Table 13.1.1 that assignment operators are evaluated from right to left:

result = *a* = *b* = 8	
b = 8	8 assigned to the variable *b*
8	8 is returned
a = 8	8 assigned to the variable *a*

```
                8      8 is returned
result  =       8      8 assigned to the variable result
     8                 8 is returned
```

This expression returns 8 and assigns this same number to the three variables.

Example 13.1.2

A variable can be initialized and used in an expression, all at the same time, as shown below:

```
result  =  (a  =  5) + (b  =  13)
           (a  =  5)                  5 is assigned to the variable a
               5
                     (b  =  13)       13 is assigned to the variable b
                            13
               5    +       13
                    18
result  =           18
     18
```

Thus this expression is, in effect, equivalent to the following three:

a = 5;
b = 13;
result = *a* + *b*;

Example 13.1.3

The assignment operator may appear as part of an argument to a function. Consider the following lines of code:

```
printf("Enter an amount > ");
scanf("%f", &amt);
growth = amt * 0.08;
printf("The expected growth is %f\n", growth);
```

The assignment operator returns a number, and it can be moved into the *printf()* statement:

```
printf("Enter an amount > ");
scanf("%f", &amt);
printf("The expected growth is %f\n", growth = amt * 0.08);
```

Assuming that the amount entered is 50, the *printf()* statement will be executed as follows:

```
printf("The expected growth is %f\n", growth = amt * 0.08);
                                               50  * 0.08
                                                  4.0
                                      growth =    4.0
                                            4.0
printf("The expected growth is %f\n",       4.0            );
```

The following message will then be displayed:

The expected growth is 4.000000

Note that the result returned by the assignment is 4.0, of type *float,* so the type of format code must agree.

EXERCISES 13.1.1

1. Is there anything wrong with any of the following code? If not, what will be displayed? Assume the declaration:

```
int   n, m, total;
float coeff;
```

a. `printf("5 multiplied by 9 is %d\n", total = (n = 5) * (m = 9));`
b. `printf("coeff is %d\n", coeff = (n = 5) * (m = 9));`
c. `printf("total is %d\n", total = (n = 5.61) * (m = 9));`
d. `printf("total is %f\n", total = 5.61 * (m = 9));`

2. Is the output from the following *printf()* predictable? If so, what is it? (***Hint:*** Read about common error 2 in Section 13.1.5.)

a.
```
n = 1;
m = 0;
printf("%d multiplied by %d is %d\n",
        n, m, total = (n = 5) * (m = 9));
```
b.
```
n = 1;
m = 0;
printf("%d multiplied by %d is %d\n",
        n = 7, m = 3, total = (n = 5) * (m = 9));
```

13.1.2 BE WARY OF SYSTEM DEPENDENCIES

The use of assignments operators within an expression is slick, but you must be careful: overusing them may lead to mind-boggling bugs. Example 13.1.4 explains.

Example 13.1.4

Assume a variable *a* contains 5. Let us evaluate the expression *result = a + (a = 10)*. It is natural to assume that the computer will evaluate it as follows:

```
result = a + (a = 10)
             (a = 10)
                10
        10 +    10
          20
result =  20
     20
```

This is because parentheses have the highest precedence. Surprisingly, some compilers will evaluate it as follows:

```
result = a + (a = 10)
         5
             (a = 10)
                10
         5 +    10
          15
result =  15
     15
```

Quite a different result! Why does this happen? The reasons are technical but you deserve some explanation. The compiler will parse the expression according to ANSI C's table of precedence while generating machine code for each operator. The problem is that no rules are specified by ANSI C for the generation of these machine codes, perhaps because this domain is system dependent—so the machine codes generated by compilers differ among manufacturers. In most cases, this never matters; in cases like the one above, it does. So how do you know if the evaluation of an expression is system dependent? Here is the rule of thumb:

> When an expression sets a variable with an assignment operator and then uses that same variable some other place within the **same** expression, its evaluation is unpredictable.

This rule applies to shorthand operators, too, which are covered in Subsection 13.1.3.

An implication of system dependency on the evaluation of an expression is that with binary operators, the order in which the operands are evaluated is not specified by ANSI C. As seen above, the result of the following expression is unpredictable.

$$result = a + (a = 10)$$

If operand 2, $(a = 10)$, is evaluated first, then *result* will receive 20; otherwise, it will receive 15.

EXERCISES 13.1.2

1. Given that the variable *num* contains 3 and *m* contains 5, is the result of each of the following expressions unpredictable? If not, what is the result of each?
   a. $(num + 1) * (num = 1)$
   b. $(num = 3) - (num = 12)$
   c. $num + (m = 6)$
   d. $num + (m = num)$
2. You most likely needed at least three separate assignment statements to solve Exercise 3.2.2, 2(a). Now combine them all into a single expression.

13.1.3 SHORTHAND ASSIGNMENT OPERATORS

Section 9.1 introduced assignment operators += and −=. These are called ***shorthand*** operators and work as follows. Assume that *age* contains 4. The following assignment has two operands: the variable *age* and the number 13:

```
age += 13
```

Two actions take place:

1. The operator is expanded as $age = age + 13$, so the number 4 + 13 = 17 is stored in the variable *age*.
2. This same number constitutes the result of the operation +=.

Let us look at a few more complex examples.

Example 13.1.5

Shorthand operators have the exact same precedence as the usual assignment operator. For example, following is the evaluation of an expression, which is evaluated from left to right. Assume that *a* contains 2.5:

```
b  =  a  +=  11.2  *  5
             11.2  *  5
                56.0
      a  +=     56.0
         58.5
b  =     58.5
 58.5
```

Note that the statement $a += 56.0$ is the same as $a = a + 56.0$.

Example 13.1.6

The assignment operators *= and /= are occasionally used as well. They work similarly. Following is the evaluation of a sample expression. Assume that *a* contains 2.5 again:

```
b  =  a  /=  5  *  5
             5  *  5
```

25
a /= 25
0.1
b = 0.1
0.1

Note that the statement *a /= 25* is the same as *a = a / 25*. Remember that these shorthand operators should be used only in the context of loops, as demonstrated in Subsection 9.1.2.

EXERCISES 13.1.3

1. Given that the variable *num* contains 3 and *m* contains 5, is the result of each of the following expressions unpredictable? If not, what is the result of each?
   a. *(num += 1) * (num + 1)*
   b. *num *= num – 12*
   c. *num *= num = 12*
   d. *num + (m /= 6)*
   e. *num + (m –= num)*
2. Are the expressions *num –= a * 5 + i* and *num = num – a * 5 + i* equivalent?

13.1.4 DEFAULT SETTING OPERATOR (OR INITIALIZATION OPERATOR)

Chapter 2 said that at the time that a variable is declared, most compilers automatically set its value to 0. (Some compilers do not set it to anything!) This is called the ***default value.*** However, you may want the variable to receive a different default value. The C language allows this, but the default value must be set at the time that the variable is declared.

Example 13.1.7

In the following declaration, the variable *height* is declared as a *float* type and is set to the default value of 1.50 meters:

```
float height = 1.50;
```

The use of the = operator tells the compiler to set the variable to 1.50.

Note that this equal sign is **not** an assignment operator. (In fact, it is not an operator at all, but we will call it that none the less.) An assignment operator can be executed at any time; the ***default setting operator*** is executed only at the time that the variable is declared, and this takes place when the function in which that variable is declared starts execution. However, a variable declared inside *main()* would be set at the time that the program's run is initiated. (Why is this so?). A variable declared globally is also set at that time.

When should a default setting be used? Most C books use the term ***initialization operator;*** but this term is slightly misleading, because the same term is also used in the context of loops. As a result of the confusion, the default setting operator is often wrongly used. The following examples illustrate this point.

Example 13.1.8

Consider the following code segment:

```
int counter = 0;

for ( ; counter < 5; counter++)
{
      printf("%d", counter);
}
```

The absence of an initialization part *(counter = 0)* in the *for* header wrongly suggests that the loop does not need initialization. The default setting operator should not be used here. The initialization code should be:

```
for (counter=0; counter < 5; counter++)
{
     printf("%d", counter);
}
```

Example 13.1.9

The following program is taken from Example 8.2.4 with two additional features: it calculates the average of the list of numbers, and it uses default setting operators. These changes are shown in bold type.

```
#include <stdio.h>

main()
{
   int    sum = 0, counter = 0, num, flag;[1]
   FILE * ifp;
   FILE * ofp;

   ifp = fopen("in.dat", "r");
   if (ifp == NULL)
   {
      printf("Could not open input file\n");
   }
   ofp = fopen("ans.out", "w");
   if (ofp == NULL)
   {
      printf("Could not open output file\n");
   }
   if (ifp != NULL && ofp != NULL)
   {
      flag = fscanf(ifp, "%d", &num);
      while (flag != EOF)[2]
      {
         sum = sum + num;
         counter = counter + 1;
         flag = fscanf(ifp, "%d", &num);
      }
      avg = sum / counter;
      fprintf(ofp, "The sum is %d and the average is %f.\n", sum, avg);
      fclose(ifp);
      fclose(ofp);
   }
}
```

Explanations

1. The default setting should not be used. The true reason that the variables *sum* and *counter* are set to zero is for the processing of the loop, so . . .
2. . . . the setting to zero should occur at the location of the loop, not at the top of the program.

EXERCISES 13.1.4

1. Make the suggested changes in Example 13.1.9 above.

2. Default settings can be used for global variables, too. Consider the following program:

```
#include <stdio.h>

int   a = 6;

void fcn1(void)
{
        printf("%d\n", a);
}

int   b = 2;

void fcn2(void)
{
        int   c = 9;

        printf("%d%d%d\n", a, b, c);
}

int   d = 12;
main()
{
        int   e = 4;

        fcn1();
        fcn2();
        printf("%d%d\n", d, e);
}
```

a. What will the program display?
b. Eliminate the use of the default settings, and use initialization statements instead.

13.1.5 COMMON ERRORS AND TRAPS

Use the following information to avoid common programming errors.

1. Do not inadvertently assign into a constant. This can happen in subtle ways. For example, look at the following expression, in which *a* contains 3:

$$result \;=\; a \;*\; 5 \;+\; b \;=\; 8$$
$$3 \;*\; 5$$
$$15$$
$$15 \;+\; b$$
$$15 \;+\; 0$$
$$15$$
$$15 \;=\; 8$$

   As the last line indicates, you cannot assign to a constant. The compiler would complain with a message such as "Lvalue expected." This means that it expected a variable as the left operand of the assignment operator.

2. Do not use the assignment operator as part of an argument to a function. This is not an error *per se,* but its overuse can trap you. For example, the following program simply asks for the cost for an item, and then it calculates Canada's provincial sales tax and goods and services tax. It displays the results for both taxes and the overall total. Note the two assignment operators within the last *printf():*

```
#include <stdio.h>

main()
{
```

```
    float cost, pst, gst;

    printf("Enter the cost of the item $ ");
    scanf("%f", &cost);


    printf("The PST is $%.2f, the GST is $%.2f, and the total is $%.2f\n",
           pst = cost * 0.09, gst = cost * 0.07, pst + gst);
}
```

A sample display from this program might look like this:

Enter the cost of the item $ 90.00
The PST is $8.10, the GST is $6.30, and the total is $14.40

Surprisingly, the results may be different when the program is run with another compiler or computer system. For example, one compiler would give the following results:

Enter the cost of the item $ 90.00
The PST is $8.10, the GST is $6.30, and the total is $0.00

Let us now look at the arguments of the *printf()* statement again:

```
printf("The PST is $%.2f, the GST is $%.2f, and the total is $%.2f\n",
       pst = cost * 0.09, gst = cost * 0.07, pst + gst);
```

It is natural to expect that the argument *pst = cost * 0.09* would be evaluated first, followed by the other two. It turns out that the order in which these three arguments are evaluated may differ across compilers. For example, they may be evaluated in the following order:

```
printf("The PST is $%.2f, the GST is $%.2f, and the total is $%.2f\n",
        pst = cost * 0.09, gst = cost * 0.07, pst + gst);
                                               0  +  0
                                                  0

                              90.0 * 0.07
                                   6.30
                         gst =     6.30
                            6.30
           90.0 * 0.09
              8.10
        pst =     8.10
           8.10
```

Then these three numbers, 8.10, 6.30, and 0, are sent to the function.

3. Do not use the default setting operator unnecessarily.

13.2 THE RELATIONAL/LOGICAL OPERATORS AND LOGICAL DATA TYPE

This section discusses the representation in memory of logical values as well as logical variables and logical expressions. (This topic could have been covered in Chapter 4, but its technical details were not needed nor wanted at the time).

13.2.1 NUMERIC VALUES OF TRUE AND FALSE

Chapter 4 mentioned the existence of two logical values: "true" and "false." It turns out that the story does not end there. Consider the following examples.

Example 13.2.1

The program below asks for a person's age and determines whether or not that person is a child:

```
#include <stdio.h>

main()
```

```
{
        int    age;

        printf("How old are you? ");
        scanf("%d", &age);
        if (age >= 2 && age <= 12)
        {
                printf("You are a child\n");
        }
        else
        {
                printf("You are not a child\n");
        }
}
```

Suppose the person's age is 14. Chapter 5 explained that the *if* condition is evaluated as follows:

```
age   >=   2   &&   age   <=   12
14    >=   2
   true
                     14   <=   12
                        false
   true       &&        false
          false
```

In the computer memory, a false result is actually stored as the number 0, whereas a true result is stored as the number 1. The evaluation actually proceeds as follows:

```
age   >=   2   &&   age   <=   12
14    >=   2
    1
                     14   <=   12
                           0
    1         &&           0
              0
```

Next the *if* receives this 0 and interprets it as false:

```
if (age   >=   2   &&   age   <=   12)

if (            0                   )
if (          false                 )
```

Example 13.2.2

To prove that the logical values are stored as 0s and 1s, the following program displays the results of each component of the condition *age >= 2 && age <= 12:*

```
#include <stdio.h>

main()
{
        int    age;

        printf("How old are you? ");
        scanf("%d", &age);
        printf("The logical value of age >= 2 is %d", age >= 2);
        printf("The logical value of age <= 12 is %d", age <= 12);
```

```
        printf("The logical value of age >= 2 && age <= 12 is %d",
               age >= 2 && age <= 12);
}
```

If *age* is 14, the display would be:

The logical value of age >= 2 is 1
The logical value of age <= 12 is 0
The logical value of age >= 2 && age <= 12 is 0

Clearly, logical values are no different in nature than any other numbers. This implies that the result from a logical expression may be stored in an integer variable, as illustrated in Example 13.2.3.

Example 13.2.3

The program above may be modified as shown below, and it will still work the same.

```
#include <stdio.h>

main()
{
     int   age, child;
     printf("How old are you? ");
     scanf("%d", &age);
     child = age >= 2 && age <= 12;¹
     if (child)²
     {
          printf("You are a child\n");
     }
     else
     {
          printf("You are not a child\n");
     }
}
```

Explanations

1. As seen in Example 13.2.2, this expression will evaluate to a 1 or 0. The variable *child* will receive a 1 or 0 for certain.
2. A 1 or a 0 is all the *if* needs to receive, so the *if* condition does not need to be *child == 1.* Both conditions are the same. Suppose that child contains 0:

```
if (child)                    if (child == 1)
if (  0  )                    if (  0   == 1)
                              if (     0     )
```

Verify for yourself the case for *child* being equal to 1.

Logical variables. Note that because the variable *child* in Example 13.2.3 is sure to receive a 0 or a 1, 1 byte is all it takes to store the logical value into it. Consequently, it is sufficient to declare the variable *child* of *char* type. We refer to variables such as *child* as ***logical variables,*** even though the C programming language does not have a built-in logical data type.

Example 13.2.4

Logical values can be read in as well, simply as numbers. Let us take the program from Example 5.2.1 to illustrate:

```
#include <stdio.h>

main()
```

```
{
     int   mark, new_mark;
     char  late;
     float correction_factor;

     printf("Enter the mark > ");
     scanf("%d", &mark);
     printf("Is it late? (yes = 1, no = 0) > ");
     scanf("%d", &late);                    /* read logical value */
     if (late)
     {
          printf("Enter the correction factor > ");
          scanf("%f", &correction_factor);
          new_mark = mark - mark * correction_factor;
          printf("The new mark is %d\n", new_mark);
     }
     else
     {
          printf("The new mark is %d\n", mark);
     }
}
```

Note that the *if* condition may be reduced from *late == 1* to simply *late.* (Why is that so?)

All this is pretty slick, but there is more! In C, logical values are extendable to much more than 0 and 1. In fact, any **whole** number can be stored in a logical variable. The number 0 means "false" and any nonzero number is interpreted as "true." Example 13.2.5 illustrates this.

Example 13.2.5

The following program sums up a list of numbers (negative or positive) until a 0 is reached:

```
#include <stdio.h>

main()
{
       int num, sum;

       sum = 0;
       printf("Enter a list of numbers (enter 0 to terminate):\n");
       scanf("%d", &num);
       while (num)
       {
              sum += num;
              scanf("%d", &num);
       }
       printf("The sum is %d\n", sum);
}
```

The condition *while (num)* means the same as *while (num != 0).* Indeed, suppose that *num* contains –71. Then these two conditions would be evaluated as follows:

```
while ( num )                        while ( num   != 0 )
while (-71)                       while (-71.52 != 0)
while ("true")                       while (     1      )
                                     while ( "true"     )
```

Truth tables revisited. Now, the truth tables for the three logical operators discussed can be generalized as shown in Table 13.2.1.

Table 13.2.1

Operand 1	||	Operand 2	Result
nonzero	||	nonzero	1
nonzero	||	0	1
0	||	nonzero	1
0	||	0	0

Operand 1	&&	Operand 2	Result
nonzero	&&	nonzero	1
nonzero	&&	0	0
0	&&	nonzero	0
0	&&	0	0

! Operand	Result
! nonzero	0
! 0	1

EXERCISES 13.2.1

1. Consider the following code segment:

```
if (!child)
{
        printf("You are not a child\n");
}
else
{
        printf("You are a child\n");
}
```

   a. Suppose that *child* contains a 0 or a 1. Is this segment valid?
   b. If it is valid, is it equivalent to the *if/else* in Example 13.2.3?
2. Evaluate the following logical expressions. Assume that the variables *i, j, a, b,* and *ok* contain the values 2, –5, 13.5, 13.5, and 1, respectively:
   a. *7 && 1*
   b. *0 || –5*
   c. *–4 && 8.15 || 0.0001*
   d. *i == j || a < b || ok*
   e. *!j && b || (a = i)*
   f. *!(i * a) + ok*
3. Assume the declaration *int stm.* Are the following always true? If not, for what values of *stm* are they true (if ever)?
   a. The logical expression *stm != 0* is equivalent to simply *stm.*
   b. The logical expression *stm > 0* is equivalent to *stm.*
   c. The logical expression *stm < 0* is equivalent to *!stm.*
   d. The logical expression *stm >= 5* is equivalent to *!(stm – 5).*
4. Redo question 3 with the declaration *float stm.*
5. Why does the following code segment always produce the output "Let's do it!" even when the user selects to exit the menu?

```
int ans;

printf("M E N U \n\n");
```

```
printf(1. Open\n");
printf(2. Close\n");
printf(3. Select\n");
printf(4. Delete\n");
printf(0. Exit\n\n");
printf("Select a number > ");
scanf("%d", &ans);
if (ans = 0)
{
        printf("Good-bye!\n");
}
else
{
        printf("Let's do it!\n");
}
```

6. Consider the programs obtained from the following exercises:
   a. Exercise 10.4.3, 5
   b. Exercise 12.1.2, 5
   c. Exercise 12.1.2, 7
   Some of the conditions in each program explicitly compare with a 0 or a 1 (whatever the case may be). Taking advantage of what you learned in this subsection, eliminate the need for such a relational operator.

13.2.2 SHORT-CIRCUIT EVALUATIONS

This subsection demonstrates shortcuts that the C language sometimes takes to evaluate logical expressions. It may be handy to know these at times.

Example 13.2.6

To illustrate, let us look at the *if/else* statement in the first program of this section.

```
af (age >= 2 && age <= 12)
{
        printf("You are a child\n");
}
else
{
        printf("You are not a child\n");
}
```

Suppose that the variable *age* is 1. The C language will evaluate the condition as follows:

```
age  >=  2  &&  age  <=  12
 1   >=  2
     0
     0       &&
             0
```

The second part of the expression, *age <=12,* will not be evaluated. It will be skipped because regardless of its logical value, the result of the && operation will be 0. (Why is that so?)

When a portion of an expression does not need to be evaluated toward its overall evaluation, then it is skipped. The overall evaluation of the expression is said to be ***short-circuited.*** Note that short-circuit evaluation can only occur with the && and || operators.

EXERCISES 13.2.2

1. a. Using the truth table for the && operator, explain why the second part of the expression above does not need to be evaluated.

b. Should *age* have been 14, would a short-circuit evaluation occur?
2. Consider the expression *age < 2 || age > 12*.
   a. Evaluate it with *age* set to 1. Does a short-circuit evaluation occur?
   b. Evaluate it with *age* set to 14. Does a short-circuit evaluation occur?
3. Reevaluate logical expressions (d) and (e) in Exercise 13.2.1, 1, taking into account short-circuit evaluation.

Bit-wise operators. There may exist rare situations when you do not want the evaluation to be short-circuited. In these cases, you must use the operators | and & instead. The | operator is called the ***bit-wise* OR** operator, while the & operator is called the ***bit-wise* AND** operator. For example, the use of these operators in the following expressions will guarantee that these expressions will never be short-circuited.

```
age  >=  2   &  age  <=  12
age  <  2    |  age  > 12
```

(A more meaningful example cannot be provided yet and will be postponed until the next section.)

Note that these bit-wise operators are **not** logical operators—they are meant to manipulate bits in memory. Consequently, they are **not** meant to be used in a logical operation, so in that context, their operation may be erroneous at times. For instance, *1 && 2* is true, while *1 & 2* is false. How do you know when it is safe to use them? As long as both operands are 0s or 1s **only,** they work the same as their logical counterparts. Remember that it is rare that logical operators will need to be replaced by these bit-wise operators.

13.2.3 LOGICAL EXPRESSIONS WITHIN ARITHMETIC EXPRESSIONS

Example 13.2.7

Remember that the program for Example 5.2.3 used a formula (totally fictional) that tells the time it takes for a chicken dish or a beef dish to cook. Only the weight of the dish needs to be known. Here is the program again:

```
#include <stdio.h>

main()
{
      float       weight, cook_time;
      int         meat_type;

      printf("Is it (1) beef or (2) chicken ? ");
      scanf("%d", &meat_type);
      printf("Enter the weight of the meat > ");
      scanf("%f", &weight);

      if (meat_type == 1)
      {
            cook_time = 40 + weight * 0.2;
      }
      else
      {
            cook_time = 20 + weight * 0.15;
      }
      printf("The dish will take %.0f minutes to cook", cook_time);
}
```

It was shown (although not recommended) that the *if/else* could be reduced to the following single expression:

```
#include <stdio.h>

main()
```

```
{
        float           weight, cook_time;
        int             meat_type;

        printf("Is it (1) beef or (2) chicken ? ");
        scanf("%d", &meat_type);
        printf("Enter the weight of the meat > ");
        scanf("%f", &weight);
        cook_time = (meat_type1) * (20 + weight * 0.15) -
                    (meat_type2) * (40 + weight * 0.2);
        printf("The dish will take %.0f minutes to cook", cook_time);
}
```

Now, because logical expressions return a number, 0 or 1, they can take part in an arithmetic expression. For instance, the expression

```
cook_time = (meat_type == 1) * (20 + weight * 0.15) +
            (meat_type == 2) * (40 + weight * 0.2)
```

does the same thing as the one shown in the above program. The use of logical expressions within arithmetic expressions obviously reduces the length of a program because they eliminate an *if/else*. Nevertheless, it is advisable to keep the *if/else* instead, since it is more readable.

EXERCISES 13.2.3

1. a. Show that the expression above works the same as that in the preceding program.
   b. The expression above is not strictly logically equivalent to the *if/else* with which we started. To see that, suppose the user entered the meat code 3 by mistake. Compare the calculation of the cook time with either method.
   c. Suggest a correction to the expression so as to make it logically equivalent to the *if/else* statement.

2. Reduce the following piece of code to a single expression:

```
if (num > 0)
{
        num = -num;
}
absolute = num;
```

3. Write a logical expression that is equivalent to the following *if/else* structures. Assume that *ok* is of type *int* and may contain a 0 or 1 only.
   a.
```
if (ok)
{
        temp = line + 2;
}
else
{
        temp = line;
}
```
   b.
```
if (ok)
{
        temp = line;
}
else
{
        temp = line + 2;
}
```

4. In question 3 above, suppose that *ok* is of type *float* and could contain any number. Would your solutions still work? If not, modify them so that they work.

5. Eliminate the use of an *if/else* chain in the following segment by replacing it with a single expression that is equivalent:

```
increase = 0.0;
if (mark <= 70 && attend >= 0.9)
{
      increase = 0.07;
}
else if (mark >= 71 && mark <= 95)
{
      increase = 0.03;
}
new_mark = mark * (1 + increase);
```

6. Eliminate the use of an *if/else* in the following segment:

```
range = income < 20000 || income > 29000;
if (range)
{
      printf("Tax is %f\n", income * 0.17 + 300);
      printf("count is now %d\n", count);
}
else
{
      printf("Tax is %f\n", income * 0.29 + 100);
      printf("count is now %d\n", count = count + 1);
}
```

13.2.4 COMMON ERRORS AND TRAPS

The following information will help you avoid making programming errors:

Do not forget the potential occurrence for a short-circuit evaluation. In some situations you will not want the evaluation to be short-circuited. (Such an example cannot be provided yet and will be postponed until the next section.)

SUPPLEMENTARY EXERCISES 13.2

1. This question is about implicit conversions, format codes, and assignment operators. Below you will find a program that reads as input your:

   - Initials
   - Salary per year
   - Education level (1 to 12)
   - Height (meters)
   - Age
   - Weight (kilos)

   If your age is 18, it sends the message "Welcome to the adult world!" It also echoes your input in the following way:

   - The initials, education level, and age are echoed as read in.
   - The height is converted and echoed in millimeters and feet. The conversions factors are: 1000 for meters to millimeters; 3.289 for meters to feet. The conversion to feet should be rounded off to the nearest integer.
   - The weight is converted and echoed in milligrams and pounds. The conversion factors are: 1000000 for kilos to milligrams; 2.205 for kilos to pounds. The conversion to pounds should be truncated to an integer.

Following is an example of what your output should look like:

Enter your initials > JPC
Enter your education level, age, and salary > 12 18 27670.08
Enter your height and weight > 1.72 74.08

Remark: Welcome to the adult world!

Echo of the data read in:

initials = JPC
education level = 12, age = 18
height: in millimeters is 1720, in feet 6 (rounded off)
weight: in milligrams is 74080, in pounds 163 (truncated)

The following program is supposed to produce this output. However, it contains many errors. (There are **no** compilation errors, though.)

```
#include <stdio.h>

#define  CONV_M_F       3.289
#define  CONV_K_P       2.205

main()
{
    int     age,    educ,   salary, temp;
    float   height, weight;
    int     c1,     c2,     c3;

    printf("%3cEnter your initials > ");
    scanf("%c%c%c", &c1, &c2, &c3);
    printf("%3sEnter your education level, age, and salary > ", ' ');
    scanf("%d%f", educ, &age, &salary);
    printf("Enter your height and weight > ", " ");
    scanf("%f",&height);
    if (age = 18)
          printf("\nRemark: Welcome to the adult world!\n");
    printf("%20s", "\nEcho of the data read in:\n\n");
    printf("initials = %s %s %s\n", c1, c2, c3);
    printf("education level = %f, age = %d", educ, age);
    printf("height: in millimeters is %5d, in feet   %3d (roundoff)",
           height * 1000, temp = height * CONV_M_F);
    printf("weight: in milligrams  is %5d, in pounds %3d (truncated)",
           weight * 1000000, weight * CONV_K_P);
}
```

Your task is to locate those places where the code fails, and fix it.
Hints:

- Many statements (perhaps even all of them?) contain at least one error, except the first six, which **do not** contain any errors.
- All of the statements are needed; they simply need to be fixed. Thus, do not strike out any statements and do not add any new ones.
- You may declare new variables, though, if you think you will need some in order to fix the statements.

2. A teacher asked her class to write a C program that calculates the net profit projection of a fictional business over a number of years. The first year saw 100 sales at $500 profit each. The number of sales will increase by 20% each year. From this, the advertising and operating costs are deducted, giving the projected net profit of each year. A student completed the following program:

```
#include <stdio.h>

main()
```

```
{
    int qty_sales = 100,profit_per_sale = 500,increase_ad = 2;
    double op_cost = 10000;
    double net_profit = 0,old_net_profit = 0,ad_cost = 1000;
    float increase_qty_sales = 1.20;
    int year = 1996;

    printf("\n\n              Net Profit Projection");
    printf("\n\n     Year    Sales          Ad Costs    Net Profit");

    printf("\n\n    %d      %4.2lf           %4.2lf          %4.2lf",
           year,qty_sales,ad_cost,
           net_profit = qty_sales * profit_per_sale
                        ad_cost  op_cost);
    do
    {
          year++;
          ad_cost *= increase_ad;
          qty_sales *= increase_qty_sales;
          old_net_profit = net_profit;
          net_profit = 0;

          net_profit = (qty_sales * profit_per_sale)
                        ad_cost  op_cost;

          printf("\n\n    %d      %4.2lf      %4.2lf"
                 "              %4.2lf",
                 year,qty_sales,ad_cost,
                 net_profit = qty_sales * profit_per_sale -
                              ad_cost  op_cost);
    }
    while (net_profit > old_net_profit);
    printf("\n The profit per sale is always %d",profit_per_sale);
    printf("\n The operating cost is %lf the first year",op_cost);
}
```

He ran this program and obtained a very troubling result:

Net Profit Projection

Year	Sales	Ad Costs	Net Profit
1996	2.00	–3.91910664854026e+202	0.00
1997	2.00	0.00	0.00
1998	2.00	3.10503618461283e+231	0.00
1999	2.00	2.00	0.00
2000	2.00	1.39234637989471e+188	0.00

The profit per sale is always 500
The operating cost is 10000.000000 the first year

He handed the program to his teacher, lamenting that he could not see why it would not work.

a. Find the problem and fix it.
b. Note that the program's coding style is quite poor. Brush it up by answering the following questions:
   i. Which of the default setting operators are appropriate?
   ii. Some variables never change. Which ones don't and what should be done with them?
   iii. Is the use of a *do/while* appropriate?
   iv. The method of generating the table is poor. Suggest a better one. Also, some of the format codes are poorly chosen.
   v. Is the use of an assignment operator in the *printf()* useful?
   vi. Improve the general layout.

EXAMPLES OF FANCY TRICKS WITH OPERATORS

This section shows some nifty tricks that involve devising expressions with assignment operators and logical expressions. These tricks enable a programmer to shorten a program further, although this is not always desirable.

Example 13.3.1

The assignment operator may also be part of a condition. For instance, the following program asks for two teams' win-loss-tie standings. Then it determines which team has the best standing.

```
#include <stdio.h>

main()
{
    int score1, score2, w1, w2, l1, l2, t1, t2;

    printf("Enter the number of wins, losses, and ties for team 1 > ");
    scanf("%d%d%d", &w1, &l1, &t1);
    printf("Enter the number of wins, losses, and ties for team 2 > ");
    scanf("%d%d%d", &w2, &l2, &t2);
    if ((score1 = 2 * w1 + t1) > (score2 = 2 * w2 + t2))
    {
          printf("Team 1 has a better standing\n");
    }
    else
    {
          printf("Team 2 has a better standing\n");
    }
    printf("The teams' scores were: Team 1 %d, Team 2 %d\n",
                score1, score2);
}
```

A win gains 2 points, a tie 1 point, and a loss no point. To see how the *if* condition is evaluated, suppose the user entered the following:

Enter the number of wins, losses, and ties for team 1 > 8 1 2
Enter the number of wins, losses, and ties for team 2 > 5 0 4

The expression in the *if* condition is evaluated as follows:

```
(score1  =  2  *  w1  +  t1)  >  (score2  =  2  *  w2  +  t2)
(score1  =  2  *  w1  +  t1)
            2  *  8
              16
              16     +  2
                  18
score1   =        18
         18
                                 (score2  =  2  *  w2  +  t2)
                                             2  *  5
                                               10
                                               10     +  4
                                                   14
                                  score2  =        14
                                          14
         18                   >           14
                              1
```

The number 18 is assigned to *score1* and 14 to *score2*. The condition is true. This condition does two things: it calculates the scores for both teams, and it compares them.

Example 13.3.2

Revisit the program of Example 3.2.12, which calculates the total weight of a wheelbarrow's contents, consisting of two boxes. One contains bricks each weighing 1,200 grams; the other contains rods each weighing 650 grams. Here is that program again:

```
#include <stdio.h>

main()
{
        int  box1, box2;
        long weight;

        printf("Enter the number of bricks in box one > ");
        scanf("%d", &box1);
        printf("Enter the number of rods in box two > ");
        scanf("%d", &box2);

        weight = box1 * 1200 + box2 * 650;
        printf("The total weight is %ld grams\n", weight);
}
```

It was explained that implicit conversions would occur in the formula that calculates the weight, as shown in Figure 13.3.1.

Figure 13.3.1

```
            Evaluation                                    Type of values

weight = box1 * 1200 + box2 * 650      weight = box1 * 1200 + box2 * 650
           24   * 1200                                 i  *   i
             28800                                        i
                         41   * 650                                   i  *   i
                           26650                                         i
             28800    +    26650                          i       +      i
                    55450                                        i[1]
```

Explanation

1. The cell allocated for the end result is of type *int.* 55450 is too big to fit in it. This is the problem.

   Example 3.2.12 showed three methods for getting around this problem. Here they are summarized:

1. Perform the calculation in three steps. Use two more *long* variables and store the results of the two multiplications in them.
2. Simply declare the variables *box1* and *box2* of type *long int,* even though their values would never exceed, say, a hundred or so.
3. Simply insert an *L* immediately to the right of the constants 1200 and 650. This tells the C compiler to store these constants in a cell of type *long int,* not *int.*

Using assignment operators within an expression gives us a fourth method, which is really a shortened version of method 1:

```
long  temp1, temp2;
weight = (temp_lg1 = box1 * 1200) + (temp_lg2 = box2 * 650);
```

EXERCISE 13.3.1

Verify that this fourth method works by evaluating it given the values 24 for *box1* and 41 for *box2.*

Example 13.3.3

The following program simply reads numbers from a file named LIST and stores the summation in a file named SUM:

```
#include <stdio.h>

main()
{
    int     sum, num;
    FILE * ifp;
    FILE * ofp;

    ifp = fopen("LIST", "r");
    if (ifp == NULL)
    {
        printf("Could not open input file\n");
    }
    ofp = fopen("SUM", "w");
    if (ofp == NULL)
    {
        printf("Could not open output file\n");
    }
    if (ifp != NULL && ofp != NULL)
    {
        sum = 0;
        while (fscanf(ifp, "%d", &num) != EOF)
        {
            sum += num;
        }
        fprintf(ofp, "The sum is %d.\n", sum);
        fclose(ifp);
        fclose(ofp);
    }
}
```

This program can be shortened. The first two *if* statements can be changed to:

```
if ((ifp = fopen("LIST", "r")) == NULL)
{
    printf("Could not open input file\n");
}
if ((ofp = fopen("SUM", "w")) == NULL)
{
    printf("Could not open output file\n");
}
```

Here is how these conditions are evaluated: Suppose that the file LIST cannot be opened, causing *fopen()* to return a 0. The *if* would then evaluate as follows:

```
if ((ifp = fopen("LIST", "r")) == NULL)
    (ifp = fopen("LIST", "r"))
           fopen("LIST", "r")
                    0
     ifp =          0
           0
           0                     == NULL
                      1
if (                  1                 )
if (               "true"               )
```

Note that 0 is assigned to *ifp*. In fact, the program can be shortened even more:

```
#include <stdio.h>

main()
{
    int     sum, num;
    FILE * ifp;      /* file pointer variables */
    FILE * ofp;

    if (((ifp = fopen("LIST", "r")) != NULL) &&
            ((ofp = fopen("SUM", "w")) != NULL))
    {
            sum = 0;
            while (fscanf(ifp, "%d", &num) != EOF)
            {
               sum += num;
            }
            fprintf(ofp, "The sum is %d.\n", sum);
            fclose(ifp);
            fclose(ofp);
    }
    else
    {
            printf("A file could not be opened\n");
    }
}
```

The *if* condition does three things in one:

1. It tries to open each file.
2. It checks if each can be opened.
3. It verifies if both files can be opened.

We have seen three examples of the inclusion of the assignment operator as part of an expression or condition. This technique should not be overused, though. In the above example, it is overused; the condition is hard to understand at first glance.

EXERCISES 13.3.2

1. Suppose that the file LIST is successfully opened but the file SUM is not. Show how the long condition above is evaluated.
2. The following segment asks the user first to enter two numbers, then to enter three others. If at least three of them were read in properly, then it issues a congratulatory message. Shorten the segment.

```
success1 = scanf("%d%d", &a, &b);
if (success1 == NULL)
{
      printf("None could be read\n");
}
success2 = scanf("%d%d%d", &c, &d, &e);
if (success2 == NULL)
{
      printf("None could be read\n");
}
if (success1 + success2 >= 3)
{
      printf("Pretty good\n");
```

```
        printf("Only %d entries could not be read\n",
              5 - (success1 + success2));
}
```

Note that the function *scanf()* always returns the number of items that it successfully read in.

3. Shorten the following segment:

```
success1 = scanf("%d%d", &a, &b);
success2 = scanf("%d%d%d", &c, &d, &e);
if (success1 > 1 || success2 >= success1)
{
        printf("Successfully read %d times, first time\n",
               success1);
        printf("Successfully read %d times, second time\n",
               success2);
}
```

Is your solution free of the side effects explained in Subsection 13.3.1?

13.3.1 COMMON ERRORS AND TRAPS

The following information will help you avoid common programming errors:

The use of assignment operators within an expression must be used carefully. Following is an example in which one is not used with such care. The following program simply asks for two numbers and then it displays their ratio. Note that it also validates the numbers. (The solution is based on that of Supplementary Exercise 8.1, 3.):

```
#include <stdio.h>

main()
{
      char   zero, fail;
      float  a, b;

      printf("Enter two numbers: ");
      while ((fail = scanf("%f%f", &a, &b) < 2) || zero = (b == 0))
      {
            if (zero)
            {
                  printf("Cannot divide by zero\n");
            }
            if (fail)
            {
                  printf("The scanf() failed\n");
            }
            printf("Enter two numbers again: ");
      }
      printf("The division is %f\n", a / b);
}
```

Suppose the program is run with the following data:

```
Enter two numbers: 7 0
Cannot divide by zero
Enter two numbers again: u 9
Cannot divide by zero
The scanf() failed
Enter two numbers again: 7 9
The division is 0.777778
```

In the second set of data, the number 9 is not zero! What happened? Here is what caused the erroneous message after the input *u 9*. The first time that the *while* condition was reached, it was evaluated as follows:

```
while ((fail = scanf("%f%f", &a, &b) < 2) || (zero = (b == 0)))
               scanf("%f%f", &a, &b) < 2
                        2            < 2
                               0
      (fail =                  0       )
                     0
                     0                        (zero = (b == 0))
                                                       0 == 0
                                                          1
                                               zero =     1
                                                      1
                     0                   ||           1
                                    1
```

The second time that the loop was executed, the condition was evaluated as follows:

```
while ((fail = scanf("%f%f", &a, &b) < 2) || (zero = (b == 0)))
               scanf("%f%f", &a, &b) < 2
                        0            < 2
                               1
      fail =                   1
                     1
                     1                   ||
```

The evaluation is short-circuited: the second operand to the || is not evaluated because it does not need to be. This implies that the variable *zero* will not be reassigned; it remains at 1, even though *b* is no longer zero. This is what caused the erroneous message. Tricky, isn't it? How do you fix the bug?

- Using the bit-wise OR operator (Subsection 13.2.2), tell the compiler not to short-circuit the evaluation. The condition will become:

  ```
  while ((fail = scanf("%f%f", &a, &b) < 2) | (zero = (b == 0)))
  ```

  No short-circuit will occur now.
- The best remedy is to simplify the condition by taking the assingments out of the condition. Do this as an exercise.

13.4 THE INCREMENT/DECREMENT OPERATORS

Section 9.1 introduced these operators in their simplest context. They may be used in more complex ways. There are two kinds of increment/decrement operators: the postfix and the prefix ones, and the outcome of each differs, as this section will show.

13.4.1 HOW THEY REALLY WORK

Three examples will illustrate how these increment/decrement operators work. (They are not as trivial as they seemed in Section 9.1!)

Example 13.4.1

Let us evaluate the expression *b* = *a*++, in which *a* and *b* are integer variables, and the ++ operator is in the postfix position. Suppose that *a* contains 3:

```
b = a++
    3                    The value of a, 3, is used; then
                         a is incremented by one, becoming 4.
```

```
b = 3                    The assignment operator is applied.
  3                      3 is returned.
```

This single expression does the same as the following two:

```
b = a;
a = a + 1;
```

When the ++ is in the prefix position, the expression is evaluated differently:

```
b = ++a
    4                    The variable a is first incremented;
                           then 4 is used.
b = 4                    The assignment operator is applied.
  4                      4 is returned.
```

This expression alone does the same as the following two:

```
a = a + 1;
b = a;
```

Of course, the decrement operator can be used similarly. For example:

```
b = --a
    2                    The variable a is first decremented;
                           then 2 is used.
b = 2                    The assignment operator is applied.
  2                      2 is returned.
```

To fully understand how these operators work, let us consider more complex expressions.

Example 13.4.2

Suppose that *a* contains 3 and *b* contains 7. Let us evaluate the expression *result* = *a*++ – *b*++. There are two increment operators. Table 13.3.1 indicated that the associativity is from right to left, so the ++ to the far right will be executed first:

```
result = a++ - b++
                 7       7 is used in the expression;
                           then b is incremented by 1.
         3               3 is used in the expression;
                           then a is incremented by 1.

         3   - 7
          -4             -4 is returned.
result =  -4
```

In effect, this expression is equivalent to the following:

```
result = a - b;
a = a + 1;
b = b + 1;
```

Example 13.4.3

Now let us change the postfix *b*++ to a prefix ++*b* and reevaluate the expression. Assume the same initial values as above:

```
result = a++ - ++b
                         b is incremented by 1;
                   8     then 8 is used in the expression.

           3             3 is used in the expression;
                         then the variable a is incremented.

         3  -  8
```

```
              -5
result =      -5
```

The result is different from the one in Example 13.4.2. In effect, this expression is equivalent to the following:

```
b = b + 1;
result = a - b;
a = a + 1;
```

EXERCISES 13.4.1

1. Write four very short expressions that each add 1 to the variable *num.*
2. Write an expression to perform each of the following:
   a. Assign the sum of *a* and *b* to *c;* then increment *b* by 1.
   b. Assign the sum of *a* and *b* to *c* after *b* is decremented by 1.
   c. Increment *a* by 1; then subtract it from *b.*
   d. Add *a* and *b,* then decrement *a* by 1.
3. What will the following program display?

```
#include <stdio.h>

main()
{
        int  num;

        num = 29;
        printf("%d\n", num++);
        printf("%d\n", num);
        printf("%d\n", ++num);
        printf("%d\n", num);
}
```

4. Evaluate the expression *--y == 8 && !(a++ <= 2),* in which *y* is 9 and *a* is 1.

13.4.2 USE INCREMENT/DECREMENT OPERATORS TO SHORTEN THE CODE

The main use of these increment/decrement operators is to shorten a program.

Example 13.4.4

Consider the following loop:

```
#include <stdio.h>

main()
{
        int sum, num;

        sum = 0;
        num = 12;
        while (num != 0)
        {
                sum = sum + num;
                num = num - 1;
        }
        printf("sum = %d", sum);
}
```

The statement *num = num – 1* is always performed just prior to reevaluating the condition *num != 0*. This means that the sequence of execution is:

Execute *num = num - 1;*
Test the condition *while (num != 0)*
Execute *sum = sum + num;*
Execute *num = num - 1;*
Test the condition *while (num != 0)*
Execute *sum = sum + num;*
etc.

The first two statements can be joined in one expression: *while (––num != 0),* right? The prefix position of the decrement operator will ensure that *num* will be decreased by 1 before the condition is evaluated. The loop is now shortened to:

```
sum = 0;
num = 13;
while --num != 0)
{
        sum = sum + num;
}
printf("sum = %d", sum);
```

Note that *num* must now be initialized to 13, not 12. (Why is that so?) Actually, the loop can be shortened much more. From Section 13.2, we now know that *while (––num != 0)* is equivalent to *while (––num).* Also the use of a *for* loop and of the shorthand operator += give us the most shortened loop, shown below:

```
for (sum = 0, num = 13; --num; sum += num) ;
printf("sum = %d", sum);
```

Notice the empty loop before the last semicolon in the first line.

We started with six lines of code and reduced them to two lines. Not bad! This still does not make this latter loop better than the former one. It is all a matter of taste. In fact, the techniques of shortening a segment of code presented in this and the previous section should be used with reserve. Often a shortened program is not highly readable.

EXERCISES 13.4.2

1. What is the value of *i* after each of the following loops is complete?

a.
```
i = 1;
while (++i <= 10) ;
```
b.
```
i = 1;
while (i++ <= 10) ;
```
c.
```
i = 0;
while (i < 5)
{
        ++i;
        j *= i;
}
```
d.
```
i = 1;
do
{
        ++i;
}
while (i++ < 10);
```
e.
```
i = 1;
while (i <= 20)
```

```
  {
          j = ++i;
          k = i++;
  }
```

f. `for (i=0; x=i++; i < 10; ++i) ;`

g. `for (sum=0, i=1; i <= 10; sum += i++) ;`

h.
```
for (++j, i+=j; i < 100; ++i)
  {
          k *= j++;
  }
```

2. Shorten the following program as much as possible:

```
i = i + 1;
while (i < r)
{
        a = a + 1;
        r = r - (a * 5 + i);
        i = i + 1;
        r = r - 1;
}
```

3. What will the following programs display?

a.
```
void increment(int a)
  {
          printf("a = %d\n", a++);
  }

  main()
  {
          int  i;

          for (i=0; i < 10; ++i)
          {
                  increment(++i);
                  printf("i = %d\n", i);
          }
  }
```

b.
```
a = 3;
  if (--a)
  {
          printf("Can't be\n");
  }
  if (a-- > 1)
  {
          printf("Hello\n");
  }
  if (a++ + 2)
  {
          printf("a = %d\n", a);
  }
```

13.4.3 BE WARY OF SYSTEM DEPENDENCIES

Be extra careful when using increment/decrement operators. Overusing them may lead to mind-boggling bugs. Their uses in the four examples above are fine. However, even a minimal change to them could cause trouble, as Example 13.4.5 illustrates.

Example 13.4.5

In Example 13.4.3, let us change the *++b* to *++a.* Assume that *a* contains 5. You would expect the evaluation of the expression to proceed exactly the same way as before:

```
result = a++ - ++a
                                  a is incremented by 1;
               6                  then 6 is used in the expression.

          6                       6 is used in the expression;
                                  then the variable a is incremented.

          6 -  6
             0
result =     0
```

The variable *a* becomes 7 when the evaluation of this expression is terminated. Surprisingly, some compilers would evaluate this expression in a different order, that is, the ++ to the left might be evaluated first:

```
result = a++ - ++a
          5                       5 is used in the expression;
                                    then a is incremented by 1.
               7                  a is incremented by 1;
                                    then 7 is used in the expression.

          5 -  7
            -2
```

The variable *a* still becomes 7 when the evaluation is terminated, but now -2, not 0, is stored in the variable *result.* In other words, the expression is **not** in effect equivalent to the following statements, even though the table of operator precedence says that it should be:

```
a = a + 1;
result = a - a;
a = a + 1;
```

Why do compilers evaluate such expressions differently? The reasons are the same as explained in Section 13.1: the evaluation of an expression is system dependent. The rule of thumb to tell if an expression involving ++ or -- is system dependent is as follows:

> When an expression uses the ++ or the -- operator on a variable and then uses that same variable some other place within the **same** expression, its evaluation is unpredictable.

Example 13.4.6

The above rule extends to function calls as well. For instance, the display from the following program is unpredictable:

```
main()
{
        int     i;

        while (i < 10)
        {
                printf("%d  %d\n", i, ++i);
        }
}
```

There is no telling which of the two arguments of the *printf()* will be evaluated first.

EXERCISES 13.4.3

1. Could any one of the following cause an unpredictable result?
   a. *x++ * --y*

b. $x = ++y - x++$
c. $fcn(j++, j++)$
d. $ans = a / 2 + 15 * (1 - a++)$
e. $ans = a / 2 + 15 * (1 - ++a)$
f. $x++ > x$

2. Suppose variable n contains 6 at the time the expression $n = n++$ is reached. What would be the value of n afterward? Answer the same question with $n += n++$.

13.4.4 COMMON ERRORS AND TRAPS

Avoid programming bugs by never overlooking the system dependency of the increment/decrement operators.

13.5 THE CONDITIONAL OPERATOR

There are some situations in which the use of the *if/else* is routinely needed. For example, it can be used to find the largest of two numbers, as shown below:

```
printf("Enter two numbers > ");
scanf("%d%d", &num1, &num2);
if (num1 > num2)
{
      max = num1;
}
else
{
      max = num2;
}
printf("The largest number is %d\n", max);
```

This *if/else* statement requires too many lines for such a common and simple operation. Therefore, the C language provides a ***conditional operator*** to abbreviate the process.

13.5.1 THE MECHANISM OF THE CONDITIONAL OPERATOR

Example 13.5.1

Let us abbreviate the *if/else* above with the use of the conditional operator, shown in the line of bold type:

```
printf("Enter two numbers > ");
scanf("%d%d", &num1, &num2);
max = num1 > num2 ? num1 : num2;
printf("The largest number is %d\n", max);
```

The conditional operator is symbolized as ?: and requires three operands, as shown in Figure 13.5.1.

Figure 13.5.1

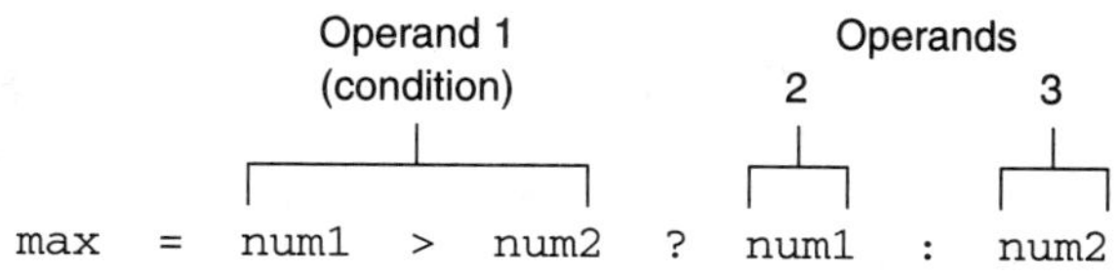

Here is how this operator works: Suppose that *num1* and *num2* contain 3 and 5, respectively. Note that operand 1 is a condition. If it is true, then the value of operand 2 is assigned to *max;* otherwise the value of operand 3 is assigned to *max.* Note that the condition is followed by a question mark and that two alternatives, operands 2 and 3, are separated by a colon.

Now let us see how the expression *max = num1 > num2 ? num1 : num2* is evaluated by the compiler. Note that three operators are present: =, > and ?:. As usual, the compiler will execute first the one with the most precedence, which is >; = has the least precedence: The evaluation of the expression is shown in Figure 13.5.2.

Figure 13.5.2

```
max = num1 > num2 ? num1 : num2
        3   >  5
             0
             0        ?  3   :   5
                      5
max =                 5
             5
```

Note the three operands 0, 3, and 5. 5 is returned because the condition *num1 > num2* is false.

Let us look at another useful application.

Example 13.5.2

The following program uses the conditional operator to display the words *yes* or *no.* Note the use of double quotation marks around the words.

```
main()
{
        char  ans;

        printf("Would you accept a bonus ticket? (y/n) ");
        scanf("\n%c", &ans);
        printf("You answered %s\n", ans == 'y' ? "yes" : "no");
}
```

EXERCISES 13.5.1

1. Change the conditional operator in Example 13.5.2 to an *if/else.*
2. Change each *if/else* statements below to a conditional operator:
   a.
```
if (sales > 10000)
{
        rate = 0.08;
}
else
{
rate = 0.10;
}
```
   b.
```
if (income >= 20000 &&
        income <= 29999)
{
        tax = 8000;
}
else
{
        tax = 2000;
}
```
   c.
```
if (a == b)
{
        flag = 1;
}
else
{
```

```
            flag = 0;
    }
```

3. Reduce the code of the following function to a simple conditional operator:

```
char  lower(char ch)
{
      if (isupper(ch))
      {
            return ch + ('a' - 'A');
      }
      else
      {
            return ch;
      }
}
```

4. Consider the following expression:

```
t = ++x < 9 ? x++ : 5
```

   a. Suppose that *x* starts as 7. Is the value stored in *t* unpredictable? What is the value of *x* afterwards?
   b. Suppose that *x* starts as 6. Is the value stored in *t* unpredictable? What is the value of *x* afterwards?

5. Modify the function *roll_dice()* developed in Exercise 10.3.1, 8, that simulates the roll of two dice. Now the function will tell if both dice showed the same number or not. Use the conditional operator. Include this function in a program that will allow the user to roll the dice repeatedly. For example:

```
I rolled the dice and got the same numbers!
Should I roll the dice again? (y/n) y
I rolled the dice and got different numbers!
Should I roll the dice again? (y/n) n
Bye
```

   [***Hint:*** Only the words *the same* and *different* differ in the message. Use the conditional operator within a *printf( ).*]

6. Write a function named *absolute()* that uses the conditional operator to return the absolute value of the argument.

13.5.2 WHEN SHOULD A CONDITIONAL OPERATOR BE USED?

The conditional operator is meant to be used only when both alternatives consist of one statement. In the following two examples, the conditional operator is inappropriate.

Example 13.5.3

The *if/else* in the following cannot be transformed into a ?: operator. (Why is that so?)

```
printf("Enter the weight of both persons > ");
scanf("%f%f", &weight1, &weight2);
if (weight1 != weight2)
{
      same = 0;
      printf("These people should be in different categories\n");
}
else
{
      same = 1;
      printf("These people may be in the same category\n");
}
```

Example 13.5.4

In fact, even when both alternatives consist of only one statement, it may not be a good idea to use a conditional operator. For example:

```
printf("Enter two numbers > ");
scanf("%d%d", &num1, &num2);
if (num1 > num2)
{
      printf("The first number is the largest\n");
}
else
{
      printf("The second number is the largest\n");
}
```

The following conditional operator will do the same job:

```
printf("Enter two numbers > ");
scanf("%d%d", &num1, &num2);
num1 > num2 ? printf("The first number is the largest\n") :
               printf("The second number is the largest\n");
```

This is a little awkward to read, so it should be avoided. Yet the conditional operator may still be a good choice if the code is looked at in a different way, as shown below:

```
printf("Enter two numbers > ");
scanf("%d%d", &num1, &num2);
printf("The %s number is the largest\n", num1 > num2 ?
                                        "first" : "second");
```

In effect, both segments do the same. If *num1* > *num2* is true, then the string "first" will be passed as the argument to *printf();* otherwise, it will be the string "second." The format code *%s* will capture whichever is there.

A conditional operator can be used as part of a larger expression, as the following example shows. This is not often advisable, though.

Example 13.5.5

Let us change the following *if/else* statement to a conditional operator:

```
if (water_usage < 1000)
{
      cost = water_usage * 0.0025 + 24;
}
else
{
      cost = water_usage * 0.0016 + 24;
}
```

Since the only information that depends on the condition is the coefficient, the *if* statement really only needs to set the coefficient to 0.0025 or 0.0016. A conditional operator (shown in bold type) can certainly do that:

```
cost = water_usage * (water_usage < 1000 ? 0.0025 : 0.0016) + 24;
```

Of course, this expression is a little difficult to read and probably should be avoided. Nevertheless, let us see how it is evaluated. Suppose that *water_usage* is 550:

```
cost = water_usage * (water_usage < 1000 ? 0.0025 : 0.0016) + 24;
                     (water_usage < 1000 ? 0.0025 : 0.0016)
                          550     < 1000
                                1
                                1         ? 0.0025 : 0.0016
```

```
                                        0.0025
           550      *                   0.0025
                        1.375
                        1.375                                     + 24
                                       25.375
cost =                                 25.375
         25.375
```

EXERCISES 13.5.2

1. The parentheses in the expression above are needed. Explain why by evaluating it without them.
2. How would you write an expression consisting of a series of conditional operators for the following *if/else* chain?

```
if (code == 1)
{
      num = 5;
}
else if (code == 2)
{
      num = 3;
}
else
{
      num = 12;
}
```

13.5.3 COMMON ERRORS AND TRAPS

Avoid a common programming error by never using the conditional operator in inappropriate ways, as explained in this section.

13.6 VARIOUS OPERATIONS WITH CHARACTERS

Section 3.3 briefly introduced the *char* type and ASCII codes. This section picks up the discussion and shows some of the things that may be done with ASCII codes. It will surprise you!

It turns out that all information, no matter the kind, is stored in the memory in form of numeric codes. These codes depend on the computer system in use. There are various coding systems in the world. In an effort to standardize character representations, two coding systems have emerged as the most popular: the EBCDIC (Extended Binary Coded Decimal Interchange Code) and ASCII (American Standard Code for Information Interchange) coding schemes. EBCDIC is used on IBM mainframes, and will not be covered in this book. The ASCII coding system is what most microcomputers and networks use. This section will therefore discuss in detail the ASCII coding scheme.

13.6.1 THE STANDARD ASCII CHARACTER CODES SEQUENCE

First, let us refresh our memory about ASCII codes.

Example 13.6.1

On a computer that operates with the ASCII coding system, the name "The Kid" is stored in memory as the following sequence of numbers:

```
84 104 101 32 75 105 100
T   h   e     K   i   d
```

These numbers are ASCII character codes taken from the ***ASCII character codes sequence.*** Each character is assigned an ASCII code. The ***standard ASCII character code sequence*** is 128 codes long, and consists of all letters, numbers, and punctuation as well as other special characters. (Appendix A includes the full list.)

How to display ASCII codes. To find the ASCII code of a particular character, you may refer to a table such as the one in Appendix A, or you may simply write a C program with a *printf()*. For instance, in the following statement,

```
printf("%d", 'a');
```

the characters *"%d"* tell the program to display the letter that follows as a number, meaning to display the ASCII code. This statement displays the number 97, the ASCII code for the letter *a*. Conversely, to find out which character has a specific ASCII code, you may use a *printf()* again. For instance, in the following statement, the characters *"%c"* tell the program to display the ASCII code that follows as a character. This statement

```
printf("%c", 97);
```

displays the character a, the character for ASCII code 97.

EXERCISES 13.6.1

1. What will the following program display? You may wish to refer to the table of ASCII codes in Appendix A.

```
char  c, d;

c = 'd';
d = 0;
printf("d = %d, c = %c\n", d, c);
c = d;
d = '0';
printf("d = %d, c = %c\n", d, c);
```

2. Write a program that asks the user to enter a character and then displays its ASCII code.
3. Write a program that asks the user to enter an ASCII code between 32 and 126 and then displays its character.
4. Run the program in question 2 through a loop so that the user is asked repeatedly to enter a character.
5. Run the program in question 3 through a loop so that the user is asked repeatedly to enter an ASCII code between 32 and 126.

Control characters. As mentioned before, any information in the computer is stored in a series of ASCII codes. This includes such keystrokes as the Enter key, the Tab key, and so on. When these keys are pressed, a character is actually sent to the screen. These characters are not graphic; they do not show any symbol on the screen. However, their effect can be seen. For example, the Enter key makes the cursor move to the beginning of the next line. These characters are sometimes called ***control characters,*** as opposed to ***printable characters*** such as letters of the alphabet. The printable characters range from codes 32 to 126. All of the others are control characters. Table 13.6.1 gives a sampling of control characters.

There are two ways that these control characters can be sent to the screen. For instance, the bell can be sent to the screen as follows:

```
printf("\a");          or          printf("%c", 7);
```

Note the *c* in the second statement. It tells the computer to display the number 7 as a character. (What would happen if you mistakenly used a *d?*) The ASCII code 7 will produce a bell sound, a rather short high-pitched sound.

Table 13.6.1

Character	ASCII code	Written in C as an escape sequence	Keystroke, if one exists
null	0	\0	
bell	7	\a	Ctrl-G**
backspace	8	\b	←**
horizontal tab	9	\t	Tab
newline	10	\n	Enter
vertical tab	11	\v	Ctrl-K**
form feed	12	\f	Ctrl-L**
carriage return	13	\r	Home**
escape	27	ESC*	Esc
delete	127	DEL*	Del**

*No escape sequence exists for this key. Instead, a symbolic constant is used.

**Machine dependent. The effect of the keystroke may differ across computer systems.

13.6.2 SOME APPLICATIONS WITH CONTROL CHARACTERS

Example 13.6.2

The following program simulates a clock countdown starting at 60 "seconds." The bell sounds every ten "seconds."

```
#include <stdio.h>

main()
{
   int   seconds;    /* just a counter */

   printf("Count down:\n");
   for (seconds=60; seconds > 0; seconds--)
   {
        printf("\rThere are %2d seconds left", seconds);
        if (seconds % 10 == 0)
        {
             printf("\a");      /* sound the bell every ten "seconds" */
        }
   }
}
```

The escape character \r in the second *printf()* simply returns the cursor at the beginning of the current line. Then the message is redisplayed on the same line. For example:

There are 60 seconds left

←——————————— The cursor is returned.

———————————→ The message is redisplayed.

The cursor sweeps back and forth, redisplaying the message every time. The cursor never moves to the next line.

EXERCISES 13.6.2

1. In Example 13.6.2, what would be displayed if the \r wasn't present?
2. Write a function named *ascii()* that returns a 1 if its argument is an ASCII code (within 0 to 127), or a 0 otherwise.
3. Write a function named *printable()* that returns a 1 if its argument is a printable, or a 0 otherwise.

Example 13.6.3

Let us modify the program of Example 13.6.2 above so that the cursor will redisplay only the part of the message that shows the seconds. It will not sweep over the whole message, as it did in Example 13.6.2. For instance:

There are 60 seconds left
← Move back the cursor.
→ Redisplay the seconds.

The trick is to display the whole message once, leaving the cursor on the same line:

There are 60 seconds left

The cursor is at the end of the message, and then it moves back under the digit 6 of the number 60. This is accomplished by using the escape character *\b* (backspace) 15 times:

There are 60 seconds left
←———————

Then the number 59 is displayed. To display the remaining numbers, the cursor is simply swept backward over the two digits by using the *\b* twice.

There are 59 seconds left
←
→

This is done over again for each second counted down. Following is the program:

```
#include <stdio.h>

main()
{
    int   seconds;

    printf("Count down:\n");
    printf("There are %2d seconds left", 60);
    printf("\b\b\b\b\b\b\b\b\b\b\b\b\b\b\b");      /* move the cursor back */
    for (seconds=60; seconds > 0; seconds--)                 /* 15 spaces */
    {
        printf("%2d\b\b", seconds);             /* display the number and */
        if (seconds % 10 == 0)                    /* move the cursor back */
        {
            printf("\a");                               /* sound the bell */
        }
    }
}
```

Although both Examples 13.6.2 and 13.6.3 produce the same display, the latter one displays the numbers faster. (Why is that so?)

EXERCISES 13.6.3

1. Modify the program in Example 10.4.9 so that, in addition to the error message, the bell will sound if a file cannot be opened.
2. Do the following two statements produce the same effect?

   `printf("\n\r\b");` and `printf("%c%c%c", 10, 13, 8);`

3. What will the following code display on the screen?

```
printf("%c%c%c%c%c%c%c%c%c%c%c%c%c%c%c",
          72, 97, 8, 105, 33, 11, 72, 97,
          9, 33, 13, 66, 121, 101, 33);
```

4. a. It was said in Subsection 3.3.5 that *putchar()* cannot be used to display numeric data, so the segment below would produce errors at the lines indicated with asterisks. Does it? Explain.

```
main()
{
        putchar('a');
        putchar('b');
        putchar(99);*
        printf("Msg1");
        putchar('\n');
        putchar('d');
        putchar(10);*
        printf("Msg2\n");
}
```

   b. Suggest a single *printf()* that can produce the same output.

5. Use the control character \v to produce a function *big_backslash()* that displays a big backslash. For instance:

```
\
    \
        \
            \
                \
```

   The number of slashes desired is passed as a argument. (***Note:*** Since the control character \v may behave differently across different systems, your system may not be able to produce the display shown here.)

13.6.3 THE EXTENDED ASCII CHARACTER CODES SEQUENCE

The English language has only 26 letters in its alphabet. They all fit nicely within the standard ASCII code sequence. For other languages, such as French and Spanish, accents may be combined with letters to form new letters, such as the *à* or *ô*. For these languages, more codes are needed beyond the first 128. These extra codes constitute the ***extended ASCII code sequence*** and it ranges from codes 128 to 255. For example, the first nine such codes are listed in Table 13.6.2.

Table 13.6.2

ASCII code	Character
128	Ç
129	ü
130	é
131	â
132	ä
133	à
134	å
135	ç
136	ê

Because these codes are not within the standard ones, the characters they represent often differ across computer systems. For instance, in the list above, these characters apply to the IBM PC and compatible computers only. On other systems, they may be entirely different.

EXERCISES 13.6.4

1. Find the extended characters on your system. Write a loop that displays the characters that correspond to ASCII codes from 128 to 256.

2. Using the extended ASCII codes you found in question 1, see if you can write a program that displays the message:

   Déjà Noël! Ça alors.

3. a. Write a function named *whatchar()* that accepts a character and lets you know whether or not it can be displayed and whether or not it is an extended character.
   b. Modify this function so that instead it has two parameters by reference: the first one receives a 1 if the character can be displayed, and a 0 otherwise; the second one receives a 1 if the character is an extended one, or a 0 otherwise.

This extended sequence is still not long enough for such languages as Japanese and Chinese. These languages have so many letters that the code sequence must be extended beyond 255. Such codes cannot fit within one byte so two bytes are needed to store them. Other characters that require two bytes are the function keys F1 to F12, and combination keystrokes involving either Ctrl or Alt and a second key. (The method of reading these keys differs across computer systems and will not be covered here.)

13.6.4 SOME OPERATIONS WITH CHARACTERS

Since characters are stored as their equivalent ASCII codes, i.e., as numbers, they can be involved in arithmetic operations as well. This subsection presents three typical applications.

Converting a letter's case. This is probably the most common application of doing arithmetic with characters.

Example 13.6.4

Let us write a function named *upper()* that simply changes a letter to uppercase. In Section 5.1.4, we saw that the function *toupper()* does precisely this. Here, we will see that this operation can be done with a single arithmetic expression! The trick is to realize that there is a difference of 32 between the ASCII codes of uppercase and lowercase letters; as seen in Table 13.6.3.

Table 13.6.3

Character	ASCII code	Character	ASCII code	Difference
A	65	a	97	97 – 65 = 32
B	66	b	98	98 – 66 = 32
C	67	c	99	99 – 67 = 32
D	68	d	100	100 – 68 = 32
E	69	e	101	101 – 69 = 32
F	70	f	102	102 – 70 = 32
G	71	g	103	103 – 71 = 32
.....	.....	.....	.....	.....

So to convert a letter to uppercase, it is only a matter of taking the lowercase letter and subtracting 32 from its ASCII code:

uppercase ASCII code = lowercase ASCII code – 32

Of course, should the argument already be in uppercase, no conversion is needed. Following is the function *upper()*:

```
char upper(char letter)
{
      char  upper_letter;
```

```
        if (letter >= 'a' && letter <= 'z')
        {
                upper_letter = letter  32;     /* convert to uppercase */
        }
        return upper_letter;
}
```

Here is how the conversion is done. Assume that the argument *letter* contains the letter 'e.' Then the expression would be evaluated as follows:

`upper_letter = letter - 32`	
`'e'  - 32`	
`101  - 32`	Use 101, the ASCII code for 'e.'
`69`	This is the ASCII code for 'E.'
`'E'`	
`upper_letter =   'E'`	'E' is stored.
`'E'`	

Note that *'A'– 'a'* equals 32, so the expression could just the same have been expressed as:

```
upper_letter = letter - ('A' - 'a');
```

Running through the alphabet. It is a very simple matter to single-step through the alphabet. To do this, let us define the functions as in Example 13.6.5.

Example 13.6.5

Let us write a function named *next_char()* that returns the character that comes immediately next after the argument in the ASCII code sequence. This function is surprisingly simple:

```
char next_char(char ch)
{
     return ch + 1;
}
```

That is all! To run through the alphabet is as simple as:

```
char ch;

for (ch='A'; ch <> 'Z'; ch = next_char(ch))
{
      printf("%c", ch);
}
```

EXERCISES 13.6.5

1. Write a function named *lower()* that converts an uppercase letter to lowercase. Do not use C library functions.
2. Evaluate the following expressions:
   a. *'f' + 4 == 'j'*
   b. *'F' + 4 == 'J'*
   c. *'a' + 'B' < 'A' + 'b'*
3. Write a program that simply lists the letters of the alphabet contained within a section specified by the user. Example:

   Enter the first and last letter
   of the section of the alphabet desired > t x

   The letters are t u v w x

Write two versions of the program:

a. Use a loop with a *char* "counter" that runs from the first letter to the last letter of the section.

b. Use a loop again, but now use the *next_char()* function above to run through the letters.

4. Consider the expressions below. Assume the declaration *char ch:*

   a. (int) 'W' – (int) 'Q'

   b. *ch = (char) ((int) 's' – 3)*

   c. *ch = (char) 67*

   Will each expression work? If so, are the cast operators necessary? Why?

5. Why does the following program always produce the message "That's Canadian," even when the currency is American?

```
#include <stdio.h>
#include <stdlib.h>

main()
{
      char currency;

      printf("Enter the currency (C=Canadian, A=American) > ");
      scanf("\n%c", &currency);
      currency = toupper(currency);
      if (currency = 'C')
      {
            printf("That's Canadian");
      }
      else
      {
            printf("That's American");
      }
}
```

6. Write a function named *position()* that returns the position of its argument in the alphabet. For example, 'e' is at position 5. The function should be case insensitive. Also if a nonletter is provided, –1 will be returned.

Encoding a message. This application may be applied to word games, but it is also used in password security systems.

Example 13.6.6

Let us write a program that encodes a message using the encryption method shown in Table 13.6.4.

Table 13.6.4

Letter in message	Changed to	Letter in message	Changed to
space	#		
a	d	A	D
b	e	B	E
c	f	C	F
etc.	etc.	etc.	etc.
x	{	X	[
y	|	Y	\
z	}	Z	]

Note the pattern: each letter is changed to the third one following. For example, look at Table 13.6.5.

Table 13.6.5

Letter in message	Changed to	Difference in code
space	#	'#' – ' ' = 35 – 32 = 3
a	d	'd' – 'a' = 100 – 97 = 3
etc.	etc.	etc.
z	}	'}' – 'z' = 125 – 122 = 3

Assume that the message contains letters (and spaces) only. Following is an example of a run:

Enter a message: Watson I want you
Encoded: Zdwvrq#L#zdqw#Irx

Here is the program that does this:

```
#include <stdio.h>

main()
{
        char  ch;
        printf("Enter a message: ");
        ch = getchar();
        printf("Encoded: ");
        while (ch != '\n' && ch != EOF)[1]
        {
                putchar(ch + ('d' - 'a'));[2]
                ch = getchar();
        }
}
```

Explanations

1. The condition reads as follows:

```
          ch  !=  '\n'  &&  ch  !=  EOF
          |__________|      |__________|
               |                 |
WHILE     Enter key     AND   CTRL-Z           THEN continue looping
          not pressed         not pressed
```

2. Note the argument of *putchar()*. It is an expression that converts the character read to the encoded character. For instance, suppose that *ch* is 'b'. It should be encoded to 'e':

```
 ch + ('d' - 'a')
      (100 - 97 )
             3
'b' +        3
98  +        3
    101
    'e'
```

Then *putchar()* displays this letter.

EXERCISES 13.6.6

1. Based on the encryption method above, write a program that decodes a message, reversing the process of the program above.

2. Write a complex condition so that the loop in Example 13.6.6 is structured as follows:

```
while (___________________________)
{
     putchar(ch - ('d' - 'a'));
}
```

A single statement remain within the body of the loop. (***Hint:*** Use an assignment statement and move the *getchar()* within the condition.)

3. Write a program that encodes a message using the following encryption method:

Letter in message	Changed to	Letter in message	Changed to
space	#		
a	d	A	D
b	e	B	E
c	f	C	F
etc.	etc.	etc.	etc.
x	a	X	A
y	b	Y	B
z	c	Z	C

This is the same encryption method as in Example 13.6.6, except that the letters 'x', 'y', 'z', 'X', 'Y', and 'Z' are encoded as letters. Assume that the message contains letters (and spaces) only. A sample run would look like this:

Enter a message: Where exit the zoo
Encoded: Zkhuh#halw#wkh#crr

4. a. The following program simply reads in a digit as a character, then uses a *switch* statement to store it as a number in the variable *num:*

```
main()
{
      char digit;
      int  num;

      printf("Enter a single digit: ");
      scanf("\n%c", &digit);
      switch(digit)
      {
            case '0': num = 0; break;
            case '1': num = 1; break;
            .....
            case '8': num = 8; break;
            case '9': num = 9; break;
      }
}
```

Replace the *switch* statement with a single very simple arithmetic expression.

b. In a similar fashion, eliminate the need for a *switch* structure in the program in Exercise 8.1.1, 10b.

5. You now know enough to write a solution for Exercise 3.3.5, 7b.
6. Write a program that encodes a message by using the following simplistic encryption method: it adds up the ASCII code from each letter from within the message. This addition constitutes the encoded message. For example:

Enter a message > Cancel exam!
The code for the message is: 1009

Indeed, the message consists of the ASCII code sequence:

```
67 97 110 99 101 108 32 101 120 97 109 33
```

from which only the characters' codes are added up:

```
67+97+110+99+101+108+101+120+97+109 = 1009
```

(***Note:*** This is a very poor encryption method. Can you see why?)

7. Modify the encoding scheme above so that the encoded message is produced by weighing the letters in base 2. The ASCII codes will be offset by 65, which is the code for 'A'. For example, the message above would be encoded as:

$2+32*2+45*2^2+34*2^3+36*2^4+43*2^5+36*2^6+55*2^7+32*2^8+44*2^9 = 7078$

(***Note:*** This is a much better encryption method. Can you see why?)

8. The program below is a special case of the encoding program above: it only encodes messages that are exactly three letters long:

```
main()
{
    char  ch;
    int   code;

    printf("Enter a message > ");
    code = getchar() + getchar() * 2 + getchar() * 4;
    printf("The code for the three-letter message is %d\n", code);
}
```

Is the code predictable? (***Hint:*** Revisit Subsection 13.1.2.)

SUPPLEMENTARY EXERCISES 13.6

1. a. Write a function named *scan_int()* that reads integers very similarly to *scanf()*. It will first read each digit of a number as characters, then these are converted to digits, then these make up the number. Finally this number is returned via a parameter by reference. Any nondigit will indicate the end of the number, at which time *scan_int()* will discard the rest of the line with *fflush(stdin)* and then terminate. Here is the outline of the code desired:

```
______ scan_int(__________________)
{
 .*
 .
 .
}

main()
{
       int  num;

       printf("Enter a number > ");
       scan_int(&num);
       printf("The number read is %d\n", num);
}
```

* Code here makes up the function.
Here is an example of a run:

Enter a number > 42091↵
The number entered is 42091

The following underlined numbers build to the number 42091:

$\underline{4} \times 10^4 + \underline{2} \times 10^3 + \underline{0} \times 10^2 + \underline{9} \times 10^1 + \underline{1} \times 10^0$

b. Add the following feature to the function: should the function hit an invalid data instead of a number, the function will return a 0; otherwise it will return a 1. Here is the *main()*:

```
main()
{
     int  num;
     char success;
     printf("Enter a number > ");
     success = scan_int(&num);
     if (success)
     {
          printf("The number read is %d\n", num);
     }
     else
     {
          printf("Invalid!\n");
     }
```

Here is an example of a run:

Enter a number > quit↵
Invalid!

But the following run is correct:

Enter a number > 17r↵
The number read is 17

In any case, whether a number is read successfully or not, it discards the rest of the line with *fflush(stdin)*.

c. By making a slight change to *scan_int()*, this function can overcome the problem encountered in Exercise 8.1.1, 10a, regardless of the number entered. How? Use that function in a program that reads a list of numbers terminated by the Enter key.

2. a. Write a function named *scan_float()* that reads real numbers just as *scanf()* does. It will read digits and convert to numbers until a dot is reached. Then it will proceed to read the decimal digits until there areno more digits. The following underlined numbers build to the number 420.91.

$$\underline{4}\times 10^2 + \underline{2}\times 10^1 + \underline{0}\times 10^0 + \underline{9}\times 10^{-1} + \underline{1}\times 10^{-2}$$

b. Improve this function so that it may also read integers.

3. a. Write a function named *echo()* that simply echoes to the screen any keystroke it detects. It does this until the end-of-file character is pressed, which is Ctrl-Z on most systems. When the function terminates, it returns the number of keystrokes it detected.

b. Modify the function above so that the nonprintable and control characters will not be echoed to the screen. Instead, a dot will be displayed.

c. Modify the function further. Now the function will terminate either when Ctrl-Z is pressed or when the number of keystrokes has reached the limit set by an argument passed to the function.

4. a. Write a program that simulates the dial of a phone number. The user will enter a phone number and the program will acknowledge the call. The phone number may also be entered with letters. For example:

Enter a phone number > LEE-FREE
You dialled 533-3733

Another example:

Enter a phone number > 4DI-LOVE
You dialled 434-5683

Define a function named *read_dials()* that reads each digit/letter dialled into a *char* variable. Use a *scanf()* with the appropriate template (see Subsection 8.2.5 for the use of templates). All digits are sent back through parameters by reference. Then, for each dial, the program will use a function named *todigit()*, which receives an argument that may be a number or a letter dialled. If it is a number, it is simply returned; otherwise, the digit corresponding to the letter is returned. Here are the letters associated with each digit:

0		5	J K L
1		6	M N O
2	A B C	7	P R S
3	D E F	8	T U V
4	G H I	9	W X Y

Finally, a function named *acknowledge_call()* will display the phone number. Assume that the number dialled is always valid.

b. Note that the letters Q and Z are not represented. If the user enters either one, the call will be invalid. For example:

```
Enter a phone number > 303-ZZ01
You dialled an invalid number
```

The function *read_dials()* should now return a –1 if any letter in the phone number is invalid.

c. A phone number never begins with a 0, so the program should flag an error if such a number is entered. Make *read_dials()* return –2 in this case. Also a phone number never begins with 555, so the program should flag an error if such a number is entered. Make *read_dials()* return –3 in this case.

d. Modify the program in (c) above so that the dash in the number may appear anywhere. For example:

```
Enter a phone number > LESS-TAX
You dialled 537-7829
```

```
Enter a phone number > WATCH-US
You dialled 928-2487
```

The *scanf()* within the function *read_dials()* can no longer be used. Instead, use a *getchar()* to read each character input individually.

14 One-Dimensional Arrays

OBJECTIVES

This chapter introduces you to the following information:

- A discussion of one-dimentional arrays and how to manipulate them.
- How to pass arrays to a function.
- Some typical applications of arrays.

INTRODUCTION

The first 13 chapters were designed to give you a solid grasp of problem solving and basic program logical structures. No doubt you are now itching for more sophisticated programming techniques, and arrays certainly open the way. When used properly, arrays will add flexibility and professionalism to your programs in ways that were not possible until now. Normally, the string, which is a special kind of array, would be covered in this chapter. However, string manipulation is such a complex topic that it deserves a separate chapter.

14.1 WHAT IS AN ARRAY?

An ***array*** is nothing more than a collection of similar data types such as integers or characters. Computer software often uses a set of identical data that have the same type and are used for the exact same purpose. For instance, a forecasting programmer may wish to keep track of the number of rainy days observed each month of the year. Suppose the programmer observed the patterns shown in Table 14.1.1.

Table 14.1.1

Month	Number of rainy days	Month	Number of rainy days
January	0	July	4
February	1	August	8
March	3	September	7
April	2	October	14
May	6	November	3
June	5	December	0

All of this data serves a common purpose, so it is natural to want to group them together in a table. In the computer's memory, it is best to store this data in adjacent memory cells. Supposing that the data for January is at address 430; in that case, we would want the memory layout shown in Figure 14.1.1.

Figure 14.1.1

Jan	Feb	Mar	Apr	May	June	July	Aug	Sept	Oct	Nov	Dec
0	1	3	2	6	5	4	8	7	14	3	0
430	432	434	436	438	440	442	444	446	448	450	452

Note that each cell occupies two bytes. (Why is that so?) This kind of arrangement is called an ***array.*** This section will explain how arrays are declared in a program, how data is stored in them, and how data is retrieved from them and displayed.

14.1.1 DECLARING AN ARRAY

Continuing with the forecasting example, let us write a program that simply asks for the data for each month, and then reports it all on the screen. For instance:

```
Enter the monthly rainy days this year > 0 1 3 2 6 5 4 8 7 14 3 0
In month 1, 0 rainy days
In month 2, 1 rainy days
In month 3, 3 rainy days
etc.
In month 11, 3 rainy days
In month 12, 0 rainy days

There were 53 rainy days
```

Note that the total number of rainy days is also reported. Two solutions will be worked out: the first solution will not use arrays, and the second one will.

Example 14.1.1

This program accomplishes the above task by using a separate variable to store the data for each month, as shown below:

```
#include <stdio.h>

main()
{
     int jan, feb, mar, apr, may, june, july, aug, sept, oct, nov, dec;
     int sum;

     /* ask for the data */

     printf("Enter the monthly rainy days this year > ");
     scanf("%d", &jan);
     scanf("%d", &feb);
     :
     etc....
     :
     scanf("%d", &dec);

     /* produce a report */

     printf("In month 1, %d rainy days\n", jan);
     printf("In month 2, %d rainy days\n", feb);
     :
```

```
        etc....
        :
        printf("In month 11, %d rainy days\n", nov);
        printf("In month 12, %d rainy days\n", dec);

        sum = jan + feb + mar + apr + may + june +
              july + aug + sept + oct + nov + dec;

        printf("There were %d rainy days\n", sum);
}
```

You can verify that this program does meet the requirements. Of course, the naming of the variables is totally arbitrary. They could just as well have been declared as:

```
int month1, month2, month3, month4, month5, month6,
    month7, month8, month9, month10, month11, month12;
```

Regardless, this solution is not at all elegant and is way too long for such a simple task. It turns out that the use of an array provides a much shorter and elegant solution, as we will shortly see.

Allocation of memory. As mentioned in the introduction of this section, an array is a set of adjacent cells in memory. The set of variables *jan, feb,* and so on in Example 14.1.1 are adjacent, so what is different? The difference is that with an array, the variables within it are accessed by **position,** not by name. This has very advantageous implications.

To illustrate, let us first allocate memory for an entire array consisting of twelve cells, one for each month of the year. This is accomplished with the declaration in Figure 14.1.2.

Figure 14.1.2

```
int month[12];
```

Type of each element of the array (→ `int`)

Array name (→ `month`)

Maximum number of elements in the array (also called array ***size***) (→ `[12]`)

This statement tells C to declare a variable called *month* to be an array that may contain no more than 12 ***elements,*** each of which must hold an integer. The ***size*** of the array is simply the maximum number of elements that it may hold, which in this case is 12. In some other context the size may also mean the number of ***bytes*** that the array occupies. In this case, since each element is of type *int,* the size is $12 \times 2 = 24$ bytes. In general, the size in bytes of an array is given by the formula:

Array size in bytes = Maximum number of elements that the array may hold × Bytes per element

The size in bytes of an array may also be provided by the operator *sizeof.* For instance, here, *sizeof(month)* is 24.

At declaration time, most compilers set all of the cells of an array to 0.

Accessing an element of an array. Now suppose that data has already been placed in the array and that you wish to access the data for October. Figure 14.1.3 shows where you would find October.

Figure 14.1.3

Array *month*: (October ↓ position 9)

Value:	0	1	3	2	6	5	4	8	7	14	3	0
Address:	430	432	434	436	438	440	442	444	446	448	450	452
Position:	0	1	2	3	4	5	6	7	8	9	10	11

Note that the first cell is at position 0, the second cell at position 1, and so on. To access the data for October, you therefore must specify that you wish to access the 10th cell of the array, which is at position 9 (**not** 10, because the first cell always starts at position 0, not 1). Figure 14.1.4 shows the notation used to identify this cell in a program. For instance, the assignment *month[9] = 2* would store the number 2 in the cell for October; the statement *printf("rain in October was %d", month[9])* would display it. The term 9 is called an ***index*** (or a ***subscript,*** which is a mathematical term). It specifies the position of the cell within the array.

Figure 14.1.4

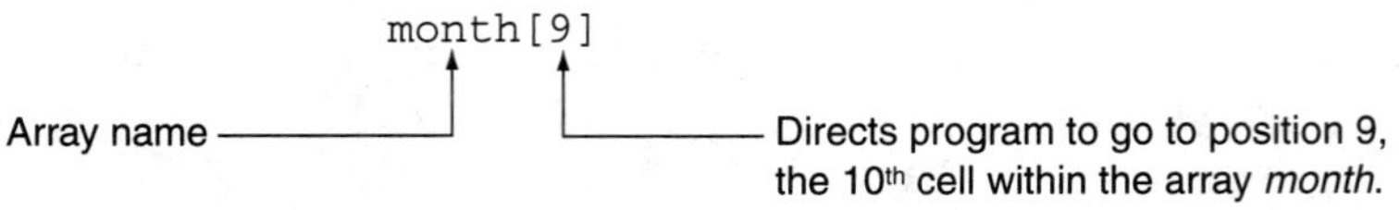

EXERCISES 14.1.1

1. For each array declaration below,
   i. *int qty[23];*
   ii. *float height[11];*
   iii. *char ch[5];*
   iv. *long int seconds[8];*
   answer the following questions:
   a. What is the name of the array?
   b. What is the size in bytes of the array?
   c. How many elements can the array hold?
   d. Specify the notation to access the 3rd element and assign the number 25 to it.
   e. Change the value of the 2nd element to that of the 5th element.
   f. Specify the notation for the last element of the array, and display it.
2. In what ways do the declarations *float age1, age2, age3, age4* and *float age[4]* differ?
3. You have the array *long jk[23].* Devise a simple formula (that involves the operator *sizeof*) that returns the number of elements contained by this array.

14.1.2 READING AND DISPLAYING ARRAYS

We are now ready for our first full program that uses an array.

Example 14.1.2

The following program accomplishes the same task as that in Example 14.1.1 but reads the data into an array and displays it:

```
#include <stdio.h>

main()
{
    int month[12];[1]   /* declare an array, one cell per month */
    int index;              /* an index variable */
    int sum;

    /* store data in each element of the array */

    printf("Enter the monthly rainy days this year > ");

    for (index=0; index < 12; index++)[2]
    {
         scanf("%d", &month[index]);
    }

    /* produce a report */

    sum = 0;
```

```
    for (index=0; index < 12; index++) [3]
    {
         printf("In month %d, %d rainy days\n", index+1, month[index]); [4]
         sum += month[index];
    }

    printf("There were %d rainy days\n", sum);
}
```

Explanations

1. The array *month* is allocated to store the data from each month.
2. Each cell needs to be accessed in order to store an element into it. The program must go through each cell of the array and store a number in it. This requires a loop, in which an ***index variable*** will run through the array from position 0 through position 11. Each time, the *scanf()* will read the user's data and store it in the cell specified by the index variable, i.e., *month[index]*. Note that the address operator in *scanf()* is &:

   ```
   scanf("%d", &month[index])
   ```

   &month[index] is the address of the cell at position *index*. For instance, if *index* is 9, the array would look like Figure 14.1.5. In this example, *&month[index]* is 448. Note that the index variable, which here is 9, must be of an integral type, meaning it cannot be of type *float* or *double*.

Figure 14.1.5

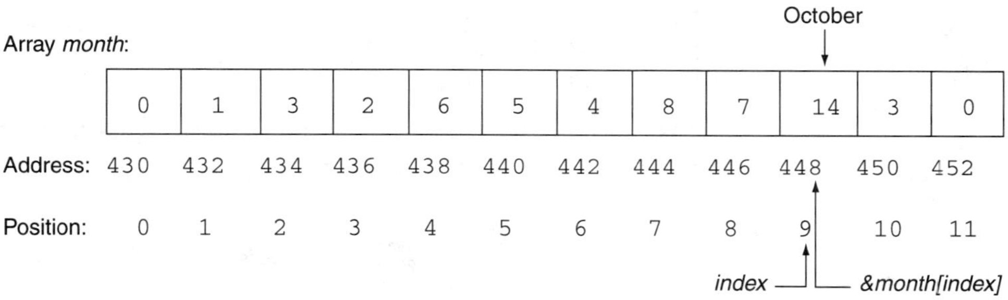

3. This loop simply displays all of the data from the array, one element at a time. The index variable *index* is run from 0 to 11, inclusive. Note that even though the variable *index* is referred to as an index, it may also be viewed as a counter running through the array.
4. Note the +1 in this code. (Why do you think it is included?)

By comparing Examples 14.1.1 and 14.1.2, it is clear that the use of an array shortened the code considerably. Arrays offer other advantages that this example does not really show, two of which are: they allow the programmer to develop more flexible programs, and the programs may be made to perform more complex and useful tasks. These last two points will be illustrated many times throughout this chapter and those following.

Frequently, programs manipulate more than one array. For instance, declarations such as:

```
int  year94[12], year95[12];
```

would be necessary if the task was to process the monthly rainfall for 1994 and 1995. As you can see, more than one array may be declared in a single declaration statement.

EXERCISES 14.1.2

1. The following loop reads the rainfall for each month of the year. Fill in the blanks.

   ```
   for (month_ctr=1; month_ctr __________; month_ctr++)
    {

          scanf("%d", &month[________]);
    }
   ```

2. After the following segment is executed, what will be the content of each cell of the array?

```
float  flt[6];
flt[0] = 2;   flt[1] = 5;   flt[4] = 8;
```

3. Revisit Example 7.3.5. There, the user was asked to enter a list of numbers. For example:

   Enter a list of grades terminated by pressing Ctrl-Z:
   61 76 63 92 50 80 70 43 79CTRL-Z↵
   The average grade is 68.22

   Store these numbers in an array of size 9. The user may enter less than nine numbers, but assume that he will never enter more than nine numbers. Develop two solutions:
   a. The grades are summed up as the numbers are read in (as done in Example 7.3.5).
   b. The grades are summed up in a separate loop after all numbers are read in.
4. Write a program that asks for the monthly rainfall for both 1994 and 1995, then adds up the rainfall of the corresponding months and displays the sum.
5. Write a program that asks the user to enter assignment marks from a student. These marks are stored in an array. Then the program asks the highest mark possible for each assignment. This is stored in a different array. Finally, the program calculates the overall average as a percent. For instance, if the marks are 48, 24, and 8 and are out of high marks of 80, 25, and 10 respectively, then the overall average is [(48/80) + (24/25) + (8/10)]/3 = 0.79.
6. Arrays may hold characters as well as numbers. Write a program that reads your initials into an array, and then displays them as follows:

   Enter your initials: JPC
   First name starts with a(n) J
   Middle name starts with a(n) P
   Last name starts with a(n) C

   Assume that initials always consist of three letters, so a loop is not needed.

14.1.3 AN ARRAY: A GROUP OF VARIABLES OF THE SAME TYPE

This section emphasizes that an array is a collection of variables of the same type and of common purpose.

A group of counters. In particular, arrays may hold a group of counters, as Example 14.1.3 illustrates.

Example 14.1.3

Suppose you are tossing a die just to kill time. You decide to write a program that will count how many times each of the six faces show. This requires a counter variable for each face. This group of six counters would fit nicely into the array shown in Figure 14.1.6.

Figure 14.1.6

count

	1	2	3	4	5	6	The face value on the die
Index:	[0]	[1]	[2]	[3]	[4]	[5]	Array index
	0	0	0	0	0	0	Initialization

The array will first be initialized to 0. Then every time the die is tossed the appropriate counter will be incremented. For instance, if the number 3 shows up, then the element *count[2]* would be incremented. Note that the index is 2, not 3. (Why is that so?) Once this game is over, the following histogram is produced:

Number	Occurrence
1	**** 4
2	*** 3
3	****** 6

4 ** 2
5 * 1
6 *** 3

Here is the program:

```
#include <stdio.h>
#include <stdlib.h>

main()
{
  int    i, index;
  int    count[6];          /* array for the 6 counters */
  int    outcome;

  for (i=0; i < 6; ++i)         /* initialize all 6 counters */
  {
       count[i] = 0;
  }

  /* Read each toss from the user. Increment the appropriate counter. */

  printf("What did you toss? ");
  while (scanf("%d", &outcome) != EOF)
  {
       ++count[outcome - 1];[1]
  }

  /* Display the histogram */

  printf("%10s%s\n\n", "Number", "Occurrence");
  for (index=0; index < 6; ++index)
  {
       printf("%10d  ", index + 1);
       for (i=0; i < count[index]; i++)
       {
           printf("*");
       }
       printf("%d\n", count[index]);
  }
}
```

Explanation

1. Note how simple and quick it is to increment the appropriate counter! This concise solution would not be possible if separate variables were used.

EXERCISES 14.1.3

1. Suppose that arrays did not exist in C. How would the above program need to be rewritten?
2. Write a program that initializes all elements of an array to 25.
3. a. Write a program that uses a loop to generate and store the following sequence in an array: 0, 1, 2, 3, 4, 5, 6, 7, 8, 9.
   b. Write a program that uses a loop to generate and store the following sequence in an array: 2, 4, 6, 8, 10, 12, 14, 16, 18, 20.
   c. Write a program that uses a loop to generate and store the following sequence in an array: 3, 5, 8, 12, 17, 23, 30, 38, 47, 57.
4. a. Write a program that uses a single loop to generate and store the following sequence in an array: 2, 10, 2, 10, 2, 10, 2, 10, 2, 10.

b. Redo (a) above with two loops: one places the 2s, the other places the 10s.

5. For each of the following situations, discuss whether it is more appropriate to store the data in an array or in individual variables, or whether either one works. The answer may also depend on the processing required on this data. Do not concern yourself with that here.

   a. The data is your age, height, and weight.

      Example: 27, 1.83 meters, 71.75 kg

   b. The data is the average gas mileage of four different car models.

      Example: 24.5 miles/gallon, 36.1, 13.6, 49.2

   c. The data is your initials, age, sex, and education level.

      Example: JPC, 33, M, 11

   d. The data is the number of people with a preference among four different car models.

6. A file named ANSWERS.CP contains multiple choice answers from exam questions. There are four possible answers: A, B, C, and D. Write a program that reads in all the answers obtained and produces a histogram. For example, the file might contain the following letters. Note that the letters are separated by a space.

```
c C A D B b C C a c A c B C A C
```

Then the histogram will be:

Letter	**Occurrence**
A	****
B	***
C	********
D	*

Note that the histogram is not case sensitive.

A counter will be needed for each of the four possible answers. Also, each counter must be initialized to 0. This group of four counters would fit nicely in an array. As the file is read, the appropriate counter, the one for 'A', 'B', 'C', or 'D', will be incremented.

7. Based on the program developed in question 6, write another that reads a student's file that contains a list of letter grades. There are five possible letter grades: A, B, C, D, and F. Again, one counter will be needed per letter. Use an array to contain these counters:

	A	B	C	D		F	
Letter	[0]	[1]	[2]	[3]	[4]	[5]	Array index
	0	0	0	0	0	0	Initialization

Note that there is no letter grade for 'E', so its cell is not needed. So why is a cell allocated for it? Simply because there was no choice: memory for an array is allocated in chunks, here from 'A' to 'F'.

8. Use the function *star_line()* from Example 10.3.1 in the program in Example 14.1.3 above.

9. Write a program that simulates the toss of a die. This program will be very similar to Example 14.1.3, except that the user will specify how many times to toss the die, and the program will use the function *rand()* to randomly generate the numbers. Finally, a histogram will summarize the number of times each face appeared. The frequency of occurrences should be similar for all faces.

A group of summation variables. An array may be used as a collection of summation variables. Consider Example 14.1.4.

Example 14.1.4

The following program reads a file containing hours worked by part-time employees on shift work during the entire month. Each record consists of an employee number from 1 to 5 (there are five employees), and the number of hours worked on that shift. For instance, the file might look like this:

4	4.5
1	8.5
2	11.5
5	2.0
3	5.0
2	8.0
5	14.5
1	5.5

and so on . . .

Then a histogram is produced that shows how many hours each employee has worked:

Employee	**Total hours worked (truncated to integer)**
1	********************************* 31
2	********************** 23
3	*** 45
4	*** 53
5	*** 51

Here is the program. It remains somewhat similar to that of Example 14.1.3, so it is presented without any explanation:

```
#include <stdio.h>
#include <stdlib.h>

main()
{
   int    i, index, sum_trunc;
   float  sum[5];          /* array for the five summation variables */
   int    emp_no;
   float  hours;
   FILE * ifp;

   for (i=0; i < 5; ++i)
   {
         sum[i] = 0;
   }

   /* Process the file. Increment the appropriate summation variable. */

   ifp = fopen("hours.wk", "r");
   while (fscanf(ifp, "%d%f", &emp_no, &hours) != EOF)
   {
      sum[emp_no] += hours;
   }
   fclose(ifp);

   /* Display the histogram */

   printf("%10s%s\n\n", "Employee", "Total hours worked");

   for (index=0; index < 5; ++index)
   {
       printf("%10d", index, ' ');
       sum_trunc = sum[index];         /* truncate the sum to integer */
       for (i=0; i < sum_trunc; i++)
       {
```

```
                printf("*");
            }
            printf("\n");
        }
        printf("\n");
    }
```

EXERCISES 14.1.4

1. Suppose that arrays did not exist in C. How would the program above need to be rewritten?
2. Add code to the program in Example 14.1.4 so that it calculates the average number of hours worked by each employee per shift. (***Hint:*** You need an additional array for counters.)

14.1.4 OUT-OF-BOUNDS ACCESS

In the program for Exercise 14.1.2, 3, you probably declared your array with nine cells, since it was assumed that the user would never enter more than nine numbers. What if the user did enter more? Well, here is what would have happened: suppose the array's name is *grade* and it contains the numbers shown in Figure 14.1.7, including one too many stored in the last cell. Surprisingly, the C language has absolutely no provision to disallow an index to go past the end of an array! The term used to signify that an index has reached past an array is ***out-of-bounds access*** or ***condition.***

Figure 14.1.7

Position:	0	1	2	3	4	5	6	7	8	9
	71	69	53	55	77	81	80	59	61	85

The effect on the program's behavior. This condition may cause the program to become unpredictable, so make every effort to avoid this mishap. Note that if the program only accesses a cell out-of-bounds, without changing what is in it, then the program likely will not misbehave. For instance, consider the following segment:

```
int  list[5];

printf("%d", list[6]);
list[6] = 14;
```

The first statement only accesses and should not cause harm. The second statement modifies the cell content. This may cause harm. This out-of-bounds condition is further discussed in Subsection 14.1.6, which you should read before moving on.

EXERCISES 14.1.5

1. Improve the program in Exercise 14.1.2, 3, so that the user will be told not to enter more than nine numbers. If the user does enter too many numbers, the extra ones will be ignored; i.e., the loop will terminate at nine numbers. Make sure that any extra numbers are cleared from the input buffer with a call to the function *fflush(stdin).*
2. Which of the code segments below produce unpredictable results? Could the program crash? If yes, at what line? Assume the array:

   ```
   double list[3];
   ```

   a.
   ```
   scanf("%f", &list[3]);
   printf("%f", list[3]);
   ```
   b.
   ```
   list[3] = 8;
   printf("%f", list[3]);
   ```

c. `printf("%f", list[62]);`

d. `scanf("%f", &list[62]);`
   `printf("%f", list[62]);`

3. The loops below have an error. What is it? Could it make the program crash? If so, when?

a.
```
float  list[15];
int    i;

for (i=0; i <= 15; i++)
{
     list[i] = 44;
}
```

b.
```
float  list[15];
int    i;

for (i=0; i <= 15; i++)
{
      list[2*i] = 44;
}
```

c.
```
float record[4];

printf("Enter your GPA > ");
scanf("%f", &record[0]);
printf("Enter your age > ");
scanf("%d", &record[1]);
printf("Enter your initials > ");
scanf("\n%c\n%c\n%c", &record[2], &record[3], &record[4]);
```

14.1.5 ARRAY INITIALIZATION

Earlier examples have shown that an array may be initialized to 0 (or any other common number) with a simple *for* loop. The following examples show a number of other ways that arrays may be initialized.

Example 14.1.5

The array *count* in Example 14.1.3 could have been initialized at declaration time (note the use of braces):

```
int count[6] = { 0, 0, 0, 0, 0, 0 };
```

Since the six elements are initialized to 0, the following will do as well:

```
int count[6] = { 0 };
```

The lone zero can be stored in *count[0]* and the missing elements will be initialized to 0 by default. For instance, the following:

```
int month[12] = { 0, 1, 3 };
```

is equivalent to the following series of individual initializations:

```
month[0] = 0;       month[1] = 1;       month[2] = 3;
month[3] = 0;       month[4] = 0;       month[5] = 0;
month[6] = 0;       month[7] = 0;       month[8] = 0;
month[9] = 0;       month[10] = 0;      month[11] = 0;
```

Example 14.1.6

The following shows the declaration and initialization of an array of characters:

```
char  vowels[5] = { 'a', 'e', 'i', 'o', 'u' };
```

Note the use of single quotation marks, **not** double quotation marks. This initialization is equivalent to the following set of instructions:

```
vowels[0] = 'a';    vowels[1] = 'e';    vowels[2] = 'i';
vowels[3] = 'o';    vowels[4] = 'u';
```

Example 14.1.7

C allows the omission of the size when an array is initialized. For example,

```
int month[] = { 0, 1, 3 };
```

Since the size is not specified in the brackets, the compiler will allocate three cells only, because only three elements are listed. This means that an array access such as *month[4] = 0* would be out-of-bounds. The omission of the size is usually not a good idea and most compilers do not allow it if it is not accompanied by an initialization. For example, *int month[];* would fail. It is always better to mention the largest size that you think the array needs.

EXERCISES 14.1.6

1. Write an array declaration, including initialization, for each of the following:
   a. A list of 12 weights, double precision. Each element is set to 1.
   b. A list of 6 ages, all integers. Each element is set to 0.
   c. The list of the four suits in a deck of cards. Use a character code for each card, such as 'H' for hearts.
2. For each declaration below, indicate the content of the array after initialization and the size in bytes of the array. Also indicate if there is any error:
   a. *float www[16] = { 9.5, 1.0, 0.3, 7.5 };*
   b. *int abc[7] = { 44 };*
   c. *double xyz[] = { 71.8, 99 };*
   d. *int s[3] = { 4, 33, 6, –77 };*
   e. *long codes[];*
   f. *float junk[6] = { 2, 6, –9, 208.62 };*
   g. *char str[6] = { 'G', 'o', 97, 116 };*

14.1.6 COMMON ERRORS AND TRAPS

Use the following information to avoid programming errors.

1. Do not access an array out-of-bounds. As was mentioned in Subsection 14.1.4, the C language cannot disallow an index to reach past the end of an array, so it is the programmer's responsibility to ensure that this does not happen. What happens if there is an out-of-bounds condition? Let us look at an example. A very common mistake is to think that, say, if an array has a size of five elements, then the last cell is at index 5:

   ```
   int   list[5];
   float f1 = 33.9, f2 = 11.1;

   list[5] = 6;    /* last element? */
   ```

   Let us see what this mistake may cause. Usually, the compiler allocates all of the variables in adjacent cells, so the variables *list, f1,* and *f2* might be stored in the arrangement below:

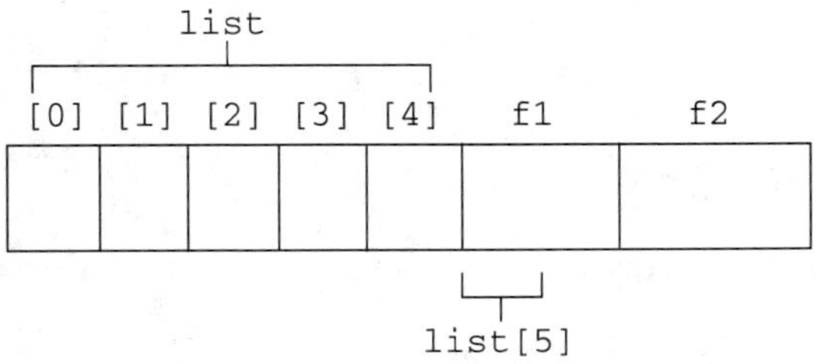

Each cell of the array *list* occupies 2 bytes, and *f1* and *f2* each occupy 4 bytes. Even though *list[5]* does not exist, the number 6 will be stored at index position 5, which is the position indicated on the figure. This position overlaps the cell for *f1*. This will cause the value inside the variable *f1* to corrupt, eventually leading to some erroneous results from the program. However, in this case, the program likely will not crash but it can have some big problems if the index goes far past the array, say, to position 25. Then what happens is anybody's guess, but a nasty crash is in the realm of possibilities.

2. Do not supply too many values in an initialization list. For example:

```
int  list[4] = { 5, 9, 8, 1, 6 };
```

The extra element 6 will cause an out-of-bounds access, which the compiler will detect (contrary to the case in common error 1).

3. Do not forget the semicolon at the end of an initialization. For example:

```
int  list[4] = { 5, 9, 8, 1, 6 }
```

The compiler will complain.

4. Do not forget to specify a size as part of the array declaration. For example:

```
int list;
list[0] = 6;
```

The compiler will complain.

5. Do not use an index that is one number off. This error often leads to an out-of-bounds condition. For example:

```
int  i, list[5];

for (i=0; i <= 5; i++)
{
      list[i] = 8;
}
```

Can you see the problem?

6. Do not use double quotation marks when initializing an array of characters. For example:

```
char  vowels[5] = { "a", "e", "i", "o", "u" };
```

As you know, single and double quotation marks carry entirely different meanings, yet some compilers may not detect this obvious error. As a result, garbage will be stored in the array. Consequently, when the array is sent to the screen, weird things may happen!

7. Do not use an increment/decrement operator in the index specification. Examples are provided in Supplementary Exercises 14.1, 2, 3, and 4.

8. Do not think that arrays start at index 1. For example:

```
int  i, list[5];

for (i=1; i <= 5; i++)
{
      list[i] = 8;
}
```

Here, *i=1* should be *i=0*. Strictly, it is not wrong to store and access an array starting at index 1, but if you do, be consistent and make sure that the size of the array is increased by 1, i.e., *int list[6]*.

9. Do not forget to initialize an array when it needs to be initialized. Although most compilers automatically set all elements of an array to 0, it is best to ensure that they are indeed set to 0. The fastest method to do this is as follows:

```
float  list[8] = { 0 };
```

The compiler will set the remaining seven elements to 0.

10. Do not forget to use an index to access an array. For example:

```
int  list[4];
list = 67;
```

The compiler will not allow such an assignment simply because it makes no sense!

SUPPLEMENTARY EXERCISES 14.1

1. Use arrays for the following problem. A fast food restaurant sells four different flavors of milk shakes. The manager wants to keep an inventory of each using the program that you are now asked to develop. It initially asks how many milk shakes there are in stock of each flavor. Then it lets the user choose one or more milk shakes. At the end of the day, the program provides a report of the inventory. Here is an example of a run:

   Enter the quantity of milk shakes available:
   Flavor 1: 150
   Flavor 2: 200
   Flavor 3: 176
   Flavor 4: 401

   Which flavor do you want? 3
   How many? 2
   Which flavor do you want? 4
   How many? 6
   etc.
   Which flavor do you want? 1
   How many? 3
   *** Only 5 left—order more
   Which flavor do you want? 1
   *** The stock ran out—sorry
   Which flavor do you want? –1

   Here is the inventory report:

   ```
   Flavor      Sold      Quantity      Comment
               Today     Left

   1           150          0          Order more
   2            82        116
   3           173          3          Order more
   4            91        310
   ```

   The program displayed a warning as soon as fewer than six milk shakes of a particular flavor are left in stock. This applied to the inventory report, too.
2. The following program lists all 15 elements of an array, three per line.

   ```
   #include <stdio.h>

   main()
   {
        long int  que[15] = { 6, 9, 3,
                              2, 4, 1,
                              10, 5, 0,
                              0, 3, 3,
                              66, 77, 99 };
        int       i;

        for (i = 0; i < 15; i++)
        {
             printf("%lu %lu %lu\n", que[i], que[++i], que[++i]);
        }
   }
   ```

   Surprisingly, the results may differ depending on the compiler used. Why? (***Hint:*** Recall common error 2 in Subsection 13.1.5.)
3. The following program displays the quotient of every adjacent pair of numbers in an array.

   ```
   #include <stdio.h>

   main()
   ```

```
{
     long int  seq[6] = { 9, 2, 4, 10, 3, 6 };
     int       i;

     i = 0;
     while (i < 15)
     {
          printf("quotient = %lu\n", seq[i] / seq[++i]);
     }
}
```

Surprisingly, the results may differ depending on the compiler used. Why? (***Hint:*** Recall Subsection 13.4.3.)

4. The following segment simply sets the elements of an array to 1, 2, 3, 4, and so on. However, the results may be unpredictable. Why? (***Hint:*** Recall Subsection 13.4.3.)

```
main()
{
     int  i;
     int  ar[15];

     i = 0;
     while (i < 15)
     {
           ar[i++] = i + 1;
     }
}
```

5. Introduce arrays where appropriate in the program in Supplementary Exercise 4.3, 4.

14.2 PASSING ARRAYS TO FUNCTIONS

In C, passing an array to a function means that the function is granted access to all of the elements of that exact array, not a copy of it. This section explains how this is possible and covers numerous applications.

14.2.1 THE MECHANISM OF PASSING ARRAYS

Example 14.2.1

Let us write a function named *display_array()* that simply displays to the screen each element of an array passed to it:

```
#include <stdio.h>

void display_array(int array[5])[1]
{
     int  i;

     for (i=0; i < 5; i++)
     {
          printf(" %d", array[i]);
     }
     printf("\n");
}

main()
{
```

```
        int  list[5] = { 3, 1, -9, 7, 1 };

        display_array(list);²
}
```

Explanations

1. The parameter *int array[5]* indicates clearly that it is an array named *array* with a size of five elements.
2. The argument to the call *display_array()* is simply the name of the array to be passed to it. The argument array *list* will be passed to the parameter *array;* then the function will handle this parameter the same as if it was used from *main()*. Passing arrays to functions is that simple!

Passing an array of any size. Note in the program above that the parameter is declared with a size of 5. Also, the *for* loop runs to index 5. These two observations show that this function *display_array()* is capable of displaying arrays of size 5 only, thereby limiting its portability. The following example shows how a simple modification to the function definition will ensure that any array may be passed to it and displayed.

Example 14.2.2

The function *display_array()* below can display an array of any size. Note the difference from the definition in Example 14.2.1.

```
void display_array(int array[], int size)¹
{
        int  i;

        for (i=0; i < size; i++)
        {
                printf(" %d", array[i]);
        }
        printf("\n");
}

main()
{
        int  list[5] = { 3, 1, -9, 7, 1 };

        display_array(list, 5);²
}
```

Explanations

1. The size specification is removed from the array parameter declaration:

   ```
   void display_array(int array[], int size)
   ```

   Since no size is mentioned in the empty brackets, this array parameter may receive an array of any size. The actual size is received from the second argument and passed to the parameter *size*.
2. In addition to the array *list*, its size is passed to the function. This way the function knows how many elements there are to display.

EXERCISES 14.2.1

1. Refer to Example 14.2.2. What will the calls below produce? Indicate if unpredictable results may occur.
   a. *display_array(list, 6);*
   b. *display_array(list, 0);*

2. a. Write a function named *add_them()* with three parameters: an array named *a1* of size 8; another array named *a2* that must be able to receive an array argument of any size; and a parameter named *size* that receives the actual size of the second array argument (passed to *a2*). Both arrays contain integers. The function will simply produce a table showing the addition of all possible pairs of numbers from both arrays. For example, suppose the following declarations:

```
int ar1[8] = {2, -5, 8, 17, 9, 9, 7, 0};
int ar2[3] = { 5, -5, 3 };
```

A call to *add_them(ar1, ar2, 3)* will produce the following table:

```
      2  -5   8  17   9   9   7   0
     -----------------------------
 5 |  7   0  13  22  14  14  12   5
-5 | -3 -10   3  12   4   4   2  -5
 3 |  5  -2  11  20  12  12  10   3
```

Make the program work for these two particular arrays.

b. Have the program ask for the numbers that make up the two arrays.

c. Improve the function *add_them()* so that it accepts an array *ar1* of any size. The size will be passed to the function. In other words, the function call becomes *add_them(ar1, 8, ar2, 3)*.

3. Write a function named *filtered_display()* that displays from any array passed to it only the elements that are greater than a number passed as a second argument.

4. Write a function named *display_columns()* that displays any array in five columns. For example, the array 5, 9, –7, 0, 2, 12, 52, 11, –91, 0, 6 would be displayed as:

```
 5      9      -7      0      2
12     52      11    -91      0
 6
```

5. What will the following program display?

```
#include <stdio.h>

int  fcn(int ar[], int n)
{
      int  i;

      for (i=0; i < n-2; i++)
      {
            ar[i+2] = 2 * ar[i+1] + ar[i];
      }
      return ar[i];
}

main()
{
      int  list[8] = { 1 };

      printf("last element = %d\n", fcn(list, 8));
      printf("last element = %d\n", fcn(list, 8));
}
```

The array is actually passed by reference. At the beginning of this section, it was stated that passing an array to a function meant that the function received all of the elements of that exact array. Let us now see how this actually happens. Could the array be passed by value? If it is, then every single element of the argument array will be copied to the parameter, as shown in Figure 14.2.1.

Figure 14.2.1

Function call: `display_list(list);`
Function header: `void display_list(int array[])`

Is every single element in *list* copied to *array?* Imagine if the array *list* had 10,000 elements. That many elements would be copied to the parameter, making array passing extremely slow. Clearly, an array should never be passed by value. Consequently, arrays are always passed by reference; that is, in Figure 14.2.1, the **address** where the array is located is copied to the parameter, **not** the array content itself.

Only the address of *list* is copied to *array.* To illustrate, suppose that the array *list* starts at address 500 (called the ***base address***). Then the array is seen in Figure 14.2.2.

Figure 14.2.2

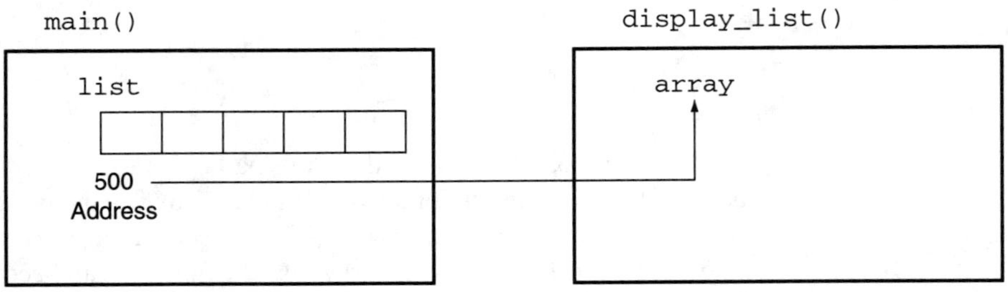

The base address of the array *list* is copied to the parameter *array.* The called function may then modify the content of any cells of that array *list,* as Example 14.2.3 shows.

Example 14.2.3

Let us write a function named *reset_list()* that resets all of the entries of an array back to 0. Here is the program:

```
#include <stdio.h>

void reset_array(int array[], int size)
{
        int  i;

        for (i=0; i < size; i++)
        {
                array[i] = 0;
        }
}

void display_array(int array[], int size)
{
        int  i;

        for (i=0; i < size; i++)
        {
                printf("%d", array[i]);
        }
}

main()
{
        int  list[5] = { 3, 1, -9, 7, 1 };

        display_array(list, 5);
        reset_array(list, 5);
}
```

Note that the address operator **must not** be used function calls, even though the array is passed by reference. This discussion on passing arrays by reference is not entirely complete. Much more needs to be explained about the topics of base addresses and array passing. However, these topics are rather advanced and will be postponed until Chapter 16, which will discuss the very close relationship between arrays and pointers and will complete the explanation undertaken here.

EXERCISES 14.2.2

1. True or false:
   a. Arrays may be passed by value.
   b. When an array is passed to a function, all of its elements are copied over to the parameters of the function.
   c. In the program in Example 14.2.2, the arrays *list* and *array* contain the same data.
   d. In the program in Example 14.2.2, the arrays *list* and *array* are not the same array.
2. Find the error(s) in the following program code:

```
void read_array(int array)
{
        int  i;

        for (i=0; i < 5; i++)
        {
                scanf("%d", array[i]);
        }
}

main()
{
        int  list[5] = { 3, 1, -9, 7, 1 };

        read_array(list[5]);
}
```

3. What will be the contents of the array *list* after the call to *augment()* in each of the following cases?

a.
```
void augment(int ar[], int value)
{
        int  i;

        for (i=0; i < 4; i++)
        {
                ar[i] += value;
        }
}

main()
{
        int  list[4] = { 11, 22, 33, 44 };

        augment(list, 6);
}
```

b.
```
void increment(int arelm, int value)
{
        arelm += value;
}

void augment(int ar[], int value)
```

```
{
        int  i;

        for (i=0; i < 4; i++)
        {
              increment(ar[i], value);
        }
}

main()
{
        int  list[4] = { 11, 22, 33, 44 };

        augment(list, 6);
}
```

4. Modify the function *reset_array()* in Example 14.2.3 so that it sets all of the elements of an array to a number passed as argument.
5. a. Write a function named *negate_array()* that negates all of the elements in the array passed to it; e.g., 8 becomes –8 and –4 becomes 4. The size of the array is also passed as argument.
   b. Modify the function so that negative numbers remain negative.
6. Write a function named *scalar_mult()* that multiplies each element of an array by a real number given by an argument. Of course, the array is also passed as an argument. For example, the call *scalar_mult(list, 3.2)* would multiply each element by 3.2.
7. The following two programs do the same thing, but in different ways. Discuss the difference in the way they proceed:

a.
```
void display_one_element(int elm)
{
        printf("element is %d\n", elm);
}

main()
{
        int list[] = { 9, 5, 9, 7, 1 };

        display_one_element(list[4]);
}
```

b.
```
void display_one_element(int array[], int index)
{
        printf("element is %d\n", array[index]);
}

main()
{
        int list[] = { 9, 5, 9, 7, 1 };

        display_one_element(list, 4);
}
```

8. a. Write a function named *read_array()* that reads a list of numbers into an array. It will then return the number of elements read back to the calling function. For example:

```
printf("Enter a list of numbers: ");
size = read_array(list);
```

   Ctrl-Z will be pressed to indicate the end of the data.
   b. Modify the code in (a) above so that the function may read no more elements than what are given by a second argument. The remaining numbers will be eliminated from the buffer with the function *fflush(stdin)*.
   c. Introduce this function in Example 14.1.2.

9. a. Modify the function *read_array()* above so that the sentinel INT_MIN is stored in the array at the end of the data.
   b. Modify the function *display_array()* in Example 14.2.3 so that the presence of the sentinel INT_MIN will terminate the loop. The parameter *size* is no longer needed. (Why is that so?)
10. Modify the function *time()* developed in Exercise 11.2.2, 25, in the following way. It will still accept a quantity value in seconds, but now it will send back the equivalent in days, hours, minutes, and seconds as part of a single array:

Days	Hours	Minutes	Seconds

11. Write a function named *basezero()* that replaces all negative elements from an array with zeros.
12. Introduce arrays in appropriate places in the program in Example 12.1.2.

Note: Unless otherwise stated, from now on, in this text any time the functions *read_array()* and *display_array()* are used in examples, their definitions will be the ones from Exercise 14.2.2, 8b and Example 14.2.2, respectively, and will no longer be included in the code. Consequently, many of the examples will be incomplete and cannot immediately be run unless the definitions of these two functions are added.

14.2.2 FUNCTION PROTOTYPES

Recall that a function prototype is needed when a function call precedes its definition. The proper syntax of a function prototype with a parameter declaration is shown in Example 14.2.4.

Example 14.2.4

Reconsider Example 14.2.1. Let us force the use of a function prototype for *display_array()* by moving its definition after *main()*. Changes from the earlier program are shown in bold type.

```
#include <stdio.h>

void display_array(int [5]);      /* function prototype */

main()
{
      int  list[5] = { 3, 1, -9, 7, 1 };

      display_array(list);
}

void display_array(int array[5])
{
      int  i;

      for (i=0; i < 5; i++)
      {
            printf("%d", array[i]);
      }
}
```

As usual, the function prototype is nearly identical to the function header. It simply omits the actual name of the parameter and ends with a semicolon:

```
void display_array(int [5]);
```

int [5] says that the parameter is an array data type with a size of 5 elements.

EXERCISE 14.2.3

Force the use of a function prototype in the programs in Examples 14.2.2 and 14.2.3.

14.2.3 BE WARY OF PARAMETER/ARGUMENT TYPE MISMATCHES

As shown in Subsection 10.2.2, the data types of the corresponding arguments and parameters should agree, although in some cases the implicit conversion incurred would be done correctly. For instance, an integer argument can safely be passed to a parameter of type *float.* With arrays, though, the C language is totally unable to perform implicit conversions correctly. Consequently, it is the responsibility of the programmer to ensure that the types of the corresponding argument and parameter agree. Example 14.2.5 shows what may happen when they do not agree.

Example 14.2.5

The following program calls a function named *setarray()* that simply resets all elements of an array to 99. Extra codes are added to show the content of the array in the output before it is passed to the function, after it is passed to the function, and after the function returns to *main()*.

```
#include <stdio.h>

void setarray(float arr[])
{
        int i;

        printf("\nWe are within setarray():\n");
        printf("The array passed to setarray():\n");
        for (i=0; i < 3; i++)
        {
            printf(" %f ", arr[i]);
        }

        for (i=0; i < 3; i++)                          2
        {
            arr[i] = 99;
        }

        printf("\nThe results of setting the array to 99:\n");
        for (i=0; i < 3; i++)
        {
            printf(" %f ", arr[i]);
        }
}

main()                                                        1
{
        int  list[3] = { 9, 8, 7 };
        int  i;

        printf("In main(), the array is:\n");
        for (i=0; i < 3; i++)
        {
            printf(" %d ", list[i]);
        }

        setarray(list);

        printf("\nBack in main(), the array is now set to:\n");
```

```
        for (i=0; i < 3; i++)                    ─┐
        {                                         ├── 3
            printf(" %d ", list[i]);              │
        }                                        ─┘
}
```

The type of the argument passed to *setarray()* is *int*, and the type of the corresponding parameter is *float*. Converting from *int* to *float* has never been a problem before, except that now the data passed is an array. Here is what is obtained from running this program:

In main(), the array is:
9 8 7[1]
We are within setarray():
The array passed to setarray():
0.000000 0.000000 0.000000[1]
The results of setting the array to 99:
99.000000 99.000000 99.000000[2]
Back in main(), the array is now set to:
0 17094 0[3]

Explanations

1. Before the function call, the array correctly contains 9, 8, 7, as can be seen in the output. Yet garbage is obtained by the parameter when this array is passed to the function *setarray()*. Clearly, the numbers 9, 8, and 7 could not be converted to *float* when passed to the function!
2. Once within the function, each element of the parameter array is set to 99 correctly . . .
3. . . . but when the program returns to *main()*, the array is not sent back correctly.

It is not important to know why an implicit conversion is impossible with arrays. Simply make sure that the types of the arrays agree. On the one hand, working with arrays is great in the sense that you may write fairly sophisticated programs. On the other hand, you better learn how to handle them, or weird and puzzling things will happen, and it will get worse when pointers (Chapter 16) and strings (Chapter 18) are involved. But take heart; in the end it will all be well worth the effort of learning!

Next we should discuss how arrays may be returned back to the calling function with the *return* statement; but this involves pointers and will be postponed until Chapter 16.

EXERCISE 14.2.4

The arguments' and parameters' types do not agree in the following function call. Nevertheless, will the results be unpredictable? Explain.

```
void augmentby(float ar_elm, float value)
{
      ar_elm += value;
}

main()
{
      int  list[] = { 7, 9, 2, 5, 4 };
      int  i;

      for (i=0; i < 5; i++)
      {
            augmentby(list[i], 3);

      }
}
```

14.2.4 COMMON ERRORS AND TRAPS

The following information will help you avoid common programming errors.

1. Do not use the address operator with an array passed to a function. For example:

```
void reset_array(int array[], int size)
{
        int  i;

        for (i=0; i < size; i++)
        {
                array[i] = 0;
        }
}


main()
{
        int  list[5] = { 3, 1, -9, 7, 1 };

        reset_array(&list, 5);
}
```

   The & address operator is never needed to pass an array. Here the compiler will probably **not** complain, but when the program is run, unpredictable things may happen. Section 11.2 mentioned that the address operator must be used in order to pass an argument by reference. True, but arrays are an exception, for they are always passed by reference.

2. Do not use brackets when passing an array to a function. For example:

```
main()
{
        int  list[5] = { 3, 1, -9, 7, 1 };

        reset_array(list[], 5);
}
```

   The brackets in the fourth line of this program code will cause a syntax error. Use brackets only when a cell within the array is being accessed via an index.

14.3 LIST OPERATIONS USING ARRAYS, PART 1

This section covers some operations on arrays that are fairly common, such as finding the average of numbers in an array and copying arrays. In almost all cases, we will define list operations solely with arrays of integers, although the same operations may be defined in just the same way for arrays of other types. In the context of a list of elements, the ***size*** of the array means the number of elements that it contains, not the number of cells. For example, the array *int list[8] = { 6, 9, 8, 1 }* is a list of size 4 elements but occupies 8 cells. In this section and Section 15.2, the term ***size*** will often have this meaning.

14.3.1 DOING STATISTICS

Example 14.3.1

Let us write a function named *find_avg()* that returns the average of the elements from an array given as an argument. The size of the array is also passed to the function. Here is the program:

```
#include <stdio.h>

float  find_avg(int array[], int size)
```

```
{
        int    i, sum;

        sum = 0;
        for (i=0; i < size; i++)
        {
                sum += array[i];
        }
        return ((float) sum) / size;
}

main()
{
        int  list[5] = { 8, -3, 11, 6, 2 };
        float avg;

        avg = find_avg(list, 5);
        printf("Average = %f\n", avg);
}
```

Note the necessary use of a cast operator with the *return* statement. (Why is it necessary?)

EXERCISES 14.3.1

1. Modify the function *find_avg()* above so that the sum is sent back by reference instead of by a *return* statement.
2. Given the definition of *find_avg()* in the example, will the following segment run correctly? Explain. (***Hint:*** Review Subsection 14.2.3.)

```
main()
{
        float  list[5] = { 8, -3, 11, 6, 2 };
        float  avg;

        avg = find_avg(list, 5);
        printf("Average = %f\n", avg);
}
```

3. a. Write a function named *find_sum()* that returns the sum of all the elements from an array given as an argument. The size of the array is also passed to the function.
   b. Use the function *find_sum()* in the program in Example 14.1.2. The output must still remain the same.
4. Use the function *find_avg()* in the program in Exercise 14.1.4, 2.
5. Write a function named *find_std()* that returns the standard deviation from an array given as an argument. The size of the array is also passed to the function. The standard deviation is a measure of the spread of the data around the average. The more spread out the data is, the larger the deviation; the more centered the data is, the smaller the deviation. Suppose that the data is in the array named *list.* The standard deviation is arrived at in three steps:
   a. The average is calculated and stored in the variable *avg.*
   b. The expression *square* += *sqr(list[i] – avg)* is executed for each element in the list; i.e., the index *i* is run through the array *list.*
   c. The standard deviation is *std* = *sqrt(square).*
6. a. Write a function named *find_sumEE()* that sums up only the even elements.
   b. Write a function named *find_sumEI()* that sums up only the elements whose index is even.
7. Assume that the arrays passed to all the *find_* functions terminate with a sentinel of INT_MIN. Modify all of these functions so that they go through the array until the sentinel is reached. The size of the array no longer needs to be passed.
8. Write a program that acts as a very simple billing system.

a. Have the program ask for a quantity of items bought and the unit price. This will be done for up to ten products. Then a bill will be shown on the screen with the heading:

```
            B I L L

Quantity        Unit Price        Cost
--------        ----------        ----
```

b. Introduce into the program the function *total()* from Example 10.4.1. Also introduce the function *find_sum()* from this section so that the sum of the cost may be displayed. ***Note:*** you must change the array parameter type to *float*.

9. a. Write a program that asks the user to enter the daily hours worked by an employee in the past week. The hours may be fractional. Assume the employee worked five days. The program will then produce a simple report including the total number of hours worked and the average per day.
   b. Have the program display the largest number of hours worked in one day.
   c. Have the program display the smallest number of hours worked in one day.
   d. Have the program display on which days these occurred.
10. Reconsider the solution of Supplementary Exercise 12.2, 7. The list of hours spent on projects will now be stored in an array. Define a function named *find_total()* that accepts this array and returns the total number of hours. There may be up to eight projects. Provide two solutions:
   a. In all records, the list of hours is terminated by a –1.
   b. The list of hours is preceded by the number of projects for the particular record.
11. Reconsider the solution of Supplementary Exercise 12.2, 8. The list of credit charges (for each purchase location) will now be stored in an array. Define a function named *find_total()* that accepts this array and returns the total amount of all credit charges made that month. Also the function *show_purchases()* will no longer read the purchase costs. It will now accept credit charges for those purchases from the array mentioned earlier. The actual reading of the credit charges will be done by a new function named *read_purchases()*.

14.3.2 COPYING AN ARRAY AND COMPARING TWO ARRAYS

Example 14.3.2

Let us write a program that asks a student to enter his student number. To make sure that it is entered correctly, the student will be asked to enter it twice. If both entries agree, then the student is allowed to enter the pub. The student number is eight digits long, which will be stored in an array, one digit per cell. Here is the program:

```
#include <stdio.h>

main()
{
    int  id1[8], id2[8];[1]
    int  i;
    char agree;

    printf("Enter your I.D.: ");
    for (i=0; i < 8; i++)
    {
        scanf("%1d", &id1[i]);[2]     /* store each digit in array 1 */
    }
    printf("Enter your I.D. again: ");
    for (i=0; i < 8; i++)
    {
        scanf("%1d", &id2[i]);      /* store each digit in array 2 */
    }

    /* check if both I.D.s are identical */
```

```
    agree = 1;3
    for (i=0; (i < 8) && agree; i++)
    {
         if (id1[i] != id2[i])
         {
              agree = 0;
         }
    }
    if (agree)
    {
         printf("You can come in the pub\n");
    }
    else
    {
         printf("Wait!\n");
    }
}
```

Explanations

1. The array *id1* will contain the digits of the I.D. and *id2* will contain a copy of it.
2. Note the format code *%1d*. The digit 1 tells *scanf()* to read one digit only. Should this 1 not be specified, the whole I.D. would be read at once as a single number.
3. The condition of the loop *(i < 8) && agree* makes the loop continue to compare corresponding digits from both arrays as long as the index is not past the array and all digits still agree.

EXERCISES 14.3.2

1. a. Based on the program above, write a function named *compare_array()* that compares two arrays passed to it. Both arrays have to be of the same size, and that size is also passed to the function. A 0 is returned if both arrays agree; otherwise, 1 is returned.
   b. Assume the arrays:

```
int  list[7]   = { 2, 4, 66, -6, 66,  3, 66 };
int  lineup[7] = { 2, 4, 66, -6, 66, 21, 14 };
int  que[5]    = { 2, 4, 66,  0, 3 };
```

   What will be the result of the following calls? Indicate if unpredictable results may occur.
   1. *compare_array(list, lineup, 7)*
   2. *compare_array(list, lineup, 5)*
   3. *compare_array(lineup, list, 5)*
   4. *compare_array(list, que, 5)*
   5. *compare_array(list, que, 3)*
   6. *compare_array(list, que, 7)*
   7. *compare_array(list, que, 90)*
2. a. Write a function named *copy_array()* that makes a copy of an array. The first argument will be the destination array (the copy) and the second argument will be the original array (the source array). The size of the original array will be the third argument.
   b. Assume the arrays:

```
int  list[7]   = { 2, 4, 66, -6, 66, 3, 66 };
int  lineup[7];
int  kly[12];
int  que[5];
```

   What will be the result of the following calls? Indicate if unpredictable results may occur.
   1. *copy_array(lineup, list, 7)*
   2. *copy_array(list, lineup, 7)*
   3. *copy_array(lineup, list, 4)*

4. *copy_array(que, list, 4)*
5. *copy_array(que, list, 7)*
6. *copy_array(kly, list, 7)*

3. Another array operation is displaying an array in reverse. Fill in the blanks in the following segment so that the array *list* is displayed in reverse. Assume that the array already contains data:

```
printf("In reverse: ");
for (i=0; i ____________; ____)
{
        printf("%d ", list[______]);
}
```

4. Based on the question above, write a program that accepts an array and displays it in reverse. For example:

   Enter a list of no more than 10 integers: <u>7 9 –5 1 0 81</u>
   In reverse: 81 0 1 –5 9 7

   Use the function *read_array()* from Exercise 14.2.2, 8b.
5. Based on the program in the question above, write a function named *display_reversed()* that displays an array reversed. The array is passed to the function as well as its size.
6. The function *display_reversed()* in question 5 does not reverse the array itself. Define a function named *reverse_itself()* that accepts an array and reverses it. It does not display it, so the function *display_array()* from Example 14.2.2 needs to be called.
7. Write a function named *reverse_array()* that reverses an array into another one also passed as an argument. Develop the following versions:
   a. Use the functions *copy_array() and reverse_itself()*.
   b. Do not use these functions.
8. Write a function named *palindrome()* that accepts an array of digits and returns 1 if it reads the same way from both ends; otherwise, it returns 0. Use the functions *reverse_array()* from question 7 above and *compare_array()* from Exercise 14.3.2, 1.

14.3.3 CONCATENATING TWO ARRAYS

When you concatenate two arrays, you join them into a single one.

Example 14.3.3

The program below stores a set of vowels and a set of consonants into two separate arrays. Then both are concatenated into a single array (Figure 14.3.1).

Figure 14.3.1

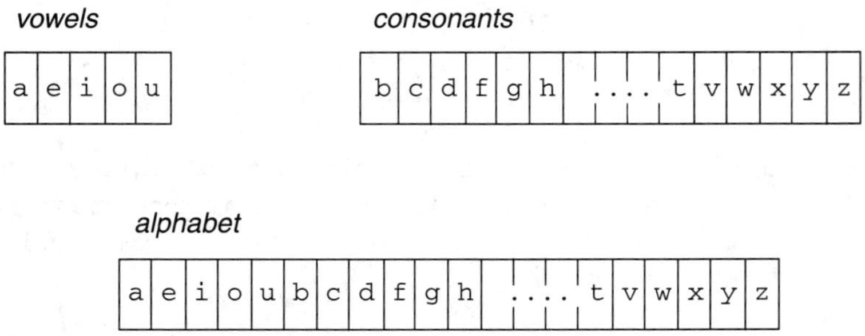

A function named *concatenate()* will take as argument the two arrays and their different sizes and concatenate them into one. Here is the program:

```
#include <stdio.h>

void concatenate(char ar1[], int size1, char ar2[], int size2,
                 char ar3[])
```

```
{
        int i;
        for (i=0; i < size1; i++)     /* copy over array ar1 */
        {
                ar3[i] = ar1[i];
        }
        for (i=0; i < size2; i++)     /* copy over array ar2 */
        {
                ar3[i+size] = ar2[i];
        }
}

main()
{
        char vowels[5] = { 'a, 'e', 'i', 'o', 'u' };
        char consonants[21] = { 'b', 'c', 'd', 'f', 'g', 'h', 'j',
                                'k', 'l', 'm', 'n', 'p', 'q', 'r',
                                's', 't', 'v', 'w', 'x', 'y', 'z' };
        char alphabet[26];
        concatenate (vowels, 5, consonants, 21, alphabet);

}
```

Figure 14.3.2 annotates the *concatenate()* function for you. Study this program before moving on. Note that we started with two sorted arrays, *vowels* and *consonants,* and the concatenation produced an unsorted array, *alphabet.* To produce a sorted array, the two initial arrays should be ***merged*** instead of concatenated. This technique is a little complex, but is explained in Supplementary Exercise 15.1, 7.

Figure 14.3.2

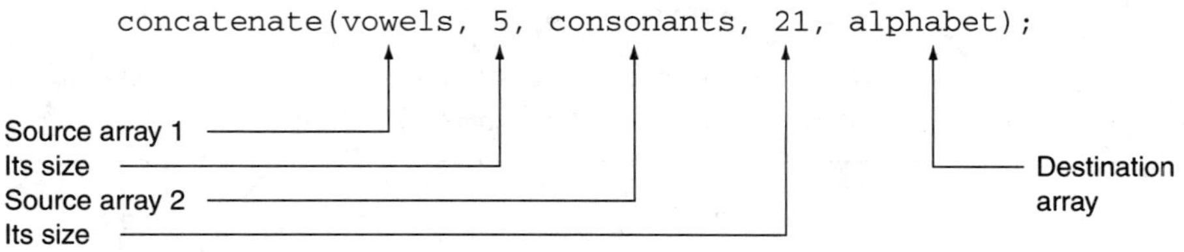

EXERCISES 14.3.3

1. Suppose the array *char alph[10].* What will be the result of the following calls? Indicate if unpredictable results may occur.
   a. *concatenate(vowels, 3, consonants, 5, alph)*
   b. *concatenate(vowels, 0, consonants, 8, alph)*
   c. *concatenate(vowels, 2, consonants, 8, alph)*
   d. *concatenate(vowels, 8, consonants, 2, alph)*
   e. *concatenate(vowels, 5, consonants, 12, alph)*
   f. *concatenate(vowels, 5, vowels, 2, alph)*
2. The function *concatenate()* is nothing more than two copy operations: one from *ar1* to *ar3,* another from *ar2* to *ar3.* So the *copy_array()* could have been used as follows:

```
void concatenate(char ar1[], int size1, char ar2[], int size2,
                 char ar3[])
{
        int i;

        copy_array(ar3, ar1, size1);
        copy_array(ar3, ar2, size2);
}
```

   Does this solution work? Explain.

3. Modify the function *concatenate()* so that array *ar2* is concatenated at the end of array *ar1* instead of into parameter *ar3*. This latter parameter is no longer needed. Be careful: the size of *ar1* must be large enough to contain the concatenation.
4. Write a function named *intcat()* that is a version of *concatenate()* (in Example 14.3.3) for integer arrays.
5. A hospital compiles the number of babies that are delivered each day during the month:

```
Enter # of babies born in week 1: 4 0 1 0 2 2 0
Enter # of babies born in week 2: 0 0 2 1 2 0 0
Enter # of babies born in week 3: 0 3 1 1 5 4 1
Enter # of babies born in week 4: 2 2 7 0 0 0 0
40 babies were born this month
```

   Assume that a month consists of exactly 28 days and exactly four weeks. Develop two versions of the program.
   a. Use the function *read_array()* to read a week's data into an array named *week*. Then call the function *intcat()* to concatenate it at the end of an array named *month*. A loop will ensure that this is done for all four weeks. In the end, the array *month* should contain the figures for all four weeks.
   b. Redo the program without the function *intcat()* to concatenate.
6. Modify the function *intcat()* so that it will assume that both arrays terminate with a sentinel of INT_MIN. Concatenation will proceed until the sentinel is found. The sizes of the arrays are no longer passed to the function.
7. Consider the following generalization to the question 5. Most months consist of more than four weeks and some weeks are not complete. For instance:

```
Enter # of babies born in week 1: 4 0 1
Enter # of babies born in week 2: 2 0 2 1 2 0 0
Enter # of babies born in week 3: 0 3 1 1 5 4 1
Enter # of babies born in week 4: 2 2 7 0 0 0 0
Enter # of babies born in week 5: 8 5 1 0 2 0
54 babies were born this month
```

   Modify the program in question 5 by using the function *read_array()* from Exercise 14.2.2, 9a and the function *intcat()* in question 6 above.

15 Why Use Arrays?

OBJECTIVES

This chapter introduces you to the following information:

- Situations in which arrays are absolutely needed.
- More typical, but more complex, applications of arrays than those in the previous chapter.

INTRODUCTION

You may already have deduced from Chapter 14 that arrays are indeed useful. This chapter goes beyond this observation, claiming that sometimes nothing else will do! It is important to know that.

15.1 WHEN NOTHING BUT ARRAYS WILL DO

Section 14.1 taught you that an array is a way of grouping together a set of variables that have a common type and purpose. The ability to access each variable using an index enables the programmer to shorten the code immeasurably. This is certainly one good reason for using arrays rather than individual variables. There are other reasons as well, as this section will demonstrate.

Essentially, the introduction of arrays increases the flexibility and capabilities of programs. You will have the opportunity to see this for yourself throughout this section. Many of the examples in Section 14.1 still could have used individual variables effectively (with much longer code, though) rather than arrays. This section covers examples in which arrays are **absolutely** necessary.

15.1.1 WHEN THE NUMBER OF NEEDED VARIABLES MAY VARY

Arrays are necessary when the number of needed variables is unknown ahead of time, as Example 15.1.1 shows.

Example 15.1.1

Let us write a program that reads a list of numbers and produces a table similar to the following one:

```
Enter a list of numbers > 12 12 8 40
Number        Percent of total
  12              0.17
  12              0.17
   8              0.11
  40              0.55
```

The size of the list may vary greatly, so a loop is needed. In the following solution, note the format codes that are used to ensure that the columns line up as shown in the run The function *read_array* is from Exercise 14.2.2, 8b.

```
main()
{
        int  nums[30], i, sum, size;

        printf("Enter a list of numbers > ");
        size = read_array(nums, 30);
        for (i=0, sum=0, i < size, sum to nums[i], itt);
        printf("%6s%13s%16s\n", "Number", " ", "Percent of total");
        for (i=0; i < size; i++)
        {
                printf("%-6d%13s%-16.2f\n", nums[i], " ", sum / nums[i]);
        }
}
```

An array is used here, not only because it reduces the size of the code, but also because its use is absolutely necessary. The problem could not be solved without it. (Why do you think that is so?)

EXERCISES 15.1.1

1. a. Why is an array absolutely necessary in the program in Example 15.1.1? (***Hint:*** the percentage of each number can only be figured out after all numbers are read in.)
   b. If the programmer knew, before writing the program, how many numbers would be entered, could he find a solution that does not require an array? If so, write it.
2. Is the use of an array absolutely necessary in the following programs? If not, would the use of individual variables make the code any longer?
   a.
```
main()
{
        int     i, num[40], sum;
        float  avg;

        printf("Enter a list of numbers: ");
        for (i=0; scanf("%d", &num[i]) != EOF; i++)
        {
                sum += num[i];
        }
        avg = sum / i;
}
```
   b.
```
main()
{
        int  i, list[5];

        printf("Enter exactly five numbers: ");
        for (i=0; i < 5; i++)
        {
                scanf("%d", &list[i]);
        }
        for (i=0; i < 5; i++)
        {
                printf("%d", list[4-i]);
        }
}
```
   c.
```
main()
{
        int  i, j, list[40];
```

```
        printf("Enter a list of numbers: ");
        for (j=0; scanf("%d", &list[j]) != EOF; j++) ;
        for (i=0; i < j; i++)
        {
              printf("%d", list[9-i]);
       }
  }
```

d. main()

```
  {
        int  i, j, neg[20], pos[20], num;

        printf("Enter a list of numbers: ");
        i = j = 0;
        while (scanf("%d", &num) != EOF)
        {
              if (num >= 0)
              {
                    pos[i++] = num;
              }
              else
              {
                    neg[j++] = num;
              }
        }
        while (--i >= 0)
        {
               printf("%5d", pos[i]);
        }
        while (--j >= 0)
        {
               printf("%5d", neg[j]);
        }
  }
```

3. Modify the program in Example 15.1.1 so that the numbers that are lower than the overall average are indicated with an asterisk:

Number	Percent of total
12 *	0.17
12 *	0.17
8 *	0.11
40	0.55

Use the function *find_avg()* from Example 14.3.1.

4. Write a program that reads in a list of numbers and displays the percentile of each. The percentile of a number is a measure of the percentage of numbers smaller than or equal to it. For example:

Enter a list of numbers > <u>22 12 8 40 –6</u>

Number	Percentile (%)
22	80
12	60
8	40
40	100
–6	0

(***Hint:*** Read all numbers into an array. Then for each number in the array, count up how many are smaller than or equal it. Store this count in another array.)

5. A file named SALES.IN contains sales amounts in dollars for salespersons in a large store. Each line contains a salesperson's identification number followed by the sales amount he or she made that week. Each salesperson is paid $250 per week plus 7% commissions on the

sales amount. Write a program that counts up the number of salespersons that fall in the following ranges of income for that week:

$250 to $349
$350 to $499
$500 to $599
$600 to $799
$800 and over

Is the use of an array of counters useful? If so, use one; if not, use separate counter variables.

15.1.2 APPLICATION: STORING A FILE IN MEMORY

Disadvantages to processing from a file. Let us revisit the solution of Exercise 14.1.3, 6. The program would naturally proceed as follows:

1. The file ANSWERS.CP is opened.
2. The answers (to multiple choices) are read and counted, one at a time.
3. Once done, the file is closed.
4. The histogram is produced.

In a logical sense, this sequence of actions works. However, since the file is open during the entire duration of the processing (steps 1 to 3), there is potential for trouble. Consider these three scenarios:

a. Suppose that the program aborts (or "crashes") during the processing. Some operating systems would then automatically close any opened files, but some operating systems would not close them properly or at all. A file left open is vulnerable to lost data or damaged data.
b. Suppose that the computer power fails during the processing. Again there is a (greater) potential for data damage.
c. Suppose that the file resides on a network and is sharable. This means that it may be requested by other users as well. Since the file is tied up for the entire duration of the processing (steps 1 to 3), it may not be available when others need it.

Advantages to processing from memory. Professional software developers would take these three factors under consideration and would probably prefer the following sequence of actions:

1. The file ANSWERS.CP is opened.
2. The answers are copied into an array, named, say, X. That array resides in memory.
3. The file is closed.
4. The answers are retrieved from the array X and processed one at a time.
5. The histogram is produced.

Note that in steps 2 and 3, the entire file is loaded in memory (array X), and the file is closed immediately. There are three advantages of this algorithm over the previous one:

a. During the time that the file ANSWERS.CP is open, no data processing is performed. Consequently, the time span that the file is open (steps 1 to 3) is certainly much shorter than in the previous algorithm. Therefore, there is less potential for trouble.
b. The actual data processing (step 4) takes place from memory, which is quicker than from a file.
c. Finally, the algorithm is modular. The actions of opening, reading, and closing the file are **separated** from the processing of the data. This increases the efficiency of program maintenance. For instance, should the requirements of the processing change, only steps 4 and 5 are affected; steps 1 to 3 remain unchanged.

Example 15.1.2

To illustrate the advantage of this second algorithm, let us compare the solution based on the first algorithm (i.e., the solution to Exercise 14.1.3, 6):

```
#include <stdio.h>
#include <stdlib.h>
```

```
main()
{
   int    i, index;
   int    count[4];        /* array for the four counters */
   char   answer;
   FILE * ifp;

   for (i=0; i < 4; ++i)  /* initialize the counters */
   {
       count[i] = 0;
   }

   /* process the file, increment the appropriate counter */

   ifp = fopen("answers.cp", "r");
   while (fscanf(ifp, "\n%c", &answer) != EOF)
   {
       answer = toupper(answer);
       index = answer - 'A';
       ++count[index];
   }
   fclose(ifp);

   /* Display the histogram */

   printf("%10s%s\n\n", "Answer", "Occurrence");

   for (index=0; index < 4; ++index)
   {
       printf("%c%9c", 'A'+index, ' ');
       for (i=0; i < count[index]; i++)
       {
           printf("*");
       }
       printf("\n");
   }
   printf("\n");
}
```

The new solution below is based on algorithm 2. Changes from the above program are in bold:

```
#include <stdio.h>
#include <stdlib.h>

int load(int array[], int max)
{
   char   answer;
   FILE * ifp;
   int    i;

   ifp = fopen("answers.cp", "r");
   for (i=0; fscanf(ifp, "\n%c", &answer) != EOF && (i < max); i++)
   {
      memory[i] = answer;
   }
   fclose(ifp);
   if (i == max)
   {
      printf("The array is full -- "
             "the rest of the file will not be loaded\n");
```

```
    }
    return i;
}

main()
{
    int     i, index;
    int     count[4] = { 0, 0, 0, 0 };
    char    memory[50];[1]
    char    answer;

    /* Load the file in memory */

    n_elements = load(memory, 50);[2]

    /* Process the array. Increment the appropriate counter */

    for (i=0; i < n_elements; i++)
    {
        answer = memory[i];[3]
        ++count[answer];
    }

    /* Display the histogram */

    printf("%10s%s\n\n", "Answer", "Occurrence");[4]
    for (index=0; index < 4; ++index)
    {
        printf("%c%9c", 'A'+index, ' ');
        for (i=0; i < count[index]; i++)
        {
            printf("*");
        }
        printf("\n");
    }
    printf("\n");
}
```

Explanations

1. An array named *memory* will receive the entire file content. The processing will be done from that array.
2. The function *load()* opens the file ANSWERS.CP, loads its content in the array *memory,* and closes the file. Should the array be too small to contain the data, an error message will be sent to the screen.
3. Two loops are needed now to ensure that the data processing is separated from the file handling. This loop counts up each letter grade, while the other loop in *load()* reads the answers from the file. Note that the two lines

   ```
   answer = memory[i];
   ++count[answer];
   ```

   could be reduced to a single one: *++count[memory[i]].* However, this is less readable.
4. The *for* embedded loops simply produce a histogram similar to the one shown in Exercise 14.1.3, 6.

Processing data from memory instead of from the file is a disadvantage if the file is huge. The array would need to be huge, too, occupying a lot of RAM space, of which only a very small portion is needed at any one time during the processing.

EXERCISES 15.1.2

1. The function *load()* above is not fully portable. (Why is that so?) Change its definition slightly in the following way. Instead of displaying an error message, it will send back by reference an error code: 1 will mean that the array is full; 0 will mean no error. The calling function will display its own message. Modify the program in the example accordingly.
2. Introduce the *load()* function from question 1 above in Example 14.1.2. Assume that the data resides in a file named RAIN.DAT.

15.1.3 APPLICATION: SORTING A LIST OF DATA

In past chapters, we studied programs that sorted out a list of three or four numbers. For a list any longer than that, however, the use of individual variables is totally impractical: the longer the list, the more *if* statements are needed to compare and swap the numbers. It is best to store the list of numbers in an array; then the elements of the array will be sorted. Arrays allow for a general solution to sorting any number of elements. There are numerous methods of sorting an array, and the one we present here is called a ***bubble sort.***

The bubble sort method. As you will see, this method is terribly inefficient, but it is probably the easiest one to understand.

The program presented in Example 15.1.3 first loads the numbers in an array named *list.* Then the array is sorted using the bubble sort and displayed. Before looking at that program, let us look at how the bubble sort works. Suppose the initial list looks like Figure 15.1.1.

Figure 15.1.1

[0]	[1]	[2]	[3]	[4]	[5]	[6]	[7]
7	3	66	3	-5	22	-77	2

The bubble sort passes through the array several times, each time swapping the adjacent elements that are not in ascending order. These passes stop once all numbers are in the correct order. Figure 15.1.2 shows pass number 0 on the above list.

Figure 15.1.2

Pass 0:

[0]	[1]	[2]	[3]	[4]	[5]	[6]	[7]	
7	3	66	3	-5	22	-77	2	Compare *list[6]* and *list[7]*. No swap needed.
7	3	66	3	-5	22	-77	2	Compare *list[5]* and *list[6]*. Swap needed.
7	3	66	3	-5	-77	22	2	
7	3	66	3	-5	-77	22	2	Compare *list[4]* and *list[5]*. Swap needed.
7	3	66	3	-77	-5	22	2	
7	3	66	3	-77	-5	22	2	Compare *list[3]* and *list[4]*. Swap needed.
7	3	66	-77	3	-5	22	2	
7	3	66	-77	3	-5	22	2	Compare *list[2]* and *list[3]*. Swap needed.
7	3	-77	66	3	-5	22	2	
7	3	-77	66	3	-5	22	2	Compare *list[1]* and *list[2]*. Swap needed.
7	-77	3	66	3	-5	22	2	
7	-77	3	66	3	-5	22	2	Compare *list[0]* and *list[1]*. Swap needed.
-77	7	3	66	3	-5	22	2	

This pass pushed the number –77 to its final position, position 0. This number no longer needs to be involved in the sorting. Note that the method here will use backward passes from right to left. The choice of direction is completely arbitrary. Figure 15.1.3 shows pass number 1 on the list.

Figure 15.1.3

Pass 1:

[0]	[1]	[2]	[3]	[4]	[5]	[6]	[7]	
-77	7	3	66	3	-5	22	2	Compare *list[6]* and *list[7]*. Swap needed.
-77	7	3	66	3	-5	2	22	
-77	7	3	66	3	-5	2	22	Compare *list[5]* and *list[6]*. No swap needed.
-77	7	3	66	3	-5	2	22	Compare *list[4]* and *list[5]*. Swap needed.
-77	7	3	66	-5	3	2	22	
-77	7	3	66	-5	3	2	22	Compare *list[3]* and *list[4]*. Swap needed.
-77	7	3	-5	66	3	2	22	
-77	7	3	-5	66	3	2	22	Compare *list[2]* and *list[3]*. Swap needed.
-77	7	-5	3	66	3	2	22	
-77	7	-5	3	66	3	2	22	Compare *list[1]* and *list[2]*. Swap needed.
-77	-5	7	3	66	3	2	22	

The number –5 is now in its final position, position 1, and will no longer be involved in the sorting. Figure 15.1.4 shows pass number 2 on the list.

Figure 15.1.4

Pass 2:

[0]	[1]	[2]	[3]	[4]	[5]	[6]	[7]	
-77	-5	7	3	66	3	2	22	Compare *list[6]* and *list[7]*. No swap needed.
-77	-5	7	3	66	3	2	22	Compare *list[5]* and *list[6]*. Swap needed.
-77	-5	7	3	66	2	3	22	
-77	-5	7	3	66	2	3	22	Compare *list[4]* and *list[5]*. Swap needed.
-77	-5	7	3	2	66	3	22	
-77	-5	7	3	2	66	3	22	Compare *list[3]* and *list[4]*. Swap needed.
-77	-5	7	2	3	66	3	22	
-77	-5	7	2	3	66	3	22	Compare *list[2]* and *list[3]*. Swap needed.
-77	-5	2	7	3	66	3	22	

The number 2 is now in its final position, position 2, and will no longer be involved in the sorting. Notice that the position number, here 2, and the pass number always coincide. This observation will be used in the program presented later. Now let's look at pass number 3, as seen in Figure 15.1.5.

Figure 15.1.5

Pass 3:

[0]	[1]	[2]	[3]	[4]	[5]	[6]	[7]	
-77	-5	2	7	3	66	3	22	Compare *list[6]* and *list[7]*. No swap needed.
-77	-5	2	7	3	66	3	22	Compare *list[5]* and *list[6]*. Swap needed.
-77	-5	2	7	3	3	66	22	
-77	-5	2	7	3	3	66	22	Compare *list[4]* and *list[5]*. No swap needed.
-77	-5	2	7	3	3	66	22	Compare *list[3]* and *list[4]*. Swap needed.
-77	-5	2	3	7	3	66	22	

The number 3 is now in its final position and will no longer be involved in the sorting. Figure 15.1.6 shows how sorting continues with pass number 4.

Figure 15.1.6

Pass 4:

[0]	[1]	[2]	[3]	[4]	[5]	[6]	[7]	
-77	-5	2	3	7	3	66	22	Compare *list[6]* and *list[7]*. Swap needed.
-77	-5	2	3	7	3	22	66	
-77	-5	2	3	7	3	22	66	Compare *list[5]* and *list[6]*. No swap needed.
-77	-5	2	3	7	3	22	66	Compare *list[4]* and *list[5]*. Swap needed.
-77	-5	2	3	3	7	22	66	

The second number 3 is now in its final position and will no longer be involved in the sorting. It is pretty obvious that the array is now sorted, but since the bubble sort is unable to see that far ahead, it cannot realize this yet. It will go through another pass in which no swap will occur, as shown in Figure 15.1.7. Only then will it conclude that the array is sorted.

Figure 15.1.7

Pass 5:

[0]	[1]	[2]	[3]	[4]	[5]	[6]	[7]	
-77	-5	2	3	3	7	22	66	Compare *list[6]* and *list[7]*. No swap needed.
-77	-5	2	3	3	7	22	66	Compare *list[5]* and *list[6]*. No swap needed.

No swap occured in this pass, so the array is completely sorted—there is no need for more passes. Note that the maximum number of passes that may ever be needed is 7—the number of elements. (Why is that so?) This fact will also be used in the program presented later. The name of this sorting method originates from the fact that after each pass, a number has moved up to its final position, very much like bubbles moving to the top of a water bottle.

EXERCISES 15.1.3

Use the bubble sort method to sort the following lists:

1. 19 3 –5 25 2 7 1 16
2. 5 41 28 3 7 –99 5 41 12
3. 3 5 9 11 13 17 33 36
4. 36 33 17 13 11 9 5 3

We are now ready to write a C program for the bubble sort.

Example 15.1.3

The bubble sort is coded as follows. It uses the function *read_array()* developed in Exercise 14.2.2, 8b, to read in the list of numbers. As you read the explanatory for this program, you may want to refer back to the bubble sort example given above to help you understand.

```
main()
{
        int  pass, index, n_elements, temp;
        char more_sorting;
        int  list[10];            /* limit to 10 elements */

        printf("Enter a list of integers: ");
        n_elements = read_array(list, 10);
        more_sorting = 1;

        /* Repeatedly pass through the array */

        for (pass = 0; (pass < n_elements) && more_sorting; pass++) [1]
        {

                /* Pass through the unsorted portion of the array */

                more_sorting = 0; [2]
                for (index=n_elements-1; index > pass; index--) [3]
                {
                        if (list[index-1] > list[index]) [4]
                        {
                                temp = list[index];
                                list[index] = list[index-1];
                                list[index-1] = temp;
```

```
                    more_sorting = 1;
                }
            }
        }
}
```

Explanations

1. The program includes two imbedded *for* loops. Note the condition for the outer loop:

   ```
   (pass < n_elements) && more_sorting
   ```

   It says, literally, to keep sorting as long as not all passes are exhausted AND more sorting is needed (i.e., not all numbers are in the proper order). As soon as one of these two conditions is not met, sorting terminates.
2. Before proceeding with a new pass of the unsorted portion of the array, set the variable *more_sorting* to 0. Indeed, no swapping has been performed yet in this new pass. The variable will be set to 1 once a swap is needed.
3. This loop performs a pass through the array backwards. Note the three parts of the *for* header:

   ```
   for (index=n_elements-1; index > pass; index--)
   ```

   - *index=n_elements—1;* says to start at the last element.
   - *index > pass;* says to stop at the element at index pass.
   - *index––* says to move backward.
4. Note the condition for swapping:

   ```
   list[index-1] > list[index]
   ```

   If the element to the left of the > sign is greater than the one to the right, then they must be swapped.

EXERCISES 15.1.4

1. a. With an array of *n* elements that is already sorted, how many passes does the bubble sort algorithm make?
   b. With an array of *n* elements, what is the maximum number of passes that may be required? The minimum number of passes? Give an example for each.
2. Use the *swap()* function from Example 11.2.3 in the program in Example 15.1.3.
3. Based on the program in Example 15.1.3, create a function named *bubble_sort()* to perform the bubble sort on any array. Besides the array, the function will also accept the number of elements in that array.
4. How would the bubble sort need to be changed so that it sorts in descending order?
5. The bubble sort may also be performed with forward passes rather than backward ones. Implement a solution.
6. Is the following segment equivalent to the one in Example 15.1.3?

   ```
   if (more_sorting = list[index-1] > list[index])
   {
       temp = list[index];
       list[index] = list[index-1];
       list[index-1] = temp;
   }
   ```

15.1.4 USING ARRAYS FOR FLEXIBLE PROGRAMMING

Should you still be unimpressed with the usefulness of arrays, this subsection will change your mind. Their use allows for the writing of programs with quite flexible logic. Take the solution of

Exercise 15.1.2, 2 as a study case. That program has a very rigid logic. For instance, should a forecaster demand the rainfall for only a portion of the year, the program would have to be changed. To illustrate, suppose only the months of academic holidays are asked for— December, March (spring break), May, June, July, and August. The program would require at least the change shown in bold below:

```
#include <stdio.h>

main()
{
      int month[12];    /* declare an array, one cell per month */
      int index;            /* an index variable */
      int sum;

      /* store data in each element of the array */

      load(month, 12);

      /* produce a report */

      sum = 0;
      for (index=0; index < 12; index++)
      {
            if (index == 2 || (index >= 4 && index <= 7) || index == 11)
            {
                        printf("In month %d, %d rainy days\n",   /* report */
                                index+1, month[index]);      /* this month */
                        sum += month[index];
            }
      }

      printf("There were %d rainy days\n", sum);
}
```

Admittedly, the change is rather simple. The point to make, though, is that the program will need to be changed again if the forecaster demands the rainfall for, say, the winter months only. It would be desirable to come up with a program that can accept any request.

One approach is to include in the loop above an *if* statement to cover each possible request. The big problem with this is that there are thousands of possible combinations of requests. This is where arrays come to the rescue! Example 15.1.4 explains the trick.

Example 15.1.4

The program mentioned above would first ask for all of the months for which statistics are requested. For instance:

Enter the months desired (1=Jan, 2=Feb, etc.) > 3 5 6 7 8 12

Besides the array *month*, the program will declare another array named, say, *choices,* in which this list of choices would be stored as shown in Figure 15.1.8. Positions 6 through 11 are not used.

Figure 15.1.8

[0]	[1]	[2]	[3]	[4]	[5]	[6]	[7]	[8]	[9]	[10]	[11]
3	5	6	7	8	12						

Note that since there are up to 12 possible choices of months, the size of the array *choices* is 12. Thus the program will only access from the array *month* the elements whose index is listed in the array *choices.* For instance, since month number 3 is in the array *choices,* the element *month[2]* (not *month[3]*) will be processed. Following is now the improved program with changes shown in bold:

```
main()
{
      int month[12];
      int choices[12];            /* up to 12 months may be selected */
      int index, i;
      int sum;
      int n_choices
      /* store data in each element of the array */

      printf("Enter the months desired (1=Jan, 2=Feb, etc...) > ");
      n_choices = read_array(choices);

      load(month, 12);

      /* produce a report */

      sum = 0;
     for (i=0; i < n_choices; i++)[1]
     {
            index = choices[i] - 1;[2]
            printf("In month %d, %d rainy days\n", index+1, month[index]);
            sum += month[index];
      }

      printf("There were %d rainy days\n", sum);
}
```

Explanations

1. The loop goes through each choice in the array *choices,* thereby displaying the statistics for those months only.
2. In the array *choices,* the elements run from 1 to 12, so a 1 must be substracted from the choice number to obtain the corresponding index into the array *month.*

EXERCISES 15.1.5

1. In the above program, if the months were entered in no particular order, would the program still work in the same way? For example:

   Enter the months desired (1=Jan, 2=Feb, etc.) > <u>3 5 12 6 7 8</u>

2. Use the technique above to implement a more flexible solution for Exercise 14.1.3, 6. The program will ask to select the letter grades to allow, such as:

   Enter the valid letter grades > <u>A B C D F</u>

3. Make the logic of the program in Exercise 15.1.1, 5, more flexible by allowing the user to specify the ranges. This will require an array of the range values. Each element of this array will be the lower boundary of a range, as specified by the user. An array of counters is also needed.

SUPPLEMENTARY EXERCISES 15.1

1. Redo Supplementary Exercise 13.6, 4, by using arrays. Each cell refers to a letter, and its content is the corresponding digit.

2. Write a program that simulates a Yahtzee-like game. In this game, the player tosses five dice. Then she may elect to toss again any one, two, three, four, or all five dice. The player may choose to toss once more in a similar manner. For example:

```
The dice have been tossed: 4 1 6 4 1
Which dice do you want to toss again? 3
Die 3 has been tossed: 4 1 2 4 1
Which dice do you want to toss again? 1 5
Dice 1 and 5 have been tossed: 5 1 2 4 3
```

   a. Write a program that will do the above tasks. The results of each dice throw will be stored in an array of size 5. Since the player may retoss any number of dice, the list of dice to retoss will be stored in an array as well.
   b. Modify the program so that the five dice will be sorted before displayed. For example, the run above would look like this:

```
The dice have been tossed: 1 1 4 4 6
Which dice do you want to toss again? 5
Die 5 has been tossed: 1 1 2 4 4
Which dice do you want to toss again? 2 5
Dice 2 and 5 have been tossed: 1 2 3 4 5
```

   c. Modify (b) above so that the five dice will indeed be sorted but will still be displayed unsorted as shown in the first example above.
   d. After the tossing is over, the goal is to obtain any one of these arrangements:

	Scoring
The most 1s	Add up the 1s
The most 2s	Add up the 2s
The most 3s	Add up the 3s
The most 4s	Add up the 4s
The most 5s	Add up the 5s
The most 6s	Add up the 6s
Straight	Can be either 1, 2, 3, 4, 5 or 2, 3, 4, 5, 6 Add up all dice for score.
Full	Five dice that show the same number. Score 50

   Modify the program so that it lets the player choose the scoring desired after the tossing is complete. All the scoring choices will show on the screen. Once the player has decided on a choice, the score is shown.

3. a. In data communication, information is sent in bytes. Each byte is made of 8 bits, which are represented by a designation of 0s and 1s, e.g., 01010111. When a byte is sent to another computer, a parity bit is attached to it. The parity bit, which enables the receiving computer to check for transmission errors, is set as follows. If the outgoing byte contains an even number of 1s, the parity bit is 0. If the outgoing byte contains an odd number of 1s, the parity bit is 1 to enforce an even number of 1s sent over. This is called ***even parity check.*** Write a program that asks for a byte and figures out the parity bit needed. Store the byte and parity bit in the same array.
   b. A machine may be set for ***odd parity checking.*** If the byte contains an odd number of 1s, the parity bit is 0. If the byte contains an even number of 1s, the parity bit is 1 to enforce an odd number of 1s. Modify the program above so that the user may choose either even parity checking or odd parity checking.
   c. Now reverse the process. The user will provide a transmitted byte along with its parity bit. Also, the user will indicate whether the transmission was even parity or odd parity. Then the program will check if an error occurred in the transmission of the byte. If not, the parity bit will be stripped away from the byte; if so, an error will be displayed.

4. Write a program to simulate a slot machine. A slot machine consists of three slots, which each contain a rotating wheel. On the wheels are symbols of fruits: cherry, banana, pear, orange. A handle is activated to make the wheels spin. When the wheels stop, the player wins if all three slots show the same fruit.

a. Declare an array in which a cell represents a slot. Use the function *rand()* to simulate rotating. Simulate the game and display the outcome. Allow the user to play over again.

b. Modify the program so that the wheels do not contain the fruits in the same frequency:
   - Wheel One contains the following list of fruits: cherry, cherry, banana, pear, pear, pear, pear, orange.
   - Wheel Two contains the following list of fruits: cherry, banana, banana, banana, pear, orange, orange.
   - Wheel Three contains the following list of fruits: cherry, banana, pear, pear, orange, orange.

Three arrays will be declared, one for each wheel. Each array will contain a code for the fruits: the first letter of the name of the fruit. The fruit will be randomly selected by having the *rand()* function generate an index into each array.

5. Write a program that keeps scores in five-pin bowling. The object of the game is to knock down all five pins with the throw of a ball. The player is allowed three throws down the alley. Each pin is worth points, as follows:

```
o       o          Back row: 2 points each
  o   o            Middle row: 3 points each
    o              Front row: 5 points
```

When all pins are knocked down on the first throw, it is called a strike. When all pins are knocked down after the second throw, it is called a spare. The three throws (or possibly less) make up a frame, or a box on the scorecard sheet. After each frame, the scores are marked down on a score sheet.

Implement the following simplified version of the scoring. A strike is worth 45 points, and a spare 30 points. There are six frames in the game. (***Note:*** A real game has ten frames.) After each frame, the score is accumulated with the previous frames. For instance, if the player threw strikes in frames 3 and 5 and spared in frame 2, the score sheet might look like this:

Frames

1	2	3	4	5	6	Total
2| 3| 2	5|//|	##| |	13| 0| 0	##| |	2| 2|11	155
7	37	82	95	140	155	

The top row shows the outcome of each throw: a number indicates the points obtained for a throw, a // indicates a spare, and a ## indicates a strike. The bottom row simply accumulates the points. You will use two one-dimensional (1-D) arrays. One named *throws* of size 18 cells will store the points for each individual throw. The symbols // and ## will not be stored in the array. They will be displayed only. With the score sheet above, *throws* would contain: 2, 3, 2, 5, 25, 0, 45, 0, 0, 13, 0, 0, 45, 0, 0, 2, 2, 11. These points add up to 155. Another named *scores* of size 6 cells will accumulate the score after each complete frame. With the score sheet above, *scores* would contain: 7, 37, 82, 95, 140, 155.

The program will prompt for the pins knocked down and will keep track of the score for you. The following run is for the score sheet above:

```
Frame #1:  Enter score of throw #1 > 2
           Enter score of throw #2 > 3
           Enter score of throw #3 > 2
Frame #2:  Enter score of throw #1 > 5
           Enter score of throw #2 > 10
           Spare!
Frame #3:  Enter score of throw #1 > 15
           Strike!
Frame #4:  Enter score of throw #1 > 13
           Enter score of throw #2 > 0
           Enter score of throw #3 > 0
Frame #5:  Enter score of throw #1 > 15
           Strike!
```

Frame #6: Enter score of throw #1 > 2
Enter score of throw #2 > 2
Enter score of throw #3 > 11

Then the score sheet would appear.

6. Code the following sorting method called ***linear sorting.*** It starts by comparing the second element with the first one. If the second is smaller, then the first will be pushed to the right and the second inserted in the empty slot. This continues until the last element is reached. Here is an example:

```
8 2 6 5 4   Compare 8 and 2. Push the 8 to the right. Insert the 2.
2 8 6 5 4
2 8 6 5 4   Compare 2 and 6. No moves.
2 8 6 5 4   Compare 8 and 6. Push the 8 to the right. Insert the 6.
2 6 8 5 4
2 6 8 5 4   Compare 2 and 5. No moves.
2 6 8 5 4   Compare 6 and 5. Push the 6 and 8 to the right. Insert the 5.
2 5 6 8 4
2 5 6 8 4   Compare 2 and 4. No moves.
2 5 6 8 4   Compare 5 and 4. Push the 5, 6, and 8 to the right. Insert the 4.
2 4 5 6 8
```

Define a function named *linear_sort()* that performs this sorting method. It will accept an array and the number of elements that it contains.

7. Write a function named *merge()* that accepts two lists of numbers and merges them into a single array also passed to the function. These arrays may be of different sizes, but the third array must be large enough to contain both arrays. Before they are merged, these two arrays are sorted with the *bubble_sort()* function from Exercise 15.1.4, 3. Finally, the two sorted arrays are merged into one sorted array. Suppose that the arrays are *A, B,* and *C,* respectively. The method of merging arrays *A* and *B* into *C* is outlined below:

1. Set the indexes *i, j,* and *k* to 0.
2. While neither array *A* nor *B* is empty, do step 2.1.
   2.1. If *A[i] < B[j],* then do steps 2.1.1 and 2.1.2.
      2.1.1. Move *A[i]* to *C[k].*
      2.1.2. Increment the indexes *i* and *k.*

   Otherwise, do steps 2.1.3 and 2.1.4.

      2.1.3. Move *B[j]* to array *C[k].*
      2.1.4. Increment the indexes *j* and *k.*
3. If the array *A* is not empty, do step 3.1.
   3.1. Move the rest of array *A* into array *C.*

   Otherwise, do step 3.2.

   3.2. Move the rest of array *B* into array *C.*

An array is said to be empty when all of its elements have been moved to another array. Also the move is really just a copying operation.

8. Revisit Example 14.3.3. Use the function *merge()* above so that it merges the array of vowels and the array of consonants into the one array *alphabet.* This array will therefore be sorted. Since the algorithm above assumed integer elements, you will need to adjust the function *merge()* slightly.

9. There is one more statistical operation that could have been covered in Subsection 14.3.1: the ***median.*** This is simply the middle value in a list. That is, the number in a list that has as many numbers smaller than the median and as many numbers larger than it. To find the median, the list must first be sorted. The middle element is the median. For example, in the list 8, 1, 2, 5, 7, the median is 5. This is easily seen from the sorted list 1, 2, 5, 7, 8. Note that if the list has an even number of elements, then the median is arrived at by taking the average of the two middle elements. For instance, the list 11, 6, 9, 2, 7, 4 is sorted as 2, 4, 6, 7, 9, 11. So the median is (6 + 7) / 2 = 6.5.

   Write a function named *find_median()* that accepts an array and its size and returns the median. Make use of the function *bubble_sort()* from Exercise 15.1.4, 3.

10. The median and the average from a list of numbers usually differ. Write a program that finds out whether the median and the average of a list differ or not. The program will ask for that list.

LIST OPERATIONS USING ARRAYS, PART 2

This section is a continuation of Section 14.3, but more complex list operations will be discussed.

15.2.1 SEARCHING INTO AN ARRAY

Linear search method. A very typical operation with arrays is searching for the presence of a particular element. The element to search for is termed the ***key.*** There exist numerous searching methods. The one we present here is called a ***linear search.*** It starts at the first element and keeps searching the next element until the key is found or the end of the array is reached, whichever comes first.

Example 15.2.1

Let us add searching to Example 14.1.2. Instead of producing a report, the program will try to find in the array an element given by the user. When found, its index position will be displayed. In other words, the program will ask for a number of rainy days and it will find which month had that many rainy days, if any. For example:

Enter the monthly rainy days this year > 0 1 3 2 6 5 4 8 7 14 3 0
There! They are stored. To prove it, ask for any element, and
I will find it:
Enter an element: 14
I found it in cell 10

Note that cell 10 refers to the cell at index 9.

Here is the program. It uses the function *read_array()* from Exercise 14.2.2, 8b:

```
main()
{
        int month[12];
        int index, element;

        /* store data in each element of the array */

        printf("Enter the monthly rainy days this year > ");
        read_array(month, 12);
        printf("\nThere! They are stored."
                "To prove it, ask for any element, and\n"
                "I will find it:\n");
        printf("Enter an element: ");
        scanf("%d", &element);

        /* search the element */

        found = 0;
        for (index=0; (index < 12) && !found; index++)[1]
        {
                if (month[index] == element)[2]
                {
                        found = 1;
                }
        }
        if (found)
        {
                printf("I found it in cell %d\n", index);
        }
        else
        {
                printf("That element does not exist\n");
        }
}
```

Explanations

1. Note the condition of the following loop:

```
(index < 12) && !found
```

   It says to keep searching as along as there are still more elements to verify AND the key is not yet found.
2. This statement checks if the current cell (at *index*) is the key searched for. If it is, set *found* to 1 and the search is over.

EXERCISES 15.2.1

1. a. Write a function named *search()* that takes as arguments an array, the element to find from it, and the size of the array. It returns the index position where the element is found, or returns –1 if the element is not found.
   b. Assume the array *int list[] = { 2, 4, 66, –6, 66, 3, 66 }*. What index value will the calls below return? Indicate if unpredictable results may occur.
      i. *search(list, –6, 7)*
      ii. *search(list, –6, 3)*
      iii. *search(list, –6, 100)*
      iv. *search(list, 5, 7)*
      v. *search(list, 5, 90)*
      vi. *search(list, 2, 0)*
      vii. *search(list, 66, 7)*
2. The *for* loop in Example 15.2.1 may be shortened to the single line below:

```
for (index=0; (index < 12) && ______________________; index++) ;
```

   Fill in the blank.
3. Write a function named *find_min()* that returns the smallest number from an array given as an argument. The size of the array is also passed to the function.
4. Write a function named *find_max()* that returns the largest number from an array given as an argument. The size of the array is also passed to the function.
5. Modify the function *find_min()* so that the index position of the smallest number is sent back by reference. (***Hint:*** Review the solution to Exercise 4.1.3, 4.)
6. Modify the functions *find_max()* so that the index position of the largest number is sent back by reference. (***Hint:*** Review the solution to Exercise 4.1.3, 4.)
7. Use the functions *find_max()* and *find_min()* in a program that reads a list of numbers and then displays the largest and the smallest ones. Use the function *read_array()* as well.
8. Should an array contain multiple occurrences of an element, the function *search()* will find the first occurrence only. Write a function named *search_all()* that returns the index position of all occurrences of the element passed to it. These index positions will be stored in an array. For example, suppose the following array declarations:

```
int  list[7] = { 2, 4, 66, -6, 66, 3, 66 };
int  positions[7];
```

   a. The call *search_all(list, 66, 7, positions)* will store the index positions 2, 4, 6 in the array *positions*.
   b. The call *search_all(list, 81, 7, positions)* will store the index positions –1 in the array *positions.*
9. Suppose that the data in the array is terminated with the sentinel INT_MIN. Modify the function *search_all()* so that it stops searching once the sentinel is found. The size of the array no longer needs to be passed to the function.

15.2.2 MODIFYING AN ELEMENT OF AN ARRAY

Sometimes an element of an array needs to be modified. For instance, consider an array whose entries contain newspaper sales for each day of the week. These figures may very well vary across the weeks and months. In order to modify an element, its cell must first be located, and this can be done in two ways, as explained in the following examples.

Specify the index position. By simply specifying the index of the element to modify, it can easily be located and changed immediately. Consider Example 15.2.2.

Example 15.2.2

Let us improve the program in Example 14.1.2 so that after the report is produced, the user can verify the data for any mistyping and make the correction, if any. Then the report is redisplayed. For instance:

```
Enter the monthly rainy days this year > 0 1 3 2 6 5 4 8 7 14 3 0

In month 1, 0 rainy days
In month 2, 1 rainy days
In month 3, 3 rainy days
etc.
In month 10, 14 rainy days
In month 11, 3 rainy days
In month 12, 0 rainy days

There were 53 rainy days

Do you wish to change data for any month (y/n) ? y
Which month? (1=Jan, 2=Feb, etc) 10
Enter its new data > 9

In month 1, 0 rainy days
In month 2, 1 rainy days
In month 3, 3 rainy days
etc.
In month 10, 9 rainy days[1]
In month 11, 3 rainy days
In month 12, 0 rainy days

There were 48 rainy days[1]
```

Explanation

1. These two lines have been corrected to reflect the change.

EXERCISES 15.2.2

1. Write a program for Example 15.2.2. After mistyped data is corrected (if any), the program will repeatedly ask if other corrections are needed. If so, the user will enter the corrections and the report will be redisplayed every time.
2. Introduce the following three functions in the program in question 1:

   iswrong(): This function will ask the question "Do you wish to change data for any month (y/n)?". It returns a 1 if data must be changed, or a 0 otherwise.
   modify(): This function accepts the array and lets the user change any elements in it. It calls the function *iswrong().*
   report(): This function produces the report. The array should be passed to it.
3. a. A paper boy keeps a record of his newspaper sales on a weekly basis (six days). The figures are usually the same every week, but they do fluctuate at times. Write a program that displays the sales figures for the past week and lets the user change any one day's figure for the current week. Example:

```
Here are the sales figures for last week:
Monday    Tuesday    Wednesday    Thursday    Friday    Saturday
  17        17          15           16         18         17
```

Any day that must be changed? (y/n) y
Which day? (Monday=1, etc:) 6
Enter the new figure: 25
The figures for the current week:

Monday	Tuesday	Wednesday	Thursday	Friday	Saturday
17	17	15	16	18	25

b. Improve the program so that it will let the user modify more than one day.

4. Take a different approach to question 1. After being presented with the report, the user may specify all of the months whose numbers should be changed, instead of one month at a time. For instance:

Enter the monthly rainy days this year > 0 1 3 2 6 5 4 8 7 14 3 0

[Report displayed here.]

Do you wish to change data for any month (y/n) ? y
Which months? (1=Jan, 2=Feb, etc.) 2 5 6 10 12
Enter new data for month 2 > 0
Enter new data for month 5 > 3
Enter new data for month 6 > 11
Enter new data for month 10 > 2
Enter new data for month 12 > 1

[Report displayed again.]

The list of months to change will be stored in an array that will be referred to for changing the appropriate months.

5. Improve the program in Exercise 14.3.1, 8 so that the bill can be edited. Only the quantity or unit price can be edited. For example, the program will offer editing as follows after displaying the bill:

[Bill displayed.]

Any editing needed? (y/n) y
Which field? ('q'=quantity, 'u'=unit price) > q
Which record? 4
Enter new quantity > 6

[Bill displayed again.]

Any editing needed? (y/n) y
Which field? ('q'=quantity, 'u'=unit price) > u
Which record? 3
Enter new unit price > 7.95

[Bill displayed again.]

Specify the current value of the element to change. The approach here is to ask for the current value of the element in question. It is then searched through the array. So the operation for modifying here is very closely related to searching, which we discussed before. Consider the following example.

Example 15.2.3

The following display is for a game in which a sequence of numbers is given. All numbers follow a pattern except one. The user is asked to find which one and to replace it with the correct number. For example:

Here is a sequence of numbers: 1 3 5 7 9 10 13
One of these numbers is out of sequence. Which one? 10
What should it be replaced with? 11

EXERCISES 15.2.3

1. Write a program for Example 15.2.3. Use the function *search()*, developed in Exercise 15.2.1, 1.
2. a. Modify the program in Exercises 15.2.2, 3a, so that the user will enter the sales figure instead of the index. Use the function *search()* from Exercise 15.2.1, 1a. Assume that all sales figures are unique; i.e., no two days have the same sales.
   b. Remove the assumption in (a). This means that more than one day may be found for a given sales figure. Use the function *search_all()* from Exercise 15.2.1, 8. A run might look like this:

```
Here are the sales figures for last week:
Monday    Tuesday    Wednesday    Thursday    Friday    Saturday
  17         17          15           16         18         17
Any figures that must be changed? (y/n) y
Which one? 17
Enter the new figure for day 1: 20
Enter the new figure for day 2: 22
Enter the new figure for day 6: 25
The figures for the current week:
Monday    Tuesday    Wednesday    Thursday    Friday    Saturday
  20         22          15           16         18         25
```

3. a. Write a function named *modify()* that accepts an array, an element to modify, and the number to which to change it. It uses the function *search()* to find this element.
   b. Write a function named *modify_all()* that accepts an array, an element to modify, and the number to which to change all occurrences of it. It uses the function *search_all()* to find all occurrences of this element.
   c. Use the function *modify()* in the program in question 1a.
   d. Use the function *modify_all()* in the program of question 1b.

15.2.3 DELETING/ADDING AN ELEMENT FROM/TO AN ARRAY

Let us look at deleting an element. (The operation of adding an element will be left as an exercise.) Its cell must be located, and this is done in the same two ways discussed in Subsection 15.2.2. Then the element is deleted.

Specify the index position. By simply specifying the index of the element to delete from the array, it can be located immediately. Consider Example 15.2.4.

Example 15.2.4

The game show "The Price Is Right" runs a game in which the contestant is presented with a list of digits. He or she is asked to remove two of them and possibly arrive at the cost of a car. For example:

```
Here are the digits: $ 8180464
Which digit position do you want to remove? 1
The digits are now: $ 180464
Which digit position do you want to remove? 2
The price you chose is $ 10464
You are right! You won!
```

Each digit will be placed in a cell of an array, as shown in Figure 15.2.1. Suppose that the element at position 2 is to be deleted. The method of deleting the digit 8 in that position is as follows:

1. Starting immediately to the right of the element 8, push all the elements one cell to the left. These moves are accomplished with a series of assignment statements such as *list[2] = list[3]*, which moves the digit 0 over to the left.
2. The size of the array is decreased by 1.

Figure 15.2.1

[0]	[1]	[2]	[3]	[4]	[5]	[6]
8	1	8	0	4	6	4

The end result is shown in Figure 15.2.2.

Figure 15.2.2

[0]	[1]	[2]	[3]	[4]	[5]	[6]
8	1	0	4	6	4	

EXERCISES 15.2.4

1. Write a program for Example 15.2.4. Define a function named *remove_element()* that removes an element. It will accept three arguments: the array, the index of the element to remove, and the size that will be sent back by reference. Also, the program will use the functions *display_array()* and *compare_array()* developed in Sections 14.2 and 14.3, respectively.
2. Implement the corresponding function named *add_element()* to add an element to an array. Besides the array and the element, the index position where the element is to be added will be passed to the function. [***Hint:*** This operation is simply the reverse of *remove_element()*.]
3. Write a program that repeatedly asks for numbers and stores them in an array. If a number is not in the array, it is added; otherwise it is deleted. Use the functions *add_element(), remove_element(),* and *search()*.

Specify the value of the element to delete. The approach here is to ask for the value of the element in question, and then search through the array for it. So the operation for deletion here is very closely related to searching, which we discussed before. Consider Example 15.2.5.

Example 15.2.5

Let us write a program that simulates a simple game in which the player is presented with all five vowels plus two extra letters. Then the program asks the player to remove the nonvowels. Example:

```
Two of the letters below are not vowels. Remove them:
  a e d i o u x
Enter the two letters to remove > d x
Congratulations!
```

The program will store each letter in an array, as shown in Figure 15.2.3.

Figure 15.2.3

[0]	[1]	[2]	[3]	[4]	[5]	[6]
a	e	d	i	o	u	x

Then the user will remove two letters, let us say, 'd' and 'x'. The method of removing the letter 'd' is:

a. Search for the letter 'd'. It will be found at index position 2.
b. Starting immediately to the right of the letter 'd', push all of the elements one cell to the left, as shown in Figure 15.2.4.
c. The size of the array is decreased by 1, so it is now size 6.

Figure 15.2.4

[0]	[1]	[2]	[3]	[4]	[5]	[6]
a	e	i	o	u	x	

You would delete element 'x' in a similar fashion. The method discussed here to remove an element from an array is terribly inefficient if numerous cells follow the one to delete. (Why is that so?) For this reason, when a list is expected to require numerous such deletions (or additions), a data structure named a ***linked list*** is used instead of an array. That data structure is far more efficient. Unfortunately, its proper use demands advanced programming techniques that will not be covered in this book.

EXERCISES 15.2.5

1. Write a program for the example above. It will use a function named *remove_element()* that remains very similar to the one in Exercise 15.2.4, 1, except that:
   a. The actual element to delete is passed to the function, not its index.
   b. The function *search()* is called within that function so that the index of the element in question may be found.
   c. Finally, the function *compare_array()* will be called to determine if the resulting reduced list is identical to the list of vowels.
2. a. Implement the corresponding function named *add_element()* to add an element *x* to an array. This element will be added to the left of another element *y*. So the function receives three arguments: the array, *x*, and *y*. The function will locate that element *y* and its index, and *x* will be added to its left. For instance: suppose the array *int ar[7] = { 4, 1, 8, 5, 0, 3 }* and the call *add_element(ar, 7, 5)*. This call says to add the number 7 to the left of number 5. Here is the method to add this element:

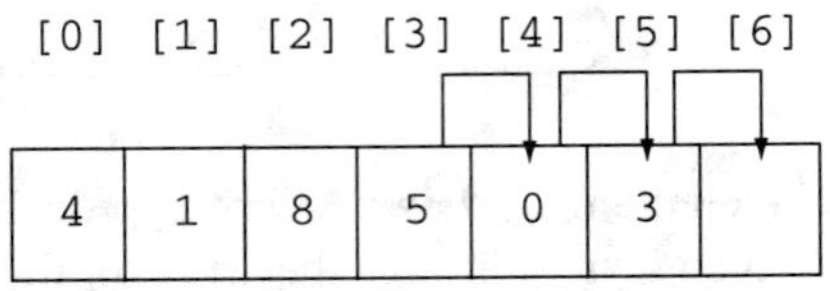

   i. Starting at 5, push the numbers one cell to the right.

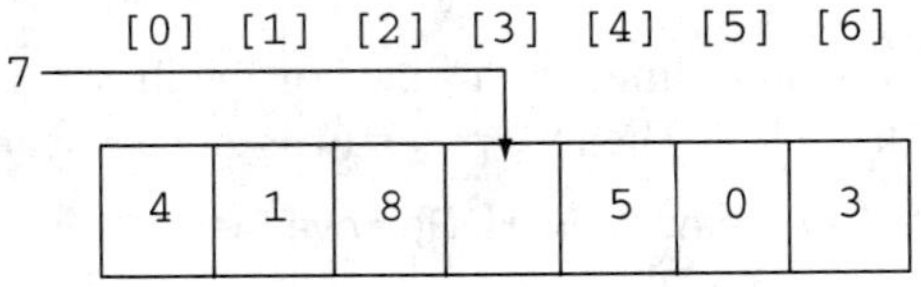

   ii. Place the number 7 into the empty cell.
   To add a number at the end of the list causes a problem: there is no number to its right! This special case will be addressed by the third argument; *add_element(ar, 7, INT_MAX)* will add the number 7 at the end of the array.

   b. Improve the function so that it returns 1 if the addition was successful or 0 otherwise. The operation is unsuccessful if the element to add to the left cannot be found. For instance, the call *add_element(ar, 7, 16)* returns 0 because 16 cannot be found.
3. Modify the program in Example 15.2.5 so that a random sequence of vowels will be presented on the screen.
   a. To this end, define a function named *gen_vowel()* that generates a vowel randomly. It simply generates a random number from 0 to 4. Then this number is used to index the array *vowels*. The resulting vowel is returned. The array *vowels* should be passed to *gen_vowel()*.
   b. In a similar fashion, define a function named *gen_consonant()*.
   c. In a similar fashion, define a function named *gen_letter()* that generates any letter.
4. a. Write a program that presents on the screen a random sequence of nine letters of the alphabet. Use the function *gen_letter()*. Then the player is asked to make the longest possible word. The original sequence is placed in an array named *sequence.* The player removes from it all the letters she wants to use to build a word. These letters are added to another array named *word.* Define the functions *add_letter()* and *remove_letter()* identical to the functions *add_element()* and *remove_element()*, except that the elements are characters. Here is an example of a run:

Here is a sequence of letters: kbxieosh
Form a word from it: boxes
Good!
Here is a sequence of letters: plgiwaor
Form a word from it: plier
The letter 'e' is not in the set

Normally, the program should also check that the word exists, but this would be too difficult.

b. Since there are only five vowels out of 26 letters, vowels will rarely be generated in the program above. To rectify this, have the program alternate the generation of vowels and consonants. Use the functions *gen_vowel()* and *gen_consonant()*.

c. Modify the program once more. The player now indicates whether he wants a vowel or a consonant.

SUPPLEMENTARY EXERCISES 15.2

1. a. Write a function named *unique()* that takes in an array of numbers and eliminates from it all multiple occurrences. For instance the list 8, 3, 13, –5, 13, 8, 8, 4, 8 would become 8, 3, 13, –5, 4.

   b. Modify the function so that it stores in a second array the elements that had duplicates. In the example above, this array would contain 8, 13.

2. Consider the following method of deletion that is faster than the one developed in this section. The element is deleted by simply marking its cell as "deleted." This can be done by storing, say, the character escape sequence *\b* in it. No elements are actually moved. For instance, suppose the array contains the following:

[0]	[1]	[2]	[3]	[4]	[5]	[6]
a	e	d	i	o	u	x

   and the element 'd' is to be deleted. The procedure is as follows:

   - Search for the letter 'd'. It will be found at index position 2.
   - Replace it with *\b*.
   - The size of the array is decreased by 1.

   Whenever the array is accessed, this cell will be skipped. Write a function named *rmv_mark()* that accepts an array, an element to delete, and the size of the array. It removes the element with the method explained above.

3. In reference to question 2 above, rewrite the following functions, which were defined earlier, so that they skip any "deleted" cells:

   a. *display_array()*

   b. *search()*

4. a. Write a function named *next_index()* that takes two arguments: an array with possibly "deleted" cells and an index in this array. The function then returns the index of the next non-"deleted" cell. For instance, with the following array *ar:*

[0]	[1]	[2]	[3]	[4]	[5]	[6]
a	e	\b	i	\b	u	\b

   the call next_index(ar, 3) returns 5.

   b. Redo question 3 above with this function.

5. The disadvantage of the function *rmv_mark()* is that it leaves empty cells that can no longer be used because they are marked "deleted." Write a function named *compress()* that removes these "deleted" cells. For instance, the array in question 4 above would be compressed into:

[0]	[1]	[2]	[3]	[4]	[5]	[6]
a	e	i	u			

6. Write a function named *rotate()* that takes in an array of numbers and its size. It then rotates it to the right a number of elements specified by a third argument. For example, assume the array *int seq[5] = { 2, 3, 5, 8, 13 }*. The call *rotate(seq, 5, 2)* will rotate the array two elements to the right: 8, 13, 2, 3, 5. The call *rotate(seq, 5, –2)* will rotate the array two elements to the left: 5, 8, 13, 2, 3.

16 Accessing Arrays with Pointers

OBJECTIVES

This chapter introduces you to the following information:

- Pointer manipulation of arrays, and the close relationship between arrays and pointers.
- Pointer arithmetic.
- Technical explanations of array passing to functions.
- How to send arrays back to the calling function.

INTRODUCTION

In Chapter 11, you saw that pointers are involved in the passing of parameters by reference to a function. You also learned that the manipulation of pointer variables is a necessary skill in the context of parameter passing by reference.

In this chapter you will see that pointers and pointer variables are also involved in accessing arrays to functions. However, unlike parameter passing by reference, learning pointer manipulation in the context of arrays is not absolutely necessary, for the involvement of pointers is all internal. As you saw, no mention of pointers was ever necessary in Chapters 14 and 15. Nevertheless, learning to access arrays with pointers remains a necessary skill to acquire in a proper education on C programming.

16.1 POINTER MANIPULATION

Arrays in C are quite loosely implemented. Not only can they be accessed via an index, they may also just as easily be accessed via a pointer variable. The mechanism of the pointer was first explored in Section 11.1. This section will cover pointer arithmetic and extend their use to accessing arrays.

16.1.1 ACCESSING A CELL VIA A POINTER

It was shown in Section 14.1 that an element of an array is accessed through an index. Since each cell has an address, it should be possible to access any cell through an address reference. Indeed, it is possible. Let us revisit the memory layout of the array *month* from Section 14.1, illustrated in Figure 16.1.1.

Figure 16.1.1

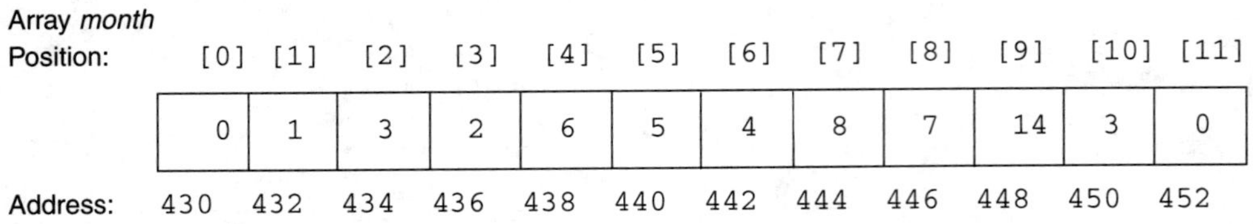

Suppose you wish to access the cell at position 8: To access this cell through a pointer, a pointer variable will of course be needed besides the array declaration:

```
int     month[12];
int   * ptr;
```

To make *ptr* point to the cell at position 8 (i.e., month[8]) is a simple matter of assigning the address of *month[8]* to *ptr:*

```
ptr = &month[8];
```

Now *ptr,* assigned the address 446, points to the cell at that address, as shown in Figure 16.1.2.

Figure 16.1.2

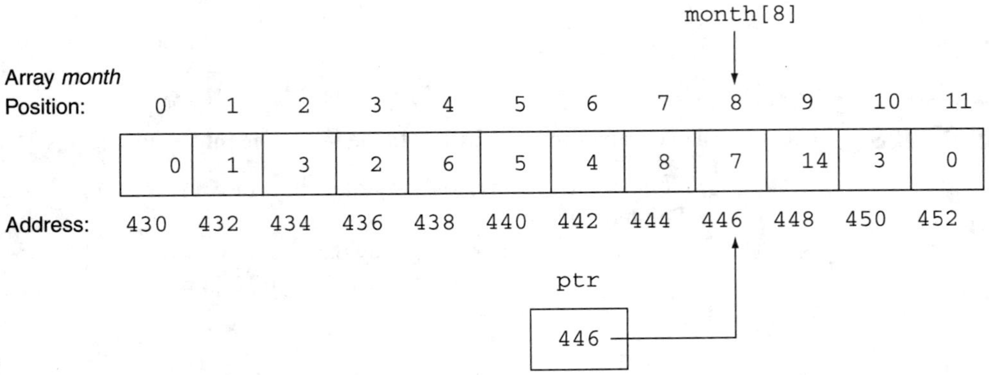

Should you wish to display the content of this cell via the pointer, simply use the dereferencing operator *, which makes the pointer go to the cell to which the operator points:

```
printf("element at position 8 is %d\n", *ptr);
```

16.1.2 MOVING TO ANOTHER CELL VIA A POINTER

In the above example, to move the pointer to the next cell, simply increment the pointer by 1:

```
ptr = ptr + 1;          or          ptr++
```

The pointer is now at position 9, as shown in Figure 16.1.3.

Figure 16.1.3

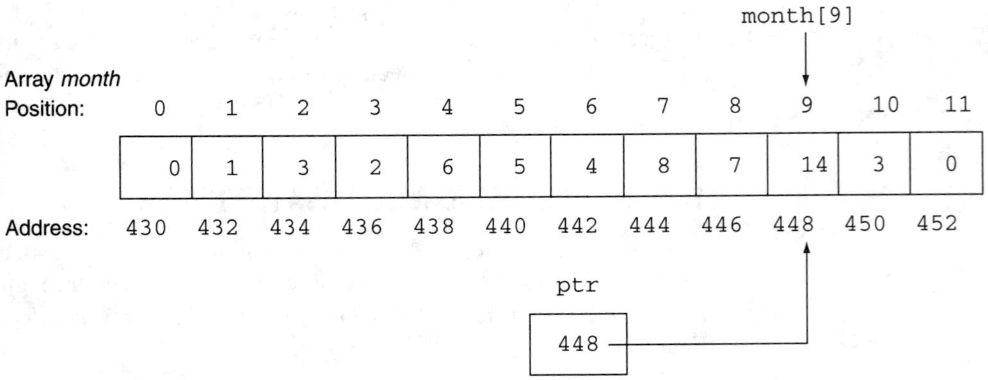

The value of *ptr* is now 448. Something does not seem to be right: only + 1 was added to it; it should now be 447. The explanation is that pointer arithmetic works a little differently. In the following expression:

```
ptr = ptr + 1;
```

the 1 tells C to move the pointer to the next cell. It does **not** mean to move to the next address, which is 447. Since a cell occupies 2 bytes, the content of the pointer is actually incremented by 2.

Example 16.1.1

Let us now recode the program in Example 14.1.2 so that a pointer is used to access each cell of the array. Here is the result, with changes in bold type:

```
#include <stdio.h>

main()
{
        int   month[12];        /* declare an array, one cell per month */
        int * ptr;1             /* a pointer variable */
        int   i, sum;

        /* store data in each element of the array */

        printf("Enter the monthly rainy days this year > ");
        for (ptr=&month[0]; ptr <= &month[11] ; ptr++)2
        {
                scanf("%d", ptr);3
        }

        /* produce a report */

        sum = 0;
        for (ptr=&month[0], i=0; ptr <= &month[11]; ptr++, i++)
        {

                printf("In month %d, %d rainy days\n", i+1, *ptr);4
                sum += *ptr;4
        }
        printf("There were %d rainy days\n", sum);
}
```

Explanations

1. A pointer will run through the array, so an index variable is not needed and has been replaced with a pointer variable declaration.
2. This *for* header ensures that the pointer *ptr* runs from the first cell to the twelfth cell of the array. Indeed, in the following statement:

   ```
   for (ptr=&month[0]; ptr <= &month[11]; ptr++)
   ```

   &month[0] is the address of the cell at position 0 (the first cell); *&month[11]* is the address of the cell at position 11 (the twelfth cell); and the ++ operator tells C to move the pointer to the next cell.
3. Note that the argument *ptr* to the *scanf()* does not use the address operator. (Why is that so?)
4. Of course, to access the element at the cell pointed to by *ptr,* it is necessary to use the dereferencing operator.

16.1.3 BASE ADDRESSES

Example 16.1.1 showed that the statement *ptr = &month[0]* sets the pointer to the address of the first element. This address is called the ***base address*** of the array. Surprisingly enough, the following statement accomplishes the same thing:

```
ptr = month;
```

This implies that the name of the array, *month,* also holds the base address of that array. In other terms, *month* is a pointer! Up to now, we always referred to the **array** *month,* not the **pointer** *month.* Strictly speaking, though, *month* is not an array; it points to an array. Figure 16.1.4 illustrates how month acts as a ponter to the array.

Figure 16.1.4

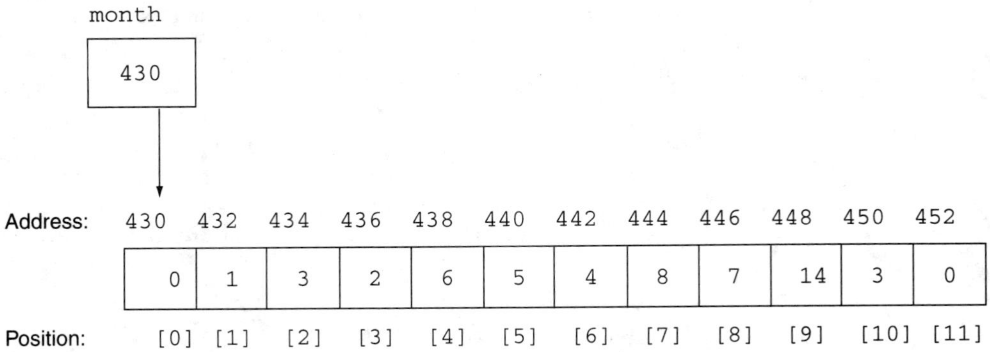

Take note that *month* is a pointer **constant, not** a pointer variable, such as *ptr* is. The variable *ptr* can be set to any cell address, but the pointer *month* cannot be changed. For instance, the following is not allowed:

```
month = ptr;
```

Remember that *sizeof(month)* returns the size in bytes of the array *month.* Given that *month* is actually a pointer constant, shouldn't *sizeof(month)* return the size of the pointer, 4 bytes? Obviously, it does not. This observation demonstrates the inconsistency in the design of the array data type in C.

EXERCISES 16.1.1

1. Given the array *float list[5] = { 4.5, –9.1, 0, 6, 7.05 }* and the pointer *float * ptr,* determine which of the following segments are valid. For those that are, what will be displayed?
   a. `ptr = &list[2];`
      `printf("%f", *ptr);`
   b. `printf("%f", list[1]);`
      `printf("%f", *list);`
   c. `ptr = list[1];`
      `printf("%f", *ptr);`
   d. `printf("%f", &list[4]);`
   e. `printf("%f", list[5]);`
   f. `ptr = &list[3];`
      `*ptr = list[1];`
      `printf("%f", *ptr);`
2. Answer true or false and justify the following:
   a. The declaration *float speed[1]* is equivalent to the declaration *float speed.*
   b. Given that *queue* and *stack* are arrays of the same size, the statement *queue = stack* automatically copies all elements from *stack* to *queue.*
3. What is wrong with the following segment?

```
float nums[4], * ptr;

nums[0] = nums[1] = nums[2] = nums[3] = 77.66;
```

```
ptr = &nums;
printf("The array starts at address %p", ptr);
```

4. Given the declaration *float list[22]* and that the array begins at address 7520, what is the value of each of the following addresses?
   a. *&list[0]*
   b. *&list[4]*
   c. *&list[22]*
   d. *list*
5. What is the error in the following segment?

```
void fcn(float ar[])
{
        printf("%f", ar);

}

main()
{
        float  list[] = { 67, 76, 69, 96 };

        fcn(*list);
}
```

6. Find all of the errors in the following segment.

```
main()
{
        int  a = 'a', b = 'b';
        char codes[4] = { 4, 3, 6, 10 };

        printf("The data is:\n");
        for (i=0; i < 4; i++)
        {
               printf("codes[%d] = %d\n", codes[i]);
        }
        printf("a = %c, b = %c\n", a, b);
        printf("This data begins at the addresses:\n");
        printf("a = %p, b = %p, codes = %p\n", a, b, codes);
}
```

7. What will be displayed by the following segment?

```
int  fcn(float list[])
{
        float * ptr;

        for (ptr = list; *ptr++; ) ;
        return (int) (ptr - list);
}

main()
{
        float arr[5] = { 8, 5, -7, 0, 3 };

        printf("%d", fcn(arr));
}
```

8. As stated in the text, *sizeof(month)* evaluates to the size in bytes of the array *month.* Can you come up with a slight modification to this expression so that it evaluates to the size in bytes of the base pointer to the array? (***Hint:*** Use a cast operator.)

16.1.4 POINTER INITIALIZATION

Example 16.1.2

The two most widely used applications of pointer initialization at declaration time are as follows:

1. A pointer variable set to the base of an array
2. A pointer variable set to zero

Here is a segment of code that illustrates both:

```
int   month[12] = { 0 };
int * ptr = month;
int * list_ptr = NULL;
```

Here *ptr* points to the array *month* as soon as it is declared, and *list_ptr* is set to zero. A pointer set to zero means that it points to nothing. By default, most compilers set pointers to zero at declaration time.

EXERCISES 16.1.2

1. What will the following segment produce?

```
int     list[] = { 11, 91, 66, 99, 77 };
int   * ptr = &list[3];

for ( ; ptr > list; ptr--)
{
        printf("%d", *ptr);
}
```

2. Assume the following declarations:

```
float  list[20];
float  * ptr = list;
```

As you know, the statement *ptr = ptr + 1;* moves the pointer to the next cell, i.e., 4 bytes ahead. Devise an expression that forces *ptr* to move up 1 byte only. (***Hint:*** Use a cast operator.)

16.1.5 DEREFERENCING AND INDEXING AT THE SAME TIME

The elements of an array may be referenced to by using more complex pointer notations than shown so far in this section. For example, consider the following three statements that display the tenth element of the array *month* via a pointer reference:

```
ptr = &month[8];
ptr = ptr + 1;
printf("%f", *ptr);
```

The second step can be merged with the third one:

```
ptr = &month[8];
printf("%f", *(ptr + 1));
```

The argument of the *printf()* works as shown below. Note that *ptr* is the pointer and 1 is the index. Keep in mind that *ptr* contains the address of the ninth element, 446.

`*(ptr  + 1)`	
`(446 + 1)`	Move the pointer to the next cell.
`448`	
`*    448`	Go to the cell with the address 448.
`14`	Number 14 is there, and is displayed.

Example 16.1.3

A pointer can be made to move back and forth through the array. The following segment illustrates this. Assume the declaration *int elm;*

```
ptr = month;              /* ptr now points to the element month[0] */
ptr = month + 3;          /* ptr now points to the element month[3] */
elm = *(month + 3);       /* same as elm = month[3] */
ptr = month;
elm = *(ptr + 3);         /* same as elm = month[3] */
ptr--;
elm = *(ptr + 2);         /* same as elm = month[4]; */
```

Go through these statements and think about what they do.

EXERCISES 16.1.3

1. Given the array *float list[5] = { 4.5, -9.1, 0, 6, 7.05 };* and the pointer *float * ptr;*, determine which of the following segments are valid. For those that are, what will be displayed?
   a.
   ```
   ptr = &list[5];
   ptr = ptr - 1;
   printf("%f", *ptr);
   ```
   b.
   ```
   ptr = &list[0];
   printf("%f", *(ptr + 3));
   ```
   c.
   ```
   ptr = list + 2;
   printf("%f", *ptr);
   ```
   d.
   ```
   ptr = list + 3;
   ptr = ptr - 2;
   printf("%f", *(ptr - 2));
   ```
2. True or false:
   a. Given *ptr = &month[1],* then ptr + 2 is equivalent to *&month[3].*
   b. *&month[3]* is equivalent to **(month + 3).*
   c. Given *ptr = month* + *2,* then *ptr* + *2* is equivalent to *&month[4].*
   d. Given *ptr = month* + *2,* then **ptr* – *2* is equivalent to *month[0].*
3. Replace the following cell references with a pointer reference.
   a. *wages[7]*
   b. *dist[90]*
   c. *fahr[41]*
   d. *step[5]*
4. Replace the following cell references with an indexed reference:
   a. **(rate + 2)*
   b. **tempo*
   c. **(course + 61)*
   d. **(list + 1)*
5. Are the following code segments valid? If so, what is displayed?
   a.
   ```
   char * ptr, grades[] = { 'a', 'b', 'c', 'f' };
   *ptr = &grades[2];
   printf("%c", *ptr);
   ```
   b.
   ```
   int whole[3] = { 7, 2, -9 };
   *whole = *(whole + 2);
   printf("%d", whole[0]);
   ```
   c.
   ```
   int whole[3] = { 7, 2, -9 };
   whole = whole + 2;
   printf("%d", whole[0]);
   ```
   d.
   ```
   int * ptr, whole[3] = { 7, 2, -9 };
   *ptr = whole + 1;
   printf("%d%d", *whole[1], *ptr);
   ```

6. Suppose the declarations *float list[22], * ptr* and the statement *ptr = &list[5]*. What is the value of each of the following addresses, assuming that the array begins at address 7520?
   a. *list + 8*
   b. *ptr + 4*
   c. *ptr – 2*

16.1.6 COMMON ERRORS AND TRAPS

Use the following information to avoid common programming errors:

1. Do not think that the parameter declarations *int list[]* and *int * list* mean the same. Although these two parameters work in the same way, the former one should be used to receive an array, and the latter one to receive a pointer to a single integer. This will be made clearer in Section 16.2.
2. Do not fail to understand that the array name holds the address of the array. It is not the array itself.
3. Do not use the address operator in an attempt to assign the address of an array to a pointer. For example:

```
int  list[5], * ptr;
ptr = &list;
```

   The compiler will complain.

16.2 PASSING ARRAY ADDRESSES TO FUNCTIONS

Now that you have learned the relationship between pointers and arrays, let us move onto discussing passing array addresses (or pointers) to a function. This topic is closely related to simply passing arrays to functions.

16.2.1 THE MECHANISM OF ARRAY PASSING EXPLAINED WITH POINTERS

Subsection 14.2.1 explained that an array is sent by reference, meaning that the base address of the array is copied to the parameter. That explanation was not entirely complete, and we are now in a position to complete it. Let us look again at the function *display_array()* from Subsection 14.2.1:

```
void display_array(int array[5])
{
        int  i;

        for (i=0; i < 5; i++)
        {
                printf(" %d", array[i]);
        }
        printf("\n");
}
```

and assume the call *display_array(list)*. From Section 16.1, we know that the array *list* is a pointer to the actual array, so what really happens is that the content (pointer) of the constant name *list* is copied to the parameter *array*, making it point to the array *list,* as shown in Figure 16.2.1. Assume that the array *list* is at address 500.

So both *list* and *array* are looking at the same array; hence the array *list* is sent by reference. It is as simple as that. Let us now look at an interesting application of this array-passing mechanism.

Figure 16.2.1

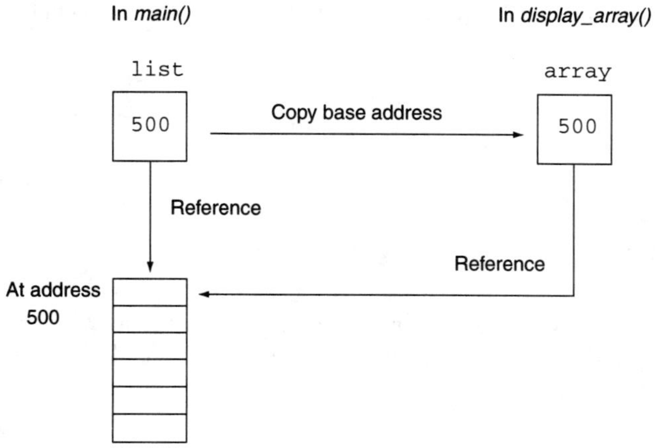

Example 16.2.1

Consider the following function that simply sums up the elements of an array:

```
int sum(int list[], int size)
{
      int i, sum;

      sum = 0;
      for (i=0; i < size; ++i)
      {
            sum += list[i];
      }
      return sum;
}
```

Since an array is nothing more than a pointer (to its first cell), it should be possible to pass to this function *sum()* not only an array, but also a pointer to any one cell from an array. The following program illustrates this.

```
main()
{
      int  ar[10] = { 2, -2, 8, 1, 0, -8, 6, 3, 9, 12 };
      int  s;

      s = sum(ar, 10);     /* s is the sum of ar[0] + ... + ar[9] */
      s = sum(ar, 5);      /* s is the sum of ar[0] + ... + ar[4] */
      s = sum(&ar[0], 8); /* s is the sum of ar[0] + ... + ar[7] */
      s = sum(&ar[2], 4); /* s is the sum of ar[2] + ... + ar[5] */
      s = sum(ar+2, 8);    /* s is the sum of ar[2] + ... + ar[9] */
}
```

It uses the function *sum()* above to calculate the sum of selected subsets from the array *ar.* To see how these calls work, consider the fourth one:

```
s = sum(&ar[2], 4)
```

At the time of the call, the array contains the data shown in Figure 16.2.2, and *&ar[2]* is the address of the third element.

Figure 16.2.2

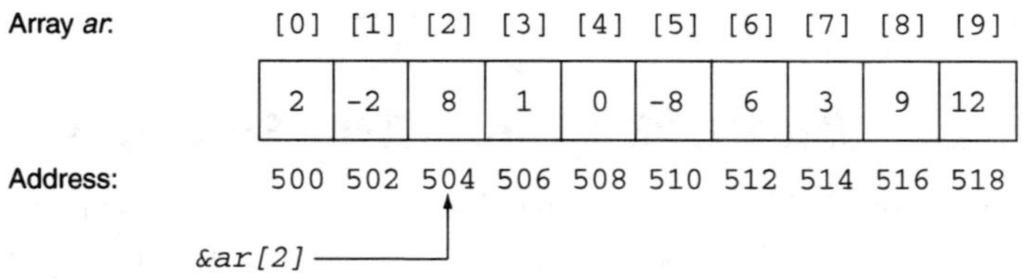

So the parameter *list* receives the address of the third element, as shown in Figure 16.2.3.

Figure 16.2.3

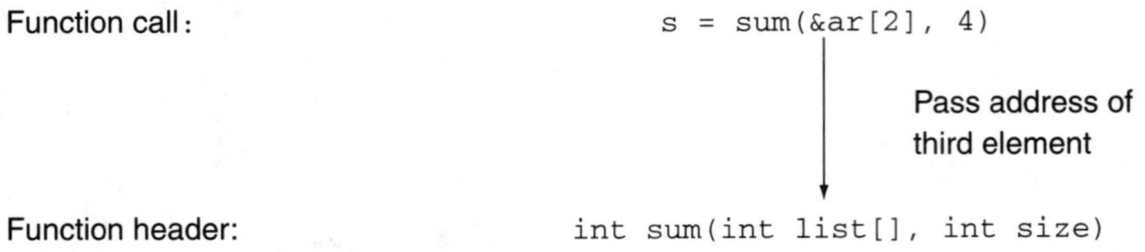

The function *sum()* views the parameter *list* as an array whose base address is 504, as shown in Figure 16.2.4. Consequently, *list[0]* is the same element as *ar[2], list[1]* is the same element as *ar[3],* and so on.

Figure 16.2.4

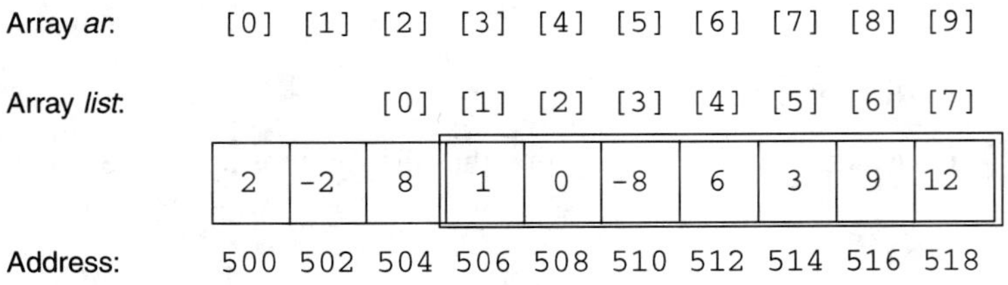

EXERCISES 16.2.1

1. What will the following program display?

```
#include <stdio.h>

int  fcn(int [], int);

main()
{
        int  list[8] = { 1 };

        printf("last element = %d\n", fcn(list+2, 6));
        printf("last element = %d\n", fcn(&list[2], 6));
        printf("last element = %d\n", fcn(list+4, 4));
}

int  fcn(int ar[], int n)
{
        int  i;

        for (i=0; i < n-2; i++)
        {
                ar[i+2] = 2 * ar[i+1] + ar[i];
        }
        return ar[i+2];
}
```

2. Reconsider Exercise 14.3.3, 2. Based on the material covered in this subsection, make all of the necessary corrections to both calls to *copy_array()* so that the function *concatenate()* will work as intended.

16.2.2 VARIATIONS IN PARAMETER DEFINITIONS

Subsection 16.2.1 showed that a pointer argument may be sent to an array parameter. The reverse is also true. This leads to a few different ways that arrays (and individual array elements) may be passed to a function and processed. Consider the following discussions.

The use of the pointer notation. Since an array is really a pointer, then a pointer parameter may be used in place of an array parameter. For instance, for the function *sum()* from Example 16.2.1, the following function header, which uses the * operator as a pointer, would do just as well.

```
int sum(int * list, int size)
```

Nonetheless, there is still a cosmetic difference between the two:

```
int sum(int list[], int size)              int sum(int * list, int size)
```

While *int list[]* in the first statement suggests that *list* is an array, *int * list* in the second statement suggests that *list* is nothing more than a pointer variable.

It does not really matter which notation you choose. Nevertheless, it is preferable to use the array notation if indeed an array is sent to the parameter. But for illustration's sake, the following example shows that *list* may be declared as an array or pointer.

Example 16.2.2

This example illustrates three different ways of defining *sum()*'s first parameter.

Solution 1:

```
int sum(int * list, int size)
{
        int i, sum;

        sum = 0;
        for (i=0; i < size; ++i)
        {
               sum += *list++;
        }
        return sum;
}
```

In this example, the parameter is a pointer, not an array. To see how the expression **list++;* works, suppose that *list* points to the first element of the array, as shown in Figure 16.2.5.

Figure 16.2.5

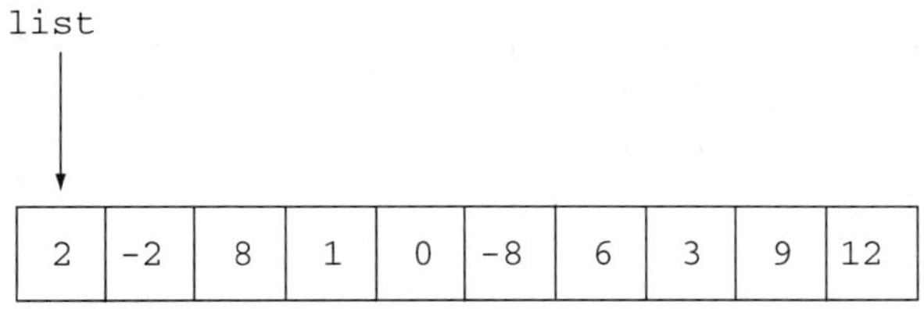

According to the operator precedence, the expression will be evaluated in the following order:

```
sum += *list++
       *list
          2
 sum +=   2
```

Because the operator ++ is in the postfix position, *list++* will take place only after the expression is evaluated. Thus, as shown in Figure 16.2.6, *list* now points to the second element. The loop will ensure that *list* will slide all the way to the end of the array while accumulating the summation.

Figure 16.2.6

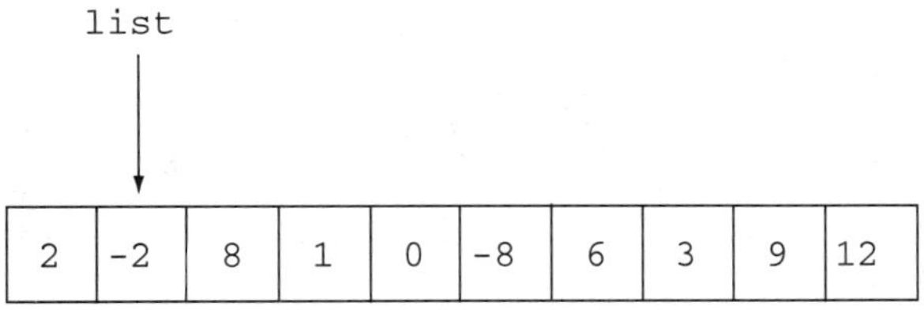

Surprisingly, even when *list* is declared as an array parameter, it can still be used as a pointer, as the following two solutions show.

Solution 2:

```
int sum(int list[], int size)
{
        int i, sum;

        sum = 0;
        for (i=0; i < size; ++i)
        {
                sum += *list++;
        }
        return sum;
}
```

Here, the parameter is an array name (first line of code), yet is used as a pointer later *(*list++;)*.

Solution 3:

```
int sum(int list[10], int size)
{
        int i, sum;

        sum = 0;
        for (i=0; i < size; ++i)
        {
                sum += *list++;
        }
        return sum;
}
```

In this solution, the parameter is an array name with a size specification *(list[10])*, yet it is used as a pointer later *(*list++;)*.

The use of the *const* keyword. It seems that even when an array size is mentioned in the parameter, the value of *list* may be incremented. Something does not seem right: at the beginning of this section, it was said that an array name is a pointer constant. How could the value of the array name *list* be modifiable? The reason is that a parameter is always a variable, never a constant, unless the qualifier *const* is used, such as in *int sum(const int list[10], int size)*. The *const* keyword is seldom used by programmers, but it can be found in the function declarations of some ANSI C functions such as *printf(const char *,...)*.

EXERCISES 16.2.2

1. Suppose that the array *long int dist[35]* is to be passed to a function. Formulate three different ways that the parameter may be declared.
2. What will the following functions do that is different from the function *sum()* in Example 16.2.2?

   a.
   ```
   int some_sum(int * ptr, int size)
   {
           int i, sum;

           sum = 0;
           for (i=0; i < size; ++i)
           {
                   sum += *++ptr;
           }
           return sum;
   }
   ```

b.
```
int some_sum(int * ptr, int size)
{
        int i, sum;

        sum = 0;
        for (i=0; i < size; ++i)
        {
                sum += (*ptr)++;
        }
        return sum;
}
```
c.
```
int some_sum(int * ptr, int size)
{
        int i, sum;

        sum = 0;
        for (i=0; i < size; ++i)
        {
                sum += ++*ptr;
        }
        return sum;
}
```
d.
```
int some_sum(int * ptr, int size)
{
       int i, sum;

       sum = 0;
       for (i=0; i < size; ++i)
       {
            sum += --*ptr++;
       }
       return sum;
}
```
3. a. Multiple pointers may run through the same array at the same time. This is precisely what the function below does. What does it produce?

```
float fcn(float * ptr, int size)
{
       float  t, * ptr2;
       int    i;

       ptr2 = ptr + (size - 1);
       for (i=0; i < size; i++)
       {
            t += *ptr++;
            t += *ptr2--;
       }
       return t;
}
```

b. Rewrite the function using indexes only.

4. Consider the following two functions:

```
void fcn1(int list[5])
{
     int i;

     for (i=0; i < 5; i++)
     {
          list[i] = i;
```

```
    }
}

void fcn2(int list[5])
{
    int i;

    for (i=0; i < 5; i++, list++)
    {
        *list = i;
    }
}
```

Given the array *int line_up[5]* stored at address 8800, answer the following questions:

a. What is the value of each element of the array *line_up* after the call *fcn1(line_up)?*
b. What is the value of each element of the array *line_up* after the call *fcn2(line_up)?* Also, since *list* is being changed within this function, will this affect the value of the pointer *line_up* after the function terminates? If so, to what address?

5. Consider the following program. In the chart below, list the functions for each global variable, that can
   a. see that variable (i.e., is visible within a function)
   b. reach that variable (i.e., its memory location is known there)

   It is totally irrelevant what the functions do, so the code within them is omitted. Remember that a variable may be reachable and yet not visible. (Refer back to Section 12.3 to brush up on these concepts.) This question is very similar to the one in Exercise 12.3.4, 2, except that arrays are now included.

```
#include <stdio.h>

int  a[6][8];
int  * b = a;

void  fcn_one(void)
{
    int b;

    .....
}

int c[5];

void  fcn_two(int c[5], int * f)
{
    int a;

    .....
}

int d;

void  fcn_three(int a, int c)
{
    .....
}


main()
{
    int a[8];
```

Global variable	Functions that can See the variable	Functions that can Reach the variable
a		
b		
c		
d		

```
        fcn_two(c, &d);
        fcn_three(c[1], *b);
    }
```

Example 16.2.3

The pointer notation of Example 16.2.2 and the index notation may be combined as shown below to run across the array:

```
int sum(int * list, int size)
{
        int i, sum;

        sum = 0;
        for (i=0; i < size; ++i)
        {
                sum += *(list + i);
        }
                return sum;
}
```

Throughout the run of the loop, the pointer variable *list* remains fixed at the first element. It is the index variable *i* that moves across the array.

EXERCISE 16.2.3

Rewrite the function in Exercise 16.2.1, 5 by using pointer and index notations.

16.3 RETURNING AN ARRAY FROM A FUNCTION

The concept of returning an array from a function, although in appearance quite trivial, had to be postponed until this section because an understanding of pointers was first needed.

16.3.1 THE MECHANISM OF RETURNING AN ARRAY

Now that you know about the equivalence between pointers and arrays, the mechanism of returning an array from a function may be discussed.

Example 16.3.1

The following program simply adds up each corresponding element from two arrays *t1* and *t2* into a third array *sum*. A function named *add_up()* is defined for this purpose. It assumes that all arrays are of the same size. Here is the program:

```
#include <stdio.h>

int * add_up(int arr1[], int arr2[], int sum[], int size)[1]
{
        int  i, j;

        for (i=0; i < size; i++)
        {
                sum[i] = arr1[i] + arr2[i];
        }
```

```
        return sum;²
}

main()
{
        int     t1[5] = { 7, 9, 0, 7, 5 },
                t2[5] = { 11, 0, 8, 81, 1 };
                sum[5];
        int * ptr;

        ptr = add_up(t1, t2, sum, 5);³
}
```

Explanations

1. Note the header:

   ```
   int * add_up(int arr1[], int arr2[], int sum[], int size)
   ```

   The function type is necessarily int *. Explanation 2 clarifies this.
2. The array *sum* is returned. Since *sum* is also the base address (i.e., a pointer), the *return* statement actually returns a pointer to an integer; hence the type of the function *int* * in explanation 1.
3. The function *add_up()* adds up the arrays *t1* and *t2* and stores the results into the array *sum.* Also, its base address is stored into *ptr.* So there are now two ways that the array *sum* may be accessed: through its name, or through the pointer *ptr.*

16.3.2 WHY SEND AN ARRAY WITH A *return* STATEMENT?

Example 16.3.1 probably made you wonder why you would return a pointer to the array when *sum* does that already! The following example illustrates a typical situation in which this is useful.

Example 16.3.2

The following segment uses the function *add_up()* from Example 16.3.1 to add up four arrays of the same size.

```
main()
{
        int     t1[5] = { 7, 9, 0, 7, 5 },
                t2[5] = { 11, 0, 8, 81, 1 },
                t3[5] = { -9, 1, 24, 81, 0 },
                t4[5] = { 0, 0, 2, 8, 71 };
                sum[5];
        int * ptr;

        ptr = add_up(t1, t2, sum, 5);
        ptr = add_up(ptr, t3, sum, 5);
        add_up(ptr, t4, sum, 5);
}
```

This code does the job! It turns out that many C functions (especially string functions) are designed to return an array as *add_up()* does here.

EXERCISES 16.3.1

1. Would the following two segments produce the same results as in Example 16.3.2?
   a. `add_up(add_up(t1, t2, sum), sum);`

b. `add_up(t1, t2, sum);`
   `add_up(sum, t2, sum);`

2. Do you see something wrong with the following segments of code? If so, what is it?

a.
```
int * copy_array(int list[5])
{
        int  i;
        int  cpy[5];

        for (i=0; i < 5; i++)
        {
                cpy[i] = list[i];
        }
        return cpy;     /* return the copy of the array */
}
```

b.
```
int * difference(int arr1[], int arr2[])
{
        int  i, j;
        int  diff[5];

        for (i=0; i < 5; i++)
        {
                diff[i] = arr1[i] + arr2[i];
        }
        return diff;
}
```

c.
```
int * difference(int arr1[], int arr2[], int diff[])
{
        int  i, j;

        for (i=0; i < 5; i++)
        {
                diff[i] = arr1[i] + arr2[i];
        }
        return diff;
}

main()
{
        int    t1[] = { 7, 9, 0, 7, 5 },
               t2[] = { 11, 0, 8, 81, 1 },
               t3[] = { -2, 0, 8, -4, 6 },
               diff[];

        difference(t1, t2, diff);
}
```

16.4 THE ARRAY ELEMENT OPERATOR

16.4.1 ITS SYNTAX AND OPERATION

There is more to say about pointer movement within an array. Consider the very simple assignment *month[3] = 7.* At first glance this expression seems to have only one operator, the assignment operator. In reality, it has a second one: the ***array element operator,*** symbolized as *[].* It requires two operands. To clearly see how it works, let us pull it out of the following expression:

```
month[3]
```

Here, *month* is operand 1, which has to be a pointer. This pointer may either be an array name, a pointer variable, or any expression that evaluates to a pointer value, such as an address.

Operand 2 (in this example, [3]) is an integer that serves as an index into the array, starting at the address evaluated in operand 1.

To illustrate, let us examine three examples. In the first example, operand 1 is an array name; in the second example, it is a pointer variable; in the third example, it is an expression.

16.4.2 WHEN THE LEFT OPERAND IS AN ARRAY NAME

Example 16.4.1

Let us evaluate the expression *month[3] = 7*. Here operand 1 of *[]* is an array name. Since the operator *[]* has a higher priority than the assignment operator, it will be evaluated first, as shown in Figure 16.4.1. This means to store 7 in the cell at address 436, which is the fourth cell.

Figure 16.4.1

```
                              month [ 3 ]   =   7
base address in month  +  3 elements
   address 430         +  3 × 2 bytes/element
   address 430         +  6 bytes
         address  436
         address  436                       =   7
```

EXERCISES 16.4.1

Assume the array declarations below:

```
int      qty[23];
float     height[11];
char      ch[5];
long int seconds[8];
```

Assume that the base addresses of these arrays are 5000, 5048, 5094, and 5100, respectively. Evaluate the following expressions, one operator at a time, as shown in the above example:

1. *qty[7]*
2. *height[10]*
3. *ch[3]*
4. *seconds[2]*

16.4.3 WHEN THE LEFT OPERAND IS A POINTER VARIABLE

Example 16.4.2

In this example, operand 1 of *[]* is a pointer variable. Suppose the declaration *int * ptr;* and that *ptr = month + 2*. So now, *ptr* points to the cell at index position 2, as shown in Figure 16.4.2.

Figure 16.4.2

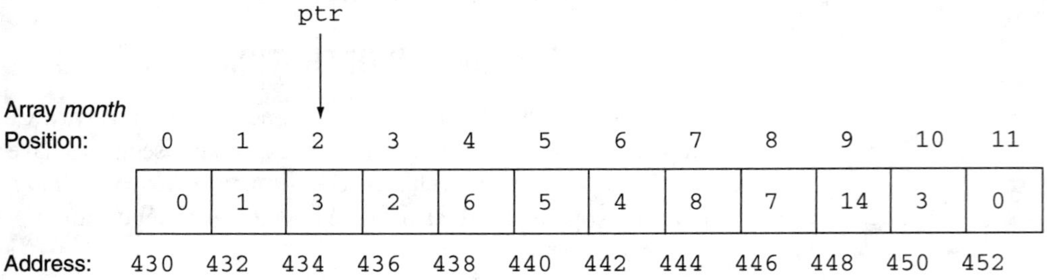

Now let us evaluate the expression *ptr[5] = 12* (Figure 16.4.3). This means to store 12 in the cell at address 444, which is the eighth element (Figure 16.4.4). So clearly *ptr[5]* is exactly the same as element *month[7]*.

Figure 16.4.3

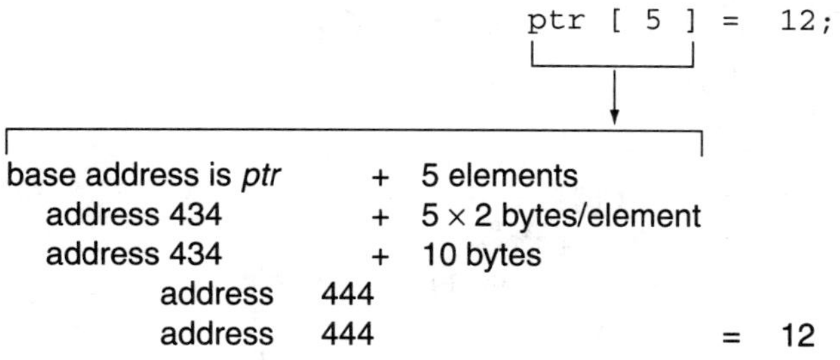

Figure 16.4.4

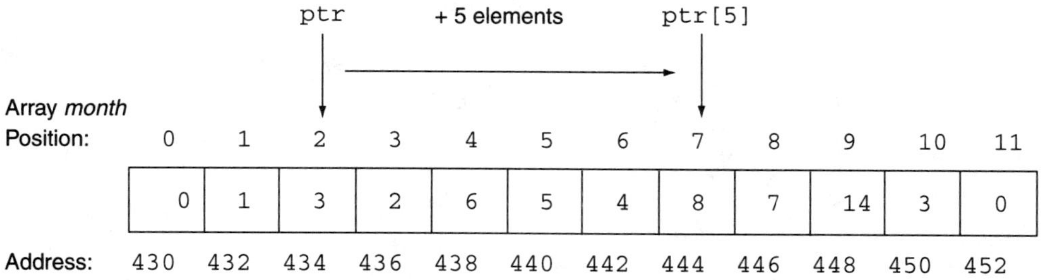

16.4.4 WHEN THE LEFT OPERAND IS AN EXPRESSION

Example 16.4.3

In this example, operand 1 of *[]* is an expression that evaluates to an address. Let us evaluate the expression *(ptr + 4)[2] = 12,* where *ptr* is the same as in Example 16.4.2. There are four operators here. The parentheses operator *()* and the array element operator *[]* both have the same precedence, but associativity says that they are evaluated from left to right; hence the operator *()* will be applied first. The evaluation is shown in Figure 16.4.5. This means to store 12 in the cell at address 446, which is the ninth element. In other terms, *(ptr + 4)[2]* is the same element as *month[8].*

Figure 16.4.5

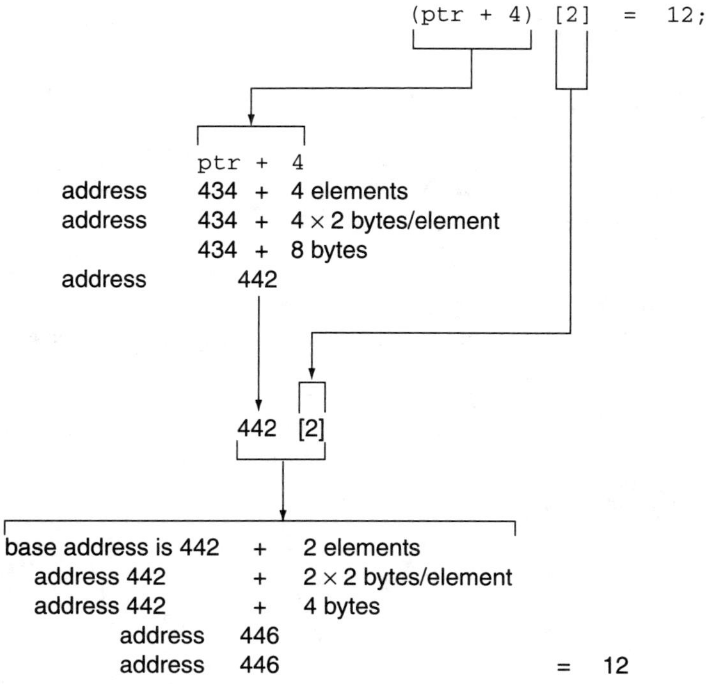

EXERCISES 16.4.2

1. Consider the array *float list[5] = { 4.5, -9.1, 0, 6, 7.05 };* and the pointer variable *float * ptr;*.
   a. Evaluate the expression within each *printf()* call below.
   b. Which *printf()*s display the content of *list[4]?*

```
   i. printf("%f", (list + 4)[0]);
  ii. ptr = list + 1;
      printf("%f", ptr[2]);
 iii. ptr = &list[2];
      printf("%f", ptr[2]);
  iv. printf("%f", (list+1)[3]);
   v. ptr = list + 3;
      printf("%f", (ptr - 3)[3]);
```

2. Will the following segment compile correctly? If so, what does it produce when run? Explain the results.

```
float   paul = 6.5, julien = 3.02, serge = 11.2, john = 2.98;
float * ptr = &paul;
int     i;

for (i=0; i < 4; i++)
{
      printf("%8.2f", ptr[i]);
}
```

In this and previous sections, you have learned different ways of accessing the cells of an array. It would be appropriate to close off this section with a summary that serves to compare them.

Example 16.4.4

All of the following loops do exactly the same thing: they all set the elements of the array *month* to 22, but they go about it in different ways. Assume the declarations *int * p, i.*

1. Using a pointer:

```
for (p=month; p < &month[12]; ++p)
{
    *p = 22;
}
```

2. Using an index:

```
for (i=0; i < 12; ++i)
{
     month[i] = 22;
}
```

3. Using a pointer and an index:
   This may be accomplished in many ways, three of which are shown here:

```
a. for (i=0; i < 12; ++i)                for (p=month, i=0; i < 12; ++i)
   {                                     {
       *(month+i) = 22;                       p[i] = 22;
   }                                     }
b. for (p=month, i=0; i < 12; ++i)
     {
          p[i] = 22;
     }
```

c.
```
for (i=0; i < 12; ++i)
{
    (month+i)[0] = 22;
}
```

Do they indeed all perform the same thing? Indeed, they do.

EXERCISES 16.4.3

1. Assume the declaration *int * ptr = &month[3]*. Which of the following expressions are equivalent to **ptr?*
   a. *month*
   b. *ptr[0]*
   c. *ptr[1]*
   d. **(month+3)*
   e. *(ptr)[0]*
   f. *(month+3)[0]*
   g. *(month+1)[2]*
   h. **(month+3)[0]*
2. Assume the declaration *int * ptr = &month[3]*. Which of the following expressions are equivalent to *month[8]?*
   a. *month+8*
   b. *(month+8)[8]*
   c. **(month+8)*
   d. *ptr+5*
   e. *ptr[5]*
   f. *(month+8)[0]*
   g. *(ptr+5)[0]*
   h. *(ptr–2)[6]*
3. What do the following loops achieve?
   a.
   ```
   for (p=month; p < &month[12]; p++)
   {
       p[0] = 0;
   }
   ```
   b.
   ```
   for (i=0; i < 12; ++i)
   {
       (month-i)[i] = 0;
   }
   ```

---

17 Two-Dimensional Arrays

OBJECTIVES

This chapter introduces you to the following information:

- What two-dimensional (2-D) arrays are and how to manipulate them.
- How to pass 2-D arrays to a function.
- The important relationship between arrays, pointers, and arrays of pointers.
- How a 2-D array is stored in memory.
- The difference between static allocation and dynamic allocation of memory.

INTRODUCTION

Two-dimensional arrays are typically used to store and manipulate two-dimensional tables of data. Nevertheless, their uses are as varied as 1-D arrays, as this chapter will illustrate.

17.1 WHAT IS A TWO-DIMENSIONAL ARRAY?

17.1.1 TWO WAYS OF LOOKING AT 2-D ARRAYS

A two-dimensional array may be looked at in different ways. First, it may be viewed as a list of one-dimensional arrays. For instance, the *month* array from Section 14.1 holds the data for one year only. What if a request comes in to store in memory the data for the past five years, as shown in Figure 17.1.1?

Figure 17.1.1

	Jan	Feb	Mar	Apr	May	June	July	Aug	Sept	Oct	Nov	Dec
Year 1	0	1	3	2	6	5	4	8	7	14	3	0
Year 2	0	0	0	2	3	5	5	4	8	7	1	0
Year 3	1	0	1	5	9	5	6	3	5	2	1	0
Year 4	0	1	0	8	4	4	4	8	7	1	1	0
Year 5	0	2	1	6	10	2	2	3	4	1	1	0

One solution is to declare five 1-D arrays, one for each year: *int year1[12], year2[12], year3[12], year4[12], year5[12];*. However, this approach suffers the same drawback as separate variable declarations: each array must be accessed by name, making a program long and inflexible. A better approach is to declare an array of arrays:

```
int  month[5][12];
```

In this statement, 5 is the number of 1-D arrays, 12 is the size of each 1-D array, and each cell contains an integer. This variable *month* as declared here is termed a ***two-dimensional (2-D) array*** because it has two dimensions: it consists of five arrays, each made of 12 cells.

Depending on the situation, a 2-D array may be interpreted differently than an array of arrays. For instance, suppose that we wish to store the chessboard in Figure 17.1.2 in memory.

Figure 17.1.2

Row \ Column	1	2	3	4	5	6	7	8
1	R	B	Kt	K	Q	Kt	B	R
2	P	P	P	P	P	P	P	P
3								
4								
5								
6								
7	P	P	P	P	P	P	P	P
8	R	B	Kt	K	Q	Kt	B	R

This board is clearly two-dimensional, but is viewed as a series of rows and columns, rather than a series of 1-D arrays. It is natural to store this board into a 2-D array such as:

```
char  board[8][8];
```

This statement says that each cell in the array contains a character, and the array has eight rows and eight columns. Now let us see how each individual cell of a 2-D array is accessed and manipulated.

17.1.2 ACCESSING TWO-DIMENSIONAL ARRAYS WITH ROW AND COLUMN INDEXES

Two-dimensional arrays are accessed in very much the same way as one-dimensional ones are, except that two indexes (one for each dimension) and two imbedded loops are needed, as Example 17.1.1 shows.

Example 17.1.1

Suppose that five international students coming from different countries—say, Canada, the U.S., Mexico, Russia, and Japan—took part in an academic competition. The competition consisted of eight assignments. The following program simply asks to enter each student's marks on those eight assignments:

Enter the results of all 8 assignments:
For student #1: 18 22 15 25 91 8 17 22
For student #2: 20 25 20 25 86 9 19 24
For student #3: 11 14 8 18 46 9 15 19
For student #4: 15 19 14 16 61 5 9 15
For student #5: 17 23 16 24 73 7 12 20

The total possible scores for each assignment are 20, 25, 20, 25, 100, 10, 20, and 25, respectively. All of these marks will be stored in a 2-D array named *table,* as shown in Figure 17.1.3.

Figure 17.1.3

Array *table*

8 assignments (columns); 5 students (rows)

18	22	15	25	91	8	17	22
20	25	20	25	86	9	19	24
11	14	8	18	46	9	15	19
15	19	14	16	61	5	9	15
17	23	16	24	73	7	12	20

A row will contain the result of all eight assignments for one student. Here is the program that accomplishes all this:

```
#include <stdio.h>

main()
{
        int  table[5][8];1
        int  i, j;

        printf("Enter the results of all 8 assignments:\n");
        for (i=0; i < 5; i++)2
        {
                printf("For student #%d: ", i+1);
                for (j=0; j < 8; j++)3
                {
                        scanf("%d", &table[i][j]);4
                }
        }
}
```

Explanations

1. A 2-D array of five rows and eight columns is needed.
2. This outer loop visits each row, one per loop. There is one row per student, so the loop will run five times. The index variable *i* refers to the row being accessed. Note that the row numbers begin at 0, not 1.
3. This inner loop runs through the columns for a particular row. There is one column per assignment, so the loop will run eight times. The index variable *j* refers to the column being accessed. Note that the column numbers begin at 0, not 1.
4. The index variable *i* refers to the row being indexed, while the index variable *j* refers to the column being indexed.

EXERCISES 17.1.1

1. For each array declaration below, answer the following questions:
   a. What is the name of the array?
   b. What is the size in bytes of the array?
   c. How many elements can the array hold?
   d. Specify the notation to access the element in the 3rd row, 7th column, and assign the number 25 to it.

e. Specify the notation for the last element of the array, and display it.
   i. *int table[3][7];*
   ii. *long int table[6][10];*
   iii. *char text[25][81];*

2. Given the array *int matrix[3][4]* that contains the following data:

81	7	38	–7
1	11	–4	20
71	3	88	–5

What is the value of the following?
a. *matrix[2][3]*
b. *matrix[0][3]*
c. The element at row 2, column 1

3. The following code asks for students' marks for all eight assignments. The data is input in exactly the same way as shown in Example 17.1.1, and the array declaration remains the same. Fill in the blanks.

```
for (student_ct = 1; student_ct __________; student_ct++)
{
        printf("For student #%d: ", __________);
        for (assign_ct = 1; assign_ct __________; assign_ct++)
        {
                scanf("%d", &table[__________][__________]);
        }
}
```

4. Suppose the embedded loop in Example 17.1.1 had been coded as the following:

```
printf("Enter the results of all 8 assignments for 5 students:\n");
for (i=0; i < 5; i++)
{
        for (j=0; j < 8; j++)
        {
                scanf("%d", &table[i][j]);
        }
}
```

and that the user entered the same data in three different ways, as shown below:

a. Enter the results of all 8 assignments for 5 students:
<u>18 22 15 25 91 8 17 22</u>
<u>20 25 20 25 86 9 19 24</u>
<u>11 14 8 18 46 9 15 19</u>
<u>15 19 14 16 61 5 9 15</u>
<u>17 23 16 24 73 7 12 20</u>

b. Enter the results of all 8 assignments for 5 students:
<u>18 22 15 25 91 8 17 22 20 25 20 25 86 9 19 24 11 14 8 18 46 9</u>
<u>15 19 15 19 14 16 61 5 9 15 17 23 16 24 73 7 12 20</u>

c. Enter the results of all 8 assignments for 5 students:
<u>18 22 15 25 91 8 17 22 20 25 20 25 86 9 19</u>
<u>24 11 14 8</u>
<u>18 46 9</u>
<u>15 19 15 19 14 16 61 5 9 15 17 23 16 24 73</u>
<u>7 12 20</u>

In all cases, would the data be stored in the same locations in the 2-D array? Explain.

Interchanging the row and column specifications. Note that our decision to declare the array *table* with five rows and eight columns is completely arbitrary. It could just as well have been declared with eight rows, five columns: *(int table[8][5])*, giving the memory layout shown in Figure 17.1.4.

Figure 17.1.4

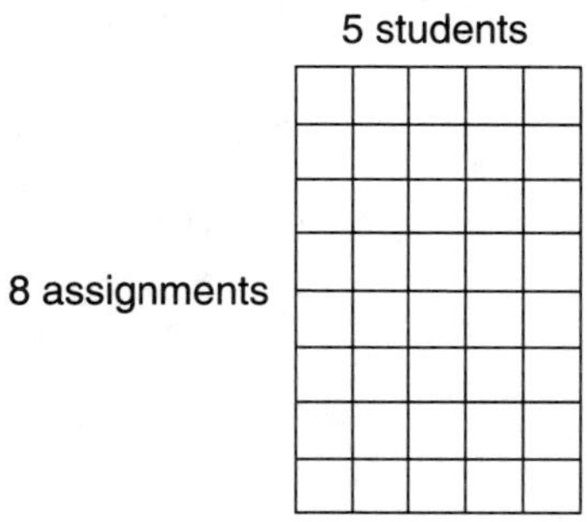

Either way is fine because the orientation of the 2-D array is not crucial. The important factor is that each element is stored in the correct entry. For instance, in the former layout (Example 17.1.1), the third assignment of the second student would be stored in the cell *table[1][2],* whereas in the latter layout (above), it would be stored in the cell *table[2][1].* Of course, the code will differ slightly from Example 17.1.1, as shown in Example 17.1.2.

Example 17.1.2

The following program shows the modifications necessary to the program from Example 17.1.1 when the array *int table[8][5]* is used rather than *int table[5][8]* (changes are shown in bold type):

```
#include <stdio.h>

main()
{
        int  table[8][5];
        int  i, j;

        printf("Enter the results of all 5 students:\n");
        for (i=0; i < 8; i++)[1]
        {
                printf("For assignment #%d: ", i+1);
                for (j=0; j < 5; j++)[2]
                {
                        scanf("%d", &table[i][j]);[3]
                }
        }
}
```

Explanations

1. This outer loop visits each row, one per loop. There is one row per **assignment,** so the loop will run eight times.
2. This inner loop runs through the columns for a particular row. Each **student** is associated with a column, so the loop will run five times.
3. The index variable *i* refers to the row being indexed, while the index variable *j* refers to the column being indexed.

EXERCISES 17.1.2

1. Rewrite the entire program in Exercise 17.1.1, 3, with the array declaration *int table[8][5].*
2. Would the following segment produce the same results as in Example 17.1.2?

```
int  table[8][5];
int  i, j;
```

```
printf("Enter the results of all 5 students:\n");

for (j=0; j < 8; j++)
{
        printf("For assignment #%d: ", j+1);
        for (i=0; i < 5; i++)
        {
                scanf("%d", &table[i][j]);
        }
}
```

3. a. Modify the program in Example 17.1.1 so that the array *table* is displayed as follows:

	Assignments							
Student	1	2	3	4	5	6	7	8
1	18	22	15	25	91	8	17	22
2	20	25	20	25	86	9	19	24
3	11	14	8	18	46	9	15	19
4	15	19	14	16	61	5	9	15
5	17	23	16	24	73	7	12	20

b. Add code to your solution so that the sums of the columns and rows will be shown:

	Assignments								
Student	1	2	3	4	5	6	7	8	Totals
1	18	22	15	25	91	8	17	22	218
2	20	25	20	25	86	9	19	24	228
3	11	14	8	18	46	9	15	19	140
4	15	19	14	16	61	5	9	15	154
5	17	23	16	24	73	7	12	20	192
Totals	81	103	73	108	357	38	72	100	932

c. Modify your solution once more so that the averages of the columns and rows will be shown instead.

d. Modify your program further so that the display is changed to the following:

	Assignments							
Student	1	2	3	4	5	6	7	8
1	18	22	15	25	91	8	17	22
2	20	25	20	25	86	9	19	24
3	11	14	8	18	46	9	15	19
4	15	19	14	16	61	5	9	15
5	17	23	16	24	73	7	12	20

Averages:

Student	1	2	3	4	5			
	27.3	28.5	17.5	19.3	24.0			
Assignment	1	2	3	4	5	6	7	8
	16.2	20.6	14.6	21.6	71.4	7.6	14.4	20.0

(***Hint:*** The vertical and horizontal averages will be stored in separate 1-D arrays as they are calculated.)

4. a. Improve the program in question 3a so that the user will be asked to enter the total possible mark for each assignment. This will be stored in a 1-D array. Using this new information, the student's average will be displayed as a percentage. All assignment have the same weight toward the calculation of this average. A sample run might look like this:

Enter the results of all 8 assignments:
For student #1: <u>18 22 15 25 91 8 17 22</u>
For student #2: <u>20 25 20 25 86 9 19 24</u>
For student #3: <u>11 14 8 18 46 9 15 19</u>
For student #4: <u>15 19 14 16 61 5 9 15</u>
For student #5: <u>17 23 16 24 73 7 12 20</u>

Highest possible mark for each assignment? 20 25 20 25 100 10 20 25

				Assignments					
Student	1	2	3	4	5	6	7	8	Percent
1	18	22	15	25	91	8	17	22	87%
2	20	25	20	25	86	9	19	24	95%
3	11	14	8	18	46	9	15	19	63%
4	15	19	14	16	61	5	9	15	62%
5	17	23	16	24	73	7	12	20	79%

b. Modify the program further so that the assignments may have different weights. The user will enter these weights as percentages (such as 0.35 meaning 35%) of the final average.

17.1.3 ROW-WISE VERSUS COLUMN-WISE ACCESS

In all the programs seen thus far, all 2-D arrays were accessed row by row. This is called ***row-wise*** access and is illustrated in Figure 17.1.5.

Figure 17.1.5

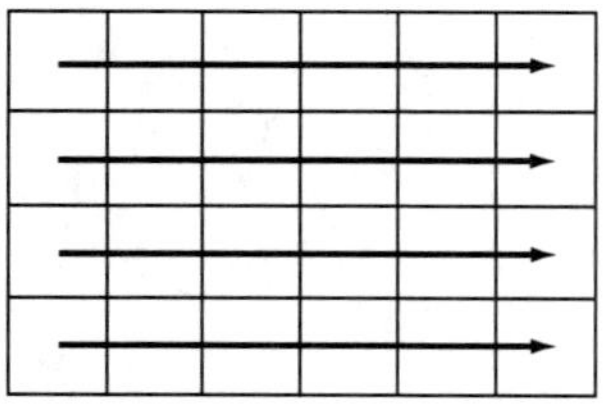

In this type of access, the inner loop runs from column 0 to the last column in each row. For instance, for the array *int table[5][8]* the loop would be as follows:

```
for (i=0; i < 5; i++)¹
{
        printf("For student #%d: ", i+1);
        for (j=0; j < 8; j++)²
        {
                scanf("%d", &table[i][j]);³
        }
}
```

Explanations

1. This outer *for* loop provides for access that runs from **row** 0 to **row** 4.
2. This inner loop provides access that runs from **column** 0 to **column** 7.
3. The index variable *i* refers to the row being indexed, while the index variable *j* refers to the column being indexed.

Yet the same 2-D arrays may also be accessed column by column, called ***column-wise*** access, as shown in Figure 17.1.6.

Figure 17.1.6

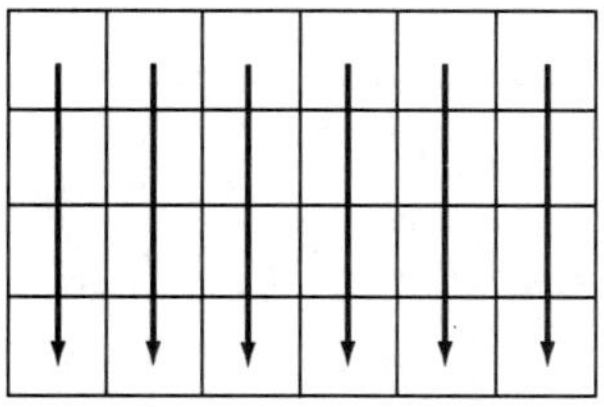

Example 17.1.3 shows how this is done.

Example 17.1.3

The 2-D array in Example 17.1.1 is accessed and read into row-wise (i.e., student-wise). Accessing it column-wise would force the user to enter the data in a different order. Instead of entering all eight assignment results for each student, the following program will ask for the results of assignment 1 from all five students, then the results of assignment 2 from all five students, and so on. This is assignment-wise. The interaction with the user should go like this:

```
Enter the results of all 5 students:
For assignment #1: 18 20 11 15 17
For assignment #2: 22 25 14 19 23
For assignment #3: 15 20  8 14 16
For assignment #4: 25 25 18 16 24
For assignment #5: 91 86 46 61 73
For assignment #6:  8  9  9  5  7
For assignment #7: 17 19 15  9 12
For assignment #8: 22 24 19 15 20
```

The program is surprisingly similar to that of Example 17.1.1 (changes are in bold):

```
#include <stdio.h>

main()
{
        int  table[5][8];1
        int  i, j;

        printf("Enter the results of all 5 students:\n");
        for (i=0; i < 8; i++)2
        {
                printf("For assignment #%d: ", i+1);
                for (j=0; j < 5; j++)2
                {
                        scanf("%d", &table[j][i]);3
                }
        }
}
```

Explanations

1. The declaration of the 2-D array does not change. Indeed, it is the access to the array that changes, not the orientation of the array in memory.
2. The boundaries change as shown. The outer loop runs through the **columns,** one for each loop. The inner loop runs through the **rows** of a particular column.
3. Probably the most important change is the interchange of the two indexes.

Note the striking similarity between this program and that of Example 17.1.2. Indeed, they both accomplish the exact same task, except that this one traverses the array column-wise, and therefore does not require a different orientation of the 2-D array.

EXERCISES 17.1.3

1. Write a segment of code that initializes to 0 a 2-D array of size 4-by-9. Do this in two ways:
   a. column-wise
   b. row-wise
2. Write a program that constructs a 2-D array of size 5-by-7 where the element at row *i*, column *j*, equals *i+j*. Do this in two ways:
   a. column-wise
   b. row-wise

3. Fill in the blanks so that each of the following segments will store the data in the same entries as did the segment in Exercise 17.1.2, 2:

a.
```
int table[5][8], i, j;

printf("Enter the results of all 8 assignments:\n");
for (i=0; i < 8; i++)
{
        for (j=0; j < 5; j++)
        {
                scanf("%d", &table[__][__]);
        }
}
```
b.
```
int table[__][__], i, j;

printf("Enter the results of all 8 assignments:\n");
for (j=0; j < 8; j++)
{
        for (i=0; i < 5; i++)
        {
                scanf("%d", &table[i][j]);
        }
}
```
c.
```
int table[8][5], i, j;
printf("Enter the result of all 8 assignments:\n");
for (i=0; i < 5; i++)
{
        for (j=0; j < 8; j++)
        {
                scanf("%d", &table[__][__]);
        }
}
```
4. Write a program that reads in the following 2-D array:

```
8 0 3 6 3
1 3 1 0 7
2 7 9 4 5
```

and displays it in the following ways:

```
a. 8 1 2          c. 2 7 9 4 5        e. 5 4 9 7 2
   0 3 7             1 3 1 0 7           7 0 1 3 1
   3 1 9             8 0 3 6 3           3 6 3 0 8
   6 0 4          d. 2 1 8
   3 7 5             7 3 0
b. 3 6 3 0 8         9 1 3
   7 0 1 3 1         4 0 6
   5 4 9 7 2         5 7 3
```

5. Redo question 4 above, storing the 2-D array in the following orientation:

```
8 1 2
0 3 7
3 1 9
6 0 4
3 7 5
```

6. a. Write a program that performs any one of the following "flips" of the letter F.

```
FFFFFFF      FFFFFFF      F                  F
F                  F      F                  F
FFFF            FFFF      FFFF            FFFF
F                  F      F                  F
F                  F      FFFFFFF      FFFFFFF
```

The letter will first be presented upright. Then the user will be given the choice to flip it in any one of the four directions.

b. Change the program so that the user will first design some pattern on the screen. The program will store it in a 2-D array of size 6-by-9. Then the program will flip it as requested by the user.

7. a. Write a program that sets the backward diagonal of a 6-by-8 2-D array to 99. Following is a sample of a backward diagonal:

```
99   8   2   5
 6  99   5   1
 2   9  99  71
 7   7   3  99
```

b. Write a program that sets the forward diagonal of a 6-by-8 2-D array to 99. Following is a sample of a forward diagonal:

```
11   8   2  99
 6   1  99   1
 2  99   9  71
99   7   3   0
```

c. Write a program that sets both diagonals of a 6-by-8 2-D array to 99.

17.1.4 INITIALIZING TWO-DIMENSIONAL ARRAYS AT DECLARATION TIME

There are two ways that 2-D arrays may be initialized at declaration time, as shown by the following examples.

Example 17.1.4

Initialization may be done the same way as with a 1-D array. For instance:

```
int  tbl[3][4] = { 8, 16, 9, 52, 3, 15, 27, 6, 14, 25, 2, 10 };
```

The 12 elements are stored in the cells row-wise; that is, the first row is filled, then the second one, and finally the third one, as shown in Figure 17.1.7.

Figure 17.1.7

Row 0	8	16	9	52
Row 1	3	15	27	6
Row 2	14	25	2	10

Initialization at declaration time is always done row-wise. (Section 17.3 will cover the technical reason for this.) Of course, for better readability, the rows should be on separate lines:

```
int  tbl[3][4] = { 8, 16,  9, 52,
                    3, 15, 27,  6,
                   14, 25,  2, 10 };
```

Example 17.1.5

Row-wise initialization may be made explicit. For instance:

```
int  tbl[3][4] = { {  8, 16,  9, 52 },
                   {  3, 15, 27,  6 },
                   { 14, 25,  2, 10 } };
```

Note that this initialization looks very similar to the one just above it. The one difference is that the numbers pertaining to the same row are enclosed in braces. Of course, the initialization could still be placed all on one line:

```
int tbl[3][4] = { { 8, 16, 9, 52 }, { 3, 15, 27, 6 }, { 14, 25, 2, 10 } };
```

This is harder to read, although the rows can still be recognized easily.

Just like 1-D arrays, elements (or a complete row) of a 2-D array may be omitted, in which case their value defaults to 0. For instance, the following declaration

```
int  tbl[3][4] = { {  8, 16 },
                   {  3, 15, 27 } };
```

would result in the storage shown in Figure 17.1.8.

Figure 17.1.8

8	16	0	0
3	15	27	0
0	0	0	0

EXERCISES 17.1.4

What will be stored in the following arrays?

1. `int map[4][8] = { { 1, 9, -8, 4 },`
   `                   { 3, 0 },`
   `                   { 17, 5, 2, -6 },`
   `                   {  0, 25, -6 } };`
2. `int list[6][3] = { 2, 0, 6, 11, 66, 23, 99, 3, 0, 0, 71, 41, 12 };`
3. `int surface[3][5] = { 4, 2, 8 };`
4. `int surface[3][5] = { { 4 }, { 2 }, { 8 } };`
5. `float flow[6][10] =  { 6.52 };`
6. `float plane[4][2] =  { 5, 9, 0.13, 2 };`

17.1.5 COMMON ERRORS AND TRAPS

Use the following information to avoid common programming errors.

1. Do not use the wrong syntax in accessing an element from a 2-D array. For example, the following segment will attempt to set the cell at row 0, column 2, to 8:

   ```
   int  table[3][5];
   table[0,2] = 8;
   ```

   Surprisingly, the compiler will not find a syntax error! This is because the comma is a valid operator in C (in fact, it is often used in the *for* header). Nonetheless the compiler will complain about an invalid type assignment. (The reason for this is too technical to explain here, so we will skip it.)
2. Do not mix up row and column indexes, thereby accessing the wrong entry.

17.2 PASSING A 2-D ARRAY TO A FUNCTION

Not surprisingly, 2-D arrays are passed to a function in a fashion similar to that used for 1-D arrays.

17.2.1 THE MECHANISM OF PASSING A 2-D ARRAY TO A FUNCTION

Example 17.2.1

To illustrate the passing of 2-D arrays to a function, let us revisit Example 17.1.1, and introduce functions into it. The following functions—*read_table()* and *display_table()*—will both accept a 2-D array of size 5-by-8. Here is the result:

```
#include <stdio.h>

void read_table(int array[5][8])[1]
{
        int  i, j;

        printf("Enter the results of all 8 assignments:\n");
        for (i=0; i < 5; i++)
        {
                printf("For student #%d: ", i+1);
                for (j=0; j < 8; j++)
                {
                        scanf("%d", &array[i][j]);
                }
        }
}

void display_table(int array[5][8])
{
        int  i, j;

        for (i=0; i < 5; i++)
        {
                for (j=0; j < 8; j++)
                {
                        printf(" %d ", array[i][j]);
                }
        }
}

main()
{
        int  table[5][8];

        read_table(table);[2]
        display_table(table);
}
```

Explanations

1. As declared, the parameter *array* is a 2-D array of size 5-by-8, and the corresponding argument has to be of the same size.
2. To send the 2-D array to the function, it is only a matter of specifying its name. We will see later that the name also holds the base address to the 2-D array, just as with 1-D arrays.

Can 2-D arrays of undetermined size be passed? The two user-defined functions above can only work with arrays of size 5-by-8. This is unacceptable because it limits their portability. Section 14.2 showed that the solution, in the case of 1-D arrays, was to omit the size of the array parameter, and add a parameter that will receive the actual size of the array. Let us now simply extend this idea to 2-D arrays:

```
void display_table(int array[][], int n_rows, int n_cols)
```

Note the empty brackets, from which the sizes have been omitted. Note also the parameters *n_rows* and *n_cols,* which are used to indicate the number of rows and columns to display. Unfortunately, the C compiler (or any other compiler) is unable to allocate space for a 2-D array parameter that has no dimension at all.[1] The compiler is only able to allocate space if the parameter is given the array's number of columns while the number of rows may be omitted. This leads us to Example 17.2.2.

Example 17.2.2

Let us make the functions *read_table()* and *display_table()* more flexible by giving them the ability to read any number of rows. Here is the result:

```
#include <stdio.h>

void read_table(int array[][8], int n_rows)1
{
        int  i, j;

        printf("Enter the results of all 8 assignments:\n");
        for (i=0; i < n_rows; i++)
        {
                printf("For student #%d: ", i+1);
                for (j=0; j < 8; j++)
                {
                        scanf("%d", &table[i][j]);
                }
        }
}

void display_table(int array[][8], int n_rows)1
{
        int  i, j;

        for (i=0; i < n_rows; i++)
        {
                for (j=0; j < 8; j++)
                {
                        printf(" %d ", table[i][j]);
                }
                printf("\n");
        }
}

main()
{
        int  table[5][8];
        int  i, j;

        read_table(table, 5);2
        display_table(table, 5);2
}
```

Explanations

1. Note the header for *read_table():*

```
void read_table(int array[][8], int n_rows)
```

[1]Actually, a solution is possible in which a parameter can receive a 2-D array of any size. Because of the technicality involved, this topic will be postponed until Section 17.4.

The empty brackets indicate that a 2-D array of any number of rows will be accepted but the *[8]* says that the array must have eight columns. The parameter *n_rows* indicates the actual number of rows to read. This header works similarly for *display_table()*.
2. The actual number of rows to display is sent to the functions.

EXERCISES 17.2.1

1. What will the calls below produce? Indicate if unpredictable results may occur.
   a. *read_table(table, 3);*
   b. *read_table(table, 12);*
   c. *read_table(table, 0);*
2. Find out if your compiler will accept the following header:

```
void read_table(int array[5][], int n_cols)
```

   Explain your finding.
3. a. Write a function that finds and displays the maximum value in a 2-D array of integers of size 10-by-20. The array should be passed to the function.
   b. Modify the function in (a) so that it may handle any number of rows. The actual number of rows is sent as an argument.
4. Write a function named *transpose()* that accepts two 2-D arrays. It then stores the transposed first array into the second array:

```
3 -9 8 5              3  0  1
0  2 7 0   ——→       -9  2  1
1  1 4 1              8  7  4
                      5  0  1
```

   Develop the following three versions:
   a. Assume that the 2-D array to transpose is always of size 3-by-4.
   b. Assume that the 2-D array to transpose always has four columns, but may have any number of rows.
   c. How would you return the transposed 2-D array?
5. Write a function named *compare_DDarray()* that compares two 2-D arrays (of the same dimensions) passed to it. The function returns 0 if both agree, or 1 otherwise. The dimensions of the first array are passed to the function.
6. Write a function named *copy_DDarray()* that makes a copy of a 2-D array. Only the dimensions of the original array are passed to the function, since the dimensions of the destination array must agree with the source's.
7. Write a function named *DDsearch()* that takes as arguments a 2-D array, the element to find from it, and the dimensions of the array. It sends back by reference the row and column positions in which the element is found and returns 1; if the element is not found, it returns 0.
8. Write a function named *DDfind_min()* that returns the smallest number from a 2-D array given as an argument. It also sends back by reference the row and column positions. The dimensions of the array are also passed to the function.
9. Write a function named *DDfind_max()* that returns the largest number from a 2-D array given as an argument. It also sends back by reference the row and column positions. The dimensions of the array are also passed to the function.
10. Use the functions *DDfind_max()* and *DDfind_min()* in a program that reads a table of numbers and then displays the largest and the smallest ones.
11. Write a function named *DDfind_avg()* that returns the average from the elements of a 2-D array given as an argument. The dimensions of the array are also passed to the function.
12. Write a function named *DDfind_sum()* that returns the average from the elements of a 2-D array given as an argument. The dimensions of the array are also passed to the function.
13. Write a function named *DDscalar_mult()* that multiplies each element of a 2-D array by any real number given as an argument. The array is also passed as an argument.

14. Write a function named *DDsort()* that sorts the 2-D array passed as an argument. Within the function, use the 2-D array as a 1-D array. Then apply the bubble sort to it. For instance, the following 2-D array:

```
 4  1   8   2   7
-1  6  -9  11   2
 5  5  -3  -2  19
```

is sorted into this:

```
-9  -3  -2  -1   1
 2   2   4   5   5
 6   7   8  11  19
```

15. Modify the program in Exercise 15.1.5, 3, so that the list of the salesperson's numbers that fall in each range is also displayed. These numbers will be stored in a 2-D array, one row for each range.

17.2.2 COMMON ERRORS AND TRAPS

Use the following information to avoid a common programming error.

When passing a 2-D array to a function, only one dimension may be omitted in the parameter declaration. The following is not allowed:

```
void  fcn(float list[][])
```

The compiler will complain. In fact only the first dimension (the number of rows) may be omitted, never the number of columns.

SUPPLEMENTARY EXERCISES 17.2

1. a. Write a function named *magic()* that determines if a 2-D array passed to it is a magic square. A magic square is one in which the summation of both diagonals, all rows, and all columns add up to the same number. For example, the square below is magic:

```
4  9  2
3  5  7
8  1  6
```

The sum is 15 in every direction. The function will return 1 if the 2-D array is magic; otherwise, it will return 0.

b. Improve the function above so that if the function returns 0, a message giving the reason will be sent back by reference. The message will appear in the form of a code number:

–1 The rows do not all add up to the same number.
–2 The columns do not all add up to the same number.
–4 The diagonals do not all add up to the same number.
–8 The summation of all of the rows agree, the summation of all the columns agree, and the summation of both diagonals agree, but these are not the same sums.

There may be a combination of reasons why a square is not a magic square, in which case, the sum of the code numbers for the reasons is returned. For instance, if a square has rows that do not add up to the same number and diagonals that don't add up correctly as well, then the code number –5 is returned (–1 + –4 = –5).

2. a. Write a program that uses a 2-D array to solve the following problem. A news magazine wants to conduct a survey of the colleges in the country. For each college, they want to gather the number of departments, the number of students (full-time and part-time separately), the percentage of failures, and the overall GPA. All of this data is to be stored in a

file named SURVEY.LIS, one record per college. Assume that the file contains no more than 50 records. The program will read them into a 2-D array and produce a report such as the following:

College	Number of departments	Number of students Full-time	Part-time	Percent Failures	Overall GPA
1	14	1807	1551	0.17	3.06
2	31	7203	8509	0.27	2.90
3	9	581	1058	0.12	3.21

The program will then calculate the average for each column and figure out the highest and the lowest values in each category. These values will be kept in an array of size 5 (one cell per column). All of this data will also be displayed at the end of the report.

b. Add the following feature to the program. An additional table will be produced below the one in question 2a that will list the top three colleges (by number) in each of the five categories (numbers of departments, full-time students, part-time students, percentage of failures, and overall GPA). For instance, assuming that the file SURVEY.LIS contained only the three colleges displayed in question 2a, the table would look like this:

	Top Three Colleges		
Number of departments	2	1	3
Number of full-time students	2	1	3
Number of fart-time students	2	1	3
Percent of failures (lowest)	3	1	2
Overall GPA (highest)	3	1	2

3. Write a program that reads in sales information about salespersons contained in a file named SALES.INF. Each salesperson has one record, which consists of the salesperson's number and the sales in dollars for four different products. Assume that the file contains no more than 20 records. The program must calculate the commission for all salespersons based on Exercise 15.1.5, 3. A report will be produced as follows:

Salesperson number	SALES Products 1	2	3	4	Commissions
6883	$ 56.99	$127.17	$ 82.61	$385.75	$???????
1592	$136.56	$127.17	$729.84	$340.02	$???????

It will summarize the report with the average for each column as well as the largest and the smallest figures. These figures will be kept in an array.

4. Write a program that simulates a random walk of a robot in the empty room below. A random walk is one where the next step taken by the robot is always randomly either to the left, right, ahead, or back.

```
   ####################
   #                  #
   #                  #
   #                  #
   #                  ——→
   #                  #
   #                  #
——→                   #
   #                  #
   ####################
```

The room will be stored in a 2-D array of size 10-by-20. This includes the walls. The initial position of the robot is at row 7, column 0, and will be marked with an 'r'. As soon as this initial position is left, the door will close; i.e., the cell will be replaced with a # sign. Define the functions *move_up(), move_down(), move_left(),* and *move_right()* to simulate a move. These functions will take the 2-D array as argument and will mark the new cell occupied with an 'r', changing the old position to an asterisk (*). Should a move be illegal, the robot will not move. A move is illegal if an attempt is made to move into the wall.

These functions must know what the current position (row and column) of the robot is at all times. To this end, define two global index variables *cur_row* and *cur_col* of the current position.

The program will let the robot walk until it finds the exit. There is a possibility that this may take quite some time, so the program will prompt for the maximum number of steps the user wants the robot to take. In the end, the room and the traces of the walk will be shown on the screen.

5. Modify the above program as follows:
   a. Allow the user to specify where the entry and exit gates are to be placed. These gates may be in the same spot.
   b. Instead of using the symbol * to form a walk trace, store a character from 0 to 9. The number will indicate the number of times that the robot went through that cell. Store an exclamation point (!) in any cell where the number exceeded 9.
6. Modify the program in question 4 above so that the robot will enter the labyrinth below and attempt to come out of it:

```
      ####################
      #   #### #      #  #
      #   #    #   ##### #
      #   ### #    #   # #
      ###     #        #   ------>
      #    ####  ####  # #
      #  ###      #      #
----->        ### ##     #
      #  #  #      ###   #
      ####################
```

   Except for the extra walls, this room is exactly the same one as shown in question 4. The entry and exit gates are at the same positions. The functions *move_up(), move_down(), move_left(),* and *move_right()* must disallow any illegal move, such as into the walls. The robot will not make an illegal move.
7. Write a program that uses a 2-D array to simulate the game of tic-tac-toe. This game requires two players. One player places the symbol 'X' in the grid, the other places an 'O'. The goal of the game is to be the first one to form a line of one's symbols in any direction on the grid. For instance, in the grid below, the player playing the 'X' wins:

```
 O | X | X
-----------
   | X | O
-----------
 X | O |
```

   Use a 2-D array to store the 'X' and 'O'. The bars are not stored and will be produced only when the array is displayed.
8. a. Write a simplified seat reservation system for a convention center. The program will show the following seating plan. The user reserves one or more seats.

```
                          Stage
     ------------------------------------------------
A  | [][][]   [][][][][][][][]   [][][] |
B  | [][][]   [][][][][][][][]   [][][] |
C  | [][][]   [][][][][][][][]   [][][] |
D  | [][][]   [][][][][][][][]   [][][] |
E  | [][][]   [][][][][][][][]   [][][] |
F  | [][][]   [][][][][][][][]   [][][] |
G  | [][][]   [][][][][][][][]   [][][] |

     1 2 3    4 5 6 7 8 9 10 11  12 13 14
```

Each pair of [] symbols indicates a seat. The rows run from A to G with 14 seats per row. Use a 2-D array for storing seat reservations. A 1 stored in a cell means that that seat is reserved; a 0 means that it is available. Here is how the program operates:

```
Welcome to the Reservation System
Enter the list of seats you want to reserve > b7 b8 b9↵
Reservation confirmed.
Enter the list of seats you want to reserve > b9 b10↵
No reservation.
  Seat B9 reserved already. Try again? (y/n) y↵
Enter the list of seats you wish to reserve > c9 c10↵
Reservation confirmed.
Enter the list of seats you wish to reserve > c7 c8 c9 c10↵
No reservation.
  Seats C9 and C10 reserved already. Try again? (y/n) n↵
Enter the list of seats you wish to reserve > ↵
Bye!
```

b. Modify the program so that a user may cancel a reservation for any number of seats.

9. a. Write a program that tabulates the results of an election. Each ward has three candidates, and there are six wards. The data will be read from a file named ELECT.RES that contains one record per vote. Each record consists of the number of the ward and the political party voted for, which is a number from 1 to 3. The tabulation will determine the winner of each ward, and will declare a majority, if there is one. For instance:

Election Results

Wards

Candidate	1	2	3	4	5	6
1	261	683	590	465	929	1177
2	20	870	461	773	782	395
3	1843	499	954	800	80	623

```
Winners:
  Ward1: Candidate 3, majority of 1562 votes
  Ward 2: Candidate 2
  Ward 3: Candidate 3
  Ward 4: Candidate 3
  Ward 5: Candidate 1, majority of 67 votes
  Ward 6: Candidate 1, majority of 159 votes
```

b. Improve the program above so that the user enters the number of wards and the maximum number of candidates in each ward.

10. Write a program that tabulates results of an opinion poll on banning smoking in public places. The results are contained in a file named SMOKE.POL. Each record consists of a single opinion: 1 indicates "in favor of," 2 for "opposed," 3 for "no opinion." Then the results are displayed. For example:

Opinion	Male	Female	Total
In favor	19	25	44
Opposed	23	24	47
No opinion	6	5	11
Total polled	48	54	102

11. a. In hockey a team earns 2 points for each win, 1 point for each tie, and no points for a loss. Consider the National Hockey League prior to 1967, when the league consisted of only six teams. Suppose at the end of each month, the league needed a summary of each team's number of games played, wins, ties, losses, total goals scored, total goals scored against them, and total points.

Write a C program to read in a file named GAMES.LIS, which consists of input lines. Each line contains the scores for one game: the visiting team initial followed by its score, then the home team initial followed by its score. After all the data has been read in, the program will print out each team name along with its number of games played, number of wins, number of ties, number of losses, total goals scored, total goals scored against them, and total points.

The teams are:

Team initial	**Team name**	**Team initial**	**Team name**
M or m	Montréal	B or b	Boston
T or t	Toronto	D or d	Detroit
N or n	New York	C or c	Chicago

Sample Input:

```
n 1 b 4
t 2 m 2
m 6 N 13
c 6 d 4
T 11 m 2
D 3 B 3
etc.
```

This is the output your program must produce:

Number of games successfully processed = 21

Team	Games played	Wins	Losses	Ties	Goals for	Goals against	Points
Montréal	7	0	6	1	24	54	1
Toronto	7	5	0	2	43	12	12
New York	5	3	1	1	26	17	7
Boston	7	2	1	4	22	16	8
Detroit	4	0	2	2	12	19	2
Chicago	6	3	3	0	23	32	6

Use a 2-D array named *standings,* which has one row for each team. Each row will hold the number of games played, number of wins, number of ties, number of losses, total goals scored, total goals scored against them, and total points for one team.

Use the following functions:

read_games(): This function will read all the games from the file. A 2-D array named *games* will be passed to it. In this array will be stored all the games read in, that is, the names of both teams and the scores. The file will never contain more than 36 games.

make_stats(): This function accepts one game (row) from the array *games* above and the 2-D array *standings.* The statistics for both teams involved in the game are gathered.

display_standing(): This function displays the standing as shown above. A single row from the 2-D array *standings* is passed.

b. Your program should incorporate error checks to make sure that all team initials are within the range and that all scores are neither less than 0 nor greater than 21. The errors will be echoed to the screen. For example:

```
Game #7: Invalid team — game not processed
Game #11: Invalid score — game not processed
Game #16: Invalid score — game not processed
Number of games successfully processed = 18
```

Then the teams' standings are displayed.

12. a. A used car dealership wants to keep the prices of their cars in the computer. These are kept in a file named CARS.PR. Each record contains the car model as a code from 1 to 5, the year built (from 1991 to 1995), and the price. The dealership needs a report. For example:

	Year				
Model of car	1991	1992	1993	1994	1995
1	$ 2400	$ 3340	$ 4100	$ 8990	$12000
2	$ 3100	$ 4540	$ 6000	$ 8630	$14581
3	$ 2320	$ 3640	$ 4680	$ 7760	$ 9958
4	$ 4400	$ 4540	$ 5000	$ 6220	$ 7790
5	$ 1700	$ 1800	$ 2200	$ 2800	$ 3310

Assume that the file contains only one car per model for each year.

b. It is likely that the dealer possesses more than one car per model for each year. Modify the program above so that the table will show the average price (rounded off to the nearest dollar) of all the cars of a given model and year.

13. a. The same car dealership conducted extensive tests on one car model that had a dubious reputation. The results are stored in a file named TESTS.CAR. Each record contains the year of the car and the rating of a particular test. There were four tests conducted, and each was conducted on a model from a particular year only once. The report that is needed for each car model might look like this:

	Year				
Test	1991	1992	1993	1994	1995
Engine	Fair	Fair	Good	Very	Very
Brakes	Fair	Good	Good	Very	Very
Wheels	Good	Very	Good	Very	Excl
Electrical system	Bad	Good	Good	Good	Good

A coding system is used for the rating. In the file is stored the following:

0 if the rating is Bad
1 if the rating is Fair
2 if the rating is Good
3 if the rating is Very good
4 if the rating is Excellent

These same codes will be stored in the 2-D array.

b. Modify the program so that an average rating is calculated for each test and each year. The averages will be fractional and need to be rounded off so that the correct rating may be displayed. With the example above, this gives us:

	Year					
Test	1991	1992	1993	1994	1995	Avg
Engine	Fair	Fair	Good	Very	Very	Good
Brakes	Fair	Good	Good	Very	Very	Good
Wheels	Good	Very	Good	Very	Excl	Good
Electrical system	Bad	Good	Good	Good	Good	Good
Average	Fair	Good	Good	Very	Very	

17.3 MEMORY LAYOUT OF A 2-D ARRAY

Section 17.4 will show that, just like 1-D arrays, 2-D arrays may also be accessed via a pointer. To understand how that works, it is necessary to first discuss how a 2-D array is actually stored in memory.

17.3.1 HOW THE CELLS ARE STORED IN MEMORY

The computer memory is one-dimensional: it simply consists of a long sequence of bytes. Consequently, a two-dimensional array has to be stored as a one-dimensional array. Here is how this is accomplished. Assume the declaration:

```
int   table[5][4] =  { { 4, 3, 2, 1 },
                       { 1, 2, 3, 4 },
                       { 5, 6, 7, 8 },
                       { 2, 5, 7, 9 },
                       { 0, 5, 9, 0 } };
```

Starting at row 0 of the 2-D array, each row is laid out in memory in sequence. The 2-D array would be laid out in memory as shown in Figure 17.3.1.

Figure 17.3.1

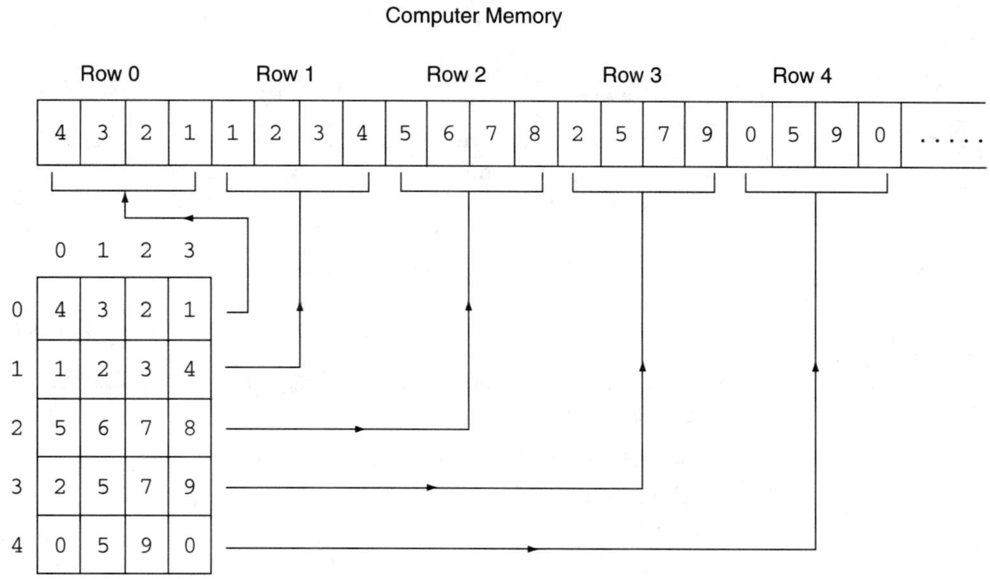

Example 17.3.1

The program below demonstrates that, indeed, the 2-D array *table* above is stored in memory sequentially. To show this, it simply displays the address of each cell.

```
#include <stdio.h>

void display_row(int row[])
{
    int i;

    for (i=0; i < 4; i++)
    {
        printf(" %d (%p) ", row[i], &row[i]);
    }
    printf("\n");
}

main()
{
    int   table[5][4] = { { 4, 3, 2, 1 },
                          { 1, 2, 3, 4 },
                          { 5, 6, 7, 8 },
                          { 2, 5, 7, 9 },
                          { 0, 5, 9, 0 } };
    int   i, j;

    printf("The 2-D array table is located at address %p\n\n", table);[1]
    printf("Content and address of each cell in the table:\n\n");
    for (i=0; i < 5; i++)
    {
        for (j=0; j < 4; j++)
        {
            printf(" %d (%p)", table[i][j], &table[i][j]);[2]
        }
        printf("\n");
    }
    printf("\nAddress of each row of the table:\n\n");
```

```
    for (i=0; i < 5; i++)
    {
        printf("address of table[%d] is %p\n", i, table[i]);[3]
    }
    printf("\nContent and address of each cell in the table from\n"
           "using the function display_row():\n\n");
    for (i=0; i < 5; i++)
    {
        display_row(table[i]);[4]
    }
}
```

Before knowing more about this program, look at its output. Each number in parentheses is an address to a cell of the 2-D array:

The 2-D array table is located at address 8426[1]

Content and address of each cell in the table:[2]

4 (8426)	3 (8428)	2 (842A)	1 (842C)
1 (842E)	2 (8430)	3 (8432)	4 (8434)
5 (8436)	6 (8438)	7 (843A)	8 (843C)
2 (843E)	5 (8440)	7 (8442)	9 (8444)
0 (8446)	5 (8448)	9 (844A)	0 (844C)

Address of each row of the table:[3]

address of table[0] is 8426
address of table[1] is 842E
address of table[2] is 8436
address of table[3] is 843E
address of table[4] is 8446

Content and address of each cell in the table from using the function display_row():[4]

4 (8426)	3 (8428)	2 (842A)	1 (842C)
1 (842E)	2 (8430)	3 (8432)	4 (8434)
5 (8436)	6 (8438)	7 (843A)	8 (843C)
2 (843E)	5 (8440)	7 (8442)	9 (8444)
0 (8446)	5 (8448)	9 (844A)	0 (844C)

Explanations

1. This *printf()* displays the value of *table* as 8426. This is precisely the address of the first element of the 2-D array. So, just as with 1-D arrays, the name of the 2-D array contains the address to it.
2. This *printf()* displays the content and the address of each cell within the 2-D array so that it can be seen where the cell is stored:

   ```
   printf(" %d (%p)", table[i][j], &table[i][j])
   ```

   The cell is designated by *table [i][j],* and its address by *&table[i][j].* Note in the output that some addresses are shown with letters such as 842C and 842E. This happens because the format code *%p* displays addresses in ***hexadecimal notation,*** a numeric system widely used to display memory addresses and contents. (This notation is explained in Appendix E.) Nevertheless, you can see that the cells are stored in sequence:

   ```
   8426  8428  842A  842C   842E  8430  8432  8434   and so on.
   |_______________________|  |_______________________|
             Row 0                      Row 1
   ```

   Note that this program was run on an Intel 80386 CPU chip. If run on another system, the addresses would likely be expressed entirely differently.
3. The code accesses each row individually.The *printf()* displays the value of the cell *table[i]:*

   ```
   printf("address of table[%d] is %p\n", i, table[i])
   ```

The format code *%p* is used because the value of *table[i]* is actually an address. Look again carefully at the output above. For instance, the value of *table[2]* is 8436, which is precisely the address of the cell *table[2][0]*. Note the pattern:

table[0] is the address of the cell *table[0][0]*
table[1] is the address of the cell *table[1][0]*
table[2] is the address of the cell *table[2][0]*
table[3] is the address of the cell *table[3][0]*

Therefore the value of *table[i]* is the address to row *i*.

4. A call to *display_row()* is made for each row. A single row is passed to the function, and it displays it. Note the argument and parameter.

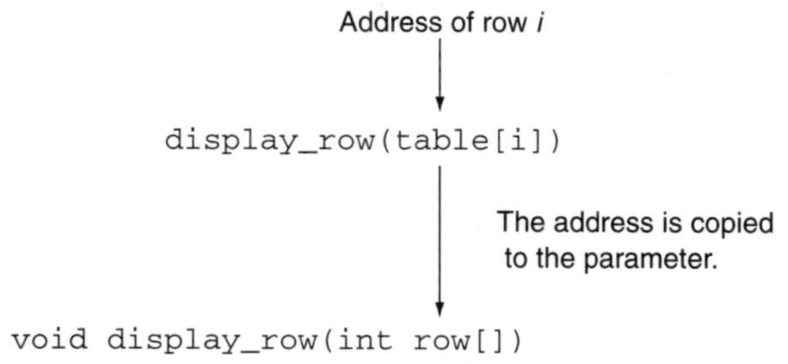

row[] is declared as a 1-D array since the row passed to it is one-dimensional.

EXERCISES 17.3.1

Given the following 2-D array that begins at address 3300, answer the questions below:

```
float matrix[3][5] = { { 9, 4, -8, 5, 0 },
                       { 11, -4, 0, 1, 5 },
                       { 3, 20, 3, 6, 3 } };
```

1. What is the address of each of the following?
   a. `matrix[0][0]`
   b. `matrix[0][4]`
   c. `matrix[2][4]`
   d. `matrix[1][1]`
2. a. What is the value of *matrix[2]?*
   b. Give an expression that is equivalent to it.
3. a. What is the value of *matrix[0]?*
   b. Give two expressions that are equivalent to it.
4. Is the expression *(matrix[1])[4]* valid? If so, why and to what element does it refer? (***Hint:*** Recall Section 16.4.)
5. Just as with 1-D arrays, a pointer may run through a 2-D array. It is only a matter of moving the pointer from one cell to the next. (You may wish to refer back to Section 16.2.) Modify the functions *read_table()* and *display_table()* so that the parameter is a pointer to the 2-D array, and this single pointer variable will run through the 2-D array.

Example 17.3.2 shows a simple application from the findings of Example 17.3.1.

Example 17.3.2

Let us write a program that reverses each row of the 2-D array *table* from Example 17.3.1. The function *reverse_itself()* developed in Exercise 14.3.2, 6 will be called to reverse individual rows. Here is the solution:

```
void display_row(int row[])
{
      int i;
```

```
        for (i=0; i < 4; i++)
        {
            printf(" %d ", row[i]);
        }
        printf("\n");
}

main()
{
        int   table[3][4] = { { 4, 3, 2, 1 },
                              { 1, 2, 3, 4 },
                              { 5, 6, 7, 8 } };
        int   i;

        for (i=0; i < 3; i++)
        {
            reverse_itself(table[i]); [1]
        }
        for (i=0; i < 3; i++)
        {
            display_row(table[i]); [1]
        }
}
```

Explanation

1. The value of *table[i]*, which is the address of row *i,* is passed to these functions. Since a row is a 1-D array, the parameter of both functions has to be a 1-D array, which it is.

EXERCISES 17.3.2

1. a. Modify the program in Example 17.2.1 as follows. The function *read_table()* will call another function named *read_row()*. This one will accept each individual row and read into it. Similarly, the function *display_table()* will call another function named *display_row()*. This one will accept each individual row and display it.
   b. Modify the program in Example 17.2.2 in a similar fashion. In addition, the function *read_row()* will be given the number of elements to read into the row (i.e., this is equivalent to the number of columns of the 2-D array). Similarly, the function *display_row()* will be given the number of elements to display from the row.
2. a. Why does the following function work, even though a 2-D array is passed to a parameter that is a 1-D array? What will be displayed?

```
void display(int list[], int length)
{
        int i;

        for (i=0; i < length; i++)
        {
                printf(" %d ", list[i]);
        }
        printf("\n");
}

main()
{
        int   table[3][4] = { { 4, 3, 2, 1 },
                              { 1, 2, 3, 4 },
```

```
                                    { 5, 6, 7, 8 } };

        display(table, 3 * 4);
}
```

b. In the function *display()*, use a pointer through the 2-D array instead of an index.

3. In Example 17.3.2, suppose that the loop inside the function *display_row()* has been mistyped as shown, with the error appearing here in bold type:

```
for (i=0; i < 7; i++)
{
     printf(" %d ", row[i]);
}
```

What would the program display?

4. Still in Example 17.3.2, suppose that the loop inside the *main()* has been mistyped as shown, with the error appearing here in bold type:

```
for (i=0; i < 6; i++)
{
     reverse_itself(table[i]);
}
```

Would the program produce unpredictable results? If so, when?

5. a. Use the function *bubble_sort()* from Exercise 15.1.4, 3, to sort each row of any 2-D array. (***Hint:*** Simply call the sort function within a loop each time a row is passed to it.)
   b. Can the *bubble_sort()* function be used in the same way to sort each column? That is, can a column be passed to the sort function? If so, show how by filling the blank below. If not, why?

```
main()
{
        int    table[3][4] = { { 4, 3, 2, 1 },
                               { 1, 2, 3, 4 },
                               { 5, 6, 7, 8 } };
        int    j;

        for (j=0; j < 4; j++)        /* for each column */
        {
               bubble_sort(_________________);
               }
}
```

6. Consider the following program:

```
void fcn(int a[3][8], int b[21])
{
       int  i, j, k;

       for (i=0, k=0; i < 3; i++)
       {
              for (j=0; j < 8; j++, k++)
              {
                     b[k] = a[i][j];
              }
}

main()
{
       int  table[3][8] = { 7, 0, 4, 33, 12, 7, 81, 8,
                            9, 0, 12, -8, 6, 23, 1, 0,
                            0, -1, 11, 77, 2, 5, 5, 5 };
```

```
        int  cpy[21];

        fcn(table, cpy);
}
```

a. What does this program do?
b. The code of *fcn()* can be reduced to a single loop and still produce the same result. How?

17.3.2 APPLICATION: SORTING A 2-D ARRAY ON A SPECIFIC ROW

Because of the 2-D array's two dimensions, the meaning of sorting a 2-D array is not clear and could be any one of the following: (1) sorting each row separately, (2) sorting each column separately, (3) sorting based on one specific row, or (4) sorting based on one specific column. Example 17.3.3 shows how to implement the fourth possibility.

Example 17.3.3

Refer back to Example 17.2.1. Suppose the task now is to display the assignments sorted by results in descending order. The user specifies on which assignment to sort the table. For instance:

```
Enter the results of all 8 assignments:
For student #1:  18  22  15  25  91  8  17  22
For student #2:  20  25  20  25  86  9  19  24
For student #3:  11  14   8  18  46  9  15  19
For student #4:  15  19  14  16  61  5   9  15
For student #5:  17  23  16  24  73  7  12  20
By which assignment would you like to have the table sorted? 7

                         Assignments
              1   2   3   4   5  6   7   8
Student #2:  20  25  20  25  86  9  19  24
Student #1:  18  22  15  25  91  8  17  22
Student #3:  11  14   8  18  46  9  15  19
Student #5:  17  23  16  24  73  7  12  20
Student #4:  15  19  14  16  61  5   9  15
```

As you can see, the column for assignment 7 is now sorted. Note that as column 7 is sorted, the other numbers on the rows follow, too; that is, when a swap of a number in column 7 is performed, the whole corresponding row is swapped, too, so the swapping is two-dimensional. Clearly the function *bubble_sort()* cannot be used here; it can only swap in one dimension. Nevertheless, the bubble sort algorithm can still be used. There is actually another reason why the function *bubble_sort()* cannot be used. A column cannot be passed as an argument to *bubble_sort()*, unlike in the solution of Exercise 17.3.2, 5a, where the row to sort could easily be passed. Consequently, the following program defines a new function named *sort()* to implement the bubble sort.

Let us first examine how the swapping may be done in two dimensions. When a mark in column 7 needs to be swapped, the whole row will be swapped:

```
                         Assignments
              1   2   3   4   5  6   7   8
Student #1:  18  22  15  25  91  8  17  22
Student #2:  20  25  20  25  86  9  19  24
Student #3:  11  14   8  18  46  9  15  19
Student #4:  15  19  14  16  61  5   9  15
Student #5:  17  23  16  24  73  7  12  20
```

Rows 2 and 3 will be swapped; then no swapping will be necessary until the last two rows:

```
                         Assignments
              1   2   3   4   5  6   7   8
Student #1:  18  22  15  25  91  8  19  22
Student #2:  20  25  20  25  86  9  17  24
```

Student #3:	11	14	8	18	46	9	15	19
Student #4:	15	19	14	16	61	5	9	15
Student #5:	17	23	16	24	73	7	12	20

Using an array of indexes for efficiency. This method is terribly inefficient because the swapping is applied to the whole row—eight numbers must be swapped every time. Fortunately, there is a better way. Instead of swapping the rows, swap the indexes of those rows stored in an ***array of indexes.*** For example, here before the sorting is underway, the index array would be initialized to the indexes shown in Figure 17.3.2, which shows the initial row position of each student.

Figure 17.3.2

`index_array`

0	1	2	3	4

When the rows for students 1 and 2 must be swapped, the first and second index in this array will be swapped as shown in Figure 17.3.3.

Figure 17.3.3

`index_array`

1	0	2	3	4

The rows themselves are never swapped. When the rows for students 4 and 5 must be swapped, the fourth and fifth index in this array are swapped as shown in Figure 17.3.4.

Figure 17.3.4

`index_array`

1	0	2	4	3

Finally, to display the sorted table, the program will first refer to this index array to find out the correct order: Row 1, Row 0, Row 2, Row 4, and Row 3, as shown in Figure 17.3.5.

Figure 17.3.5

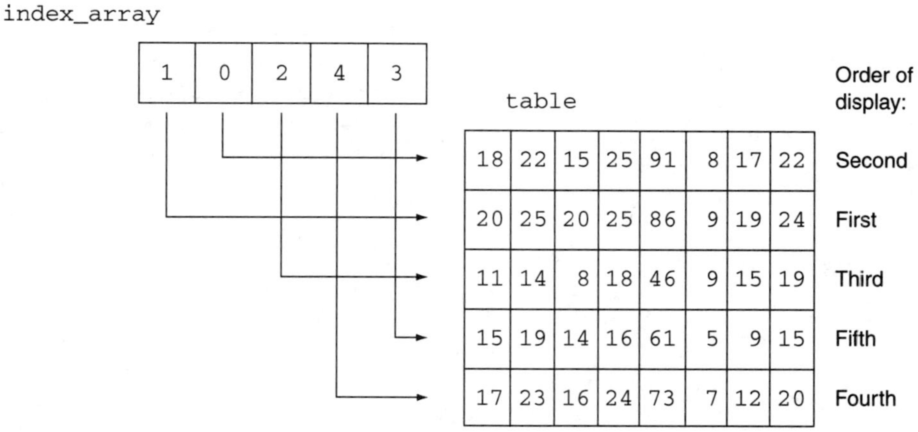

Following is the complete solution. The function *read_table()* does not change, but other changes occur.

```
#include <stdio.h>

void read_table(int array[5][8])
{
     int  i, j;
```

```
    printf("Enter the results of all 8 assignments:\n");
    for (i=0; i < 5; i++)
    {
        printf("For student #%d: ", i+1);
        for (j=0; j < 8; j++)
        {
            scanf("%d", &table[i][j]);
        }
    }
}

void display_table(int array[5][8], int index[5])
{
    int  i, j;

    for (i=0; i < 5; i++)
    {
        for (j=0; j < 8; j++)
        {
            printf(" %d ", table[index[i]][j]);1
        }
    }
}

void sort(int table[5][8], int col, int index[5])
{
    int  row, pass;
    char more_sorting;

    more_sorting = 1;
    for (pass=0; (pass < 5) && more_sorting; pass++)
    {
        more_sorting = 0;
        for (row=0; row < pass; row++)
        {
            if (table[row][col] > table[row+1][col])2
            {
                more_sorting = 1;
                temp = index[row];3
                index[row] = index[row+1];
                index[row+1] = temp;
            }
        }
    }

}

main()
{
   int  table[5][8];
   int  index[5];
   int  assign_no;

   read_table(table);
   printf("By which assignment would you like to have the table sorted? ");
   scanf("%d", &assign_no);
   sort(table, assign_no, index);4
   display_table(table, index);5
}
```

Explanations

1. Each element of the 2-D array is displayed via the array of indexes. This ensures that the rows appear in the correct order determined by the function *sort()*:

   ```
   printf(" %d ", table[index[i]][j]);
   ```

   index[i] contains the index of the row to display.
2. The sorting is done on column number *col,* which is also the assignment number passed to the function. The sorting algorithm compares pairs of numbers in this column by changing the row number (designated by *[row]* and *[row+1],* but leaving the column fixed at *col:*

   ```
   if (table[row][col] > table[row+1][col])
   ```

3. When it is found that a swap is necessary, the corresponding indexes from the array of indexes are swapped. Again, the rows of the table are never swapped.
4. The function *sort()* requires the 2-D array *table,* the column number *assign_no,* on which to sort, and the array of indexes in which will be stored the proper order of the rows to display.
5. The function *display_table()* displays the whole sorted table. It requires the 2-D array and the array of indexes.

EXERCISES 17.3.3

1. Add a loop to the program above so that the user may sort the table on different columns.
2. Refer back to Example 17.2.1. Write a program that sorts the columns on the basis of a particular assignment. For instance:

   ```
   Enter the results of all 5 students:
   For assignment #1:  18  20  11  15  17
   For assignment #2:  22  25  14  19  23
   For assignment #3:  15  20   8  14  16
   For assignment #4:  25  25  18  16  24
   For assignment #5:  91  86  46  61  73
   For assignment #6:   8   9   9   5   7
   For assignment #7:  17  19  15   9  12
   For assignment #8:  22  24  19  15  20

   By which assignment would you like to have the table sorted? 7

                                 Student
                        2   1   3   5   4

   Assignment #1:      20  18  11  17  15
   Assignment #2:      25  22  14  23  19
   Assignment #3:      20  15   8  16  14
   Assignment #4:      25  25  18  24  16
   Assignment #5:      86  91  46  73  61
   Assignment #6:       9   8   9   7   5
   Assignment #7:      19  17  15  12   9
   Assignment #8:      24  22  19  20  15
   ```

   Note that the columns are swapped, too. Base your solution on the one provided in Example 17.3.3.
3. Reconsider the file CARS.PR from Supplementary Exercise 17.2, 12b. Write a program that displays the report in ascending order of any one of the years, as specified by the user.

17.4 ARRAYS OF POINTERS

What do arrays of pointers have to do with 2-D arrays? On the one hand, they may be viewed as a generalization of 2-D arrays in that all rows do not necessarily have the same number of columns. On the other hand, a 2-D array may be viewed as a special kind of array of pointers. This section explains and illustrates this.

17.4.1 HOW ARRAYS OF POINTERS ARE STORED IN MEMORY

Example 17.4.1

Reconsider Example 17.1.1. The disadvantage of using a 2-D array is that there is no explicit mention of the countries in the declaration *int table[5][8]*. It might be better to declare a separate array for each country. Then the array *table* could be reduced to a 1-D array of pointers to these arrays. Here is that program, with changes shown in bold type:

```
#include <stdio.h>

main()
{
     int    Canada[8];          /* separate */
     int    US[8];              /* array */
     int    Mexico[8];          /* for */
     int    Russia[8];          /* each */
     int    Japan[8];           /* country */
     int  * table[5] = { Canada, US, Mexico, Russia, Japan };[1]
     int    i, j;

     printf("Enter the results of all 8 assignments:\n");
     for (i=0; i < 5; i++)
     {
          printf("For student #%d: ", i+1);
          for (j=0; j < 8; j++)
          {
               scanf("%d", &table[i][j]);[2]
          }
     }
}
```

Explanations

1. The array *table* is now a 1-D array of pointers:

   ```
   int  * table[5] = { Canada, US, Mexico, Russia, Japan };
   ```

   In this array, *int* * indicates pointers to an integer, while *table[5]* notes that the array *table* is of size 5. The names of the countries are the names of the arrays and also pointers to them.

   Although this 1-D array looks rather different than all the ones seen so far, it remains nothing more than a 1-D array whose elements are pointers to 1-D arrays. Indeed, recall that the name of an array is also a pointer to it. For instance, suppose that *Canada* is stored at address 2200, *US* is stored at address 2218, *Mexico* at address 2236, *Russia* at address 2254 and *Japan* at 2272. Then the cell *table[0]* is made to point to address 2200, the cell *table[1]* is made to point to address 2218, and so on. This is all set automatically at declaration time, as illustrated below.

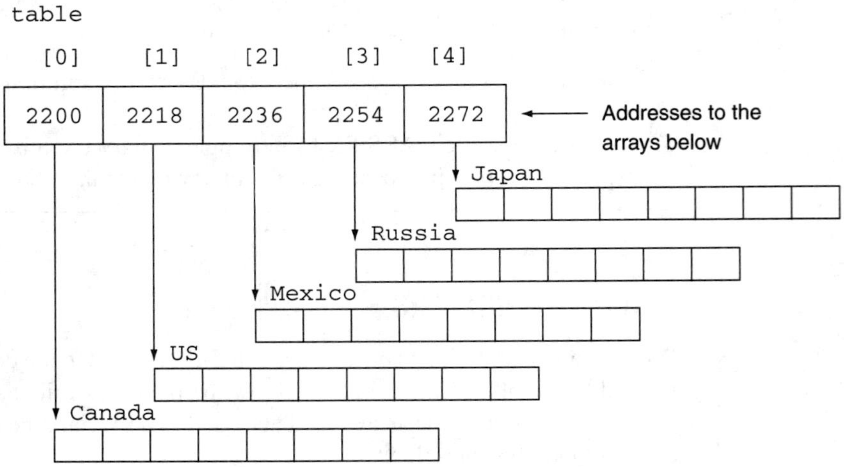

2. Note that the elements from each one of the five arrays are accessed through the *table* array in exactly the same way as if *table* was a 2-D array: with two indexes. In fact, an array of pointers and a 2-D array are very nearly the same thing. Indeed, by reorganizing Figure 17.4.1 a little, it may be made to look very much like the 2-D array shown here:

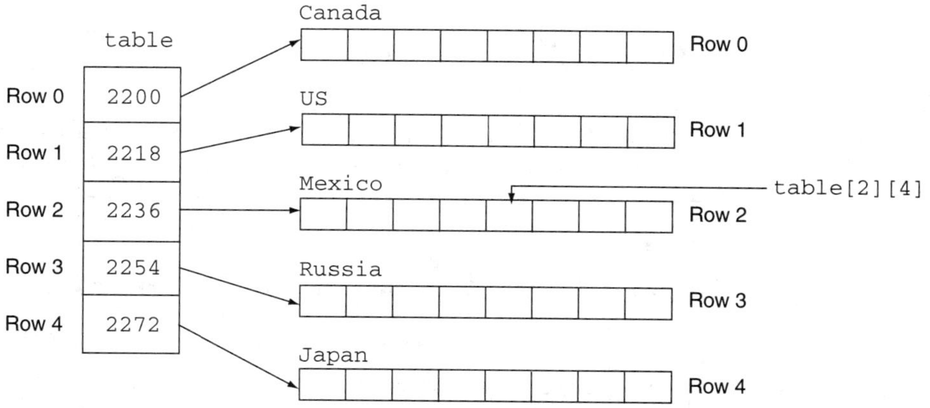

In this regard, each array may be viewed as a row of a 2-D array, and all corresponding elements from each array may be viewed as a column. For instance, the element *table[2][4]* is located as shown in the illustration. Note that the element *Mexico[4]* is exactly the same cell!

Last, note that the size of the array of pointers may be omitted as in:

```
int  * table[] = { Canada, US, Mexico, Russia, Japan };
```

EXERCISES 17.4.1

1. Consider these declarations:

```
float high[6] = { 3.30, 2.84, 3.90, 2.00, 1.93, 3.10 };
float college[6] = { 1.70, 2.25, 2.91, 3.57, 3.99, 4.00 };
float university[6] = { 2.88, 2.99, 2.72, 3.08, 3.11, 3.78};
float class[3] = { high, college, university };
```

These arrays are stored respectively at the addresses 6500, 6526, 6552, and 6578.

a. Draw a memory layout for these arrays like the one in Example 17.4.1.

b. What is the value of the following cells, and at what addresses are they located?

   i. *class[1][5]*

   ii. *class[2][1]*

c. Formulate an equivalent notation for the following entities:

   i. *college[4]*

   ii. *class[2][3]*

   iii. *high[3]*

   iv. *class[2]*

   v. *university*

2. Consider the following segment:

```
ptr1 = &table;
ptr2 = table;
```

Here *table* is declared as in Example 17.4.1. What are the proper declarations for *ptr1* and *ptr2?*

3. Discuss the differences and similarities among the following declarations:

a. *int table[5]* c. *int ** table*

b. *int * table[5]* d. *int * table*

4. Will the program below work? If not, explain what is wrong and suggest changes to make it work.

```
main()
{
      int  * list[5];
```

```
        for (i=0; i < 5; i++)
        {
                for (j=0; j < 4; j++)
                {
                        list[i][j] = 0;
                }
        }
}
```

5. Implement the solution of Example 17.3.3 by using an array of pointers instead of an array of indexes. The array of pointers will be made of pointers to rows of the 2-D array.

17.4.2 ARRAYS OF POINTERS VS. 2-D ARRAYS

There are two important differences between a 2-D array and an array of pointers:

1. With a 2-D array all rows are adjacent, whereas with an array of pointers, the "rows" do not have to be adjacent at all. Indeed, the pointer may be assigned to point to an arbitrary location.
2. With a 2-D array, all rows are of same length, whereas with an array of pointers, the "rows" may differ in size.

These two differences are clarified in Example 17.4.2.

Example 17.4.2

Reconsider Example 17.4.1 again. Suppose that some countries did not complete all assignments. For instance, suppose Canada finished six assignments, Mexico finished five assignments and Japan finished seven assignments. These countries require smaller arrays, as shown below:

```
#include <stdio.h>

main()
{
    int     Canada[6];
    int     US[8];
    int     Mexico[5];
    int     Russia[8];
    int     Japan[7];
    int   * table[5] = { Canada, Mexico, Japan, US, Russia };[1]
    int     i, j, num;

    printf("Enter the results of all 8 assignments:\n");
    for (i=0; i < 5; i++)
    {
        printf("How many assignments completed for student #%d: ", i+1);
        scanf("%d", &num);
        for (j=0; j < num; j++)
        {
            scanf("%d", &table[i][j]);[2]
        }
    }
}
```

Explanations

1. Note the order in which the arrays are listed in the array *table.* They are listed in a different order than they were in Example 17.4.1. Clearly, the rows are no longer adjacent. Assuming

that the arrays are stored at the same addresses as in Example 17.4.1, the memory layout would now look like this.

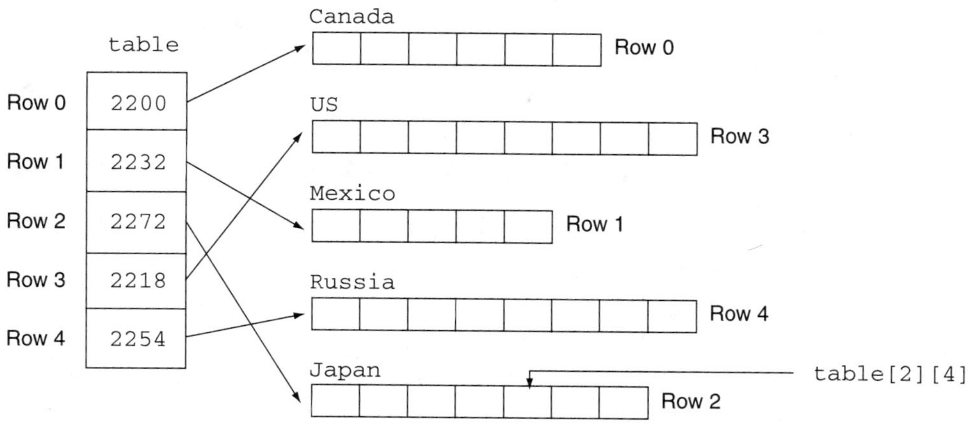

As you can see, the rows are no longer adjacent. Also each row has a different number of columns. With this new arrangement, the element *table[2][4]* refers to a different element than in Example 17.4.1, even though it is still at row 2, column 4.

2. The index *j* accesses a different number of columns, depending on the row *i*. Note that, despite changes, entries are still accessed as if the 1-D array table were still a 2-D array!

EXERCISES 17.4.2

1. Consider the following declarations:

```
float high[6] = { 3.30, 2.84, 3.90, 2.00, 1.93, 3.10 };
float college[6] = { 1.70, 2.25, 2.91, 3.57, 3.99, 4.00 };
float university[6] = { 2.88, 2.99, 2.72, 3.08, 3.11, 3.78};
float class[3] = { college, university, high };
```

These arrays are stored at the addresses 6500, 6526, 6552, and 6578, respectively, as in Exercise 17.4.1, 1. But now, these arrays are accessed by the array *class* in a different order.

a. Draw a memory layout for these arrays like the one in Example 17.4.2.
b. What is the value of the cells below, and at what addresses are they located?
   i. *class[1][5]*
   ii. *class[2][1]*
c. Formulate an equivalent notation for the following entities:
   i. *college[4]*
   ii. *class[2][3]*
   iii. *high[3]*
   iv. *class[2]*
   v. *university*

2. The city of Los Angeles has a professional team in each of the following sports: basketball, baseball, football, and hockey. A news station keeps a record of the scores for the most recent game played in each sport. This data is stored in a file named SPORTS.SCR:

```
3 7 11 0 23
1 45 29 33 26
4 1 0 3
2 0 0 2 0 1 1 0 0 4
```

The first number of each record is a code for the sport: 1 for basketball, 2 for baseball, 3 for football, and 4 for hockey. The numbers that follow are the scores for each period of play. As you can see, basketball has 4 periods, baseball has 9 innings, football has 4 quarters, and hockey has 3 periods. Write a program that simply reads the file into memory and displays the data to the screen in a well-organized, user-friendly manner. Develop the following two solutions:

a. Store the data in a 2-D array of size 4-by-9.
b. The solution in (a) is a memory waster! Much of the 2-D array is never used. Use an array of pointers and individual arrays for each sport in a way that no memory will be unused.

17.4.3 PASSING AN ARRAY OF POINTERS TO A FUNCTION

Passing an array of pointers to a function is done in the same way as any other array, as Example 17.4.3 illustrates.

Example 17.4.3

Reconsider Example 17.2.1. Let us use the same functions as we did then, except we will use an array of pointers instead of a 2-D array. Here is the new program:

```
#include <stdio.h>

void read_table(int * array[5])[1]
{
        int  i, j;

        printf("Enter the results of all 8 assignments:\n");
        for (i=0; i < 5; i++)
        {
                printf("For student #%d: ", i+1);
                for (j=0; j < 8; j++)
                {
                        scanf("%d", &array[i][j]);[2]
                }
        }
}

void display_table(int * array[5])[1]
{
        int  i, j;

        for (i=0; i < 5; i++)
        {
                for (j=0; j < 8; j++)
                {
                        printf(" %d ", array[i][j]);[2]
                }
        }
}

main()
{
        int     Canada[8];
        int     US[8];
        int     Mexico[8];
        int     Russia[8];
        int     Japan[8];
        int   * table[5] = { Canada, US, Mexico, Russia, Japan };[1]

        read_table(table);[2]
        display_table(table);[2]
}
```

Explanations

1. Except for the array declarations and the parameter declarations, nothing has changed from the programin Example 17.2.1.
2. The array *table* is still passed to the functions the same way and is referred to in the same way! However, the parameter declaration is now an array of five pointers.

   Note that should a function prototype be needed for, say, *read_table()*, it would be formulated as follows:

   ```
   void read_table(int * [5]);
   ```

Application: Passing a 2-D array of undetermined size. Recall that prior to Example 17.2.2, it was mentioned that it was not possible to send a 2-D array of any size to a function. Actually, it is possible when the 2-D array is viewed as an array of pointers. Example 17.4.4 shows how.

Example 17.4.4

The following program is a generalization of Example 17.2.2 in that it may accept a 2-D array of any size. Explanations follow:

```
#include <stdio.h>

void read_table(int * array[], int rows, int cols) [1,2]
{
      int  i, j;

      printf("Enter the results of all 8 assignments:\n");
      for (i=0; i < rows; i++)
      {
            printf("For student #%d: ", i+1);
            for (j=0; j < cols; j++)
            {
                  scanf("%d", &array[i][j]);
            }
      }
}

void display_table(int * array[], int rows, int cols) [2]
{
      int  i, j;

      for (i=0; i < rows; i++)
      {
            for (j=0; j < cols; j++)
            {
                  printf(" %d ", array[i][j]);
            }
      }
}

main()
{
      int  table[5][8];

      read_table(table, 5, 8); [3]
      display_table(table, 5, 8); [3]
}
```

Explanations

1. Note the parameter declarations to both functions:

   ```
   void display_table(int * array[], int rows, int cols)
   ```

In this statement, *int * arrays* indicates the array of pointers, and *int rows* and *int cols* indicates the dimensions of the arrays.

2. Of course, the functions *read_table()* and *display_table()* must be given the actual dimensions of the array actually sent, so that they know how many rows and columns to go through. This is accomplished with the use of *int rows* and *int cols*. Note that the first parameter could have been declared to the equivalent *int ** array*. (Why is that so?)
3. The 2-D array *table* is still passed the same way as usual, so it is the header of the functions that makes all the difference. How can that allow the function to receive a 2-D array of any size? There are two reasons:
   a. Because the parameter array (of pointers) is not given a size, it may accept any number of elements (here, pointers). This is equivalent to saying that it may accept any number of rows from the 2-D array *table*.
   b. Any given pointer within *array* may point to an array of any size. This is equivalent to saying that it may accept any number of columns from the 2-D array *table*.

EXERCISES 17.4.3

1. Rewrite the program for Supplementary Exercise 17.2, 11b by using an array of pointers. You will need one array for each team. Each array will hold the number of games played, number of wins, number of ties, number of losses, total goals scored, total goals scored against the team, and total points for one team. The array of pointers will point to these arrays. Use the same functions as before, although the parameters declarations may need to be changed.
2. Rewrite the program for the Supplementary Exercise 17.2, 12, by using an array of pointers. You will need one array for each car model.
3. Rewrite the program for Supplementary Exercise 17.2, 13, by using an array of pointers. You will need one array for each test type.

Although presented in this chapter, arrays of pointers are much more widely used to store character strings, which is the topic of Chapter 18.

17.5 DYNAMIC MEMORY ALLOCATION

There are two ways data (variables, arrays, and so on) are allocated memory: statically and dynamically. Both ways are illustrated in the following examples. Both programs simply allocate and initialize each cell of a 1-D array named *one_d* to 99 and each cell of a 2-D array named *two_d* to 66.

17.5.1 WHAT IS DYNAMIC MEMORY?

This question will be answered with the following examples.

Example 17.5.1

In this example, both arrays are allocated memory at the time that they are declared. But the size of both arrays was decided at the time that the programmer wrote the program (at compile time). This type of memory allocation is called ***static memory allocation.*** Following is the program:

```
#include <stdio.h>

main()
{
     int  one_d[10], two_d[5][8];
     int  i, j;

     for (i=0; i < 10; i++)
```

```
        {
                one_d[i] = 99;
        }

        for (i=0; i < 5; i++)
        {
                for (j=0; j < 8; j++)
                {
                        two_d[i][j] = 66;
                }
        }
}
```

The line in bold type indicates static memory allocation. You will notice that there is nothing new in this example. We have always used static memory allocation up to this point; consequently, this program requires no further explanations. However, we have not yet encountered the second kind of memory allocation, which is introduced in Example 17.5.2.

Example 17.5.2

In this example, both arrays are allocated memory only at the time that the user requests it at run time. At the time that the programmer wrote the program, the amount of memory to allocate was still unknown. This type of memory allocation is called ***dynamic memory allocation.*** Following is the program, which makes use of a function named *calloc()* that will be explained:

```
#include <stdio.h>
#include <stdlib.h>


main()
{
        int  * one_d, (*two_d)[];[1]
        int  i, j;
        int  size1D, row, column;

        printf("Enter size of the 1-D array to allocate > ");
        scanf("%d", &size1D);

        one_d = calloc(size1D, sizeof(int));[2]
        printf("Enter size of the 2-D array to allocate > ");
        scanf("%d%d", &row, &column);2

        two_d = calloc(row * column, sizeof(int));[2]

        for (i=0; i < size1D; i++)
        {
                one_d[i] = 99;[3]
        }

                for (i=0; i < row; i++)
                {
                        for (j=0; j < column; j++)
                        {
                                two_d[i][j] = 66;[3]
                        }
                }
                free(one_d);[4]
                free(two_d);[4]
}
```

Explanations

1. Note that the array declarations differ when dynamically allocated instead of statically allocated. Compare the two types in Table 17.5.1.

Table 17.5.1

Static allocation	Dynamic allocation
int one_d[10];	int *one_d;
int two_d[5][8];	int (*two_d)[];

Of course, with dynamic allocation the sizes should not be specified, because it is the user who will decide at run time what size to allocate. The declaration *int (*two_d)[]* means that *two_d* is a pointer to a list of arrays. The * symbol is the pointer, and the [] indicates the array. For example, *int (*two_d)[5]* would mean that *two_d* is a pointer to five arrays, as shown below:

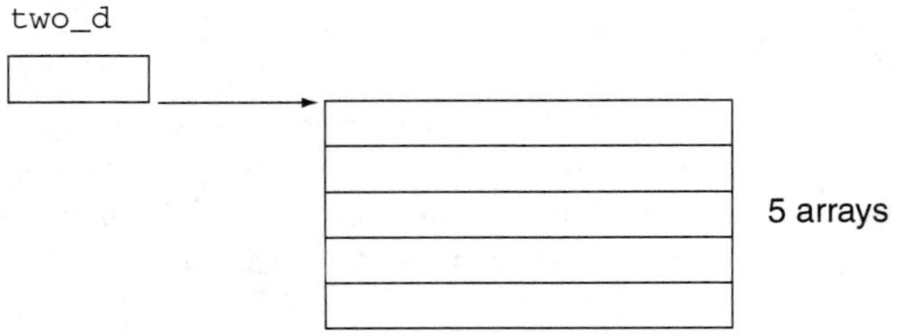

This figure suggests that *two_d* may be viewed as a pointer to a 2-D array. Indeed so! It is better, though, to omit any size specifications so that a 2-D array of any size may be dynamically allocated. Note that *one_d* and *two_d* are pointer variables, not pointer constants, such as *int one_d[10]* would be. It is necessary that they both be pointer variables (as explanation 2 will clarify).

2. The call to the function *calloc()* ensures that enough memory is allocated for the arrays. The first call allocates memory for the 1-D array pointed to by *one_d*. Note that *size1D* indicates the number of elements, and *sizeof(int)* stands for the size of each element.

```
one_d = calloc(size1D, sizeof(int));
```

So *size1D * sizeof(int)* bytes will be allocated. For instance, if the user entered 12 in the variable *size1D*, then 12 * 2 = 24 bytes would be allocated.

The second call allocates memory for the 2-D array pointed to by *two_d*. Note that *row * column* stands for the number of elements and *sizeof(int)* stands for the size of each element.

```
two_d = calloc(row * column, sizeof(int));
```

So *row * column * sizeof(int)* bytes will be allocated. Note that since *one_d* and *two_d* are assigned an address, they had to be declared pointer variables, not pointer constants.

3. Each element of the 1-D array and the 2-D array are accessed exactly as if *one_d* and *two_d* were array names! Slick!
4. The functions to release memory previously allocated are *free(one_d);* and *free(two_d);*, where *one_d* and *two_d* point to the first element of the blocks of memory to release. Before terminating, a program should always release memory that it had allocated dynamically. Should the *free()* calls be omitted, the operating system usually releases the memory automatically. Nevertheless, use the *free()* function anyway—it is better practice.

EXERCISES 17.5.1

1. Discuss the differences among the following declarations:
   a. *int table[5]*
   b. *int * table[5]*
   c. *int (*table)[5]*
   d. *int * table;*

2. Change the following program into one that allocates the 2-D array dynamically:

```
main()
{
    float   wages[7][15];
    int     i, j, depts, empls;

    printf("Enter the number of departments: ");
    scanf("%d", &depts);
    printf("Enter the number of employees per department: ");
    scanf("%d", &empls);
    for (i=0; i < depts; i++)
    {
          printf("Dept #%d: Enter the wages for all %d employees:\n",
                 depts, empls);
          for (j=0; j < empls; j++)
          {
                scanf("%f", &wages[i][j]);
          }
      }
}
```

The *calloc()* and *malloc()* C functions. In general, the syntax of *calloc()* is as follows:

```
pointer_var = calloc(number of elements, size of each element);
```

1. It allocates *(number of elements)* × *(size of each element)* bytes.
2. *pointer_var* points to the first one of those bytes.
3. All elements are automatically initialized to 0.
4. If the allocation fails for any reason, 0 is stored in *pointer_var.*

Many other C functions allocate memory, such as the *malloc()* function. Here is how it could be used to allocate memory for the 2-D array *two_d:*

```
two_d = malloc(row * column * sizeof(int));
```

1. This call allocates *row * column * sizeof(int)* bytes, which is the argument sent to *malloc().*
2. *two_d* points to the first cell of the 2-D array.
3. Unlike *calloc()*, the elements are **not** automatically initialized to 0.
4. If the allocation fails for whatever reason, 0 is stored into *two_d.*

EXERCISES 17.5.2

1. Change the following segment of code into one that uses the *calloc()* function:

```
float    (*table)[];
int      row, col;

printf("Enter the dimensions of the matrix: ");
scanf("%d%d", &row, &col);
table = malloc(row * col * sizeof(float));
for (i=0; i < row; i++)
{
      for (j=0; j < col; j++)
      {
            table[i][j] = 0;
      }
}
free(table);
```

2. Is there anything wrong with the segment below?

```
main()
{
    float   list[23];
    float * line_up[5];
    int     i;

    for (i=0; i < 23; i++)
    {
            list[i] = i;
    }
    line_up = malloc(5 * 3);    /* allocate a 5 x 3 array */
    free(list);
}
```

3. This is a technical question: can you think of one reason why the functions *calloc()* and *malloc()* do not have the same parameters? (***Hint:*** The former function has to initialize each element of the array.)

Advantages of dynamic allocation. The advantage of using dynamic allocation is obvious. In most situations, the size of memory needed cannot be known at compile time (static allocation), when the program is written. It is only determined when the program is run (dynamic allocation). Dynamic allocation allows delaying the allocation until the block of memory is indeed needed. This makes for more memory-efficient programs. For instance, a word processor will allocate memory only when a file is to be loaded in, and it releases the memory when it is done with the file.

17.5.2 ALLOCATING MEMORY SAFELY

The program in Example 17.5.2 is not very safe. Should a *calloc()* fail to allocate memory to, say, array *two_d,* subsequent access to it will quite likely lead to unpredictable results. It is safest to verify the successful allocation of an array before moving on to use it. This is done with an *if* statement:

```
if ((two_d = calloc(row * column, sizeof(int))) == NULL)
{
       printf("Oops! Out of memory!");
       free(one_d);
       exit(EXIT_FAILURE);
}
```

The *if* condition does three things: it attempts to allocate memory, it sets a pointer to it, and it verifies if the allocation was successful. An unsuccessful allocation is usually caused by a out-of-memory condition, so there is usually no point in continuing. The program should therefore terminate in a friendly manner, closing any opened files (if any) and releasing any memory previously dynamically allocated (if any), and only then should it terminate.

Termination may be achieved in two ways:

1. Use an embedded *if/else* construct, or
2. Call the *exit()* function, declared in the header file *stdlib.h.*

The *exit()* function immediately terminates the program and sends the argument it received to the operating system. In the segment above, the argument is *EXIT_FAILURE,* which tells the operating system that the program failed.

EXERCISES 17.5.3

1. Without using the *exit()* function, suggest a way to make the program terminate as soon as a memory allocation fails. (***Hint:*** Use an embedded *if/else.*)

2. Use dynamically allocated memory for all arrays in the following exercises:
   a. Exercise 17.1.2, 3a
   b. Exercise 17.1.2, 3d
   c. Supplementary Exercise 17.2, 3
   d. Supplementary Exercise 17.2, 9
   e. Supplementary Exercise 17.2, 12
3. The program in Exercise 17.5.1, 2, assumes that all departments have the same number of employees. Of course, this is totally unrealistic. Make the program more flexible so that the memory for each department is allocated separately. For example:

   ```
   Enter the number of departments: 3
   Enter the number of employees for department #1: 6
   Enter the wages for all 6 employees:
   661.50 279.92 501.46 538.82 199.20 700.00
   Enter the number of employees for department #2: 2
   Enter the wages for all 2 employees:
   146.21 822.22
   Enter the number of employees for department #3: 4
   Enter the wages for all 4 employees:
   366.15 266.29 450.14 586.23
   ```

   Define an array of pointers, whose allocation will occur at the time that the user indicates how many departments there are. Each pointer of the array will point to another array that will be allocated for the wages of each department.

17.5.3 COMMON ERRORS AND TRAPS

Do not fail to realize the difference between the declaration of an array of pointers, such as *int * list[4],* and a pointer to a list of arrays, such as *int (*list)[ ].*

18 Character Strings

OBJECTIVES

This chapter introduces you to the following information:

- The definition of a character string.
- The various ways to declare string variables.
- How to read and display a string from and to the screen.
- How to use standard C string functions.

INTRODUCTION

A character string is a special kind of 1-D array, so it should probably have been covered in Chapter 14. However, strings deserve special attention for three reasons: (1) string processing is complex enough to warrant a separate chapter; (2) numerous interesting applications exist with strings, many of which will be seen in this chapter; and (3) the C standard library contains numerous useful functions for manipulating strings.

18.1 WHAT IS A STRING?

A string (or character string) is simply a ***sequence*** of characters, such as a person's name, address, city, or any text in general. Just like other data types, strings may be read, processed, and displayed. This section will discuss reading and displaying only. There are numerous functions for the reading and displaying of strings. For now, only four of them will be covered. (The discussion will remain nontechnical so that someone wishing to learn only about reading and displaying text may read this section immediately after Section 3.3. This section's topic, including technical details, will be undertaken again in Section 18.2.)

18.1.1 READING AND DISPLAYING STRINGS WITH *scanf()* AND *printf()*

Example 18.1.1

Let us modify the program of Example 3.3.1 once more. This time, a name, not the initials, will be read and displayed. Here is an example:

Enter your name > Jamie↵
Enter the hourly wage > 7.05↵
Enter the total work hours per week > 35↵

Enter the number of weeks of work > 10↵

Jamie, You will make $ 2467.50 this summer

How can the name be read? One way is to read each letter into a separate *char* variable:

```
char letter1, letter2, letter3, letter4, letter5;
```

(Program continues.)

```
scanf("\n%c\n%c\n%c\n%c\n%c",
          &letter1, &letter2, &letter3, &letter4, &letter5);
```

There are two obvious problems with this approach: many extra variables are needed, and it works only with names of five letters.

The best solution is to use a ***string variable,*** a special kind of array. A single string variable can store names of various sizes. Let us now use this approach in the following program, with the modifications shown in bold:

```
#include <stdio.h>

main()
{
    float   hourly_rate;
    int     hours_per_week;
    float   total_income;
    int     num_weeks;
    char    name[9];[1]

    printf("Enter your name > ");
    scanf("%s", name);[2]
    printf("Enter the hourly wage > ");
    scanf("%f", &hourly_rate);
    printf("Enter the total work hours per week > ");
    scanf("%d", &hours_per_week);
    printf("Enter the number of weeks of work > ");
    scanf("%d", &num_weeks);

    total_income = hourly_rate * hours_per_week * num_weeks;

    printf("%s, You will make $ %.2f this summer", name, total_income);[3]
}
```

Explanations

1. This declaration says to the compiler that the variable *name* is a string variable and occupies nine cells (9 bytes). Remember that a character occupies 1 byte in memory. All cells are automatically set to the number 0 (**not** the character '0') at declaration time, as shown below:

name

0	0	0	0	0	0	0	0	0

2. This *scanf()*, of course, reads a name into the string variable *name.* Note that the format code to use is *%s* when a character string is to be scanned. Note also that there is **no** symbol & preceding the variable. This exception applies to string variables (and arrays) only.

   For example, from the run illustrated above, the *scanf()* would store the name "Jamie" in the string variable *name,* as shown below:

name

J	a	m	i	e	0	0	0	0

The cells that are not used remain occupied by zeros. In string parlance, a cell that contains a zero is said to be an ***empty cell.***

3. Note that the format code *%s* is also necessary in the *printf()* to display the content of the string variable.

Choosing the string variable size. Suppose the name entered in the example above had been "François." Then *name* would contain the following:

name

F	r	a	n	ç	o	i	s	0

Only one cell remains empty now. It turns out (for reasons explained in Section 18.2) that there **must always be at least one empty cell** to the right of the name. Therefore, even though the string variable *name* is declared as *char name[9],* it is capable of holding **one less** character than what is indicated (i.e., it can hold only eight letters, **not** nine). The data stored in a string variable is called a ***character string*** or simply a ***string.***

Be wary of *scanf()* —again! Recall that Section 3.3 gave a stiff warning about reading single characters with *scanf().* Now even stranger news: bizarre program behavior may arise when a program reads character strings, **if the strings are not entered exactly as *scanf()* expects them.**

For instance, with the program above, suppose that the user entered a name longer than eight letters. The string variable *name* can only hold eight letters. Despite this, *scanf()* will let you enter more letters anyway, but later the program may exhibit bizarre behavior! (This is explained in more detail in Subsection 18.1.5.)

The best way to avoid such mishaps is to give the string variable *name* as much space as may be needed. How much is that? Well, the computer screen is 80 columns wide, so surely a name could not be longer than one line's width. Consequently, declaring a string variable as wide as the screen will ensure that the string variable *name* will be able to hold any name. The declaration should therefore be *char name[81].* (Why is that so?)

Example 18.1.2

A string variable may be used for many purposes other than storing names. In the following program, it holds a license plate number:

```
#include <stdio.h>

main()
{
       char plate[8];

       printf("Enter your license plate number > ");
       scanf("%s", plate);
       printf("You entered %s\n", plate);
}
```

A sample run might look like this:

Enter your license plate number > LAV–871
You entered LAV–871

Note that the string variable *plate* may hold seven characters, which is the length of the license plate number in this example.

EXERCISES 18.1.1

1. Write a program that asks for your first name and your lover's first name. (If you do not have one, make up a name!) It then displays a secret message with both names in it. For example:

   Enter your first name > Oliver
   Enter your lover's first name > Maria

   Oliver should take Maria for a stroll in the park . . .

2. How long a string can the following string variables hold?
   a. `char msg[20];`
   b. `char letter[1];`
3. Is there any data that could make the following code segments misbehave?
   a.
```
char german[26];

printf("Enter a long German word: ");
scanf("%s", german);
printf("The word is : %s\n", german);
```
   b.
```
char word[12];

printf("Enter a word: ");
scanf("%s", word);
printf("Word is : %s\n", word)
```
4. Is there anything wrong in the following code segments?
   a.
```
char age[4];

printf("Enter your age: ");
scanf("%s", age);
printf("Age is : %d\n", age)
```
   b.
```
char letter[1];

printf("Enter a single letter: ");
scanf("%s", letter);
printf("Letter is : %c\n", letter)
```
   c.
```
char  answer[1];

printf("Do you like C programming (y/n) > ");
scanf("\n%c", answer);
```
   d.
```
char  answer[1];

printf("Do you like C programming (y/n) > ");
scanf("\n%s", answer);
```

Reading more than one word at a time. Let's go back to Example 18.1.1. What if the first and last name were entered? For instance, suppose the name entered was Blaise Pascal. Here is what would happen:

Enter your name > Blaise Pascal↵
Enter the hourly wage > Enter the total work hours per week >
Enter the number of weeks of work >

Blaise, You will make $ 0.00 this summer

What a mess! The first *scanf()* read the first name **only,** leaving "Pascal" unread! The second *scanf()* was meant to read a number, but instead it found "Pascal" in the input buffer. This caused it to panic, which made the remaining *scanf()*s panic as well. (Recall the discussion of *scanf()* panics in Section 2.2.4.)

Evidently, the format code *%s* in the *scanf()* reads one word only, which here was the first name. A second format code [or a second *scanf()*] is therefore needed to read the last name. We are now ready for Example 18.1.3.

Example 18.1.3

Let us modify the program in Example 18.1.1 to allow the user to enter the full name. A sample run might look like this:

Enter your name > Jamie MacClan↵
Enter the hourly wage > 7.05↵

Enter the total work hours per week > 35↵
Enter the number of weeks of work > 10↵

Jamie MacClan, You will make $ 2467.50 this summer

Two string variables are needed, one for each name. Following is the new program, with the latest modifications in bold type:

```
#include <stdio.h>

main()
{
    float  hourly_rate;
    int    hours_per_week;
    float  total_income;
    int    num_weeks;
    char   first_name[9], last_name[9];

    printf("Enter your name > ");
    scanf("%s%s", first_name, last_name);
    printf("Enter the hourly wage > ");
    scanf("%f", &hourly_rate);
    printf("Enter the total work hours per week > ");
    scanf("%d", &hours_per_week);
    printf("Enter the number of weeks of work > ");
    scanf("%d", &num_weeks);

    total_income = hourly_rate * hours_per_week * num_weeks;

    printf("%s%s, You will make $ %.2f this summer",
           first_name, last_name, total_income);
}
```

EXERCISES 18.1.2

1. Redo Exercise 3.3.3, 1, this time using one *scanf()* to read each word. All three words appear on the same line. Then the program will display “Toe, Tac, Tic.”
2. Redo Exercise 3.3.3, 1 again, this time using a single *scanf()* to read all of the words.

18.1.2 READING AND DISPLAYING STRINGS WITH *gets()* AND *puts()*

Unlike *scanf()* and *printf()*, the functions *gets()* and *puts()* are exclusively designed to read and display strings only. They will not work with any other data types. The function *gets()* is particularly useful because it may read more than one word into the same string variable [which the format code *%s* in *scanf()* cannot do].

Example 18.1.4

The following program illustrates the use of the functions *gets()* and *puts()*:

```
#include <stdio.h>

main()
{
      char msg[81];

      printf("Enter some message > ");
      gets(msg);[1]
```

```
        printf("The following: ");
        puts(msg);²
        printf("is what I received");³
}
```

Here is a sample run:

Enter some message > <u>Round-up party on Friday</u>
The following: Round-up party on Friday
is what I received

Explanations

1. The call *gets(msg)* stores the **entire line** "Round-up party on Friday," not just the first word, into the string variable *msg*. Consequently, *gets(msg)* does **not** have the same effect as *scanf("%s", msg)*. You must still ensure that the string variable is long enough to hold the line of text. *gets()* will not warn you if the variable is short of space.
2. The call *puts(msg)* displays the whole message "Round-up party on Friday" from the string variable *msg* to the screen.
3. The message from this *printf()* appears on the next line, even though there is no *\n* to have caused the cursor to move to the next line! The explanation is that the *puts()* from the line above automatically moved the cursor to the next line, after its message was displayed. In other terms, *puts(msg)* has the same effect as *printf("%s\n", msg)*. Note the *\n*, and note that any text enclosed in double quotation marks, such as "milk shake," is a character string, more precisely a ***string constant,*** as opposed to a string variable. Therefore *puts()* can also accept text in double quotation marks and display it, as Example 18.1.5 shows.

Example 18.1.5

The following program is the equivalent of Example 18.1.4. It uses all *puts()*s instead of *printf()*s:

```
#include <stdio.h>

main()
{
        char msg[81];

        puts("Enter some message > ");
        gets(msg);
        puts("The following: ");
        puts(msg);
        puts("is what I received");
}
```

Since *puts()* automatically moves the cursor to the next line after displaying its message, the output will differ slightly from that of Example 18.1.4:

Enter some message >
<u>Round-up party on Friday</u>
The following:
Round-up party on Friday
is what I received

Note that the cursor moved to the next line after each display of "Round-up party on Friday."

EXERCISES 18.1.3

1. Rewrite the following program by replacing all I/O functions with *scanf()*s and *printf()*s in the segment. The resulting program must preserve the exact same output. Because the *scanf()* reads using format codes, you need to know how many items the input contains. So assume that the input line contains six words, each separated by a space.

```
char line[81];

puts("Hello! There");
puts("Enter anything...");
gets(line);
puts("I got ");
puts(line);
```

2. Is there any data that could make this code misbehave? If so, give an example.

```
char full_address[18];

printf("Enter your address: ");
gets(full_address);
printf("Address is: ");
puts(full_address);
```

3. Can the following segments be replaced by *gets()*s and *puts()*s and still produce the exact same display? If so, give the solution. If not, explain.
   a. `float level;`

   ```
   scanf("%f", &level);
   printf("level = %f", level);
   ```

   b. `char line[81];`

   ```
   printf("Enter some text: ");
   scanf("%s", line);
   printf("The line is %s, isn't it?", line);
   ```

4. Is a solution for Exercise 18.1.2, 1, feasible in which one *gets()* is used for each word?
5. Consider the two segments below:

```
printf("Enter some data: ");
scanf("%s", subject);
scanf("%d%f", &num1, &num2);
scanf("%s%f", name, &num3);
```

```
printf("Enter some data: ");
gets(subject);
scanf("%d%f", &num1, &num2);
scanf("%s%f", name, &num3);
```

Suppose that the input for the subject consists of a single word. Will both segments produce the same result:

a. When all of the data is entered on the same line?
b. When the data is entered on three separate lines?

18.1.3 READING STRINGS WITH *sscanf()*

In Chapter 2, it was explained that when a *scanf()* fails (because of incorrectly coded or mistyped data), then all the subsequent *scanf()*s will fail, even if their code and input data are correct. The reason for this chain reaction was that the input buffer becomes corrupted as soon as the first error is encountered. (Recall the discussion of *scanf()* failures in Section 2.4.4.)

If you are one of the numerous programmers who hate *scanf()*, I now suggest the function *sscanf()* as a nice alternative. When used in conjunction with *gets()*, this function ensures that the input buffer is never corrupted. The reason is that it reads the data from within the memory instead of the input buffer. Example 18.1.6 shows how it works.

Example 18.1.6

The program below uses the function *sscanf()* to perform the exact same task as in Example 3.3.1:

```
#include <stdio.h>

main()
{
    float  hourly_rate;
```

```
    int    hours_per_week;
    float  total_income;
    int    num_weeks;
    char   letter1, letter2, letter3;
    char   line[81];

    printf("Enter your initials > ");
    gets(line);[1]
    sscanf(line, "\n%c\n%c\n%c", &letter1, &letter2, &letter3);[2]
    printf("Enter the hourly wage > ");
    gets(line);[3]
    sscanf(line, "%f", &hourly_rate);[4]
    printf("Enter the total work hours per week > ");
    gets(line);
    sscanf(line, "%d", &hours_per_week);
    printf("Enter the number of weeks of work > ");
    gets(line);
    sscanf(line, "%d", &num_weeks);

    total_income = hourly_rate * hours_per_week * num_weeks;

    printf("%c%c%c, You will make $ %.2f this summer",
           letter1, letter2, letter3, total_income);
}
```

Explanations

1. The call *gets(line)* will read all of the data (here, the initials) from the input buffer into the string variable *line*. At this point, the buffer is empty and therefore is not corrupted.
2. This line will read the input data from the string variable *line*, not from the buffer, but from memory, as shown below:
   Observe the syntax of *sscanf()*, as shown below:

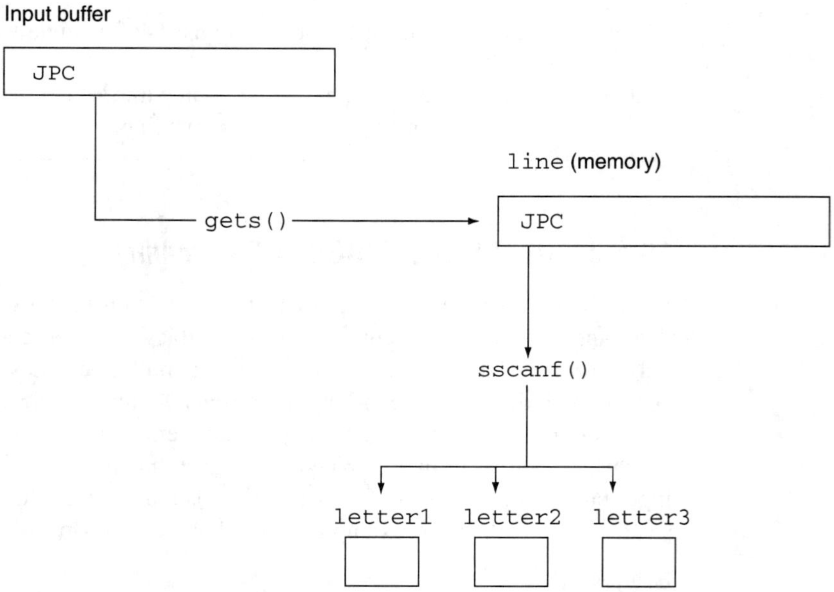


```
sscanf(line, "\n%c\n%c\n%c", &letter1, &letter2, &letter3);
```

Here, *line* is the variable string in memory, while the data that follows is the format string and variables. This function uses the format string to read off the data in the **exact** same way as *scanf()* [or *fscanf()*] does. Nonetheless, there are two very important differences. With *sscanf():*
a. The format codes take action in memory (e.g., the string variable *line*) instead of in the

input buffer.

b. The reading always begins at the beginning of the string, whereas with *scanf()*, reading takes place wherever the buffer pointer happens to be.

(Difference (a) has already been mentioned. Difference (b) is more complex and is dealt with below.)

3. Another *gets()* is called to capture the input from the second prompt.
4. Then a *sscanf()* will extract from the string the hourly rate. Similar steps are taken for the next two prompts.

Comparing the functionality of *scanf()* and *sscanf()*. To illustrate difference (b), consider the following two segments of code. Both segments read the following data from the screen:

Enter I.D. number, followed by the name, age, and height:
<u>8651 Quinn 49 1.99</u>

The first segment reads the data using a sequence of *scanf()*s:

```
float  height;
int    id, age;
char   name[81];

printf("Enter I.D. number, followed by the name, age, and height:\n");
scanf("%d", &id);
scanf("%s", name);
scanf("%d%f", &age, &height);
printf("I.D.=%d, name=%s, age=%d, height=%f\n",
       id, name, age, height);
```

Clearly, this segment works as expected. The output is:

I.D.=8651, name=Quinn, age=49, height=1.99

In the second segment, the *scanf()*s are simply replaced with *sscanf()*s:

```
char  line[81];

printf("Enter I.D. number, followed by the name, age, and height:\n");
gets(line);
sscanf(line, "%d", &id);
sscanf(line, "%s", name);
sscanf(line, "%d%f", &age, &height);
printf("I.D.=%d, name=%s, age=%d, height=%f\n",
       id, name, age, height);
```

Here is what is obtained with this second segment:

I.D.=8651, name=8651, age=8651, height=0.000000

What happened? The function *gets()* reads the whole data into the string variable *line*. Then every single call to *sscanf()* starts reading the string *line* at its **first** entry, which was 8651. Each call to *sscanf()* kept reading the number 8651 over again. That's the way *sscanf()* always works, and it is important to realize this.

Why *sscanf()* should be preferred over *scanf()*. Another thing that is important to realize is that *sscanf()* is not a magic cure for input reading failure. If the user enters the data incorrectly, this data will be copied into the string variable *line* incorrectly. Therefore, *sscanf()* won't be able to read them correctly either. For instance, suppose the program in Example 18.1.6 was run with the incorrect data below:

Enter your initials > <u>J-P,C</u>
Enter the hourly wage > <u>seven</u>
Enter the total work hours per week > <u>35</u>
Enter the number of weeks of work > <u>10</u>

J-P, You will make $ 0.00 this summer

The results are still wrong. One good thing remains though: the subsequent *scanf()*s did not panic, and that is a good enough reason for using *sscanf()*, isn't it? (Compare this sample run with the disastrous one in Example 2.2.5.)

EXERCISES 18.1.4

1. Change the sequences of codes below into *sscanf()*s. Suppose that all variables are declared appropriately:
   a.
   ```
   printf("Enter some data: ");
   scanf("%d%f", &num1, &num2);
   scanf("%f", &num3);
   ```
   b.
   ```
   printf("Enter some data: ");
   scanf("%s", subject);
   scanf("%d%f", &num1, &num2);
   scanf("%s%f", name, &num3);
   ```
   c. Could a single *sscanf()* suffice in (a) or (b)? If so, make the changes.
2. Provide a solution for Exercise 18.1.2, 1, using *sscanf()* and *gets()*.
3. Back in Example 18.1.6, the uses of \n in the following statement:

   ```
   sscanf(line, "\n%c\n%c\n%c", &letter1, &letter2, &letter3);
   ```

   are totally redundant, unlike when used in a *scanf()*. Can you see why?
4. Now that you know that *sscanf()* returns the number of items it successfully read, introduce it in the program of Supplementary Exercise 8.1, 3.

18.1.4 DISPLAYING STRINGS WITH FORMAT CODES

Just like the other format codes we have seen in Chapters 2 and 3, a width and precision may be added to *%s* to allow various displays. The precision number has an entirely different meaning with strings, though. Consider the following examples.

Example 18.1.7

Suppose the string variable *msg* contains the string "Constitutional." The following statement:

```
printf("The message %20s is received\n", msg);
```

will display:

```
The message ␣␣␣␣␣␣Constitutional is received
```

The display zone is 20 spaces wide.

Note that the string is right-aligned within the display zone.

Example 18.1.8

The following statement:

```
printf("The message %20.5s is received\n", msg);
```

will display:

```
The message ␣␣␣␣␣␣␣␣␣␣␣␣␣␣␣Const is received
```

The first five letters are right-aligned.

The display zone is 20 spaces wide.

Therefore, in *%20.5s,* the *5* means to display only the first five characters from the variable *msg.*

Example 18.1.9

The following statement:

```
printf("The message %.5s is received\n", msg);
```

will display:

```
The message Const is received
```

First five characters

Since no width is specified in *%.5s,* the display zone will only be as large as necessary.

Example 18.1.10

The following statement:

```
printf("The message %4s is received\n", msg);
```

will display:

```
The message Constitutional is received
```

The display zone is 14 spaces wide.

The width specification in *%4s* is too small to display the variable's content, so the display zone will default to whatever size it needs.

Example 18.1.11

The following statement:

```
printf("The message %-20s is received\n", msg);
```

will display:

```
The message Constitutional␣␣␣␣␣␣ is received
```

The display zone is 20 spaces wide.

As you can see, the minus sign in *%-20s* told the program to display the string left-aligned within the display zone.

Example 18.1.12

The following statement:

```
printf("The message %-20.5s is received\n", msg);
```

will display:

```
The message Const␣␣␣␣␣␣␣␣␣␣␣␣␣␣␣ is received
```

The first five letters are left-aligned.

The display zone is 20 spaces wide.

Rules for the format code *%s*. To summarize the discussion on output formatting for strings, Figure 18.1.1 shows the rules, using *%7.3s* as an example.

Figure 18.1.1

`%-7.3s`

Format code	Meaning	Default (No code specified)
`s`	Display the argument as a *string.*	None. The code *s* is needed.
`.3`	Display the first three characters. If the argument has less than three characters, fill in with blanks. If the argument has more than three characters, display the first three characters only.	Display all the characters until display zone is full.
`7`	Use a display zone width of seven spaces. If the argument needs more space give it what it needs to show correctly. Otherwise: Fill the zone with **leading** blank spaces (unless a minus sign present, then fill the zone with **trailing** blank spaces).	Use whatever print zone width is needed to show the string correctly.
`-`	If a minus sign is present: Display left-aligned. Otherwise: Display right-aligned.	Display right-aligned.
`%`	Begin formatting of the argument.	None. The code % is needed.

EXERCISES 18.1.5

1. Fill in the following table:

Argument	**%s**	**%.5s**	**%8.5s**	**%–8.5s**	**%5.0s**
over there					
at the					
abcd					

2. Write a program that asks for the name, education level, age, and height for four people who have been accepted at a fitness academy. Then dispaly a table. Use appropriate format codes so that the table will look like those shown below:

a.

```
                   New Students
 Name              Education          Age     Height
 Serge Latimer     Grade 12           18      1.72
 Trevor Kea        One year college   20      1.59
 Lucie Taylor      Grade 10           19      1.60
 Bob Maximillian   University         24      2.06
```

b.

```
                   New Students
             Name  Education          Age     Height
    Serge Latimer  Grade 12           18      1.72
       Trevor Kea  One year college   20      1.59
     Lucie Taylor  Grade 10           19      1.60
  Bob Maximillian  University         24      2.06
```

c.

```
                       New Students
          Name          Education     Age    Height
         Serge           Grade 12     18     1.72
        Trevor   One year college     20     1.59
         Lucie           Grade 10     19     1.60
           Bob         University     24     2.06
```

18.1.5 COMMON ERRORS AND TRAPS

Use the following information to avoid common programming errors.

1. Do not use a & when reading into a string variable. For example:

   ```
   scanf("%s", &name);
   ```

   Some compilers may not detect this error at all! As a result, the name will not be stored properly inside the cells of the string variable *name*. The program may even crash as a result!
2. Do not store a string too big to fit in the string variable. Let us consider two cases using Example 18.1.1.
   a. Suppose the name Jean-Paul was stored in the string variable *name*:

J	e	a	n	-	P	a	u	l

   The name does fit in the nine cells, but no empty cells remain to the right. Remember that at least one empty cell must be present at the end of the string. This oversight can easily cause the program to misbehave. In particular, the display of the name could be erroneous.
   b. Suppose the name Marguerithe was stored in *name*:

M	a	r	g	u	e	r	i	t	h	e

   The name goes past the last cell. For the same reason as in (a), this can cause the display of the name to be erroneous. Furthermore, since the name exceeds the space allotted for it, this error is a little more serious, and the program could even crash without any explanation.
3. Do not attempt to read two words at the same time with a single *%s* in the *scanf()*. It only reads one; the other would remain in the buffer, and that can lead to trouble.
4. Do realize that the input functions *scanf()* and *gets()* do not check to see if the text entered is too large to fit inside the string variable.
5. Do not use the format code *%c* to read and/or display a string. For example:

   ```
   scanf("%c", name);
   ```

   (Program continues here.)

   ```
   printf("%c, You will make $ %.2f this summer",
          name, total_income);
   ```

   The compiler will not detect these errors, yet the program will likely misbehave.
6. Do realize that *gets()* reads a whole line of data, all at once, not just the first item.
7. Do realize that *puts()* moves the cursor to the beginning of the next line after its data is displayed.

18.2 WHAT IS A STRING—TECHNICALLY?

This section discusses the concepts covered in Section 18.1 in full technical detail. A prior reading of Section 14.1 is essential, and please read all of Chapters 14 through 17 before tackling the remaining sections of this present chapter.

A ***string*** is a special kind of 1-D array: it is an array of (any ASCII) characters terminated with the character '\0' (null character). This null character serves as a sentinel to indicate the end of the string. The sentinel is important because all C string functions expect its presence. A ***string constant*** is any sequence of characters enclosed in **double** quotation marks, such as "Welcome back!" Note that the C compiler does not have a built-in string type in the same respect as, say, *int* or *char.* In other words, you may not declare a string variable as *string message.*

18.2.1 STRING INITIALIZATION

Not surprisingly, a string variable is initialized in a manner that is very similar to that of arrays, yet a little more complex. Unless initialized, a string variable is always automatically set to empty. For example, the declaration *char msg[10]* sets *msg* to all null characters, as shown below:

\0	\0	\0	\0	\0	\0	\0	\0	\0	\0

Example 18.2.1

String variables may be initialized in two ways, both at declaration time.

1. Declare an array of characters and initialize it. For example:

```
char  name[7] = "Joseph";
char  name[7] = "Sam";
```

When the compiler sees the double quotation marks, it automatically sees a string and attaches a '\0' at the end of it. Therefore, you must make sure there is a cell reserved for this '\0'. Consequently, the size of the array must be at least **one more** than the number of characters within the double quotes. For instance, the following declaration is incorrect:

```
char name[3] = "Rod";
```

2. Declare a pointer variable of type *char,* and initialize it to a string constant. For example:

```
char * name_ptr = "sam";
```

The string constant "sam" will be stored somewhere in memory, say, starting at address 7050. Then *name_ptr* is made to point to this string, that is, the address 7050 is copied into *name_ptr,* as shown in Figure 18.2.1.

Figure 18.2.1

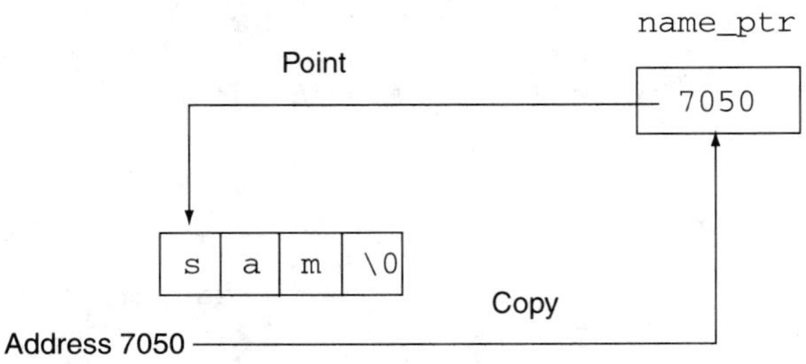

Note that the declaration *char * name_ptr = "sam"* seems to indicate that the variable *name_ptr* is assigned the string "sam." This is incorrect. It is instead assigned the **address** 7050 where that string is located. Whenever a string is used in a program, it is actually the address to it that is manipulated, never the string itself. This is precisely what happens in every call to a *printf( ).* For instance:

```
printf("Hello there");
```

The address to this message ("Hello there") is passed to *printf(),* not the message itself. Indeed, a look at the function declaration for *printf()* in *stdio.h* will reveal that *printf(const char *, . . .).*

A string is not quite the same as an array of characters. Perhaps it should be mentioned that some books explain that a string variable may be initialized one character at a time. For example:

```
char  name[7] = { 'J', 'o', 's', 'e', 'p', 'h', '\0' };
char  name[7] = { 'S', 'O', 'S', '\0' };
```

This method of initializing should be avoided simply because it is awkward. Another reason to avoid it is that the compiler will not realize you are initializing a string, since no double quotation marks are present. Therefore it will not automatically insert a null character at the end. You must again ensure that a cell in the array is reserved for the null character. For instance, the two declarations above are large enough for a null character to fit in. But the following two initializations are incorrect:

```
char  city[8] = { 'M', 'o', 'n', 't', 'r', 'e', 'a', 'l' };
char  sport[6] = { 'h', 'o', 'c', 'k', 'e', 'y' };
```

EXERCISES 18.2.1

1. Fill in the blanks appropriately:
   a. `char  greetings[____] = "Hello there!";`
   b. `char  greetings[____] = { 'H', 'e', 'l', 'l', 'o' };`
   c. `char  greetings[____] = { 'B', 'y', 'e', 0, 0 };`
2. Which of the following declare a string improperly?
   a. `int   array[4] = { 8, 7, 3, 0 };`
   b. `char  array[4] = "the";`
   c. `char  array[4] = { 't', 'h', 'e' };`
   d. `int   array[4] = { 't', 'h', 'e', '\0' };`
   e. `char  array[4] = { 't', 'h', 'e', '\0' };`
   f. `char  array[4] = { '\0' };`
   g. `char  array[4] = { 8, 7, 3, 0 };`
   h. `char  array[4] = { 65, 66, 67, 0 };`
   i. `char  array[4] = "Data Structures";`
   j. `char  array[4] = { 't', 2, 'e', '\0' };`
   k. `char  array[4] = { 't' };`
3. Is there any difference between the pair of declarations below?
   a. `char  name[] = "Rex Humbard";`
      `char  * name = "Rex Humbard";`
   b. `char  num = -51.8;`
      `char  * num = "-51.8";`
4. Is the declaration and initialization below equivalent to that of *char * name_ptr = "Rex"*? If not, is it valid?

```
char * name_ptr;

*name_ptr = 'R';           *(name_ptr + 1) = 'e';
*(name_ptr + 2) = 'x';     *(name_ptr + 3) = '\0';
```

5. Determine the value of **text, *(text+3), *(text+12), text[1],* and *text[9],* assuming that *text* is a string variable and the following has been stored in it:
   a. "now is the time"
   b. "Happy Days with Data Structures"
   c. "So long!"
6. Consider the following program:

```
#include <stdio.h>

main()
{
    char   msg[10];
    char * p;

    msg = "Bonjour";
    p = "Bonjour";
    printf("msg = <%s>, p = <%s>\n", msg, p);
}
```

   The compiler will complain at *msg = "Bonjour"* but will not complain at *p = "Bonjour"*. Explain.

7. Consider the following segment:

```
char  line[81], first[25], last[30], sin[12];

printf("Enter your first and last name and social security #:\n");
gets(line);
sscanf(line, "%s", first);
sscanf(line, "%s", last);
sscanf(line, "%s", ssn);
printf("Name: %s %s, SSN: %s\n", first, last, ssn);
```

Here is an example of a run:

```
Enter your first and last name and social security #:
Joe Lane 634–903–931
Name: Joe Joe, SSN: Joe
```

a. Explain these wrong results. (***Hint:*** Review Subsection 18.1.3.)

b. While still using three *sscanf()*s, change the segment so that it will run. (***Hint:*** Instead of passing *line* to *sscanf(),* pass a pointer that keeps track of where the next data is to be scanned from the string *line.*)

8. By looking at the declaration of *scanf()* in the header file *stdio.h,* explain exactly how the following format string is passed to *scanf():*

```
scanf("\n%c", &ch);
```

9. Early in this subsection, it was mentioned, that at the sight of text in double quotation marks, the compiler manipulates the address to that constant string rather than the string itself. To prove this, run the following segment and explain the result:

```
main()
{
      printf("%c", *("abcdef" + 3));
}
```

10. In this book, the first argument to a *printf()* has always been a format string in double quotation marks. Yet, would the uses of *printf()* in the following segments work?

a.
```
char  line[81];

printf("Enter a line of text:\n");
gets(line);
printf(line);
```

b.
```
char  word[81];
char  format[12] = "%s%d";
int   count;

printf("Enter a word followed "
            "by the number of letters it contains:\n");
scanf(format, word, count);
printf(format, word, count);
```

18.2.2 STRING LENGTH VS. ITS ARRAY SIZE

The ***length*** of a string is the count of the number of characters preceding the first null character. It is important to realize that this definition differs from the ***size*** of the array, as Example 18.2.2 distinguishes.

Example 18.2.2

Consider the following declarations:

1. `char  name[6] = "Pete";`
   The array size of 6 bytes appears in brackets; the length of the string is four characters ("Pete").

2. `char name[6] = { 's', 'a', 'm', '\0' , '\0', '\0' };`
   The size of the array is 6 bytes; the string length is three characters ('s', 'a', 'm'); and the first null character terminates the string.
3. `char name[6] = { 'J', 'o', 's', '\0' , 'p', 'h' };`
   The size of the array is 6 bytes; the string length is three characters ('J', 'o', 's'); and the null character terminates the string.

It is also important to understand the difference between the *string* and the *array* that contains it. As the above examples show, the string does not necessarily occupy the whole array. So an array can be thought of as a cigar box, while a string is the cigars contained in the box.

When a string variable is initialized at declaration time, the size specification may be omitted. In that case, the size in bytes that the compiler will allot to the array depends on to what the array is initialized. Consider Example 18.2.3.

Example 18.2.3

Consider the same three declarations above, but with the size specification missing:

1. `char name[] = "Pete";`
   The length of four characters ("Pete") + 1 byte for the null character = the size of 5 bytes allocated.
2. `char name[] = { 's', 'a', 'm', '\0' , '\0', '\0' };`
   The length of three characters ('s', 'a, 'm') + 3 bytes = the size of 6 bytes allocated.
3. `char name[] = { 'J', 'o', 's', '\0' , 'p', 'h' };`
   The length of three characters ('J', 'o, 's') + 3 bytes = the size of 6 bytes allocated.

As shown in Subsection 3.1.3, the operator *sizeof* is handy for finding out the size in bytes of a data type, which may also be an array. For instance, with the following declaration:

```
char name[] = { 'J', 'o', 's', '\0' , 'p', 'h' };
```

sizeof(name) is 6. Note that a string declaration that lacks a size specification should always be accompanied by an initialization. For instance, avoid a declaration such as *char s3[];* because the compiler does not know what size to give the array. In fact, many compilers do not accept such a declaration.

Finding out the length of a string. If you are not sure about the length of a string, the predefined string function *strlen()* may be used to determine its length. For instance, *strlen(name)* returns 3 in the final example above. This function is declared in the header file *string.h.*

Note that the size of a string variable is always determined at declaration time and can never be changed thereafter, unless it is dynamically allocated. Of course, the length of the string variable may be set and changed at will, simply by changing its content.

EXERCISES 18.2.2

1. Fill in the entries to the left for the declarations to the right in the table below. Use the symbol ? for any values that are undetermined, and use the designation N/A for entries that are not applicable.

Size	Length	Declarations
		a. `char name[35];`
		b. `int table[];`
		c. `char name[];`
		d. `int table[] = { 4, -8, 0 };`
		e. `char name[] = "Mine";`
		f. `char name[] = { 'M', 'i', 'n', 'e' };`
		g. `char name[] = { 'M', 'i', 'n', 'e', '\0' };`
		h. `char name[50] = { 'M', 'e', '\0', 'e', 'w', ' ' };`

2. The difference between the size of an array and the length of a string within it may be best illustrated with the following program. It simply initializes six string variables, *s1, s2, s3, s4, s5,* and *s6* to the word "The" by using the different methods shown in this subsection.

```
#include <stdio.h>
#include <string.h>

main()
{
    char s1[] = "The";
    char s2[] = { 'T', 'h', 'e', '\0' };
    char s3[] = { 'T', 'h', 'e' };
    char s4[4] = { 'T', 'h', 'e' };
    char s5[4] = "The";
    char s6[];

    s6[0] = 'T'; s6[1] = 'h'; s6[2] = 'e'; s6[3] = '\0';
    printf("s1: length = %d, size = %d\n", strlen(s1), sizeof(s1));
    printf("s2: length = %d, size = %d\n", strlen(s2), sizeof(s2));
    printf("s3: length = %d, size = %d\n", strlen(s3), sizeof(s3));
    printf("s4: length = %d, size = %d\n", strlen(s4), sizeof(s4));
    printf("s5: length = %d, size = %d\n", strlen(s5), sizeof(s5));
    printf("s6: length = %d, size = %d\n", strlen(s6), sizeof(s6));
    s2[0] = 'a'; s2[1] = 's'; s2[2] = '\0';
    printf("s2: length = %d, size = %d\n", strlen(s2), sizeof(s2));
}
```

Note: Some compilers may not accept the declaration *char s6[];*. If so, simply remove it. Now, run this program and explain the results.

3. Are the following segments of code correct? If so, what is displayed? If not, what is wrong?

a.
```
char  msg[] = { 'h', 'e', 'c', 'k' };

printf("length = %d", strlen(msg));
```

b.
```
char  msg1[] = "", * msg2;

printf("length = %d", strlen(msg1));
printf("length = %d", strlen(msg2));
```

18.2.3 READING AND DISPLAYING STRINGS—A TECHNICAL DISCUSSION

This subsection discusses in technical detail how the functions *scanf()*, *printf()*, *gets()*, and *puts()* work with respect to strings.

Using strings with *scanf()* and *printf()*. It is all a matter of realizing that it is the format code *%s* that does the operation.

Example 18.2.4

This example explains how *scanf()* reads strings and how *printf()* displays them.

```
#include <stdio.h>

main()
{
      char name[20];

      printf("Enter your full name > ");
      scanf("%s", name);
      printf("You entered %s", name);
}
```

Let us use Figure 18.2.2 to explain how the format code *%s* reads and displays a name. Note that the format code *%s* in *printf()* always expects its corresponding argument to be either a string variable, a pointer to a character, or a string constant.

Figure 18.2.2

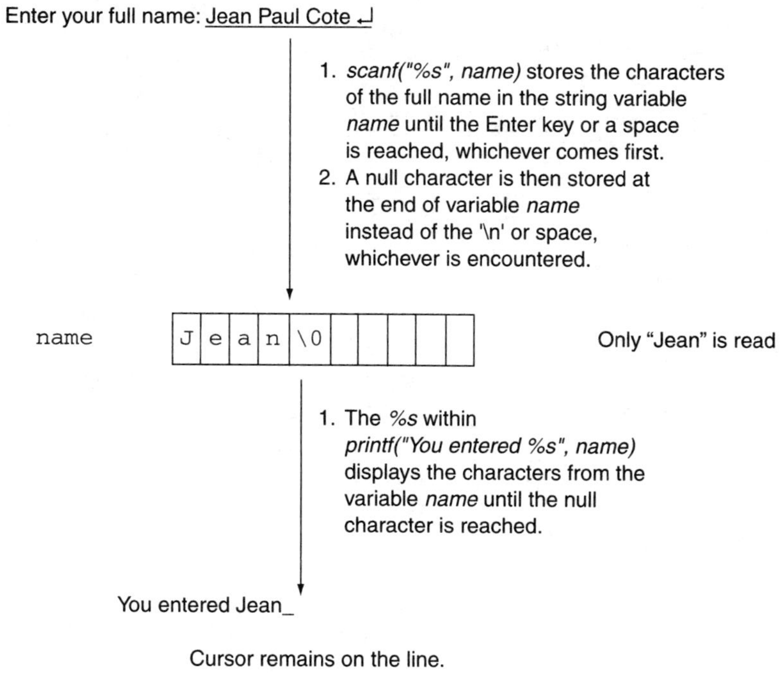

EXERCISES 18.2.3

1. Can you see a problem with the following segments?

a.
```
char  * ptr = "Such is life";

printf("Message for you: %s\n", *ptr);
```
b.
```
char text[] = "Have a good day!";

printf("%c", text);
```

2. Will the following segment compile correctly? Is so, what will it display?

```
char  msg[26] = "Such is life";

printf("Message for you: %s\n", msg);
printf("Message for you: %s\n", msg + 8);
printf("Message for you: %s\n", &msg[6]);
```

Using strings with *gets()* and *puts()*. These two functions do not make use of format codes to read data, as the example below shows.

Example 18.2.5

This example explains how *gets()* reads strings and how *puts()* displays them.

```
#include <stdio.h>

main()
{
      char name[20];
```

```
        printf("Enter your full name > ");
        gets(name);
        printf("You entered ");
        puts(name);
}
```

Figure 18.2.3 shows how the name will be read and displayed.

Figure 18.2.3

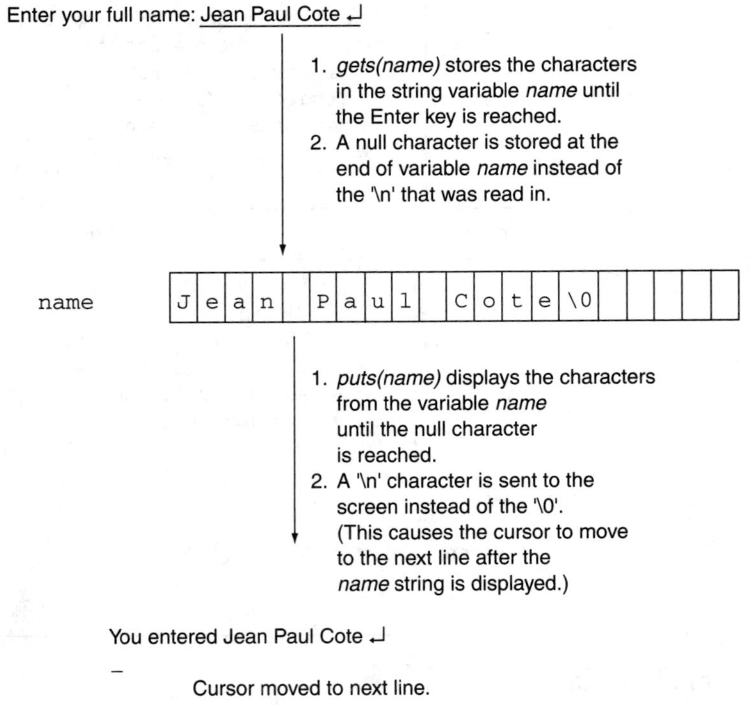

EXERCISES 18.2.4

1. Improve the program in Example 10.4.9 so that the names of the files are provided by the user (i.e., the program reads them in).
   a. Use *scanf()*
   b. Use *gets()*
2. a. Modify the program in Exercise 4.3.2, 9, so that it asks for the last name of the individual, rather than the initials, as in the following run:

   What is your name? Anderson
   Are you a male or a female? (m=male, f=female) f
   How many children do you have? 3

   Ms. Anderson has 3 children.

   b. Modify the program further so that it asks for the full name.
3. Modify Exercise 6.1.7, 17, so that the full name is entered instead of the initials.

18.2.4 BE WARY OF SLIGHT DIFFERENCES BETWEEN *scanf()* AND *gets()*

Using the Enter key. It is important to notice that *scanf()* and *gets()* do not deal with the *\n* character the same way. This makes them slightly incompatible. Consequently, when used together, unpredictable things may happen. To illustrate, compare the following two segments. This first one works perfectly well:

```
main()
{
        char name[20];
```

```
        printf("Enter your full name > ");
        gets(name);
        printf("Enter your age > ");
        scanf("%d", &age);
        printf("You entered ");
        puts(name);
        printf("Age = %d", age);
}
```

Following is an example of a run:

Enter your full name > Richard Ricchi
Enter your age > 27
You entered Richard Ricchi
Age = 27

The second segment below is exactly the same as the first, except that the first two prompts have been switched, as indicated in bold type. (Note that *scanf()* and *gets()* have been switched, too, of course.)

```
main()
{
        char name[20];

        printf("Enter your age > ");
        scanf("%d", &age);
        printf("Enter your full name > ");
        gets(name);
        printf("You entered ");
        puts(name);
        printf("Age = %d", age);
}
```

A very minor change, yet watch what happens when this program is run:

Enter your age > 27
Enter your full name > You entered
Age = 27

Oops! The program did not let the user enter the name! Here is what happened: The *scanf()* read the number 27 and returned, thereby leaving the *\n* in the input buffer, which was then picked up by *gets()*. As a result, the string variable *name* remained empty. (Why is that so?)

The problem here is that input functions in C are not entirely compatible with each other; the same goes for output functions. Two remedies are possible here:

1. Use *gets()* and *sscanf()* only to read any data—a string, text, or a number, or
2. Use *fflush(stdin)* to remove any leftover data in the buffer prior to calling *gets()*.

Method 1 has already been illustrated in Subsection 18.1.3, so Example 18.2.6 will show how Method 2 is implemented.

Example 18.2.6

To continue with the program above, the modification shown below correctly makes calls to *gets()* and *scanf()* by clearing the input buffer when necessary.

```
main()
{
        char name[20];

        printf("Enter your age > ");
        scanf("%d", &age);
        printf("Enter your full name > ");
        fflush(stdin);
```

```
        gets(name);
        printf("You entered ");
        puts(name);
        printf("Age = %d", age);
}
```

Using the Ctrl-Z combination keys. Both *scanf()* and *gets()* handle the Ctrl-Z marker the same way at the input buffer level. However, they notify the program of its presence in a different way. This is worth noting, for it is often a source of confusion. When Ctrl-Z is pressed, *gets()* returns NULL, not EOF [as with *scanf()* and *getchar()*].

EXERCISES 18.2.5

1. In the following segment, the user is asked to enter a social security number. Since such a number is nine digits long, the *%9d* within the *scanf()* ensures that only that many will be read; the others remain in the buffer until *fflush(stdin)* flushes them out.

```
printf("Enter a social security number > ");
scanf("%9d", &ssn);
fflush(stdin);
```

   Write an equivalent segment that uses *gets()* and *sscanf()*. Do you still need the *fflush(stdin)?*

2. The following two loops do exactly the same thing: they simply read in characters and echo them to the screen. Assume that the variables are appropriately declared:

   a.
```
printf("Enter some characters (press Enter to end)\n");
gets(msg);
i = 0;
while ((ch = msg[i++]) != '\0')
{
        putchar(ch);
}
```
   b.
```
printf("Enter some characters (press Enter to end)\n");
while ((ch = getchar()) != '\n')
{
        putchar(ch);
}
```

   The user entered data and then made the mistake of pressing Ctrl-Z instead of Enter. Below is what was observed for each loop respectively:

   i. The program still worked.
   ii. The program looped forever.

   Explain the behavior of both programs.

3. Will the following loop run properly? If not, why?

```
int   i;
char  city[25], state[25];
long  pop;

i = 0;
do
{
      printf("Enter the city name > ");
      gets(city);
      printf("Enter the population > ");
      scanf("%d", &pop);
      printf("Enter the state > ");
      gets(state);
}
while (i++ < 5);
```

4. a. Write a program that uses *gets()* to read lines of text until Ctrl-Z is pressed.
   b. Write a version that uses *scanf()* instead.

18.2.5 A TYPICAL APPLICATION WITH *gets()*

Example 18.2.7

A very useful application of *gets()* is to allow the user to skip a prompt when she does not wish to enter data there. For instance, suppose a program asks for such personal information as:

Enter the name > Victorine Hugo
Enter the age > ↵
Enter the gender > ↵

You entered: Name: Victorine Hugo
Age: N/A
Gender: N/A

The user chose to skip the prompts for the age and the gender. Here is the program that accomplishes this.

```
#include <stdio.h>
#include <string.h>

main()
{
        char  name[51], gender[8], str[4];
        int   age = -1;1

        printf("Enter the name > ");
        gets(name);
        printf("Enter the age > ");2
        gets(str);
        if (strlen(str))
        {
                sscanf(str, "%d", &age);
        }
        printf("Enter the gender > ");
        gets(gender);
        printf("You entered:       Name: %s\n", name);
        if (age != -1)3
        {
                printf("                   Age: %d\n", age);
        }
        else
        {
                printf("                   Age: N/A\n");
        }
        if (strlen(gender))4
        {
                printf("                   Gender: %s\n", gender);
        }
        else
        {
                printf("                   Gender: N/A\n");
        }
}
```

Explanations

1. The variable *age* is set to an invalid value such as –1. Any other invalid value would also do, as explained below.
2. It is necessary that the age be first read as a string using *gets()*. This is so because the use of *scanf("%d", &age)* would force the user to enter data; thus, skipping this entry would not be an option. Next the string function *strlen()* is called and returns 0 if the string *str* is empty, and the value of *age* remains –1. If *str* is not empty, then *sscanf()* is called to pull the age number out of the string *str* into the variable *age*.
3. If the value of *age* is no longer –1, this means that the prompt for the age was answered, not skipped.
4. The variable *gender* started out as empty, hence a length of 0. If it has a length at this point, then its prompt was answered.

EXERCISES 18.2.6

1. The above program is slightly inconsistent. If the user does not enter a name, the program will not display "N/A". For example:

   ```
   Enter the name > ↵
   Enter the age > ↵
   Enter the gender > ↵

   You entered:     Name:
                    Age: N/A
                    Gender: N/A
   ```

   Modify the solution so that a "N/A" will show on the "Name" line.
2. Modify the program in Example 18.2.7 so that the name must be entered, but either of the other two prompts may still be skipped. For instance:

   ```
   Enter the name > ↵
   A name must be entered
   Enter the name > ↵
   A name must be entered.
   Enter the name > Tillier Alex
   Enter the age > ↵
   Enter the gender > male

   You entered:     Name: Tillier Alex
                    Age: N/A
                    Gender: male
   ```

18.2.6 COMMON ERRORS AND TRAPS

Use the following information to avoid common programming errors.

1. Do not store a string too big to fit in a string variable. This is the same error mentioned in Section 18.1, except now a technical discussion is possible. Suppose you have the following program:

```
#include <stdio.h>

main()
{
        char name[9];

        printf("Enter your name: ");
        gets(name);
        puts(name);
}
```

Suppose the user enters the name "Marguerithe." At 11 letters, this name will not fit into the variable *name:*

```
|M|a|r|g|u|e|r|i|t|h e
```

In addition, no room is left for the null character, and the name "trespasses" outside its allowed memory space. These two mishaps will likely cause the *puts()* to fail, mainly because *puts()* will be looking for a null character that is not there. The same nasty outcome would likely occur if *printf()* was used instead.

2. In initializing a string variable, allow for a space in which the compiler can store the null character.
3. Do not confuse a string variable with a pointer to a string. For instance, in the following declaration:

   ```
   char * text = "Patience is a virtue";
   ```

   text is a pointer to a string, **not** a string variable.
4. Do not fail to distinguish between a string and an array of characters. For example:

   ```
   char grade[5] = { 'A', 'B', 'C', 'D' };
   char name[14] = "Brenda";
   ```

   Because of the way these variables are declared, the programmer does not intend to use the variable *grade* as a string, but he does intend that use for *name.*

18.3 STANDARD OPERATIONS WITH STRINGS

The standard C library comes with a long list of string functions, all of them declared in the header file *string.h.* This section covers uses for some of the more popular functions.

18.3.1 COPYING STRINGS WITH *strcpy()* AND *strncpy()*

There are two functions to copy strings, as explained in Example 18.3.1.

Example 18.3.1

The following program simply displays copies of the message "The game is underway."

```
#include <stdio.h>
#include <string.h>

main()
{
      char msg[25] = "The game is underway";
      char copy[25];

      strcpy(copy, msg);[1]
      printf("The first copy gave  |%s|\n", copy);
      strncpy(copy, msg, 11);[2]
      printf("The second copy gave |%s|\n", copy);
      strncpy(copy, msg, 7);[3]
      printf("The third copy gave  |%s|\n", copy);
}
```

The output produced is:

The first copy gave |The game is underway|
The second copy gave |The game is|
The third copy gave |The gam|

Explanations

1. The syntax of the function *strcpy()* is:

```
strcpy(copy, msg)
```

copy is the destination, and *msg* is the source. The string in the variable *msg* is copied character by character into the variable *copy* until a null character within *msg* is encountered.

2. The statement

```
strncpy(copy, msg, 11)
```

works exactly like *strcpy()* except that it copies only the first 11 characters from the variable *msg* into the variable *copy*. Should this number be equal or larger than the length of the source string, then the whole string is copied. For example, *strncpy(copy, msg, 25)* is equivalent to *strcpy(copy, msg)*.

3. The statement *strncpy(copy, msg, 7)* copies the first seven characters from the variable *msg* into the variable *copy*.

EXERCISES 18.3.1

1. What is stored in the string variable *char cpy[30]* for each call below? Indicate if some unpredictable results may occur.
   a. `strcpy(cpy, "Alternative life styles")`
   b. `strncpy(cpy, "Alternative life styles", 6)`
   c. `strncpy(cpy, "Alternative life styles", 34)`
   d. `strcpy(cpy, "To be or not to be, that is the question")`
2. Write a program that reads any message and displays it one character at a time. For example:

```
Enter a message: In the den
I
In
In
In t
In th
In the
In the
In the d
In the de
In the den
```

3. a. The following program simply makes a copy of three variables into temporary variables and displays them.

```
int   years = 96, t1;
float kms = 201.7, t2;
char  projectile[24] = "a rock", t3[24];

t1 = years;
t2 = kms;
t3 = projectile;
printf("t1 = %d, t2 = %f, t3 = %s\n", t1, t2, t3);
```

   Answer these questions:
   i. Will this segment compile correctly?
   ii. If yes, will it run correctly?
   iii. If you answered no to either (i) or (ii), then fix the error.

   b. Suppose that the declaration for *t3* is changed to:

```
char  * t3;
```

   Answer (i), (ii) and (iii) again.

These copy functions return a pointer. What for? Note that both copy functions also return a pointer to the destination string variable. Indeed, the function declarations found in *string.h* are:

```
char * strcpy(char str1[], char str2[])
char * strncpy(char str1[], char str2[], int n)
```

char * indicates the type of data returned, while *str1* is the string destination and *str2* is the string source. Also, the data returned is the address of the destination string. Thus the program in Example 18.3.1 could just as well have been written as follows:

```
#include <stdio.h>
#include <string.h>

main()
{
        char msg[25] = "The game is underway";
        char copy[25], * ptr;

        ptr = strcpy(copy, msg);[1]
        printf("The first copy gave  |%s|\n", ptr);[2]
        ptr = strncpy(copy, msg, 11);
        printf("The second copy gave |%s|\n", ptr);
        ptr = strncpy(copy, msg, 7);
        printf("The third copy gave  |%s|\n", ptr);
}
```

Explanations

1. The pointer *ptr* is made to point to the destination array *copy.*
2. The format code *%s* displays the string at the address indicated by *ptr.*

From this code, you may be thinking that it is rather pointless for the function *strcpy()* to return the pointer to the destination string *copy,* since the first argument is already that very string. Indeed! This program fails to truly show the advantage of returning this pointer. The advantage is that it allows you to make the program shorter, as shown in Example 18.3.2.

Example 18.3.2

Following is the same program as above but a little shorter.

```
#include <stdio.h>
#include <string.h>

main()
{
        char msg[25] = "The game is underway";
        char copy[25];

        printf("The first copy gave  |%s|\n", strcpy(copy, msg));
        printf("The second copy gave |%s|\n", strncpy(copy, msg, 11));
        printf("The third copy gave  |%s|\n", strncpy(copy, msg, 7));
}
```

In all three statements, the format code *%s* will display the string at the address returned by the *strcpy()* or *strncpy()* function.

18.3.2 COMPARING STRINGS WITH *strcmp()* AND *strncmp()*

Example 18.3.3

Let us write a program that tests typing abilities. It will ask the user to enter a sentence twice. Then it will check if both are typed the same. Here is a run of the program:

Enter a sentence > Little house on the prairie
Enter it again > Litle house onthe prarie
Bad typing!

Here is the program:

```
#include <stdio.h>
#include <string.h>

main()
{
      char str1[81], str2[81];
      int  diff;

      printf("Enter a sentence > ");  [1]
      gets(str1);
      printf("Enter it again > "); [1]
      gets(str2);
      diff = strcmp(str1, str2); [2]
      if (diff == 0)
      {
      printf("Good typing--both sentences are the same\n");
      }
      else
      {
      printf("Bad typing!\n");
      }
}
```

Explanations

1. The sentences are first entered.
2. They are then compared using the statement:

```
diff = strcmp(str1, str2)
```

This function returns a 0 if both strings are identical; otherwise it returns a nonzero number. Hence, the condition *diff == 0* is true only when both strings are identical.

How *strcmp()* operates. Internally, the function *strcmp()* operates by comparing corresponding characters from both strings. It keeps doing this until either:

1. The end of the string *str1* or *str2* is encountered, or
2. A mismatch is found.

Here are a few examples to cover all possible situations:

1. `strcmp("april fool's day", "april foil's day")`
   Corresponding characters are compared until this mismatch (fool's, foil's) is encountered. A nonzero number will be returned.
2. `strcmp("avril fool's day", "april fool's day")`
   Corresponding characters are compared until this mismatch (avril, april) is encountered. A nonzero number will be returned.
3. `strcmp("april fool", "april fool's day")`
   All characters up to the end of the first string match. However, since both strings are not of the same length, they cannot be considered equal. A nonzero number will be returned.
4. `strcmp("APRIL", "april")`
   This call will return a nonzero number because string comparisons in C are always case sensitive; **all** ANSI C string functions are case sensitive.

Sometimes you may wish to compare only a portion of a string. In this case, the function *strncmp()* is used. See Example 18.3.4.

Example 18.3.4

The following program asks the user to enter any two words with two-letter prefixes. Then it determines if they have the same prefix. For example:

Enter two words > unrelated unseen
They have the same two-letter prefix.

Here is the program:

```
#include <stdio.h>

main()
{
        char word1[30], word2[30];
        int  diff;

        printf("Enter two words > ");
        scanf("%s%s", word1, word2);
        diff = strncmp(word1, word2, 2);
        if (diff == 0)
        {
                printf("They have the same two-letter prefix\n");
        }
        else
        {
                printf("They have different two-letter prefixes\n");
        }
}
```

Note the statement for comparing the prefixes:

```
diff = strncmp(word1, word2, 2)
```

String 1 is *word1,* string 2 is *word2,* and the number of characters to compare is 2, the length of the prefix. Only the first two characters from both words will be compared. If they are the same, a 0 is returned, otherwise a nonzero number is returned.

EXERCISES 18.3.2

1. Using the program in Example 18.3.4, determine whether or not the following function calls return a zero:
   a. `strcmp("flavored", "favored")`
   b. `strcmp("flavored", "flavor")`
   c. `strcmp("flavored", "flavor", 4)`
   d. `strncmp("flavored", "favored", 1)`
   e. `strncmp("flavored", "flavor", 6)`
   f. `strncmp("lunar", "lunar", 7)`
   g. `strncmp("Lunar", "lunar", 7)`
2. Write a program that asks for the name of an input file and an output file. The input file contains a list of numbers from which the average must be found. This average will then be stored in the output file. Of course the program should not allow the user to enter the same name for both files. For instance:

   Enter the input file name > class.95
   Enter the output file name > class.95
   Cannot use the same file
   Enter the input file name > class.95
   Enter the output file name > avg.95

3. The functions *stricmp()* and *strnicmp()* work precisely like *strcmp()* and *strncmp()*, except that they are case insensitive. They are, however, not ANSI C standard. If your compiler allows it, use them in the programs in Examples 18.3.3 and 18.3.4 so that they become case insensitive.
4. a. Modify the program in Exercise 6.1.7, 16, so that the words "his" or "her" and "Ms" or "Mr" are stored in a string variable, and then later displayed.
   b. Modify the program in Exercise 6.1.7, 17, in a similar way. In addition, the appropriate word "has" or "have" will be stored in a variable, and later displayed.

Application: Sorting words. An interesting application to *strcmp()* is to sort strings, as Example 18.3.5 shows.

Example 18.3.5

The following program asks the user to enter two last names, and then displays them in ascending order. A sample run might look like this:

Enter two last names > Kline Briere
In ascending order: Briere Kline

Here is the program:

```
#include <stdio.h>

main()
{
	char name1[30], name2[30];
	int  diff;

	printf("Enter two last names > ");
	scanf("%s%s", name1, name2);
	diff = strcmp(name1, name2);¹
	if (diff < 0)²
	{
		printf("In ascending order: %s %s\n", name1, name2);
	}
	else
	{
		printf("In ascending order: %s %s\n", name2, name1);
	}
}
```

Explanations

1. In the expression *diff = strcmp(name1, name2)*, the function *strncmp()* returns:
   a. a negative number if *name1* is smaller than *name2*.
   b. a positive number if *name1* is greater than *name2*.
   c. a zero if *name1* and *name2* are the same.
   One word is said to be smaller than another one if it comes first in alphabetical order, or more precisely in the ASCII sequence. For example "rain" comes before "raisin" so *strcmp("rain", "raisin")* returns a negative number. What number, you might wonder? This is not important to know for now. Nevertheless, Exercise 19.1.1, 9, describes how it is found.
2. Note the condition for testing the order: *diff < 0*. This tests if *word1* is less than *word2*.

EXERCISES 18.3.3

1. Using the program in Example 18.3.5, determine if the following function calls return a negative or a positive number or a zero:
   a. `strcmp("flavored", "favored")`
   b. `strcmp("flavored", "flavor")`

c. strcmp("flavored", "flavor", 4)
d. strncmp("flavored", "favored", 1)
e. strncmp("flavored", "flavor", 6)
f. strncmp("lunar", "lunar", 7)
g. strcmp(" lunar", "lunar")

2. Write a program that sorts out three words in alphabetical order. Use the same technique as with numbers, i.e., swap the words via a temporary string variable. [***Hint:*** Besides *strcmp()*, use the function *strcpy()*.]

18.3.3 CONCATENATING STRINGS WITH *strcat()* AND *strncat()*

Concatenating two strings simply means placing them together into a single string. Following is an example of this.

Example 18.3.6

The following program simply asks for a person's first and last names. These names are stored in separate variables, and then concatenated together in a third variable and displayed.

```
#include <stdio.h>
#include <string.h>

main()
{
      char first[25], last[25], full_name[50];

      printf("Enter your first and last names > ");
      scanf("%s%s", first, last);
      strcpy(full_name, first);[1]
      strcat(full_name, " ");
      strcat(full_name, last);[2]
      printf("The full name is %s\n", full_name);
}
```

Explanations

1. Suppose that the name entered was "Valerie MacMaster." The function *strcpy()* copies the variable *first* into the variable *full_name:*

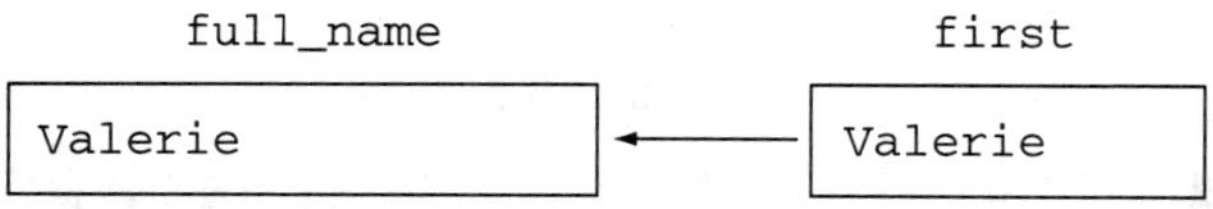

2. The function *strcat()* concatenates the variable *last* at the end of the variable *full_name,* right next to the first name, as shown below:

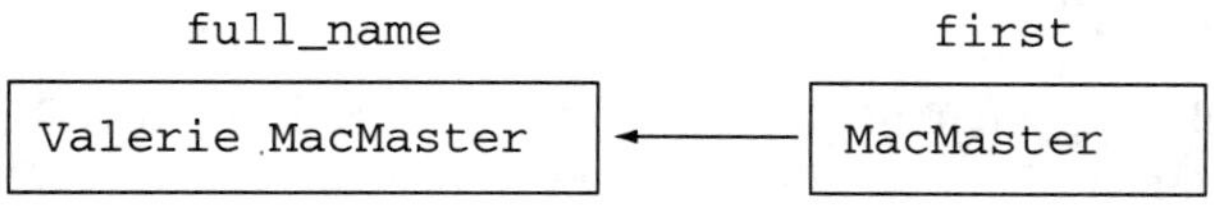

Note that a space was inserted in the variable *full_name* prior to concatenating the last name.

The function *strncat()* catenates only a portion of a string. For instance, in *strncat(full_name, last, 3),* only the first three letters of the variable *last* are concatenated. If the number is larger than the length of the string variable *last* [e.g., *strncat(full_name, last, 53*], the function will terminate after reaching the end of the string *last.* Note that both *strcat()* and *strncat()* return a pointer to the destination string (here, the address of the string *full_name* is returned).

EXERCISES 18.3.4

1. Assume the string variable *char msg[30] = "After"*. What is the content of this variable after each call below? Indicate if some unpredictable results may occur.
   a. `strcat(msg, "wards")`
   b. `strcat(msg, "wards, let us have some desserts")`
   c. `strncat(msg, "wards, let us have some desserts", 5)`
   d. `strncat(msg, "wards", 15)`
2. a. Write a program that uses the function *scanf()* to read each word of a sentence. As each is read, it is concatenated with the others. The sentence is ended with the Enter key.
   b. Rewrite the program with *gets()* and *sscanf()* instead.
3. A user enters in pairs a list of cities and their countries: Berlin Germany Paris France Tokyo Japan.
   a. Write a program that uses the function *scanf()* to read each pair. As each is read, the city will be concatenated into the string variable *cities,* and the country will be concatenated into the string variable *countries.* Make sure that these destination variables are large enough. Also assume that city and country names are each one word only.
   b. Rewrite the program with *gets()* and *sscanf()* instead.
4. Can you see a potential problem with the following segment? If not, what does it produce?

```
char * ptr, line[81];

ptr = strcpy(line, strcat("Joe ", "Smith"));
puts(ptr);
```

   Hint: When a function call terminates, all of its memory is released. This includes that of the parameter.
5. a. Is the syntax of the following segment correct? If so, what does it produce?

```
printf(strcat(strcpy(line, "Breakfast with "), " the family"));
```

   b. Break it down into three separate statements.
6. Back to question 4: While still keeping *strcpy()* and *strcat()* within the same statement, re-arrange it so that it will be free of problems.
7. The following four statements are taken from Example 18.3.6:

```
strcpy(full_name, first);
strcat(full_name, " ");
strcat(full_name, last);
printf("The full name is %s\n", full_name);
```

   Merge them into a single statement.

18.3.4 LOCATING A CHARACTER OR STRING WITHIN ANOTHER STRING

Using the *strstr()* function. This function helps locate a string within another string. Consider the example below.

Example 18.3.7

The following program asks the user to enter a street address. Then it determines if it contains the prefix "Saint". For example:

Enter a street address > <u>71 Saint-Paul Street</u>
The street name contains the prefix "Saint"

Here is the program:

```
#include <stdio.h>
#include <string.h>

main()
```

```
{
    char name[80], * substr;

    printf("Enter a street address > ");
    gets(name);
    substr = strstr(name, "Saint");[1]
    if (substr != NULL)[2]
    {
        printf("The street name contains the prefix \"Saint\"");
    }
    else
    {
        printf("The street name does NOT contain the prefix \"Saint\"");
    }
}
```

Explanations

1. In the following statement:

   ```
   substr = strstr(name, "Saint")
   ```

   the function *strstr()* tries to find the substring "Saint" within the string variable *name*. If it does find it, the address of the first character of this substring (i.e., 'S'), is returned; otherwise NULL is returned. In the run above, *substr* will point to 'S' in the substring "Saint-Paul Street" as shown below:

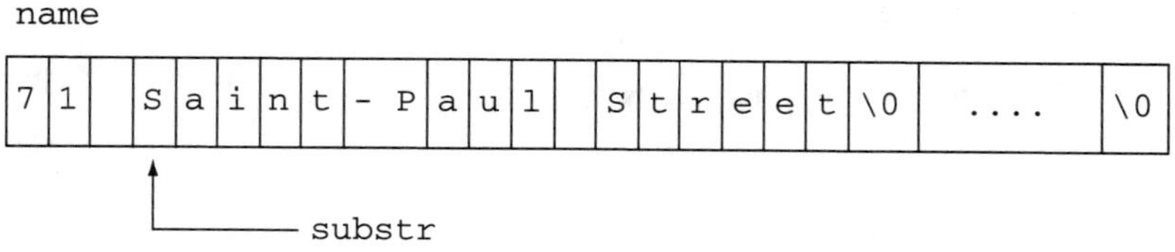

   Note that the function *strstr()* does not guarantee that the "Saint" it locates is indeed a prefix to a street name. For instance, in the street address "203 Domain-of-the-Saint Street", "Saint" is not a prefix.
2. If *substr* is not NULL, then the substring "Saint" has been found; otherwise it could not be found.

Note that *substr* **has** to be a **pointer** variable, not a string variable. (Why is that the case?) Note also that the function *strstr()* locates only the first occurrence of the substring. To find all occurrences, a loop is needed, as Example 18.3.8 illustrates.

Example 18.3.8

The following program finds all occurrences of the word "ion" in a sentence given by the user. For instance:

Enter a sentence: <u>For ions, creation of new fashions, a passion</u>
4 occurrences of "ion" have been found.

Here is the program:

```
#include <stdio.h>
#include <string.h>

main()
{
        char sentence[81], * ion_ptr;

        printf("Enter a sentence > ");
        gets(sentence);
```

```
        ion_ptr = strstr(sentence, "ion");[1]
        for (ct = 0; ion_ptr != NULL; ct++)[2]
        {
             ion_ptr = strstr(ion_ptr, "ion");[3]
        }
        printf("%d occurrences of \"ion\" have been found.", ct);
}
```

Explanations

1. This initial call to *strstr()* locates the first occurrence of "ion". Hence, the pointer *ion_ptr* is located as shown:

```
    |
    v
For ions, creation of new fashions, a passion
```

2. The condition of the loop checks if *ion_ptr* is NULL. If so then no more occurrences of "ion" will be found; otherwise the loop continues.
3. This call to *strstr()* is repeated until no more occurrences of "ion" are found. It takes in the current position of *ion_ptr* and returns the new one:

```
New position             Current position
   |                        |
   v                        v
 ion_ptr = strstr(ion_ptr, "ion")
```

The pointer *ion_ptr* is now located as shown:

```
                    |
                    v
For ions, creation of new fashions, a passion
```

EXERCISES 18.3.5

1. Replace the loop in the example above with a *do/while* loop.
2. Is there anything wrong with the following segment?

```
char sentence[80], word[25];

gets(sentence);
word = strstr(sentence, "all");
puts(word);
```

Using the *strchr()* and the *strrchr()* functions. The following example illustrates two new string functions: *strchr()* and *strrchr()*. Rather than locating a whole substring within a string, these look for a single character. Consider Example 18.3.9 below.

Example 18.3.9

The following program lets the user enter a message; then it attempts to find from it the first and the last occurrences of a letter also given by the user. A sample run looks like this:

Enter a message > From the depth of the sea
What is the letter you want me to find? e
I found its first occurrence at position 7
I found its last occurrence at position 23

Here is the program:

```
#include <stdio.h>

main()
{
      char ch;
      char msg[81], *ptr;

      printf("Enter a message > ");
      gets(msg);
      printf("What is the letter you want me to find? ");
      scanf("\n%c", &ch);
      ptr = strchr(msg, ch);[1]
      printf("I found its first occurrence at position %d\n",
             (int) (ptr - msg));[2]
      ptr = strrchr(msg, ch);[3]
      printf("I found its last occurrence at position %d\n",
             (int) (ptr - msg));
}
```

Explanations

1. The function *strchr()* locates the first occurrence of the letter in *ch,* here 'e', within the string *msg* (in the first "the"). It returns the address, not the index, of that letter.
2. Note the formula that is used to obtain the index position of the letter:

   ```
   (int) (ptr - msg)
   ```

   The difference of these two addresses (*ptr* and *msg*) constitutes the index position, but is expressed as an address value. It must be converted to *int* before it may be displayed.
3. The function *strrchr()* locates the last occurrence of the letter in *ch,* 'e', within the string *msg.* It returns the address, not the index, of that letter (in the word "sea").

EXERCISES 18.3.6

1. In the above example, replace the call to *strchr()* with a call to *strstr().* Also replace the call to *strrchr()* with a series of calls to *strstr()* within a loop.
2. Write a program that accepts a line of text. Then the user will replace every occurrence of a letter with another one. For instance:

   Enter some text: threw, flew, and blew
   Enter the letter to replace, and its substitute > e o
   throw, flow, and blow

3. a. Write a program that reads in a sentence and echoes the word, or words, contained within a set of double quotation marks. For instance:

   Enter a sentence: Stop "goofing up", the teacher warned
   goofing up

   Assume that one and only one set of such quotation marks is ever present.

   b. Modify the program so that it will work even when no quotation marks are present. If this is the case, it will simply echo "No quotation marks found."

4. a. Write a program that asks you to enter a sentence in which no letter is used twice. For instance:

   Enter a sentence in which letters are used once:
   This is too hard
   Wrong! Some letters appeared more than once.

(***Hint:*** Call *strchr()*, then *strrchr()*. If both point to the same location, then the letter is unique.) Note that the program should be case insensitive.

b. Improve the program so that the letters at fault will be listed:

   Enter a sentence in which letters are used once:
   This is too hard
   Wrong! These letters appeared more than once:
   t h i s o

Using the *strspn()* function. Let us look at a last substring function, the *strspn()* function. It is typically used to test the membership of a character in a set. Consider Example 18.3.10.

Example 18.3.10

The following program asks the user to enter multiple-choice answers from ten questions in a quiz. The set of allowed answers is a, b, c, or d. The program is to stop processing the answers as soon as one is found to be invalid. For example:

Enter your answers (do not space them out) > dbbfaefa
The answer to question 4 is invalid

Here is the program:

```
#include <stdio.h>
#include <string.h>

main()
{
    char set[4] = "abcd";
    char answer[10];

    printf("Enter your answers (do not space them out) > ");
    gets(answer);
    correct = strspn(answer, set);[1]
    if (correct != 10)[2]
    {
        printf("The answer to question %d is invalid %d\n", correct+1);
    }
}
```

Explanations

1. In this expression, the function *strspn()* takes the first letter in the string *answer,* 'd', and checks if it is in the string *set.* It is, so it moves onto the next letter and finds that it is also in the string *set,* so it moves onto the next letter, 'b', and finds that it is also in the string *set.* When it moves to the letter 'f', it does not find it in the string *set*. This causes the function to terminate, and it returns the count of the number of answers that were found valid this far (3). This count will be stored in the variable *correct.*
2. If all answers were valid, then the count that *strspn()* will return is 10 (the total number of questions in the quiz). So if the variable *correct* is not 10, then the answer at position *correct+1* is invalid.

   Note that there are other invalid answers in the run above, but *strspn()* stops at the first one.

EXERCISES 18.3.7

1. a. In the example above, why does the prompt warn the user not to space out the answers? What would happen if they were spaced out?

b. Modify the program so that spaces may be inserted anywhere and will not affect the outcome. (***Hint:*** Only a very minor change is necessary.)

2. What will the following calls return?
   a. `strspn("873h60f", "03678")`
   b. `strspn("h60f", "03678")`
   c. `strspn("h60f", "03678")`
   d. `strspn("ooff! It's hot!", "abcdefghijklmnopqrstuvwxyz")`
   e. `strspn("ooff! It's hot!", "abcdefghijklmnopqrstuvwxyz ")`
   f. `strspn("ooff! It's hot!", "abcdefghijklmnopqrstuvwxyz !'")`
   g. `strspn("shredded wheat", "bcdfghjklmnpqrstvw")`
3. The use of *strspn()* helps reduce the size of a program. To see that, rewrite the program in Example 18.3.10 without the help of this function.
4. Add a loop to the program in Example 18.3.10 above so that all invalid answers will be found.
5. a. Write a program that reads in a positive whole number and tells if it was entered incorrectly. For instance, –23.9 or 2,45 are incorrect. [***Hint:*** Use *gets()* and, of course, *strspn().*]
   b. Extend the program to allow it to read negative numbers as well. For positive numbers, the plus sign may now be specified.
   c. Extend the program to allow it to read real numbers in decimal form, such as 352.84.
6. Improve the program in Example 18.3.10 so that it reports the position of all the answers that are invalid. (***Hint:*** Use a technique somewhat similar to that of Example 18.3.8. A pointer variable will move along the string of answers and will continually be fed to the function *strspn()* to find the next invalid answer.)
7. a. Use the function *strspn()* in the program in Example 5.1.6 to check the secretary code. Also add two new codes: 'S' for School secretary and 'C' for CEO secretary.
   b. In a similar fashion, modify Example 6.1.5.

18.3.5 STRING CONVERSIONS

Although the variables *char num[6] = "–51.8"* and *int num = –51.8* appear to contain the same information, they do not. In the former, –51.8 is stored as a string, not a number. So what if the string "–51.8" is needed as a number? Call a standard C library function to convert it. Conversely, there are other C functions that convert a number into a string. Some of those functions are covered below.

From a string to a number. The standard C library contains functions specific to converting from a string to a number, as Example18.3.11 shows.

Example 18.3.11

The following program accepts a number and displays it. If the number is not entered correctly, the program warns the user.

```
#include <stdio.h>
#include <stdlib.h>

main()
{
       char   line[20];
       float  num;

       printf("Enter a number > ");
       gets(line);
       num = atof(line);
       if (num)
       {
              printf("The number is %f\n", num);
       }
       else
```

```
        }
                printf("There was some error in entering the number\n");
        }
}
```

In *num = atof(line),* the function *atof()* converts the string within *line* to a *float* number, which is then stored in *num.* If that string contained a number incorrectly entered, then *atof()* would return a 0. Likewise, there is a function named *atoi()* that converts a string to an integer value. Note that these *ato* functions are declared in *stdlib.h.*

EXERCISES 18.3.8

1. What will the following calls return?
   a. `atof("7105.41")`
   b. `atof("7105")`
   c. `atof("0.00")`
   d. `atof("zero")`
   e. `atoi("zero")`
   f. `atoi("7105")`
   g. `atoi("7105.41")`
2. In Example 18.1.6, use the functions *atof()* and *atoi()* instead of *sscanf()* wherever appropriate.

From a number to a string. The standard C library contains the function *sprintf()* that may be used to convert a number into a string. At first, conversion from number to string appears rather useless, but it is not quite, as shown below.

Suppose that over the summer an amateur scientist conducted experiments to measure the speeds of snails, of hair growth, of dragonflies, and of propellers. He wrote a program in which he stored directly in two arrays the growth or distance covered in meters for each specimen and the time it took in seconds. Then the program generated a table showing the speeds. Here is the program. (Note that the scientist entered the data into arrays of declaration time.)

```
#include <stdio.h>

main()
{
     float distance[4] = { 0.72, 0.0134, 20, 3.1 };
     float seconds[4] = { 610, 4665600, 2.6, 0.02 };
     float speed;
     int   i;

     printf("%10s%5s%10s%5s%20s\n", "Distance", "Time", "Speed");
     for (i=0; i < 4; i++)
     {
         speed = distance[i] / seconds[i];
         printf("%10g%5s%10g%5s%20g m/s\n",
                 distance[i], " ", seconds[i], " ", speed);
     }
}
```

Note the format code *%g* in the *printf().* Recall from Example 2.4.8 that *%g* displays a number either in decimal form or exponential form, depending on its magnitude. Here is the run of the program:

Distance	Time	Speed
0.72	610	0.00118 m/s
0.0134	4665600	2.872085e009 m/s
20	2.6	7.692308 m/s
3.1	0.02	155 m/s

In the right column, the speeds are spread in a wide range, causing the second one to show in exponential form. Now suppose that this program was written for the general public. Many people either do not know exponential notation, or do not feel comfortable with it. Example 18.3.12 shows how *sprintf()* can help make this program a little more user friendly.

Example 18.3.12

The following program shows the changes in bold that will ensure that numbers in exponential form will not show. Instead, the message "Very tiny" will show.

```
#include <stdio.h>

main()
{
     float distance[4] = { 0.72, 0.0134, 20, 3.1 };
     float seconds[4] = { 610, 4665600, 2.6, 0.02 };
     char  strspeed[21];
     float speed;
     int   i;

     for (i=0; i < 4; i++)
     {
         speed = distance[i] / seconds[i];
         sprintf(strspeed, "%20g", speed);[1]
         if (strchr(strspeed, 'e') || strchr(strspeed, 'E'))[2]
         {
             strcpy(strspeed, "Very tiny");[3]
         }
         printf("%10g%5s%10g%5s%20s m/s\n",
                distance[i], " ", seconds[i], " ", strspeed);[4]
     }
}
```

Explanations

1. Before sending the calculation of the speed to the screen, the function *sprintf()* sends the display to memory first:

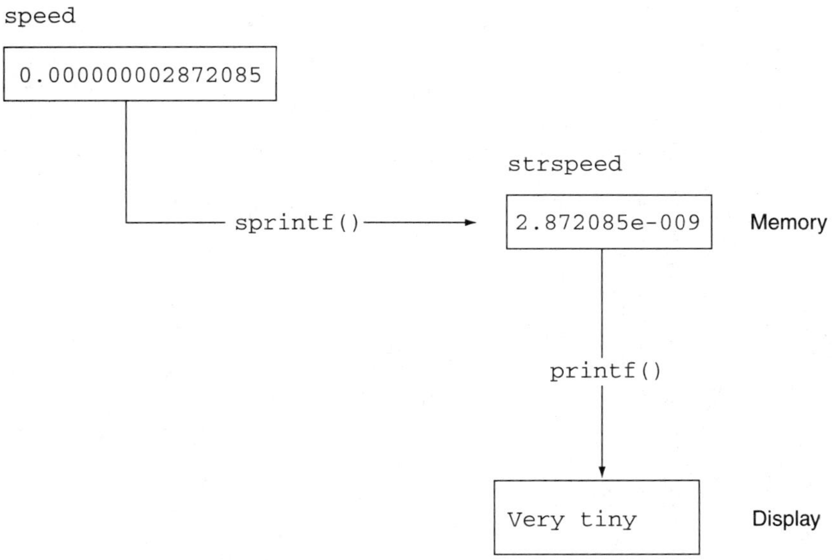

   Observe the syntax of *sprintf()*:

```
sprintf(strspeed, "%20g", speed)
```

Here, *strspeed,* is the variable string in memory, *%20g* is the format string, and *speed* is the variable.

This function uses the format string in the **exact** same way as *printf()* [or *fprintf()*] does. This means that the number in *speed* will be stored in the variable *strspeed* in exactly the same form as on the screen. The format string may consist of more than one format code, of course.

Nonetheless, there are two very important differences. With *sprintf():*

a. The format codes take action in memory (e.g., the string variable *strspeed*) instead of from the screen.
b. The storing of the "display" always begins at the beginning of the string, whereas with *printf(),* the display begins wherever the cursor happens to be.

2. This condition checks if the letter 'e' or 'E' is in the string *strspeed.* If so, then the "display" is in exponential notation, such as 2.872085e – 009, and should not be sent to the screen.
3. If 'e' or 'E' is found, the display will change to "Very tiny"; otherwise, do nothing.
4. The string inside *strspeed* is displayed instead of the number *speed.* This is because *strspeed* contains what is to be displayed, whether it is the speed or the message "Very tiny." Note that the format code is changed to *%20s*.

EXERCISES 18.3.9

1. Given the following declarations:

```
char msg[81];
int  num[6] = { 3, 5, 11, 19, 23, 33 }, bonus = 17;
```

What will the segments below display?

a.
```
sprintf(msg, "%d-%d-%d\n", num[0], num[1], num[2]);
printf("%s\n", msg);
sprintf(msg, "%d-%d-%d\n", num[3], num[4], num[5]);
printf("\n%s", msg);
```
b.
```
sprintf(msg, "The winning numbers ");
sprintf(msg, "for the lottery");
sprintf(msg, "%3d, %3d, %3d followed by ", num[0], num[1], num[2]);
sprintf(msg, "by %3d, %3d, %3d", num[3], num[4], num[5]);
sprintf(msg, "\nand the bonus is %5d\n", bonus);
printf("%s", msg);
```
c.
```
sprintf(msg, "The winning numbers for the lottery"
             %3d, %3d, %3d followed by %3d, %3d, %3d",
              "\nand the bonus is %5d\n",
           num[0], num[1], num[2],
           num[3], num[4], num[5], bonus);
printf("%s", msg);
```

2. The following segment simply displays a column of random numbers:

```
#include <stdio.h>
#include <stdlib.h>

main()
{
     int i;

     printf("%6s%10s\n\n", "Loop #", "Generated");
     for (i=0; i < 8; i++)
     {
          printf("%6d%6s%4d\n", i+1, " ", rand());
     }
}
```

Here is an example of a run:

Loop #	Generated
1	0
2	4310
3	24759
4	15029
5	17457
6	7174
7	1541
8	22245

Some numbers do not line up; these are the ones that need more spaces than *%4d* allows. Modify the program so that these misaligned numbers will not show. Instead "****" will be displayed:

1	0
2	4310
3	****
4	****
5	****
6	7174
7	1541
8	****

This may be done in various ways, but do it with *sprintf()* this time.

18.3.6 COMMON ERRORS AND TRAPS

Do not forget that the C string functions do not check if the destination string variable is large enough to contain the result. For example:

```
char  name[8];
strcpy(name, "Brenslisky");
```

The variable *name* is too small to contain "Brenslisky." Yet the function will copy it anyway. Later, when *name* is displayed, weird things may happen to your output.

19 User-Defined String Functions

OBJECTIVES

This chapter introduces you to the following information:

- How to pass strings to functions.
- How to write string processing functions of your own.
- The criteria for writing portable functions so that they may be used across programs.

INTRODUCTION

Functions may be defined for specific string handling and processing not provided by standard functions. The concept and technique appear to be the same as for arrays. This chapter covers many situations in which it may be desirable to define user-defined string functions.

19.1 PASSING/RETURNING STRINGS TO/FROM A FUNCTION

The standard functions covered in Section 18.3 barely scratch the surface of string-processing applications. Numerous—in fact countless—other operations may be applied to strings. In this section you will learn how to write functions to customize string processing to the user's needs.

19.1.1 JUST AS WITH ANY OTHER 1-D ARRAY . . .

Since strings are simply a special kind of array, anything that may be done with an array may be done with a string. In particular, each character of a string may be accessed individually via either an index or a pointer, and a string may be passed to a function. This section focuses on these two capabilities and addresses the issue of good programming practices in writing string functions. The following examples start us off.

Example 19.1.1

The function *open_input_safely()* in Example 10.4.9 can open the file IN.DAT only. Of course, it is desirable for the function to open any file. This is only a matter of passing its name to the function. Here is the new function:

```
FILE * open_input_safely(char name[])
{
   FILE * fp;

   fp = fopen(name, "r");
```

```
    if (fp == NULL)
    {
        printf("Could not open input file %s\n", name);
    }
    return fp;
}
```

This function is now portable. Back in Example 10.4.9, the call simply needs to change to *open_input_safely("in.dat")*. But the real advantage of passing a string here is that the user may open any file just by supplying a string variable containing the file name, such as:

```
printf("Enter the input file to open > ");
scanf("%s", filename);
ifp = open_input_safely(filename);
```

The function *open_output_safely()* may be modified similarly. Now, the example below shows that characters within a string may be accessed and processed individually.

Example 19.1.2

Let us write a function named *my_strcpy()* that performs the exact same task as the standard function *strcpy()*:

```
char * my_strcpy(char str1[], char str2[])
{
        int  i;

        for (i=0; str2[i] != '\0'; i++)
        {
                str1[i] = str2[i];
        }
        str1[i] = '\0';
        return str1;
}
```

The source string *str2* and the destination string *str1* are passed to the function. Inside it, a loop copies each entry *str2[i]* into *str1[i]* until the null character from *str2* is reached. Note that the string *str1* (i.e., its address) is also returned; and make sure the destination string is terminated with a null character ('\0').

EXERCISES 19.1.1

1. Do the following segments compile correctly? If not, why?
   a.
   ```
   char  train[6] = "Ciuf! Ciuf!";
   char  toy[6];

   toy = strcpy(toy, train);
   ```
   b.
   ```
   char  train[6] = "Ciuf! Ciuf!";
   char  * toy;

   toy = strcpy(toy, train);
   ```
2. In Example 19.1.2 above, since *str1* is returned, it should no longer be necessary to send it by reference. That is, the following code should do just as well:

   ```
   char * my_strcpy(char str2[])
   {
           int  i;
           char str1[81];

           for (i=0; str2[i] != '\0'; i++)
   ```

```
        {
                str1[i] = str2[i];
        }
        str1[i] = '\0';
        return str1;
}
```

Should it? Explain.

3. In Example 19.1.2, since the purpose of the *for* loop is to copy each character from the source string to the destination string, it should be more logical that it also copies the null character from *str2* as part of the loop, not after it. Suggest a loop that ensures this. (***Hint:*** Use a *do/while* loop.)
4. Write a function named *my_strlen()* that does exactly the same thing as *strlen()* does.
5. Write a function to count the total number of characters, excluding blanks, contained in a string. Do not use the *strlen()* library function.
6. Write a function named *strempty()* that sets the string variable sent to it to empty. A string is empty when its length is 0.
7. a. Back to Example 19.1.1: There is really no need to have two separate functions to open files. Merge the operations of the functions *open_input_safely()* and *open_output_safely()* into one named *open_safely()*. In addition to the file name, this function will accept the access mode (i.e., "r" or "w"). For instance a call might be *open_safely("in.dat", "r")*. If the file cannot be opened, the message "Could not open input file IN.DAT" would show. If the call *open_safely("out.dat", "w")* failed, the message would be "Could not open output file OUT.DAT."
   b. Add code to the function above so that the user will be repeatedly asked to reenter the proper file name, if the file cannot be opened.
   c. Add this function to the program in Example 10.4.9.
8. a. Write a function named *mirror()* that takes in a string, reverses it, and puts the result back in the same parameter.
   b. Modify the function so that the result is stored in a second parameter. This string is also returned.
9. a. Write a function named *my_strcmp()* that works exactly like *strcmp()*, as was explained in Subsection 18.3.2. There, it was explained that a nonzero number is returned when the two strings differ. It was never explained, though, what that number was. It is simply the difference between the ASCII code of the last pair of characters compared. Here are a few examples:

```
strcmp("april fool's day", "april foil's day")
```

Returns 'o' – 'i'
111 – 105 = 6

```
strcmp("avril fool's day", "april fool's day")
```

Returns 'v' – 'p'
118 – 112 = 6

```
strcmp("april fool", "april fool's day")
```

Returns '\0' – '\''
0 – 39 = –39

   b. Modify the function above so that it is case insensitive.

19.1.2 MANIPULATING STRINGS VIA INDEXES AND POINTERS

Just like other arrays, strings may be accessed via indexes and pointers. With this in mind, let us look at a couple of other ways that the function *my_strcpy()* may be coded.

Example 19.1.3

Note that by using some tricks learned in Chapter 13 you can shorten the code of *my_strcpy()* to:

```
char * my_strcpy(char str1[], char str2[])
{
      int  i;

      for (i=0; str1[i] = str2[i]; i++) ;
      return str1;
}
```

This is the shortest solution possible for copying strings: a single line! The condition does two things: it assigns *str2[i]* into *str1[i]*, and it checks if the character assigned is a null character. For instance, suppose that the source string *str2* contains the word "BLUES". Figure 19.1.1 shows what that would entail. Of course, the parameters may be declared with the pointer notation as follows: *char * my_strcpy(char * str1, char * str2).* The rest of the function will work just the same.

Figure 19.1.1

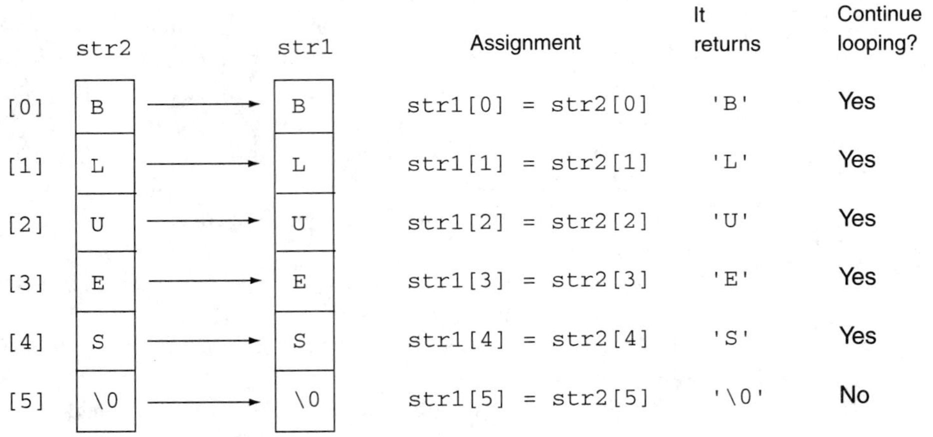

Example 19.1.4

Just like other arrays, strings may be traversed with a pointer instead of an index. For instance, the function *my_strcpy()* could be written as follows:

```
char * my_strcpy(char * ptr1, char * ptr2)
{
      for ( ; *ptr1++ = *ptr2++; ) ;
      return ptr1;
}
```

Let us see how the condition works. Suppose that *ptr1* contains the address 5510 and *ptr2* contains 3304; i.e., the strings sent to this function are located at addresses 5510 and 3304, respectively, as shown in Figure 19.1.2.

Figure 19.1.2

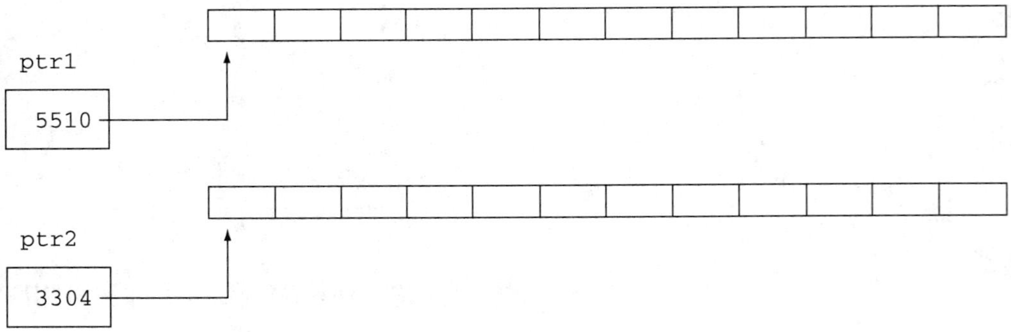

In **ptr1++ = *ptr2++*, you can see that the postfix incrementations *ptr1++* and *ptr2++* take place after the condition is evaluated, so the dereferencing will take place first: **ptr1 = *ptr2*. This assigns the content of the cell pointed to by *ptr2* to the cell pointed to by *ptr1*. Then the pointers are moved to the next cell. This will continue until the condition is false, which occurs when *ptr2* points to the null character.

EXERCISES 19.1.2

1. Do the following functions correctly copy the string *str2* into *str1*?

   a.
   ```
   char * my_strcpy(char str1[], char str2[])
   {
           int  i;

           for (i=0; str1[i] = str2[i++]; ) ;
           return str1;
   }
   ```
   b.
   ```
   char * my_strcpy(char str1[], char str2[])
   {
           int  i;

           for (i=0; str1[i++] = str2[i]; ) ;
           return str1;
   }
   ```
   c.
   ```
   char * my_strcpy(char str1[], char str2[])
   {
           int  i;

           for (i=0; str1[i] = str2[++i]; ) ;
           return str1;
   }
   ```
   d.
   ```
   char * my_strcpy(char * ptr1, char * ptr2)
   {
           for ( ; *++ptr1 = *++ptr2); ) ;
           return ptr1;
   }
   ```
2. Rewrite the function *my_strlen()* from Exercise 19.1.1, 4, by using pointers instead of indexes.
3. Write a function named *display_vert()* that accepts a string and displays it one character per line. Do not use the *strlen()* function.
   a. Develop a solution using index notation.
   b. Develop a solution using pointer notation.
   c. Develop a solution that uses the *strlen()* function to indicate the end of the string.
4. Write a function named *display_subi()* that accepts a string and displays a substring of it as specified by two boundary indexes. For example, with the declaration *char msg[] = "Sign of things to come"*, the call to *display_subi(msg, 8, 16)* will display "things to."
   a. Develop a solution using index notation.
   b. Develop a solution using pointer notation.
5. Write a function named *display_subl()* that accepts a string and displays a substring of it as specified by a starting index and how many characters to display. For example, with the declaration *char msg[] = "Sign of things to come"*, the call to *display_subl(msg, 8, 9)* will display "things to."
   a. Develop a solution using index notation.
   b. Develop a solution using pointer notation.
6. Write a function named *palindrome()* that accepts a string and returns 1 if it is a palindrome or 0 otherwise. A palindrome string is one that reads the same in both directions, such as the word "deed."

7. Write a function named *charcount()* to count the total number of characters, excluding blanks, contained in a string. Do not use the *strlen()* library function.
8. Write a function *strupper()* that changes to uppercase all letters in the string sent to it.
9. Is the function below coded correctly?

```
void fcn(char * str)
{
        printf("length = %d", strlen(*str));
}
```

10. The function below displays its argument in uppercase. Fill in the blank.

```
void upper(char str[])
{
        while (*str != '\0')
        {
        printf("%c", ___________________);
        }
}
```

11. Do the following functions perform exactly the same thing?

a.
```
void fcn(char * s)
{
        while (*s)
        {
                putchar(*s++);
        }
}
```

b.
```
void fcn(char * s)
{
        while (*s++)
        {
                putchar(*s);
        }
}
```

12. Write a function named *isvowel()* that returns 1 if the character sent to it is a vowel or returns 0 otherwise. Use the string function *strspn()*.
13. Write a function named *isconsonant()* that returns 1 if the character sent to it is a consonant or returns 0 otherwise. Use the string function *strspn()*.

19.1.3 COMMON ERRORS AND TRAPS

Use the following information to avoid common programming errors.

1. In manipulating a string internally, do not forget to store a '\0' at the end of the string.
2. Do not write a function that returns the address of a string declared locally. The trap is that this string will be deallocated after the function returns, making access to it invalid.

SUPPLEMENTARY EXERCISE 19.1

Modify the program in Exercise 10.1.1, 6, so that the banner is displayed horizontally:

```
*    *              *
*    *   *   *      *   ****   ****
*    *       *      *   *  *   *  *
******   *   *      *   *  *   ****
*    *   *       *  *   *  *   *
*    *   *   *   ****   ****   ****
```

A loop is necessary to draw one line at a time for each letter. Of course, a different pattern of stars will be displayed for each line. The *main()* will remain very similar to that of Exercise 10.1.1, 6. Use the same letter functions, except that a parameter is needed to receive the line number to draw. For example, if the letter read is 'A', the function *A(3)* will draw the third line of the letter 'A':

```
     **
    *  *
   *    *   <------------ Third line
  ********
 *        *
*          *
```

19.2 HOW TO WRITE PROPER USER-DEFINED STRING FUNCTIONS

Section 12.2 discussed how to write user-defined functions. It should not be surprising that the exact same discussion applies to defining string functions as well. However, at that time, we had not yet covered arrays. This section will continue the discussion, and in particular, the issue of portability and efficiency of a string function.

19.2.1 THE MOST COMMON APPROACHES TO WRITING STRING FUNCTIONS

To better learn how to write good string functions, we will first look at common approaches, both good and bad, that are often taken to write string functions.

Example 19.2.1

Let us write a function that processes a line of text. We have encountered this kind of processing before, notably in Subsection 7.3.3, but never in the context of string functions. The program will read a sentence from the terminal and display it to the screen, one word per line. The sentence is terminated with Ctrl-Z. For example:

Enter a sentence: <u>C pgming. Ah! this is the life</u>
C
pgming.
Ah!
this
is
the
life.

Assume that the words are always separated by one blank space only. Define a function *strlines()* that takes the sentence and pulls the words out of it. Three of the most often attempted solutions are provided below.

Solution 1. In this solution the function *strlines()* does everything except display the prompt:

```
void strlines(void)
{
      char  ch;

      while ((ch = getchar()) != EOF)
      {
         if (isspace(ch))  /* if it is a space, then end of the word */
         {
               putchar('\n');          /* move cursor to a new line */
         }
         putchar(ch);                     /* echo the character read */
      }
}
```

```
main()
{
        printf("Enter a sentence: ");
        strlines();
}
```

The reason that the prompt is left out of *strlines()* is that the function is then portable: the programmer can call *strlines()* as is, while providing her own prompt.

Solution 2. A *scanf()* is used to read each word.

```
void strlines(void)
{
        char  word[81];

        while (scanf("%s", word) != EOF)
        {
                printf("%s\n", word);
        }
}

main()
{
        printf("Enter a sentence: ");
        strlines();
}
```

This is undoubtedly the easiest solution, because *scanf()* does most of the work for you. Again, the prompt is kept outside the function *strlines()*.

Solution 3. The reading of the string is performed in the *main()*. Then the function *strlines()* receives that string for processing:

```
void strlines(char line[])
{
        char  ch;
        int   i;

        for (i=0; (ch = line[i]) != '\0'; i++)
        {
                if (isspace(ch))
                {
                        putchar('\n');
                }
                putchar(ch);
        }
}

main()
{
        char  sentence[81];

        printf("Enter a sentence: ");
        gets(sentence);
        strlines(sentence);
}
```

Perhaps the reason a programmer would choose this third solution over the other two is that it makes more sense to have the prompt and the read statement together. The next subsection will come back to these three solutions and conclude that they lack modularity and efficiency. A better solution will be offered.

EXERCISES 19.2.1

1. Remove the assumption made in Example 19.2.1 that the words are separated with a single space. Implement the necessary changes to solutions 1 and 3. Of course, solution 2 needs no changes. (Why is that the case?)
2. Back to Example 19.2.1: Perhaps a fourth solution could have been suggested:

```
void strlines(char line[])
{
        char  word[51];

        while (sscanf(line, word) != EOF)
        {
                printf("%s\n", word);
        }
}
```

   This solution is very similar to solution 2, with two differences: the *scanf()* has been replaced by a *sscanf()* function, and the function assumes that the sentence has already been read in *main()* and passed into the parameter *line*.
   a. Would this solution work? Explain.
   b. If not, make it work by passing a pointer to *sscanf()* instead of *line*. (***Hint:*** Use the same idea as in Exercise 18.2.1, 7b.)
3. a. Revisit the program in Example 8.1.3. Introduce a function named *compress()* that compresses the sentence.
   b. Revisit the program in Exercise 8.1.2, 2. Introduce a function named *letters()* that removes all nonletters from the sentence. Note that the function should also call the function *compress()*.
   c. Revisit the program in Exercise 8.1.2, 3. Introduce a function named *reverse_case()* that reverses the case of the letters of the sentence. Note that the function should also call the function *compress()*.
   d. Revisit the program in Exercise 8.1.2, 4. Introduce a function named *collapse()* that collapses the sentence.
   e. Revisit the program in Exercise 8.1.2, 5. Introduce a function named *up_low()* that capitalizes the first letter of a word and puts the other letters in lowercase.
   f. Revisit the program in Exercise 8.1.2, 6. Introduce a function named *count_ldps()* that counts the number of letters, the number of digits, the number of punctuations, and the number of spaces in a sentence.

19.2.2 A CRITIQUE OF THE MOST COMMON APPROACHES

So there are many ways to approach a solution, as Example 19.2.1 showed. Nonetheless, some are better than others. Now that you know about the technical aspect of writing string functions, it is time to teach you about some good programming practices in writing such functions. These focus on making sure that a function is portable.

Example 19.2.2

Reconsider the solutions in Example 19.2.1. All three solutions, although in perfect working order, are somewhat inefficient and lack modularity. Here is a critique for each.

Solution 1. This first solution seems fine. Nevertheless, a closer look reveals three disadvantages:

1. *getchar()* is called for every single character. Since I/O operations are slow in comparison to the CPU, this approach slows down the program needlessly.
2. This solution is not modular. Everything is done within the function *strlines()*. The program should be broken down into smaller tasks.

3. The calls to *getchar()* and *putchar()* reduce this function's portability. Indeed, what if the sentence is to be read from a file?

Solution 2. This solution suffers from disadvantages 2 and 3 above.

Solution 3. *putchar()* is called for every single character. Too slow. It also suffers from disadvantages 2 and 3 above.

The best solution, which avoids these disadvantages, is to move all I/O operations out of the function *strlines()*. The idea is that the function's purpose should be to extract the words and nothing else. The reading of the sentence and the displaying of the words should be the responsibility of another function, in this case, the *main()*. This gives us the following solution, number 4:

Solution 4. The *main()* reads the sentence and passes it to the function *strlines()*. This one extracts the words and sends them **all** back within the **same** string named *words* to *main()*, which finally displays them all at once. For instance, suppose the sentence is "It is bed time," as shown in Figure 19.2.1.

Figure 19.2.1

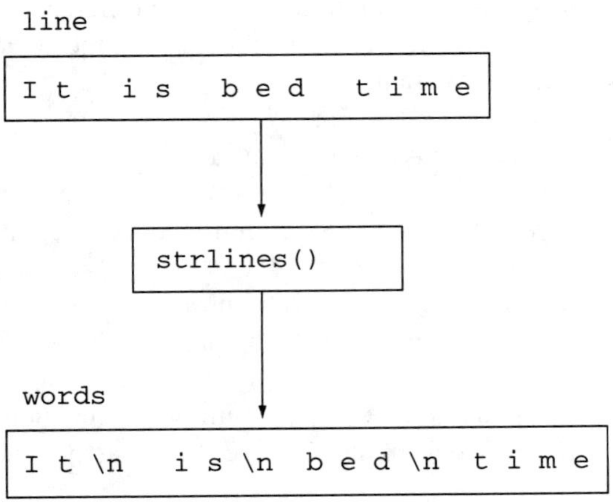

As each word is found and copied into the variable *words,* a \n is inserted immediately after it. This ensures that the statement *printf(words)* will cause all words to appear on separate lines. Two versions of this approach are shown below.

Version 1. Each character is processed individually.

```
void strlines(char line[], char words[])
{
        char  ch;
        int   i, j;

        for (i=0, j=0; (ch = line[i]) != '\0'; i++)
        {
                if (isspace(ch))                /* is end of word found? */
                {
                        words[j++] = '\n';
                }
                words[j++] = ch;                /* copy the character over */
        }
        words[j] = '\0';
}

main()
{
        char  sentence[81], words[81];
```

```
        printf("Enter a sentence: ");
        gets(sentence);
        strlines(sentence, words);
        printf(words);
}
```

Study this first version carefully before moving on to the second version below.

Version 2. Each **word** is processed individually. This version uses the predefined functions *sscanf()* and *strcat()* to do this:

```
void strlines(char line[], char words[])
{
   char  word[81], * word_ptr;

   for (word_ptr = line;              /* set the pointer to first cell */
     sscanf(word_ptr, "%s", word);     /* scan at the pointer location */
     word_ptr += strlen(word))        /* move the pointer past the word */
   {
     strcat(word, "\n");              /* concatenate the \n to the word */
     strcat(words, word);               /* then this word to the others */
    }
}
```

This is more concise code! This solution shares some similarity with the one asked for in Exercise 19.2.1, 2, so it is left for you to study.

Either version is just fine, except that version 2 is somewhat slower. (Why is that so?) It is also perhaps harder to understand at first glance. The important thing is that the function *strlines()* is now totally portable: it does not depend on any I/O operations. A sentence may now be read from a file or wherever and the words may be sent to wherever, and all the while this function can be used without ever needing a change. Also, it is fast because the string is accessed from memory at the time that the words are extracted.

19.2.3 TWO DISTINCT APPROACHES TO WRITING STRING FUNCTIONS

Now let us summarize what has been said about the four solutions. Essentially, there are two approaches to writing string functions:

1. Read and process the string one character at the time. As the string is processed, the results are progressively sent to the screen one character at a time, as shown in Figure 19.2.2. This is usually the approach taken by most beginners and not-so-beginners! Unfortunately, it leads to slower, and most importantly, unmodular programs, as discussed earlier in Section 19.2.

Figure 19.2.2

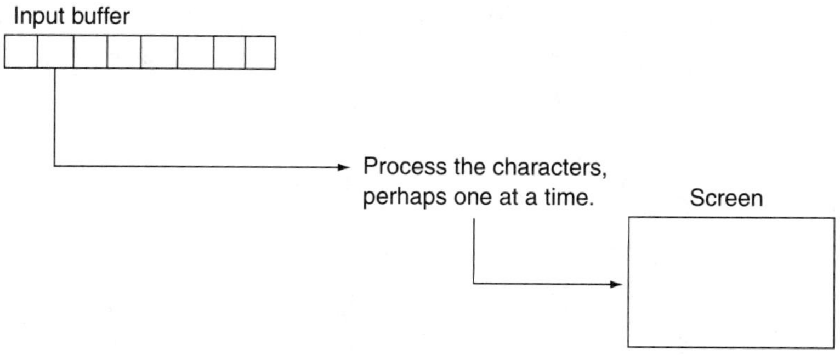

2. Read the whole string into memory first, i.e., into a string variable named, say, *in_str.* Do the whole processing from that string variable into another string variable named, say, *out_str.* When done, that string variable is then sent as a whole to the screen, as shown in Figure 19.2.3.

Figure 19.2.3

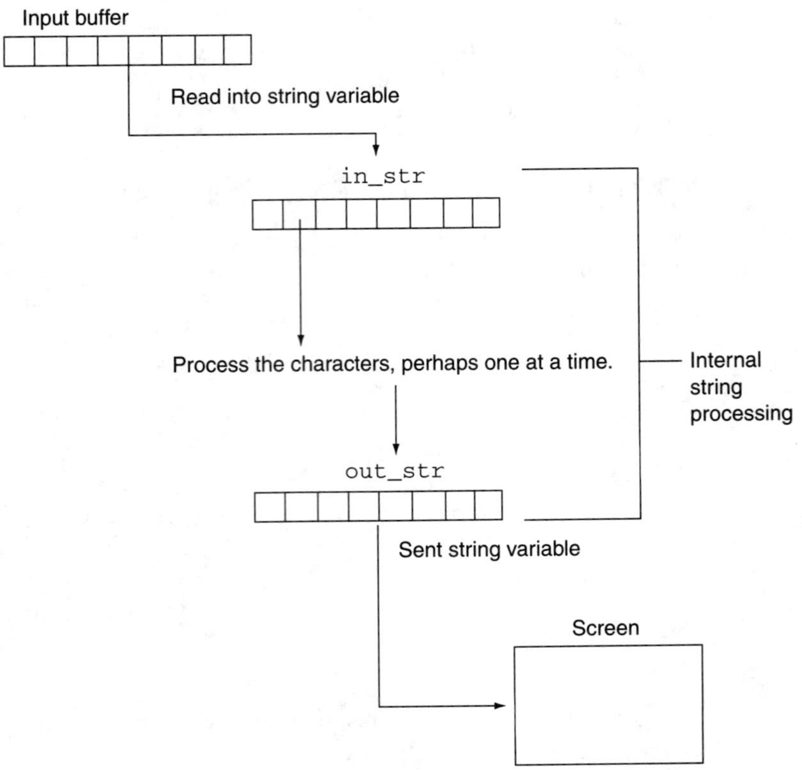

Advantages of internal string processing. Internal string processing (approach 2 above) offers obvious advantages over processing from the input device (approach 1):

1. The string is read and output as a whole. This is more efficient than reading one character at a time, because there is an overhead every time an I/O operation is performed. Since I/O operations are always slower than memory access, the string should be processed internally.
2. It facilitates modular programming, because the following three steps are automatically separated: reading in the string, processing the screen, and outputting the string.
3. The program is easier to maintain. Should any one of these three steps need modifications, the other two are not affected, making program maintenance more efficient. For example, should the message to read be stored in a file, only step 1 needs to be changed; steps 2 and 3 remain the same. (This idea will come handy in Section 20.2.)

EXERCISES 19.2.2

1. The following program reads in a message and then displays the vowels only and in uppercase, all separated by a space. The end of the message is indicated with the Enter key.

```
void display_vowels(void)
{
    char  c;

    while ((c = toupper(getchar())) != '\n')
    {
          switch(c)
          {
            case 'A': case 'E': case 'I': case 'O': case 'U':
                putchar(c);
                putchar(' ');
                break;
          }
    }
```

```
    putchar('\n');
}

main()
{
    printf("Enter some message: ");
    display_vowels();
}
```

Change the program so that the function *display_vowels()* processes the string internally. The I/O operations will be performed in the *main()*.

2. a. The following program simply reads in a line of text and echoes it, one letter per line:

```
signed char ch;
ch = getchar();
while (ch != '\n' && ch != EOF)
{
     putchar(ch);
     putchar('\n');
     ch = getchar();
}
```

The input may be terminated by pressing either the Enter key or Ctrl-Z. Change the loop so that the processing is now internal. Fill in the blanks below:

```
____________________;
for (______;__________________________;______)
{
     out_str[i] = ch;
     ______________;
}
____________________;
```

   b. Would the following loop be guaranteed to work in the same way as the one in (a)?

```
while ((ch = getchar()) != '\n' && ch != EOF)
{
     putchar(ch);
     putchar('\n');
}
```

3. Write a program named *capital_words()* that accepts a string of characters from the terminal and displays to the screen only the words that begin with a capital letter. Provide two solutions using the approaches to writing string functions explained in Subsection 19.2.2.
   a. Use approach 1.
   b. Use approach 2.
4. a. Is the function that you wrote for Exercise 19.2.1, 3a portable?
   b. If not, then make it so. (***Hint:*** Do all of the string processing internally and send the result back by reference into a second argument with the *return* statement.)
   c. Do the same for the functions in the following exercises:
      i. Exercise 19.2.1, 3b
      ii. Exercise 19.2.1, 3c
      iii. Exercise 19.2.1, 3d
      iv. Exercise 19.2.1, 3e
      v. Exercise 19.2.1, 3f
5. Write a function named *rtrim()* that deletes all trailing blanks from a string, passed as a parameter. The function returns the string.
   a. Write the function using pointers.
   b. Write the function using indexes.
6. Write a function named *ltrim()* that deletes all leading blanks from a string, passed as a parameter. The function returns the string.
   a. Write the function using pointers.

b. Write the function using indexes.
c. Introduce that function in a program that accepts a message and displays it without any leading blanks.

7. The following program simply asks for a message terminated by the Enter key. Then it creates a copy of it.

```
char * my_strcpy(char str[])
{
      int  i;
      char ch;

      for (i=0; (ch = getchar()) != '\n'; i++)
      {
            str[i] = ch;
      }
      str[i] = '\0';
      return str;
}

main()
{
      char copy[81];

      printf("Enter a message > ");
      stringcp(copy);
}
```

a. Does the program work?
b. If it does, discuss a number of disadvantages for the way the function *stringcp()* is defined.
c. Come up with a better, more efficient, and modular solution.

8. The following function simply skips a number of lines as specified by the parameter:

```
void skip(int n_lines)
{
      for ( ; n_lines--; )
      {
            printf("\n");
      }
}
```

a. This solution is inefficient. Explain why.
b. Suggest an alternative that uses a string in a way that will speed up the function manifolds.

9. a. Write a program that reads in a censored message, in which some of its letters are replaced with nonalphabetic characters. The program counts how many letters have not been replaced. If at least 50% of the letters are replaced, the censored message is approved. For instance:

   Enter a censored message > <u>&a%n $#c@ the **#r&</u>
   There are 7 letters not replaced in this message.
   57% covered -- message approved.

   Use the function *isalpha()* to determine if a character is a letter or not. But do not define any functions.

   b. Introduce a function named *censor()* that processes the message. Ensure that the function is portable and efficient.

10. Revisit Example 18.3.12. Write a function named *format()* that accepts the speed calculated and the width of the display zone. Then it will determine if the number or the message "very tiny" should be displayed. The function must be fully portable. Also, it must be defined in such a way that it may be used within a *printf()*. For instance:

```
printf("Mortgage rate = %s", format(7.25, 8, ________))
```

would produce the output "Mortgage rate =   7.25," but

```
printf("An atom is %s mm wide", format(2e-12, 6, ________))
```

would produce the output "An atom is very tiny mm wide" where the blank spaces should be occupied by an argument. What kind of argument? Note that whenever the function *format()* is used, the format code must be *%s.*

11. Suppose that the following problem is given to a student. If you are given one dollar the first day of the month, two dollars the second day, four dollars the third, and so on, how much money would you have at the end of the month? The student finds out with the following program:

```
#include <stdio.h>

main()
{
        int  day;
        long money;

        for (money=1, day = 0; day <= 30; day++, money *= 2)
        {
             printf("On day %2d, $ %4ld money to give\n", day, money);
        }
}
```

He decided to give two spaces for the number of the day and four spaces for the amount of money. Yet an outline of its output shows that, when needed, more spaces were given to the money amount:

```
On day  0, $    1 money to give
On day  1, $    2 money to give
On day  2, $    4 money to give
On day  3, $    8 money to give
On day  4, $   16 money to give
```

(Program continues.)

```
On day 13, $ 8192 money to give
On day 14, $ 16384 money to give
On day 15, $ 32768 money to give
On day 16, $ 65536 money to give
On day 17, $ 131072 money to give
```

(Program continues.)

```
On day 29, $ 536870912 money to give
On day 30, $ 1073741824 money to give
```

What happened? As you may recall from Section 2.4, a number that is wider than its format code's width specification is fully displayed anyway. If this program was written for an electronic spreadsheet, asterisks would show for the numbers that are wider than four spaces. The output above would be:

```
On day  0, $    1 money to give
On day  1, $    2 money to give
On day  2, $    4 money to give
On day  3, $    8 money to give
On day  4, $   16 money to give
```

(Program continues.)

```
On day 13, $ 8192 money to give
On day 14, $ **** money to give
On day 15, $ **** money to give
On day 16, $ **** money to give
On day 17, $ **** money to give
```

(Program continues.)

```
On day 29, $ **** money to give
On day 30, $ **** money to give
```

Write a function named *display()* that decides whether a number or asterisks should be displayed. This function may be called from within a *printf()*, much as shown in the question above.

12. Modify the loop in Exercise 7.3.6, 5. This time the processing will be done internally by using an input string called *line_in* and an output string called *line_out.* The input is read into *line_in,* one line at a time using *gets().* For every line, as the characters are processed they are copied into *line_out.* Once the processing is done with that line, the output is sent from *line_out* to the screen using *puts(). **Note:** line_out* must also include characters such as *\n* or > (prompt) so that when the string is sent to the screen, the display will be as it was in the original loop.

19.3 MORE COMPLEX USER-DEFINED STRING FUNCTIONS

When it comes to writing string functions, the sky is the limit! The domains of applications are only limited by your imagination. This section presents some typical but more complex applications.

Example 19.3.1

Let us construct a function named *strmv_chars()* that removes a portion of a string passed to it. The function takes three arguments: the string, the starting point in the string where characters should be deleted, and the number of characters to delete. The function returns the modified string. For instance, with the declaration *char line[30] = "ANSI C++ programming";*:

```
strmv_chars(line, 5, 3)
```

will return the string "ANSI programming," because the 5 tells it to start at the fifth character, and the 3 tells it to delete three characters from that point.

Following are three ways that this function may be coded. It is a good gymnastic exercise for the mind to study more than one solution.

Solution 1. This solution is very similar to the function *remove_element()* developed in Exercise 15.2.4, 1. It differs in two ways, though: more than one element is removed, and a null character must be reinserted.

```
char * strmv_chars(char str[], int start, int shift)
 {
       int   index;

       for (index=start-1; str[shift+index] != NULL; index++)
       {
             str[index] = str[shift+index];
       }
       str[index] = '\0';
       return str;
}
```

This solution uses an index variable to run through the string *str.* It starts at the first character to delete, at position *start–1,* all the way to the end of the string. For each execution of the loop, a character is shifted *shift* cells to the left, as shown in Figure 19.3.1.

Figure 19.3.1

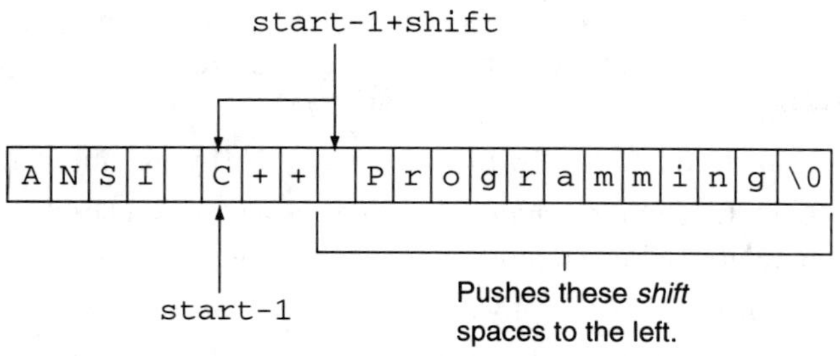

Here are two solutions in which the *for* loop uses a counter instead of an index.

Solution 2.

```
char * strmv_chars(char str[], int start, int shift)
{
        int    ctr;

        for (ctr=0; str[start-1+shift+ctr] != NULL; ctr++)
        {
                str[start-1+ctr] = str[start-1+shift+ctr];
        }
        str[start-1+ctr] = '\0';
        return str;
}
```

Solution 3.

```
char * strmv_chars(char str[], int start, int shift)
{
        int    ctr, l_str;

        l_str = strlen(str);
        loop = (l_str - shift) - start;
        for (ctr=0; ctr <= loop; ctr++)
        {
                str[start-1+ctr] = str[start-1+shift+ctr];
        }
        return str;
}
```

EXERCISES 19.3.1

1. Use the function *strmv_chars()* in a program that asks for its three arguments as follows:

   Enter a message > <u>The moon is a bright grey</u>
   Starting position > <u>13</u>
   Number of characters to delete > <u>8</u>

   The message is now: The moon is grey

2. Write a function *add_char()* that inserts a string into another string. The function takes three arguments: the original string, the string to be inserted, and the position where the insertion begins. For example, with the declaration *char line[30] = "ANSI programming";*,

   add_char(line, "C++ ", 6) will return "ANSI C++ programming."

3. Write a function called *remove()* that removes all occurrences of a character from a string. The function takes two arguments: the string and the character to be removed. For example, with the declaration: *char line[30] = "ANSI C++ programming";*,

   remove(line, 'g') will return "ANSI C++ prorammin."

4. Write a function called *strrmv()* that removes a substring from a string. The function takes two arguments: the string and the substring to be removed. For example, with the declaration: *char line[30] = "ANSI C++ programming";*,

   strrmv(line, "C++")   will return   "ANSI programming."

5. a. Write a function *strcenter()* that receives a string and centers the text inside it. The string is then returned. For example, with the declaration

   char line[81] = "   ANSI C   programming   ";,

   strcenter(line)   will return   "   ANSI C   programming   ."

   b. Modify the function so that it will center on the basis of the length of the resulting string desired. For example, with the declarations

   char line[81] = "ANSI C   programming", center[38];,

   strcenter(line, center, 37) will return

   "   ANSI C   programming   " which is of length 37.

   c. Use the function *strcenter()* in the segment below so that the text will be centered:

```
printf("      Welcome to\n\n");
printf(" Rumoli's Italian Restaurant\n\n");
printf("         7172 5th Street West\n\n");
printf("        Open daily from 8am to 10pm        \n\n");
```

6. a. Write a function *strdot()* that receives a fractional number within a string and aligns it on the decimal point. The first argument is the number (in a string), the second is the string variable to contain the result, the third argument is the position where the decimal point, or dot, should be placed, and the last argument is the length of the resulting string. The result is also returned. For example, with the following declaration:

   char answer[15] = "–4851.07", aligned[81];,

   strdot(answer, aligned, 13, 18) will return

   "   –4851.07   " which is of length 18, and the decimal point will be aligned at cell 13. Assume that the number contains a decimal point.

   b. Remove the assumption. If no decimal point is present, the function will insert one.

   c. Use the function to produce the following display:

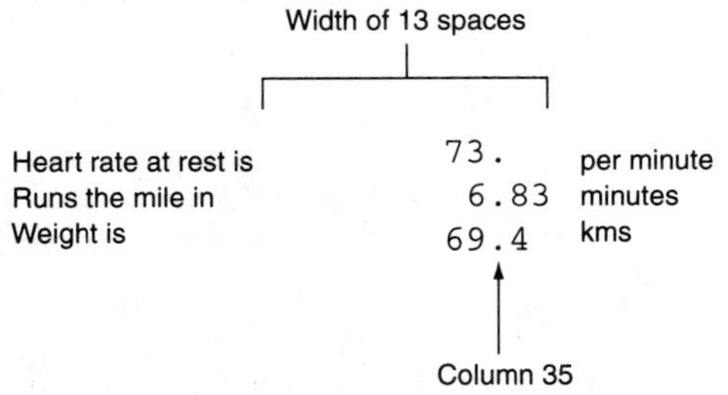

7. Develop a solution for *strmv_chars()* that uses a pointer to access each cell.

8. a. Determine what the following program does exactly. To help, go through the code by hand with the sentence: "It ain't just the same."

```
#include <stdio.h>
#include <ctype.h>

#define MAX_SIZE   81

main()
{
   char    line[MAX_SIZE];
   char  * change(char *);

   printf("Enter a message: ");
```

```
    gets(line);
    printf("Here it is changed somewhat:\n%s", change(line));
}

char * change(char * s)
{
    char   new_s[MAX_SIZE];
    char * ptr, temp;

    ptr = new_s;
    *ptr++ = '\t';
    for ( ; *s ; ++s)
    {
        if ((temp = toupper(*s)) == 'A' || temp == 'E' ||
              temp == 'I' || temp == 'O' || temp == 'U')
        {
            *ptr++ = toupper(*s);
        }
        else if (*s == ' ')
        {
            *ptr++ = '\n';
            *ptr++ = '\t';
        }
        else
        {
            *ptr++ = *s;
        }
    }
    return new_s;
}
```

b. Would it produce the same results with the sentence: "It   ain't   just   the   same."?

c. You may not have noticed yet, but, although its logic is spotless, this program actually contains three very subtle technical errors that may make the program produce erroneous results. Locate them.

d. Introduce the function *isvowel()* (developed in Exercise 19.1.2, 12) in the program above.

e. The size of the program can be shortened if *scanf()* is used to scan each word and then have each word sent to the function *change()*. Make all of the necessary changes.

9. a. Determine what the following function does exactly. To help, go through the code by hand with the sentence: "It ain't just the same." This sentence would constitute the first argument of the function.

```
int process (int * p, int * nch_ptr, int * nlet_ptr, int * nwo_ptr)
{
   for (*nch = 0; *p != '\0'; )
   {
        for ( ; isspace(*p) && *p != '\0'; *nch++, p++) ;
        if (*p != '\0')
        {
             for ( ; isalpha(*p) && *p != '\0'; *nch++, ++*nlet_ptr, p++) ;
             ++*nwo_ptr;
        }
}
```

b. Include this function in a working program that will repeatedly read a sentence terminated with the Enter key. For each sentence, the program will echo what this function produces. All this will be repeated until Ctrl-Z is pressed.

20 More Complex Applications for Strings

OBJECTIVES

This chapter introduces you to the following information:

- The definintion of arrays of strings and their applications.
- How to process text either from the screen or from a file.
- How to process file involving strings.
- How to create your own commands that may be issued from the command line.

INTRODUCTION

Not surprisingly, countless applications for string processing exist. Just think of your own personal computer, if you own one. String processing occurs virtually every time you provide input, regardless of the software you use. This chapter covers only a few typical applications.

20.1 ARRAYS OF STRINGS

So far we have seen arrays of integers, of real numbers, of characters, and of pointers. Arrays of strings are like these other arrays, although technically they are more complicated. There are two ways to declare arrays of strings, but there is a common way to use them.

20.1.1 AS A 2-D ARRAY OF CHARACTERS

Example 20.1.1

Let us write a program that simply lets the user enter the name of her native language. Then the program gives a greeting in that language:

```
#include <stdio.h>

main()
{
      char greeting[4][13] = { "Good morning",
                               "Bonjour",
                               "Bongiorno",
                               "Buenos dias" };[1]
```

```
        char lang;

        printf("What is your native language:\n");
        printf("1. English  2. French  3. Italian  4. Spanish\n");
        printf("> ");
        scanf("%d", &lang);
        printf("%s", greeting[lang-1]);[2]
}
```

Explanations

1. Look at the following declaration statement for the 2-D array of characters. Note that the number of strings is indicated as 4 and the size of each array (in which each string resides) is indicated as 13.

```
char greeting[4][13] = { "Good morning",        Row 0
                         "Bonjour",             Row 1
                         "Bongiorno",           Row 2
                         "Buenos dias" };       Row 3
```

The array *greeting* is stored in memory as shown in Figure 20.1.1.

Figure 20.1.1

greeting[0]	G	o	o	d		m	o	r	n	i	n	g	\0
greeting[1]	B	o	n	j	o	u	r	\0	\0	\0	\0	\0	\0
greeting[2]	B	o	n	g	i	o	r	n	o	\0	\0	\0	\0
greeting[3]	B	u	e	n	o	s		d	i	a	s	\0	\0

Note that when the compiler sees a string constant such as "Good Morning," it fills in the rest of the array with null characters. Note also that, just like any other 2-D array, *greeting[i]* is a pointer to row *i* (recall Subsection 17.3.1). This 2-D array is truly structured in the same way as were other 2-D arrays we saw in Chapter 17. In fact, it can be initialized the same way, one element at a time:

```
char greetings[4][13] = { 'G', 'o', 'o', 'd', ' ', 'm', 'o', 'r', 'n', 'i', 'n', 'g', '\0' },
                        { 'B', 'o', 'n', 'j', 'o', 'u', 'r', '\0' },
                        { 'B', 'o', 'n', 'g', 'i', 'o', 'r', 'n', 'o', '\0' },
                        { 'B', 'u', 'e', 'n', 'o', 's', ' ', 'd', 'i', 'a', 's', '\0' };
```

But do this only if you like pain!

2. To access a specific string within the array, it is only a matter of referring to its row number. For instance, the following statement selects the appropriate greeting, given the language code:

```
printf("%s", greeting[lang-1])
```

greeting[lang–1] refers to the line number *lang–1* within the 2-D array *greeting*. *greeting[lang–1]* is actually a pointer to the text of the greeting for language code *lang–1*.

As you realize by now, the use of an array of strings eliminated the need for a *switch* statement.

EXERCISES 20.1.1

1. Consider the declaration:

```
char  line[4][20] = { "Hay, Hey, Hi and Ha",
                      "Wow and Whee",
                       "Hurray and Hurrah!" };
```

Answer these questions:

a. What is the content of the following cells?
   i. *line[1][6]*
   ii. *line[0][15]*
   iii. *line[2][1]*
   iv. *line[1][13]*
   v. *line[3][0]*
b. Supposing that the 2-D array starts at address 2200, what is the content of:
   i. *line[1]*
   ii. *line[3]*
c. What is the length of the string in:
   i. *line[1]*
   ii. *line[3]*
d. What is the size of the string in:
   i. *line[1]*
   ii. *line[3]*

2. Rewrite the program in Example 20.1.1 without the use of arrays.
3. Write two versions of a program that asks for a month of the year, and then it tells its season:
   a. Store the appropriate seasons in words, such as "Winter," in an array of 12 strings, one for each month.
   b. Rewrite the program without any arrays.
4. In the following program, we want to enter one line of text in each row of the 2-D array *line.* Fill in the spaces by answering the questions below.

```
main ()
{
        int  i;
        char line[10][80];

        for (i=0; i < ________; i++)
        {
                printf("Enter a line of text: ");
                gets(__________);
        }
}
```

   a. What is the maximum number of lines that can be entered in the array?
   b. What is the maximum length a line can be?
   c. What should be the argument to *gets()*?

Modifying a string within the array. The concept here is the same as modifying an element in an array of, say, integers: you simply need to specify the row number of the greeting to modify. Let us look at two simple examples.

Example 20.1.2

The following program is the one from Example 20.1.1, but it allows the user to change the phrasing of the greeting. Changes are shown in bold type.

```
#include <stdio.h>
#include <ctype.h>

main()
{
        char greeting[4][13] = { "Good morning",
                                 "Bonjour",
                                 "Bongiorno",
                                 "Buenos dias" };
        char lang, ans;
```

```
        printf("What is your native language:\n");
        printf("1. English  2. French  3. Italian  4. Spanish\n");
        printf("> ");
        scanf("%d", &lang);
        printf("%s", greeting[lang-1]);
        printf("Would you like to change that greeting? (y/n) ");
        scanf("\n%c", &ans);
        if (toupper(ans) == 'Y')
        {
                printf("Enter new greeting > ");
                gets(greeting[lang-1]);
        }
}
```

The cell *greeting[lang–1]* is a pointer to the string for the language code *lang–1.* Thus the greeting at that language will be changed. For instance, if *lang* is 2, then the string pointed to by *greeting[1]* would be changed, as shown in Figure 20.1.2. The user must ensure that the greeting is not longer than 12 characters.

Figure 20.1.2

greeting[0]	G	o	o	d		m	o	r	n	i	n	g	\0
greeting[1]													
greeting[2]	B	o	n	g	i	o	r	n	o	\0	\0	\0	\0
greeting[3]	B	u	e	n	o	s		d	i	a	s	\0	\0

Example 20.1.3

In this example, the array of strings *greeting* starts off empty. The user is then asked to enter his own greetings for all four languages:

```
#include <stdio.h>
#include <ctype.h>

main()
{
        char greeting[4][13];

        printf("Enter a greeting in the following languages:\n");
        printf("1. English > ");
        gets(greeting[0]);
        printf("2. French > ");
        gets(greeting[1]);
        printf("3. Italian > ");
        gets(greeting[2]);
        printf("4. Spanish > ");
        gets(greeting[3]);
}
```

EXERCISES 20.1.2

1. The four *printf()*s and *gets()*s in Example 20.1.3 are rather repetitive. Modify the program so that a loop will be executed four times to produce the same results. (***Hint:*** Use an array of strings for displaying the prompts.)

2. Given the following declarations:

```
char msg[5][81];
int  num[6] = { 3, 5, 11, 19, 23, 33 }, bonus = 17;
int  i;
```

what will the segment below display?

```
sprintf(msg[0], "The winning numbers ");
sprintf(msg[1], "for the lottery");
sprintf(msg[2], "%3d, %3d, %3d followed ",
        num[0], num[1], num[2]);
sprintf(msg[3], "by %3d, %3d, %3d",
        num[3], num[4], num[5]);
sprintf(msg[4], "\nand the bonus is %5d\n", bonus);
for (i=0; i < 5; i++)
{
      printf("%s", msg[i]);
}
```

20.1.2 AS A 1-D ARRAY OF POINTERS TO STRINGS

The method of declaring an array of strings as a 2-D array has one disadvantage: all strings occupy the same space, even though some require less or more space. In Section 17.4 we saw that arrays of pointers do not have this memory restriction. They are the best method to use here, but the difference is that each pointer of the array will point to a character instead of a number. Example 20.1.4 shows how to proceed.

Example 20.1.4

Let us rewrite the program in Example 20.1.1 by declaring an array of pointers instead (changes are shown in bold type):

```
#include <stdio.h>

main()
{
      char * greeting[4] = { "Good morning",
                             "Bonjour",
                             "Bongiorno",
                             "Buenos dias" };
      char   lang;

      printf("What is your native language:\n");
      printf("1. English  2. French  3. Italian  4. Spanish\n");
      printf("> ");
      scanf("%d", &lang);
      printf("%s", greeting[lang-1]);
}
```

Note the following declaration:

```
char * greeting[4]
```

This says that *greeting* is a 1-D array *(greeting[4])* of pointers to characters *(char *)*.

Now let us turn our attention to the initialization that accompanies this declaration. The compiler will store each string in some location—say 2200 for "Good morning," 2214 for "Bonjour," 2223 for "Bongiorno," and 2236 for "Buenos dias." The array *greeting* is constructed as shown in Figure 20.1.3.

Figure 20.1.3

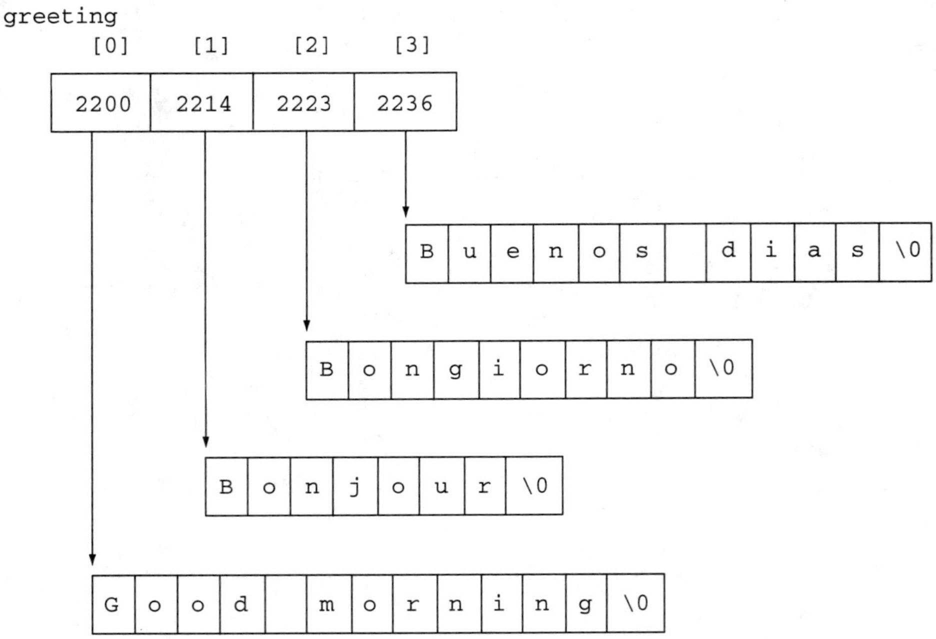

The cell *greeting[0]* is made to point to the address 2200, the cell *greeting[1]* is made to point to the address 2214, and so on. All this is done automatically at declaration time.

The advantages of arrays of pointers over 2-D arrays of characters. As you can see, each string is allocated only the space that it needs. Note that although they are adjacent here, the strings do not need to be adjacent at all. (Why is that so?) Note also that in the declaration of *greeting,* the size of the array may be omitted:

```
char * greeting[] = { "Good morning",
                      "Bonjour",
                      "Bongiorno",
                      "Buenos dias" };
```

Its size would automatically be set to four cells, one for each pointer. Also, the individual characters can still be accessed. For example, *greeting[2][6]* is the letter 'r' in "Bongiorno." Regardless, then, of how the array of strings is declared, each row or individual cell is accessed in the same way.

EXERCISES 20.1.3

1. Consider the following declaration:

```
char  * line[4] = { "Hay, Hey, Hi and Ha",
                    "Wow and Whee",
                    "Hurray and Hurrah!" };
```

Answer these questions:

a. What is the content of the following cells? Indicate if the operation is unpredictable.
   i. *line[1][6]*
   ii. *line[0][15]*
   iii. *line[2][1]*
   iv. *line[1][13]*
   v. *line[3][0]*

b. Supposing that the 2-D array starts at address 2200, what is the content of the following?
   i. *line[1]*
   ii. *line[3]*

c. What is the length of the string in the following arrays? Indicate if the operation is unpredictable.
   i. *line[1]*
   ii. *line[3]*
d. What is the size of the string in the following arrays? Indicate if the operation is unpredictable.
   i. *line[1]*
   ii. *line[3]*

2. Rewrite the program in Exercise 20.1.1, 3a, with an array of pointers.
3. The program below simply reads some lines of text into an array of strings and then it echoes that array. The end of the text is marked with Ctrl-Z.

```
#include <stdio.h>

main()
{
        char * line[100];

        printf("Enter some text:\n");
        for (i=0; gets(line[i]) != NULL; i++) ;
        for ( ; i--; )
        {
                puts(line[i]);
        }
}
```

Answer the following questions:
a. What is the maximum number of lines that may be entered?
b. What is the maximum length that a line can be?
c. Will this program work? If not, why? Suggest a solution.

Well, there are always different ways of writing programs. The one in Example 20.1.4 is no exception, as Example 20.1.5 explains.

Example 20.1.5

The program in Example 20.1.4 can be written in a different way while still using an array of pointers. The following version declares four 1-D arrays, one for each language. Then the array of pointers is made to point to each:

```
#include <stdio.h>

main()
{
        char   english[] = "Good morning";
        char   french[] = "Bonjour";
        char   italian[] = "Bongiorno";
        char   spanish[] = "Buenos dias";
        char * greeting[4] = { english, french, italian, spanish };[1]
        char   lang;

        printf("What is your native language:\n");
        printf("1. English  2. French  3. Italian  4. Spanish\n");
        printf("> ");
        scanf("%d", &lang);
        printf("%s", greeting[lang-1]);
}
```

Explanation

1. Note the declaration of the array of strings. Recall that the name of an array is also its address, so this declaration is interpreted as follows: *english* is the address to "Good Morning," *french* is the address to "Bonjour," and so on. So an array of strings is actually an array of pointers to each string. Note again that nothing else in the program needs to be changed.

EXERCISES 20.1.4

1. Consider the following declarations:

```
char    ack[20] = { "Hay, Hey, Hi and Ha" };
char    happy[12] = { "Wow and Wee" };
char    success[19] = { "Hurray and Hurrah!" };
char  * line[4] = { ack, happy, success };
```

   Answer these questions:

   a. What is the content of the following cells? Indicate if the operation is unpredictable.
      i. *line[1][6]*
      ii. *line[0][15]*
      iii. *line[2][1]*
      iv. *line[1][13]*
      v. *line[3][0]*
   b. Back in (a), give an equivalent name for each cell, if one exists.
   c. Give an equivalent name for the cells below:
      i. *happy[4]*
      ii. *ack[12]*
   d. What is the length of the string in the arrays below? Indicate if the operation is unpredictable.
      i. *line[1]*
      ii. *line[3]*
   e. What is the size of the string in the arrays below? Indicate if the operation is unpredictable.
      i. *line[1]*
      ii. *line[3]*
2. Rewrite the programs in the following exercises by using individual arrays as shown in the example above:
   a. Exercise 20.1.2, 1.
   b. Exercise 20.1.3, 2.
3. Reconsider Example 17.4.1. By using a new array of strings named *country*, have the program display the names of the countries instead of a student number. For example:

   Enter the results of all 8 assignments:
   For Canada: <u>18 22 15 25 91 8 17 22</u>
   For US: <u>20 25 20 25 86 9 19 24</u>
   For Mexico: <u>11 14 8 18 46 9 15 19</u>
   For Russia: <u>15 19 14 16 61 5 9 15</u>
   For Japan: <u>17 23 16 24 73 7 12 20</u>

20.1.3 ADVANTAGES TO USING ARRAYS OF STRINGS

The following examples illustrate the best two advantages of using arrays of strings.

They reduce the size of a program. As Example 20.1.6 will show, in some cases arrays of strings may be used to eliminate the need for decision structures such as *if/else*s. This often leads to a reduction in the program's size.

Example 20.1.6

Reconsider the simplified tax information system presented in Example 4.4.1:

Tax Information System

Select your civil status:

(1) Married
(2) Single
(3) Widowed
(4) Divorced

Enter here > 2

You must fill out form TX-113-2

Here again is its solution:

```
#include <stdio.h>

main()
{
      int civil_code;

      printf("%s%s%s%s%s%s%s",
             "          Tax Information System\n\n",
             "          Select your civil status:\n\n",
             "          (1)     Married\n",
             "          (2)     Single\n",
             "          (3)     Widowed\n",
             "          (4)     Divorced\n\n",
             "          Enter here > ");
      scanf("%d", &civil_code);

      switch(civil_code)
      {
          case 1:
                 printf("\nYou must fill out form TX-120-9\n");
                 break;

         case 2: case 4:
                 printf("\nYou must fill out form TX-113-2\n");
                 break;
         case 3:
                 printf("\nYou must fill out form TX-121-7\n");
                 break;
         default:
                 printf("\nInvalid code.");
                 break;
      }
}
```

As was stated in Chapter 17, the introduction of arrays in a program usually results in its size being reduced considerably. With the program here, by storing the tax form codes in an array of strings, the *switch* is no longer needed:

```
#include <stdio.h>

main()
{
```

```
    int civil_code;
    char * form[4] = { "TX-120-9", "TX-113-2",
                       "TX-121-7", "TX-113-2" };

    printf("%s%s%s%s%s%s%s",
        "              Tax Information System\n\n",
        "              Select your civil status:\n\n",
        "              (1)     Married\n",
        "              (2)     Single\n",
        "              (3)     Widowed\n",
        "              (4)     Divorced\n\n",
        "              Enter here > ");
    scanf("%d", &civil_code);

    if (civil_code >= 1 && civil_code <= 4)
    {
        printf("\nYou must fill out form %s\n",
               form[civil_code-1]);
    }
    else
    {
        printf("\nInvalid code.");
    }
}
```

In fact, the *if/else* construct can also be eliminated by storing the list of all five possible messages displayed by *printf()* in an array of strings. Then this also enables a simple conditional operator to replace the *if/else* statement we first used:

```
#include <stdio.h>

main()
{
    int    civil_code;
    char * msg[5] = { "\nYou must fill out form TX-120-9",
                      "\nYou must fill out form TX-113-2",
                      "\nYou must fill out form TX-121-7",
                      "\nYou must fill out form TX-113-2",
                      "\nInvalid code."
                    };

    printf("%s%s%s%s%s%s%s",
        "              Tax Information System\n\n",
        "              Select your civil status:\n\n",
        "              (1)     Married\n",
        "              (2)     Single\n",
        "              (3)     Widowed\n",
        "              (4)     Divorced\n\n",
        "              Enter here > ");
    scanf("%d", &civil_code);

    civil_code = civil_code >= 1 && civil_code <= 4 ? civil_code : 5;
    printf(msg[civil_code-1]);
}
```

In this case, the program is now a few lines shorter than the one with which we started. The last solution above is questionable, though, because it is less readable.

EXERCISES 20.1.5

1. Revisit Example 8.2.5. There, a long *switch* statement was needed to determine which of the months to store in the file. Define an array of strings containing the name of each month. This array, when indexed, may be used in place of a *switch* statement. (How?) As a result, the program will be much reduced in size.
2. Revisit Exercises 6.1.7, 18. Its program asks for a date and gives a choice of how to display it. For instance:

   ```
   Enter the day (1 to 31) > 7
   Enter the month (1 to 12) > 1
   Enter the year (1900 to 1999> 18

   How do you wish the date to be displayed?
   (a)  Verbalized
   (b)  DD/MM/YY
   (c)  MM/DD/YY
   (d)  DD-MMM-YY
   (e)  MMM-DD-YY
   Enter selection > d
   The date is 07-Jan-18
   ```

   Rewrite the program using arrays of strings. The menu will be stored in one array, and the format strings will be stored in another. To display the date, the appropriate format string will be passed to *printf()*.

They make the program more flexible. Another advantage of arrays of pointers is that they may increase the flexibility of a program, as Example 20.1.7 shows.

Example 20.1.7

Let us continue with the last program version in Example 20.1.6. Suppose that the programmer decides to include other civil status possibilities such as (5) Common-law, (6) Living with partner, and (7) Living with parents. Every time that you load this program, this long menu of seven options will always appear. Since most of those civil status conditions may not apply in your home, it would be better if the program allows you to customize the menu. Here is an example of a desirable run:

```
Tax Information System

Here is the main menu:

        (1)  Married
        (2)  Single
        (3)  Widowed
        (4)  Divorced
        (5)  Common-law
        (6)  Living with partner
        (7)  Living with parents

        Enter the options that you want to use > 256

Here is your customized menu:

Select your civil status:

        (2)  Single
        (5)  Common-law
        (6)  Living with partner

        Enter here > 6
You must fill out form TX-141-1
```

This is easily achievable with the use of arrays of pointers, as the following program shows:

```
#include <stdio.h>

main()
{
      int     civil_code, i;
      char    options[7];
      char * msg[8] = { "\nYou must fill out form TX-120-9",
                        "\nYou must fill out form TX-113-2",
                        "\nYou must fill out form TX-121-7",
                        "\nYou must fill out form TX-113-2",
                        "\nYou must fill out form TX-131-1",
                        "\nYou must fill out form TX-141-1",
                        "\nYou must fill out form TX-161-2",
                        "\nInvalid code."};

      char * menu[7] = { "          (1)      Married\n",
                         "          (2)      Single\n",
                         "          (3)      Widowed\n",
                         "          (4)      Divorced\n",
                         "          (5)      Common-law\n",
                         "          (6)      Living with partner\n",
                         "          (7)      Living with parents\n\n"};[1]
      char * custom_menu[7];[2]

      printf("          Tax Information System\n\n");
      printf("Here is the main menu:\n\n");
      for (i=0; i < 7; i++)
      {
          printf(menu[i]);
      }
      printf("          Enter the options that you want > ");
      scanf("%s", options);[3]
      for (i=0; options[i]; i++)
      {
          custom_menu[i] = menu[options[i] - '0' - 1];[4]
      }
      printf("\nHere is your customized menu:\n\n");
      printf("Select your civil status:\n\n");
      for (i=0; i < 7; i++)
      {
          printf(custom_menu[i]);
      }
      printf("          Enter here > ");
      scanf("%d", &civil_code);

      civil_code = civil_code >= 1 && civil_code <= 7 ? civil_code : 8;
      printf(msg[civil_code-1]);
}
```

Explanations

1. The array *menu* contains all seven options. Note that row 0 contains option 1, row 1 contains option 2, and so on.
2. The array *custom_menu* is initially empty. Eventually, the options that the user requests will be stored in it.
3. The options selected by the user are read in as a string of digits.

4. This statement prepares the custom menu, one item at a time. Each digit from the string *options* is accessed in order to determine which options the user wants to be stored in the customized menu array *custom_menu.* For instance, suppose that the user stored menu options 2, 5, and 6 in the array *options,* as shown below:

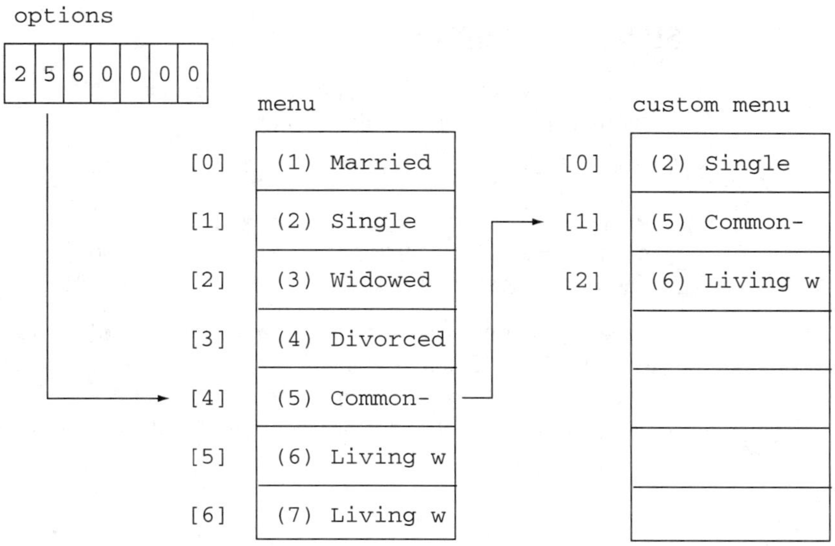

Let us go through Figure 20.1.4 when i=1, that is with the second option, *options[1],* which contains the character '5'. This leads to the option in *menu[4],* which is then copied into *custom_menu[1].* All this is done in a single statement, the evaluation of which is shown below:

```
custom_menu[i] = menu[options[i]   -   '0' - 1]
custom_menu[1] = menu[options[1]   -   '0' - 1]
                 menu[    '5'      -   '0' - 1]
                 menu[    53       -   48  - 1]
                 menu[          5          - 1]
                 menu[             4          ]
custom_menu[1] = menu[4]
```

The assignment says that option 5 will be our second option in the custom menu. Strictly speaking, it is actually the address of the string that is assigned to *custom_menu[1],* not the string itself.

EXERCISES 20.1.6

1. The program above has one flaw. In the customized menu, the user can still choose an option that is not listed without the program flagging an error. For instance, in the custom menu in the example above, the options 1, 3, 4, and 7 could have been selected, but they should be considered invalid. Modify the program to fix this. Do not use any *if/else* or *switch* statements. (***Hint:*** Use the string function *strspn()* covered in Subsection 18.3.4.)
2. The customized menu shows gaps in the option numbers. For instance, the menu below lists 2, 5 and 6.

Here is your customized menu:

Select your civil status:

(2) Single
(5) Common-law
(6) Living with partner

Enter here > 6
You must fill out form TX-141-1

Modify the program so that the customized menu will number the options starting at 1, in increments of 1.

SUPPLEMENTARY EXERCISES 20.1

1. Use an array of strings in Supplementary Exercise 17.2, 12, so that a name will be listed for the car model instead of a number. For example:

Model of car	1991	1992	1993	1994	1995
Stampeder	$ 2400	$ 3340	$ 4100	$ 8990	$12000
4-D Country	$ 3100	$ 4540	$ 6000	$ 8630	$14581
The Turbo Boost	$ 2320	$ 3640	$ 4680	$ 7760	$ 9958

Make up your own model names. (***Note:*** The file content remains as it was in Supplementary Exercise 17.2, 12; that is, the model number is read, not its name.)

2. Use an array of strings in Supplementary Exercise 17.2, 9, so that the name of the candidate will be listed, as well as the number of the ward. For example:

ELECTION RESULTS

Wards

Candidate	1	2	3	4	5	6
Douglas	261	683	590	465	929	1177
Klought	20	870	461	773	782	395
Yestman	1843	499	954	800	80	623

Winners:
Ward 1: Yestman, majority of 1562 votes
Ward 2: Klought
Ward 3: Yestman
Ward 4: Yestman
Ward 5: Douglas, majority of 67 votes
Ward 6: Douglas, majority of 159 votes

Make up your own names. (***Note:*** The file content remains as in Supplementary Exercise 17.2, 9; that is, the candidate's number is read, not his or her name.)

3. Use an array of strings in Supplementary Exercise 17.2 , 3, so that the name of the products will be listed. Make up your own names. (***Note:*** The file content remains as in Supplementary Exercise 17.2, 3; that is, the product number is read, not its name.)
4. Use an array of strings in Supplementary Exercise 17.2, 2, so that the name of the colleges will be listed. Make up your own names. (***Note:*** The file content remains as in Supplementary Exercise 17.2, 2; that is, the college number is read, not its name.)
5. The following function simply tabulates the interest earned over a period of time:

```
void table(float fund, float rate, int year, int period)
{
      float interest;
      int   ct;

      printf("       Year              Interest         Fund\n"
             "       ----              --------         ----\n\n");
      for (ct=0; ct < period; ct++)
      {
            interest = fund * rate;
            fund += interest;
            printf("      %d                 %.2f          %.2f\n",
```

```
                    year+ct, interest, fund);
        }
}
```

Suppose now that you have been asked to store the table in a file. The obvious problem is that this function sends the table to the screen. Also, this function is not entirely portable. Make it so by following the changes below:

a. Use the function *sprintf()* instead of *printf()*. This way, the display will be stored in a string, one line at a time. (***Hint:*** This is similar to Exercise 20.1.2, 2.)
b. Change the header to the following:

```
void table(float fund, float rate, int year, int period,
     char photo[][81])
```

The parameter *photo* will receive all of the lines of the display. Consequently, it needs to be a 2-D array.

c. Test the function with a program that stores the table in a file.

20.2 FILE PROCESSING INVOLVING STRINGS

Strings stored in files are read in in almost exactly the same way as they are read from the screen. The most visible differences are the functions' names and syntaxes. The file functions *fscanf()* and *fprintf()* have already been covered in Sections 2.5 and 8.2. They read and store strings in exactly the same manner as *scanf()* and *printf()* do; thus, they will not be covered in this section. The standard C library (in *stdio.h*) provides two functions specialized to read and store strings to and from files: *fgets()* and *fputs()*. They are the parallels to *gets()* and *puts()*, with some subtle differences as we shall see. We will look at a few other file I/O functions as well.

20.2.1 FILE I/O STRING OPERATIONS WITH *fgets()* AND *fputs()*

Example 20.2.1

The following program simply makes a copy of a file's content into another file. Both the source and the destination files are provided by the user.

```
#include <stdio.h>

main()
{
      char   line[81];
      char   source[20], dest[20];
      FILE * sfp;
      FILE * dfp;

      printf("Enter the source file name: ");
      scanf("%s", source);
      printf("Enter the destination file name: ");
      scanf("%s", dest);
      sfp = fopen(source, "r");
      dfp = fopen(dest, "w");
      while (fgets(line, 81, sfp) != NULL)[1]
      {
            fputs(line, dfp);[2]
      }
      fclose(sfp);
      fclose(dfp);
}
```

Explanations

1. The condition does two things: it reads a chunk of 80 characters at a time from the input file, and it checks to see if the end of the file has been reached:

   ```
   fgets(line, 81, sfp)
   ```

   Here, *line* is the string variable that receives the data; *81* is the maximum number of characters to read, plus 1; and *sfp* is the file pointer to the source file. This function reads 80 characters (**not** 81) into the string variable *line* or reads until a *\n* is reached, whichever occurs first. The number 81 refers to the size that the string variable *line* has to be in order to be able to store all 80 characters. Note that unlike *gets()*, the *\n* is stored in the string variable. *fgets()* returns NULL when the end-of-file marker is reached.
2. This function call results in the storage of the string *line* into the output file:

   ```
   fputs(line, dfp)
   ```

   line is the string to send out, and *dfp* is the file pointer to the destination file. Each character from the string *line* is stored in the destination file until a null character is reached. The null character is not stored in the file. Note that unlike *puts()*, *fputs()* does **not** send a *\n* to the file.

Be wary of subtle differences from *gets()* and *puts()*. The subtle differences between the functions *gets()* and *fgets()*, and *puts()* and *fputs()*, are quite important to remember. Figure 20.2.1 summarizes their differences.

Figure 20.2.1

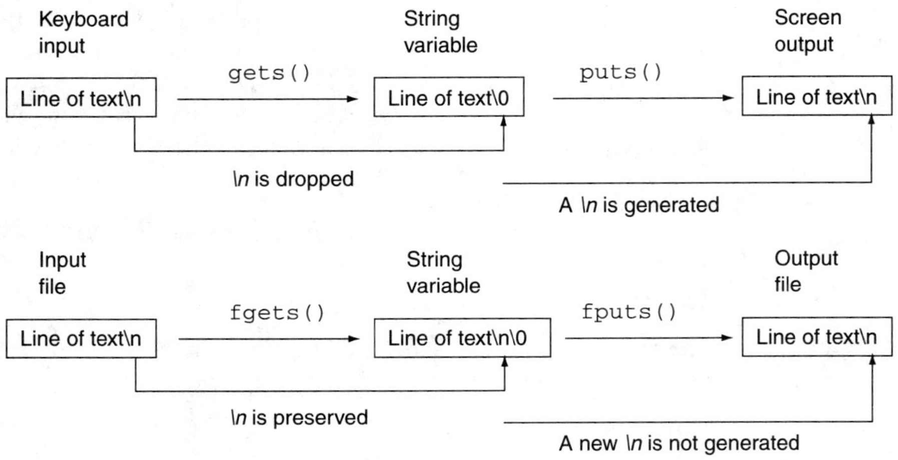

EXERCISES 20.2.1

1. Let us say the content of the source file in Example 20.2.1 is the following:

   Here's an unusual opportunity for everyone who
   is determined to get ahead in business.
   Just print your name and address on the special shipping label.

   Given the sequence of *fgets()* and *fputs()* below, what would be stored in the destination file?

   ```
   fgets(line, 11, sfp);
   fputs(line, dfp);
   fgets(line, 51, sfp);
   fputs(line, dfp);
   fgets(line, 133, sfp);
   fputs(line, dfp);
   fgets(line, 41, sfp);
   fputs(line, dfp);
   fgets(line, 41, sfp);
   fputs(line, dfp);
   ```

2. a. List the three conditions that make a call to *fgets()* terminate.
   b. List the two conditions that make a call to *gets()* terminate.
3. Write a program that accepts lines of text from the keyboard and stores them in a file provided by the user. Use *gets()* and *fputs()*. The text must be stored in the file exactly as entered at the keyboard.
4. Write a program that displays to the screen the content of a file provided by the user. Use *fgets()* and *puts()*. The text must be displayed to the screen exactly as read from the file.
5. Modify the solution of Supplementary Exercise 8.2, 1, so that the full name is read from the screen and stored in the file LETTERS.LIS.

20.2.2 TWO SIMPLE APPLICATIONS

Section 18.1 warned that *gets()* does not check to make sure that the string variable is long enough to receive the input; it keeps reading from the keyboard until a *\n* is reached, regardless of whether or not this may cause an out-of-bounds condition on the string variable. To avoid this, the *fgets()* may be used instead. It can be coded to ensure that the string variable will never receive more data than it can hold. Example 20.2.2 illustrates this.

Example 20.2.2

The following program asks for a customer name to be stored in a string variable that will hold up to 15 characters (plus 1 for the null character). The *fgets()* function is used to ensure that no more than 15 characters are stored:

```
#include <stdio.h>

main()
{
      char   cust_name[16];

      printf("Enter the customer name > ");
      fgets(cust_name, 16, stdin);¹
      printf("The name %s was stored in memory\n", cust_name);
      fflush(stdin);²
}
```

Here is an example of a run:

Enter the customer name > Dimitri Costomopoulous
The name Dimitri Costomo was stored in memory

Note that only the first 15 characters (Dimitri Costomo) are stored.

Explanations

1. The file pointer sent to the function *fgets()* is *stdin,* the file pointer for the standard input, the keyboard. This ensures that *fgets()* will read from the keyboard instead of a file.
2. Since only the first 15 characters are read into the string variable, the rest of the name remains in the input buffer. This data definitely should be flushed out with *fflush(stdin).*

EXERCISES 20.2.2

1. a. In Example 20.2.2, could the *fgets()* be replaced by the following statement and still produce the same result?

   ```
   scanf("%15s", cust_name);
   ```

   b. While using *gets(),* devise a way to ensure that the name entered is truncated to 15 characters. [***Hint:*** Also use *strncpy().*] Is *fflush(stdin)* still needed?

2. The following segment of code reads only the first five digits of a number:

```
printf("Enter a number > ");
scanf("%5d", &num);
fflush(stdin);
```

a. Using *fgets()* and *atoi()*, devise a way to perform the same task as the above code does. Is *fflush(stdin)* still needed?
b. Using *gets()*, *strncpy()* and *atoi()*, devise a way to perform the same task as the above code does. Is *fflush(stdin)* still needed?
c. Using *gets()* and *sscanf()*, devise a way to do the same. Is *fflush(stdin)* still needed?

Let us look at another interesting application of the functions covered.

Example 20.2.3

Let us write a program to display the text in a file called LETTER.TXT in capital letters and double spaced. Following is an example of a run. Assume the file LETTER.TXT contains the following text:

```
I WANT to apply for this job!
YOU BETTER take me or else *&%^&$!
Sincerely yours,

Mr. Blewit
```

The text will be displayed in capital letters and double spaced as follows:

```
I WANT TO APPLY FOR THIS JOB!

YOU BETTER TAKE ME OR ELSE *&%^&$!

SINCERELY YOURS,



MR. BLEWIT
```

As discussed in Section 19.2, string processing should be done internally for the sake of program portability and efficiency. This means that a whole line of text will be read into a string variable named *in_str*. Then the conversions to uppercase letters and double-spaced lines will be stored in the string variable *out_str*. Finally, that string will be sent to the screen. Here is the solution:

```
#include <stdio.h>
#include <ctype.h>
#define  LEN_LINE      80
#define  LEN_FILENAME  12

main()
{
     char     ch;
     int      i_in, i_out;
     FILE   * ifp, * ofp;
     char     in_str[LEN_LINE+1], out_str[LEN_LINE+1];
     char     ifname[LEN_FILENAME+1];

     printf("Enter input file > ");
     scanf("%s", ifname);
     ifp = fopen(ifname, "r");
     while (fgets(in_str, LEN_LINE+1, ifp) != NULL)[1]
     {
     /* process the line */
```

```
        for (i_in=i_out=0; (ch = in_str[i_in]) != '\0'; i_in++)[2]
        {
             if (islower(ch))
             {
                  out_str[i_out++] = toupper(ch);
             }
             else
             {
                  out_str[i_out++] = ch;
             }
         }
         out_str[i_out] = '\0';[3]
         puts(out_str);[4]
    }
    fclose(ifp);
}
```

Explanations

1. A whole line is read in at a time.
2. Process the string until reaching its end.
3. Make sure that the output string is terminated with a '\0'.
4. The *fgets()* preserves the '\n' and *puts()* sends an additional one. So the screen will receive two '\n' codes, accounting for the double spacing.

EXERCISES 20.2.3

1. Modify the program in Example 8.2.1 so that the full name is stored in the file.
2. Modify Exercise 8.2.3, 2, so that the full name (instead of initials) is stored in the file PARENTS.KDS. Exactly 25 spaces are reserved for this name.
3. Modify the program in Example 8.2.5 so that the full name is stored in the file.

20.2.3 FILE I/O CHARACTER OPERATIONS WITH *fgetc()* AND *fputc()*

The four I/O functions seen so far in this section perform I/O in a block; that is, an entire chunk of characters is read or output from or to a file. Characters may also be read and stored individually, as Example 20.2.4 shows.

Example 20.2.4

The program below does essentially the same thing as that in Example 20.2.1, except that every single character is read and stored individually rather than line by line.

```
#include <stdio.h>

main()
{
      signed char  chr;
      FILE *       sfp;
      FILE *       dfp;

      printf("Enter the source file name: ");
      scanf("%s", source);
      printf("Enter the destination file name: ");
      scanf("%s", dest);
      sfp = fopen(source, "r");
```

```
        dfp = fopen(dest, "w");
        while ((chr = fgetc(sfp)) != EOF)¹
        {
              fputc(chr, dfp);²
        }
        fclose(source);
        fclose(dest);
}
```

Explanations

1. The condition does two things: it reads a single character from the input file into the variable *chr,* and it checks to see if the end-of-file marker is reached. When this happens, EOF is stored in the variable *chr.* Since EOF is the number –1, *chr* has to be declared *signed char.*
2. This function simply sends the character in *chr* to the output file.

Every single character is processed. It is important to understand that the function *fgetc()* reads every single character from the input file and that the function *fputc()* sends out every single character received. This implies that, unlike *gets(), fgetc()* does read the \n into the variable. Also the function *fputc(),* unlike *puts(),* does not add a new \n to the output. Finally note that this program is slower than the one in Example 20.2.1. (Why is that so?)

EXERCISES 20.2.4

1. Redo the program in Example 20.2.3 with *fgetc()* and *fputc()* only.
2. Make the necessary modifications to the program in Example 20.2.3 so that the lines are not double spaced.
3. Consider the following program:

```
main()
{
   char   ch;
   char   filename[20];
   FILE * ifp;
   int    r;

   printf("Enter the file name: ");
   scanf("%s", filename);
   ifp = fopen(filename, "r");
   r = fscanf(ifp, "%c", &ch);
   while (r != EOF && ch != '\n')
   {
         printf("%c", ch);
         r = fscanf(ifp, "%c", &ch);
   }
   fclose(ifp);
}
```

   a. Rewrite it using *fgetc()* and *putchar().*
   b. This code is rather inefficient. Rectify this, and at the same time, shorten the code.

20.2.4 A SUMMARY OF I/O C FUNCTIONS

The main difficulty with I/O functions in C arises from the handling of the character \n. Some keep it, some drop it, and some generate a new one. What a mess! To help, Table 20.2.1 summarizes the various I/O functions seen in this book. In the left column are listed the functions for ***file input/output.*** The right column lists the functions for the ***keyboard/screen input/output.***

Each row contains the two homologous functions for file I/O and keyboard/screen I/O, respectively [for instance, *fputc()* is to file I/O what *putchar()* is to screen I/O].

Table 20.2.1

File I/O	**Keyboard/Screen I/O**
fputc(ch, fp); Characters are never converted or discarded.	*putchar(ch);* Characters are never converted or discarded.
fputs(str, fp); The null character is discarded. In particlular: 1. \0 –X–>[1] \n 2. \0 –X–> \0	*puts(str);* The null character is converted as follows: \0 ---> \n
ch[2] = fgetc(fp); 1. Characters are never converted or discarded. 2. If EOF (–1) is stored in the variable *ch,* then end-of-file marker is reached.	*ch[2]= getchar();* 1. Characters are never converted or discarded. 2. If EOF (–1) is stored in the variable *ch,* then the end of input is reached.
check = fgets(str, size, fp); 1. Reads *size–1* characters or until \n reached or until end-of-file marker is reached. 2. If NULL (0) is stored in the variable *check,* then end-of-file marker is reached. 3. The newline character is kept: \n --->[1] \n	*check = gets(str);* 1. Reads characters until \n reached or until the end of input is reached. 2. If NULL (0) is stored in the variable *check,* then the end of input is reached. 3. The newline character is converted: \n ---> \0

[1]---> stands for "changed into"; –X–> stands for "**not** changed into." For instance, \0 –X–> \n means that the null character is not changed into a newline character during a particular I/O operation. The notation \n ---> \n would mean that the newline character is kept during the I/O operation.

[2]*ch* **must** be declared as a *signed* variable. For example, if you decide to make it of type *char,* its declaration would be *signed char ch;*

20.2.5 COMMON ERRORS AND TRAPS

Do not fail to realize the subtle differences between *gets()* and *fgets(),* and *puts()* and *fputs().*

SUPPLEMENTARY EXERCISES 20.2

1. Rewrite the loop from Exercise 19.2.2, 12, again, this time reading the input from a file called DATA.IN. Use *fgets()* and *fputs().* Since the input is no longer received at the keyboard, discard the code that displays the prompts. You will need to open the file, but do not include code to verify if it opened correctly. (***Hint:*** Few—but important—changes are needed.)
2. a. Write a function named *fngets()* that works exactly the same as *fgets(),* except that it does not preserve the *\n.* [***Hint:*** Use *strchr()* to locate *\n;* then change it to *\0.*]
   b. Write a function named *fnputs()* that works exactly the same as *fputs(),* except that it generates a *\n.*
   c. Use these two new functions in Example 20.2.1.
3. Revisit Supplementary Exercises 20.1, 1 to 4. The names of models, candidates, and so on, that were chosen should now be stored in the file and read from there into the program.
4. Write a function named *read_dfile()* that reads in the following file:

```
J. Corr               629 Treeman St.      Moose Jaw
K. Beans              1001 Tremp           Moose Jaw
B. J. Wilson          2 Victoire St.       Weyburn
Y. Boon               14 3rd St.           Swift Current
```

1 Name 22	23 Address 42	43 City 60

Note the columns occupied by each field, shown below the file text.

a. The names are to be stored in a 2-D array, one name per row. The addresses and cities are to be read in 2-D arrays also, one per row. All of these arrays are passed to the function, as is the input file pointer. Assume the file is already open. [***Hint:*** Use the *fgets()* function to read each field. Your function must be able to read any number of records.]

b. Rewrite the code so that the address is stored in two different arrays: the number is to be read into a 1-D array and the street name into another array (2-D).

5. Modify the program in Exercise 14.3.1, 10, so that the employee names are also stored in the file WORK.DAT. They will be stored in their respective output files.
6. Modify the program in Exercise 14.3.1, 11, so that the purchase location names are stored in the input file as follows:

```
4510
Sears                      20.77
Toyota                     361.02
Coles Bookstore            72.81
Chez Jacques Restaurant    55.12
–1
Computer Corner            1178.09
Shell                      31.03
–1
```

The location name occupies 40 spaces.

20.3 TEXT PROCESSING

The manipulation of text such as margin setting, centering text, deletion of words and paragraphs, and so on, is called ***text processing.*** Text processing is probably the most common type of software application. Of course, text editors and word processors use it, but so do time management planners and games. This section is a very brief introduction to text processing.

20.3.1 TOKEN EXTRACTION USING THE *strtok()* FUNCTION

Even at its simplest, text processing is possible only when the program has the ability to extract every single entity from the text in order to manipulate it. An entity may be a word, a number, an acronym, and so on. In computer terms, the word ***token*** is used instead of entity. For instance, the line below contains ten tokens, "e.g.," "5.245690612," "×," "1026," "which," "now," "has," "a," "fractional," and "part."

e.g., 5.245690612 × 1026,   which now has a   fractional part.

As you can see, tokens are separated by at least one space. How can a token be extracted? We saw in Example 19.2.1 that *scanf()* can do it. However Example 19.2.2 pointed out that *scanf()* needs to be called for every single word to extract, which is slow. It was concluded that string processing is desirable internally. The standard C library includes the function *strtok()* that is specialized for this exact purpose. It is declared in the header file *string.h.* The string is first read in with, say, *gets();* then *strtok()* extracts each word, one at a time. Example 20.3.1 shows how this is done.

Example 20.3.1

The following program performs the same task as programs in Examples 19.2.1 and 19.2.2, but this one uses *strtok():*

```
#include <stdio.h>
#include <string.h>

void strlines(char line[], char tokens[])
{
      char * token_ptr, token[81];
```

```
        token_ptr = strtok(line, " ");[1]
        while (token_ptr)[5]
        {
                strcpy(token, token_ptr);[2]
                strcat(tokens, strcat(token, "\n"));[3]
                token_ptr = strtok(NULL, " ");[4]
        }
}

main()
{
        char sentence[81], words[81];

        printf("Enter a sentence: ");
        gets(sentence);
        strlines(sentence, words);
        puts(words);
}
```

A sample run may look like this:

```
Enter a sentence: Ooff! one, two, three; are we done yet?
Ooff!
one,
two,
three;
are
we
done
yet?
```

Explanations

1. Each call to *strtok()* results in the next token being extracted from the string *line*. The first call extracts the first token:

   ```
   token_ptr = strtok(line, " ")
   ```

   token_ptr is the pointer to the token extracted; *line* is the string from which tokens are extracted; and the blank character (“ ”) delimits each token. Each time *strtok()* is called, all blanks are skipped until the next token is reached. Then the address to that token is returned. For instance, you can see where *token_ptr* would point to after the first call:

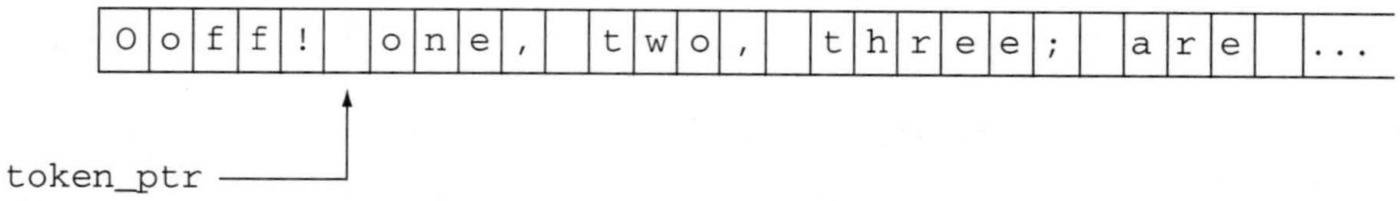

2. It turns out that a copy of the token at *token_ptr* should always be made as soon as a token is extracted. Only the copy should be handled, and **never** *token_ptr* itself. Why? Because unpredictable things may occur if the program attempts to modify in any way the string at *token_ptr.* The precise reason for this is too technical to be discussed here.
3. As a token is found, it is appended to the string *tokens.* This is accomplished in two steps, as shown below:

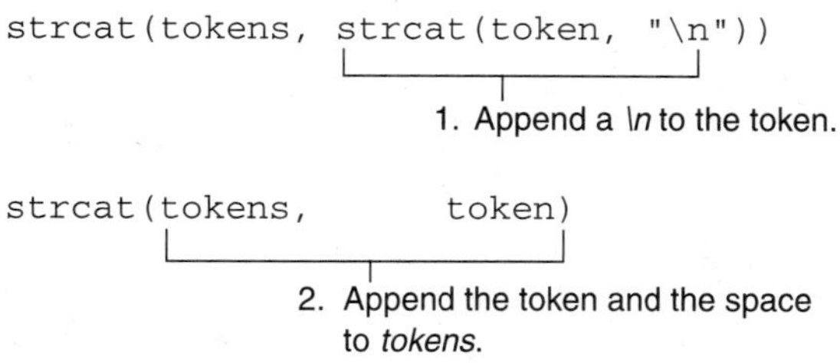

As a result, *tokens* contains the text shown:

O	o	f	f	!	\n	\0	...

4. The subsequent calls to *strtok()* extract the other tokens within the string *line:*

```
token_ptr = strtok(NULL, " ")
```

The NULL indicates to *strtok()* to extract tokens still from the string *line,* as opposed to another string. The string from which to extract tokens must be specified only in the very first call to *strtok()*. After this second call, *token_ptr* points to the space following the next token, as shown:

O	o	f	f	!		o	n	e	,		t	w	o	,		t	h	r	e	e	;		a	r	e	...
										↑ token_ptr																

Then the statement *strcat(tokens, strcat(token, "\n"))* appends "one," to the string *tokens,* as shown:

O	o	f	f	!	\n	o	n	e	,	\0	...

5. An so on, until *strtok()* reaches the end of the string *line*, at which time *token_ptr* is NULL.

EXERCISES 20.3.1

1. What do you think the following segments will produce?
   a.
```
char   line[] = "Four hundred and thirty two";

printf("Word 1 is %s\n", strtok(line, " "));
printf("Word 2 is %s\n", strtok(line, " "));
printf("Word 3 is %s\n", strtok(NULL, " "));
printf("Word 4 is %s\n", strtok(NULL, " "));
```
   b.
```
char   line[] = "Four-hundred and thirty-two";

printf("Word 1 is %s\n", strtok(line, " "));
printf("Word 2 is %s\n", strtok(line, " "));
printf("Word 3 is %s\n", strtok(NULL, " "));
printf("Word 4 is %s\n", strtok(NULL, " "));
```
2. Would the following statement also correctly append a token to *line_out?*

```
strcat(strcat(line_out, token), " ")
```

3. The function below may produce unpredictable results. Locate the problem.

```
void strlines(char line[], char tokens[])
{
      char * token_ptr;

      token_ptr = strtok(line, " ");
      while (token_ptr)
      {
            strcat(tokens, strcat(token_ptr, "\n"))
            token_ptr = strtok(NULL, " ");
      }
}
```

4. Example 19.2.2 showed that *sscanf()* may also be used to extract words and, just like *strtok()*, process a string internally. Rewrite the program in Example 20.3.1 so that it uses *sscanf()*.

20.3.2 WORD EXTRACTION

Example 20.3.2

The program in Example 20.3.1 does not truly extract words: the punctuation marks, such as .,;?!, are appended to the words. It would be desirable to extract the words only. Surprisingly, the changes required are minimal. It is only a matter of changing the second argument to every call to *strtok()* as follows:

```
token_ptr = strtok(line, " .,;?!");
token_ptr = strtok(NULL, " .,;?!");
```

All of the characters included in this second argument will be skipped from the input line. Note that a blank space has to remain.

EXERCISES 20.3.2

1. What do you think the following segments will produce?
   a.
   ```
   char   line[] = "Four-hundred and thirty-two";

   printf("Word 1 is %s\n", strtok(line, "-"));
   printf("Word 2 is %s\n", strtok(line, "-"));
   printf("Word 3 is %s\n", strtok(NULL, "-"));
   printf("Word 4 is %s\n", strtok(NULL, "-"));
   ```
   b.
   ```
   char   line[] = "Four-hundred and thirty-two";

   printf("Word 1 is %s\n", strtok(line, " -"));
   printf("Word 2 is %s\n", strtok(line, " -"));
   printf("Word 3 is %s\n", strtok(NULL, " -"));
   printf("Word 4 is %s\n", strtok(NULL, " -"));
   ```
2. a. Write a program that uses the function *strtok()* to extract and display to the screen every single item in the following list:

   Enter identification information:
   Stephen Spline,28,1.79,73.8,10/04/66
   Name: Stephen Spline
   Age: 28
   Height: 1.79
   Weight: 73.8
   Birth: 10/04/66

   b. Modify the program so that the birth will be extracted in three parts. Hence the output will be:

   Name: Stephen Spline
   Age: 28
   Height: 1.79
   Weight: 73.8
   Birth: Month: 10
   Day: 04
   Year: 1966

3. a. Write a function named *find_next_token()* that does the same thing as *strtok()* used above. It will have three arguments:
   i. The string from which to extract tokens.
   ii. The current index position inside this string at the time of the call. This argument will be sent by reference, since its position will inevitably move past the word that is being extracted.
   iii. The token found, if any.

   This function will return the value 1 if a token was found; otherwise it will return 0.

   b. Rewrite the program in Examples 20.3.1 and 20.3.2 using the function *find_next_ token()*.

4. Extend the capabilities of text processing in Examples 20.3.1 and 20.3.2 to processing a whole file. The program will accept a file (perhaps a letter) and compress it. That is, all multiple lines and multiple spaces will be eliminated.

   The program will read one line at a time and store it in a variable string named *line_in.* Processing will be performed on it. The characters will be copied into another string variable *line_out.* Lines of text will be read repeatedly into *line_in* and concatenated into *line_out* until either:

   a. The length of the string in *line_out* is too large to contain another token.

   b. A blank line from the input file has been reached.

   In both cases, *line_out* will be sent to the screen.

   Compressing a file is quite a complex operation. The following algorithm should help you get started:

   1. Reset the string *prev_out* to empty.
   2. While the end of the file is not reached, do steps 2.1 to 2.5.
      - 2.1. Read a line of text from the input into *line_in.*
      - 2.2. Reset *line_out* to empty.
      - 2.3. While not all tokens are extracted from *line_in,* do steps 2.3.1 to 2.3.3.
        - 2.3.1. Extract a token.
        - 2.3.2. If inserting this token into the output string, *line_out,* would cause the width to exceed the maximum; do steps 2.3.2.1 and 2.3.2.2.
          - 2.3.2.1. Send *line_out* to the screen without the new token.
          - 2.3.2.2. Reset *line_out* to empty.
        - 2.3.3. Insert the new token into *line_out,* leaving one space after it.
      - 2.4. If either *line_out* is not empty or *prev_out* is not empty, do steps 2.4.1 and 2.4.2.
        - 2.4.1. Send *line_out* to the screen.
        - 2.4.2. Reset *line_out* to empty.
      - 2.5. *line_out* is now the new *prev_out.*

20.4 COMMAND LINE ARGUMENTS

A very useful application to arrays of strings is the access of ***command line arguments.*** The command line is the place on the screen where the operating system's prompt appears and waits for commands. For instance, the following command tells the operating system VMS to mail a letter stored in the file LETTER.OUT. The dollar sign ($) is the VMS system prompt, and *mail letter.out* is the command line:

```
$ mail letter.out
```

Some operating systems do not use a command line interface. Examples include Windows NT, Windows 95, and OS/2. These operating systems use a graphic or windowing interface. If you use this kind of interface rather than a command line interface, then you may skip this section entirely. For those who wish to continue, let us assume we are using the MS-DOS operating system throughout this section.

A command consists of a command verb followed by optional arguments. The command verb refers to the program that executes the command. For instance, in MS-DOS, the command line shown in Figure 20.4.1 lists all of the places in the file LETTER.TXT where the word "Xmas" is found.

Figure 20.4.1

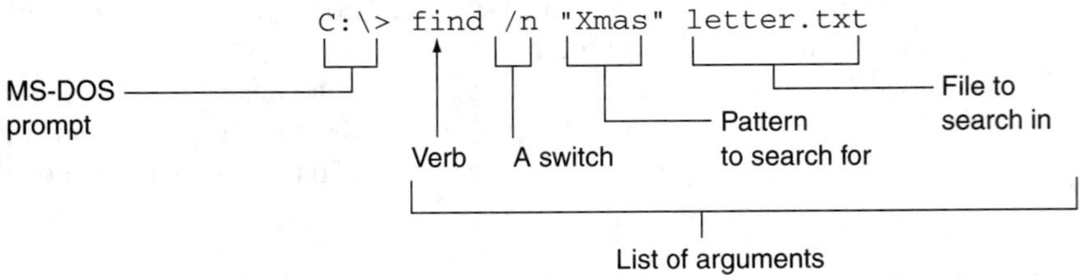

When this command is issued, MS-DOS reads each component as a separate string and puts them in memory, forming an array of strings, as shown in Figure 20.4.2.

Figure 20.4.2

Arguments

0	1	2	3
FIND.EXE	/n	"Xmas"	LETTER.TXT

At this point, as far as C is concerned, each component of the command line, including the verb, is called an ***argument*** [sent to *main()*]. Note that this list of strings is totally external to the program: the operating system looks after it for you. Yet the following example shows one technique that allows your program to access it anyway. Not all operating systems allow a C program to access the command line in the way that will be shown in this section.

20.4.1 THE *argc* AND *argv* PARAMETERS

Example 20.4.1

The following program simply accesses each string from the command line and displays them on the screen. Let us store this program in a file named ECHO_LINE.C.

```
#include <stdio.h>

main(int argc, char * argv[])[1]
{
      int  ctr;

      for (ctr = 0; ctr < argc; ctr++)
      {
            printf("argument #%d is -> |%s|\n", ctr, argv[ctr]);[2]
      }
}
```

When compiled and linked in MS-DOS, this program can be run, and may be provided with arguments:

```
C:\> echo_line   oh! "my", the Canadiens won    3   to   2
argument #0 is -> |C:\ECHO_LINE.EXE|
argument #1 is -> |oh!|
argument #2 is -> |"my",|
argument #3 is -> |the|
argument #4 is -> |Canadiens|
argument #5 is -> |won|
argument #6 is -> |3|
argument #7 is -> |to|
argument #8 is -> |2|
```

Explanations

1. As soon as the program is run, the operating system sends all of the command line arguments to two parameters of the *main()* function:

   ```
   main(int argc, char * argv[])
   ```

   The parameter *argv* holds the number of arguments received, while the parameter *argv* is the list of the arguments; i.e., here it is a list of strings.

With the run above, the parameters are as shown below:

agrc

9

argv	[0]	[1]	[2]	[3]	[4]	[5]	[6]	[7]	[8]
	ECHO_LINE.EXE	oh!	"my",	the	Canadiens	won	3	to	2

2. The counter *ctr* runs from 0 to *argc–1,* which is 8 here. For each execution of the loop, the command line argument *argv[ctr]* is displayed. This is simply a string, so the format code *%s* is needed. In the output, the vertical bars surrounding each string clearly show that the arguments do not contain any blanks. Indeed, in forming the argument list, MS-DOS automatically skips all blanks separating the arguments. For instance, the command line

```
C:\> echo_line      oh!      "my", the Canadiens won         3 to 2
```

would produce the same output as above. Finally, note that the first argument is "ECHO_LINE.EXE," not "echo_line." The content of the first argument is always system dependent, but it also always reflects the verb.

EXERCISES 20.4.1

1. a. Write a command named *my_echo* that simply echoes to the screen whatever is typed on the command line. Example:

```
C:\> echo_line      oh!      "my", the Canadiens won         3 to 2
oh! "my", the Canadiens won 3 to 2
```

   b. Note that the message is compressed automatically. What causes that? Can you think of any way to cancel compression?
2. Write a program that simulates the reading of a command by the operating system. Your program will display a "system" prompt, and then the cursor will wait for a command. Once provided, each component of the command line will be stored in an array of strings. Finally, the content of this array will be echoed to the screen. For instance:

```
%% show users /all/full

Argument 0: "show"
Argument 1: "users"
Argument 2: "/all/full"
```

Do not concern yourself with the meaning of whatever command you provide. Your program is not expected to understand and act upon the command anyway. (***Note:*** No arguments to *main()* are required.)

Example 20.4.1, which was meant solely to explain command line arguments, makes use of them in the simplest possible way. Example 20.4.2 begins to show the true usefulness of the technique: the creation of your own commands!

Example 20.4.2

Let us write a command verb named *compute* that may be used to display the result of a single arithmetic operation. For instance:

```
C:\> compute 9.2 * 2.1
answer = 19.32
```

The procedure has two steps:

The first step is to write a C program that accesses the command line arguments and manipulates them as required. This program **has** to be stored in the file named COMPUTE.C. This will ensure that the command verb generated in the next step will be "compute":

```
#include <stdio.h>
#include <string.h>
#include <stdlib.h>

main(int argc, char *argv[])[1]
{
      float  op1, op2, answer;
      char   operator[2];

      op1 = atof(argv[1]);[2]
      op2 = atof(argv[3]);
      strcpy(operator, argv[2]);
      if (strcmp(operator, "+") == 0)
      {
            answer = op1 + op2;
      }
      else if (strcmp(operator, "-") == 0)
      {
            answer = op1 - op2;
      }
      else if (strcmp(operator, "*") == 0)
      {
            answer = op1 * op2;
      }
      else if (strcmp(operator, "/") == 0)
      {
            answer = op1 / op2;
      }
      printf("Answer = %f\n", answer);
}
```

Explanations

1. The content of the parameters is shown below:

agrc

4

argv

[0]	[1]	[2]	[3]
COMPUTE.EXE	9.2	*	2.1

Note that the names of the parameters *argc* and *argv* were chosen totally arbitrarily; any other name will do. However, they have become standard names, and **you are expected to use them.**

2. The arguments are immediately copied into temporary variables. This is a better practice; the arguments *argc* and *argv* have rather meaningless names.

The second step in the procedure is to compile and link the file COMPUTE.C. The result is the file COMPUTE.EXE. At this point, the command may be used as shown in the above example.

EXERCISES 20.4.2

1. Modify the command *compute* above so that it will be able to perform the following operations:

Operation	Symbol
Exponentiation	**
Quotient	div
Remainder	mod

For instance:

```
C:\> compute 8.3 div 1.9
Answer = 4
C:\> compute 8.3 mod 1.9
Answer = 0.7
```

The remainder is arrived at by the following procedure: 8.3 is divided by 1.9, which results in the answer 4.368421053. Then 4 is subtracted from the answer, which results in the number 0.368421053. Finally, this number is multiplied by 1.9, which gives the remainder 0.7. You may use standard arithmetic functions provided by your C compiler if you wish.

2. a. Modify the command *echo_line* in Exercise 20.4.1, 1, so that if the user does not enter any message, he will be prompted for one. For example:

```
C:\> echo_line
Enter a message:
     oh!      "my", the Canadiens won        3 to 2
oh! "my", the Canadiens won 3 to 2
```

Note that when the message is provided on the command line, its echo on the screen will be compressed automatically, but such is not the case if the message is provided at the prompt "Enter a message:". In that case, your program must perform the compression. (***Hint:*** Use *strtok()* or the method used in Exercise 19.2.1, 3, whichever you prefer.)

b. Include a loop to the program so that the user may enter many messages.

3. a. Create a command named *mycopy* that copies a file. Both the source and the destination file names must be on the command line. (***Hint:*** You may start off with the program in Example 20.2.1.) The two files cannot have the same name.

b. Modify the command so that the user may omit the destination or both file names. The user will be prompted for the missing file names.

4. Return to Example 20.4.2, and note that the conditions to check the operator are rather awkward and long. Indeed, the following solution is much shorter:

```
switch (operator)
{
  case '+': answer = op1 + op2; break;
  case '-': answer = op1 - op2; break;
  case '*': answer = op1 * op2; break;
  case '/': answer = op1 / op2; break;
}
```

but it requires further changes to the code:

a. What should the new declaration be for *operator?*

b. How should *argv[2]* be assigned to it?

SUPPLEMENTARY EXERCISES 20.4

1. Create a command named *tformat* for Exercise 20.3.2, 4, so that the file name and the margin specifications may be entered on the command line. If any argument is not mentioned on the command line, the user will be prompted for it.
2. Create a command named *search* that lists on the screen every line of a file that contains a certain word. The file name and the word for which to search may be entered on the command line. If any argument is not mentioned, the user will be prompted for it.

21 Structures and Enumerated Types

OBJECTIVES

This chapter introduces you to the following information:

- The definition of a structure and how it differs from an array.
- How to use structures in programs.
- Purposes of structures.
- The definition and purposes of enumerated types.
- How to define your own data types.

INTRODUCTION

As programs grow larger and larger, it becomes necessary to find ways to shorten them and make them easier to read. Previous chapters have shown some methods for doing that. This chapter shows how structure data types and enumerated types can also help in that direction. They may especially improve the modularity of a program.

21.1 WHAT IS A STRUCTURE?

A ***structure*** is a collection of data types such as integers or characters. You might notice that this description sounds very similar to that of an array. The fundamental difference is that a structure may group together data of **different** types. Structures are typically used when reading records from a file, but there are other uses as well.

21.1.1 STRUCTURE: A GROUP OF DATA TYPES

Example 21.1.1

Let us write a program that simply asks for your birthdate and then displays it. To appreciate what a structure is, we will look at two solutions that do not use a structure and then a third one that does.

Solution 1. The month, day, and year of birth are stored in separate variables.

```
#include <stdio.h>

main()
{
        int month;          /* date */
        int day;            /* of */
```

```
        int year;          /* birth */

        printf("Enter your birthdate MM/DD/YY > ");
        scanf("%d/%d/%d", &month, &day, &year);
        printf("Your birthdate is %d/%d/%d", month, day, year);
}
```

Solution 2. The month, day, and year of birth are stored in an array.

```
#include <stdio.h>

main()
{
        int date[3];       /* date of birth */

        printf("Enter your birthdate MM/DD/YY > ");
        scanf("%d/%d/%d", &date[0], &date[1], &date[2]);
        printf("Your birthdate is %d/%d/%d", date[0], date[1], date[2]);
}
```

Solution 3. The month, day, and year of birth are stored in a structure.

```
#include <stdio.h>

main()
{
        struct[1]
        {
              int month;
              int day;
              int year;
        } birth;

        printf("Enter your birthdate MM/DD/YY > ");
        scanf("%d/%d/%d", &birth.month, &birth.day, &birth.year);
        printf("Your birthdate is %d/%d/%d",
               birth.month, birth.day, birth.year);[2]
}
```

Explanations

The following explanations are for Solution 3 only.

1. This declaration says that the variable *birth* contains within it the three variables *month, day,* and *year.* These are stored in memory as follows:

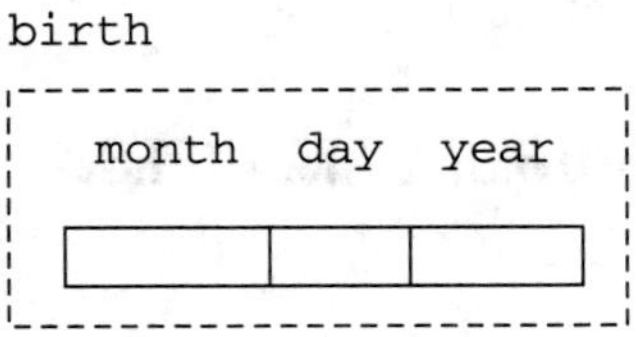

The variable *birth* is like a box with smaller boxes within it. Compare the memory organization of this variable with that of the previous two solutions:

Solution 1

Separate variables:

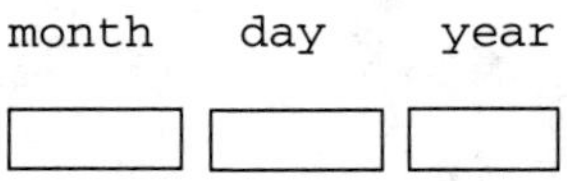

Solution 2

With array:

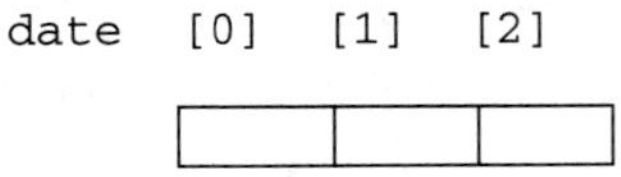

As you can see, the variable *birth* offers the best of both methods of data storage:

a. It has the memory layout of an array (all three variables are adjacent to each other), and
b. It has the advantage of separate variable names that are indicative of the kind of data they hold.

The three variables *month, day,* and *year* make up the structure of the variable *birth;* hence *birth* is called a ***structure variable*** (for brevity's sake, sometimes the term "variable" will be dropped). Also, the three variables within it are called ***members*** of the structure. The syntax of the structure definition is summarized as follows:

```
struct
{
    int month;
    int day;
    int year;
} birth;
```

struct ← Signals the beginning of a structure definition

The actual structure definition: { int month; int day; int year; }

int month; int day; int year; — The members of the structure

} birth; ← Structure variable

The list of all the member definitions is called a ***structure template.***

2. The *printf()* displays the content of the three variables within the structure variable *birth.* The syntax used to identify each variable is as follows:

```
birth.month
```

In this example, *birth* is the name of the box (a structure variable), and *month* is the name of the variable within the box (a member). The dot is actually a binary operator called the ***member reference*** operator. This operator requires the left operand to be a structure variable and the right operand to be a member of that structure. The member operator is used to access a variable within a structure.

EXERCISES 21.1.1

1. In the program above, if the members of the structure were switched as follows:

```
struct
{
    int day;
    int month;
    int year;
} birth;
```

would any changes be necessary in the rest of the program?

2. Suppose a structure variable *measurement* is stored in memory as follows:

measurement

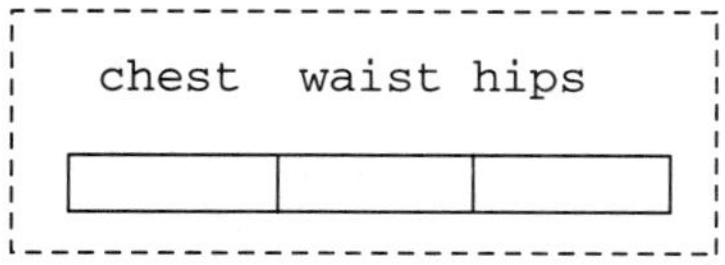

The three variables are of type *float.*
a. Write the declaration for *measurement.*
b. Write the expression to access the variable *waist* and store 29.4 inches in it.

3. The segment below will not compile. Why?

```
main()
{
        struct
        {
                long micro;
                long energy;
        } impact;
```

```
        scanf("%ld%ld", &micro, &energy);
        printf("%ld, %ld", micro, energy);
}
```

4. a. Write a program that uses a structure to store and display time in the format HH:MM:SS.
   b. Improve the program so that it indicates if that time is morning (am) or evening (pm). For instance:

   Enter a time (HH:MM:SS) > <u>15:34:02</u>
   The time is 3:34:02 pm

In Example 21.1.1, all three members of the structure are of the same type. Structures can also contain data of different types. Consider Example 21.1.2.

Example 21.1.2

Let us modify the program of Example 21.1.1 so that the user will also enter his name, age, and height. These three data will be included in the structure:

```
#include <stdio.h>

main()
{
      struct[1]
      {
            char  name[41];
            int   age;
            float height;
            int   month;
            int   day;
            int   year;
      } you;

      printf("Enter your name > ");
      gets(you.name);[2]
      printf("Enter your age > ");
      scanf("%d", &you.age);[2]
      printf("Enter your height > ");
      scanf("%f", &you.height);
      printf("Enter your birthdate MM/DD/YY > ");
      scanf("%d/%d/%d", &you.month, &you.day, &you.year);
     printf("%s, your birthdate is %d/%d/%d",
             you.name, you.month, you.day, you.year);
}
```

Explanations

1. The structure variable *you* will be stored in memory as shown below:

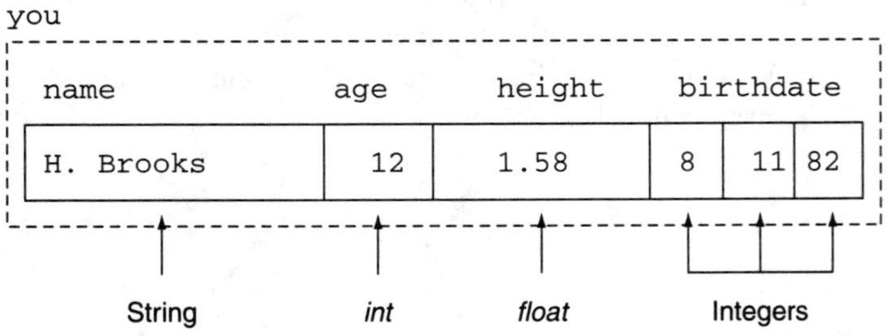

Notice the **different** data types all within the same structure variable *you.* This is probably the main advantage of structures over arrays (which cannot mix types). A structure is said to be a

derived data type because it is constructed from other data types. In contrast, a ***basic data type*** is one that is not derived from other types. For instance, *int* is a basic data type.

2. The name is read into the variable *you.name.* This is the variable *name* within the structure variable *you.* The variable *you.name* is therefore a string variable just like any others we saw in Chapter 18. This implies that the address operator should not be used with *scanf(),* and that each individual character may be accessed. For instance, the character at index 4 is accessed as *you.name[4],* which is the letter 'r' in the illustration.

EXERCISES 21.1.2

1. What are the two main advantages of structures over arrays?
2. Suppose a structure variable *engine* is stored in memory as follows:

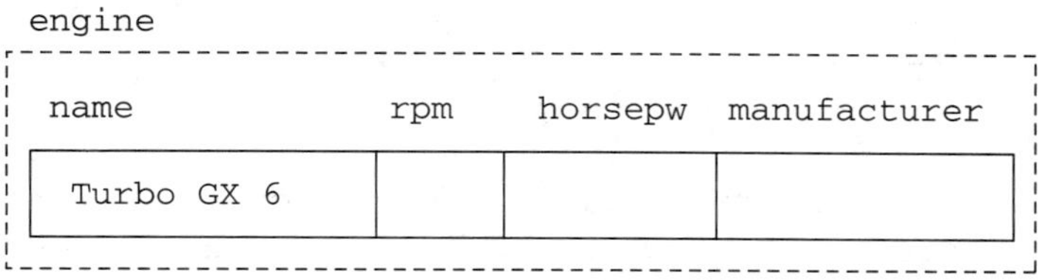

   a. Write the declaration for *engine.*
   b. Write the expression to access the variable *rpm* and store 3400 in it.
   c. Write the expression to access the variable *manufacturer* and store "Douglas" in it.
   d. What is the value of *engine.name[2]?*
3. Write a program that uses a structure to read and display each record below:
   a. A student name, a final mark, and a G.P.A.
   b. A political candidate's name, age, occupation, party represented, and hobby.
   c. A part identification, part name, quantity on stock, cost per unit, and supplier's name.
   d. An author's name, book title, number of pages, publisher's name, and price.
   e. A license number, date of birth, eye color, and height.
   f. An employee's name, occupation, immediate supervisor's name, number of years served, and exact time reported to work today.
   g. An athlete's first and last name, age, date of birth, measurements (chest, waist, hips), height, weight, and country of birth.
   h. A city name, population, and location (longitude and latitude both expressed in degrees, minutes, and seconds and N, W, E, or S).

Structure variables with common member names. Consider the example below.

Example 21.1.3

The following program shows that more than one structure variable may be declared and used:

```
#include <stdio.h>

main()
{
        struct
        {
                int month;
                int day;
                int year;
        } birth, anniv;[1]

        printf("Enter your birthdate MM/DD/YY > ");
        scanf("%d/%d/%d", &birth.month, &birth.day, &birth.year);
```

```
    printf("Enter your anniversary date MM/DD/YY > ");
    scanf("%d/%d/%d", &anniv.month, &anniv.day, &anniv.year);

    printf("Your birthdate is %d/%d/%d",
           birth.month, birth.day, birth.year);
    printf("Your anniversary is on %d/%d/%d",
           anniv.month, anniv.day, anniv.year);
}
```

Explanation

1. The two structure variables will be stored in memory as shown below:

Each has its **own** set of variables *month, day,* and *year.* Even though the variables have the same name, they are stored in different boxes; hence, they cannot be the same variables. Note that structure variables cannot be compared. For instance:

```
if (birth == anniv)
```

is not allowed. However, a whole structure variable may be copied using the assignment operator:

```
struct
{
   int month;
   int day;
   int year;
} anniv, temp;

temp = anniv;
```

The assignment *temp = anniv* copies each member into its corresponding destination member to the left. However, such an assignment is possible only if both variables share the **exact** same structure.

EXERCISES 21.1.3

1. a. Is the following sequence of structures allowed? If so, is there a shorter way of declaring the variables *husband* and *wife?*

```
struct
{
      char name[21];
      int  age;
} husband;

struct
{
      char name[21];
      int  age;
} wife;
```

   b. What is a shorter way of doing the following?

```
strcpy(husband.name, wife.name);
husband.age = wife.age;
```

2. In the following segments, will the compiler complain because the variable *driver* is used twice?

a.
```
struct
{
      float alcohol_level;
      char  driver[31];
} accused;
char driver[31];
```
b.
```
strcpy(accused.driver, driver);
```
c.
```
struct
{
      float alcohol_level;
      char  name[31];
} driver;
char driver[31];
```
3. Back in Exercises 21.1.2, 3, modify each program so that two records are read in and displayed.
4. Modify each program from question 3 above so that the two structure variables are displayed in ascending order determined by a key member. Here is the key to use for each structure:
   a. The student name
   b. The party represented
   c. The part identification
   d. The price of the book
   e. The license number
   f. The exact time reported to work today
   g. The athlete's last name
   h. The city name
5. Extend each program from question 4 to three structure variables.

21.1.2 INTRODUCING STRUCTURES INTO AN ALREADY EXISTING PROGRAM

Sometimes it is better to use a structure than individual variables; other times it is not. This section investigates this quandry, taking a program from a previous chapter and determining whether the use of a structure will be appropriate or not.

Example 21.1.4

Let us rewrite the program in Example 4.3.1 using a structure variable. Here again is that program:

```
#include <stdio.h>

main()
{
    float  hourly_rate;
    int    hours_per_week;
    float  total_income;
    int    num_weeks;
    float  minimum;

    printf("Enter the minimum income acceptable > ");
    scanf("%f", &minimum);
    printf("Enter the hourly wage > ");
    scanf("%f", &hourly_rate);
    printf("Enter the total work hours per week > ");
    scanf("%d", &hours_per_week);
    printf("Enter the number of weeks of work > ");
    scanf("%d", &num_weeks);

    total_income = hourly_rate * hours_per_week * num_weeks;
```

```
    if (total_income >= minimum)
    {
       printf("Take the job!\n");
       printf("You will make $ %.2f this summer\n", total_income);
    }
    else
    {
       printf("Look someplace else for a job.\n");
    }
}
```

We simply need to decide if any variables constitute a group. The variables *hourly_rate, hours_per_week,* and *num_weeks* probably could be grouped because they relate to the specifics of the wages for the job. Let us then put them in a structure variable named *job.* Following is the new program, with changes in bold:

```
#include <stdio.h>

main()

    struct
    {
        float  hourly_rate;
        int    hours_per_week;
        int    num_weeks;
    } job;
    float  total_income;
    float  minimum;

    printf("Enter the minimum income acceptable > ");
    scanf("%f", &minimum);
    printf("Enter the hourly wage > ");
    scanf("%f", &job.hourly_rate);
    printf("Enter the total work hours per week > ");
    scanf("%d", &job.hours_per_week);
    printf("Enter the number of weeks of work > ");
    scanf("%d", &job.num_weeks);

    total_income = job.hourly_rate * job.hours_per_week * job.num_weeks;

    if (total_income >= minimum)   /* if this is true, do next two steps */
    {
        printf("Take the job!\n");
        printf("You will make $ %.2f this summer\n", total_income);
    }
    else   /* otherwise, do the following step */
    {
       printf("Look someplace else for a job.\n");
    }
}
```

It is pleasantly surprising that so few changes are necessary! Admittedly, this example will not convince you of the usefulness of structures. Its purpose is only to show that structures may be used to put related variables together. The question of why and when structures are useful will be fully answered later in the chapter.

EXERCISES 21.1.4

1. For the following programs, would the introduction of a structure be appropriate? If so, name the members and make all the necessary changes. If not, explain.
   a. Example 5.1.1

b. Exercise 4.3.2, 9
c. Example 5.1.2
d. Example 5.1.4
e. Exercise 5.1.7, 5
f. Example 6.1.2
g. Exercise 14.1.2, 3. Also, the program should find the smallest and the largest grade.
h. Exercise 14.1.2, 5. Also, the program should find the smallest and the largest grade.
i. Example 12.1.2
j. Exercises 8.2.3, 4

2. Change the program of Exercise 14.1.3, 7, so that the histogram will look like this:

```
Stacked Histogram
++++***########&
4   3 8        1
```

The program will read all of the grades and increment the counters, exactly as done currently, except that the array of counters will be a member of a structure. Another member will be an array of symbols, one for each letter grade.

21.1.3 EMBEDDED STRUCTURES AND TAGS

Declaring embedded structures. The following example introduces embedded structures and how they are declared.

Example 21.1.5

In the structure definition of Example 21.1.2, it is no longer obvious that the members *month, day,* and *year* make up a birthdate:

```
struct
{
      char  name[41];
      int   age;
      float height;
      int   month;
      int   day;
      int   year;
} you;
```

It would be best to keep these three variables in the structure variable called *birth* that we had earlier. This leads to the following program:

```
#include <stdio.h>

main()
{
      struct
      {
            char  name[41];
            int   age;
            float height;
            struct[1]
            {
                  int   month;
                  int   day;
                  int   year;
            } birth;
      } you;

      printf("Enter your name > ");
      gets(you.name);
```

```
        printf("Enter your age > ");
        scanf("%d", &you.age);
        printf("Enter your height > ");
        scanf("%f", &you.height);
        printf("Enter your birthdate MM/DD/YY > ");
        scanf("%d/%d/%d", &you.birth.month,
                          &you.birth.day, &you.birth.year);[2]
        printf("%s, your birthdate is %d/%d/%d",
                you.name,
               you.birth.month, you.birth.day, you.birth.year);
}
```

Explanations

1. A structure variable *birth* is defined within the structure variable *you;* i.e., it is an ***embedded structure.*** The memory layout is now as shown below:

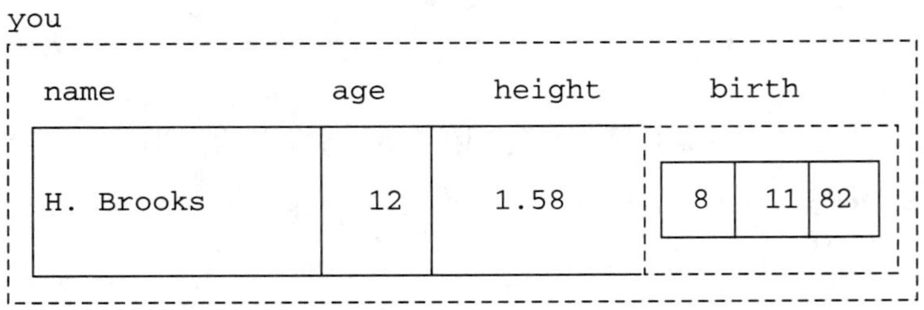

2. The data is stored within the variables *month, day,* and *year* as follows:

   `you.birth.month`

   The variable *month* is within the structure variable *birth,* which is within the structure variable *you.* Note that the member reference operator (the dot) needs to be used twice in order to reach the variable *month.*

EXERCISES 21.1.5

1. a. For which structure definitions in Exercises 21.1.2, 3e to h, would the introduction of embedded structures be appropriate? What would the embedded definition be?
   b. Redo the corresponding programs from Exercise 21.1.3, 5, with these new structures defined in (a).
2. Are the following structure definitions allowed? If so, write the expression that leads to each of the members.
   a.
```
struct
{
        char name[21];
        int  education_level;
        struct
        {
              int  age;
              char name[21];
        } patient;
} doctor;
```
   b.
```
struct
{
        long id;
        int  age;
        struct
        {
```

```
                int age[5];
                char name[5][21];
            }
            children;
        }
        babysitter;
```

Defining tags. Tags may be used as a means of identifying structure templates. Consider the example below.

Example 21.1.6

In Example 21.1.5, the declaration of the structure variable *you* is now a little too long. Also, since the date structure (month, day, year) is very commonly used, it should not be made an integral part of the structure variable *you.* Rather, it should be defined separately. This way, it may be used in any structure. This leads to the following modified program:

```
#include <stdio.h>

main()
{
        struct date1
        {
                int   month;
                int   day;
                int   year;
        } ;
        struct person
        {
                char  name[41];
                int   age;
                float height;
                struct date birth;2
        } ;
        struct person you;2

        printf("Enter your name > ");3
        gets(you.name);
        printf("Enter your age > ");
        scanf("%d", &you.age);
        printf("Enter your height > ");
        scanf("%f", &you.height);
        printf("Enter your birthdate MM/DD/YY > ");
        scanf("%d/%d/%d", &you.birth.month,
                          &you.birth.day, &you.birth.year);
        printf("%s, your birthdate is %d/%d/%d",
                you.name,
                you.birth.month, you.birth.day, you.birth.year);
}
```

Explanations

1. The approach here is to define the structure **templates** and the declaration of the structure **variables** separately. First the templates are defined. The two *struct* statements define the structure templates tagged *date* and *person:*

```
struct date ◄──────────────── Tag
{
      int   month;
      int   day;
      int   year;
} ; ◄──────────────────────── Note: no variable
struct person ◄────────────── Tag
{
      char  name[41];
      int   age;
      float height;
      struct date birth;
} ; ◄──────────────────────── Note: no variable
```

At this point, no variables are defined yet. The compiler is waiting for variables to use these templates.

2. These tags are then referred to in order to define the structure variables. For instance, the declaration:

   ```
   struct person you;
   ```

   declares a structure variable *you* of type *struct person,* where *person* is the tag referring to the structure above. Another way to phrase this is: the variable *you* is an ***instance*** of the structure tagged by *person.* The structures themselves do not occupy any memory; an instance of it does. Picture the structure template as the blueprint of a house; the structure variable is the house once it is built.
3. Note that the rest of the program does not change at all! Members of the structure variable *you* are still accessed in the exact same way as in Example 21.1.5. Can you see how it is so?

EXERCISES 21.1.6

1. a. What is a tag? What is it used for?
   b. What is a structure template? How does it differ from a structure variable?
2. The use of tags makes a program more flexible. In Example 21.1.5, the structure for the date (month, day, year) is a structure very commonly needed. For example, let's look at a structure that gathers the date of various important events at a college, such as the registration deadline, the commencement of classes, and the end of classes:

   ```
   struct
   {
         char college_name[81];
         char address[81];
         struct
         {
               int month;
               int day;
               int year;
         } registration;
         struct
         {
               int month;
               int day;
               int year;
         } start_classes;
         struct
         {
               int month;
               int day;
               int year;
   ```

```
        } end_classes;
    } events;
```

This declaration is cumbersome. Define a tagged structure and simplify this code.

3. In Examples 21.1.1 and 21.1.2, would the use of a tag be advantageous?
4. Redo Exercise 21.1.5, 1, so that tagged structures are defined.
5. Redefine the structures in Exercise 21.1.5, 2, using tagged structures.
6. Redefine the structures in Exercise 21.1.4, 1, using tagged structures.

Be wary of self-referential structures. Remember that ***self-referential*** structures are not allowed. For instance:

```
struct family
{
     char name[81];
     int  num_children;
     struct family in_law;
} ;
```

struct family in_law; is of type *struct family,* the same type as the structure of which it is a member. This sort of self-referential declaration is not allowed.

Scope of tags. The example below will show that tags obey the same scoping rules as do variables.

Example 21.1.7

The program below is the same as that of Example 21.1.6, except that the structure templates are defined globally, not locally to *main().*

```
#include <stdio.h>

struct date
{
      int   month;
      int   day;
      int   year;
} ;

struct person
{
      char   name[41];
      int    age;
      float  height;
      struct date birth;
} ;

main()
{
      struct person you;

      printf("Enter your name > ");
      gets(you.name);
      printf("Enter your age > ");
      scanf("%d", &you.age);
      printf("Enter your height > ");
      scanf("%f", &you.height);
      printf("Enter your birthdate MM/DD/YY > ");
      scanf("%d/%d/%d", &you.birth.month,
                        &you.birth.day, &you.birth.year);
}
```

Why define structure templates globally? Because they become visible to the whole program. The exact same scoping rules covered in Chapters 10 and 11 apply to structure template definitions as well.

EXERCISE 21.1.7

Is there anything wrong with the following program?

```
struct meeting
{
        char  place[41];
        struct time in, out;
} ;

struct time
{
        int   hour;
        int   min;
        int   sec;
} ;

main()
{
        struct meeting annual;

        printf("Enter the place of the meeting > ");
        gets(annual.place);
        printf("Enter the starting time > ");
        scanf("%d:%d:%d", &annual.in.hour,
                          &annual.in.min, &annual.in.min);
        printf("Enter the finish time > ");
        scanf("%d:%d:%d", &annual.out.hour,
                          &annual.out.min, &annual.out.min);
}
```

21.1.4 INITIALIZATION OF STRUCTURES

A structure may be initialized either at declaration time or later. The following examples show various ways to initialize a structure.

At declaration time. The examples below show how to initialize a structure at declaration time.

Example 21.1.8

Back in Example 21.1.2, the structure variable *you* could be initialized as follows:

```
struct
{
        char  name[41];
        int   age;
        float height;
        int   month;
        int   day;
        int   year;
} you = { "H. Brooks", 12, 1.58, 8, 11, 82 };
```

The structure variable is initialized with a list of data within braces in exactly the same way as an array is initialized. Each data in the list initializes the corresponding member.

Example 21.1.9

In Example 21.1.6, the variables *you* and *me* could have been initialized as follows:

```
struct person you = { "H. Brooks", 12, 1.58, { 8, 11, 82 } },
              me = { "A. Fisher", 9, 1.38, { 1, 29, 85 } };
```

Note the use of embedded braces. They indicate the initialization of the structure variable *birth* within the structure variables *you* and *me.*

At run time. Example 21.1.10 shows how to initialize a structure at run time.

Example 21.1.10

Of course, each member of a structure may be initialized separately using the assignment operator:

```
strcpy(you.name, "H. Brooks");
you.age = 12;
you.height = 1.58;
you.birth.day = 8;
you.birth.month = 11;
you.birth.year = 82;
```

Example 21.1.11

Naturally, members may be omitted in an initialization; in that case, their value defaults to 0 (or empty for strings). For example:

```
struct person you = { "H. Brooks", 12, 1.58 },
              me = { "A. Fisher", 9, 1.38, { 1, 29 } };
```

is equivalent to:

```
strcpy(you.name, "H. Brooks");       strcpy(me.name, "A. Fisher");
you.age = 12;                        you.age = 9;
you.height = 1.58;                   you.height = 1.38;
you.birth.day = 0;                   you.birth.day = 1;
you.birth.month = 0;                 you.birth.month = 29;
you.birth.year = 0;                  you.birth.year = 0;
```

The process of initializing a structure, whether at declaration time or later, is termed ***populating*** the structure.

EXERCISES 21.1.8

1. Initialize the structure in Exercises 21.1.3, 3a to d, to the data below:
   a. A student name of "Stephane Smith," a final mark of 81, and a G.P.A. of 3.63
   b. An candidate name of "Vladimir Ruskim," 46 years old, teacher, Communist Party, hobby is making vodka
   c. A part identification of 10038, part name of water filter, 13 of them in stock, $180.99 per unit, the supplier is "Aquafine"
   d. The author's name is "McLeod, book title is "The Joy of C," 750 pages, publisher's name is "Westman and Co.," $47.99
2. Initialize at declaration time the structures used in Exercise 21.1.6, 4, to the following:
   a. A license number of 676501, date of birth 08/21/66, eye color green, and a height of 1.79 meters
   b. Employee name of "Maluski," occupation of "Decorator," immediate supervisor's name is "Clark," 12 years served, reported to work today at 7:59:34
   c. An athlete's first and last name of "Chris" and "Meehan," 12 years old, born on 11/31/76, measurements of 42, 33, and 38 inches, height of 1.95 meters, 75 kg, born in Canada

d. A city name of "Springfield"; population of 93,305; longitude 59 degrees, 28 minutes, 3 seconds N, latitude 38 degrees, 18 minutes, 55 seconds

3. Initialize the structures in questions 1 and 2 using a sequence of assignments.

21.1.5 COMMON ERRORS AND TRAPS

Use the following information to avoid common programming errors:

1. Do not initialize the structure instead of the structure **variable.** For example:

```
struct
{
        char  name[41] = "H. Brooks";
        int   age = 12;
        float height = 1.58;
        int   month = 8;
        int   day = 11;
        int   year = 82;
} you;
```

   This is not valid because the structure template itself does not occupy any memory. It is **not** a variable; *you* is.

2. Do not initialize at the wrong place. For example:

```
struct
{
        char name[41];
        int   age;
        float height;
        int   month;
        int   day;
        int   year;
} you;

you = { "H. Brooks", 12, 1.58, 8, 11, 82 };
```

   The compiler will complain. This sort of initialization is allowed only at declaration time.

3. Do not think that a tag is a variable. For example:

```
struct person me;
strcpy(person.name, "Ted");
```

   The compiler will complain. Although it looks like *person* is a variable, you have to visualize it as a tag that identifies the structure template that it represents.

4. Do not think that a tag is a type. For example:

```
struct date
{
        int month;
        int day;
        int year;
} ;

date birth;
```

   The tag *date* by itself is rather meaningless. The keyword *struct* must accompany it.

5. Do not forget the semicolon at the end of a structure definition. For example:

```
struct date
{
        int month;
```

```
        int day;
        int year;
}
```

The ; is missing on the last line of code.

6. Do not attempt to compare two structures as a unit. This cannot be done. Each member must be compared separately.
7. Do not attempt to read or display a structure's content with a single I/O statement. For example:

```
struct date birth;

printf("Enter your birthdate MM/DD/YY > ");
scanf("%d/%d/%d", &birth);
```

Each member **must** be read into and displayed individually.

8. Do not define a structure that is self-referential.

21.2 MISCELLANEOUS ISSUES CONCERNING STRUCTURES

Many other miscellaneous issues about structures have been grouped into this section.

21.2.1 AN ARRAY OF STRUCTURES

An array of structures is no different in concept than an array of any other data type. It is simply a grouping of structure variables in memory. Such an array is ideal for reading in records from a file into memory (more on that in Section 22.2). The example below shows how an array of structures is accessed.

Example 21.2.1

The following program simply displays the content of an array of structures previously initialized. The structure templates used are the same as in the previous section.

```
#include <stdio.h>

struct date
{
        int   month;
        int   day;
        int   year;
} ;

struct person
{
        char  name[41];
        int   age;
        float height;
        struct date birth;
} ;

main()
{
        int           i;
        struct person list[4] = { { "Dooley", 33, 1.62, { 10, 23, 62 } },
                                  { "Leach", 22, 1.55, { 3, 7, 73 } },
                                  { "Presley", 42, 1.66, { 1, 1, 52 } },
                                  { "Corey", 18, 1.78, { 8, 4, 76 } } };[1]
```

```
        for (i=0; i < 4; i++)
        {
              printf("Record #%d\n", i+1);
              printf("Name: %s\n", list[i].name);
              printf("Age: %d , height: %7.2f\n", list[i].age,
                     list[i].height);
              printf("Birthdate MM/DD/YY: %d/%d/%d\n",
                     list[i].birth.month, list[i].birth.day,
                     list[i].birth.year);[2]
        }
}
```

Explanations

1. The array *list* consists of four elements of type *struct person.* In other terms, it consists of four structures.
2. The loop asks for the data to be stored in each structure of the array. The index *i* identifies the structure into which data is being stored. For instance, with *i* equal to 1, the term *list[1]* refers to a whole structure and the variable *list[1].birth.month* refers to variable *month* within that structure, as shown below:

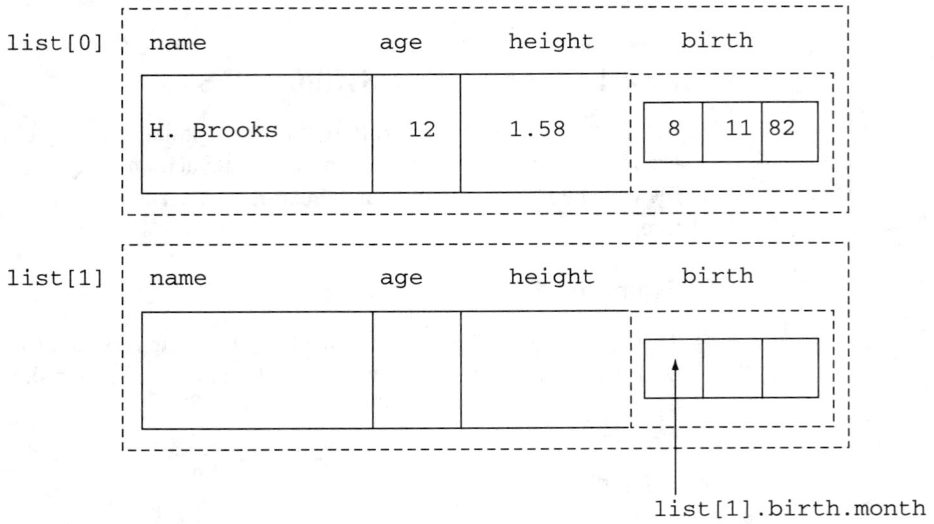

and so on. Thus, an array of structures is somewhat like a generalized 2-D array containing different data types: each structure constitutes a row, and across the array, members of the same name constitute a column.

EXERCISES 21.2.1

1. Consider the following declaration:

```
struct
{
      char   name[41];
      float  salary;
      char   duties_desc[4][81];
} employee, list[50];
```

a. Explain the difference between *employee.name[5]* and *employee[5].name.* Which one is valid here?
b. What is the expression for the 21st character in the text description for the second duty of the variable *employee?*

c. What is the expression for the 21st character in the text description for the second duty of the 49th employee in the array *list?*

2. Suppose an array of structures named *stock* is stored in memory as shown:

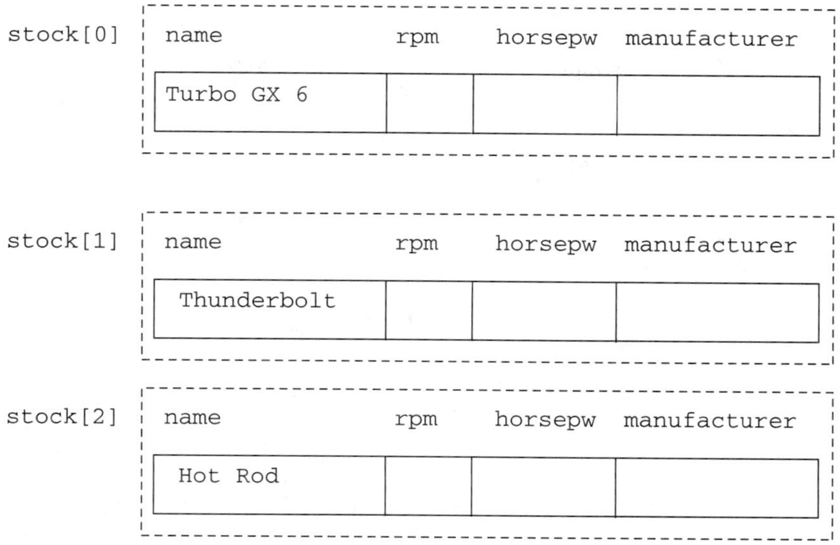

a. Write the declaration for *stock.*

b. Write the expression to access the variable *rpm* of the second structure and store 3400 in it.

c. Write the expression to access the variable *manufacturer* of the third structure and store "Douglas" in it.

d. What is the value of *stock[2].name[6]?*

3. Describe a few similarities and differences between a 2-D array and an array of structures.

4. Change the following structure variable into an array of structures that can still retain the same information:

```
struct
{
        char    city_name[8][51];
        int     population[8];
        float   area[8];
        int     age[8];
} cities;
```

5. The situation in Exercise 21.1.4, 2, may be approached differently. Define an array of four structures, one for each letter grade. Each structure will consist of a counter and the symbol to use to form the bar. Make the necessary modifications to the program.

Example 21.2.1 showed how to display data from an array of structures. The following example simply shows how to read data into an array of structures.

Example 21.2.2

Let us modify the program in Example 21.2.1 so that it reads the data from the screen:

```
#include <stdio.h>


struct date
{
        int    month;
        int    day;
        int    year;
} ;
```

```
struct person
{
      char  name[41];
      int   age;
      float height;
      struct date birth;
} ;
main()
{
      struct person list[4];[1]
      int           i;

      for (i=0; i < 4; i++)
      {
            printf("Enter a name > ");
            gets(list[i].name);[2]
            printf("Enter the age > ");
            scanf("%d", &list[i].age);[2]
            printf("Enter the height > ");
            scanf("%f", &list[i].height);
            printf("Enter the birthdate MM/DD/YY > ");
            scanf("%d/%d/%d", &list[i].birth.month,
                              &list[i].birth.day, &list[i].birth.year);
      }
}
```

Explanations

1. Of course, the array need not be initialized.
2. Note the placement of the address operator:

   ```
   &list[i].age
   ```

   This is the address of the variable *age* within the structure *list[i]*. To enforce that the address operator be applied correctly, the parentheses may be used—*&(list[i].age)*—although this is unnecessary. Note also the absence of the address operator with the member *name*: *list[i].name*. Of course, this is because *name* is a string variable; hence it already contains the address.

EXERCISES 21.2.2

1. Define an array of structures of the kind used in Exercises 21.1.2, 3a to d. Data from a file will be stored in these structures.
2. Define an array of structures of the kind used in Exercise 21.1.6, 3. Data from a file will be stored in these structures.

21.2.2 ACCESSING AN ARRAY OF STRUCTURES VIA A POINTER

Using the pointer operator. In Chapter 16 we saw that an array may be accessed via a pointer. Thus, it should be possible to do the same with an array of structures. The following examples illustrate this concept.

Example 21.2.3

Let us modify the program in Example 21.2.1 so that the structure array *list* is traversed via a pointer instead of an index:

```
#include <stdio.h>

struct date
```

```
{
    int   month;
    int   day;
    int   year;
} ;


struct person
{
    char  name[41];
    int   age;
    float height;
    struct date birth;
} ;

main()
{
    struct person * ptr;[1]
    int             i;
    struct person   list[4] = { { "Dooley", 33, 1.62, { 10, 23, 62 } },
                                { "Leach", 22, 1.55, { 3, 7, 73 } },
                                { "Presley", 42, 1.66, { 1, 1, 52 } },
                                { "Corey", 18, 1.78, { 8, 4, 76 } } };

    for (i=0, ptr=&list[0]; ptr <= &list[3]; ptr++, i++)[2]
    {
          printf("Record #%d\n", i+1);
          printf("Name: %s\n", ptr->name);[3]
          printf("Age: %d , height: %7.2f\n", ptr->age, ptr->height);
          printf("Birthdate MM/DD/YY: %d/%d/%d\n",
                 ptr->birth.month, ptr->birth.day, ptr->birth.year);
    }
}
```

Explanations

1. The variable *ptr* is meant to point to a data of type *struct person;* i.e., it points to a structure.
2. The pointer is made to start at the address of the first structure and move all the way to the last one:

   ```
   for (i=0, ptr=&list[0]; ptr <= &list[3]; ptr++, i++)[2]
   ```

   &list[0] is the address of the first structure; *&list[3]* is the address of the last structure, and *ptr++* moves the pointer to the next structure.
3. To access the members of a particular structure, simply make the pointer *ptr* go to it with the ***pointer operator*** (–>). For instance, suppose that *ptr* points to *list[0];* then *ptr–>birth.month* is as shown below:

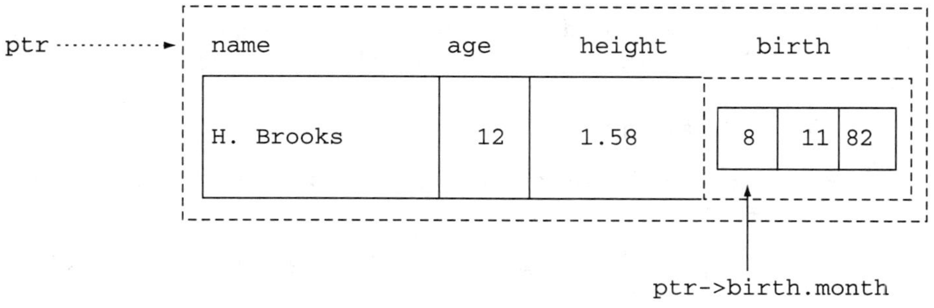

Note that the value of *ptr* remains fixed during this particular access.

Example 21.2.4

Let us modify the program in Example 21.2.2 so that the structure array *list* is traversed via a pointer instead of an index:

```
#include <stdio.h>

struct date
{
      int   month;
      int   day;
      int   year;
} ;
struct person
{
      char  name[41];
      int   age;
      float height;
      struct date birth;
} ;

main()
{
      struct person   list[4];
      struct person * ptr;

      for (ptr=&list[0]; ptr <= &list[3]; ptr++)
      {
            printf("Enter a name > ");
            gets(ptr->name);
            printf("Enter the age > ");
            scanf("%d", &ptr->age);1
            printf("Enter the height > ");
            scanf("%f", &ptr->height);
            printf("Enter the birthdate MM/DD/YY > ");
            scanf("%d/%d/%d", &ptr->birth.month,
                              &ptr->birth.day, &ptr->birth.year);
            fflush(stdin);          /* remove the trailing '\n' */
      }
}
```

Explanation

1. Note the placement of the address operator:

   `&ptr->age`

   This is the address of the variable *age* within the structure *list[i]*, to which *ptr* points. To enforce that the address operator is applied correctly, the parentheses may be used—*&(ptr–>age)* —although it is unnecessary.

Using the dereferencing operator. The dereferencing operator * may be used in place of the pointer operator –>, as Example 21.2.5 shows.

Example 21.2.5

The following segment is taken from Example 21.2.4. The pointer operator is replaced with the dereferencing operator:

```
      for (ptr=&list[0]; ptr <= &list[3]; ptr++)
      {
            printf("Enter a name > ");
            gets((*ptr).name);1
```

```
            printf("Enter the age > ");
            scanf("%d", &(*ptr).age);
            printf("Enter the height > ");
            scanf("%f", &(*ptr).height);
            printf("Enter the birthdate MM/DD/YY > ");
            scanf("%d/%d/%d", &(*ptr).birth.month,
                              &(*ptr).birth.day, &(*ptr).birth.year);
            fflush(stdin);
        }
}
```

Explanation

1. The expression *(*ptr).name* is evaluated in two parts: The parentheses force **ptr* to be evaluated first. This tells the pointer to go to the structure it is pointing to; then *.name* tells the program to go to the member for the name. The pointer operator –> performs these two steps all at once, so it is preferred.

EXERCISES 21.2.3

1. Rewrite the following segments without the use of a pointer:
   a.
   ```
   struct person   george;
   struct person * ptr = &george;

   printf("What is his name > ");
   gets(ptr->name);
   printf("Enter his age > ");
   scanf("%d", &ptr->age);
   ```
   b.
   ```
   struct person   class[25];
   struct person * ptr = &class[24];

   printf("What is his name > ");
   gets((*ptr).name);
   printf("Enter his age > ");
   scanf("%d", &(*ptr).age);
   ```
2. Given the following declarations:
   ```
   struct person list[4] = { { "Dooley", 33, 1.62, { 10, 23, 62 } },
                             { "Leach", 22, 1.55, { 3, 7, 73 } },
                             { "Presley", 42, 1.66, { 1, 1, 52 } },
                             { "Corey", 18, 1.78, { 8, 4, 76 } } };
   struct person * ptr = &list[0];
   ```
   what will be displayed for each of the following segments? Indicate any errors.
   a. `printf("%s", ptr->name);`
   b. `printf("%s", (*ptr).name);`
   c. `ptr = ptr + 2;`
      `printf("%d", ptr->age);`
   d. `printf("%c", *ptr->name);`
   e. `ptr = ptr + 1;`
      `printf("%c", *ptr.name);`
   f. `printf("%f", (ptr+2)->height);`
   g. `ptr = list + 2;`
      `printf("%c", *(ptr->name + 6));`
3. Is each expression below valid? If so, display the equivalence using the dereferencing operator:
   a. `ptr->name`
   b. `(ptr+3)->age`
   c. `*ptr->name`
   d. `(*ptr)->height`

21.2.3 PASSING/RETURNING A STRUCTURE TO/FROM A FUNCTION

Passing the structure by value (and returning). Again, this process is accomplished just as with any other array. A single example will suffice.

Example 21.2.6

Back in the program from Example 21.1.7, let us introduce a function named *read_struct()* that stores the data into a structure and then returns it, and a function named *display_struct()* that displays the information within a structure passed to it. Here is what we get:

```
#include <stdio.h>

struct date[1]
{
      int   month;
      int   day;
      int   year;
} ;
struct person
{
      char  name[41];
      int   age;
      float height;
      struct date birth;
} ;

struct person read_struct(void)[2]
{
      struct person temp;

      printf("Enter your name > ");
      gets(temp.name);
      printf("Enter your age > ");
      scanf("%d", &temp.age);
      printf("Enter your height > ");
      scanf("%f", &temp.height);
      printf("Enter your birthdate MM/DD/YY > ");
      scanf("%d/%d/%d", &temp.birth.month,
                        &temp.birth.day, &temp.birth.year);
      return temp;[3]
}

void display_struct(struct person some)[4]
{
      printf("Name: %s\n", some.name);
      printf("Age: %d , height: %7.2f\n", some.age, some.height);
      printf("Birthdate MM/DD/YY: %d/%d/%d\n",
             some.birth.month, some.birth.day, some.birth.year);
}

main()
{
      struct person you;

      you = read_struct();[3]
      display_struct(you);[4]
}
```

Explanations

1. Note that the structure templates have to be declared globally. (Why is this the case?)
2. The header of the function *read_struct()* indicates that it returns a data of type *struct person.*
3. The whole structure *temp* is returned and copied into the variable structure *you.* That is, each member is copied as shown below:

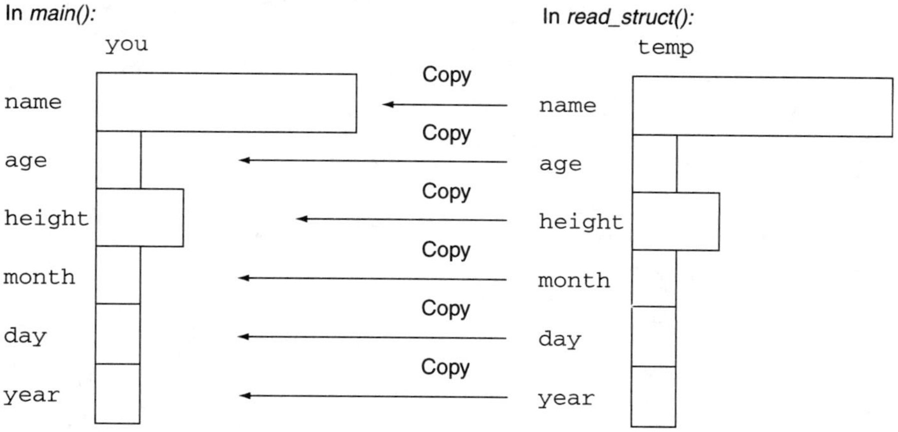

4. Similarly, when a structure is passed to a parameter, the whole structure, here *you,* is copied to the parameter *some.* Unlike arrays, the address is not passed; instead, the whole structure is passed.

In conclusion, even though a structure variable contains variables within it, it is passed and returned to and from a function in exactly the same way as an individual variable would be passed and returned.

EXERCISES 21.2.4

1. What will the following program display?

```
struct rec
{
      char occupation[30];
      int  children;
} b = { "teacher", 3 };

fcn1(struct rec a)
{
      a.children = 5;
}

fcn2(struct rec b)
{
      strcpy(b.occupation, "Homemaker");
      fcn1(b);
}

main()
{
      fcn2(b);
      printf("%s  %d", b.occupation, b.children);
}
```

2. Is there anything wrong with the program below?

```
struct meeting read(void)
{
```

```
        struct meeting ans;

        printf("Enter the place of the meeting > ");
        gets(ans.place);
        printf("Enter the starting time > ");
        scanf("%d:%d:%d", &ans.in.hour,
                          &ans.in.min, &ans.in.min);
        printf("Enter the finish time > ");
        scanf("%d:%d:%d", &ans.out.hour,
                          &ans.out.min, &ans.out.min);
        return ans;
}

main()
{
        struct meeting
        {
                char  place[41];
                struct time in, out;
        } ;

        struct time
        {
                int   hour;
                int   min;
                int   sec;
        } ;

        struct meeting annual;

        annual = read();
}
```

3. Define similar *read_struct()* and *display_struct()* functions for the programs of Exercises 21.1.6, 3 and 4.
4. a. Define a structure template tagged *fraction* to represent a fraction $^a/_b$.
   b. Write a function named *decimal()* that takes a fraction (i.e., a structure as defined in 4a) and returns the decimal equivalent. For instance, the decimal equivalent of $^3/_8$ is 0.375.
   c. Write a function named *numerator()* that returns the numerator of the fraction passed to it.
   d. Write a function named *denominator()* that returns the denominator of the fraction passed to it.
   e. Write a function named *tofraction()* that accepts two numbers and returns the corresponding fraction.
   f. Write a function named *add()* that accepts two fractions and adds them. The result is returned as a fraction.
   g. Write a function named *sub()* that accepts two fractions and subtracts the second one from the first. The result is returned as a fraction.
   h. Write a function named *mult()* that accepts two fractions and multiplies them. The result is returned as a fraction.
   i. Write a function named *div()* that accepts two fractions and divides them. The result is returned as a fraction.
5. Rewrite the functions from the exercises below so that the data passed to and sent back is stored in a structure as appropriate:
   a. The function *in_seconds()* in Supplementary Exercise 10.4, 1. The hours, minutes, and seconds will be in a structure, as well as the total in seconds.
   b. The function *hypothenuse()* in Exercise 11.2.2, 14. All three sides will be in a structure.

c. The function *liquid()* in Exercise 11.2.2, 24. The gallons, quarts, and pints will be in a structure, as well as the total quantity in pints.
d. The function *time()* in Exercise 11.2.2, 25. The days, hours, minutes, and seconds will be in a structure, as well as the total number of seconds.
e. The function *days()* in Exercise 11.2.2, 26. The years, months, and days will be in a structure, as well as the total number of days.
f. The function *money()* in Exercise 11.2.2, 27. The dollars, quarters, dimes, nickels, and pennies will be in a structure, as well as the total amount of money in pennies.

6. Redo Exercise 11.2.2, 28, using the functions in (d) and (e) above.

Passing the structure by reference. Once more, this task is done just as if it were any other array. Consider the example below.

Example 21.2.7

Let us modify the function *read_struct()* from Example 21.2.6 so that the structure is passed as an argument by reference. The function *display_struct()* and the structure templates remain the same, so they are omitted here so that you may concentrate on the codes that do change.

```
/* Template definitions from Example 21.2.6 would go here */

void read_struct(struct person * ptr) [1]
{
        printf("Enter your name > ");
        gets(ptr->name); [2]
        printf("Enter your age > ");
        scanf("%d", &ptr->age); [2]
        printf("Enter your height > ");
        scanf("%f", &ptr->height);
        printf("Enter your birthdate MM/DD/YY > ");
        scanf("%d/%d/%d", &ptr->birth.month,
                          &ptr->birth.day, &ptr->birth.year);
}

/* The display_struct() definition from Example 21.2.6 would go here */

main()
{
        struct person you;

        read_struct(&you); [1]
        display_struct(you);
}
```

Explanations

1. The address of the structure is passed to the function. This means that the parameter must be declared as a pointer to the structure. Suppose that the structure variable *you* begins at address 3250. Here is what happens:

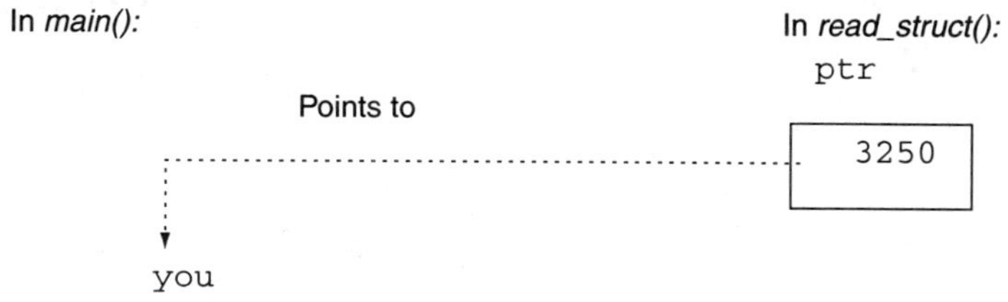

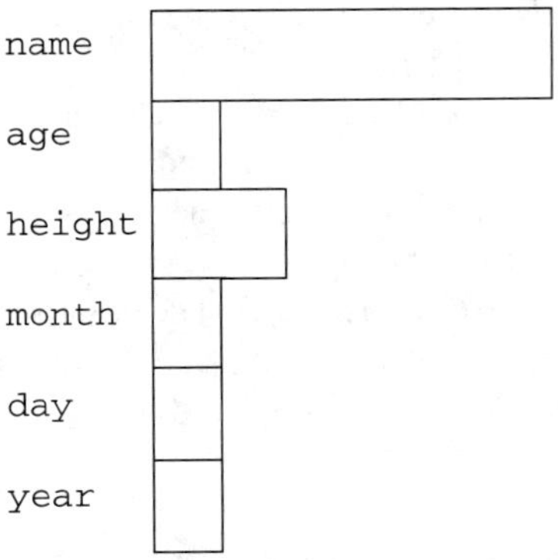

2. Because *ptr* is a pointer, the operator –> (or *) must be used in order to access each member of the structure variable *you.*

EXERCISES 21.2.5

1. a. Define functions *read_struct()* and *display_struct()* appropriate for the problems in Exercises 21.1.2, 3a to d.
   b. Define functions *read_struct()* and *display_struct()* appropriate for the problems in Exercise 21.1.5, 1.
2. Redo Exercises 21.2.4, 5 and 6, with the structure sent back by reference.

21.2.4 INTRODUCING STRUCTURES INTO AN ALREADY EXISTING PROGRAM

In Section 21.1.2, we had already begun this topic of introducing structures into existing programs. Let us now discuss this a little further. Many programs that you have seen and written in the previous 20 chapters could easily have employed structure variables. It is thus fitting that we briefly discuss how structures may be incorporated into these programs. In the process, you will inevitably better understand the true purpose of structures.

Example 21.2.8

Let us introduce an appropriate structure in Example 10.4.1. Here is that program again:

```
#include <stdio.h>

float total(int qty, float unit_cst)
{
   return qty * unit_cst;
}

main()
{
     int   items;
     float cost, owe;

     printf("Enter the number of items bought > ");
     scanf("%d", &items);
     printf("Enter the cost of each item > ");
     scanf("%f", &cost);

     owe = total(items, cost);

     printf("You owe $ %8.2f\n", owe);
}
```

Let us decide that the structure will consist of the number of items, the unit cost, and the total cost. Here is the result, with changes in bold type:

```
#include <stdio.h>

struct bill
{
    int   items;
    float cost, owe;
} ;

float total(struct bill payment)
{
   return payment.items * payment.cost;
}

main()
{
    struct bill pay;

    printf("Enter the number of items bought > ");
    scanf("%d", &pay.items);
    printf("Enter the cost of each item > ");
    scanf("%f", &pay.cost);

    pay.owe = total(pay);

    printf("You owe $ %8.2f\n", pay.owe);
}
```

Note that the template is defined globally. Note also the way that the data is passed to and returned from the function *total()*.

EXERCISES 21.2.6

1. In the program above, introduce a function named *populate()* that asks for the data to be stored in the structure. The structure will be passed to it by reference so that it can be populated.
2. Modify Supplementary Exercise 17.2, 5, so that the coordinates are kept in a structure tagged *coord*. The members will be *x* and *y*.
3. Fill in the blanks so that the member *birth* of the structure *you* is sent be reference to *setdate()*:

```
struct date
{
      int   month;
      int   day;
      int   year;
} ;

struct person
{
      char  name[41];
      int   age;
      float height;
      struct date birth;
} ;

void setdate(______________________________)
{
```

```
        scanf("%d/%d/%d", _______________________________);
}

main()
{
        struct person you;

        setdate(______________________________);
}
```

4. Another very useful application of structures involves situations in which too many arguments are to be passed to a function. Consider Example 12.3.2. The use of global variables allowed the reduction in arguments to be passed. However, global variables are too dangerous, for reasons discussed in Section 12.3. Devise a solution that does not use these nasty variables. Instead, define a structure that has as members the appropriate variables. The structure, rather than the list of variables, will be passed. (***Hint:*** If your answer to Exercise 21.1.4, 1i, is correct, then the structure definition here should be similar, except that the member for the number of dependents is not used in this present question.)
5. Introduce appropriate structures into the program in Exercise 21.1.4, 1j, in order to reduce the number of arguments to send to functions.
6. Introduce appropriate structures into the program in Supplementary Exercise 20.2, 5.
7. Introduce appropriate structures into the program in Supplementary Exercise 20.2, 6.

21.2.5 PASSING AN ARRAY OF STRUCTURES TO A FUNCTION

Arrays of structures are passed to functions in the exact same way as arrays of basic data types. Example 21.2.9 illustrates this concept.

Example 21.2.9

The following program is a modification of the program in Example 21.2.7. It now reads a list of records, not just a single record, into an array:

```
#include <stdio.h>

struct date
{
     int   month;
     int   day;
     int   year;
} ;
struct person
{
     char  name[41];
     int   age;
     float height;
     struct date birth;
} ;

void read_struct(struct person array[], int size)[1]
{
     int           i;

     for (i=0; i < size; i++)
     {
          printf("Enter your name > ");
          gets(array[i].name);
          printf("Enter your age > ");
```

```
            scanf("%d", &array[i].age);
            printf("Enter your height > ");
            scanf("%f", &array[i].height);
            printf("Enter your birthdate MM/DD/YY > ");
            scanf("%d/%d/%d", &array[i].birth.month,
                                &array[i].birth.day, &array[i].birth.year);
            fflush(stdin);
      }
}

void display_struct(struct person array[], in size)[1]
{
      int             i;

      for (i=0; i < size; i++)
      {
            printf("Name: %s\n", array[i].name);
            printf("Age: %d , height: %7.2f\n",
                   array[i].age, array[i].height);
            printf("Birthdate MM/DD/YY: %d/%d/%d\n",
                        array[i].birth.month, array[i].birth.day,
                        array[i].birth.year);
      }
}

main()
{
      struct person list[4];

      read_struct(list, 4);[2]
      display_struct(list, 4);[2]

}
```

Explanations

1. The parameter is defined as an array of structures. Note that the size of the array is also passed.
2. The array of structures is passed to the functions in the same way as would be done with an array of basic data type: only the name of the array is passed. Do not use the address operator.

EXERCISES 21.2.7

1. Rewrite the function *read_struct()* above with pointer notation rather than array notation.
2. Rewrite the function *display_struct()* above with pointer notation rather than array notation.

21.2.6 APPLICATION: THE TIME STRUCTURE AS PREDEFINED IN *time.h*

The time structure is a predefined structure found in the header file *time.h*. It is tagged *tm* and contains the following 12 members:

```
struct tm
{
      int tm_sec;       /* seconds (0 to 59) */
      int tm_min;       /* minutes (0 to 59) */
      int tm_hour;      /* hours (0 to 23) */
      int tm_mday;      /* day of the month (1 to 31) */
```

```
        int tm_mon;        /* months since January (0 to 11) */
        int tm_year;       /* year (since 1900) */
        int tm_wday;       /* days since Sunday (0 to 6) */
        int tm_yday;       /* days since January first (0 to 365) */
        int tm_isdst;      /* Daylight Saving Time flag */
} ;
```

This structure is used by many functions declared in *time.h,* only two of which will be explained here. These functions are quite useful, perhaps as useful as a watch!

Example 21.2.10

The program below uses the *tm* structure and two time functions to display today's time and date:

```
#include <stdio.h>
#include <time.h>

main()
{
        struct tm * hold_ptr;
        time_t      elapse;

        time(&elapse);[1]
        hold_ptr = localtime(&elapse);[2]
        printf("min=%d, hour=%d, day=%d, month=%d, year=%d",
               hold_ptr>tm_min, hold_ptr>tm_hour,[3]
               hold_ptr>tm_mday, hold_ptr>tm_mon, hold_ptr>tm_year);[3]
}
```

Here is a sample run:

min=49, hour=8, day=18, month=6, year=95

In simple language, this says: 49 minutes, 8 o'clock, 18th day of month, 6 (July) 1995

Explanations

1. The function *time(),* declared in the file *time.h,* returns the number of seconds elapsed since January 1, 1980. This is stored in the variable *elapse* of type *time_t.* This type is also defined in the file *time.h.* Note that the variable *elapse* must be sent by reference.
2. Then this variable must be sent again by reference to the function *localtime(),* also declared in the file *time.h.* This function takes the number of seconds and figures from this the data for the 12 members of the structure tagged *tm.* It returns the pointer to the structure, **not** the structure itself.
3. This *printf()* simply displays the content of some of the members of that structure.

EXERCISES 21.2.8

1. a. Write a function named *getdate()* that returns the current date in a structure with three members: the day, the month, and the year.
   b. Rewrite this function so that the current date is sent by reference.
2. a. Write a function named *gettime()* that returns the current time in a structure with three members: the seconds, the minutes, and the hour.
   b. Rewrite this function so that the current time is sent by reference.
3. Revisit Supplementary Exercise 2.4, 4. Currently, the time and date must be entered by the checkout clerk. Modify the program so that the computer will provide the time and date using the functions *gettime()* and *getdate()* above.
4. Just as in question 3 above, modify the program in Exercise 21.2.6, 6, so that the date of processing is stored in the file CHECK.DAT.
5. Just as in question 4 above, modify the program in Exercise 21.2.6, 7, so that the date of processing is stored in each output file.

6. a. Write a function named *DOStime()* that works exactly as the DOS *time* command. Base your solution on Exercise 9.2.2, 11. In addition, the real current time will be retrieved instead of a random one.
   b. Now, build a command named *my_time* that calls the function above. Refer to Section 20.4 to recall how to do this.
7. a. Write a function named *DOSdate()* that works exactly as the DOS *date* command.
   b. Now, build a command named *my_date* that calls the function above.

21.2.7 ALLOCATING STRUCTURES DYNAMICALLY

Arrays of structures are often used to load massive amounts of data in memory. Usually, the memory is allocated dynamically. To allocate memory for structures at run time, naturally, the functions *calloc()* or *malloc()* are used. For instance, to allocate memory for one instance of the structure *struct person* would be done as follows:

```
struct person * ptr;
ptr = calloc(1, sizeof(struct person));
```

The *sizeof(struct person)* is the size in bytes of an instance of the structure *struct person*, as shown in Figure 21.2.1.

Figure 21.2.1

```
struct person
{
        char  name[41];      <--------   sizeof(name)                  = 41
        int   age;           <-------- + sizeof(age)                   =  2
        float height;        <-------- + sizeof(height)                =  4
        struct date birth;   <-------- + sizeof(struct date)   3 x 2   =  6
                                                                        --
                                                                     53 bytes
```

Note that the *struct date* is made of three integer variables, each 2 bytes. The pointer *ptr* would point to a block of 53 bytes. Arithmetically, the structure should occupy 53 bytes, but in reality, it will likely occupy more. This is because some computers require all data to be stored at even addresses, a condition called ***memory alignment.*** Assuming that the structure above begins at address 5000, Figure 21.2.2 shows how it would fit in memory. An extra byte has been allocated to ensure that the variable *age* (and the following ones) are stored at even addresses.

Figure 21.2.2

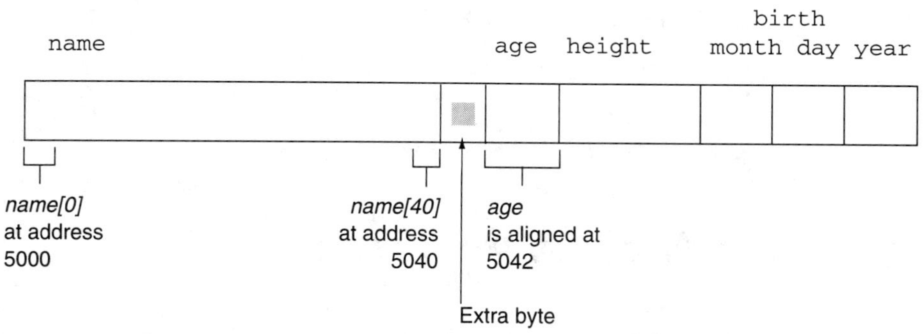

EXERCISES 21.2.9

1. Calculate the memory requirements of the following structures, assuming that no alignment takes place:
   a. struct

```
{
        int   id;
        char  name[21];
        char  address[41];
```

```
            float wages;
    } employee;
```
b.
```
  struct
    {
            char  id;
            char  name[21];
            char  address[41];
            float wages;
    } employee;
```
c.
```
  struct
    {
            char  id[7];
            char  name[21];
            char  address[41];
    } boss;
```
d.
```
  struct
    {
            char  id[8];
            char  name[22];
            char  address[42];
    } boss;
```
2. How much memory will the structures in question 1 actually occupy if memory alignment is performed by the compiler?
3. Write a program that dynamically allocates memory to the list of structures in Example 21.2.9.

21.2.8 COMMON ERRORS AND TRAPS

Use the following information to avoid common programming errors:

1. Do not insert a space between – and > as in *ptr – > name*.
2. Do not forget to use parentheses when referring to a member of a structure via a pointer, such as **ptr.name*.
3. Do not mix up the order in which the operators & and * are applied, as in *&ptr –> age* or *(*ptr) –> age*.
4. Remember that a structure is not automatically passed by reference to a function, as an array is. The address operator must be used.
5. Do not specify the index specification in the wrong location when accessing an array within an array of structures. For example:

   ```
   struct person class[24];
   class.age[0] = 35;
   ```

   when it is meant to access *class[0].age*.

21.3 ENUMERATED DATA TYPES

An enumerated data type is one that accepts only a finite set of values, as specified by the programmer. This section illustrates the mechanics of this data type and its proper use.

21.3.1 DECLARING AN ENUMERATED-TYPE VARIABLE

Example 21.3.1

The following program simply asks for the current season and your favorite season and then displays a message:

```
#include <stdio.h>

main()
```

```
{
      enum[1]
      {
            FALL,
            WINTER,
            SPRING,
            SUMMER
      } this_season, favorite;

   printf("What season are we in (fall=0, winter=1, spring=2, summer=3) ");
   scanf("%d", &this_season);[2]
   printf("What is your favorite season? ");
   scanf("%d", &favorite);[2]
   switch(this_season)
   {
     case FALL: printf("The leaves are falling\n");
                break;
     case WINTER: printf("Bright, white, fluffy snow everywhere\n");
                  break;
     case SPRING: printf("Colorful flowers are coming out\n");
                  break;
     case SUMMER: printf("Let's go to the beach!\n");
                  break;
   }
   if (this_season == favorite)
   {
         printf("This is your favorite season!\n");
   }
}
```

Explanations

1. Note the variable declarations shown below:

```
enum  <-------------------------------- Keyword
{
      FALL,      <---------------- 0  ┐
      WINTER,    <---------------- 1  ├─ Set of valid values
      SPRING,    <---------------- 2  │  (enumerators)
      SUMMER     <---------------- 3  ┘
} this_season, favorite;  <-------- The variables
```

   This statement says that the variables *this_season* and *favorite* may be assigned the names listed within the braces only. These are called the ***enumerators.***
2. Since the content of an enumerated-type variable is really a number (more on this in the paragraph below), *scanf()* is used in the same way as when reading in an integer variable.

Initializing/assigning enumerated-type variables. Enumerated-type variables are initialized and assigned to just as numeric variables are. For instance:

```
this_season = SPRING;
favorite = FALL;
```

are possible assignments. When the compiler sees these statements, it substitutes the names of the enumerators with their respective number in the range of 0 to 3. Here 3 would replace *SPRING* and 0 would replace *FALL.* Thus, the statements

```
this_season = 3;
favorite = 0;
```

are allowed as well, even though the literals 0 and 3 are not in the list of enumerators. However, the following are not acceptable because no enumerators stand for those numbers:

```
this_season = 4;
this_season = 19;
```

Yet, surprisingly, the compiler will not complain! This means that it is the responsibility of the programmer to ensure that only valid values are assigned.

EXERCISES 21.3.1

1. What will be displayed by the following code?

```
enum
{
        red,
        yellow,
        green,
        none
} light, seen;

light = green;
seen = 12;
printf("%d %d %d", light, seen, none);
```

2. Write a program that uses an enumerated-type variable to run the menu for the program in Example 4.4.2. Use appropriate names for the enumerators.

21.3.2 WHY USE ENUMERATED-TYPE VARIABLES?

Since the compiler does not enforce the assignment of valid values into an enumerated-type variable, defining an enumerated type appears useless. Actually, this is not so, for the two reasons given below.

Increased readability. The example below shows that the presence of enumerated-type variables may make a program easier to read.

Example 21.3.2

Consider the following program:

```
main()
{
    int this_season, favorite;

    printf("What season are we in (fall=0, winter=1, spring=2, summer=3) ");
    scanf("%d", &this_season);
    printf("What is your favorite season? ");
    scanf("%d", &favorite);
    switch(this_season)
    {
      case 0: printf("The leaves are falling\n");
              break;
      case 1: printf("Bright, white, fluffy snow everywhere\n");
              break;
      case 2: printf("Colorful flowers are coming out\n");
              break;
      case 3: printf("Let's go to the beach!\n");
              break;
    }
    if (this_season == favorite)
```

```
    {
        printf("This is your favorite season!\n");
    }
}
```

No enumerated-type variable is used, yet the program remains equivalent to that of Example 21.3.1. The main reason for using an enumerated type is that it enables the program to look more meaningful, and hence it becomes easier to read. The advantage of enumerated-type variables is that the names of the enumerators carry the meaning of the numbers for which they stand; i.e., they make the readability of a program more intuitive. Note that usually the enumerators are in capital letters. This practice is followed for the same reason it is followed for symbolic constants, that is, to clearly differentiate them from variables.

A comparison with *#define*. The advantage of enumerated-type variables mentioned above is identical to that of symbolic constants. So which method to use? Example 21.3.3 helps you decide for yourself.

Example 21.3.3

The *#define* preprocessor command is an alternative to an enumerated type. Thus the program in Example 21.3.1 could be coded as follows:

```
#include <stdio.h>

#define FALL    0
#define WINTER  1
#define SPRING  2
#define SUMMER  3

main()
{
   int  this_season, favorite;

   printf("What season are we in (fall=0, winter=1, spring=2, summer=3) ");
   scanf("%d", &this_season);
   printf("What is your favorite season? ");
   scanf("%d", &favorite);
   switch(this_season)
   {
     case FALL: printf("The leaves are falling\n");
                break;
     case WINTER: printf("Bright white, fluffy snow everywhere\n");
                break;
     case SPRING: printf("Colorful flowers are coming out\n");
                break;
     case SUMMER: printf("Let's go to the beach!\n");
                break;
   }
   if (this_season == favorite)
      {
         printf("This is your favorite season!\n");
      }
}
```

Indeed, it does not really matter which approach is taken. Nevertheless, keep the following two observations in mind:

1. With an enumerated type, the enumerators are automatically assigned values.
2. Symbolic constants defined with *#define* do not necessarily occupy the same amount of memory as their *enum* counterparts. They usually occupy less space.

21.3.3 SETTING THE VALUES OF THE ENUMERATORS

Example 21.3.4

By default, the enumerators are always set 0, 1, 2, 3, etc. The programmer may change this, however. Here are two examples:

```
1. enum season { FALL=1,              Set to 1
                 WINTER,              Set to 2
                 SPRING,              Set to 3
                 SUMMER               Set to 4
               } this_season;
2. enum season { FALL=7,              Set to 7
                 WINTER,              Set to 8
                 SPRING=3,            Set to 3
                 SUMMER               Set to 4
               } this_season;
```

The enumerators that are not explicitly set to a number will receive a number that follows the ascending sequence that starts with the last enumerator explicitly set. The exercises below will give you a chance to better understand this. Note that the enumerators also may all be listed on one line:

```
enum season { FALL=7, WINTER, SPRING=3, SUMMER } this_season;
```

EXERCISES 21.3.2

1. What will be displayed by the following code segments?

a.
```
enum
{
      red,
      yellow = 4,
      green,
      blink = 1,
      none
} light, seen;

light = green;
seen = red + 8 * yellow;
printf("%d %d %d", light, seen, none);
```

b.
```
enum
{
      red = 'R',
      yellow = 'W',
      green = 'G',
      blink = 'B',
      none
} light, seen;

light = green;
seen = red + 8;
printf("%d %d %d", light, seen, none);
```

2. Using the *#define* preprocessor command, rewrite the two segments of code in question 1.
3. Write a program that uses an enumerated-type variable to run the menu for the program in Example 4.4.1.
4. Assume the folowing declarations:

```
enum
{
      SMALL,
      MEDIUM,
```

```
        LARGE
} size = LARGE;
char  qty;
```

Would the compiler issue an error of incompatible types for the assignment below, since variable *qty* is not declared as an enumerated type?

```
qty = size;
```

5. A novice programmer defined the following enumerated-type variable *set.* The compiler rejected it because the enumerators must be identifiers, not numbers.

```
enum
{
        3,
        5,
        7,
        9
} set;
```

Even if the compiler had accepted it, such a definition would be foolish. Explain why.

6. Would it be useful to use an enumerated-type variable in the segment in Exercise 4.4.1, 2?
7. Introduce an enumerated-type variable to the following exercises:
   a. Exercise 4.4.1, 6
   b. Exercise 4.4.1, 7
8. Run the following program:

```
#include <stdio.h>

#define  PLANE   1
#define  BIRD    2

main()
{
        enum
        {
                CAR,
                BUS,
                BICYCLE
        } vehicle;

        printf("%d %d", sizeof(PLANE), sizeof(CAR));
}
```

   a. What numbers does the *printf()* display?
   b. Are both numbers the same? If so, do you think that would always be so, regardless of the system on which this program is run?

21.3.4 USE OF TAGS

For the same reasons as with structures, it is a better practice to define a tag for an enumerated type. Consider the following example.

Example 21.3.5

The program below is the same as in Example 21.3.1, plus it uses a tag and the enumerated type is declared globally:

```
#include <stdio.h>

enum season[1]
{
```

```
    FALL,
    WINTER,
    SPRING,
    SUMMER
} ;

main()
{
    enum season this_season, favorite;2

    printf("What season are we in (fall=0, winter=1, spring=2, summer=3) ");
    scanf("%d", &this_season);
    printf("What is your favorite season? ");
    scanf("%d", &favorite);
    switch(this_season)
    {
      case FALL: printf("The leaves are falling\n");
                 break;
      case WINTER: printf("Bright, white, fluffy snow everywhere\n");
                 break;
      case SPRING: printf("Colorful flowers are coming out\n");
                 break;
      case SUMMER: printf("Let's go to the beach!\n");
                 break;
    }
    if (this_season == favorite)
    {
         printf("This is your favorite season!\n");
    }
}
```

Explanations

1. This statement defines an enumerated-type tag globally with the name *season.* This tag may then be used to define variables. Note that no variable is declared yet.
2. Note the syntax of the enumerated-type variable declared below:

   ```
   enum season this_season, favorite;
   ```

   In this code segment, *enum season* is the type, *season* is the tag, and *this_season, favorite* is the list of variables. The rest of the program does not change from Example 21.3.1.

21.3.5 PASSING/RETURNING AN ENUMERATED-TYPE VARIABLE TO/FROM A FUNCTION

Since an enumerated-type variable contains nothing more than an integer, the mechanism of passing and returning an enumerated-type variable to or from a function is absolutely **identical** to that of a variable of an integral type. (Let us look at an example anyway!)

Example 21.3.6

The following program illustrates both the passing of an enumerated-type variable to a function and the return of an enumerated-type variable from the same function. The program asks for two seasons and displays the next ones. It uses the same enumerated type *enum season* found in Example 21.3.5:

```
#include <stdio.h>

enum season
{
      FALL,
      WINTER,
```

```
        SPRING,
        SUMMER
} ;


enum season find_next(enum season s)1
{
    enum season next_s;

    switch(s)
    {
        case FALL:   next_s = WINTER; break;
        case WINTER: next_s = SPRING; break;
        case SPRING: next_s = SUMMER; break;
        case SUMMER: next_s = FALL;   break;
        default: break;
    }
    return next_s;
}

main()
{
    enum season s1, s2;

    printf("Enter two seasons (0=fall, 1=winter, 2=spring, 3=summer) > ");
    scanf("%d %d", &s1, &s2);
    if (s1 == s2)
    {
        printf("You entered the same season\n");
    }
    else
    {
        printf("You entered different seasons\n");
    }
    printf("The next seasons are: %d and %d\n", find_next(s1), find_next(s2));
}
```

Explanation

1. As you see, you can simply mention the type *enum season* of the data received by the function and sent. This works just like any one of the basic types. Of course, an enumerated-type variable may also be sent by reference.

EXERCISES 21.3.3

1. Using the *#define* preprocessor command, rewrite the program in Example 21.3.6 so that the symbolic constant *SEASON* will replace *enum season.*
2. Rewrite the program in the same example so that the next season is sent back by reference.
3. Introduce an appropriate enumerated data type to Exercise 10.2.4, 1.

21.3.6 COMMON ERRORS AND TRAPS

Use the following information to avoid common programming errors:

1. Do not think that a tag is a type name.
2. Do not think that a tag is a variable.
3. Do not think that an enumerator is a variable. Not so! Its value cannot be changed.

22 User-Defined Types and Applications

OBJECTIVES

This chapter introduces you to the following information:

- How to define your own data types.
- How to write applications that use your own types, such as a simple database management system (DBMS).
- The definition and uses of object-oriented programming.

INTRODUCTION

This chapter is a continuation of Chapter 21. User-defined data types allow the programmer to tailor data representation to a particular application. Just as the name of a variable should be indicative of the information it holds, the same holds true for data types. For instance, the data type *char* is not always a proper name; one example is a logical variable declaration. User-defined data types are also useful for collecting a group of other related data types, treating them as a unit. In the last two sections of the chapter, we will look at a few typical applications in which user-defined types will be quite handy.

22.1 THE *typedef* STATEMENT

22.1.1 DEFINING A SYNONYM FOR A DATA TYPE

Chapter 21 showed how to create user-defined types such as structure and enumerated types. These types are usually accompanied by a tag. This tag forces the data type to be expressed in two words, such as *struct person* or *enum season.* In would be better if we could refer to types as a single word. For instance, instead of the declaration

```
enum season winter, spring;
```

The following declaration would be better:

```
season winter, spring;
```

Let us look at two approaches to achieve this.

Using *#define*. It is only a matter of defining a symbolic constant for the two-word type, as Example 22.1.1 illustrates.

Example 22.1.1

Consider Example 21.3.1 again. Let us define a symbolic one-word constant named *SEASON* and use it as shown below:

```
#include <stdio.h>

#define SEASON enum season

enum season
{
   FALL,
   WINTER,
   SPRING,
   SUMMER
} ;

main()
{
   SEASON this_season, favorite;
   printf("What season are we in (fall=0, winter=1, spring=2, summer=3) ");
   scanf("%d", &this_season);
   printf("What is your favorite season? ");
   scanf("%d", &favorite);
   switch(this_season)
   {
     case FALL: printf("The leaves are falling\n");
                 break;
     case WINTER: printf("Bright, white, fluffy snow everywhere\n");
                 break;
     case SPRING: printf("Colorful flowers are coming out\n");
                 break;
     case SUMMER: printf("Let's go to the beach!\n");
                 break;
   }
   if (this_season == favorite)
   {
         printf("This is your favorite season!\n");
   }
}
```

Indeed, the one-word "type" *SEASON* is more convenient to use.

EXERCISE 22.1.1

Use the *#define* preprocessor command and rewrite the program in Example 21.2.6. Replace *struct person* with *PERSON* and *struct date* with *DATE*.

Using *typedef* for enumerated types. Example 22.1.1 above made a successful attempt at replacing the type *enum season* with the single word, *SEASON*. However, *SEASON* was only a symbolic constant, not truly a type in every sense of the word. The statement *typedef* allows the programmer to define a brand new user-defined one-word type. Following are two examples.

Example 22.1.2

Let us use this *typedef* statement in the program in Example 21.3.1. Changes are shown in bold type.

```
#include <stdio.h>

enum season
```

```
{
   FALL,
   WINTER,
   SPRING,
   SUMMER
} ;

typedef enum season SEASON

main()
{
   SEASON this_season, favorite;

   printf("What season are we in (fall=0, winter=1, spring=2, summer=3) ");
   scanf("%d", &this_season);
   printf("What is your favorite season? ");
   scanf("%d", &favorite);
   switch(this_season)
   {
     case FALL: printf("The leaves are falling\n");
              break;
     case WINTER: printf("Bright, white, fluffy snow everywhere\n");
              break;
     case SPRING: printf("Colorful flowers are coming out\n");
              break;
     case SUMMER: printf("Let's go to the beach!\n");
              break;
   }
   if (this_season == favorite)
   {
         printf("This is your favorite season!\n");
   }
}
```

Very little has changed. The following *typedef* statement:

```
typedef enum season SEASON
```

defines the new data type *SEASON* to be nothing more than a synonym for the type *enum season;* i.e., it is the exact same type as *enum season.* Note the syntax: the existing type is listed first *(enum season)* followed by the new type (*SEASON*). *typedef,* the keyword, is different from *#define:* it informs the compiler that *SEASON* is a ***new type*** in the same respect as *int* or *float,* for instance. This has advantageous applications, which will be discussed later.

EXERCISES 22.1.2

1. Use the *typedef* statement to define the new types below:
   a. The type *real* as a synonym for *float*
   b. The type *whole* as a synonym for *int*
   c. The type *byte* as a synonym for *char*
   d. The type *small* as a synonym for *char*
   e. The type *chptr* as a synonym for *char **
   f. The type *uint* as a synonym for *unsigned int*
   g. The type *luint* as a synonym for *long unsigned int*
2. Consider the following segment:

```
struct hotel
{
      char  name[30];
```

```
        char  address[45];
        int   n_rooms;
} ;

typedef struct hotel HOTEL;
```

a. What is the difference between the terms *hotel* and *HOTEL?*
b. Are the following declarations identical?

```
struct hotel choices[5];
HOTEL        choices[5];
```

c. Is the expression *sizeof(HOTEL)* allowed? If so, what is its value? Assume that no alignment is enforced.

3. Define appropriate new types for the structures in the following programs:
   a. Example 21.2.1
   b. Example 21.2.4
   c. Example 21.2.6
   d. Example 21.2.7
4. The following program reads in a 0 or a 1 for true or false:

```
BOOLEAN answer;

printf("The Golden Gate Bridge is in Boston (1=true, 0=false) > ");
scanf("%d", &answer);
if (answer == TRUE)
{
      printf("Wrong!");
}
else
{
      printf("Right!");
}
```

   Provide a type definition for *BOOLEAN* so that this segment will compile and run correctly.

5. The following program reads in a 0 or a 1 for yes or no:

```
ANSWER proposal;

printf("Will you marry me? (y/n) > ");
scanf("\n%c", &proposal);
proposal = tolower(proposal);
if (proposal == YES)
{
      printf("Hurray!");
}
else
{
      printf("Sigh!");
}
```

   Provide a type definition for *ANSWER* so that this segment will compile and run correctly.

Since a user-defined type is regarded by the compiler in the same way as the basic types, then a user-defined type may be used in any place where it is syntactically valid to have a basic type. Consider Example 22.1.3 below.

Example 22.1.3

The following program accomplishes the same task as that of Example 21.3.6, but it uses the *typedef* statement:

```c
#include <stdio.h>

enum  season
{
      FALL,
      WINTER,
      SPRING,
      SUMMER
} ;

typedef  enum season  season_type;


season_type find_next(season_type s)
{
   season_type next_s;

   switch(s)
   {
      case FALL:    next_s = WINTER; break;
      case WINTER: next_s = SPRING; break;
      case SPRING: next_s = SUMMER; break;
      case SUMMER: next_s = FALL;   break;
      default: break;
   }
   return next_s;
}

main()
{
   season_type s1, s2;

   printf("Enter two seasons (0=fall, 1=winter, 2=spring, 3=summer) > ");
   scanf("%d %d", &s1, &s2);
   if (s1 == s2)
   {
      printf("You entered the same season\n");
   }
   else
   {
      printf("You entered different seasons\n");
   }
   printf("The next seasons are: %d and %d\n", find_next(s1), find_next(s2));
}
```

Now a single name, *season_type,* identifies the data type. The same effect can be achieved with a *#define* directive as in Exercise 21.3.3, 1. Note that it is a better practice to end a user-defined type with "*_type*" or "*_t*", especially if the type is not defined in uppercase. This way, they are more easily distinguishable as user-defined types.

Using *typedef* for structure types. Of course, *typedef* is also quite useful to define structure types, and Example 22.1.4 shows how to do this.

Example 22.1.4

Reconsider the program in Example 21.2.6, shown below, in which two structure types named *DATE* and *PERSON* are defined:

```c
#include <stdio.h>

struct date
```

```
{
     int   month;
     int   day;
     int   year;
} ;

typedef struct date DATE; [1]

struct person
{
     char  name[41];
     int   age;
     float height;
     DATE birth;
} ;

typedef struct person PERSON; [1]

PERSON read_struct(void) [2]
{
     PERSON temp;

     printf("Enter your name > ");
     gets(temp.name);
     printf("Enter your age > ");
     scanf("%d", &temp.age);
     printf("Enter your height > ");
     scanf("%f", &temp.height);
     printf("Enter your birthdate MM/DD/YY > ");
     scanf("%d/%d/%d", &temp.birth.month,
                       &temp.birth.day, &temp.birth.year);
     fflush(stdin);
     return temp;
}

void display_struct(PERSON some) [2]
{
     printf("Name: %s\n", some.name);
     printf("Age: %d , height: %7.2f\n", some.age, some.height);
     printf("Birthdate MM/DD/YY: %d/%d/%d\n",
               some.birth.month, some.birth.day, some.birth.year);
}

main()
{
     PERSON you;

     you = read_struct();
     display_struct(you);
}
```

Explanations

1. The first *typedef* defines the structure type *DATE*. Note that this statement had to appear prior to the definition of *struct person*. (Why is that the case?) Then the structure type *PERSON* is defined.
2. *PERSON* replaces *struct person* everywhere it appeared earlier. It's that simple!

EXERCISES 22.1.3

1. Redo Exercises 21.2.4, 4, 5, and 6, with *typedef.*
2. Use the newly defined types *DATE* and *PERSON* in the program in Example 21.2.7.
3. Redo Exercises 21.2.5, 1 and 2, with *typedef.*

Defining a tag and the new type simultaneously. Back to Example 22.1.1: Note that the *typedef* and the *enum* declarations could have been put together:

```
typedef enum season
{
  FALL,
  WINTER,
  SPRING,
  SUMMER
  SEASON;
}
```

This statement defines the new tag *season,* the new enumerators, and the enumerated type *SEASON* all at the same time. Programmers often create their user-defined types this way. This *typedef* statement still has the same syntax as all the others did. Perhaps this is more easily seen if this definition is rearranged as follows:

```
typedef enum season { FALL, WINTER, SPRING, SUMMER } SEASON;
```

EXERCISES 22.1.4

1. Redo Exercise 22.1.2, 3, by putting the tag and the type statements together.
2. The type *FILE* that we have been using is actually a type defined in the file *stdio.h.* Locate it there and answer the following questions:
   a. Is it a derived type, i.e., a structure type, or an enumerated type, or a synonym for a basic data type?
   b. If it is a structure type, how many members does it have? Is a tag defined?
   c. For the declaration *FILE * fp,* give an expression that accesses each member. (***Note:*** Usually, you should never access the members directly.)
3. a. Back to Exercise 22.1.2, 2: Put the definition of the structure and the *typedef* statement together.
   b. Is the tag *hotel* necessary now?

22.1.2 WHY USE *typedef?*

For improved readability. Typically, the *typedef* statement is used to define and name complex types used in the context of linked lists for example. As we saw in Example 22.1.1, *typedef* helps clarify the meaning of a program, thus making its readability intuitive.

For increased portability. Another reason for the use of *typedef* is that it helps to support the portability of a program. Consider Example 22.1.5.

Example 22.1.5

Some computers allocate 4 bytes for a variable of type *int,* whereas others allocate 2 bytes only. For instance, suppose that Computer A allocates 4 bytes and Computer B allocates 2 bytes. The following program has a potential for producing incorrect results with Computer B:

```
#include <stdio.h>

main()
```

```
{
      int  a, b, c;

      printf("Enter two numbers > ");
      c = a * b;
}
```

The result of the multiplication may be too large to fit in variable *c*. The solution is to define your own type that always allocates 4 bytes, regardless of the system:

```
#include <stdio.h>

typedef long int   INTEGER;[1]
/* typedef int  INTEGER; */[2]

main()
{
      INTEGER  a, b, c;

      printf("Enter two numbers > ");
      c = a * b;
}
```

Explanations

1. Use this one when run on Computer B.
2. Use this one when run on Computer A.

This simplistic example fails to show the usefulness of the technique. With very large software development projects, the use of *typedef* is very valuable. Such a system would contain numerous such user-defined types. They would perhaps all be stored in a header file, say, *mydefs.h*. For instance:

```
#include <stdio.h>
#include "mydefs.h"

main()
{
      INTEGER  a, b, c;

      printf("Enter two numbers > ");
      c = a * b;
}
```

When a change is requested for a particular type, only this header file would need to be retouched. Nothing else would need changing, regardless of the size of the system!

EXERCISE 22.1.5

The following program will cause portability problems. Why?

```
#include <stdio.h>

typedef long int   INTEGER;
/* typedef int  INTEGER; */

main()
{
      INTEGER  a, b, c;
```

```
        printf("Enter two numbers > ");
        c = a * b;
        printf("The result = %d\n", c);
}
```

How can this be fixed? (***Hint:*** Use a *#define.*)

22.1.3 *typedef* GOES BEYOND *#define*

You may still be thinking that *#define* and *typedef* are equivalent methods of declaring synonymous user-defined types. There are two important differences:

1. As mentioned before, *#define* only makes a substitution—the new type never reaches the compiler; *typedef* does. It informs the compiler of a new type.
2. Because *typedef* carries the meaning of the new type to the compiler, more complex types may be defined. The examples below illustrate how this is done.

Defining an array type. Let us look at two typical applications of user-defined types.

Example 22.1.6

Assume the declaration:

```
float emp_sal[10], emp_height[10], emp_weight[10];
```

It is somewhat cumbersome to have to mention the size of each array. When your program uses many variables of the same type, you may wish to define your own type to simplify or shorten the declaration. In this case, since all arrays are to be of size 10, one could define a type of "array of 10 floats":

```
typedef float  ARRAY[10];
```

This definition says that *ARRAY* is a data type array of 10 *float*s. The identifier *ARRAY* is **not** a variable; it is a data type and is used to declare variables. The above variables would be declared as:

```
ARRAY  emp_sal, emp_height, emp_weight;
```

These three variables are declared of type *ARRAY*. That is, they are of type "array of 10 *float*s." Since the type *ARRAY* implicitly stands for an array of size 10, the size should not be mentioned beside the variables. Note that *emp_sal*, *emp_height* and *emp_weight* are constant pointers. (Why is that the case?) Their values cannot be changed.

Example 22.1.7

Let us define the type named *YEAR* in Example 14.1.2. This type will mean "array of 12 integers."

```
#include <stdio.h>

typedef int MONTH[12];1

main()
{
        MONTH month;1
        int index;
        int sum;

        printf("Enter the monthly rainy days this year > ");

        for (index=0; index < 12; index++)2
        {
                scanf("%d", &month[index]);
        }
```

```
    sum = 0;
    for (index=0; index < 12; index++)
    {
          printf("On month %d, %d rainy days\n", index+1, month[index]);2
          sum += month[index];
    }
    printf("There were %d rainy days\n", sum);
}
```

Explanations

1. The definition of the new type and the declaration of the array *month* are without a size specification.
2. It is important to understand that, even though the size is no longer mentioned in the declaration of *month,* its elements are still accessed via an index. *typedef* changes the way a variable is declared, but never the way that this variable is operated on.

Defining a pointer type. Pointer declaration is another area that can benefit from user-defined types. Again, consider two examples.

Example 22.1.8

Consider the declaration:

```
int   * ptr1, * ptr2, * ptr3;
```

As mentioned in Section 11.1, the * is **not** part of the variable name, even though one needs to be placed besides each variable. The * is really part of the type. The *typedef* may be used to eliminate the need to mention these confusing asterisks. Here it is:

```
typedef  int *  ptr_int;
```

The identifier *ptr_int* is a pointer type to integers. Since the asterisk is now an integral part of the type *ptr_int,* the three variable pointers may now be declared without it:

```
ptr_int  ptr1, ptr2, ptr3;
```

This is less confusing, is it not?

Example 22.1.9

Let us define a new type named *fptr* for Example 11.2.1. This type will be a pointer to a *float*.

```
#include <stdio.h>
typedef float * fptr;1

void total(int qty, float unit_cst, fptr owe_addr, fptr tax_addr)
{
   *owe_addr = qty * unit_cst;2
   *tax_addr = qty * unit_cst * 0.05;2
}

main()
{
    int   items;
    float cost, owe, tax_owe;

    printf("Enter the number of items bought > ");
    scanf("%d", &items);
    printf("Enter the cost of each item > ");
    scanf("%d", &cost);
```

```
    total(items, cost, &owe, &tax_owe);³

    printf("You owe $ %8.2f, with tax %8.2f\n", owe, tax_owe);
}
```

Explanations

1. This is the definition of the new type and the declaration of the pointer parameters without an asterisk.
2. It is important to understand that even though the asterisk is no longer mentioned in the declaration of these parameters the dereferencing operator is still needed.
3. The address operator is still needed as well.

EXERCISES 22.1.6

1. Does the following declaration:

   ```
   ptr_int  ptr1, ptr2, ptr3;
   ```

   preserve the same meaning as in Example 22.1.8, in which *ptr_int* was defined with *#define ptr_int int ** rather than *typedef?*
2. Given the type declaration *typedef long int ar_type[6],* answer the following questions:
   a. Which of the following variable declarations correctly declare a variable array of six long integers?
      i. `ar_type list;`
      ii. `ar_type list[6];`
      iii. `long    list;`
      iv. `long    list[6];`
   b. Is the declaration *ar_type list[10]* allowed? If so, what does it say?
   c. Is the declaration *ar_type * list* allowed? If so, what does it say?
3. Given the type declaration *typedef char * ch_type*, answer the following questions:
   a. Which of the following variable declarations correctly declare a variable pointer to a pointer to a character?
      i. `ch_type list;`
      ii. `ch_type *  list;`
      iii. `char    list;`
      iv. `char    ** list;`
   b. Is the declaration *ch_type list[5]* allowed? If so, what does it say?
4. True or false: The definition *typedef int [10] list* is equivalent to *typedef int list[10].*
5. Each of the following segments runs correctly, as long as the type *string* is defined appropriately. What is the *typedef* used?
   a. `string  name;`
      `name = "Joseph Mathieu";`
   b. `string name;`
      `strcpy(name, "Joseph Mathieu");`
6. Define a data type named *LIST* in the following programs so that the size no longer needs to be mentioned in the declarations:
   a. Example 14.2.2
   b. Exercise 14.2.2, 6
   c. Exercise 14.2.2, 8b
7. Define a data type named *PTR* in the following programs so that the asterisk no longer needs to be mentioned in the declarations:
   a. Example 11.2.3
   b. Example 11.2.4
   c. Example 11.2.5
8. Back in Example 11.2.6, define a data type named *file* so that the parameter of the functions *open_input_safely()* and *open_output_safely()* will be declared as *file * fp*.

9. Is there anything wrong with the following segments?

a.
```
typedef  float  list_type[25];

list_type  table1, table2;

printf("%f", list_type[0]);
table1 = table2;
```
b.
```
typedef  int  list_type[6][20];

list_type  a, b[4], * c;
```
c.
```
typedef  char  list_type[5];

list_type a, * b;
```
d.
```
typedef  char *  list_type[5];

list_type a, * b;

a = "Alleluia";
b = "Bla";
```
e.
```
typedef  char * string;
string a, b;
a = "Alleluia";
strcpy(b, a);
```

22.1.4 COMMON ERRORS AND TRAPS

The following information will help you avoid common programming errors.

1. Do not think that *typedef* defines a variable. For example:

```
typedef struct
{
      int mon;
      int day;
      int year;
} DATE;
```

   DATE is not a variable. It is a type that defines a structure. A variable of that type would be declared as *DATE birth*.
2. Do not confuse the terms *tag, type,* and *variable.*

22.2 APPLICATION: DATABASE MANAGEMENT SYSTEMS

The first section of this chapter for the most part covered the mechanics, the syntax, and the properties of structures with little emphasis on their purpose. This section and the next will fill you in on that topic.

Here we will reduce the meaning of the term ***database*** to that of a single file of data. You may already have heard or used a database management system (DBMS). They are designed to create a database, modify records, add records, search records, generate reports, and so on. This section will teach you how to design and build a very simple database management system. Functions and techniques learned in the previous chapter will be instrumental here.

22.2.1 CREATING A DATABASE FILE

There are various methods for storing data in a file. Some use fairly sophisticated data structures such as B-trees. Our DBMS will simply store the data in a plain ASCII file in tabular form, which is clearly the simplest approach.

Example 22.2.1

Let us write a program that creates a database file named CUST.DBF and lets the user enter records in it. Each record will contain the following fields:

Field	Type	Width
Employee I.D.	integer	8 spaces
Employee name	string	20 spaces
Salary	float	8 spaces, 2 decimals

At the time of entry, truncation of the data may be required to ensure that it fits within the fields. For instance:

Do you wish to create the database CUST.DBF (y/n) ? y
Enter a record: Employee I.D. > 8917027243
Employee name > Pierre-Jacques Levasseur
Salary > 109962.09
Another record (y/n) ? n

The employee I.D. would be truncated to eight digits: 89170272; the employee name would be truncated to "Pierre-Jacques Levas," and the salary would be stored as 109962.00, eliminating the decimal digit 9.

The one-to-one relationship between structures and records. Now let us look at how a program may be written for the database entering system above. A function named *read_data()* will store the data provided by the user into memory. The data will be stored in memory into an array of structures named *mem*. Each structure will consist of three members: employee I.D., employee name, and salary. Then the data from each structure will be stored into the appropriate field in the file, one record at a time, as Figure 22.2.1 illustrates.

Figure 22.2.1

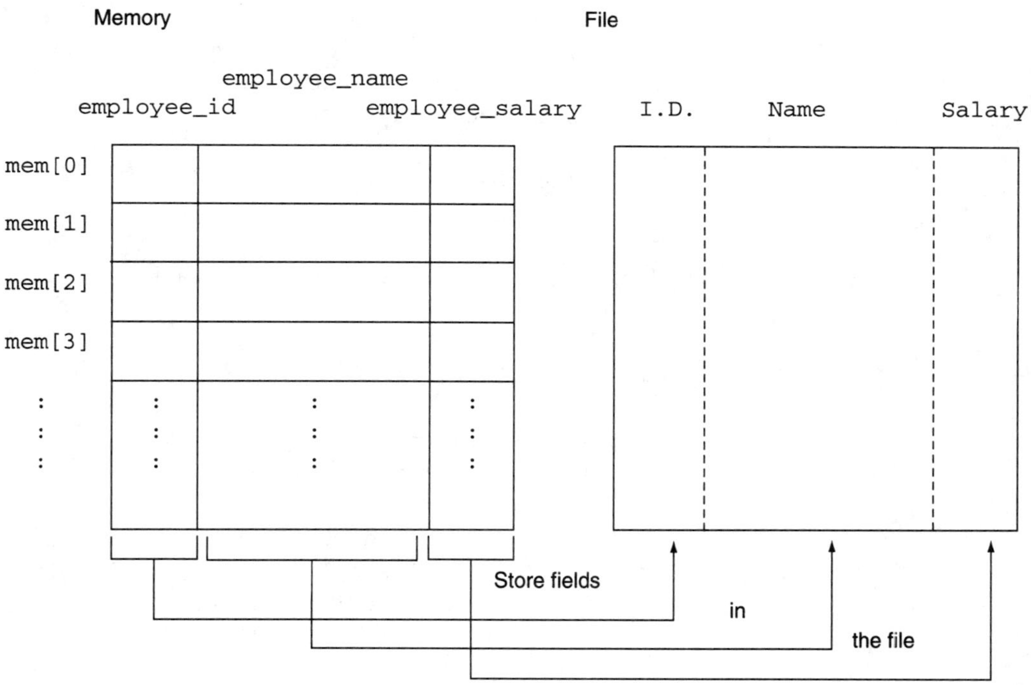

Clearly, a structure corresponds exactly to one record in a file. This is why they are used here. Note the striking resemblance between an array of structures and a 2-D array. A function named *save_dfile()* will then store the data from memory into the file CUST.DBF. Here is the program:

```
#define  MAX_RECS  40   /* assume maximum # of records to store is 40 */
#define  NAME_LEN  20

struct record¹
{
```

```
    int   employee_id;
    char  employee_name[NAME_LEN+1];
    float employee_salary;
} ;

void read_data(struct record list[], int * num_rec_ptr)2
{
   char   ans;
   int    i;
   int    id;                    /* these three are */
   float  salary;                /* temporary */
   char   name[LEN_NAME+1];      /* variables */

   i = 0;
   do
   {
      printf("Enter a record: Employee I.D. > ");3
      scanf("%8d", &id);
      fflush(stdin);
      printf("                Employee name > ");
      fgets(name, LEN_NAME+1, stdin);
      fflush(stdin);
      printf("                Salary > ");
      scanf("%8f", &salary);
      fflush(stdin);
      list[i].employee_id = id;
      strcpy(list[i].employee_name, name);
      list[i].employee_salary = salary;
      i++;
      printf("Another record (y/n) ? ");
      scanf("\n%c", &ans);
   }
   while (toupper(ans) == 'Y');
}

void save_dfile(char filename[], struct record list[], int num_rec)4
{
   int    i;
   FILE * dbfp;

   dbfp = fopen(filename, "r");
   for (i=0; i < num_rec; i++)
   {
      fprintf(dbfp, "%8d%20s%8.2f\n",
                    list[i].employee_id, list[i].employee_name,
                    list[i].employee_salary);
   }
   fclose(dbfp);
}

main()
{
    char            ans;
    int             num_rec;
    int             dbf_name[13] = "CUST.DBF";
    struct record mem[MAX_RECS];5
```

```
    printf("Do you wish to create the database CUST.DBF (y/n) ? ");
    scanf("\n%c", &ans);
    if (toupper(ans) == 'Y')
    {
        read_data(mem, &num_rec);
        save_dfile(dbf_name, mem, num_rec);
    }
}
```

Explanations

1. Note that this is a structure definition of *struct record* only—no variables are declared yet.
2. The function *read_data()* reads data from the screen into the structure array *mem*. It also sends back by reference the number of records read.
3. The information is read and then stored in the structure array *mem*.
4. The function *save_dfile()* takes the information from the structure array *list* (which is really *mem*) into the file with the name *filename*.
5. *mem* is an array of *NUM_RECS* structures of type *struct record*.

EXERCISES 22.2.1

1. For the structure template below:

```
struct record
    {
    int   employee_id[NUM_RECS];
    char  employee_name[NUM_RECS][NAME_LEN+1];
    float employee_salary[NUM_RECS];
} ;
```

   a. Rewrite the program in the above example using this template.
   b. Comment on either approach. Which one is better?
2. How would you write the program in the above example if structures did not exist in C? (***Hint:*** Use an array for each field.)
3. In the above example, some may argue that the file should be part of the structure as well because it is directly related to the memory content of the array structure *mem*. Consider the embedded structure declarations below that reflect this:

```
struct record
{
    int   employee_id;
    char  employee_name[NAME_LEN+1];
    float employee_salary;
} ;

struct dbase
{
    FILE *          dbfp;
    char            filename[81];
    struct record mem[NUM_RECS];
} ;
```

   Make all of the necessary changes to the program in Example 22.2.1 to include these structures.
4. Define a data type named *DBASE* for the program in Example 22.2.1. This type will be a synonym for an array of *MAX_RECS* structures. Make all other necessary changes.

5. Write a program that creates a database file named STUDENTS.DBF. Each record consists of a student I.D. number, a number of credits completed, and a cumulative grade point average:

Student I.D. Number:	4 digits
Number of Credits Completed:	2 digits
Grade Point Average:	5 spaces, 2 decimals

6. Write a program that creates a database file named STOCKS.DBF. Each record consists of an integer part number, a part description, a number of parts in inventory, and an integer reorder number:

Part Number:	5 digits
Description:	15 characters
Number in Stock:	3 digits
Reorder Number:	3 digits

7. Write a program that creates a database file named MAILING.DBF. Each record consists of a name, a street address, a city, a state or province, and a ZIP or postal code.

Name:	25 characters
Street Address:	20 characters
City:	20 characters
State or Province:	2 characters
ZIP or Postal Code:	7 characters

8. How would the programs in the previous three questions need to be modified if structures were not available in C?
9. Write a function named *sort_db()* that accepts an array of structures of type *struct person* and sorts them by name. An array of indexes will also be passed in which the new order will be stored. (***Hint:*** This function remains similar to the solution provided in Example 17.3.3.)
10. Redo Supplementary Exercise 20.2, 4, using structures wherever appropriate.
11. Write a program that reads in records from the database file CUST.DBF (in Example 22.2.1) and produces a list of the records. Two new functions will be defined: a function named *load_dfile()* will read the data from the file and store it in memory. Make sure that all necessary parameters are defined. Also *fscanf()* will be called twice to read the numeric fields Employee I.D. and Salary; a *fgets()* is needed to read the employee name. Another function named *db_list()* will produce a simple report of the data. Here is an example of a run:

Employee Database

Record#	Employee_ID	Employee_Name	Salary
1	30949916	Fabien Duschene	47772.90
2	89170272	Pierre-Jacques Levas	109962.00
3	89172243	Peter Leach	1062.09
4	22300011	Mike Pilsner	95081.37

12. In the function *load_dfile()* from the above question, some may feel that it should be feasible to read each field of the file CUST.DBF using the same function instead of the two different functions *fscanf()* and *fgets()*. Investigate this possibility in three ways:
    a. Could a single *fscanf()* read in all three fields, i.e., would the following loop read the records correctly too?

```
for (i=0;
     fscanf(dbfp, "%8ld%20s%8f",
        &emp_id[i], emp_name[i], &salary[i]) != EOF;
     i++) ;
```

    b. In the above question, you were told to use a *fgets()* to read the name. Could *fscanf()* also be used? (***Hint:*** The name may be made of multiple words.)
    c. Still in the question above, you were told to use a *fscanf()* to read the employee I.D. and salary. Could a *fgets()* also be used? (***Hint:*** They would then need to be converted to numeric characters.)
13. Write a program that loads the database file STUDENTS.DBF from Exercise 22.2.1, 5, and lists it on the screen.

14. Write a program that loads the database file STOCKS.DBF from Exercise 22.2.1, 6, and lists it on the screen.
15. Write a program that loads the database file MAILING.DBF from Exercise 22.2.1, 7 and lists it on the screen.
16. Write a function named *append_records()* that lets the user append new records to a database file. This function will work in very much the same way as the function *read_data()* (in Example 22.2.1), except that the file will be opened with the permissible mode "a" (refer to Subsection 8.2.2 to recall what this means). The following example shows how the function *append_records()* should interact with the user:

```
Enter a new record: Employee I.D. > 89172243
                    Employee name > Peter Leach
                    Salary > 1062.09
Append another record (y/n) ? n
```

17. Based on the program in Example 22.2.1, create a command named *dsave* so that the file name may be entered on the command line. If it is not there, the user will be prompted for it. Refer back to Section 20.4 to recall how to create a command.
18. Based on the program in question 5 above, create a command named *dload* so that the file name may be entered on the command line. If it is not there, the user will be prompted for it. Refer back to Section 20.4 to recall how to create a command.

22.2.2 EDITING RECORDS

Editing a record requires the following steps:

1. Editing is done in memory, so the file must first be loaded in.
2. Some key information, such as an I.D., must be provided; this determines which record is to be edited.
3. The record is searched.
4. Once found, selected fields from the record may be modified.
5. The changes are saved back to the file.

Example 22.2.2 illustrates all these steps.

Example 22.2.2

Let us continue with Example 22.2.1. The program would load the file CUST.DBF into memory, and then it would let the user edit any records. The user must specify the employee I.D. of the record to edit; this is the key. Then the program would find it through a simple linear search. The program would use a function named, say, *load_dfile()*, to load the data in memory, a function named *edit_data()* to edit records, and the function *save_dfile()* to save the changes. The function *edit_data()* would contain a loop to let the user edit any number of records until she no longer wishes to edit any more. Here is an example of a run:

```
File CUST.DBF loaded.
Enter the employee I.D. to search for > 95105
Below is the record found:
      Employee I.D. > 95105
      Employee name > Bryan Muhler
      Salary > 471.09

Edit the fields:
      Employee name > Bryan Muhler
      Salary > 505.97

Do you wish to edit another record (y/n) ? n
```

Note that the field "Employee I.D." is not editable. That should make sense, since the I.D. never changes. For the other fields, the new information is entered. That goes also for the fields that do not require editing, such as the name. In this case, you simply type the same name over again, which is not terribly user-friendly. An exercise below gives you the opportunity to improve this.

EXERCISES 22.2.2

1. Write a program for Example 22.2.2.
2. The function *edit_data()* in the program above assumes that the employee I.D. will always be found. Make modifications so that it will skip out of editing any more records if the employee I.D. cannot be found.

   Define a function named *seek_employee_id()* that searches the record, given the key. It *returns* the record number if found, otherwise it returns –1. This function will be called by the function *edit_data()*.
3. Modify the function *edit_data()* so that fields that do not require editing will not need to be retyped—they may be skipped. For example:

   ```
   Enter the employee I.D. to search for > 95105
   Below is the record found. Edit any fields.
   Press Enter to skip the fields you do not want to edit:

           Employee I.D. > 95105
           Employee name > Bryan Muhler
           Salary > 471.09
   ```

   The cursor displays the prompt and data for the first field. Then the cursor backs up to the beginning of the field data as shown (in the Employee I.D. field). (***Hint:*** In a loop, send a \b repeatedly to move the cursor back.) The user has the choice of pressing Enter to skip editing this field, or to enter the new data and then press Enter. Therefore, the program must detect if new data is entered. (***Hint:*** Refer back to Example 18.2.7 to recall how to do this.) Once the user presses Enter, the prompt and data for the next field will appear. Again, once the user presses Enter, the prompt and data for the last field will appear.
4. Write a program that loads the database file STUDENTS.DBF from Exercise 22.2.1, 13, lets the user edits records, and then saves the changes.
5. Write a program that loads the database file STOCKS.DBF from Exercise 22.2.1, 14, lets the user edits records, and then saves the changes.
6. Write a program that loads the database file MAILING.DBF from Exercise 22.2.1, 15, lets the user edits records, and then saves the changes.

22.2.3 DELETING RECORDS

The following steps are required to delete records:

1. Deleting is first done in memory, so the file must be loaded in *a priori*.
2. Some key information, such as an I.D., must be provided; this determines which record is to be deleted.
3. The record is searched.
4. Once found, the record is deleted.
5. Decrease the number of record by one.
6. The changes are saved back to the file.

There are two approaches to deleting records, and they were presented in Chapter 15! Indeed, Subsection 15.2.3 described one method of deleting an element, and Supplementary Exercise 15.2, 2, described another. A record of a file may be seen as an element of a list, so the methods of deletion described there may be applied here too. Let us see which one is best.

Physically removing the structure from memory. Consider the file CUST.DBF again. We will use the employee I.D. to identify the record to delete. This first method consists of moving up all of the records that are below the one deleted, as shown in Figure 22.2.2.

Obviously, this method is terribly slow, and we will not even write a program for it. The method described below must be adopted.

Figure 22.2.2

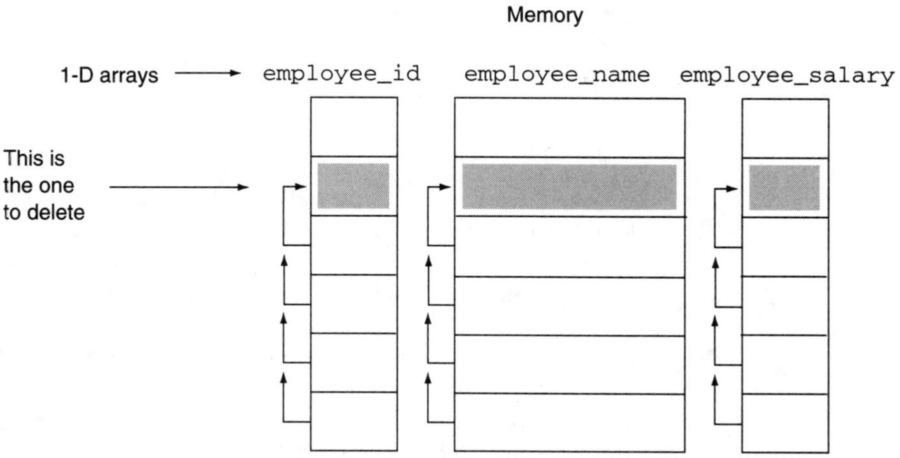

Tagging the structure in question as deleted. With this method, the record to delete is simply marked as "deleted" and is not removed. To this end, a new array named *deleted* will be added. The cell *deleted[i]* will correspond to the record *i*. As shown in Figure 22.2.3, a 1 stored in that cell will indicate that its corresponding record is deleted.

Figure 22.2.3

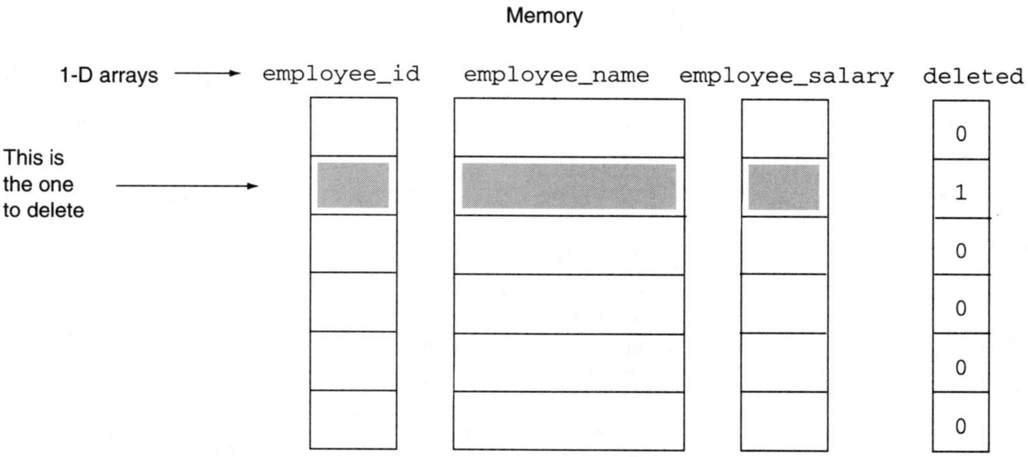

EXERCISES 22.2.3

1. Write a program that implements the algorithm of the second method described above.
2. Write a program that loads the database file STUDENTS.DBF from Exercise 22.2.1, 13, lets the user delete records, and then saves the changes.
3. Write a program that loads the database file STOCKS.DBF from Exercise 22.2.1, 14, lets the user delete records, and then saves the changes.
4. Write a program that loads the database file MAILING.DBF from Exercise 22.2.1, 15, lets the user delete records, and then saves the changes.

SUPPLEMENTARY EXERCISES 22.2

1. Build a complete database management system for the database file CUST.DBF by putting all of the pertinent functions defined in this section in a single program. Here is an example of a run:

   Database Management System

   (1) Create a database
   (2) Load a database
   (3) Append data

(4) Edit data
(5) Delete records
(6) Produce a report
(7) Exit

Enter your choice > 1

Now try to use the function *strcenter()* from Exercise 19.3.1, 5b, to center the title.

2. Build a database management system for the database file STUDENTS.DBF from Exercise 22.2.1, 5.
3. Build a database management system for the database file STOCKS.DBF from Exercise 22.2.1, 6.
4. Build a database management system for the database file MAILING.DBF from Exercise 22.2.1, 7.
5. Modify questions 2, 3, and 4 above. Using *typedef,* define your own type called *string* that is to be used to declare all string variables.
6. Write a simple DBMS for a file named WATER.PYT. This file contains water payments from city residents. Here is a sample:

Customer number	Customer name	Address Number	Street name	City	Payment
43171	Le Funes	207	Champs Elysee	Paris	230.40
43000	LeVasseur	7	Gregoire	Ste Victoire	1.04
13001	Clousseau	3336	Becancour	Paris	272.30
20011	Sarto Fourn	12	Bozo	Zozo	230.40
01	10	24	31	47	62

Columns

The reporting must be presented as follows:

Customer 1: 43000 Name: Le Vesseur
Address: 7 Gregoire Ste Victoire
Payment received: $ 1.04

Customer 2: 13001 Name: Clousseau
Address: 3336 Becancour Paris
Payment received: $ 272.30

Customer 3: 20011 Name: Sarto Fourn
Address: 12 Bozo Zozo
Payment received: $ 230.40

7. For each database file described below, develop a DBMS with a menu:

DBMS for *filename*

(1) Create the database
(2) Add records
(3) Delete records
(4) Modify records
(5) Make a report
(6) Sort the database

a. Each record of a file named PLANETS.DBF contains the following fields:

Name	Length
Planet Name	20
Diameter (kms)	8 spaces, 2 decimals
Weight (kgs)	12 spaces, exponential
Distance (from sun)	12 spaces, exponential
Number of Moons	3 spaces

b. Each record of a file named SUSPECTS.DBF contains the following fields:

Name	Length
Suspect's Name	40
Height	5 spaces
Weight	5 spaces
Eye Color	2 spaces
Age	3 spaces
Sex	2 spaces

c. Each record of a file named RESTAUR.DBF contains the following fields:

Name	Length
Restaurant Name	40
Type of Food Served	2
Rating	2
Address	30
Capacity	4

d. Each record of a file named MULTIPLE.DBF contains the following fields:

Name	Length
Question	As many lines as needed
Multiple Choices	Up to 5 choices, each on separate lines
Answer	2 spaces

8. Create a command for all of the questions above. If the database file name is specified on the command line, the menu options "(1) Create a database" and "(2) Load a database" will not be presented.

22.3 APPLICATION: OBJECT-ORIENTED PROGRAMMING

Another area in which structures are very useful is in object-oriented programming (OOP). This is an exciting, novel method of programming that has become popular in recent years. Unfortunately, the C language is not designed for OOP. Nevertheless, many concepts of OOP may still be explained and illustrated with all of the tools that you have learned in this book.

This book has taught you ***procedural-based programming*** (PBP), which is based on the development of algorithms that manipulate variables. PBP forces the programmer to concentrate heavily on **how** to accomplish a task.

Object-oriented programming (OOP) is a method of developing computer programs based on constructing and manipulating classes of objects rather than individual variables. OOP recognizes that the world is made of objects. People are much more comfortable with objects than they are with algorithms and variables. OOP lets the programmer concentrate on **what** the specifics of a task are.

This section is intended to introduce you to some basic concepts and programming skills in OOP. We will continue to use the C language here, although C is not designed for OOP. To do otherwise would require covering technical details beyond the intent of this section.

22.3.1 WHAT IS AN OBJECT?

An object is a member of a class. The three examples below illustrate this concept.

Example 22.3.1

Suppose you are asked to write a program that simulates a car. OOP takes the following approach. An object has properties and characteristics called ***attributes*** and a behavior dictated by whatever operation is applied to it. Two questions need to be asked:

1. Of **what** is a car made? To list just a few items in this category: a car is made of (1) a make and model, (2) doors, (3) a color, (4) a top or lack thereof (i.e., a convertible), (5) an engine, and (6) a gas tank. These are called the ***attributes of the object.***

2. **What** can be done with a car? Again, to list just a few things in this category: a car may be (1) driven, (2) turned to the right or left, (3) backed up, or (4) filled up. These are called ***operations from the outside*** (i.e., by the driver), each of which forces upon the object a determined ***behavior.*** For instance, the operation to "drive" brings upon the behavior of "moving."

Note that with PBP these questions can also be asked. The difference is that a lot more effort would need to be directed at **how** to implement the answers to both questions. An OOP language is already designed around building objects. There is a one-to-one correspondence with the attributes, operations, and behaviors listed above and the way that they are coded in the program.

Example 22.3.2

Suppose that you are asked to write a program that simulates a stove. The same two questions are asked again:

1. Of **what** is a stove made? Some of the attributes are: (1) a make (company), (2) burners, (3) dials to turn them on, and (4) a color.
2. **What** can be done with a stove? Some of the operations are: (1) turn a burner on or off, (2) set a pot on a burner, (3) plug the stove into the power source. Sometimes there may be more than one possible behavior for one operation. For instance, the operation "turn burner on" may bring the behavior of heating up to "red hot" or "moderate."

Example 22.3.3

A rectangle can clearly be seen as an object. Its attributes would be: (1) its width, (2) its height, and (3) the color of its borders. Its operations could include: (1) setting its width and height, and (2) drawing its borders.

Note that the attributes and operations in the three examples above do not describe a specific object. In Example 22.3.1, any car fits the description; the same may be said for Example 22.3.2 and 22.3.3. These attributes and operations describe a **type** of object, not an actual object. In OOP, the term used is a ***class*** of objects. Therefore the three examples above define classes of objects. To describe an actual object, the attributes of the class must be set to specific values. Consider Example 22.3.4.

Example 22.3.4

Let us make an actual object from the classes described in Examples 22.3.1, 22.3.2, and 22.3.3:

An actual car object could be: (1) a Ford Taurus, (2) with four doors, (3) of blue color, (4) with a top, and (5) with a V6 engine.

An actual stove object could be: (1) made by General Electric, (2) with four burners, (3) of white color, and (4) with four dials.

An actual rectangle object could be: (1) dimension of 12 inches wide by 5 inches high, with (2) its borders traced in green.

EXERCISES 22.3.1

1. Answer the following questions:
   a. What is a class?
   b. What is an object?
   c. What is an operation?
   d. What is a behavior?
   e. What is the relationship between an operation and its corresponding behavior(s)?
2. For each of the following classes,
   - Make a list of some attributes describing the class.
   - Make a list of some operations describing the class.
   - For each operation, give a list of possible behaviors.
   - Give an example of an object of the class.
     a. A cigarette lighter
     b. A cigarette box

c. A book
d. A pen
e. A radio
f. A cassette tape player
g. A cassette
h. A bottle
i. A computer printer
j. A die
k. A window
l. A television
m. A ball

Why learn OOP? OOP has been one of the most exciting developments in software engineering and has been receiving a lot of public attention since the early 1990s. There are good reasons for that:

1. The popularity of OOP is in part due to the emergence of graphic and windowing applications and systems. OOP makes it easy to manipulate windows, because they are coded as objects rather than unrelated lines, boxes, and colors.
2. Because of the way in which OPP compilers are designed, they encourage the creation of code that is reusable and portable. These qualities were stressed in Sections 12.2 and 19.2. Systems built in this manner are easier to maintain.
3. Typically, the level of abstraction in OOP allows programmers to develop a system much more quickly.
4. OOP makes ***visual programming*** possible. In this kind of programming, programs are built from visual objects as well as conventional coding.

Numerous software development packages that exclusively use OOP are now coming onto the market. As mentioned in Chapter 1, C++ is one of them. C++ may also be used as an improved version of C (for instance by the use of such objects as *cin* and *cout)*. Even though C is not designed to support OOP, *struct* type variables may be used to emulate some capabilities of OOP. This is the purpose of the remainder of this section.

22.3.2 HOW IS AN OBJECT PROGRAMMED?

OOP is carried out differently than PBP. For those accustomed to PBP, it takes a while to form an object-oriented frame of mind. The following examples of C programs should help.

Example 22.3.5

Let us write a program that emulates a car of the class described in Example 22.3.1. We will limit ourselves to the following four attributes: A car (1) has a color, (2) has two or four doors, (3) has a gas tank, and (4) has an engine with some gas consumption rate. Let us say that a car (1) can be built, (2) can be filled up, and (3) can be driven. These are the operations; here is the program:

```
#include <stdio.h>

typedef enum
{
      WHITE,
      RED,
      BLUE,
      BLACK
} COLOR;

typedef struct[1]
{
      COLOR body;
      int   doors;
      float tank;
      float consumption_rate;
```

```
} CAR;

void build(CAR * this, COLOR paint, int drs, float cons)[2]
{
      this->body = paint;
      this->doors = drs;
      this->tank = 0;
      this->consumption_rate = cons;
}

void fillup(CAR * this, float gas)
{
      this->tank += gas;
}

void drive(CAR * this, float distance)
{
      float gas_consumed;

      gas_consumed = (this->consumption_rate / 100) * distance;
      this->tank -= gas_consumed;
}

main()
{
      CAR mine;[3]

      build(&mine, BLACK, 4, 11.3);[4]
      fillup(&mine, 50);[5]
      drive(&mine, 228.4);[6]
}
```

Because C is not an object-oriented language, technically, this program is procedural based. However, the approach remains object oriented. For this reason, explanations will be given for both approaches in Table 22.1.1. You will see that the terms employed differ between the two approaches. These terms are highlighted in bold in the table. The numbers in the table refer to the superscript numbers in the program.

Table 22.1.1

Explanations

Procedural-Based Approach	Object-Oriented Approach
1. This defines the ***type*** named *CAR.* It consists of three ***members*** that any ***variable*** of this ***type*** has. Note that this ***type*** does not define an actual ***variable,*** for none has been "allocated" yet. (As was mentioned in Section 21.1, *struct* does not allocate memory to a structure. Memory is only allocated to a variable of that structure.) 2. These are the three ***functions*** that may manipulate a ***variable*** of the ***type*** *CAR.* 3. This declares a ***variable,*** named *mine,* of the ***type*** *CAR. mine* is not ***populated*** yet. 4. This ***function populates*** the actual ***variable*** called *mine.* That is, its ***members*** are set to specific values. 5. This ***function*** emulates the filling up of the car *mine.* 6. This ***function*** emulates the driving of the car *mine.*	1. This defines the ***class*** named *CAR.* It consists of three ***attributes*** that any ***object*** in this ***class*** has. Note that this ***class*** does not define an actual ***object,*** for none has been "allocated" yet. 2. These are the three ***operations*** that may manipulate an ***object*** in the ***class*** *CAR.* 3. This declares an ***instance,*** named *mine,* of the ***class*** *CAR. mine* is not an ***object*** yet. 4. This ***operation builds*** the actual ***object*** called *mine.* That is, its ***attributes*** are set to specific values. Up until this point, no actual car existed yet. 5. This ***operation*** emulates the filling up of the car *mine.* 6. This ***operation*** emulates the driving of the car *mine.*

General terms used in OOP. By comparing both approaches, the following practical OOP definitions may be made, using C as a basis:

1. A ***class*** is a user-defined structure type. The class *CAR* may be viewed as a ***type*** in the same respect as *int* or *float.* To be strictly correct, though, a class definition consists of a *struct* statement and a set of function definitions (operations).
2. An ***attribute*** is a member of a structure.
3. An ***object*** is a structure variable that has been populated.
4. An ***instance*** of a class is a structure variable that may not have been populated yet.
5. ***Building*** an object means populating a structure variable.
6. Applying an ***operation*** to an object means calling a function that manipulates a structure variable.

Some terms employed here may not be standard to all books on object-oriented programming, except of course the terms ***class*** and ***object.***

22.3.3 TWO SIMPLE APPLICATIONS

The range of applications of OOP is boundless. Even abstract concepts, such as a date, may be viewed as objects. Consider Example 22.3.6.

Example 22.3.6

A date such as the one manipulated in Example 21.1.1 may be viewed as an object. You only need to ask yourself two questions: What is it made of (i.e., what are its attributes?), and what operations can be done with it?

First, what is it made of? Obviously a date is made of a month, day, and year. Second, what are the operations that may be applied to this object? Example 21.1.1 showed that a date may be set and looked at.

With this object-oriented approach in mind, the program in Example 21.1.1 becomes:

```
#include <stdio.h>

enum
{
      JAN = 1, FEB, MAR, APR, MAY, JUNE, JULY, AUG, SEPT, OCT, NOV, DEC
} MONTH;

typedef struct[1]
{
      MONTH month;
      int   day;
      int   year;
} DATE;

void setdate(DATE * dt, MONTH mon, int dy, int yr)[2]
{
      dt->month = mon;
      dt->day = dy;
      dt->yr = year;
}

void lookdate(DATE * dt, MONTH * pmon, int * pdy, int * pyr)
{
      *pmon = dt->month;
      *pdy = dt->day;
      *pyr = dt->yr;
}

main()
{
```

```
        DATE  birth;[3]
        MONTH mon, dy, yr;

        printf("Enter your birthdate MM/DD/YY > ");
        scanf("%d/%d/%d", &mon, &dy, &yr);
        setdate(&birth, mon, dy, yr);[4]
        lookdate(&birth, &mon, &dy, &yr);[5]
        printf("Your birthdate is %d/%d/%d", mon, dy, yr);
}
```

Explanations

1. This is the definition for the class *DATE.*
2. These are the two operations that may be applied to an object in the class *DATE.*
3. This declares an instance of the class *DATE.* It is not a date object yet.
4. This operation builds the actual object called *birth.* Up to this point, no actual date yet existed.
5. This operation emulates the action of looking at the date.

OOP may be used for just about any situation. In particular, any program in this book could be rewritten into one that uses the object-oriented approach. However, sometimes the attempt may seem rather fruitless, as Example 22.3.7 below illustrates.

Example 22.3.7

Suppose that you are asked to write an OOP program that simply asks for the following information:

Enter your name > Paul Baxter

A prompt may indeed be viewed as an object. To define it, simply answer the usual two questions:

1. What is it made of; i.e., what are its attributes? Let us decide that a prompt consists of three parts:

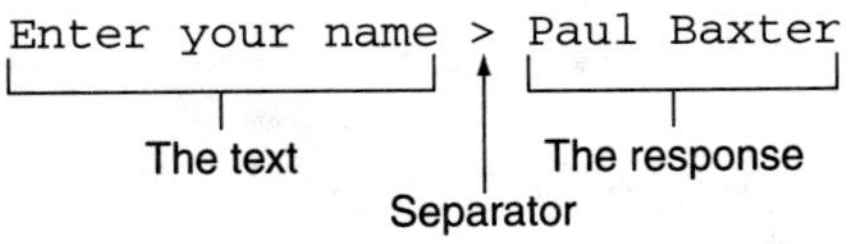

2. What operations can be done with it? Let us decide that a prompt may be identified (i.e., text is given to it), may be displayed, and may accept data.

Following is the object-oriented solution. Similar explanations to the ones from the previous two examples apply to this solution, so it is left for you to study:

```
#include <stdio.h>

typedef struct
{
      char text[81];
      char separator[4];
      char response[81];
} PROMPT;
```

The definition of the class *PROMPT*

```
void identify_prompt(PROMPT * pt, char txt[], char sep[])
{
      strcpy(pt->text, txt);
      strcpy(pt->separator, sep);
}

void display_prompt(PROMPT * pt)
{
      printf("%s%s", pt->text, pt->separator);
}
```

The operations belonging to the class *PROMPT*

```
void accept_response(PROMPT * pt, char * name)
{
        gets(pt->response);
        strcpy(name, pt->response);
}

main()
{
        PROMPT name;           <------------- An instance of the class PROMPT
        char   response[81];

        identify_prompt(&name, "Enter your name", " > ");   ┐  Operations
        display_prompt(&name);                              ├─ applied to
        accept_response(&name, response);                   ┘  the object
}                                                              name
```

At this point, you may be thinking: why bother with this complex solution? After all, the following code does exactly the same thing:

```
printf("Enter your name > ");
gets(name);
```

True. The OOP approach here is nevertheless the correct one! Unfortunately, the power of OOP becomes more apparent with bigger and more complex programs, which we will not get into here.

22.3.4 SOME PRINCIPLES OF GOOD OOP PRACTICES

Three important observations should be made about the three examples above:

Encapsulation. Subsection 22.3.1 pointed out that a class is defined by its attributes **and** its operations. Yet this is not reflected in above three examples. Only the attributes are included in the class definition. For instance:

```
typedef struct
{
        COLOR body;
        int   doors;
        float tank;
        float consumption_rate;
} CAR;
```

The operations *build()*, *fillup()*, and *drive()* of this class *CAR* should be part of this definition too. If C++ was used here, indeed, we would have done so. Unfortunately, the C language is not equipped to allow this. The action of integrating both the attributes and the operations into a class definition is called ***encapsulation.***

Passing objects to their operations. The objects *mine, birth,* and *name* were always sent to the operations by reference, even when it was unnecessary [for instance, in *look(&birth, &mon, &dy, &yr)* or in *display_prompt(&name)*]. The reason for this is to enforce consistency in passing objects to its operations. The more consistent a program is, the less frequent are occurrences of coding errors.

Information hiding. The individual attributes from either the object *mine, birth,* or *name* are accessed inside the operations **only,** not in the *main()*. This is a principle of OOP: an object should be manipulated via its operations only. For instance, the following segment violates this:

```
main()
{
        DATE  birth;
        MONTH mon, dy, yr;

        printf("Enter your birthdate MM/DD/YY > ");
```

```
        scanf("%d/%d/%d", &mon, &dy, &yr);
        setdate(&birth, mon, dy, yr);

        birth.day = birth.day + 2;

        lookdate(&birth, &mon, &dy, &yr);
        printf("Your birthdate is %d/%d/%d", mon, dy, yr);
}
```

The statement *birth.day = birth.day + 2* requires the programmer to know that the object *birth* has a member named *day*. This means that the programmer had to know some details about the implementation of the object. This is in violation of OOP. A programmer should not need to know how the inside of an object is made. This principle is called ***information hiding.*** An object should be viewed as an entity and manipulated as such. Any manipulation of an object should be done via an operation only. For example, a radio is manipulated via its buttons only. Nobody needs to know, or should need to know, anything about the inside of the radio in order to operate it!

EXERCISES 22.3.2

1. a. Write an object-oriented program that reads in a baby's birthdate and an anniversary date and displays both. Of course, use the class *DATE.*
   b. Define a new operation named *cmpdate()* that compares two date objects. A 0 is returned if they are both the same; a –1 is returned if the first date is less than the second; and otherwise, a 1 is returned.
   c. Test this new operation with the program in (a). The program will display the message "Baby born before marriage" or "Baby born after marriage."
   d. Modify the operation *cmpdate()* so that the difference in days between the two dates will be returned. For instance the number –17 would mean that the first date is 17 days behind the other. (To simplify the operation, disregard the possibility of leap years.)
2. Write an object-oriented program that reads in your first name and last name on a separate prompt. Use the class *PROMPT.*
3. a. Define a class named *TIME* with the operations *settime()* and *looktime()*. (***Hint:*** The implementation is one-to-one with the class *DATE.)*
   b. Test both operations with a simple program.
   c. Define a new operation named *cmptime()* that compares two time objects. A 0 is returned if they are both the same; a –1 is returned if the first time is less than the second; and otherwise, a 1 is returned.
   d. Test this new operation with a program that asks for the time that a work shift begins and the time that the worker actually reported for work. An appropriate message will be displayed.
   e. Modify the operation *cmptime()* so that the difference in seconds between the two times will be returned.
4. a. Define a class named *RECTANGLE* with the operations *setdimensions(), setborder(),* and *lookrect()*. The operation *setdimensions()* sets the width and height of the object; the operation *setborder()* sets the style of the border. This will be dotted '.', dashed '–', double-dashed '=' or with stars '*'; the operation *lookrect()* simply displays the object.
   b. Test all three operations with a simple program.
   c. Define a new operation named *placerect()* that places a rectangle in any reasonable place on the screen. The user will provide the coordinates of the upper left corner. This means that the attributes' line number and column for this corner must be added to the class *RECTANGLE*. Assume that the user will never specify coordinates that would cause the rectangle to show only partially.
5. a. Add an operation named *lookgas()* to the class *CAR.* It will simulate the driver looking at the gas gauge to see how much gas there is left. The amount of gas left will be returned.
   b. Modify the operation *drive()* so that it detects if the car runs out of gas. If so, the number 0 is returned; otherwise, 1 is returned.

c. Write an object-oriented program that drives two cars to a distance set by the two drivers. Then it displays how much gas each has left.

6. A fraction $^{a}/_{b}$ may be thought of as an object. Revisit Exercise 21.2.4, 4, and make the modifications necessary so that a OOP approach is taken. That is:
   a. Define the class named *FRACTION.*
   b. Modify all of the functions so that they become operations on objects of the class *FRACTION.*
   c. Write a program that tests each of these operations.
7. a. Write an operation named *read_frac()* that reads in a fraction and returns it. The fraction is entered as follows: 2/5, 3/7, and so on.
   b. Write an operation named *display_frac()* that displays a fraction passed to it. The fraction is displayed as follows 2/5, 3/7, and so on.
   c. Transform the following segment into one that uses the class *FRACTION:*

```
main()
{
        float  a, b, c;

        printf("Enter two fractional numbers: ");
        scanf("%f%f", &a, &b);
        c = a + b;
        printf("Their sum is %f\n", c);
}
```

8. Write an object-oriented program for each class defined in Exercise 22.3.1, 2. Also, define appropriate operations.
9. a. Define a class named *MY_FLOAT* that is the class of real numbers. This class has two attributes: (1) the whole part, and (2) the fractional part of the number.
   b. Define the arithmetic operations for addition and subtraction in this class.
   c. Define the operations for reading and displaying objects in this class. They are entered in this manner: 3 1/4, 91 5/7, and so on, and displayed similarly.
   d. Write a program that tests each of these operations.
   e. How do you change the program so that the fractional part may be ignored? In such a case, the fractional part will be set to 0.
10. a. Define a class named *STRING* that has the following attributes: (1) a 1-D array of characters, and (2) a length determined by the presence of a '\0'.
    b. Define the operations copy, concatenate, and finding the length. **Do not** use the standard C functions. They cannot work here because the operations are to work on an object (structure), not a string, as defined and used in Chapter 18.
11. Define a class named *LIST* that has the following attributes: (1) a 1-D array of integers, and (2) a size. Its operations will be (1) add an element, (2) delete an element, (3) modify an element, and (4) compare two lists. These are basically the functions from Sections 14.3 and 15.2, which you are now asked to implement in a OOP environment.

APPENDIX A
ASCII Character Codes

The ASCII (American Standard Code for Information Interchange) coding scheme is a method of representing information in a computer. This topic is thoroughly covered in Section 13.6. Table A.1 lists the standard ASCII codes.

Table A.1

	0	1	2	3	4	5	6	7	8	9
0	null	soh	stx	etx	eot	enq	ack	bell	bcksp	ht
1	newl	vt	ff	cr	so	si	dle	dc1	dc2	dc3
2	dc4	nak	syn	etb	can	em	sub	esc	fs	gs
3	rs	us	space	!	"	#	$	%	&	'
4	(	)	*	+	,	–	.	/	0	1
5	2	3	4	5	6	7	8	9	:	;
6	<	=	>	?	@	A	B	C	D	E
7	F	G	H	I	J	K	L	M	N	O
8	P	Q	R	S	T	U	V	W	X	Y
9	Z	[	\	]	^	_	`	a	b	c
10	d	e	f	g	h	i	j	k	l	m
11	n	o	p	q	r	s	t	u	v	w
12	x	y	z	{	|	}	~	Del		

Many of the codes between 0 and 31 are used for communication controls over networks. The set of extended ASCII codes (beyond code 127) vary depending on the computer system used, so no table will be presented for them.

APPENDIX B
Operator Precedence and Associativity

Operators were covered in Chapters 2, 3, and 13. Table B.1 lists the precedence and associativity of every operator in the C language. It also indicates the sections in this book that discusses each. (Note that not all operators are covered in this book.)

Table B.1

Order	Operator	Description		Associativity	Sections in text
1	()	Parentheses	unary	Left	3.2.3
	[]	Array element operator	binary	to	16.4
	–>	Pointer operator	binary	right	21.2.2
	.	Member operator	binary		21.1.1
2	++	Increment	unary		9.1.2, 13.4
	––	Decrement	unary		9.1.2, 13.4
	–	Negative sign	unary		3.2.1
	+	Positive sign	unary		3.2.1
	!	Logical negation	unary	Right	4.1.3
	(*type*)	Cast operator	unary	to	3.2.6
	sizeof	Size (in bytes)	unary	left	3.1.3, 14.1.1, 21.2.7
	&	Address of	unary		11.1, 11.2, 16.1, 21.2
	*	Dereference	unary		11.1, 11.2, 16.1, 21.2
	~	One's complement	unary		Not covered
3	*	Arithmetic multiplication	binary		2.2, 3.2
	/	Arithmetic division	binary		3.2
	%	Remainder operator	binary		3.2.1
4	+	Arithmetic addition	binary		2.2.1, 3.2
	–	Arithmetic subtraction	binary		2.2.1, 3.2
5	<<	Left shift	binary		Not covered
	>>	Right shift	binary		Not covered
6		Relational operators:			
	<	Less than	binary		4.1.1
	<=	Less than or equal	binary	Left	4.1.1
	>	Greater than	binary	to	4.1.1
	>=	Greater than or equal	binary	right	4.1.1

(continued on next page)

Order	Operator	Description		Associativity	Sections in Text
7	==	Relational equality	binary		4.1.1
	!=	Relational inequality	binary		4.1.1
8	&	Bitwise AND	binary		6.3.2
9	^	Bitwise exclusive OR	binary		Not covered
10	|	Bitwise inclusive OR	binary		13.3.1
11	&&	Logical AND	binary		5.1.2, 5.1.4
12	||	Logical OR	binary		5.1.1, 5.1.4
13	? :	Conditional	ternary		13.5
14	=	Assignment	binary		2.2.1, 13.1.1
	+=	Shorthand assignment		Right	
	-=	(arithmetic)	binary	to	9.1.2, 13.1.3
	*=	"		left	
	/=	"			
	%=	"			
	^=	"			
	&=	Shorthand assignment			
	|=	(bitwise)	binary		Not covered
	<<=	"			
	>>=	"			
15	,	Comma operator	binary	Left to right	9.1.1

APPENDIX C
Preprocessor Directives

As explained in Sections 2.3 and 12.4, a C program goes through a preprocessor before being compiled. This preprocessor manipulates the program text by executing any directives that it may contain. These ***preprocessing directives*** are positioned on lines beginning with a *#*. Once manipulated, the program text is handed down to the compiler for the actual compilation.

An ANSI C compiler comes with numerous preprocessor directives. This book covers only two directives: the *#include* and the *#define*. The purpose of this appendix is to cover a few others. Note that the preprocessor is not really part of the C compiler; it does not "know" C.

C.1 CONDITIONAL DIRECTIVES

The following example illustrates a practical use of the conditional directives.

Example C.1

Example 22.1.5 showed the program below:

```
#include <stdio.h>

typedef long int    INTEGER;¹
/* typedef int  INTEGER; */²


main()
{
      INTEGER  a, b, c;

      printf("Enter two numbers > ");
      c = a * b;
}
```

Explanations

1. Use this one when run on computer B.
2. Use this one when run on computer A.

It was explained in Example 22.1.5 that the programmer defines the symbolic constant *INTEGER* differently depending on the machine on which the program is compiled and run. To this end, the programmer needs to edit and comment out the appropriate *typedef* whenever the program is run on a different machine. This becomes cumbersome after a while. The use of the *#if* directive eliminates the need for editing. The new program below shows how:

```
#include <stdio.h>

#ifdef MACHINE_B[1]
typedef long int   INTEGER;
#endif
#ifdef MACHINE_A[2]
typedef int  INTEGER;
#endif

main()
{
      INTEGER  a, b, c;

      printf("Enter two numbers > ");
      c = a * b;
}
```

Explanations

1. The *#ifdef* directive checks if the symbol *MACHINE_B* is defined. If so, then the statement *typedef long int INTEGER;* will be passed to the compiler.
2. If the symbol *MACHINE_A* is defined, the statement *typedef int INTEGER;* will be passed to the compiler.

Note that the program makes use of two symbolic constants: *MACHINE_B* and *MACHINE_A*. Note also that no *#define* directives are present to define them. It turns out that a symbolic constant may also be defined externally, as is the case here. This is accomplished in various ways depending on the compiler package used. For instance, Borland C would define a symbolic constant as follows:

```
bcc somefile.c -DMACHINE_A
```

This command calls the compiler and would be issued at the command line. The option –DMACHINE_A tells the compiler to define the symbolic constant *MACHINE_A*. This is what you would want if the program is to run on machine A. If it is to run on machine B, the symbolic constant *MACHINE_B* will be defined and *MACHINE_A* will be left undefined. This kind of definition is identical to the *#define* except that it occurs "dynamically from outside the program."

The *#ifdef* directive allows for what is called ***conditional compilation.*** A block of code is compiled only if a certain condition is met. This block of code would be surrounded with an *#ifdef* and *#endif*, as shown in Figure C.1.

Figure C.1

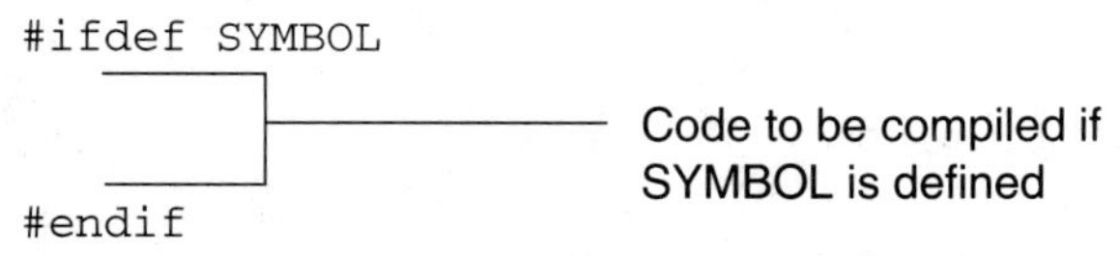

EXERCISES C.1

1. a. What does the following segment produce?

```
#define XT   1

main()
```

```
{
#ifdef XT
        printf("I am an XT machine\n");
#else
        printf("What am I?\n");
#endif
}
```

b. What would the segment produce if the *#define* was:
   i. `#define XT  0`
   ii. `#define XT`

2. a. Is there any significant difference between the program in the question above and the one below?

```
char  XT = 1;

main()
{
        if (XT)
        {
                printf("I am an XT machine\n");
        }
        else
        {
                printf("What am I?\n");
        }
}
```

b. Which program is preferable?

3. a. Use a symbol called *TESTING* in the program in Example 6.2.8 so that the testing *printf()* statements will be compiled only when the symbol *TESTING* is defined.
   b. Compare this with the method illustrated in Example 12.3.1. Which one is preferable?

C.2 MACROS

The *#define* directive may also be used to define ***macros.*** A macro is a symbolic constant that uses arguments. Consider Example C.2.

Example C.2

The program below uses a macro to find the minimum of two numbers:

```
#include <stdio.h>

#define MIN(x, y)    x < y ? x : y[1]

main()
{
        int num1, num2, min;

        num1 = 4;
        num2 = 7;
        min = MIN(num1, num2);[2]
}
```

Explanations

1. This directive defines *MIN* to be a symbolic constant that receives two arguments. These arguments are then used as specified in the expression to the right: *x < y ? x : y.*

2. Here a macro substitution occurs. Argument equivalences are made: *x* with *num1* and *y* with *num2*. The result is that the preprocessor will substitute the macro "call" *MIN(num1, num2)* with *num1 < num2 ? num1 : num2*. This is the expression that the compiler receives.

EXERCISES C.2

1. a. Offhand, to what do you think the following macro substitutions should evaluate?
   i. `MIN(num1 = 7, num2 = 5)`
   ii. `MIN(7 + 4, 5 - 1)`
   b. Now write a program to test them.
   c. You should find that the results may not be what you first expected in (a). Explain why and suggest a simple modification to the macro definition so that this sort of error never occurs.
2. Are there any significant differences between:
   a. A function call and a macro "call"?
   b. A function definition and a macro definition?
3. Define a macro named *MAX(x, y)* that is a substitute for an expression that finds the largest of the two arguments.
4. a. Define a macro named *PERIM(w, l)* that is a substitute for the formula that finds the perimeter of a rectangle.
   b. Use this macro in the following program:

```
main()
{
      float  perim, width, length;

      width = 15.3;
      length = 4.8;
      perim = 2 * (width + length);
}
```

5. Define a macro named *ABS(x)* that is a substitute for an expression that finds the absolute value of the argument.
6. A useful property of macros is that the arguments received by the macro may be of any type (which does not necessarily work with functions). For instance, the macro *MIN* in Example C.2 may be given arguments of type *float* just the same:

```
#include <stdio.h>

#define MIN(x, y)     x < y ? x : y

main()

      float f1, f2, min;

      f1 = 4.55
      f2 = 4.9;
      min = MIN(f1, f2);
}
```

   a. Can you see why the data type of the arguments does not matter?
   b. Given the variable *char first[25]*, would the following code work? Explain.

```
first = MIN("Aaron", "Andrew");
```

APPENDIX D
Static Variables

Section 3.1.1 explained that at the time of declaration, a variable is given

- a name
- a type
- a cell in memory
- a storage class

At the time, we avoided a discussion of the storage class of a variable. In most cases, the programmer does not need to worry about it! Nevertheless, its discussion remains a part of a proper computer programming education, so an appendix appears appropriate on the subject. To put it simply, the storage class indicates the degree of life span of a variable. By default, variables "live" only the duration of a function call and execution. Variables that are given a storage class of *static* "live" through the entire duration of a program. Rather than presenting a general discussion of ***static variables,*** this appendix will focus on one of its applications.

D.1 THE LIFE SPAN OF A LOCAL VARIABLE

Before discussing static variables, we need to fully understand the life span of a local variable. When a function is called, space is allocated in memory for it and for its arguments. This is briefly explained in Section 10.2. When the function is exited, all of that space is released. For instance, consider the program in the following example.

Example D.1

Let us define a function named *move_robot()* that simulates a robot moving horizontally while leaving a '+' in its trail:

int move_robot(int num)[1]

```
{
      int  counter;

      for (counter=0; counter < num; counter++)
      {
         printf("+");
         if (counter > 80)
         {
              printf("\n");
```

```
        }
    }
    printf("\n");
    return counter;
}

main()
{
    int   distance;

    distance = move_robot(4);²
    printf("Distance travelled: %d\n", distance);
    distance = move_robot(7);
    printf("Distance travelled: %d\n", distance);
    distance = move_robot(2);
    printf("Distance travelled: %d\n", distance);
}
```

The program will run as follows:

```
++++
Distance travelled: 4
+++++++
Distance travelled: 7
++
Distance travelled: 2
```

Explanations

1. At the time that the function *move_robot()* is called, space is allocated in memory for:
   a. Its function body (its executable code)
   b. Its parameters, here *num*
   c. Its local variables, here *counter* only
2. The function *move_robot()* is called three times. The robot first moves four steps, then seven steps, and finally two steps. Each time, '+' signs are left behind. Note that the function *move_robot()* also returns the distance travelled, which is simply the number of '+' signs displayed.

When the function is exited, all of that memory is released. The implication of this is that each subsequent function call to *move_robot()* cannot recall how much distance the robot covered so far. For instance, the function call *move_robot(7)* has no way of knowing that the robot had already moved four steps. In other terms, the run below cannot be arrived at:

```
++++
Distance travelled so far: 4
+++++++
Distance travelled so far: 11
++
Distance travelled so far: 13
```

But there are ways around this problem, as the section below explains.

D.2 HOW TO PRESERVE A LOCAL VARIABLE'S VALUE

There are various methods that ensure that *move_robot()* can be made to keep track of the accumulated distance travelled. Below are two of these.

Example D.2

One method is to pass a summation variable by reference to *move_robot()*. The distance travelled would be accumulated into it. Here is the solution:

```
int move_robot(int num, int * dist_ptr)
{
```

```
    int  counter;

    for (counter=0; counter < num; counter++)
    {
        printf("+");
        if (counter > 80)
        {
            printf("\n");
        }
    }
    printf("\n");
    *dist_ptr += counter;
    return *dist_ptr;
}

main()
{
    int   distance;

    printf("Distance travelled so far: %d\n", move_robot(4, &distance));
    printf("Distance travelled so far: %d\n", move_robot(7, &distance));
    printf("Distance travelled so far: %d\n", move_robot(2, &distance));
}
```

The disadvantage here is that an **external** variable, *distance,* is needed for a task that is solely **internal** to *move_robot().* The need for such an accumulator should therefore be hidden from *main().* This leads to the more modular solution in the example below.

Example D.3

Since the accumulator *distance* only has a purpose within *move_robot,* it should be declared locally to that function rather than within *main().* But then how can its value be preserved across different calls? Look at the following program for an answer:

```
int move_robot(int num)
{
    int        counter;
    static int distance = 0;

    for (counter=0; counter < num; counter++)
    {
        printf("+");
        if (counter > 80)
        {
            printf("\n");
        }
    }
    printf("\n");
    distance += counter;
    return distance;
}

main()
{
    printf("Distance travelled: %d\n", move_robot(4));
    printf("Distance travelled: %d\n", move_robot(7));
    printf("Distance travelled: %d\n", move_robot(2));
}
```

The qualifier *static* ensures that the variable *distance* is never removed from memory, even after the function *move_robot()* returns. This way, during the next call, *distance*'s value is preserved from the previous call. The variable *distance* is appropriately called a ***static variable.*** Any variable that does not have such a qualifier is called an ***automatic variable.*** The terms "static" and "automatic" refer to what is called ***storage classes.*** Much more could be said about storage classes, but that would be beyond the scope of this book.

Finally, let us look at an application.

Example D.4

Let us write a program that reads in a list of names and simply echoes them to the screen. Adjacent names are separated by the same character. Usually the separator chosen is a space, but it could be a comma or some other character, as specified by the user.

Here are two examples of a run:

Example 1

What is the delimiting character? ,↵
Enter the list of the names > Joe,Tim,Sylvia,Mimi↵
The names read in are:
    Joe
    Tim
    Sylvia
    Mimi

Example 2

What is the delimiting character? ↵
Enter the list of the names > Joe Tim Sylvia Mimi↵
The names read in are:
    Joe
    Tim
    Sylvia
    Mimi

The names are all read into a single string. Then a function named *extract()* will extract the words from the string, one per call. Let us look at two implementations of this function. This first one does not make use of a *static* variable.

```
#include <stdio.h>

char * extract(char line[], char separator, int * p_ptr, char name[])1
{
    char  ch;
    int   i;

    while (line[(*p_ptr)++] == separator) ;2
    for (i=0; (ch = line[(*p_ptr)++] != separator) && ch != NULL; i++)3
    {
          name[i] = ch;
    }
    name[i] = '\0';
    return name;
}

main()
{
    int  pos;
    char input[81], name[81], separator;

    printf("What is the delimiting character? ");
    scanf("\n%c", &separator);
    printf("Enter the list of the names > ");
    gets(input);
    printf("The names read in are:\n");
    while (extract(input, separator, &pos, name))4
```

```
        {
                printf("\t%s", name);
        }
}
```

Explanations

1. The function *extract()* finds a name from the parameter *line* and returns it. It also sends it back by reference through the parameter *name.*
2. This *while* loop skips separators as it searches for the beginning of the next name.
3. This *for* loop runs over the name, stores it, and stops past the end of it.
4. Note that the *main()* uses an index variable *pos* that is fed into the function *extract().* It runs through the string *input* in search of names. Hence its value changes after each call. The next call to *extract()* must use the latest value of *pos.* Therefore, *pos* must be sent by reference.

Study this program carefully before moving on.

Note that the index variable *pos* has a purpose only within the function *extract(),* yet it is declared in *main()!* The solution below fixes this by defining the index variable inside the function *extract()* as a *static* variable so that its value is never lost across different calls:

```
#include <stdio.h>

char * extract(char line[], char separator, char name[])
{
        char        ch;
        int         i;
        static int pos = 0;1

        while (line[pos++] == separator) ;
        for (i=0; (ch = line[pos++] != separator) && ch != NULL; i++)
        {
                name[i] = ch;
        }
        name[i] = '\0';
        return name;
}

main()
{
        char input[81], name[81], separator;

        printf("What is the delimiting character? ");
        scanf("\n%c", &separator);
        printf("Enter the list of the names > ");
        gets(input);
        printf("The names read in are:\n");
        while (extract(input, separator, name))2
        {
                printf("\t%s", name);
        }
}
```

Explanations

1. Note the declaration of a *static* variable.
2. The index into the string *input* no longer needs to be passed. (Why is that so?)

The actual logic of the program does not change, so no more explanations are needed! Note that static variables may either be declared inside a function's body or outside. In any case, the need for *static* variables is rather rare. In most situations, their use is not a good idea!

EXERCISES D.1

1. Write a function named *strtoken()* that works in exactly the same way as the library function *strtok()*. This function was used in Section 20.3, but an in-depth explanation of its internal mechanism was avoided. You are now asked to come up with the coding of that mechanism, with the help of the following algorithm. Assume the function prototype *char * strtok(char p[], char s[])*. The function *strtok()* works as follows:

   1. If the string *p* is not *NULL*, do step 1.1.
      1.1. If a token *t* is found in *p*, do steps 1.1.1 to 1.1.3.
         1.1.1. In the string *p*, the character immediately following the token *t* is overwritten with a null character.
         1.1.2. The remainder of *p* is copied into a local *static* string variable named *h*.
         1.1.3. The address of the token *t* found in the string *p* is returned.
      Otherwise, do step 1.1.4.
         1.1.4. Return *NULL*.
      Otherwise, do step 1.2.
      1.2. If a token *t* is found in *h*, do steps 1.2.1 to 1.2.2.
         1.2.1. In the string *h*, the character immediately following the token *t* is overwritten with a null character.
         1.2.2. The address of the token *t* found in the string *h* is returned.
      Otherwise, do step 1.2.3.
         1.2.3. Return *NULL*.

2. Reconsider the function *format()* in Exercise 19.2.2, 10. It is used as follows:

```
char  display[10];
printf("An atom is %s mm wide", format(2e-12, 6, display))
```

   The string variable *display* would hold the formatted number or the message "Very tiny," whichever the case may be. In the case here, the display would be "Very tiny." Note that the function *format()* returns that string too. So why send it back by reference too? The reason is that a string is always returned by pointer reference, and that pointer must be provided via an argument by reference.

   It is a common mistake to forget to include this string argument simply because the following use of *format()* comes more naturally:

```
printf("An atom is %s mm wide", format(2e-12, 6))
```

   Make the necessary changes to *format()* so that it may be called as shown here. [***Hint:*** Declare a *static* string variable within the function *format()*.]

APPENDIX E
Hexadecimal Number Representation

Technically minded programmers such as engineers often use the C programming language to manipulate the hardware, such as the memory boards and I/O ports, directly. In such situations, it is more appropriate to express data in hexadecimal notation rather than in decimal notation. This is because hexadecimal notation is closest to the computer machine language. The purpose of this appendix is to define what hexadecimal numbers are and how they may be used in a C program.

E.1 BITS AND BYTES

Programs and data travel through a computer system in binary form, which consists of 0s and 1s. For instance, the word "Kid" is stored in memory as:

```
01001011 01101001 01100100
```

Eight bits are needed to code an individual letter, and a sequence of 8 bits is called a ***byte.*** Above, each group of 8 bits represents a letter of the alphabet. These 3 bytes make up the word "Kid."

In the very early days of computers, programmers had the daunting task of programming at that level of 0s and 1s. Soon a numeric system called ***hexadecimal*** was invented in order to abbreviate long sequences of 0s and 1s into shorter and easier-to-read sequences. For instance, in hexadecimal notation, "Kid" would be represented as 4B 69 64. To arrive at that, the sequence of bits that makes up the word is split into groups of four. Then each group is given a code, as shown in Figure E.1.

Figure E.1

```
01001011 01101001 01100100
   |  |     |  |     |  |
   4  B     6  9     6  4
```

Thus the 4B is the ASCII code in hexadecimal notation for the letter 'K,' and so on for the other two letters. Each group of 0s and 1s is replaced by a symbol running from 0 to F, as shown in Table E.1.

Table E.1

Pattern	Symbol	Pattern	Symbol
0000	0	1000	8
0001	1	1001	9
0010	2	1010	A
0011	3	1011	B
0100	4	1100	C
0101	5	1101	D
0110	6	1110	E
0111	7	1111	F

EXERCISES E.1

1. Find the hexadecimal notation for each sequence of bits below:
   a. `001000100111011010100011 1010`
   b. `11111101101101110000000101011`
2. What sequences of 0s and 1s do the hexadecimal numbers below represent?
   a. `8A0FFA470`
   b. `60CD1C9A`

The C language allows programming at the very low level where individual bits are manipulated. In such cases, programmers prefer to express numerals in hexadecimal notation when these numerals need to be manipulated bitwise. For instance, instead of defining a symbolic constant as *#define ESC 27,* the hexadecimal notation *#define ESC 0x1B* may be preferred. The hexadecimal numeral *0x1B* is equivalent to the number *27*. But how does one obtain this equivalence? Read on.

E.2 CONVERSIONS TO HEXADECIMAL NOTATION AND VICE VERSA

The purpose of this subsection is to learn how to convert decimal numbers to hexadecimal numbers and vice versa. The hexadecimal system operates with 16 symbols; hence it is said to operate in base 16, as opposed to the base 10 to which we are accustomed. The symbols used are 0 to F, as shown before. Table E.2 shows how the hexadecimal notation compares to values in base 10.

Table E.2

Symbol	Value in base 10	Symbol	Value in base 10
0	0	8	8
1	1	9	9
2	2	A	10
3	3	B	11
4	4	C	12
5	5	D	13
6	6	E	14
7	7	F	15

For instance, F5C is a hexadecimal number. Its value in base 10 is calculated as follows:

$$\begin{array}{ccccc} F \times 16^2 & + & 5 \times 16^1 & + & C \times 16^0 \\ 15 \times 16^2 & + & 5 \times 16^1 & + & 12 \times 16^0 \\ 15 \times 256 & + & 5 \times 16 & + & 12 \times 1 \\ 3840 & + & 80 & + & 12 \\ & & 3932 & & \end{array}$$

EXERCISES E.2

Find the decimal equivalents of these hexadecimal numbers:

1. 3AF7
2. 10827
3. ABC0DEF

To convert a decimal number into its equivalent hexadecimal, the process explained above is reversed. The number is repeatedly divided by 16. Figure E.2 uses the number 3932 to show how this works.

Figure E.2

Quotient

3932 ÷ 16 = 245, with remainder of 12 which is the symbol **C**

245 ÷ 16 = 15, with remainder of **5**

15 ÷ 16 = 0, with remainder of 15 which is the symbol **F**

The division continues until the quotient is zero. The hexadecimal equivalent of 3932 is F5C.

EXERCISES E.3

Find the hexadecimal equivalents of these decimal numbers:

1. 10832
2. 14
3. 98760654

E.3 THE USE OF HEXADECIMAL NUMBERS IN C PROGRAMS

A hexadecimal number is expressed in C by preceding it with a *0x,* as Example E.1 illustrates.

Example E.1

This program simply shows how to display the decimal equivalent of an hexadecimal number:

```
#include <stdio.h>

#define  ESC      0x1b[1]

main()
{
      printf("The ASCII code for the ESCAPE key is %d", ESC);[2]
}
```

Explanations

1. The literal *0x1b* represents the hexadecimal number 1B, which is 27 in decimal.
2. The message output will be:

   The ASCII code for the ESCAPE key is 27

Note that the format code *%d* displays the hexadecimal number *0x1b* in decimal. To display it in hexadecimal notation, use the format code *%x:*

```
printf("The ASCII code for the ESCAPE key is %x", ESC);
```

The display will be:

The ASCII code for the ESCAPE key is 1b

To display a hexadecimal number in uppercase, use the format *%X:*

```
printf("The ASCII code for the ESCAPE key is %X", ESC);
```

The display will be:

The ASCII code for the ESCAPE key is 1B

EXERCISES E.4

1. The numbers below are specified in base 10:

   ```
   int num1, num2, num3;

   num1 = 70361;
   num2 = 44800;
   num3 = 102821;
   ```

   Change them into their hexadecimal equivalents.
2. What number will be stored in the variable *float res?*
   a. *res = 0x2ad / 0xa*
   b. *res = 0xfa * 0xb*
3. The code below is meant to add the two hexadecimal numbers A2 and B6 together. Will it compile correctly? If not, fix it.

   ```
   int  res;
   res = a2 + b6;
   ```

4. Write a program that displays a table of the hexadecimal equivalences for the decimal numbers from 0 to 999. (***Hint:*** Use the format code *%X* to display the numbers in hexadecimal notation.)
5. Write a program that displays a table of the decimal equivalences of the hexadecimal numbers from 0 to FFF. (***Hint:*** Use the format code *%d* to display the numbers in decimal.)

APPENDIX F
The Input Mechanism

In order to fully understand how input functions [such as *scanf( ), getchar( ),* and so on] work, it is quite useful to examine the internals of the input mechanism over which they operate. In doing so, you will be able to better understand why *scanf( )* fails in some situations, as extensively illustrated in Section 2.2.

F.1 FROM THE KEYBOARD TO THE C PROGRAM

This input mechanism is a combination of hardware (keyboard) and software (input stream) that permits the transmission of keystrokes from the keyboard to the C program. Example F.1 shows how this happens.

Example F.1

Consider the following program:

```
#include <stdio.h>

main()
{
    float move;

    printf("What's the percentage change in the stock market today? ");
    scanf("%f", &move);
}
```

Suppose that the user enters the number –4.62. Figure F.1 shows how this number ends up in the program. As you can see, there are four components involved: the keyboard, the input buffer, the input stream, and a call to *scanf( )*.

Input buffer. The key '–' is pressed. It is automatically stored into the input buffer. Similarly the keys '4', '.', '6' and '2' are pressed and stored in sequence in the input buffer. At this point the buffer contains the data shown in Figure F.2.

Figure F.1

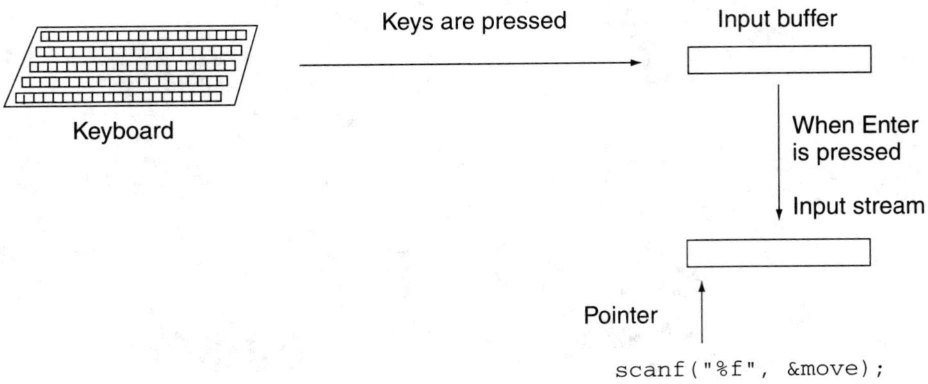

Figure F.2

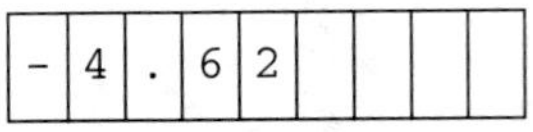

Note that every keystroke is stored as a character, never as a number, so the number –4.62 is stored as the sequence of characters "–4.62."

Input stream. When the user presses the Enter key, the whole content of the input buffer is moved into the input stream, as shown in Figure F.3.

Figure F.3

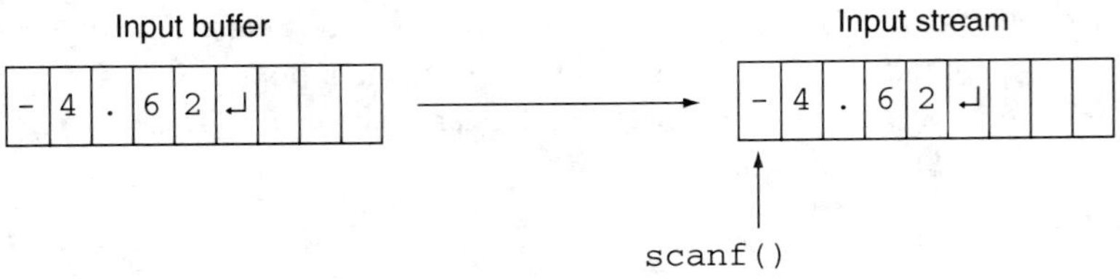

Input stream pointer. At this point, the *scanf()* can access this data. More precisely, it is the format string that tells *scanf()* how to scan the data from within the input stream. A pointer moves across the input stream in a way determined by the format codes contained in the format string. In this case, since the format code is *%f,* the pointer will scan all the characters making up –4.62, therefore **excluding** the Enter characters, as shown in Figure F.4.

Figure F.4

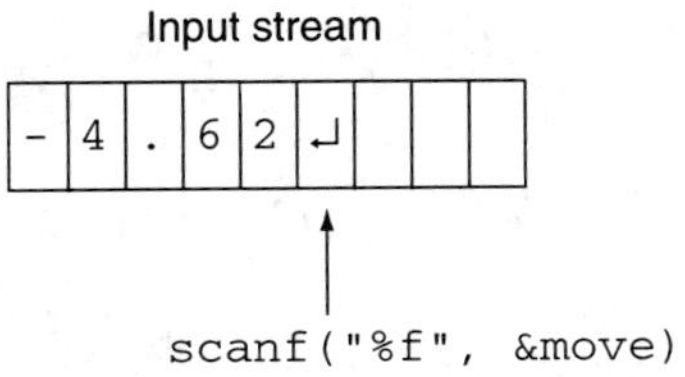

Finally *scanf()* stores this data into the variable *move.*

F.2 MORE ON THE INPUT STREAM POINTER

As mentioned above, the format codes dictate to the input stream pointer how to scan the data from the input stream. Here is how the input stream pointer moves around, given what is inside the format string:

1. One or more blank spaces placed in the format string will cause the pointer to move to the first nonblank character in the input stream. Note that white spaces, such as *\n* and *\t,* are considered blanks too.
2. The presence of *\n* tells the pointer to skip any newline character(s), as well as any white spaces, as explained in (1).

3. If the format code is:
   a. *%d.* The pointer scans an integer, skipping leading white spaces if any are found. If the pointer encounters a character (hence not part of an integer), it immediately stops under this character, thereby terminating scanning of this particular number.
   b. *%f.* The pointer scans a number. This number could be formatted as a floating-point number, a fractional number, or even an integer. Again leading white spaces (if any) are skipped. If the pointer encounters a character that is not part of an integer, a fractional number or a floating-point number, it immediately stops under this character, thereby terminating scanning of this particular number.
   c. *%c.* The pointer scans the next character (the one it is currently pointing at) into the program. Note that even if the character is a white space, it is scanned, never skipped.
4. The pointer always stops at the character immediately following the scanned datum.

Note that these rules are in fact simplified from the real ones! Let us now look at Example F.2 which illustrates some of these rules.

Example F.2

Let us write a C program that prompts the user to enter some information about an employee. Then the program will print it out:

```
#include <stdio.h>

main()
{
   int   age, educ, code;
   float height, salary;
   char  c1, c2, c3;

   printf("Enter your employee code and initials > ");
   scanf("%d\n%c%c%c", &code, &c1, &c2, &c3);

   printf("Enter your education level and age > ");
   scanf("%d%d", &educ, &age);

   printf("Enter your height and salary > ");
   scanf("%f%f", &height, &salary);

   printf("\ncode = %d, initials = %c%c%c\n"
          "educ = %d, age = %d, height = %4.2f, "
          "salary = $ %6.0f\n",
           code, c1, c2, c3, educ, age, height, salary);
}
```

Suppose that the input provided is:

Enter your employee code and initials > 2092 JPC↵
Enter your education level and age > 13 21↵
Enter your height and salary > 1.68 409.81↵

Let us now walk through each step taken by the input mechanism to store this data into the appropriate variable. After the user presses Enter at the first prompt, the input stream will contain the data shown in Figure F.5, with the input pointer reset at the start.

Figure F.5

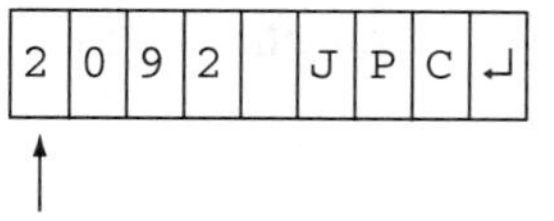

Then the format string in *scanf("%d\n%c%c%c", &code, &c1, &c2, &c3)* would make the pointer move as shown in Table F.1.

Table F.1

Input stream after datum read	Format code acted upon	Data stored code	c1	c2	c3
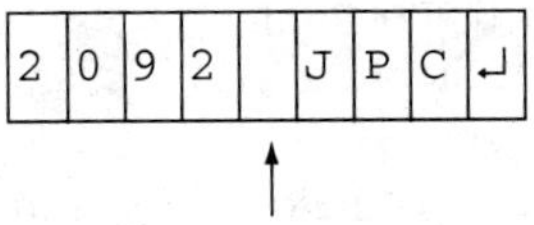	%d	2092			
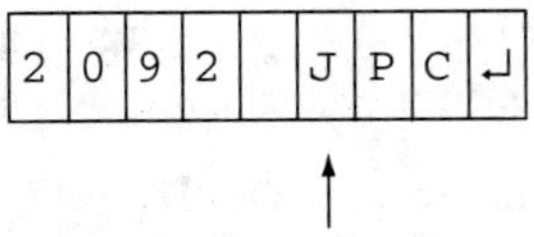	\n	2092			
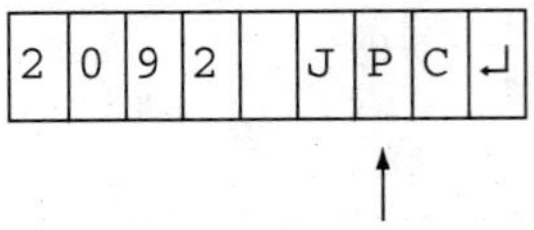	%c	2092	J		
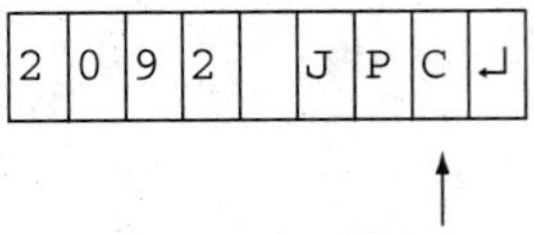	%c	2092	J	P	
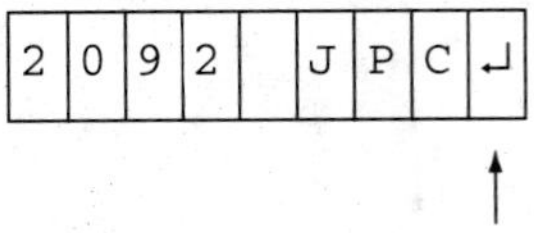	%c	2092	J	P	C

Then the next *scanf("%d%d", &educ, &age)* executes. Note that the input pointer is still at the ↵ character, as shown in Figure F.6.

Figure F.6

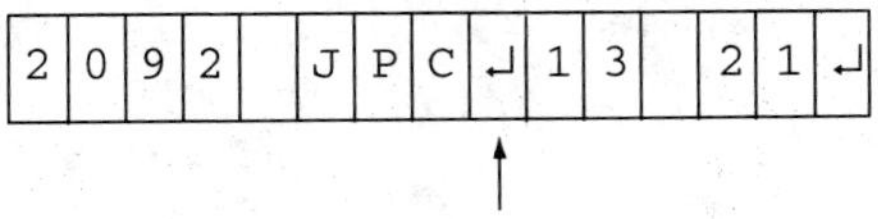

The pointer is **not** reset. To reset it—thereby erasing all data in the input stream—the function *fflush(stdin)* would have to be called, but it was not called in this program. Here is how the second *scanf()* will scan the data, as shown in Table F.2.

Table F.2

Input stream after datum read	Format code acted upon	Data stored educ	age
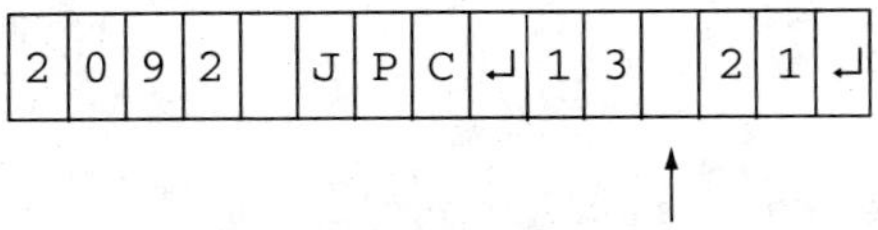	%d	13	
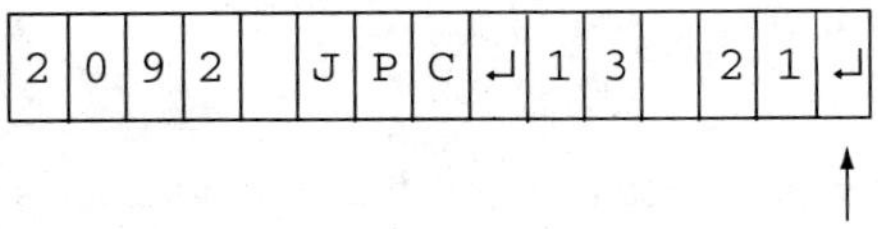	%d	13	21

As you can see, after the data is read, the Enter key (↵) remains in the stream and may need to be dealt with also. This is often overlooked. The last *scanf("%f%f", &height, &salary)* is left for you as an exercise. In the end the output produced by the program would be as expected:

```
code = 2092, initials = JPC
educ = 13, age = 21, height = 1.68, salary = $ 410.
```

EXERCISES F.1

1. A user is prompted to enter data, and he or she wants to key in the following data:

```
1   -2 3↵
4-5 6↵
7            -8      -9↵
```

Suppose the declaration: *int num1, num2, num3, num4;*
What values will be assigned to these variables when each of the following statements is executed?

a. `scanf("%d%d%d%d", &num1, &num2, &num3, &num4);`

b.
```
scanf("%d%d", &num1, &num2);
scanf("%d", &num3);
scanf("%d", &num4);
```

2. The program in Example F.2 may just as well have asked to enter the data in a different way than shown, as each segment below illustrates. For each segment, walk through each step taken by the input mechanism to store the data in the appropriate variable.

a.
```
printf("Enter your employee code > ");
scanf("%d", &code);

printf("Enter your initials > ");
scanf("\n%c", &c1);
scanf("%c", &c2);
scanf("%c", &c3);

printf("Enter your education level > ");
scanf("%d", &educ);

printf("Enter your age > ")
scanf("%d", &age);

printf("Enter your height > ");
scanf("%f", &height);

printf("Enter your salary > ");
scanf("%f", &salary);
```

Data is entered as follows:

Enter your employee code > 2092↵
Enter your initials > JPC↵
Enter your education level > 13↵
Enter your age > 21↵
Enter your height > 1.68↵
Enter your salary > 409.81↵

b.
```
printf("Enter your employee code, initials,\n"
       "       education level, age, height,"
       " and salary:\n");
scanf("%d\n%c%c%c%d%d%f%f",
      &code, &c1, &c2, &c3,
      &educ, &age, &height, &salary);
```

Data is entered as follows:

Enter your employee code, initials,
      education level, age, height, and salary:
2092 JPC 13 21 1.68 409.81↵

F.3 *scanf()* FAILURES EXPLAINED

Mistyping input data, even slightly, can cause it to be read incorrectly. This was shown many times over in Chapter 2. We are now in a position to explain why. Consider Example F.3.

Example F.3

Suppose that the following data was entered:

Enter your employee code, initials,
    education level, age, height and salary:
<u>2092↵</u>
<u>J P C13↵</u>
<u>21 1.68 409.81↵</u>

How will the program behave? After the first Enter is pressed, the input stream will contain the data shown in Figure F.7.

Figure F.7

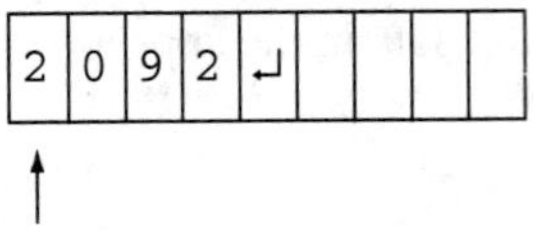

The first *scanf("%d\n%c%c%c", &code, &c1, &c2, &c3)* scans the data as shown in Table F.3.

Table F.3

Input stream after datum Read	Format code acted upon	Data stored `code`
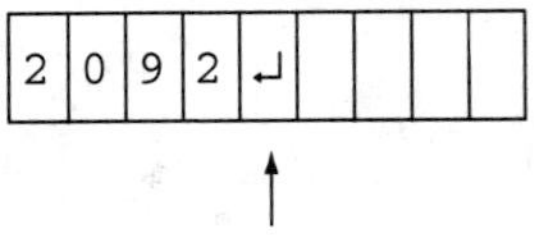	`%d`	`2092`

The *scanf()* wants to scan more data, so it waits for the user. When the user enters the second line, *J P C13*↵, Table F.4 shows what happens.

Table F.4

Input stream after datum read	Format code acted upon	Data stored `c1`	`c2`	`c3`
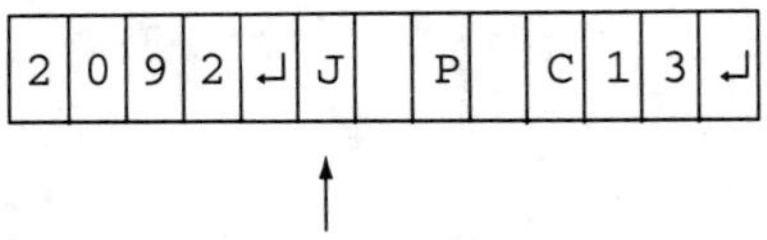	`\n`			
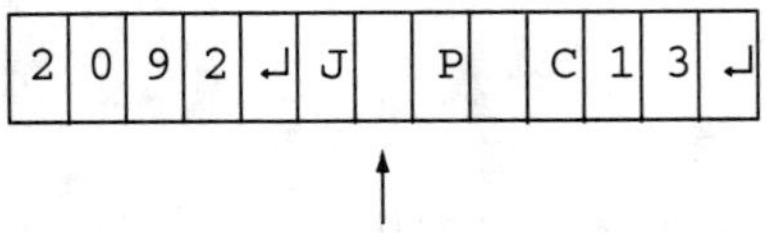	`%c`	`J`		
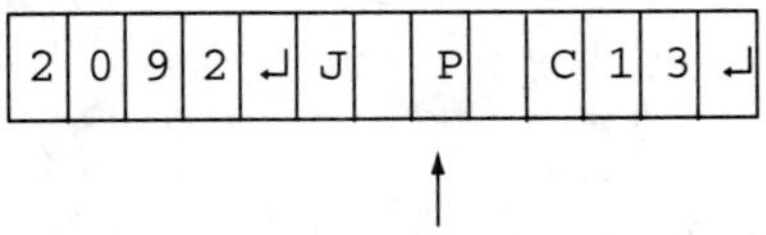	`%c`	`J`	`' '`	
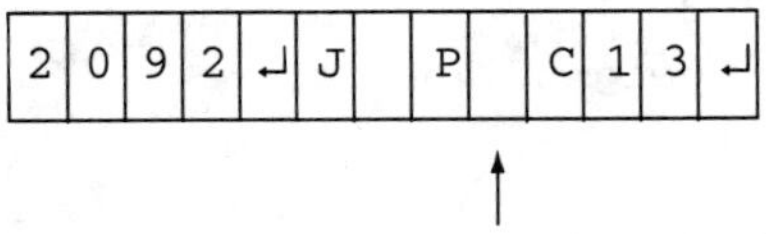	`%c`	`J`	`' '`	`P`

Then the second *scanf("%d%d", &educ, &age)* continues the scanning, but fails, as Table F.5 illustrates.

Table F.5

Input stream after datum read	Format code acted upon	Data stored educ	age
`2 0 9 2 ↵ J _ P _ C 1 3 ↵` (pointer ↑ at C)	`%d`		

The pointer skipped the space (which is normal), but then it encountered a 'C' instead of a number. As a consequence, the *scanf()* fails and immediately terminates. Note that the pointer still remains at the location of the failure. Then the third *scanf("%f%f", &height, &salary)* takes over, but it wants to read a number too, and it also fails! When we run this program with this input data, we see the following output:

code = 2092, initials = J P
educ = 9952, age = –32268, height = 0.00, salary = $ 2844821520
68527323000000.

This is quite silly! Once a format code fails, the others in the current *scanf()* and subsequent ones likely will fail too. This accounts for all of the bad data.

EXERCISES F.2

1. a. Continuing with the example above, walk through each step taken by the input mechanism and with the data below locate where the input will fail:

   Enter your employee code, initials,
   education level, age, height, and salary:
   <u>2092.1↵</u>
   <u>JPC13↵</u>

   b. Run the program, and explain what happens.
2. a. With the segment in Exercise F.1, 2a, walk through each step taken by the input mechanism, and locate where the input will fail with the data below:

   i. Enter your employee code > <u>2092↵</u>
   Enter your initials > <u>J P C↵</u>
   Enter your education level > <u>12↵</u>
   Enter your age > <u>21.5↵</u>
   Enter your height > <u>1.68↵</u>
   Enter your salary > <u>871.1↵</u>

   ii. Enter your employee code > <u>2092↵</u>
   Enter your initials > <u>JPC↵</u>
   Enter your education level > <u>12↵</u>
   Enter your age > <u>21.5↵</u>
   Enter your height > <u>1.68↵</u>
   Enter your salary > <u>871.1↵</u>

   b. Run the program, and explain what happens.
3. Suppose that the following was entered in the segment in Exercise F.1, 2b. Would the data be read correctly? Explain.

   a. Enter your employee code, initials,
   education level, age, height, and salary:
   <u>2092JPC↵</u>
   <u>13↵</u>
   <u>21↵</u>
   <u>1.68↵</u>
   <u>409.81↵</u>

b. Enter your employee code, initials,
    education level, age, height, and salary:

<u>2092↵</u>
<u>JPC13↵</u>
<u>21↵</u>
<u>1.68 409.81↵</u>

4. When prompted for data by the program in Example F.2, suppose an absent-minded user entered all data at the first prompt:

   Enter your employee code and initials > <u>2092 JPC 13 21 1.68 409.81↵</u>

   Would the data still be read in correctly? How would the program behave exactly on the screen?

5. A user is prompted to enter data. He plans to enter the folllowing:

```
123    45.6↵
↵
x78   -909.8 7↵
- 65$    432.10↵
```

   It is not important to know what that data is all about. Suppose the declarations:

```
int     n1, n2, n3, n4;
float   f1, f2, f3, f4;
char    c1, c2, c3, c4;
```

   What values will be assigned to these variables when each of the following statements is executed with the input shown above? Where would the input fail, if at all?

   a. `scanf("%d%f", &n1, &f1);`
      `scanf("%c%c%d", &c1, &c2, &n2);`
      `scanf("%f", &f2);`
      `scanf("%c%d%c", &c3, &n3, &c4);`

   b. `scanf("%d%f%c%c%c%d%f%d%f%c",`
      `&n1, &f1, &c1, &c2, &c3, &n2, &f2, &n3, &f3, &c4);`

   c. `scanf("%f%d%f\n%c%d %c %f %d %d",`
      `&f1, &n1, &f2, &c1, &n2, &c2, &f3, &n3, &n4);`

6. Assume the same declarations as above, with the content of the input stream as follows:

5	4		3	2	e	1	↵	-	6	.	7	8	$	9	0	↵	↵		1	↵
↑																				

   What values will be assigned to these variables when each of the following statements is executed?

   a. `scanf("%d%d%c%c%f%c%d", &n1, &n2, &c1, &c2, &f1, &c3, &n3);`

   b. `scanf("%d%f%f%c%c%c%d", &n1, &f1, &f2, &c1, &c2, &c3, &n2);`

APPENDIX G
Some Input/Output Objects from C++

Increasingly, C programming development is being done with a C++ compiler. There are many reasons for this preference, three of which are:

- The C++ compiler is a superset of C. Consequently, any C program may be compiled with a C++ compiler and run normally.
- The C++ compiler is better at detecting errors than C is.
- The C++ compiler includes the objects *cin* and *cout,* which are supersets of *scanf()* and *printf(),* respectively. The C++ compiler uses ***objects*** instead of functions (recall the exact definition of an object from Subsection 22.3.1). Objects are much less error prone than their function counterparts.

Much more can be done with *cin* and *cout* than *scanf()* and *printf().* Still, this appendix will only cover the equivalences in functionality between the two sets. This will be accomplished by simply presenting a C program, followed immediately by its equivalent C++ version and explanations. We will also cover similar objects for reading from and storing into files

It is important to understand that this appendix is not a substitute to studying C I/O functions such as *scanf()* and *printf().* In fact, it is assumed that these functions are studied first. Then if you wish, refer to this appendix to study the equivalences in C++. To ease the effort, this appendix has been subdivided into sections by relevant chapters. Finally, contrary to the chapters, this appendix offers few exercises. You are instead encouraged to select any programs that you developed using C in the course of this book and convert them into C++.

G.1 STANDARD I/O OBJECTS: *cin* AND *cout* (CHAPTER 2)

Example G.1 illustrates the use of the object *cout.*

Example G.1

Consider the following C program:

```
#include <stdio.h>

main()
{
      printf("Cze the future!");
```

```
        printf("\nI C C there\n");
        printf("So C now. Don't be a CC\n");
}
```

Its equivalent program in C++ is:

```
#include <iostream.h>[1]

main()
{
        cout << "Cze the future!";[2]
        cout << "\nI C C there\n";
        cout << "So C now. Don't be a CC\n";
}
```

Explanations

1. Notice the header file to include is no longer *stdio.h* but *iostream.h.* It contains the definitions for the objects *cin* and *cout.*
2. This statement simply sends the message in double quotation marks to the screen. Actually, the message is sent to the object *cout,* which represents the screen.

```
cout << "Cze the future!";
```

The object *cout* is the screen object and the << symbol sends the message to *cout.* Note that the three *cout* statements could have been replaced with this single one:

```
cout << "Cze the future!"
     << "\nI C C there\n"
     << "So C now. Don't be a CC\n";
```

or all on a single line:

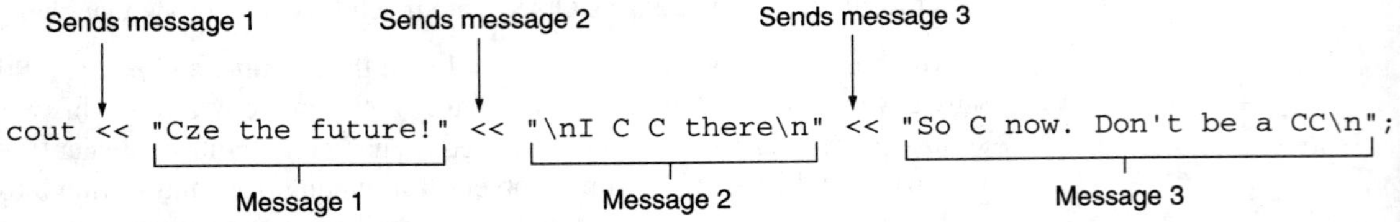

Note that a << is needed to the left of each message to be sent to the object *cout.*

EXERCISES G.1

1. What are the equivalent *printf()* statements for the two *cout* statements above?
2. Rewrite the following segment using *cout:*

```
printf("Here's an unusual opportunity for everyone who\n"
       "is determined to get ahead in business.\n"
       "Just print your name and address\n"
       "on the special shipping label.\n\n");
```

3. Find the error in each statement below:
   a. `cout >> "Tuesday's meeting\n" >> " is cancelled";`
   b. `cout < "World trade";`
   c. `cout << "Forecast tomorrow", " is for ", "gusting winds";`

The next two examples illustrate the use of the object *cin* and some more of the object *cout.*

Example G.2

Consider the program below:

```
#include <stdio.h>

main()
{
    int    num_weeks;
    float  pay_rate;

    printf("Enter the number of weeks of work > ");
    scanf("%d", &num_weeks);
    printf("What's the pay rate? ");
    scanf("%f", &pay_rate);
    printf("You will work %d weeks ", total_income);
    printf(" paid at %f an hour", pay_rate);
}
```

Its equivalent program in C++ is:

```
#include <iostream.h>

main()
{
    int    num_weeks;
    float  pay_rate;

    cout << "Enter the number of weeks of work > ";
    cin  >> num_weeks;[1]
    cout << "What's the pay rate? ";
    cin  >> pay_rate;[1]
    cout << "You will work " << num_weeks << " weeks";[2]
    cout << " paid at " << pay_rate << " an hour";[2]
}
```

Explanations

1. The object *cin* reads a number and stores it into the variable *num_weeks.* The >> symbol sends the data into the variable *num_weeks.* The object *cin* represents the keyboard. Similarly *cin >> pay_rate* reads the pay rate and stores it into the variable *pay_rate.* Note that no format codes are needed! The object *cin* is clever enough to know how to read data, any data, whether it is data of type *int, float,* or whatever else. How pleasant!
2. This statement sends three items to the object *cout:*

```
cout << "You will work " << num_weeks << " weeks";
```

Item 1 (message) — "You will work "
Item 2 (variable) — num_weeks
Item 3 (message) — " weeks"

For instance, the output might be "You will work 12 weeks." The statement *cout << " paid at " << pay_rate << " an hour"* works similarly. Note that no format codes are needed to display the variables' content. The object *cout* is also clever enough to know how to display data, any data, whether it is data of type *int, float,* or whatever.

Example G.3

Consider the following program:

```
#include <stdio.h>

main()
```

```
{
    int num1, num2, num3, sum, product;

    printf("Enter two numbers: ");
    scanf("%d%d%d", &num1, &num2, &num3);
    sum = num1 + num2 + num3;
    product = num1 * num2 * num3;
    printf("sum = %d, product = %d", sum, product);
}
```

Its equivalent program in C++ is:

```
#include <iostream.h>

main()
{
    int num1, num2, num3, sum, product;

    cout << "Enter two numbers: ";
    cin  >> num1 >> num2 >> num3;
    sum = num1 + num2 + num3;
    product = num1 * num2 * num3;
    cout << "sum = " << sum << " product = " << product;
}
```

The object *cin* can read more than one datum at a time, and because no format codes are needed, this operation is less error prone than *scanf("%d%d%d", &num1, &num2, &num3).*

EXERCISES G.2

1. Convert the C program below into a C++ program:

```
#include <stdio.h>

main()
{
     float  hourly_rate;
     int    hours_per_week;
     float  total_income;
     int    num_weeks;

     printf("Enter the hourly wage,\n"
            "the total work hours per week, and\n"
            "the number of weeks of work > ");
     scanf("%f%d%d", &hourly_rate, &hours_per_week, &num_weeks);

     total_income = hourly_rate * hours_per_week * num_weeks;

     printf("You will make $ %f in %d weeks this summer",
             total_income, num_weeks);
}
```

2. Write a program in C++ that reads in a name of four letters, such as Mike, and displays it backwards, i.e., ekiM.

Although *cout* does not require format codes, sometimes you may want to format the display of the data in a particular way. Consider Example G.4.

Example G.4

Here is a C program that demonstrates output formatting with format codes:

```
#include <stdio.h>

main()
{
    int    num_weeks;
    float  pay_rate;

    printf("Enter the number of weeks of work > ");
    scanf("%d", &num_weeks);
    printf("What's the pay rate? ");
    scanf("%f", &pay_rate);
    printf("You will work %5d weeks ", total_income);
    printf(" paid at %7.2f an hour", pay_rate);
}
```

Let us compare this with its equivalent program in C++:

```
#include <iostream.h>
#include <iomanip.h>1

main()
{
    int    num_weeks;
    float  pay_rate;

    cout << "Enter the number of weeks of work > ";
    cin  >> num_weeks;
    cout << "What's the pay rate? ";
    cin  >> pay_rate;
    cout << "You will work " << setw(5) << total_income << " weeks";2
    cout << " paid at "
         << setw(7) << setprecision(2) << pay_rate << " an hour";3
}
```

Explanations

1. When formatting of data is desired, the header file *iomanip.h* must be included. It contains functions for formatting data.
2. This statement displays the number in *total_income* inside a display zone of five spaces:

   ```
   cout << "You will work " << setw(5) << total_income << " weeks";
   ```

   The function *setw(5)* is called a ***format manipulator.*** << *setw(5)* sets the width of the display zone to five spaces, and then the variable *total_income* is displayed inside this zone.
3. This statement displays the number in *pay_rate* inside a display zone of seven spaces. Also the format manipulator *setprecision(2)* is called to set the precision to two digits after the point:

   ```
   cout << " paid at "
   << setw(7) << setprecision(2) << pay_rate << " an hour";
   ```

   setw(7) sets the width of the display zone to seven spaces, while *setprecision(2)* sets the precision to two digits after the point. Then the variable *pay_rate* is displayed inside this zone.

Thus *printf()* uses format codes while *cout* uses format manipulators. The formatting rules with *cout* are the same ones as for *printf()*. Given the same format, both *cout* and *printf()* display a number in the same way. Here are a few more examples showing the equivalences:

1. `cout << "|" << setw(12) << setprecision(3) << total_income << "|";`

displays the same as:

```
printf("|%12.3f|", total_income);
```

2. `cout << "|" << setprecision(3) << total_income << "|";`

   displays the same as:

   ```
   printf("|%.3f|", total_income);
   ```

   Note that the width specification is missing from both statements.

3. `cout << "|" << setw(12) << total_income << "|";`

   displays the same as:

   ```
   printf("|%12f|", total_income);
   ```

4. `cout << "|" << setw(12) << num_weeks << "|";`

   displays the same as:

   ```
   printf("|%12d|", num_weeks);
   ```

5. `printf("|%e|", total_income);`

   may be changed to the equivalent statement:

   ```
   cout << "|" << setiosflag(ios::scientific) << total_income << "|";
   ```

   The flag *ios::scientific* sent to the manipulator *setiosflag()* instructs the object *cout* to display the variable *total_income* in exponentional (i.e., scientific) notation. This is precisely what *%e* does.

6. `printf("|%-12f|", total_income);`

   may be changed to the equivalent statement:

   ```
   cout << "|" << setw(12) << setiosflag(ios::left) << total_income << "|";
   ```

   The flag *ios::left* sent to the manipulator *setiosflag()* instructs the object *cout* to display the variable *total_income* left justified. There is also the flag *ios::right* to display the number right justified, which is also the default.

EXERCISES G.3

1. Convert the following statements into C++:
   a. `printf("%6.2f and %6.2f makes %8.2f", 18, 4, 18 + 4);`
   b. `printf("%.2f and %.2f makes %.2f", 18, 4, 18 + 4);`
   c. `printf("Judy will work %6d weeks", 14);`
   d. `printf("Judy will work %7.5d weeks", 14);`
2. Suppose the number given to *cout* is –702.0166. Indicate the format manipulator(s) required for the following to be displayed in the display zone:
   a. –702.0
   b. __–702.01660
   c. ____–702.0167
   d. –702.02

G.2 READING/DISPLAYING ARRAYS (CHAPTERS 14 AND 15)

Consider the two examples below.

Example G.5

Take a look at the following C program from Example 14.1.2:

```
#include <stdio.h>

main()
```

```
{
      int month[12];
      int index, sum;

      printf("Enter the monthly rainy days this year > ");
      for (index=0; index < 12; index++)
      {
          scanf("%d", &month[index]);
      }
      sum = 0;
      for (index=0; index < 12; index++)
      {
          printf("In month %d, %d rainy days\n", index+1, month[index]);
          sum += month[index];
      }
      printf("There were %d rainy days\n", sum);
}
```

Its equivalent program in C++ is:

```
#include <iostream.h>

main()
{
      int month[12];
      int index;
      int sum;

      cout << "Enter the monthly rainy days this year > ";
      for (index=0; index < 12; index++)
      {
          cin >> month[index];
      }
      sum = 0;
      for (index=0; index < 12; index++)
      {
          cout << "In month " << index+1 << ", "
                << month[index] << " rainy days\n";
          sum += month[index];
      }
      cout << "There were " << sum << " rainy days\n";
}
```

As you can see, displaying an element of an array is a snap!

Displaying a memory address. The simple example below will suffice to illustrate how to display memory addresses.

Example G.6

Displaying addresses of arrays and other variables is just as easy. Here is a program in C that displays addresses:

```
#include <stdio.h>

main()
{
       int   month[12];
       int   index;

       printf("Address of the array month is %p", month);
```

```
        printf("Address of the index is %p", &index);
}
```

Its equivalent program in C++ is:

```
#include <iostream.h>

main()
{
        int   month[12];
        int   index;

        cout << "Address of the array month is " << month;
        cout << "Address of the index is " << &index;
}
```

Notice that no format codes are needed. *cout* is smart enough to know that *&index* refers to an address! If you had accidentally omitted the address operator, the *cout* object would have issued an error (unlike C, which would simply leave you puzzled). How refreshing!

EXERCISES G.4

1. Use the objects *cin* and *cout* in the program in Exercise 14.1.2, 5.
2. Use the objects *cin* and *cout* in the program in Exercise 17.1.2, 3d.
3. Use the objects *cin* and *cout* in the program in Example 17.3.1.

G.3 READING/DISPLAYING CHARACTERS AND STRINGS (CHAPTER 18)

Just as in C, C++ offers various methods to read and display characters and strings. Consider the three examples below.

Example G.7

The following C program reads a name and displays it:

```
#include <stdio.h>

main()
{
        char name[81];

        printf("Enter your name: ");
        scanf("%s", name);
        printf("Your name is %s", name);
}
```

Its equivalent program in C++ is:

```
#include <iostream.h>

main()
{
        char name[81];

        cout << "Enter your name: ";
        cin  >> name;
        cout << "Your name is " << name;
}
```

Again, there is no need for a format code to tell *cin* or *cout* how to read and display the string. It should be pointed out that *cin* reads strings just as *scanf()* does: it stops scanning when it hits a space or a *\n*. Only the first name will be read, and the last name remains in the input buffer.

Example G.8

This example shows how *cin* may be made to read a whole line at the time. Recall that a C program uses *gets()* to do this:

```
#include <stdio.h>

main()
{
      char name[81];

      printf("Enter your name: ");
      gets(name);
      printf("Your name is %s", name);
}
```

Its equivalent program in C++ is:

```
#include <iostream.h>

main()
{
      char name[81];

      cout << "Enter your name: ";
      cin.getline(name, 81);
      cout << "Your name is " << name;
}
```

The function *cin.getline()* works exactly as *gets()* does, except that a second argument, here *81*, may be passed to it. It specifies the maximum number of characters that may be read, minus 1. Note the placement of the dot:

```
cin.getline(name, 81);
```

This dot indicates that *getline()* is actually a member function **within** the object *cin*. Indeed, if you recall from Section 22.3, an object contains functions that may be called to operate on it.

Actually *cin.getline()* really works like *fgets(name, 81, stdin)*.

Example G.9

C++ can also read one character at a time. First look at the C program that uses *getchar()* to do this:

```
#include <stdio.h>
#include <ctype.h>

main()
{
      signed char  ch;

      while ((ch = getchar()) != '\n')
      {
            if (islower(ch))
            {
                  putchar(ch);
            }
      }
}
```

Its equivalent program in C++ is:

```
#include <iostream.h>
#include <ctype.h>

main()
{
      signed char  ch;

      while ((ch = cin.get()) != '\n')[1]
      {
            if (islower(ch))
            {
                  cout.put(ch);[2]
            }
      }
}
```

Explanations

1. The function *cin.get()* works exactly like *getchar()*. Need we say more?
2. Similarly, the function *cout.put()* works exactly as *putchar()* does.

EXERCISES G.5

1. Convert each C program below into C++. Decide whether it is better to use *cin*, *cin.getline()*, or *cin.get()*:
   a. Exercise 18.1.1, 1
   b. Exercise 18.1.2, 1
   c. Exercise 18.1.2, 2
   d. Example 18.1.4
   e. Example 18.2.7
   f. All solutions of Example 19.2.1
   g. Example 20.1.2
2. In C++, formatting of data may be applied to strings as well as numbers. The syntax remains the same. Write a C++ program that reads in a full name in a single string and displays it as part of a statement, as follows:

```
Enter your full name: Jennifer Linda Handley
Hello Jennifer Linda Handley. How are you?
Hello Jennifer Lin. How are you?
Hello         Jennifer Lin. How are you?
Hello Jennifer Lin         . How are you?
```

   Hint: Use all of the appropriate format manipulators discussed in Section G.1.

G.4 FILE HANDLING (CHAPTERS 2 AND 8)

In C, a file pointer **variable** is used to access a file. In C++, a file **object** is used instead. Yet the underlying input/output mechanism remains the same. The four examples below illustrate file handling in C++.

Example G.10

The following C program simply makes a copy of a list of numbers from the file IN.DAT into the file OUT.DAT:

```
#include <stdio.h>

main()
```

```
{
      FILE * ifp;
      FILE * ofp;
      int    num;

      ifp = fopen("in.dat", "r");
      ofp = fopen("out.dat", "w");
      while (!feof(ifp))
      {
            fscanf(ifp, "%d", &num);
            fprintf(ofp, "%d", num);
      }
      fclose(ifp);
      fclose(ofp);
}
```

Its equivalent program in C++ is:

```
#include <fstream.h>[1]

main()
{
      fstream ifp;
      fstream ofp;[2]
      int     num;

      ifp.open("in.dat", ios::in);[3]
      ofp.open("out.dat", ios::out);[3]
      while (!ifp.eof())[4]
      {
            ifp >> num;[5]
            ofp << num;[6]
      }
      ifp.close();[7]
      ofp.close();[7]
}
```

Explanations

1. The header file *fstream.h* contains the class definition for *fstream.*
2. These two statements declare the file **objects** *ifp* and *ofp.* These are **not** variables, but objects from the ***class*** *fstream.* Classes are the equivalent of types in C, except that they are far more sophisticated. To put it simply, a type is to variables what a class is to objects. Note that the file objects *ifp* and *ofp* are not pointers either, contrary to the case in the C program. So perhaps their names should have been changed to, say, *ifo* (for input file object) and *ofo* (for output file object) respectively, to better reflect this. However, for the sake of easier one-to-one comparison with the C program, their names were purposely left the same. Note that the objects *cin* and *cout* are also of class *fstream.* This implies that any function that is a member of these objects, such as *cin.get(),* is also passed down (inherited) to the objects *ifp* and *ofp.* We will see a few examples later.
3. This function call opens the file IN.DAT and links the object *ifp* with it. At this point, this object represents the file. The second argument is the access mode *ios::in.* This mode says that the file IN.DAT is open for reading. Compare with *fopen():*

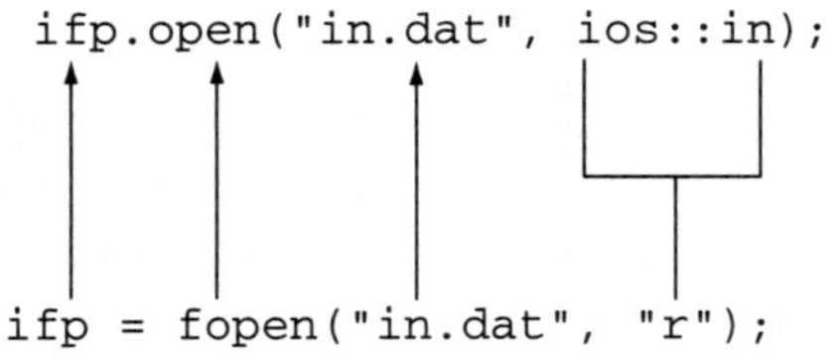

4. The function call *ifp.eof()* returns 1 if the end-of-file marker is reached; it returns 0 otherwise.
5. The syntax used to read the numbers from the input file is the same as it was with *cin.* Regardless of the actual I/O device accessed, the syntax is always the same. This is a strong point in favor of C++ I/O operations.
6. Similarly, the syntax used to store the numbers into the output file is exactly the same as with *cout.*
7. Of course, these two function calls close the files.

The class *fstream* offers the append mode too. Hence the call *ofp = fopen("out.dat", "a");* has the equivalent function call *ofp.open("out.dat", ios::app);*

Example G.11

The C program below does the same thing as the one above except that *fscanf()* is used to check for the end-of-file marker and to read each individual number:

```
#include <stdio.h>

main()
{
        FILE * ifp;
        FILE * ofp;
        int    num;

        ifp = fopen("in.dat", "r");
        ofp = fopen("out.dat", "w");
        while (fscanf(ifp, "%d", &num) != EOF)
        {
                fprintf(ofp, "%d", num);
        }
        fclose(ifp);
        fclose(ofp);
}
```

Its equivalent program in C++ is:

```
#include <fstream.h>

main()
{
        fstream  ifp;
        fstream  ofp;
        int      num;
        char     ch;

        ifp.open("in.dat", ios::in);
        ofp.open("out.dat", ios::out);
        while ((ch = ifp.peek()) != EOF)1
        {
                ifp >> num;2
                ofp << num;
        }
        ifp.close();
        ofp.close();
}
```

Explanations

1. The function *ifp.peek()* takes a peek at the next character from the input file. If that character is the EOF, the loop terminates; otherwise, it continues. Note that *ifp.peek()* does not read any data, it only looks at it; thus the data remain in the input buffer.
2. This statement does the actual reading.

EXERCISES G.6

Convert the programs below into C++:

1. Example 8.2.1
2. Example 8.2.2
3. Example 8.2.3

Example G.12

The C program below simply attempts to open a file and then verifies if the operation was successful:

```
#include <stdio.h>

main()
{
	FILE * ifp;

	ifp = fopen("in.dat", "r");
	if (ifp == 0)
	{
		printf("The file could not be opened\n");
	}
	else
	{
		fclose(ifp);
	}
}
```

Its equivalent program in C++ is:

```
#include <fstream.h>

main()
{
	fstream ifp;

	ifp.open("in.dat", ios::in);
	if (ifp == 0)
	{
		cout << "The file could not be opened\n";
	}
	else
	{
		ifp.close();
	}
}
```

The object *ifp* receives a value of 0 if the file cannot be opened.

EXERCISE G.7

Convert the program in Example 8.2.4 into C++.

Example G.13

The C language has the function *fgets()* to read a field from a record, a whole record, or a whole line from an input file. For instance, the following C program reads records one at a time and displays them:

```
#include <stdio.h>

main()
{
        FILE * ifp;
        FILE * ofp;
        char   line[81];

        ifp = fopen("letter.txt", "r");
        ofp = fopen("copy.txt", "w");
        while (fgets(line, 81, ifp) != EOF)
        {
                fputs(line, ofp);
        }
        fclose(ifp);
        fclose(ofp);
}
```

Its equivalent program in C++ is:

```
#include <fstream.h>

main()
{
        fstream  ifp;
        fstream  ofp;
        char     ch;
        char     line[81];

        ifp.open("letter.txt", ios::in);
        ofp.open("copy.txt", ios::out);
        while (ifp.getline(line, 81) != EOF)
        {
                ofp << line;
        }
        ifp.close();
        ofp.close();
}
```

The function call *ifp.getline(line, 81)* works exactly as the *fgets()* does in the C program. Note that a function named *ifp.get()* exists that could be used to read one character at a time. It works exactly the same way as *cin.get()*. In fact, any function member of the object *cin* is also a member of the object *ifp*. This is because the objects *cin* and *ifp* are both of class *fstream*.

EXERCISES G.8

Convert the programs below into C++:

1. Example 20.2.1
2. Exercise 20.2.1, 3
3. Exercise 20.2.1, 4
4. Example 20.2.2
5. Example 20.2.4

G.5 PASSING FILES TO AND FROM FUNCTIONS (CHAPTERS 10 AND 11)

Argument passing in C++ is more sophisticated than in C. In C++, data may be passed by declaring the parameter as a copy of the argument (by value); as a pointer reference to the argument;

or as a ***reference*** to the argument. The first two methods are common to C and C++, but the third method is unique to C++ and will not be discussed here.

Passing a file as an argument to a function. Example G.14 illustrates how to pass a file object by reference to a function. If you chose to skip Subsection 11.2.4, then you should skip this example.

Example G.14

The C program below uses a function named *open_output_safely()* from Example 11.2.6 to open an output file:

```
#include <stdio.h>

int open_output_safely(FILE ** fp)
{
   *fp = fopen("out.dat", "w");
   if (*fp == 0)
   {
       printf("The file could not be opened\n");
       return 0;
   }
   return 1;
}

main()
{
   FILE * ofp;

   if (open_output_safely(&ofp))
   {
       fprintf(ofp, "It's working");
       fclose(ofp);
   }
   return 0;
}
```

Its equivalent program in C++ is:

```
#include <fstream.h>
#include <iostream.h>

int open_output_safely(fstream * fp)1
{
   (*fp).open("in.dat",ios::out);2
   if (*fp == 0)
   {
       cout << "The file could not be opened\n";
       return 0;
   }
   return 1;
}


main()
{
   fstream ofp;

   if (open_output_safely(&ofp))3
   {
```

```
        ofp << "It's working";
        ofp.close();
    }
    return 0;
}
```

Explanations

1. The file parameter *fp* is declared as a pointer so that it may receive the address of the object *ofp*. For instance, assuming that the object *ofp* is at address 5500:

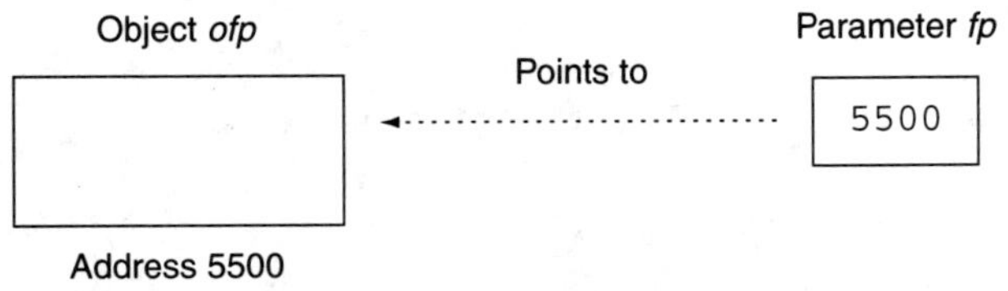

2. The dereferencing operator must be applied to the pointer *fp* in order to reach the object *ofp*. Then the *open()* function within that object opens the file.
3. The object *ofp* is to be passed via a pointer reference so that the function *open_output_safely()* may assign a file to it.

Returning a file object. The following example illustrates how to return a file object from a function.

Example G.15

The C program below uses a function named *open_output_safely()* from Example 10.4.8 to open an output file. The file pointer is returned:

```
#include <stdio.h>

FILE * open_output_safely(void)
{
    FILE * fp;

    fp = fopen("out.dat", "w");
    if (fp == 0)
    {
        printf("The file could not be opened\n");
    }
    return fp;
}

main()
{
    FILE * ofp;

    if (ofp = open_output_safely())
    {
        fprintf(ofp, "It's working");
        fclose(ofp);
    }
    return 0;
}
```

Its equivalent program in C++ is:

```
#include <fstream.h>
#include <iostream.h>
```

```
fstream * open_output_safely(void)[1]
{
   static fstream fp;[2]

   fp.open("out.dat", ios::out);[3]
   if (fp == 0)
   {
       cout << "The file could not be opened\n";
   }
   return &fp;[4]
}

main()
{
   fstream * ofp;[5]

   if (ofp = open_output_safely())[6]
   {
       *ofp << "It's working";[7]
       (*ofp).close();[7]
   }
   return 0;
}
```

Explanations

1. Note that the type of the function *open_output_safely()* is *fstream **. This is so because it returns a pointer to a file object of class *fstream.* This action will be necessary as mentioned in (5) below.
2. This declares the file object *fp* that is to access the file. This object will be needed outside this function too, so the qualifier *static* must be present. A detailed explanation of what this qualifier does and why it is needed here can be found in Appendix D. Note that the file object *fp* is not a pointer, contrary to the case in the C program. So perhaps its name should have been changed to, say, *fo* (for file object) to better reflect this. However, for the sake of easier one-to-one comparison with the C program, the name was purposely left the same.
3. The file OUT.DAT is opened and linked into the file object *ofp.*
4. The address of the file object is returned, not the object itself.
5. In C++, an object cannot be sent back with a *return* statement. So a pointer to the object, here named *ofp,* is sent instead.
6. This function call creates a file object and returns a pointer to it.
7. The file object *fp,* although declared inside *open_output_safely(),* may be used outside it. A pointer reference to it is needed, however; hence the use of the pointer *ofp* and the dereferencing operator.

EXERCISE G.9

Convert the program in Example 10.4.9 into a C++ program.

Index